Lecture Notes in Computer Science 3288

Commenced Publication in 1973
Founding and Former Series Editors:
Gerhard Goos, Juris Hartmanis, and Jan van Leeuwen

Paolo Atzeni Wesley Chu
Hongjun Lu Shuigeng Zhou
Tok Wang Ling (Eds.)

Conceptual Modeling – ER 2004

23rd International Conference on Conceptual Modeling
Shanghai, China, November 8-12, 2004
Proceedings

Springer

Volume Editors

Paolo Atzeni
Universtità Roma Tre, Dipart Informatica e Automazione
Via Vasca Navale, 79 00146 Roma, Italy
E-mail: atzeni@dia.uniroma3.it

Wesley Chu
University of California, Computer Science Department
3731 Boelter Hall, Los Angeles, CA, 90095, USA
E-mail: wwc@cs.ucla.edu

Hongjun Lu
Hong Kong University of Science and Technology, Department of Computer Science
Clear Water Bay, Kowloon, Hong Kong, China
E-mail: luhj@cs.ust.hk

Shuigeng Zhou
Fudan University, Department of Computer Science and Engineering
220 Handan Road, Shanghai, 200433, China
E-mail: sgzhou@fudan.edu.cn

Tok Wang Ling
National University of Singapore, School of Computing
3 Science Drive 2, Singapore 117543
E-mail: lingtw@comp.nus.edu.sg

Library of Congress Control Number: 2004114106

CR Subject Classification (1998): H.2, H.4, F.4.1, I.2.4, H.1, J.1, D.2, C.2

ISSN 0302-9743
ISBN 3-540-23723-2 Springer Berlin Heidelberg New York

Springer is a part of Springer Science+Business Media

springeronline.com

Typesetting: Camera-ready by author, data conversion by Olgun Computergrafik
Printed on acid-free paper SPIN: 11335221 06/3142 5 4 3 2 1 0

Foreword

On behalf of the Organizing Committee, we would like to welcome you to the proccedings of the 23rd International Conference on Conceptual Modeling (ER 2004). This conference provided an international forum for technical discussion on conceptual modeling of information systems among researchers, developers and users. This was the third time that this conference was held in Asia; the first time was in Singapore in 1998 and the second time was in Yokohama, Japan in 2001. China is the third largest nation with the largest population in the world. Shanghai, the largest city in China and a great metropolis, famous in Asia and throughout the world, is therefore a most appropriate location to host this conference.

This volume contains papers selected for presentation and includes the two keynote talks by Prof. Hector Garcia-Molina and Prof. Gerhard Weikum, and an invited talk by Dr. Xiao Ji.

This volume also contains industrial papers and demo/poster papers. An additional volume contains papers from 6 workshops.

The conference also featured three tutorials: (1) Web Change Management and Delta Mining: Opportunities and Solutions, by Sanjay Madria, (2) A Survey of Data Quality Issues in Cooperative Information Systems, by Carlo Batini, and (3) Visual SQL – An ER-Based Introduction to Database Programming, by Bernhard Thalheim.

The technical program of the conference was selected by a distinguished program committee consisting of three PC Co-chairs, Hongjun Lu, Wesley Chu, and Paolo Atzeni, and more than 70 members. They faced a difficult task in selecting 57 papers from many very good contributions. This year the number of submissions, 293, was a record high for ER conferences. We wish to express our thanks to the program committee members, external reviewers, and all authors for submitting their papers to this conference.

We would also like to thank: the Honorary Conference Chairs, Peter P. Chen and Ruqian Lu; the Coordinators, Zhongzhi Shi, Yoshifumi Masunaga, Elisa Bertino, and Carlo Zaniolo; Workshop Co-chairs, Shan Wang and Katsumi Tanaka; Tutorial Co-chairs, Jianzhong Li and Stefano Spaccapietra; Panel Co-chairs, Chin-Chen Chang and Erich Neuhold; Industrial Co-chairs, Philip S. Yu, Jian Pei, and Jiansheng Feng; Demos and Posters Co-chair, Mong-Li Lee and Gillian Dobbie; Publicity Chair, Qing Li; Publication Chair cum Local Arrangements Chair, Shuigeng Zhou; Treasurer, Xueqing Gong; Registration Chair, Xiaoling Wang; Steering Committee Liaison, Arne Solvberg; and Webmasters, Kun Yue, Yizhong Wu, Zhimao Guo, and Keping Zhao.

We wish to extend our thanks to the Natural Science Foundation of China, the ER Institute (ER Steering Committee), the K.C. Wong Education Foundation in Hong Kong, the Database Society of the China Computer Federation, ACM SIGMOD, ACM SIGMIS, IBM China Co., Ltd., Shanghai Baosight Software Co., Ltd., and the Digital Policy Management Association of Korea for their sponsorships and support.

At this juncture, we wish to remember the late Prof. Yahiko Kambayashi who passed away on February 5, 2004 at age 60 and was then a workshop co-chair of the conference. Many of us will remember him as a friend, a mentor, a leader, an educator, and our source of inspiration. We express our heartfelt condolence and our deepest sympathy to his family.

We hope that the attendees found the technical program of ER 2004 to be interesting and beneficial to their research. We trust they enjoyed this beautiful city, including the night scene along the Huangpujiang River and the postconference tours to the nearby cities, leaving a beautiful and memorable experience for all.

November 2004

Tok Wang Ling
Aoying Zhou

Preface

The 23rd International Conference on Conceptual Modeling (ER 2004) was held in Shanghai, China, November 8–12, 2004. Conceptual modeling is a fundamental technique used in analysis and design as a real-world abstraction and as the basis for communication between technology experts and their clients and users. It has become a fundamental mechanism for understanding and representing organizations, including new e-worlds, and the information systems that support them.

The International Conference on Conceptual Modeling provides a major forum for presenting and discussing current research and applications in which conceptual modeling is the major emphasis. Since the first edition in 1979, the ER conference has evolved into the most prestigious one in the areas of conceptual modeling research and applications. Its purpose is to identify challenging problems facing high-level modeling of future information systems and to shape future directions of research by soliciting and reviewing high-quality applied and theoretical research findings. ER 2004 encompassed the entire spectrum of conceptual modeling. It addressed research and practice in areas such as theories of concepts and ontologies underlying conceptual modeling, methods and tools for developing and communicating conceptual models, and techniques for transforming conceptual models into effective information system implementations.

We solicited forward-looking and innovative contributions that identify promising areas for future conceptual modeling research as well as traditional approaches to analysis and design theory for information systems development.

The Call for Papers attracted 295 exceptionally strong submissions of research papers from 36 countries/regions. Due to limited space, we were only able to accept 57 papers from 21 countries/regions, for an acceptance rate of 19.3%. Inevitably, many good papers had to be rejected. The accepted papers covered topics such as ontologies, patterns, workflows, metamodeling and methodology, innovative approaches to conceptual modeling, foundations of conceptual modeling, advanced database applications, systems integration, requirements and evolution, queries and languages, Web application modeling and development, schemas and ontologies, and data mining.

We are proud of the quality of this year's program, from the keynote speeches to the research papers, with the workshops, panels, tutorials, and industrial papers. We were honored to host the outstanding keynote addresses by Hector Garcia-Molina and Gerhard Weikum. We appreciate the hard work of the organizing committee, with interactions around the clock with colleagues all over the world. Most of all, we are extremely grateful to the program committee members of ER 2004 who generously spent their time and energy reviewing submitted papers. We also thank the many external referees who helped with the review process. Last but not least, we thank the authors who wrote high-quality research papers and submitted them to ER 2004, without whom the conference would not have existed.

November 2004

Paolo Atzeni, Wesley Chu, and Hongjun Lu

ER 2004 Conference Organization

Honorary Conference Chairs

Peter P. Chen	Louisiana State University, USA
Ruqian Lu	Fudan University, China

Conference Co-chairs

Aoying Zhou	Fudan University, China
Tok Wang Ling	National University of Singapore, Singapore

Program Committee Co-chairs

Paolo Atzeni	Università Roma Tre, Italy
Wesley Chu	University of California at Los Angeles, USA
Hongjun Lu	Univ. of Science and Technology of Hong Kong, China

Workshop Co-chairs

Shan Wang	Renmin University of China, China
Katsumi Tanaka	Kyoto University, Japan
Yahiko Kambayashi[1]	Kyoto University, Japan

Tutorial Co-chairs

Jianzhong Li	Harbin Institute of Technology, China
Stefano Spaccapietra	EPFL Lausanne, Switzerland

Panel Co-chairs

Chin-Chen Chang	Chung Cheng University, Taiwan, China
Erich Neuhold	IPSI, Fraunhofer, Germany

Industrial Co-chairs

Philip S. Yu	IBM T.J. Watson Research Center, USA
Jian Pei	Simon Fraser University, Canada
Jiansheng Feng	Shanghai Baosight Software Co., Ltd., China

[1] Prof. Yahiko Kambayashi died on February 5, 2004.

Demos and Posters Chair

Mong-Li Lee — National University of Singapore, Singapore
Gillian Dobbie — University of Auckland, New Zealand

Publicity Chair

Qing Li — City University of Hong Kong, China

Publication Chair

Shuigeng Zhou — Fudan University, China

Coordinators

Zhongzhi Shi — ICT, Chinese Academy of Science, China
Yoshifumi Masunaga — Ochanomizu University, Japan
Elisa Bertino — Purdue University, USA
Carlo Zaniolo — University of California at Los Angeles, USA

Steering Committee Liaison

Arne Solvberg — Norwegian University of Sci. and Tech., Norway

Local Arrangements Chair

Shuigeng Zhou — Fudan University, China

Treasurer

Xueqing Gong — Fudan University, China

Registration

Xiaoling Wang — Fudan University, China

Webmasters

Kun Yue — Fudan University, China
Yizhong Wu — Fudan University, China
Zhimao Guo — Fudan University, China
Keping Zhao — Fudan University, China

Program Committee

Jacky Akoka	CNAM & INT, France
Hiroshi Arisawa	Yokohama National University, Japan
Sonia Bergamaschi	Università di Modena e Reggio Emilia, Italy
Mokrane Bouzeghoub	Université de Versailles, France
Diego Calvanese	Università di Roma La Sapienza, Italy
Cindy Chen	University of Massachusetts at Lowell, USA
Shing-Chi Cheung	Univ. of Science and Technology of Hong Kong, China
Roger Chiang	University of Cincinnati, USA
Stefan Conrad	Heinrich-Heine-Universität Düsseldorf, Germany
Bogdan Czejdo	Loyola University, New Orleans, USA
Lois Delcambre	Oregon Health Science University, USA
Debabrata Dey	University of Washington, USA
Johann Eder	Universität Klagenfurt, Austria
Ramez Elmasri	University of Texas at Arlington, USA
David W. Embley	Brigham Young University, USA
Johann-Christoph Freytag	Humboldt-Universität zu Berlin, Germany
Antonio L. Furtado	PUC Rio de Janeiro, Brazil
Andreas Geppert	Credit Suisse, Switzerland
Shigeichi Hirasawa	Waseda University, Japan
Arthur ter Hofstede	Queensland University of Technology, Australia
Matthias Jarke	Technische Hochschule Aachen, Germany
Christian S. Jensen	Aalborg Universitet, Denmark
Manfred Jeusfeld	Universiteit van Tilburg, Netherlands
Yahiko Kambayashi	Kyoto University, Japan
Hannu Kangassalo	University of Tampere, Finland
Kamalakar Karlapalem	Intl. Institute of Information Technology, India
Vijay Khatri	Indiana University at Bloomington, USA
Dongwon Lee	Pennsylvania State University, USA
Mong-Li Lee	National University of Singapore, Singapore
Wen Lei Mao	University of California at Los Angeles, USA
Jianzhong Li	Harbin Institute of Technology, China
Qing Li	City University of Hong Kong, Hong Kong, China
Stephen W. Liddle	Brigham Young University, USA
Ee-Peng Lim	Nanyang Technological University, Singapore
Mengchi Liu	Carleton University, Canada
Victor Zhenyu Liu	University of California at Los Angeles, USA
Ray Liuzzi	Air Force Research Laboratory, USA
Bertram Ludäscher	San Diego Supercomputer Center, USA
Ashok Malhotra	Microsoft, USA
Murali Mani	Worcester Polytechnic Institute, USA
Fabio Massacci	Università di Trento, Italy
Sergey Melnik	Universität Leipzig, Germany

Xiaofeng Meng	Renmin University of China, China
Renate Motschnig	Universität Wien, Austria
John Mylopoulos	University of Toronto, Canada
Sham Navathe	Georgia Institute of Technology, USA
Jyrki Nummenmaa	University of Tampere, Finland
Maria E. Orlowska	University of Queensland, Australia
Oscar Pastor	Universidad Politécnica de Valencia, Spain
Jian Pei	Simon Fraser University, Canada
Zhiyong Peng	Wuhan University, China
Barbara Pernici	Politecnico di Milano, Italy
Dimitris Plexousakis	FORTH-ICS, Greece
Sandeep Purao	Pennsylvania State University, USA
Sudha Ram	University of Arizona, USA
Colette Rolland	Univ. Paris 1 Panthéon-Sorbonne, France
Elke Rundensteiner	Worcester Polytechnic Institute, USA
Peter Scheuermann	Northwestern University, USA
Keng Siau	University of Nebraska-Lincoln, USA
Janice C. Sipior	Villanova University, USA
Il-Yeol Song	Drexel University, USA
Nicolas Spyratos	Université de Paris-Sud, France
Veda C. Storey	Georgia State University, USA
Ernest Teniente	Universitat Politècnica de Catalunya, Spain
Juan C. Trujillo	Universidad de Alicante, Spain
Michalis Vazirgiannis	Athens Univ. of Economics and Business, Greece
Dongqing Yang	Peking University, China
Jian Yang	Tilburg University, Netherlands
Ge Yu	Northeastern University, China
Lizhu Zhou	Tsinghua University, China
Longxiang Zhou	Chinese Academy of Science, China
Shuigeng Zhou	Fudan University, China

External Referees

A. Analyti
Michael Adams
Alessandro Artale
Enrico Blanzieri
Shawn Bowers
Paolo Bresciani
Linas Bukauskas
Ugo Buy
Luca Cabibbo
Andrea Calì
Cinzia Cappiello
Alain Casali
Yu Chen
V. Christophidis
Fang Chu
Valter Crescenzi
Michael Derntl
Arnaud Giacometti
Paolo Giorgini
Cristina Gómez
Daniela Grigori
Wynne Hsu
Stamatis Karvounarakis
Ioanna Koffina
George Kokkinidis
Hristo Koshutanski
Kyriakos Kritikos
Lotfi Lakhal
Domenico Lembo
Shaorong Liu
Stéphane Lopes
Bertram Ludaescher
Chang Luo
Gianni Mecca
Massimo Mecella
Carlo Meghini
Paolo Merialdo
Antonis Misargopoulos
Paolo Missier
Stefano Modafferi
Wai Yin Mok
Enrico Mussi
Noel Novelli
Alexandros Ntoulas
Phillipa Oaks
Seog-Chan Oh
Justin O'Sullivan
Manos Papaggelis
V. Phan-Luong
Pierluigi Plebani
Philippe Rigaux
Nick Russell
Ulrike Sattler
Monica Scannapieco
Ka Cheung Sia
Riccardo Torlone
Goce Trajcevski
Nikos Tsatsakis
Haixun Wang
Moe Wynn
Yi Xia
Yirong Yang
Fan Ye

Co-organized by

Fudan University of China
National University of Singapore

In Cooperation with

Database Society of the China Computer Federation
ACM SIGMOD
ACM SIGMIS

Sponsored by

National Natural Science Foundation of China (NSFC)
ER Institute (ER Steering Committee)
K.C. Wong Education Foundation, Hong Kong

Supported by

IBM China Co., Ltd.
Shanghai Baosight Software Co., Ltd.
Digital Policy Management Association of Korea

Table of Contents

Keynote Addresses

Entity Resolution: Overview and Challenges 1
Hector Garcia-Molina

Towards a Statistically Semantic Web 3
Gerhard Weikum, Jens Graupmann, Ralf Schenkel, and Martin Theobald

Invited Talk

The Application and Prospect of Business Intelligence in Metallurgical Manufacturing Enterprises in China 18
Xiao Ji, Hengjie Wang, Haidong Tang, Dabin Hu, and Jiansheng Feng

Conceptual Modeling I

Conceptual Modelling – What and *Why* in Current Practice 30
Islay Davies, Peter Green, Michael Rosemann, and Stan Gallo

Entity-Relationship Modeling *Re*-revisited 43
Don Goelman and Il-Yeol Song

Modeling Functional Data Sources as Relations 55
Simone Santini and Amarnath Gupta

Conceptual Modeling II

Roles as Entity Types: A Conceptual Modelling Pattern 69
Jordi Cabot and Ruth Raventós

Modeling Default Induction with Conceptual Structures 83
Julien Velcin and Jean-Gabriel Ganascia

Reachability Problems in Entity-Relationship Schema Instances 96
Sebastiano Vigna

Conceptual Modeling III

A Reference Methodology for Conducting Ontological Analyses 110
Michael Rosemann, Peter Green, and Marta Indulska

Pruning Ontologies in the Development of Conceptual Schemas of Information Systems 122
Jordi Conesa and Antoni Olivé

Definition of Events and Their Effects
in Object-Oriented Conceptual Modeling Languages 136
Antoni Olivé

Conceptual Modeling IV

Enterprise Modeling with Conceptual XML 150
David W. Embley, Stephen W. Liddle, and Reema Al-Kamha

Graphical Reasoning for Sets of Functional Dependencies 166
János Demetrovics, András Molnár, and Bernhard Thalheim

ER-Based Software Sizing for Data-Intensive Systems 180
Hee Beng Kuan Tan and Yuan Zhao

Data Warehouse

Data Mapping Diagrams for Data Warehouse Design with UML 191
Sergio Luján-Mora, Panos Vassiliadis, and Juan Trujillo

Informational Scenarios for Data Warehouse Requirements Elicitation 205
Naveen Prakash, Yogesh Singh, and Anjana Gosain

Extending UML for Designing Secure Data Warehouses 217
Eduardo Fernández-Medina, Juan Trujillo, Rodolfo Villarroel, and Mario Piattini

Schema Integration I

Data Integration with Preferences Among Sources 231
Gianluigi Greco and Domenico Lembo

Resolving Schematic Discrepancy in the Integration
of Entity-Relationship Schemas 245
Qi He and Tok Wang Ling

Managing Merged Data by Vague Functional Dependencies 259
An Lu and Wilfred Ng

Schema Integration II

Merging of XML Documents 273
Wanxia Wei, Mengchi Liu, and Shijun Li

Schema-Based Web Wrapping 286
Sergio Flesca and Andrea Tagarelli

Web Taxonomy Integration Using Spectral Graph Transducer 300
Dell Zhang, Xiaoling Wang, and Yisheng Dong

Data Classification and Mining I

Contextual Probability-Based Classification ... 313
Gongde Guo, Hui Wang, David Bell, and Zhining Liao

Improving the Performance of Decision Tree: A Hybrid Approach ... 327
LiMin Wang, SenMiao Yuan, Ling Li, and HaiJun Li

Understanding Relationships: Classifying Verb Phrase Semantics ... 336
Veda C. Storey and Sandeep Purao

Data Classification and Mining II

Fast Mining Maximal Frequent ItemSets Based on FP-Tree ... 348
Yuejin Yan, Zhoujun Li, and Huowang Chen

Multi-phase Process Mining: Building Instance Graphs ... 362
B.F. van Dongen and W.M.P. van der Aalst

A New XML Clustering for Structural Retrieval ... 377
Jeong Hee Hwang and Keun Ho Ryu

Web-Based Information Systems

Link Patterns for Modeling Information Grids and P2P Networks ... 388
Christopher Popfinger, Cristian Pérez de Laborda, and Stefan Conrad

Information Retrieval Aware Web Site Modelling and Generation ... 402
Keyla Ahnizeret, David Fernandes, João M.B. Cavalcanti, Edleno Silva de Moura, and Altigran S. da Silva

Expressive Profile Specification and Its Semantics for a Web Monitoring System ... 420
Ajay Eppili, Jyoti Jacob, Alpa Sachde, and Sharma Chakravarthy

Query Processing I

On Modelling Cooperative Retrieval Using an Ontology-Based Query Refinement Process ... 434
Nenad Stojanovic and Ljiljana Stojanovic

Load-Balancing Remote Spatial Join Queries in a Spatial GRID ... 450
Anirban Mondal and Masaru Kitsuregawa

Expressing and Optimizing Similarity-Based Queries in SQL ... 464
Like Gao, Min Wang, X. Sean Wang, and Sriram Padmanabhan

Query Processing II

XSLTGen: A System for Automatically Generating XML Transformations via Semantic Mappings ... 479
Stella Waworuntu and James Bailey

Efficient Recursive XML Query Processing in Relational Database Systems ... 493
Sandeep Prakash, Sourav S. Bhowmick, and Sanjay Madria

Situated Preferences and Preference Repositories for Personalized Database Applications ... 511
Stefan Holland and Werner Kießling

Web Services I

Analysis and Management of Web Service Protocols ... 524
Boualem Benatallah, Fabio Casati, and Farouk Toumani

Semantic Interpretation and Matching of Web Services ... 542
Chang Xu, Shing-Chi Cheung, and Xiangye Xiao

Intentional Modeling to Support Identity Management ... 555
Lin Liu and Eric Yu

Web Services II

WUML: A Web Usage Manipulation Language for Querying Web Log Data ... 567
Qingzhao Tan, Yiping Ke, and Wilfred Ng

An Agent-Based Approach for Interleaved Composition and Execution of Web Services ... 582
Xiaocong Fan, Karthikeyan Umapathy, John Yen, and Sandeep Purao

A Probabilistic QoS Model and Computation Framework for Web Services-Based Workflows ... 596
San-Yih Hwang, Haojun Wang, Jaideep Srivastava, and Raymond A. Paul

Schema Evolution

Lossless Conditional Schema Evolution ... 610
Ole G. Jensen and Michael H. Böhlen

Ontology-Guided Change Detection to the Semantic Web Data ... 624
Li Qin and Vijayalakshmi Atluri

Schema Evolution in Data Warehousing Environments – A Schema Transformation-Based Approach ... 639
Hao Fan and Alexandra Poulovassilis

Conceptual Modeling Applications I

Metaprogramming for Relational Databases ... 654
Jernej Kovse, Christian Weber, and Theo Härder

Incremental Navigation: Providing Simple and Generic Access to Heterogeneous Structures ... 668
Shawn Bowers and Lois Delcambre

Agent Patterns for Ambient Intelligence ... 682
Paolo Bresciani, Loris Penserini, Paolo Busetta, and Tsvi Kuflik

Conceptual Modeling Applications II

Modeling the Semantics of 3D Protein Structures ... 696
Sudha Ram and Wei Wei

Risk-Driven Conceptual Modeling of Outsourcing Decisions ... 709
Pascal van Eck, Roel Wieringa, and Jaap Gordijn

A Pattern and Dependency Based Approach to the Design of Process Models ... 724
Maria Bergholtz, Prasad Jayaweera, Paul Johannesson, and Petia Wohed

UML

Use of Tabular Analysis Method to Construct UML Sequence Diagrams ... 740
Margaret Hilsbos and Il-Yeol Song

An Approach to Formalizing the Semantics of UML Statecharts ... 753
Xuede Zhan and Huaikou Miao

Applying the Application-Based Domain Modeling Approach to UML Structural Views ... 766
Arnon Sturm and Iris Reinhartz-Berger

XML Modeling

A Model Driven Approach for XML Database Development ... 780
Belén Vela, César J. Acuña, and Esperanza Marcos

On the Updatability of XML Views Published over Relational Data ... 795
Ling Wang and Elke A. Rundensteiner

XBiT: An XML-Based Bitemporal Data Model ... 810
Fusheng Wang and Carlo Zaniolo

Industrial Presentations I: Applications

Enterprise Cockpit for Business Operation Management 825
Fabio Casati, Malu Castellanos, and Ming-Chien Shan

Modeling Autonomous Catalog for Electronic Commerce 828
Yuan-Chi Chang, Vamsavardhana R. Chillakuru, and Min Wang

GiSA: A Grid System for Genome Sequences Assembly 831
Jun Tang, Dong Huang, Chen Wang, Wei Wang, and Baile Shi

Industrial Presentations II: Ontology in Applications

Analytical View of Business Data: An Example 834
Adam Yeh, Jonathan Tang, Youxuan Jin, and Sam Skrivan

Ontological Approaches to Enterprise Applications 838
Dongkyu Kim, Yuan-Chi Chang, Juhnyoung Lee, and Sang-goo Lee

FASTAXON: A System for FAST (and Faceted) TAXONomy Design 841
Yannis Tzitzikas, Raimo Launonen, Mika Hakkarainen, Pekka Korhonen, Tero Leppänen, Esko Simpanen, Hannu Törnroos, Pekka Uusitalo, and Pentti Vänskä

CLOVE: A Framework to Design Ontology Views 844
Rosario Uceda-Sosa, Cindy X. Chen, and Kajal T. Claypool

Demos and Posters

iRM: An OMG MOF Based Repository System with Querying Capabilities 850
Ilia Petrov, Stefan Jablonski, Marc Holze, Gabor Nemes, and Marcus Schneider

Visual Querying for the Semantic Web 852
Sacha Berger, Franois Bry, and Christoph Wieser

Query Refinement by Relevance Feedback in an XML Retrieval System ... 854
Hanglin Pan, Anja Theobald, and Ralf Schenkel

Semantics Modeling for Spatiotemporal Databases 856
Peiquan Jin, Lihua Yue, and Yuchang Gong

Temporal Information Management Using XML 858
Fusheng Wang, Xin Zhou, and Carlo Zaniolo

SVMgr: A Tool for the Management of Schema Versioning 860
Fabio Grandi

GENNERE: A Generic Epidemiological Network for Nephrology and Rheumatology 862
Ana Simonet, Michel Simonet, Cyr-Gabin Bassolet, Sylvain Ferriol, Cédric Gueydan, Rémi Patriarche, Haijin Yu, Ping Hao, Yi Liu, Wen Zhang, Nan Chen, Michel Forêt, Philippe Gaudin, Georges De Moor, Geert Thienpont, Mohamed Ben Saïd, Paul Landais, and Didier Guillon

Panel

Beyond Webservices – Conceptual Modelling for Service Oriented Architectures 865
Peter Fankhauser

Author Index 867

Entity Resolution: Overview and Challenges

Hector Garcia-Molina

Stanford University, Stanford, CA, USA
hector@cs.stanford.edu

Entity resolution is a problem that arises in many information integration scenarios: We have two or more sources containing records on the same set of real-world entities (e.g., customers). However, there are no unique identifiers that tell us what records from one source correspond to those in the other sources. Furthermore, the records representing the same entity may have differing information, e.g., one record may have the address misspelled, another record may be missing some fields. An entity resolution algorithm attempts to identify the matching records from multiple sources (i.e., those corresponding to the same real-world entity), and merges the matching records as best it can. Entity resolution algorithms typically rely on user-defined functions that (a) compare fields or records to determine if they match (are likely to represent the same real world entity), and (b) merge matching records into one, and in the process perhaps combine fields (e.g., creating a new name based on two slightly different versions of the name).

In this talk I will give an overview of the Stanford SERF Project, that is building a framework to describe and evaluate entity resolution schemes. In particular, I will give an overview of some of the different entity resolution settings:

- *De-duplication versus fidelity enhancement.* In the de-duplication problem, we have a single set of records, and we try to merge the ones representing the same real world entity. In the fidelity enhancement problem, we have two sets of records: a base set of records of interest, and a new set of acquired information. The goal is to coalesce the new information into the base records.
- *Clustering versus snapping.* With snapping, we examine records pair-wise and decide if they represent the same entity. If they do, we merge the records into one, and continue the process of pair-wise comparisons. With clustering, we analyze all records and partition them into groups we believe represent the same real world entity. At the end, each partition is merged into one record.
- *Confidences.* In some entity resolution scenarios we must manage confidences. For example, input records may have a confidence value representing how likely it is they are true. Snap rules (that tells us when two records match) may also have confidences representing how likely it is that two records actually represent the same real world entity. As we merge records, we must track their confidences.
- *Schema Mismatches.* In some entity resolution scenarios we must deal, not just with resolving information on entities, but also with resolving discrepancies among the schemas of the different sources. For example, the attribute names and formats from one source may not match those of other sources.

In the talk I will address some of the open problems and challenges that arise in entity resolution. These include:

P. Atzeni et al. (Eds.): ER 2004, LNCS 3288, pp. 1–2, 2004.

- *Performance.* Entity resolution algorithms must perform very large number of field and record comparisons (via the user provided functions), so it is critical to perform only the absolutely minimum number of invocations to the comparison functions. Developing efficient algorithms is analogous to developing efficient join algorithms for relational databases.
- *Confidences.* Very little is understood as to how confidences should be manipulated in an entity resolution setting. For example, say we have two records, one reporting that "Joe" uses cell phone 123, and the other reporting that "Joseph" uses phone 456. The first record has confidence 0.9 and the second one 0.7. A snap rule tells us that "Joe" and "Joseph" are the same person with confidence 0.8. Do we assume this person has been using two phones? Or that 123 is the correct number because that record has a higher confidence? If we do merge the records, what are the resulting confidences?
- *Metrics.* Say we have two entity resolution schemes, A and B. How do we know if A yields "better" results and compared to B? Or say we have one base set of records, and we wish to enhance its fidelity with either new set X or new set Y. Since it costs money to acquire either new set, we only wish to use one. Based on samples of X and Y, how do we decide which set is more likely to enhance our base set? To address questions such as these we need to develop metrics that quantify not just to performance of entity resolution, but also its accuracy.
- *Privacy.* There is a strong connection between entity resolution and information privacy. To illustrate, say Alice has given out two records containing some of her private information: Record 1 gives Alice's name, phone number and credit card number; record 2 gives Alice's name, phone and national identity number. How much information has actually "leaked" depends on how well and adversary, Bob, can piece together these two records. If Bob can determine that the records refer to the same person, then he knows Alice's credit card number *and* her national identity number, opening the door for say identity theft. If the records do not snap together, then Bob knows less and we have a smaller information leak. We need to develop good ways to model information leakage in an entity resolution context. Such a model can lead us, for example, to techniques for quantifying the leakage caused by releasing one new fact, or the *decrease* in leakage caused by releasing disinformation.

Additional information on our SERF project can be found at

http://www-db.stanford.edu/serf

This work is joint with Qi Su, Tyson Condie, Nicolas Pombourcq, and Jennifer Widom.

Towards a Statistically Semantic Web

Gerhard Weikum, Jens Graupmann, Ralf Schenkel, and Martin Theobald

Max-Planck Institute of Computer Science
Saarbruecken, Germany

Abstract. The envisioned Semantic Web aims to provide richly annotated and explicitly structured Web pages in XML, RDF, or description logics, based upon underlying ontologies and thesauri. Ideally, this should enable a wealth of query processing and semantic reasoning capabilities using XQuery and logical inference engines. However, we believe that the diversity and uncertainty of terminologies and schema-like annotations will make precise querying on a Web scale extremely elusive if not hopeless, and the same argument holds for large-scale dynamic federations of Deep Web sources. Therefore, ontology-based reasoning and querying needs to be enhanced by statistical means, leading to relevance-ranked lists as query results.

This paper presents steps towards such a "statistically semantic" Web and outlines technical challenges. We discuss how statistically quantified ontological relations can be exploited in XML retrieval, how statistics can help in making Web-scale search efficient, and how statistical information extracted from users' query logs and click streams can be leveraged for better search result ranking. We believe these are decisive issues for improving the quality of next-generation search engines for intranets, digital libraries, and the Web, and they are crucial also for peer-to-peer collaborative Web search.

1 The Challenge of "Semantic" Information Search

The age of information explosion poses tremendous challenges regarding the intelligent organization of data and the effective search of relevant information in business and industry (e.g., market analyses, logistic chains), society (e.g., health care), and virtually all sciences that are more and more data-driven (e.g., gene expression data analyses and other areas of bioinformatics). The problems arise in intranets of large organizations, in federations of digital libraries and other information sources, and in the most humongous and amorphous of all data collections, the World Wide Web and its underlying numerous databases that reside behind portal pages. The Web bears the potential of being the world's largest encyclopedia and knowledge base, but we are very far from being able to exploit this potential.

Database-system and search-engine technologies provide support for organizing and querying information; but all too often they require excessive manual preprocessing, such as designing a schema and cleaning raw data or manually classifying documents into a taxonomy for a good Web portal, or manual postprocessing such as browsing through large result lists with too many irrelevant items or surfing in the vicinity of promising but not truly satisfactory approximate matches. The following are a few example queries where current Web and intranet search engines fall short or where data

P. Atzeni et al. (Eds.): ER 2004, LNCS 3288, pp. 3–17, 2004.

integration techniques and the use of SQL-like querying face unsurmountable difficulties even on structured, but federated and highly heterogeneous databases:

Q1: Which professors from Saarbruecken in Germany teach information retrieval and do research on XML?

Q2: Which gene expression data from Barrett tissue in the esophagus exhibit high levels of gene A01g? And are there any metabolic models for acid reflux that could be related to the gene expression data?

Q3: What are the most important research results on large deviation theory?

Q4: Which drama has a scene in which a woman makes a prophecy to a Scottish nobleman that he will become king?

Q5: Who was the French woman that I met in a program committee meeting where Paolo Atzeni was the PC chair?

Q6: Are there any published theorems that are equivalent to or subsume my latest mathematical conjecture?

Why are these queries difficult (too difficult for Google-style keyword search unless one invests a huge amount of time to manually explore large result lists with mostly irrelevant and some mediocre matches)? For Q1 no single Web site is a good match; rather one has to look at several pages together within some bounded context: the homepage of a professor with his address, a page with course information linked to by the homepage, and a research project page on semistructured data management that is a few hyperlinks away from the homepage. Q2 would be easy if asked for a single bioinformatics database with a familiar query interface, but searching the answer across the entire Web and Deep Web requires discovering all relevant data sources and unifying their query and result representations on the fly. Q3 is not a query in the traditional sense, but requires gathering a substantial number of key resources with valuable information on the given topic; it would be best served by looking up a well maintained Yahoo-style topic directory, but highly specific expert topics are not covered there. Q4 cannot be easily answered because a good match does not necessarily contain the keywords "woman", "prophecy", "nobleman", etc., but may rather say something like "Third witch: All hail, Macbeth, thou shalt be king hereafter!" and the same document may contain the text "All hail, Macbeth! hail to thee, thane of Glamis!". So this query requires some background knowledge to recognize that a witch is a woman, "shalt be" refers to a prophecy, and thane is a title for a Scottish nobleman. Q5 is similar to Q4 in the sense that it also requires background knowledge, but it is more difficult because it additionally requires putting together various information fragments: conferences on which I served on the PC found in my email archive, PC members of conferences found on Web pages, and detailed information found on researchers' homepages. And after having identified a candidate like Sophie Cluet from Paris, one needs to infer that Sophie is a typical female first name and that Paris most likely denotes the capital of France rather than the 500-inhabitants town of Paris, Texas, that became known through a movie. Q6 finally is what some researchers call "AI-complete", it will remain a challenge for a long time.

For a human expert who is familiar with the corresponding topics, none of these queries is really difficult. With unlimited time, the expert could easily identify relevant pages and combine semantically related information units into query answers. The challenge is to automate or simulate these intellectual capabilities and implement them so that they can handle billions of Web pages and petabytes of data in structured (but schematically highly diverse) Deep-Web databases.

2 The Need for Statistics

What if all Web pages and all Web-accessible data sources were in XML, RDF, or OWL (a description-logic representation) as envisioned in the Semantic Web research direction [25, 1]? Would this enable a search engine to effectively answer the challenging queries of the previous section? And would such an approach scale to billions of Web pages and be efficient enough for interactive use? Or could we even load and integrate all Web data into one gigantic database and use XQuery for searching it?

XML, RDF, and OWL offer ways of more explicitly structuring and richly annotating Web pages. When viewed as logic formulas or labeled graphs, we may think of the pages as having "semantics", at least in terms of model theory or graph isomorphisms[1]. In principle, this opens up a wealth of precise querying and logical inferencing opportunities. However, it is extremely unlikely that all pages will use the very same tag or predicate names when they refer to the same semantic properties and relationships. Making such an assumption would be equivalent to assuming a single global schema: this would be arbitrarly difficult to achieve in a large intranet, and it is completely hopeless for billions of Web pages given the Web's high dynamics, extreme diversity of terminology, and uncertainty of natural language (even if used only for naming tags and predicates). There may be standards (e.g., XML schemas) for certain areas (e.g., for invoices or invoice-processsing Web Services), but these will have limited scope and influence. A terminologically unified and logically consistent Semantic Web with billions of pages is hard to imagine.

So reasoning about diversely annotated pages is a necessity and a challenge. Similarly to the ample research on database schema integration and instance matching (see, e.g., [49] and the references given there), knowledge bases [50], lexicons, thesauri [24], or *ontologies* [58] are considered as the key asset to this end. Here an ontology is understood as a collection of *concepts* with various *semantic relationships* among them; the formal representation may vary from rigorous logics to natural language. The most important relationship types are hyponymy (specialization into narrower concepts) and hypernymy (generalization into broader concepts).

To the best of my knowledge, the most comprehensive, publicly available kind of ontology is the WordNet thesaurus hand-crafted by cognitive scientists at Princeton [24]. For the concept "woman" WordNet lists about 50 immediate hyponyms, which include concepts like "witch" and "lady" which could help to answer queries like Q4 from the previous section. However, regardless of whether one represents these hyponymy relationships in a graph-oriented form or as logical formulas, such a rigid "true-or-false" representation could never discriminate these relevant concepts from the other 48 irrelevant and largely exotic hyponyms of "woman". In information-retrieval (IR) jargon, such an approach would be called Boolean retrieval or Boolean reasoning; and IR almost always favors *ranked retrieval* with some quantitative relevance assessment. In fact, by simply looking at statistical correlations of using words like "woman" and "lady" together in some text neighborhood within large corpora (e.g., the Web or large digital libraries) one can infer that these two concepts are strongly related, as opposed to concepts like "woman" and "siren". Similarly, mere statistics strongly suggests that

[1] Some people may argue that all computer models are mere syntax anyway, but this is in the eye of the beholder.

a city name "Paris" denotes the French capital and not Paris, Texas. Once making a distinction of strong vs. weak relationships and realizing that this is a full spectrum, it becomes evident that the significance of semantic relationships needs to be quantified in some manner, and the by far best known way of doing this (in terms of rigorous foundation and rich body of results) is by using probability theory and statistics.

This concludes my argument for the necessity of a "statistically semantic" Web. The following sections substantiate and illustrate this point by sketching various technical issues where statistical reasoning is key. Most of the discussion addresses how to handle non-schematic XML data; this is certainly still a good distance from the Semantic Web vision, but it is a decent and practically most relevant first step.

3 Towards More "Semantics" in Searching XML and Web Data

Non-schematic XML data that comes from many different sources and inevitably exhibits heterogeneous structures and annotations (i.e., XML tags) cannot be adequately searched using database query languages like XPath or XQuery. Often, queries either return too many or too few results. Rather the ranked-retrieval paradigm is called for, with relaxable search conditions, various forms of similarity predicates on tags and contents, and quantitative relevance scoring. Note that the need for ranking goes beyond adding Boolean text-search predicates to XQuery. In fact, similarity scoring and ranking are orthogonal to data types and would be desirable and beneficial also on structured attributes such as time (e.g., approximately in the year 1790), geographic coordinates (e.g., near Paris), and other numerical and categorical data types (e.g., numerical sensor readings and music style categories).

Research on applying IR techniques to XML data has started five years ago with the work [26,55,56,60] and has meanwhile gained considerable attention. This research avenue includes approaches based on combining ranked text search with XPath-style conditions [4,13,35,11,31,38], structural similarities such as tree-editing distances [5,54,69,14], ontology-enhanced content similarities [60,61,52], and applying probabilistic IR and statistical language models to XML [28,2].

Our own approach, the XXL[2] query language and search engine [60,61,52], combines a subset of XPath with a similarity operator $\sim$ that can be applied to element or attribute names, on one hand, and element or attribute contents, on the other hand. For example, the queries Q1 and Q4 of Section 1 could be expressed in XXL as follows (and executed on a heterogeneous collection of XML documents):

```
Q1: Select * From Index
    Where ~professor As P
    And P = "Saarbruecken"
    And P//~course = "~IR"
    And P//~research = "~XML"
```

```
Q4: Select * From Index
    Where ~drama//scene As S
    And S//~speaker = "~woman"
    And S//~speech = "king"
    And S//~person = "~nobleman"
```

Here XML data is interpreted as a directed graph, including href or XLink/XPointer links within and across documents that go beyond a merely tree-oriented approach. End nodes of connections that match a path condition such as `drama//scene` are bound to node variables that can be referred to in other search conditions. Content conditions

[2] Flexible XML Search Language.

such as = "~woman" are interpreted as keyword queries on XML elements, using IR-style measures (based on statistics like term frequencies and inverse element frequencies) for scoring the relevance of an element. In addition and most importantly, we allow expanding the query by adding "semantically" related terms taken from an ontology. In the example, "woman" could be expanded into "woman wife lady girl witch ...". The score of a relaxed match, say for an element containing "witch", is the product of the traditional score for the query "witch" and the *ontological similarity* of the query term and the related term, $sim(woman, witch)$ in the particular example. Element (or attribute) name conditions such as ~course are analogously relaxed, so that, for example, tag names "teaching", "class", or "seminar" would be considered as approximate matches. Here the score is simply the ontological similarity, for tag names are only single words or short composite words. The result of an entire query is a ranked list of subgraphs of the XML data graph, where each result approximately matches all query conditions with the same binding of all variables (but different results have different bindings). The total score of a result is computed from the scores of the elementary conditions using a simple probabilistic model with independence assumptions, and the result ranking is in descending order of total scores.

Query languages of this kind work nicely on heterogeneous and non-schematic XML data collections, but the Web and also large fractions of intranets are still mostly in HTML, PDF, and other less structured formats. Recently we have started to apply XXL-style queries also to such data by automatically converting Web data into XML format. The COMPASS[3] search engine that we have been building supports XML ranked retrieval on the full suite of Web and intranet data including combined data collections that include both XML documents and Web pages [32]. For example, query Q1 can be executed on an index that is built over all of DBLP (cast into XML) and the crawled homepages of all authors and other Web pages reachable through hyperlinks. Figure 1 depicts the visual formulation of query Q1. Like in the original XXL engine, conditions with the similarity operator ~ are relaxed using statistically quantified relationships from the ontology.

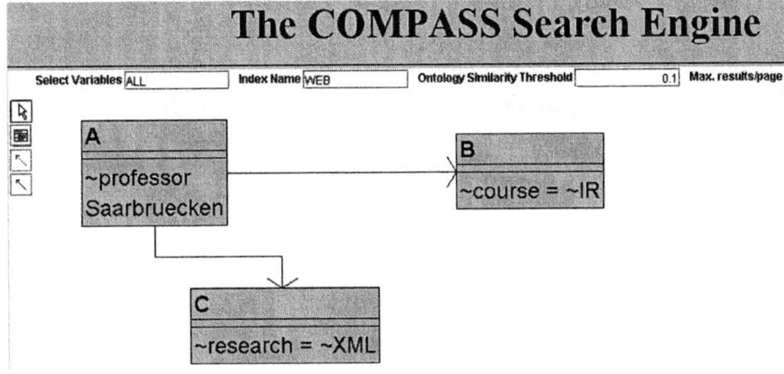

Fig. 1. Visual COMPASS Query

[3] Concept-oriented Multi-format Portal-aware Search System.

The conversion of HTML and other formats into XML is based on relatively simple heuristic rules, for example, casting HTML headings into XML element names. For additional automatic annotation we use the information extraction component ANNIE that is part of the GATE System developed at the University of Sheffield [20]. GATE offers various modules for analyzing, extracting, and annotating text; its capabilities range from part-of-speech tagging (e.g., for noun phrases, temporal adverbial phrases, etc.) and lexicon lookups (e.g., for geographic names) to finite state transducers for annotations based on regular expressions (e.g., for dates or currency amounts). One particularly useful and fairly light-weight component is the Gazetteer Module for named entity recognition based on part-of-speech tagging and a large dictionary containing names of cities, countries, person names (e.g., common first names), etc. This way one can automatically generate tags like `<location>` and `<person>`. For example, we were able to annotate the popular Wikipedia open encyclopdia corpus this way, generating about 2 million person and location tags. And this is the key for more advanced "semantics-aware" search on the current Web. For example, searching for Web pages about the physicist Max Planck would be phrased as `person = "Max Planck"`, and this would eliminate many spurious matches that a Google-style keyword query "Max Planck" would yield about Max Planck Institutes and the Max Planck Society[4].

There is a rich body of research on information extraction from Web pages and wrapper generation. This ranges from purely logic-based or pattern-matching-driven approaches (e.g., [51, 17, 6, 30]) to techniques that employ statistical learning (e.g., Hidden Markov Models) (e.g., [15, 16, 39, 57, 40]) to infer structure and annotations when there is too much diversity and uncertainty in the underlying data. As long as all pages to be wrapped come from the same data source (with some hidden schema), the logic-based approaches work very well. However, when one tries to wrap all homepages of DBLP authors or the course programs of all computer science departments in the world, uncertainty is inevitable and statistics-driven techniques are the only viable ones (unless one is willing to invest a lot of manual work for traditional schema integration, writing customized wrappers and mappers).

Despite advertising our own work and mentioning our competitors, the current research projects on combining IR techniques and statistical learning with XML querying is still in an early stage and there are certainly many open issues and opportunities for further research. These include better theoretical foundations for scoring models on semistructured data, relevance feedback and interactive information search, and, of course, all kinds of efficiency and scalability aspects. Applying XML search techniques to Web data is in its infancy; studying what can be done with named-entity recognition and other automatic annotation techniques and understanding the interplay of queries with such statistics-based techniques for better information organization are widely open fields.

4 Statistically Quantified Ontologies

The important role of ontologies in making information search more "semantics-aware" has already been emphasized. In contrast to most ongoing efforts for Semantic-Web on-

[4] Germany's premier scientific society, which encompasses 80 institutes in all fields of science.

tologies, our work has focused on quantifying the strengths of semantic relationships based on corpus statistics [52, 59] (see also the related work [10, 44, 22, 36] and further references given there). In contrast to early IR work on using thesauri for query expansion (e.g., [64]), the ontology itself plays a much more prominent role in our approach with carefully quantified statistical similarities among concepts.

Consider a graph of concepts, each characterized by a set of synonyms and, optionally, a short textual description, connected by "typed" edges that represent different kinds of relationships: hypernyms and hyponyms (generalization and specialization, aka. is-a relations), holonyms and meronyms (part-of relations), is-instance-of relations (e.g., Cinderella being an instance of a fairytale or IBM Thinkpad being a notebook), to name the most important ones.

The first step in building an ontology is to create the nodes and edges. To this end, existing thesauri, lexicons, and other sources like geographic gazetteers (for names of countries, cities, rivers, etc. and their relationships) can be used. In our work we made use of the WordNet thesaurus [24] and the Alexandria Digital Library Gazetteer [3], and also started extracting concepts from page titles and href anchor texts in the Wikipedia encyclopedia. One of the shortcomings of WordNet is its lack of instances knowledge, for example, brand names and models of cars, cameras, computers, etc. To further enhance the ontology, we crawled Web pages with HTML tables and forms, trying to extract relationships between table-header column and form-field names and the values in table cells and the pulldown menus of form fields. Such approaches are described in the literature (see, e.g., [21, 63, 68]). Our experimental findings confirmed the potential value of these techniques, but also taught us that careful statistical thresholding is needed to eliminate noise and incorrect inferencing, once again a strong argument for the use of statistics.

Once the concepts and relationships of a graph-based ontology are constructed, the next step is to quantify the strengths of semantic relationships based on corpus statistics. To this end we have performed focused Web crawls and use their results to estimate statistical correlations between the characteristic words of related concepts. One of the measures for the similarity of concepts $c1$ and $c2$ that we used is the Dice coefficient

$$Dice(c1, c2) = \frac{2|\{docs\ with\ c1\} \cap \{docs\ with\ c2\}|}{|\{docs\ with\ c1\}| + |\{docs\ with\ c2\}|}$$

In this computation we represent concept c by the terms taken from its set of synonyms and its short textual description (i.e., the WordNet gloss). Optionally, we can add terms from neighbors or siblings in the ontological graph. A document in the corpus is considered to contain concept c if it contains at least one word of the term set for c, and considered to contain both $c1$ and $c2$ if it contains at least one word from each of the two term sets. This is a heuristics; other approaches are conceivable which we are investigating.

Following this methodology, we constructed an ontolgy service [59] that is accessible via Java RMI or as a SOAP-based Web Service described in WSDL. The service is used in the COMPASS search engine [32], but also in other projects. Figure 2 shows a screenshot from our ontology visualization tool.

One of the difficulties in quantifying ontological relationships is that we aim to measure correlations between *concepts* but merely have statistical information about

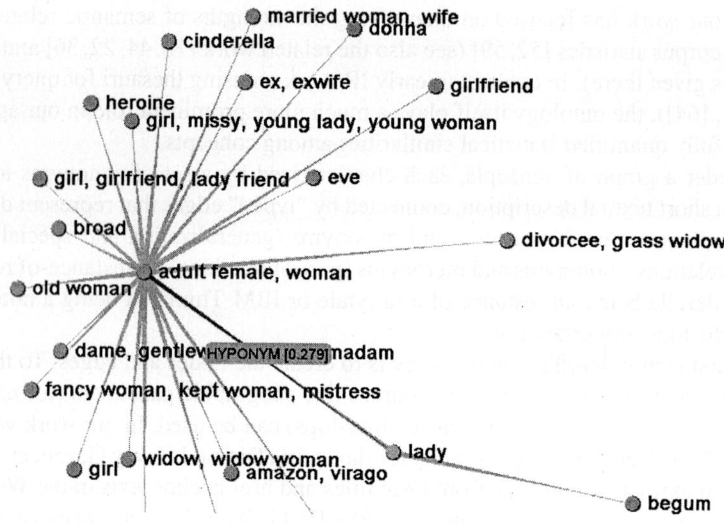

Fig. 2. Ontology Visualization

correlations between *words*. Ideally, we should first map the words in the corpus onto the corresponding concepts, i.e., their correct meanings. This is known as the *word sense disambiguation* problem in natural language processing [45], obviously a very difficult task because of polysemy. If this were solved it would not only help in deriving more accurate statistical measures for "semantic" similarities among concepts but could also potentially boost the quality of search results and automatic classification of documents into topic directories. Our work [59] presents a simple but scalable approach to automatically mapping text terms onto ontological concepts, in the context of XML document classification. Again, statistical reasoning, in combination with some degree of natural language parsing, is key to tackling this difficult problem.

Ontology construction is a highly relevant research issue. Compared to the ample work on knowledge representations for ontological information, the aspects of how to "populate" an ontology and how to enhance it with quantitative similarity measures have been underrated and deserve more intensive research.

5 Efficient Top-k Query Processing with Probabilistic Pruning

For ranked retrieval of semistructured, "semantically" annotated data, we face the problem of reconciling efficiency with result quality. Usually, we are not interested in a complete result but only in the top-k results with the highest relevance scores. The state-of-the-art algorithm for top-k queries on multiple index lists, each sorted in descending order of relevance scores, is the Threshold Algorithm, TA for short [23, 33, 47]. It is applicable to both relational data such as product catalogs and text documents such as Web data. In the latter case, the fact that TA performs random accesses on very long, disk-resident index lists (e.g., all URLs or document ids for a frequently occurring word), with only short prefixes of the lists in memory, makes TA much less attractive, however.

In such a situtation, the TA variant with sorted access only, coined NRA (no random accesses), stream-combine, or TA-sorted in the literature, is the method of choice [23, 34]. TA-sorted works by maintaining lower bounds and upper bounds for the scores of the top-k candidates that are kept in a priority queue in memory while scanning the index lists. The algorithm can safely stop when the lower bound for the score of the rank-k result is at least as high as the highest upper bound for the scores of the candidates that are not among the current top-k. Unfortunately, albeit theoretically instance-optimal for computing a precise top-k result [23], TA-sorted tends to degrade in performance when operating on a large number of index lists. This is exactly the case when we relax query conditions such as `~speaker = ~woman` using semantically related concepts from the ontology[5]. Even if the relaxation uses a threshold for the similarity of related concepts, we may often arrive at query conditions with 20 to 50 search terms.

Statistics about the score distributions in the various index lists and some probabilistic reasoning help to overcome this efficiency problem and re-gain performance. In TA-sorted a top-k candidate d that has already been seen in the index lists in $E(d) \subseteq [1..m]$, achieving score $s_j(d)$ in list j $(0 < s_j(d) \leq 1)$, and has unknown scores in the index lists $[1..m] - E(d)$, satisfies:

$$lowerb(d) = \sum_{j \in E(d)} s_j(d) \leq s(d) \leq \sum_{j \in E(d)} s_j(d) + \sum_{j \notin E(d)} high_j = upperb(d)$$

where $s(d)$ denotes the total, but not yet known, score that d achieves by summing up the scores from all index lists in which d occurs, $lowerb(d)$ and $upperb(d)$ are the lower and upper bounds of d's score, and $high_j$ is the score that was last seen in the scan of index list j, upper-bounding the score that any candidate may obtain in list j. A candidate d remains a candidate as long as $upperb(d) > lowerb(rank\text{-}k)$ where $rank\text{-}k$ is the candidate that currently has rank k with regard to the candidates' lower bounds (i.e., the worst one among the current top-k). Assuming that d can achieve a score $high_j$ in all lists in which it has not yet been encountered is conservative and, almost always, overly conservative. Rather we could treat these unknown scores as random variables S_j $(j \notin E(d))$, and estimate the probability that d's total score can exceed $lowerb(rank\text{-}k)$. Then d is discarded from the candidate list if

$$P[lowerb(d) + \sum_{j \notin E(d)} S_j > lowerb(rank\text{-}k)] < \delta$$

with some pruning threshold δ.

This probabilistic interpretation makes some small, but precisely quantifiable, potential error in that it could dismiss some candidates too early. Thus, the top-k result computed this way is only approximate. However, the loss in precision and recall, relative to the exact top-k result using the same index lists, is stochastically bounded and can be set according to the application's needs. A value of $\delta = 0.1$ seems to be acceptable in most situations. Technically, the approach requires computing the convolution

[5] Note that the TA and TA-sorted algorithms can be easily modified to handle both element-name and element-contents conditions (as opposed to mere keyword sets in standard IR and Web search engines).

of the random variables S_j, based on assumed distributions (with parameter fitting) or precomputed histograms for the individual index lists and taking into account the current $high_j$ values, and predicting the (1-δ)-quantile of the sum's distribution. Details of the underlying mathematics and the implementation techniques for this *Prob-sorted* method can be found in [62]. Experiments with the TREC-12 .Gov corpus and the IMDB data collection have shown that such a probabilistic top-k method gains about a factor of ten (and sometimes more) in run-time compared to TA-sorted.

The outlined algorithm for approximate top-k queries with probabilistic guarantees is a versatile building block for XML ranked retrieval. In combination with ontology-based query relaxation, for example, expanding ~`woman` into `(woman or wife or witch)`, it can add index lists dynamically and incrementally, rather than having to expand the query upfront based on thresholds. To this end, the algorithm considers the ontological similarity $sim(i, j)$ between concept i from the original query and concept j in the relaxed query, and multiplies it with the $high_j$ value of index list j to obtain an upper bound for the score (and characterize the score distribution) that a candidate can obtain from the relaxation j. This information is dynamically combined with the probabilistic prediction of the other unknown scores and their sum.

The algorithm can also be combined with distance-aware path indexes for XML data (e.g., the HOPI index structure [53]). This is required when queries contain element-name and element-contents conditions as well as path conditions of the form `professor//course` where matches for "course" that are close to matches for "professor" should be ranked higher than matches that are far apart. Thus, the Prob-sorted algorithm covers a large fraction of an XML ranked retrieval engine.

6 Exploiting Collective Human Input

The statistical information considered so far refers to data (e.g., scores in index lists) or metadata (e.g., ontological similarities). Yet another kind of statistics is information about user behavior. This could include relatively static properties like bookmarks or embedded hyperlinks pointing to high-quality Web pages, but also dynamic properties inferred from query logs and click streams. For example, Google's PageRank views a Web page as more important if it has many incoming links and the sources of these links are themselves high authorities [9, 12]. Technically, this amounts to computing stationary probabilities for a Markov-chain model that mimics a "random surfer". What PageRank essentially does is to exploit the intellectual endorsements that many human users (or Web administrators on behalf of organizations) provide by means of hyperlinks.

This rationale can be carried over to analyzing and exploiting entire surf trails and query logs of individual users or an entire user community. These trails, which can be gathered from browser histories, local proxies, or Web servers, capture implicit user judgements. For example, suppose a user clicks on a specific subset of the top 10 results returned by a search engine for a query with several keywords, based on having seen the summaries of these pages. This implicit form of relevance feedback establishes a strong correlation between the query and the clicked-on pages. Further suppose that the user refines a query by adding or replacing keywords, e.g., to eliminate ambiguities in the previous query. Again, this establishes correlations between the new keywords and the subsequently clicked-on pages, but also, albeit possibly to a lesser extent, between the original query and the eventually relevant pages.

We believe that observing and exploiting such user behavior is a key element in adding more "semantic" or "cognitive" quality to a search engine. The literature contains some very interesting work in this direction (e.g., [19, 65, 67]), but is rather preliminary at this point. Perhaps, the difficulties in obtaining comprehensive query logs and surf trails outside of big service providers is a limiting factor in this line of experimental research. Our own, very recent, work generalizes the notion of a "random surfer" into a "random expert user" by enhancing the underlying Markov chain to incorporate also query nodes and transitions from queries to query refinements as well as clicked-on documents. Transition probabilities are derived from the statistical analysis of query logs and click streams. The resulting Markov chain converges to stationary authority scores that reflect not only the link structure but also the implicit feedback and collective human input of a search engine's users [43].

The de-facto monopoly that large Internet service providers have on being able to observe user behavior and statistically leverage this valuable information may be overcome by building next-generation Web search engines in a truly decentralized and ideally self-organized manner. Consider a peer-to-peer (P2P) system where each peer has a full-fledged Web search engine, including a crawler and an index manager. The crawler may be thematically focused or crawl results may be postprocessed so that the local index contents reflects the corresponding user's interest profile. With such a highly specialized and personalized "power search engine" most queries should be executed locally, but once in a while the user may not be satisfied with the local results and would then want to contact other peers. A "good" peer to which the user's query should be forwarded would have thematically relevant index contents, which could be measured by statistical notions of similarity between peers. These measures may be dependent on the current query or may be query-independent; in the latter case, statistics is used to effectively construct a "semantic overlay network" with neighboring peers sharing thematic interests [8, 42, 48, 18, 7, 66]. Both query routing and "statistically semantic" networks could greatly benefit from collective human inputs in addition to standard IR measures like term and document frequencies or term-wise score distributions: knowing the bookmarks and query logs of thousands of users would be a great resource to build on.

Further exploring these considerations on P2P Web search should become a major research avenue in computer science. Note that our interpretation of Web search includes ranked retrieval and thus is fundamentally more difficult than Gnutella-style file sharing or simple key lookups via distributed hash tables. Further note that, although query routing in P2P Web search resembles earlier work on metasearch engines and distributed IR (see, e.g., [46] and the references given there), it is much more challenging because of the large scale and the high dynamics of the envisioned P2P system with thousands or millions of computers and users.

7 Conclusion

With the ongoing information explosion in all areas of business, science, and society, it will be more and more difficult for humans to keep information organized and extract valuable knowledge in a timely manner. The intellectual time for schema design, schema integration, data cleaning, data quality assurance, manual classification, directory and search result browsing, clever formulation of sophisticated queries, etc. is already the major bottleneck today, and the situation is likely to become worse. In my opinion, this will render all attempts to master Web-scale information in a perfectly consistent, purely logic-based manner more or less futile. Rather, the ability to cope with uncertainty, diversity, and high dynamics will be mandatory. To this end, statistics and their use in probabilistic inferences will be key assets.

One may envision a rich probabilistic algebra that encompasses relational or even object-relational and XML query languages, but interprets all data and results in a probabilistic manner and always produces ranked result result lists rather than Boolean result sets (or bags). There are certainly some elegant and interesting, but mostly theoretical, approaches along these lines (e.g., [27, 29, 37]). However, there is still a long way to go towards practically viable solutions. Among the key challenges that need to be tackled are customizability, composability, and optimizability.

- *Customizability:* The appropriate notions of ontological relationships, "semantic" similarities, and scoring functions are dependent on the application. Thus, the envisioned framework needs to be highly flexible and adaptable to incorporate application-specific or personalized similarity and scoring models.
- *Composability:* Algebraic building blocks like a top-k operator need to be composable so as to allow the construction of rich queries. The desired property that operators produce ranked list with some underlying probability (or "score mass") distribution poses a major challenge, for we need to be able to infer these probability distributions for the results of complex operator trees. This problem is related to the difficult issues of selectivity estimation and approximate query processing in a relational database, but goes beyond the state of the art as it needs to incorporate text term distributions and has to yield full distributions at all levels of operator trees.
- *Optimizability:* Regardless of how elegant a probabilistic query algebra may be, it would not be acceptable unless one can ensure efficient query processing. Performance optimization requires a deep understanding of rewriting complex operator trees into equivalent execution plans that have significantly lower cost (e.g., pushing selections below joins or choosing efficient join orders). At the same time, the top-k querying paradigm that avoids computing full result sets before applying some ranking is a must for efficiency, too. This combination of desiderata leads to a great research challenge in query optimization for a ranked retrieval algebra.

References

1. Karl Aberer et al.: Emergent Semantics Principles and Issues, International Conference on Database Systems for Advanced Applications (DASFAA) 2004
2. Mohammad Abolhassani, Norbert Fuhr: Applying the Divergence from Randomness Approach for Content-Only Search in XML Documents, ECIR 2004
3. Alexandria Digital Library Project, Gazetteer Development, http://www.alexandria.ucsb.edu/gazetteer/

4. Shurug Al-Khalifa, Cong Yu, H. V. Jagadish: Querying Structured Text in an XML Database, SIGMOD 2003
5. Sihem Amer-Yahia, Laks V. S. Lakshmanan, Shashank Pandit: FleXPath: Flexible Structure and Full-Text Querying for XML, SIGMOD 2004
6. Arvind Arasu, Hector Garcia-Molina: Extracting Structured Data from Web Pages, SIGMOD 2003
7. Mayank Bawa, Gurmeet Singh Manku, Prabhakar Raghavan: SETS: Search Enhanced by Topic Segmentation, SIGIR 2003
8. Matthias Bender, Sebastian Michel, Gerhard Weikum, Christian Zimmer: Bookmark-driven Query Routing in Peer-to-Peer Web Search, SIGIR Workshop on Peer-to-Peer Information Retrieval 2004
9. Sergey Brin, Lawrence Page: The Anatomy of a Large-Scale Hypertextual Web Search Engine, WWW Conference 1998
10. Alexander Budanitsky, Graeme Hirst: Semantic Distance in WordNet: An Experimental, Application-oriented Evaluation of Five Measures, Workshop on WordNet and Other Lexical Resources 2001
11. David Carmel, Yoëlle S. Maarek, Matan Mandelbrod, Yosi Mass, Aya Soffer: Searching XML Documents via XML Fragments, SIGIR 2003
12. Soumen Chakrabarti: Mining the Web: Discovering Knowledge from Hypertext Data, Morgan Kaufmann Publishers, 2002
13. T. Chinenyanga, N. Kushmerick: An Expressive and Efficient Language for XML Information Retrieval, Journal of the American Society for Information Science and Technology (JASIST) 53(6), 2002
14. Sara Cohen, Jonathan Mamou, Yaron Kanza, Yehoshua Sagiv: XSEarch: A Semantic Search Engine for XML, VLDB 2003
15. William W. Cohen, Matthew Hurst, Lee S. Jensen: A Flexible Learning System for Wrapping Tables and Lists in HTML Documents, in: A. Antonacopoulos, J. Hu (Editors), Web Document Analysis: Challenges and Opportunities, Word Scientific Publishing, 2004
16. William W. Cohen, Sunita Sarawagi: Exploiting Dictionaries in Named Entity Extraction: Combining Semi-markov Extraction Processes and Data Integration Methods, KDD 2004
17. Valter Crescenzi, Giansalvatore Mecca, Paolo Merialdo: RoadRunner: Towards Automatic Data Extraction from Large Web Sites, VLDB 2001
18. Arturo Crespo, Hector Garcia-Molina: Semantic Overlay Networks, Technical Report, Stanford University, 2003.
19. Hang Cui, Ji-Rong Wen, Jian-Yun Nie, Wei-Ying Ma: Query Expansion by Mining User Logs, IEEE Transactions on Knowledge and Data Engineering 15(4), 2003
20. Hamish Cunningham. GATE, a General Architecture for Text Engineering, Computers and the Humanities 36, 2002
21. Hasan Davulcu, Srinivas Vadrevu, Saravanakumar Nagarajan, I. V. Ramakrishnan: OntoMiner: Bootstrapping and Populating Ontologies from Domain-Specific Web Sites, IEEE Intelligent Systems 18(5), 2003
22. Anhai Doan, Jayant Madhavan, Robin Dhamankar, Pedro Domingos, Alon Y. Halevy: Learning to Match Ontologies on the Semantic Web, VLDB Journal 12(4), 2003
23. Ronald Fagin, Amnon Lotem, Moni Naor: Optimal Aggregation Algorithms for Middleware, Journal of Computer and System Sciences 66(4), 2003
24. Christiane Fellbaum (Editor): WordNet: An Electronic Lexical Database, MIT Press, 1998
25. Dieter Fensel, Wolfgang Wahlster, Henry Lieberman, James A. Hendler (Editors): Spinning the Semantic Web: Bringing the World Wide Web to Its Full Potential, MIT Press, 2002
26. Norbert Fuhr, Kai Großjohann: XIRQL – An Extension of XQL for Information Retrieval, SIGIR Workshop on XML and Information Retrieval 2000

27. Norbert Fuhr: Probabilistic Datalog: Implementing Logical Information Retrieval for Advanced Applications, Journal of the American Society for Information Science (JASIS) 51(2), 2000
28. Norbert Fuhr, Kai Großjohann: XIRQL: A Query Language for Information Retrieval in XML Documents, SIGIR 2001
29. Lise Getoor, Nir Friedman, Daphne Koller, Avi Pfeffer: Learning Probabilistic Relational Models, in: S. Dzeroski, N. Lavrac (Editors), Relational Data Mining, Springer, 2001
30. Georg Gottlob, Christoph Koch, Robert Baumgartner, Marcus Herzog, Sergio Flesca: The Lixto Data Extraction Project – Back and Forth between Theory and Practice, PODS 2004
31. Torsten Grabs, Hans-Jörg Schek: Flexible Information Retrieval on XML Documents. in: H. Blanken et al. (Editors), Intelligent Search on XML Data, Springer, 2003
32. Jens Graupmann, Michael Biwer, Christian Zimmer, Patrick Zimmer, Matthias Bender, Martin Theobald, Gerhard Weikum: COMPASS: A Concept-based Web Search Engine for HTML, XML, and Deep Web Data, Demo Program, VLDB 2004
33. Ulrich Güntzer, Wolf-Tilo Balke, Werner Kießling: Optimizing Multi-Feature Queries for Image Databases, VLDB 2000
34. Ulrich Güntzer, Wolf-Tilo Balke, Werner Kießling: Towards Efficient Multi-Feature Queries in Heterogeneous Environments, International Symposium on Information Technology (ITCC) 2001
35. Lin Guo, Feng Shao, Chavdar Botev, Jayavel Shanmugasundaram: XRANK: Ranked Keyword Search over XML Documents, SIGMOD 2003
36. Maria Halkidi, Benjamin Nguyen, Iraklis Varlamis, Michalis Vazirgiannis: THESUS: Organizing Web Document Collections Based on Link Semantics, VLDB Journal 12(4), 2003
37. Joseph Y. Halpern: Reasoning about Uncertainty, MIT Press, 2003
38. Raghav Kaushik, Rajasekar Krishnamurthy, Jeffrey F. Naughton, Raghu Ramakrishnan: On the Integration of Structure Indexes and Inverted Lists, SIGMOD 2004
39. Nicholas Kushmerick, Bernd Thomas: Adaptive Information Extraction: Core Technologies for Information Agents. in: M. Klusch et al. (Editors), Intelligent Information Agents, Springer, 2003
40. Kristina Lerman, Lise Getoor, Steven Minton, Craig A. Knoblock: Using the Structure of Web Sites for Automatic Segmentation of Tables, SIGMOD 2004
41. Zhenyu Liu, Chang Luo, Junghoo Cho, Wesley W. Chu: A Probabilistic Approach to Metasearching with Adaptive Probing, ICDE 2004
42. Jie Lu, James P. Callan: Content-based Retrieval in Hybrid Peer-to-peer Networks, CIKM 2003
43. Julia Luxenburger, Gerhard Weikum: Query-log Based Authority Analysis for Web Information Search, submitted for publication
44. Alexander Maedche, Steffen Staab: Learning Ontologies for the Semantic Web, International Workshop on the Semantic Web (SemWeb) 2001
45. Christopher D. Manning, Hinrich Schütze: Foundations of Statistical Natural Language Processing, MIT Press, 1999
46. Weiyi Meng, Clement T. Yu, King-Lup Liu: Building Efficient and Effective Metasearch Engines, ACM Computing Surveys 34(1), 2002
47. Surya Nepal, M. V. Ramakrishna: Query Processing Issues in Image (Multimedia) Databases, ICDE 1999
48. Henrik Nottelmann, Norbert Fuhr: Combining CORI and the Decision-Theoretic Approach for Advanced Resource Selection, ECIR 2004
49. Erhard Rahm, Philip A. Bernstein: A Survey of Approaches to Automatic Schema Matching, VLDB Journal 10(4), 2001
50. Stuart J. Russell, Peter Norvig: Artificial Intelligence - A Modern Approach, Prentice Hall, 2002

51. Arnaud Sahuguet, Fabien Azavant: Building Light-weight Wrappers for Legacy Web Datasources using W4F, VLDB 1999
52. Ralf Schenkel, Anja Theobald, Gerhard Weikum: Ontology-Enabled XML Search. in: H. Blanken et al. (Editors), Intelligent Search on XML Data, Springer, 2003
53. Ralf Schenkel, Anja Theobald, Gerhard Weikum: An Efficient Connection Index for Complex XML Document Collections, EDBT 2004
54. Torsten Schlieder, Holger Meuss: Querying and Ranking XML Documents, Journal of the American Society for Information Science and Technology (JASIST) 53(6), 2002
55. Torsten Schlieder, Holger Meuss: Result Ranking for Structured Queries against XML Documents, DELOS Workshop: Information Seeking, Searching and Querying in Digital Libraries, 2000
56. Torsten Schlieder, Felix Naumann: Approximate Tree Embedding for Querying XML Data, SIGIR Workshop on XML and Information Retrieval, 2000
57. Marios Skounakis, Mark Craven, Soumya Ray: Hierarchical Hidden Markov Models for Information Extraction, IJCAI 2003
58. Steffen Staab, Rudi Studer (Editors): Handbook on Ontologies, Springer 2004
59. Martin Theobald, Ralf Schenkel, Gerhard Weikum: Exploiting Structure, Annotation, and Ontological Knowledge for Automatic Classification of XML Data, International Workshop on Web and Databases (WebDB) 2003
60. Anja Theobald, Gerhard Weikum: Adding Relevance to XML. International Workshop on Web and Databases (WebDB) 2000, extended version in: LNCS 1997, Springer, 2001.
61. Anja Theobald, Gerhard Weikum: The Index-based XXL Search Engine for Querying XML Data with Relevance Ranking, EDBT 2002
62. Martin Theobald, Gerhard Weikum, Ralf Schenkel: Top-k Query Evaluation with Probabilistic Guarantees, VLDB 2004
63. Yuri A. Tijerino, David W. Embley, Deryle W. Lonsdale, George Nagy: Ontology Generation from Tables, WISE 2003
64. Ellen M. Voorhees: Query Expansion Using Lexical-Semantic Relations. SIGIR 1994
65. Ji-Rong Wen, Jian-Yun Nie, Hong-Jiang Zhang: Query Clustering Using User Logs, ACM TOIS 20(1), 2002
66. Linhao Xu, Chenyun Dai, Wenyuan Cai, Shuigeng Zhou, Aoying Zhou: T owards Adaptive Probabilistic Search in Unstructured P2P Systems. Asia-Pacific Web Conference (APWeb) 2004
67. Gui-Rong Xue, Hua-Jun Zeng, Zheng Chen, Wei-Ying Ma, Hong-Jiang Zhang, Chao-Jun Lu: Implicit Link Analysis for Small Web Search, SIGIR 2003
68. Shipeng Yu, Deng Cai, Ji-Rong Wen, Wei-Ying Ma: Improving Pseudo-Relevance Feedback in Web Information Retrieval Using Web Page Segmentation, WWW Conference 2003
69. Pavel Zezula, Giuseppe Amato, Fausto Rabitti: Processing XML Queries with Tree Signatures. in: H. Blanken et al. (Editors), Intelligent Search on XML Data, Springer, 2003

The Application and Prospect of Business Intelligence in Metallurgical Manufacturing Enterprises in China

Xiao Ji, Hengjie Wang, Haidong Tang, Dabin Hu, and Jiansheng Feng

Data Strategies Dept, Shanghai Baosight Software Co., Ltd
Shanghai 201203, China

Abstract. This paper introduces the application of Business Intelligence (BI) technologies in metallurgical manufacturing enterprises in China. It sets forth the development procedure and successful cases of BI in Shanghai Baoshan Iron & Steel Co., Ltd (Shanghai Basteel in short), and puts forward the methodology adaptable to the construction of BI systems in the metallurgical manufacturing enterprises in China. Finally, it prospects the next generation of BI technologies in Shanghai Baosteel. It should be mentioned as well that it is the Data Strategies Dept of Shanghai Baosight Software Co., Ltd (Shanghai Baosight in short) and the Technology Center of Shanghai Baoshan Iron & Steel Co., Ltd. that supports and does research works on BI solutions in Shanghai Baosteel.

1 Introduction

1.1 The Application of BI Technologies in Metallurgical Manufacturing Enterprises in the World

The executives of enterprises sometimes are totally at a loss when they face with the explosive increasing data from different kinds of application systems with different levels such as MES, ERP, CRM, SCM, etc. Statistics show that the amount of data will be doubled within eighteen months. But among them, how much do we really need, and how much do we really can use for the further analysis? The main advantage of BI technologies is to discover and turn these massive data into the useful information for enterprise decision-making.

The researches and application of BI have become a hot topic in global IT area since the term of BI technology was first brought forward by Howard Dresner from Gartner Group in 1989. Through our years practice, we consider BI a concept rather than an information technology. It is a business concept in solving the problems for enterprise production, operation, management, and etc. Taking enterprise data warehouse as basis, the BI technologies uses professional

P. Atzeni et al. (Eds.): ER 2004, LNCS 3288, pp. 18–29, 2004.

knowledge and special data mining technologies to disclose key factors in solving business problems, and assisting operational management and decision-making.

As the most advanced metallurgical manufacturing enterprise in China, Shanghai Baosteel has begun to use BI technologies in solving some key problems in daily production and management since last decade. It has applied BI technologies such as data analysis and data mining in both self-motion and self-consciousness since the development of Solution of Iron Ores Mixing in1995, and thereafter quality control system, SPC, IPC, and finally the large-scale enterprise data warehouse nowadays. In the meantime, Shanghai Baosight has formed its own characteristics of applying BI in metallurgical manufacturing enterprises, especially in quality control area. In addition, Shanghai Baosight has cultivated its experienced professional team in system development and project management. Following are the some achievements in specific areas.

Data Warehouse: Considering the size, complexity and technical level, Shanghai Baosteel enterprise data warehouse system is a rare and advanced system in China. As a successful BI case, such data warehouse system has become a model in metallurgical manufacturing today.

Quality Control and Analysis: In such area, many data mining techniques with high level technologies and characteristics have been widely applied for quality improvement, and can be extended to other manufacturing enterprises as well.

SPC and IPC: As basis of quality control, SPC and IPC systems with special characteristics are commonly used in Shanghai Baosteel. Of course they are fitted to the other manufacturing enterprises too.

The achievements in the above three areas prove that Shanghai Baosteel is leading in BI application in metallurgy and manufacturing enterprises in China. And with experience transfer, the others metallurgy manufacturing enterprises will follow the step of Shanghai Baosteels. And Shanghai Baosight will go further too in the related BI application areas.

Comparing with international craft brothers such as POSCO and the United States Steel Corporation (UEC), Shanghai Baosteel is also among the top in BI application. UEC once invited Shanghai Baosteel to introduce its experience in building metallurgical manufacturing enterprise.

1.2 The Information System Development of Shanghai Baosteel

Shanghai Baosteel is the largest and the most modernized iron and steel complex in China. Baosteel has established its status as a world steel-making giant with comprehensive advantages in its reputation, talents, innovation, management and technology. According to the publication "Guide to the World Steel Industry", Shanghai Baosteel ranks among the first three of the most competitive steel-makers worldwide, and is also believed as the most potentially competitive iron and steel enterprise in the future.

Shanghai Baosteel specializes in producing high-tech and high-value-added steel products. Meanwhile it has become the main steel supplier to automobile industries, household appliances, container, oil and natural gas exploration, and pressure vessel in China. Meanwhile, Shanghai Baosteel exports its products to over forty countries and regions including Japan, South Korea and countries in Europe and America.

All the facilities that the company possesses are based on the advanced technologies of contemporary steel smelting, cold and hot processing, hydraulic sensing, electronic control, computer and information communications. They feature large-scale, continuity and automation, and are kept the most advanced technology in the world.

Shanghai Baosteel possesses tremendous strength of research and development. It has made great efforts in developing new technology, new products and new equipment, and has accumulated vigorous driving force for company's further development.

Shanghai Baosteel is located in Shanghai, China. Its first phase construction project began on the 23rd of December in 1978, and was completed and put into production on the 15th of September in 1985. Its second phase project went into operation in June, 1991 and third phase project was completed before the end of 2000. Shanghai Baosteel turned to be a stock company officially on the 3rd of February in 2000, and was successfully listed in Shanghai Security Exchange on the 12th December in the same year.

In the early days when Shanghai Baosteel was setting up in 1978, the sponsors considered that they should build up computer systems to assist management. They realized it should import the most advanced equipments, techniques and management at the time from Japan, and take some factories of the Nippon Steel as models.

In May 1981, with the impelling of the minister from the Ministry of the Metallurgy and Manufacturing, Shanghai Baosteel finished the "the Feasible Research of the Synthetic Computer System", and lodged to build Shanghai Baosteel information system with five-level computer structures by setting up four area-control computer systems between the L3 systems and the central management information system.

On the 15th February 1996, Shanghai Baosteel and IBM contracted to import the advanced computer system of IBM 9672 from the US as the area level management information system of hot and cold rolling areas in phase three project, changing the way in phase two project that there were two respective management systems within hot rolling areas and cool rolling areas. The decision was a revolution on information system construction in Shanghai Baosteel. And in the coming days, the executives of Shanghai Baosteel decided to build the comprehensive information system using IBM 9672 to integrate the whole distributed information systems. They then cancelled the fifth-level management information system, and the new system was put into production in March 1998, ensuring the proper production of 1580 hot rolling mill, 1420 cold rolling mill, and following second steel-making system.

In May 2001, Shanghai Baosteel raised new strategic concept of Enterprise System Innovation. The ESI system included a three level architecture. First to rebuild the business processes of Shanghai Baosteel to bring up new effective ones; second, to reconstruct the organizational structure on the basis of new business processes; third to build corresponding information systems to assist to realize the new business processes. The main objective of ESI system is to help Shanghai Baosteel to realize its business target, and to be a good competitor in steel enterprises, and to prepare to face the overall challenges after China becomes a member of WTO.

The above ESI decision was prospectively made by the executives of Shanghai Baosteel, to help Baosteel to realize its modernized management, and to be one of the Global 500 in the world.

And now Shanghai Baosteel has successfully finished its third phase information system development. In the first phase project, several process control systems, self-developed central management system (IBM 4341) with batch processing, and PC networks were set up. In the second phase project, process control systems and product control systems, imported technology based management information system (IBM 4381) for 2050 hot rolling mill, self-developed management information system (IBM RS6000) for 2030 cold rolling mill, iron-making regional management information system, steel-making regional management information system were built. In the third phase project, better configured process control systems, production control systems for 1580 hot rolling mill, and 1420, 1550 cold rolling mills, enterprise-wide OA and human resource management system, and ERP system which included integrated production and sales system and equipment management system, were successfully developed.

After the three phase project construction, Shanghai Baosteel has formed its four-level production computer system. In recent years, with ESI concept, many assisted information systems were set up as well, such as integrated equipment maintenance management system, data warehouse and data mining applications, information services system for mills and departments, e-business platform - BSTEEL.COM online, and Supply Chain Management, etc.

The architecture of Shanghai Baosteel's information system can be illustrated as followed.

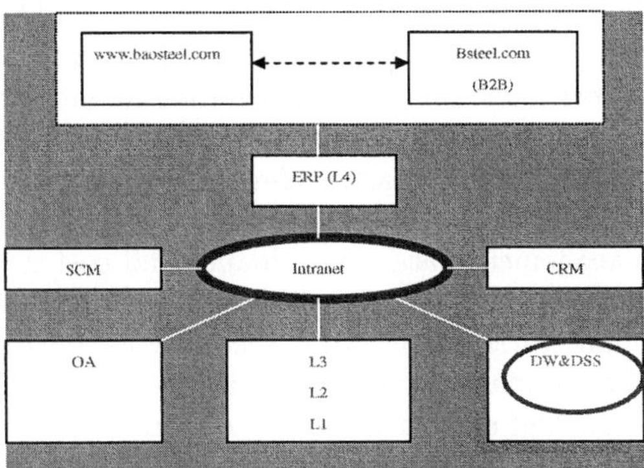

Fig. 1. Information Architecture of Shanghai Baosteel

2 Application of Business Intelligence in Shanghai Baosteel

2.1 The Application and Methodology of Business Intelligence in Shanghai BaoSteel

As one of the most advanced metallurgical manufacturing enterprises in China, Shanghai Baosteel is now in its rapid development age. In order to continuously reduce cost and improve competitiveness in the international or the domestic markets, executives strongly realize the importance of the followings:

- To speed up the logistic turnover, and to improve the level of the products turnover.
- To stabilize and improve the products quality.
- To promote the sales and related capabilities to expand markets sharing.
- To strengthen the infrastructure of cost and finance.
- To optimize the allocation of enterprise resources, which farthest satisfies the markets' requirements.

In order to achieve the above objectives, the requirement to build an enterprise data warehouse system has been raised. In order to satisfy the strategy of Shanghai Baosteel's information development, the data warehouse system should help Shanghai Baosteel to organize every kind of data required by the enterprise analysts and to transfer all needed information to end users. Then Shanghai Baosteel and Shanghai Baosight started to evaluate and plan the data warehouse system. The evaluation estimates the current enterprise infrastructure and the operational environments of Shanghai Baosteel. As the high level of information development, the data warehouse system could be built, and planned to build the first data warehouse subject area for Shanghai Baosteel - the technique and quality management data mart.

Currently Shanghai Baosteel builds the enterprise data warehouse system on two IBM S85 machine with major data source from the ERP system. This data warehouse system includes ODS data stores, and perfectly integrated subject data stores according to the "Quick Data Warehouse Building" methodology. The first quality management data mart has accumulated much experience, and it has included the decision supporting information about the related products and their quality management. Nowadays, the system has already built the enterprise statistics management data mart, technique and quality management data mart, sales and marketing management data mart, production management data mart, equipment management data mart, finance and cost data mart which includes planning values, metal balancing, cost analysis, BUPC, finance analysis, and production administration information system, enterprise guidelines system, manufacturing mill area analysis which includes steel-making, hot rolling, cold rolling, etc. The amount of current data in the system is around 2TB, and the ETL task deals with about 3GB data everyday, and the newly appended data are about 1GB. In addition, nearly 1700 static analytical reports are produced each day, and 1600 kinds of dynamic queries are provided synchronously.

At the same time, through many years' practice and researches, Shanghai Baosight has abstracted a set of effective business intelligence solutions for manufacturing industry. This solution is significant for product designing, quality management, cost management in the metallurgical manufacturing enterprise. Typically, the implement of business intelligence for metallurgical manufacturer consists of the following 6 processes that offer the logical segmentation of works, and check whether the project is built steadily. The following flow chart illustrates the overview and work flow for the development phrases of this methodology.

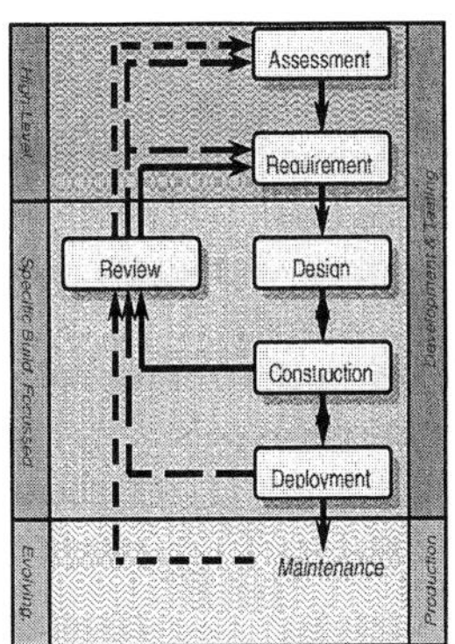

Fig. 2. The Methodology of the BI construction

1. Assessment
   Within this phrase the users' current situations and conditions should be studied. These factors will absolutely affect the data warehouse solutions. The target of phase is to analyze the users' problems and the methods to resolve them. The initial assessment should identify and clarify the targets, and the requirements for the research for clarifying the targets. This kind of assessment will result in the decision of starting, delaying or the canceling of a project.
2. Requirements investigation
   In this phrase, the project group gathers the high level requirements in the aspects of operation and information technology (IT), and collects the information required by the departments' targets. The result of this phrase is to submit a report, which identifies the business purpose, meanings, information requirements and the user interfaces. These requirements are also going to be used in other phases of the project and the design of data warehouse. In addition, the topic data model and data warehouse subject of enterprise level are accomplished in this phrase.
3. Design
   In the side of subject selection, the item group fasten on the collection detailed information request and designing of the scheme of the data flat roof

include data, process, application modeling. In this phrase, many kinds of methods of collect information and test, such as data modeling, processing modeling, meeting, prototype presentation are used.
Item group evaluate the technology scheme, business request and information request. Now, the difference between the IT scheme and the requested IT scheme is very outstanding. So it is advised that an appropriate data warehouse design and scheme should be applied.

4. Construction
This phrase includes creating physical databases and data gathering, application testing and code review. The manager of the data warehouse and the leader of end-user should know well the system. After successfully test, the data platform can be used.
5. Deployment and maintenance
In this phrase, the data warehouse and BI system can be displayed to business users. At the same time, trainings to the users should start too. After deployment, maintenance and users opinions should be considered.
6. Summary
In this phrase, the whole project should be evaluated, and it consists of three steps. The first is to sum up the success and lessons learned. Second is to check whether the configuration is realized as expected. If needed, plans should be changed. The third is to evaluate the influence and the benefit to the company.

2.2 Successful cases of Shanghai Baosteel's BI application

Shanghai Baosteel's BI involves knowledge not only data warehouse, mathematics and statistics, data mining and knowledge discovery, but also professional knowledge of metallurgy, automatic control, management, etc. These are the main characteristics of Shanghai Baosteel's BI application. And there are many successful cases in Shanghai Baosteel till now.

- The Production Administration System Based on Data Warehouse
  As a metallurgical manufacturing enterprise, rational production and proper administration is required in Shanghai Baosteel. According to the management requirement, in order to report the latest production status to the high level executives and get the latest guides from top managers, managers from all mills and functional departments must take part in the morning conference, which is presided by the general manager assistant or the vice general manager. Before the data warehouse system is built, the corresponding staff has to go to the production administration center everyday. And all conference information was organized by a Foxpro system with manual input, and the data mainly came from the phone and ERP system. The new production administration system then take the most advantages of enterprise data warehouse system. Based on the product information collected by data warehouse system, the system can automatically organize on Web daily information of production administration, material flow chart, quality analysis results, etc., to support the daily production administration and routine

executives' morning conference. And now with the online meeting system on Baosteel intranet, the managers can even take part in the conference and get all kinds of information in their offices. After the system has been put into production, it has won itself good reputation.

- Integrated Process Control Systems

  Quality is the life of the enterprise. In order to challenge the furious competition from the market, continuous improvement on the quality control is needed. The IPC systems have realized the improvement of the quality during the productions with lowest cost, and form the core ability of Shanghai Baosteel's QA management - Know How.

  As a supporting analysis system, IPC system assists the quality manager's control abilities during production processes, advances the technical person's statistical and analysis abilities, and provides more accurate, convenient and institutional approaches for the operational manipulators to inspect products. These systems integrate both high visualized functions and multi-layered data mining functions in a subtle way.

- The Quality Data Mining System

  The quality data mart was the first BI system that brought benefits for Shanghai Baosteel, and it plays a more and more important role in daily management. On one side, it provides daily reports, and the analysis functions as online quality analysis, capability changing analysis, quality exception analysis, finished product quality analysis, quality cost statistics, index data maintenance, integrate analysis, KIV-KOV modeling, and so on. On the other side the data mart supports well the quality data mining.

  Quality data mining system based on data warehouse is strongly aid to the metallurgy industry. There are many cases of data mining and knowledge discovery, such as reducing sampling of steel ST12, improve the bend strength of the hot-dip galvanized products of the steel ST06Z, material calculation design based on knowledge. In the case of reducing the sampling of steel ST12, the original specification required that it must do sampling at both head and tail. It cost very much manpower and equipment. After the analysis of some key indexes such as the bend strength, tensile strength, etc., some

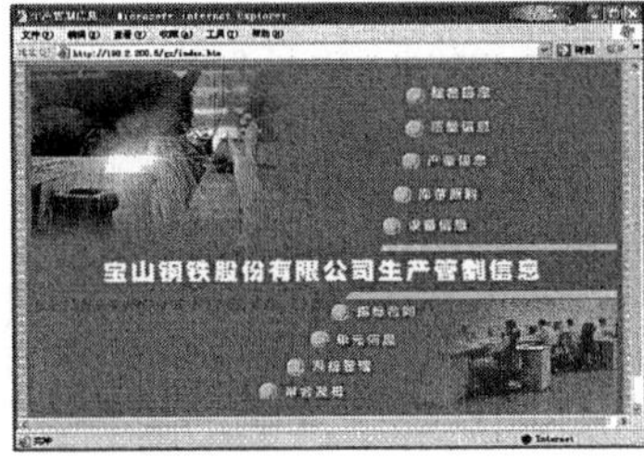

Fig. 3. The Production Administration System of Shanghai Baosteel.

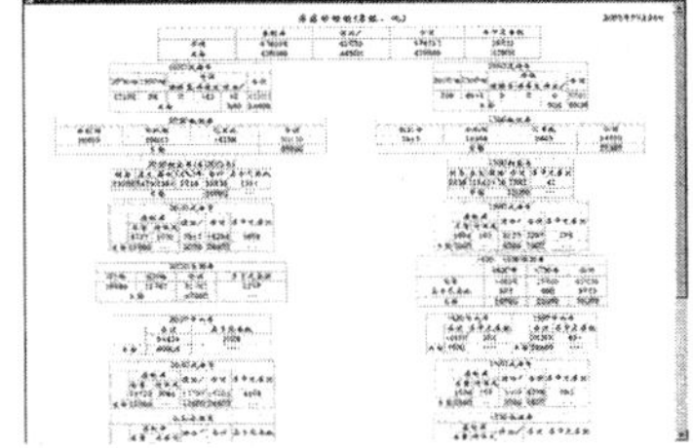

Fig. 4. The Web Page of the Storage Presentation.

similar analysis results of the head sampling and the tail sampling have been found out, and the tail sampling was a little bit worse. Through the reviews of some experts and testing practice, after the April of 2004 Shanghai Baosteel released a new operational specification to test only the tail sampling for steel ST12. As a result, it reduces cost RMB$2.60m annually.

– The Iron Ore Mixing System

  Raw material mixing is one of the most important jobs at the beginning of the steel-making. Shanghai Baosteel once faced many problems, such as how to evaluate a new ore that was not listed in the original ore mixing scheme? Which sintering ore mostly affect the final quality? Is there one scheme that can fit all different needs? Can we improve the quality of sintering mine while at the same time reduce the cost of sinter?

  Data mining in the Iron Ore Mixing System is to find out ways to meet the need of all kinds of sintering ores. The system forecasts the sinter quality through modeling, supports the mixing method with low cost, creates iron ore mixing knowledge database, and also provides friendly user interface.

  The data mining of iron ore mixing is in four steps: data preparation, iron ore evaluation with clustering analysis, modeling with neural networks, optimization. The evaluation results from the system are almost the same as those from experts. The forecasting accuracy reaches above 85

– A Defect Diagnosis Expert System

  The defect diagnosis is an important basis of reliability engineering, and is and important component and key technology of total quality control. Computer aided defect diagnosis can reduce and prevent the same defects from occurring repeatedly. It can also assist to provide information for decision-making.

  The system comes from experiments and massive data made by technicians after real accidents happen. It was developed with computer technologies, statistics analysis, data mining technologies, and artificial intelligence, and is consisted of data storage, statistics analysis, knowledge repository, and defect diagnosis. The system contains both high generalized visualized functions and multi-layered data mining functions.

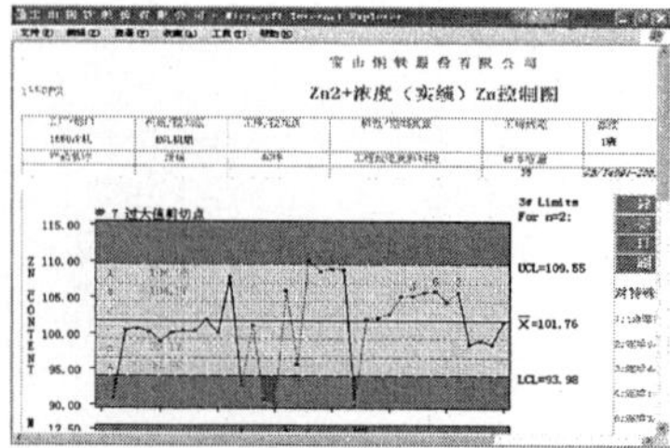

Fig. 5. The Quality Control of IPC.

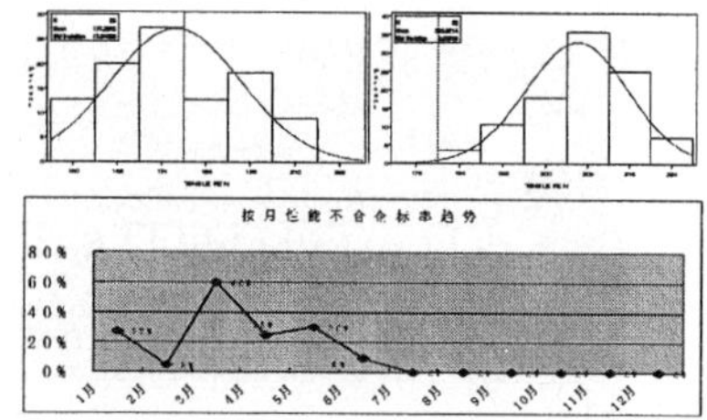

Fig. 6. Improvement the Bend Strength of the Steel ST06Z Products.

3 The Next Generation of Business Intelligence in Shanghai Baosteel

Shanghai Baosteel is the main body of Shanghai Baosteel Group. As Shanghai Baosteel Group became the Fortune's 2003 Global 500, the application of BI in Shanghai Baosteel will be strengthened and developed further. Followings are the tasks to perform.

3.1 Carrying out the Application in Department Level

Shanghai Baosteel will persist in developing its own characteristics of BI, and will take quality control and synthetic reports as its main goal, and will extend the combination of IPC, data warehouse and data mining. Quality control is the everlasting subject in manufacturing and is a durative market in which product design and development should be strengthened. Nowadays enterprises emphasize strategies particularly on process improvement in response to both daily improvements from client's requirements and drastic competitive market. In the industrial manufacturing, especially metallurgical manufacturing, there are many factors that cause quality problems, such as equipment invalidation, staff's carelessness, parameter abnormal, raw material differences, fluctuating settings. Especially in large steel enterprises with complicated business and technical flows, "Timely finding and forecasting exceptions, promptly controlling and quality analysis" is a necessity.

Therefore based on the quality control notion of 6 sigma, the application which based on data warehouse technologies, together with process control, fuzzy control, neural networks, expert system, data mining, can be applied in complicated working procedure as blast furnace, iron- making, steel-making, continuous casting, steel rolling. It is certainly the road to develop further the BI in department level.

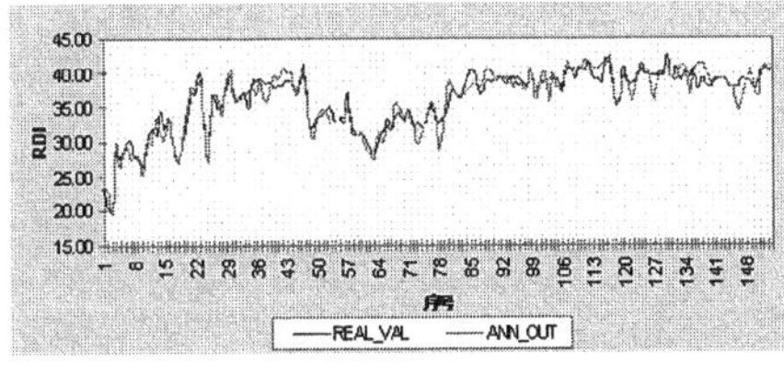

Fig. 7. The Forecast of the RDI in the Iron Ore.

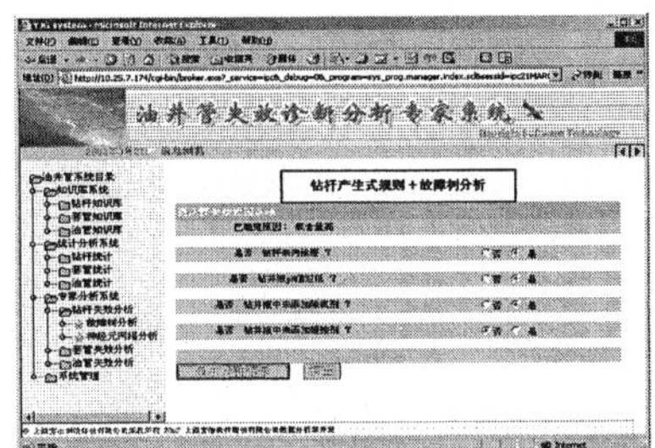

Fig. 8. The Diagnosis Expert System of the Steel Tube.

3.2 Strengthening Researches on Application of BI in Enterprise Level

In enterprise level there are many requirements, which can lead to data warehouse based EIS, Key Performance Indexes (KPI) system, etc.

KPI is a measurable management target which can set, sample, calculate and analyze the key parameters of the internal organization flow's input and output. It is a tool that can decompose the organizational strategic goal to the operational tasks, and is the basis of the organizational performance management. It can make the definite responsibilities to a department manager, and extend to the staff in the department. So building a definite credible KPI system is the sticking point for a good performance management.

3.3 Following up the Technical Tide of BI and Applying New Technologies into Industry

BI is a subject which overlaps many disciplines. Shanghai Baosteel and Shanghai Baosight are actively following up the technical tide of BI and researching new BI techniques in the metallurgical manufacturing among fields as stream data management, text (message) data mining, KPI practice in manufacturing, customized information based on position, knowledge management, etc.

Stream data management: Data which from L3 system (production control system) has the characteristics of stream data, so the knowledge of stream data management can be applied when IPC systems need to analyze timely and do data mining on the production line.

Text (message) data mining: Data communication between the ERP system and other information systems of Shanghai Baosteel are implemented by messages. All the messages have been extracted and loaded into data warehouse system. So how to use text mining techniques to analyze and solve exceptions quickly will be a new challenge.

The practice of KPI in manufacturing, customized information based on position, and knowledge management are new subjects and trends to provide extensive BI application in metallurgical manufacturing.

Meanwhile, Shanghai Baosight and Technology Center of Shanghai Baosteel are fully taking the advantage of the previous experience to develop the data mining tools which have independent knowledge property rights. Practical Miner from Technology Center has been popular in Shanghai Baosteel for years, while Shanghai Baosight is developing a data mining tool according to the standards of CWM1.1 and CORBA, and is expected to release early in 2005.

4 Conclusions

Shanghai Baosteel is leading in Chinese metallurgical manufacturing industry, while it is a leader in BI application as well. With many years' application and practice, it has benefited much from BI. And it will pursue an even further goal in BI in the near future.

References

1. Inmon Bill, Data mart does not equal data warehouse, DM Direct,Nov.1997.
2. Inmon W.H., Building the data warehouse (Second Edition), John Wiley & Sons, Inc, New York, 1996.
3. Ji Xiao, Yu Ge, Application of SAS software in the establishment of a data mart for quality analysis system in the metallurgical industry, Proc. of the 25th Annual SUGI Conf., USA. 2000. 4.
4. Kollios George, Gunopulos Dimitrios, Tsotras Vassilis J.On Indexing Mobile Objects. PODS 1999: 261-272.
5. Ji Xiao, Zhou Shichun, Data warehousing helps enterprise improve quality management, Proc. of the 26th Annual SUGI Conf., USA. 2001. 4.
6. Ji Xiao, Yu Ge, Bao Yubin, et al. Data warehousing and its application for procuct quality analysis in metallurgical enterprises, Proc. of 2000 Int. conf. on AMSMA, Guangzhou, China. 2000.
7. SAS Institute Inc., Rapid Warehousing Methodology. Cary, NC: SAS Institute Inc., 2000: 20-40.
8. Tang Haidong, Ji Xiao, Tracking your data warehouse using SAS software, Proc. of the 20th Annual SEUGI Conf., Paris. 2001. 12.
9. Theodoratos D, Sellis T., Designing data warehouses configuration, Proc. of the 23rd Intl. VLDB, 1997: 126-135.
10. Wang Daling, Bao Yubin, Ji Xiao, et al. Development of a data mining system supporting quality control in metallurgy enterprise, Proc. of 16th World Computer Congress 2000 on IIP, Beijing, China. 2000: 578-581.
11. Wang Daling, Bao Yubin, Ji Xiao, Wang Guoren, Integrated classification rule management system for data mining, Second Int. Conf. (WAIM 2001) Proceedings, 2001. 7. 122-129.
12. Wang Guoren, Yu Ge, Zhang Bin,et al. Schema integration architecture for multi-database systems, The 21st Annual Int. Computer Software and Application Conf. (IEEE Compsac97). Washington, DC, Aug. 1997.IEEE Computer Society, 1997: 200-203.
13. Widom J., Research problems in data warehousing, Proc. of the 4th Int. Conf. on Information and Knowledge Management (CIKM), Balthore MD USA. November 1995: 25-30.
14. Wu M C, Buchmann A. Encoded, bitmap indexing for data warehouses, Proc. of ICDE 1998: 220-230.
15. Yu Ge, Wang Guoren, Zheng Huaiyuan, et al. Transform more semantics from relational databases to object-oriented database. Proc. of the 4th Int. Conf. on Database Systems for Advanced Application (DASEFAA) Apr1995. Singapore. 300-307.

Conceptual Modelling – What and *Why* in Current Practice

Islay Davies[1], Peter Green[2], Michael Rosemann[1], and Stan Gallo[2]

[1] Centre for Information Technology Innovation
Queensland University of Technology
Brisbane, Australia
{ig.davies,m.rosemann}@qut.edu.au

[2] UQ Business School
University of Queensland
Ipswich, Australia
{p.green,s.gallo}@uq.edu.au

Abstract. Much research has been devoted over the years to investigating and advancing the techniques and tools used by analysts when they model. As opposed to what academics, software providers and their resellers promote as should be happening, the aim of this research was to determine whether practitioners still embraced conceptual modelling seriously. In addition, what are the most popular techniques and tools used for conceptual modelling? What are the major purposes for which conceptual modelling is used? The study found that the top six most frequently used modelling techniques and methods were ER diagramming, data flow diagramming, systems flowcharting, workflow modelling, RAD, and UML. However, the primary contribution of this study was the identification of the factors that uniquely influence the continued-use decision of analysts, viz., communication (using diagrams) to/from stakeholders, internal knowledge (lack of) of techniques, user expectations management, understanding models integration into the business, and tool/software deficiencies.

1 Introduction

The areas of business systems analysis, requirements analysis, and conceptual modelling are well-established research directions in academic circles. Comprehensive analytical work has been conducted on topics such as data modelling, process modelling, meta modelling, model quality, and the like. A range of frameworks and categorisations of modelling techniques have been proposed (*e.g.* [6, 9]). However, they mostly lack an empirical foundation. Thus, it is difficult to provide solid statements on the importance and potential impact of related research on the actual practice of conceptual modelling.

More recently, Wand and Weber [13, p. 364] assume "the importance of conceptual modelling" and they state "Practitioners report that conceptual modelling is difficult and that it often falls into disuse within their organizations." Unfortunately, anecdotal feedback to us from information systems (IS) practitioners confirmed largely the assertion of Wand and Weber [13]. Accordingly, as researchers involved in attempting to advance the theory of conceptual modelling in organisations, we were concerned to determine that practitioners still found conceptual modelling useful and that they were indeed still performing conceptual modelling as part of their business systems analysis processes. Moreover, if practitioners still found modelling useful, why

P. Atzeni et al. (Eds.): ER 2004, LNCS 3288, pp. 30–42, 2004.

did they find it useful and what were the major factors that inhibited the wider use of modelling in their projects. In this way, the research that we were performing would be relevant for the practice of information systems development (See the IS Relevance debate on ISWorld, February 2001).

Hence, the research in this paper is motivated in several ways. First, we want to obtain empirical data that conceptual modelling is indeed being performed in IS practice in Australia. Such data will give overall assurance to the practical relevance of the research that we perform in conceptual modelling. Second, we want to find out what are the principal tools, techniques, and purposes for which conceptual modelling is performed currently in Australia. In this way, researchers can obtain valuable information to help them direct their research towards aspects of conceptual modelling that contribute most to practice. Finally, we were motivated to perform this study so that we could gather and analyse data on major problems and benefits *unique* to the task of conceptual modelling in practice.

So, this research aims to provide current insights into actual modelling practice. The underlying research question is "Do practitioners actually use conceptual modelling in practice?" The derived and more detailed questions are:

What are popular tools and techniques used for conceptual modelling in Australia?
What are the purposes of modelling?
What are major problems and benefits *unique* to modelling?

In order to provide answers for these questions, an empirical study using a web-based questionnaire has been designed. The goal was to determine what modelling practices are being used in business, as opposed to what academics, software providers and their resellers believe should be used. In summary, we found that the current state of usage of business systems/conceptual modelling in Australia is: ER diagramming, data flow diagramming, systems flowcharting, and workflow modelling being most frequently used for database design and management, software development, documenting and improving business processes. Moreover, this modelling work is supported in most cases by the use of Visio (in some version) as an automated tool. Furthermore, planned use of modelling techniques and tools into the short-term future appears to be expected to reduce significantly compared to current usage levels.

The remainder of the paper unfolds in the following manner. The next section reviews the related work in terms of empirical data in relation to conceptual modelling practice. The third section explains briefly the instrument and methodology used. Then, an overview of the quantitative results of the survey is given. The fifth section presents succinctly the results of the analysis of the textual data on the problems and benefits of modelling. The last section concludes and gives an indication of further work planned.

2 Related Work

Over the years, much work has been done on how to do modelling – the quality, correctness, completeness, goodness of representation, understandability, differences between novice and expert modellers, and many other aspects (*e.g.*, [7]). Comparatively little empirical work however has been undertaken on modelling in practice. Floyd [3] and Necco *et al.* [8] conducted comprehensive empirical work into the use of modelling techniques in practice but that work is now considerably dated. Batra and Marakas [1] attempted to address this problem of a lack of current empirical evidence however their work focused on comparing the perspectives of the academic and practitioner communities regarding the applications of conceptual data modelling. Indeed, these authors simply reviewed the academic and practitioner literatures without actually collecting primary data on the issue. Moreover, their work is now dated. However, it is interesting that they (p. 189) observe "there is a general lack of any substantive evidence, anecdotal or empirical, to suggest that the concepts are being widely used in the applied design environment." Batra and Marakas [1, p. 190] state that "Researchers have not attempted to conduct case or field studies to gauge the cost-benefits of enterprise-wide conceptual data modelling (CDM)." This research has attempted to address the problems alluded to by Batra and Marakas [1].

Iivari [4] provided some data on these questions in a Finnish study of the perceptions of effectiveness of CASE tools. However, he found the adoption rate of CASE tools by developers in organisations very low (and presumably the extent of conceptual modelling to be low as well). More recently, Persson and Stirna [10] noted the problem, however, their work was limited in that it was only an exploratory study into practice. Most recently, Chang *et al.* [2] conducted 11 interviews with experienced consultants in order to explore the perceived advantages and disadvantages of business process modelling. This descriptive study did not, however, investigate the critical success factors of process modelling. Sedera *et al.* [11] have conducted three case studies to determine a process modeling success model, however they have not yet reported on a planned empirical study to test this model. Furthermore, the studies by Chang *et al.* [2] and Sedera *et al.* [11] are limited to the area of process modeling.

3 Methodology

This study was conducted in the form of a web-based survey issued with the assistance of the Australian Computer Society (ACS) to its members. The survey consisted of seven pages[1]. The *first page* explained the objectives of our study. It also highlighted the available incentive, *i.e.,* free participation in one of five workshops on business process modelling. The *second page* asked for the purpose of the modelling activities. In total, 17 purposes (*e.g.,* database design and management, software development) were made available. The respondents were asked to evaluate the relevance of each of these purposes using a five-point Likert scale ranging from 1 (not relevant) to 5 (highly relevant). The *third page* asked for the modelling techniques[2] used by the respondent. It provided a list of 18 different modelling techniques ranging from data flow diagram and ER diagrams, to the various IDEF standards, up to UML. For each modelling technique, the participants had to provide information about the past, current and future use of the modelling technique. It was possible to differentiate between infrequent and frequent use. Furthermore, participants could indicate whether they knew the technique or did not use it at all. It was possible also to add further modelling techniques that they used. The *fourth page* was related to the modelling tools. Following the same structure as for the modelling technique, a list of 24 modelling tools was provided. A hyperlink provided a reference to the homepage of each tool provided. It was clarified also if a tool had been known under a different name

---

1 A copy of the survey pages is available from the authors on request.

2 'Technique' here is used as an umbrella term referring to the constructs of the technique, their rules of construction, and the heuristics and guidelines for refinement.

(*e.g.*, Designer2000 for the Oracle9i Developer Suite). The *fifth page* explored qualitative issues. Participants were asked to list major problems and issues they had experienced with modelling as well as perceived key success factors. On the *sixth page*, demographic data was collected. This data included person type (practitioner, academic or student), years of experience in business systems analysis and modelling, working area (business or IT), training in modelling and the size of the organisation. The *seventh page* allowed contact details for the summarised results of the study and the free workshop to be entered. The instrument was piloted with 25 members of two research centres as well as with a selected group of practitioners. Minor changes were made based on the experiences within this pilot.

A major contribution of this paper is an examination of the data gathered through the *fifth* page of the survey. This section of the survey asked respondents to list critical success factors for them in the use of conceptual modelling and problems or issues they encountered in successfully undertaking modelling in their organisations. The phenomena that responses to these questions allowed us to investigate were why do we continue/discontinue to use a technical method (implemented using a technological tool) – conceptual modelling. To analyse these phenomena, we used the following procedure:

1. What responses confirm the factors we already know about in regard to these phenomena; and
2. What responses are identifying new factors that are unique to the domain of conceptual modelling?

To achieve step 1, we performed a review of the current thinking and literature in the areas of adoption and continued use of a technology. Then, using Nvivo 2, one researcher classified the textual comments, where relevant, according to these known factors. This researcher's classification was then reviewed and confirmed with a second researcher. The factors identified from the literature and used in this first phase of the process are summarised and defined in Table 1.

After step 1, there remained factors that did not readily fit into one or other of the known factor categories. These unclassified responses had the potential to provide us with insight on factors unique and important to the domain of conceptual modelling. However, the question was how to derive this information in a relatively objective and unbiased manner from the textual data. We used a new state-of-the-art textual content analysis tool called Leximancer[3]. Using this tool, we identified from the unclassified text five new factors specific to conceptual modelling. Subsequently, one researcher again classified the remaining responses using these newly identified factors. His classification was reviewed and confirmed by a second researcher. Finally, the relative importance of each of the new factors was determined.

3.1 Why Use Leximancer?

The Leximancer system allows its users to analyse large amounts of text quickly. The tool performs this analysis both systematically and graphically by creating a map of the constructs – the document map – that are displayed in such a manner that links to related subtext may be subsequently explored. Each of the words on the document map represents a concept that was identified. The concept is placed on the map in

[3] For more information on Leximancer, see www.leximancer.com

Table 1. Summary of Factors identified for initial analysis

Factor	Definition	Source(s)
Relative Advantage	The degree to which adopting/using the technique is perceived as being better than using the practise it supersedes.	Karahanna *et al,* [5]
Image	The degree to which adoption/usage of the technique is perceived to enhance ones image or status.	Karahanna *et al,* [5]
Compatibility	The degree to which adopting the technique is compatible with the individual's job responsibilities and value system.	Tan and Teo, [12]
Complexity	The degree to which using a particular technique is free from effort.	Karahanna *et al,* [5]
Trialability	The degree to which one can experiment with the technique on a limited basis before making an adoption or rejection decision.	Karahanna *et al,* [5]
Risk	The degree of perceived risk that accompanies the adoption of the technique.	Tan and Teo, [12]
Visibility	The degree to which the technique is visible within the organisation.	Karahanna *et al,* [5]
Results Demonstrability	The degree to which results of adopting/using the technique are observable and communicable to others.	Karahanna *et al,* [5]
Subjective Norms	Generated by the normative beliefs that a respondent attributes to what relevant others (colleagues/peers/respected management) expect them to do with respect to adopting the technique as well as their motivation to comply with those beliefs.	Karahanna *et al,* [5]
Self Efficacy	Self-confidence in a participant's own ability to perform a behaviour.	Tan and Teo, [12]
Facilitating Conditions	Availability of and ease of access to, technological infrastructure and support.	Tan and Teo, [12]
Internalisations	Degree to which decisions are motivated by accepting information from expert sources and integrating it into ones cognitive system.	Karahanna *et al,* [5]
Identification	Decisions resulting from feeling some bond with a likeable source.	Karahanna *et al,* [5]
Compliance	Degree of influence that is produced by a powerful source having control over the respondent in the forms of rewards and punishments.	Karahanna *et al,* [5]
Top management support	Degree of support for the project from middle and upper management of the organisation.	
Communication Issues	Degree to which the decisions or attitudes were affected by communications problems between the respondents and key stakeholders within the organisation.	

proximity of other concepts in the map through a derived combination of the direct and indirect relationships between those concepts. Essentially, the Leximancer system is a machine-learning technique based on the Bayesian approach to prediction. The procedure used for this is a self-ordering optimisation technique and does not use neural networks. Once the optimal weighted set of words is found for each concept, it is used to predict the concepts present in fragments of related text. In other words, each concept has other concepts that it attracts (or is highly associated with contextually) as well as concepts that it repels (or is highly disassociated with contextually). The relationships are measured by the weighted sum of the number of times two concepts are found in the same 'chunk'. An algorithm is used to weight them and determine the confidence and relevancy of the terms to others in a specific chunk and across chunks.

Leximancer was selected for this qualitative data analysis for several reasons:

- Its ability to derive the main concepts within text and their relative importance using a scientific, objective algorithm;
- Its ability to identify the strengths between concepts (how often they co-occur) – centrality of concepts;
- Its ability to assist the researcher in applying grounded theory analysis to a textual dataset;
- Its ability to assist in visually exploring textual information for related themes to create new ideas or theories; and
- Its ability to assist in identifying similarities in the context in which the concepts occur – contextual similarity.

4 Survey Results and Discussion

From 674 individuals who started to fill out the survey, 370 actually completed the entire survey, which leads to a completion rate of 54.8%. Moreover, of the 12,000 members of the ACS, 1,567 indicated in their most recent membership profiles that they were interested in conceptual modelling/business systems analysis. Accordingly, our 370 responses indicate a relevant response rate of 23.6%, which is very acceptable for a survey. Moreover, we offered participation in one of five seminars on business process modelling free of charge as an inducement for members to participate. This offer was accepted by 186 of 370 respondents. Corresponding with the nature of the ACS as a professional organisation, 87% of the participants were practitioners. The remaining respondents were academics (6%) and students (7%). It is also not a surprise that 85% of the participants characterised themselves as an IT service person while only 15% referred to themselves as a businessperson or end user.

Sixty-eight percent of the respondents indicated that they gained their knowledge in Business Systems Analysis from University. Further answers were TAFE (Technical and Further Education) (6%), ACS (3%). Twenty-three percent indicated that they did not have any formal training in Business Systems Analysis. Forty percent of the respondents indicated that they have less than five years experience with modelling. Thirty-eight percent have between 5 and 15 years of experience. A significant proportion, 22%, has more than 15 years of experience with modelling. These figures indicate that the average expertise of the respondents is supposedly quite high. Twenty-eight percent of respondents indicated that they worked in firms employing less than 50 people, most likely small software consulting firms. However, a quarter of the respondents worked in organisations with 1000 or less employees. So, by Australian standards, they would be involved in software projects of reasonable size.

We were concerned to obtain information in three principle areas of conceptual modelling in Australia *viz.*, what techniques are used currently in practice, what tools are used for modelling in practice, and what are the purposes for which conceptual modelling is used.

Table 2 presents from the data the top six most frequently used modelling techniques. It describes the usage of techniques as *not known or not used*, *infrequently used* (which in the survey instrument was defined as used less than five times per week), and *frequently used*. The table clearly demonstrates that the top six most frequently used (used 5 or more times a week) *techniques* are ER diagramming, data flow diagramming, systems flowcharting, workflow modelling (range of workflow modelling techniques), RAD, and UML. It is significant to note that even though object-oriented analysis, design, and programming has been the predominant paradigm for systems development over the last decade 64 percent of respondents either did not know or did not use UML. While not every conceptual modelling technique available was named in the survey, the eighteen techniques used were selected based on their popularity reported in prior literature. It is interesting again to note that approximately 40 percent of respondents (at least) do either not know or use any of the 18 techniques named in the survey.

Table 2. Top six modelling techniques most frequently used

Description	Not Known/ Not Used	%	Infrequently Used	%	Frequently Used	%
ER diagram	154	42%	70	19%	146	39%
Data flow diagram	152	41%	91	25%	127	34%
System flowcharts	153	43%	94	26%	112	31%
Workflow modelling	187	52%	88	24%	86	24%
RAD (rapid application development)	227	63%	55	15%	79	22%
UML (unified modelling language)	232	64%	60	16%	72	20%

Moreover, while not explicitly reported in Table 2, this current situation of non-usage appears to be set to increase into the short-term future (next 12 months) as the planned frequent use of the top four techniques is expected to drop to less than half its current usage, *viz.*, ER diagramming (17 percent), data flow diagramming (15 percent), systems flowcharting (10 percent), and workflow modelling (12 percent). Furthermore, no increase in the intention to use any of the other techniques was reported, to balance this out. Perhaps, this short-term trend reflects the perception that the current general downturn in the IT industry will persist into the future. Accordingly, respondents perceive a significant reduction of new developmental work requiring business systems modelling in the short-term future. It may also just reflect the lack of planning of future modelling activities.

Our work was also interested in what tools were used to perform the conceptual modelling work that was currently being undertaken. Table 3 presents the top six most frequently used tools when performing business systems analysis and design. The data is reported using the same legend as that used for Table 2.

Again, while not every conceptual modelling tool available was named in the survey, the twenty-four tools were selected based on their popularity reported in prior literature. Table 3 clearly indicates that Visio (58 percent – both infrequent and frequent use) is the preferred tool of choice for business systems modelling currently. This result is not surprising as the top four most frequently used techniques are well supported by Visio (in its various versions). A long way second in frequent use is Rational Rose (19 percent – both infrequent and frequent use) reflecting the current level of use of object-oriented analysis and design techniques. Again, at least 40 percent of respondents (approximately) do either not know or use any of the 24 tools named in the survey – even a relatively simple tool like Flowcharter or Visio.

Table 3. Top six most frequently used tools

Description	Not Known/ Not Used	%	Infrequently Used	%	Frequently Used	%
Visio	150	42%	57	16%	148	42%
Rational Rose	285	81%	33	9%	36	10%
Oracle9i Developer Suite	302	85%	31	9%	21	6%
iGrafx FlowCharter	284	80%	49	14%	22	6%
AllFusion ERwin Data Modeler	333	94%	12	3%	10	3%
WorkFlow Modeler	346	97%	2	1%	7	2%

Moreover, while not explicitly reported in Table 3, into the short-term future (next 12 months), the planned frequent use of the top two tools is expected to drop significantly from their current usage levels, *viz.*, Visio (21 percent) and Rational Rose (8 percent) with no real increase reported for planned use of other tools to compensate for this drop. Again, this trend in planned tool usage appears to reflect the fact that respondents expect a significant reduction in new developmental work requiring business systems modelling in the short-term future.

Business systems modelling (conceptual modelling) must be performed for some purpose. Accordingly, we were interested in obtaining data on the various purposes for which people might be undertaking modelling. Using a five-point Likert scale (where 5 indicates Very Frequent Use), Table 4 presents (in rank order from the highest to the lowest score) the average score for purpose of use from the respondents.

Table 4. Average use score for modelling purpose (in rank order)

Description	Average Score	Standard Deviation
Database design and management	3.9	1.2
Improvement of internal business processes	3.7	1.2
Software development	3.7	1.2
Business process documentation	3.7	1.2
Workflow management	3.4	1.2
Improvement of collaborative business processes	3.4	1.3
Design of Enterprise Architecture	3.4	1.3
Change management	3.3	1.3
Knowledge management	3.2	1.3
End user training	3.1	1.3
Software configuration	3.1	1.3
Software selection	2.9	1.3
Certification / quality management	2.8	1.3
Activity-based costing	2.6	1.4
Human resource management	2.6	1.3
Auditing	2.5	1.3
Simulation	2.5	1.3

Table 4 indicates that database design and management remains the highest average *purpose* for use of modelling techniques. This fact links to the earlier result of ER diagramming being the most frequently used modelling technique. Moreover, software development as a purpose would support the high usage of data flow diagramming and ER diagramming noted earlier. Indeed, the relatively highly regarded purposes of documenting and improving business processes, and managing workflows, would support further the relatively high usage of workflow modelling and flowcharting indicated earlier. The more specialised tasks like identifying activities for activity-based costing and internal control purposes in auditing appear to be relatively infrequently used purposes for modelling. This fact however may derive from the type of population that was used for the survey, *viz.*, members of the Australian Computer Society.

5 Textual Analysis Results and Discussion

Nine hundred and eighty (980) individual comments were received across the questions on critical success factors and problems/issues for modelling. Using the known factors (Table 1) influencing continued use of new technologies in firms, Table 5 shows the classification of the 980 comments after phase 1 of the analysis using Nvivo.

Table 5. Results of classification by key factors influencing continued use (after phase 1)

Key	Percentage	Totals
Relative Advantage/Usefulness	45%	441
Complexity	8%	74
Compatibility	7%	69
Internalisations	6%	54
Top Management Support	5%	48
Facilitating Conditions	4%	42
Image	0%	0
Trialability	0%	4
Risk	1%	11
Visibility	0%	2
Results Demonstrability	1%	5
Subjective Norms	2%	22
Self-Efficacy	1%	14
Identification	0%	2
Compliance	0%	2
Communication Issues	3%	25
Unclassified	***17%***	***165***
Total (All records)	**100.00%**	**980**

Clearly, relative advantage (disadvantage)/usefulness from the perspective of the analyst was the major driving factor influencing the decision to continue (discontinue) modelling. Does conceptual modelling (and/or its supporting technology) take too much time, make my job easier, make my job harder, and make it easier/harder for me to elicit/confirm requirements with users? Such comments typically contributed to this factor. Furthermore, it is not surprising to see that complexity of the method and/or tool, compatibility of the method and/or tool with the responsibilities of my job, the views of "experts", and top management support were other major factors driving analysts' decisions on continued use. Prior literature had told us to expect these results, in particular, the key importance of top management support to the continued successful use of such key business planning and quality assurance mechanisms as conceptual modelling for systems.

However, nearly one-fifth of the comments remained unclassified. Were there any new, important factors unique to the conceptual modelling domain contained in this data? Fig. 1 shows a document (concept) map produced by Leximancer from the unclassified comments.

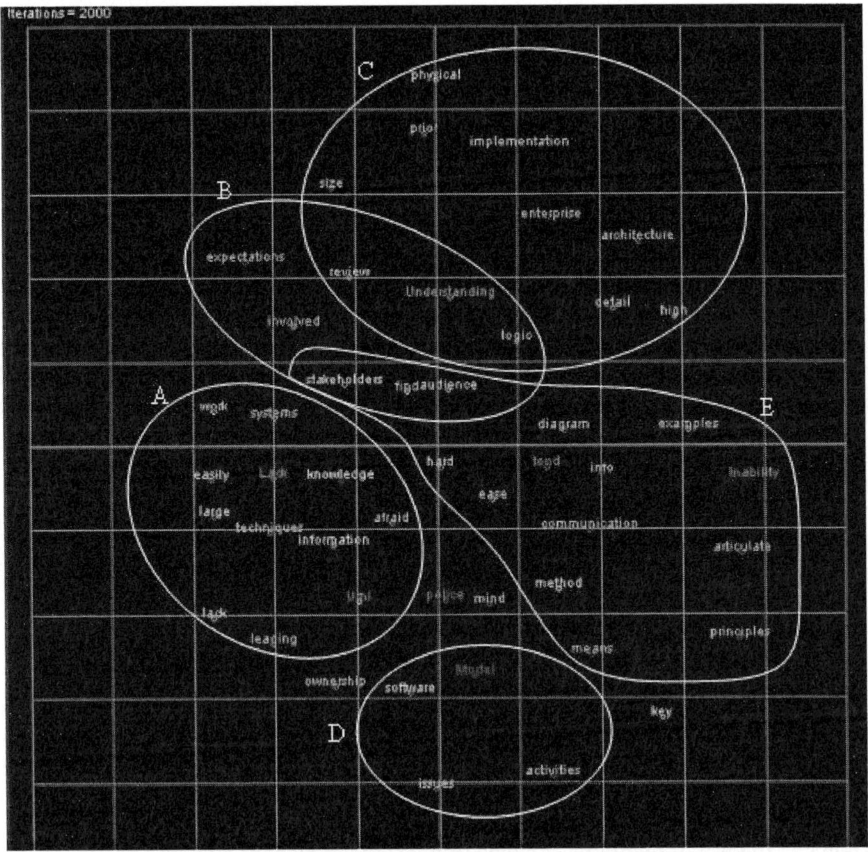

Fig. 1. Concept map produced by Leximancer on the unclassified comments

Five factors were identified from this map using the centrality of concepts and the relatedness of concepts to each other within identifiable 'chunks'. While the resolution of the Leximancer generated concept map (Fig. 1) may be difficult to read on its own here, the concepts (terms) depicted are referred to within the discussion of the relevant factors below.

A. Internal Knowledge (Lack of) of Techniques
This group centred on such concepts as knowledge, techniques, information, large, easily and lack. Related concepts were work, systems, afraid, UML and leading. Accordingly, we used these concepts to identify this factor as the degree of direct/indirect knowledge (or lack of) in relation to the use of effective modelling techniques. Highlighted inadequacies raise issues of the modeller's skill level and questions of insufficient training.

B. User Expectations Management
This group centred on such concepts as expectations, stakeholders, audience and review. Understanding, involved, logic and find were related concepts. Consequently, we used these items to identify this factor as issues arising from the need to manage the expectations of users as to what they expect conceptual modelling to do for them and to produce. In other words, the analyst must ensure that the stakeholders/audience for the outputs of conceptual modelling have a realistic understanding of what will be achieved. Continued (discontinued) use of conceptual modelling may be influenced by difficulties experienced (or expected) with users over such issues as acceptance, understanding and communication of the outcomes of the modelling techniques.

C. Understanding the Models Integration into the Business
This group centred on understanding, enterprise, high, details, architecture, logic, physical, implementation and prior. Accordingly, we identified a factor as the degree to which decisions are affected by stakeholder/modeller's perceived understanding (or lack of) in relation to the models integration into business processes (initial and ongoing). In other words, for the user, to what extent do the current outputs of the modelling process integrate with the existing business processes and physical implementations to support the goals of the overall enterprise architecture?

D. Tool/Software Deficiencies
This group was focused on such concepts as software, issues, activities, and model. Subsequently, a factor was identified as the degree to which decisions are affected by issues relating directly to the perceived lack of capability of the software and/or the tool design.

E. Communication (Using Diagrams) to/from Stakeholders
This final group involved such concepts as diagram, information, ease, communication, method, examples, and articulate. Related concepts were means, principals, inability, hard, audience, find, and stakeholders. From these key concepts, we deduced a factor as the degree to which diagrams can facilitate effective communication between analysts and key stakeholders in the organisation. In other words, to what extent can the use of diagrams enhance (hinder) the explanation to, and understanding by, the stakeholders of the situation being modelled?

Using these five new factors, we revisited the unclassified comments and, using the same dual coder process as before, we confirmed a classification for those outstanding comments easily. Table 6 presents this classification and the relative importance of those newly identified factors.

Table 6. Relative importance of factors unique to conceptual modelling

Key	Percentage	Total
Communication (Diagrams) to/from Stakeholders	28%	46
Internal Knowledge (Lack of) of Techniques	27%	44
User Expectations Management	18%	30
Understanding models integration into the business	17%	28
Tool/Software deficiencies	10%	17
Total:	100%	**165**

As can be seen from Table 6, communication using diagrams and internal knowledge (lack of) of the modelling techniques are major issues specific to the continued use of modelling in organisations. To a lesser degree, properly managing users' expectations of modelling and ensuring users understand how the outcomes of a specific modelling task support the overall enterprise systems architecture are important to the continued use of conceptual modelling. Deficiencies in software tools that support conceptual modelling frustrate the analyst's work occasionally.

6 Conclusions and Future Work

This paper has reported the results of a survey conducted nationally in Australia on the status of conceptual modelling. It achieved 370 responses and a relevant response rate of 23.6 percent. The study found that the top six most frequently used modelling techniques were ER diagramming, data flow diagramming, systems flowcharting, workflow modelling, RAD, and UML. Furthermore, it found that clearly Visio is the preferred tool of choice for business systems modelling currently. Rational Rose and Oracle Developer suite were a long way second in frequent use. Database design and management remains the highest average *purpose* for use of modelling techniques. This fact links to the result of ER diagramming being the most frequently used modelling technique. Moreover, software development as a purpose would support the high usage of data flow diagramming and ER diagramming. A major contribution of this study is the analysis of textual data concerning critical success factors and problems/issues in the continued use of conceptual modelling. Clearly, relative advantage (disadvantage)/usefulness from the perspective of the analyst was the major driving factor influencing the decision to continue (discontinue) modelling. Moreover, using a state-of-the-art textual analysis and machine-learning software package called Leximancer, this study identified five factors that uniquely influence the continued use decision of analysts, *viz.*, communication (using diagrams) to/from stakeholders, internal knowledge (lack of) of techniques, user expectations management, understanding models integration into the business, and tool/software deficiencies.

The results of this work are limited in several ways. Although every effort was taken to mitigate potential limitations, it still suffers from the usual problems with surveys, most notably, potential bias in the responses and lack of generalisability of the results to other people and settings. More specifically, in relation to the qualitative analysis, even though a form of dual coding (with confirmation) was employed, there still remains subjectivity in the classification of comments. Furthermore, while the members of the research team all participated, the identification of the factors using the Leximancer document map and the principles of relatedness and centrality remains arguable.

We intend to extend this work in two ways. First, we will analyse the data further investigating cross-tabulations and correlations between the quantitative data and the qualitative results reported in this paper. For example, do the factors influencing the continued-use decision vary by the demographic dimensions of source of formal training, years of modelling experience, and the like. Second, we want to administer the survey in other countries (Sweden and Netherlands already) to address the issues of lack of generalisability in the current results and cultural differences in conceptual modelling.

References

1. Batra, D., Marakas, G. M.: Conceptual data modelling in theory and practice. European Journal of Information Systems, Vol. 4 Nr. 3 (1995) 185-193
2. Chang, S., Kesari, M., Seddon, P.: A content-analytic study of the advantages and disadvantages of process modelling. 14th Australasian Conference on Information Systems. Eds.: J. Burn., C. Standing, P. Love. Perth (2003)
3. Floyd, C.: A comparative evaluation of system development methods. Information Systems Design Methodologies: Improving the Practice. North-Holland, Amsterdam (1986) 19-37
4. Iivari, J.: Factors affecting perceptions of CASE Effectiveness. IEEE Softwarc. Vol. 4 (1995) 143-158
5. Karahanna, E., Straub, D. W., Chervany, N. L.: Information Technology Adoption Across Time: A Cross-Sectional Comparison of Pre-Adoption and Post-Adoption Beliefs. MIS Quarterly, Vol. 23 Nr. 2 (1999) 183-213
6. Karam, G. M., Casselman, R. S.: A cataloging framework for software development methods. IEEE Computer, Feb., (1993) 34-46
7. Lindland, O. I., Sindre, G., Solvberg, A.: Understanding Quality in Conceptual Modeling. IEEE Software, March, (1994) 42-49
8. Necco, C. R., Gordon, C. L., Tsai, N. W.: Systems analysis and design: Current practices. MIS Quarterly, Dec., (1987) 461-475
9. Olle, T. W., Hagelstein, J., Macdonald, I. G., Rolland, C., Sol, H. G., M.van Assche, F. J., Verrijn-Stuart, A. A.: Information Systems Methodologies: A Framework for Understanding. Addison-Wesley, Wokingham (1991)
10. Persson, A., Stirna, J.: Why Enterprise Modelling? An Explorative Study Into Current Practice. 13th Conference on Advanced Information Systems Engineering, Switzerland (2001) 465-468
11. Sedera, W., Gable, G., Rosemann, M., Smyth, R.: A success model for business process modeling: findings from a multiple case study. 8th Pacific Asia Conference on Information Systems (PACIS'04). Eds.: Liang T.P., Zheng, Z.: Shanghai (2004)
12. Tan, M., Teo, T. S. H.: Factors Influencing the Adoption of Internet Banking. Journal of the Association for Information Systems, Vol. 1 (2000) 1-43
13. Wand, Y., Weber, R.: Research Commentary: Information Systems and Conceptual Modeling – A Research Agenda. Information Systems Research. Vol. 13 Nr. 4 (2002) 363-376.

Entity-Relationship Modeling *Re*-revisited

Don Goelman[1] and Il-Yeol Song[2]

[1] Department of Computer Science
Villanova University
Villanova, PA 19085
don.goelman@villanova.edu

[2] College of Information Science and Technology
Drexel University
Philadelphia, PA 19104
song@drexel.edu

Abstract. Since its introduction, the Entity-Relationship (ER) model has been the vehicle of choice in communicating the structure of a database schema in an implementation-independent fashion. Part of its popularity has no doubt been due to the clarity and simplicity of the associated pictorial Entity-Relationship Diagrams ("ERD's") and to the dependable mapping it affords to a relational database schema. Although the model has been extended in different ways over the years, its basic properties have been remarkably stable. Even though the ER model has been seen as pretty well "settled," some recent papers, notably [4] and [2 (from whose paper our title is derived)], have enumerated what their authors consider serious shortcomings of the ER model. They illustrate these by some interesting examples. We believe, however, that those examples are themselves questionable. In fact, while not claiming that the ER model is perfect, we do believe that the overhauls hinted at are probably not necessary and possibly counterproductive.

1 Introduction

Since its inception [5], the Entity-Relationship (ER) model has been the primary approach for presenting and communicating a database schema at the "conceptual" level (i.e., independent of its subsequent implementation), especially by means of the associated Entity-Relationship Diagram (ERD). There's also a fairly standard method for converting it to a relational database schema. In fact, if the ER model is in some sense "correct," then the associated relational database schema should be in pretty good normal form [15]. Of course, there have been some suggested extensions to Chen's original ideas (e.g., specialization and aggregation as in [10, 19]), some different approaches for capturing information in the ERD, and some variations on the mapping to the relational model, but the degree of variability has been relatively minor. One reason for the remarkable robustness and popularity of the approach is no doubt the wide appreciation for the simplicity of the diagram. Consequently, the desirability of incorporating additional features in the ERD must be weighed against the danger of overloading it with so much information that it loses its visual power in communicating the structure of a database. In fact, the model's versatility is also evident in its relatively straightforward mappability to the newer Object Data Model [7]. Now admittedly an industrial strength ERD reflecting an actual enterprise would necessarily be some order of magnitude more complex than even the production numbers in standard texts [e.g., 10]. However, this does not weaken the ability of a simple ERD to

P. Atzeni et al. (Eds.): ER 2004, LNCS 3288, pp. 43–54, 2004.

capture local pieces of the enterprise, nor does it lessen the importance of ER-type thinking in communicating a conceptual model.

Quite recently, however, both Camps and Badia have demonstrated [4, and 2 (from whose paper the title of this one is derived)] some apparent shortcomings in the ER model, both in the model itself and in the processes of conversion to the relational model and its subsequent normalization. They have illustrated these problems through some interesting examples. They also make some recommendations for improvements, based on these examples. However, while not claiming that the ER model can be all things to all users, we believe that the problems presented in the examples described in those two papers are due less to the model and more to its incorrect application.

Extending the ERD to represent complex multi-relation constraints or constraints at the attribute level are interesting research topics, but are not always desirable. We claim that representing them would clutter the ERD as a conceptual model at the enterprise level; complex constraints would be better specified in a textual or language-oriented format than at the ERD level.

The purpose of this paper is to take these examples as a starting point to discuss the possible shortcomings of the ER model and the necessity, or lack thereof, for modifying it in order to address them. We therefore begin by reviewing and analyzing those illustrations. Section 2 describes and critiques Camps' scenarios; Section 3 does Badia's. Section 4 considers some related issues, most notably a general design principle only minimally offered in the ER model. Section 5 concludes our paper.

2 The Camps Paper

In [4], the author begins by describing an apparently simple enterprise. It has a straightforward ERD that leads to an equally straightforward relational database schema. But Camps then escalates the situation in stages, to the point where the ER model is not currently able to accommodate the design, and where normalizing the associated relational database schema is also unsatisfying. Since we are primarily concerned with problems attributed to the ER model, we will concentrate here on that aspect of the paper. However, the normalization process at this point is closely tied to that model, so we will include some discussion of it as well. We now give a brief recapitulation, with commentary.

At first, Camps considers an enterprise with four ingredients: **Dealer**, **Product**, **State**, and **Concession**, where **Concession** is a ternary relationship among the other three, implemented as entity types. Each ingredient has attributes with fairly obvious semantics, paraphrased here: d-Id, d-Address; p-Id, p-Type; s-Id, s-Capital; and c-Date. The last attribute's semantics represents the date on which a given state awards a concession to a given dealer for a given product. As for functional dependencies, besides the usual ones, we are told that for a given state/product combination, there can only be one dealer. Thus, a minimal set of dependencies is as follows:

{s-Id, p-Id} → d-Id
{s-Id, p-Id} → c-Date
d-Id → d-Address (A)
p-Id → p-Type
s-Id → s-Capital

An ERD for this is given in Figure 1 (attributes are eliminated in the figures, for the sake of clarity), and the obvious relational database schema is as follows:

State(s-Id, s-Capital
Product(p-Id, p-Type)
Dealer(d-Id, d-Address)
Concession(s-Id, p-Id, d-Id, c-Date) (B)

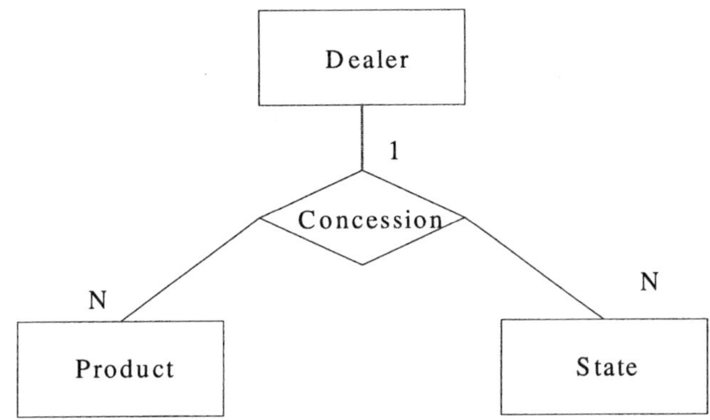

Fig. 1. Example of 1:N:N relationship (from Figure 1 in [4], modified)

The foreign key constraints derive here from the two components of Concession's key, which are primary keys of their native schemas. Since the only functional dependencies are those induced by keys, the schema is in BCNF. Here Camps imposes further constraints:

p-Id → d-Id
s-Id→d-Id

In other words, if a product is offered as a concession, then it can only be with a single dealer **regardless of the state**; and analogously on the state-dealer side. The author is understandably unhappy about the absence of a standard ERD approach to accommodate the resulting *binary constraining relationships* (using the language of [12]), which he renders in a rather UML-like fashion [17], similar to Figure 2. At this point, in order to highlight the generic structure, he introduces new notation (A, B, C, D for State, Dealer, Product, Concession, respectively). However, we will keep the current ones for the sake of comfort, while still pursuing the structure of his narrative. He notes that the resulting relational database schema includes the non-3NF relation schema Concession(s-Id,p-Id,d-Id,c-Date). Further, when Camps wishes to impose the constraints that a state (respectively product) instance can determine a dealer if and only if there has been a concession arranged with some product (respectively state), he expresses them with these conditions:

$$\pi_{\text{s-Id,d-Id}}(\text{Concessions}) = \pi_{\text{s-Id,d-Id}}(\text{State})$$
$$\pi_{\text{p-Id,d-Id}}(\text{Concessions}) = \pi_{\text{p-Id,d-Id}}(\text{Product}) \qquad \text{(C)}$$

Each of these can be viewed as a double inclusion dependency and must be expressed using the **CHECK** construct in SQL.

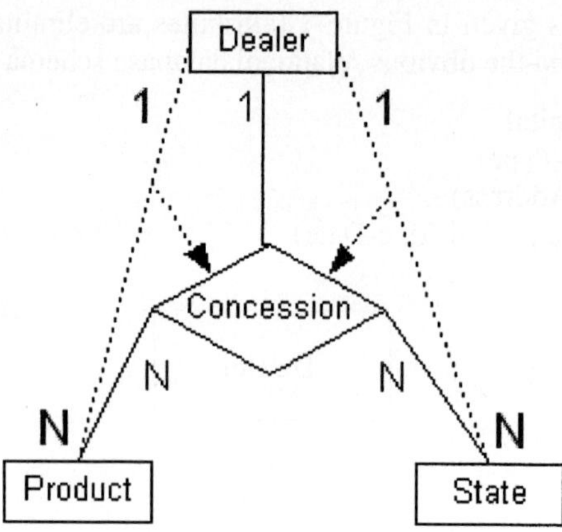

Fig. 2. Two imposed FDs (from Figure 2 of [4])

Now we note that it is actually possible to capture the structural properties of the enterprise at this stage by the simple (i.e., ternary-free) ERD of either Figure 3a [13] or Figure 3b [18]. The minimal set of associated functional dependencies in Figure 3a is as follows:

s-Id → s-Capital
p-Id → p-Type
d-Id → d-Address
s-Id → d-Id (D)
p-Id → d-Id
{s-Id, p-Id} → c-Date

One, therefore, obtains the following relational database schema, which is, of course, in BCNF, since all functional dependencies are due to keys:

State(<u>s-Id</u>,s-Capital,d-Id)
Product(<u>p-Id</u>,p-Type,d-Id)
Dealer(<u>d-Id</u>,d-Address) (E)
Concession(<u>s-Id,p-Id</u>,c-Date)

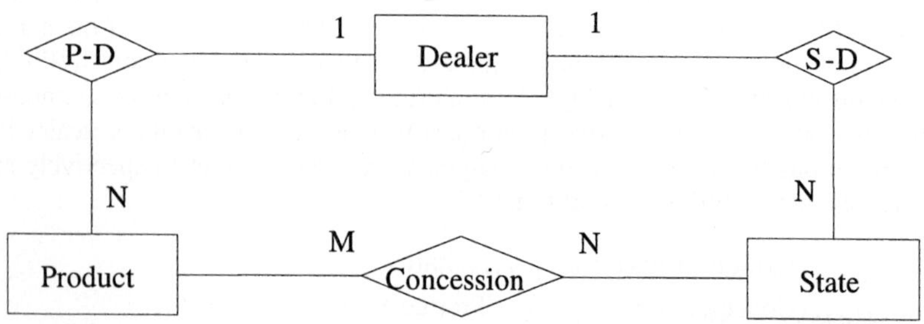

Fig. 3a. A binary model of Figure 2 with Concession as a M:N relationship

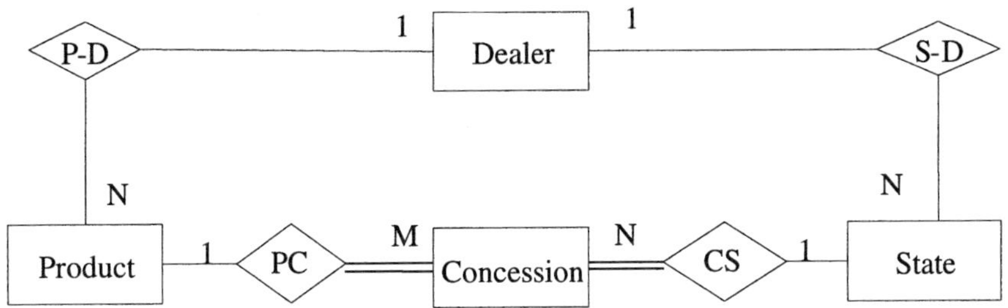

Fig. 3b. A binary model of Figure 2 with Concession as an intersection (associate) entity

Admittedly, this approach loses something: the ternary character of **Concession**. However, any dealer-relevant information to a concession instance can be discovered by a simple join; a view can also be conveniently defined. The ternary relationship in Figure 2 is therefore something of a red herring when constraining binary relationships are imposed to a ternary relationship. In other words, it is possible that an expansion of the standard ERD language to include n-ary relationships' being constrained by m-ary ones might be a very desirable feature, but its absence is not a surprising one.

Jones and Song showed that the ternary schema with FDs imposed in Figure 2 can have lossless decomposition, but cannot have an FD-preserving schema (Pattern 11 in [13]). Camps now arrives at the same schema (E) (by normalizing his non-3NF one, not by way of our ERD in Figure 3a). The problem he sees is incorporating the semantics of (C). The constraints he develops are:

$$\pi_{\text{s-Id, p-Id}}\text{(Concessions)} \subseteq \pi_{\text{s-Id, p-Id}}\text{(State*Product)}$$
$$\pi_{\text{s-Id}}\text{(State)} \subseteq \pi_{\text{s-Id}}\text{(Concessions) iff State.d-Id is not null} \qquad \text{(F)}$$
$$\pi_{\text{p-Id}}\text{(Product)} \subseteq \pi_{\text{p-Id}}\text{(Concessions) iff Product.d-Id is not null}$$

The last two conditions seem not to make sense syntactically. The intention is most likely the following (keeping the first condition and rephrasing the other two):

$$\pi_{\text{s-Id, p-Id}}\text{(Concessions)} \subseteq \pi_{\text{s-Id, p-Id}}\text{(State*Product)}$$
$$(\forall s_0 \in \pi_{\text{s-Id}}\text{(State)})(s_0 \in \pi_{\text{s-Id}}\text{(Concessions) iff } (\exists d_0)(<s_0,d_0> \in \pi_{\text{s-Id, d-Id}}\text{(State)})) \qquad \text{(G)}$$
$$(\forall p_0 \in \pi_{\text{p-Id}}\text{(Product)})(p_0 \in \pi_{\text{p-Id}}\text{(Concessions) iff } (\exists d_0)(<p_0,d_0> \in \pi_{\text{p-Id, d-Id}}\text{(Product)}))$$

At any rate, Camps shows how SQL can accommodate these conditions too using **CHECK**s in the form of ASSERTIONS, but he considers any such effort (to need any conditions besides key dependencies and inclusion constraints) to be anomalous. We feel that this is not so surprising a situation after all. The complexity of real-world database design is so great that, on the contrary, it is quite common to encounter a situation where many integrity constraints are not expressible in terms of functional and inclusion dependencies alone. Instead, one must often use the type of constructions that Camps shows us or use triggers to implement complex real-world integrity constraints.

3 The Baida Paper

In his paper [2] in turn, Badia revisits the ER model because of the usefulness and importance of the ER model. He contends that, as database applications get more complex and sophisticated and the need for capturing more semantics is growing, the ER model should be extended with more powerful constructs to express powerful semantics and variable constraints. He presents six scenarios that apparently illustrate some inadequacies of the ER model; he classifies the first five as **relationship constraints** that the model is not up to incorporating and the sixth as an **attribute constraint**. We feel that some of the examples he marshals, described below in 3.3 and 3.6, are questionable, leading us to ask whether they warrant extending the model. Badia does discuss the down side of overloading the model, however, including a thoughtful mention of tradeoffs between **minimality** and **power**. In this section we give a brief recapitulation of the examples, together with our analyses.

3.1 Camps Redux

In this portion of his paper, Badia presents Camps' illustrations and conclusions, which he accepts. We've already discussed this.

3.2 Commutativity in ERD's

In mathematical contexts, we call a diagram commutative [14] if all different routes from a common source to a common destination are equivalent. In Figure 4, from Badia's paper (there called Figure 1), there are two different ways to navigate from **Course** to **Department**: directly, or via the **Teacher** entity. To say that this particular diagram commutes, then, is to say that for each course, its instructor must be a faculty member of the department that offers it. Again, there is a SQL construct for indicating this. Although Badia doesn't use the term, his point here is that there is no mechanism for ERD's to indicate a commutativity constraint. This is correct, of course. Consider the case of representing this kind of multi-relation constraints in the diagram with over just 50 entities and relationships, which are quite common in real-world applications. We believe, therefore, that this kind of a multi-relation constraint is better to be specified as a textual or a language-oriented syntax, such as OCL [17], rather than at a diagram level. In this way, a diagram can clearly deliver its major semantics without incurring visual overload and clutter.

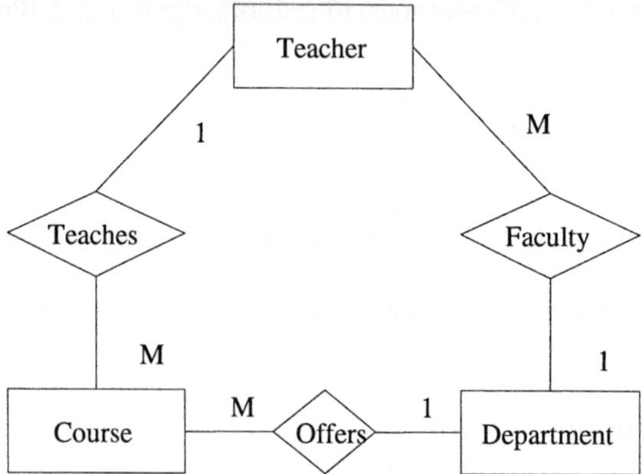

Fig. 4. An example of multi-paths between two entities (from Figure 1 in [2])

In certain limited situations [8] the **Offers** relationship might be superfluous and recovered by composing the other two relationships (or, in the relational database schema, by performing the appropriate joins). We would need to be careful about dropping **Offers**, however. For example, if a particular course were at present unstaffed, then the **Teaches** link would be broken. This is the case when **Course** entity has partial (optional) participation to **Department** entity. Without an explicit **Offers** instance, we wouldn't know which department offers the course. This is an example of a **chasm trap** which requires an explicit **Offers** relationship [6]. Another case where we couldn't rely on merely dropping one of the relationship links would arise if a commutative diagram involved the composition of two relationships in each path; then we would surely need to retain them both and to implement the constraint explicitly.

We note that allowing cycles and redundancies in ERD's has been a topic of research in the past. Atzeni and Parker [1] advise against it; Markowitz and Shoshani [15] feel that it is not harmful if it is done right. Dullea and Song [8, 9] provide a complete analysis of redundant relationships in cyclic ERD's. Their decision rules on redundant relationships are based on both maximum and minimum cardinality constraints.

3.3 Acyclicity of a Recursive Closure

Next, Badia considers the recursive relationship **ManagerOf** (on an **Employee** entity). He would like to accommodate the hierarchical property that nobody can be an indirect manager of oneself. Again, we agree with this observation but can't comment on how desirable such an ER feature would be at a diagram level. Badia points out that this is a problem even at the level of the relational database, although some Oracle releases can now accommodate the constraint.

3.4 Fan Traps

At this point the author brings Figure 5 (adapted from [6], where it appears as Figure 11.19(a); for Badia it is Figure 2) to our attention. (The original figure uses the "Merise," or "look here" approach [17]; we've modified it to make it consistent with the other figures in this paper.) The problem, called a **fan trap** arises when one attempts to enforce a constraint that a staff person must work in a branch operated by her/his division. This ER anomaly percolates to the relational schemas as well. Further, if one attempts to patch things up by including a third binary link, between **Staff** and **Branch**, then one is faced with the commutativity dilemma of Section 3.2. In general fan traps arise when there are two 1:N relationships from a common entity type to two different destinations. The two typical solutions for fan traps are either to add a third relationship between the two many-side entities or rearrange the entities to make the connection unambiguous. The problem in Figure 5 here is simply caused by an incorrect ERD and can be resolved by rearranging entities as shown in Figure 6. Figure 6 avoids the difficulties at both the ER and relational levels. In fact, this fix is even exhibited in the Connolly source itself. We note that the chasm trap discussed in Section 3.2 and the fan trap are commonly called **connection traps** [6] which make the connection between two entities separated by the third entity ambiguous.

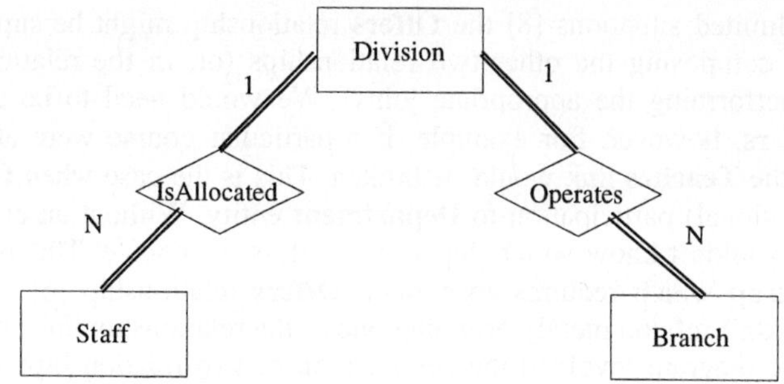

Fig. 5. A semantically wrong ERD with a fan trap (from Figure 2 in [2] and Figure 11.19(a) from [6])

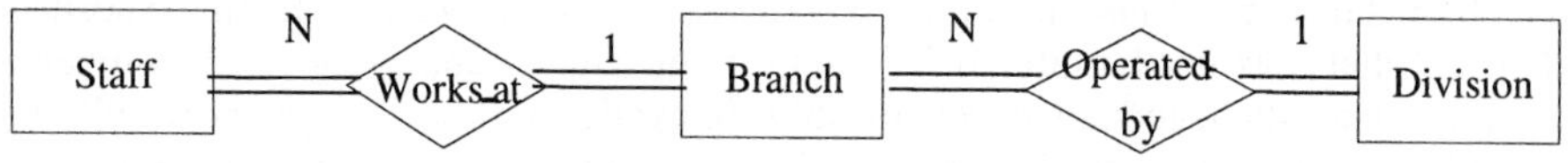

Fig. 6. A correct ERD of Figure 5, after rearranging entities

3.5 Temporal Considerations

Here Badia looks at a **Works-in** relationship, M:N between **Employee** and **Project**, with attributes **start-date** and **end-date**. A diagram for this might look something like Figure 7b; for the purposes of clarity, most attributes have been omitted. Baida states that the rule that *even though en employee may work in many projects, an employee may not work in two projects at the same time* may not be represented in an ERD. It appears impossible to express the rule, although the relationship is indeed M:N. But wouldn't this problem be solved by creating a third entity type, **TimePeriod**, with the two date attributes as its composite key, and letting **Works-in** be ternary? The new relationship would be M:N:1, as indicated in Figure 7c, with the 1 on the **Project** node, of course. In figures of 7a through 7d, we show several variations of this case related to capturing the history of works-in relationships and the above constraint. We'll comment additionally on this in Section 4.

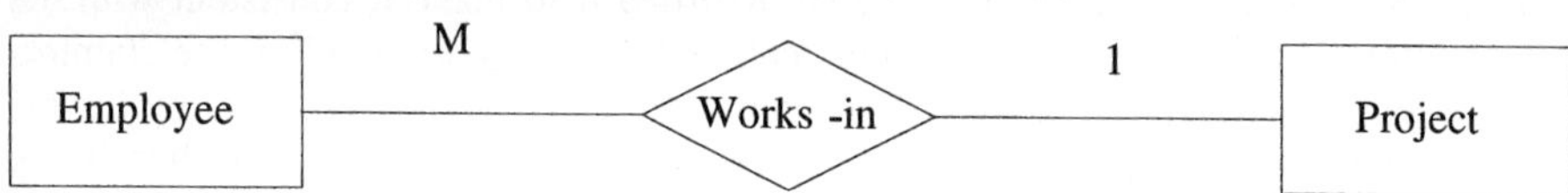

Fig. 7a. An employee may work in only one project and each project can have many employees. The diagram already assumes that an employee must work for only one project at a time. This diagram is **not** intended to capture any history of *works-in* relationship

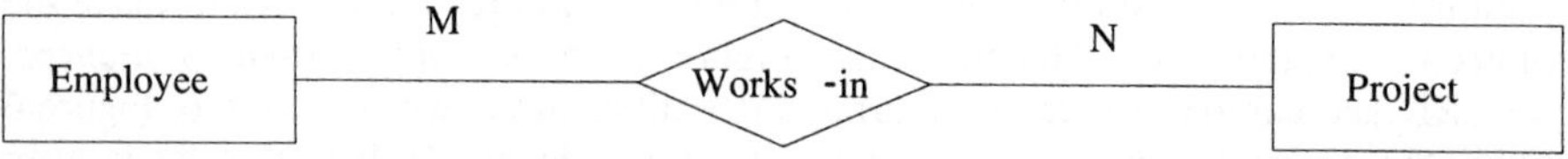

Fig. 7b. An employee may work in many projects and each project may have many employees. The diagram assumes that an employee may work for many projects at the same time. This diagram is also **not** intended to capture any history of *works-in* relationship

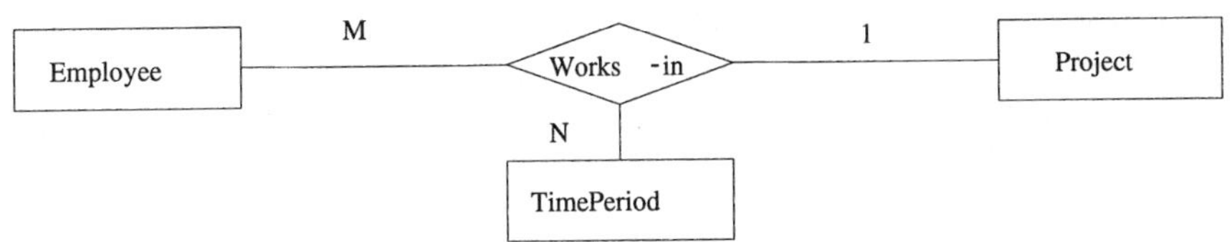

Fig. 7c. An employee may work in only one project at a time. This diagram can capture a history of *works-in* relationship of an employee for projects and still satisfies the constraint that an employee may work in only one project at a time

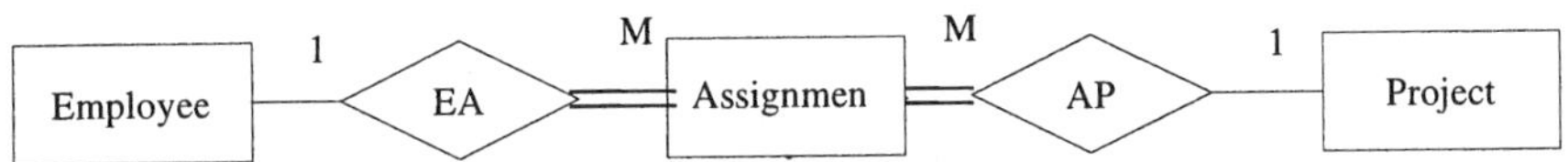

Fig. 7d. In Figure 7.c, if entity TimePeriod is not easily materialized, we can reify the relationship Works-in to an intersection entity. This diagram can capture the history of works-in relationship, but does not satisfy the constraint that an employee may work in only one project

3.6 Range Constraints

While the five previous cases exemplify what Badia calls **relationship constraints**, this one is an **attribute constraint**. The example given uses the following two tables:

Employee (<u>employee_id</u>, rank_id, salary, ...)
Rank (<u>rank_id</u>, max_salary, min_salary)

The stated problem is that the ERD that represents the above schema cannot express the fact that the salary of an employee must be within the range determined by his or her rank. Indeed, in order to enforce this constraint, explicit SQL code must be generated. Baida correctly sates that the absence of information at the attribute level is a limitation and cause difficulty in solving semantic heterogeneity. We believe, however, that information and constraints at the attribute level could be expressed at the data dictionary level or in a separate low level diagram below the ERD level. Again, this will keep an ERD as a *conceptual model* at enterprise level without too much clutter. Consider the complexity of representing attribute constraints in ERDs for real-world applications that have over 50 entities and several hundreds of attributes. The use of a CASE tool that supports a conceptual ERD with its any low level diagram for attributes and/or its associated data dictionary should be a right direction for this problem.

4 General Cardinality Constraints

While on the whole, as indicated above, we feel many of the alleged shortcomings of the ER model claimed in recent papers are not justified, some of those points have been well taken and are quite interesting. However, there is another important feature of conceptual design that we shall consider here, one that the ER model really does lack. In this section, we briefly discuss McAllister's general cardinality constraints [16] and their implications.

McAllister's setting is a general n-ary relationship **R**. In other words, R involves **n** different **roles**. This term is used, rather than **entity types**, since the entity types may not all be distinct. For example, a recursive relationship, while binary in the mathematical sense, involves only a single entity type. Given two disjoint sets of roles A and B, McAllister defines **Cmax(A,B)** and **Cmin(A,B)** as follows: for a tuple <a>, with one component from each role in A, and a tuple <b>, with one component from each role in B, let us denote by <a,b> the tuple generated by the two sets of components; we recall that A and B are disjoint. Then Cmax(A,B) (respectively Cmin(A,B)) is the maximum allowable cardinality over all <a> of the set of tuples <b> such that $<a,b> \in \pi_{A \cup B}$ (R). For example, consider the **Concession** relationship of Figure 1. Then to say that

Cmax({State, Product},{Dealer}) = 1 is to express the fact that {s-Id, p-Id} →d-Id. And the condition **Cmin({Product},{State,Dealer}) = 1** is equivalent to the constraint that **Product** is total on **Concession**. Now, as we see from these examples, Cmax gives us information about functional dependencies and Cmin about participation constraints. When B is a singleton set and A its complement, this is sometimes called the "Chen" approach to cardinality [11] or "look across"; when A is a singleton set and B its complement, it is called the "Merise" approach [11] or "look here." All told, McAllister shows that there are 3^n-2^{n+1}+1 different combinations possible for A and B, where n is the number of different roles.

Clearly, given this explosive growth, it is impractical to include all possible cardinality constraints in a general ERD, although McAllister shows a tabular approach that works pretty well for ternary relationships. He shows further that there are many equalities and inequalities that must hold among the cardinalities, so that the entries in the table are far from independent. The question arises as to which cardinalities have the highest priorities and should thus appear in an ERD. It turns out that the Merise and Chen approaches give the same information in the binary case but not in the ternary one, which becomes the contentious case (n>3 is rare enough not to be a serious issue). In fact one finds both Chen [as in 10] and Merise [as in 3] systems in practice. In his article, Genova feels that UML [17] made the wrong choice by using the Chen method for its Cmin's, and he suggests that class diagrams include <u>both</u> sets of information (but only when either A or B is singleton). That does not seem likely to happen, though.

Still, consideration of these general cardinality constraints and McAllister's axioms comes in handy in a couple of the settings we have discussed. The general setting helps understand connections between, for example, ternary and related binary relationships as in Figure 2 and [12]. And it similarly sheds light on preservation (and loss) of information in Section 3.5 above, when a binary relationship is replaced by a ternary one. Finally, we believe that it also provides the deep structural information for describing the properties of decompositions of the associated relation schemas. It is therefore indisputable in our opinion that these general cardinality constraints do much to describe the fundamental structure of a relationship in the ER model; only portions of which, like the tip of an iceberg, are currently visible in a typical ERD. And yet we are not claiming that such information should routinely be included in the model.

5 Conclusion

We have reviewed recent literature ([4] and [2]) that illustrate through some interesting examples areas of conceptual database design that are not accommodated sufficiently at the present time by the Entity-Relationship model. However, some of these examples seem not to hold up under scrutiny.

Capabilities that the model does indeed lack are constraints on commutative diagrams (Section 3.2 above), recursive closures (3.3), and some range conditions (3.6) as pointed out by Badia. Another major conceptual modeling tool missing in the ER model is that of general cardinality constraints [16]. These constraints are the deep structure that underlies such more visible behavior as constraining and related relationships, Chen and Merise cardinality constraints, functional dependencies and decompositions, and participation constraints. How many of these missing features should actually be incorporated into the ER model is pretty much a question of triage, of weighing the benefits of a feature against the danger of circuit overload.

We believe that some complex constraints such as multi-relation constraint are better to be represented as a textual or a language-oriented syntax, such as OCL [17], rather than at the ER diagram level. We also believe that information and constraints at the attribute level could be expressed at the data dictionary level or in a separate low level diagram below the ERD level. In these ways, we will keep an ERD as a *conceptual model* at enterprise level to deliver major semantics without visual overload and too much clutter. Consider the complexity of an ERD for a real-world application that has over 50 entities and hundreds of attributes and representing all those complex multi-relation and attribute constraints in the ERD. The use of a CASE tool that supports a conceptual ERD with its any low level diagram for attributes and/or its associated data dictionary should be a right direction for this problem.

We note that we do not claim that some research topics suggested by Baida, such as relationships over relationships and attributes over attributes, are not interesting or worthy. Research in those topics would bring interesting new insights and powerful ways of representing complex semantics. What we claim here is that the ERD itself has much value as it is now, especially for relational applications, where all the examples of Baida indicate. We believe, however, that extending the ER model to support new application semantics such as biological applications should be encouraged.

The "D" in ERD connotes to many researchers and practitioners the simplicity and power of communication that account for the model's popularity. Indeed, as the Entity-Relationship model nears its 30th birthday, we find its robustness remarkable.

References

1. 1.Atzeni, P. and Parker, D.S., "Assumptions in relational database theory", in *Proceedings of the 1st ACM Symposium on Principles of Database Systems*, March 1982.
2. Badia, A. "Entity-Relationship Modeling Revisited", *SIGMOD Record,* 33(1), March 2004, pp. 77-82.
3. Batini, C., Ceri, S., and Navathe, S., *Conceptual Database Design*, Benjamin/Cummings, 1992.
4. Camps Paré, R. "From Ternary Relationship to Relational Tables: A Case against Common Beliefs", *SIGMOD Record*, 31(20), June 2002, pp. 46-49.
5. Chen, P. "The Entity-Relationship Model – towards a Unified View of Data", *ACM Transactions on Database Systems,* 1(1), 1976, pp. 9-36.
6. Connolly, T. and Begg, C., *Database Systems*, 3d Edition, Addison-Wesley, 2002.
7. Dietrich, S. and Urban, S., *Beyond Relational Databases*, Prentice-Hall, to appear.
8. Dullea, J. and Song, I.-Y., "An Analysis of Cardinality Constraints in Redundant Relationships," *in Proceedings of Sixth International Conferences on Information and Knowledge Management (CIKM97),* Las Vegas, Nevada, USA, Nov. 10-14, 1997, pp. 270-277.

9. Dullea, J., Song, I.-Y., and Lamprou, I., "An Analysis of Structural Validity in Entity-Relationship Modeling," *Data and Knowledge Engineering*, 47(3), 2003, pp. 167-205.
10. Elmasri, R. and Navathe, S.B., *Fundamentals of Database Systems*, 4th Ed., Addison-Wesley, 2003.
11. Genova, G., Llorenz, J., and Martinez, P., "The meaning of multiplicity of n-ary associations in UML", Journal of Software and Systems Modeling, 1(2), 2002.
12. Jones, T. and Song, I.-Y., "Analysis of binary/ternary cardinality combinations in entity-relationship modeling", *Data & Knowledge Engineering*, 19(1), 1996, pp. 39-64.
13. Jones, T. and Song, I.-Y., "Binary Equivalents of Ternary Relationships in Entity-Relationship Modeling: a Logical Decomposition Approach." *Journal of Database Management*, 11(2), 2000, (April-June, 2000), pp. 12-19.
14. MacLane, S., *Categories for the Working Mathematician*, Springer-Verlag, 1971.
15. Markowitz, V. and Shoshani, A., "Representing Extended Entity-Relationship Structures in Relational Databases: A Modular Approach", *ACM Transactions on Database Systems*, 17(3), 1992, pp. 423-464.
16. McAllister, A., "Complete rules for n-ary relationship cardinality constraints", *Data & Knowledge Engineering*, 27, 1998, pp. 255-288.
17. Rumbaugh, J., Jacobson, I., and Booch, G., *The Unified Modeling Language Reference Manual*, Addison-Wesley, 1999.
18. Song, I.-Y., Evans, M., and Park, E.K., "A Comparative Analysis of Entity-Relationship Diagrams," *Journal of Computer and Software Engineering*, 3(4) (1995), pp. 427-459.
19. Teorey, T., *Database Modeling & Design*, 3d Edition, Morgan Kaufmann, 1999.

Modeling Functional Data Sources as Relations

Simone Santini and Amarnath Gupta*

University of California, San Diego

Abstract. In this paper we present a model of functional access to data that, we argue, is suitable for modeling a class of data repositories characterized by functional access, such as web sites. We discuss the problem of modeling such data sources as a set of relations, of determining whether a given query expressed on these relations can be translated into a combination of functions defined by the data sources, and of finding an optimal plan to do so.

We show that, if the data source is modeled as a single relation, an optimal plan can be found in a time linear in the number of functions in the source but, if the source is modeled as a number of relations that can be joined, finding the optimal plan is NP-hard.

1 Introduction

These days, we see a great diversification in the type, structure, and functionality of the data repositories with which we have to deal, at least when compared with as little as fifteen or twenty years ago. Not too long ago, one could quite safely assume that almost all the data that a program had both the need and the possibility to access were stored in a relational database or, were this not the case, that the amount of data, their stability, and their format made their insertion into a relational database feasible.

As of today, such a statement would be quite undefensible. A large share of the responsibility for this state of affairs must be ascribed, of course, to the rapid diffusion of data communication networks, which created a very large collection of data that a person or a program might want to use. Most of the data available on data communication networks, however, are not in relational form [1] and, due to the volume and the instability of the medium, the idea of storing them all into a stable repository is quite unfeasible.

The most widely known data access environment of today, the *world-wide web*, was created with the idea of displaying reasonably well formatted pages of material to people, and of letting them "jump" from one page to another. It followed, in other words, a rather procedural model, in which elements of the page definition language (*tags*) often stood for actions: a link specified a "jump" from one page to another. While a link establishes a connection between two pages, this connection is not symmetric (a link that carries you from page A to page B will not carry you from page B to page A) and therefore is not a *relation* between two pages (in the sense in which the term

* The work presented in this paper was done under the auspices and with the funding of NIH project NCRR RR08 605, *Biomedical Informatics Research Network*, which the authors gratefully acknowledge.

P. Atzeni et al. (Eds.): ER 2004, LNCS 3288, pp. 55–68, 2004.

"relation" is used in databases), but rather a *functional connection* that, given page A, will produce page B.

In addition to this basic mechanism, today many web sites that contain a lot of data allow one to specify search criteria using the so-called *forms.* A form is an input device through which a fixed set of values can be assigned to an equally fixed set of parameters, the values forming a search criterion against which the data in the web site will be matched, returning the data that satisfy the criterion.

Consider the web site of a public library (an example to which we will return in the following). Here one can have a form that, given the name of an author returns a *web page* (or other data structures) containing the titles of the books written by that author. This doesn't imply that a corresponding form will exist that, given the title of a book, will return its author. In other words, the dependence author$\longrightarrow$book is not necessarily invertible. This limitation tells us that we are not in the presence of a set of relations but, rather, in the presence of a data repository with *functional access*. The diffusion of the internet as a source of data has, of course, generated a great interest in the conceptual modeling of web sites [2–4]. In this paper we present a formalization of the problem of representing a functional data source as a set of relations, and of translating (whenever possible) relational queries into sequences of functions.

2 The Model

For the purpose of this work, a *functional data source* is a set of procedures that, given a number of attributes whose value has been fixed, instructs us on how to obtain a data structure containing further attributes related to the former.

To fix the ideas, consider again the web site of a library. A procedure is defined that, given the name of an author, retrieves a data structure containing the titles of all the books written by that author. The procedure for doing so looks something like this:

Procedure 1: author -> set(title)

- i) go to the "search by author" page;
- ii) put the desired name into the "author" slot of the form that you find there;
- iii) press the button labeled "go";
- iv) look at the page that will be displayed next, and retrieve the list of titles.

Getting the publisher and the year of publication of a book, given its author and title is a bit more complicated:

Procedure 2: author, title -> publisher, year

- i) execute procedure 1 and get a list of titles;
- ii) search the desired title in the list;
- iii) if found then
  - iii.1) access the book page, by clicking on the title;
  - iii.2) search the publisher and year, and return them;
- iv) else fail.

On the other hand, in most library web pages there is no procedure that allows one to obtain a list of all the books published by a given publisher in a given year, and a query asking for such information would be impossible to answer.

We start by giving an auxiliary definition, and then we give the definition of the kind of functional data sources that we will consider in the rest of the paper.

Definition 1. *A* data sort *S is a pair (N,T), written $S = N : T$, where N is the* name *of the sort, and T its* type. *Two data sorts are equal if their names and their types coincide.*

A data sort, in the sense in which we use the term here, is not quite a "physical" data type. For instance, *author:string* and *title:string* are both of the same data type (string) but they represent different data sorts[1].The set of *complex sorts* is the transitive closure of the set of data sorts with respect to Cartesian product of sorts and the formation of collection types (sets, bags, and lists).

Definition 2. *A* functional data source *is a pair (S,F) where $S = \{S_1,\ldots,S_n\}$ is a set of* data sorts, *$F = \{f_1,\ldots,f_m\}$ is a set of functions $\alpha \xrightarrow{f} \beta$, where both α and β are composite sorts made of sorts in S.*

In the library web site, *author:string*, and *year:int* are examples of data sorts. The procedures are instantiations of functions. Procedure 1, for example, instantiates a function author:string$\xrightarrow{f}$title:string.

The elements "author:string" and "title:string" are examples of composite sorts. Sometimes, when there is no possibility of confusion, we will omit the type of the sort. Our goal in this paper is to model a functional data source like this one in a way that resembles a set of relations upon which we can express our query conditions. To this end, we give the following definition.

Definition 3. *A* relational model *of a functional data source is a set of relations $R = \{R_1,\ldots,R_p\}$ where $R_i \subseteq S_{i_1} \times \cdots \times S_{i_q}$ and all the S_i's are sorts of the functional data source. The relation R_i is called a* relational façade *for the underlying data source, and will sometimes be indicated as $R_i(N_{i_1} : T_{i_1},\ldots,N_{i_q} : T_{i_q})$.*

The problems we consider in this paper are the following: (1) Given a model R of a functional data source (S,F) and a query on the model, is it possible to answer the query using the procedures f_i defined for the functional data source?, and (2) if the answer to the previous question is "yes," is it possible to find an optimal sequence of procedures that will answer the query with minimal cost?

It goes without saying that not all the queries that are possible on the model are also possible on the data source. Consider again the library web site; a simple model for this data source is composed of a single relation, that we can call "book," and defined as:

book(name:string, title:string, publisher:string, year:int).

[1] The entities that we call data sorts are known in other quarters as "semantic data types." This name, however, entails a considerable epistemological commitment, quite out of place for a concept that, all in all, has nothing semantic about it: an *author:string* is as syntactic an entity as any abstract data type, and does not require extravagant semantic connotations.

A query like

(N, T) :- book(N, T, 'dover', 1997),

asking for the author and title of all books published by dover in 1997 is quite reasonable in the model, but there are no procedures on the web site to execute it.

We will assume, to begin with, that the model of the web site contains a single relation. In this case we can also assume, without loss of generality, that the relation is defined in the Cartesian product of all the sorts in the functional data source: $R(S_1, \ldots, S_n)$. Throughout this paper, we will only consider non-recursive queries. It should be clear in the following that recursive queries require a certain extension of our method, but not a complete overhaul of it. Also, we will consider conjunctive queries[2], whose general form can be written as:

$$(S_{k_1}, \ldots, S_{k_p}) : -R(S_1, \ldots, S_n), S_{j_1} = c_1, \ldots, S_{j_q} = c_q, \phi_1(S_{11}, S_{12}), \ldots, \phi_1(S_{u1}, S_{u2}) \quad (1)$$

where $c_1, \ldots, c_q$ are constants, all the S's come from the sorts of the relation R, and the ϕ_i's are comparison operators drawn from a suitable set, say $\phi_i \in \{<, >, =, \neq, \leq, \geq\}$.

We will for the moment assume that the functional data source provides no mechanism for verifying conditions of the type $\phi_1(S_{11}, S_{12})$. The only operations allowed are retrieving data by entering values (constants) in a suitable field of a form or traversing a link in a web site with a constant as a label (such as the title of a book in the library example). Given the query (1) in a data source like this, we would execute it by first determining whether the function $f : S_{j_1} \times \cdots \times S_{j_n} \rightarrow \{S_{k_1} \times \cdots \times S_{k_p} \times S_{11} \times \cdots \times S_{u2}\}$ can be computed. If it can, we compute $f(c_1, \ldots, c_q)$ and, for each result returned, check whether the conditions $\phi_i(S_{i1}, S_{i2})$ are verified.

The complicated part of this query schema is the first step: the determination of the function f that, given the constants in the query, allows us to obtain the query outputs $\{S_{k_1}, \ldots, S_{k_p}\}$, augmented with all the quantities needed for the comparisons.

3 Query Translation

Informally, the problem that we consider in this section is the following. We have a collection of data sorts $S = \{S_1, \ldots, S_n\}$. Given two data sorts α, β, defined as Cartesian products of elements of S ($\alpha = S_{\alpha_1} \times \cdots \times S_{\alpha_a}$ and $\beta = S_{\beta_1} \times \cdots \times S_{\beta_b}$) one can define a formal (and unique) *correspondence function* $f_{\alpha\beta} : \alpha \rightarrow \beta$. This function operates on the model of the data source (this is why we used the adjective "formal" for it: it is not necessarily a function that one can compute) and, given the values $\{S_{\alpha_1}, \ldots, S_{\alpha_a}\}$, returns the corresponding values $\{S_{\beta_1}, \ldots, S_{\beta_b}\}$. If $\{v_1, \ldots, v_a\}$ are the input values, this function computes the relational algebra operation

$$\pi_{N_{\beta_1}, \ldots, N_{\beta_b}} \circ \sigma_{S_{\alpha_1} = v_1 \ldots, S_{\alpha_a} = v_a} \quad (2)$$

where the N's are the names of the sorts S, as per definition 1. A correspondence function can be seen, in other words, as the functional counterpart of the query (2)

[2] Any query can, of course, be translated in a disjunctive normal form, that is, in a disjunction of conjunctive queries. The system in this case will simply pose all the conjunctive queries and then take the union of all the results.

which, on a single table, is completely general. (Remember that we don't yet consider conditions other than the equality with a constant.)

The set $F = \{f_{\alpha\beta}\}$ of all correspondence functions contains the grounding of all queries that we might ask on the model. The functional data source, on the other hand, has procedures P_i, each one of which implements a specific function $f_{\alpha\beta}$, a situation that we will indicate with $P_i \rightsquigarrow f_{\alpha\beta}$. The set of all implemented correspondence functions if $F_{|\rightsquigarrow} = \{f | \exists P : P \rightsquigarrow f\}$. Our query implementation problem is then, given a query q, with the relative correspondence function f, to find a suitable combination of functions in $F_{|\rightsquigarrow}$ that is equal to f. In order to make this statement more precise, we need to clarify what do we mean by "suitable combination of functions" that is, we need to specify a function algebra. We will limit our algebra to three simple operations that create sequences of functions, as shown in Table 1. (We assume, pragmatically, that more complex manipulations are done by the procedures P_i.)

Table 1. Operators of the function algebra.

Operation	Definition	Description	Typing
$f \circ g$	$(f \circ g)(x) = f(g(x))$	function composition	$\frac{f:\alpha\to\beta \quad g:\gamma\to\alpha}{f\circ g:\gamma\to\beta}$
$\langle f, g\rangle$	$\langle f, g\rangle(x) = (f(x), g(x))$	cartesian composition	$\frac{f:\alpha\to\beta \quad g:\alpha\to\gamma}{\langle f,g\rangle:\alpha\to\beta\times\gamma}$
$f \times g$	$(f \times g)(x, y) = (f(x), g(y))$	cartesian product	$\frac{f:\alpha\to\beta \quad g:\delta\to\gamma}{f\times g:\alpha\times\delta\to\beta\times\gamma}$

A function $f \in F_{|\rightsquigarrow}$ for which a procedure is defined, and that transforms a data sort S into a data sort P can be represented as a diagram

$$S \xrightarrow{f} P. \tag{3}$$

The operators of the function algebra generate diagrams like those in the first and third column of Table 2. In order to obtain the individual data types, we introduce the formal operator of projection. The projection is "formal" in that it exists only in the diagrams: in practice, when we have the data type $P \times Q$ we simply select the portion of it that we need. The projections don't correspond to any procedure and their cost is zero. The dual of the projection operator is the Cartesian product which, given two data of type A and B produces from them a datum of type $A \times B$. This is also a formal operator with zero cost. where the dotted line with the $\times$ symbols is there to remind us that we are using a Cartesian product operator, and the arrow goes from the type that will appear first in the product to the type that will appear second (we will omit the arrow when this indication is superfluous).

The Cartesian product of the functions $S \xrightarrow{f} P$ and $Q \xrightarrow{g} R$ is represented as

$$S \times Q \xrightarrow{f \times g} P \times R \tag{4}$$

With these operations, and the corresponding diagrams, in place, we can arrange the correspondence functions $f \in F_{|\rightsquigarrow}$ in a diagram, which we call the *computation diagram* of a data source.

Definition 4. *The* computation diagram *of a functional data source is a graph* $G = (N, E)$ *with nodes labeled by a labeling function* $\lambda_n : N \to S$, S *being the set of composite data sorts of the source, and edges labeled by the labeling function* $\lambda_e : E \to F_{|\leadsto}$ *such that each edge is one of the following:*

1. *A function edge, such that if the edge is* (n_1, n_2)*, then* $\lambda_E((n_1, n_2)) : \lambda_n(n_1) \to \lambda_n(n_2)$*, and represented as in (3);*
2. projection edges,
3. cartesian product edges

Let us go back now to our original problem. We have a query and a correspondence function $S_1 \times \cdots \times S_n \xrightarrow{f} P_1 \times \cdots \times P_m$ that we need to compute, where $S_1, \ldots, S_n$ are the data sorts for which we give values, and $P_1, \ldots, P_m$ are the results that we desire. In order to see whether the computation is possible, we adopt the following strategy: first, build the computation diagram of the data source, then we add a node called s to the graph, and connect it to $S_1, \ldots, S_n$, as well as a node d, with edges coming from $P_1, \ldots, P_m$; finally, we check whether a path exists from s to d.

If we are to find an optimal solution to the grounding of a correspondence function f, we need to assign a cost to each node of the graph and, in order to do this, we need to determine the cost of traversing an edge. The cost functions of the various combinations that appear in a computation graph are defined in table 2.

Table 2. Cost of the functional operations in terms of graph path.

Operation	Cost	Operation	Cost
$A \xrightarrow{f} B$	$C(B) = C(A) + C(f)$	$A \searrow \times \swarrow B$ into $A \times B$	$C(A \times B) = C(A) + C(B)$
$A \times B$ with π_2 to A and π_1 to B	$C(A) = C(B) = C(A \times B)$	$A \xrightarrow{f_1} D \xleftarrow{f_2} B$	$C(D) = \min(C(A) + c(f_1), C(B) + c(f_2))$

The problem of finding the optimal functional expression for a given query can therefore be reduced to that of finding the shortest path in a suitable function graph, a problem that we will now briefly elucidate. Let G be a function graph, $G.V$ the set of its vertices, and $G.E$ the set of its edges.

For every node $u \in G.V$, let $u.\kappa$ be the distance between u and the source of the path, $u.\pi$ the predecessor(s) of u in the minimal path, and $u.\nu$ the set of nodes adjacent to u (accounting for the edge directions)

In addition, a *cost* function c : vertex $\times$ vertex $\to$ real is defined such that $c(u, v)$ is the cost of the edge (u, v). If $(u, v) \notin G.E$, then $c(u, v) = \infty$.

The algorithm in table 3 uses the Djikstra's shortest path algorithm to build a function graph that produces a given set of output from a given set of input, if such a graph exists: the function dijkstra(G, c, s) returns the set of nodes in G where, for each node n, $n.\kappa$ is set to the cost of the path from s to n according to the cost function c. Dijkstra's algorithm is a standard one and is not reported here.

Table 3. Algorithm for the creation of function graphs.

```
make_graph(I : {vertex}, O : {vertex}, G : graph, c : vertex × vertex → real) : graph
    s, d : vertex;
    G.V := G.V ∪ {s, d};
    forall u in I do G.E := G.E ∪ {(s, u)}; od
    forall u in O do G.E := G.E ∪ {(u, d)}; od;
    S := dijkstra(G, c, s);
    Q : graph;
    T, P : {vertex};
    S := S − {s, d}; Q.V := ∅; T := O; P := O;
    while T ≠ ∅ do
        u := element(T);
        if u.ν ≠ s ∧ u.ν ≠ ∅ do
            forall v in I do
                Q.V := Q.V ∪ {v};
                if v ∉ P do T := T ∪ {v} fi
                P := P ∪ {v}; Q.E := Q.E ∪ {(v, u)};
            od;
            T := T − {u};
        fi;
    od;
    return Q;
```

4 Relaxing Some Assumptions

The model presented so far is a way of solving a well known problem: given a set of functions, determine what other functions can be computed using their combination; our model is somewhat more satisfying from a modeling point of view because of the explicit inclusion of the cartesian product of data sorts and the function algebra operators necessary to take them into account but, from an algorithmic point of view, what we are doing is still finding the transitive closure of a set of functional dependencies. We will now try to ease some of the restrictions on the data source. These extensions, in particular the inclusion of joins, can't be reduced to the transitive closure of a set of functional dependencies, and therein lies, from our point of view, the advantage of the particular form of our model.

Comparisons. The first limitation that we want to relax is the assumption that the data source doesn't have the possibility of expressing any of the predicates $\phi_i(S_{i1}, S_{i2})$ in the query (1). There are cases in which some limited capability in this sense is available.

We will assume that the following limitations are in place: firstly, the data sources provides a finite number of predicate possibilities; secondly each predicate is of the form $\phi(S, R) = S \text{ op } R$, where S and R are fixed data sorts, and "op" is an operator that can be chosen amongst a finite number of alternative. The general idea here comes, of course, from an attempt to model web sites in which conditions can be expressed as part of "forms."

In order to incorporate these conditions into our method, one can consider them as data sorts: each condition $\phi(S, R)$ is a data sort that takes values in the set of triples (s, r, op), with s of sort S and r of sort R. In other words, indicating a sort as a pair $N : T$, where N is the name and T the data type of the sort, a comparison data sort $\mathfrak{C}(S_1, S_2)$ is isomorphic to $N_1 : T_1 \times N_2 : T_2 \times (T_1 \times T_2 \to \mathbf{2})$ where $\mathbf{2}$ is the data type of the booleans. A procedure that accepts in input a value of a data sort S_1, and a condition on the data sorts S_2, S_3, would be represented as

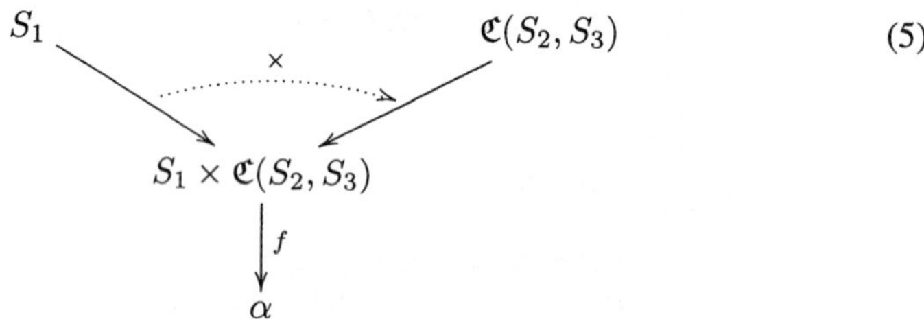

(5)

The only difference between condition data sorts and regular data sorts is that conditions can't be obtained as the result of a procedure, so that in a computation graph a condition should not have any incoming edge.

Joins. Let us consider now the case in which the model of the functional data source consists of a number of relations. We can assume, for the sake of clarity, that there are only two relations in the model:

$$\begin{array}{l} R_1(N_1 : T_1, \ldots, N_p : T_p) \\ R_2(M_1 : Q_1, \ldots, M_v : Q_v). \end{array} \tag{6}$$

Each of these relations supports intra-relational queries that can be translated into functions and executed using the computation graph of that part of the functional source that deals with the data sorts in the relation. In addition, however, we have now queries that need to *join* data between the two relations. Consider the relations: $R_1(X_1, X_2, X_3)$, $R_2(Y_1, Y_2, Y_3)$ and the following query:

$$(A, B) : -R_1(X, \text{'x'}, A), R_2(Y, \text{'y'}, B), A = B. \tag{7}$$

We can compute this query in two ways. The first makes use of the following two correspondence functions:

$$\begin{array}{l} X_2 \xrightarrow{f_1} X_1 \times X_3 \\ Y_2 \times Y_3 \xrightarrow{f_2} Y_1 \,. \end{array} \tag{8}$$

To implement this query, we adopt the following procedure:

Procedure 3:

i) use the computation graph of R_1 to compute f_1('x'), returning a set of pairs $(a : X_1, b : X_2)$;

ii) for each pair (a, b) returned:

 ii.1) compute f_2('y', b) using the graph of R_2, obtaining a set of results $(c : Y_1)$;

 ii.2) for each c, form the pair (a, c), and add it to the output.

The procedure can be represented using a computation graph in which the graphs that compute f_1 and f_2 are used as components. Let us indicate the graph that computes the function f as:

$$\alpha \longrightarrow (f) \longrightarrow \beta \tag{9}$$

Then a join like that in the example is computed by the following diagram:

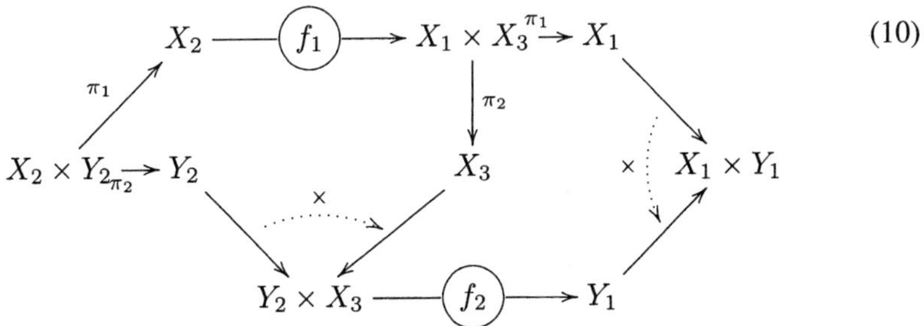

(10)

The second possibility to compute the join is symmetric. While in this case we used the relation R_1 to produce the variable on which we want to join and the relation R_2 to impose the join condition, we will now do the reverse. We will use the functions

$$\begin{aligned} Y_2 &\xrightarrow{f_3} Y_1 \times Y_3 \\ X_2 \times X_3 &\xrightarrow{f_4} X_1 . \end{aligned} \tag{11}$$

and a computation diagram similar to the previous one. Checking whether the source can process the join, therefore, requires checking if either the pairs of functions (f_1, f_2) or (f_3, f_4) can be computed. The concept can be easily extended to a source with many relations and a query with many joins as follows.

Take a conjunctive query, and let $J = \{J_1, \ldots, J_n\}$ the set of its joins, with $J_i : (X_i = Y_i)$. We can always rewrite a query so that each variable X will appear in only one relation, possibly adding some join conditions. Consider, for example, the fragment $R(A, X), P(B, X), Q(C, X)$, which can be rewritten as

$$R(A, X_1), P(B, X_2), Q(C, X_3), X_1 = X_2, X_2 = X_3. \tag{12}$$

We will assume that all queries are normalized in this way. Given a variable X, let $\mathfrak{s}(X)$ be the relation in which X appear. Also, given a relation R in the query, let $\mathfrak{i}(R)$ the Cartesian product of its input sorts, and $\mathfrak{o}(R)$ the Cartesian product of its output sorts.

Table 4. Algorithm for the verification of the join conditions.

check(I : {vertex}, O : {vertex}, G : graph, c : vertex × vertex → real) : real
  s, d : vertex;
  $G.V := G.V \cup \{s, d\}$;
  forall u in I do $G.E := G.E \cup \{(s, u)\}$ od;
  forall u in O do $G.E := G.E \cup \{(u, d)\}$ od;
  $S :=$ dijkstra(G, c, s);
  return $(d.\kappa < \infty)$;

The algorithm for query rewriting is composed of two parts. The first is a function that determines whether a function from a given set of input to a given set of outputs can be implemented, and represented in Table 4. The second finds a join combination that satisfies the query. It is assumed that a set of the join conditions that appear in the query $J = \{(X_1, Y_1), \ldots, (X_n, Y_n)\}$ is given. The algorithm, reported in table 5 returns a computation graph that computes the query with all the required joins.

Table 5. Join determination algorithm.

joins(J : {vertex × vertex}, G : graph, c : vertex × vertex → real) : graph
1. $I := \emptyset$
2. forall (X, Y) in J do
    $R := \mathfrak{s}(X); Q := \mathfrak{s}(Y)$;
    if check$(\mathfrak{i}(R), \mathfrak{o}(R) \cup \{X\}, G, c) \wedge$ check$(\mathfrak{i}(Q) \cup \{Y\}, \mathfrak{o}(Q), G, c)$ do
      $I := I \cup \{(X, Y)\}$
    elseif check$(\mathfrak{i}(Q), \mathfrak{o}(Q) \cup \{Y\}, G, c) \wedge$ check$(\mathfrak{i}(R) \cup \{R\}, \mathfrak{o}(R), G, c)$ do
      $I := I \cup \{(Y, X)\}$
    fi od;
3. $Q :=$ make_graph$(\bigcup_i \mathfrak{i}(R_i) \cup \{X | (X, Y) \in I\}, \bigcup_i \mathfrak{o}(R_i) \cup \{Y | (X, Y) \in I\}, G, c)$;
4. forall u in O do $Q.E := Q.E \cup \{(X, Y)\}$ od;
5. if cycle(Q) do error fi;
6. return Q;

The correctness of the algorithm is proven in the following proposition:

Proposition 1. *Algorithm 1 succeeds if and only if the query with the required joins can be executed.*

The proof can be found in [5].

While the algorithm "joins" is an efficient (linear in the number of joins) way of finding *a* plan whose correctness is guaranteed, finding an *optimal* plan is inherently harder:

Theorem 1. *Finding the minimal set of functions that implements all the joins in the query is NP-hard.*

Proof. We prove the theorem with a reduction from *graph cover*. let $G = (V, E)$ be a graph, with sets of nodes $V = \{v_1, \ldots, v_n\}$, edges $E = \{e_1, \ldots, e_m\}$, and with

$e_i = (v_{i_1}, v_{i_2})$, $v_{i_1}, v_{i_2} \in V$. Given such a graph, we build a functional source and a query as follows.

For each node v_i define a sort X_i and a function $f : I \to X_i$. All the sorts are of the same data type. For each edge (v_h, v_k) define a condition $X_h = X_k$. Also, define a function $g : X_i \times \cdots \times X_n \to Y$. Finally, define the relations $R_1(I, X_1)$, $R_2(X_1, X_2), \ldots, R_{n+1}(X_n, Y)$ and the query

$$\begin{aligned} \text{ans}(Y) : -R_1(I, X_1), R_2(X_1, X_2), \ldots, R_{n+1}(X_n, Y), \\ I =' i', X_{1_1} = X_{1_2}, \ldots, X_{m_1} = X_{m_2} \end{aligned} \tag{13}$$

where the equality conditions are derived from the edges of the graph. The reduction procedure is clearly polynomial so, in order to prove the theorem we only need to prove that a solution of graph cover for G exists if and only if a cost-bound plan can be found for the query.

1. Suppose that a query plan for the query exists that uses $B + 1$ functions: $P = \{f_1, \ldots, f_B, g\}$ (the function g must obviously be part of every plan, since it is the only function that gives us the required output Y). Consider the set $S = \{v_i | f_i \in P\}$, which contains, clearly, B nodes, and the edge (v_{i_1}, v_{i_2}) of the graph. This edge is associated to a condition $X_{i_1} = X_{i_2}$ in the query and, since the query has been successfully planned, either the function f_{i_1} or f_{i_2} are in the plan. Consequently, either v_{i_1} or v_{i_2} are in the set, and the edge (v_{i_1}, v_{i_2}) is covered.
2. let now $S = \{v_1, \ldots, v_B\}$ be a covering and consider the plan $P = \{f_i | v_i \in S\} \cup \{g\}$. The output is clearly produced correctly as long as all the join conditions are satisfied. let $X_{i_1} = X_{i_2}$ be a join condition. This corresponds to an edge (v_{i_1}, v_{i_2}) and, since S is a covering, either v_{i_1} or v_{i_2} are in S. Assume that it is v_{i_1} (if it is v_{i_2} we can clearly carry out a similar argument). Then the plan contains the function f_{i_1}, which computes X_{i_1} so that the variables X_{i_1} and X_{i_2} and the join are determined by the following graph fragment

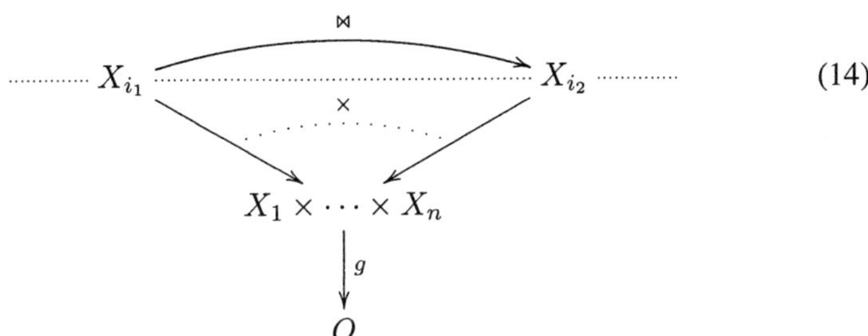

(14)

5 Related Work

The idea of modeling certain types of functional sources using a relational façade (or some modification thereof) is, of course, not new. The problem of conciliating the broad matching possibilities of a relation with the constraints deriving from the source has been solved in various ways the most common of which, to the best of our knowledge, is by the use of *adornments* [6,7], which also go under the name of *binding patterns*.

Given a relation $R(X_1, \ldots, X_n)$, a binding pattern is a classification of the variables $X_1, \ldots, X_n$ into *input* variables (which must be "bound" when the relation is accessed in the query, hence the name of the technique), *output* variables (which must be free when the relation is accessed), and *dyadic* variables, which can be indifferently inputs or outputs. Any query that accesses the relation by assigning values to the input variables and requiring values for some or all the output variables can be executed on that relation façade. A relational façade can, of course, have multiple binding patterns. If the relational façade is used to model an n-ary relation isomorphic to it, for instance, it allows all the 2^n possible bound/free binding patterns on its variables or, equivalently, all its variables are dyadic. In the following, a binding pattern for any n-ary relation will be represented as a string $b \in \{i, o, d\}$ (where i, o, and d stand for *input*, *output*, and *dyadic*, respectively, although dyadic variables will not appear in the examples that follow). Unlike our techinque, which determines query feasibility at run time, binding patterns are determined as part of the model. This difference results in a number of limitations of binding patterns, some examples of which are given below.

Multiple relations with hidden sorts. Consider a source with five sorts, X, Y, P, W, Q, and the functional dependencies shown in the following diagram

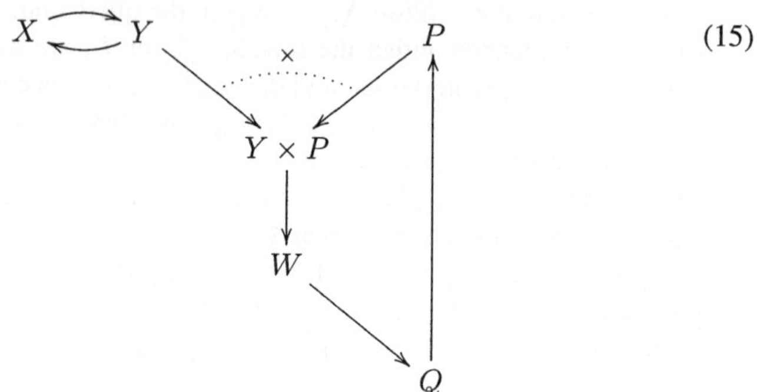

(15)

We want to model this source as a pair of relations: $R_1(X, Y)$ and $R_2(P, Q)$, while the sort W should not be exported. Considering the two relations and the functions needed to answer queries on them, we can see that the relation R_1 has two binding patterns: (i, o) and (o, i), while R_2 has only (o, i). A query such as "ans(Q) : $-R_1(X, y), R_2(X, Q)$" would be rejected by the binding pattern verification system because R_1 produces a set of X values from the query constant y, but R_2 can't take the X's as an input, Mapping the query to a functional diagram, however, produces

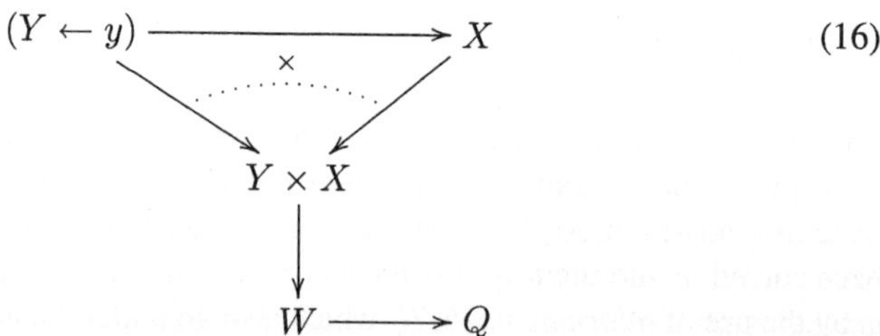

(16)

which is computable. Therefore, the query can be answered using the model presented in this paper.

Non-binding conditions. Binding patterns are based, as the name suggests, on the idea of binding certain variables in a relation, that is, on the idea of assigning them specific values. Because of these foundations, binding pattern models are ill-equipped to deal with non-binding conditions (that is, essentially, with all conditions except equality and membership in a finite set).

As an example, consider a source with three sorts, A, B, and C, and a function $A \times B \to C$. in addition, the source has a comparison capability which allows it to compare B with a fourth sort D and return C's for a specified value of A such that a specified condition $\mathfrak{C}(B, D)$ is verified: $A \times \mathfrak{C}(B, D) \to C$. the diagram of this source is:

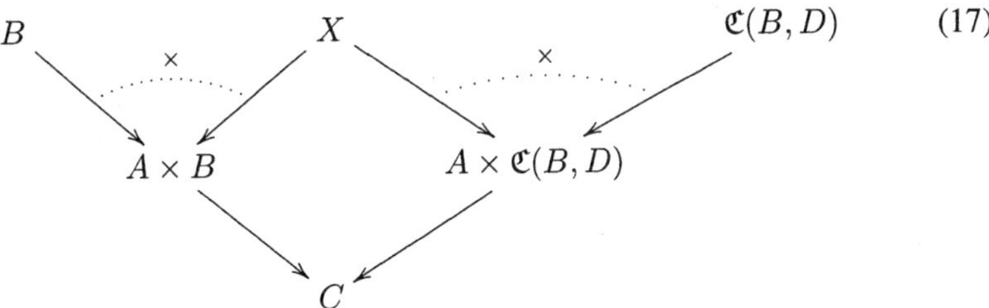

Because the condition $\mathfrak{C}(B, D)$ is non-binding, it doesn't contribute any binding pattern to the relation $R(A, B, C)$ for which the only binding pattern is, therefore, (i, i, o). A query such as "ans(C) : $-R(a, B, C), B < v$" where "<" is one of the operators allowed for $\mathfrak{C}(B, D)$ is not allowed in the binding pattern model, while it can be executed with the model presented here.

These examples highlight an important general difference between methods, such as binding patterns, that encode the satisfiability of functional constraints in the model, and methods such as ours that verify them when a query is executed: the latter class of methods can take advantage of rewriting opportunities that arise from the specific form of the query, even if they do not apply to a class of queries that can be identified at modeling time.

6 Conclusions

In this paper, we have considered the modeling of data sources for which a relational model doesn't apply, but that can be as a set of functions that, given certain constants and certain conditions, return a set of "corresponding" values. We were interested in modeling these sources as relations, and to find algorithms to translate queries on these relations into combinations of functions provided by the source.

The simplest form of the model that we have presented here is, mutatis mutandis, an instance of the problem of finding the closure of a set of functional dependencies and, in this sense, a rather classic one. The framework introduced in that section, however, allowed us to extend the formalism to other problems that either from a modeling point of view (the inclusion of data sorts representing conditions) of algorithmic (the inclusion of joins) go beyond the transitive closure problem.

In these conclusions, we would like to propose a further interpretation of the work presented here, an interpretation that, we believe, is more likely to generate interesting developments. The functions defined for the data source can be seen as atomic statements in a query planning language in which we want to translate our queries, and the function algebra that we have defined constitutes the structural statements of this planning language.

The problem that we have is therefore that of "implementing" queries in a language of fixed structure, but whose primitives change from source to source. In this framework, we can start asking questions such as the optimal structure of the language in order to manage the variability of the statement while still preserving the possibility of easy optimization, or the minimal characteristics of the primitive statements that allow the creation of interesting plans.

Finally, the nature of our method might make static planning (planning done separately from the execution) impossible, because there is no a priori indication of what queries will be feasible and which won't. it is not clear, at this time, whether static optimal planning is possible for sources with restrictions modeled this way, or if it is necessary to resort to some form of on-the-fly planning as the query is being executed.

These we regard as promising future directions for our work.

References

1. E. Damiani and L. Tanca, "Semantic approaches to structuring and querying web sites," in *DS-7*, 1997.
2. Z. Liu, F. Li, and W. K. Ng, "Wiccap data model: Mapping physical websites to logical views," in *Proceedings of ER 2002: 21st International Conference on Conceptual Modeling, Tampere, Finland*, pp. 120–134, October 2002.
3. A. S. da Silva, I. M. Evangelista Filha, A. H. F. Laender, and D. W. Embley, "Representing and querying semistructured web data using nested tables with structural variants," in *Proceedings of ER 2002: 21st International Conference on Conceptual Modeling, Tampere, Finland*, pp. 135–151, October 2002.
4. V. Zadorozhny, L. Raschid, M.-E. Vidal, T. Urhan, and L. Bright, "Efficient evaluation of queries in a mediator for websources," in *Proceedings of ACM SIGMOD*, 2002.
5. S. Santini, "Notes on a relational model of functional data sources," tech. rep., BIRN-CC, University of California, San Diego, 2003. http://ssantini.ucsd.edu/personal/bibliography/all-by-year/2003/s426long.pdf.
6. R. Yerneni, C. Li, H. Garcia-Molina, and J. Ullman, "Computing capabilities of mediators," in *Proceedings of ACM SIGMOD*, pp. 443–454, 1999.
7. Z. Li and H. Chen, "Computing strong/weak bisimulation equivalences and observation congruence for value-passing processes," *Lecture Notes in Computer Science*, vol. 1579, pp. 300–314, 1999.

Roles as Entity Types: A Conceptual Modelling Pattern

Jordi Cabot[1,2] and Ruth Raventós[2]

[1] Estudis d'Informàtica i Multimèdia, Universitat Oberta de Catalunya
jcabot@uoc.edu

[2] Dept. Llenguatges i Sistemas Informàtics, Universitat Politècnica de Catalunya
raventos@lsi.upc.es

Abstract. Roles are meant to capture dynamic and temporal aspects of real-world objects. The role concept has been used with many semantic meanings: *dynamic class, aspect, perspective, interface* or *mode*. This paper identifies common semantics of different role models found in the literature. Moreover, it presents a conceptual modelling pattern for the role concept that includes both the static and dynamic aspects of roles. A conceptual modelling pattern is aimed at representing a specific structure of knowledge that appears in different domains. In particular, we adapt the pattern to UML. The use of this pattern eases the definition of roles in conceptual schemas. In addition, we describe the design of schemas defined using our pattern in order to implement them in any object-oriented language. We also discuss the advantages of our approach over previous ones.

1 Introduction

Accurate and complete conceptual modelling is an essential premise for a correct development of an information system. Reusable conceptual schemas facilitate this difficult and time-consuming activity. The use of patterns is a key aspect to increase the reusability in all stages of software development.

A pattern identifies a problem and provides the specification of a generic solution to that problem. The definition of patterns in conceptual modelling may be regarded in two different ways: conceptual modelling patterns and analysis patterns.

In this paper, we distinguish between a conceptual modelling pattern that is aimed at representing a specific structure of knowledge encountered in different domains (for instance the *MemberOf* relationship), and an analysis pattern that specifies a generic and domain-dependent knowledge required to develop an application for specific users (for instance a pattern for electronic marketplaces). Authors do not always make this distinction. For example, to Fowler, in [9], patterns correspond to our conceptual modelling patterns while to Fernandez and Yuan, in [8], patterns correspond to our definition of analysis patterns. For a further discussion on analysis patterns see Teniente in [30].

The goal of this paper is to propose a conceptual modelling pattern for roles. A role is meant to capture dynamic and temporal aspects of real-world objects. There are some dynamic situations from the real world that are not well suited just with the basic modelling language constructs. For example, when we want to model situations where an entity can present different properties depending on the context where it is used.

P. Atzeni et al. (Eds.): ER 2004, LNCS 3288, pp. 69–82, 2004.

Although definitions of the role concept abound in the literature of conceptual modelling [2][4][6][9][14][25][26] a non-uniform and globally accepted definition is given. Roles are difficult to represent. They are not merely reified names for the participants in events. As we show in section 3, they can neither be represented as subtypes of other entity types even assuming multiple classification and inheritance. Rather, roles have their own characteristics that require them to be specified with a particular language construct in conceptual schemas.

We identify common semantics of role models found in the literature and present a pattern that fulfils them. The use of this pattern eases the definition of roles in conceptual schemas. Moreover, we also discuss the design and the implementation of conceptual schemas that use our pattern to facilitate their implementation in object-oriented languages. We adapt the pattern to UML [20]. As far as we know, ours is the first approach that allows the definition of roles by using the standard UML.

The rest of this paper is organized as follows: the next section presents the *Roles as entity types* Pattern. Section 3 comments related work and compare it with our proposal. Finally, conclusions and further work are presented.

2 *Roles as entity types* Pattern

In order to describe the role pattern we adopt the template proposed by Geyer-Schulz and Hahsler in [12] to describe conceptual modelling patterns (called by the authors analysis patterns). They adopt a uniform and consistent format, in contrast to Fowler in [9] who uses a very free format for pattern writing. Geyer-Schulz and Hahsler stress that adhering to a structure for writing patterns is essential since patterns are easier to teach, learn, compare, write and use once the structure has been understood.

Their template preserves the typical context/problem/forces/solution structure of design patterns but adapted for the description of conceptual modelling patterns. The template includes the following sections: (1) Pattern Name. (2) Intent: what the pattern does and what problems it addresses. (3) Motivation: a scenario that illustrates the problem and how the pattern contributes to the solution in the specific scenario. (4) Forces and Context that should be resolved by the pattern. (5) Solution: description of all relevant structural and behavioural aspects of the pattern. (6) Consequences: how the pattern achieves its objectives and the existing trade-off. (7) Design and implementation: how the pattern can be realized in the design stage. (8) Known uses: examples of the pattern.

Note that, in the same way design patterns include the outline of possible implementations of the pattern [11], our conceptual modelling pattern includes the outline of the design of the pattern.

Following this template, next sections present the *Roles as entity types* Pattern.

2.1 Intent

The intent is the representation of roles that entities play through their life span and the control of their evolution.

2.2 Motivation

The role concept appears very frequently in conceptual modelling. However, the possibilities that offer conceptual modelling languages to deal with them are very limited and cover only a small part of the role features (see, for example, what UML supports in [7] and [28]).

There is not a uniform and globally accepted definition of roles. We illustrate here some of the most relevant ones:

- "Role classes capture the temporal and evolutionary aspects of the real-word objects", Dahchour et al. in [6].
- "Roles allow an object to receive and send different messages at different stages of evolution", Pernici in [25].
- "Role is a defined behaviour pattern which may be assumed by entities of different kinds", Bachman and Daya in [1].
- "Roles are founded; defined in terms of relationship to other things, and lacks of "semantics rigidity" (something is semantically rigid if its existence is tied to its class)", Guarino in [14].

To summarize the above definitions, we could say that roles are useful to model the properties and behaviour of entities that evolve over time. The entity type *Person* is an illustrative example. During his or her life, a person may play different roles, for example he or she may become a student, an employee, a project manager, and so forth. Besides this, a person may have different properties and behaviour depending on the role or roles he/she is playing in a certain instant of time.

For instance, consider the following scenario: let Maria be a person who starts studying at a University (Maria plays the role of student). After some years of study she registers to a second university degree (Maria plays twice the role of student) and starts to work in a company (Maria plays the role of employee). In that company she may become a project manager (now, Maria through her employee role, plays the role of project manager). Note that, in this scenario, if we ask for the telephone number of Maria, the answer is not trivial since depending on the role she is playing it may be her personal or her company phone number.

Taking into account the complexity of the notion of role and the lack of support for roles in present conceptual modelling languages, it is clear that a pattern to define such a common construct is needed in conceptual modelling.

2.3 Forces and Context

Our definition of the role concept is refined by describing the set of features that roles must meet, most of which have been identified by Steinmann [27]. In our case, these features are the forces that influence and should be resolved by the pattern.

We describe them using some examples over the scenario introduced above:

1. Ownership. A role comes with its own properties [16][6][15][31], i.e., an instance of *Employee* has its own properties which may be different to the ones of the entity type that plays such a role.

2. Dependency. An instance of a role is related to a unique instance of its entity type and its existence depends on the entity type to which it is associated to [16][4][6], i.e., it is not possible to have an instance of *Student* not related to an instance of *Person.*
3. Diversity. An entity may play different roles simultaneously [16][6][13][25][15][31][32], i.e., an instance of *Person* may play simultaneously the role of *Student* and *Employee.*
4. Multiplicity. An instance of an entity type may play several instances of the same role type at the same time [16][6][13][15][25][31][32]. For instance, a person that registers to more than a University have multiple instaces of *Student* related to it.
5. Dynamicity. An entity may acquire and relinquish roles dynamically [1][16][6][13][15][23], i.e., a person may become a student, after some years become an employee, finish his/her studies, become a project manager, start another degree and so forth.
6. Control. The sequence in which roles may be acquired and relinquished can be subject to restrictions [6][25][31], i.e., a person may not become an employee when he/she is older than 65 years.
7. Roles can play roles [16][4][6][31][32]. This mirrors that an instance of *Person* can play the role of *Employee* and an instance of *Employee* can also play de role of *ProjectManager.*
8. Role identity [31]. Each instance of a role has its own role identifier, which is different from that of all other instances of the entity to which is associated with. This solves the so-called *counting problem* introduced by Wieringa et al in [31]. It refers to the fact that we need to distinguish the instances of the roles from the instances of the entity types that play them. For example, if we want to count the number of people that are students in a university (i.e. every person who is registered to at least a program in such university), the total number is less than the number of registered students in such university (in this case a person is counted twice if he or she is registered at two programs).
9. Adoption. Roles do not inherit from their entity types [16][13]. Instead, instances of roles have access to some properties of their corresponding entities i.e., *Student* may adopt *name* and *address* properties of *Person* but neither *religion* nor *marital status* properties. Therefore, the *Student* role cannot use the last two referred properties.

2.4 Solution

We divide the solution of our role pattern in two subsections. The first one deals with the structural aspects of roles while the second one deals with their evolution.

2.4.1 Structural Aspects of Roles

We believe there is not a fundamental difference between roles and entity types since roles have their own properties and identity. Therefore, we represent roles as entity types with their own attributes, relationships and generalisation/specialisation hierarchies. For practical reasons we call *role entity* types (or simply role if the context is clear) the entity types that represent roles and *natural entity types*[1] (or simply entity types) the entity types that may play those roles.

We define the relationship between a role entity type and its natural entity type by means of a *RoleOf* relationship. This special relationship relates a natural entity type with a role entity type to indicate that the natural entity type may play the role represented by the role entity type. In the relationship we also specify the properties (attributes and associations) of the natural entity type that are adopted by the role entity type.

Note that, since roles may play other roles, the same entity type may appear as a role entity type in a *RoleOf* relationship and as a natural entity type in a different *RoleOf* relationship.

Although this representation may be expressed in many conceptual modelling languages, in this work, we only adapt it to UML. In particular, we use UML 2.0 [20] and OCL 2.0 [19] versions.

To be able to represent the *RoleOf* relationship we use the extension mechanisms provided by UML, such as stereotypes, tags and constraints. Stereotypes allow us to define (virtual) new subclasses of metaclasses by adding some additional semantics. A stereotype may also define additional constraints on its base class and add some new properties through the use of tags.

The <<RoleOf>> stereotype allows us to define a *RoleOf* relationship between the natural and role entity types. The base class of the stereotype is the *Association* metaclass, which represents association relationships among classes. The <<RoleOf>> stereotype also includes the properties[2] the role adopts from the natural entity type. They are represented with a multivalued tag, called *adoptedProperties*. We may pack this stereotype in a new UML Profile [20] for Roles. Figure 1 shows the definition of the <<RoleOf>> stereotype.

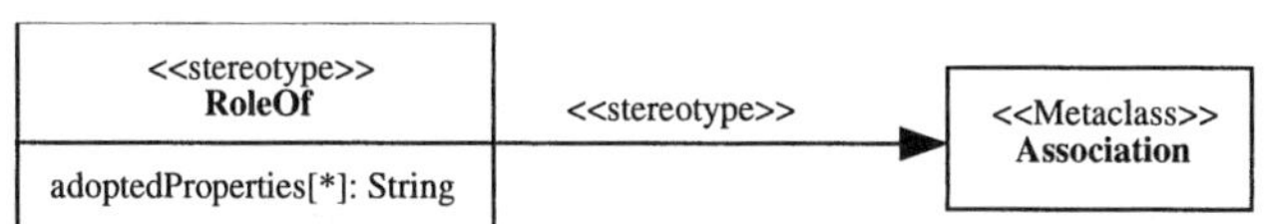

Fig. 1. Definition of the RoleOf stereotype

The multiplicity of the role towards its entity type is '1' (since a role can only be related to a single instance of the entity type) and its settability is *readOnly* (the role instance must always be related to the same instance of the entity type).

As an example, figure 2 shows the extended example introduced in section 2.2 specified in UML. The figure illustrates a natural entity type, *Person*, with its own properties, playing two roles: *Student* and *Employee*. The role *Student* is a generalisation of domestic and foreign students. The role *Employee* may play also the role of *ProjectManager*, who manages a set of tasks. *Student* adopts properties name, phone

[1] The *natural entity type* of a role relationship has sometimes been called *object class* [6] [31] *ObjectWithRoles* [13], *natural type* [14] [27], *base class* [4], *entity type* [1], *entity class* [2], *base role* [24], or *core object* [3].

[2] A property in UML 2.0 [20] represents both the attributes and associations of an entity type.

number and country (represented as attributes) and address (represented as an association) from *Person*, and *Employee* adopts the name and the derived age attribute. *ProjectManager* adopts name, employee number and the contract expiration date from *Employee*.

Note that *Employee* has its own phone number different from the *Person*'s phone number, i.e., *Employee* does not adopt the phone number attribute from *Person*. Therefore the answer to the question: "which is the phone number of Maria?" will vary depending on whether we are considering Maria as an instance of *Person* or *Employee*. The stereotyped operations shown in the figure will be taken up in the following section.

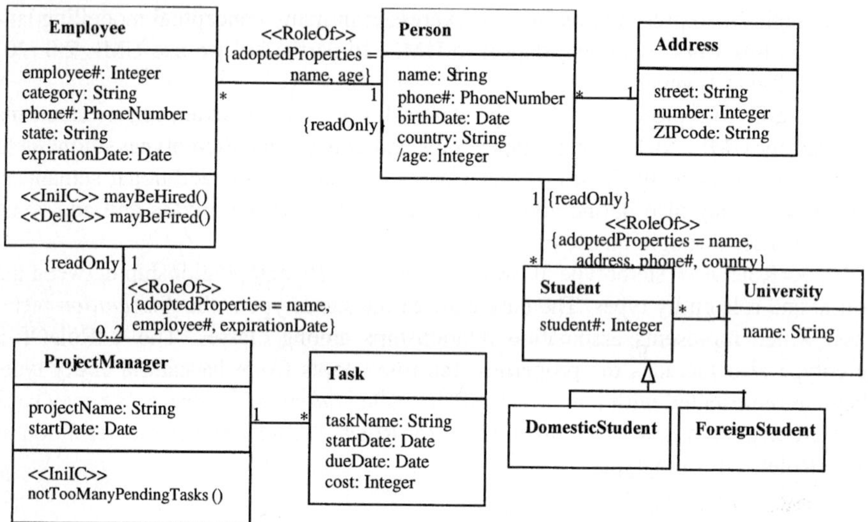

Fig. 2. Example of *RoleOf* relationhips in the UML

To complete the definition of the static aspects of roles we must attach some constraints to the <<RoleOf>> stereotype in order to control the correctness of its use. The constraints are the following:

- A stereotyped <<RoleOf>> association is a binary association with multiplicity '1' and settability *readOnly* in a member end.
- Each value of the *adoptedProperty* tag must coincide with the name of a property of the natural entity type.
- A role entity type can only be related throughout a *RoleOf* relationship to at most a natural entity type.
- No cycles of roles are permitted; a role entity type may not be related throughout a direct or indirect *RoleOf* relationship to itself.

Adopted properties by the role from its natural entity type may be considered as implicit properties of the role entity type. Nevertheless, in order to facilitate the use of these adopted properties (for instance, when writing OCL expressions) we may need to include them explicitly in the role entity type. In this case, we add an extra property in the role entity type for each adopted property. These extra properties are labeled with the <<adopted>> stereotype to distinguish them from the own properties of the role entity type. In addition, they are derived. Their derivation rule always follows the general form:

context *RoleEntityType::adoptedPropertyX: Type*
derive*: naturalEntityType.propertyX*

Note that, to facilitate the work of designers, these added properties can be automatically generated. Figure 3 extends a subset of the previous example illustrating the *Student* role entity type including its adopted properties.

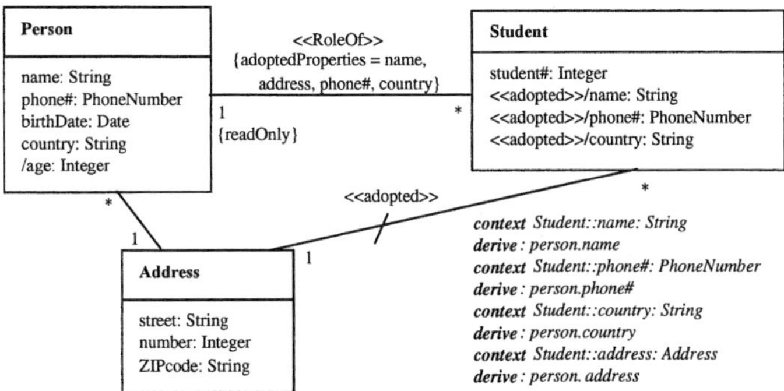

Fig. 3. Example of the *Student* role entity type

2.4.2 Role Acquisition and Relinquishment

So far, we have introduced a representation of the static part of the *Roles as entity types* Pattern. Nevertheless, this is not enough since role instances may be added or removed dynamically from an entity during its lifecycle and this addition or removal may be subjected to user-defined restrictions.

Since roles are represented as entity types we may define constraints on roles in the same way as we define constraints on entity types. Some of the constraints are inherent to our role representation (for example, that a person must play the role of *Employee* to play the role of *ProjectManager*, is already enforced by the schema). Other restrictions involved may be expressed by means of the predefined constraints of UML. For example, to restrict that an *Employee* cannot play more than twice the *ProjectManager* role simultaneously, it is enough to define a cardinality constraint in the relationship. The definition of the rest of constraints requires the use of a general-purpose language, commonly OCL in the case of UML. For instance, we could specify OCL constraints to control that:

- A *person* can only play the role of *Employee* if he/she is between 18 and 65 years old:

  context *Employee* ***inv****:*

  self.age>=18 and self.age<=65

- Any task of a ProjectManager must finish before his contract expires

  context *Task* ***inv****:*

  self.dueDate<self.projectManager.expirationDate

These OCL constraints are static, and thus, the role instances must satisfy them at any time. However, many of the restrictions that may be involved in the evolution of roles only apply at particular times, concretely they only need to be satisfied when the role is acquired or when it is relinquished. To specify such constraints we use the notion of creation-time constraints defined by Olivé in [18] and, in a similar way, we define the deletion-time constraints.

Creation-time constraints must hold when the instances of some entity type are created (in our case when the role is created). Deletion-time constraints must hold when the instances of some entity type are deleted (in our case when the role is deleted). These constraints are represented as operations, also called *constraint* operations, attached to the entity types and identified by a special stereotype. The creation-time constraint operations are marked with the stereotype <<IniIC>>. We define the stereotype <<DelIC>> for the deletion-time constraint operations.

These operations return a boolean that must be true to indicate that the constraint is satisfied. If the operation returns false (i.e., the constraint is not satisfied) then the creation or deletion event of the role is not accomplished. When appropriate, the operations are automatically executed by the information system.

As an example, we have defined the following restrictions in figure 2:

- A person cannot become an employee if he/she is studying two university degrees simultaneously. Note that this does not imply that a person that is already an employee may apply for two degrees.

  ```
  context Employee :: mayBeHired () : Boolean
  body: self.person.student->size()<2
  ```

- An employee may not be fired if he or she is in maternity leave.

  ```
  context Employee :: mayBeFired () : Boolean
  body: self.state<>'MaternityLeave'
  ```

- An employee may not become a new project manager if he/she still holds more than ten pending tasks.

  ```
  context ProjectManager:: notTooManyPendingTasks(): Boolean
  body self.employee.projectManager.tasks->
                       select(dueDate>Today)->size()<=10
  ```

2.5 Consequences

Our pattern of roles achieves the objectives proposed in Section 2.3 since it fulfils the role features outlined before:

- Ownership. As roles are represented as entity types, they may have their own properties.
- Dependency. The cardinality '1' with the tag {readOnly} ensures that all role instances depend on a unique instance of the natural entity type.
- Diversity. As the *RoleOf* relationship is an association, entity types may have many *RoleOf* relationships.
- Multiplicity. This is obtained by the cardinality at the *RoleOf* relationship.
- Dinamicity. Entities are related to their roles through an association. Thus, an entity may acquire or retract instances of a role many times.

- Control. The sequence in which roles may be acquired and relinquished can be subjected to restrictions.
- Roles can play roles. Roles are represented by ordinary classes. So, they can be participants of a *RoleOf* relationship.
- Role identity. As roles are represented as entity types, their instances have their own identifier.
- Adoption. The *adoptedProperty* tag of the *RoleOf* relationship allows the definition of this mechanism.

A trade-off that one may find in our representation is that we do not consider that roles can be associated to different natural entity types. We believe this situation may be solved by defining a common supertype for all the natural entity types that play such role. For instance, if we need *Client* to be role of both *Company* and *Person* (understood as a physical person), we could define a common supertype for *Company* and *Person*, called *LegalPerson*, which plays the role of *Client*.

On the other hand, we do not allow roles to remain unconnected to any entity, as for instance, *Employee* understood as a vacant position not played by any *Person*. This approach is commonly used when considering roles just as interfaces. We discuss the limitations of this approach in Section 3.

2.6 Design and Implementation

There are some design patterns useful for designing and implementing roles in object oriented languages [9]. However, most of them are unable to deal with our proposed role semantics completely. A well-known pattern close to our role defined semantics is the *Role Object Pattern* [3]. This pattern is especially well suited for role implementation when roles are deemed as a specialization (or a kind of specialization) of its entity type (see Pelechano et al. in [24] as an example).

Nevertheless, this pattern is not entirely appropriate for designing our conceptual modelling pattern. We encounter two main problems in the *Role Object Pattern*. First, it uses a common superclass for all the roles of the entity type. In our approach, roles are independent entity types with not necessarily any common properties that justify this superclass. Secondly, all the roles are forced to have the same inherited properties; it is not possible to define different adopted properties for each role.

This is the reason why we advocate here for an adapted version of this pattern that takes into account our complete role semantics, including the adoption mechanism and the creation-time and deletion-time constraints.

Given a natural entity type and the set of its roles, we create a class for the natural entity type and a class for each role. We create a different relationship between the natural entity type and each of its roles. This relationship will be used to navigate from the natural entity type to its roles and vice versa. We add to the natural entity type two new operations *addRole* and *deleteRole* in charge of adding (deleting) roles to the natural entity after checking the creation-time (deletion-time) constraints. We could also add other useful operations when dealing with roles, such as *hasRole* (to check whether an entity plays a role) or *getRole* (to obtain a role played by the entity).

The problem of the design of the adopted properties may be regarded as the same problem as designing derived information. In general, from a design and/or implementation point of view, there are two different approaches to deal with derived information. The attributes may be computed if they are calculated by means of an operation or may be materialized if they are explicitly stored in the class. In this case, for each adopted property we add an extra operation to the role class that returns the value of the property of the natural entity type. The operation accesses the property of the natural entity type navigating through the relationship.

Figure 4 summarizes our proposal. In figure 5 we apply the proposed design pattern to a part of the conceptual schema of figure 2. Note that *Employee* is both a role for the *Person* entity type and a natural entity type for the *ProjectManager* role, and thus, it presents both a reference to *Person* (as a role entity type) and the operations *addRole* and *deleteRole* (as a natural entity type). Additionally, *Employee* includes also the *name* and *age* operations to get this information from *Person*.

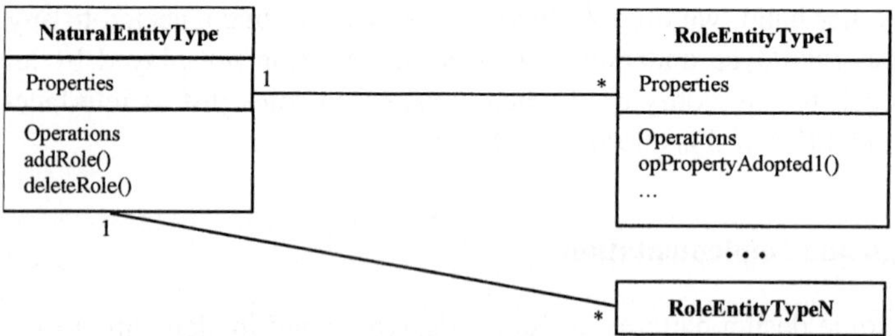

Fig. 4. Summarized class diagram of the design

This structure can be directly implemented in any common object-oriented language. An example of the implementation in the Java Language can be found in [4].

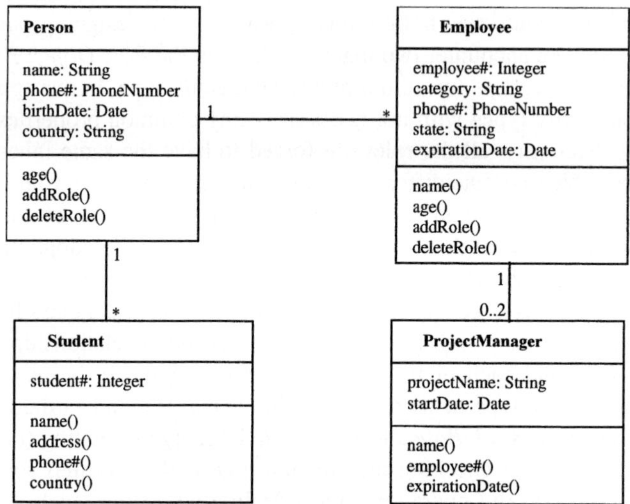

Fig. 5. Example of an application of the design

2.7 Known Uses

The role concept appears frequently in many different domains of the real world, since in each domain we can find entity types that present some properties that evolve over time.

Papazoglou et al. in [23] note that roles can be useful for several types of applications based on the use of object-oriented technology and they describe two examples of broad types of application that need role support: *security* and *workflows*. Some more examples are discussed by Jodlowski et al. in [15].

3 Related Work

Previous research can be grouped in four basic approaches to represent roles. We discuss the major drawbacks of each approach according to our role defined semantics. However, they may suffice when considering more limited semantics.

The first approach represents a role as a label assigned to a participant in an event [20]. This representation does not achieve our objectives because roles come with their own properties different from those of the entity types playing them, which cannot be defined within the label.

A second approach considers that roles and entity types can be combined into a single hierarchy [1][4][26]. Role entity types are represented as subtypes of the natural entity type. For instance, if *Person* were a natural entity type, then *Student, Employee* and *ProjectManager* roles would appear as subtypes. Quite obviously, such a solution requires dynamic and multiple classification, since a person can change his/her role and play several roles simultaneously. However we would like to make emphasis of three important features that specialization does not cover. First, what we have defined as multiplicity: an entity may play the same role more than once at the same time (i.e., specializations does not allow to define a *Person* playing simultaneously twice the role of *Employee*). The second one is adoption; with specialization we cannot restrict which attributes are adopted by the roles because they inherit all the attributes of their supertype. And finally, with specialization the role and the entity type have the same identifier, therefore the counting problem mentioned before is not solved. A further discussion on this topic can be seen in [27] and [15].

A third approach suggests that roles are only partial specifications of the entities playing them, and then the features of roles are the very features of interfaces (interfaces as types, in the sense of Java and UML) as Steimann in [29] or Lea and Marlowe in [17]. This alternative does not solve the multiplicity feature since an entity may not play the same interface more than once at the same time. On the other hand, roles do not have their own separated state (the whole state is shared in the natural entity type), since interfaces do not have their own attributes. Besides, when an instance of the natural entity type is created it acquires automatically all the roles, and thus, we cannot control nor restrict the evolution of the roles the instance of the natural entity type plays. Therefore, we consider that interfaces do not cover everything one might expect from the role concept.

The last approach, and also our approach, represents a role as a distinct element from an entity type but coupled to it [6][16][22][25][27]. However, most of these approaches use different semantics that the ones presented in this paper. For instance, some solutions are based on the fact that the instance of a natural entity type and its role instances share the same object identifier as Papazoglou et al in [22], among others. These solutions neither solve the counting problem mentioned before. Others, as Pernici in [25] do not allow roles to play roles. Our alternative suggesting roles as separated entity types fulfils the role semantics.

We believe one of the main advantages of our approach over previous ones is that we handle the complexity of role semantics in a very simple manner since we represent roles and its evolution with already existing elements (entity types and constraints) without adding completely new language constructs. Therefore, the designer can easily use the pattern to specify roles in conceptual schemas. In addition to this, our pattern describes a representation of roles in the standard UML, and thus, the pattern can be directly incorporated into current UML CASE tools.

We would also like to remark that our approach is complete and feasible in the sense that includes the design and the implementation of the pattern, in contrast to most of previous approaches that do not state how this could be achieved.

4 Conclusions and Further Work

This paper identifies the most important features of roles and presents the *Roles as entity types* pattern, a conceptual modelling pattern for roles. We have adapted the pattern to allow the specification of roles in UML conceptual schemas. To our knowledge, ours is the first standard extension to UML to define roles in conceptual schemas in this language. The pattern can be easily implemented in any UML CASE tool in order to allow designers to use the role concept.

The pattern includes the static aspects of roles as well as their evolution. We define roles as entity types (role entity types) related to natural entity types by means of a *RoleOf* relationship that includes the adoption of properties from the natural entity types by the role entity types. We have extended UML by means of the <<*RoleOf*>> stereotype to be able to represent such kind of relationships. To specify the role evolution we use two special kinds of constraints: creation-time constraints and deletion-time constraints. We have also discussed the design and implementation of conceptual schemas specified using the pattern.

It would be interesting to study which taxonomies appearing in conceptual schemas should be better specified by using *RoleOf* relationships. This could be done by comparing the specification of the same case study with and without the use of roles. Moreover, we would like to automatize our approach by means of an application that given a conceptual schema (for instance, represented in XMI [21]) would generate automatically the corresponding classes in the target object oriented language. These are directions in which we plan to continue our work.

Acknowledgements

We would like to thank people of the GMC group for their many useful comments to previous drafts of this paper. This work has been partially supported by the Ministerio de Ciencia y Tecnologia and FEDER under project TIC2002-00744.

References

1. Albano, R. Bergamini, G. Ghelli, R. Orsini, "An Object Data Model with Roles", Proceedings of the 19th VLDB Conference. Morgan Kaufmann, 1993, pp. 39-51.
2. C.W. Bachman, M. Daya. "The Role Concept in Data Models", Proceedings of the Third International Conference on Very Large Databases, 1977, pp. 464-476.
3. D. Bäumer, D. Riehle, W. Wiberski, M. Wulf. "The Role Object Pattern", Proceedings of PLoP '97. Technical Report WUCS-97-34. Washington University Dept.
4. J.Cabot, R. Raventos, "Roles as Entity Types: A Conceptual Modelling Pattern", Technical Report No. LSI-03-55-R, UPC, December 2003.
5. W.W. Chu, G. Zhang, "Associations and Roles in Object-oriented Modeling", Proceedings of the 16th Int. Conf. on Conceptual Modeling (ER'97), LNCS 1331, Springer, pp. 257-270.
6. M. Dahchour, A. Pirotte, E. Zimányi, "A role model and its metaclass implementation", Information Systems, 29 (2004) pp. 235-270.
7. R.Depke, G.Engels, J.M. Küster, "On the Integration of Roles in the UML", Technical Report No. 214, Universityof Paderborn, August 2000.
8. E. B. Fernandez; X. Yuan. "Semantic Analisis Patterns", Proceedings of the 19th Int. Conf. on Conceptual Modeling (ER'00), LNCS 1920, Springer 2000, pp. 183-195.
9. M. Fowler, "Dealing with Roles", PLoP '97 and EuroPLoP '97 Conference, Technical Report #wucs-97-34, Dept. of Computer Science, Washington University, 1997.
10. M. Fowler, "Analysis Patterns: Reusable Object Models", Addison-Wesley, 1997.
11. E.Gamma, R.Helm, R.Johnson, J. Vlissides, "Design Patterns – Elements of Reusable Object-Oriented Software", Addison-Wesley, 1994.
12. A. Geyer-Schulz, M. Hahsler, "Software Reuse with Analysis Patterns", Proceedings of AMCIS 2002, August 2002.
13. G. Gottlob, M. Schrefl, B. Röck, "Extending Object-oriented Systems with Roles", ACM Transactions on Information Systems 14 (3), 1996, pp. 268-296.
14. N. Guarino, "Concepts, Attributes and Arbitrary Relations", Data & Knowledge Engineering 8, 1992, pp. 249-261.
15. A. Jodłowski, P. Habela, J. Płodzien, C. Subieta, "Extending OO Metamodels towards Dynamic Object Roles", R. Meersman et al. (Eds.): CoopIS/DOA/ODBASE 2003, LNCS 2888, pp. 1032–1047, 2003.
16. B.B. Kristensen, Object Oriented Modeling with Roles, Proceedings of the 2nd Int. Conf. on Object-Oriented Information Systems (OOIS'95), 1995
17. D. Lea, J. Marlowe, "Interface-Based Protocol Specification of Open Systems using PSL", 9th European Conference ECOOP'95 - Object-Oriented Programming, LNCS 952 Springer 1995, pp. 374-398.
18. A. Olivé, "Integrity Constraints Definition in Object–Oriented Conceptual Modeling Languages", Proceedings of the 22th Int. Conf. on Conceptual Modeling (ER'03), LNCS 2813, 2003, pp.349-362.
19. Object Management Group, OMG Adopted Specification, "UML 2.0 OCL", October 2003.
20. Object Management Group, OMG Adopted Specification. "UML 2.0 Superstructure Specification", August 2002.
21. Object Management Group, "OMG XML Metadata Interchange Specification", v.1.2, January 2002.
22. M.P. Papazoglou, B.J. Krämer, "A database model for object dynamics", The VLDB Journal (6), January 1997, pp. 73-96.

23. M. P. Papazoglou, "Modeling Object Dynamics", in. M.P. Papazoglou, S. Spaccapietra, Z.Tari (Eds.), Advances in Object-Oriented Data Modeling. MIT Press 2000, pp. 195-217.
24. V. Pelechano, M. Albert, E. Campos, O. Pastor, "Automating the Code Generation of Role Classes in OO Conceptual Schemas", , Proceedings of the 4st Int. Conf. on Enterprise Information Systems (ICEIS 2002), 2002, pp. 656-686.
25. Pernici, "Objects with Roles", Proceedings of the Conference on Office Information Systems, SIGOIS Bulletin, vol. 11, no. 2/3, ACM Press, New York, 1990, pp. 205-215.
26. J. Sowa, "Conceptual Structures: Information Processing in Mind and Machine. Addison-Wesley Publishing Company, New York, 1984.
27. F. Steimann, "On the Representation of Roles in Object-oriented and Conceptual Modelling", Data & Knowledge Engineering 35, 2000, pp. 83-106.
28. F. Steimann, "A Radical Revision of UML's Role Concept", UML 2000: The Unified Modelling Language, LNCS 1939, Springer, pp. 194-209.
29. F. Steimann, "Role=Interface", Journal of Object-Oriented Programming, October/November 2001, Vol. 14, Num. 14, pp. 23-32.
30. E. Teniente, "Analysis Pattern Definition in the UML", Proceedings IRMA'2003, Idea Group Pub., pp. 774–777.
31. R.Wieringa, W. de Jonge. P. Spruit., "Using Dynamic Classes and Role Classes to Model Object Migration",Theory and Practice of Object Systems, 1(1), 1995, pp. 61-83.
32. R. K. Wong, H. L. Chau, F. H. Lochovsky, "A Data Model and Semantics of Objects with Dynamic Roles", 13th International Conference on Data Engineering, IEEE Computer Society, pp. 402-411.

Modeling Default Induction with Conceptual Structures

Julien Velcin and Jean-Gabriel Ganascia

LIP6, Université Paris VI
8 rue du Capitaine Scott
75015 Paris, France
{julien.velcin,jean-gabriel.ganascia}@lip6.fr

Abstract. Our goal is to model the way people induce knowledge from rare and sparse data. This paper describes a theoretical framework for inducing knowledge from these incomplete data described with conceptual graphs. The induction engine is based on a non-supervised algorithm named default clustering which uses the concept of stereotype and the new notion of default subsumption, the latter being inspired by the default logic theory. A validation using artificial data sets and an application concerning an historic case are given at the end of the paper.

1 Introduction

We aim to model the way it is possible to induce knowledge from rare and sparse data using a default reasoning. In this way, we propose a new induction engine using non-supervised learning techniques and the conceptual graph formalism as described by J. Sowa [1]. The induction mechanism is based on the notion of default subsumption, the latter having been inspired from the default logic theory of R. Reiter [2]. This new model has been designed both to deal with heterogeneous and incomplete databases and to understand the way people build stereotypes from incomplete information, as it can be found for example in newspaper articles.

On the one hand, such databases have to be automatically completed with a default reasoning to become comparable. On the other hand, our hypothesis is that popular inductions are not only due to the lack of facts, but also to the poor description of the existing facts. This sparseness is particularly favorable to the use of background knowledge –like theories– and to the elaboration of caricatural representations we called *stereotypes.*

In such cases, we simulate the erection of categories from incomplete information by using machine learning and data mining techniques. These categories are formed with a new relation we introduce, the default subsumption, and named thanks to the concept of stereotype, which is defined below. In the past, some meaningful results have been obtained by using supervised learning techniques and applying them to model pre-scientific reasoning both in the field of medicine and in some cases of dissemination of social misrepresentations [3, 4].

P. Atzeni et al. (Eds.): ER 2004, LNCS 3288, pp. 83–95, 2004.

Our paper is divided in two parts. The first section presents the logical framework modeling inductive reasoning from sparse descriptions. This framework makes use both of the notion of default subsumption, which is analogous to default logic, and of the concept of stereotype, which models the way sparse descriptions may be categorized. Details tools and strategies are then detailed in order to build such sets of stereotypes. The second section is dedicated to the validation of the model from artificial data sets and to a real application dealing with social misrepresentations.

2 Logical Framework

2.1 Default Logic

During the eighties, there were many attempts to model deductive reasoning in presence of implicit informations. A lot of formalisms [5, 6, 2] have been developed to encompass the inherent difficulties of such models, especially their non-monotony: close-world assumption, circumscription, default logic, etc. Since our goal here is to model the way people induce empirical knowledge from partially and non homogeneously described facts, we face a very similar problem: in both cases, it is to reason in presence of implicit information. Therefore, it is natural to make use of similar formalisms.

In this case, we choose the default logic formalism, which were developed in the eighties by R. Reiter [2]. This logic for default reasoning is based on the notion of default rules, which permits to infer new formulas when the hypotheses are not inconsistent.More generally, a default rule has always the following form: $A : B_1, B_2, ...B_n/C$ where A is called the prerequisite, B_i the justifications and C the conclusion. This default rule can be interpreted as follows: if A is known to be true and if it is consistent to assume $B_1, B2, ...B_n$ then conclude C.

For instance, let us consider the next default rule:

`politician(X) ∧ introducedAbroad(X) : ¬ diplomat(X) / traitor(X)`

This rule translates a usual way of reasoning for people living in France during the end of the 19th century; it means that one can suspect all politicians who are introduced abroad to be traitors towards their own countries, except for diplomats. In other words, it expresses that the conclusion traitor(X) can be derived if X is a politician who is known to be introduced abroad while we cannot prove that he is a diplomat.

Let us note that information conveyed by default rules refers to implicit connotations. As example, the antinomy among patriots and internationalists or the rule that assimilates almost all the politicians involved with foreigners to traitors correspond to connotations and may facilitate the completion of partial descriptions. The key idea is that people have in mind stereotypes that correspond to strong images stored in memory and that partial descriptions evoke such stereotypes. The following sections are dedicated to this concept of stereotype; before, it is necessary to introduce the notion of default subsumption.

In the rest of this section, we use the framework designed by Sowa in [1]. A short introduction can be found at [7].

2.2 Default Subsumption

First of all, let us assume that a stereotype is a specific description, which will be in this paper a conceptual graph, and consider the description function $\delta : F \to D$ which associates a conceptual graph $\delta(f) \in D$ to each fact f from the set of initial facts F. Let us next consider that a fact subsumes another fact if it is the result of the generalization operators.

A stereotype stored in the memory is said to subsume a fact by default if it has no contradictory features with the description of the fact considered, i.e. $\delta(f)$. So it can be used to complete this description without adding any incoherence. In other words, the fact can be completed in such a way that its description can now be subsumed by the stereotype.

Let us consider now the graph g associated with a fact in which there is a very large number of missing data. The missing data can be guessed and completed to obtain a more specific graph g_S. We follow here the notations given by Sowa in [1] (definition 3.5.1): $g_S \leq g$ means that g_S is a specialization of g and g is a generalization of g_S, i.e. g subsumes g_S. Now, let s be one stereotype belonging to the structured memory. If this stereotype is more general than g_S, ie $g_S \leq s$, then it subsumes g *by default.* More formally:

Definition 1. *Let f be a fact represented by the conceptual graph $g = \delta(f)$ and s a stereotype. s* subsumes g by default *if and only if there exists a graph g_S with $g_S \leq g$ and $g_S \leq s$. g_S is therefore a graph formed by the join operator performed on the graphs g and s.*

Fig. 1 presents the fact *The meal of Jules is composed of steak, red wine, and ends with a cup of very hot coffee* which can be subsumed by default by the stereotype *The meal is composed of steak with potatoes and French bread, and ends with a cup of coffee* because the fact can be completed to *The meal of Jules is composed of steak with potatoes and French bread, red wine, and ends with a cup of very hot coffee.* If the stereotype had presented a meal ending with a liqueur, it would not match the fact and so could not subsume it by default.

Property 1. The notion of default subsumption is more general than that of classic subsumption. Let g and g' be two conceptual graphs. If g subsumes g' then g subsumes g' by default.

Property 2. The default subsumption is a symmetrical relation. Let u_1 and u_2 be two conceptual graphs. If u_1 subsumes u_2 by default, then u_2 subsumes u_1 by default too.

Let us note that the notion of default subsumption may appear strange for people accustomed to classical subsumption since it is symmetrical. As a consequence, it does not define an ordering relationship on the space of description.

2.3 Concept of Stereotype

Eleanor Rosch saw the categorization itself as one of the most important issues in cognitive science [8]. She observed that children learn how to classify first

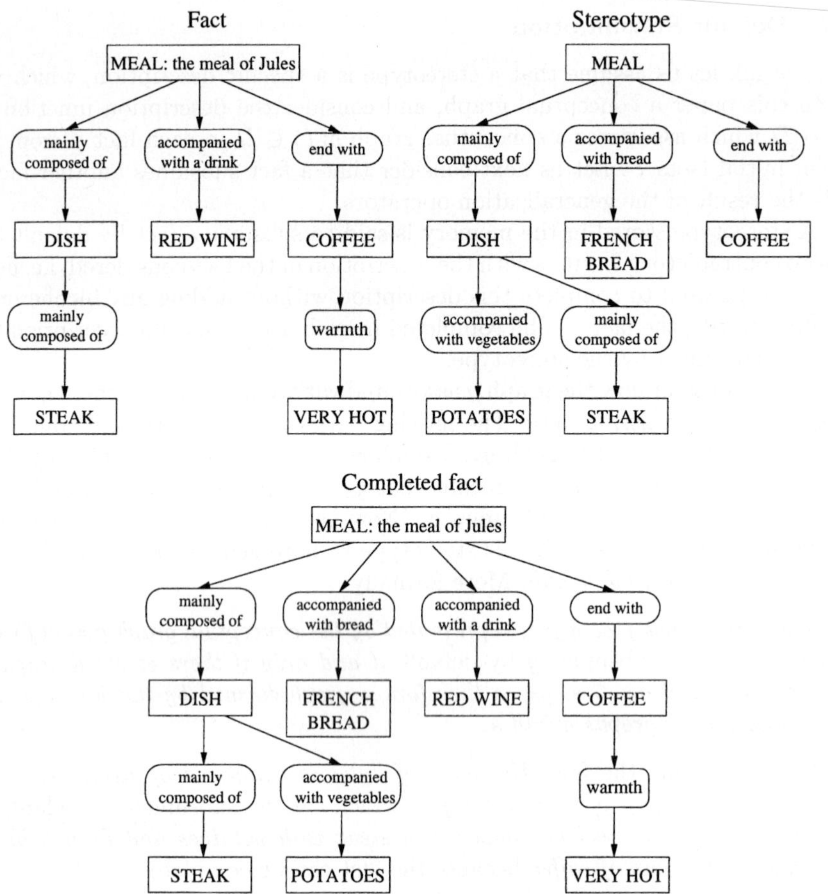

Fig. 1. The stereotype *subsumes by default* the fact description. The description below is the result of the join operator, i.e. the completed fact.

in terms of concrete cases rather than through defining features. She therefore introduced the concept of prototype as the ideal member of a category. Ownership to a class is then defined by the proximity to the prototype and not by the number of shared features.

For example, a robin is closer to the bird prototype than an ostrich, but they are both closer to it than they are to the prototype of a fish, so we call them both birds. However, it takes longer to say an ostrich is a bird than it takes to say a robin is a bird because the ostrich is further from the prototype. Sowa defines a prototype as a typical instance formed by joining one or more schemata. Instead of describing a specific individual, it describes a typical or "average" individual.

From a computational point of view the concept of prototype is difficult to manage since many complete observations have to be considered in order to construct such an ideal fact. Furthermore, it is not really appropriate in order to classify new observations and predict missing information. We therefore propose to adopt the concept of stereotype, which is quite close to that of prototype but more adapted to missing values.

The concept of stereotype was introduced by W. Lippman in a book about public opinion [9]. We define it here as a specific and imaginary fact that combines features found in the facts it subsumes by default. Since there is no contradiction between a fact and its related stereotype, it may be used to complete its description. In other words, a stereotype s is said to cover a fact described by g if and only if s subsumes by default the graph g. As a consequence, g may be completed by the conceptual graph s. This point will be detailed later.

2.4 Set of Stereotypes

Groups of people share implicit knowledge, which makes them able to understand each other without having to express everything explicitly. This sort of knowledge can be expressed in terms of erudite theories (e.g. the "blocking perspiration" theory in [3]) or use a more "naive" formulation. Our second hypothesis is that this implicit knowledge can be stored in terms of sets of stereotypes. This means that many people have in mind the sets of stereotypes and that they use them to reason in a stereotyped way by associating new facts to stereotypes they have in mind.

To formalize this idea, let first suppose that a description space D and a set of facts F are given. Then, a measure of dissimilarity M_D is defined on D. Previous work deals with graph matching and an interesting method to calculate the similarity between two conceptual graphs is proposed in [10]. However, in the present context we consider sufficient a simplier measure that adds the differences between graphs.

First let us recall the definition of *compatibility* given in [1]:

Definition 2. *Let conceptual graphs u_1 and u_2 have a common generalization v with projections $\pi_1 : v \longrightarrow u_1$ and $\pi_2 : v \longrightarrow u_2$. The two projections are said to be* compatible *if for each concept c in v, the following conditions are true:*

1. *$type(\pi_1 c) \cap type(\pi_2 c) > \bot$.*
2. *The referents of $\pi_1 c$ and $\pi_2 c$ conform to $type(\pi_1 c) \cap type(\pi_2 c)$.*
3. *If $referent(\pi_1 c)$ is the individual marker i, then $referent(\pi_2 c)$ is either i or $*$.*

We now consider that there is always only one least common generalization, i.e. only two projections that are compatible and maximally extended. It is easy to generalize our model with graphs having several least common generalizations.

The following theorem is stated in order to link the notions of compatibility and default subsumption:

Theorem 1. *Let conceptual graphs u_1 and u_2 have the least common generalization v with projections $\pi_1 : v \longrightarrow u_1$ and $\pi_2 : v \longrightarrow u_2$. π_1 and π_2 are compatible if and only if u_1 subsumes u_2 by default.*

Proof. If π_1 and π_2 are compatible then there exists a common specialization w of u_1 and u_2 (cf. theorem 3.5.7). According to definition 1, u_1 subsumes u_2 by default. Reciprocally, if u_1 subsumes u_2 by default then there exists a common specialization w. Suppose that π_1 and π_2 are not compatible. There therefore exists at least one concept in v with $type(\pi_1 c) \cap type(\pi_2 c) = \perp$, or with the referent of $\pi_1 c$ or $\pi_2 c$ not conform to $type(\pi_1 c) \cap type(\pi_2 c)$, or with $referent(\pi_1 c) = i$ and $referent(\pi_2 c) = j$, $i \neq j$. These three cases are absurd because they contradict the construction of w. Therefore, π_1 and π_2 are compatible.

Consider now the measure M_D counting the dissimilarities between two graphs u_1 and u_2. Let v be the least common generalization graph with projections $\pi_1 : v \rightarrow u_1$ and $\pi_2 : v \rightarrow u_2$. If π_1 and π_2 are not compatible then the measure $M_D(u_1, u_2)$ is fixed by convention with an infinite value noted M_∞ because one graph can't be subsumed by default by the second one (cf. theorem 1). Otherwise $M_D(u_1, u_2)$ counts all the differences between the concepts and relations of u_1 and those of u_2. The measure is thus defined:

Definition 3. *Let conceptual graphs u_1 and u_2 have the least common generalization v with projections $\pi_1 : v \rightarrow u_1$ and $\pi_2 : v \rightarrow u_2$. The* measure of dissimilarities *$M_D(u_1, u_2)$ is equal to:*

1. *M_∞ if π_1 and π_2 are not compatible.*
2. *$C + T(u_1) + T(u_2)$ otherwise, where:*
   - *$C = |\{concept\ c \in v / type(\pi_1 c) \neq type(\pi_2 c)\ or\ referent(\pi_1 c) \neq referent(\pi_2 c)\}|$.*
   - *$T(u) = card(u) - card(v)$; $card(g)$ corresponds to the number of nodes (concepts and relations) of graph g.*

This measure presents the following properties:

Property 3. For any conceptual graph u, $M_D(u, u) = 0$.

Property 4. For any conceptuals graphs u and v, $M_D(u, v) = M_D(v, u)$.

Let us now define what is a set of stereotypes:

Definition 4. *In the framework of the conceptual graphs, a set of stereotypes is a tuple of n graphs $(s_1, s_2, ...s_n)$.*

2.5 Completion of Facts

Being given a set of facts F and a set of stereotypes $(s_1, s_2, ...s_n)$, it is possible to complete the descriptions of almost any fact f. More precisely, the completion is possible when there exists at least one stereotype s_i belonging to the set of stereotype $(s_1, s_2, ...s_n)$ such that s_i subsumes by default the description $\delta(f)$ of the fact f. In other words, thinking by stereotypes is possible when new descriptions are so sparse that they seem consistent with existing stereotypes. This capacity to classify and to complete the descriptions is characteristic of the concept of stereotype as introduced by Lippman.

When one and only one stereotype s_i covers by default the fact f, the description of f, $\delta(f)$, may be completed by the stereotype s_i. However, it happens that facts may be covered by two or more stereotypes s_i. Then, the stereotype associated with a fact f is the one that minimizes the measure of disimilarity M_D, i.e. it is the stereotype s_i which both covers $\delta(f)$ by default and minimizes $M_D(\delta(f), s_i)$. It is called the relative cover of f, thanks to the measure of dissimilarity M_D and to a set of stereotypes $S = (s_1, s_2, ...s_n)$.

Definition 5. *In a more formal way, the relative cover of a fact f, with respect to a set of stereotype $S = (s_1, s_2, ...s_n)$, noted $C_S(e)$, is the stereotype s_i if and only if:*

1. $s_i \in (s_1, s_2, ...s_n)$,
2. $M_D(\delta(f), s_i) \neq M_\infty$,
3. $\forall k \in [1, n], k \neq i, M_D(\delta(f), s_i) < M_D(\delta(f), s_k)$.

It may also happen that no stereotype covers the new fact f, which means that $\delta(f)$, the description of f, is inconsistent with all s_i. In this case, there may not be any completion and thinking by stereotype is impossible.

2.6 Extraction of Stereotypes

Implicit reasoning is formalized here with both the default subsumption and sets of stereotypes which structure our memory. Up to now, these sets of stereotypes were supposed to be given. This section shows how our memories can be organized into sets of stereotypes. In other words, it is to model the way facts aggregate into structures which render implicit reasoning possible. From a technical point of view, this memory organization process can be seen as a non-supervised learning task we call *default clustering*, which can be summarized as follows.

Being given a set of facts F described with conceptual graphs, a non-supervised learning algorithm is supposed to organize the initial set of facts F into a structure, for instance a hierarchy, a lattice or a pyramid. In the present case, we restrain to partitions of the training set, which correspond to sets of stereotypes. Let us recall that $(F_1, F_2, ...Fn)$ constitutes a partition of the set F if and only if:

1. $\forall i \in [1, n], F_i \subset F$
2. $\cup_{i \in [1,n]}, F_i = F$
3. $\forall (i, j) \in [1, n]^2, F_i \cap F_j = \emptyset$

This partition may be generated by n conceptual graphs $\{g_1, g_2, ...g_n\}$: it is sufficient to associate to each g_i the set F_i of facts belonging to F and covered by g_i relative to $(g_1, g_2, ...g_n)$.

To choose among the numerous possible structures, even with simple structures like partitions, a non-supervised algorithm requires a distance. The usual way is to minimize the so-called intra-class distance – i.e. the average distance between examples belonging to the same class – and/or to maximize the inter-class distance – i.e. the sum of distances between pairs of examples belonging to different classes. – The key point is to have a distance among examples of the learning set and to extend it to intra and inter-class distances.

The first distance considered used probabilities. It is very similar to the Category Utility measure [12] which is used in the COBWEB system [13] to evaluate good partitions. But in practice this measure is not really appropriate for sparse descriptions. Moreover, runtime cost was rather high, which made the learning algorithm very inefficient.

Referring to the definition of both "sets of stereotypes" and the relative cover, it appears natural to make use of a distance close to the measure of dissimilarity M_D. This is exactly what we do by introducing a cost function h based on M_D:

Definition 6. *F being a set of facts, the so-called training set, $S = (s_1, s_2, ...s_n)$ a set of stereotypes and C_S the function that associates to each fact f its relative cover, i.e. its closest stereotype with respect to M_D and S, the cost function h is defined as follows:*

$$h(S) = \sum_{f \in F} M_D(\delta(f), C_S(f))$$

Once the cost function h has been defined, the non-supervised learning algorithm has to build the set of stereotypes $(s_1, s_2, ...s_n)$ that minimizes h. In other words, the non-supervised learning problem is reduced to an optimization problem.

There are several methods for exploring such search space. One is incremental and very similar to the one used by Fisher in COBWEB. It starts from an empty set with no stereotypes, considers at each step a new individual to be covered and updates the set of stereotypes with some specific operators. For instance, one of them creates a new stereotype equal to the considered individual; another modifies one existing stereotype to cover it; the "merge" operator merges two stereotypes belonging to the set of stereotypes and the "split" operator splits one active stereotype. The search in COBWEB is a "hill-climbing" strategy; its robustness is largely due to these last two specific operators, the "merge" and the "split". However, in case of sparse descriptions and especially with graphs, the "merge" and "split" operators cannot be easily implemented. Therefore, it is difficult to apply this algorithm here.

The second option is to search for the best set of stereotypes using general optimization techniques. We chose a "tabu" strategy, which is a classical meta-heuristic technique used in operational research. It seems quite well adapted to solve our problem, as we shall see in the next section. From a technical point of view, a neighborhood is calculated from the current solution with the assistance of permitted movements. These movements can be of low influence (enrich one stereotype with a descriptor, remove a descriptor from another) or of high influence (add or retract one stereotype from the current set of stereotypes). As in almost all local search techniques, there is a trade-off between exploitation, i.e. choosing the best movement, and exploration, i.e. choosing a non optimal state. The search uses short and long-term memory to avoid loops and to intelligently explore the search space. We shall not detail here the "tabu" search algorithm since it is a classical one (see [11]); we shall just evaluate its robustness on artificial data in the next section.

3 Experiments

This section validates our approach in the Attributes/Values formalism, before proposing a real application dealing with a famous French affair translated into conceptual graphs.

3.1 Validation on Artificial Data Sets

Evaluation validates on artificial data sets the robustness of the non-supervised learning algorithm, which builds sets of stereotypes from a learning set F and a description language D. Let us recall that stereotypes are supposed to be more or less shared by many people living in the same society. Since use of stereotypes is the way to model implicit reasoning, it could explain why prejudges and presupposes are almost identical in a group. Our second hypothesis is that people reason from sparse descriptions that they are always able to complete and to organize into a set of stereotypes in their memory. These two hypotheses entail that people, who shared different experiences, and who read different news, are able to build very similar sets of stereotypes from very different learning sets. Therefore, our attempt to model construction of sets of stereotypes with a non-supervised learning algorithm ought to have this stability property. We evaluate it here on artificial data.

Let us now consider the Attributes/Values formalism. Being given this description language, we introduce some full consistent descriptions, e.g. (d_1, d_2, d_3), which stand for the description of a set of stereotypes. Let us note as n_s the number of such descriptions. These n_s descriptions may be randomly generated; the only points are that they need to be full and consistent.

The second step of the artificial set generation is to duplicate these description n_d times, for instance, 50 times, making $n_s \times n_d$ artificial examples. Then, these $n_s \times n_d$ descriptions are arbitrarily degraded: descriptors belonging to these duplications are chosen randomly to be destroyed. The only parameter is the percentage of degradation, i.e. the ratio of the number of destroyed descriptors on the total number of descriptors. The generated learning set contains $n_s \times n_d$ example descriptions, which all correspond to degradations of the n_s initial descriptions.

The default clustering algorithm is tested on these artificially generated and degraded learning sets. Then, the stability property is evaluated by weighing the set of stereotypes built by the non-supervised algorithm against the n_s descriptions initially given when generating the artificial learning set.

Our first evaluation consists in comparing the quality –i.e. the percentage of descriptors– and the number of generated stereotypes to the initial descriptions,

n_s, while the percentage of degradation increases from 0% up to 100%. It appears that up to more than 85% of degradation, the sets of stereotypes corresponds most of the time to the initial ones (see figure 2).

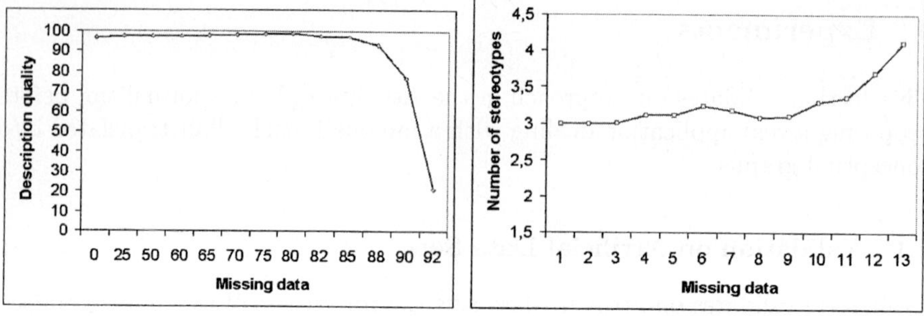

Fig. 2. Quality and number of stereotypes discovered.

The second test counts the classification error rate, i.e. the rate of degraded facts that are not covered by the right stereotype. We mean by "right stereotype" the discovered description that corresponds to the initial fact the degraded facts come from. Fig. 3 shows the results of our program P.R.E.S.S. relatively to three classic algorithm for classification: k-means, COBWEB and EM. These experiments clearly state that the results of P.R.E.S.S. are really good with a very stable learning process: up to 75% of degradation, the error rate is less than 10% and best as the three others.

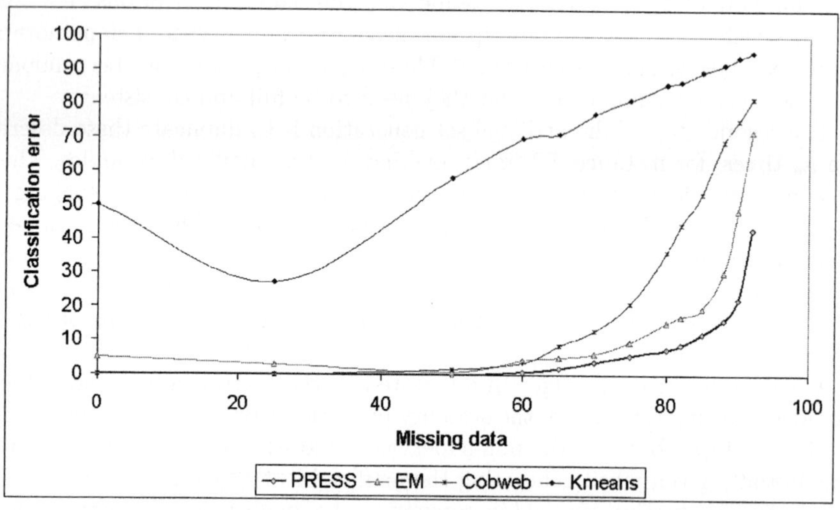

Fig. 3. Classification error of degraded examples.

3.2 Studying Social Misrepresentation

The application we propose deals with an historic event, the famous miscarriage of justice known as the Dreyfus Affair which occurred at the end of the 19th century in France. In 1894 Captain Alfred Dreyfus, an officer on the French general staff, was accused of spying for Germany, France's opponent in the previous war. There were many articles about this very complex affair, bringing different views depending on the date, recent events, the newspaper political leanings. Thus, the liberal pro-Dreyfus *Le Siècle* expressed opinions which were diametrically opposed to those of the conservative anti-Dreyfus *L'éclair*. The facts we considered have been taken from these articles and translated into conceptual graphs, in order to build automatically a simplified model of the affair. The objective is to understand the influence of the press on the mental representations during this period.

Type hierarchies including 399 concepts and 174 relations were built for this specific context. In addition, a typical graph was proposed in order to translate the articles into facts. Fig. 4 shows an example of a graph. It represents an article from the newspaper *L'éclair* using the CoGITaNT library implemented by D. Genest and E. Salvat [14]. This library in C++ manipulating conceptual graphs was chosen because of the gnu public licence, its great flexibility and the quality of the available documentation.

It could be summarized as follows: *the article taken from the newspaper* L'éclair *explicitly asserts that Alfred Dreyfus is guilty because Esterhazy was*

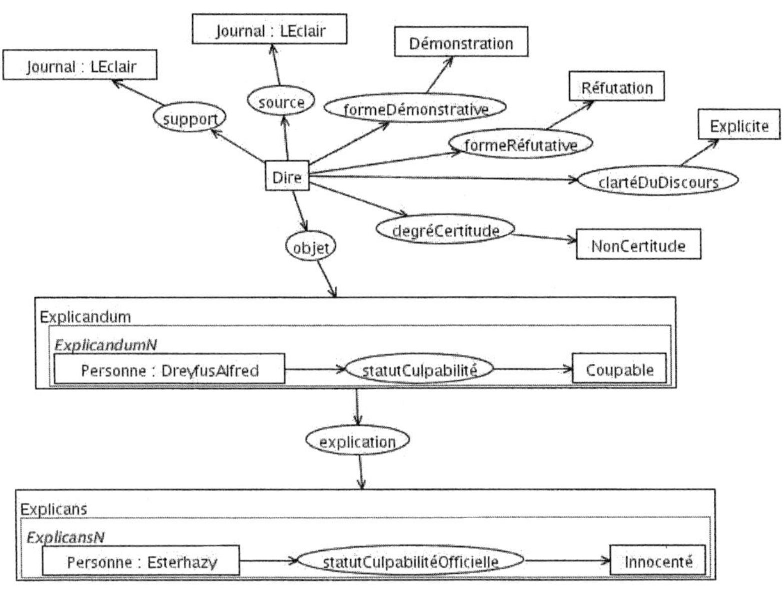

Fig. 4. A conceptual graph which translates a newspaper article.

proved innocent by the courts. Once several articles have been translated in this way, stereotypes can be discovered using the methods proposed earlier.

4 Conclusion

Flows of information play a key role in today's society. However, the value of information depends on its being interpreted correctly, and implicit knowledge has a considerable influence on this interpretation. This is the case in many today's heterogeneous databases that are far to be complete and, consequently, need special techniques to be automatically completed. This is particularly true of the media, such as newspapers, radio and television, where the information given is always sparse.

In this context we propose a cognitive model based on sets of stereotypes which summarize facts by "guessing" the missing values. Stereotypes are an alternative to prototypes and are more suitable in the categorization of sparse descriptions. They rely on the notion of default subsumption which relaxes constraints and makes possible the manipulation of such descriptions. Descriptions are then completed according to the closest stereotypes, with respect to the dissimilarity measure M_D. Very good results have been found in the Attributs/Values formalism with artificial data sets. Our interest is now focused on a real application using conceptual graphs.

This work relates to the domain of social representations as introduced by Serge Moscovici in [15]. According to him, social representations are a sort of "common sense" knowledge which aims at inducing behaviors and allows communication between individuals. We think that social representations can be constructed with the help of sets of stereotypes. The way these representations change can be studied through the media over different periods and social groups in comparison with such sets. This represents an unexplored way for enriching historical and social analysis.

Finally, this paper emphasizes the danger related to a conceptualization not really adapted to a particular problem. Missing data might induce bad interpretations and lead to erroneous results. This is also what we show with the concept of stereotypes and the notion of default subsumption.

Acknowledgments

The authors would particularly like to thank David Genest for his patience and useful advice concerning the CoGITaNT library and Anne Remillieux for constructing the type hierarchies and graph examples.

References

1. Sowa, J.F.: Conceptual Structures: Information Processing in Mind and Machine, Addison-Wesley Publishing Company (1984), Massachusetts, The Systems Programming Series.

2. Reiter, R.: A logic for default reasoning. In: Artificial Intelligence, number 13 (1980) 81–132.
3. Corruble, V., Ganascia, J.-G.: Induction and the discovery of the causes of scurvy: a computational reconstruction. In: Artificial Intelligence Journal, Special issue on scientific discovery. Elsevier Press (1997) 205–223.
4. Velcin J.: Reconstruction rationnelle des mentalités collectives: deux études sur la xénophobie, DEA report, Internal Report University Paris VI, Paris (2002).
5. McDermott, D., Doyle, J.: Nonmonotonic logic 1. In: Artificial Intelligence, number 13 (1980) 41–72.
6. McCarthy, J.: Circumscription: a form of non-monotonic reasoning. In: Artificial Intelligence, number 13 (1980) 27–39, 171–172.
7. http://www.cs.uah.edu/ delugach/CG/.
8. Rosch, E.: Cognitive representations of semantic categories. In: Journal of Experimental Psychology: General, number 104 (1975) 192–232.
9. Lippman, W.: Public Opinion, Ed. MacMillan (1922), NYC.
10. Zhong, J., Zhu H., Li J., Yu Y.: Conceptual Graph Matching for Semantic Search. In: Proceedings of the 10th International Conference on Conceptual Structures: Integration and Interfaces, Spring-Verlag (2002) 92–106.
11. Glover, F., Laguna, M.: In: Tabu Search, Kluwer Academic Publishers (1997).
12. Corter, J.E., Gluck, M.A.: Information, uncertainty, and the utility of categories, In: Proceedings of the Seventh Annual Conference of the Cognitive Science Society. Lawrence Erlbaum Associates (1985) 283–287.
13. Fisher, D.H.: Knowledge Acquisition Via Incremental Conceptual Clustering. In: Machine Learning, number 2 (1987) 139–172.
14. Genest, D., Salvat, E.: A platform allowing typed nested graphs: How cogito became cogitant. In: Proceedings of the Sixth International Conference on Conceptual Structures, Springer-Verlag (1998), Berlin.
15. Moscovici, S.: La psychanalyse: son image et son public. PUF (1961), Paris.

Reachability Problems in Entity-Relationship Schema Instances

Sebastiano Vigna

Dipartimento di Scienze dell'Informazione, Università degli Studi di Milano
vigna@acm.org

Abstract. Recent developments in reification of ER schemata include automatic generation of web-based database administration systems [1, 2]. These systems enforce the schema cardinality constraints, but, beyond unsatisfiable schemata, this feature may create *unreachable instances.* We prove sound and complete characterisations of schemata whose instances satisfy suitable reachability properties; these theorems translate into linear algorithms that can be used to prevent the administrator from reifying schemata with unreachable instances.

1 Introduction

Web-based database administration systems are becoming extremely popular as a mean to access database information without the need to deploy a specific, architecture-bound client. In particular, recent research focuses on systems that are automatically generated from a specification in the language of entity-relationship (ER) schemata[1] [1,2]. The administrator specifies a schema in a suitable language, and the system generates an SQL implementation and an application running server side that presents the user with suitable forms for editing the database.

An important feature of ER schemata is the possibility of specifying *cardinality constraints*, that is, constraints on the number of relationships involving a certain entity. They are particularly important in the case of content management (i.e., database administration for content to be published on the web), because relying on the constraints leads to simpler HTML generation (e.g., special cases or missing relationships do not need to be checked). For this reason, ER-based database administration systems enforce cardinality constraints: when modifying the database, the user is prevented from moving the database form a legal configuration to an illegal one.

Cardinality constraints, however, cannot be imposed lightly, as they can easily lead to problems when the schema is poorly designed. The first systematic study of this issues can be found in a seminal paper by Lenzerini and Nobili [5], which gave necessary and sufficient conditions for a schema to have an instance at all (a condition called *satisfiability*), or to have non-empty instances (*strong*

[1] ER schemata are a popular conceptual model originally introduced by Chen [3], and later extended in several ways [4].

P. Atzeni et al. (Eds.): ER 2004, LNCS 3288, pp. 96–109, 2004.

satisfiability). This is the first, necessary step to ensure that the schema definition has any sense. Later, the results were further extended to schemata with ISA [6], albeit the extension did not take into consideration type features, such as disjunctive subtyping.

Even if a schema has non-empty instances, however, there is another orthogonal problem: modifications to the schema instance (i.e., to a database) are usually constrained (e.g., a user can modify just a subset of the instance in a transaction), and thus the existing instances may be "too far" to make the user actually able to modify one into another.

A typical case is one in which we have entity types E and F and mandatory relationship types R from E to F and S from F to E. In this case, there is no way to move from the empty instance (without any entity or relationship) to any nonempty instance *using only local modifications*, that is, inserting, deleting or updating at most one entity and its relationships at a time (as indeed happens in web-based content management). In other word, the schema happily passes all *static* satisfiability conditions, but it is in practice unusable.

The purpose of this paper is to present sound and complete algorithms that statically check an ER schema for instance reachability conditions. In particular, we present an algorithm guaranteeing that all instances are mutually reachable, and an algorithm guaranteeing that all *everywhere nonempty* instances are mutually reachable. The second case is useful when a pre-populated database needs very stringent constraints that do not pass the first check (as it happens in the previous example). These results complements the static satisfiability aforementioned results: all instances of a schema *with no instance at all*, for instance, are by definition mutually reachable, so satisfiability tests are necessary, but, as shown in our previous examples, instances of fully satisfiable schemata may be mutually unreachable.

To make our reasoning precise, we need a completely formal definition and semantics of ER schemata that refers only to sets, elements and functions (as proposed, for instance, in [7]); as a by-product, our results are valid independently of the kind of DBMS that is used to implement the schema semantics[2].

The main motivation for this work is ERW (`http://erw.dsi.unimi.it/`), a reification tool developed by the author that creates a complete web-based database administration system starting from a schema definition. ERW supports sophisticated features such as weak entities, multiple inheritance, user authentication and authorisation, etc. It has been in use for the last two years to manage the web site of the Computer Science Department of the Università degli Studi di Milano; recently, other departments and universities in Italy have refactored their databases to use ERW. Since its public release in February 2002 there have been more than 10 000 accesses to the ERW home page.

[2] In general, ER-based management systems should be based on a formal, abstract semantics of schema instances and transactions so that different database models (i.e., relational or object-oriented) and different DBMS can be used to implement the abstract semantics.

ERW is based on the abstract semantics described in this paper. In particular, before creating the actual database administration system it performs a number of checks on the validity of the schema. One of the algorithms solves the problem of *double ownership*, that is, the problem of identifying weak entities, and has been described in [2]. In this paper, we describe the techniques by which we prevent administrators from creating databases that can lock the user in unmodifiable configurations.

No published solution to these problems is known to the author. To be true, only a small part of the work on conceptual modeling is formalised mathematically, and this makes it difficult, if not impossible, to develop algorithms and prove their correctness. Moreover, the problem of reachability was born with stateless web interactions: the usual notion of database transaction is stateful, so reachability is not a problem in that case.

Note that general techniques for satisfiability problems in first-order (but possibly more general than entity-relationship schemata) theories are useless here, because we the problem we study is inherently of higher order—we want to prove statements about the *models* of the theory.

First, we introduce briefly the semantics for schemata with binary relationship types that we proposed in [2]; it extends the original one given by Chen [3], but adds typing and inheritance (the original ER proposal did not include explicit subtyping information). Moreover, it introduces *multirelations* as the abstract semantics of relationship types (with respect to the formulation given in [2], we add a new notion, that of *abstract entity types*, motivated partly by ontological reasons and partly by the need of representing complete disjunctive types).

Once the semantics is set up, we introduce a notion of *isomorphism of instances* that allows us to define precisely when two schema instances are equivalent modulo the particular elements used in representing them, and of *local modification*, which models stateless interaction with a web client.

At this point, we discuss two notions of reachability and characterise them mathematically in a sound and complete way. From the characterisation it is immediate to derive linear check algorithms. However, the characterisation is given for schemata without `ISA` relationship types (i.e., without subtyping). Thus, we conclude discussing some techniques that should be applied when subtyping is present. We also discuss extensions to n-ary relationship types.

A Java implementation of the algorithms described in this paper and in [2] is available as free software by the author at the URI above.

2 Schemata

We note first that we do not need to introduce attributes in our schema definition. Since we have to discuss just cardinality issues, it is sufficient to be able to speak of sets and elements (one can of course add an attribute map for every set involved and easily discuss keys, attribute constraints and so on). Moreover, for simplicity we present the algorithm for binary relationship types, and discuss at the end of the paper the (easy) extension for types of arbitrary arity.

An EER schema (of binary relations) $\mathscr{S}$ is given by a set $\mathscr{E}$ of entity types, a set $\mathscr{R}$ of relationship types, a source function $s : \mathscr{R} \to \mathscr{E}$ and a target function

$t : \mathscr{R} \to \mathscr{E}$ (note that in order to give a formal semantics to an EER schema without roles you need to consider relationship types as directed). An entity type may be *abstract*. Moreover, each relationship type has a source and a target *cardinality constraint*, which is a symbol out of `(0:1)`, `(1:1)`, `(0:N)`, `(1:N)`, `(0:M)`, `(1:M)`. The ordered pair of cardinality constraint of a relationship type is usually written as `(-:-)`→`(-:-)`. Finally, a relationship type may be marked optionally either `ISA`, in which case its constraint must be `(1:1)`→`(0:1)`[3].

Whenever there is an `ISA` relationship type from E to F, E is said to be a *direct subtype* of F, and F a *direct supertype* of E. A *subtype* of E is either E or a direct subtype of a subtype of E (analogously for supertypes).

Note that there are two new cardinality types: `(0:M)` and `(1:M)`. The `M` indicates that we are actually requiring a multirelation.

The notion of abstract entity type is a new extension with respect to the definition presented in [2], and it is borrowed from object-oriented languages (notably Java). The idea is that it should be used for types which are necessary for a correct structuring of the type hierarchy, but that are "universals" (in the ontological sense) and thus have no instance themselves—they can be just instantiated through their subtypes. We shall see that this extension allows one to implement some additional type constructs (at the price of a more complex interaction between types and constraints).

3 Instances

To define a schema instance, one introduces multirelations in the spirit of bicategory theory [8, 9]:

Definition 1. *A (binary) multirelation from set X to set Y is a set M endowed with two functions, the* left leg M_0 *and the* right leg M_1*:*

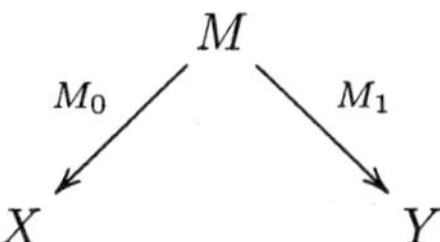

Two elements $x \in X$ and $y \in Y$ are related if there is an $r \in M$ such that $M_0(r) = x$ and $M_1(r) = y$, a condition that we write in short with the notation $r(x, y)$. The reader should notice that it can happen that there are two elements $r, s \in M$ such that $r(x, y)$ and $s(x, y)$. In this case, the elements x and y are related "more than once". If this never happens, then M is a standard relation represented in tabular form (if you start from a relation as a subset of $X \times Y$ the two legs are just the projections).

Definition 2. *An instance σ for a schema $\mathscr{S}$ is given by a map σ assigning to each entity type E in $\mathscr{E}$ a set $\sigma(E)$ and to each relationship type R in $\mathscr{R}$ a multirelation $\sigma(R)$ satisfying the following properties:*

---

[3] For completeness, we should introduce the `WEAK` labelling for arcs that represent identification functions, but this has no effect on the present discussion.

1. *The left leg of $\sigma(R)$ must end in $\sigma(s(E))$, and the right leg in $\sigma(t(E))$; in other words, if R is a relationship type from entity type E to entity type F, then $\sigma(R)$ must be a multirelation*

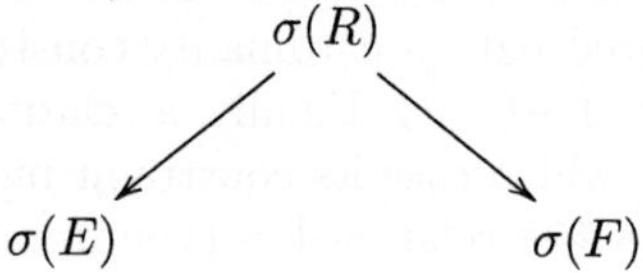

that is, a multirelation with a left leg ending in $\sigma(E)$ and a right leg ending in $\sigma(F)$.

2. *A cardinality constraint of the form* `(1:-)` *requires that the corresponding leg be a surjective function.*
3. *A cardinality constraint of the form* `(-:1)` *requires that the corresponding leg be an injective function.*
4. *A cardinality constraint of the form* `(-:N)` *requires that the multirelation is actually a relation (i.e., nothing is related twice).*
5. *Whenever a relationship type is marked* `ISA`*, the first leg is the identity and the second leg is an inclusion map, so that that source entity set is a subset of the target entity set.*
6. *Whenever entity types E and F have a common supertype and $x \in \sigma(E) \cap \sigma(F)$, there is a common subtype G of E and F such that $x \in \sigma(G)$*[4].
7. *If E is abstract, $\sigma(E)$ is exactly the union of $\sigma(F)$ when F ranges through the proper subtypes of E.*

The wording of cardinality constraints may seem a bit unorthodox: however, it is easy to see that it is exactly equivalent to the standard *participation interpretation* of constraints, and moreover extends immediately to n-ary relationship types.

Condition (6) is important as it forces *definite typing.* Essentially, every entity must have a type: if, for instance, `man` and `woman` are subtypes of `person`, it is not possible that x belongs to $\sigma($`man`$)$ *and* $\sigma($`woman`$)$ (unless you add a common subtype `hermaphrodite` of both `man` and `woman`).

An *entity* is now a pair (E, x) such that E is the type of x. Note that we did not restrain entity sets to be disjoint, so an x whose type is E and an x whose type is F are actually *distinct entities*[5].

Finally, condition (7) gives a precise semantics to abstract entity types: their instances are all subtype instances. In particular, an abstract entity type without subtypes cannot have instances.

Abstract types are useful as they allow one to model *complete disjunctive subtyping.* Getting back to the example above, by making `person` abstract we force every person to be either a man or a woman.

[4] The last two conditions are an elementary phrasing of a *stability* condition on suitably defined maps—see [2].

[5] This feature parallels the common usage of numerical identifiers to represent set elements in SQL databases—the identifiers are not necessarily distinct in different tables.

4 Local Modifications

To formalise reachability problems, we introduce *local modifications*, which parallel the action of a user interacting with a database by means of a web browser (and thus, essentially, statelessly).

Definition 3. *A* local modification *of an instance σ of the schema $\mathscr{S}$ is one of the following operations:*

1. *adding an entity* e *of type* E*, together with relationships involving* e *and another entity;*
2. *adding a relationship;*
3. *deleting an entity* e *of type* E *and all relationships involving* e*;*
4. *deleting a relationship.*

If τ is derived by σ by means of a local modification, we write $\sigma \to \tau$. We write $\sigma \Rightarrow \tau$ if there is a chain

$$\sigma = \upsilon_0 \to \upsilon_1 \to \cdots \to \upsilon_n = \tau$$

of instances.

Note that the previous definition is targeted to the applications we have in mind: stateless interaction with a server does not allow to access data stored client-side until there is a commit (if we are interacting to create e we cannot access e as if it was already on the server). This is the reason why the notion of addition and of deletion of an entity are not symmetric.

5 Isomorphism of Instances

To discuss reachability problems, it is important to identify instances which differ only for the set-theoretical identity of their elements, but for not their relational structure, as shown in the example of Fig. 1.

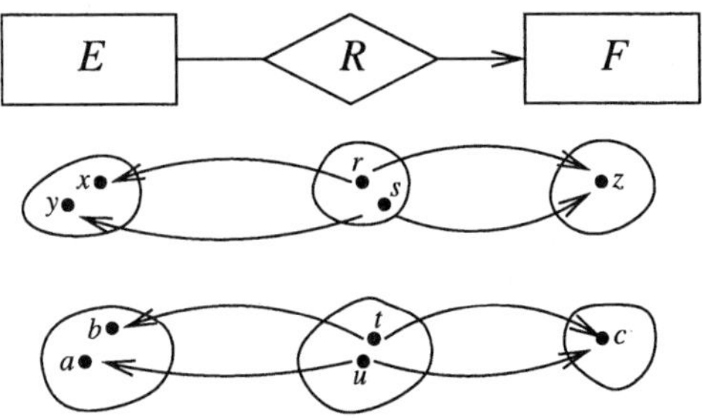

Fig. 1. Isomorphic instances.

Definition 4. *We say that instances σ and τ of a schema $\mathscr{S}$ are* isomorphic *if we have for each entity type $E \in \mathscr{E}$ and for each non-ISA relationship type $R \in \mathscr{R}$ bijections $\iota_E : \sigma(E) \to \tau(E)$ and $\iota_R : \sigma(R) \to \tau(R)$ such that*

$$r(x, y) \in \sigma(R) \iff \iota_R(r)(\iota_{s(R)}(x), \iota_{t(R)}(y)) \in \tau(R).$$

The definition above could be rephrased by saying that the entity and relationship sets must be in bijection, and the bijections must commute with the multirelations (more precisely, with their legs)[6]. In particular, we notice that every instance in which all entity and relationship sets contain at most one element is unique up to isomorphism.

6 Full Reachability

We can now formalise our problem in its most general form:

Problem 1. Given a class of instances $\mathscr{C}$ of the schema $\mathscr{S}$, is it true that for every pair of instances $\sigma, \tau \in \mathscr{C}$ we have, up to isomorphism, $\sigma \Rightarrow \tau$?

This question is important: if, for instance, there is no path out of the empty instance, then it is impossible to populate the instance by means of local modifications, that is, using a web-based database administration system. As we discussed in the introduction, if we have two entity types E and F, and two relationship types R from E to F and S from F to E, and both R and S have constraints `(1:N)`$\to$`(0:N)`, then no local modification is possible on the empty instance (as adding an entity to E or F would violate a cardinality constraint). However, in this case, it is easy to see that *all nonempty instances are mutually reachable.*

The situation is very different if we instead assume `(1:1)`$\to$`(1:N)` as constraint of R and S. In this case, *all instances are mutually unreachable.* This happens because every instance contains a cycle of *surjective functions*, and a trivial counting argument shows that *all entity sets along such a cycle must have the same cardinality* (assuming, of course, the entity sets are finite). This forbids *any* local modification. Clearly we want to avoid this case.

To give our results, we set up a few terms that will be useful: a schema is said to be *flat* if it contains neither `ISA` relationship types nor abstract entity types; an *endorelationship* of an entity e is a relationship of the form $r(e, e)$.

Definition 5. *Given a flat schema $\mathscr{S}$, the graph $\Gamma(\mathscr{S})$ is defined as follows: the set of nodes of $\Gamma(\mathscr{S})$ is the set of entity types $\mathscr{E}$, and there is an arc from E to F whenever there is a relationship type with constraint of the form* $(- : -) \to$ $(1 : -)$ *from E to F or a relationship type with constraint of the form* $(1 : -) \to$ $(- : -)$ *from F to E.*

[6] The notion of instance can be easily seen to be a special case of the notion of *pseudo-functor* between bicategories [8, 10]; the notion of isomorphism above is just an elementary restatement of the definition of functor isomorphism.

The graph $\Gamma(\mathscr{S})$ embodies the mandatoriness constraints in a form that makes it easy to check whether they are contradictory:

Theorem 1. *Let $\mathscr{S}$ be a flat schema. Then all instances of $\mathscr{S}$ are mutually reachable if and only if $\Gamma(\mathscr{S})$ is acyclic (i.e., it contains no cycles).*

Proof. We start by proving the right-to-left implication. It is sufficient to show that from an instance σ we can reach the empty instance by means of reversible local modifications. To do so, it is sufficient to show that we can always reversibly delete an entity from any given instance.

The only local modification that is not reversible in general is deletion of an entity e that has endorelationships. However, since by hypothesis the type of those endorelationships cannot be mandatory (or there would be a loop), we can obtain the same result by first deleting all endorelationships, and then finally deleting e (the last step is reversible, as all relationships at this point involve some other entity).

Consider now a nonempty instance σ, and an entity e of type E of σ. Then, either e can be deleted without breaking any cardinality constraint, or there must be a relationship type, say from E to $F \neq E$ with constraint $(- : -) \to (1 : -)$ satisfied by e (the dual case of a relationship type from F to E with constraint $(1 : -) \to (- : -)$ can be treated analogously). Thus, there must be an arc of $\Gamma(\mathscr{S})$ from E to F, and an entity f of type F which is in relation with e. We can iterate this procedure on f, but since $\Gamma(\mathscr{S})$ contains no cycle after a finite number of steps we must get to an entity that can be deleted.

For the other implication, consider a cycle in $\Gamma(\mathscr{S})$, to which we can associate a sequence E_0, R_0, E_1, R_1, $\ldots$, R_n, E_0 of mandatory relationship types[7]. If $n > 0$, given an instance σ such that $\sigma(E_i) = \varnothing$ for all i, there is no local modification that can change this condition, as adding an entity of any of the $\sigma(E_i)$'s would imply adding at the same time other n entities, which is not allowed by the definition of local modification. If $n = 0$, adding an entity would imply adding at the same time an endorelationship or other entities, which again is not allowed by the definition of local modification.

7 Almost Full Reachability

There are situations in which the previous check is too strict (for instance, if we start from a pre-populated database, which is never meant to be empty). A reasonable relaxing of full reachability is requiring that all instances in which all entity sets are nonempty are mutually reachable. We give a formal definition of this fact:

Definition 6. *A schema instance σ is* everywhere nonempty *if for every $E \in \mathscr{E}$ we have $\sigma(E) \neq \varnothing$, that is, if all its entity sets are nonempty.*

[7] To simplify the proof, we assume without loss of generality that all mandatory types involved are "in the right direction".

In this case, we have to look for *injective mandatory relations.* A relationship that is injective and mandatory, that is, such that every entity is in relation with some other entity and such that two entities are never related to the same entity, imposes a cardinality bound on the size of the source and target entity set (the first one must be smaller than or equal to the second one). If we get a cycle of such constraints, we may be in trouble (the fact that cycles of injective relations can be substituted with cycles of bijections without changing the allowable instances was already noticed in [4]).

Again, we build a graph that embodies the combinatorial bounds imposed by cardinality constraints:

Definition 7. *Given a flat schema $\mathscr{S}$, we define the graph $A(\mathscr{S})$ as follows: the set of nodes of $A(\mathscr{S})$ is the set of entity types $\mathscr{E}$, and there is an arc from E to F whenever there is a relationship type with constraint of the form* $(- : 1) \to (1 : -)$ *from E to F or a relationship type with constraint of the form* $(1 : -) \to (- : 1)$ *from F to E.*

Theorem 2. *Let $\mathscr{S}$ be a flat schema. Then all everywhere nonempty instances of $\mathscr{S}$ are mutually reachable if and only if $A(\mathscr{S})$ contains no cycles.*

Proof. Analogously to the proof of Theorem 1, for the right-to-left implication we show that from an instance σ we can reach a fixed instance (up to isomorphism) having exactly one entity per entity type and one relationship per relationship type. Such an instance certainly satisfies all cardinality constraints (as all multirelations are bijections).

We notice again that all entity deletions performed in the proof will be reversible. Indeed, if we have to delete $e \in \sigma(E)$, with $|\sigma(E)| > 1$, and e is involved in endorelationships, we can certainly either delete them (because their type is not mandatory), or modify them so to relate to some other element of the same type of e (because they are not injective); otherwise, the types of those relationships would generate a loop in $A(\mathscr{S})$.

Consider now an everywhere nonempty instance σ, an entity set $\sigma(E)$ with more than one element and an entity e of type E. If e can be deleted without breaking any cardinality constraint, we are done. If e cannot be deleted, this must happen because it is the only entity associated to one or more other entities f_0, $f_1, \ldots, f_n$ of type $F_0, F_1, \ldots, F_n$ and there are mandatory relationship types $R_0, R_1, \ldots, R_n$ from each of $F_0, F_1, \ldots, F_n$ to E, satisfied by association with e.

However, if these relationship types are not injective (i.e., if their cardinality constraints are *not* of the form $(- : -) \to (- : 1)$, then we can first make a finite number of modifications associating $f_0, f_1, \ldots, f_n$ to a different element of E, and then delete e. Otherwise, we take an element f_i of type F_i, where R_i has a constraint of the form $(1 : -) \to (- : 1)$, and iterate the above operations (note that $\sigma(F_i)$ must contain more than one element, or we could delete e without breaking any constraint of R_i). In doing so, we have followed an arc of $A(\mathscr{S})$, so we can iterate a finite number of times. At the last step, we obtain an entity that can be deleted.

For the other implication, consider a cycle in $A(\mathscr{S})$, to which we can associate a sequence E_0, R_0, E_1, R_1, ..., R_n, E_0 of mandatory injective relationship types. If $n > 0$, given an instance σ such that $|\sigma(E_i)| = k > 0$ for all i, there is no local modification that can change this condition, as adding an entity to any of the $\sigma(E_i)$'s would imply either adding a relationship from e to itself (if $n = 0$) or otherwise adding at the same time other $n > 0$ entities. Indeed, e must be associated in R_0 to some other entity, but we cannot use any other previously existing entities, or we would violate injectivity (since all $\sigma(E_i)$'s have the same cardinalities, the $\sigma(R_i)$'s are all bijections).

8 Arbitrary Arity

In general, one would like to handle relationship types of arbitrary arity. To this purpose we slightly (but naturally) extend the definition of schema and instances.

Definition 8. *A (n-ary) multirelation between the sets X_0, X_1, ..., X_{n-1} is a set M endowed with n functions, the* legs, *M_0, M_1, ..., M_{n-1}*

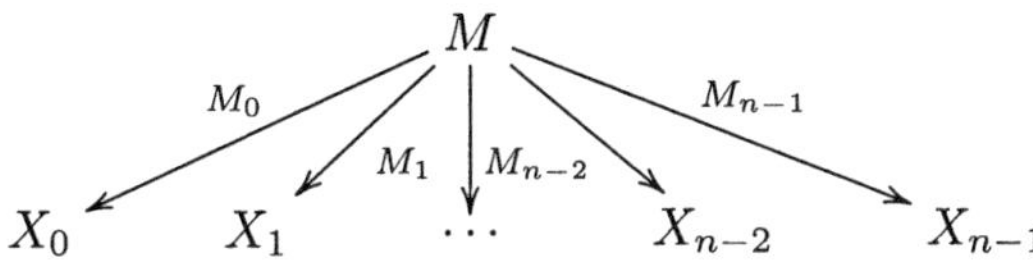

We can now easily extend the definition of schema by allowing n-ary relationship types in the obvious way, and by giving their semantics using n-ary multirelations.

Definition 9. *An n-ary schema is given by a set of entity types $\mathscr{E}$ and a set of relationship types $\mathscr{R}$. Each type $R \in \mathscr{R}$ is endowed with a list E_0, E_1, ..., E_{n-1} of $n \geq 2$* component types *and a list of n cardinality constraints. In this case, we say that R is n-ary, or of arity n.*

Extending corresponding the definition of instances is now trivial. Note that the definition of cardinality constraints remains valid also in this case.

To extend our results to n-ary schemata, all we need to do is to rephrase correctly the construction of the graphs $\Gamma(\mathscr{S})$ and $A(\mathscr{S})$. At that point it is not difficult to show that Theorem 1 and Theorem 6 remain true.

Theorem 3. *Given an n-ary schema $\mathscr{S}$, we define the graph $\Gamma(\mathscr{S})$ as follows: the set of nodes of $A(\mathscr{S})$ is the set of entity types $\mathscr{E}$, and there is an arc from F to G whenever there is a relationship type R with component types E_0, E_1, ..., E_{n-1}, indices $i \neq j$ such that $E_i = F$, $E_j = G$, and the j-th constraint is of the form (1:-). Then, all instances of $\mathscr{S}$ are mutually reachable if and only if $\Gamma(\mathscr{S})$ is acyclic.*

The construction above puts an arc in $A(\mathscr{S})$ from F to G whenever F and G are connected by a relationship type in such a way that to each entity of type G we must associate an entity of type F. In particular, this means that you cannot have a ternary relationship type that is mandatory on *two* component types (as you would create a cycle of length two).

Note also the careful wording of the definition: an apparently similar definition claiming that we should insert an arc whenever there is a relationship type R whose component type include F and G, where the constraint of G is the form `(1:-)`, would erroneously include the case that F is equal to G *and in the same position in the component list.* This of course is wrong, as we would add an an arc from E to E for a relationship type with list of component types E, F which is mandatory in E (the only correct one would be from F to E). The position of a type in the component list act as a *role*; roles are usually specified using identifiers, but from a mathematical viewpoint it is much more manageable to use the position in the component list (this is also the approach taken in [4]).

Analogously, we can give a suitable redefinition of $A(\mathscr{S})$:

Theorem 4. *Given an n-ary schema $\mathscr{S}$, we define the graph $A(\mathscr{S})$ as follows: the set of nodes of $A(\mathscr{S})$ is the set of entity types $\mathscr{E}$, and there is an arc from F to G whenever there is a relationship type R with component types E_0, E_1, ..., E_{n-1}, indices $i \neq j$ such that $E_i = F$, $E_j = G$, the i-th constraint is of the form (-:1), and the j-th constraint is of the form (1:-). Then, all everywhere nonempty instances of $\mathscr{S}$ are mutually reachable if and only if $A(\mathscr{S})$ is acyclic.*

In this case, we put from F to G whenever F and G are connected by a relationship type in such a way that to each entity of type G we must associate a *distinct entity of type F.*

9 Considerations on Subtypes

In the previous sections valid and complete checks for full and almost full reachability were provided. Turning these checks into algorithms is of course trivial, as cycle detection is linear. However, the theorem were given for schemata *without subtyping.* When subtyping is taken into consideration, the combinatorics of the problem becomes much more entangled, as we will try to explain using a few examples, and obtaining sound and complete results becomes much more difficult.

First of all, *there is no canonical everywhere nonempty instance.* The heart of the proof of Theorem 6 is that we have a unique (up to isomorphism) simple instance to work with. If subtypes are present, this is no longer true.

Consider the schema shown in Fig. 2. If there are k entities in D, there must be at least k entities in both A and B. But this means that there must be at least $2k$ entities in C (because of definite typing) and thus at least $2k$ elements in D (because of T). This set of constraints reduces to $k \leq 0$, and thus it is satisfied *by the empty instance only.*

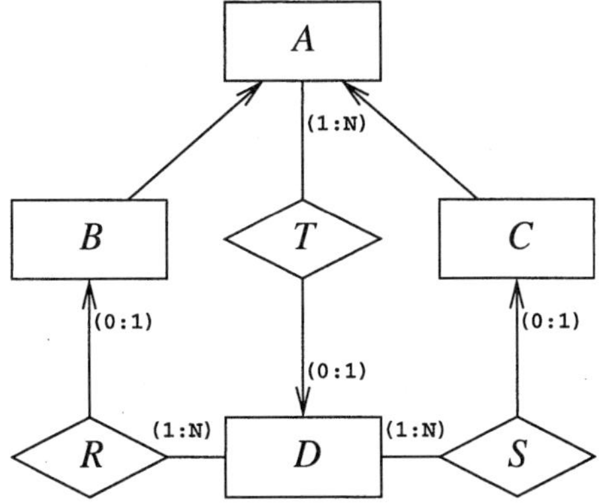

Fig. 2. A diagram without nonempty instances.

If we eliminate T, things get better, but it is easy to see that there is no everywhere nonempty canonical instance, as if we put one entity in B and C we are forced to put two in A; more complex type hierarchies may create extremely entangled combinatorial constraints.

One could think that at least the left-to-right implications of Theorems 1 and 6 should continue to hold (of course, all ISA relationship types will end up in both $\Gamma(\mathscr{S})$ and $A(\mathscr{S})$). However, there are certainly situations in which this is not true. Consider the diagram in Fig. 3, where dashed entities are abstract. It would pass all of our checks. Nonetheless, an instance in which every type has exactly one element (i.e., $\sigma(A) = \sigma(B) = \sigma(C) = \{x\}$, $\sigma(E) = \sigma(F) = \sigma(G) = \{y\}$, $\sigma(T) = \{t(y,x)\}$ and $\sigma(S) = \{s(x,y)\}$) has no legal modification.

The point is that *relationship types are inherited.* Since C is a subtype of A, also elements of type C may participate to a relationship of type T. Moreover, since A is abstract, each entity of type A must also be of type C. All in all, we get a cycle analogous to the ones used in the proof of Theorem 6.

Abstractness here plays a fundamental rôle: should not A be abstract, we could add an entity z to A, change the relationship $t(y,x)$ to $t(y,z)$, delete x and its adjacent relationship $s(x,y)$, delete y and its adjacent relationship $t(y,z)$, and finally z, getting to the empty instance.

Indeed, cycles of this kind can be built only using *forced subtypes* (E is a *forced subtype* of F if every entity of type F is also of type E). For a graph-

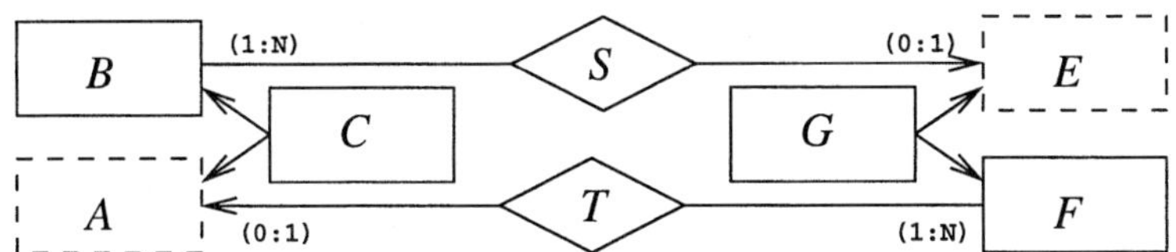

Fig. 3. An apparently innocuous diagram fragment.

theoretical viewpoint, an entity type E is a forced subtype of F if and only if E is the only minimal (i.e., without proper subtypes) subtype of F and all sequences of ISA relationship types going from E to F traverse abstract entity types only (including F, but except possibly for E).

Forced subtyping is important for reachability because cycles of mandatory (and possibly injective) *inherited* relationships can usually be broken by inserting suitable entities, as we pointed out in our last example, but this does not happen if inheritance (on the non-mandatory side of the relationship type) is by forced subtypes.

Nonetheless, forced subtyping is a pathological condition that should not appear in a schema as much as abstract entity types without subtypes. Both pathologies can be filtered before performing the acyclicity check; under the hypothesis that no forced subtype exists, one can prove the following one-sided theorem, using the same techniques of Theorem 1 and 6:

Theorem 5. *If all instances of a schema $\mathscr{S}$ without forced subtypes are mutually reachable, then $\Gamma(\mathscr{S})$ is acyclic. If all everywhere nonempty instances are mutually reachable, then $A(\mathscr{S})$ is acyclic.*

10 Conclusions

We have presented the first sound and complete algorithms to check instance reachability in entity-relationship schemata. Since the algorithms are acyclicity tests on a graph whose size in linearly bounded by the schema size, they are linear by definition.

It would be interesting to extend these results to schemata with ISA arcs *and a type system* as described in Definition 2, or, at least, for type constructors with disjunctive types (albeit the former definition is more general). It would be more cautious, however, to start first with an extension in this direction of the results given in [5], as the problem seems to be already tough enough in that case.

References

1. Ceri, S., Fraternali, P., Bongio, A.: Web Modeling Language (WebML): a modeling language for designing web sites. In: Proc. Ninth World Wide Web Conference. (2000)
2. Vigna, S.: Multirelational semantics for extended entity-relationship schemata with applications. In: Conceptual Modeling—ER 2002. 21st International Conference on Conceptual Modeling. Number 2503 in Lecture Notes in Computer Science, Springer–Verlag (2002) 35–49
3. Chen, P.P.S.: The entity-relationship model: Toward a unified view of data. ACM Transactions on Database Systems **1** (1976) 9–36
4. Thalheim, B.: Entity-Relationship Modeling. Springer–Verlag (2000)
5. Lenzerini, M., Nobili, P.: On the satisfiability of dependency constraints in entity-relationship schemata. Information Systems **15** (1990) 453–461

6. Calvanese, D., Lenzerini, M.: On the interaction between ISA and cardinality constraints. In Elmagarmid, A.K., Neuhold, E., eds.: Proceedings of the 10th International Conference on Data Engineering, Houston, TX, IEEE Computer Society Press (1994) 204–213
7. Gogolla, M., Hohenstein, U.: Towards a semantic view of an extended entity-relationship model. ACM Transactions on Database Systems (TODS) **16** (1991) 369–416
8. Bénabou, J.: Introduction to bicategories. In: Reports of the Midwest Category Seminar. Number 47 in Lecture Notes in Mathematics. Springer–Verlag (1967) 1–77
9. Bruni, R., Gadducci, F.: Some algebraic laws for spans (and their connections with multirelations). In Kahl, W., Parnas, D., Schmidt, G., eds.: Relational Methods in Software. Volume 44.3 of Electronic Notes in Theoretical Computer Science., Elsevier (2001)
10. Borceux, F.: Handbook of Categorical Algebra 1. Volume 50 of Encyclopedia of Mathematics and Its Applications. Cambridge University Press (1994)

A Reference Methodology for Conducting Ontological Analyses

Michael Rosemann[1], Peter Green[2], and Marta Indulska[2]

[1] Centre for Information Technology Innovation
Queensland University of Technology
126 Margaret Street, Brisbane QLD 4000
m.rosemann@qut.edu.au

[2] UQ Business School, The University of Queensland
11 Salisbury St, Ipswich QLD 4305, Australia
{p.green,m.indulska}@business.uq.edu.au

Abstract. The ontological analysis of conceptual modelling techniques is of increasing popularity. Related research did not only explore the ontological deficiencies of classical techniques such as ER or UML, but also business process modelling techniques such as ARIS or even Web services standards such as BPEL4WS. While the selected ontologies are reasonably mature, it is the actual process of an ontological analysis that still lacks rigor. The current procedure leaves significant room for individual interpretations and is one reason for criticism of the entire ontological analysis. This paper proposes a procedural model for the ontological analysis based on the use of meta models, the involvement of more than one coder and metrics. This model is explained with examples from various ontological analyses.

1 Popularity of Ontological Analyses

As techniques for conceptual modelling, enterprise modelling, and business process modelling have proliferated over the years (e.g., [12]), researchers and practitioners alike have attempted to determine objective bases on which to compare, evaluate, and determine when to use these different techniques (e.g., [4, 11]). Throughout the 80's, 90's, and into the new millennium however, it has become increasingly apparent to many researchers that without a theoretical foundation on which to base the specification for these various modelling techniques, incomplete evaluative frameworks of factors, features, and facets would continue to proliferate. Furthermore, without a theoretical foundation, one framework of factors, features, or facets is as justifiable as another for use (e.g., [2]).

Wand and Weber [19-23] have investigated the branch of philosophy known as ontology as a foundation for understanding the process in developing an information system. Ontology is a well-established theoretical domain within philosophy dealing with identifying and understanding elements of the real world. Today however, interest in, and the applicability of, ontologies extends to areas far beyond modelling. As Gruninger and Lee [9, p.13] point out, "…a Web search engine will return over 64,000 pages given "ontology" as a keyword…the first few pages are phrases such as "enabling virtual business", "gene ontology consortium, and "enterprise ontology"." The usefulness of ontology as a theoretical foundation for knowledge representation and natural language processing is a fervently debated topic at the present time in the

P. Atzeni et al. (Eds.): ER 2004, LNCS 3288, pp. 110–121, 2004.

artificial intelligence research community [10]. The popularity of using ontologies as a basis for the analysis of techniques that purport to assist analysts to develop models that emulate portions of the real world has been growing steadily. The Bunge-Wand-Weber (BWW) ontological models [24], for example, have been applied extensively in the context of the analysis of various modelling techniques. Wand and Weber [19-23] and Weber [24] have applied the BWW representation model to the "classical" descriptions of entity-relationship (ER) modelling and logical data flow diagramming (LDFD). Weber and Zhang [25] also examined the Nijssen Information Analysis Method (NIAM) using the ontology. Green [5] extended the work of Weber and Zhang [25] and Wand and Weber [22-23] by analysing various modelling techniques as they have been extended and implemented in upper CASE tools. Furthermore, Parsons and Wand [15] proposed an initial model of objects and they use the ontological models to identify representation-oriented characteristics of objects. Along similar lines, Opdahl and Henderson-Sellers [13] have used the BWW representation model to examine the individual modelling constructs within the OPEN Modelling Language (OML) version 1.1 based on "conventional" object-oriented constructs. Green and Rosemann [6] have extended the analytical work into the area of integrated process modelling based on the techniques presented in Scheer [17]. Most recently, Green *et al.* [8] have extended the use of this evaluative base into the area of enterprise systems interoperability using business process modelling languages like ebXML, BPML, BPEL4WS, and WSCI.

Clearly, ontology is a fruitful theoretical basis on which to perform such analyses. However, while ontological analyses are frequently utilised, particularly in the area of conceptual modelling technique analysis, the actual process of performing the analysis remains problematic. The current process of ontological analysis is open to the individual interpretations of the researchers who undertake the analysis. Consequently, such analyses are criticised as being subjective, *ad hoc*, and lacking in relevance. There is a need, therefore, for the systematic identification of shortcomings of the current ontological analysis process. The identification of such weaknesses, and their subsequent mitigation, will lead to a more rigorous, objective, and replicable analytical process.

Accordingly, this paper has several objectives. First, we aim to identify comprehensively the shortcomings in the current practice of ontological analysis. The identification of such shortcomings will provide a basis upon which the practice of ontological analysis can be improved. Second, we want to develop several propositions and methodology extensions that enhance the ontological analysis process by making it more objective and structured.

There are several contributions that this paper aims to make. They are based on previous experiences with ontological analyses as well as observations derived from published analyses. First, the work presents a detailed analysis of the actual process of performing an ontological evaluation. The presented work identifies eight shortcomings of the current ontological analysis process, *viz.,* lack of understandability, lack of comparability, lack of completeness, lack of guidance, lack of objectivity, lack of adequate result representation, lack of result classification, lack of relevance. Each of the identified shortcomings is classified then as belonging to one of three phases of analysis, *viz.,* input, process, and output. Second, the paper presents recommendations on how each of the shortcomings in the three phases can be overcome. The recommendations, *inter alia,* include an extended methodology for the improvement of the objectivity of the analysis as well as a weighting model that aims to improve the classification of the results of any ontological analysis.

The remainder of this paper is structured as follows. The next section identifies eight current shortcomings of ontological analyses that are classified with respect to the three phases of analysis, *viz.*, input, process and output. The third section provides recommendations concerning how to overcome the identified shortcomings in each of the three phases. The final section provides a brief summary of this work and outlines future research in this area.

2 Shortcomings of Current Ontological Analyses

An ontological analysis is in principle the evaluation of a selected modelling grammar from the viewpoint of a pre-defined and well-established ontology. The current focus of ontological analyses is on the bi-directional comparison of ontological constructs with the elements of the modelling grammar that is under analysis. Weber [24] clarifies two major situations that may occur when a grammar is analysed according to an ontology. After a particular grammar has been analysed, predictions on the modelling strengths and weaknesses of the grammar can be made according to whether some or any of the following situations arise out of the analysis.

1. *Ontological Incompleteness (or Construct Deficit)* exists unless there is at least one grammatical construct for each ontological construct.
2. *Ontological Clarity* is determined by the extent to which the grammar does not exhibit one or more of the following deficiencies:
   - *Construct Overload* exists in a grammar if one grammatical construct represents more than one ontological construct.
   - *Construct Redundancy* exists if more than one grammatical construct represents the same ontological construct.
   - *Construct Excess* exists in a grammar when a grammatical construct is present that does not map to any ontological construct.

Though this type of ontological analyses is widely established, it still has a range of shortcomings. These shortcomings can be categorised into the three main phases of an ontological analysis, *i.e.* preparation of the input data, the process of conducting the analysis, and the evaluation and interpretation of the results.

The first two identified shortcomings refer to the quality of the input data.

2.1 Lack of Understandability

Most of the ontologies that are currently used for analysis of modelling grammars have been specified in formal languages. While such a formalisation is beneficial for a complete and precise specification of the ontology, it is not naturally a very intuitive specification. An ontology that is not clear and intuitive can lead to misinterpretations as the involved stakeholders have problems with the specifications. Furthermore, it forms a hurdle for the application of the ontology as it requires a deep understanding of the formal language in which it is specified.

2.2 Lack of Comparability

The specification of an ontology requires typically a formal syntax, which allows the precise specification of the elements and relationships of the ontology. Such specifications are required, but not necessarily intuitive. Consequently, textual descriptions of the ontology in 'plain English' often extend the formal specification.

However, even if an ontology is specified in an intuitive and understandable language, the actual comparison with the selected modelling grammar remains a problem. Unless the ontology and the grammar are specified in the *same* language, it will be up to the coder to 'mentally convert' the two specifications into each other, which adds a subjective element to the analysis. Different languages can also lead to different levels of detail and further complicate the analysis. In any case, they make a more automated comparison practically impossible. This is the typical situation in nearly all previous analyses.

The further three shortcomings identified below are related to the process of the ontological analysis and refer to what should be analysed, how it should be analysed as well as who should conduct the analysis.

2.3 Lack of Completeness

The first decision that has to be made in the process of an ontological analysis is on the scope and depth of the analysis. Even if most ontologies have been discussed for many decades they still undergo modifications and extensions. It is up to the researcher to clearly specify the selected version of the ontology and the scope and level of detail of the analysis. In our work in the area of Web Services, for example, it was often not clear what constructs form the core of the standard. Two researchers who conducted independent analyses of the same Web Services standard, selected consequently a different number of constructs.

Moreover, many ontological analyses solely focus on the constructs of the ontology and the constructs of the grammar but do not sufficiently consider the relationships between these constructs. The difficulty in clearly specifying the boundaries of the analysis as well as the limited consideration of relationships between the ontological constructs lead to a lack of completeness.

2.4 Lack of Guidance

After the scope and the level of detail of the analysis have been specified, it is typically up to the coder to decide on the procedure of the analysis, i.e. in what sequence will the ontological constructs and relationships be analysed? Currently, there are hardly any recommendations on where to start the analysis. This lack of procedural clarity underlies most analyses and has two consequences. First, a novice analyst lacks guidance in the process of conducting the ontological evaluation. Second, the procedure of the analysis can potentially have an impact on the results of the analysis. Thus, it is possible that two analyses that follow a different process may lead to different outcomes.

2.5 Lack of Objectivity

An ontological analysis of a grammar requires not only detailed knowledge of the selected ontology and grammar but also a good understanding of the languages in which the ontology and the grammar are specified. This requirement explains why most analyses are carried out by single researchers as opposed to research teams. Consequently, these analyses are based on the individual interpretations of the involved researcher, which adds significant subjectivity to the results. This problem is further compounded by the fact that, unlike other qualitative research projects, ontological analyses typically do not include attempts to further validate the results.

The five shortcomings identified above have a common flavour in that they heavily depend on the researcher conducting the ontological evaluation. Three further shortcomings have been identified, *viz.*, lack of result representation, lack of result classification and lack of relevance. These shortcomings are detailed below and refer to the outcomes of the analysis.

2.6 Lack of Adequate Result Representation

The results of a complete ontological analysis, i.e. representation mapping and interpretation mapping, are typically summarised in two tables. These tables list all ontological constructs (first table) and all grammatical constructs (second table) and the corresponding constructs of the other meta model. Such tables can become quite lengthy and are typically not sorted in any particular order. They don't provide any insights into the importance of identified deficiencies and they also don't cluster the findings.

2.7 Lack of Result Classification

As indicated above, it is common practice to derive ontological deficiencies based on a comparison of the constructs in the ontology and the grammar. Ontological weaknesses are identified when corresponding constructs are missing in the obtained mapping between the ontology and the grammar or 1-many (or many-1 or even many-many) relationships exist. Such identified deficiencies are the typical starting point for the derivation of propositions and then hypotheses. In general, the ontological analysis does not make any statements regarding the relative importance of these findings in comparison with each other. Though this seems to be the established practice, it lacks more detailed insights into the significance of the results. It is expected, however, that the missing support for a core construct of an ontology can be rated higher than a missing corresponding construct for a minor ontological construct or a relationship. This lack of a more detailed statement regarding the significance of a potential shortcoming makes it difficult to judge quickly the outcomes of the results of two different sets of analyses, e.g. an ontological analysis of ARIS in comparison with an ontological analysis of UML.

2.8 Lack of Relevance

Finally, the results of an ontological analysis should be perceived as relevant by the related stakeholders. However, if an ontological analysis leads, for example, to the outcome that Entity Relationship Models do not support the description of behaviour, then it is not surprising that the IS community develops a rather critical opinion. It seems that an ontological analysis has to consider the purpose of the grammar as well as the background of the modeller who is applying this grammar. The application of a high-level and generic ontology does not consider this individual context and there is a danger that the outcomes can be perceived as trivial.

3 Reference Methodology for Conducting Ontological Analyses

The above identified shortcomings motivated the development of an enhanced methodology for ontological analyses. The main purpose of this methodology is to increase the rigour, the overall objectivity and the level of detail of the analysis. The proposed methodology for ontological analyses is structured in three phases, *viz.*, input, process and output.

3.1 Input

The formal specification of ontologies, together with the differences in the languages used to specify the ontologies and the grammars under analysis, have been classified as issues pertaining to the lack of understandability and comparability.

In order to overcome these shortcomings, it is proposed to convert the ontology as well as the selected modelling grammar to meta models using the same language (e.g. ER Models or UML Class Diagram). This facilitates a pattern-matching approach towards the ontological analyses of completeness and clarity of a grammar. As a first step we converted, for example, the Bunge-Wand-Weber ontology into an ER-based meta model. This meta model includes 50 entity types and 92 relationship types. It has clusters such as system, property or class/kind. Such a meta model explains, in a language familiar to the Information Systems (IS) community, the core constructs of the ontology. It also highlights the underlying focus of the ontology. In the case of the BWW model, for example, it is obvious from the visual inspection of the meta model that the ontology is centred around the existence of a *thing*, which is the central entity type in the meta model.

The obtained meta model can now be used for a variety of ontological analyses. Moreover, it allows a critical review of the BWW model by a wider community. The approach, however, is not without its limitations. Commonly used modelling techniques such as ER or UML are often widely accepted, however, they have not been designed for the purposes of meta modelling. Thus, they lack occasionally the required expressiveness. Fig. 1 provides an impression of the size and complexity of the meta model for the BWW ontology.

While an ER-based meta model helps to overcome issues related to the understandability of an ontology, a corresponding meta model of the analysed grammar is required to deal with the lack of comparability issue. Many popular modelling techniques (e.g. ARIS or UML, and also interoperability standards such as ebXML) are already specified in meta models using ER-notations or UML Class Diagrams. If the meta models for the ontology and the modelling technique are specified in the same language, the ontological analyses turns into a comparison of two conceptual models. As part of the analyses, it will be required to identify corresponding entity types and relationship types in both models. It also becomes immediately obvious, if the paradigm of the analysed grammar differs from the ontology. In the case of ARIS or many web services standards, for example, the meta models are centred around *functions* or *activities* instead of being centred around *things*.

3.2 Process

Issues related to the process of conducting an ontological analysis have been described as lack of completeness, lack of guidance and lack of objectivity.

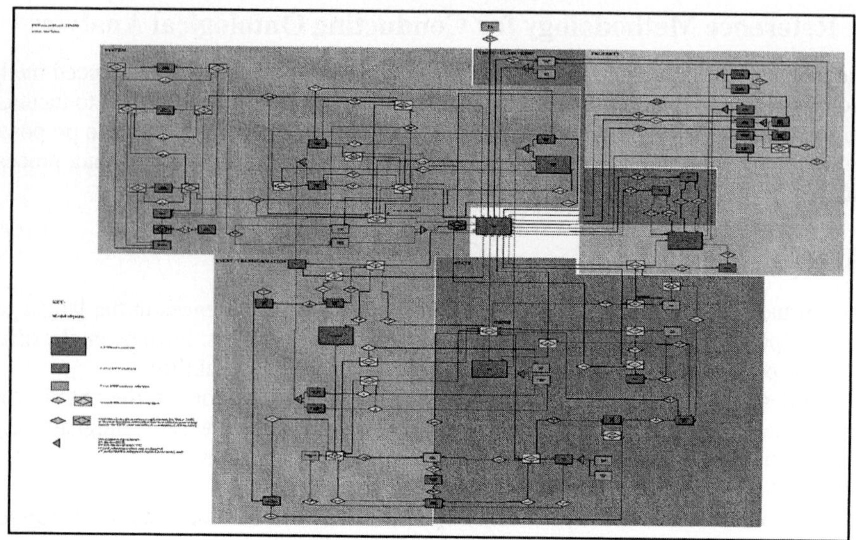

Fig. 1. The BWW meta model

Based on the assumption that corresponding meta models for the ontology and the analysed grammar are available, it is possible to clearly specify the scope of an analysis using those meta models. Such a selection of clusters, entity types and relationship types would define all elements that are to be perceived of relevance for a complete analysis. An analysis of an ER-based notation, for example, could be focused on the BWW clusters *thing*, *system* and *property* and could exclude the more behavioural-oriented clusters *event* and *state*. Such boundaries of an analysis could be easily visualised in the meta model and would provide a clear description of the comprehensiveness of the analysis.

The existence of two corresponding meta models and a clear definition of the scope of the analysis is a necessary but not a sufficient criteria for a well-guided process. Further guidelines are required regarding the starting point of such a process and the actual sequence of activities. Based on our experiences, we recommend starting with the representation mapping, i.e. selecting the meta model of the ontology and subsequently identifying the corresponding elements in the modelling grammar. The first construct to be analysed should be the most central entity type, i.e. in the case of the BWW models the entity type *thing*. Our previous work provides a strong argument that this analysis if followed by a cluster-by-cluster approach. Starting with the core constructs in a cluster, this allows a more structured and focused analysis of the completeness of a modelling grammar. The analysis of the entity types is followed by the relationships and the cardinalities. Constructs in the meta model that only have been introduced for the correctness of the meta model, but that do not reflect ontological constructs are excluded from the analysis. The representation mapping is followed by an analysis of the clarity, i.e. the interpretation mapping. In this case the meta model of the grammar under analysis is the starting point. The general procedure is similar. A main advantage of a cluster-based analysis is that the structure of the two meta models provides valuable input for the ontological analysis. An example is the analysis of generalisation-specialisation relationships in the meta model of the grammar. We propose to ontologically classify the super-type first and then to inherit this ontological classification to all sub-types. This streamlines the process of the analyses and increases the consistency.

The lack of objectivity issue, on the other hand, frequently stems from the analysis being performed by a single researcher. The situation results in an analysis that is almost certainly biased by the researcher's background as well as their interpretation of the specification of the grammar. In order to improve the validity of the analysis, a research methodology can be adopted that undertakes individual analyses of a particular grammar by at least two members of a research team, followed by consensus as to the final analysis by the entire team of researchers. The methodology consists of three steps:

Step 1: Using the specification of the grammar in question, at least two researchers separately read the specification and interpret, select and map the ontological constructs to candidate grammatical constructs to create individual first drafts of the analysis.

Step 2: The researchers involved in Step 1 of the methodology, meet to discuss and defend their interpretations of the representation modelling analysis. This meeting leads to an agreed second draft version of the analysis that incorporates elements of each of the researchers' first draft analyses. The overlap in the selection of the constructs and in the actual ontological analysis can be quantified by various figures that are used in content analysis and other more qualitative research.

Step 3: The second draft version of the analysis for each of the interoperability candidate standards is used as a basis for defence and discussion in a meeting involving the entire research team. The outcome of this meeting forms the final analysis of the grammar in question.

Such a methodology was employed in a project that sought to apply the BWW representation model analysis to a number of the leading potential Web Service standards, *viz.*, ebXML, BPML, BPEL4WS and WSCI. The project team was composed of four researchers and the standards were analysed in the order: ebXML → BPML → BPEL4WS → WSCI. Two researchers were involved in steps 1 and 2 of the methodology, *i.e.* the individual analysis of a standard followed by a meeting of the two researchers in order to obtain an agreed mapping. This was followed by a meeting of the entire team in order to discuss the mapping and arrive at the final analysis. The process was performed for each of the four standards.

Table 1 shows the recorded agreement statistics at the second step of the applied methodology while Table 2 shows the recorded agreement statistics at the third step of the methodology.

Table 1. Summary of Step 2 mapping agreement between both researchers

Web Service Language	Construct Mapping agreed upon by both researchers	Total number of specification constructs identified	Mapping conference
ebXML	43	51	84%
BPML	36	46	78%
BPEL4WS	30	47	63%
WSCI	39	49	79%

Table 2. Summary of Step 3 mapping agreement

Web Service Language	Construct Mapping agreed upon by the team	Total number of specification constructs identified	Mapping conference
ebXML	49	51	96%
BPML	41	46	89%
BPEL4WS	42	47	89%
WSCI	46	49	94%

The adoption of such a methodology is seen to have greatly improved the objectiveness of the carried out analyses.

3.3 Output

The three main shortcomings related to the outcome of an ontological analysis have been characterised as the lack of adequate result representation, lack of result classification and the lack of relevance.

The meta models, which have been used as input for the ontological analyses, are an appropriate medium to visualise the outcomes of the entire analysis process. In our work on the analysis of ARIS, we derived a meta model of the BWW model that highlighted all constructs of the ontology that do not have a corresponding construct in the grammar under analysis, *i.e.* we visualised incompleteness in the model using simple colour coding. In a similar way, we derived three ARIS meta models that highlighted excess, overload and redundancy in ARIS. Such models form a very intuitive way of representing the identified ontological shortcomings. The underlying clustering of the models also helps to quickly comprehend the main areas of shortcomings.

At present time, the process of an ontological analysis results in the identification of ontological incompleteness and ontological clarity through the identification of missing, overloaded or redundant grammatical constructs. While the end result identifies such problems, it fails to account for their relative importance. For example, *thing* is one of the fundamental constructs of the BWW model. The lack of mapping for the construct should, therefore, be considered more important than the lack of mapping for the *well-defined event* construct for example. There is a need for the development of a scoring model that enables the calculation of the 'goodness' of a grammar with respect to the ontology. In such a scoring model, each of the ontological constructs has a value assigned to it that reflects the relative importance of the construct in the ontology. Core constructs would therefore have high weightings whereas less important constructs would attract lower values of weightings. Following an ontological analysis of a particular grammar, the weighting of all missing constructs would be calculated to arrive at one value that generally reflects the outcome of the analysis.

An example for such a classification could have the following structure. All core constructs of an ontology (and the modelling grammar) would get the value 1. All other constructs represented as an entity type in the meta model of the ontology would receive the value 0.7, and all other constructs get the value 0.3. Such a weighting would then be applied to the outcomes of the ontological analysis. The scores would be aggregated across the ontology and modelling grammar. They also would be calculated separately for completeness, excess, overload and redundancy. Furthermore, they could be aggregated per cluster, which allows a more differentiated view on the particular strengths of a modelling grammar. Though the consolidated score of such an evaluation should not be overrated, it provides better insights into the characteristics of the ontological deficiencies and provides a first rating of the significance and importance of the identified shortcomings.

Apart from the lack of result classification that is addressed by the scoring model, another problem with the outcome of the analyses has been the perceived lack of relevance. Since most modelling grammars focus on modelling a sub-set of the phenomena that occurs in the real world, it would follow that not *all* constructs of an ontology are necessary in order to analyse such a grammar. If the full ontology is used in the analysis, the result may identify potential problems that would not, in reality, occur, because the modelling grammar is not used to model any phenomena described by the missing constructs. Further, there may also be a need for specialisation of some of the ontological constructs in order to enhance analysis of a grammar pertaining to a particular domain. The concept of a focussed ontology is shown in Fig. 2.

Indeed, the outcomes of the ontological analyses of different modelling grammars to date appear to support the need for a focused ontology, which consists of different subsets of the ontological constructs for different domains. The analyses of the examined grammars consistently show that the constructs *conceivable state space, conceivable event space* and *lawful event space*, for example, have no representative constructs in the grammars. Such missing constructs, if identified to be unnecessary for the particular domain, can be ignored leading to a simpler analysis that does not consider phenomena that are deemed to be outside of the scope of the domain.

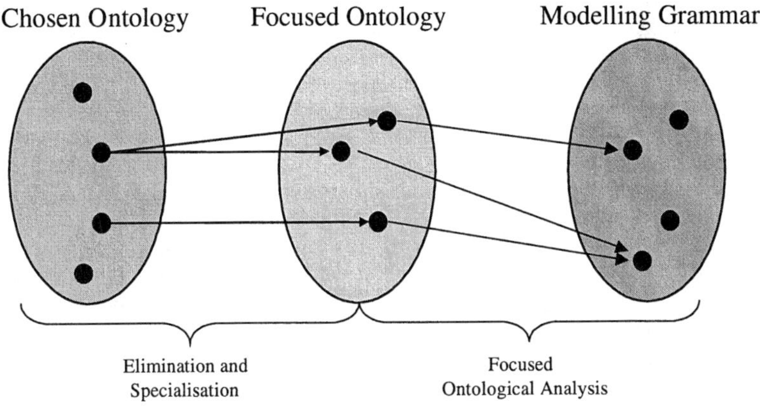

Fig. 2. An extension of ontological analysis through the use of focused ontologies

4 Summary and Future Work

There has been a marked increase in the popularity of the application of ontologies for the purposes of modelling grammar analysis. For example, a literature review identified more than 25 papers that applied the Bunge-Wand-Weber ontology for the analysis of modelling grammars such as ER (e.g., [19, 22-23], OMT, UML (e.g., [3, 14, 18], Petri-Nets, ARIS (e.g., [6-7, 16] or Web Services standards such as ebXML, BPEL4WS, BPML or WSCI (e.g., [1, 26, 8]. In general, selected ontologies and their interpretations, from an Information Systems viewpoint, are reasonably advanced.

However, the actual process of conducting an ontological analysis is still rather premature. At this stage, the process is focused on the identification of the cardinality of the relationships between corresponding elements in the ontology and the modelling grammar under analysis.

In total, eight shortcomings of the current process of ontological analysis have been identified and categorised into issues related to the input, process and output of the analysis.

This paper proposed to further enhance the current process of ontological analyses. The objectives of such a methodology are

- to provide guidance for researchers who are interested in conducting ontological analyses,
- to add rigour to the entire process and reduce the dependence on the subjective interpretations of the involved researcher, and
- to overall increase the credibility of the ontological analysis.

Examples from our ontological analyses of ARIS and various Web Services standards have been used to exemplify this methodology. As a consequence, we hope that the presented more rigorous process will increase the overall acceptance of using ontologies for the analysis, comparison and engineering of various grammars.

References

1. van der Aalst, W. M. P., Dumas M., ter Hofstede, A.H.M. et al.: Pattern Based Analysis of BPML (and WSCI). Brisbane, Queensland University of Technology (2002)
2. Bansler, J. P. and Bodker K.: A reappraisal of structured analysis: Design in an organizational context. ACM Transactions on Information Systems, Vol. 11. Nr. 2 (1993) 165-193
3. Burton-Jones, A., Meso P.: How good are these UML diagrams?: An empirical test of the Wand and Weber good decomposition model. in: Proc. 23rd International Conference on Information Systems, Barcelona (2002)
4. Gorla, N., Pu H.-C., Rom W.O.: Evaluation of process tools in systems analysis. Information and Software Technology, Vol. 37, Nr. 2 (1995) 119-126
5. Green, P. F.: Use of Information Systems Analysis and Design (ISAD) Grammars in Combination in Upper CASE Tools - An Ontological Evaluation. in: Proc. 2nd CaiSE/IFIP8.1 International Workshop on the Evaluation of Modeling Methods in Systems Analysis and Design, Barcelona (1997) 1-12
6. Green, P. F., Rosemann M.: Integrated Process Modelling: An Ontological Evaluation. Information Systems, Vol. 25, Nr. 2 (2000) 73-87
7. Green, P. F., Rosemann M.: Perceived ontological weaknesses of process modeling techniques: Further evidence. in: Proc. 10th European Conference on Information Systems, Poland (2002) 312-321
8. Green, P., Rosemann, M., Indulska, M. et al.: Candidate Interoperability Standards: An Ontological Overlap Analysis, Working Paper, The University of Queensland (2003)
9. Gruninger, M., Lee J.: Ontology: Applications and Design. Communications of the ACM, Vol. 45, Nr 2 (2002) 39-41
10. Guarino, N., Welty C.: Evaluating Ontological Decisions with OntoClean. Communications of the ACM, Vol. 45, Nr. 2 (2002) 61-65
11. Karam, G. M., Casselman, R.S.: A cataloging framework for software development methods. IEEE Computer, February, (1993) 34-46
12. Olle, T. W., Hagelstein, J., Macdonald, I.G., et al.: Information Systems Methodologies: A Framework for Understanding. Wokingham, Addison-Wesley (1991)
13. Opdahl, A. L., Henderson-Sellers, B.: Grounding the OML metamodel in ontology. Journal of Systems and Software, Vol. 57, Nr. 2 (2001) 119-143

14. Opdahl, A. L., Henderson-Sellers, B.: Ontological evaluation of the UML using the Bunge-Wand-Weber Model. Software and Systems Modeling, Vol. 1, Nr. 1 (2002) 43-67
15. Parsons, J., Wand, W.: Using objects in systems analysis. Communications of the ACM, Vol. 40, Nr. 12, (1997) 104-110
16. Rosemann, M., Green, P.: Developing a meta model for the Bunge-Wand-Weber ontological constructs. Information Systems, Vol. 27, Nr. 2 (2002) 75-91
17. Scheer, A.-W.: ARIS - Business Process Modeling. Heidelberg, Springer: Berlin (2000)
18. Shanks, G., Tansley, E., Nuredini, J., et al.: Representing part-whole relationships in conceptual modelling: An empirical evaluation. in: Proc. 23rd International Conference on Information Systems, Barcelona (2002)
19. Wand, Y., Weber, R.: An ontological evaluation of systems analysis and design methods. Information System Concepts: An In-depth Analysis. E. D. Falkenberg and P. Lindgreen, North-Holland (1989) 79-107
20. Wand, Y., Weber, R.: Mario Bunge's Ontology as a formal foundation for information systems concepts. Studies on Mario Bunge's Treatise. P. Weingartner and G. J. W. Dorn. Atlanta, Rodopi (1990) 123-149
21. Wand, Y., Weber, R.: An ontological model of an information system. IEEE Transactions on Software Engineering, Vol. 16, Nr. 11 (1990) 1281-1291
22. Wand, Y., Weber, R.: On the ontological expressiveness of information systems analysis and design grammars. Journal of Information Systems, Vol. 3, Nr. 4 (1993) 217-237
23. Wand, Y., Weber, R.: On the deep structure of information systems. Information Systems Journal, Vol. 5 (1995) 203-223
24. Weber, R.: Ontological Foundations of Information Systems. Melbourne, Vic., Coopers & Lybrand and the Accounting Association of Australia and New Zealand (1997)
25. Weber, R., Zhang, Y.: An analytical evaluation of NIAM's grammar for conceptual schema diagrams. Information Systems Journal, Vol. 6, Nr. 2 (1996) 147-170
26. Wohed, P., van der Aalst, W.M.P., Dumas, M., et al.: Pattern Based Analysis of BPEL4WS. Brisbane, Queensland University of Technology (2002)

Pruning Ontologies in the Development of Conceptual Schemas of Information Systems

Jordi Conesa and Antoni Olivé

Universitat Politècnica Catalunya
Departament de Llenguatges i Sistemes Informàtics
Jordi Girona 1-3 E08034 Barcelona (Catalonia)
{jconesa,olive}@lsi.upc.es

Abstract. In the past, most conceptual schemas of information systems have been developed essentially from scratch. Currently, however, several research projects are considering an emerging approach that tries to reuse as much as possible the knowledge included in existing ontologies. Using this approach, conceptual schemas would be developed as refinements of (more general) ontologies. However, when the refined ontology is large, a new problem that arises using this approach is the need of pruning the concepts in that ontology that are superfluous in the final conceptual schema. This paper proposes a new method for pruning ontologies in this approach. We show the advantages of our method with respect to similar pruning methods developed in other contexts. Our method is general and it can be adapted to most conceptual modeling languages. We give the complete details of its adaptation to the UML. On the other hand, the method is fully automatic. The method has been implemented. We illustrate the method by means of its application to a case study that refines the Cyc ontology.

1 Introduction

Most conceptual schemas of information systems have been developed essentially from scratch. The current situation is not very different: most industrial information systems projects are being developed using a methodology that assumes that the conceptual schema is created every time from scratch. However, it is well-known that substantial parts of conceptual schemas can be reused in different projects, and that such reuse may increase the conceptual schema quality and the development productivity [13].

Several research projects explore alternative approaches that try to reuse conceptual schemas as much as possible [3, 12, 21, 22]. The objective is similar to that of projects in the artificial intelligence field that try to reuse ontologies. There are several definitions of the term "ontology". We adopt here the one proposed in [7, 24], in which an ontology is defined as the explicit representation of a conceptualization. A conceptualization is the set of concepts (entities, attributes, processes) used to view a domain. An ontology is the specification of a conceptualization in some language. In this paper, we consider a conceptual schema as the ontology an information system needs to know.

Ontologies can be classified in terms of their level of generality into [8]:

- *Top-level* ontologies, which describe domain-independent concepts such as space, time, etc.

P. Atzeni et al. (Eds.): ER 2004, LNCS 3288, pp. 122–135, 2004.

- *Domain* and *task* ontologies which describe, respectively, the vocabulary related to a generic domain and a generic task.
- *Application* ontologies, which describe concepts depending on a particular domain and task.

We call top-level, domain and task ontologies *general* ontologies. One example of general ontology is Cyc [11].

General ontologies can play several roles in conceptual modeling [22]. One of them is the base role. We say that a general ontology plays a base role when it is the basis from which the conceptual schema is developed. In general, the development requires three main activities: refinement, pruning and refactoring [5] which are reviewed in the next section. The objective of the refinement activity is to extend the base ontology with the particular concepts needed in a conceptual schema, and that are not defined in that ontology.

In general, when the base ontology is large, the extended ontology cannot be accepted as the final conceptual schema because it includes many superfluous concepts. The objective of the pruning activity is then to prune the unnecessary concepts. In this paper, we propose a new method for pruning ontologies in the development of conceptual schemas. To the best of our knowledge, ours is the first method that is independent of the conceptual modeling language used and of the base ontology. The method can be used in other contexts as well, and we will show that it has several advantages over similar existing methods ([23, 20]). Our method can be adapted to most languages, and we give the complete details of its adaptation to the UML [17]. We illustrate the method by means of its application to a case study that refines the Cyc ontology. The case study deals with the directory of an organization (departments, persons, assignment of persons to departments, contact locations, etc.). The complete details of the case study are reported in [4].

The structure of the paper is as follows. In the next section we review the three main activities in the development of a conceptual schema from a base ontology, with the objective of defining the context of the pruning activity, the focus of this paper. Section 3 presents the pruning method we propose. Section 4 compares our method with similar ones. Finally, Section 5 gives the conclusions and points out future work.

2 The Context

In this section we briefly review the three activities required to develop a conceptual schema from a general ontology: refinement, pruning and refactoring. Normally, these activities will be performed sequentially (see Fig. 1), but an iterative development is also possible [5].

2.1 Refinement

Normally, a general ontology O_G will not include completely the conceptual schema CS required by a particular information system. The objective of the refinement activity is then to obtain an extended ontology O_X such that:

- O_X is an extension of O_G, and
- O_X includes the conceptual schema CS.

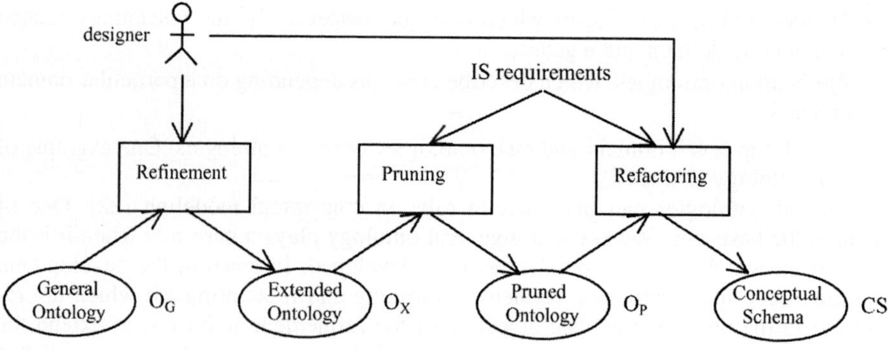

Fig. 1. The three activities in the development of conceptual schemas from general ontologies

The refinement is performed by the designer. S/he analyzes the IS requirements, determines the knowledge the system needs to know to satisfy those requirements, checks whether such knowledge is already in O_G and, if not, makes the necessary extensions to O_G, thus obtaining O_X.

In our case study, we adopted as general ontology O_G *OpenCyc* [18], the public version of the *Cyc* ontology. *OpenCyc* includes over 2900 entity types and over 1300 relationship types. Even if these numbers are large (and even larger in other ontologies such as *Cyc*) it is likely that additional entity or relationship types may be needed for the CS of a particular IS.

For example, our case study deals with an organization, its departments and the people working in them. A department is a sub-organization, part of the organization to which it belongs, and it performs some of the activity of that organization. The organizational structure is hierarchical, with some departments reporting directly to the organization itself, while others report to another department. However, the concept of *Department* does not exist[1] in *OpenCyc*, so we have to add it. We have added the entity type *Department*, as a subtype of the pre-existing *Organization* (an indirect subtype of *Agent*), the relationship type *HasDepartments* (see Figure 2), and the constraint that the organizational structure is hierarchical.

As another example, *OpenCyc* includes the relationship type *HasWorkers* between two *Agents*. The meaning is that an agent (*worker*) regularly works for the other (*work*). A person may be worker of several agents. *HasWorkers* has a supertype (*WorksWith*) and a subtype (*HasEmployees*). The relationship type that fits best our needs is *HasWorkers*. However, in our case study, the participants are *Person* and *Organization*. We have then refined *HasWorkers* in *Person* so that the work must be instance of *Organization*. On the other hand, in our case study, the participation of a person in *HasWorkers* is mandatory (multiplicity 1..* in *work* role, see Figure 2).

The complete refinement of *OpenCyc* for the case study is described in [4]. In summary, we have added one entity type (*Department*), one attribute (attribute *name* of *Agent*, shown in Figure 2) and two associations (one of them is *HasDepartments* in Figure 2). We have added also one refinement of attributes, one of associations (shown in Figure 2) and four general integrity constraints.

[1] In fact, it appears in the documentation, but it is not included yet in the public download.

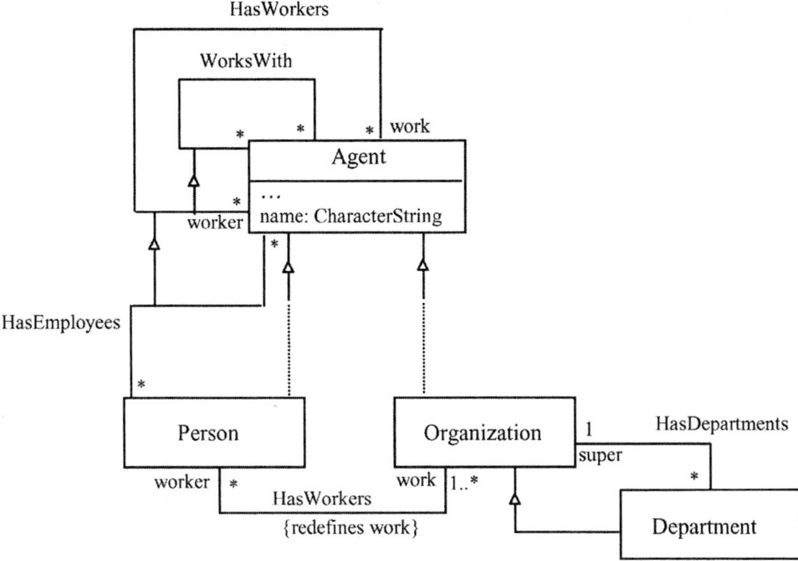

Fig. 2. (Partial) refinement of OpenCyc in the case study

2.2 Pruning

Normally, an extended ontology O_X will contain many irrelevant concepts for a particular information system. The objective of the pruning activity is then to obtain a pruned ontology O_P such that:

- O_P is a subset of O_X, and
- O_P includes the conceptual schema *CS*, and
- the concepts in O_X but not in O_P would have an empty extension in the information system (i.e. they are irrelevant).

In the case study, we find that the *OpenCyc* ontology contains thousands of concepts irrelevant for organizational directory management. For example, the entity and relationship types dealing with Chemistry. Our information system is not interested in these concepts and, therefore, their extension in the information base would be empty. The objective of the pruning activity is to remove such concepts from O_X. In the next section we present a method for the automatic pruning of ontologies. The input of the method is either the formal specification of the IS requirements (domain events, queries) or the explicit definition of the concepts (entity and relationship types) of interest.

2.3 Refactoring

Normally, a pruned ontology O_P cannot be accepted as a final CS because it can be improved in several respects. The objective of the refactoring activity is then to obtain a conceptual schema *CS* that is externally equivalent to O_P yet improves its structure. The purpose of ontology (or conceptual schema) refactoring is equivalent to that of software refactoring [6]. The refactoring is performed by the designer, but important parts of the activity can be assisted or automated, provided that the IS requirements are formalized. Refactoring consists in the application of a number of refactoring operations to parts of an ontology. Many of the software refactoring operations can be adapted to conceptual modeling, but this will not be explored in this paper.

3 Pruning the Extended Ontology

In this section, we define the problem of pruning the extended ontology and we propose a new method for its solution. The starting point of the pruning activity is an extended ontology O_X and the functional requirements of the IS.

3.1 The Extended Ontology

We assume that, in the general case, an ontology O_X consists of sets of the following elements:

- Concepts. There are two kinds of concepts:
  - Entity types.
  - Relationship types. We will denote by $R(p_1{:}E_1,\ldots,p_n{:}E_n)$ a relationship type R with participant entity types $E_1, \ldots, E_n$ playing roles $p_1, \ldots, p_n$ respectively.
- Generalization relationships between concepts. We denote by $IsA(C_1,C_2)$ the generalization relationship between concepts C_1 and C_2. IsA^+ will be the transitive closure of *IsA*. We admit multiple specialization and multiple classification.
- Integrity constraints[2].

Adaptation to the UML. In the UML an ontology O_X consists of sets of the following elements (see Figure 2):

- Concepts:
  - Entity types.
  - Data types.
  - Attributes.
  - N-ary associations.
  - Association classes, which reify associations. An association class and its reifying association are a single element.
- Generalization relationships between de above concepts. Attributes cannot be generalized.
- Constraints.

In the UML, some constraints are predefined (they have a particular language construct) and others may be user-defined. In our method we deal with constraints of the following kinds:

- Cardinality constraints of associations and attributes.
- Completeness and disjointness of sets of generalizations.

[2] The generalization relationships are (inclusion) constraints also, but we give them an special treatment due to its prominent role in ontologies and in conceptual modeling.

– Redefinitions of association ends and attributes (refinement constraints). Figure 2 shows an example of association redefinition: the association *HasWorkers* is redefined in *Person*.
– General constraints. We assume that general constraints are defined by constraint operations and specified in the OCL, as explained in [16]. The adaptation of our method to constraints defined as invariants is straightforward. An example is the constraint that the name of agents must be unique. Its formal specification is:

```
Context Agent::uniqueName():Boolean
   body Agent.allInstances() -> isUnique(name)
```

In the case study, O_X consists of:

– 2,697 Entity types and 255 Data types.
– 266 Attributes and 1,446 Associations.
– 4 general integrity constraints.

3.2 Concepts of Direct Interest

Usually, the extended ontology O_X will be (very) large, and only a (small) fraction of it will be needed for the CS of a particular IS. The objective of the pruning activity, as we will define it below, is to remove some non-needed elements from O_X.

The pruning activity needs to know which concepts from O_X are of direct interest in the IS. A concept is of direct interest in a given IS if its users and designers are interested in representing its population in the Information Base of the IS.

When the functional requirements of an IS are formally specified, then the concepts of direct interest *CoI* may be automatically extracted from them [22]. The details of the extraction process depend on the method and language used for that specification. We explain here the process when the IS behavior is specified by system operations, as is done in many methods such as Larman's method [10], the B method [1] or Fusion [2]. A similar process can be used when the behavior is specified by statecharts, event operations or other equivalent methods.

In general, the formal specification of a system operation consists of:

– A signature (name, parameters, and result). The types of the parameters and the result are entity types defined in O_X.
– A set of preconditions. Each precondition is a boolean expression involving concepts defined in O_X.
– A set of postconditions. As above, each postcondition is a boolean expression involving concepts defined in O_X.

The concepts of direct interest *CoI* are then defined as:

– The types of the parameters and result of the system operations.
– The concepts appearing in the pre or postconditions.

In some cases the formal specification may not be available or may be incomplete. In these cases, the designers may wish to define the concepts *CoI* explicitly or to add new concepts to those determined from the functional specification. Given that our pruning method needs to know these concepts, independently of how they have been obtained, we allow designers to define them explicitly, either in total or in part.

If a relationship type is a concept of direct interest then we require that its participant entity types are in *CoI* also. Formally, we say that a set of concepts of direct interest *CoI* is *complete* if for each relationship type $R(p_1:E_1,\ldots,p_n:E_n) \in CoI$ the participant entity types $\{E_1, \ldots, E_n\} \subset CoI$.

In O_X there may be some concepts that generalize those in *CoI* and which are not part of *CoI*. We are interested in these generalized concepts because they may be involved in constraints that affect instances of the concepts *CoI*. To this end, we call set of *generalized* concepts of interest *G*(*CoI*) the concepts of a complete set *CoI* and their generalizations. Formally:

$$G(CoI) = \{c \mid c \in CoI \vee \exists sub\ (\text{IsA}^+(sub,c) \wedge sub \in CoI)\}$$

Adaptation to the UML. The adaptation is straightforward. We assume that the pre/postconditions are written in the OCL. For example, consider the system operation *changeSuper*, whose purpose is to change the super of a given department. Its formal specifications may be:

```
Context System::changeSuper(sub:Department, super:Organization)
  pre:  super <> sub.super
  post: sub.super = super
```

The *CoI* inferred from this operation are: *Department*, *Organization* and *HasDepartments*.

3.3 Constrained Concepts

We call constrained concepts of an integrity constraint *ic*, *CC*(*ic*), the set of concepts appearing in the formal expression of *ic*. By abuse of notation we write *CC*(*O*) to denote the set of concepts constrained by all the integrity constraints defined in ontology *O*. Formally,

$$CC(O) = \{c \mid c \text{ is a concept} \wedge c \in O \wedge \exists ic\ (ic \text{ is a constraint} \wedge ic \in O \wedge c \in CC(ic))\}$$

Adaptation to the UML. If *ic* is a cardinality constraint of an attribute or association, then *CC*(*ic*) will be the attribute or association, and the entity and data types involved in it.

If *ic* is a completeness constraint with a common supertype *super* and subtypes $sub_1, \ldots, sub_n$, then $CC(ic) = \{super, sub_1, \ldots, sub_n\}$.

A disjointness constraint with a common supertype *super* and subtypes $sub_1, \ldots, sub_n$, corresponds to $n(n\text{-}1)/2$ disjunction constraints each of which constraints two subtypes, sub_i and sub_j, and *super*. Strictly speaking, these constraints do not involve the supertype *super*, but in the UML they are attached to sets of generalizations having the same supertype.

If *ic* is a redefinition of an association or attribute then *CC*(*ic*) will be the redefined association or attribute, and the entity and data types involved in the association or attribute.

The constrained concepts of a general constraint will be the entity types, data types, attributes, associations and association classes appearing in the OCL expression that defines it. For example, if *uniqueName* is the general constraint defined in 3.1, then CC(*uniqueName*) = {*Agent*, *name*}.

3.4 The Pruning Problem

Given an extended ontology O_X and a complete set of concepts of direct interest *CoI*, as explained above, the pruning problem consists in obtaining a pruned ontology O_P such that:

(a) The elements in O_P are a subset of those in O_X. We do not want to add new elements to O_X in the pruning activity. Additions can be done in the refinement or in the refactoring activities.

(b) O_P includes the concepts of direct interest *CoI*. These concepts must be included in O_P because they are referred to in the specification of the system operations.

(c) If C_1 and C_2 are two concepts in O_P and there is a direct or indirect generalization relationship between them in O_X, then such relationship must also exist in O_P. Formally:

$$\forall c_1,c_2 \ (c_1 \in O_P \wedge c_2 \in O_P \wedge IsA^+(c_1,c_2) \in O_X \rightarrow IsA^+(c_1,c_2) \in O_P)$$

(d) O_P includes all constraints defined in O_X whose constrained concepts are in *G*(*CoI*). The rationale is that the constraints in O_X which constraint the Information Base of O_P must be part of it. The constraints in O_X that involve one or more concepts not in *G*(*CoI*) cannot be enforced and, therefore, are not part of O_P.

(e) O_P is consistent, that is, it is a valid instance of the conceptual modeling language in which it is specified (metamodel).

(f) O_P is minimal, in the sense that if any of its elements is removed from it, the resulting ontology does not satisfy (b-e) above.

For each O_X and *CoI* there is at least an ontology O_P that satisfies the above conditions and, in the general case, there may be more than one.

To the best of our knowledge, there does not exist a method that obtains O_P automatically in a context similar to ours. In what follows we describe a method for the problem. In the next section we will compare it with existing similar methods.

3.5 The Pruning Algorithm

Our algorithm obtains O_P in three steps. The algorithm begins with an initial ontology O_0 which is exactly O_X (that is, $O_0 := O_X$) and obtains O_P. The steps are:

- Pruning irrelevant concepts and constraints. The result is the ontology O_1.
- Pruning unnecessary parents. The result is the ontology O_2.
- Pruning unnecessary generalization paths. The result is O_P.

Pruning irrelevant concepts and constraints. The concepts of direct interest for the IS are given in the set *CoI*, and *G*(*CoI*) is the set of concepts in which the IS is directly or indirectly interested in. However, O_0 may include other concepts, which are irrelevant for the IS. Therefore, in the first step we prune from O_0 all concepts which are not in *G*(*CoI*), that is, we prune the set of concepts:

$$\text{IrrelevantConcepts} = \{c \mid c \text{ is a concept } \wedge c \in O_0 \wedge c \notin G(CoI)\}$$

Pruning a concept implies the pruning of all generalization relationships in which that concept participates.

Similarly, we prune the constraints in O_0 that are not relevant for the IS, because they constraint one or more concepts not in $G(CoI)$. That is, we prune the set of constraints:

IrrelevantConstraints =
$\{ic \mid ic$ is a constraint $\wedge\ ic \in O_0 \wedge \exists c\ (c \in CC(ic) \wedge c \notin G(CoI))\}$

The result of this step is the ontology O_1:

$$O_1 = O_0 - \text{IrrelevantConcepts} - \text{IrrelevantConstraints}$$

In the example of Figure 2, we have that *HasWorkers* is a concept of interest and, therefore, $\{HasWorkers, WorksWith\} \subseteq G(CoI)$. However, *HasEmployees*, a subtype of *HasWorkers*, is not a member of $G(CoI)$ and it is then pruned in this step. Likewise, *Person* is a concept of interest but its subtypes (*Student*, *HumanChild*, *HumanAdult*, *FemalePerson*, *MalePerson*, etc. not shown in Figure 2) are not, and therefore they are also pruned in this step. The same happens to "lateral" concepts such as *Atom* or *Electron*.

In the case study, after the application of this step we have an ontology O_1 consisting of:

- 96 Entity types and 8 Data types.
- 6 Attributes and 21 Associations.
- 4 general integrity constraints.

Pruning unnecessary parents. After the previous step, the concepts of the resulting ontology (O_1) are exactly $G(CoI)$. However, not all of them are needed in the CS. The concepts strictly needed are given by:

$$NeededConcepts = CoI \cup CC(O_1)$$

The other concepts (i.e. those given by $G(CoI) - NeededConcepts$) are potentially not needed. We can prune the parents of *NeededConcepts* which are not children of some concept in *NeededConcepts*. Formally,

UnnecessaryParents =
$\{c \mid c \notin \text{NeededConcepts} \wedge \neg\exists c'\ (c' \in \text{NeededConcepts} \wedge \text{IsA}^+(c,c'))\}$

As we have said before, the pruning of a concept implies the pruning of all generalization relationships in which that concept participates.

The result of this step is the ontology O_2:

$$O_2 = O_1 - \text{UnnecessaryParents}$$

In Figure 2, an example of unnecessary parent is the association *WorksWith*. In the case study, *WorksWith* neither is a needed concept of O_1 nor is a child of some needed concept, and therefore it is pruned in this step.

In the case study, after the application of this step we have an ontology O_2 consisting of:

- 23 Entity types and 6 Data types.
- 6 Attributes and 5 Associations.
- 4 general integrity constraints.

Pruning unnecessary generalization paths. In some cases, the ontology O_2 may contain generalization paths between two concepts such that not all of them are necessary. The purpose of the third step is to prune these paths.

We say that there is a generalization path between C_1 and C_n if:

- C_1 and C_n are two concepts from O_2,
- $IsA^+(C_1,C_n)$ and
- The path includes two or more generalization relationships $IsA(C_1,C_2)$, …, $IsA(C_{n-1},C_n)$.

A generalization path $IsA(C_1,C_2)$, …, $IsA(C_{n-1},C_n)$ between C_1 and C_n is potentially redundant if none of the intermediate concepts C_2, …, C_{n-1}:

- Is member of the set $CoI \cup CC(O_2)$
- Is the super or the sub of other generalization relationships.

A potentially redundant generalization path between concepts C_1 and C_n is redundant if there are other generalization paths between the same pair of concepts. In this case, we prune the concepts C_2, …, C_{n-1} and all generalization relationships in which they participate. Note that, in the general case, this step is not determinist.

The output of this step is the pruned ontology, O_P.

Figure 3 shows two generalization paths between the concepts of interest *Person* and *Agent*. None of the four intermediate concepts is member of $CoI \cup CC(O_2)$. However, *SocialBeing* is the super of a generalization of *Organization*. Therefore, the only potentially redundant generalization path is *IsA(Person,Animal)*, *IsA(Animal, PerceptualAgent)*, *IsA(PerceptualAgent,Agent)*, and it can be pruned from the ontology.

In the case study, after the application of this step we have an ontology O_P consisting of (see Figure 4):

- 10 Entity types and 6 Data types (not shown in the Figure).
- 6 Attributes and 5 Associations.
- 4 general integrity constraints.

4 Comparison with Previous Work

The need for pruning an ontology has been described in several research works in the fields of information systems and knowledge bases development. We may mention Swartout et al. [23], Knowledge Bus [20], Text-To-Onto [9, 14], Wouters et al. [26], the ODS (Ontology-Domain-System) approach [25], and OntoLearn [15].

Even if the above works differ in the context in which the need for pruning arises, the ontology language, the particular ontology used as base, or the selection of the concepts of interest, we believe that (at least parts of) our pruning method can be adapted to be used successfully in all those works. The reason are: (1) we deal with any base ontology; (2) our method can be adapted to any ontology language; (3) we take into account the specificity of entity types, relationship types, generalizations and constraints present in all complete conceptual modeling languages; and (4) we may obtain the concepts of interest from the functional specifications. In the following we

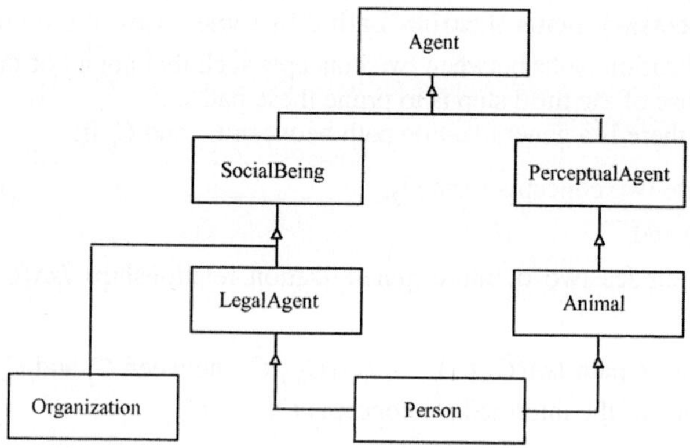

Fig. 3. Two generalization paths between *Person* and *Agent*

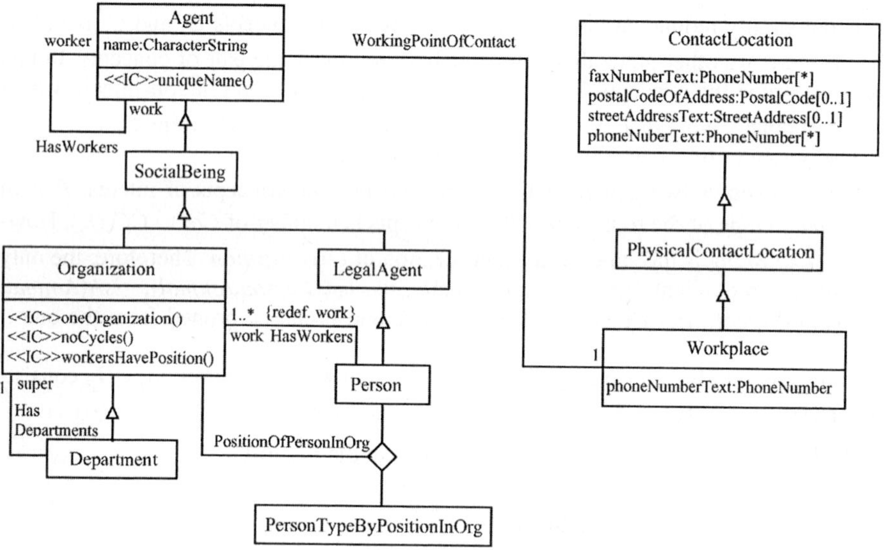

Fig. 4. The pruned ontology in the case study

give some comments on the first two works, which are the more closely related to ours, and that describe a comparable pruning method.

The purpose of Swartout et al. [23] is the development of specialized, domain specific ontologies from a large base ontology. The base ontology is Sensus, a natural language based ontology containing well over 50,000 concepts. The elements of the ontology are only entity types and generalization relationships. The concepts of interest are assumed to be a set of entity types (called the "seed") selected explicitly by domain experts, and all entity types that generalize them. The pruning method corresponds roughly to our first step (pruning irrelevant concepts and constraints). Using our method, the domain experts could select the seed, as before, but also the generalized entity types of interest. The two other steps of our method could then be applied here, thus obtaining more specific domain ontologies.

The purpose of Knowledge Bus [20] is to generate information systems from application-focused subsets of a large ontology. The base ontology is Cyc, and the ontology language is CycL. The concepts of interest are assumed to be the set of entity types defined in a context (a subset of Cyc), also called the "seed" set, and all the entity and relationship types that can be "navigated" directly or indirectly from them. For example, with reference to Figure 2, if the seed set were only {*Organization*} then all entity and relationship types shown in that figure would be considered concepts of interest. If we consider not only the fragment shown in that figure but the complete OpenCyc, then over 700 entity types and 1300 relationship types would be considered concepts of interest. The pruning method (called the sub-ontology extractor) corresponds here also to our first step (pruning irrelevant concepts and constraints). The result is that (as the authors recognize) many superfluous types are extracted from Cyc. Using our method, the domain experts can be more precise with respect to the concepts of interest. They could select the seed, as before, but also the generalized entity and relationship types of interest. The two other steps of our method could then be applied here as well, thus improving the specificity of the sub-ontology extraction process.

5 Conclusions

We have tried to contribute to the approach of developing conceptual schemas of information systems by reusing existing ontologies. We, as many others, believe that this approach offers a great potential for increasing both the conceptual schema quality and the development productivity.

We have focused on the problem of pruning ontologies. The problem arises when the reused ontology is large and it includes many concepts which are superfluous for the final conceptual schema. The objective of the pruning activity is to remove these superfluous concepts.

We have presented a new formal method for pruning an ontology. The input to our method is the ontology and the set of concepts of interest. When the functional requirements are formally specified, the concepts of interest can be automatically extracted from them. Otherwise, the designer has to define them explicitly. From this input, our method obtains automatically a pruned ontology, in which most of the superfluous concepts have been removed.

We have formalized the method independently of the conceptual modeling language used. However, the method can be adapted to most languages. We have shown the details of its adaptation to the UML. On the other hand, our method can be used with any ontology. We have illustrated the method by means of its application to a case study that refines the public version of the Cyc ontology. We have shown that our method improves on similar existing methods, due to its generality and greater pruning effectiveness.

We plan to continue our work in (at least) three directions. First, our method assumes the pruning activity in the context of the development of a conceptual schema, but the method can be used in other contexts as well. In particular, we would like to use it in the development of domain ontologies. Second, we would like to adapt the method to other general languages such as the OWL (Web Ontology Language) [19]. Finally, we plan to work on the activity that follows pruning: refactoring. The large amount of existing work on schema transformation can be “reused” for that purpose.

Acknowledgments

I would like to thank Jordi Cabot, Xavier de Palol, Dolors Costal, Cristina Gómez, Anna Queralt, Ruth Raventós, Maria Ribera Sancho and Ernest Teniente for their many useful comments to previous drafts of this paper.

This work has been partly supported by the Ministerio de Ciencia y Tecnologia and FEDER under project TIC2002-00744.

References

1. Abrial, J.R. The B-Book. Cambridge University Press, 1996, 779 p.
2. Coleman, D.; Arnold, P.; Bodoff, S.; Dollin, C.; Gilchrist, H.; Hayes, F.; Jeremaes, P. Object-Oriented Development. The Fusion Method. Prentice Hall, 1994, 316p.
3. Castano, S.; De Antonellis, V.; Zonta, B. "Classifying and Reusing Conceptual Schemas", Proc. ER'92, LNCS 645, pp. 121-138.
4. Conesa, J. "A Case Study on Pruning General Ontologies for the Development of Conceptual Schemas". Technical Report LSI-04-18-R, UPC, 2004.
5. Conesa, J.; de Palol, X.; Olivé, A. "Building Conceptual Schemas by Refining General Ontologies". Proc. DEXA 2003. LNCS 2736, Springer, pp. 693-702.
6. Fowler, M. Refactoring. Improving the Design of Existing Code. Addison-Wesley, 2000, 431 p.
7. Gruber, T.R. "Toward Principles for the Design of Ontologies used for Knowledge Sharing". International Journal of Human and Computer Studies, vol. 43 (5/6), 1995, pp. 907 - 928.
8. Guarino, N. "Formal Ontology and Information Systems", Proc. FOIS'98, Trento, IOS Press, pp. 3-15.
9. Kietz, J-U.; Maedche, A.; Volz, R. "A Method for semi-automatic ontology acquisition from a corporate intranet". In Proc. of EKAW'2000, France, 2000.
10. Larman, C. Applying UML and Patterns. Prentice Hall, Second Edition, 2002.
11. Lenat, D.B.; Guha, R.V.; Pittman, K.; Pratt, D.; Shepherd, M. "CYC: Towards Programs with Common Sense", Comm. ACM, 33(8), pp. 30-49.
12. Lloyd-Williams, M. "Exploiting domain knowledge during the automated design of O-O databases", Proc. ER'97, LNCS 1331, pp. 16-29.
13. Mili, H.; Mili, F.; Mili, A. "Reusing Software: Issues and Research Directions", IEEE TSE, 21(6), 1995, pp. 528-562.
14. Maedche, A.; Staab, S. "Ontology Learning for the Semantic Web". IEEE Intelligent Systems, March/April 2001, pp. 72-79.
15. Navigli, R. Automatically Extending, Pruning and Trimming General Purpose Ontologies. Proc. of 2nd IEEE International Conference on Systems, Man and Cybernetics (SMC 2002), Tunisy, October 6-9th, 2002.
16. Olivé, A. "Integrity Constraints Definition in Object-Oriented Conceptual Modeling Languages". Proc. ER 2003, LNCS 2813, Springer, pp. 349-363.
17. OMG. UML 2.0 Superstructure Specification, 2003.
18. Opencyc, http://www.opencyc.org, 2004.
19. W3C. OWL Web Ontology Language Reference. http://www.w3.org/TR/owl-ref/, 2004.
20. Peterson, B.J.; Andersen, W.A.; Engel, J. "Knowledge Bus: Generating Application-focused Databases from Large Ontologies". Procs. 5th KRDB Worshop Seattle, May 1998
21. Storey, V.; Chiang, R.; Dey, D.; Goldstein, R.; Sundaresan, S. "Database Design with Common Sense Business Reasoning and Learning", ACM TODS 22(4), 1997 pp. 471-512.
22. Sugumaran, V.; Storey, V.C. "Ontologies for conceptual modeling: their creation, use and management". Data & Knowledge Engineering, 42 (2002), pp. 251-271.

23. Swartout, B.; Patil, R.; Knight, K.; Russ, T. "Toward Distributed Use of Large-Scale Ontologies", Proc. 10th. KAW'96, 1996, Canada.
24. Uschold, M.; Gruninger, M. "Ontologies: principles, methods and applications", The Knowledge Engineering Review, 11(2), 1996, pp. 93-136.
25. Wang, X.; Chan, C.W.; Hamilton, H.J. "Design of Knowledge-Based Systems with the Ontology-Domain-System Approach". Proc. SEKE'02, Italy, pp. 233-236.
26. Wouters, C.; Dillon, T.; Rahayu, W.; Chang, E. "A Practical Walkthrough of the Ontology Derivation Rules", Proc. DEXA 2002, LNCS 2453, pp. 259-268.

Definition of Events and Their Effects in Object-Oriented Conceptual Modeling Languages

Antoni Olivé

Dept. Llenguatges i Sistemes Informàtics
Universitat Politècnica de Catalunya
08034 Barcelona (Catalonia)
olive@lsi.upc.es

Abstract. Most current conceptual modeling languages and methods do not model events as entities. We argue that, at least in Object-Oriented (O-O) languages, modeling events as entities provides substantial benefits. We show that a method for behavioral modeling that deals with event and entity types in a uniform way may yield better behavioral schemas. The proposed method makes an extensive use of language constructs such as constraints, derived types, derivation rules, type specializations and operations, which are present in all complete O-O conceptual modeling languages. The method can be adapted to most O-O languages. In this paper we explain its adaptation to the UML.

1 Introduction

According to the well-known 100 Percent (or completeness) principle, a conceptual schema must include all relevant general static and dynamic aspects [18]. The part of a conceptual schema that deals with static aspects is called the structural schema (or subschema), and the part that deals with dynamic aspects is called the behavioral schema. This paper focuses on behavioral schemas.

The approaches to behavioral modeling taken by conceptual modeling languages are diverse. The main differences are due to the style in which each language is based (logic, structured, object-oriented (O-O), temporal, Petri nets, etc.) and to the degree of formalization (informal, semiformal, formal) they aim at. These approaches have been surveyed and compared in (among many others) [12,34,2,25].

In O-O languages, an important classification of behavioral modeling approaches is with respect to whether or not they model events as entities (objects or individuals). When events are entities, they are modeled in a way similar to ordinary entities: they are instance of event types (a special kind of entity types), they may participate in relationships, they can be specialized or generalized, and so on. When events are not considered entities, they are modeled by means of other language constructs, usually as invocations of operations or actions.

Most current conceptual modeling languages and methods do not model events as entities. Among them, we may mention the well-known Syntropy [8], Fusion [7], Object-oriented SSADM [30], ROOM [32], B [1], TROLL [19], Statecharts [16], IDEA [6], Catalysis [10], IDEFIX [17], Larman's method [20] and Executable UML [23].

P. Atzeni et al. (Eds.): ER 2004, LNCS 3288, pp. 136–149, 2004.

In this paper we argue that, at least in O-O languages, modeling events as entities provides substantial benefits. We show that a method for behavioral modeling that deals with event and entity types in a uniform way may yield better behavioral schemas.

The idea that events can be modeled as objects is not new in the conceptual modeling field. It was suggested in the beginning of the 80's [3,4,24], and it was (at least partially) adopted in a few languages and methods developed around the early 90's, such as OSA [13], KAOS [11], IFO_2 [33], and Martin and Odells' method [21]. However, later methods have advocated approaches to behavioral modeling that use (only) state transition diagrams and/or operations.

Currently, there does not exist any UML-based method that models events as entities. The UML language distinguishes four kinds of events: (1) call events, which are invocations of operations; (2) signal events, which are similar to objects, but are limited and intended for asynchronous communication between objects; (3) change events, which are satisfaction of boolean conditions; and (4) time events, which are satisfaction of time expressions [29, 31]. Therefore the UML does not provide an appropriate construct for modeling events as objects at the conceptual level. Change and time events are useful constructs in conceptual modeling, but they can be used only in state transition diagrams.

We propose a new method that makes an extensive use of language constructs such as constraints, derived types, derivation rules, type specializations and operations, which are present in all complete modern conceptual modeling languages. The method can be adapted to most O-O languages. We explain in this paper its adaptation to the UML.

The structure of the paper is as follows. Next Section defines the terminology we use, and delimits the scope of our work. Section 3 presents the basics of the method we propose. Section 4 describes a useful extension to the basic method. Finally, Section 5 summarizes the conclusions and points out to future work. The examples in the paper will be about a fragment of an elementary version of a Material Requirements Planning (MRP) system. Figure 1 shows the structural schema of that fragment. The details are introduced where they arise.

2 Events

In this section, we introduce the terminology, definitions and classifications of events used in the paper, and we delimit the scope of our method [21].

2.1 Domain Events

An Information System (IS) maintains a representation of the state of a domain in its Information Base (IB). The state of a domain at some time point is the set of instances of the relevant entity and relationship types that exist in the domain at that time. The state of the domain at time *t* changes if the domain state at that time, *t,* is different from the domain state at the previous time, *t-1*. A state change consists in a set of one or more structural events. A **structural event** is an elementary change in the population of an entity or relationship type [9]. The precise number and meaning of structural events depend on the conceptual modeling language used. In the logic language, there are only two kinds of structural events: insertion and removal of facts. In the UML, there are nine kinds of structural events: create object, reclassify object, etc. [29, p.203+]. A **domain event** is a state change that consists of a set of structural events that are perceived or considered as a single change in the domain. The time at which the change occurs is the **occurrence time** of the event. In principle, two or more domain events may occur at the same time.

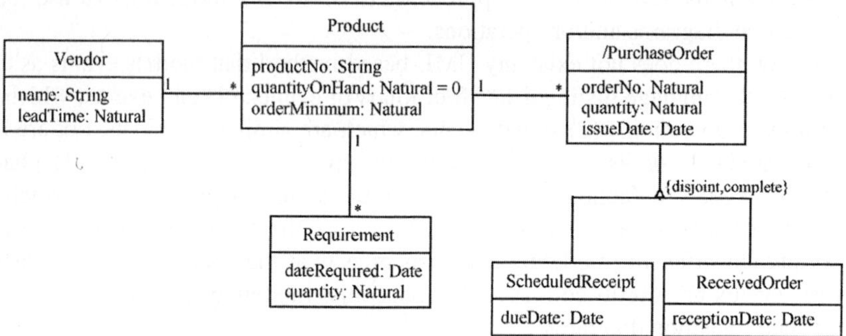

Fig. 1. Fragment of the structural schema for an MRP application

Usually, domain events are caused by actions performed in the domain. However, in some cases the users may delegate the task of producing some domain events to the IS. We can then classify the domain events in terms of where (the source) they have been produced: either in the domain or in the IS. They are called external and generated domain events, respectively. Some of the external events are produced by just the passing of time, and they are called temporal domain events. We briefly review these three kinds of domain events in the following.

An **external** domain event is caused by an action performed in the domain. The event occurs independently from the IS. An example of external domain event is the reception of a scheduled receipt.

A **temporal** domain event is caused by the passing of time. The domain is in some state and the simple passing of time changes it. The event occurs independently from the IS. An example of temporal domain event could be the arrival of the day after the due date of a scheduled receipt. The scheduled receipt becomes an overdue order by just the passing of time (the entity type *OverdueOrder*, subtype of *ScheduledReceipt*, is not shown in Figure 1).

A **generated** domain event is caused by actions performed by the IS itself. Generated domain events are caused when some generating condition *C* is satisfied. The IS detects when *C* is satisfied and, at that time, it generates the corresponding domain event. In principle, the generating condition might take any form. However, the most widely used particular forms are:

- *State-based.* The change of the truth value of a boolean condition over the IB in two consecutive states.
- *Event-based.* The occurrence of an event, when the IB satisfies a given condition.

An example of generated domain event with a state-based generating condition could be the automatic generation of purchase order releases. The generating condition could be: "The quantity on hand plus the total expected receipts of a product is equal or greater than the sum of the required quantities of that product". When the truth value of the condition changes between two consecutive states (from true to false) the system must generate a "purchase order release" for the corresponding product.

2.2 Query Events

A **query** event is a request for information to which an IS must respond. Query events are not changes in the domain state represented in the IB. The source of query events may be external to the IS or the IS itself. They are then called external or generated query events, respectively.

An **external** query event is issued by an actor. Most query events are external. A **generated** query event is an implicit request for information issued by the IS itself. Similar to generated domain events, an IS may generate a query event when a generating condition is satisfied. In principle, the generating condition might take any form. However, two particular forms are widely used:

- *State-based.* The change of the truth value of a boolean condition over the IB in two consecutive states. For example, sending an automatic reminder notice to a vendor when a scheduled receipt is approaching its due date.
- *Event-based.* The occurrence of an event, when the IB satisfies a given condition.

2.3 Scope of This Paper

This paper deals with domain and query events that are external or generated with an event-based generating condition. The reason for leaving aside domain and query events that are generated with a state-based generating condition, and the temporal domain events, is that their definition in most O-O languages (including the UML) requires the use of state transition diagrams, which are not discussed here.

3 The Basics of the Method

3.1 Events as Entities

Our method adopts the view that events are similar to ordinary entities and, therefore, that events can be modeled as a special kind of entities, which we call event entities [3,4,24]. Event entities are instance of event types. An event type is a concept whose instances, at a given time, are identifiable events that occur at that time. Like any other entity, event entities may participate in relationships.

In non-temporal IBs, event entities exist in the IB only during its occurrence time. It is assumed that events are instantaneous, that the IS response to them is also instantaneous, and that after the response (and before the next time tick) the events are removed from the IB. In this paper we do not deal with temporal IBs.

The adaptation of our method to a particular O-O language requires a linguistic construct to define event types. In the UML, we use for this purpose a new stereotype, that we call <<*event*>>. A type with this stereotype defines an event type.

Like any other entity type, event types may be specialized and/or generalized. This will allow us to build a taxonomy of event types, where common elements are defined only once. It is convenient to define a root entity type, named *Event*, as shown in Figure 2. All event types are direct or indirect subtypes of *Event*. In fact, *Event* is defined as derived by union of its subtypes. We define in this event type the attribute *time*, which gives the occurrence time of each event. We define also the abstract operation *effect*, whose purpose will be made clear later. It is not necessary to stereotype event types as <<*event*>> because all direct or indirect subtypes of *Event* will be considered event types.

The view of events as entities is not restricted to domain events. We apply it also to query events.

3.2 Event Characteristics

The characteristics of an event are the set of relationships in which it participates. There is at least one relationship between each event entity and a time point, representing the event occurrence time. We assume that the characteristics of an event are determined when the event occurs, and remain fixed.

In a particular language, the characteristics of events should be modeled like those of ordinary entities. In the UML, we model them as attributes or associations. Figure 2 shows the definition of the external domain event type *NewProduct*, with four attributes (including time) and an association with *Vendor*. The immutability of characteristics can be defined by setting their *isReadOnly* property to *true* (not shown in the Figure) [29, p. 89+].

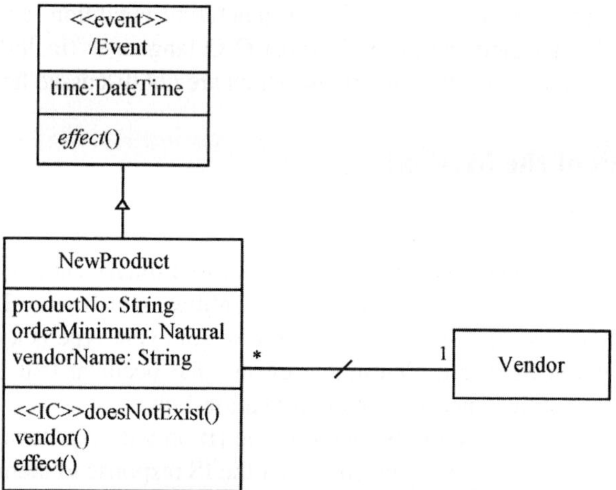

Fig. 2. Definition of event type *NewProduct*

Event characteristics may be derived. The value for a derived characteristic may be computed from other characteristics and/or the state of the IB when the event occurs, as specified by the corresponding derivation rule. The practical importance of derived characteristics is that they can be referred to in any expression (integrity constraints, effect, etc.) exactly as the base ones, but their definition appears in a single place (derivation rule).

In the UML, derived elements (attributes, associations, entity types) are marked with a slash (/). We define derivation rules by means of defining operations [26]. In the example of Figure 2, attribute *vendorName* gives the name of the vendor that will supply the new product. The association between *NewProduct* and *Vendor* may be derived from the vendor's name. The defining operation: `NewProduct::vendor(): Vendor` gives the vendor associated with an event instance. In the UML 2.0, the result of operations is specified by a *body* expression [29, p. 76+]. Using the OCL, the formal specification of the above operation may be:

```
context NewProduct::vendor() : Vendor
  body: Vendor.allInstances() -> any (name = self.vendorName)
```

3.3 Event Constraints

An event constraint is a condition an event must satisfy to occur [8]. An event constraint involves the event characteristics and the state of the IB before the event occurrence. It is assumed that the state of the IB before the event occurrence satisfies all defined constraints. Therefore, an event *E* can occur when the domain is in state *S* if: (1) state *S* satisfies all constraints, and (2) event *E* satisfies its event constraints.

An IS checks event constraints when the events occur and the values of their characteristics have been established, but before the events have any effect in the IB or produce any answer. Events that do not satisfy their constraints are not allowed to occur and, therefore, they must be rejected. Event constraints checking is (assumed to be) done instantaneously.

In a particular conceptual modeling language, event constraints can be represented like any other constraint. In the UML, they can be expressed as invariants or as constraint operations [27]. Event constraints are always creation-time constraints because they must be satisfied when events occur. Here we will define constraints by operations, called constraint operations, and we specify them in the OCL. In the UML, we show graphically constraint operations with the stereotype <<IC>>. The result of the evaluation of constraint operations must be *true*.

A constraint of the *NewProduct* event (Figure 2) is that the product being added cannot exist already. We define it with the constraint operation *doesNotExist*. The specification in the OCL is:

```
context NewProduct::doesNotExist() : Boolean
  body: not Product.allInstances() ->
                         exists (productNo = self.productNo)
```

On the other hand, the vendor must exist. This is also an event constraint. However, in this case the constraint can be expressed as a cardinality constraint. The multiplicity *1* in the vendor role requires that each instance of *NewProduct* must be linked to exactly one vendor. The constraint is violated if the *vendor*() operation does not return an instance of *Vendor*.

An event constraint defined in a supertype applies to all its direct and indirect instances. This is one of the advantages of defining event taxonomies: common constraints can be defined in a generalized event type. Figure 3 shows an example. The event type *ExistingProductEvent* is defined as the union of *NewRequirement, PurchaseOrderRelease* and *ProductDetails*. The constraint that the product must exist is defined in *ExistingProductEvent*, and it applies to all its indirect instances. Note that the constraint has been defined by a cardinality constraint, as explained above. Although it is not shown in Figure 3, the event type *ExistingProductEvent* is a subtype of *Event*.

Figure 3 shows also the constraint *validDate* in *NewRequirement*. The constraint is satisfied if *dateRequired* is greater than the event date.

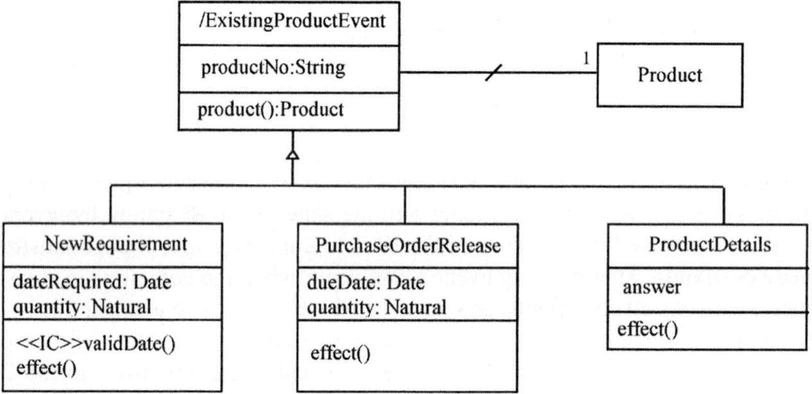

Fig. 3. *ExistingProductEvent* is asubtype of *Event* (not shown here) and a common supertype of domain event types. *NewRequirement* and *PurchaseOrderRelease* and of the query event type *ProductDetails*

3.4 Query Events Effects

The effect of a query event is an answer providing the requested information. The effect is specified by an expression whose evaluation on the IB gives the requested information. The query is written in some language, depending on the conceptual modeling language used. In the UML, we can represent the answer to a query event and the query expression in several ways. We explain one of them here, which can be used as is, or as a basis for the development of alternative ways.

The answer to a query event is modeled as one or more attributes and/or associations of the event, with some predefined name. In the examples, we shall use names starting with *answer*. An alternative could be the use of a stereotype to indicate that an attribute or association is the answer of the event.

Now, we need a way to define the value of the answer attributes and associations. To this end, we use the operation *effect* that we have defined in *Event*. This operation will have a different specification in each event type. For query events, its purpose is to specify the values of the answer attributes and associations. The specification of the operation can be done by means of postconditions, using the OCL.

Figure 3 shows the representation of external query event type *ProductDetails*. The answer is given by attribute:

```
answer : TupleType(qoh:natural, vendorName:String)
```

The specification of the *effect* operation may be:

```
context ProductDetails::effect()
  post: answer = Tuple(qoh = product.quantityOnHand,
                       vendorName = product.vendor.name)
```

Alternatively, in O-O languages the answer to a query event could be specified as the invocation of some operation. The effect of this operation would then be the answer of the query event.

3.5 Domain Events Effects: The Postcondition Approach

The effect of a domain event is a set of structural events. There are two main approaches to the definition of that set: the postconditions and the structural events approaches [25]. These approaches are called declarative and imperative specifications, respectively, in [34]. In the former, the definition is a condition satisfied by the IB after the application of the event effect. In the latter, the definition is an expression whose evaluation gives the corresponding structural events. Both approaches can be used in our method, although we (as many others) tend to favor the use of postconditions. We deal with the postcondition approach in this subsection, and the structural events approach in the next one.

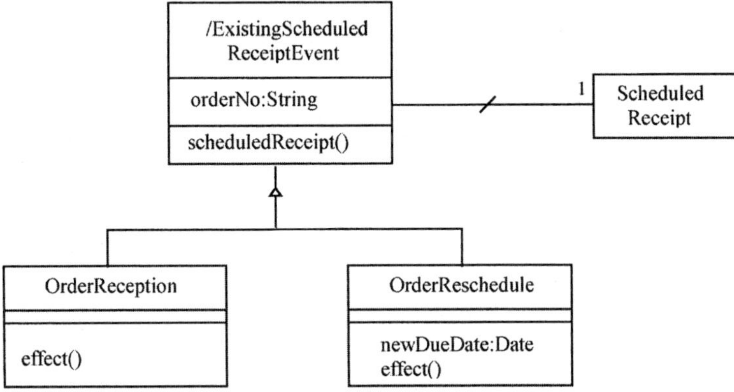

Fig. 4. Definition of *OrderReception* and *OrderReschedule* event types

In the postcondition approach, the effect of an event *Ev* is defined by a condition *C* over the IB. The idea is that the event *Ev* leaves the IB in a state that satisfies *C*. It is also assumed that the state after the event occurrence satisfies all constraints defined over the IB. Therefore, the effect of event *Ev* is a state that satisfies condition *C* and all IB constraints.

In an O-O language, we can represent the effect of a domain event in several ways. As we did for query events, we explain one way here, which can be used as is, or as a basis for the development of alternative ways. We define a particular operation in each domain event type, whose purpose is to specify the effect. To this end, we use the operation *effect* that we have defined in *Event*. This operation will have a different specification in each event type. Now, the postcondition of this operation will be exactly the postcondition of the corresponding event. As we have been doing until now, in the UML we also use the OCL to specify these postconditions formally.

As an example, consider the external domain event type *NewRequeriment*, shown in Figure 3. The effect of one instance of this event type is the addition of one instance into entity type *Requirement* (see Figure 1). Therefore, in this case the specification of the *effect* operation is:

```
context NewRequirement::effect()
  post ThereIsANewInstanceOfRequirement:
          r.oclIsNew() and
          r.oclIsTypeOf(Requirement) and
          r.dateRequired = dateRequired and
          r.quantity = quantity and
          r.product = product
```

In our method, we do not define preconditions in the specification of *effect* operations. The reason is that we *implicitly* assume that the events satisfy their constraints *before* the application of their effect. In the example, we assume implicitly that a *NewRequirement* event references an existing product, and that its required date is valid. The postcondition states simply that a new instance of *Requirement* has been created in the IB, with the corresponding values for its attributes and association. Any implementation of the *effect* operation that leaves the IB in a state that satisfies the postcondition and the IB constraints is valid.

Another example is the external domain event type *OrderReception* (see Figure 4). An instance of *OrderReception* occurs when a scheduled receipt is received. The event effect is that the purchase order now becomes *ReceivedOrder* (see Figure 1), and that the quantity on hand of the corresponding product is increased by the quantity received. We specify this effect with two postconditions of *effect*() in *OrderReception*:

```
context OrderReception::effect()
  post TheOrderIsNowReceived:
 scheduledReceipt.oclIsTypeOf(ReceivedOrder) and
 scheduledReceipt.oclAsType(ReceivedOrder).receptionDate =
          CurrentDate
 post TheQuantityOnHandIsIncreased:
          scheduledReceipt.product.quantityOnHand =
             scheduledReceipt.product.quantityOnHand@pre +
             scheduledReceipt.quantity
```

3.6 Domain Events Effects: The Structural Events Approach

In the structural events approach, the effect of an event *Ev* is defined by an expression written in some language. The idea is that the evaluation of the expression gives the set *S* of structural events corresponding to the event *Ev* effect. The application of *S* to the previous state of the IB produces the new state. The new state of the IB is the previous state plus the entities or relationships inserted, and minus the entities or relationships deleted. This approach is in contrast with the previous one, which defines a condition that characterizes the state of the IB after the event. It is assumed that the set *S* is such that it leaves the IB in a new state that satisfies all the constraints. Therefore, when defining the expression, one must take into account the existing constraints, and to ensure that the new state of the IB will satisfy all of them.

Our method could be used in O-O languages that follow the structural events approach. The idea is to provide a method for the *effect* operations. The method is a procedural expression, written in the corresponding language, whose evaluation yields the structural events.

3.7 Comparison with Previous Work

In most current conceptual modeling methods and languages, events are not considered objects. Instead of this, events are represented as invocations of actions or operations, or the reception of signals or messages. Event types are defined by means of operations (with their signatures) or an equivalent construct.

We believe that the view of events as entities (albeit of a special kind) provides substantial benefits to behavioral modeling. The reason is that the uniform treatment of event and entity types implies that most (if not all) language constructs available for entity types can be used also for event types. In particular: (1) Event types with common characteristics, constraints, derivation rules and effects can be generalized, so that common parts are defined in a single place, instead of repeating them in each event type. We have found that, in practice, many event types have characteristics, constraints and derivation rules in common with others [14]; (2) The graphical notation related to entity types (including attributes, associations, multiplicities, generalization, packages, etc.) can be used also for event types; and (3) Event types can be specialized in a way similar to entity types, as we explain in the next section.

4 Event Specialization

One of the fundamental constructs of O-O conceptual modeling languages is the specialization of entity types. When we consider events as entities, we have the possibility of defining specializations of event types. We may use these specializations when we want to define an event type whose characteristics, constraints and/or effect are extensions and/or specializations of another event type.

For example, assume that some instances of *NewRequirement* are special because they require a large quantity of their product and, for some reason, the quantity required must be ordered immediately to the corresponding vendor. This special behavior can be defined in a new event type, *SpecialRequirement*, defined as a specialization of *NewRequirement*, as shown Figure 5.

Note that *SpecialRequirement* redefines the constraint *validDate*, and adds a new constraint called *largeQuantity*. The required date of the new events must be beyond

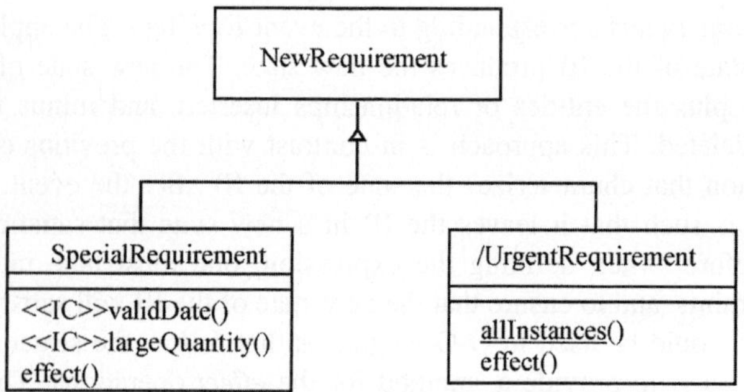

Fig. 5. Two specializations of the event type *NewRequirement* (Fig. 3)

the current date plus the vendor's lead time, and the quantity required must be at least ten times the product order minimum.

In the UML, the body of operations may be overridden when an operation is redefined, whereas preconditions and postconditions can only be added [29, p. 78]. Therefore, we redefine *validDate* as:

```
context SpecialRequirement::validDate() : Boolean
    body: dateRequired > time.date + product.vendor.leadTime
```

The new constraint *largeQuantity* can be defined as:

```
context SpecialRequirement::largeQuantity() : Boolean
    body: quantity > product.orderMinimum * 10
```

The effect of a *SpecialRequirement* is the same as that of a *NewRequirement*, but we want the system to generate an instance of *PurchaseOrderRelease* (see Figure 3). We define this extension as an additional postcondition of the *effect* operation:

```
context SpecialRequirement::effect()
  post CreateAnInstanceOfEventTypePurchaseOrderRelease :
   pOR.oclIsNew() and
   pOR.oclIsTypeOf(PurchaseOrderRelease)and
   pOR.productNo = self.productNo and
   pOR.quantity = self.quantity and
   pOR.dueDate = self.dateRequired
```

On the other hand, we can define event types *derived by specialization.* A derived event type is an event type whose instances at any time can be inferred by means of a derivation rule. An event type *Ev* is derived by specialization of event types Ev_1, ..., Ev_n when *Ev* is derived and their instances are also instance of Ev_1, ..., Ev_n [28]. We may use event types defined by specialization when we want to define particular constraints and/or effect for events that satisfy some condition.

For example, suppose that some instances of *NewRequirement* are urgent because they are required within the temporal horizon of the current MRP plan (seven days), and therefore they could not have been taken into account when the plan was generated. We want a behavior similar to the previous example. The difference is that now we determine automatically which are the urgent requirements. We define a new event type, *UrgentRequirement*, shown Figure 5, defined as derived by specialization of *NewRequirement.*

In the UML, the name we give to the defining operations for derived entity types is *allInstances* [26]. In this case, *allInstances* is a class operation that gives the population of the type. The derivation rule of *UrgentRequirement* is then:

```
context UrgentRequirement::
                        allInstances() : Set(UrgentRequirement)
    body: NewRequirement.allInstances() ->
                           select(dateRequired < time.date + 7)
```

The effect of an urgent requirement is the same as that of a new requirement, but again we want the system to generate an instance of *PurchaseOrderRelease* (see Figure 3). We would define this extension as an additional postcondition of the *effect* operation, as we did in the previous example.

Comparison with Previous Work. Event specialization is not possible when events are seen as operation invocations. The consequence is that this powerful modeling construct cannot be used in methods like those mentioned in the Introduction.

5 Conclusions

In the context of O-O conceptual modeling languages, we have proposed a method that models events as entities (objects), and event types as a special kind of entity types. The method makes an extensive use of language constructs such as constraints, derived types, derivation rules, type specializations, operations and operation redefinition, which are present in all complete conceptual modeling languages. The method can be adapted to most O-O languages. In this paper we have explained in detail its adaptation to the UML. The method is fully compatible with the UML-based CASE tools, and thus it can be adopted in industrial projects, if it is felt appropriate.

The main advantage of the method we propose is the uniform treatment we give to event and entity types. The consequence is that most (if not all) language constructs available for entity types can be used also for event types. Event types may have constraints and derived characteristics, like entity types. Characteristics, constraints and effects shared by several event types may be defined in a single place. Event specialization allows the incremental definition of new event types, as refinements of their supertypes. Historical events ease the definition of constraints, derivation rules and event effects. In summary, we believe that the view of events as entities provides substantial benefits to behavioral modeling.

Among the work that remains to be done, there is the integration of the proposed method with the state transition diagrams. These diagrams allow defining the kinds of events that were beyond the scope of this paper.

Acknowledgements

I would like to thank Jordi Cabot, Jordi Conesa, Dolors Costal, Xavier de Palol, Cristina Gómez, Anna Queralt, Ruth Raventós, Maria Ribera Sancho and Ernest

Teniente for their help and many useful comments to previous drafts of this paper. This work has been partly supported by the Ministerio de Ciencia y Tecnologia and FEDER under project TIC2002-00744.

References

1. Abrial, J-R. The B-Book. Cambridge University Press, 1996, 779p.
2. Bonner, A.J.; Kifer, M. "The State of Change: A Survey". LNCS 1472, 1998, pp. 1-36.
3. Borgida, A.; Greenspan, S. "Data and Activities: Exploiting Hierarchies of Classes". Workshop on Data Abstraction, Databases and Conceptual Modelling, 1980, pp. 98-100.
4. Bubenko, J.A.jr. "Information Modeling in the Context of System Development". Proc. IFIP 1980, North-Holland, 1980, pp. 395-411.
5. Cabot, J.; Olivé, A.; Teniente, E. "Representing Temporal Information in UML". Proc. UML'03. LNCS 2863, pp. 44-59.
6. Ceri, S.; Fraternalli, P. Designing Database Applications with Objects and Rules. The IDEA Methodology. Addison-Wesley, 1997, 579p.
7. Coleman, D.; Arnold, P.; Bodoff, S.; Dollin, C.; Gilchrist, H.; Hayes, F.; Jeremaes, P. Object-Oriented Development. The Fusion Method. Prenticel Hall, 1994, 316p.
8. Cook, S.; Daniels, J. Designing Object Systems. Object-Oriented Modelling with Syntropy. Prentice Hall, 1994, 389 p.
9. Costal, D.; Olivé, A.; Sancho, M-R. "Temporal Features of Class Populations and Attributes in Conceptual Models". Proc. ER'97, LNCS 1331, Springer, pp. 57-70.
10. D'Souza, D.F.; Wills, A.C. Objects, Components and Frameworks with UML. The Catalysis Approach. Addison-Wesley, 1999, 785 p.
11. Dardenne, A.; van Lamsweerde, A.; Fickas, S. "Goal-directed requirements acquisition". Science of Computer Programming, 20(1993), pp. 3-50.
12. Davis, A.M. Software Requirements. Objects, Functions and States. Prentice-Hall, 1993.
13. Embley, D.W.; Kurtz, B.D.; Woodfield, S.N. Object-Oriented System Analysis. A Model-Driven Approach. Yourdon Press, 1992, 302 p.
14. Frias, L.; Olivé, A.; Queralt, A. "EU-Rent Car Rentals Specification". UPC, Research Report LSI 03-59-R, 2003, 159 p., http: //www.lsi.upc.es/dept/techreps/techreps.html.
15. Gamma, E.; Helm, R.; Johnson, R.; Vlissides, J. Design Patterns. Elements of Reusable Object-Oriented Software. Addison-Wesley, 1995, 395 p.
16. Harel, D.; Gery, E. "Executable Object Modeling with Statecharts". IEEE Computer, July 1997, pp. 31-42.
17. IEEE. IEEE Standard for Conceptual Modeling Language Syntax and Semantics for IDEF1X97 (IDEFobject). IEEE Std 1320.2-1998, 1999.
18. ISO/TC97/SC5/WG3. "Concepts and Terminology for the Conceptual Schema and the Information Base", J.J. van Griethuysen (ed.), March, 1982.
19. Jungclaus, R.; Saake, G.; Hartmann, T.; Sernadas, C. "TROLL-A Language for Object-Oriented Specification of Information Systems". ACM TOIS, 14(2), 1996, pp. 175-211.
20. Larman, C. Applying UML and Patterns. Prentice Hall, 2002, 627 p.
21. Martin, J.; Odell, J.J. Object-Oriented Methods: A Foundation. Prentice Hall, 1995, 412 p.
22. Martin, R.C. Agile Software Development, Principles, Patterns and Practices. Prentice Hall, 2003, 529p.
23. Mellor, S.J.; Balcer, M.J. Executable UML. A Foundation for Model-Driven Architecture. Addison-Wesleyy, 2002, 368p.
24. Mylopoulos, J.; Bernstein, P.A.; Wong, H.K.T. "A Language Facility for Designing Database-Intensive Applications". ACM TODS, 5(2), pp. 185-207, 1980.

25. Olivé, A. "Time and Change in Conceptual Modeling of Information Systems". In Brinkkemper, S.; Lindencrona, E.; Solvberg, A. "Information Systems Engineering. State of the Art and Research Themes", Springer, 2000, pp. 289-304.
26. Olivé, A. "Derivation Rules in Object-Oriented Conceptual Modeling Languages". Proc. CAiSE 2003, LNCS 2681, pp. 404-420.
27. Olivé, A. "Integrity Constraints Definition in Object-Oriented Conceptual Modeling Languages". Proc. ER 2003, LNCS 2813, pp. 349-362, 2003.
28. Olivé, A.; Teniente, E. "Derived types and taxonomic constraints in conceptual modeling". Information Systems, 27(6), 2002, pp. 391-409.
29. OMG. UML Superstructure 2.0 Final Adopted Specification, 2003, http://www.omg.org/cgi-bin/doc?ptc/2003-08-02.
30. Robinson, K.; Berrisford, G. Object-oriented SSADM. Prentice Hall, 1994, 524p.
31. Rumbaugh, J.; Jacobson, I.; Booch, G. The Unified Modeling Language Reference Manual. Addison-Wesley, 1999, 550 p.
32. Selic,B.; Gullekson, G.; and Ward, P.T. Real-Time Object-Oriented Modeling. John Wiley & Sons, 1994, 525p.
33. Teisseire, M; Poncelet, P.; Cichetti, R. "Dynamic Modelling with Events", Proc. CAiSE'94, LNCS 811, pp. 186-199, 1994.
34. Wieringa, R. "A survey of structured and object-oriented software specification methods and techniques". ACM Computing Surveys, 30(4), December 98, pp. 459-527.

Enterprise Modeling with Conceptual XML

David W. Embley[1], Stephen W. Liddle[2], and Reema Al-Kamha[1]

[1] Department of Computer Science
Brigham Young University, Provo, Utah 84602, USA
{embley,reema}@cs.byu.edu
[2] School of Accountancy and Information Systems
Brigham Young University, Provo, Utah 84602, USA
liddle@byu.edu

Abstract. An open challenge is to integrate XML and conceptual modeling in order to satisfy large-scale enterprise needs. Because enterprises typically have many data sources using different assumptions, formats, and schemas, all expressed in – or soon to be expressed in – XML, it is easy to become lost in an avalanche of XML detail. This creates an opportunity for the conceptual modeling community to provide improved abstractions to help manage this detail. We present a vision for Conceptual XML (C-XML) that builds on the established work of the conceptual modeling community over the last several decades to bring improved modeling capabilities to XML-based development. Building on a framework such as C-XML will enable better management of enterprise-scale data and more rapid development of enterprise applications.

1 Introduction

A challenge [3] for modern enterprise modeling is to produce a simple conceptual model that: (1) works well with XML and XML Schema; (2) abstracts well for conceptual entities and relationships; (3) scales to handle both large data sets and complex object interrelationships; (4) allows for queries and defined views via XQuery; and (5) accommodates heterogeneity.

The conceptual model must work well with XML and XML Schema because XML is rapidly becoming the de facto standard for business data. Because conceptualizations must support both high-level understanding and high-level program construction, the conceptual model must abstract well. Because many of today's huge industrial conglomerations have large, enterprise-size data sets and increasingly complex constraints over their data, the conceptual model must scale up. Because XQuery, like XML, is rapidly becoming the industry standard, the conceptual model must smoothly incorporate both XQuery and XML. Finally, because we can no longer assume that all enterprise data is integrated, the conceptual model must accommodate heterogeneity. Accommodating heterogeneity also supports today's rapid acquisitions and mergers, which require fast-paced solutions to data integration.

We call the answer we offer for this challenge *Conceptual XML* (*C-XML*). C-XML is first and foremost a conceptual model, being fundamentally based on object-set and relationship-set constructs. As a central feature, C-XML supports

P. Atzeni et al. (Eds.): ER 2004, LNCS 3288, pp. 150–165, 2004.

high-level object- and relationship-set construction at ever higher levels of abstraction. At any level of abstraction the object and relationship sets are always first class, which lets us address object and relationship sets uniformly, independent of level of abstraction. These features of C-XML make it abstract well and scale well. Secondly, C-XML is "model-equivalent" [9] with XML Schema, which means that C-XML can represent each component and constraint in XML Schema and vice versa. Because of this correspondence between C-XML and XML Schema, XQuery immediately applies to populated C-XML model instances and thus we can raise the level of abstraction for XQuery by applying it to high-level model instances rather than low-level XML documents. Further, we can define high-level XQuery-based mappings between C-XML model instances over in-house, autonomous databases, and we can declare virtual views over these mappings. Thus, we can accommodate heterogeneity at a higher level of abstraction and provide uniform access to all enterprise data.

Besides enunciating a comprehensive vision for the XML/conceptual-modeling challenge [3], our contributions in this paper include: (1) mappings to and from C-XML and XML Schema, (2) defined mechanisms for producing and using first-class, high-level, conceptual abstractions, and (3) XQuery view definitions over both standard and federated conceptual-model instances that are themselves conceptual-model equivalent. As a result of these contributions, C-XML and XML Schema can be fully interchangable in their usage over both standard and heterogeneous XML data repositories. This lets us leverage conceptual model abstractions for high-level understanding while retaining all the complex details involved with low-level XML Schema intricacies, view mappings, and integration issues over heterogeneous XML repositories.

We present the details of our contributions as follows. Section 2 describes C-XML. Section 3 shows that C-XML is "model-equivalent" with XML Schema by providing mappings between the two. Section 4 describes C-XML views. We report the status of our implementation and conclude in Section 5.

2 C-XML: Conceptual XML

C-XML is a conceptual model consisting of object sets, relationship sets, and constraints over these object and relationship sets. Graphically a C-XML model instance M is an augmented hypergraph whose vertices and edges are respectively the object sets and relationship sets of M, and whose augmentations consist of decorations that represent constraints. Figure 1 shows an example.

In the notation boxes represent *object sets* – dashed if lexical and not dashed if nonlexical because their objects are represented by object identifiers. With each object set we can associate a data frame (as we call it) to provide a rich description of its value set and other properties. A data frame lets us specify, for example, that *OrderDate* is of type *Date* or that *ItemNr* values must satisfy the value pattern "[A-Z]{3}-\d{7}". Lines connecting object sets are *relationship sets*; these lines may be hyper-lines (hyper-edges in hyper-graphs) with diamonds when they have more than two connections to object sets. Optional

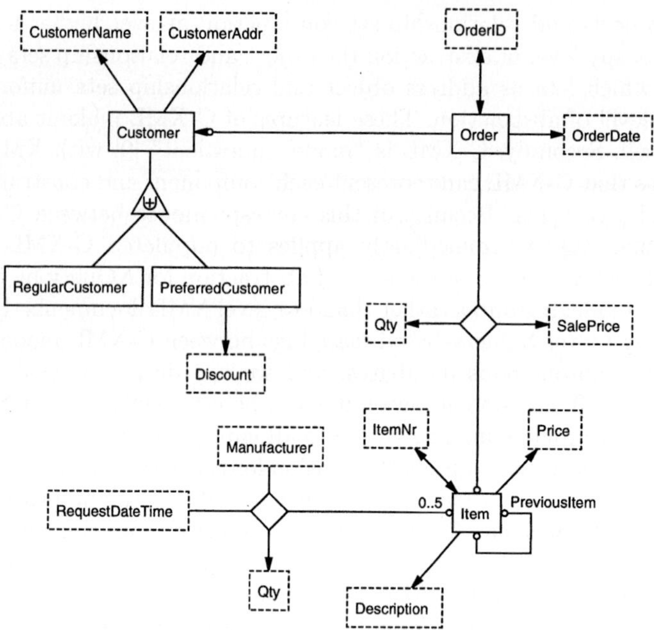

Fig. 1. Customer/Order C-XML Model Instance.

or mandatory *participation constraints* respectively specify whether objects in a connected relationship may or must participate in a relationship set (an "o" on a connecting relationship-set line designates *optional* while the absence of an "o" designates *mandatory*). Thus, for example, the C-XML model instance in Figure 1 declares that an *Order* must include at least one *Item* but that an *Item* need not be included in any *Order*. Arrowheads on lines specify *functional constraints*. Thus, Figure 1 declares that an *Item* has a *Price* and a *Description* and is in a one-to-one correspondence with *ItemNr* and that an *Item* in an *Order* has one *Qty* and one *SalePrice*. In cases when optional and mandatory participation constraints along with functional constraints are insufficient to specify minimum and maximum participation, explicit *min..max* constraints may be specified. Triangles denote *generalization/specialization hierarchies*. We can constrain ISA hierarchies by partition ($\uplus$), union ($\cup$), or mutual exclusion (+) among specializations. Any object-set/relationship-set connection may have a role, but a role is simply a shorthand for an object set that denotes the subset consisting of the objects that actually participate in the connection.

3 Translations Between C-XML and XML Schema

Many translations between C-XML and XML Schema are possible. In recent ER conferences, researchers have described varying conceptual-model translations to and/or from XML or XML DTD's or XML-Schema-like specifications. (See, for example, [4,6,10].) It is not our purpose here to argue for or against a particular translation. Indeed, we would argue that a variety of translations may be desirable. For any translation, however, we require information and constraint preservation. This ensures that an XML Schema and a conceptual instantiation of an XML Schema as a C-XML model instance correspond and that a system can reflect manipulations of the one in the other.

To make our correspondence exact, we need information- and constraint-preserving translations in both directions. We do not, however, require that translations be inverses of one another – translations that generate members of an equivalence class of XML Schema specifications and C-XML model instances are sufficient. In Section 3.1 we present our C-XML-to-XML-Schema translation, and in Section 3.2 we present an XML-Schema-to-C-XML translation. In Section 3.3 we formalize the notions of information and constraint preservation and show that the translations we propose preserve information and constraints.

3.1 Translation from C-XML to XML Schema

We now describe our process for translating a C-XML model instance C to an XML Schema S_C. We illustrate our translation process with the C-XML model instance of Figure 1 translated to the corresponding XML Schema excerpted in Figure 2.

Fully automatic translation from C to S_C is not only possible, but can be done with certain guarantees regarding the quality of S_C. Our approach is based on our previous work [8], which for C generates a forest of scheme trees F_C such that (1) F_C has a minimal number of scheme trees, and (2) XML documents conforming to F_C have no redundant data with respect to functional and multi-valued constraints of C. For our example in Figure 1, the algorithms in [8] will generate the following two nested scheme trees.

$(Customer, CustomerName, CustomerAddr, Discount$
$\quad (Order, OrderID, OrderDate,$
$\qquad (Item, SalePrice, Qty)*)*)*$
$(Item, ItemNr, Description, Price,$
$\quad (PreviousItem)*, (Manufacturer, RequestDateTime, Qty)*)*$

Observe that the XML Schema in Figure 2 satisfies these nesting specifications. *Item* in the second scheme tree appears as an element on Line 8 with *ItemNr*, *Description*, and *Price* defined as its attributes on Lines 28–30. *PreviousItem* is nested, by itself, underneath *Item*, on Line 18, and *Manufacturer*, *Request-DateTime*, and *Qty* are nested underneath *Item* as a group on Lines 13–15. The XML-Schema notation that accompanies these C-XML object-set names obscures the nesting to some extent, but this additional notation is necessary either to satisfy the syntactic requirements of XML Schema or to allow us to specify the constraints of the C-XML model instance.

As we continue, recall first that each C-XML object set has an associated data frame that contains specifications such as type declarations, value restrictions, and any other annotations needed to specify information about objects in

```
...
<xs:element name="Document">
  <xs:complexType>
    <xs:choice minOccurs="0" maxOccurs="unbounded">
      <xs:element ref="Customer"/>
      <xs:element name="Item">
        <xs:complexType>
          <xs:sequence>
            <xs:element name="ItemMR" minOccurs="0" maxOccurs="5">
             <xs:complexType>
              <xs:attribute name="Manufacturer" type="xs:string" use="required"/>
              <xs:attribute name="RequestDateTime" type="xs:date" use="required"/>
              <xs:attribute name="Qty" type="xs:positiveInteger" use="required"/> ...
            <xs:element name="PreviousItem" minOccurs="0" maxOccurs="unbounded">
              <xs:complexType>
                <xs:attribute name="ItemNr" type="xs:positiveInteger" use="required"/> ...
              <xs:keyref name="r1" refer="ItemKey">
                <xs:selector xpath="."/>
                <xs:field xpath="@ItemNr"/> ...
          <xs:attribute name="ItemNr" type="xs:positiveInteger" use="required"/>
          <xs:attribute name="Description" type="xs:string" use="required"/>
          <xs:attribute name="Price" type="xs:decimal" use="required"/> ...
  <xs:key name="OrderKey"><xs:selector xpath=".//Order"/><xs:field xpath="@OrderID"/> ...
  <xs:key name="ItemKey"><xs:selector xpath=".//Item"/><xs:field xpath="@ItemNr"/> ...
<xs:element name="Customer" abstract="true"/>
<xs:element name="PreferredCustomer" substitutionGroup="Customer">
  <xs:complexType>
    <xs:group ref="CustomerDetails"/>
    <xs:attribute name="Discount" type="xs:string" use="required"/> ...
<xs:element name="RegularCustomer" substitutionGroup="Customer">
  <xs:complexType><xs:group ref="CustomerDetails"/></xs:complexType> ...
<xs:group name="CustomerDetails">
  <xs:sequence>
    <xs:element name="CustomerName" type="xs:string"/>
    <xs:element name="CustomerAddr" type="xs:string"/>
    <xs:element name="Order" minOccurs="0" maxOccurs="unbounded">
      <xs:complexType>
        <xs:sequence>
          <xs:element name="OrderItem" minOccurs="0" maxOccurs="unbounded">
            <xs:complexType>
              <xs:attribute name="Qty" type="xs:positiveInteger" use="required"/> ...
            <xs:keyref name="r3" refer="ItemKey">
              <xs:selector xpath="."/>
              <xs:field xpath="@ItemNr"/> ...
      <xs:attribute name="OrderID" type="xs:positiveInteger" use="required"/>
      <xs:attribute name="OrderDate" type="xs:date" use="required"/> ...
```

Fig. 2. XML Schema Excerpt for the C-XML Model Instance in Figure 1.

the object set. For our work here, we let the kind of information that appears in a data frame correspond exactly to the kind of data constraint information specifiable in XML Schema. One example we point out explicitly is order information, which is usually absent in conceptual models, but is unavoidably present in XML. Thus, if we wish to say that *CustomerName* precedes *CustomerAddr*, we add the annotation "$\prec$ *CustomerAddr*" to the *CustomerName* data frame and add the annotation "$\succ$ *CustomerName*" to the *CustomerAddr* data frame. In our discussion, we assume that these annotations are in the data frames that accompany the object sets *CustomerName* and *CustomerAddr* in Figure 1.

Our conversion algorithm preserves all annotations found in C-XML data frames. This is where we obtain all the type specifications in Figure 2. We capture the order specification, $CustomerName \prec CustomerAddr$, by making *CustomerName* and *CustomerAddr* elements (rather than attributes) and placing them, in order, in their proper place in the nesting – for our example in Lines 58 and 59 nested under *CustomerDetails.*

In the conversion from C-XML to XML Schema we use attributes instead of elements where possible. An object set can be represented as an attribute of an element if it is lexical, is functionally dependent on the element, and has no order annotations. The object sets *OrderID* and *OrderDate*, for example, satisfy these conditions and appear as attributes of an *Order* element on Lines 75 and 76. Both attributes are also marked as "*required*" because of their mandatory connection to *Order* as specified by the absence of an "o" on their connection to *Order* in Figure 1.

When an object set is lexical but not functional and order constraints do not hold, the object set becomes an element with minimum and maximum participation constraints. *PreviousItem* in Line 18 has a minimum participation constraint of 0 and a maximum of *unbounded.*

Because XML Schema will not let us directly specify n-ary relationship sets ($n \geq 2$), we convert them all to binary relationship sets by introducing a tuple identifier. We can think of each diamond in a C-XML diagram as being replaced by a nonlexical object set containing these tuple identifiers. To obtain a name for the object set containing the tuple identifiers, we concatenate names of non-functionally dependent object sets. For example, given the n-ary relationship set for *Order*, *Item*, *SalePrice*, and *Qty*, we generate an *OrderItem* element (Line 63). If names become too long, we abbreviate using only the first letter of some object-set names. Thus, for example, we generate *ItemMR* (Line 11) for the relationship set connecting *Item*, *Manufacturer*, *RequestDateTime*, and *Qty*.

When a lexical object set has a one-to-one relationship with a nonlexical object set, we use the lexical object set as a surrogate for the nonlexical object set and generate a key constraint. In our example, this generates key constraints for *Order*/*OrderID* in Line 35 and *Item*/*ItemNr* in Line 39. We also use these surrogate identifiers, as needed, to maintain explicit referential integrity. Observe that in the scheme trees above, *Item* in the first tree references *Item* in the root of the second scheme tree and also that *PreviousItem* in the second scheme tree is a role and therefore a specific specialization (or subset) of *Item* in the root. Thus, we generate *keyref* constraints, one in Lines 69–72 to ensure the referential integrity of *ItemNr* in the *OrderItem* element and another in Lines 22–25 for the *PreviousItem* element.

Another construct in C-XML we need to translate is generalization/specialization. XML Schema uses the concept of *substitution groups* to allow the use of multiple element types in a given context. Thus, for example, we generate an abstract element for *Customer* in Line 44, but then specify in Lines 45–55 a substitution group for *Customer* that allows *RegularCustomer* and *PreferredCustomer* to appear in a *Customer* context. We model content that would normally be associated with the generalization by generating a *group* that is referenced in each specialization (in Lines 47 and 52). In our example, we generate the group

CustomerDetails and nest the details of *Customer* such as *CustomerName*, *CustomerAddr*, and *Orders* under *CustomerDetails* as we do beginning in Line 56. Further, we can nest any information that only applies to one of the specializations directly with that specialization; thus, in Line 48 we nest *Discount* under *PreferredCustomer*.

Finally, XML documents need to have a single content root node. Thus, we assume the existence of an element called *Document* (Line 4) that serves as the universal content root.

3.2 Translation from XML Schema to C-XML

We translate XML Schema instances to C-XML by separating structural XML Schema concepts (such as elements and attributes) from non-structural XML Schema concepts (such as attribute types and order constraints). Then we generate C-XML constructs for the structural concepts and annotate generated C-XML object sets with the non-structural information.

We can convert an XML Schema S to a C-XML model instance C_S by generating object sets for each element and attribute type connected by relationship sets according to the nesting structure of S. Figure 3 shows the result of applying our conversion process to the XML Schema instance of Figure 2. Note that we nest object and relationship sets inside one another corresponding to the nested element structure of the XML Schema instance. Whether we display C-XML object sets inside or outside one another has no semantic significance. The nested structure, however, is convenient because it corresponds to the natural XML Schema instance structure.

The initial set of generated object and relationship sets is straightforward. Each element or attribute generates exactly one object set, and each element that is nested inside another element generates a relationship set connecting the two. Each attribute associated with an element e always generates a corresponding object set a and a relationship set r connecting a to the object set generated by e. Participation constraints for attribute-generated relationship sets are always *1..** on the a side and are either *1* or *0..1* on the e side. Participation constraints for relationship sets generated by element nesting require a bit more work. If the element is in a *sequence* or a *choice*, there may be specific minimum/maximum occurrence constraints we can use directly. For example, according to the constraints on Line 60 in Figure 2 a *CustomerDetails* element may contain a list of 0 or more *Order* elements. However, an *Order* element must be nested inside a *CustomerDetails* element. Thus, for the relationship set connecting *CustomerDetails* and *Order*, we place participation constraints of *0..** on the *CustomerDetails* side, and *1* on the *Order* side.

In order to make the generated C-XML model instance less redundant, we look for certain patterns and rewrite the generated model instance when appropriate. For example, since *ItemNr* has a key constraint, we infer that it is one-to-one with *Item*. Further, the keyref constraints on *ItemNr* for *PreviousItem* and *OrderItem* indicate that rather than create two additional *ItemNr* object sets, we can instead relate *PreviousItem* and *OrderItem* to the *ItemNr* nested in *Item*.

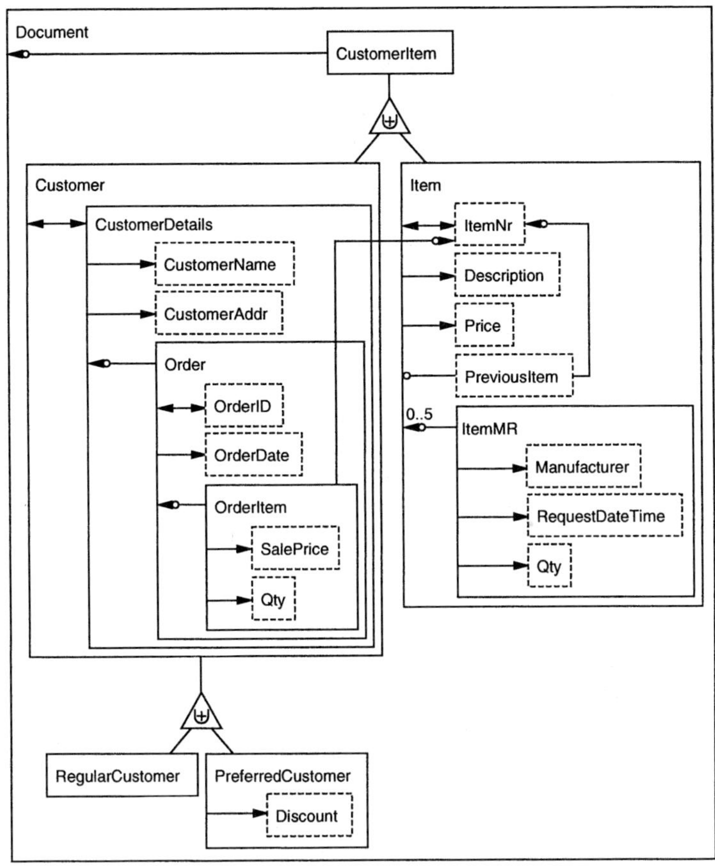

Fig. 3. C-XML Model Instance Translated from Figure 2.

Another optimization is the treatment of substitution groups. In our example, since *RegularCustomer* and *PreferredCustomer* are substitutable for *Customer*, we construct a generalization/specialization for the three object sets and factor out the common substructure of the specializations into the generalization. Thus, *CustomerDetails* exists in a one-to-one relationship with *Customer*.

Another complication in XML Schema is the presence of anonymous types. For example, the complex type in Line 5 of Figure 2 is a choice of 0 or more *Customer* or *Item* elements. We need a generalization/specialization to represent this, and since C-XML requires names for object sets, we simply concatenate all the top-level names to form the generalization name *CustomerItem*.

There are striking differences between the C-XML model instances of Figures 1 and 3. The translation to XML Schema introduced new elements *Document*, *CustomerDetails*, *OrderItem*, and *ItemMR* in order to represent a top-level root node, generalization/specializations, and decomposed n-ary relationship sets. If we knew that a particular XML Schema instance was generated from an original C-XML model instance, we could perform additional optimizations. For example, if we knew *CustomerDetails* was fabricated by the translation to XML Schema, we could observe that in the reverse translation to C-XML it is superfluous because it is one-to-one with *Customer*. Similarly, we could recognize that *Document* is a fabricated top-level element and omit it from the reverse translation; this would also eliminate the need for *CustomerItem* and its generalization/specialization. Finally, we could recognize that n-ary relationship sets have been decomposed, and in the reverse translation reconstitute them. The original C-XML to XML Schema translation could easily place annotation objects in the generated XML Schema instance marking elements for this sort of optimization.

3.3 Information and Constraint Preservation

To formalize information and constraint preservation for schema translations, we use first-order predicate calculus. We represent any schema specification in predicate calculus by generating an n-place predicate for each n-ary tuple container and a closed formula for each constraint [7]. Using the closed-world assumption, we can then populate the predicates to form an interpretation. If all the constraints hold over the populated predicates, the interpretation is valid.

For any schema specification S_A of type A there is a corresponding valid interpretation I_{S_A}. We can guarantee that a translation T translates a schema specification S_A to a constraint-equivalent schema specification S_B by checking whether the constraints of the generated predicate calculus for the schema specification of type B imply the constraints of the generated predicate calculus for the schema specification of type A. A translation T that translates a schema specification S_A into a schema translation S_B induces a translation T' from an interpretation I_{S_A} for a schema of type A to an interpretation I_{S_B} for a schema of type B. We can guarantee that a T-induced translation T' translates any valid interpretation I_{S_A} into an information equivalent valid interpretation I_{S_B} by translating both of the corresponding valid interpretations to predicate calculus interpretations $I_{S_A^{PC}}$ and $I_{S_B^{PC}}$ and checking for information equivalence.

Definition 1. *A translation T from schema specification S_A to a schema specification S_B* preserves information *if there exists a procedure P that for any valid interpretation I_{S_A} corresponding to S_A computes I_{S_A} from I_{S_B} where I_{S_B} is the interpretation corresponding to S_B induced by T.* □

Definition 2. *A translation T from schema specification S_A to a schema specification S_B* preserves constraints *if the constraints of S_B imply the constraints of S_A.* □

Lemma 1. *Let $I_{S_{C-XML}}$ be a valid interpretation for a populated C-XML model instance S_{C-XML}. There exists a translation t_{C-XML} that correctly represents $I_{S_{C-XML}}$ as a valid interpretation $I_{S^{PC}_{C-XML}}$ in predicate calculus*[1].

[1] Due to space constraints, we have omitted all proofs in this paper.

Lemma 2. *Let $I_{S_{XMLSchema}}$ be an XML document that conforms to an XML Schema instance $S_{XMLSchema}$. There exists a translation $t_{XMLSchema}$ that correctly represents $I_{S_{XMLSchema}}$ as a valid interpretation $I_{S^{PC}_{XMLSchema}}$ in predicate calculus.*

Theorem 1. *Let T be the translation described in Section 3.1 that translates a C-XML model instance S_{C-XML} to an XML Schema instance $S_{XMLSchema}$. T preserves information and constraints.*

Theorem 2. *Let T be the translation described in Section 3.2 that translates an XML Schema instance $S_{XMLSchema}$ to a C-XML model instance S_{C-XML}. T preserves information and constraints.*

4 C-XML Views

This section describes three types of views – simple views that help us scale up to large and complex XML schemas, query-generated views over a single XML schema, and query-generated views over heterogeneous XML schemas.

4.1 High-Level Abstractions in C-XML

We create simple views in two ways. Our first way is to nest and hide C-XML components inside one another [7]. Figure 3 shows how we can nest object sets inside one another. We can pull any object set inside any other connected object set, and we can pull any object set inside any connected relationship set so long as we leave at least two object sets outside (e.g. in Figure 1 we can pull *Qty* and/or *SalePrice* inside the diamond). Whether an object set appears on the inside or outside has no effect on the meaning. Once we have object sets on the inside, we can implode the object set or relationship set and thus remove the inner object sets from the view. We can, for example, implode *Customer*, *Item*, and *PreferredCustomer* in Figure 3, presenting a much simpler diagram showing only five object sets and two generalization/specialization components nested in *Document*. To denote an imploded object or relationship set, we shade the object set or the relationship-set diamond. Later, we can explode object or relationship sets and view all details. Since we allow arbitrary nesting, it is possible that relationship-set lines may cross object- or relationship-set boundaries. In this case, when we implode, we connect the line to the imploded object or relationship set and make the line dashed to indicate that the connection is to an interior object set.

Our second way to create simple views is to discard C-XML components that are not of interest. We can discard any relationship set, and we can discard all but any two connections of an n-ary relationship set ($n > 2$). We can also discard any object set, but then must discard (1) any connecting binary relationship sets, (2) any connections to n-ary relationship sets ($n > 2$), and (3) any specializations and relationship sets or relationship-set connections to these specializations. Figure 4 shows an example of a high-level abstraction of Figure 1. In

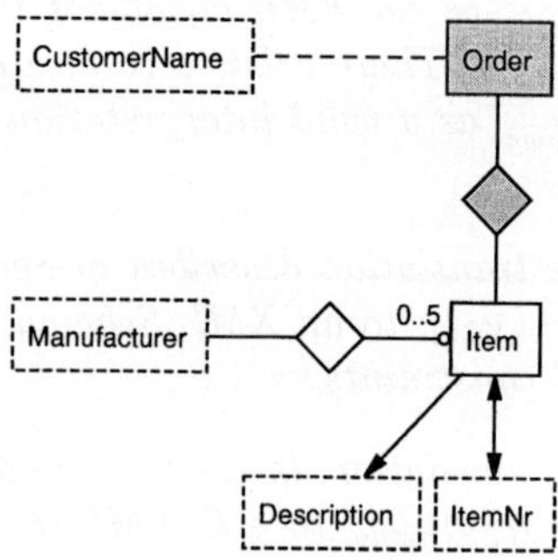

Fig. 4. High-Level View of Customer/Order C-XML Model Instance.

Figure 4 we have discarded *Price* and its associated binary relationship set, the relationship set for *PreviousItem*, and the connections to *RequestDateTime* and *Qty* in the *n*-ary relationship set involving *Manufacturer*. We have also hidden *OrderID*, *OrderDate*, and all customer information except *CustomerName* inside *Order*, and we have hidden *SalePrice* and *Qty* inside the *Order-Item* relationship set. Note that both the *Order* object set and the *Order-Item* relationship set are shaded, indicating the inclusion of C-XML components; that neither the *Item* object set nor the *Item-Manufacturer* relationship set are shaded, indicating that the original connecting information has been discarded rather than hidden within; and that the line between *CustomerName* and *Order* is dashed, indicating that *CustomerName* connects, not to *Order* directly, but rather to an object set inside *Order*.

Theorem 3. *Simple, high-level views constructed by properly discarding C-XML components are valid C-XML model instances.*

Corollary 1. *Any simple, high-level view can be represented by an XML Schema.*

4.2 C-XML XQuery Views

We now consider the use of C-XML views to generate XQuery views. As other researchers have pointed out [2, 5], XQuery can be hard for users to understand and manipulate. One reason XQuery can be cumbersome is because it must follow the particular hierarchical structure of an underlying XML schema, rather than the simpler, logical structure of an underlying conceptual model. Further, different XML sources might specify conflicting hierarchical representations of the same conceptual relationship [2]. Thus, it is highly desirable to be able to construct XQuery views by generating them from a high-level conceptual model-based description. [5] describes an algorithm for generating XQuery views from ORA-SS descriptions. [2] also describes how to specify XQuery views by writing *conceptual XPath* expressions over a conceptual schema and then automatically generating the corresponding XQuery specifications. In a similar fashion, we can

```
define view CustomersByItemsOrdered
{   for $item in Item
    return
    <Item>
        {$item/ItemNr, $item/Description}
        {   for $customer in $item/Order/Customer
            return
            <Customer>
                {$customer/CustomerName, $customer/CustomerAddr}
                {   for $order in $customer/Order,
                        $item2 in $order/Item
                    where $item2 = $item
                    return
                    <Order>
                        {$order/OrderDate, $item2/Qty, $item2/SalePrice}
                    </Order>
                }
            </Customer>
        }
    </Item>
}
```

Fig. 5. C-XQuery View of Customers Nested within Items Ordered.

generate XQuery views directly from high-level C-XML views. In some situations a graphical query language would be an excellent choice for creating C-XML views [9], but in keeping with the spirit of C-XML we define an XQuery-like textual language called C-XQuery.

Figure 5 shows a high-level view written in C-XQuery over the model instance of Figure 1. We introduce a view definition with the phrase *define view*, and specify the contents of the view with FLWOR (for, let, where, order by, return) expressions [14]. The first *for $item in Item* phrase creates an iterator over objects in the *Item* object set. Since there is no top-level *where* clause, we iterate over all the items. Also, since C-XML model instances do not have "root nodes" the idea of context is different. In this case, *Item* defines the *Item* object set as the context of the path expression. For each such item, we return an *<Item>* ... *</Item>* structure populated according to the nested expressions.

C-XQuery is much like ordinary XQuery, with the main distinguishing factor that our path expressions are conceptual, and so, for example, they are not concerned with the distinction between attributes and elements. Note particularly that for the data fields, such as *ItemNr*, *CustomerName*, and *OrderDate*, we do not care whether the generated XML treats them as attributes or elements. A more subtle characteristic of our conceptual path expressions is that since they operate over a flat C-XML structure, we can traverse the conceptual-model graph more flexibly, without regard for hierarchical structure. Thus, we generalize the notion of a path expression so that the expression *A//B* designates the path from *A* to *B* regardless of hierarchy or the number of intervening steps in the path [9]. This can lead to ambiguity in the presence of cycles or multiple paths between nodes, but we can automatically detect ambiguity and require the user to disambiguate the expression (say, by designating an intermediate node that fixes a unique path).

```
define view RecentNitrogenFertilizerCustomers
{   for $i in CustomersByItemsOrdered/Item
    where $i/Description = "Nitrogen Fertilizer"
    return
    <Customer>
        {   for $c in $i/Customer
            let $total := sum( for $o in $c/Order
                               where $o/OrderDate > add-days(current-date(),-90)
                               return $o/Qty * $o/SalePrice )
            return
            {$c/CustomerName, Total=$total}
        }
    </Customer>
}

for $c in RecentNitrogenFertilizerCustomers/Customer
where $c/total > 300
return
<PotentialThreatCustomer>
    {$c/CustomerName, $c/Total}
</PotentialThreatCustomer>
```

Fig. 6. C-XQuery over the View of Customers Nested within Items Ordered.

Given a view definition, we can write queries against the view. For the view in Figure 5, for example, the query in Figure 6 finds customers who have purchased more than $300 worth of nitrogen fertilizer within the last 90 days. To execute the query, we unfold the the view according to the view definition and minimize the resulting XQuery. See [13] for a discussion of the underlying principles.

The view in Figure 6 illustrates the use of views over views. Indeed, applications can use views as first-class data sources, just like ordinary sources, and we can write queries against the conceptual model and views over that model. In any case, we translate the conceptual queries to XQuery specifications over the XML Schema instance generated for the C-XML conceptual model.

Theorem 4. *A C-XQuery view Q over a C-XML model instance C can be translated to an XQuery query Q_C over an XML Schema instance S_C.*

Observe that by the definition of XQuery [14], any valid XQuery instance generates an underlying XML Schema instance. By Theorem 4, we thus know that for any C-XQuery view we retain a correspondence to XML Schema. In particular, this means we can compose views of views to an arbitrary depth and still retain a correspondence to XML Schema.

4.3 XQuery Integration Mappings

To motivate the use of views in enterprise conceptual modeling, suppose through mergers and acquisitions we acquire the catalog inventory of another company. Figure 7 shows the C-XML for this assumed catalog. We can rapidly integrate this catalog into the full inventory of the parent company by creating a mapping from the acquired company's catalog to the parent company's catalog. Figure 8 shows such a mapping. In order to integrate the source (Figure 7) with the target (Figure 1), the mapping needs to generate target names in the source. In

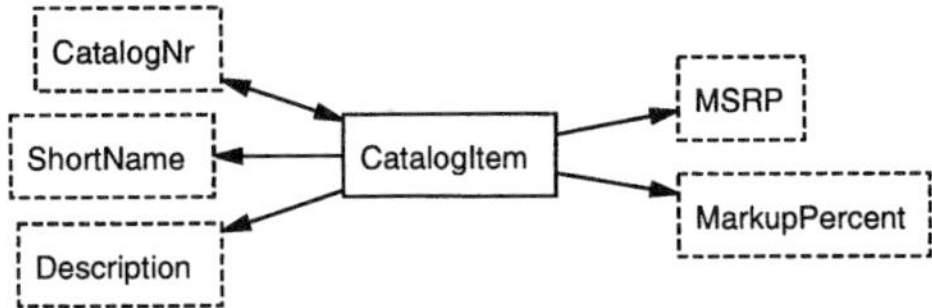

Fig. 7. C-XML Model Instance for the Catalog of an Acquired Company.

```
define view CatalogItemToItem
{   for $cItem in CatalogItem
    let $itemNr := CatalogNr-to-ItemNr($cItem)
    let $price := $cItem/MSRP * (1 + $cItem/MarkupPercent)
    return
        <Item>
            <ItemNr>{$itemNr}</ItemNr>
            <Description>{$cItem/ShortName}</Description>
            <Price>{$price}</Price>
        </Item>
}
```

Fig. 8. C-XQuery Mapping for Catalog Integration.

this example, *CatalogItem*, *CatalogNr*, and *ShortName* correspond respectively to *Item*, *ItemNr*, and *Description*. We must compute *Price* in the target from the *MSRP* and *MarkupPercent* values in the source, as Figure 8 shows. We assume the function *CatalogNr-to-ItemNr* is either a hand-coded lookup table, or a manually-programmed function to translate source catalog numbers to item numbers in the target. The underlying structure of this mapping query corresponds directly to the relevant section of the C-XML model instance in Figure 1, so integration is now immediate.

The mapping in Figure 8 creates a target-compatible C-XQuery view over the acquired company's catalog in Figure 7. When we now query the parent company's items, we also query the acquired company's catalog. Thus, the previous examples are immediately applicable. For example, we can find those customers who have ordered more than $300 worth of nitrogen fertilizer from either the inventory of the parent company or the inventory of the acquired company by simply issuing the query in Figure 6. With the acquired company's catalog integrated, when the query in Figure 6 iterates over customer orders, it iterates over data instances for both *Item* in Figure 1 and *CatalogItem* in Figure 8. (Now, if the potential terrorist has purchased, say $200 worth of nitrogen fertilizer from the original company and $150 worth from the acquired company, the potential terrorist will appear on the list, whereas the potential terrorist would have appeared on neither list before.)

We could also write a mapping query going in the opposite direction, with Figure 1 as the source and Figure 7 as the target. Such bidirectional integration is useful in circumstances where we need to shift between perspectives, as is often the case in enterprise application development. This is especially true because all enterprise data is rarely fully integrated.

In general it would be nice to have a mostly automated tool for generating integration mappings. In order to support such a tool, we require two-way mappings between both schemas and data elements. Sometimes we can use automated element matchers [1, 12] to help us with the mapping. However, in other cases the mappings are intricate and require programmer intervention (e.g. calculating *Price* from *MSRP* plus a *MarkupPercent* or converting *CatalogNr* to *ItemNr*). In any case, we can write C-XQuery views describing each such mapping, with or without the aid of tools (e.g. [11]), and we can compose these views to provide larger C-XQuery schema mappings. Of course there are many integration details we do not address here, such as handling dirty data, but the approach of integrating by composing C-XQuery views is sound.

Theorem 5. *A C-XQuery view Q over a C-XML model instance C of an external, federated XML Schema can be translated to an XQuery query* Q_C *over an XML Schema instance* S_C.

5 Concluding Remarks

We have offered Conceptual-XML (C-XML) as an answer to the challenge of modern enterprise modeling. C-XML is equivalent in expressive power to XML Schema (Theorems 1 and 2). In contrast to XML Schema, however, C-XML provides for high level conceptualization of an enterprise. C-XML allows users to view schemas at any level of abstraction and at various levels of abstraction in the same specification (Theorem 3), which goes a long way toward mitigating the complexity of large data sets and complex interrelationships. Along with C-XML, we have provided C-XQuery, a conceptualization of XQuery that relieves programmers from concerns about the often arbitrary choice of nesting and arbitrary choice of whether to represent values with attributes or with elements. Using C-XQuery, we have shown how to define views and automatically translate them to XQuery (Theorem 4). We have also shown how to accommodate heterogeneity by defining mapping views over federated data repositories and automatically translate them to XQuery (Theorem 5).

Implementing C-XML is a huge undertaking. Fortunately, we have a foundation on which to build. We have already implemented tools relevant to C-XML include graphical diagram editors, model checkers, textual model compilers, a model execution engine, and several data integration tools. We are actively continuing development of an Integrated Development Environment (IDE) for modeling-related activities. Our strategy is to plug new tools into this IDE rather than develop stand-alone programs. Our most recent implementation work consists of tools for automatic generation of XML normal form schemes. We are now working on the implementation of the algorithms to translate C-XML to XML Schema, XML Schema to C-XML, and C-XQuery to XQuery.

Acknowledgements

This work is supported in part by the National Science Foundation under grant IIS-0083127 and by the Kevin and Debra Rollins Center for eBusiness at Brigham Young University.

References

1. J. Biskup and D. Embley. Extracting information from heterogeneous information sources using ontologically specified target views. *Information Systems*, 28(3):169–212, 2003.
2. S. Camillo, C. Heuser, and R. dos Santos Mello. Querying heterogeneous XML sources through a conceptual schema. In *Proceedings of the 22nd International Conference on Conceptual Modeling (ER2003), Lecture Notes in Computer Science 2813*, pages 186–199, Chicago, Illinois, October 2003.
3. M. Carey. Enterprise information integration – XML to the rescue! In *Proceedings of the 22nd International Conference on Conceptual Modeling (ER2003), Lecture Notes in Computer Science 2813*, page 14, Chicago, Illinois, October 2003.
4. Y. Chen, T. Ling, and M. Lee. Designing valid XML views. In *Proceedings of the 21st International Conference on Conceptual Modeling (ER'02)*, pages 463–477, Tampere, Finland, October 2002.
5. Y. Chen, T. Ling, and M. Lee. Automatic generation of XQuery view definitions from ORA-SS views. In *Proceedings of the 22nd International Conference on Conceptual Modeling (ER2003), Lecture Notes in Computer Science 2813*, pages 158–171, Chicago, Illinois, October 2003.
6. R. Conrad, D. Scheffner, and J. Freytag. XML conceptual modeling using UML. In *Proceedings of the Ninteenth International Conference on Conceptual Modeling (ER2000)*, Salt Lake City, Utah, October 2000. 558–571.
7. D. Embley, B. Kurtz, and S. Woodfield. *Object-oriented Systems Analysis: A Model-Driven Approach.* Prentice Hall, Englewood Cliffs, New Jersey, 1992.
8. D. Embley and W. Mok. Developing XML documents with guaranteed 'good' properties. In *Proceedings of the 20th International Conference on Conceptual Modeling (ER2001)*, pages 426–441, Yokohama, Japan, November 2001.
9. S. Liddle, D. Embley, and S. Woodfield. An active, object-oriented, model-equivalent programming language. In M. Papazoglou, S. Spaccapietra, and Z. Tari, editors, *Advances in Object-Oriented Data Modeling*, pages 333–361. MIT Press, Cambridge, Massachusetts, 2000.
10. M. Mani, D. Lee, and R. Muntz. Semantic data modeling using xml schemas. In *Proceedings of the 20th International Conference on Conceptual Modeling (ER2001)*, pages 149–163, Yokohama, Japan, November 2001.
11. R. Miller, L. Haas, and M. Hernandez. Schema mapping as query discovery. In *Proceedings of the 26th International Conference on Very Large Databases (VLDB'00)*, pages 77–88, Cairo, Egypt, September 2000.
12. E. Rahm and P. Bernstein. A survey of approaches to automatic schema matching. *The VLDB Journal*, 10:334–350, 2001.
13. I. Tatarinov and A. Halevy. Efficient query reformulation in peer data management systems. In *Proceedings of the 2004 ACM SIGMOD International Conference on Management of Data*, 2004. (to appear).
14. XQuery 1.0: An XML Query Language, November 2003. URL: http://www.w3.org/TR/xquery/.

Graphical Reasoning for Sets of Functional Dependencies

János Demetrovics[1], András Molnár[2], and Bernhard Thalheim[3]

[1] MTA SZTAKI, Computer and Automation Institute
of the Hungarian Academy of Sciences
Kende u. 13-17, H-1111 Budapest, Hungary
demetrovics@sztaki.hu

[2] Department of Information Systems, Faculty of Informatics,
Eötvös Loránd University Budapest
Pázmány Péter stny. 1/C, H-1117 Budapest, Hungary
modras@elte.hu

[3] Computer Science and Applied Mathematics Institute, University Kiel,
Olshausenstrasse 40, 24098 Kiel, Germany
thalheim@is.informatik.uni-kiel.de

Abstract. Reasoning on constraint sets is a difficult task. Classical database design is based on a step-wise extension of the constraint set and on a consideration of constraint sets through generation by tools. Since the database developer must master semantics acquisition, tools and approaches are still sought that support reasoning on sets of constraints. We propose novel approaches for presentation of sets of functional dependencies based on specific graphs. These approaches may be used for the elicitation of the full knowledge on validity of functional dependencies in relational schemata.

1 Design Problems During Database Semantics Specification and Their Solution

Specification of database structuring is based on three interleaved and dependent parts [9]:

Syntactics: Inductive specification of structures uses a set of base types, a collection of constructors and an theory of construction limiting the application of constructors by rules or by formulas in deontic logics. In most cases, the theory may be dismissed.

Semantics: Specification of admissible databases on the basis of static integrity constraints describes those database states which are considered to be legal.

Pragmatics: Description of context and intension is based either on explicit reference to the enterprise model, to enterprise tasks, to enterprise policy, and environments or on intensional logics used for relating the interpretation and meaning to users depending on time, location, and common sense.

P. Atzeni et al. (Eds.): ER 2004, LNCS 3288, pp. 166–179, 2004.

Specification of syntactics is based on the database modeling language. Specification of semantics requires a logical language for specification of classes of constraints. Typical constraints are dependencies such as functional, multivalued, and inclusion dependencies, or domain constraints. Specification of pragmatics is often not explicit. The specification of semantics is often rather difficult due to the complexity. For this reason, it must be supported by a number of solutions supporting acquisition and reasoning on constraints.

Prerequisites of Database Design Approaches

Results obtained during database structuring are evaluated on two main criteria: *completeness* [8] of and *unambiguity* of specification.

Completeness requires that all constraints that must be specified are found. Unambiguity is necessary in order to provide a reasoning system. Both criteria have found their theoretical and pragmatical solution for most of the known classes of constraints. Completeness is, however, restricted by the human ability to survey large constraint sets and to understand all possible interactions among constraints.

Theoretical Approaches to Problem Solution: A number of normalization and restructuring algorithms have been developed for functional dependencies. We do not know simple representation systems for surveying constraint sets and for detecting missing constraints beyond functional dependencies yet.

Pragmatical Approaches to Problem Solution: A step-wise constraint acquisition procedure has been developed in [7, 10, 12]. The approach is based on the separation of constraints into:

The set of valid functional dependencies Σ_1**:** All dependencies that are known to be valid and all those that can be implied from the set of valid and excluded functional dependencies.

The set of excluded functional dependencies Σ_0**:** All dependencies that are known to be invalid and all those that are invalid and can be implied from the set of valid and excluded functional dependencies.

This approach leads to the following simple elicitation algorithm:

1. *Basic step: Design obvious constraints.*
2. *Recursion step: Repeat until the constraint sets* Σ_0 *and* Σ_1 *do not change.*
   - *Find a functional dependency* α *that is neither in* Σ_1 *nor in* Σ_0*.* *If* α *is valid then add* α *to* Σ_1*. If* α *is invalid then add* α *to* Σ_0*.*
   - *Generate the logical closures of* Σ_0 *and* Σ_1*.*

This algorithm can be refined in various ways. Elicitation algorithms know so far are all variation of this simple elicitation algorithm.

However, neither the theoretical solutions nor the pragmatical approach provides a solution to problem 1:

Define a pragmatical approach that allows simple representation of and reasoning on database constraints.

This problem becomes more severe in association with the following problems.

Complexity of Semantics

Typical algorithms such as normalization algorithms can only generate a correct result if specification is complete. Such completeness is not harmful as long as constraint sets are small. The number of constraints may however be exponential in the number of attributes [3]. Therefore, specification of the *complete set of functional dependencies* may be a task that is `infeasible`. This problem is closely related to another well-known combinatoric problem presented by János Demetrovics during MFDBS'87 [11] and that is still only partially solved:

Problem 2. What is the size of sets of independent functional dependencies for an n-ary relation schema?

Inter-dependence Within a Constraint Set

Constraints such as functional dependencies are not independent from each other. Typical axiomatizations use rules such as the union, transitivity and path rules. Developers do not reason this way. Therefore, the impact of adding, deleting or modifying a constraint within a constraint set is not easy to capture. Therefore, we need a system for reasoning on constraint sets.

Theoretical Approaches to Problem Solution: [14] and [1] propose to use a graph-based representation of sets of functional dependencies. This solution provides a simple survey as long as constraints are simple, i.e., use singleton sets for the left sides. [13] proposes to use a schema architecture by developing first elementary schema components and constructing the schema by application of composition operations which use these components. [4] propose to construct a collection of interrelated lattices of functional dependencies. Each lattice represents a component of [13]. The set of functional dependencies is then constructed through folding of the lattices.

Pragmatical Approaches to Problem Solution: [6] proposes to use a fact-based approach instead of modeling of attributes. Elementary facts are 'small' objects that cannot be decomposed without loosing meaning.

We, thus, must solve **problem 3.**

Develop a reasoning system that support easy maintenance and development of constraint sets and highlight logical inter-dependence among constraints.

Instability of Normalization

Normalization is based on the completeness of constraint sets. This is impractical. Althouth database design tools can support completeness, incompleteness of specification should be considered the *normal* situation. Therefore, normalization approaches should be robust with regard to incompleteness.

Problem 4.[12] Find a normalization theory which is robust for incomplete constraint sets or robust according to a class of changes in constraint sets.

Problems That Currently Defy Solution

Dependency theory consists of work on about 95 different classes of dependencies, with a very few classes that have been treated together. Moreover, properties of sets of functional dependencies remain still unknown.

In most practical cases several negative results obtained in the dependency theory do not restrict the common utilization of several classes. The reason for this is that the used constraint sets do not have these properties. Therefore, we need other classification principles for describing 'real life' constraint sets.

Problem 5. [12] Classify 'real life' constraint sets which can be easily maintained and specified.

This problem is related to one of the oldest problems in database research expressed by Joachim Biskup in the open problems session [11] of MFDBS'87:

Problem 6. Develop a specification method that supports consideration of sets of functional dependencies and derivation of properties of those sets.

Outline of the Paper[1] and the Kernel Problem Behind Open Problems

The six problems above can be solved on one common basis:

Find a simple and sophisticated representation of sets of constraints that supports reasoning on constraints.

This problem is infeasible in general. Therefore, we provide first a mechanism to reason on sets of functional dependencies defined on small sets of attributes. Geometrical figures such as polygons or tetrahedra nicely support reasoning on constraints. Next we demonstrate the representation for attribute sets consisting of three or four attributes. Finally we introduce the implication system for graphical representations and show how these representations lead to a very simple and sophisticated treatment of sets of functional dependencies.

2 Sets of Functional Dependencies for Small Relation Schemata

2.1 Universes of Functional Constraints

Besides functional dependencies (FDs), we use *excluded functional constraints* (also called *negated functional dependencies*): eg. $X \not\rightarrow Y$ states that the functional dependency $X \longrightarrow Y$ is not valid.

Treating sets of functional constraints becomes simpler if we avoid dealing with obviously redundant constraints. In our notation, a *trivial* constraint (a functional dependency or an excluded functional constraint) is a constraint with

[1] Due to the lack of space, this paper does not contain proofs or the representation of all possible sets of functional dependencies. All technical details as well as some other means of representation can be read in a technical report available under [5].

at least one attribute of its left-hand side and right-hand side in common or has the empty set as its right-hand side. Furthermore, a *canonical (singleton)* functional dependency or a singleton excluded functional constraint has exactly one attribute on its right-hand side. We introduce the notations $\mathbb{D}$, $\mathbb{D}^+$ and $\mathbb{D}_c^+$ for the universes of functional dependencies, non-trivial functional dependencies and non-trivial canonical (singleton) functional dependencies, respectively, over a fixed underlying domain of attribute symbols. Similarly, $\mathbb{E}$, $\mathbb{E}^+$ and $\mathbb{E}_c^+$ denote the universes of excluded functional constraints, non-trivial excluded constraints and non-trivial singleton excluded functional constraints (negated non-trivial, canonical dependencies) over the same set of attribute symbols, respectively. The traditional universe of functional constraints (including functional dependencies and excluded constraints) is $\mathbb{D} \cup \mathbb{E}$, while our graphical representations deal with sets of constraints over $\mathbb{D}_c^+ \cup \mathbb{E}_c^+$. In other words, the graphical representations we present in this paper deal with non-trivial canonical functional dependencies and non-trivial singleton excluded functional constraints only. It will be shown that we do not loose relevant deductive power applying this restriction to the universe of functional constraints.

In most of the cases, we focus on *closed* sets of functional dependencies. A finite set $\mathcal{F} \subset \mathbb{D}_c^+$ is closed (over $\mathbb{D}_c^+$) iff $\mathcal{F}^+ = \mathcal{F}$ where $\mathcal{F}^+$ is the closure of $\mathcal{F}$, ie. $\mathcal{F}^+ = \{\delta \in \mathbb{D}_c^+ \mid \mathcal{F} \models \delta\}$.

2.2 The Notion of Dimension

For the classification of functional constraints and the attributes they refer to, we introduce the notion of dimension first. The dimension of a constraint is simply the size of its left-hand side, i.e. the number of attributes on its left-hand side.

For a functional dependency $X \to A \in \mathbb{D}_c^+$ denote by $[X \to A]$ its *dimension*, defined as

$$[X \to A] \stackrel{\text{def}}{=} |X|$$

(the dimension of an excluded functional constraint can be defined similarly). For a single attribute A, given a set of functional dependencies $\mathcal{F} \subset \mathbb{D}_c^+$, the *dimension of* A is denoted by $[A]_\mathcal{F}$ (or just simply $[A]$) and defined as

$$[A]_\mathcal{F} \stackrel{\text{def}}{=} \min_{X \to A \in \mathcal{F}^+} |X|$$

This definition is extended with $[A]_\mathcal{F} \stackrel{\text{def}}{=} \infty$ for the case when no $X \to A$ exists in $\mathcal{F}^+$. The dimensions of attributes classify the sets of functional dependencies.

2.3 Summary of the Number of Closed Sets

Let n be the number of attributes of the considered relation schema. Denote by $\mathcal{SD}_n$ the set of closed sets of (singleton, non-trivial) functional dependencies for this n (with constant attributes disallowed). Defining τ as the equivalence relation on these sets classifying them into different types or cases (for two equivalent sets there exists a permutation of attributes transforming one set to another), the set of different classes is $\mathcal{SD}_n/\tau$. We are focusing on these different classes and the size of this set. Another possibility is to let the attributes to be stated as constants. Performing this extension to $\mathcal{SD}_n$ we get a larger set, denoted by $\mathcal{SD}_n^0$. The different cases (types) of functional dependency sets taking these zero-dimensional constraints into account form the set $\mathcal{SD}_n^0/\tau$. It can be easily verified that $|\mathcal{SD}_{n+1}^0/\tau| = |\mathcal{SD}_{n+1}/\tau| + |\mathcal{SD}_n^0/\tau|$ holds for each $n \in \mathbb{N}^+$.

With these notations, Table 1 shows the number of closed sets of functional dependencies for unary, binary, ternary, quaternary and quinary relational schemata and demonstrates the combinatorial of the search space.

Table 1. Number of closed sets of functional dependencies for n attributes

n	$\|\mathcal{SD}_n\|$	$\|\mathcal{SD}_n/\tau\|$	$\|\mathcal{SD}_n^0\|$	$\|\mathcal{SD}_n^0/\tau\|$
1	1	*1*	2	2
2	4	*3*	7	5
3	45	*14*	61	19
4	2 271	*165*	2 480	184
5	1 373 701	*14 480*	1 385 552	14 664

3 The Graphical Representation of Sets of Functional Dependencies

There have been several proposals for graphical representation of sets of functional dependencies. Well-known books such as [1] and [14] have used a graph-theoretic notion. Nevertheless, these graphical notations have not made there way into practice and education. The main reason for this failure is the complexity of representation. Graphical representations are simple as long as the set of functional dependencies are not too complex. [2] has proposed a representation for the ternary case based on either assigning an N-notation if nothing is known or assigning a 1-notation to an edge from X to Y at the Y end if the functional dependency $X \to Y$ is valid. This representation is simple enough but already redundant in the case of ternary relationship types. Moreover, it is not generalizable to cases of n-ary relationship types with $n > 3$.

We use a simpler notation which reflects the validity of functional dependencies in a simpler and better understandable fashion.

We distinguish two kinds of functional dependencies for $n = 3$:

One-dimensional (singleton left sides): Functional dependencies of the form $\{A\} \to \{B, C\}$ can be decomposed to canonical functional dependencies $\{A\} \to \{B\}$ and $\{A\} \to \{C\}$. They are represented by endpoints of binary edges (1D shapes) in the triangular representation.

Two-dimensional (two-element left sides): Functional dependencies with two-element left-hand sides $\{A, B\} \to \{C\}$ cannot be decomposed. They are represented in the triangular (2D shape) on the node relating their right side to the corner.

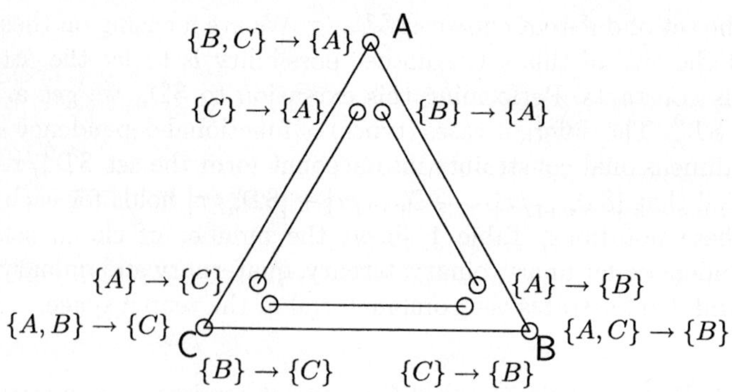

Fig. 1. Triangular representation of sets of functional dependencies for the ternary case

We may represent also candidates for excluded functional dependencies by

crossed circles for the case that we know that the corresponding functional dependency is not valid in applications or by

small circles for the case that we do not know whether the functional dependency holds or does not hold.

We use now the following notations in the figures:

Basic functional dependencies are denoted by filled circles.

Implied functional dependencies are denoted by circles.

Negated basic functional dependencies are either denoted by dots or by crossed filled circles.

Implied negated functional dependencies are either denoted by dots or by crossed circles.

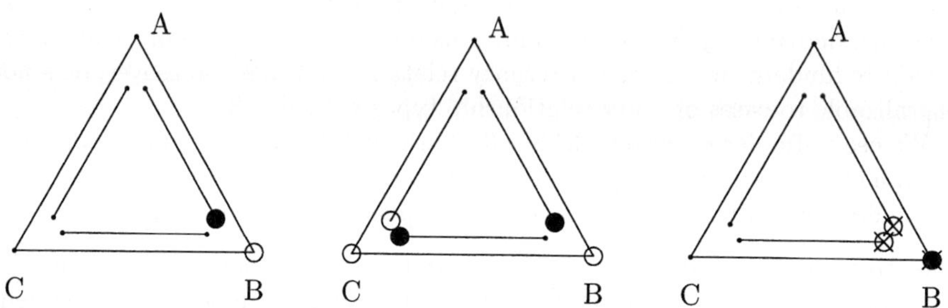

Fig. 2. Examples of the triangular representation

Figure 2 shows some examples of the triangular representation. The functional dependency $\{A\} \to \{B\}$ and the implied functional dependency $\{A,C\} \to \{B\}$ are shown in the left part. The functional dependencies $\{A\} \to \{B\}$, $\{B\} \to$

$\{C\}$ and their implied functional dependencies are pictured in the middle triangle. The negated functional dependency $\{A,C\} \not\rightarrow \{B\}$ and the implied negated functional dependencies $\{A\} \not\rightarrow \{B\}$ and $\{C\} \not\rightarrow \{B\}$ are given in the right picture.

As mentioned above, the triangular representation can be generalized to higher number of attributes. Generalization can be performed in two directions: representation in a higher-dimensional space (3D in the case of 4 attributes, resulting the *tetrahedral* representation) or constructing a planar (2D, *quadratic*) representation. We use the same approach as before in the case of three attributes. An example is displayed in Figure 3 (implication is explained later). In this paper we concentrate on the 2D representation.

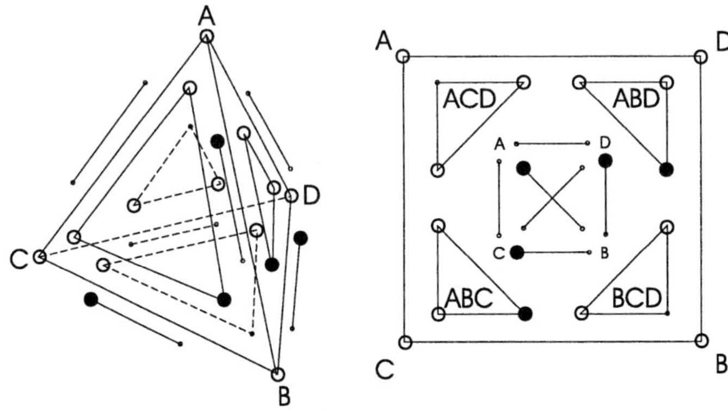

Fig. 3. The tetraherdal and quadratic representations of the set generated by $\{ B \rightarrow C, B \rightarrow D, B \rightarrow A, AD \rightarrow B, AC \rightarrow B\}$

This representation can be generalized to the case of 5 attributes.

4 Implication Systems for the Graphical Representations

Excluded functional constraints and functional dependencies are axiomatizable by the following formal system [12].

Axioms

$$XY \rightarrow Y$$

Rules

$$(1)\ \frac{X \longrightarrow Y}{XVW \longrightarrow YV} \qquad (2)\ \frac{X \longrightarrow Y,\ Y \longrightarrow Z}{X \longrightarrow Z}$$

$$(3)\ \frac{X \longrightarrow Y,\ X \not\longrightarrow Z}{Y \not\longrightarrow Z} \qquad (4)\ \frac{X \not\longrightarrow Y}{X \not\longrightarrow YZ} \qquad (5)\ \frac{XZ \not\longrightarrow YZ}{XZ \not\longrightarrow Y}$$

$$(6)\ \frac{X \longrightarrow Z,\ X \not\longrightarrow YZ}{X \not\longrightarrow Y} \qquad (7)\ \frac{Y \longrightarrow Z,\ X \not\longrightarrow Z}{X \not\longrightarrow Y}$$

The universe of the extended Armstrong implication system is $\mathbb{D} \cup \mathbb{E}$ (see Section 2.1) while our graphical and spreadsheet representations deal with sets of constraints over $\mathbb{D}_c^+ \cup \mathbb{E}_c^+$ [2]. However, the axiom and rules of the extended Armstrong implication system do not correspond to this restriction. It will be shown that an equivalent implication system can be constructed if these restrictions are applied to the universe of constraints. We develop a new implication system for graphical reasoning:

$$(S)\ \frac{Y \to B}{YC \to B} \qquad (T)\ \frac{Y \to A,\ YA \to B}{Y \to B} \qquad (P)\ \frac{YC \not\to B}{Y \not\to B}$$

$$(Q)\ \frac{Y \to A,\ Y \not\to B}{YA \not\to B} \qquad (R)\ \frac{YA \to B,\ Y \not\to B}{Y \not\to A} \qquad (\square)\ \neg(Y \to B,\ Y \not\to B)$$

The rules presented here can directly be applied for deducing consequences of a set of constraints given in terms of the graphical or spreadsheet representation. We use the following two implication systems:

- the *ST implication system* over $\mathbb{D}_c^+$ with rules (S) and (T) and no axioms,
- the *PQRST implication system* over $\mathbb{D}_c^+ \cup \mathbb{E}_c^+$ with all the presented rules and the symbolic axiom ($\square$), which is used for indicating contradiction.

These systems are sound and complete for deducing non-trivial, singleton constraints.

Theorem 1 The ST system is sound and complete over $\mathbb{D}_c^+$, ie. $\mathfrak{F} \vdash_{ST} \delta \iff \mathfrak{F} \models \delta$ for each finite subset $\mathfrak{F}$ of $\mathbb{D}_c^+$ and $\delta \in \mathbb{D}_c^+$.

Theorem 2 Let $\mathfrak{F}$ be a finite subset of $\mathbb{D}_c^+ \cup \mathbb{E}_c^+$ and $\delta \in \mathbb{D}_c^+ \cup \mathbb{E}_c^+$.
The PQRST system without ($\square$) is sound over $\mathbb{D}_c^+ \cup \mathbb{E}_c^+$ and complete with the restriction that $\mathfrak{F}$ cannot be contradictory, ie. $\mathfrak{F} \vdash_{PQRST} \delta \iff \mathfrak{F} \models \delta$ for each non-contradictory $\mathfrak{F}$. Moreover, $\neg(\square)$ can be derived iff $\mathfrak{F}$ is contradictory.

The implication systems introduced above have the advantage of the existence of a specific order of rules which provides a complete algorithmic method for getting all the implied functional dependencies and excluded functional constraints starting with an initial set, allowing one to determine the possible types of relationships the initial set of dependencies defines.

Theorem 3[3]

1. Let $\mathfrak{F}$ and $\mathfrak{G}$ be finite subsets of $\mathbb{D}_c^+$. If $\mathfrak{F} \vdash_{ST} \mathfrak{G}$ then all elements of $\mathfrak{G}$ can be deduced starting with $\mathfrak{F}$ by using the rules (S) and (T) the way that no application of (T) precede any application of (S).

[2] For example, $X \to AB$ is represented as $X \to A$ and $X \to B$. Excluded functional constraints with more than one attribute on their right-hand sides can not be eliminated this way. However, omitting these can also be achieved (see [5]).

[3] Proofs of the theorems are given in [5].

2. If $\mathcal{F}$ and $\mathcal{G}$ are finite subsets of $\mathbb{D}_c^+ \cup \mathbb{E}_c^+$ and $\mathcal{F} \vdash_{PQRST} \mathcal{G}$ then all elements of $\mathcal{G}$ can be deduced starting with $\mathcal{F}$ by using the rules (S), (T), (R), (P) and (Q) the way that no application of (T) precede any application of (S), no application of (R) precede any application of (T) and no application of (P) or (Q) precede any application of (R). Order of (P) and (Q) is arbitrary. Furthermore, (R) is needed to be applied at most once if $|\mathcal{G}| = 1$.

5 Graphical Reasoning

Rules of the PQRST implication system support graphical reasoning. We will discuss first the case of $n = 3$.

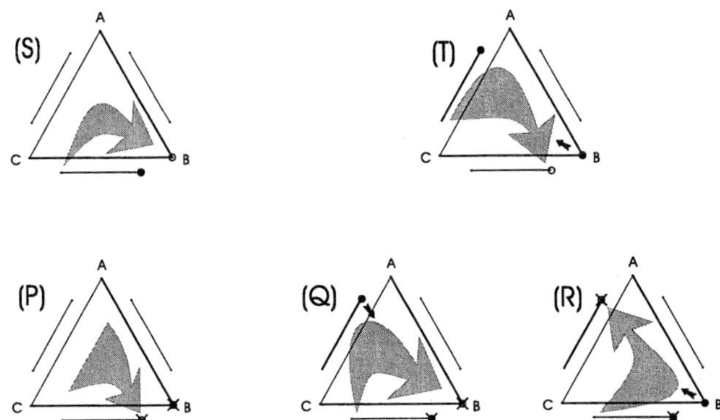

Fig. 4. Graphical versions of rules (S), (T) and (P), (Q), (R)

Graphical versions of rules are shown on Figure 4 for the triangular representation (case $Y = \{C\}$). The small black arrows indicate support (necessary context) while the large grey arrows show the implication effects. Rule (S) is a simple extension rule and rule (T) can be called as "rotation rule" or "reduction rule". We may call the left-hand side of a functional dependency the *determinant* of it and the right-hand side the *determinate.* Rule (S) can be used to extend the determinant of a dependency resulting another dependency with one dimension higher, while rule (T) is used for *rotation*, that is, to replace the determinate of a functional dependency by the support of another functional dependency with one dimension higher (the small black arrow at B indicates support of $AC \to B$). Another possible way to interpret rule (T) is for reduction of the determinant of a higher-dimensional dependency by omitting an attribute if a dependency holds among the attributes of the determinant.

For excluded functional constraints, rule (Q) acts as the extension rule (needs support of a positive constraint, ie. functional dependency) and (R) as the rotation rule (needs a positive support too). These two rules can also be viewed as negations of rule (T). Rule (P) is the reduction rule for excluded functional constraints, with the opposite effect of rule (Q) (but without the need of support). Rule (Q) is also viewed as the negation of rule (S).

These graphical rules can be generalized to higher dimensional cases, where the number of attributes is more than 3. Figure 5 shows the patterns of rules (S) and (T) for the case $n = 4$. We use two or three patterns for a single case since we need a way to survey constraint derivation by (not completely symmetric) 2D diagrams. We differentiate between the case that the rules (S) and (T) use functional dependencies consisting of singleton left sides and the case that the minimum dimension of functional dependencies is two.

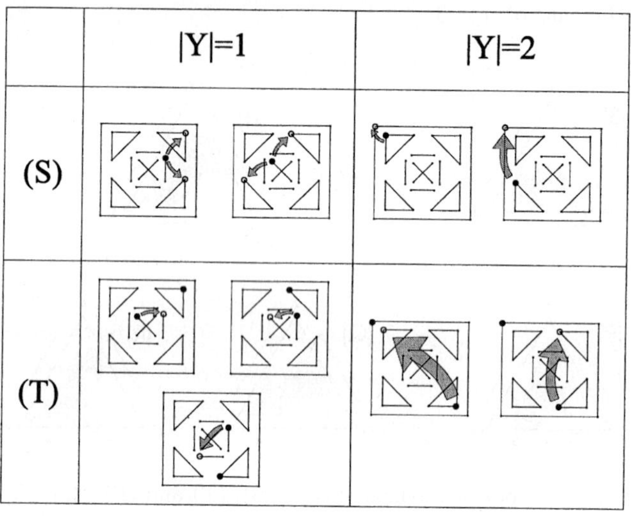

Fig. 5. Patterns of graphical rules (S) and (T) for the quadratic representation

Theorem 3 in Section 4 shows that for positive dependencies, using (S) first as many times as possible and using (T) as many times as possible afterwards is a complete method for obtaining all non-trivial positive consequences of a given set of constraints. We may call it *ST algorithm*[4]. This can be extended for the case with excluded functional constraints. We now present it as an algorithm for FD derivation based on the graphical representation:

The STRPQ Algorithm for Sets of Both Positive and Negative Constraints. Rules (P), (Q) and (R) can be applied as complements of rules (S) and (T), resulting the following algorithm called *STRPQ algorithm* (based on part 2 of Theorem 3):

[4] With some modifications, this algorithm has been used for generating and counting all sets of functional dependencies (see Section 2.3) with a PROLOG program.

1. Starting with the given initial set of non-trivial, singleton functional dependencies and excluded functional constraints as input,
2. extend the determinants of each dependency using rule (S) as many times as possible, then
3. apply rule (T) until no changes occur,
4. apply rule (R) until no changes occur,
5. reduce and extend the determinants of excluded constraints using rules (P) and (Q) as many times as possible.
6. Output the generated set.

The algorithm just presented can be used for reasoning on sets of functional constraints, especially in terms of the graphical representations. The structure of the generalized triangular representations (2D–triangular, 3D–tetrahedral, etc.) may also be used for designing a data structure representing sets of functional constraints for the algorithms.

6 Applying Graphical Reasoning to Sets of Functional Dependencies

Let us consider a more complex example discussed in [12]. We are given a part of the Berlin airport management database for scheduling flights and pilots at one of its airports. Flights depart at one departure time and to one destination. A flight can get different pilots and can be assigned to different gates each day of a week. In the given application we observe the following functional dependencies for the attributes *Flight#, (Chief)Pilot#, Gate#, Day, Hour, Destination*:

{ *Flight#, Day* } → { *Pilot, Gate#, Hour* }
{ *Flight#* } → { *Destination, Hour* }
{ *Day, Hour, Gate#* } → { *Flight#* }
{ *Pilot#, Day, Hour* } → { *Flight#* }

As noticed in [12] we can model this database in a five very different ways. Figure 6 displays one of the solutions. All types in Figure 6 are in the third normal form. Additionally, the following constraints are valid for solution in Figure 6:

flies : { *GateSchedule.Time, Pilot.#* } ⟶ { *GateSchedule* }.

The two schemata have additionally transitive path constraints, e.g.:

flies: { *GateSchedule.Time,Day, Flight.#* } ⟶ { *GateSchedule.Gate.#* }.

But the types are still in third normal form since for each functional dependency defined for the types $X \to Y$ either X is a key or Y is a part of a key.
The reason for the existence of rather complex constraints is the twofold usage of *Hour*. For instance, in our solution we find the equality constraint:

flies.Flight.Hour = *flies.GateSchedule.Time.Hour*.

We must know now whether the set of functional dependencies is complete. The combinatorial complexity of brute-force consideration of dependency sets is overwhelming.

Let us now apply our theoretical findings to cope with the complexity and to reason on the sets of functional dependencies. We may use the following algorithm:

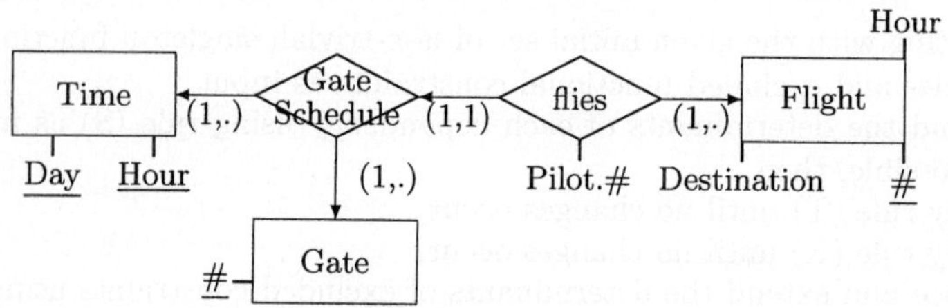

Fig. 6. An extended ER Schema for the airline database with transitive path constraints

1. Consider attributes which are not used in any left side of a functional dependency whether they are really dangling. This is done by using the **STRPQ** algorithm with each of the attributes and the rest of other attributes. We may strip out dangling attributes not loosing the reasoning power. In the example we strip out *Destination.*
2. Combine attributes to groups such that they appear together in left sides of functional dependencies. Consider first the relations among those attribute groups using the **STRPQ** algorithm. In our example we consider the groups (A) *Day, Hour*, (B) *Flight#, Day*, (C) *(Chief)Pilot#*, and (D) *Gate#*. The result is shown on Figure 3.
3. Recursively now apply the **STRPQ** algorithm to decompositions of attribute groups.

The example shows how graphical reasoning can be directly applied to larger sets of attributes which have complex relations among them and can be expressed through functional dependencies.

7 Conclusion

The problem whether there exists a simple and sophisticated representation of sets of constraints that supports reasoning on constraints is solved in this paper by introducing a more surveyable means for the representation of constraint sets: the graphical representation. It requires a different implication system than the classical Armstrong system. We, thus, introduced another system and could show (Theorem 1 and 2) its soundness and completeness.

This system has another useful property (Theorem 3): Constraint derivation may be ordered on the basis of sequences of rules. Derivation rule application can be described using the regular expression $(S)^*; (T)^*; (R)^*; ((P)\|(Q))^*$. This order of rule application is extremely useful whenever we want to know whether the set of generated functional constraints is full (closed), i.e., consists of all (positive or both positive and negative) dependencies that follow from the given initial system of functional constraints. Based on this, we were able to generate all possible sets of initial functional dependencies for $n = 3, 4, 5$.

Graphical reasoning supports a simpler style of reasoning on constraint sets. Completeness and soundness of systems of functional dependencies and excluded functional dependencies becomes surveyable. Since database design approaches rely on completeness and soundness of constraint sets, our approach enables database designers to obtain better database design results.

Acknowledgements

We would like to thank Tibor Ásványi for his help in improving the efficiency of our PROLOG program, which generates the sets of functional dependencies and Zoltán Csaba Regéci for his assistance in running the program at MTA SZTAKI. We are also grateful to Andrea Molnár for her valuable comments on the illustration of the graphical rules and the tetrahedral representation.

References

1. P. Atzeni and V. De Antonellis. *Relational database theory.* Addison-Wesley, Redwood City, 1993.
2. R. Camps. From ternary relationship to relational tables: A case against common beliefs. *ACM SIGMOD Record, 31(2)*, pages 46–49, 2002.
3. J. Demetrovics and G. O. H. Katona. Combinatorial problems of database models. In *Colloquia Mathematica Societatis Janos Bolyai 42, Algebra, Combinatorics and Logic in Computer Science*, pages 331–352, Györ, Hungary, 1983.
4. J. Demetrovics, L. O. Libkin, and I. B. Muchnik. Functional dependencies and the semilattice of closed classes. In *Proc. MFDBS'89, LNCS 364*, pages 136–147, 1989.
5. J. Demetrovics, A. Molnar, and B. Thalheim. Graphical and spreadsheet reasoning for sets of functional dependencies. Technical Report 0402, Kiel University, Computer Science Institute,
http://www.informatik.uni-kiel.de/reports/2004/0402.html, 2004.
6. T. A. Halpin. *Conceptual schema and relational database design.* Prentice-Hall, Sydney, 1995.
7. M. Klettke. *Akquisition von Integritätsbedingungen in Datenbanken.* DISBIS 51. infix-Verlag, St. Augin, 1998.
8. O.I. Lindland, G. Sindre, and A. Solvberg. Understanding quality in conceptual modeling. *IEEE Software*, 11(2):42–49, 1994.
9. C.W. Morris. Foundations of the theory of signs. In *International Encyclopedia of Unified Science.* University of Chicago Press, 1955.
10. V.C. Storey, H.L. Yang, and R.C. Goldstein. Semantic integrity constraints in knowledge-based database design systems. *Data & Knowledge Engineering*, 20:1–37, 1996.
11. B. Thalheim. Open problems in relational database theory. *Bull. EATCS*, 32:336 – 337, 1987.
12. B. Thalheim. *Entity-relationship modeling – Foundations of database technology.* Springer, Berlin, 2000.
See also http://www.informatik.tu-cottbus.de/~thalheim/HERM.htm.
13. B. Thalheim. Component construction of database schemes. In *Proc. ER'02, LNCS 2503*, pages 20–34, 2002.
14. C.-C. Yang. *Relational Databases.* Prentice-Hall, Englewood Cliffs, 1986.

ER-Based Software Sizing for Data-Intensive Systems

Hee Beng Kuan Tan and Yuan Zhao

School of Electrical and Electronic Engineering, Block S2,
Nanyang Technological University
Nanyang Avenue, Singapore 639798
ibktan@ntu.edu.sg

Abstract. Despite the existence of well-known software sizing methods such as Function Point method, many developers still continue to use ad-hoc methods or so called "expert" approaches. This is mainly due to the fact that the existing methods require much implementation information that is difficult to identify or estimate in the early stage of a software project. The accuracy of ad-hoc and "expert" methods also has much problem. The entity-relationship (ER) model is widely used in conceptual modeling (requirements analysis) for data-intensive systems. From our observation, the characteristic of a data-intensive system, and therefore the source code of its software, is well characterized by the ER diagram that models its data. Based on this observation, this paper proposes a method for building software size model from extended ER diagram through the use of regression models. We have collected some real data from the industry to do a preliminary validation of the proposed method. The result of the validation is very encouraging. As software sizing is an important key to software cost estimation and therefore vital to the industry for managing their software projects, we hope that the research and industry communities can further validate the proposed method.

1 Introduction

Estimating project size is a crucial task in any software project. Overestimates may lead to the abortion of projects or loss of projects to competitors. Underestimates pressurize project teams and may also adversely affect the quality of projects.

Despite the existence of well known software sizing methods such as Function Point method [1], [10] and the more recent Full Function Point method [7], many practitioners and project managers continue to produce estimates based on ad-hoc or so called "expert" approaches [2], [8], [15]. This is mainly due to the fact that existing sizing methods require much implementation information that is not available in the earlier stage of a software project. However, the accuracy of ad-hoc and expert approaches also has much problem that results to questionable project budgets and schedules.

The entity-relationship (ER) model originally proposed by Chen [5] is generally regarded as the most widely used tool for the conceptual modeling of data-intensive systems. An ER model is constructed to depict the ideal organization of data, independent of the physical organization of the data and where and how data are used.

Indeed, much requirement of data-intensive systems is reflected from their ER models that depict their data conceptually. This paper proposes a novel method for

P. Atzeni et al. (Eds.): ER 2004, LNCS 3288, pp. 180–190, 2004.

building software size model to estimate the size of source code for a data-intensive system based on extended ER diagram. It also discusses the validation effort conducted by us to validate the proposed method for building software size models for data-intensive systems written in Visual Basic and Java languages.

The paper is organized as follows. Section 2 gives the background information of the paper. Section 3 discusses our observation and its rationale. Section 4 presents the proposed method for building software size models to estimate the sizes of source codes for data-intensive systems. Section 5 discusses our preliminary validation of the proposed method. Section 6 concludes the paper and compares the proposed method with related methods.

2 Background

Entity-relationship (ER) model was originally proposed by Chen [5] for data modeling. And, it has been extended by Chen and others subsequently [17]. In this paper, we refer to the extended ER model that has the same set of concepts as the class diagram in terms of data modeling. In summary, the extended ER model uses the concept of entity, attribute and relationship to model the conceptual data for a problem. Each entity has a set of attributes each of which is an entity's property or characteristic that is concerned by the problem. Relationships can be classified into three types: association, aggregation and generalization.

There are four main stages in developing software systems: requirements capture, requirements analysis, design and implementation. The requirements are studied and specified in the requirements capture stage. They are realized conceptually in the requirements analysis. The design for implementing the requirements with the target environments taken into considerations is constructed in the design stage. In the implementation stage, the design is coded using the target programming language and the resulting code is tested to ensure its correctness.

Though UML (Unified Modeling Language) has gained its popularity as a standard software modeling language, many data-intensive systems are still developed in the industry through some form of data-oriented approach. In such an approach, some form of extended entity-relationship (ER) model is constructed to model the data conceptually in the requirements capture and analysis stages. And, the subsequent design and implementation activities are very much based on the extended ER model. For projects that use UML, a class diagram is usually constructed in the requirements analysis stage. Indeed, for a data intensive system, the class diagram constructed can be viewed as an extended ER model with the extension of behavioral properties (processing). Therefore, in the early stage of software development, some form of extended ER model is more readily available than information such as external inputs, outputs and inquiries, and external logical files and external interface files that are required for the computation of function points.

3 Our Observation

Data-intensive systems constitute one of the largest domains in software. These systems usually maintain large amount of structured data in a database built using a database management system (DBMS). And, it provides operational, control and management support to end-users through referencing and analyzing these data. The support is usually accomplished through accepting inputs from user, processing inputs, updating databases, printing of reports, and providing inquiries to help users in the management and decision making processes.

The proposed method for building software size model for data-intensive systems is based on our observation of these systems. Next, we shall discuss the observation and its rationale.

The Observation: Under the same development environment (that is, a particular programming language and tool used), the size of source codes for a data-intensive system usually depends on the extended ER diagram that models its data.

Rationale: The constituents of the data-intensive system can be classified into the following:

1) Support business operations through accepting inputs to maintain entities modeling in the ER diagram.
2) Support decision making processes through producing outputs from information possessed by entities modeled in the ER diagram.
3) Implement business logic to support the business operation and control.
4) Reference to entities modeled in the ER diagram to support the first three constituents.

Since the first two and the last constituents are based on the ER diagram, as such, they depend on the ER diagram. At the first glance, it seems that the third constituent may not depend on the ER diagram. However, since a data-intensive system usually does not perform complex computation within the source code (any complex computation is usually achieved through calling pre-developed function), business logic in the source code is mainly for the navigation between entities via relationship types with simple computation. For example, for the business logic that if a customer has two overdue invoices, then no further orders will be processed, the source code for implementing the business logic retrieves overdue invoices in the Invoice entity type for the customer in the Customer entity type via the relationship type that associates a customer with its invoices. There is no complex computation involved. Therefore, it is reasonable to assume that usually, the implementation of business logic in a data-intensive system also depends on the ER diagram. This completes the rationale of the observation. ❑

4 The Proposed Software Sizing

From the observation discussed in the previous section, the size of the source code for a data-intensive system usually depends and only depends on the structure and size of an extended ER diagram that models its data. Furthermore, ER diagram has been widely and well use in the requirements modeling and analysis stages. Thus, it is more suitable to base on extended ER diagram for the estimation of the size of source code for a data-intensive system. Therefore, we propose a novel method for building software size model based on extended ER diagram. This section discusses the method.

The proposed method builds software size models through well-known linear regression models. For a data-intensive system, the variables that sufficiently characterize the extended ER diagram for the system form the independent variables. The dependent variable is the size of its source code in thousand lines of code (KLOC). Note that in this case, the extended ER diagram is implemented and is only implemented by the system. That is, the extended ER diagram and the system must coincide and have a one-to-one correspondence. As such, any source code that references or updates the database that is designed from the extended ER diagram must be included as part of the source code.

In the proposed approach, a separate software size model should be built for each different development environment (that is, each programming language and tool used). For example, different software size models should be built for systems written in Visual Basic with VB Script and SQL, and systems written in Java with JSP, Java Script and SQL. In the most precise case, the independent variables that characterize the extended ER diagram comprise of the following:

1) Total number of entity types.
2) Total number of attributes.
3) Total numbers of association types classified based on their degrees and multiplicities: Usually, the degrees can be classified in exact for those below an upper limit. The remaining can all be lumped into one. Multiplicities can be classified into zero-or-one, one and many. More precise classification can also be tried.
4) Total numbers of aggregation types classified based on their degrees and multiplicities: Same as the association types.
5) Total numbers of generalization types classified based on the number of sub-classes: Usually, the number of sub-classes can be classified in exact for those below an upper limit. The remaining can all be lumped into one.

However, we do not propose to build a software size model based on a fixed set of independent variables. It all depends on the kind of ER diagrams used in organizations for which we develop the software size model. Note that the above-mentioned association refers to association that is not aggregation. The separation of relationship types into associations, aggregations and generalizations is because of the differences in their semantics. These differences may result to some differences in navigation and updating needs in the database.

We propose that the independent variables should be defined according to the type of ER diagram constructed during the requirements modeling and analysis stages. So, at least the data required for software sizing is readily available in the early stage of requirements analysis. From our experience in building proposed software size models using the data collected from the industry, hardly any relationship type is ternary or higher order. And, most of the ER diagrams do not classify their relationship types into association, aggregation and generalization. The precision of the independent variables depends on the types of extended ER diagram constructed in the requirements modeling and analysis stages in the organization. However, a larger set of independent variables will require a larger set of data for building and evaluating the model.

The steps for building proposed software size models are as follows:

1) Independent variables identification: Based on the type of data model (a class or ER diagram) constructed during requirements modeling and analysis, we identify a set of independent variables that sufficiently characterize the diagram.
2) Data collection: Collect ER diagrams and sizes of source codes (in KLOC) of sufficient data-intensive systems. A larger set of independent variables will require a larger set of data. There are many free tools available for the automated extraction of source code size.
3) Model building and evaluation: There are quite a number of commonly used regression models [16]. Both linear and non-linear models can be considered. The size of source code (in KLOC) and the independent variables identified in the first step form the dependent and the independent variables respectively for the model. Statistical packages (e.g., SAS) should be used for the model building. Ideally, we should have separate data sets for modeling building and evaluation. However, if the data is limited, the same data set may also be used for model building and evaluation. Let n be the number of data points and k be the number of independent variables. Let y_i and $\hat{y}_i$ are the real and the estimate values respectively of a project. Let $\bar{y}$ be the mean of all y_i. The evaluation of model goodness can be done according to the examination of the following parameters:
   - Magnitude of relative error, MRE, and mean magnitude of relative error, MMRE: They are defined as follows:

$$MRE = \left| \frac{y_i - \hat{y}_i}{y} \right| \tag{1}$$

$$MMRE = \frac{1}{n} \sum_{i=1}^{n} MRE_i \tag{2}$$

   If the MMRE is small, then we have a good set of predictions. A usual criterion for accepting a model as good is that the model has a MMRE ≤ 0.25.
   - Prediction at level l – Pred(l) – where l is a percentage: It is defined as the ratio of number of cases in which the estimates are within the l absolute limit of the actual values divided by the total number of cases. A standard criteria for considering a model as acceptable is Pred(0.25) ≥ 0.75.
   - Multiple coefficient of determination, R^2, and adjusted multiple coefficient of determination, R_a^2: These are some usual measures in regression analysis, denoting the percentage of variance accounted for by the independent variables used in the regression equations. They are computed as follows:

$$R^2 = \frac{\textit{Explained}\ \mathrm{var}\,\textit{iablity}}{\textit{Total}\ \mathrm{var}\,\textit{iablity}} = \frac{SS_{yy} - SSE}{SS_{yy}} = 1 - \frac{SSE}{SS_{yy}} \tag{3}$$

   and

$$R_a^2 = 1 - \left[\frac{(n-1)}{n-(k+1)} \right] \left(\frac{SSE}{SS_{yy}} \right) \tag{4}$$

where sum of squared errors $SSE = \sum_{i=1}^{n}(y_i - \hat{y}_i)^2$ and $SS_{yy} = \sum_{i=1}^{n}(y_i - \bar{y})^2$.

In general, the larger the value of R^2 and R_a^2, the better fit of the data. $R^2 = 1$ implies a perfect fit of the model passing through every data point. However, R^2 can only be used as a measure to access the usefulness of the model if the number of data points is substantially more than the number of independent variables.

If the same data set is used for both model building and evaluation, we can further examine the following parameters to evaluate the model goodness:

- Relative root mean squared error, $\overline{RMS}$, is defined as follows [6]:

$$\overline{RMS} = \frac{\sqrt{\frac{SSE}{n-(k+1)}}}{\bar{y}} \tag{5}$$

where $SSE = \sum_{i=1}^{n}(y_i - \hat{y}_i)^2$. A model is considered acceptable if $\overline{RMS} \leq 0.25$.

- Prediction sum of squares, PRESS [16]: PRESS is a measure of how well the use of the fitted values for a subset model can predict the observed responses y_i. The error sum of squares, $SSE = \sum(y_i - \hat{y}_i)^2$, is also such a measure. The PRESS measure differs from SSE in that each fitted value $\hat{y}_i$ for the PRESS is obtained by deleting the i th case from the data set, estimating the regression function for the subset model from the remaining n - 1 cases, and then using the fitted regression function to obtain the predicted $\hat{y}_{i(i)}$ for the ith case. That is, it is defined as follows:

$$PRESS = \sum_{i=1}^{n}(y_i - \hat{y}_{i(i)})^2 \tag{6}$$

Models with smaller PRESS values are considered good candidate models. The PRESS value is always larger than SSE because the regression fit for the i th case is included. A smaller PRESS value supports the validity of the model built.

5 Preliminary Validation

As ER diagrams constructed in most projects in the industry do not classify relationship types into associations, aggregations and generalizations, a complete validation of the proposed method is not possible. We have spent much effort to pursue organizations in the industry to supply us their project data for the validation of the proposed software sizing method. As such, the whole validation took about one and a half year. This section discusses our validation.

Due to the above-mentioned constraint, the independent variables for characterizing an ER diagram in our validation is simplified as follows:

1) Number of entity types (*E*)
2) Number of attributes (*A*)
3) Number of relationship types (*R*)

These variables provide a reasonable and concise characterization of the ER diagram.

Our validation bases on the following linear regression models [14]:

$$Size = \beta_0 + \beta_1 E + \beta_2 R + \beta_3 A \quad (7)$$

where *Size* is the total KLOC (thousand lines of code) of all the source code that is developed based on the ER diagram and β_i ($0 \le i \le 3$) is a coefficient to be determined.

5.1 The Dataset

We collected three datasets from multiple organizations in the industry including software house and end-users such as public organizations and insurance companies. These projects cover a wide range of application domains including freight management, administrative and financial systems. The first dataset comprises 14 projects that were developed using Visual Basic with VB Scripts and SQL. The second dataset comprises 10 projects that were developed using Java with JSP, Java Script and SQL. Table 1 and 2 show the details of the two data sets. The first and second datasets are for the building of software size models for the respective development environments. The third dataset comprises of 8 projects developed using the same Visual Basic development environment as the first dataset. Table 3 shows the details of the third dataset.

5.2 The Resulting Models

From the Visual Basic based project data set (Table 1), the resulting first order model that we built for estimating the size of source code (in KLOC) developed using Visual Basic with VB Script and SQL is as follows:

$$Size = 6.788 - 0.062E + 2.169R - 0.007A \quad (8)$$

Adjusted multiple coefficient of determination R_a^2 for this model is 0.84. The value of R_a^2 is reckoned as good.

From the Java based project data set (Table 2), the resulting first order model that we built for estimating the size of source code (in KLOC) developed using Java with JSP, Java Script and SQL is as follows:

$$Size = 4.678 + 1.218E + 0.028R + 0.023A \quad (9)$$

Adjusted multiple coefficient of determination R_a^2 for this model is 0.99 for this model. The value of R_a^2 is reckoned as very good.

Table 1. The VB based project dataset

Project No.	Actual Size (KLOC)	E	R	A
1	42.1	19	25	314
2	72	36	37	540
3	29.52	16	16	441
4	42.82	38	20	779
5	16.73	6	5	112
6	196.22	64	83	1524
7	67.31	29	11	351
8	52.76	31	24	330
9	46.92	29	24	201
10	37.54	27	8	216
11	14.723	8	6	203
12	24.667	12	10	203
13	30.464	27	23	764
14	109.659	96	63	1471

Table 2. The Java based project dataset

Project No.	Actual Size (KLOC)	E	R	A
1	14.89	7	6	40
2	12.62	6	5	37
3	20.53	10	11	75
4	23.68	16	19	61
5	31.69	19	20	91
6	20.45	11	11	56
7	84.89	49	22	889
8	104.539	64	167	765
9	194.37	125	180	1400
10	19.29	9	8	62

5.3 Model Evaluation

For the first order model that we built for estimating size of source code (in KLOC) developed using Visual Basic with VB Script and SQL, we managed to collect a separate data set for the evaluation of the model. Note that R_a^2 for this model has already been computed during model building and is 0.84, which is reckoned as good. MMRE and Pred (0.25) computed from the evaluation data set are 0.16 and 0.88 respectively. These values fall well within the acceptable level. The detailed results of the evaluation are shown together with the evaluation dataset in Table 3. Therefore, the evaluation results support the validity of the model built.

For the first order model that we built for estimating the size of source code (in KLOC) developed using Java with JSP, Java Script and SQL, we did not manage to collect a separate data set for the evaluation of the model. As such, we used the same data set for the evaluation. Note that R_a^2 for this model has already been computed during model building and is 0.99, which is reckoned as very good. MMRE, Pred (0.25), SSE and PRESS computed from the same data set are 0.07, 1.00, 10.04 and 556.84 respectively. The detailed results of the evaluation is shown in Table 4. Both MMRE and Pred(0.25) fall well within the acceptable level. Although there is a difference between SSE and PRESS, the difference is not too substantial too. Note that $\overline{RMS}$ computed from SSE in this case is 0.02. If we replace SSE by PRESS in the computation of $\overline{RMS}$, then the value of $\overline{RMS}$ is 0.18. Both of these values fall well below the acceptable level 0.25. Therefore, the evaluation results support the validity of the model built.

Table 3. The VB based project evaluation dataset

Project No.	Actual Size (KLOC)	E	R	A	Estimated Size	MRE
1	30	13	12	209	30.547	0.02
2	13.3	5	4	130	14.244	0.07
3	64.33	20	28	553	62.409	0.03
4	59.02	25	32	656	70.054	0.19
5	48.64	16	25	126	59.139	0.22
6	117.03	96	68	1718	136.302	0.16
7	23.58	6	5	157	16.162	0.31
8	43.95	15	13	167	32.886	0.25
MMRE = 0.16, Pred (0.25) = 0.88						

Table 4. The evaluation result of Java based model

Project No.	Actual Size (KLOC)	Estimated Size	MRE
1	14.89	14.292	0.04
2	12.62	12.977	0.03
3	20.53	18.891	0.08
4	23.68	26.101	0.10
5	31.69	30.473	0.04
6	20.45	19.672	0.04
7	84.89	85.423	0.01
8	104.539	104.901	0.00
9	194.37	194.168	0.00
10	17.29	17.29	0.00
MMRE = 0.03, Pred (0.25) = 1.00, SSE = 10.04, PRESS = 556.84			

Though we managed to build only simplified software size models from the proposed approach due to the limitation in the industry practice, the evaluation results have already supported the validity of the models built. As such, our empirical validation supports the validity of the proposed method for building software size models.

6 Comparative Discussion

We have proposed a novel method for building software size models for data-intensive systems. Due to the lack of complete data for validating the proposed method from completed projects in the industry, we only managed to do a validation based on building and evaluating simplified proposed software size models. The statistical evaluation supports the validity of the proposed method.

Due to the above-mentioned simplification and limited size of our dataset, we do not claim that the models built in this paper are ready for use. However, at least, we believe that our work has shown some promise to study the proposed method for software sizing further. Software size estimation is an important key to project estimation, which in turn is vital for project control and management [3], [4], [11]. There is much problem in existing software size estimation methods. As the software estimation community requires totally new datasets for the building and evaluation of software size models built using the proposed method, we call for collaborations between the industry and the research communities to validate the proposed method further and more comprehensively. From the history in establishing of Function Point method, without such effort, it is not likely to succeed in building usable software size model.

As discussed in [15], most of the existing software sizing methods [9], [12], [13], [18] require much implementation information that is not available and is difficult to predict in the early stage of a software project. The information is not even available after the requirements analysis stage. It is only available in the design or implementation stage. For example, Function Point method is based on external inputs, outputs and inquiries, and external logical files and external interface files. Such implementation details are not even available at the end of requirements analysis stage. ER diagram has been well used in the conceptual modeling for developing data-intensive systems. Some proposals for software projects have also included ER diagrams as part of project requirement. As such, ER diagrams are at least practically available after the requirements analysis stage. Once the ER diagram is constructed, the proposed software size model can be applied without much difficulty. Therefore, in the worst case, we can apply the proposed approach after the requirements analysis stage. Ideally, a brief extended ER model should be constructed during the project proposal or planning stage. And, the proposed software size model can be applied to estimate the software size to serve as an input for project effort estimation. Subsequently, when a more accurate extended ER model is available, the model can be reapplied for more accurate project estimation. A final revision of project estimation should be carried out at the end of requirements analysis stage, in which an accurate extended ER diagram should be available.

The well-known Function Point method is also mainly for data-intensive systems. As such, the domain of application for the proposed method for software sizing is similar to that of Function Point method.

Acknowledgement

We would like to thank IPACS E-Solution (S) Pte Ltd, Singapore Computer Systems Pte Ltd, NatSteel Ltd, Great Eastern Life Assurance Co. Limited, JTC Corporation and National Computer Systems Pte Ltd for providing the project data. Without their support, this work would not be possible.

References

1. A.J. Albrecht, and J. E. Gaffney, Jr., "Software function, source lines of code, and development effort prediction: a software science validation," in IEEE Trans. Software Eng., vol. SE-9, no. 6, Nov. 1983, pp. 639-648.
2. P. Armour, "Ten unmyths of project estimation: reconsidering some commonly accepted project management practices," in Comm. ACM 45(11), Nov. 2002, pp. 15-18.
3. B.W. Boehm, and R. E. Fairley, "Software estimation perspectives," in IEEE Software, Nov./Dec. 2000, pp. 22-26.
4. B.W. Boehm et al., Software Cost Estimation with COCOMO II, Prentice Hall, 2000.
5. P.P. Chen, "The entity-relationship model - towards a unified view of data," in ACM Trans. Database Syst. 1(1), Mar. 1976, pp. 9-36.
6. S.D. Conte, H. E. Dunsmore, and V. Y. Shen, Software Engineering Metrics and Models, Benjamin/Cummings, 1986.
7. COSMIC-Full Functions – Release 2.0, September 1999.
8. J.J. Dolado, "A validation of the component-based method for software size estimation," in IEEE Trans. Software Eng., vol. SE-26, no.10, Oct. 2000, pp. 1006-1021.
9. Daniel. V. Ferens, "Software Size Estimation Techniques," Proceedings of the IEEE NAECON 1988 701-705.
10. D. Garmus, and D. Herron, Function Point Analysis: measurement practices for successful software projects, Addison Wesley, 2000.
11. C.F. Kemerer, "An empirical validation of software project cost estimation models," in Comm. ACM 30(5), May 1987, pp. 416-429.
12. R. Lai, and S. J. Huang, "A model for estimating the size of a formal communication protocol application and its implementation," in IEEE Trans. Software Eng., vol. 29, no. 1, pp. 46-62, Jan, 2003.
13. L.A. Laranjeira, "Software Size Estimation of Object-Oriented Systems," in IEEE Trans. Software Eng., vol. 16, no. 5, May 1990, pp. 510-522.
14. J.T. McClave, and T. Sincich, Statistics, 9th Ed, Prentice Hall, 2003.
15. E. Miranda, "An evaluation of the paired comparisons method for software sizing," Proc. Int. Conf. On Software Eng., 2000, pp. 597-604.
16. J. Neter, M. H. Kutner, C. J. Nachtsheim, and W. Wasserman, Applied Linear Regression Models, IRWIN, 1996.
17. T.J. Teorey, D. Yang, and J. P. Fry, "A logical design methodology for relational databases using the extended entity-relationship model," in ACM Computing Surveys 18(2), June, 1986, pp. 197-222.
18. J. Verner, and G. Tate, "A software size model," in IEEE Trans. Software Eng., vol. SE-18, no. 4, Apr. 1992, pp. 265-278.

Data Mapping Diagrams for Data Warehouse Design with UML

Sergio Luján-Mora[1], Panos Vassiliadis[2], and Juan Trujillo[1]

[1] Dept. of Software and Computing Systems
University of Alicante, Spain
{slujan,jtrujillo}@dlsi.ua.es

[2] Dept. of Computer Science
University of Ioannina, Hellas
pvassil@cs.uoi.gr

Abstract. In Data Warehouse (DW) scenarios, ETL (Extraction, Transformation, Loading) processes are responsible for the extraction of data from heterogeneous operational data sources, their transformation (conversion, cleaning, normalization, etc.) and their loading into the DW. In this paper, we present a framework for the design of the DW back-stage (and the respective ETL processes) based on the key observation that this task fundamentally involves dealing with the specificities of information at very low levels of granularity including transformation rules at the attribute level. Specifically, we present a disciplined framework for the modeling of the relationships between sources and targets in different levels of granularity (including coarse mappings at the database and table levels to detailed inter-attribute mappings at the attribute level). In order to accomplish this goal, we extend UML (Unified Modeling Language) to model attributes as first-class citizens. In our attempt to provide complementary views of the design artifacts in different levels of detail, our framework is based on a principled approach in the usage of UML packages, to allow zooming in and out the design of a scenario.

Keywords: data mapping, ETL, data warehouse, UML

1 Introduction

In Data Warehouse (DW) scenarios, ETL (Extraction, Transformation, Loading) processes are responsible for the extraction of data from heterogeneous operational data sources, their transformation (conversion, cleaning, normalization, etc.) and their loading into the DW. DWs are usually populated with data from different and heterogeneous operational data sources such as legacy systems, relational databases, COBOL files, Internet (XML, web logs) and so on. It is well recognized that the design and maintenance of these ETL processes (also called DW back stage) is a key factor of success in DW projects for several reasons, the most prominent of which is their critical mass; in fact, ETL development can take up as much as 80% of the development time in a DW project [1, 2].

Despite the importance of designing the mapping of the data sources to the DW structures along with any necessary constraints and transformations,

P. Atzeni et al. (Eds.): ER 2004, LNCS 3288, pp. 191–204, 2004.

unfortunately, there are few models that can be used by the designers to this end. The front end of the DW has monopolized the research on the conceptual part of DW modeling, while few attempts have been made towards the conceptual modeling of the back stage [3, 4]. Still, to this day, there is no model that can combine (a) the desired detail of modeling data integration at the attribute level and (b) a widely accepted modeling formalism such as the ER model or UML. One particular reason for this, is that both these formalisms are simply not designed for this task; on the contrary, they treat attributes as second-class, weak entities, with a descriptive role. Of particular importance is the problem that in both models attributes cannot serve as an end in an association or any other relationship.

One might argue that the current way of modeling is sufficient and there is no real need to extend it in order to capture mappings and transformations at the attribute level. There are certain reasons that we can list against this argument:

- The design artifacts are acting as blueprints for the subsequent stages of the DW project. If the important details of this design (e.g., attribute interrelationships) are not documented, the blueprint is problematic. Actually, one of the current issues in DW research involves the efficient documentation of the overall process. Since design artifacts are means of communicating ideas, it is best if the formalism adopted is a widely used one (e.g., UML or ER).
- The design should reflect the architecture of the system in a way that is formal, consistent and allows the what-if analysis of subsequent changes. Capturing attributes and their interrelations as *first-class modeling elements* (FCME, also known as first-class citizens) improves the design significantly with respect to all these goals. At the same time, the way this issue is handled now would involve a naive, informal documentation through UML notes.
- In previous lines of research [5], we have shown that by modeling attribute interrelationships, we can treat the design artifact as a graph and actually measure the aforementioned design goals. Again, this would be impossible with the current modeling formalisms.

To address all the aforementioned issues, in this paper, we present an approach that enables the tracing of the DW back-stage (ETL processes) particularities at various levels of detail, through a widely adopted formalism (UML). This is enabled by an additional view of a DW, called the *data mapping diagram*. In this new diagram, we treat attributes as FCME of the model. This gives us the flexibility of defining models at various levels of detail. Naturally, since UML is not initially prepared to support this behavior, we solve this problem thanks to the extension mechanisms that it provides. Specifically, we employ a formal, strict mechanism that maps attributes to proxy classes that represent them. Once mapped to classes, attributes can participate in associations that determine the inter-attribute mappings, along with any necessary transformations and constraints. We adopt UML as our modeling language due to its wide acceptance and the possibility of using various complementary diagrams for modeling different system aspects. Actually, from our point of view, one of the main advantages of the approach presented in this paper is that it is totally integrated in a global approach that allows us to accomplish the conceptual, logical and the corresponding physical design of all DW components by using the same notation ([6–8]).

The rest of the paper is structured as follows. In Section 2, we briefly describe the general framework for our DW design approach and introduce a motivating example that will be followed throughout the paper. In Section 3, we show how attributes can be represented as FCME in UML. In Section 4, we present our approach to model data mappings in ETL processes at the attribute level. In Section 5, we review related work and finally, in Section 6 we present the main conclusions and future work.

2 Framework and Motivation

In this section we discuss our general assumptions around the DW environment to be modelled and briefly give the main terminology. Moreover, we define a motivating example that we will consistently follow through the rest of the paper.

The architecture of a DW is usually depicted as various layers of data in which data from one layer is derived from data of the previous layer [9]. Following this consideration, we consider that the development of a DW can be structured into an integrated framework with five stages and three levels that define different diagrams for the DW model, as explained in Table 1.

Table 1. Data warehouse development framework

- **Phases**: we distinguish five stages in the definition of a DW:
  - Source: it defines the data sources of the DW, such as OLTP systems, external data sources (syndicated data, census data), etc.
  - Integration: it defines the mapping between the data sources and the DW.
  - Data Warehouse: it defines the structure of the DW.
  - Customization: it defines the mapping between the DW and the clients' structures.
  - Client: it defines special structures that are used by the clients to access the DW, such as data marts or OLAP applications.
- **Levels**: each stage can be analyzed at three levels or perspectives:
  - Conceptual: it defines the DW from a conceptual point of view.
  - Logical: it addresses logical aspects of the DW design, such as the definition of the ETL processes.
  - Physical: it defines physical aspects of the DW, such as the storage of the logical structures in different disks, or the configuration of the database servers that support the DW.
- **Diagrams**: each stage or level require different modeling formalisms. Therefore, our approach is composed of 15 diagrams, but the DW designer does not need to define all the diagrams in each DW project. In our approach, we use UML [10] as the modeling language, because its expressive power is sufficient for the modeling of all the diagrams of the framework. But as UML is a general modeling language, we need to use the UML extension mechanisms to adapt UML to specific domains.

In previous works, we have presented some of the diagrams (and the corresponding profiles), such as the *Multidimensional Profile* [6,7] and the *ETL Profile* [4]. In this paper, we introduce the *Data Mapping Profile.*

To motivate our discussion we will introduce a running example where the designer wants to build a DW from the retail system of a company. Naturally, we consider only a small part of the DW, where the target fact table has to contain only the quarterly sales of the products belonging to the computer category, whereas the rest of the products are discarded.

In Fig. 1, we zoom-in the definition of the SCS (Source Conceptual Schema), which represents the sources that feed the DW with data. In this example, the data source is composed of four entities represented as UML classes: Cities, Customers, Orders, and Products. The meaning of the classes and their attributes, as depicted in Fig. 1 is straightforward. The "..." shown in this figure simply indicates that other attributes of these classes exist, but they are not displayed for the sake of simplicity (this use of "..." is not a UML notation).

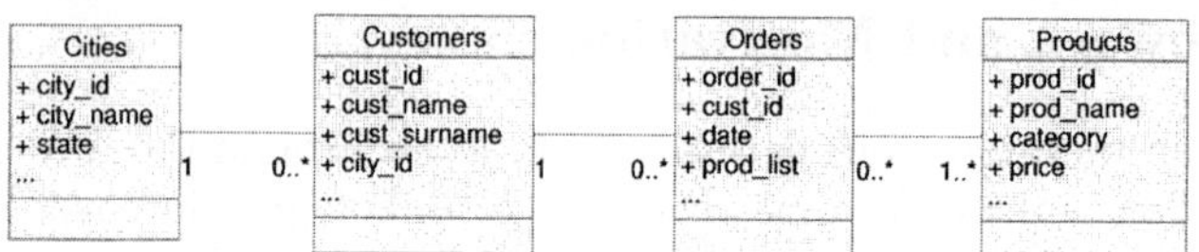

Fig. 1. Source Conceptual Schema (SCS)

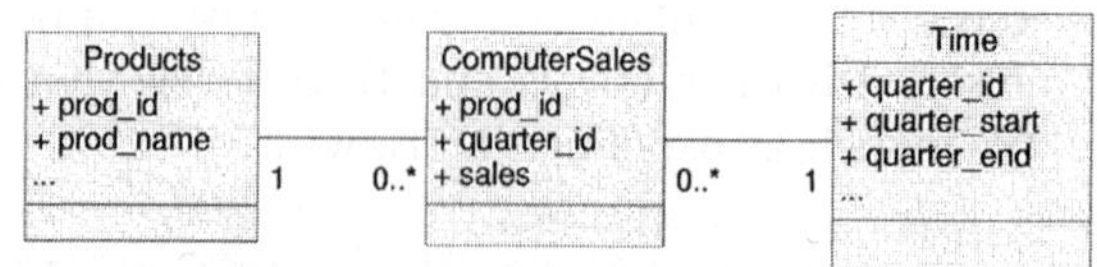

Fig. 2. Data Warehouse Conceptual Schema (DWCS)

Finally, the DWCS (Data Warehouse Conceptual Schema) of our motivating example is shown in Fig. 2. The DW is composed of one fact (ComputerSales) and two dimensions (Products and Time).

In this paper, we present an additional view of a DW, called the *Data Mapping* that shows the relationships between the data sources and the DW and between the DW and the clients' structures. In this new diagram, we need to treat attributes as FCME of the models, since we need to depict their relationships at attribute level. Therefore, we also propose a UML extension to accomplish this goal in this paper. To the best of our knowledge, this is the first proposal of representing attributes as FCME in UML diagrams.

3 Attributes as First-Class Modeling Elements in UML

Both in the Entity-Relationship (ER) model and in UML, attributes are embedded in the definition of their comprising "element" (an entity in the ER or a class in UML), and it is not possible to create a relationship between two attributes. As we have already explained in the introduction, in some situations (e.g., data integration, constraints over attributes, etc.) it is desirable to represent attributes as FCME. Therefore, in this section we will present an extension of UML to accommodate attributes as FCME. We have chosen UML instead of

ER on the grounds of its higher flexibility in terms of employing complementary diagrams for the design of a certain system.

Throughout this paper, we frequently use the term *first-class modeling elements* or *first-class citizens* for elements of our modeling languages. Conceptually, FCME refer to fundamental modeling concepts, on the basis of which our models are built. Technically, FCME involve an identity of their own, and they are possibly governed by integrity constraints (e.g., relationships must have at least two ends refering to classes.). In a UML class diagram, two kinds of modeling elements are treated as FCME. Classes, as abstract representations of real-world entities are naturally found in the center of the modeling effort. Being FCME, classes stand-alone entities also acting as attribute containers. The relationships between classes are captured by associations. Associations can be also FCME, called association classes. Even though an association class is drawn as an association and a class, it is really just a single model element [10]. An association class can contain attributes or can be connected to other classes. However, the same is not possible with attributes.

Naturally, in order to allow attributes to play the same role in certain cases, we propose the representation of attributes as FCME in UML. In our approach, classes and attributes are defined as normally in UML. However, in those cases where it is necessary to treat attributes as FCME, classes are imported to the *attribute/class diagram*, where attributes are automatically represented as classes; in this way, the user only has to define the classes and the attributes once. In the importing process from the class diagram to the attribute/class diagram, we refer to the class that contains the attributes as the *container class* and to the class that represents an attribute as the *attribute class*. In Table 2, we formally define attribute/class diagrams, along with the new stereotypes, ≪Attribute≫ and ≪Contain≫.

4 The Data Mapping Diagram

Once we have introduced the extension mechanism that enables UML to treat attributes as FCME, we can proceed in defining a framework on its usage. In

Table 2. Definitions

Definition 1 *Attribute classes are materializations of the ≪Attribute≫ stereotype, introduced specifically for representing the attributes of a class.* The following constraints apply for the correct definition of an attribute class as a materialization of an ≪Attribute≫ stereotype:

- *Naming convention*: the name of the attribute class is the name of the corresponding container class, followed by a dot and the name of the attribute.
- *No features*: an attribute class can contain neither attributes nor methods.
- *Tag definitions*: an attribute class contains the following tag definitions that represent the properties of an attribute model element (according to the UML Specification [10]): changeability, initialValue, multiplicty, ordering, ownerScope, property-string, stereotype, type, and visibility.

Definition 2 *A contain relationship is a composite aggregation between a container class and its corresponding attribute classes, originated at the end near the container class and highlighted with the ≪Contain≫ stereotype.*

Definition 3 *An attribute/class diagram is a regular UML class diagram extended with ≪Attribute≫ classes and ≪Contain≫ relationships.*

this section, we will introduce the *data mapping diagram*, which is a new kind of diagram, particularly customized for the tracing of the data flow, at various degrees of detail, in a DW environment. Data mapping diagrams are complementary to the typical class and interaction diagrams of UML and focus on the particularities of the data flow and the interconnections of the involved data stores. A special characteristic of data mapping diagrams is that a certain DW scenario is practically described by a set of complementary data mapping diagrams, each defined at a different level of detail. In this section, we will introduce a principled approach to deal with such complementary data mapping diagrams.

To capture the interconnections between design elements, in terms of data, we employ the notion of *mapping*. Broadly speaking, when two design elements (e.g., two tables, or two attributes) share the same piece of information, possibly through some kind of filtering or transformation, this constitutes a semantic relationship between them. In the DW context, this relationship, involves three logical parties: (a) the *provider* entity (schema, table, or attribute), responsible for generating the data to be further propagated, (b) the *consumer*, that receives the data from the provider and (c) their intermediate *matching* that involves the way the mapping is done, along with any transformation and filtering.

Since a data mapping diagram can be very complex, our approach offers the possibility to organize it in different levels thanks to the use of UML packages. Our layered proposal consists of four levels (see Fig. 3), as it is explained in Table 3.

Table 3. Data mapping levels

Database Level (or **Level 0**). In this level, each schema of the DW environment (e.g., data sources at the conceptual level in the SCS, conceptual schema of the DW in the DWCS, etc.) is represented as a package [8]. The mappings among the different schemata are modeled in a single mapping package, encapsulating all the lower-level mappings among different schemata.
Dataflow Level (or **Level 1**). This level describes the data relationship among the individual source tables of the involved schemata towards the respective targets in the DW. Practically, a data mapping diagram at the database level is zoomed-in to a set of more detailed data mapping diagrams, each capturing how a target table is related to source tables in terms of data.
Table Level (or **Level 2**).Whereas the mapping diagram of the dataflow level describes the data relationships among sources and targets using a single package, the data mapping diagram at the table level, details all the intermediate transformations and checks that take place during this flow. Practically, if a data mapping is simple, a single package that represents the data mapping can be used at this level; otherwise, a set of packages is used to segment complex data mappings in sequential steps.
Attribute Level (or **Level 3**). In this level, the data mapping diagram involves the capturing of inter-attribute mappings. Practically, this means that the diagram of the table is zoomed-in and the mapping of provider to consumer attributes is traced, along with any intermediate transformation and cleaning. As we shall describe later, we provide two variants for this level.

At the leftmost part of Fig. 3, a simple relationship among the DWCS and the SCS exists: this is captured by a single Data Mapping package and these three design elements constitute the data mapping diagram of the database level (or Level 0). Assuming that there are three particular tables in the DW that we would like to populate, this particular Data Mapping package abstracts the fact that there are three main scenarios for the population of the DW, one for each of this tables. In the dataflow level (or Level 1) of our framework, the data relationships among the sources and the targets in the context of each of the scenarios, is practically modeled by the respective package. If we zoom in one of these scenarios, e.g., Mapping 1, we can observe its particularities in terms of data transformation and cleaning: the data of Source 1 are transformed in two steps (i.e., they have undergone two different transformations), as shown in Fig. 3. Observe also that there is an Intermediate data store employed, to hold the output of the first transformation (Step 1), before passed on to the second one (Step 2). Finally, at the right lower part of Fig. 3, the way the attributes are mapped to each other for the data stores Source 1 and Intermediate is depicted. Let us point out that in case we are modeling a complex and huge DW, the attribute transformation modelled at level 3 is hidden within a package definition, thereby avoiding the use of cluttered diagrams.

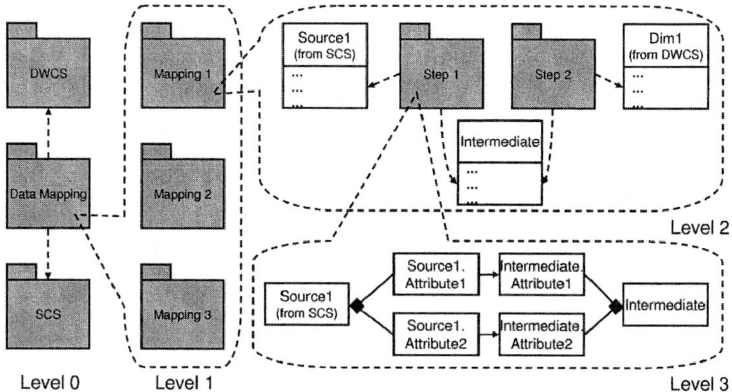

Fig. 3. Data mapping levels

The constructs that we employ for the data mapping diagrams at different levels are as follows:

- The database and dataflow diagrams (Levels 0 and 1) use traditional UML structures for their purpose. Specifically, in these diagrams we employ (a) packages for the modeling of data relationships and (b) simple dependencies among the involved entities. The dependencies state that the mapping packages are dependent upon the changes of the employed data stores.
- The table level (Level 2) diagram extends UML with three stereotypes: (a) ≪Mapping≫, used as a package that encapsulates the data interrelationships among data stores, (b) ≪Input≫ and ≪Output≫ which explain the roles of providers and consumers for the ≪Mapping≫.
- The diagram at the attribute level (Level 3) is also using several newly introduced stereotypes, namely ≪Map≫, ≪MapObj≫, ≪Domain≫, ≪Range≫, ≪Input≫, ≪Output≫, and ≪Intermediate≫ for the definition of data mappings.

We will detail the stereotypes of the table level in the next section and defer the discussion for the stereotypes of the attribute level to subsection 4.2.

4.1 The Data Mapping Diagram at the Table Level

During the integration process from data sources into the DW, source data may undergo a series of transformations, which may vary from simple algebraic operations or aggregations to complex procedures. In our approach, the designer can segment a long and complex transformation process into simple and small parts represented by means of UML packages that are materialization of a ≪Mapping≫ stereotype and contain an attribute/class diagram. Moreover, ≪Mapping≫ packages are linked by ≪Input≫ and ≪Output≫ dependencies that represent the flow of data. During this process, the designer can create *intermediate classes*, represented by the ≪Intermediate≫ stereotype, in order to simplify or clarify the models. These classes represent intermediate storage that may or may not exist actually, but they help to understand the mappings.

In Fig. 4, a schematic representation of a data mapping diagram at the table level is shown. This level specifies data sources and target sources, to which these data are directed. At this level, the classes are represented as usually in UML with the attributes depicted inside the container class. Since all the classes are imported from other packages, the legend (from ...) appears below the name of each class. The mapping diagram is shown as a package decorated with the ≪Mapping≫ stereotype and hides the complexity of the mapping, because a vast number of attributes can be involved in a data mapping. This package presents two kinds of stereotyped dependencies: ≪Input≫ to the data providers (i.e., the data sources) and ≪Output≫ to the data consumers (i.e., the tables of the DW).

4.2 The Data Mapping Diagram at the Attribute Level

As already mentioned, in the attribute level, the diagram includes the relationships between the attributes of the classes involved in a data mapping. At this level, we offer two design variants:

- Compact variant: the relationship between the attributes is represented as an *association*, and the semantic of the mapping is described in a UML *note* attached to the target attribute of the mapping.
- Formal variant: the relationship between the attributes is represented by means of a *mapping object*, and the semantic of the mapping is described in a *tag definition* of the mapping object.

With the first variant, the data mapping diagrams are less cluttered, with less modeling elements, but the data mapping semantics are expressed as UML notes that are simple comments that have no semantic impact. On the other hand, the size of the data mapping diagrams obtained with the second variant is larger, with more modeling elements and relationships, but the semantics are better defined as tag definitions. Due to the lack of space, in this paper we will only focus on the compact variant. In this variant, the relationship between the attributes is represented as an association decorated with the stereotype ≪Map≫, and the semantic of the mapping is described in a UML note attached to the target attribute of the mapping.

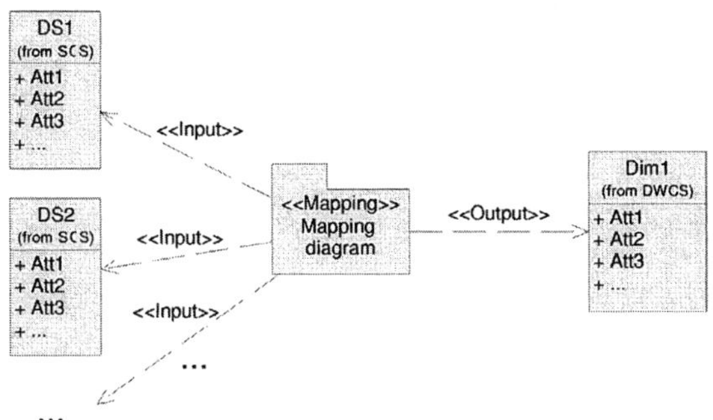

Fig. 4. Level 2 of a data mapping diagram

The content of the package Mapping diagram from Fig. 4 is defined in the following way (recall that Mapping diagram is a ≪Mapping≫ package that contains an attribute/class diagram):

- The classes DS1, DS2, ..., and Dim1 are imported in Mapping diagram.
- The attributes of these classes are suppressed because they are shown as ≪Attribute≫ classes in this package.
- The ≪Attribute≫ classes are connected by means of association relationships and we use the navigability property to specify the flow of data from the data sources to the DW.
- The association relationships are adorned with the stereotype ≪Map≫ to highlight the meaning of this relationship.
- A UML note can be attached to each one of the target attributes to specify how the target attribute is obtained from the source attributes. The language for the expression is a choice of the designer (e.g., a LAV vs. a GAV approach [11] can be equally followed).

4.3 Motivating Example Revisited

From the DW example shown in Fig.s 1 and 2, we define the corresponding data mapping diagram shown in Fig. 5. The goal of this data mapping is to calculate the quarterly sales of the products belonging to the computer category. The result of this transformation is stored in ComputerSales from the DWCS. The transformation process has been segmented in three parts: Dividing, Filtering, and Aggregating; moreover, DividedOrders and FilteredOrders, two ≪Intermediate≫ classes, have been defined.

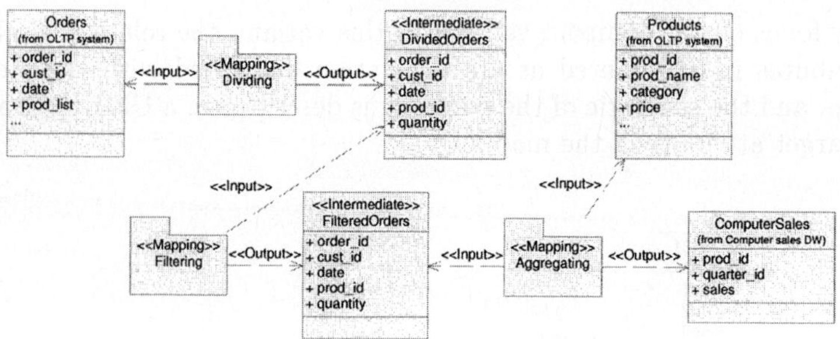

Fig. 5. Level 2 of a data mapping diagram

Following with the data mapping example shown in Fig. 5, attribute prod_list from Orders table contains the list of ordered products with product ID and (parenthesized) quantity for each. Therefore, Dividing splits each input order according to its prod_list into multiple orders, each with a single ordered product (prod_id) and quantity (quantity), as shown in Fig. 6. Note that in a data mapping diagram the designer does not specify the processes, but only the data relationships. We use the one-to-many cardinality in the association relationships between Orders.prod_list and DividedOrders.prod_id and DividedOrders.quantity to indicate that one input order produces multiple output orders. We do not attach any note in this diagram because the data are not transformed, so the mapping is direct.

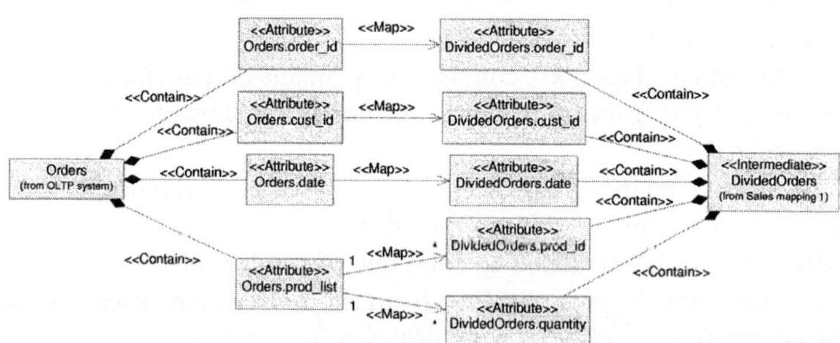

Fig. 6. Dividing Mapping

Filtering (Fig. 7) filters out products not belonging to the computer category. We indicate this action with a UML note attached to the prod_id mapping, because it is supposed that this attribute is going to be used in the filtering process.

Finally, Aggregating (Fig. 8) computes the quarterly sales for each product. We use the many-to-one cardinality to indicate that many input items are needed to calculate a single output item. Moreover, a UML note indicates how the ComputerSales.sales attribute is calculated from FilteredOrders.quantity

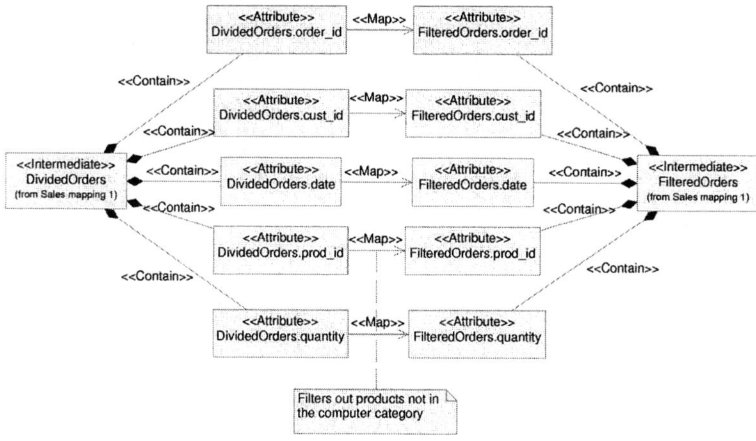

Fig. 7. Filtering Mapping

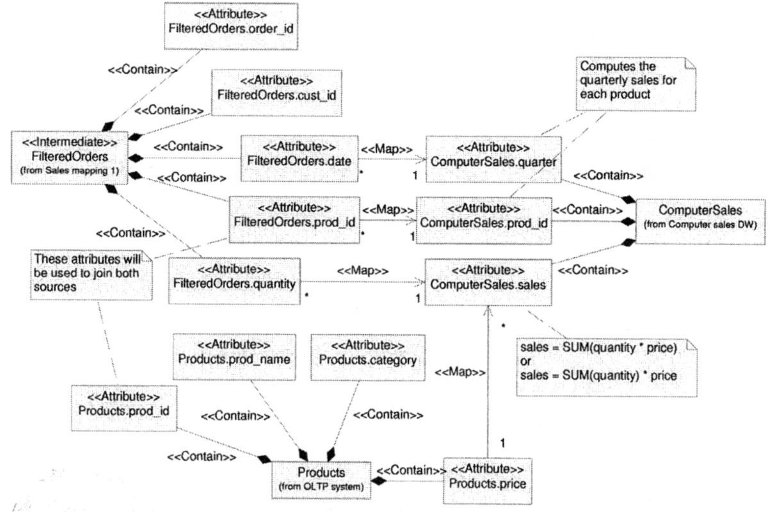

Fig. 8. Aggregating Mapping

and Products.price. The cardinality of the association relationship between Products.price and ComputerSales.sales is one-to-many because the same price is used in different quarters, but to calculate the total sales of a particular product in a quarter we only need one price (we consider that the price of a product never changes along time).

5 Related Work

There is a relatively small body of research efforts around the issue of conceptual modeling of the DW back-stage.

In [12, 13], the *model management*, a framework for supporting meta-data related applications where models and mappings are manipulated is proposed. In [13], two scenarios related to loading DWs are presented as case studies: on the one hand, the mapping between the data sources and the DW, on the other hand, the mapping between the DW and a data mart. In this approach, a mapping is a model that relates the objects (attributes) of two other models; each object in a mapping is called a *mapping object* and has three properties: *domain* and *range*, which point to objects in the source and the target respectively, and *expr*, which is an expression that defines the semantics of that mapping object. This is an isolated approach in which authors propose their own graphical notation for representing data mappings. Therefore, from our point of view, there is a lack of integration with the design of other parts of a DW.

In [3] the authors attempt to provide a first model towards the conceptual modeling of the DW back-stage. The notion of provider mapping among attributes is introduced. In order to avoid the problems caused by the specific nature of ER and UML, the authors adopt a generic approach. The static conceptual model of [3] is complemented in [5] with the logical design of ETL processes as data-centric workflows. ETL processes are modeled as graphs composed of activities that include attributes as FCME. Moreover, different kinds of relationships capture the data flow between the sources and the targets.

Regarding data mapping, in [14] authors discuss issues related to the data mapping in the integration of data. A set of mapping operators is introduced and a classification of possible mapping cases is presented. However, no graphical representation of data mapping scenarios is provided, thereby making difficult using it in real world projects.

The issue of treating attributes as FCME has generated several debates from the beginning of the conceptual modeling field [15]. More recently, some object-oriented modeling approaches such as OSM (Object Oriented System Model) [16] or ORM (Object Role Modeling) [17] reject the use of attributes (*attribute-free models*) mainly because of their inherent instability. In these approaches, attributes are represented with entities (objects) and relationships. Although an ORM diagram can be transformed into a UML diagram, our *data mapping diagram* is coherently integrated in a global approach for the modeling of DW's [6, 7], and particularly, of ETL processes [4]. In this approach, we have used the extension mechanisms provided by UML to adapt it to our particular needs for the modeling of DW's. In this case, we always use formal extensions of the UML for modeling all parts of DWs.

6 Conclusions and Future Work

In this paper, we have presented a framework for the design of the DW back-stage (and the respective ETL processes) based on the key observation that this task fundamentally involves dealing with the specificities of information at very low levels of granularity. Specifically, we have presented a disciplined framework for the modeling of the relationships between sources and targets in different levels of granularity (i.e., from coarse mappings at the database level to detailed inter-attribute mappings at the attribute level). Unfortunately, standard modeling languages like the ER model or UML are fundamentally handicapped in treating low granule entities (i.e., attributes) as FCME. Therefore, in order to formally accomplish the aforementioned goal, we have extended UML to model attributes as FCME. In our attempt to provide complementary views of the design artifacts in different levels of detail, we have based our framework on a principled approach in the usage of UML packages, to allow zooming in and out the design of a scenario.

Although we have developed the representation of attributes as FCME in UML in the context of DW, we believe that our solution can be applied in other application domains as well, e.g., definition of indexes and materialized views in databases, modeling of XML documents, specification of web services, etc. Currently, we are extending our proposal in order to represent attribute constraints such as uniqueness or disjunctive values.

References

1. SQL Power Group: How do I ensure the success of my DW? Internet: http://www.sqlpower.ca/page/dw_best_practices (2002)
2. Strange, K.: ETL Was the Key to this Data Warehouse's Success. Technical Report CS-15-3143, Gartner (2002)
3. Vassiliadis, P., Simitsis, A., Skiadopoulos, S.: Conceptual Modeling for ETL Processes. In: Proc. of 5th Intl. Workshop on Data Warehousing and OLAP (DOLAP 2002), McLean, USA (2002) 14–21
4. Trujillo, J., Luján-Mora, S.: A UML Based Approach for Modeling ETL Processes in Data Warehouses. In: Proc. of the 22nd Intl. Conf. on Conceptual Modeling (ER'03). Volume 2813 of LNCS., Chicago, USA (2003) 307–320
5. Vassiliadis, P., Simitsis, A., Skiadopoulos, S.: Modeling ETL Activities as Graphs. In: Proc. of 4th Intl. Workshop on the Design and Management of Data Warehouses (DMDW'02), Toronto, Canada (2002) 52–61
6. Luján-Mora, S., Trujillo, J., Song, I.: Extending UML for Multidimensional Modeling. In: Proc. of the 5th Intl. Conf. on the Unified Modeling Language (UML'02). Volume 2460 of LNCS., Dresden, Germany (2002) 290–304
7. Luján-Mora, S., Trujillo, J., Song, I.: Multidimensional Modeling with UML Package Diagrams. In: Proc. of the 21st Intl. Conf. on Conceptual Modeling (ER'02). Volume 2503 of LNCS., Tampere, Finland (2002) 199–213
8. Luján-Mora, S., Trujillo, J.: A Comprehensive Method for Data Warehouse Design. In: Proc. of the 5th Intl. Workshop on Design and Management of Data Warehouses (DMDW'03), Berlin, Germany (2003) 1.1–1.14
9. Jarke, M., Lenzerini, M., Vassiliou, Y., Vassiliadis, P.: Fundamentals of Data Warehouses. 2 edn. Springer-Verlag (2003)
10. Object Management Group (OMG): Unified Modeling Language Specification 1.4. Internet: http://www.omg.org/cgi-bin/doc?formal/01-09-67 (2001)
11. Lenzerini, M.: Data Integration: A Theoretical Perspective. In: Proceedings of the Twenty-first ACM SIGACT-SIGMOD-SIGART Symposium on Principles of Database Systems, Madison, Wisconsin, USA (2002) 233–246

12. Bernstein, P., Levy, A., Pottinger, R.: A Vision for Management of Complex Models. Technical Report MSR-TR-2000-53, Microsoft Research (2000)
13. Bernstein, P., Rahm, E.: Data Warehouse Scenarios for Model Management. In: Proc. of the 19th Intl. Conf. on Conceptual Modeling (ER'00). Volume 1920 of LNCS., Salt Lake City, USA (2000) 1–15
14. Dobre, A., Hakimpour, F., Dittrich, K.R.: Operators and Classification for Data Mapping in Semantic Integration. In: Proc. of the 22nd Intl. Conf. on Conceptual Modeling (ER'03). Volume 2813 of LNCS., Chicago, USA (2003) 534–547
15. Falkenberg, E.: Concepts for modelling information. In: Proc. of the IFIP Conference on Modelling in Data Base Management Systems, Amsterdam, Holland (1976) 95–109
16. Embley, D., Kurtz, B., Woodfield, S.: Object-oriented Systems Analysis: A Model-Driven Approach. Prentice-Hall (1992)
17. Halpin, T., Bloesch, A.: Data modeling in UML and ORM: a comparison. Journal of Database Management **10** (1999) 4–13

Informational Scenarios for Data Warehouse Requirements Elicitation

Naveen Prakash[1], Yogesh Singh[2], and Anjana Gosain[2]

[1] JIIT A10, Sector 62, Noida 201307, India
praknav@hotmail.com
[2] USIT, GGSIP University, Kashmere Gate, Delhi 110006, India
ys66@rediffmail.com, anjana_gosain@hotmail.com

Abstract. We propose a requirements elicitation process for a data warehouse (DW) that identifies its information contents. These contents support the set of decisions that can be made. Thus, if the information needed to take every decision is elicited, then the total information determines DW contents. We propose an Informational Scenario as the means to elicit information for a decision. An informational scenario is written for each decision and is a sequence of pairs of the form $< Query, Response >$. A query requests for information necessary to take a decision and the response is the information itself. The set of responses for all decisions identifies DW contents. We show that informational scenarios are merely another sub class of the class of scenarios.

1 Introduction

In the last decade, great interest has been shown in the development of data warehouses (DWs). We can look at data warehouse development at the design, the conceptual, and the requirements engineering levels. Two different approaches for the development of DWs have been proposed at the design level. These are the data-driven [9], and the requirements-driven [2, 12, 8, 19] approaches. Given data needs, these approaches identify the logical structure of the DW.

Jarke et al. [11] propose to add a conceptual layer on top of the logical layer. Whereas they propose the basic notion of the conceptual layer, it is assumed that the conceptual objects represented in the Enterprise Model can be determined but the question of what are useful conceptual objects for a DW and how these are to be determined is not addressed. Thus, the conceptual level does not take into account the larger context in which the DW is to function.

A relationship of the Data Warehouse to the organizational context is established at the requirements level. Fabio Rilson and Jaelson Freire [7] adapt traditional requirements engineering techniques to Data Warehouses. This approach starts with Requirements Management Planning phase, for which the authors propose guidelines concerning acquisition, documentation and control of selected requirements. The second phase talks about a) Requirements Specification, which includes Requirements elicitation through, interviews, workshops,

P. Atzeni et al. (Eds.): ER 2004, LNCS 3288, pp. 205–216, 2004.

prototyping and scenarios, b) Requirements Analysis and c) Requirements Documentation. In third and fourth phases, requirements are conformed and validated respectively.

The proposal of [7] is a "top" level proposal that builds a framework for DW requirements engineering. While providing pointers to RE approaches that may be applicable, this proposal does not establish their feasibility and also does not consider any detailed technical solutions.

Boehnein et al. [3] presents a goal-driven approach that is based on the SOM (Semantic object Model) process modeling technique. It starts with the determination of two kinds of goals- one specifies the product and services to be provided whereas the other determines the extent to which the goal is to be pursued. Information requirements are derived by analyzing business processes in increasing details and by transforming relevant data structures of business processes into data structures of the data warehouse. According to [19], since data warehouse systems are developed to support exclusively decision processes, a detailed business process analysis is not feasible for decision processes because the respective tasks are unique and often not structured. Moreover, sometimes knowledge workers refuse to disclose their process in detail.

The proposal of [14] aims to identify the decisional information to be kept in the Data Warehouse. This process starts with determination of the goals of an organization, uses these to arrive at its decision-making needs, and finally, identifies the information needed for the decisions to be supported. Therefore, the requirements engineering product is a Goal-Decision-Information (GDI) diagram that uses two associations 1) goal-decision coupling, and 2) decision- information coupling respectively. Whereas this proposal relates DW information contents to its decision-making capability as embedded in organizational goals, it is not backed up by a requirement elicitation process.

In this paper, we look at requirement elicitation process for arriving at the GDI diagram. The total process is a two-part one. In the first part, the goal-decision coupling is elicited. That is, the set of decisions that can fulfill the goals of an organization are elicited. Thereafter, in the second part, from elicited decisions, the decision-information coupling can yield decisional information. **Here, we deal with the second part of this process.**

We base our proposal on the notion of scenarios [13, 16, 6, 10, 18]. A scenario has been considered as a typical interaction between a user and the system to be developed. We treat this as the generic notion of a scenario. This is shown in Fig.1 as the root node of the scenario typology hierarchy. We refer to traditional scenarios as transactional scenarios since they reveal the system functionality needed in the new system. We propose a second kind of scenarios called Data Warehouse scenarios. In consonance with our two-part process, for goal-decision coupling we propose decisional scenarios and for decision-information coupling we postulate informational scenarios (see Fig. 1). **As mentioned earlier, our interest in this paper is in informational scenarios.**

Informational scenarios reveal the information contents of a system. An informational scenario represents a typical interaction between a decision-maker

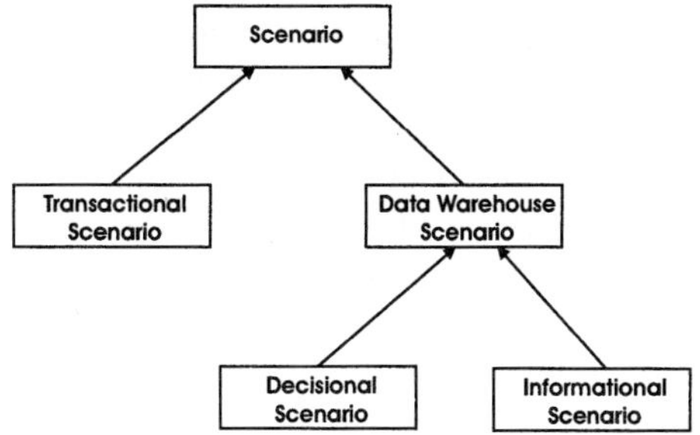

Fig. 1. Scenario Typology.

and the decisional system. This interaction is a sequence of pairs $< Q, R >$, where Q represents the query input to the system by the decision-maker and R represents the response obtained. This response yields the information to be kept in the decisional system, the data warehouse.

In the next section we present the GDI model. In section 3, we define and illustrate informational scenarios. In subsection 3.1, we position them in the 4-dimensional classification system of scenarios. In subsection 3.2, we show elicitation of decisions from an informational scenario. The paper ends with a conclusion.

2 The GDI

The Goal-Decision-information (GDI) model is shown in Fig.2. In accordance with goal-orientation [1, 4], we view a goal as an aim or objective that is to be met. A goal is a passive concept and unlike an activity/process/event it cannot perform or cause any action to be performed. A goal is set, and once so defined it needs an active component to realize it. The active component is decision. Further to fulfil the decisions appropriate information is required.

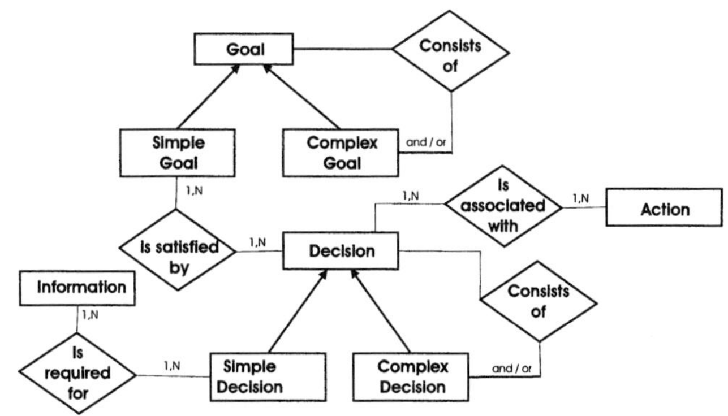

Fig. 2. GDI Diagram.

As shown in Fig.2 a goal can be either simple or complex. A simple goal cannot be decomposed into simpler ones. A complex goal is built out of other goals which may themselves be simple or complex. This makes a goal hierarchy. The component goals of a complex one may be mandatory or optional.

A decision is a specification of an active component that causes goal fulfillment. It is not the active component itself: when a decision is selected for implementation then one or more actions may be performed to give effect to it. **In other words, a decision is the intention to perform the actions that cause its implementation**. Decision-making is an activity that results in the selection of the decision to be implemented It is while performing this activity that information to select the right decision is needed. As shown in Fig.2, a decision can be either simple or complex. A simple decision cannot be decomposed into simpler ones whereas a complex decision is built out of other simple or complex decisions. Fig.2 shows that there is an association '*is satisfied by*' between goals and decisions. This association identifies the decisions which when taken can lead to goal satisfaction.

Knowledge necessary to take decisions is captured in the notion of decisional information shown in Fig.2. This information is a specification of the data that will eventually be stored in the Data Warehouse. Fig.2 shows that there is an association '*is required for*' between decisions and decisional information. This association identifies the decisional information required to take a decision.

An instance of the GDI diagram, the GDI schema is shown in Fig.4. It shows a goal hierarchy (solid lines between '*Maximize profit*' and '*increase the no. of customers*', and '*increase sales*') and a decision hierarchy(solid lines between '*improve the quality of the product*' and '*introduce statistical quality control techniques*' and '*use better quality material*') for a given set of goals and decisions. The figure shows the '*is satisfied by*' relationship between the goal '*increase sales*' and decisions '*open new sales counter*' and '*improve the quality of the product*' by dashed lines. The '*is required for*' relationship between decisions and associated information is shown by dotted lines.

The dynamics of the interaction between goals, decisions and information is shown in Fig. 3. A goal suggests a set of decisions that lead to its satisfaction. A decision can be taken after consulting the information relevant to it and available in the decisional system. In the reverse direction, information helps in selecting a decision, which in turn satisfies a goal.

For example the goal '*increase sales*' suggests the decisions '*improve the quality of the product*' and '*open new sales counter*'. These decisions may modify

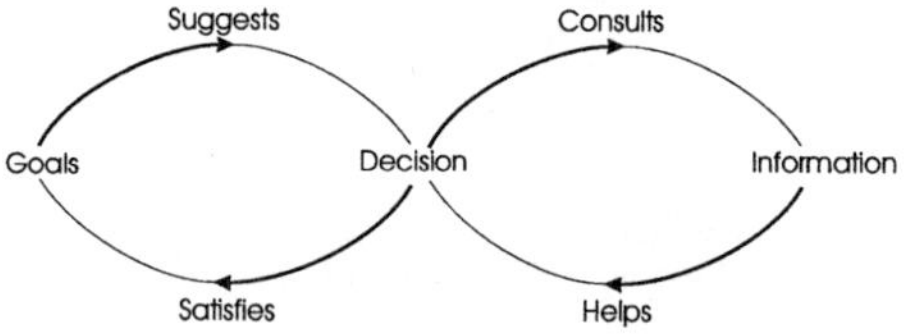

Fig. 3. The Interaction Cycle.

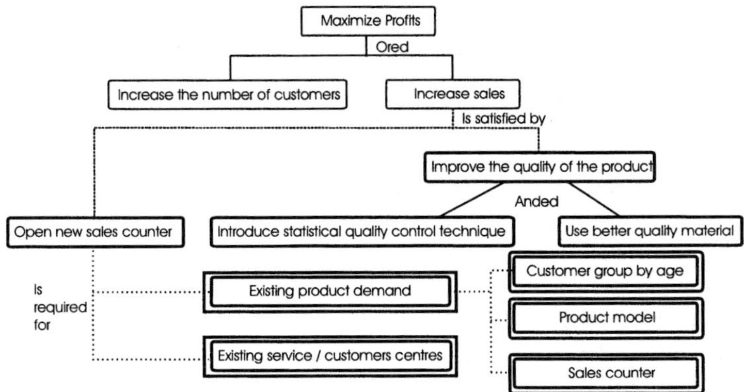

Fig. 4. A GDI Schema.

the goal state. To implement the decision '*open new sales counter*' it consults the information '*Existing product demand*' and '*Existing service/customer centers*'.

3 Informational Scenario

In this section, we show elicitation of decisional information. The decision-information coupling suggests that the information needed to select a decision can be obtained from the knowledge of the decision itself. Thus, if we focus attention on a decision then through a suitable elicitation mechanism, we can obtain the information relevant to it. Our informational scenario is one such elicitation mechanism. It can be seen that the informational scenario is an expression of the '*is required for*' relationship between a simple decision and information of the GDI diagram(see fig.2)

An informational scenario is a typical interaction between the decision-maker and the decisional system. An informational scenario is written for each simple decision of the GDI diagram, and is a sequence of pairs $< Q, R >$, where Q represents the query input to decisional system and R represents the response of the decisional system. An informational scenario is thus of the form

$< Q_1, R_1 >$
$< Q_2, R_2 >$
.
.
.
$< Q_n, R_n >$

The set of queries, Q_1 through Q_n, is an expression of the information relevant to the decision of the scenario. The information contents of the data warehouse can be derived from set of responses R_1 through R_n. We represent query Q_i in SQL and a response R_i is represented as a relation (r_i).

Once a response has been received, it can be used in two ways (a) the relation attributes identify the information type to be maintained in the warehouse, and

(b) the tuple values can suggest the formulation of supplementary queries to elicit additional information. It is possible that, all values in all tuples may be non-null. Therefore, there is full knowledge of the data and a certain supplementary query sequence follows from this. We refer to such a $< Q, R >$ sequence as a normal scenario (see Fig.6). In case a tuple contains a null value then this 'normal' sequence will not be followed and the next query may be formulated to explore the null value more deeply. This results in the breaking of the normal thought process and results in a different sequence of $< Q, R >$. We call this sequence as an exceptional scenario. Fig.5 shows these two types of informational scenarios.

Let us illustrate the notion of normal and exceptional scenarios. Let us be given a decision "*Open new sales counter*". In order to make this decision, the decision maker would like to know the units sold for different products at the various sales counters of each region. After all, a new sales counter makes sense in an area where (a) units sold is so high that existing counters are overloaded or (b) in a region where units sold is very low and this could be merely due to the absence of a sales outlet. So, the first query is formulated to reveal this information:

Q$_1$: How many units of different products have been sold at various sales counters in each region?

This query shows that Region, Sales counter, Product and Number of units sold must be made available in the data warehouse.

```
Select regions, sales counter, product, units sold  From sales, region
```

R$_1$: Let the response be as follows:

Regions	*Sales Counter*	*Product*	*Units Sold*
NR	Null	Radio	Null
NR	Null	TV	Null
SR	Lata	Radio	90
SR	Lata	TV	200
SR	Lata	Fridge	200
SR	Kanika	Radio	Null
SR	Kanika	TV	110
SR	Kanika	Fridge	110
ER	Rubina	Radio	80
ER	Rubina	TV	250
ER	Rubina	Fridge	230
CR	Null	Radio	Null
CR	Null	TV	Null

Let it be that the decision-maker is not interested in exploring '**null**' for the moment. Instead, he wishes to see if unsold stock exists in some large quantity. If so, then the opening of a sales counter might help in clearing unsold stock. So, the decision-maker may asks for the number of units manufactured. If the manufactured quantity is not sold then he may think of opening new sales counter in a particular region. This query and its response is shown in Fig. 7a. This results in the normal scenario $< \mathbf{Q}_1, \mathbf{R}_1 >$, $< \mathbf{Q}_2, \mathbf{R}_2 >$ shown in Fig. 6.

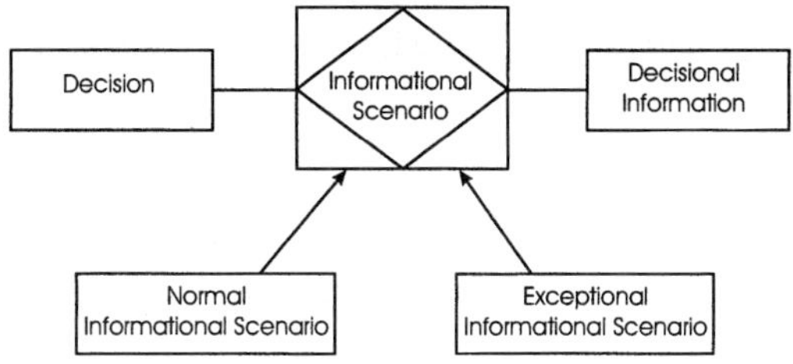

Fig. 5. An Information Scenario.

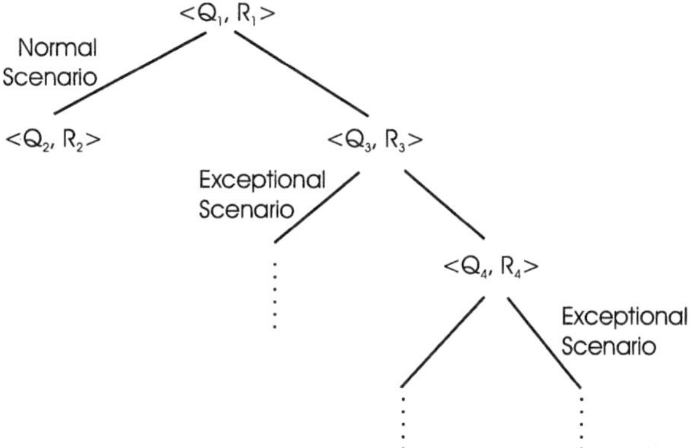

Fig. 6. Normal and Exceptional Scenario.

Suppose that the decision-maker wishes to explore '**null**' values found in sales counter of regions. The reasoning followed is that if there are service centers in the regions NR and CR which are, in fact, servicing a number of company products then there is sufficient demand in these regions. This may call for the opening of sales counters. This query and its response is shown in Fig. 7b. The sequence $< \mathbf{Q}_3, \mathbf{R}_3 >$ and any further $< \mathbf{Q}, \mathbf{R} >$ pairs following from this constitute exceptional scenario shown in fig. 6.

In fig. 7b, if the response $\mathbf{R}_3$ contains null values for service centers for any region, and the decision-maker again wishes to explore 'null' values found in services center of regions. The reasoning followed is that if there are sales counter and no service centers in the region CR then to take the decision open new sales counter in CR, he may ask for the number of sales counter of other companies manufacturing the same products. This query and its response is shown in Fig. 7c. The sequence $< \mathbf{Q}_4, \mathbf{R}_4 >$ and any further $< \mathbf{Q}, \mathbf{R} >$ pairs following from this constitute another exceptional scenario. It also shows that an exceptional scenario can lead to another exceptional scenario and so on.

3.1 Positioning of Informational Scenario

Here we show that an informational scenario is a subclass of the class of in the 4-dimensional scenario classification framework proposed by [17].

Q$_2$: Provide number of units manufactured, number of units sold and product.

```
Select units manufactured, product From  Product
```

R$_2$: Let the response be as follows:

Product	*No. of units manufactured*
TV	700
Radio	700
Fridge	400

Fig.7a

Q$_3$: Provide number of service centers, number of customers in the regions where there are no sales counters.

```
Select count(servicecenter), count(customer)
```

R$_3$: Let the response be as follows:

Regions	*No. of service Centers*	*No. of Customers*
NR	4	100
CR	0	40

Fig.7b

Q$_4$: Provide number of sales counter of different companies manufacturing same product in different regions.

```
Select count(sales counter), company, region
From  manufacturing company
```

R$_4$: Let the response be as follows:

Company	*Region*	*No. of sales counter*
Philips	CR	4
Philips	NR	2
Samsung	CR	3
Samsung	NR	2

Fig.7c

The 4-dimensional framework considers scenarios along four different views, each view allowing to capture a particular relevant aspect of the scenarios. The

Form view deals with the expression mode of a scenario. The Contents view concern the kind of knowledge which is expressed in a scenario. The Purpose view is used to capture the role that a scenario is aiming to play in the requirements engineering process. The Lifecycle view suggests to consider scenarios as artifacts existing and evolving in time through the execution of operations during the requirements engineering process.

A set of facets is associated with each view. Facets are considered as viewpoints suitable to characterize and classify a scenario according to this view. A facet has a metric attached to it. Each facet is measured by a set of relevant attributes. Table 1 shows the views, facets, attributes and possible values of these attributes in the 4-dimensional framework together with attribute values that our informational scenario takes on. Consider the level of formalism attribute of the Form view. This takes on the value Formal because of the use of SQL and relations in the scenario expression. It is possible to express a scenario less formally by using free format. Were such a scenario to exist, its level of Formalism would have the value Informal.

Information scenario proposed by us is also characterized according to these four views.

3.2 Elicitation of Decisions

In this section we show that informational scenarios can help in eliciting decisions as well. These decisions are suggested by an analysis of $< Q, R >$ sequence of the scenario.

Let us consider the decision "*Open new sales counter*" again. Let the decision-maker makes a query as follows:

$\mathbf{Q}_1$: What are the units sold for different products at various sales counters in each region?

$\mathbf{R}_1$: Let the response be as follows:

Regions	*Sales Counter*	*Product*	*Units Sold*
SR	Lata	Radio	30
SR	Lata	TV	100
SR	Lata	Fridge	90
SR	Kanika	Radio	25
SR	Kanika	TV	90
SR	Kanika	Fridge	90
ER	Rubina	Radio	40
ER	Rubina	TV	120
ER	Rubina	Fridge	100

The response shows that number of product units sold for different products is very low. Now the decision-maker may no longer be interested in continuing with the decision "*open new sales counter*" any more. Since number of units sold is low, the decision-maker may now be interested in improving product sales. This leads to the elicitation of new decision '*Improve Product Sales*'. Informational scenario is now written out for this decision.

Table 1. Positioning of Informational Scenario in 4-Dimensional Framework.

View	Facets	Attributes	Possible values	Informational Scenario Values
Form View	1)Description	i)Level of Formalism	a)Informal b)Semiformal c)Formal	Formal
		ii) Medium	a)Text b)Graphics c)Images d)Video e)S/W Prototypes	Text
	2)Presentation	i)Animation	a)Boolean	False
		ii)Interactivity	a)None b)Hypertext (refinement, exploration links, tracebility links) c)Advanced	Refinement
Content View	1)Abstraction	i)Concrete	a)Boolean	True
		ii)Abstract	a)Boolean	False
		iii)Mixed	a)Boolean	False
	2) Context	i)System Internal	a)Boolean	False
		ii)System Interaction	a)Boolean	True
		iii)Organizational context	a)Boolean	False
		iv)Organizational Environment	a)Boolean	False
	3)Argumentation	i)Positions	a)Boolean	True
		ii)Arguments	a)Boolean	False
		iii)Issues	a)Boolean	False
		iv)Decisions	a)Boolean	False
	4) Coverage	i)Functional	Set(Structure, Function, Behaviour)	{ }
		ii)Non-Functional	Set(Performance, Time constraints, etc.)	{ }
		iii)Intentional Aspect	Set(Goal, Problem Cause etc.)	<Decision, Information>
Purpose View	1)Role	i) Descriptive	a)Boolean	True
		ii) Exploratory	a)Boolean	False
		iii)Explanatory	a)Boolean	False
Life Cycle View	1)Life span	i)Life Span	a)Transient Persistent	b)Persistent
	2)Operation	i)Refinement	a)Boolean	False
		ii)Integration	b)Boolean	False
		iii)Expansion	c)Boolean	False
		iv)Delete	d)Boolean	False
		v)Capture	e)From_scratch, By_reuse	From_scratch

Thus it is possible to move in both directions in the decision-information coupling. An informational scenario is written is for a given decision, which may lead to elicitation of other decisions which, leads to informational scenarios.

4 Conclusions

Information Systems/Software Engineering moved from early 'code and fix' approaches through design to requirements engineering. Thus considerable exploration of the problem space is performed before implementation. We can see the same evolution in DW engineering: as mentioned in the Introduction, attempts have been made to introduce the design and conceptual layers. This evolution has the same expectations as before, namely, development systems that better-fit organisation needs and user requirements. Thus, we expect that today's practice where analysts understand DW use after it has been implemented /used will give way to a systematic approach satisfying the various stakeholders. Analysts will understand DW use partly through the argumentation and reasoning process of requirements engineering and partly through the use of the prototyping process model.

Just as traditional scenarios elicit the functional requirements of transactional sys-tems, informational scenarios elicit the informational requirements of decisional sys-tems. Both these belong to general class of scenarios and represent typical interac-tions between the user and the system to be developed. In traditional scenarios the interest is in functional interaction: if the user does this then the system does that. In informational scenarios the interest is in obtaining information and we have an infor-mation seeking interaction: if I ask for this information, what do I get.

Information may be missing or available. Depending upon this the user may for-mulate other information seeking interactions. We have used this to classify scenarios as exceptional or normal. Finally, it is possible that informational scenarios may sug-gest new decisions, thus helping in decision elicitation.

We are working on framing of guidelines for informational scenarios. Future work also concerns decision elicitation by exploiting the goal-decision coupling.

References

1. Anton, A.I. : Goal based requirements analysis. Proceedings of the 2nd International Conference on Requirements Engineering ICRE'96, (1996) 136-144.
2. Ballard, C., Herreman, D., Schau, D., Bell, R., Kim, E., Valencic, A. : Data Modeling Techniques for Data Warehousing, redbooks.ibm.com (1998).
3. Boehnlein, M., Ulbrich vom Ende, A.: Business Process Oriented Development of Data Warehouse Structures. Proceedings of Data Warehousing 2000, Physica Verlag (2000).
4. Bubenko, J., Rolland, C., Loucopoulos, P., De Antonellis, V. : Facilitating 'fuzzy to formal' requirements modelling. IEEE 1st Conference on Requirements Engineering, ICRE'94 (1994) 154–158.

5. Cockburn, A. : Structuring use cases with goals. Technical report. Human and Technology, 7691 Dell Rd, Salt Lake City, UT 84121, HaT.TR.95.1 (1995).
6. Dano, B., Briand, H., Barbier, F.: A use case driven requirements engineering process. Third IEEE International Symposium On Requirements Engineering RE'97, Antapolis, Maryland, IEEE Computer Society Press (1997).
7. Rilson, F., Freire, J.: DWARF: AN Approach for Requirements Definition and Management of Data Warehouse Systems. Proceeding of the 11th IEEE International Requirements Engineering Conference, September 08 - 12 (2003), 1090-1099.
8. Golfarelli, M., Maio, D., Rizzi, S.: Conceptual Design of Data Warehouses from E/R Schemes. Proceedings of the 31 st HICSS, IEEE Press (1998).
9. Inmon, W.H. : Building the Data Warehouse. John Wiley and Sons, (1996).
10. Jacobson, I. : The use case construct in object-oriented software Engineering. In *Scenario-based design: envisioning work and technology in system development*, J. M. Carroll (ed.), John Wiley and Sons, (1995) 309–336.
11. Jarke, M., Jeusfeld, A., Quix, C., Vassiliadis, P.: Architecture and Quality in Data Warehouses. Proceedings 10th CAiSE Conference (1998) 93–113.
12. Poe, V. : Building a Data Warehouse for Decision Support. Prentice Hall (1996).
13. Potts, C., Takahashi, K., Anton, A. I. : Inquiry-based requirements analysis. IEEE Software **11(2)**, (1994) 21-23.
14. Prakash, N., Gosain, A.: Requirements Engineering for Data warehouse Development. Proceedings of CAiSE03 Forum (2003).
15. Bruckner, R. M., List, B. : Developing requirements for data warehouses using use cases. Seventh Americas Conference on Information Systems (2003).
16. Rolland, C., Souveyet, C., Achour, C. B.: Guiding goal modelling using scenarios. IEEE Transactions on Software Engineering, Special Issue on Scenario Management. **24(12)** (1998).
17. Rolland, C., Grosz, G., Kla, R. : A proposal for a scenario classification framework. Journal of Requirements Engineering (RE'98), (1998).
18. Rubin, K. S., Golberg, A.: Object behavior analysis. Communications of the ACM. **35(9)** (1992) 48–62.
19. Winter, R., Strauch, B.: A Method for demand driven information requirements analysis in data warehouse projects. Proceeding of the Hawai International conference on system sciences. January 6-9, (2003).

Extending UML for Designing Secure Data Warehouses

Eduardo Fernández-Medina[1], Juan Trujillo[2], Rodolfo Villarroel[3], and Mario Piattini[1]

[1] Dep. Informática, Univ. Castilla-La Mancha, Spain
{Eduardo.FdezMedina,Mario.Piattini}@uclm.es
[2] Dept. Lenguajes y Sistemas Informáticos, Univ.Alicante, Spain
jtrujillo@dlsi.ua.es
[3] Dept. Comput. e Informática, Univ. Católica del Maule, Chile
rvillarr@spock.ucm.cl

Abstract. Data Warehouses (DW), Multidimensional (MD) Databases, and On-Line Analytical Processing Applications are used as a very powerful mechanism for discovering crucial business information. Considering the extreme importance of the information managed by these kinds of applications, it is essential to specify security measures from early stages of the DW design in the MD modeling process, and enforce them. In the past years, there have been some proposals for representing main MD modeling properties at the conceptual level. Nevertheless, none of these proposals considers security measures as an important element in their models, so they do not allow us to specify confidentiality constraints to be enforced by the applications that will use these MD models. In this paper, we discuss the confidentiality problems regarding DW's and we present an extension of the Unified Modeling Language (UML) that allows us to specify main security aspects in the conceptual MD modeling, thereby allowing us to design secure DW's. Then, we show the benefit of our approach by applying this extension to a case study. Finally, we also sketch how to implement the security aspects considered in our conceptual modeling approach in a commercial DBMS.

Keywords: Secure data warehouses, UML extension, multidimensional modeling, OCL

1 Introduction

Multidimensional (MD) modeling is the foundation of Data Warehouses (DW), MD Databases and On Line Analytical Processing Applications (OLAP). These systems are used as a very powerful mechanism for discovering crucial business information in strategic decision making processes. Considering the extreme importance of the information that a user can discover by using these kinds of applications, it is crucial to specify confidentiality measures in the MD modeling process, and enforce them.

On the other hand, information security is a serious requirement which must be carefully considered, not as an isolated aspect, but as an element presented in all stages of the development lifecycle, from the requirement analysis to implementation and maintenance[4, 6]. To achieve this goal, different ideas for integrating security in the system development process are proposed [2, 8], but they only considered information security from a cryptographic point of view, and without considering database and DW specific issues.

There are some proposals that try to integrate security into conceptual modeling. UMLSec [9], where UML is extended to develop secure systems, is probably the most

P. Atzeni et al. (Eds.): ER 2004, LNCS 3288, pp. 217–230, 2004.

relevant one. This approach is very interesting, but it only deals with information systems (IS) in general, whilst conceptual database and DW design are not considered. A methodology and a set of models have recently been proposed [5] in order to design secure databases to be implemented with Oracle9i Label Security (OLS) [11]. This approach, based on the UML, is important because it considers security aspects in all stages of the development process, from requirement gathering to implementation. Together with the previous methodology, the proposed Object Security Constraint Language (OSCL) [14], based on the Object Constraint Language (OCL) [19] of UML, allows us to specify security constraints in the conceptual and logical database design process, and to implement these constraints in a concrete database management system (DBMS) such as OLS. Nevertheless, the previous methodology and models do not consider the design of secure MD models for DW's.

In the literature, we can find several initiatives to include security in DW [15, 16]. Many of them are focused on interesting aspects related to access control, multilevel security, its applications to federated databases, applications using commercial tools and so on. These initiatives refer to specific aspects that allow us to improve DW security in acquisition, storage, and access aspects. However, neither of them considers the security aspects comprising all stages of the system development cycle nor considers security in the MD conceptual modeling.

Regarding the conceptual modeling of DW's, various approaches have proposed to represent main MD properties at the conceptual level (due to space constraints, we refer the reader to [1] for a detail comparison between the most relevant ones). These proposals provide their own non-standard graphical notations, and none of them has been widely accepted as a standard conceptual model for MD modeling. Recently, another approach [12, 18] has been proposed as an object-oriented conceptual MD modeling approach. This proposal is a profile of the UML [13], which uses its standard extension mechanisms (stereotypes, tagged values and constraints). However, none of these approaches considers security as an important issue in their conceptual models, so they do not solve the problem of security in DW's.

In this paper, we present an extension of the UML (profile) that allows us to represent main security information of data and their constraints in the MD modeling at the conceptual level. The proposed extension is based on the profile presented in [12] for the conceptual MD modeling because it allows us to consider main MD modeling properties as well as it is based on the UML (designers avoid learning a new specific notation or language). We consider the multilevel security model [17], but focusing on considering aspects regarding *read* operations because this is the most common operation for final user applications. This model allows us to classify both information and users into security classes, and enforce the mandatory access control [17]. By using this approach, we are able to implement secure MD models with any commercial DBMS that is able to implement multilevel databases, such as OLS [11] or DB2 Universal Database (UDB) [3].

The remainder of this paper is structured as follows: Section 2 briefly summarizes the conceptual approach for MD modeling in which we based on. Section 3 proposes the new UML extension for secure MD modeling. Section 4 presents a case study and apply our UML extension for secure MD modeling, Section 5 sketches some further implementation issues. Finally, Section 6 presents the main conclusions and introduces immediate our future work.

2 Object-Oriented Multidimensional Modeling

In this section, we outline our approach, based on the UML [12, 18], for DW conceptual modeling. This approach has been specified by means of a UML profile that contains the necessary stereotypes to represent all main features of MD modeling at the conceptual level [7]. In this approach, structural properties are specified by a UML class diagram in which information is organized into facts and dimensions.

Facts and dimensions are represented by means of fact classes and dimension classes respectively. Fact classes are defined as composite classes in shared aggregation relationships of n dimension classes. The *many-to-many* relations between a fact and a specific dimension are specified by means of the multiplicity 1..* on the role of the corresponding dimension class. In our example in Fig. 1, we can see how the *Sales* fact class has a *many-to-many* relationship with the *Product* dimension.

A fact is composed of measures or fact attributes. By default, all measures are considered to be additive. For non-additive measures, additive rules are defined as constrains. Moreover, derived measures can also be explicitly represented (by /) and their derivation rules are placed between braces near the fact class. Our approach also allows the definition of identifying attributes in the fact class (stereotype OID). In this way *degenerated dimensions* can be considered [10], thereby representing other fact features in addition to the measures for analysis. For example, we could store the ticket number (*ticket_number*) as degenerated dimensions, as reflected in Fig. 1.

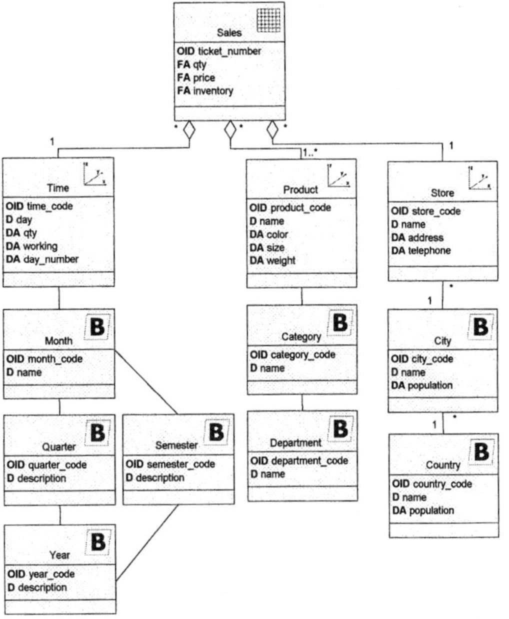

Fig. 1. Multidimensional modeling using the UML

Regarding dimensions, each level of a classification hierarchy is specified by a base class (stereotype Base). An association of base classes specifies the relationship between two levels of a classification hierarchy. These classes must define a Directed Acyclic Graph (DAG) rooted in the dimension class (DAG constraint). The DAG structure can represent both multiple and alternative path hierarchies. Every base class must also contain an identifying attribute (OID) and a descriptor attribute[1] (stereotype D). These attributes are necessary for an automatic generation process into commercial OLAP tools, as these tools store this information on their metadata.

[1] A descriptor attribute will be used as the default label in the data analysis in OLAP tools.

We can also consider non-strict hierarchies (an object at a hierarchy's lower level belongs to more than one higher-level object) and complete hierarchies (all members belong to one higher-class object and that object consists of those members only). These characteristics are specified by means of the multiplicity of the roles of the associations and defining the constraint {completeness} in the target associated class role respectively. See *Store* dimension in Fig. 1 for an example of all kinds of classification hierarchies. Lastly, the categorization of dimensions is considered by means of the generalization / specialization relationships of UML.

3 UML Extension for Secure Multidimensional Modeling

The goal of this UML extension is to allow us to design MD conceptual models, but classifying the information in order to define which properties users must own to be entitled to access the information. Therefore, we have to consider three main stages:

1. Defining precisely the organization of the users that will have access to the MD system. We can define a precise level of granularity considering three ways of organizing the users: Security hierarchy levels (which indicates the clearance level of the user), user Compartments (which indicates a horizontal classification of users), and user Roles (which indicates a hierarchical organization of users according to their roles or responsibilities into the organization).
2. Classifying the information into the MD model. We can define the security information for each element of the model (fact class, dimension class, etc.) by using a tuple composed of a sequence of security levels, a set of user compartments, and a set of user roles. We can also specify security constraints considering this security information. This security information and constraints indicate the security properties that users must own to be able to access the information.
3. Enforcing the mandatory access control (AC). The typical operations executed by final users in this type of systems are query operations. So, the mandatory access control has to be enforced for the *read* operations, whose access control rule is as follows: A user can access to an information only if, a) the security level of the user is greater or equal than the security level of the information, b) all the user compartments that have been defined for the information is owned by the user, and, c) at least one of the user roles defined for the information, is played by the user.

In this paper, we will only focus on the second stage by defining a UML extension that allows us to classify the security elements in a conceptual MD model and to specify security constraints. Furthermore, in Section 5, we sketch a prominent work to deal with the third stage by generating the needed structures in the target DBMS to consider all security aspects represented in the conceptual MD model. Finally, let us point out that the first stage concerns with security policies defined in the organization by managers, and it is out of the scope of this paper.

We define our UML extension for secure conceptual MD modeling following the schema composed of these elements: description, prerequisite extensions, stereotypes/tagged values, well-formedness rules, and comments. For the definition of the stereotypes, we consider an structure that is composed of a name, the base metaclase, the description, the tagged values and a list of constraints defined by means of OCL. For the definition of tagged values, the type of the tagged values, the multiplicity, the description, and the default value are defined.

3.1 Description

This UML extension reuses a set of stereotypes previously defined in [12], and defines new tagged values, stereotypes, and constraints, which enables us to define secure MD models. The 20 tagged values we have defined are applied to certain components that are specially particular to MD modeling, allowing us to represent them in the same model and in the same diagrams that describe the rest of the system. These tagged values will represent the sensitive information for the different elements of the MD modeling (fact class, dimension class, etc.), and they will allow us to specify security constraints depending on this security information and on the value of certain attributes of the model. The stereotypes will help us identify a special class that will define the profile of the system users. A set of inherent constraints are specified in order to define well-formedness rules. The correct use of our extension is assured by the definition of constraints in both natural language and OCL [19].

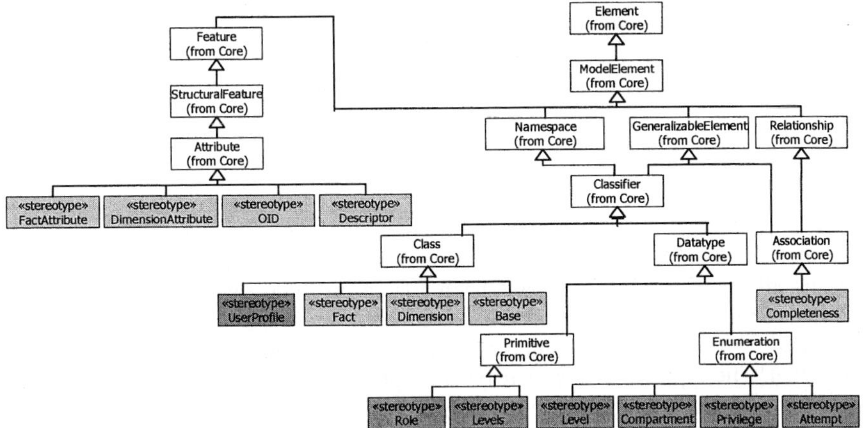

Fig. 2. Extension of the UML with stereotypes

Thus, we have defined 7 new stereotypes: one specializes in the Class model element, two specializes in the Primitive model element and four specialize in the Enumeration model element. In Fig. 2, we have represented portions of the UML metamodel[2] to show where our stereotypes fit. We have only represented the specialization hierarchies, as the most important fact about a stereotype is the base class that the stereotype specializes. In these figures, new stereotypes are colored in a dark grey, whereas stereotypes we reuse from our previous profile [27] are in a light grey and classes from the UML metamodel remain white.

3.2 Prerequisite Extensions

This UML profile reuses stereotypes previously defined in another UML profile [12]. This profile provided the needed stereotypes, tagged values, constraints to accomplish

2 All the metaclasses come from the *Core Package*, a subpackage of the *Foundation Package*. We based our extension on the UML 1.5 as this is the current accepted standard. To the best of our knowledge, the current UML 2.0 is not the final accepted standard yet.

the MD modeling properly, allowing us to represent main MD properties at the conceptual level. To facilitate the comprehension of the UML profile we present and use in this paper, we provide a brief description of the of these stereotypes in Table 1.

Table 1. Stereotype from the UML profile for conceptual MD modeling [12].

Name	Base Class	Description
Fact	Class	Classes of this stereotype represent facts in a MD model
Dimension	Class	Classes of this stereotype represent dimensions in a MD model
Base	Class	Classes of this stereotype represent dimension hierarchy levels in a MD model
OID	Attribute	Attributes of this stereotype represent OID attributes of Facts, Dimensions or Base classes in a MD model
Fact Attributes	Attribute	Attributes of this stereotype represent attributes of Fact classes in a MD model
Descriptor	Attribute	Attributes of this stereotype represent descriptor attributes of Dimension or Base classes in a MD model
Dimension-Attribute	Attribute	Attributes of this stereotype represent attributes of Dimension or Base classes in a MD model
Comple-teness	Association	Associations of this stereotype represent the completeness of an association between a Dimension class and a Base class or between two Base classes

3.3 Datatypes

First of all, we need the definition of some new data types to be used in our tagged values definitions. The type Level (Fig. 3 (a)) will be the ordered enumeration composed by all security levels that have been considered (these values, tipically are unclassified, confidential, secret and top secret, but they colud be different). The type Levels (Fig. 3 (b)) will be an interval of levels composed by a lower level and an upper level. The type Role (Fig. 3 (c)) will represent the hierarchy of user roles that can be defined for the organization. The type Roles is a set of role trees or subtrees. The type Compartment (Fig. 3 (d)) is the enumeration composed by all user compartments that have been considered for the organization. The type compartments is a set of user compartments. The type Privilege (Fig. 3 (e)) will be an ordered enumeration composed by all different privileges that have been considered (these values, typically are read, inserte, delete, update, and all). The type Attempt Fig. 3 (f) wille be an ordered enumeration composed by all different access attempt that have been considered (these values are typically none, all, frustratedAttempt, sucessfullAccess, but they could be different.

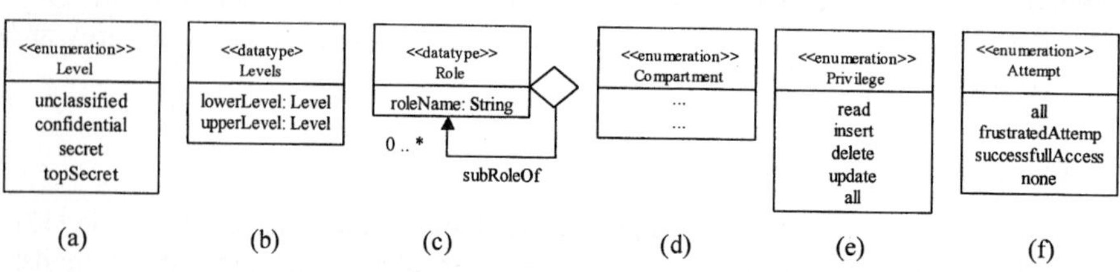

Fig. 3. New Data types

In Fig. 2 we can see the base classes these new stereotypes are specialized from. All the information surrounded in these new stereotypes has to be defined for each

MD model depending on its confidentiality properties, and on the number of users and complexity of the organization in which the MD model will be operative. Finally, we need some syntactic definitions that are not considered in the standard OCL. Particularly, we need the new collection type *Tree* with its typical operations.

3.4 Tagged Values

In this section, we provide the definition of several tagged values for the model, classes, attributes, instances and constraints.

Table 2. Stereotypes of the new data types.

Tagged Values of the Model			
Name	Type	M[a]	Description
classes	Set(OclType)	1..*	It specifies all classes of the model. This new tagged value is useful in order to navigate through all classes of the model
securityLevels	Sequence (Levels)	1..*	It specifies all security levels (ordered from less to more restrictive) that can be used by the model elements
securityRoles	Role	0..*	It specifies the hierarchical role structure that has been definedfor the organization. This type will be managed as a tree
security-Compartments	Set (Compartment)	0..*	It specifies the set of compartments that have been defined for the organization
Tagged Values of the Class			
Name	Type	M	Description
SecurityLevels	Levels	1..*	It specifies the interval of possible security level values, that aninstance of this class can receive. If the upper and lower security levels are the same, all instances will have the same security level. Otherwise, the concrete instance security level will be defined according to a security constraint
SecurityRoles	Set(Role)	0..*	It specifies a set of user roles. Each role is the root of a subtree of the general user role hierarchy defined for the organization. All instances of this class can have the same user roles, or maybe subtrees of the roles that have been defined for the class. A security constraint can decide the user roles for each instance according to the value of some attributes of the instance
Security-Compartments	Set (Compartment)	0..*	It specifies a set of compartments. All instances of this class can have the same user compartments, or a subset of them. A security constraint can decide the user compartments for each instance according to the value of some attribute of the instance
LogType	Attempt	0..1	It specifies whether the access has to be recorded: none, all access, only frustrated accesses, or only successful accesses
LogCond	OCLExpression	0..1	It specifies whether the access has to be recorded
Involved-Classes	Set(OclType)	1..*	It specifies the classes that have to be involved in a query to be enforced in an exception
ExceptSign	{+,-}	0..1	It specifies if an exception permit (+) or deny (-) the access to instances of this class to a user or a group of users
Except-Privilege	Set(Privilege)	1..*	It specifies the privileges the user can receive or remove
ExceptCond	OCLExpression	0..*	It specifies the condition that users have to fulfill to be affectedby this exception

Tagged Values of the Attribute			
Name	Type	M	Description
SecurityLevels	Levels	1..*	Due to space constraints, we do not include the descriptions of the tagged values of attributes as they are similar to their counterpart tagged values of classes.
SecurityRoles	Set(Role)	0..*	
Security-Compartments	Set (Compartment)	0..*	

Table 2. (Continued)

Tagged Values of the Instance			
Name	Type	M[a]	Description
SecurityLevel	Level	1..*	It specifies the security level of an instance
SecurityRoles	Set(Role)	0..*	It specifies a set of user roles for this instance. Each role is a subtree of the user role hierarchy defined for the organization.
Security-Compartments	Set (Compartment)	0..*	It specifies the set compartments for an instance
Tagged Values of the Constraint			
Name	Type	M	Description
Involved-Classes	Set(OCLType)	0..1	It specifies the classes, that are involved in a query, to be enforced in the constraint

[a] M stands for Multiplicity

Table 2 shows the tagged values of all elements in this extension. All default values of security tagged values of the model are empty collections. On the other hand, the default value of security tagged values for each class is the less restrictive (the lower security level, the security role hierarchy that has been defined for the model and the empty set of compartments). The default value of the security tagged values for attributes is inherited from the class they belong.

If we need to specify the situation in which accesses to the information of a class have to be recorded in a log file for future audit, we should use *LogType* and *LogCond* tagged values together in that class. By default, the value of *LogType* is *none*, so audit is not necessary by default. On the other hand, if we need to specify a security constraint, we can use OCL and the *InvolvedClasses* tagged value to specify in which situation the constraint has to be enforced. By default, the value of this tagged value is the class to which the constraint is associated. Finally, if we need to specify a special security constraint in which a user/s (depending on a condition) can or cannot access to the corresponding class, independently of the security information of that class, we should use *exceptions* together with the following tagged values: *InvolvedClasses, ExceptSign, ExceptPrivilege* and *ExceptCond*. The default value of *InvolvedClasses* is the own class. The default value for *ExceptSign* is +, and for *ExceptPrivilege* is Read.

3.5 Stereotypes

By using all these tagged values, we can specify security constraints on a MD model depending on the values of attributes and tagged values. In this extension, we need to define one stereotype in order to specify other types of security constraints (Table 3). The stereotype *UserProfile* can be necessary to specify constraints depending on a particular information of a user or a group of users, e.g., depending on citizenship, age, etc. Then, the previously-defined data types and tagged values will be used on the *fact*, *dimension* and *base* stereotypes in order to consider other security aspects.

3.6 Well-Formedness Rules

We can identify and specify in both natural language and OCL constraints some well-formedness rules. These rules are grouped in Table 4.

Table 3. Stereotype *UserProfile* of our extension.

Name	**UserProfile**
Base class	Class
Description	Classes of this stereotype contain all the properties that the systems manage from users
Constraints	– This class has no associations to another classes Self.AssociationsEnd.size()=0 – There is no more than one class of this type **Context** Model **Inv** self.classes->forAll(oclisTypeOf(UserProfile))->size()<=1 – The name of a class of this stereotype will be *UserProfile* self.className=*UserProfile*
Tagged Values	None
Icon	

Table 4. Well-Formedness constraints.

– Correct value of the tagged values:
The security levels defined for each class of the model (fact, dimension, and base classes) and for each attribute of each class (OID, FactAttribute, Descriptor, and DimensionAttribute) has to belong to the sequence of security levels that has been defined for the model.
context Model **inv** self.classes-> forAll(c | self.securityLevels -> includesAll(subSequence [a] (c.securityLevels.lowerLevel, c.securityLevels.upperLevel)) **inv** self.classes-> forAll(c | c.attributes-> forAll(a | self.securityLevels-> includesAll(subSequence(a.securityLevels.lowerLevel, a.securityLevels.upperLevel)))
The set of user roles defined for each class and attribute of the model has to be a subtree of the roles tree that has been defined for the model.
context Model **inv** self.classes-> forAll(c | c.Roles-> forAll(r | self.Role->includesAll(r))) **inv** self.classes-> forAll(c | c.attributes-> forAll(a | a.Roles-> forAll (r | self.Role-> includesAll(r))))
The set of user compartments defined for each class and attribute of the model has to be a subset of the compartments that have been defined for the model.
context Model **inv** self.classes-> forAll(c | c.Compartments-> forAll(comp | self.Compartments->includes(comp))) **inv** self.classes-> forAll(c | c.attributes-> forAll(a | a.Compartments-> forAll (comp | self.Compartments-> includes(comp))))
– The security information of instances:
The security level of the instance of a class has to be included in the ranking of security levels that has been defined for the class. The same rule is applicable for the instances of attributes.
context Model **inv** self.classes-> forAll(c | c.allInstances -> forAll (i | self.securityLevels-> subSequence(c.securityLevels.lowerLevel, c.securityLevels.upperLevel)-> includes(i.securityLevel)))
The user roles of an instance of a class, has to be subtress of the roles trees that have been defined for the class. The same rule is applicable for the instance of attributes.
context Model **inv** self.classes-> forAll(c | c.allInstances -> forAll (i | c.securityRoles-> includesAll(i.securityRoles)))
The user compartments of an instance of a class, has to be a subset of the compartments that have been defined for the class. The same rule is applicable for the instance of attributes.
context Model **inv** self.classes-> forAll(c | c.allInstances -> forAll (i | i.securityCompartments-> includesAll(i.securityCompartments)))
– Relationship between the security information of classes and its attributes:
The security levels defined for an attribute have to be equal or more restricted that the security levels defined for its class. The same rule is applicable for the role hierarchies and user compartments.
context Model **inv** self.classes-> forAll(c | c.attributes-> forAll(a | self.securityLevels-> subSequence(c.securityLevels.lowerLevel, a.securityLevels.upperLevel)-> includesAll(self.securityLevels-> subSequence(a.securityLevels.lowerLevel,a.securityLevels.upperLevel))) **inv** self.classes-> forAll(c | c.attributes-> forAll (a | c.securityRoles-> includesAll(a.securityRoles))) **inv** self.classes-> forAll (c | c.attributes-> forAll (a | c.securityCompartments-> includesAll(a.securityCompartments)))

[a] The type of the arguments of *subSequence* collection is integer, but for the sake of readability, we consider that the arguments can be elements of the subSequence. The correct expression should be subSequence(self.securityLevels->indexOf(c.securityLevels.lowerLevel),self.securityLevels ->indexOf (c.securityLevels.upperLevel). We consider this simplification in all uses of *subSequence* operation.

Table 4. (Continued)

– Categorization of dimensions:
When a dimension class is specialized in several base classes, the security levels of the subclasses have to be equal or more restrictive that the security levels of the superclass. The same rule is applicable for role hierarchies and user compartments.
context Model **inv** self.classes-> forAll(c | c.subClasses-> forAll(s | self.securityLevels-> subSequence(c.securityLevels.lowerLevel, s.securityLevels.upperLevel)-> includesAll(self.securityLevels-> subSequence (s.securityLevels.lowerLevel,s.securityLevels.upperLevel)) **inv** self.classes-> forAll(c | c.subClasses-> forAll (s | c.securityRoles-> includesAll(s.securityRoles)) **inv** self.classes-> forAll (c | c.subClasses-> forAll (s | c.securityCompartments-> includesAll(s.securityCompartments)))
– Classification hierarchies. As a general rule, we can consider that the more specific the information is, the more restricted its access is:
If the class A has a 1..* association with the class B, means that information of A groups information of B, so B is more specific than A. The security level defined for the class B has to be more restrictive than the security level defined for the class A. This rule is also applicable for user roles and compartments.
context Model **inv** self.classes-> forAll(c | c.associationEnd-> forAll (a | c.a.multiplicity>1 implies self.securityLevels-> subsequence(c.securityLevels.lowerLevel, a.securityLevels.upperLevel)-> includesAll(self.securityLevels-> subSequence(a.securityLevels.lowerLevel, a.securityLevels.upperLevel)) **inv** self.classes-> forAll(c | c.associationEnd-> forAll (a | c.a.multiplicity>1 implies c.securityRoles-> includesAll(a.securityRoles)) **inv** self.classes-> forAll(c | c.associationEnd-> forAll (a | c.a.multiplicity>1 implies c-securityCompartments-> includesAll (a.securityCompartments)))
If the class A has a *..* association with the class B, the designer has to decide which class contains the most specific information. This well-formedness rule cannot be specified because it depends of design decisions.
– Derived attributes:
The security levels of a derived attribute have to be equal or more restricted than the attributes which it is based on. The same rule is applicable for user roles and compartments. By default, the derived attributed inherit the security information of the attribute it is based on.
context Model **inv** self.classes-> forAll(c | c.attributes -> forAll(a | a.derived implies a.derivedFrom-> forAll (d | self.securityLevels-> subsequence(a.securityLevels.lowerLevel, d.securityLevels.upperLevel)-> includesAll(self.securityLevels-> subSequence(d.securityLevels.lowerLevel, d.securityLevels.upperLevel)) **inv** self.classes-> forAll(c | c.attributes -> forAll(a | a.derived implies a.derivedFrom-> forAll (d | d.securityRoles -> includesAll (a.securityRoles) **inv** self.classes-> forAll(c | c.attributes -> forAll(a | a.derived implies a.derivedFrom-> forAll (d | d.securityCompartments -> includesAll (a.securityCompartments)
– Combination of dimensions:
A query on the fact class has to consider the security information that has been defined for that class.
A query that involves the combination of a dimension class (or maybe a base class) and a fact class has to consider the combination of the security information on the dimension (or base) class and on the fact class. The security levels of the combination will be the most restrictive from the security levels of the dimension (or base) class and the fact class. The same rule is applicable for the user roles and compartments.
A query that involves the combination of several dimension classes, and the fact class, has to consider the combination of the security information of all classes. The security levels of the combination will be the most restrictive one from the security levels of all classes. The same rule is applicable for the user roles and compartments.

3.7 Comments

Many of the previous constraints are very intuitive, although we have to ensure its fulfillment, otherwise the system can be inconsistent. Moreover, the designer can specify security constraints with OCL. If the security information of a class or an attribute depends on the value of an instance attribute, it can be specified as an OCL expression (Fig. 4). Normally, security constraints defined for stereotypes of classes (fact, dimension and base) will be defined by using a UML note attached to the corresponding class instance. We do not impose any restriction on the content of these notes in order to allow the designer the greatest flexibility, only those imposed by the tagged values definitions. The connection between a note and the element it applies to is shown by a dashed line without an arrowhead as this is not a dependency [13].

4 A Case Study Applying Our Extension for Secure MD Modeling

In this section, we apply our extension to the conceptual design of a secure DW in the context of a reduced health-care system. The simplified hierarchy of the system user roles is as follows: *HospitalEmployees* are classified into *health* and *non-health* users, *health* users can be *Doctors* or *Nurses* and *non-health* users can be *Maintenance* or *Administrative*. The defined security levels are *unclassified*, *secret* and *topSecret*.

1. Fig. 4 shows an MD model that includes a fact class (*Admission*), two dimensions (*Diagnosis* and *Patient*), two base classes (*Diagnosis_group* and *City*), and a class (*UserProfile*). *UserProfile* class (stereotype *UserProfile*) contains the information of all users who will have access to this MD model. *Admission* fact class - stereotype *Fact*- contains all individual admissions of patients in one or more hospitals, and can be accessed by all users who have *secret* or *top secret* security levels -tagged value *SecurityLevels (SL) of classes*-, and play *health* or *administrative* roles -tagged value *SecurityRoles (SR) of classes*-. Note that the *cost* attribute can only be accessed by users who play *administrative* role -tagged value *SR of attributes*- *Patient* dimension contains the information of hospital patients, and can be accessed by all users who have *secret* security level –tagged value *SL*-, and play *health* or *administrative* roles –tagged value *SR*-. The *Address* attribute can only be accessed by users who play *administrative* role –tagged value *SR* of attributes-. *City* base class contains the information of cities, and it allows us to group patients by cities. Cities can be accessed by all users who have *confidential* security level – tagged value *SL*-. *Diagnosis* dimension contains the information of each diagnosis, and can be accessed by users who play *health* role –tagged value *SR*-, and have *secret* security level –tagged value *SL*-. Finally, *Diagnosis_group* contains a set of general groups of diagnosis. Diagnosis groups can be accessed by all users who have *confidential* security level –tagged value SLs-.

Several security constraints have been specified by using the previously defined constraints, stereotypes and tagged values (the number of each numbered paragraph corresponds to the number of each note in Fig. 4):

2. The security level of each instance of *Admission* is defined by a security constraint specified in the model. If the value of the *description* attribute of the *Diagnosis_group* which belongs to the *diagnosis* that is related to the *Admission* is *cancer* or *AID*, the security level –tagged value *SL*- of this admission will be *top secret*, otherwise *secret*. This constraint is only applied if the user makes a query whose the information comes from the *Diagnosis* dimension or *Diagnosis_ group* base classes together with the *Patient* dimension –tagged value *involvedClasses*-.
3. The security level –tagged value *SL*- of each instance of *Admission* can also depend on the value of the *cost* attribute, which indicates the price of the admission service. In this case, the constraint is only applicable for queries that contain information of the *Patient* dimension –tagged value *involvedClasses*-.
4. The tagged value *logType* has been defined for the *Admission* class, specifying the value *frustratedAttempts*. This tagged value specifies that the system has to record, for future audit, the situation in which a user tries to access to information of this fact class, and the system denies it because of lack of permissions.

5. For confidentiality reasons, we could deny access to admission information to users whose working area is different than the area of a particular admission instance. This is specified by another exception in *Admission* fact class, considering tagged values *involvedClasses, exceptSign* and *exceptCond.*

If patients are special users of the system, they could access to their own information as patients (e.g., for querying their personal data). This constraint is specified by using the *excepSign* and *exceptCond* tagged values in the *Patient* class.

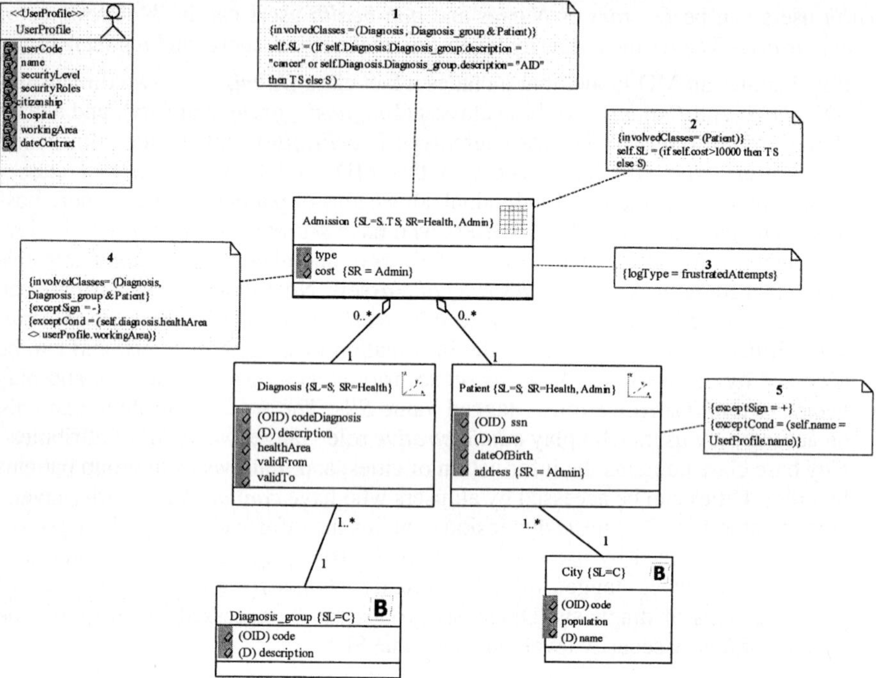

Fig. 4. Example of multidimensional model with security information and constraints[3]

5 Implementation

Oracle*9i* Label Security [11] allows us to implement multilevel databases. It defines labels that are assigned to the rows and users of a database that contain confidentiality information and authorization information for rows and users respectively. Moreover, OLS allows us to specify labeling functions and predicates that are triggered when an operation is executed, and which define the value of security labels.

A secure MD model can be implemented by OLS. The two main security elements that we include in this UML extension are confidentiality information of data, and security constraints. The basic concepts of a MD model (facts, dimension and base classes) are implemented as tables in a relational database. The security information

[3] Version 2 of OCL considers a special syntaxis for enumerations (EnumTypeName::Enum Literal-Value), but in this example, for the sake of readability, we consider only EnumLiteralValue.

of the MD model can be implemented by the security labels of OLS, and the security constraints can be implemented by labeling functions and predicates of OLS.

For instance, we could consider the table *Admission* with *CodeAdmission, Type, Cost, CodeDiagnosis* and *PatientSSN* columns. This table will have a special column to store the security label for each instance. For each instance, this label will contain the security information that has been specified in Fig. 4 (Security *Level=Secret.. TopSecret; SecurityRoles=Health, Admin*). But this security information depends on several security constraints that can be implemented by labeling functions. Table 5 (1) shows an example in which we implement the security constraints labeled with number 2 in Fig. 4. If the value of *Cost* column is greater than 10000 then the security label will be composed of *TopSecret* security level and *Health* and *Admin* user roles, else the security label will be composed of *Secret* security level and the same user roles. Table 5 (2) shows how to link this labeling function with *Admission* table.

Table 5. Example of labeling function in OLS.

```
(1) CREATE FUNCTION Which_Cost (Cost: Integer) Return LBACSYS.LBAC_LABEL
    As MyLabel varchar2(80);
    Begin
       If Cost>10000 then MyLabel := 'TS::Health,Admin'; else MyLabel := 'S::Health,Admin'; end if;
       Return TO_LBAC_DATA_LABEL('MyPolicy', MyLabel);
    End;
(2) APPLY_TABLE_POLICY ('MyPolicy', 'Admission', 'Scheme',, 'Which_Cost')
```

6 Conclusions and Future Work

In this paper, we have presented an extension of the UML that allows us to represent main security aspects in the conceptual modeling of Data Warehouses. This extension contains the needed stereotypes, tagged values and constraints for a complete and powerful secure MD modeling. These new elements allow us to specify security aspects such as security levels on data, compartments and user roles on the main elements of a MD modeling such as facts, dimensions and classification hierarchies. We have used the OCL to specify the constraints attached to these new defined elements, thereby avoiding an arbitrary use of them. We have also sketched how to implement a secure MD model designed with our approach in a commercial DBMS. The main relevant advantage of this approach is that it uses the UML, a widely-accepted object-oriented modeling language, which saves developers from learning a new model and its corresponding notations for specific MD modeling. Furthermore, the UML allows us to represent some MD properties that are hardly considered by other conceptual MD proposals.

Our immediate future work is to extend the implementation issues presented in this paper to allow us to use the considered security aspects when querying a MD model from OLAP tools. Moreover, we also plan to extend the set of privileges considered in this paper to allow us to specify security aspects in the ETL processes for DWs.

Acknowledgements

This research is part of the CALIPO and RETISTIC projects, supported by the Dirección General de Investigación of the Ministerio de Ciencia y Tecnología.

References

1. Abelló, A., Samos, J., and Saltor, F., *A Framework for the Classification and Description of Multidimensional Data Models.* 12th International Conference on Database and Expert Systems Aplications. LNCS 2113., 2001: pp. 668-677.
2. Chung, L., Nixon, B., Yu, E., and Mylopoulos, J., *Non-functional requirements in software engineering.* 2000, Boston/Dordrecht/London: Kluwer Academic Publishers.
3. Cota, S., *For Certain Eyes Only.* DB2 Magazine, 2004. **9**(1): pp. 40-45.
4. Devanbu, P. and Stubblebine, S., *Software engineering for security: a roadmap*, in *The Future of Software Engineering*, Finkelstein, A., Editor. 2000, ACM Press. pp. 227-239.
5. Fernández-Medina, E. and Piattini, M., *Designing Secure Database for OLS*, in *Database and Expert Systems Applications: 14th International Conference (DEXA 2003)*, Marik, V., Retschitzegger, W., and Stepankova, O., Editors. 2003, Springer. LNCS 2736: Prague, Czech Republic. pp. 886-895.
6. Ferrari, E. and Thuraisingham, B., *Secure Database Systems*, in *Advanced Databases: Technology Design*, Piattini, M. and Díaz, O., Editors. 2000, Artech House: London.
7. Gogolla, M. and Henderson-Sellers, B. *Analysis of UML Stereotypes within the UML Metamodel.* in UML'02. Springer, LNCS 2460. pp. 84-99. Dresden, Germany.
8. Hall, A. and Chapman, R., *Correctness by Construction: Developing a Commercial Secure System.* IEEE Software, 2002. **19**(1): pp. 18-25.
9. Jürjens, J., *UMLsec: Extending UML for secure systems development*, in *UML'02* Springer. LNCS 2460.: Dresden, Germany. pp. 412-425.
10. Kimball, R., *The data warehousing toolkit. 2 edn.* 1996: John Wiley.
11. Levinger, J., *Oracle label security. Administrator's guide. Release 2 (9.2).* 2002: http://www.csis.gvsu.edu/GeneralInfo/Oracle/network.920/a96578.pdf.
12. Luján-Mora, S., Trujillo, J., and Song, I.Y. *Extending the UML for Multidimensional Modeling.* in *UML'02.* Springer, LNCS 2460. pp. 290-304. Dresden, Germany.
13. OMG, *Object Management Group: Unified Modeling Language Specification 1.5.* 2004.
14. Piattini, M. and Fernández-Medina, E. *Specification of Security Constraint in UML.* in *35th Annual 2001 IEEE Intl. Carnahan Conf.on Security Technology.* London pp. 163-171
15. Priebe, T. and Pernul, G. *Towards OLAP Security Design - Survey and Research Issues.* in *3rd ACM International Workshop on Data Warehousing and OLAP (DOLAP'00).* Washington DC, USA. pp. 33-40
16. Rosenthal, A. and Sciore, E. *View Security as the Basic for Data Warehouse Security.* in *2nd International Workshop on Design and Management of Data Warehouse (DMDW'00).* Sweden. pp. 8.1-8.8
17. Samarati, P. and De Capitani di Vimercati, S., *Access control: Policies, models, and mechanisms*, in *Foundations of Security Analysis and Design*, Focardi, R. and Gorrieri, R., Editors. 2000, Springer: Bertinoro, Italy. pp. 137-196.
18. Trujillo, J., Palomar, M., Gómez, J., and Song, I.Y., *Designing Data Warehouses with OO Conceptual Models.* IEEE Computer, special issue on DWs, 2001(34): pp. 66-75.
19. Warmer, J. and Kleppe, A., *The Object Constraint Language Second Edition. Getting Your Models Ready for MDA.* 2003: Addison Wesley.

Data Integration with Preferences Among Sources*

Gianluigi Greco[1] and Domenico Lembo[2]

[1] Dip. di Matematica, Università della Calabria, Italy
ggreco@mat.unical.it

[2] Dip. di Informatica e Sistemistica, Università di Roma "La Sapienza", Italy
lembo@dis.uniroma1.it

Abstract. Data integration systems represent today a key technological infrastructure for managing the enormous amount of information even more and more distributed over many data sources, often stored in different heterogeneous formats. Several different approaches providing transparent access to the data by means of suitable query answering strategies have been proposed in the literature. These approaches often assume that all the sources have the same level of reliability and that there is no need for preferring values "extracted" from a given source. This is mainly due to the difficulties of properly translating and reformulating source preferences in terms of properties expressed over the global view supplied by the data integration system. Nonetheless preferences are very important auxiliary information that can be profitably exploited for refining the way in which integration is carried out. In this paper we tackle the above difficulties and we propose a formal framework for both specifying and reasoning with preferences among the sources. The semantics of the system is restated in terms of preferred answers to user queries, and the computational complexity of identifying these answers is investigated as well.

1 Introduction

The enormous amount of information even more and more distributed over many data sources, often stored in different heterogeneous formats, had boosted in recent years the interest for data integration systems. Roughly speaking, a data integration system offers transparent access to the data by providing users with the so-called global schema, which they can query in order to extract data relevant for their aims. Then, the system is in charge of accessing each source separately, and combining local results into the global answer. The means that the system exploit to answer users' queries is the mapping specifying the relationship between the sources and the global schema [16].

However, data at the sources, may result mutually inconsistent, because of the presence of integrity constraints specified on the global schema in order to

* This work has been partially be supported by the European Commission FET Programme Project IST-2002-33570 INFOMIX.

P. Atzeni et al. (Eds.): ER 2004, LNCS 3288, pp. 231–244, 2004.

enhance its expressiveness. To remedy this problem, several papers (see, e.g., [3, 6, 4, 11]) proposed to handle the inconsistency by suitably "repairing" retrieved data. Basically, such papers extend to data integration systems previous studies focused on a single inconsistent database or on the merging of mutually inconsistent databases in a single consistent theory [2, 14, 17]. Intuitively, one aspect deserving particular care, which characterizes the inconsistency problem in data integration with respect to the latter works, is the presence of the mapping relating data stored at the sources with the elements of the (virtual) global schema, over which constraints of interest for the integration application are issued.

Here, the suitability of a possible repair depends on the underlying semantic assumptions which are adopted for the mapping and on the type of constraints on the global schema. Roughly speaking, the assumptions for the mapping provide the means for interpreting data at the sources with respect to the intended extension of the global schema. In this respect, mappings are in general considered sound, i.e., data that it is possible to retrieve from the sources through the mapping are assumed to be a subset of the intended data of the corresponding global elements [16]. This is for example the mapping interpretation adopted in [3, 6, 4], where soundness is exploited for constructing those database extensions for the global schema that are enforced by the data stored at the sources and the mapping. Since obtained global databases may result inconsistent with respect to global constraints, suitable repairs (basically deletions and additions of tuples) are performed to restore consistency.

None of the above mentioned works takes into account preference criteria when trying to solve inconsistencies among data sources. We could say that they implicitly assume that all the sources have the same level of reliability, and that there is no reason for preferring values coming from a source with respect to data retrieved from another source. On the other hand, in practical applications it often happens that some sources are known to be more reliable than others, thus determining some potentially useful criteria exploitable to establish the suitability of a repair. In other words, besides the semantic assumption on the mapping, also preference criteria expressed among sources should be taken into account when solving inconsistency.

Despite the wide interest in this field, few efforts have been paid for enriching the data integration setting with qualitative or quantitative descriptions of the sources. The first (and almost isolated) attempt is in [18], where the authors introduce two parameters for characterizing each source: the *soundness*, which is used for assessing the confidence we can place in the answers provided by the source, and the *completeness*, which is used for measuring how many relevant information is stored in the source. However, the framework proposed does not fit the requirements of typical data integration systems, since it does not admit constraints over the global schema, and since it is only focused on the consistency problem, i.e., determining whether a global database exists that is consistent with all the claims of soundness and completeness of individual sources.

Other works (see, e.g., [14, 10, 15]) deal instead with special cases, where preferences are defined among repairs of a single database, and, hence, they do not capture the many facets of the data integration setting. In other words, such approaches do not tackle inconsistency in the presence of a mapping between the database schema, that has to be maintained consistent, and information sources that provide possibly inconsistent data. This is instead the challenging setting when tackling inconsistency in data integration in the presence of source preferences, which calls for suitable translations and reformulations, in which preferences between sources are mapped into preferences between repairs.

In this paper, we face this problem by proposing a formal framework for both specifying and reasoning on preferences among sources. Specifically, the main contributions of this paper are the following.

- ▷ We introduce a new semantics which is based on the repair of data stored at the sources in the presence of global inconsistency, rather than considering the repair of global database instances constructed according to the mapping. This approach is essentially a form of abductive reasoning [19], since it directly resolves the conflicts by isolating their causes at the sources. This part is described in Section 3.
- ▷ We show that our novel repair semantics allow us to properly take into account source preferences. Following the extensive literature (see, e.g., [8, 7] and the references therein) from database community, prioritized logics, logic programming, and decision theory, we exploit two different approaches for specifying preferences among sources. Specifically, we consider *unary* and *binary constraints* for defining quantitative properties and relationships between sources, respectively.
- ▷ We show how preferences expressed over the sources can be exploited for refining the way of answering queries in data integration systems. To this aim, we introduce the concept of *strongly preferred answers*, characterizing the answers that can be obtained after the system is repaired according to users' preferences. Actually, we also investigate a weaker semantics that looks for *weakly preferred answers*, i.e., answers that are as close as possible to any strong preferred one. This part and the above one are described in Section 4.
- ▷ Finally, the computational complexity of computing both strongly and weakly preferred answers is studied, by considering the most common integrity constraints that can be issued on relational databases. We show that computing strongly preferred answers is co-NP-compete, and hence it is as difficult as computing answers without additional constraints [5]. However, while turning to the weak semantics, we evidence a small increase in complexity that does not lift the problem to higher levels of the polynomial hierarchy. Indeed, the problem is complete for the class $\mathrm{P}^{\mathrm{NP}}[\mathrm{O}(\log n)]$. Computational complexity is treated in Section 5.

2 Relational Databases

In this section we recall the basic notions of the relation model with integrity constraints. For further background on relational database theory, we refer the reader to [1].

We assume a (possibly infinite) fixed database domain Γ whose elements can be referenced by constants $c_1, \ldots, c_n$ under the *unique name assumption*, i.e. different constants denote different objects. A *relational schema* $\mathcal{RS}$ is a pair $\langle \Psi, \Sigma \rangle$, where: Ψ is a set of relation symbols, each with an associated arity that indicates the number of its attributes, and Σ is a set of *integrity constraints*, i.e., assertions that have to be satisfied by each database instance.

We deal with quantified constraints [1], i.e., first order formulas of the form:

$$\forall \boldsymbol{x}. \bigwedge_{i=1}^{l} A_i \supset \exists \boldsymbol{y}. \bigvee_{j=1}^{m} B_j \vee \bigvee_{k=1}^{n} \phi_k \tag{1}$$

where $l+m>0$, $n \geq 0$, $A_1, \ldots A_l$ and $B_1, \ldots B_m$ are positive literals, $\phi_1, \ldots \phi_n$ are built-in literals, $\boldsymbol{x}$ is a list of distinct variables, $\boldsymbol{y}$ is a list of variables occurring in $B_1, \ldots B_m$ only. Notice that classical constraints issued on a relational schema, as functional, exclusion, or inclusion dependencies, can be expressed in the form 1. Furthermore, they are also typical of conceptual modelling languages.

A *database instance* (or simply *database*) $\mathcal{DB}$ for a schema $\mathcal{RS} = \langle \Psi, \Sigma \rangle$ is a set of facts of the form $r(t)$ where r is a relation of arity n in Ψ and t is an n-tuple of constants of Γ. We denote as $r^{\mathcal{DB}}$ the set $\{t \mid r(t) \in \mathcal{DB}\}$. A database $\mathcal{DB}$ for a schema $\mathcal{RS}$ is said to be *consistent* with $\mathcal{RS}$ if it satisfies (in the first order logic sense) all constraints expressed on $\mathcal{RS}$.

A *relational query* (or simply *query*) over $\mathcal{RS}$ is a formula that is intended to extract tuples of elements of Γ. We assume that queries over $\mathcal{RS} = \langle \Psi, \Sigma \rangle$ are *Union of Conjunctive Queries* (UCQs), i.e., formulas of the form $q(\boldsymbol{x}) \leftarrow conj_1(\boldsymbol{x}, \boldsymbol{y}_1) \vee \cdots \vee conj_m(\boldsymbol{x}, \boldsymbol{y}_m)$, where, for each $i \in \{1, \ldots, m\}$, $conj_i(\boldsymbol{x}, \boldsymbol{y}_i)$ is a conjunction of atoms whose predicate symbols are in Ψ, and involve $\boldsymbol{x} = X_1, \ldots, X_n$ and $\boldsymbol{y}_i = Y_{i,1}, \ldots, Y_{i,n_i}$, where n is the arity of the query, and each X_k and each $Y_{i,\ell}$ is either a variable or a constant of Γ. $q(\boldsymbol{x})$ is called the head of q. Given a database $\mathcal{DB}$ for $\mathcal{RS}$, the answer to a UCQ q over $\mathcal{DB}$, denoted $q^{\mathcal{DB}}$, is the set of n-tuples of constants $\langle c_1, \ldots, c_n \rangle$, such that, when substituting each X_i with c_i, the formula $\exists \boldsymbol{y}_1 . conj_1(\boldsymbol{x}, \boldsymbol{y}_1) \vee \cdots \vee \exists \boldsymbol{y}_m . conj_m(\boldsymbol{x}, \boldsymbol{y}_m)$ evaluates to true in $\mathcal{DB}$.

3 Data Integration Systems

Framework. A data integration system $\mathcal{I}$ is a triple $\langle \mathcal{G}, \mathcal{S}, \mathcal{M} \rangle$, where $\mathcal{G}$ is the global (relational) schema of the form $\mathcal{G} = \langle \Psi, \Sigma \rangle$, $\mathcal{S}$ is the source (relational) schema of the form $\mathcal{S} = \langle \Psi', \emptyset \rangle$, i.e., there are no integrity constraints on the sources, and $\mathcal{M}$ is the mapping between $\mathcal{G}$ and $\mathcal{S}$. We assume that the mapping is specified in the *global-as-view* (GAV) approach [16], where every relation of the global schema is associated with a view, i.e., a query, over the source schema. Therefore, $\mathcal{M}$ is a set of UCQs expressed over $\mathcal{S}$, where the predicate symbol in the head is a relation symbol of $\mathcal{G}$.

Example 1 Consider the data integration system $\mathcal{I}_0 = \langle \mathcal{G}_0, \mathcal{S}_0, \mathcal{M}_0 \rangle$ where the global schema $\mathcal{G}_0$ consists of the relation predicates $employee(Name, Dept)$ and

$boss(Employee, Manager)$. The associated set of constraints Σ_0 contains the two following assertions (quantifiers are omitted)

$$employee(X,Y) \wedge boss(X_1,Y_1) \supset X \neq Y_1; \qquad boss(X,Y) \wedge boss(X_1,Y_1) \supset Y_1 \neq X,$$

stating that managers are never employees. The source schema $\mathcal{S}_0$ comprises the relation symbols s_1, s_2, s_3, and the mapping $\mathcal{M}_0$ contains the following UCQs

$$employee(X,Y) \leftarrow s_1(X,Y); \qquad boss(X,Y) \leftarrow s_2(X,Y) \vee s_3(X,Y).$$ □

We call any database $\mathcal{D}$ for the source schema $\mathcal{S}$ a *source database* for $\mathcal{I}$. Based on $\mathcal{D}$, we specify the semantics of $\mathcal{I}$, which is given in terms of database instances for $\mathcal{G}$, called *global databases* for $\mathcal{I}$. In particular, we construct a global database by evaluating each view in the mapping $\mathcal{M}$ over $\mathcal{D}$. Such a database is called *retrieved global database*, and is denoted by $ret(\mathcal{I}, \mathcal{D})$.

Example 1 (contd.) Let $\mathcal{D}_0 = \{s_1(Mary, D1), s_2(John, Mary), s_3(Albert, Bill)\}$ be a source database. Then, thc evaluation of each view in the mapping over $\mathcal{D}_0$ is $ret(\mathcal{I}_0, \mathcal{D}_0) = \{employee(Mary, D1), boss(John, Mary), boss(Albert, Bill)\}$. □

In general, the retrieved global database is not the only database that we consider to specify the semantics of $\mathcal{I}$ w.r.t. $\mathcal{D}$, but we account for all global databases that contain $ret(\mathcal{I}, \mathcal{D})$. This means considering *sound* mappings: data retrieved from the sources by the mapping views are assumed to be a subset of the data that satisfy the corresponding global relation. This is a classical assumption in data integration, where sources in general do not provide all the intended extensions of the global schema, hence extracted data are to be considered sound but not necessarily complete. Next, we formalize the notion of mapping satisfaction.

Definition 1. Given a data integration system $\mathcal{I} = \langle \mathcal{G}, \mathcal{S}, \mathcal{M} \rangle$, and a source database $\mathcal{D}$ for $\mathcal{I}$, a global database $\mathcal{B}$ for $\mathcal{I}$ *satisfies the mapping* $\mathcal{M}$ *w.r.t.* $\mathcal{D}$ if $\mathcal{B} \supseteq ret(\mathcal{I}, \mathcal{D})$. □

Notice that databases that satisfy the mapping might be inconsistent with respect to dependencies in Σ, since data stored in local and autonomous sources are not in general required to satisfy constraints expressed on the global schema. Furthermore, cases might arise in which no global database exists that satisfies both mapping and constraints over $\mathcal{G}$ (for example when a key dependency on $\mathcal{G}$ is violated by data retrieved from the sources). On the other hand, constraints issued over the global schema must be satisfied by those global databases that we want to consider "legal" for the system [16].

Repairing global databases. In order to solve inconsistency, several approaches have been recently proposed, in which the semantics of a data integration system is given in terms of the *repairs* of the global databases that the mapping forces to be in the semantic of the system [3, 5, 4]. Such papers extend to data integration previous proposals given in the field of inconsistent databases [12, 2, 14], by considering a sound interpretation of the mapping. In this context, repairs are obtained by means of addition and deletion of tuples over the inconsistent database. Modifications are performed according to minimality criteria that are specific for each approach. Analogously, works on inconsistency in data integration basically propose to properly repair the global databases that satisfy the mapping in order to make them satisfy constraints on the global schema. In this respect, we point out that [3, 4] consider *local-as-view* (LAV) mappings, where, conversely to the GAV approach, each source relation is associated with a query over the global schema. In such papers, the notion of retrieved global database is replaced with the notion of *minimal global databases* that can be constructed according to the mapping specification and data stored at the sources. Then, a global database satisfies the mapping if it contains at least one minimal global database. Repairs computed in [3, 5, 4] are in general global databases that do not satisfy the mapping. Furthermore, they cannot always be retrieved through the mapping from a source database instance. According to [16], we could say that in these approaches, constraints are considered strong, whereas the mapping is considered soft.

Example 2 Consider the simple situation in which the global schema of a data integration system $\mathcal{I} = \langle \mathcal{G}, \mathcal{S}, \mathcal{M} \rangle$ contains two relation symbols g_1 and g_2 both of arity 1, that are mutually disjoint, i.e., the constraint $\forall X, Y. g_1(X) \wedge g_2(Y) \supset X \neq Y$ is issued over $\mathcal{G}$. Assume that the mapping $\mathcal{M}$ comprises the queries $g_1(X) \leftarrow s(X)$ and $g_2(X) \leftarrow s(X)$ where s is a unary source relation symbol. Let $\mathcal{D} = \{s(a)\}$ be the source database for $\mathcal{I}$. Then, $ret(\mathcal{I}, \mathcal{D}) = \{g_1(a), g_2(a)\}$ is inconsistent w.r.t. the global constraint. In this case, the above mentioned approaches propose to repair $ret(\mathcal{I}, \mathcal{D})$ by eliminating from each database satisfying the mapping either $g_1(a)$ or $g_2(a)$ (but not both), thus producing in the two cases two different classes of global databases that are in the semantics of the system. Notice, however, that each global database that contains only $g_1(a)$ or only $g_2(a)$ does not satisfy the soundness of the mapping, and cannot be retrieved from any source database for $\mathcal{I}$. □

Even if effective for repairing global database instances in the presence of inconsistency, the above approaches do not seem appropriate when preferences specified over the sources should be taken into account for solving inconsistency. Indeed, in these cases, one would prefer, for example, to drop tuples coming from less reliable source relations rather than considering all possible repairs to be at the same level of reliability. Nonetheless, it is not always easy to understand how preferences over tuples stored at the sources could be mapped on preferences over tuples of the global schema.

Example 3 Consider for example the simple data integration system in which the mapping contains the query $g(X, Y) \leftarrow (s_1(X, Z) \wedge s_2(Z, Y)) \vee s_3(X, Y)$, and a constraint stating that the first component of the global relation g is the key of g. Assume to have the source database $\mathcal{D} = \{s_1(a, b), s_2(b, c), s_3(a, d)\}$, and to know that source relation s_3 is more reliable than source relation s_2. Then, $ret(\mathcal{I}, \mathcal{D}) = \{g(a, c), g(a, d)\}$ violates the key constraint on g, and it seems reasonable to prefer dropping the fact $g(a, c)$, in order to guarantee consistency, rather than $g(a, d)$, according to source preferences. However, we do not have a preference specified between this two global facts in such a way that we can adopt this choice. □

The above example shows that we should need some mechanism to infer preferences over tuples of the global schema starting from preferences at the sources. On the other hand, it is not always obvious or easy to define such a mechanism. A different solution could be to move the focus, when repairing, from tuples of the global schema to tuples of the sources, i.e., minimally modify the source database. In this way, we could compare two repairs (at the sources) on the basis of the preferences established over the source relations.

Repairing the sources. The idea at the basis of our approach consists in finding the proper set of facts at the sources that imply as a consequence a global database that satisfy the integrity constraints. Basically, such a way of proceeding is a form of abductive reasoning [19]. Notice also that, according to this approach we consider "strong" both the mapping and the constraints, i.e., we take into account only global databases that satisfy both the mapping and the constraints on the global schema. Furthermore, each global database that we consider, can be computed by means of the mapping from a suitable source database. Let us now precisely characterize the ideas informally described above.

Definition 2. Given a data integration system $\mathcal{I} = \langle \mathcal{G}, \mathcal{S}, \mathcal{M} \rangle$, where $\mathcal{G} = \langle \Psi, \Sigma \rangle$, and a source database $\mathcal{D}$ for $\mathcal{I}$, $\mathcal{I}$ is *satisfiable w.r.t.* $\mathcal{D}$ if there exists a global database $\mathcal{B}$ for $\mathcal{I}$ such that

- $\mathcal{B}$ satisfies Σ w.r.t. $\mathcal{D}$, and
- $\mathcal{B}$ satisfies the mapping $\mathcal{M}$. □

We next introduce a partial order between source databases for which the system in satisfiable.

Definition 3. Given a data integration system $\mathcal{I} = \langle \mathcal{G}, \mathcal{S}, \mathcal{M} \rangle$, where $\mathcal{G} = \langle \Psi, \Sigma \rangle$. Given two source databases $\mathcal{D}_1, \mathcal{D}_2 \subseteq \mathcal{D}$ for $\mathcal{I}$ such that $\mathcal{I}$ is satisfiable w.r.t. $\mathcal{D}_1$ and $\mathcal{D}_2$. Then, we say that $\mathcal{D}_1 \leq_{(\mathcal{I},\mathcal{D})} \mathcal{D}_2$ if $\mathcal{D}_1 \cap \mathcal{D} \supseteq \mathcal{D}_2 \cap \mathcal{D}$. Furthermore, $\mathcal{D}_1 <_{(\mathcal{I},\mathcal{D})} \mathcal{D}_2$ if $\mathcal{D}_1 \leq_{(\mathcal{I},\mathcal{D})} \mathcal{D}_2$ and does not hold $\mathcal{D}_2 \leq_{(\mathcal{I},\mathcal{D})} \mathcal{D}_1$. □

We say that a source database $\mathcal{D}'$ is *minimal w.r.t.* $\leq_{(\mathcal{I},\mathcal{D})}$, if there does not exist $\mathcal{D}''$ such that $\mathcal{D}'' \leq_{(\mathcal{I},\mathcal{D})} \mathcal{D}'$. Furthermore, we indicate with $min_{\leq_{(\mathcal{I},\mathcal{D})}}$ the set of source databases that are minimal w.r.t. $\leq_{(\mathcal{I},\mathcal{D})}$.

Example 1 (contd.) The retrieved global database violates the constraints on the global schema witnessed by the facts *employee*(*Mary*, *D1*) and *boss*(*John*, *Mary*) for which Mary is both an employee and a manager. Therefore, $\mathcal{I}_0$ is not satisfiable w.r.t. $\mathcal{D}_0$. Then, $min_{\leq_{(\mathcal{I}_0,\mathcal{D}_0)}} = \{\mathcal{D}_1, \mathcal{D}_2\}$ where $\mathcal{D}_1 = \{s_1(\mathit{Mary}, \mathit{D1}), s_3(\mathit{Albert}, \mathit{Bill})\}$ and $\mathcal{D}_2 = \{s_2(\mathit{John}, \mathit{Mary}), s_3(\mathit{Albert}, \mathit{Bill})\}$. □

We are now able to define the semantics of a data integration system.

Definition 4. Given a data integration system $\mathcal{I} = \langle \mathcal{G}, \mathcal{S}, \mathcal{M} \rangle$, where $\mathcal{G} = \langle \Psi, \Sigma \rangle$, and given a source database $\mathcal{D}$ for $\mathcal{I}$, a global database $\mathcal{B}$ is *legal* for $\mathcal{I}$ w.r.t. $\mathcal{D}$ if

- $\mathcal{B}$ satisfies Σ,
- $\mathcal{B}$ satisfies the mapping $\mathcal{M}$ w.r.t. a minimal source database $\mathcal{D}'$ w.r.t. $\leq_{(\mathcal{I},\mathcal{D})}$, i.e., there exists $\mathcal{D}' \in min_{\leq_{(\mathcal{I},\mathcal{D})}}$ such that $\mathcal{B} \supseteq ret(\mathcal{I}, \mathcal{D}')$.

□

The set of all the legal databases is denoted by $Leg(\mathcal{I}, \mathcal{D})$. We point out that, under the standard *cautious* semantics, answering a query posed over the global schema $\mathcal{G}$ amounts to evaluate it on every legal database $\mathcal{B} \in Leg(\mathcal{I}, \mathcal{D})$.

Example 1 (contd.) The set $Leg(\mathcal{I}_0, \mathcal{D}_0)$ contains all global databases that satisfy the global schema and that contain either $ret(\mathcal{I}_0, \mathcal{D}_1) = \{employee(Mary, D1), boss(Albert, Bill)\}$ or $ret(\mathcal{I}_0, \mathcal{D}_2) = \{boss(John, Mary), boss(Albert, Bill)\}$. Then, the answer to the user query $q(X) \leftarrow boss(X, Y)$, which asks for all employees that have a boss, is $\{\langle Albert \rangle\}$. □

Summarizing, our approach consists in properly repairing the source database $\mathcal{D}$ in order to obtain another source database $\mathcal{D}'$ such that $\mathcal{I}$ is satisfiable w.r.t. $\mathcal{D}'$. Obviously, if $\mathcal{I}$ is satisfiable w.r.t. $\mathcal{D}$, we do not need to repair $\mathcal{D}$.

Before concluding, we point out that the set $Leg(\mathcal{I}, \mathcal{D})$ is in general different from the set of global databases that can be obtained by repairing the retrieved global database instead of repairing the source database $\mathcal{D}$. This results evident in Example 2, in which repairing is performed by dropping $s(a)$ at the sources, therefore legal databases exist that neither contain $g_1(a)$ nor $g_2(a)$.

We conclude this section by considering the difficulty of checking whether a global database is indeed a repair. Such a difficulty will be evaluated by following the *data complexity* approach [20], i.e., by considering a given problem instance having as its input the source database — this is, in fact, the approach we shall follow in all the complexity results presented in the paper.

Theorem 4 (Repair Checking). *Let $\mathcal{I} = \langle \mathcal{G}, \mathcal{S}, \mathcal{M} \rangle$ be a data integration systems with $\mathcal{G} = \langle \Psi, \Sigma \rangle$, $\mathcal{D}$ a source database for $\mathcal{I}$, and $\mathcal{B}$ a global database for $\mathcal{I}$. Then, checking whether $\mathcal{B}$ is legal is feasible in polynomial time.*

4 Formalizing Additional Properties of the Sources

In many real world applications, users often have some additional knowledge about data sources besides the mapping with the global schema, which can be modelled in terms of preference constraints specified over source relations. In this scenario, the aim is to exploit preference constraints for query answering in the presence of inconsistency.

The framework we have introduced in Section 3 allows us to easily take into account information on such preferences when trying to solve inconsistency, since repairing is performed by directly focusing on the sources, whose integration has caused inconsistency.

Intuitively, when a data integration system $\mathcal{I} = \langle \mathcal{G}, \mathcal{S}, \mathcal{M} \rangle$ is equipped with some additional preference constraints, we can easily exploit these further requirements for identifying, given a source database $\mathcal{D}$, those elements of $min_{\leq(\mathcal{I},\mathcal{D})}$ which are preferred for answering a certain query. In this respect, we distinguish between *unary constraints*, i.e., properties which characterize a given data source, and *binary constraints*, i.e., properties which are expressed over pairs of relations in the source schema $\mathcal{S}$.

4.1 Unary and Binary Constraints

As already evidenced in [18], in order to provide accurate query answering, each relation $r \in \mathcal{S}$ can be equipped with two parameters: the *soundness measure* and the *completeness measure*. The former is used for assessing the confidence that we place in the answers provided by r, whereas the latter is used for evaluating how much relevant information is contained in r. In [18], the problem of querying partially sound and complete data sources has been studied in the context of data integration systems with LAV mapping and without integrity constraints on the global schema. In such a setting, it has been shown that deciding the existence of a global database satisfying some assumptions is NP-complete.

Here, we extend such analysis for sound GAV mappings, in our repair semantics for data integration systems. In this framework, we observe that the completeness measure is of no practical interest, since each $\mathcal{B} \in Leg(\mathcal{I}, \mathcal{D})$ is such that $\mathcal{B} \supseteq ret(\mathcal{I}, \mathcal{D})$. Therefore, constraints that can be satisfied by adding tuples to $ret(\mathcal{I}, \mathcal{D})$, can be seen as "automatically repaired". Indeed, in our repair semantics we do consider addition of tuples at the sources in order to repair constraints on the global schema. Therefore, we are actually interested in bounding only the number of tuple deletions required at the sources in order to repair the system. Then, for each source relation $r \in \mathcal{S}$, we denote by r_s the value of such bound, also called *soundness constraint*, whose semantics is as follows.

Definition 5. Let $\mathcal{I} = \langle \mathcal{G}, \mathcal{S}, \mathcal{M} \rangle$ be a data integration system, $\mathcal{D}$ a source database for $\mathcal{I}$, r a relation symbol in $\mathcal{S}$, and r_s a soundness constraint for r. Then, a source database $\mathcal{D}' \in min_{\leq(\mathcal{I},\mathcal{D})}$ *satisfies* r_s if

$$\frac{|r^{\mathcal{D}-\mathcal{D}'}|}{|r^{\mathcal{D}}|} \leq r_s$$

□

Even though in several situations the soundness measure is not directly available for characterizing a source relation in an absolute way, the user might be able to compare the soundness of two different sources. For instance, he might not know the soundness constraint for source relations r_1 and r_2, but he might have observed that "r_1 is more reliable than r_2". Such intuition is formalized by the notion of binary constraints.

Let r_1 and r_2 be two relation symbols of $\mathcal{S}$, and let A denote a set of pairs $\{P^1, ..., P^n\}$, such that $P^i = (A^i_{r_1}, A^i_{r_2})$, with $A^i_{r_1}$ and $A^i_{r_2}$ attributes of r_1 and

r_2, respectively. Any expression of the form $r_1 \prec_A r_2$ is a *binary constraint* over $\mathcal{S}$, and its semantics is as follows.

Definition 6. Let $\mathcal{I} = \langle \mathcal{G}, \mathcal{S}, \mathcal{M} \rangle$ be a data integration system and $\mathcal{D}$ a source database for $\mathcal{I}$. Then, a source database $\mathcal{D}' \in min_{\leq(\mathcal{I},\mathcal{D})}$ *satisfies a binary constraint* of the form $r_1 \prec_{\{P^1,\ldots,P^n\}} r_2$ with $P^i = (A^i_{r_1}, A^i_{r_2})$ for $i = 1..n$, if

$$\forall t_1 \in r_1^{\mathcal{D}-\mathcal{D}'},\ \exists\, t_2 \in r_2^{\mathcal{D}-\mathcal{D}'} \text{ with } \pi_{A^1_{r_1},\ldots,A^n_{r_1}}(t_1) = \pi_{A^1_{r_2},\ldots,A^n_{r_n}}(t_2)$$

where $\pi_{A_1,\ldots,A_n}(t_i)$ indicates the projection of the tuple t_i on $A_1, \ldots, A_n$. □

Roughly speaking, $\mathcal{D}'$ satisfies $r_1 \prec_A r_2$ if for each tuple t_1 that has been deleted from $r_1^{\mathcal{D}}$ in order to obtain $\mathcal{D}'$, a tuple t_2 sharing the same values on the attributes in A has been deleted from $r_2^{\mathcal{D}}$. This behavior guarantees that r_1 is modified only if there is no way for repairing the data integration system by modifying r_2 only.

Example 1 (contd.) Assume now to specify the binary constraint $s_2 \prec_{(\$2,\$1)} s_1$ over the source schema $\mathcal{S}$, where \$2 indicates the second attribute of s_2 and \$1 the first attribute of s_1. Then, $\mathcal{D}_1 = \{s_1(\mathit{Mary}, \mathit{D1}), s_3(\mathit{Albert}, \mathit{Bill})\}$ violates the constraint, since it is obtained by dropping from $\mathcal{D}$ the fact $s_2(\mathit{John}, \mathit{Mary})$, whose second component coincides with the first component of $s_1(\mathit{Mary}, \mathit{D1})$, which conversely has not been dropped. On the contrary, it is easy to see that $\mathcal{D}_2 = \{s_2(\mathit{John}, \mathit{Mary}), s_3(\mathit{Albert}, \mathit{Bill})\}$ satisfies the constraint. □

4.2 Soft Constraints

As defined in the section above, unary and binary constraints often impose very severe restrictions on the possible ways repairs can be carried out. For instance, it might even happen that no minimal source database exists that satisfies such constraints, thereby leading to a data integration system with an empty semantics. In order to face such situations, whenever it is necessary we can also turn to "weak" semantics that looks for repairs as close as possible to the preferred ones. In this respect, preference constraints are interpreted in a soft version, and we aim at minimizing the number of violations, rather than imposing the absence of such violations.

Definition 7 (Satisfaction Factor). Let $\mathcal{I} = \langle \mathcal{G}, \mathcal{S}, \mathcal{M} \rangle$ be a data integration system, $\mathcal{D}$ a source database for $\mathcal{I}$, and $\mathcal{D}'$ be a source database in $min_{\leq(\mathcal{I},\mathcal{D})}$. Then, the *satisfaction factor* $w_{\mathcal{D}}(p, \mathcal{D}')$ for a constraint p is

- $|r^{\mathcal{D}-\mathcal{D}'}|$, if p is of the form r_s and $\mathcal{D}'$ does not satisfies r_s, or
- the number of tuples $t_1 \in r_1^{\mathcal{D}-\mathcal{D}'}$ such that $\nexists t_2 \in r_2^{\mathcal{D}-\mathcal{D}'}$ with $\pi_{A^1_{r_1},\ldots,A^n_{r_1}}(t_1) = \pi_{A^1_{r_2},\ldots,A^n_{r_n}}(t_2)$, if p has the form $r_1 \prec_{\{P^1,..,P^n\}} r_2$ with $P^i = (A^i_{r_1}, A^i_{r_2})$. □

Finally, the *satisfaction factor* of a set of constraints $\mathcal{P}$ is the value $w_{\mathcal{D}}(\mathcal{P}, \mathcal{D}') = \sum_{p \in \mathcal{P}} w_{\mathcal{D}}(p, \mathcal{D}')$.

4.3 Preferred Answers

After unary and binary constraints have been formalized, we next show how they can be practically used for pruning the set of legal databases of a data integration system. Specifically, we first focus on the definition of preferred legal databases, and we next show how this notion can be exploited for defining preferred answers.

In the following, given a data integration system $\mathcal{I}$, we denote by $constr(\mathcal{I})$ the set of preference constraints defined over $\mathcal{S}$. Then, the pair $\mathcal{I}^c = \langle \mathcal{I}, constr(\mathcal{I}) \rangle$ is also said to be a *constrained data integration system*. The semantics of the system is provided in terms of those legal databases that are "retrieved" from source databases of $min_{\leq_{(\mathcal{I},\mathcal{D})}}$ that satisfy $constr(\mathcal{I})$.

Definition 8. Let $\mathcal{I}^c = \langle \mathcal{I}, constr(\mathcal{I}) \rangle$ be a constrained data integration system with $\mathcal{I} = \langle \mathcal{G}, \mathcal{S}, \mathcal{M} \rangle$ and $\mathcal{G} = \langle \Psi, \Sigma \rangle$, and let $\mathcal{D}$ be a source database for $\mathcal{I}$. Then, a global database $\mathcal{B}$ is a *(weakly) preferred legal database for $\mathcal{I}^c$ w.r.t. $\mathcal{D}$* if

- $\mathcal{B}$ satisfies Σ,
- $\mathcal{B} \supseteq ret(\mathcal{I}, \mathcal{D}')$, where $\mathcal{D}'$ is a minimal source database w.r.t. $\leq_{(\mathcal{I},\mathcal{D})}$ such that no minimal source database $\mathcal{D}''$ exists with $w_{\mathcal{D}}(p, \mathcal{D}'') < w_{\mathcal{D}}(p, \mathcal{D}')$.

If $w_{\mathcal{D}}(p, \mathcal{D}') = 0$, then $\mathcal{B}$ is a *strongly preferred legal database* for $\mathcal{I}^c$ w.r.t. $\mathcal{D}$. □

We next provide the notion of answers to a query posed to a constrained data integration system.

Definition 9. Given a constrained data integration system $\mathcal{I}^c = \langle \mathcal{I}, constr(\mathcal{I}) \rangle$ with $\mathcal{I} = \langle \mathcal{G}, \mathcal{S}, \mathcal{M} \rangle$, a source database $\mathcal{D}$ for $\mathcal{I}$, and a query q of arity n over $\mathcal{G}$, the set of the *weakly preferred answers* to q, denoted $ans^{\sim}(q, \mathcal{I}, \mathcal{D})$, is

$$\{\langle c_1, \ldots, c_n \rangle \mid \langle c_1, \ldots, c_n \rangle \in q^{\mathcal{B}} \text{ for each weakly preferred legal database } \mathcal{B}\ \}$$

The set of the *strongly preferred answers* to q, denoted $ans^{*}(q, \mathcal{I}, \mathcal{D})$, is

$$\{\langle c_1, \ldots, c_n \rangle \mid \langle c_1, \ldots, c_n \rangle \in q^{\mathcal{B}} \text{ for each strongly preferred legal database } \mathcal{B}\ \}$$ □

Example 1 (contd.) Consider again the constraint $s_2 \prec_{(\$2,\$1)} s_1$. We have already observed that only $\mathcal{D}_2$ satisfies such requirement. Then, the set of strongly preferred databases is $\{\mathcal{B} \mid \mathcal{B} \supseteq ret(\mathcal{I}, \mathcal{D}_2)\}$. Therefore, for the query $q(X) \leftarrow boss(X, Y)$, $ans^{*}(q, \mathcal{I}_0, \mathcal{D}_0) = \{\langle Albert \rangle, \langle John \rangle\}$. □

We conclude this section by observing that the constraints we have defined can be evaluated in polynomial time on a given global database. However, they suffice for blowing up the intrinsic difficulty of identifying (preferred) global databases.

Theorem 5 (Preferred Repair Checking). *Let $\mathcal{I}^c = \langle \mathcal{I}, constr(\mathcal{I}) \rangle$ and let $\mathcal{D}$ be a source database for $\mathcal{I}$. Then, checking whether a global database $\mathcal{B}$ is (strongly) preferred for $\mathcal{I}^c$ w.r.t. $\mathcal{D}$ is* NP*-hard.*

Proof (Sketch). NP-hardness can be proven by a reduction of three colorability problem to our problem. Indeed, given a graph G we can build a data integration system $\mathcal{I}^c(G)$, a source database $\mathcal{D}$ and a legal database $\mathcal{B}$ for $\mathcal{I}$ such that $\mathcal{B}$ is preferred $\Leftrightarrow$ G is 3-colorable. □

5 Complexity Results

We next study the computational complexity of query answering in a constrained data integration system $\mathcal{I}^c$ under the novel semantics proposed in the paper. Our aim is to point out the intrinsic difficulty of dealing with constraints at the sources. Specifically, given a source database $\mathcal{D}$ for $\mathcal{I}^c$, we shall face the following problems:

- `StronglyAnswering`: given a UCQ q of arity n over $\mathcal{G}$ and an n-tuple t of constants of $\Gamma_{\mathcal{D}}$, is $t \in ans^*(q, \mathcal{I}^c, \mathcal{D})$?
- `WeaklyAnswering`: given a UCQ q of arity n over $\mathcal{G}$ and an n-tuple t of constants of $\Gamma_{\mathcal{D}}$, is $t \in ans^{\sim}(q, \mathcal{I}^c, \mathcal{D})$?

where $\Gamma_{\mathcal{D}}$ are constant of the domain Γ which occur also in tuples of $\mathcal{D}$.

We shall consider the (common) case in which $\mathcal{G} = \langle \Psi, \Sigma \rangle$ is such that Σ contains only key dependencies (KDs), functional dependencies (FDs) and exclusion dependencies (EDs). We recall that these are classical constraints issued on a relational schema, and that they can be expressed in the form (1) introduced in Section 2. We also point out that violations of constraints of such form, e.g., two global tuples violating a key constraint, lead always to inconsistency in our framework, since they can be repaired only by means of tuple deletions from the source database. We are now ready to provide the first result of this section.

Theorem 6. *Let $\mathcal{I}^c = \langle \mathcal{I}, constr(\mathcal{I}) \rangle$ be a constrained data integration system with $\mathcal{I} = \langle \mathcal{G}, \mathcal{S}, \mathcal{M} \rangle$ where $\mathcal{G} = \langle \Psi, \Sigma \rangle$ in which Σ contains only FDs and EDs, and let $\mathcal{D}$ be a source database for $\mathcal{I}^c$. Then, the* `StronglyAnswering` *problem is* co-NP*-complete. Hardness holds even if Σ contains either only KDs or only EDs, and if $constr(\mathcal{I})$ is empty.*

Proof (Sketch). As for the membership, we consider the dual problem of deciding whether $t \notin ans^*(q, \mathcal{I}, \mathcal{D})$, and we show that it is feasible in NP. In fact, we can guess a source database $\mathcal{D}'$ obtained by removing tuples of $\mathcal{D}'$ only. Then, we can show how to verify that $\mathcal{D}'$ is minimal w.r.t. $\leq_{(\mathcal{I},\mathcal{D})}$ in polynomial time.

Hardness for the general case can be derived from the results reported in [5] and in [9] (where the problem of query answering under different semantics in the presence of KDs is studied). Hardness for EDs only can be proven in an analogous way by a reduction from the three colorability problem to the complement of our problem. □

The above result suggests that adding constraints to the sources, enriches the representation features of a data integration systems, and it is well-behaved from a computational viewpoint. In fact, selecting preferred answers is as difficult as selecting answers without additional preference constraints, whose complexity has been widely studied in [5].

We next turn to the `WeaklyAnswering` problem, in which a weaker semantics is considered. Intuitively, this scenario provides an additional source of complexity, since finding weakly preferred global databases amount at solving an implicit (NP) optimization problem. Interestingly, the increase in complexity is rather small and does not lift the problem to higher levels of the polynomial hierarchy.

Actually, the problem stays within the polynomial time closure of NP, i.e., P^{NP}. More precisely, it is complete for the class $\mathrm{P}^{\mathrm{NP}}[\mathrm{O}(\log n)]$, in which the NP oracle access is limited to $\mathrm{O}(\log n)$ queries, where n is the size of the source database in input.

Theorem 7. *Let $\mathcal{I}^c = \langle \mathcal{I}, constr(\mathcal{I}) \rangle$ be a constrained data integration system with $\mathcal{I} = \langle \mathcal{G}, \mathcal{S}, \mathcal{M} \rangle$ where $\mathcal{G} = \langle \Psi, \Sigma \rangle$ in which Σ contains only FDs and EDs, and let $\mathcal{D}$ be a source database for $\mathcal{I}^c$. Then, the* `WeaklyAnswering` *problem is $\mathrm{P}^{\mathrm{NP}}[\mathrm{O}(\log n)]$-complete.*

Proof (Sketch). For the membership, we can preliminary compute the maximum value, say max, that the satisfaction factor for any source database may assume. Then, by a binary search in $[0, max]$, we can compute the best satisfaction factor, say c: at each step of this search, we are given a threshold s and we call an NP oracle to know whether there exists a source database $\mathcal{D}'$ such that $w_{\mathcal{D}}(p, \mathcal{D}') < s$. Finally, we ask an other NP oracle for checking whether there exists a source database $\mathcal{D}''$ with satisfaction factor c such that t does not belong to $q^{\mathcal{B}}$, for the minimal $\mathcal{B} \supseteq ret(\mathcal{I}, \mathcal{D}'')$ satisfying the constraints in $\mathcal{G}$.

Hardness can be proved by a reduction from the following problem: Given a formula Φ in conjunctive normal form on the variables $Y = \{Y_1, ..., Y_n\}$, a subset $\mathcal{X} \subseteq Y$, and a variable Y_i, decide whether Y_i is true in all the $\mathcal{X}$-MAXIMUM models, where a model M (satisfying assignment) is $\mathcal{X}$-MAXIMUM if it has the largest $\mathcal{X}$-part, i.e., if the number of variables in the set $\mathcal{X}$ that are true w.r.t. M is the maximum over all the satisfying assignments. □

6 Conclusions

In this paper we have introduced and formalized the problem of enriching data integration systems with preferences among sources. Our approach is based on a novel semantics which relies on repairing the data stored at the sources in the presence of global inconsistency. Repairs performed at the sources allow us to properly take into account preference expressed over the sources when trying to solve inconsistency. Exploiting the presence of preference constraints, we have introduced the notion of (strongly and weakly) preferred answers. Finally, we have studied the computational complexity of computing both strongly and weakly preferred answers for classes of key, functional end exclusion dependencies, which are relevant classes of constraints for relational databases as well as conceptual modelling languages.

Complexity results given in this paper can be easily extended to the presence of also inclusion dependencies on the global schema in the cases in which the problem of query answering is decidable, which have been studied in [5]. To the best of our knowledge, the present work is the first one that provide formalizations and complexity results to the problem of dealing with inconsistencies by taking into account preferences specified among data sources in a pure GAV data integration framework. Only recently, the same problem has been studied for LAV integration systems in [13].

References

1. S. Abiteboul, R. Hull, and V. Vianu. *Foundations of Databases.* Addison Wesley Publ. Co., Reading, Massachussetts, 1995.
2. M. Arenas, L. E. Bertossi, and J. Chomicki. Consistent query answers in inconsistent databases. In *Proc. of PODS'99*, pages 68–79, 1999.
3. L. Bertossi, J. Chomicki, A. Cortes, and C. Gutierrez. Consistent answers from integrated data sources. In *Proc. of FQAS'02*, pages 71–85, 2002.
4. L. Bravo and L. Bertossi. Logic programming for consistently querying data integration systems. In *Proc. of IJCAI'03*, pages 10–15, 2003.
5. A. Calì, D. Lembo, and R. Rosati. On the decidability and complexity of query answering over inconsistent and incomplete databases. In *Proc. of PODS'03*, pages 260–271, 2003.
6. A. Calì, D. Lembo, and R. Rosati. Query rewriting and answering under constraints in data integration systems. In *Proc. of IJCAI'03*, pages 16–21, 2003.
7. J. Chomicki. Preference formulas in relational queries. Technical Report cs.DB/0207093, arXiv.org e-Print archive. ACM Trans. on Database Systems.
8. J. Chomicki. Querying with intrinsic preferences. In *Proc. of EDBT'02*, pages 34–51, 2002.
9. J. Chomicki and J. Marcinkowski. On the computational complexity of consistent query answers. Technical Report cs.DB/0204010 v1, arXiv.org e-Print archive, Apr. 2002. Available at `http://arxiv.org/abs/cs/0204010`.
10. P. Dell'Acqua, L. M. Pereira, and A. Vitória. User preference information in query answering. In *Proc. of FQAS'02*, pages 163–173, 2002.
11. T. Eiter, M. Fink, G. Greco, and D. Lembo. Efficient evaluation of logic programs for querying data integration systems. In *Proc. of ICLP'03*, volume 2237 of *Lecture Notes in Artificial Intelligence*, pages 348–364. Springer, 2003.
12. R. Fagin, J. D. Ullman, and M. Y. Vardi. On the semantics of updates in databases. In *Proc. of PODS'83*, pages 352–365, 1983.
13. G. D. Giacomo, D. Lembo, M. Lenzerini, and R. Rosati. Tackling inconsistencies in data integration through source preferences. In *In Proc. of the SIGMOD Int. Workshop on Infomration Quality in Information Systems*, 2004.
14. G. Greco, S. Greco, and E. Zumpano. A logic programming approach to the integration, repairing and querying of inconsistent databases. In *Proc. of ICLP'01*, volume 2237 of *Lecture Notes in Artificial Intelligence*, pages 348–364. Springer, 2001.
15. S. Greco, C. Sirangelo, I. Trubitsyna, and E. Zumpano. Preferred repairs for inconsistent databases. In *Proc. of IDEAS'03*, pages 202–211, 2003.
16. M. Lenzerini. Data integration: A theoretical perspective. In *Proc. of PODS'02*, pages 233–246, 2002.
17. J. Lin and A. O. Mendelzon. Merging databases under constraints. *Int. J. of Cooperative Information Systems*, 7(1):55–76, 1998.
18. A. O. Mendelzon and G. A. Mihaila. Querying partially sound and complete data sources. In *Proc. of PODS'01*, pages 162–170, 2001.
19. C. S. Peirce. Abduction and induction. *In Philosophical Writings of Peirce*, pages 150–156, 1955.
20. M. Y. Vardi. The complexity of relational query languages. In *Proc. of STOC'82*, pages 137–146, 1982.

Resolving Schematic Discrepancy in the Integration of Entity-Relationship Schemas

Qi He and Tok Wang Ling

School of Computing, National University of Singapore
{heqi,lingtw}@comp.nus.edu.sg

Abstract. In schema integration, schematic discrepancies occur when data in one database correspond to metadata in another. We define this kind of semantic heterogeneity in general using the paradigm of context that is the meta information relating to the source, classification, property etc of entities, relationships or attribute values in entity-relationship (ER) schemas. We present algorithms to resolve schematic discrepancies by transforming metadata into entities, keeping the information and constraints of original schemas. Although focusing on the resolution of schematic discrepancies, our technique works seamlessly with existing techniques resolving other semantic heterogeneities in schema integration.

1 Introduction

Schema integration involves merging several schemas into an integrated schema. More precisely, [4] defines schema integration as "the activity of integrating the schemas of existing or proposed databases into a global, unified schema". It is regarded as an important work to build a *heterogeneous database system* [6, 22] (also called *multidatabase system* or *federated database system*), to integrate data in a data warehouse, or to integrate user views in database design. In schema integration, people have identified different kinds of semantic heterogeneities among component schemas: naming conflict (homonyms and synonyms), key conflict, structural conflict [3, 15], and constraint conflict [14, 21].

A less touched problem is schematic discrepancy, i.e., the same information is modeled as data in one database, but metadata in another. This conflict arises frequently in practice [11, 19]. We adopt a semantic approach to solve this issue. One of the outstanding features of our proposal is that we preserve the cardinality constraints in the transformation/integration of ER schemas. Cardinality constraints, in particular, functional dependencies (FDs) and multivalued dependencies (MVDs), are useful in verifying lossless schema transformation [10], schema normalization and semantic query optimization [9, 21] in multidatabase systems. The following example illustrates schematic discrepancy in ER schemas. To focus our contribution and simplify the presentation, in the example below, schematic discrepancy is the only kind of conflicts among schemas.

Example 1. Suppose we want to integrate supply information of products from several databases (Fig. 1). These databases record the same information, i.e., product numbers, product names, suppliers and supplying prices in each month, but have discrepant schemas. In DB1, suppliers and months are modeled as entity types. In DB2, months are modeled as meta-data of entity types, i.e., each entity type models

P. Atzeni et al. (Eds.): ER 2004, LNCS 3288, pp. 245–258, 2004.

the products supplied in one month, and suppliers are modeled as meta-data of attributes, e.g., the attribute S1_PRICE records the supplying prices by supplier *s1*[1]. In DB3, months are modeled as meta-data of relationship types, i.e., each relationship type models the supply relation in one month. We propose (in Section 4) to resolve the discrepancies by transforming the metadata into entities, i.e., transforming DB2 and DB3 into a form of DB1. The statements on the right side of Fig. 1 provide the semantics of the constructs of these schemas using ontology, which will be explained in Section 3.□

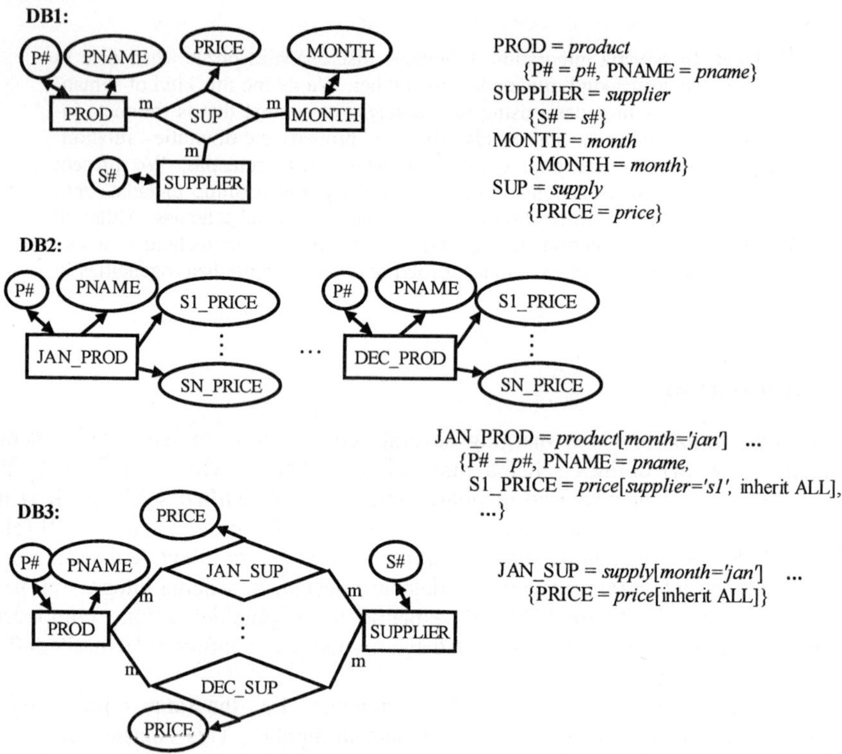

Fig. 1. Schematic discrepancy: months and suppliers modeled differently in DB1, DB2 and DB3

Paper organization. The rest of the paper is organized as follows. Section 2 is an introduction to the ER approach. Section 3 and 4 are the main contributions of this paper. In Section 3, we first introduce the concepts of ontology and context, and the mappings from schema constructs of ER schemas onto types of ontology. Then we define schematic discrepancy in general using the paradigm of context. In Section 4, we present algorithms to resolve schematic discrepancies in schema integration, without any loss of information and cardinality constraints. In Section 5, we compare our work with related work. Section 6 concludes the whole paper.

---

[1] Without causing confusion, we blur the difference on entities and identifiers of entities. E.g., we use supplier number *s1* to refer to a supplier with identifier S# = *s1*, i.e., *s1* plays both the roles of an attribute value of S# and an entity of supplier.

2 ER Approach

In the ER model, an entity is an object in the real world and can be distinctly identified. An *entity type* is a collection of similar entities that have the same set of predefined common *attributes*. Attributes can be *single-valued*, i.e., 1:1 (one-to-one) or m:1 (many-to-one), or *multivalued*, i.e., 1:m (one-to-many) or m:m (many-to-many). A minimal set of attributes of an entity type E which uniquely identifies E is called a *key* of E. An entity type may have more than one key and we designate one of them as the *identifier* of the entity type. A relationship is an association among two or more entities. A *relationship type* is a collection of similar relationships that satisfy a set of predefined common attributes. A minimal set of attributes (including the identifiers of participating entity types) in a relationship type R that uniquely identifies R is called a *key* of R. A relationship set may have more than one key and we designate one of them as the *identifier* of the relationship type.

The cardinality constraints of ER schemas incorporate FDs and MVDs. For example, given an ER schema below, let K1, K2 and K3 be the identifiers of E1, E2 and E3, we have:

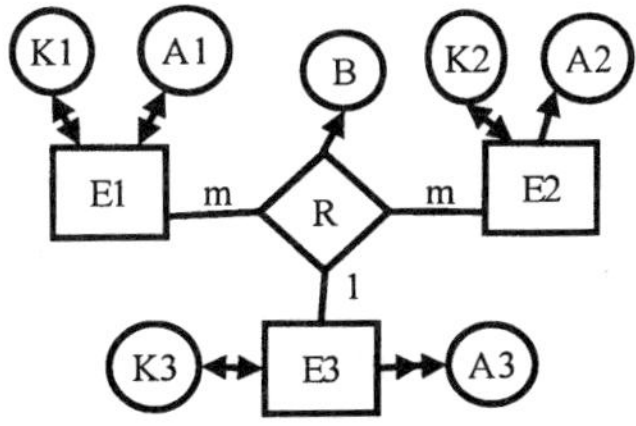

K1→A1 and A1→K1, as A1 is a 1:1 attribute of E1;
K2→A2, as A2 is a m:1 attribute of E2;
K3 $\twoheadrightarrow$ A3, as A3 is a m:m attribute of E3;
{K1, K2}→K3, as the cardinality of E3 is 1 in R;
{K1, K2}→B, as B is a m:1 attribute of R.

3 Ontology and Context

In this section, we first represent the constructs of ER schemas using ontology, then define schematic discrepancy in general based on the schemas represented using ontology. In this paper, we treat ontology as the specification of a representational vocabulary for a shared domain of discourse which includes the definitions of types (representing classes, relations, and properties) and their values. We present ontology at a conceptual level, which could be implemented by an ontology language, e.g., OWL [20].

For example, suppose ontology *SupOnto* describes the concepts in the universe of product supply. It includes the following types: *product, month, supplier, supply* (i.e., the supply relations among products, months and suppliers), *price* (i.e. the supplying prices of products), *p#, pname, s#,* etc. It also includes the values of these types, e.g. *jan, ..., dec* for *month*, and *s1, ..., sn* for *supplier*. Note we use lower case italic words to represent types and values of ontology, in contrast to capitals for schema constructs of an ER schema. By use of OWL expression, *product, month, supplier* and *supply* would be declared as classes, *p#* and *pname* as properties of *product*, *s#* as a property of *supplier*, and *price* as a property of *supply*.

Conceptual modeling is always done within a particular context. In particular, the context of an entity type, relationship type or attribute is the meta-information relating to its source, classification, property etc. Contexts are usually at four levels: *database, object class, relationship type* and *attribute*. An entity type may "inherit" a context from a database (i.e., the context of a database applies to the entities), and so on. In general, the inheritance hierarchy of contexts at different levels is:

4 Resolving Schematic Discrepancies in the Integration of ER Schemas

In this section, we resolve schematic discrepancies in schema integration. In particular, we present four algorithms to resolve schematic discrepancies for entity types, relationship types, attributes of entity types and attributes of relationship types respectively. This is done by transforming discrepant meta-attributes into entity types. The transformations keep the cardinalities of attributes and entity types, and therefore preserve the FDs and MVDs. Note in the presence of context, the values of an attribute depend on not only the identifier of an entity type/relationship type, but also the metadata of the attribute. To simplify the presentation, we only consider the discrepant meta-attributes of entity types, relationship types and attributes, leaving the other meta-attributes out as they will not change in schema transformation.

In the rest of this section, we first present Algorithm TRANS_ENT and TRANS_REL, the resolutions of discrepancies for entity types and relationship types in Section 4.1, and then TRANS_ENT_ATTR and TRANS_REL_ATTR, the resolutions for attributes of entity types and attributes of relationship types in Section 4.2. Examples are provided to understand each algorithm.

4.1 Resolving Schematic Discrepancies for Entity Types/Relationship Types

In this sub-section, we first show how to resolve discrepancies for entity types using the schema of Fig. 1, then present Algorithm TRANS_ENT in general. Finally, we describe the resolution of discrepancies for relationship types by an example, omitting the general algorithm which is similar to TRANS_ENT.

As an example to remove discrepancies for entity types, we transform the schema of DB2 in Fig. 1 below.

Example 3 (Fig. 2). In Step 1, for each entity type of DB2, say JAN_PROD, we represent the meta-attribute *month* as an entity type MONTH consisting of the only entity *jan* that is the metadata of JAN_PROD. We change the entity type JAN_PROD into PROD after removing the context, and construct a relationship type R to associate the entities of PROD and the entity of MONTH. Then we handle the attributes of JAN_PROD. As PNAME has nothing to do with the context *month* = *'jan'* of the entity type, it becomes an attribute of PROD. However, S1_PRICE, ..., SN_PRICE inherit the context of month; they become the attributes of the relationship type R. Then in Step 2, the corresponding entity types, relationship types and attributes are merged respectively. The merged entity type of MONTH consists of all the entities {*jan, ..., dec*} of the original MONTH entity types, so do the entity type PROD, relationship type R and their attributes.□

Then we give the general algorithm below.

Algorithm TRANS_ENT

Input: an elevated schema DB.

Output: a schema DB' transformed from DB such that all the discrepant meta-attributes of entity types are transformed into entity types.

Step 1: Resolve the discrepant meta-attributes of an entity type.

Let $E = E_{ont}[C_1=c_1, \ldots, C_m=c_m]$ be an entity type of DB, for E_{ont} a type in the ontology and discrepant meta-attributes $C_1, \ldots, C_m$ with the values $c_1, \ldots, c_m$. Let K be the global identifier of E.

Step 1.1: Transform discrepant meta-attributes $C_1, \ldots, C_m$ into entity types.

Construct an entity type $E' = E_{ont}$ with the global identifier K. E' consists of the entities of E without any context.

Construct entity types $E_{C_i} = C_i$ with identifier $K_{C_i} = C_i$ for each meta-attribute $C_i \in \{C_1, \ldots, C_m\}$. Each E_{C_i} contains one entity c_i.

//Construct a relationship type to represent the associations among the entities of E and the values of $C_1, \ldots, C_m$.

Construct a relationship type R connecting the entity types E' and $E_{C_1}, \ldots, E_{C_m}$.

Step 1.2: Handle the attributes of E.

Let A be an attribute (not part of the identifier) of E, and selfCnt, a set of meta-attributes with values, be the self context of A.

If A is a m:1 or m:m attribute, **then**

Case 1: attribute A has nothing to do with the context of E. Then A becomes an attribute of E'.

Case 2: attribute $A = A_{ont}$[selfCnt, inherit ALL] inherits all the context $\{C_1=c_1, \ldots, C_m=c_m\}$ from E. Then $A' = A_{ont}$[selfCnt] becomes an attribute of R.

Case 3: attribute $A = A_{ont}$[selfCnt, inherit S] inherits some discrepant meta-attributes $S \subset \{C_1, \ldots, C_m\}$ with the values from E, $S \neq \emptyset$. Then construct a relationship type R_A connecting E' and those E_{C_i} for each meta-attribute $C_i \in S$. Attribute $A' = A_{ont}$[selfCnt] becomes an attribute of R_A.

Else *// A is a 1:1 or 1:m attribute, i.e., the values of A determine the entities of E in the context. In this case, A should be modeled as an entity type to preserve the cardinality constraint. We keep the discrepant meta-attributes of A, and delay the resolution in Alg. TRANS_ENT_ATTR, the resolution for attributes of entity types.*

Construct an attribute $A' = A_{ont}$[Cnt] of E', with Cnt the (self and inherited) context of A as the (self) context of A'.

Step 1.3: Handle relationship types involving entity type E in DB.

Let R1 be a relationship type involving E in DB.

Case 1: R1 has nothing to do with the context of E. Then replace E with E' in R1.

Case 2: R1 inherits all the context $\{C_1=c_1, \ldots, C_m=c_m\}$ from E. Then replace E with R (i.e., treat R as a high level entity type) in R1.

Case 3: R1 inherits some discrepant meta-attributes $S \subset \{C_1, \ldots, C_m\}$ with the values from E, $S \neq \emptyset$. Then construct a relationship type R2 connecting E' and those E_{C_i} for each meta-attribute $C_i \in S$. Replace E with R2 in R1.

Step 2: Merge the entity types, relationship types and attributes respectively which correspond to the same ontology type with the same context, and union their domains.□

In the resolution of schematic discrepancies for relationship types, we should deal with a set of entity types (participating in a relationship type) instead of individual ones. The steps are similar to those of Algorithm TRANS_ENT, but without Step 1.3.

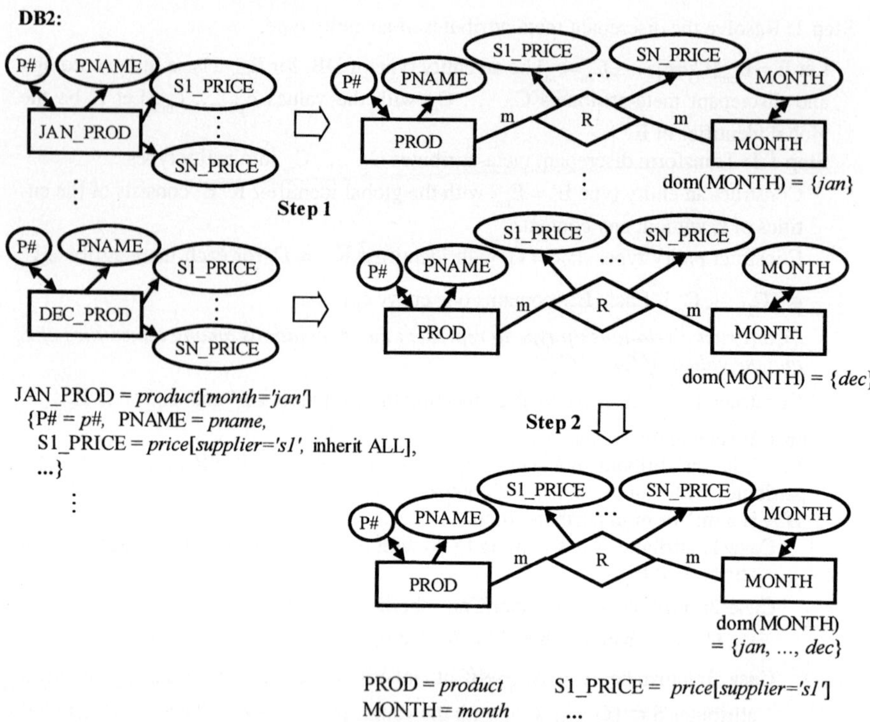

Fig. 2. Resolve schematic discrepancies for entity types

We omit the resolution algorithm TRANS_REL for lack of space, but explain it by any example below, i.e., transforming the schema of DB3 in Fig. 1.

Example 4 (Fig. 3). In Step 1, for each relationship type of DB3, say JAN_SUP, we represent the meta-attribute *month* as an entity type MONTH consisting of the only entity *jan* that is the metadata of JAN_SUP. We change JAN_SUP into the relationship type SUP after removing the context, and relate the entity type MONTH to SUP. Attribute PRICE of JAN_SUP inherits the context *month='jan'* from the relationship type, and therefore it becomes an attribute of SUP in the transformed schema. Then in Step 2, the MONTH entity types are merged into one consisting of all the entities {*jan*, ..., *dec*}; the SUP relationship types are also merged, and get the schema of DB1 in Fig. 1. □

4.2 Resolving Schematic Discrepancies for Attributes

In this sub-section, we first show how to resolve discrepancies for attributes of entity types using an example, then present Algorithm TRANS_ENT_ATTR in general. Finally, we describe the resolution of discrepancies for attributes of relationship types by an example, omitting the general algorithm which is similar to TRANS_ENT_ATTR.

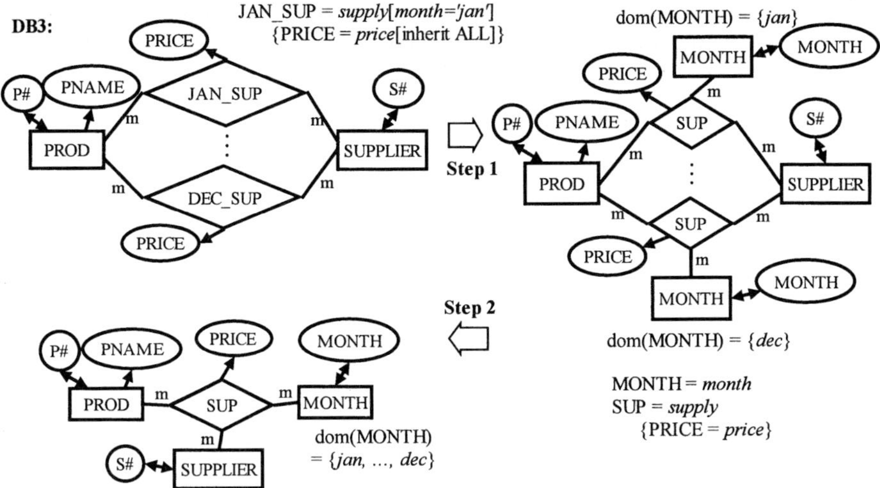

Fig. 3. Resolve schematic discrepancies for relationship types

The following example shows how to resolve discrepancies for attributes of entity types. Note the discrepancies of entity types should be resolved before this step.

Example 5 (Fig. 4). Suppose we have another database DB4 recording the supplying information, in which all the suppliers and months are modeled as contexts of the attributes in an entity type PROD. The transformation is given in Fig. 4. In Step 1, for each attribute with discrepant meta-attributes, say S1_JAN_PRICE, the meta-attributes *supplier* and *month* are represented as entity types SUPPLIER and MONTH consisting of one entity *s1* and *jan* respectively. A relationship type SUP is constructed to connect PROD, MONTH and SUPPLIER. After removing the context, we

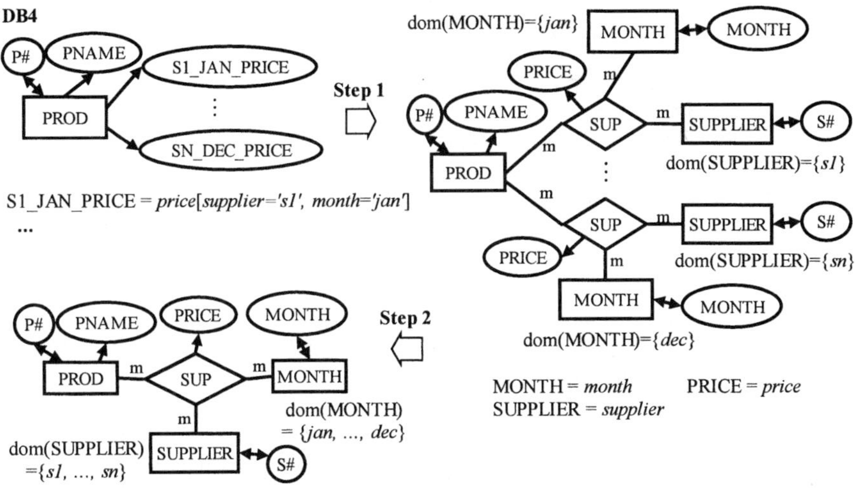

Fig. 4. Resolve schematic discrepancies for attributes of entity types

change S1_JAN_PRICE into PRICE, an attribute of the relationship type SUP. Then in Step 2, we merge all the corresponding entity types, relationship types and attributes, and get the schema of DB1 in Fig. 1. □

Then we give the general algorithm below.

Algorithm TRANS_ENT_ATTR

Input: an elevated schema DB.

Output: a schema DB' transformed from DB such that all the discrepant meta-attributes of attributes of entity types are transformed into entity types.

Step 1: Resolve the discrepant meta-attributes of an attribute in an entity type.

Given an entity type E of DB, let $A = A_{ont}[C_1=c_1, \ldots, C_m=c_m]$ be an attribute (not part of the identifier) of E, for A_{ont} a type in the ontology, and $C_1, \ldots, C_m$ the discrepant meta-attributes with the values $c_1, \ldots, c_m$. *// Note A has no inherited context which has been removed in Algorithm TRANS_ENT if any.*

// Represent the discrepant meta-attributes as entity types.

Construct entity types $E_{C_i} = C_i$ with identifiers $K_{C_i} = C_i$ for each meta-attribute $C_i \in \{C_1, \ldots, C_m\}$. Each E_{C_i} contains one entity c_i.

If A is a m:1 or m:m attribute, **then**

//Construct a relationship type to represent the associations among the entities of E and the values of $C_1, \ldots, C_m$.

Construct a relationship type R connecting the entity types E and $E_{C_1}, \ldots, E_{C_m}$.

Attribute $A' = A_{ont}$ becomes an attribute of R.

Else *// A is a 1:1 or 1:m attribute, i.e., the values of A determines the entities of E in the context. A should be modeled as an entity type to preserve the cardinality constraint.*

Construct $E_{A'} = A_{ont}$ with the identifier $A' = A_{ont}$.

Construct a relationship type R connecting the entity types E, $E_{A'}$, and $E_{C_1}, \ldots, E_{C_m}$.

Represent the FD $\{A', C_1, \ldots, C_m\} \rightarrow K$ as the cardinality constraint on R.

If A is a 1:1 attribute, also represent the FD $\{K, C_1, \ldots, C_m\} \rightarrow A'$ on R.

Step 2: Merge the entity types, relationship types and attributes respectively which correspond to the same ontology type with the same context, and union their domains.□

The resolution of schematic discrepancies for the attributes of relationship types is similar to that for the attributes of entity types, as a relationship type could be treated as a high level entity type. We omit the resolution algorithm TRANS_REL_ATTR for lack of space, but explain it by an example below.

Example 6 (Fig. 5). Given the transformed schema of Fig. 2, we transform the attributes of the relationship type R as follows. In Step 1, for each attribute of R, say S1_PRICE, we represent the meta-attribute *supplier* as an entity type SUPPLIER with one entity *s1*, and construct a relationship type SUP to connect the relationship type R and entity type SUPPLIER. After removing the context, we change S1_PRICE into PRICE, an attribute of SUP. Then in Step 2, we merge the SUPPLIER entity types and SUP relationship types respectively. In the merged schema, the relationship type R is redundant as it is a projection of SUP and has no attributes. Consequently, we remove R and get the schema of DB1 in Fig. 1. □

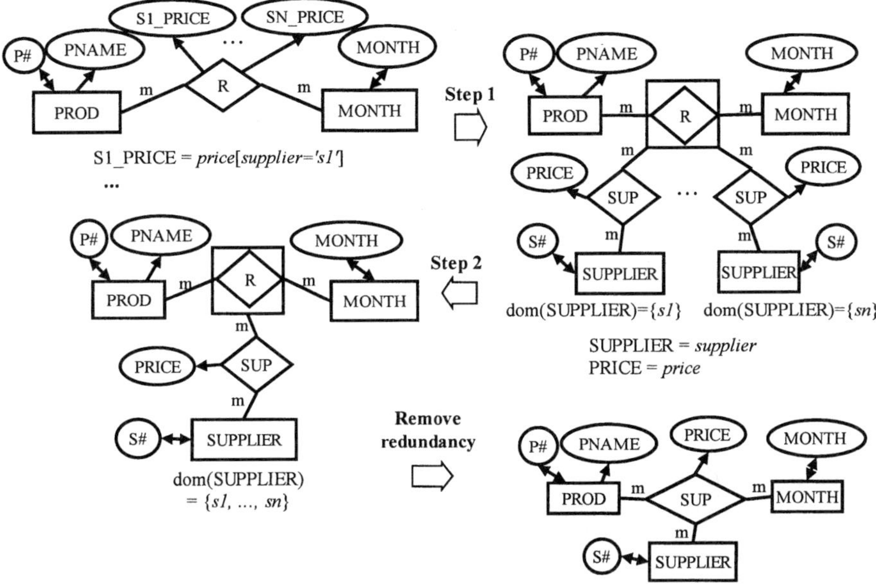

Fig. 5. Resolve schematic discrepancies for attributes of relationship types

The transformations of the algorithms (in Section 4.1 and 4.2) correctly preserve the FDs/MVDs in the presence of context, as shown in the following proposition.

Proposition 1. Let $\mathcal{E}$ be a set of similar entity types (or relationship types) with the same set of discrepant meta-attributes, and K be the global identifier of $\mathcal{E}$ (or a set of global identifiers of entity types if $\mathcal{E}$ is a set of relationship types). Suppose each entity type (or relationship type) of $\mathcal{E}$ has a set of attributes with the same cardinality:

$$\mathcal{A} = \{A \mid A = A_{ont}[C_1=c_1, \ldots, C_m=c_m, \text{inherit } C_{m+1}, \ldots, C_n], c_i \in dom(C_i) \text{ for } 1 \le i \le m\}.$$

Then in the transformed schema, $C_1, \ldots, C_n$ are modeled as entity types, and the following FDs/MVDs hold:

Case 1: $\mathcal{A}$ are m:1 attributes. Then A_{ont} is modeled as an attribute $A' = A_{ont}$, and a FD $\{K, C_1, \ldots, C_n\} \rightarrow A'$ holds.

Case 2: $\mathcal{A}$ are m:m attributes. Then A_{ont} is modeled as an attribute $A' = A_{ont}$, and a MVD $\{K, C_1, \ldots, C_n\} \twoheadrightarrow A'$ holds.

Case 3: $\mathcal{A}$ are 1:1 attributes. Then A_{ont} is modeled as an entity type with the identifier $A' = A_{ont}$, and FDs $\{K, C_1, \ldots, C_n\} \rightarrow A'$ and $\{A', C_1, \ldots, C_n\} \rightarrow K$ hold.

Case 4: $\mathcal{A}$ are 1:m attributes. Then A_{ont} is modeled as an entity type with the identifier A'= A_{ont}, and a FD {A', C_1, …, C_n} → K holds. □

For lack of space, we only prove Case 1 when $\mathcal{E}$ is a set of entity types. In a transformed schema, given two relationships with values on A': (k, c_1, …, c_m, a) and (k', c_1', …, c_m', a') for k and k' values (or value sets) of K, c_1, …, c_m and c_1', …, c_m' values of C_1, …, C_m, and a and a' values of A'. If k=k', c_1=c_1', c_2=c_2',…, c_m=c_m', then in the original schemas, the two relationships correspond to the same entity and same attribute, say A1∈$\mathcal{A}$. As A is a m:1 attribute, we have a=a'. That is, the FD {K, C_1, …, C_n} → A' holds in the transformed schema.

In schema integration, schematic discrepancies of different schema constructs should be resolved in order, i.e., first for entity types, then relationship types, finally attributes of entity types and attributes of relationship types. The resolutions for most of the other semantic heterogeneities (introduced in Section 1) follow the resolution of schematic discrepancies.

5 Related Work

Context is the key component in capturing the semantics related to the definition of an object or association. The definition of context as a set of meta-attributes with values is originally adopted in [7, 23], but is used to solve different kinds of semantic heterogeneities. Our work complements rather than competes with theirs. Their work is based on the context at the attribute level only. We consider the contexts at different levels, and the inheritance of context.

A special kind of schematic discrepancy has been studied in multidatabase interoperability, e.g. [11, 12, 16, 17, 19], and [2]. They dealt with the discrepancy when schema labels (e.g., relation names or attribute names) in one database correspond to attribute values in another. However, we use contexts to capture meta-information, and solve a more general problem in the sense that schema constructs could have multiple (instead of single) discrepant meta-attributes. Furthermore, their works are at the "structure level", i.e., they did not consider the constraint issue in the resolution of schematic discrepancies. However, the importance of constraints can never be overestimated in both individual and multidatabase systems. In particular, we preserve FDs and MVDs during schema transformation, which are expressed as cardinality constraints in ER schemas.

The purposes are also different. Previous works focused on the development of a multidatabase language by which users can query across schematic discrepant databases. However, we try to develop an integration system which can detect and resolve schematic discrepancies automatically given the meta-information on source schemas.

The issue of inferring view dependencies was introduced in [1, 8]. However, their works are based on the views defined using relational algebra. In other words, they did not solve the inference problem in the transformations between schematic discrepant schemas. In [14, 21, 24], people have begun to focus on the derivation of constraints for integrated schemas from constraints of component schemas in schema integration. However, these works failed to consider schematic discrepancy in schema integration. Our work complements theirs.

6 Conclusions and Future Works

Information integration provides a competitive advantage to businesses, and becomes a major area of investment by software companies today [18]. In this paper, we resolve a common problem in schema integration, schematic discrepancy in general, using the paradigm of context. We define context as a set of meta-attributes with values, which could be at the levels of databases, entity types, relationship types, and attributes. We design algorithms to resolve schematic discrepancies by transforming discrepant meta-attributes into entity types. The transformations preserve information and cardinality constraints which are useful in verifying lossless schema transformation, schema normalization and query processing in multidatabase systems.

We have implemented a schema integration tool to semi-automatically integrate schematic discrepant schemas from several relational databases. Next, we'll try to extend our system to integrate databases in different models and semi-structured data.

References

1. S. Abiteboul, R. Hull, and V. Vianu: Foundations of databases. Addison-Wesley, 1995, pp 216-235
2. R. Agrawal, A. Somani, Y. Xu: Storing and querying of e-commerce data. VLDB, 2001, pp 149-158
3. C. Batini, M. Lenzerini: A methodology for data schema integration in the Entity-Relationship model. IEEE Trans. on Software Engineering, 10(6), 1984
4. C. Batini, M. Lenzerini, S. B. Navathe: A comparative analysis of methodologies for database schema integration, ACM Computing Surveys, 18(4), 1986, pp 323-364
5. P. P. Chen: The entity-relationship model: toward a unified view of data. TODS 1(1), 1976
6. A. Elmagarmid, M. Rusinkiewicz, A. Sheth: Management of heterogeneous and autonomous database systems. Morgan Kaufmann, 1999
7. C. H. Goh, S. Bressan, S. Madnick, and M. Siegel: Context interchange: new features and formalisms for the intelligent integration of information. ACM Transactions on Information Systems, 17(3), 1999, pp 270-293
8. G. Gottlob: Computing covers for embedded functional dependencies. SIGMOD, 1987
9. C. N. Hsu and C. A. Knoblock: Semantic query optimization for query plans of heterogeneous multidatabase systems. TKDE 12(6), 2000, pp 959-978
10. Qi He, Tok Wang Ling: Extending and inferring functional dependencies in schema transformation. Technical report, TRA3/04. School of Computing, National University of Singapore, 2004
11. R. Krishnamurthy, W. Litwin, W. Kent: Language features for interoperability of databases with schematic discrepancies. SIGMOD, 1991, pp 40-49
12. V. Kashyap, A. Sheth: Semantic and schematic similarity between database objects: a context-based approach. The VLDB Journal 5, 1996, pp 276-304
13. Tok Wang Ling, Mong Li Lee: Issues in an entity-relationship based federated database system, CODAS, 1996, pp 60-69
14. Mong Li Lee, Tok Wang Ling: Resolving constraint conflicts in the integration of entity-relationship schemas. ER, 1997, pp 394-407
15. Mong Li Lee, Tok Wang Ling: A methodology for structural conflicts resolution in the integration of entity-relationship schemas. Knowledge and Information Sys., 5, 2003, pp 225-247
16. L. V. S. Lakshmanan, F. Sadri, S. N. Subramanian: On efficiently implementing schemaSQL on SQL database system. VLDB, 1999, pp 471-482
17. L. V. S. Lakshmanan, F. Sadri, S. N. Subramanian: SchemaSQL – an extension to SQL for multidatabase interoperability. TODS, 2001, pp 476-519

18. N. M. Mattos: Integrating information for on demand computing. VLDB, 2003, pp 8-14
19. R. J. Miller: Using schematically heterogeneous structures. SIGMOD, 1998, pp 189-200
20. Web ontology language, W3C recommendation. http://www.w3.org/TR/owl-guide/
21. M. P. Reddy, B.E.Prasad, Amar Gupta: Formulating global integrity constraints during derivation of global schema. Data & Knowledge Engineering, 16, 1995, pp 241-268
22. A. P. Sheth and S. K. Gala: Federated database systems for managing distributed, heterogeneous, and autonomous databases. ACM Computing surveys, 22(3), 1990
23. E. Sciore, M. Siegel, A. Rosenthal: Using semantic values to facilitate interoperability among heterogeneous information systems, TODS, 19(2), 1994, pp 254-290
24. M. W. W. Vermeer and P. M. G. Apers: The role of integrity constraints in database interoperation. VLDB, 1996, pp 425-435
25. Xiaoying Wu, Tok Wang Ling, Mong Li Lee, and Gillian Dobbie: Designing Semistructured Databases Using ORA-SS Model. WISE, 2001, pp 171-180

Managing Merged Data by Vague Functional Dependencies*

An Lu and Wilfred Ng

Department of Computer Science
The Hong Kong University of Science and Technology
Hong Kong, China
{anlu,wilfred}@cs.ust.hk

Abstract. In this paper, we propose a new similarity measure between vague sets and apply vague logic in a relational database environment with the objective of capturing the vagueness of the data. By introducing a new vague Similar Equality (S_{EQ}) for comparing data values, we first generalize the classical Functional Dependencies (FDs) into Vague Functional Dependencies (VFDs). We then present a set of sound and complete inference rules. Finally, we study the validation process of VFDs by examining the satisfaction degree of VFDs, and the merge-union and merge-intersection on vague relations.

1 Introduction

The relational data model [8] has been extensively studied for over three decades. This data model basically handles precise and exact data in an information source. However, many real life applications such as merging data from many sources involve imprecise and inexact data. It is well known that Fuzzy database models [11, 2], based on the fuzzy set theory by Zadeh [13], have been introduced to handle inexact and imprecise data. In [5], Gau et al. point out that the drawback of using the single membership value in fuzzy set theory is that the evidence for $u \in U$ and the evidence against $u \in U$ are in fact mixed together. (Here U is a classical set of objects, called the universe of discourse. An element of U is denoted by u.) Therefore, they propose vague sets, which is similar to that of intuitionistic fuzzy sets proposed in [1]. A true membership function $\alpha_V(u)$ and a false membership function $\beta_V(u)$ are used to characterize the lower bound on $\mu_F(u)$. (Here V means a vague set and F means a fuzzy set.) The lower bounds are used to create a subinterval $[\alpha_V(u), 1 - \beta_V(u)]$ of the unit interval [0,1], where $0 \leq \alpha_V(u) \leq \mu_F(u) \leq 1 - \beta_V(u) \leq 1$, in order to generalize the membership function of fuzzy sets.

There have been many studies which discuss the topic concerning how to measure the degree of similarity or distance between vague sets or intuitionistic fuzzy sets [3, 4, 7, 9, 12, 6]. However, the proposed methods have some limitations.

* This work is supported in part by grants from the Research Grant Council of Hong Kong, Grant Nos HKUST6185/02E and HKUST6165/03E.

P. Atzeni et al. (Eds.): ER 2004, LNCS 3288, pp. 259–272, 2004.

For example, Hong's similarity measure in [7] means that the similarity measure between the vague value with the most imprecise evidence (the precision of the evidence is 0) and the vague value with the most precise evidence (the precision of the evidence is 1) is equal to 0.5. In this case, the similarity measure should be equal to 0. Our view is that the similarity measure should include two factors of vague values. One is the difference between the evidences contained by the vague values; another is the difference between the precisions of the evidences. However, the proposed measures or distances consider only one factor (e.g. in [3, 4]) or do not combine both the factors appropriately (e.g. in [7, 9, 12, 6]). Our new similarity measure is able to return a more reasonable answer.

In this paper, we extend the classical relational data model to deal with vague information. Our first objective is to extend relational databases to include vague domains by suitably defining the *Vague Functional Dependencies* ($VFDs$) based on our notion of similarity measure. A set of sound and complete inference rules for $VFDs$ is then established. We discuss the satisfaction degree of $VFDs$ and apply $VFDs$ in merged vague relations as the second objective. The main contributions of the paper are as follows: (1) A new similarity measure between vague sets is proposed to remedy some problems for similar definitions in literature. We argue that our measure gives a more reasonable estimation; (2) A VFD is proposed in order to capture more semantics in vague relations; (3) The satisfaction degree of $VFDs$ in merged vague relations is studied.

The rest of the paper is organized as follows. Section 2 presents some basic concepts related to databases and the vague set theory. In Section 3, we propose a new similarity measure between vague sets. In Section 4, we introduce the concept of a *Vague Functional Dependency* (VFD) and the associated inference rules. We then explain the validation process which determines the satisfaction degree of $VFDs$ in vague relations. In Section 5, we give the definitions of merge operators of vague relations and discuss the satisfaction degree of $VFDs$ after merging. Section 6 concludes the paper.

2 Preliminaries

In this section, some basic concepts related to the classical relational data model and the vague set theory are given.

2.1 Relational Data Model

We assume the readers are familiar with the basic concepts of the relation data model [8]. There are two operations on relations that are particularly relevant in subsequent discussion: *projection* and *natural join*. The projection of a relation r of *R(XYZ)* over the set of attributes X is obtained by taking the restriction of the tuples of r to the attributes in X and eliminating duplicate tuples in what remains. This operation is denoted by $\pi_X(r) = \{t[X] \mid t \in r\}$. Let r_1 and r_2 be two relations of *R(XY)* and *R(XZ)*, respectively. The natural join $r_1 \bowtie r_2$ is a relation over *R(XYZ)* defined by $r = r_1 \bowtie r_2 = \{t \mid t[XY] \in$

r_1 and $t[YZ] \in r_2\}$. *Functional Dependencies* (*FDs*) are important integrity constraints in relational databases. An FD is a statement, $X \rightarrow Y$, where X and Y are sets of attributes. A relation r satisfies the FD, if for all t_p and t_q in r, $t_p[X] = t_q[X]$ implies $t_p[Y] = t_q[Y]$.

2.2 Vague Data Model

Let U be a classical set of objects, called the universe of discourse, where an element of U is denoted by u.

Definition 1. (Vague Set) *A vague set V in a universe of discourse U is characterized by a true membership function, α_V, and a false membership function, β_V, as follows: $\alpha_V : U \rightarrow [0,1], \beta_V : U \rightarrow [0,1]$, and $\alpha_V(u) + \beta_V(u) \leq 1$, where $\alpha_V(u)$ is a lower bound on the grade of membership of u derived from the evidence for u, and $\beta_V(u)$ is a lower bound on the grade of membership of the negation of u derived from the evidence against u.*

Suppose $U = \{u_1, u_2, \ldots, u_n\}$. A vague set V of the universe of discourse U can be represented by $V = \sum_{i=1}^{n}[\alpha(u_i), 1 - \beta(u_i)]/u_i$, where $0 \leq \alpha(u_i) \leq 1 - \beta(u_i) \leq 1$ and $1 \leq i \leq n$.

This approach bounds the grade of membership of u to a subinterval $[\alpha_V(u), 1 - \beta_V(u)]$ of $[0,1]$. In other words, the exact grade of membership $\mu_V(u)$ of u may be unknown, but is bounded by $\alpha_V(u) \leq \mu_V(u) \leq 1 - \beta_V(u)$, where $\alpha_V(u) + \beta_V(u) \leq 1$. We depict these ideas in Fig. 1. Throughout this paper, we simply use α and β for u if no ambiguity of V arising.

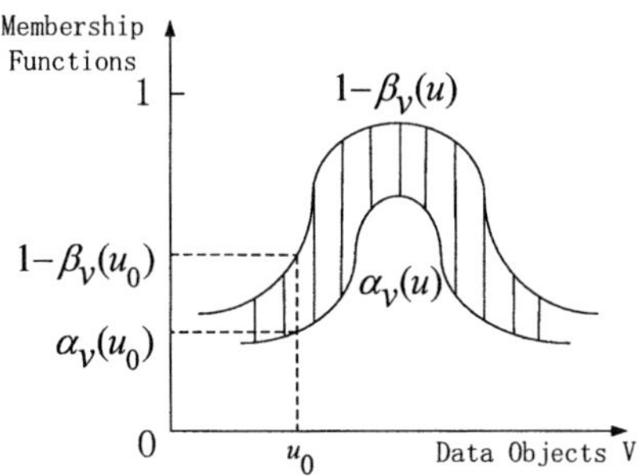

Fig. 1. The true (α) and false (β) membership functions of a vague set

For a vague set $[\alpha(u), 1 - \beta(u)]/u$, we say that the interval $[\alpha(u), 1 - \beta(u)]$ is the vague value to the object u. For example, if $[\alpha(u), 1 - \beta(u)] = [0.6, 0.9]$, then we can see that $\alpha(u) = 0.6$, $1 - \beta(u) = 0.9$ and $\beta(u) = 0.1$. It is interpreted as "the degree that object u belongs to the vague set V is 0.6, the degree that object u does not belong to the vague set V is 0.1." In a voting process, the vague value [0.6,0.9] can be interpreted as " the vote for resolution is 6 in favor, 1 against, and 3 neutral (abstentious)."

The precision of the knowledge about u is characterized by the difference $(1 - \beta(u) - \alpha(u))$. If this is small, the knowledge about u is relatively precise; if it is large, we know correspondingly little. If $(1 - \beta(u))$ is equal to $\alpha(u)$, the knowledge about u is exact, and the vague set theory reverts back to fuzzy set theory. If $(1 - \beta(u))$ and $\alpha(u)$ are both equal to 1 or 0, depending on whether u does or does not belong to V, the knowledge about u is very exact and the theory reverts back to ordinary sets. Thus, any crisp or fuzzy value can be regarded as a special case of a vague value. For example, the ordinary set $\{u\}$ can be presented as the vague set $[1, 1]/u$, while the fuzzy set $0.8/u$ (the membership of u is 0.8) can be presented as the vague set $[0.8, 0.8]/u$.

Definition 2. (Empty Vague Set) *A vague set V is an empty vague set, if and only if, its true membership function $\alpha = 0$ and false membership function $\beta = 1$ for all u. We use $\emptyset$ to denote it.*

Definition 3. (Complement) *The complement of a vague set V is denoted by V' and is defined by $\alpha_{V'}(u) = \beta_V(u)$, and $1 - \beta_{V'}(u) = 1 - \alpha_V(u)$.*

Definition 4. (Containment) *A vague set A is contained in another vague set B, $A \subseteq B$, if and only if, $\alpha_A(u) \leq \alpha_B(u)$, and $1 - \beta_A(u) \leq 1 - \beta_B(u)$.*

Definition 5. (Equality) *Two vague sets A and B are equal, written as $A = B$, if and only if, $A \subseteq B$ and $B \subseteq A$; that is $\alpha_A(u) = \alpha_B(u)$, and $1 - \beta_A(u) = 1 - \beta_B(u)$.*

Definition 6. (Union) *The union of two vague sets A and B is a vague set C, written as $C = A \cup B$, whose true membership and false membership functions are related to those of A and B by $\alpha_C(u) = max(\alpha_A(u), \alpha_B(u))$, and $1 - \beta_C(u) = max(1 - \beta_A(u), 1 - \beta_B(u)) = 1 - min(\beta_A(u), \beta_B(u))$.*

Definition 7. (Intersection) *The intersection of two vague sets A and B is a vague set C, written as $C = A \cap B$, whose true membership and false membership functions are related to those of A and B by $\alpha_C(u) = min(\alpha_A(u), \alpha_B(u))$, and $1 - \beta_C(u) = min(1 - \beta_A(u), 1 - \beta_B(u)) = 1 - max(\beta_A(u), \beta_B(u))$.*

Definition 8. (Cartesian Product) *Let $U = U_1 \times U_2 \times \cdots \times U_m$, be the Cartesian product of m universes, and $A_1, A_2, \ldots, A_m$ be the vague sets in their corresponding universe of discourse $U_1, U_2, \cdots, U_m$, respectively, $u_i \in U_i, i = 1, \ldots, m$. The Cartesian product $A = A_1 \times A_2 \times \cdots \times A_m$ is defined to be a vague set of $U = U_1 \times U_2 \times \cdots \times U_m$, where the memberships are defined as follows: $\alpha_A(u_1 \cdots u_m) = min\{\alpha_{A_1}(u_1), \ldots, \alpha_{A_m}(u_m)\}$, and $1 - \beta_A(u_1 \cdots u_m) = min\{(1 - \beta_{A_1}(u_1)), \ldots, (1 - \beta_{A_m}(u_m))\} = 1 - max\{\beta_{A_1}(u_1), \ldots, \beta_{A_m}(u_m)\}$.*

2.3 Vague Relations

Definition 9. (Vague Relation) *A vague relation r on a relation scheme $R = \{A_1, A_2, \ldots, A_m\}$ is a vague subset of $Dom(A_1) \times Dom(A_2) \times \cdots \times Dom(A_m)$. A tuple $t = (a_1, a_2, \ldots, a_m)$ in $Dom(A_1) \times Dom(A_2) \times \cdots \times Dom(A_m)$ is a vague subset of $U = U_1 \times U_2 \times \cdots \times U_m$.*

A relation scheme R is denoted by $R\{A_1, A_2, \ldots, A_m\}$ or simply by R if the attributes are understood. Corresponding to each attribute name $A_i, 1 \leq i \leq m$, the domain of A_i is written as $Dom(A_i)$. However, unlike classical and fuzzy relations, in vague relations, we define $Dom(A_i)$ as a set of vague sets. Vague relations may be considered as an extension of classical relations and fuzzy relations, which can capture more information about imprecision.

Example 1. Consider the vague relation r over Product(ID, Weight, Price) given in Table 1. In r, $Weight$ and $Price$ are vague attributes. To make the attribute ID simple, we express it as the ordinary value. The first tuple in r means the product with $ID = 1$ has the weight of $[1,1]/10$ and the price of $[0.4, 0.6]/50 + [1,1]/80$, which are vague sets. In the vague set $[1,1]/10$, $[1,1]$ means the evidence in favor "the weight is 10" is 1 and the evidence against it is 0.

Table 1. A Product Relation r

ID	Weight	Price
1	[1,1]/10	[0.4,0.6]/50+[1,1]/80
2	[1,1]/20	[1,1]/100+[0.6,0.8]/150
3	[1,1]/20	[1,1]/100+[0.6,0.8]/150
4	[1,1]/10+[0.6,0.8]/15	[1,1]/80+[0.6,0.8]/100
5	[0.6,0.8]/10+[1,1]/15+[0.6,0.8]/20	[0.6,0.8]/60+[1,1]/90

3 Similarity Measure Between Vague Sets

In this section, we review the notions of similarity measures between vague sets proposed by Chen [3, 4], Hong [7] and Li [9], together with distances between intuitionistic fuzzy sets proposed by Szmidt [12] and Grzegorzewski [6]. We show by some examples that these measures are not able to reflect our intuitions. A new similarity measure between vague sets is proposed to remedy the limitations.

3.1 Similarity Measure Between Two Vague Values

Let x and y be two vague values to a certain object such that $x = [\alpha_x, 1 - \beta_x]$, $y = [\alpha_y, 1 - \beta_y]$. In general, there are two factors should be considered in measuring the similarity between two vague values. One is the difference between the difference of the true and false membership values, which is given by $D_d = |(\alpha_x - \beta_x) - (\alpha_y - \beta_y)|/2 = |(\alpha_x - \alpha_y) - (\beta_x - \beta_y)|/2$, such that $0 \leq D_d \leq 1$; another is the difference between the sum of the true and false membership values, which is given by $D_s = |(\alpha_x + \beta_x) - (\alpha_y + \beta_y)| = |(\alpha_x - \alpha_y) + (\beta_x - \beta_y)|$, such that $0 \leq D_s \leq 1$. The first factor implies the difference between the evidences contained by the vague values, and the second factor implies the difference between the precisions of the evidences.

In [3, 4], Chen defines a similarity measure between two vague values x and y as follows:

$$M_C(x, y) = 1 - \frac{|(\alpha_x - \alpha_y) - (\beta_x - \beta_y)|}{2}, \tag{1}$$

which is equal to $(1-D_d)$. This similarity measure ignores the difference between the precisions of the evidences (D_s). For example, consider $x = [0,1], y = [a, 1-a], 0 < a \leq 0.5$,

$$M_C(x,y) = 1 - \frac{|(0-a)-(0-a)|}{2} = 1. \quad (2)$$

This means that x and y are equal. On the one hand, $x = [0,1]$ means $\alpha_x = 0$ and $\beta_x = 0$, that is to say, we have no information about the evidence, and the precision of the evidence is zero. On the other hand, $y = [a, 1-a]$ means $\alpha_x = a$ and $\beta_x = a$, that is to say, we have some information about the evidence, and the precision of the evidence is not zero. So it is not intuitive to have the similarity measure of x and y being equal to 1.

In order to solve this problem, Hong et al. [7] propose another similarity measure between vague values as follows:

$$M_H(x,y) = 1 - \frac{|\alpha_x - \alpha_y| + |\beta_x - \beta_y|}{2}. \quad (3)$$

However, this definition also has some problems. Here is an example.

Example 2. The similarity measure between $[0,1]$ and $[a,a], 0 \leq a \leq 1$ is equal to 0.5. This means that the similarity measure between the vague value with the most imprecise evidence (the precision of the evidence is equal to zero) and the vague value with the most precise evidence (the precision of the evidence is equal to one) is equal to 0.5. However, our intuition shows that the similarity measure in this case should be equal to 0.

Li et al. in [9] also give a similarity measure in order to remedy the problems in Chen's definition as follows:

$$M_L(x,y) = 1 - \frac{|(\alpha_x - \alpha_y) - (\beta_x - \beta_y)| + |\alpha_x - \alpha_y| + |\beta_x - \beta_y|}{4}. \quad (4)$$

It can be checked that $M_L(x,y) = (M_C(x,y) + M_H(x,y))/2$. This means Li's similarity measure is just the arithmetic mean of Chen's and Hong's. So Li's similarity measure still contains the same problems.

[12, 6] adopt Hamming distance and Euclidean distance to measure the distances between intuitionistic fuzzy sets as follows:

1. Hamming distance is given by

$$D_H(x,y) = \frac{|\alpha_x - \alpha_y| + |\beta_x - \beta_y| + |(\alpha_x - \alpha_y) + (\beta_x - \beta_y)|}{2}; \quad (5)$$

2. Euclidean distance is given by

$$D_E(x,y) = \sqrt{\frac{(\alpha_x - \alpha_y)^2 + (\beta_x - \beta_y)^2 + ((\alpha_x - \alpha_y) + (\beta_x - \beta_y))^2}{2}}. \quad (6)$$

These methods also have some problems. Here is an example.

Example 3. We still consider the vague values x, y_1 and y_2 in Example 2. For the Hamming distance, it can be calculated that $D_H(x, y_1) = D_H(x, y_2) = 0.6$. This means that the Hamming distance between x and y_1 are equal to that between x and y_2. In a voting process, as mentioned in Example 2, since both x and y_2 have identical votes in favor and against, the Hamming distance between x and y_2 should be less than that between x and y_1. For the Euclidean distance, consider the Euclidean distance between $[0, 1]$ and $[a, a], 0 \leq a < 1$, which is equal to $(\sqrt{a^2 - a + 1})$. This means that the distance between the vague value with the most imprecise evidence and the vague value with the most precise evidence is not equal to 1. (Actually, the Euclidean distance in this case is in the interval $[\frac{\sqrt{3}}{2}, 1)$.) However, our intuition shows that the distance in this case should always be equal to 1.

In order to solve all the problems mentioned above, we define a new similarity measure between the vague values x and y as follows:

Definition 10. (Similarity Measure Between Two Vague Values)

$$\begin{aligned} M(x,y) &= \sqrt{(1 - D_d)(1 - D_s)} \\ &= \sqrt{(1 - \frac{|(\alpha_x - \alpha_y) - (\beta_x - \beta_y)|}{2})(1 - |(\alpha_x - \alpha_y) + (\beta_x - \beta_y)|)}. \end{aligned} \quad (7)$$

Furthermore, we define a distance between the vague values x and y as $D(x, y) = 1 - M(x, y)$.

The similarity measure given in Definition 10 takes into account of both the difference between the evidences contained by the vague values and the difference between the precisions of the evidences. Here is an example.

Example 4. We still consider the vague values x, y_1 and y_2 in Example 2. It can be calculated that $M(x, y_1) = 0.53$, $M(x, y_2) = 0.63$. So $M(x, y_1) < M(x, y_2)$. This means that the similarity measures between x and y_1 are less than that between x and y_2. As mentioned in Example 2, this result is accordant to our intuition. Another example is the similarity measure between $[0, 1]$ and $[a, a], 0 \leq a \leq 1$, which is equal to 0. This means that the similarity measure between the vague value with the most imprecise evidence and the vague value with the most precise evidence is equal to 0. This result is also accordant to our intuition.

From Definition 10, we can obtain the following theorem.

Theorem 1. *The following statements are true:*

1. *The similarity measure is bounded, i.e., $0 \leq M(x, y) \leq 1$;*
2. *$M(x, y) = 1$, if and only if, the vague values x and y are equal (i.e., $x = y$);*
3. *$M(x, y) = 0$, if and only if, the vague values x and y are $[0, 0]$ and $[1, 1]$ or $[0, 1]$ and $[a, a], 0 \leq a \leq 1$;*
4. *The similarity measure is commutative, i.e., $M(x, y) = M(y, x)$.*

3.2 Similarity Measure Between Two Vague Sets

We generalize the similarity measure to two given vague sets.

Definition 11. (Similarity Measure Between Two Vague Sets) *Let X and Y be two vague sets, where $X = \sum_{i=1}^{n}[\alpha_X(u_i), 1-\beta_X(u_i)]/u_i$, and $Y = \sum_{i=1}^{n}[\alpha_Y(u_i), 1-\beta_Y(u_i)]/u_i$. The similarity measure between the vague sets X and Y can be evaluated as follows:*

$$M(X,Y) = \frac{1}{n}\sum_{k=1}^{n} M([\alpha_X(u_k), 1-\beta_X(u_k)], [\alpha_Y(u_k), 1-\beta_Y(u_k)])$$

$$= \frac{1}{n}\sum_{k=1}^{n}\sqrt{(1-\frac{|(\alpha_X(u_k)-\alpha_Y(u_k))-(\beta_X(u_k)-\beta_Y(u_k))|}{2})}\cdot$$

$$\sqrt{(1-|(\alpha_X(u_k)-\alpha_Y(u_k))+(\beta_X(u_k)-\beta_Y(u_k))|)}. \quad (8)$$

Similarly, we give the definition of distance between two vague sets as $D(X,Y) = 1 - M(X,Y)$.

From Definition 11, we obtain the following theorem for vague sets, which is similar to Theorem 1.

Theorem 2. *The following statements related to $M(X,Y)$ are true:*

1. *The similarity measure is bounded, i.e., $0 \le M(X,Y) \le 1$;*
2. *$M(X,Y) = 1$, if and only if, the vague sets X and Y are equal (i.e., $X = Y$);*
3. *$M(X,Y) = 0$, if and only if, all the vague values $[\alpha_X(u_k), 1-\beta_X(u_k)]$ and $[\alpha_Y(u_k), 1-\beta_Y(u_k)]$ are $[0,0]$ and $[1,1]$ or $[0,1]$ and $[a,a], 0 \le a \le 1$;*
4. *The similarity measure is commutative, i.e., $M(X,Y) = M(Y,X)$.*

4 Vague Functional Dependencies and Inference Rules

In this section, we first give the definition of *Similar Equality* (S_{EQ}) of vague relations, which can be used to compare vague relations. Then we present the definition of a *Vague Functional Dependency* (VFD). Next, we present a set of sound and complete inference rules for *VFDs*, which is an analogy to Armstrong's Axiom for classical *FDs*.

4.1 Similar Equality of Vague Relations

Similar Equality (S_{EQ}) of vague relations defined below can be used as a vague similarity measure to compare elements of a given domain. Suppose t_p and t_q are any two tuples in a relation r over the scheme R.

Definition 12. (Similar Equality of Tuples) *The Similar Equality of two vague tuples t_p and t_q on the attribute A_i in a vague relation is given by:*

$$S_{EQ}(t_p[A_i], t_q[A_i])$$

$$= \frac{1}{n}\sum_{k=1}^{n}\sqrt{(1-\frac{|(\alpha_{t_p[A_i]}(u_k)-\alpha_{t_q[A_i]}(u_k))-(\beta_{t_p[A_i]}(u_k)-\beta_{t_q[A_i]}(u_k))|}{2})}\cdot$$

$$\sqrt{(1-|(\alpha_{t_p[A_i]}(u_k)-\alpha_{t_q[A_i]}(u_k))+(\beta_{t_p[A_i]}(u_k)-\beta_{t_q[A_i]}(u_k))|)}. \quad (9)$$

The Similar Equality of two vague tuples t_p and t_q on attributes $X = \{A_1, \ldots, A_n\}$ $(X \subseteq R)$ in a vague relation is given by:

$$S_{EQ}(t_p[X], t_q[X]) = S_{EQ}(t_p[A_1 \cdots A_n], t_q[A_1 \cdots A_n]) \\ = min\{S_{EQ}(t_p[A_1], t_q[A_1]), \ldots, S_{EQ}(t_p[A_n], t_q[A_n])\}. \quad (10)$$

From Definition 12 and Theorem 2, we have the following theorem.

Theorem 3. *The following statements of the properties of $S_{EQ}(t_p[X], t_q[X])$ are true:*

1. *The similar equality is bounded: $0 \leq S_{EQ}(t_p[X], t_q[X]) \leq 1$;*
2. *$S_{EQ}(t_p[X], t_q[X]) = 1$, if and only if, all vague sets $t_p[A_s]$ and $t_q[A_s]$ $(i \leq s \leq j)$ are equal (i.e., $t_p[A_s] = t_q[A_s], i \leq s \leq j$);*
3. *$S_{EQ}(t_p[X], t_q[X]) = 0$, if and only if, $\exists A_i \in X$, $S_{EQ}(t_p[A_i], t_q[A_i]) = 0$, if and only if, $\exists A_i \in X$, all the vague values $[\alpha_{t_p[A_i]}(u_k), 1 - \beta_{t_p[A_i]}(u_k)]$ and $[\alpha_{t_q[A_i]}(u_k), 1 - \beta_{t_q[A_i]}(u_k)]$ are $[0, 0]$ and $[1, 1]$, or $[0, 1]$ and $[a, a]$, where $0 \leq a \leq 1$;*
4. *The similar equality is commutative: $S_{EQ}(t_p[X], t_q[X]) = S_{EQ}(t_q[X], t_p[X])$.*

4.2 Vague Functional Dependencies

Informally, a VFD captures the semantics of the fact that, for given two tuples, Y values should not be less similar than X values. We now give the following definition of a VFD.

Definition 13. (Vague Functional Dependency) *Given a relation r over a relation schema $R(A_1, A_2, \ldots, A_m)$, where $Dom(A_i)$ $(i = 1, \ldots, m)$ are sets of vague sets, a Vague Functional Dependency (VFD) $X \hookrightarrow Y$ where $X, Y \subseteq R$ holds over r, if for all tuples t_p and t_q in r, we have $S_{EQ}(t_p[X], t_q[X]) \leq S_{EQ}(t_p[Y], t_q[Y])$.*

In the database literature [8], a set of inference rules is generally used to derive new data dependencies from the given set of dependencies. We now present a set of sound and complete inference rules for $VFDs$, which is similar to Armstrong's Axiom for FDs.

Definition 14. (Inference Rules) *Let us consider a relation scheme $R(A_1, A_2, \ldots, A_m)$ and a set of $VFDs$ F. Let X, Y, and Z be subsets of the relation scheme R. We define a set of inference rules as follows:*

1. *Reflexivity: If $Y \subseteq X$, then $X \hookrightarrow Y$;*
2. *Augmentation: If $X \hookrightarrow Y$ holds, then $XZ \hookrightarrow YZ$ also holds;*
3. *Transitivity: If $X \hookrightarrow Y$ and $Y \hookrightarrow Z$ hold, then $X \hookrightarrow Z$ holds.*

The following theorem follows by assuming that there are at least two elements a and b in each data domain such that $S_{EQ}(a, b) = 0$.

Theorem 4. *The inference rules given in Definition 14 are sound and complete.*

The Union, Decomposition, Pseudotransitivity rules follow from these three rules, as in the case of functional dependencies [8]. We skip the proof due to space limitation.

4.3 Validation of VFDs

In this section, we study the validation issues of $VFDs$. We relax the notion that if a VFD does not hold for a pair of tuples in r, then the VFD does not hold. We allow the VFD to hold with a certain satisfaction degree over r. The validation process and the calculation of the satisfaction degree of the VFD $X \hookrightarrow A$ are given as follows:

1. For every attribute A_i in $X \cup A$, we calculate $S_{EQ}(t_p[A_i], t_q[A_i])$ between every pair of tuples t_p and t_q in r by constructing two $n \times n$ (n is the cardinality of r) upper triangular matrices X and A. The row and column represent a comparison of different tuples. We ignore the lower part of the matrix and the diagonal, since S_{EQ} is commutative. Thus we get $n(n-1)/2$ entries in the matrix. Each entry is the comparison of a pair of tuples;
2. We check $S_{EQ}(t_p[X], t_q[X]) \leq S_{EQ}(t_p[A], t_q[A])$ for every t_p, t_q in r. If true, then we say that the VFD $X \hookrightarrow A$ holds (with the satisfaction degree of 1). We construct a matrix $W = X - A$ to check this;
3. If the result in Step 2 is not true, in the matrix W, we count the number of entries (denoted by s) which are less than or equal to 0. The satisfaction degree SD of the VFD $X \hookrightarrow A$ in r can be calculated as follows:

$$SD = \frac{s}{(\frac{n(n-1)}{2})}. \tag{11}$$

Obviously, if the inequality given in Definition 13 holds for all tuples in r, the satisfaction degree calculated by (11) is equal to 1.

Suppose there are many $VFDs$ hold over relation r, say $f_1, f_2, \ldots, f_n$, with the satisfaction degrees $SD_1, SD_2, \ldots, SD_n$ respectively. We use a VFD set $F = \{f_1, f_2, \ldots, f_n\}$ to present this. Then the satisfaction degree of the VFD set F over relation r can be calculated by the arithmetic mean of the satisfaction degrees of F as follows:

$$SD_F = \frac{SD_1 + SD_2 + \cdots + SD_n}{n}. \tag{12}$$

Here is an example to illustrate the validation process and the calculation of the satisfaction degree of the VFD.

Example 5. Consider the vague relation r presented in Table 1, it can be checked that the VFD $Weight \hookrightarrow Price$ holds to a certain satisfaction degree.

In step 1, we calculate $S_{EQ}(t_p[A_i], t_q[A_i])$ for attributes $X = Weight$ and $A = Price$ and the results are shown by matrix X and A or Tables 2 and 3.

In step 2, we check $S_{EQ}(t_p[X], t_q[X]) \leq S_{EQ}(t_p[A], t_q[A])$ by taking the difference between the two matrices X and A. The result is shown by matrix W or Table 4.

Since $S_{EQ}(t_p[X], t_q[X]) \leq S_{EQ}(t_p[A], t_q[A])$ does not hold for every p, q, we go to step 3.

In step 3, we get $s = 5$. So the satisfaction degree SD can be calculated as follows:

Table 2. Weight

$$\mathbf{X} = \begin{pmatrix} - & 0 & 0 & 0.74 & 0.41 \\ - & - & 1 & 0.16 & 0.41 \\ - & - & - & 0.16 & 0.41 \\ - & - & - & - & 0.66 \\ - & - & - & - & - \end{pmatrix}$$

Tuples	1	2	3	4	5
1	-	0	0	0.74	0.41
2	-	-	1	0.16	0.41
3	-	-	-	0.16	0.41
4	-	-	-	-	0.66
5	-	-	-	-	-

Table 3. Price

$$\mathbf{A} = \begin{pmatrix} - & 0.28 & 0.28 & 0.71 & 0.28 \\ - & - & 1 & 0.41 & 0.24 \\ - & - & - & 0.41 & 0.24 \\ - & - & - & - & 0.24 \\ - & - & - & - & - \end{pmatrix}$$

Tuples	1	2	3	4	5
1	-	0.28	0.28	0.71	0.28
2	-	-	1	0.41	0.24
3	-	-	-	0.41	0.24
4	-	-	-	-	0.24
5	-	-	-	-	-

$$SD = \frac{s}{(\frac{n(n-1)}{2})} = \frac{5}{(\frac{5(5-1)}{2})} = 0.5. \tag{13}$$

Therefore, the *VFD* $Weight \hookrightarrow Price$ over relation r holds with the satisfaction degree 0.5.

Furthermore, for the zero entries in W, we check the corresponding values in the matrix X. If the values are equal to 1, all vague sets ($t_p[A_i]$ and $t_q[A_i]$) (A_i in X) are equal according to Theorem 3. Thus, we can remove some redundancies by decomposing the original relation into two relations.

For instance, there is a value in position (3,2) is 0 in W above. We check the corresponding value in position (3,2) in matrix X, and find the value is 1. So the vague relation in Table 1 can be decomposed into two relations *IW(ID, Weight)*, *WP(Weight,Price)* (Tables 5 and 6), and some redundancies have been removed.

5 Merge Operations of Vague Relations

In this section, we first give the definition of merge operators of vague relations and then discuss the evaluation of the satisfaction degree of $VFDs$ over the merged vague relations.

Table 4. Weight-Price

$$\mathbf{W} = \begin{pmatrix} - & -0.28 & -0.28 & 0.03 & 0.13 \\ - & - & 0 & -0.25 & 0.17 \\ - & - & - & -0.25 & 0.17 \\ - & - & - & - & 0.42 \\ - & - & - & - & - \end{pmatrix}$$

Tuples	1	2	3	4	5
1	-	-0.28	-0.28	0.03	0.13
2	-	-	0	-0.25	0.17
3	-	-	-	-0.25	0.17
4	-	-	-	-	0.42
5	-	-	-	-	-

Table 5. IW

ID	Weight
1	[1,1]/10
2	[1,1]/20
3	[1,1]/20
4	[1,1]/10+[0.6,0.8]/15
5	[0.6,0.8]/10+[1,1]/15+[0.6,0.8]/20

Table 6. WP

Weight	Price
[1,1]/10	[0.4,0.6]/50,[1,1]/80
[1,1]/20	[1,1]/100+[0.6,0.8]/150
[1,1]/10+[0.6,0.8]/15	[1,1]/80+[0.6,0.8]/100
[0.6,0.8]/10+[1,1]/15 +[0.6,0.8]/20	[0.6,0.8]/60+[1,1]/90

5.1 Merge Operators

Generally speaking, when multiple data sources merge together, the result may contain objects of three cases [10]: (1) an attribute value is not provided; (2) an attribute value is provided by exactly one source; (3) an attribute value is provided by more than one source. When merging vague data, in the first case, we use an empty vague set to express the unavailable value; in the second case, we keep the original vague set; in the third case, we take the union of the vague sets provided by the source. We now define two new merge operators to serve our purpose.

Definition 15. (Join Merge Operator) *Let t_r be a tuple in the vague relation r over scheme $R = (A_1, A_2, \ldots, A_m)$ and t_s be a tuple in the vague relation s over scheme $S = (A_1, A_i, \ldots, A_n)$. r and s have a common ID attribute A_1. The attributes $A_i, \ldots, A_m$ are common in both vague relations. Then we define the* join merge *of r and s, denoted by $r \wedge s$, as follows: $r \wedge s = \{t | \exists t_r \in r, t_s \in s$ with $t[A_1] = t_r[A_1] = t_s[A_1], t[A_j] = t_r[A_j], j = 2, \ldots, i-1; t[A_j] = t_r[A_j] \cup t_s[A_j], j = i, \ldots, m; t[A_j] = t_s[A_j], j = m+1, \ldots, n\}$, where $t_r[A_j] \cup t_s[A_j]$ means the union of two vague sets as defined in Definition 6.*

Definition 16. (Union Merge Operator) *Let $r' = r - \pi_R(r \wedge s)$, $s' = s - \pi_S(r \wedge s)$. Then we define the union merge of r and s, denoted by $r \vee s$, as follows: $r \vee s = (r \wedge s) \cup \{t | \forall t_{r'} \in r'$ with $t[A_j] = t_{r'}[A_j], j = 1, \ldots, m; t[A_j] = \emptyset, j = m+1, \ldots, n\} \cup \{t | \forall t_{s'} \in s'$ with $t[A_1] = t_{s'}[A_1], t[A_j] = \emptyset, j = 2, \ldots, i-1; t[A_j] = t_{s'}[A_j], j = i, \ldots, n\}$, where $\emptyset$ means an empty vague set.*

Since vague sets have the property of associativity given in [5], the join merge operator and the union merge operator also have the property of associativity. That is to say, $r \wedge (s \wedge t) = (r \wedge s) \wedge t$ and $r \vee (s \vee t) = (r \vee s) \vee t$ (recall that r, s, t are vague relations). We can also generalize Definitions 15 and 16 to more than two data sources. Definition 16 guarantees that every tuple is contained in the new merged relation. For example, consider the following vague relations r and s given in Tables 7 and 8. We then have $(r \wedge s)$ and $(r \vee s)$ as given in Tables 9 and 10.

5.2 Satisfaction Degree of Merged Relations

Suppose we have m data sources represented by the vague relations $r_1, \ldots, r_m$. Each relation r_i $(1 \leq i \leq m)$ has a set of $VFDs$, F_i $(1 \leq i \leq m)$, with

Table 7. Vague Relation r

A_1	A_2	A_3
1	[1,1]/2	∅
2	∅	[0.3,0.7]/a+ [0.6,0.8]/c
3	[0.2,0.3]/6+ [0.5,0.7]/8	[0.7,0.9]/b+ [0.5,0.9]/d

Table 8. Vague Relation s

A_1	A_3	A_4
1	[0.1,0.4]/a	[1,1]/x+[0.6,0.8]/z
3	[0.2,0.8]/a+ [0.6,0.8]/d	∅
5	[0.2,0.3]/b+ [0.5,0.7]/f	[0.7,0.9]/s+ [0.5,0.6]/t

Table 9. Vague Relation $r \wedge s$

A_1	A_2	A_3	A_4
1	[1,1]/2	[0.1,0.4]/a	[1,1]/x+[0.6,0.8]/z
3	[0.2,0.3]/6+[0.5,0.7]/8	[0.2,0.8]/a+[0.7,0.9]/b+[0.6,0.9]/d	∅

the satisfaction degree SD_{F_i} defined in (12). By the union merge operator, we get a new relation $r = r_1 \vee \cdots \vee r_m$. We can also get a new VFD set $F = F_1 \cup F_2 \cup \cdots \cup F_m$ over r. For each VFD in F, we can calculate the new satisfaction degree over r by the validation process proposed in Sect. 4. Then the satisfaction degree SD_F of the new VFD set F over relation r can be calculated by (12).

In the case of non-overlapping sources, we can simplify the calculation as follows. Assume two data sources represented by the vague relations, r_1 and r_2, which have the same $VFD\ X \hookrightarrow A$ on a common schemas. We let the satisfaction degree be SD_1 and SD_2, and the cardinalities of r_1 and r_2 are c_1 and c_2. (As the sources are non-overlapping, there exists no tuple which has the same value of A_1 (the ID attribute) in both r_1 and r_2.) This implies that the cardinality of $r_1 \vee r_2$ is $(c_1 + c_2)$. In order to calculate the new SD of $X \hookrightarrow A$ over $r_1 \vee r_2$, we need to construct two new $(c_1 \times c_2)$ matrices, X' and A', to calculate the S_{EQ} of every pair of tuples between r_1 and r_2. Then we need to construct a matrix $W' = X' - A'$ and count the number of entries (denoted by s'), which are less than or equal to 0 in W'. According to (11), the satisfaction degree SD of the $VFD\ X \hookrightarrow A$ over $r_1 \vee r_2$, where $C = (c_1 + c_2)(c_1 + c_2 - 1)$, can be calculated as follows:

$$SD = \frac{c_1(c_1 - 1)}{C} SD_1 + \frac{c_2(c_2 - 1)}{C} SD_2 + \frac{2s'}{C}. \tag{14}$$

Table 10. Vague Relation $r \vee s$

A_1	A_2	A_3	A_4
1	[1,1]/2	[0.1,0.4]/a	[1,1]/x+[0.6,0.8]/z
2	∅	[0.3,0.7]/a+[0.6,0.8]/c	∅
3	[0.2,0.3]/6+[0.5,0.7]/8	[0.2,0.8]/a+[0.7,0.9]/b+[0.6,0.9]/d	∅
5	∅	[0.2,0.3]/b+[0.5,0.7]/f	[0.7,0.9]/s+[0.5,0.6]/t

6 Conclusions

In this paper, we incorporate the notion of vagueness into the relational data model, with an objective to provide a generalized approach for treating imprecise data. We propose a new similarity measure between vague sets, which gives more reasonable estimation than those proposed in literature. We apply *Similar Equality*(S_{EQ}) in vague relations. The equality measure can be used to compare elements of a given vague data domain. Based on the concept of similar equality of attribute values in vague relations, we develop the notion of *Vague Functional Dependencies* ($VFDs$), which is a simple and natural generalization of classical or fuzzy functional dependencies. In spite of this generalization, the inference rules for $VFDs$ share the simplicity of Armstrong's axiom for classical FDs. We also present the validation process of $VFDs$ and the formula to determine the satisfaction degree of $VFDs$. Finally, we give the definition of merge operators of vague relations and discuss the satisfaction degree of $VFDs$ over the merged vague data. As a future work, we plan to extend the merge operations over vague data, which provide a flexible means to merge data in modern applications, such as querying internet sources and merging the returned result. We are also studying the notion of *Vague Inclusion Dependencies*, which is useful to generalize the foreign keys in vague relations.

References

1. Atanassov, K.: Intuitionistic Fuzzy Sets. Fuzzy Sets and Systems **20(1)** (1986) 87–96
2. Buckles, B.P., Petry F.E.: A Fuzzy Representation of Data for Relational Databases. Fuzzy Sets and Systems **7** (1982) 213–226
3. Chen, S.M.: Similarity Measures Between Vague Sets and Between Elements. IEEE Transactions on System, Man and Cybernetics **27(1)** (1997) 153–159
4. Chen, S.M.: Measures of Similarity Between Vague Sets. Fuzzy Sets and Systems **74(2)** (1995) 217–223
5. Gau, W.L., Danied, J.B.: Vague Sets. IEEE Transactions on Systems, Man, and Cybernetics **23(2)** (1993) 610–614
6. Grzegorzewski, P.: Distances Between Intuitionistic Fuzzy Sets and/or Interval-valued Fuzzy Sets Based on the Hausdorff Metric. Fuzzy Sets and Systems (2003)
7. Hong, D.H., Kim, C.: A Note on Similarity Measures Between Vague Sets and Between elements. Information Sciences **115** (1999) 83–96
8. Levene, M., Loizou, G.: A Guided Tour of Relational Databases and Beyond. Springer-Verlag, Berlin Heidelberg New York (1999)
9. Li, F., Xu, Z.: Measures of Similarity Between Vague sets. Journal of Software **12(6)** (2001) 922–927
10. Naumann, F., Freytag, J.C.: Completeness of Information Sources. Ulf Leser Workshop on Data Quality in Cooperative Information Systems 2003 (DQCIS) (2003)
11. Raju, K.V.S.V.N., Majumdar, A.K.: Fuzzy Functional Dependencies and Lossless Join Decomposition of Fuzzy Relational Database Systems. ACM Transactions on Database Systems **13(2)** (1988) 129–166
12. Szmidt, E., Kacprzyk, J.: Distances Between Intuitionistic Fuzzy Sets. Fuzzy Sets and Systems **114** (2000) 505–518
13. Zadeh, L.A.: Fuzzy Sets. Information and Control **8(3)** (1965) 338–353

Merging of XML Documents

Wanxia Wei, Mengchi Liu, and Shijun Li

School of Computer Science, Carleton University,
Ottawa, Ontario, Canada, K1S 5B6
{wwei2,mengchi,shj_li}@scs.carleton.ca

Abstract. How to deal with the heterogeneous structures of XML documents, identify XML data instances, solve conflicts, and effectively merge XML documents to obtain complete information is a challenge. In this paper, we define a merging operation over XML documents that can merge two XML documents with different structures. It is similar to a full outer join in relational algebra. We design an algorithm for this operation. In addition, we propose a method for merging XML elements and handling typical conflicts. Finally, we present a merge template XML file that can support recursive processing and merging of XML elements.

1 Introduction

Information about real world objects may spread over heterogeneous XML documents. Moreover, it is critical to identify XML data instances representing the same real world object when merging XML documents, but each XML document may have different elements and/or attributes to identify objects. Furthermore, conflicts may emerge when merging these XML documents.

In this paper, we present a new approach to merging XML documents. Our main contributions are as follows. First, we define a merging operation over XML documents that is similar to a full outer join in relational algebra. It can merge two XML documents with different structures. We design an algorithm for this operation. Second, we propose a method for merging XML elements and handling typical conflicts. Finally, we present a merge template XML file that can support recursive processing and merging of XML elements.

The rest of the paper is organized as follows. Section 2 defines the merging operation and presents the algorithm for this operation. Section 3 studies the mechanism for identifying XML instances. Section 4 examines XML documents that this algorithm produces. Section 5 demonstrates the method for merging elements and handling conflicts. Section 6 describes the merge template XML file. Section 7 discusses related work. Finally, Section 8 concludes this paper.

2 Our Approach

The merging operation to be defined can merge two XML documents that have different structures, and create one single XML document. We assume that two

P. Atzeni et al. (Eds.): ER 2004, LNCS 3288, pp. 273–285, 2004.

```
<Factory Name="Red Cap">
 <Department DName="Production">
  <Employees>
   <Employee>
    <Name>Paul Smith</Name>
    <Age>35</Age>
    <Contact>
     <Phone>5555</Phone><Phone>1111</Phone>
     <Address><Number>78</Number>
      <Street>Main Street</Street></Address>
     <Email>paul@redcap.ca</Email>
    </Contact>
   </Employee>
  </Employees>
 </Department>
 <Department DName="Sales">
  <Employees>
   <Employee>
    <Name>Paul Smith</Name>
    <Age>40</Age>
    <Contact>
     <Phone>8888</Phone>
     <Address><Number>10</Number>
      <Street>Prince Road</Street></Address>
     <Email>paul2@redcap.ca</Email>
    </Contact>
   </Employee>
  </Employees>
 </Department>
</Factory>
```

Fig. 1. F_1: the first XML document to be merged.

XML documents to be merged share many tag names and also have some tags with different tag names. We also assume that two tags that share the same tag name in these two XML documents describe the same kind of objects in the real world but their corresponding elements may have different structures.

This merging operation can be formally represented as:

$$F_3 := \text{merging } (F_1, F_2) \text{ on } (D_1, D_2, P_1, P_2, E_1, E_2)$$

where F_1 and F_2 are two input XML documents to be merged and F_3 is the merged XML document; D_1 and D_2 are the DTDs of F_1 and F_2; P_1 and P_2 are absolute location paths (paths for short) in XPath that designate the elements to be merged in F_1 and F_2 respectively; E_1 and E_2 are Boolean expressions that are used to control merging of XML elements in F_1 and F_2.

Boolean expression E_1 is used to identify XML instances when merging F_1 and F_2. Also, it is used for merging of XML elements and handling conflicts. It consists of a number of conditional expressions connected by Boolean operator $\wedge$. Let e_1 be one of the elements whose path is P_1 in F_1 and e_2 one of the elements whose path is P_2 in F_2. E_1 determines if e_1 in F_1 and e_2 in F_2 describe the same object. As long as E_1 is true, e_1 in F_1 and e_2 in F_2 describe the same object and they are merged. We say that e_1 in F_1 and e_2 in F_2 are *matching elements* if they describe the same object. Boolean expression E_2 is used to determine if e_2 in F_2 that does not have a matching e_1 in F_1 will be incorporated into F_3. It consists of several conditional expressions connected by Boolean operator $\wedge$.

```
<FactoryInfo>
 <Introduction>Found in 2000</Introduction>
 <People>
  <Person PName="Paul Smith">
   <WorkIn><Factory>Red Cap</Factory>
    <Unit>Production</Unit>
    <Group>One</Group></WorkIn>
   <Age>36</Age>
   <Position>Engineer</Position>
   <Phone>1111</Phone>
   <Address><Number>78</Number>
    <Street>Main Street</Street>
    <PostCode>K5S 8E2</PostCode></Address>
  </Person>
  <Person PName="Alice Bush">
   <WorkIn><Factory>Red Cap</Factory>
    <Unit>Production</Unit>
    <Group>Two</Group></WorkIn>
   <Age>45</Age>
   <Position>Technician</Position>
   <Phone>7777</Phone>
   <Address><Number>10</Number>
    <Street>Kingsway</Street>
    <PostCode>L5S 8E2</PostCode></Address>
  </Person>
 </People>
</FactoryInfo>
```

Fig. 2. F_2: the second XML document to be merged.

Example 1. The two input XML documents F_1 and F_2 in Figures 1 and 2 have different structures. They describe employees by different elements: *Employee* elements in F_1 and *Person* elements in F_2. F_1 and F_2 are merged into F_3 shown in Figure 3. The merge conditions are as follows:
P_1 = */Factory/Department/Employees/Employee.*
P_2 = */FactoryInfo/People/Person.*
E_1 = (:: *Department/@DName* = *WorkIn/Unit*) $\wedge$ (*Name* = *@PName*).
E_2 = (:: *Department/@DName* = *WorkIn/Unit*).

According to the above P_1 and P_2, *Employee* elements in F_1 and *Person* elements in F_2 are merged into the result XML document F_3. Thus, for this example, e_1 is any *Employee* element in F_1 and e_2 is any *Person* element in F_2.

In the above E_1, ::*Department/@DName* represents the attribute *DName* of the ancestor *Department* of *Employee* element in F_1 and *WorkIn/Unit* denotes the child *Unit* of the child *WorkIn* of *Person* element in F_2 (:: and @ denote an ancestor and an attribute respectively). According to E_1, an *Employee* element in F_1 and a *Person* element in F_2 describe the same employee and are merged into an *Employee* element in F_3 if the value of the attribute *DName* of the ancestor *Department* of an *Employee* is the same as the content of the descendant *Unit* of a *Person*, and the content of the child *Name* of an *Employee* is the same as the value of the attribute *PName* of a *Person*. Note that the child *Name* of an *Employee* cannot identify an *Employee* in F_1 because two *Department* elements may have *Employee* descendants that have the same content for the child *Name*.

```
<Factory Name="Red Cap">
 <Department DName="Production">
  <Employees>
   <Employee PName="Paul Smith">
    <Age>35|36</Age>
    <Contact>
     <Phone>5555</Phone> <Phone>1111</Phone>
     <Address> <Number>78</Number>
      <Street>Main Street</Street>
      <PostCode>K5S 8E2</PostCode></Address>
     <Email>paul@redcap.ca</Email>
    </Contact>
   <WorkIn> <Group>One</Group> </WorkIn>
    <Position>Engineer</Position>
   </Employee>
   <Employee PName="Alice Bush">
    <WorkIn> <Group>Two</Group> </WorkIn>
    <Age>45</Age>
    <Position>Technician</Position>
    <Phone>7777</Phone>
    <Address> <Number>10</Number>
      <Street>Kingsway</Street>
      <PostCode>L5S 8E2</PostCode></Address>
   </Employee>
  </Employees>
 </Department>
 <Department DName="Sales">
  <Employees>
   <Employee PName="Paul Smith">
    <Age>40</Age>
    <Contact>
     <Phone>8888</Phone>
     <Address> <Number>10</Number>
      <Street>Prince Road</Street></Address>
     <Email>paul2@redcap.ca</Email>
    </Contact>
   </Employee>
  </Employees>
 </Department>
</Factory>
```

Fig. 3. F_3: the resulting single XML document.

According to E_2, if there exists a *Department* in F_1 that has an attribute *DName* whose value is the same as the content of the descendant *Unit* of a non-matching *Person*, this non-matching *Person* is incorporated into F_3. Otherwise, this non-matching *Person* cannot be incorporated into F_3 because no element in F_1 can have this *Person* as a descendant.

In relational algebra, a full outer join extracts the matching rows of two tables and preserves non-matching rows from both tables. Analogously, the merging operation defined merges XML documents F_1 and F_2 that have different structures and creates an XML document F_3. It merges e_1 in F_1 and its matching e_2 in F_2 according to D_1, D_2, and E_1. It incorporates each modified non-matching e_1 in F_1 and some modified non-matching e_2 elements in F_2 based on D_1, D_2, E_1, and E_2. Moreover, it incorporates the elements in F_1 that do not need merging.

Path α is the *prefix path* of path β if α is the left part of β or α is equal to β. For example, $/x$ is the prefix path of $/x/y$. It is obvious that the path of any

```
<Factory Name="Red Cap">
 <Department DName="Production">
  <Employees>
   <Employee PName="Paul Smith">
    <Age>35|36</Age>
    <Contact>
     <Phone>5555</Phone><Phone>1111</Phone>
     <Address><Number>78</Number>
      <Street>Main Street</Street>
      <PostCode>K5S 8E2</PostCode></Address>
     <Email>paul@redcap.ca</Email>
    </Contact>
    <WorkIn><Group>One</Group></WorkIn>
    <Position>Engineer</Position>
   </Employee>
  </Employees>
 </Department>
 <Department DName="Sales">
  <Employees>
   <Employee PName="Paul Smith">
    <Age>40</Age>
    <Contact>
     <Phone>8888</Phone>
     <Address><Number>10</Number>
      <Street>Prince Road</Street></Address>
     <Email>paul2@redcap.ca</Email>
    </Contact>
   </Employee>
  </Employees>
 </Department>
</Factory>
```

Fig. 4. F_{LOJ}: the XML document procedure *LeftOuterJoin* produces for Example 1.

ancestor of an element is the prefix path of the path of this element. Path γ is the *parent path* of path δ if γ is the prefix path of δ and δ contains one more element name than γ. For Example 1, */Factory/Department/Employees* is the parent path of P_1.

The algorithm for the merging operation is as follows.

Algorithm **xmlmerge**
Input: F_1, F_2, D_1, D_2, P_1, P_2, E_1, and E_2.
Output: F_3.
  r_{F_1} := the root element of F_1;
  call *LeftOuterJoin* (F_1, F_2, r_{F_1}, D_1, D_2, P_1, P_2, E_1, F_{LOJ});
    /* F_{LOJ} is the XML document generated by procedure *LeftOuterJoin* */
  $r_{F_{LOJ}}$:= the root element of F_{LOJ};
  call *FullOuterJoin* (F_{LOJ}, F_1, F_2, $r_{F_{LOJ}}$, D_1, D_2, P_1, P_2, E_1, E_2, F_3)
End of algorithm xmlmerge

Algorithm *xmlmerge* merges F_1 and F_2, and generates an XML document F_3, which contains every element merged from e_1 in F_1 and its matching e_2 in F_2, each modified non-matching e_1 in F_1, and some modified non-matching e_2 elements. Also, F_3 incorporates the elements in F_1 that do not need merging.

Algorithm *xmlmerge* calls two recursive procedures *LeftOuterJoin* and *FullOuterJoin*. We explain *FullOuterJoin* in Section 4. *LeftOuterJoin* is as follows.

```
Procedure LeftOuterJoin (F1, F2, eF1, D1, D2, P1, P2, E1, FLOJ)
 if the path of eF1 in F1 is not equal to P1
 then
  output the start tag of eF1 to FLOJ;
  output all the attributes of eF1 to FLOJ;
  for each child element c of eF1
   if the path of c is the prefix path of P1
   then call LeftOuterJoin (F1, F2, c, D1, D2, P1, P2, E1, FLOJ)
   else copy c to FLOJ;
  output the end tag of eF1 to FLOJ
 else
  if eF1 has a matching element eF2 in F2
  then
   output the start tag of eF1 to FLOJ;
   for every attribute a1 of eF1 call processa1 (eF2, a1, D1, D2, E1, FLOJ);
   for every attribute a2 of eF2 call processa2 (eF1, a2, D1, D2, E1, FLOJ);
   for every child element c1 of eF1
        call processc1 (eF1, eF2, c1, D1, D2, E1, FLOJ);
   for every child element c2 of eF2
        call processc2 (eF1, eF2, c2, D1, D2, E1, FLOJ);
   output the end tag of eF1 to FLOJ
  else
   output the start tag of eF1 to FLOJ;
   output all the attributes of eF1 to FLOJ;
   for every child element c of eF1
    if c has a semantically corresponding attribute a that is an attribute of e2
    then
     output an attribute to FLOJ whose attribute name is that of a and
     whose value is the content of c;
   for every child element c of eF1
    if c does not have a semantically corresponding attribute that is an
       attribute of e2
    then copy c to FLOJ;
   output the end tag of eF1 to FLOJ;
End of procedure LeftOuterJoin
```

Procedure *LeftOuterJoin* merges e_1 in F_1 and its matching e_2 in F_2 and resolves conflicts by calling procedures *processa1*, *processa2*, *processc1*, and *processc2*, and produces an XML document F_{LOJ}, which contains every element merged from e_1 in F_1 and its matching e_2 in F_2, every modified non-matching e_1 in F_1, and the elements in F_1 that do not need merging. For Example 1, XML document F_{LOJ} that *LeftOuterJoin* produces is presented in Figure 4.

3 Instance Identification

A Skolem function returns a value for an object as the identifier of this object [4]. The computation of Boolean expression E_1 has the equivalent effects as a Skolem function does. For Example 1, the constructed Skolem function concatenates the attribute *DName* of the ancestor *Department* and the child *Name* of an *Employee* element in F_1, or the descendant *Unit* and the attribute *PName* of a *Person* element in F_2 and returns this concatenated value for an object as the identifier. As long as two identifiers for two objects described in F_1 and F_2 are equivalent, these two objects are the same object.

4 The Generated XML Documents

In *LeftOuterJoin* (F_1, F_2, e_{F_1}, D_1, D_2, P_1, P_2, E_1, F_{LOJ}), e_{F_1} is the currently processed element in F_1 and it always has the property: e_{F_1} is one of the elements in F_1 that need merging, or e_{F_1} does not need merging but some of the descendants of e_{F_1} need merging.

Assume y is an element in F_1 that needs merging, and x is an element in F_1 that does not need merging and x is not a descendant of y. We consider the relationship between x and y in F_1. There are four cases:

(1) x is an ancestor of y. (2) x is a sibling of an ancestor of y.
(3) x and y are siblings. (4) x is a descendant of a sibling of y.

For these four cases, y is merged with its matching element in F_2 and x is incorporated into F_{LOJ}. When y does not have a matching element in F_2, y is modified and incorporated into F_{LOJ}. We consider Example 1. The *Employee* in F_{LOJ} that has "Paul Smith" as the attribute *PName* and "Production" as the attribute *DName* of the ancestor *Department* is merged from the *Employee* in F_1 that has "Paul Smith" as the child *Name* and "Production" as the attribute *DName* of the ancestor *Department* and the matching *Person* in F_2 that has "Paul Smith" as the attribute *PName* and "Production" as the descendant *Unit*. The *Employee* in F_1 that has "Paul Smith" as the child *Name* and "Sales" as the attribute *DName* of the ancestor *Department* is a non-matching *Employee*. It is modified and incorporated into F_{LOJ}. Its child *Name* is changed to attribute *PName* to obey the structure of the merged *Employee* in F_{LOJ}. *Department* and *Employees* do not need merging and they are incorporated into F_{LOJ}.

FullOuterJoin incorporates every element in F_{LOJ} into XML document F_3, and modifies some non-matching e_2 elements and inserts the modified non-matching e_2 elements into F_3 as child elements of some elements whose path is the parent path of P_1. *FullOuterJoin* modifies some non-matching e_2 elements in order to resolve conflicts and make the non-matching e_2 elements obey the structure of the merged element in F_{LOJ}. Let us examine Example 1. The *Person* in F_2 that has "Alice Bush" as the attribute *PName* and "Production" as the descendant *Unit* is a non-matching *Person*. This non-matching *Person* in F_2 and the *Employees* in F_{LOJ} that has the ancestor *Department* that has the attribute *DName* with value "Production" make Boolean expression E_2 true. Therefore, this non-matching *Person* is modified and embodied into F_3 as a child element of this *Employees*. The element name of this non-matching *Person* is changed to *Employee*. The child *WorkIn* of this non-matching *Person* is modified.

5 Merging XML Elements and Handling Typical Conflicts

First, we rephrase the assumptions about F_1 and F_2.

(1) F_1 and F_2 share many tag names and also have some tags with different tag names.
(2) Two tags that share the same tag name in F_1 and F_2 describe the same kind of objects in the real world, but the corresponding elements can have the same structure or have different structures.
(3) For tags with different tag names in F_1 and F_2, some of them can still describe the same kinds of objects. In this case, Boolean expression E_1 indicates that they describe the same kinds of objects.
(4) For two tags in F_1 and F_2 that describe the same kind of objects, the corresponding elements have the same cardinality.
(5) For two elements whose tags describe the same kind of objects in F_1 and F_2, their two attributes have the same attribute type and the same default value if these two attributes have the same attribute name in F_1 and F_2.

Then, we introduce several notions.

Elements whose tags describe the same kind of objects in F_1 and F_2 can be classified into two categories: *semantically identical elements* and *semantically corresponding elements*. Two elements in F_1 and F_2 are *semantically identical elements* if their tags describe the same kind of objects and they have the same structure. Two semantically identical elements can have different element names. In this case, E_1 indicates they describe the same kind of objects. Two elements in F_1 and F_2 are *semantically corresponding elements* if their tags describe the same kind of objects but they have different structures. Also, two semantically corresponding elements can have different element names. In this case, E_1 indicates they describe the same kind of objects. It is true that e_1 in F_1 and e_2 in F_2 are semantically corresponding elements because they actually express the same kind of objects and they describe the same object if they make E_1 true.

Two attributes in F_1 and F_2 are said to be *semantically identical attributes* if they have the same name, and one is an attribute of an element in F_1 and the other is an attribute of the semantically identical or corresponding element of this element in F_2. Similarly, two semantically identical attributes can have different names. In this case, they are specified as semantically identical attributes in E_1. An attribute in one XML file to be merged can have a semantically corresponding element in another XML file to be merged. An attribute and an element are *a pair of semantically corresponding attribute and element* if the name of this attribute is the same as the name of this element, this attribute is an attribute of element g in one XML file and this element is a child element of the semantically corresponding element of element g in another XML file, this attribute is a required attribute and of type CDATA, and this element is specified as a parsed character data element with cardinality 1 and it does not have any attribute. Also, the attribute name and element name of a pair of semantically corresponding attribute and element can be different. In this case, E_1 indicates they are a pair of semantically corresponding attribute and element.

We present the method for merging elements and handling conflicts.

Conflicts may emerge when *LeftOuterJoin* merges e_{F_1} in F_1 and its matching e_{F_2} in F_2 into an element in F_{LOJ}. Let a_1 be an attribute of e_{F_1} and a_2 an attribute of e_{F_2}. Let c_1 be a child element of e_{F_1} and c_2 a child element of e_{F_2}. Typical conflicts are: conflicts between a_1 and a_2, conflicts between a_1 and c_2, conflicts between c_1 and a_2, conflicts between c_1 or a descendant of c_1 and c_2 or a descendant of c_2, and conflicts between c_2 or a descendant of c_2 and an ancestor of e_{F_1}.

If attribute a_1 of e_{F_1} in F_1 has a semantically identical attribute that is an attribute of e_{F_2} in F_2, a_1 and its semantically identical attribute should be merged into an attribute. If a_1 and its semantically identical attribute are consistent with each other, redundancy is eliminated by merging them into one attribute; otherwise, a conflict is indicated in the merged attribute. Similarly, if attribute a_1 of e_{F_1} in F_1 has a semantically corresponding element that is a child element of e_{F_2} in F_2, a_1 and its semantically corresponding element are merged into an attribute. Procedure *processa1* accomplishes these tasks.

In Example 1, the child element *Name* of *Employee* in F_1 and the attribute *PName* of *Person* in F_2 are semantically corresponding element and attribute because (*Name* = *@PName*) is specified in Boolean expression E_1. They are combined into the attribute *PName* of the merged *Employee* element in F_{LOJ}.

The relationship between a descendant of e_{F_1} and a descendant of e_{F_2} is illustrated in Figure 5 where (e) shows no correspondence of an element and its semantically identical or corresponding element is found.

Assume that d_1 is a descendant of e_{F_1}, d_2 is a descendant of e_{F_2}, and d_1 and d_2 are semantically corresponding or identical elements. Based on the assumptions about the two XML documents to be merged, d_1 and d_2 have the same cardinality. If the cardinality is not greater than 1, d_1 and d_2 are merged into an element and conflicts between them are reported. Otherwise, d_1 and d_2 cannot be simply merged into an element. When d_1 and d_2 describe the same object, they are merged into an element; conversely, both d_1 and d_2 are incorporated into the merged element in F_{LOJ}. Moreover, when d_1 and d_2 are semantically corresponding elements that represent the same object, if d_2 has some attributes and/or descendants that d_1 does not have, an element that has both the attributes and descendants of d_1 and the extra attributes and/or descendants of d_2 is incorporated into the merged element in F_{LOJ} as a descendant.

Recursive procedure *processc1* is responsible for completing the above tasks. We consider Example 1 again. The child *Age* of *Employee* in F_1 and the child *Age* of *Person* in F_2 are semantically identical elements with cardinality 1. They

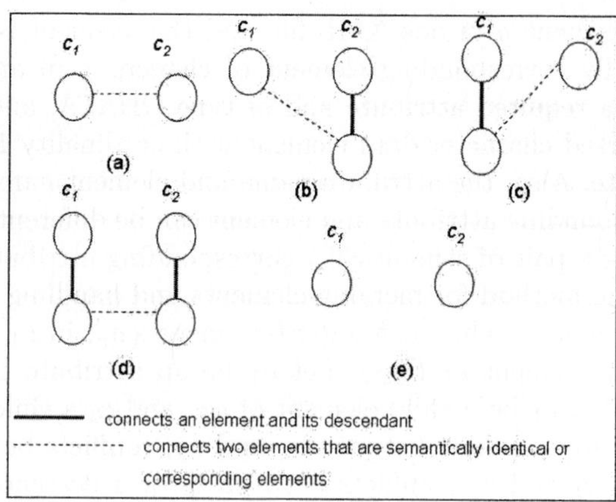

Fig. 5. The relationship between c_1 and c_2.

are combined into the child *Age* of the merged *Employee* in F_{LOJ}. F_{LOJ} reports a conflict: the child *Age* of the merged *Employee* in F_{LOJ} has content "35|36". The content "35|36" is an or-value and it implies it is not clear which one is the correct one [7]. The child *Contact* of *Employee* in F_1 contains *Phone, Address, Email* child elements. The child *Phone* of *Contact* and the child *Phone* of *Person* are semantically identical elements. The cardinality of *Phone* is greater than 1, so the child *Phone* of the child *Contact* and the child *Phone* of *Person* are usually fused into the *Phone* child elements of the child *Contact* of the merged *Employee* element in F_{LOJ}. The child *Address* of the child *Contact* of *Employee* and the child *Address* of *Person* are semantically corresponding elements with cardinality 1. There are no conflicts between them, and the child *Address* of *Person* has a child *PostCode* that the child *Address* of *Contact* does not have, and as a result, this child *PostCode* is added to the child *Address* of the child *Contact* of the merged *Employee* in F_{LOJ}. The child *Email* of the child *Contact* of *Employee* is embodied in the child *Contact* of the merged *Employee* in F_{LOJ}.

Assume that descendant d of e_{F_2} has a semantically corresponding or identical element that is an ancestor of e_{F_1} in F_1. To deal with d, two solutions are possible. One is to simply include d into the merged element in F_{LOJ}. This results in a typical conflict: a conflict between c_2 or a descendant of c_2 and an ancestor of e_{F_1}. Another is to simply exclude d. This also has a problem: if d contains some descendants that are not semantically corresponding or identical elements of any ancestors of e_{F_1}, the information about these descendants of d is lost in the merged element in F_{LOJ}. It is appropriate to reconcile these two opposing solutions by modifying d and incorporating this modified d into the merged element in F_{LOJ}.

Recursive procedure *processc2* carries out the tasks described above. Let us examine Example 1. The child *WorkIn* of *Person* in F_2 has *Factory, Unit,* and *Group* child elements. The child *Factory* of the child *WorkIn* of *Person* in F_2 and the ancestor *Factory* of *Employee* in F_1 are semantically corresponding elements. Also, the child *Unit* of the child *WorkIn* of *Person* in F_2 and the ancestor *Department* of *Employee* are semantically corresponding elements because (::*Department*/@*DName* = *WorkIn*/*Unit*) is specified in Boolean expression E_1. Consequently, *WorkIn* that has only child element *Group* is included into the merged *Employee* in F_{LOJ} as a child element.

6 A Merge Template XML File

In our implementation, a merge template XML file is created to express P_1, P_2, E_1, and E_2. Figure 6 shows an example merge template XML file for Example 1 where *MergeTemplate* has three child elements: *P1*, *P2*, and *Key*. *P1* and *P2* indicate the paths of elements to be merged in F_1 and F_2 respectively. *Key* gives the information for identifying XML instances and handling typical conflicts.

The order of element names in P_1 or P_2 is significant. The first one is the name of the root element of the corresponding XML document and the last

```
<MergeTemplate>
 <P1 Path="/Factory/Department/Employees/Employee"/>
 <P2 Path="/FactoryInfo/People/Person"/><Key>
  <Factor Name1="::Department/@DName" Name2="WorkIn/Unit"
     Selected="Yes"/>
  <Factor Name1="Name" Name2="@PName" Function="samename"/></Key>
</MergeTemplate>
```

Fig. 6. An example merge template XML file.

one indicates the name of the elements to be merged. Moreover, each pair of consecutive element names in a path is associated with a pair of a parent and a child in the corresponding XML document, and the child element in each pair of a parent and a child in F_1 associated with a pair of consecutive element names in P_1 is the only kind child that needs merging or has descendant elements that require merging. All these characteristics are used to support recursive processing of XML elements in F_1 and merging of designated elements in F_1 and F_2.

Each child *Factor* of *Key* describes a conditional expression in E_1 and a *Factor* that has a *Selected* attribute with value "Yes" also describes a conditional expression in E_2. In Sections 2 and 3, we assume that XML data in F_1 and XML data in F_2 specified in each conditional expression in E_1 have the same representations. In fact, they may have different formats. We define Boolean functions to solve this problem. Consequently, the mechanism presented combines Skolem function and user-defined Boolean functions to identify XML instances. Boolean function *samename (n1, n2)* specified in Figure 6 returns true if *n1* and *n2* actually refer to the same name although they have different formats.

7 Related Work

Bertino et al. point out that XML data integration involves reconciliation at data model level, data schema level, and data instance level [2]. In this paper, we mainly focus on reconciliation at data instance level to merge XML documents that have different structures.

A lot of research in semantic integration of XML data has been conducted [3, 10]. Castano et al. propose a semantic approach to integration of heterogeneous XML data by building a domain ontology [3]. Rodríguez-Gianolli et al. present a framework that can provide a tool to integrate DTDs into a common conceptual schema [10]. Several systems for processing XML or XML streams are developed [8, 9]. The Niagara system focuses on providing query capabilities for XML documents and can handle infinite streams [9]. Lore is a semi-structured data repository that builds a database system to query XML data [8]. The merging operation defined in this paper is not available in any of these works or systems.

A lot of research in merging or integration of XML data that has similar or identical structures has been done [6, 7]. A data model for semi-structured data is introduced and an integration operator is defined in [7]. This operator integrates similarly structured XML data. Lindholm designs a 3-way merging algorithm for XML files that comply with an identical DTD [6]. The mechanism proposed in this paper can merge two XML documents that have different structures.

Merge Templates that specify how to recursively combine two XML documents are introduced by Tufte et al. [12]. Our work is different from their work in several aspects. First, the Merge operation proposed by Tufte et al. combines two similarly structured XML documents to create aggregates over streams of XML fragments. Second, a method for merging XML elements and handling typical conflicts is proposed in this paper.

When merging XML documents, it is critical to identify XML data instances representing the same object of the real world. Albert uses the term *instance identification* to refer to this problem [1]. This problem has been investigated [1, 5]. These papers propose different methods to deal with this problem. A universal key is used in [1]. Lim et al. define the union of keys of the data sources [5]. However, these works deal with databases and support typed data. Skolem function is introduced in [4]. It returns a value for an object as the identifier of this object. Saccol et al. present a proposal for instance identification based on Skolem function [11]. The mechanism presented in this paper combines Skolem function and Boolean functions defined for designers [11] to identify XML instances.

8 Conclusion

We have defined a merging operation over XML documents that is similar to a full outer join in relational algebra. It can merge two XML documents with different structures. We have implemented a prototype to merge XML documents.

We plan to investigate other operations over XML documents, such as intersection and difference.

References

1. J. Albert. Data Integration in the RODIN Multidatabase System. In *Proceedings of the First IFCIS International Conference on Cooperative Information Systems (CoopIS'96)*, pages 48–57, Brussels, Belgium, June 19-21 1996.
2. E. Bertino and E. Ferrari. XML and Data Integration. *IEEE Internet Computing*, 5(6):75–76, 2001.
3. S. Castano, A. Ferrara, G. S. Kuruvilla Ottathycal, and V. De Antonellis. Ontology-based Integration of Heterogeneous XML Datasources. In *Proceedings of the 10th Italian Symposium on Advanced Database Systems - SEBD'02*, pages 27–41, Isola d'Elba, Italy, June 2002.
4. J. L. Hein. *Discrete Structures, Logic, and Computability.* Jones and Bartlett Publishers, USA, 1995.
5. E. Lim, J. Srivastava, S. Prabhakar, and J. Richardson. Entity Identification in Database Integration. In *Proceedings of the Ninth International Conference on Data Engineering*, pages 294–301, Vienna, Austria, April 19-23 1993. IEEE Computer Society.
6. T. Lindholm. A 3-way Merging Algorithm for Synchronizing Ordered Trees–the 3DM Merging and Differencing Tool for XML. Master's thesis, Helsinki University of Technology, Department of Computer Science, 2001.
7. M. Liu and T. W. Ling. A Data Model for Semi-structured Data with Partial and Inconsistent Information. In *Proceedings of the Seventh International Conference on Extending Database Technology (EDBT 2000)*, pages 317–331, Konstanz, Germany, March 27-31 2000. Springer.
8. J. McHugh, S. Abiteboul, R. Goldman, D. Quass, and J. Widom. Lore: A Database Management System for Semistructured Data. *SIGMOD Record*, 26(3):54–66, September 1997.
9. J. Naughton, D. DeWitt, D. Maier, and et al. Niagara Internet Query System. *IEEE Data Engineering Bulletin*, 24(2):27–33, June 2001.
10. R. Rodríguez-Gianolli and J. Mylopoulos. A Semantic Approach to XML-based Data Integration. In *Proceedings of the 20th International Conference on Conceptual Modelling (ER)*, pages 117–132, Yokohama, Japan, November 27-30 2001.
11. D. B. Saccol and C. A. Heuser. Integration of XML Data. In *Efficiency and Effectiveness of XML Tools and Techniques and Data Integration over the Web: VLDB 2002 workshop EEXTT and CAiSE 2002 workshop DIWeb*, pages 68–80. Springer, 2003.
12. K. Tufte and D. Maier. Merge as a Lattice-Join of XML Documents. In *Proceedings of the 28th VLDB Conference*, Hong Kong, China, 2002.

Schema-Based Web Wrapping

Sergio Flesca and Andrea Tagarelli

DEIS, University of Calabria, Italy
{flesca,tagarelli}@deis.unical.it

Abstract. An effective solution to automate information integration is represented by *wrappers*, i.e. programs which are designed for extracting relevant contents from a particular information source, such as web pages. Wrappers allow such contents to be delivered through a self-describing and easily processable representation model. However, most existing approaches to wrapper designing focus mainly on how to generate extraction rules, while do not weigh the importance of specifying and exploiting the desired *schema* of the extracted information. In this paper, we propose a new wrapping approach which encompasses both extraction rules and the schema of required information in wrapper definitions. We investigate the advantages of suitably exploiting extraction schemata, and we define a clean declarative wrapper semantics by introducing (preferred) extraction models for source HTML documents with respect to a given wrapper.

1 Introduction

Information available on the Web is mainly encoded into the HTML format. Typically, HTML pages follow source-native and fairly structured styles, thus are ill-suited for automatic processing. However, the need for extracting and integrating information from different sources into a structured format has become a primary requirement for many information technology companies. For example, one would like to monitor appealing offers about books concerning specific topics. Here, an interesting offer may consist in finding highly-rated books.

In this context, an effective solution to automate information integration is related to the exploitation of *wrappers*. Essentially, wrappers are programs designed for extracting relevant contents from a particular information source (e.g. HTML pages), and for delivering such contents through a self-describing and easily processable representation model. XML [19] is widely known as the standard for representing and exchanging data through the web, therefore successfully fulfills the above requirements for a wrapping environment.

Generally, a wrapper consists of a set of extraction rules which are used both to recognize relevant content portions within a document and to map them to specific semantics. Several wrapping technologies have been recently developed: we mention here *TSIMMIS* [8], *FLORID* [15], *DEByE* [13], *W4F* [18], *XWrap* [14], *RoadRunner* [2], and *Lixto* [1] as exemplary systems proposed by the research community. Traditional issues concerning wrapper systems are the

P. Atzeni et al. (Eds.): ER 2004, LNCS 3288, pp. 286–299, 2004.

development of powerful languages for expressing extraction rules and the capability of generating these rules with the lowest human effort. Such issues can be addressed by a number of approaches, such as wrapper induction based on learning from annotated examples [6, 9, 12, 17] and the visual specification of wrappers [1]. The first approach suffers from negative theoretical results on the expressive power of learnable extraction rules, while visual wrapper generation allows the definition of more expressive rules [7]. However, although the schema of the required information should be carefully defined at the time of wrapper generation, most existing wrapper designing approaches focus mainly on how to specify extraction rules. Indeed, while generating wrappers, such approaches ignore the potential advantages coming from the specification and usage of the *extraction schema*, that is the desired schema of the documents to be created to contain the extracted information. A specific extraction schema can aid to recognize and discard irrelevant or noisy information from documents resulting from the data extraction, thus improving the accuracy of a wrapper. Furthermore, the extracted information can be straightforwardly used in the data integration process, since it follows a specific organization best reflecting user requirements.

As a running example, consider an excerpt of *Amazon* page displayed in Fig.1, and suppose we would like to extract the title, the author(s), the customer rate (if available), the price proposed by the Amazon site, and the publication year, for any book listed in the page. The extraction schema for the above information can be suitably represented by the following DTD:

```
<!ELEMENT doc (store)>
<!ELEMENT store (book+)>
<!ELEMENT book (title, author+, (customer_rate | no_rate), price, year)>
<!ELEMENT title (#PCDATA)>
<!ELEMENT author (name)>
<!ELEMENT name (#PCDATA)>
<!ELEMENT customer_rate (rate)>
<!ELEMENT no_rate EMPTY>
<!ELEMENT rate (#PCDATA)>
<!ELEMENT price (#PCDATA)>
<!ELEMENT year (#PCDATA)>
```

It is easy to see that such a schema allows the extraction of structured information with multi-value attributes (operator `+`), missing attributes (operator `?`), and variant attribute permutations (operator `|`).

As mentioned above, existing wrappers are not able to specify and exploit extraction schemata. Some full-fledged systems describe a hierarchical structure of the information to be extracted [1, 17], and they are mostly capable of specifying constraints on the cardinality of the extracted sub-elements. However, no such system allows complex constraints to be expressed: for instance, it is not possible to require that element `customer_rate` may occur alternatively to element `no_rate`. As a consequence, validating the extraction of elements with complex contents is not allowed.

Two preliminary attempts of exploiting information on extraction schema have been recently proposed in the information extraction [10] and wrapping [16] research areas. In the former work, schemata represented as tree-like structures do not allow alternative subexpressions to be expressed. Moreover, a heuristic approach is used to make a rule fit to other mapping rule instances: as a con-

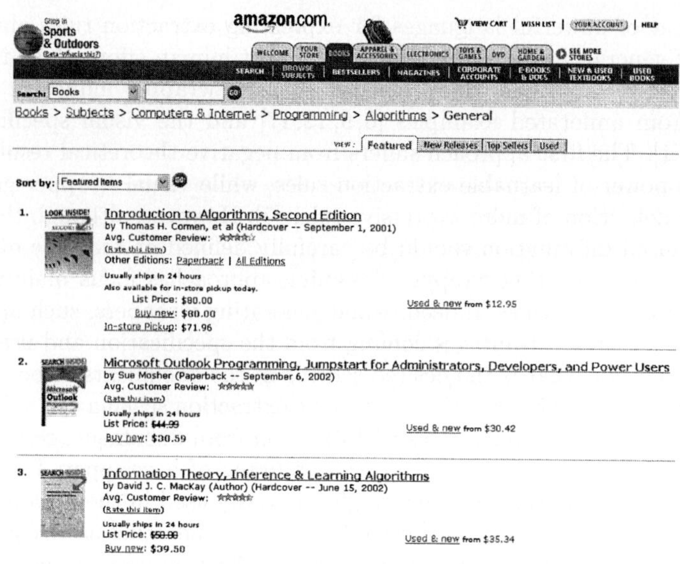

Fig. 1. Excerpt of a sample *Amazon* page from `www.amazon.com`

sequence, rule refinement based on user feedback is needed. In [10], DTD-style extraction rules exploiting enhanced content models are used in both learning and extracting phases.

[3] is related to a particular direction of research: turning the schema matching problem into an extraction problem based on inferring the semantic correspondence between a source HTML table and a target HTML schema. The proposed approach differs from the previous ones related to schema mapping since it entails elements of table understanding and extraction ontologies. In particular, table understanding strategies are exploited to form attribute-value pairs, then an extraction ontology performs data extraction.

It is worth noticing that all the above approaches lack a rigorous formalism for the specification of extraction rules. Moreover, they do not define any model for the construction of the documents into which the extracted information has to be inserted.

Our contributions can be summarized as follows. We propose a novel wrapping approach which improves standard approaches based on hierarchical extraction by introducing the presence of extraction schema in the wrapper generation. Indeed, a wrapper is defined by specifying, besides a set of extraction rules, the desired schema of the XML documents to be built from the extracted information. The schema availability not only allows the extracted XML documents to be effectively used for further processing, but also allows the exploitation of simpler rules for extracting the desired information. For instance, to extract `customer_rate` from a book, a standard approach should express a rule extracting the third row of a book table only if this row contains an image displaying the "rate". The presence of the extraction schema allows the definition of two simple rules, one for `customer_rate` element and one for its `rate` subelement: the former extracts the third row of the book table, while the latter extracts an image. Moreover, our approach in principle does not rely on any particular form of extraction rules, that is any preexisting kind of rules can be easily plugged in; however, we show that XPath extraction rules are particularly suitable for our purposes. Finally, we define a clean declarative semantics of schema-based wrappers: this is accomplished by introducing the concept of *extraction models* for source documents with respect to a given wrapper, and by identifying a *unique preferred model*.

2 Preliminaries

Any XML document can be associated with a document type definition (DTD) that defines the structure of the document and what tags might be used to encode the document. A DTD is a tuple $\mathcal{D} = \langle El, P, e_r \rangle$ where: *i)* El is a finite set of element names, *ii)* P is a mapping from El to *element type definitions*, and *iii)* $e_r \in El$ is the root element name. An element type definition is a one-unambiguous regular expression α defined as follows[1]:

- $\alpha \rightarrow \alpha_1 \,||\, \alpha_2$,
- $\alpha_1 \rightarrow (\alpha_1) \,||\, \alpha_1 | \alpha_1 \,||\, \alpha_1, \alpha_1 \,||\, \alpha_1? \,||\, \alpha_1* \,||\, e$,
- $\alpha_2 \rightarrow$ `ANY` || `EMPTY` || `#PCDATA`,

where $e \in El$, `#PCDATA` is an element whose content is composed of character data, `EMPTY` is an element without content, and `ANY` is an element with generic content. An element type definition specifies an element-content model that constrains the allowed types of the child elements and the order in which they are allowed to appear. A recursive DTD is a DTD with at least a recursive element type definition, i.e. an element whose definition refers to itself or an element that can be its ancestor. In other terms, a recursive DTD admits documents such that an element e may contain (directly or indirectly) an element of the same type. For the sake of presentation clarity, we refer to DTDs which do not contain attribute lists. As a consequence, we consider a simplified version of XML documents, whose elements have no attributes.

In our domain, the application of a wrapper to a source document can produce several candidate document results. A desirable property of a wrapping framework should be that of producing results that are ordered with respect to some criteria in order to identify a unique preferred extraction document.

We accomplish this objective by exploiting *partially ordered regular expressions* [4], i.e. an extension of regular expressions where a partial order between strings holds. A *partially ordered language* over a given alphabet Σ is a pair $\langle L, >_L \rangle$, where L is a (standard) language over Σ (a subset of Σ^+) and $>_L$

[1] The symbol || denotes different productions with the same left part. Here we do not consider *mixed content* of elements [19].

is a partial order on the strings of L. Ordered regular expressions are defined by adapting classical operations for standard languages to partially ordered languages. In particular, a new set of strings and a partial order on this set can be defined for the operations of *prioritized union*, *concatenation*, and *prioritized closure* between languages [4].

Let Σ be an alphabet. The *ordered regular expressions* over Σ, and the sets that they denote, are defined recursively as follows:

1. $\emptyset$ is a regular expression and denotes the empty language $\langle \emptyset, \emptyset \rangle$;
2. for each $a \in \Sigma$, a is a regular expression and denotes the language $\langle \{a\}, \emptyset \rangle$;
3. if α_1 and α_2 are regular expressions denoting languages $L(\alpha_1)$ and $L(\alpha_2)$, respectively, then *i)* $\alpha_1 + \alpha_2$ denotes the prioritized union language $L(\alpha_1) \oplus L(\alpha_2)$, *ii)* $\alpha_1\alpha_2$ denotes the concatenation language $L(\alpha_1)L(\alpha_2)$, *iii)* $\alpha_1^{\triangleright}$ denotes the prioritized closure language $L(\alpha_1)^{\triangleright}$.

Proposition 1. Let α be a one-unambiguous ordered regular expression. The language $L(\alpha)$ is linearly ordered. □

3 Schema-Based Wrapping Framework

In the following we describe our proposal to extend traditional hierarchical wrappers in such a way they can effectively benefit from exploiting extraction schemata. To this purpose, we do not focus on a particular extraction language, but investigate how to build documents, for the extracted information, that are valid with respect to a predefined schema. Indeed, our approach can profitably employ different kinds of extraction rules. Therefore, before describing the schema-based wrapping approach in more detail, we introduce a general notion of extraction rule.

We assume any source HTML document is represented by its parse tree, also called as XHTML document. Generally, each extraction rule works on a sequence of nodes of an HTML parse tree, providing a sequence of sequences of nodes. Notice that working on a tree-based model for HTML data is not a strong requirement, and can be easily relaxed. However, for the sake of simplicity, we do not refer to string-based extraction rules like those introduced in [1, 11, 17].

Definition 1 (Extraction rule). Given an HTML parse tree *doc* and a sequence s_p of nodes in *doc*, an *extraction rule* r is a function associating s_p with a sequence S of node sequences. □

Extraction rules so defined can be seen as a generalization of Lixto extraction filters. The main difference with respect to Lixto filters is that our rules allow the extraction of non-contiguous portions of an HTML document. However, an extraction rule is not able to contain references to elements extracted by different rules.

Moreover, we define a special type of extraction rules which turn out to be particularly useful to address the problem of wrapper evaluation [5].

Definition 2 (Monotonic extraction rule). Given a sequence s_p of nodes in an HTML parse tree *doc*, a *monotonic extraction rule* r is a function associating s_p with a sequence S of node sequences such that, for each sequence $s \in S$ and for each node $n \in s$, there exists $n' \in s_p$ which is ancestor of n. □

Let us now introduce our notion of wrapper. A *wrapper* is essentially composed of: *i)* the desired schema $\mathcal{D}$ of the information to be extracted from HTML documents, and *ii)* a set $\mathcal{R}$ of extraction rules. As in most earlier approaches (such as [1, 17]), the extraction of the desired information proceeds in a hierarchical way. The formal definition of a wrapper is provided below.

Definition 3 (Wrapper). Let $\mathcal{D} = \langle El, P, e_r \rangle$ be a DTD, $\mathcal{R}$ be a set of extraction rules, and w be a function associating each pair (e_i, e_j) of elements $e_i, e_j \in El$ with a rule $r \in \mathcal{R}$. A *wrapper* is defined as $\mathcal{WR} = \langle \mathcal{D}, w \rangle$. □

In practice, a wrapper associates the root element e_r of the DTD with the root of the HTML parse tree to be processed, then it recursively builds the content of e_r by exploiting the extraction rules to identify the sequences of nodes that should be extracted. In other terms, once an element e has been associated with a sequence s of nodes of the source document, an extraction rule r is applied to s to identify the sequences that can be associated with the children of e.

In order to devise a complete specification of a wrapper, we further propose an effective implementation of extraction rules based on the *XPath* language [20].

3.1 XPath Extraction Rules

The primary syntactic construct in XPath is the *expression*. An expression is evaluated to yield an ordered collection of nodes without duplicates, i.e. a sequence of nodes. In this work, we consider XPath expressions with variables. The evaluation of an XPath expression occurs with respect to a *context* and a *variable binding*. Variable bindings represent mappings from variable names to sequences of objects. Formally, given a variable binding θ and a variable name $\$v$, we denote with $\theta(\$v)$ the sequence associated to $\$v$ by θ. Moreover, given two disjoint variable bindings θ_1 and θ_2, we denote with $\theta_1 \circ \theta_2$ a variable binding such that, for each $\$v$, $\theta_1 \circ \theta_2(\$v) = \theta_1(\$v)$ (resp. $\theta_1 \circ \theta_2(\$v) = \theta_2(\$v)$) if $\theta_1(\$v)$ (resp. $\theta_2(\$v)$) is defined, otherwise $\theta_1 \circ \theta_2(\$v)$ is undefined. Given an XPath expression p, an XHTML document *doc*, a sequence of nodes s, and a variable binding θ, $p(s, \theta, doc)$ denotes the sequence of nodes provided by p when p is evaluated on *doc*, starting from s and according to θ.

The relation between the result of an XPath expression and a variable is represented by the concept of *XPath predicate*, which is formally defined as follows.

Definition 4 (XPath predicate). Given a set $\{\$v_1, \ldots, \$v_n, \$c, \$u\}$ of variables and an XPath expression p using the variables $\$v_1, \ldots, \$v_n$, we denote an *XPath predicate* with $\$c : p \rightarrow \$u$. Moreover, we denote a *subsequence XPath predicate* with $\$c : p \twoheadrightarrow \$u$.

Given an XHTML document *doc* and a variable binding θ, an XPath predicate $\$c : p \rightarrow \$u$ is true with respect to θ if $\theta(\$u) = p(\theta(\$c), \theta, doc)$. Analogously, a subsequence XPath predicate $\$c : p \twoheadrightarrow \$u$ is true with respect to θ if $\theta(\$u)$ is a subsequence of $p(\theta(\$c), \theta, doc)$. □

Moreover, we consider an order on node sequences which is defined according to the document order. Given two sequences $s' = [n'_1, \ldots, n'_k]$ and $s'' = [n''_1, \ldots, n''_h]$, s_1 precedes s_2 ($s_1 \prec s_2$) if there exists an index i such that $n'_j = n''_j$ and $n'_i < n''_i$, for each $j < i$, or s' is a prefix of s''. Given an XHTML document *doc*, a variable binding θ and a subsequence XPath predicate $\$c : p \twoheadrightarrow \$u$, we denote with $eval(\$c : p \twoheadrightarrow \$u, \theta)$ the sequence of node sequences $[s_1, \ldots, s_k]$ such that $s_i \prec s_j$, for each $i < j$, and $\$c : p \twoheadrightarrow \$u$ is true with respect to $\theta \circ \{\$u/s_i\}$, for each i.

XPath predicates are the basis of more complex concepts, such as extraction filters and extraction rules. An extraction filter is defined over both a target predicate and a set of other predicates which act as filter conditions.

Definition 5 (XPath extraction filter). Given a set of variables $\{\$v_1, \ldots, \$v_n, \$u\}$, an *XPath extraction filter* is defined as a tuple $f = \langle tp, \mathcal{P} \rangle$, where:

- tp is a target predicate, that is a subsequence XPath predicate defining variable $\$u$ on the empty set of variables;
- $\mathcal{P}$ is a conjunction of predicates defined on variables $\{\$v_1, \ldots, \$v_n, \$u\}$. □

The application of an XPath extraction filter $f = \langle tp, \mathcal{P} \rangle$ to a sequence $s = [n_1, \ldots, n_k]$ of nodes yields a sequence of node sequences $f(s) = [s_1, \ldots, s_k]$ where: *1)* $s_i \prec s_j$, for each $i < j$, *2)* $s_i \in eval(tp, \{\$u/s\})$, for each $i \in [1..k]$, and *3)* there exists a substitution θ, which is disjoint with respect to $\{\$u/s, \$c/s_i\}$, such that each XPath predicate in $\mathcal{P}$ is true with respect to $\theta \circ \{\$u/s, \$c/s_i\}$.

We devise any *extraction rule* as a composition of two kinds of filters: extraction filters and external filters. The latter specify conditions on the size of the extracted sequences. In particular, we consider the following external filters:

- an *absolute size condition* filter as specified by bounds (min, max) on the size of a node sequence s, that is $as(s)$ is true if $min \leq size(s) \leq max$;
- a *relative size condition* filter rs specified by policies $\{\mathsf{minimize}, \mathsf{maximize}\}$, that is, given a sequence S of node sequences and a sequence $s \in S$, $rs(s, S)$ is true if $rs = \mathsf{minimize}$ (resp. $rs = \mathsf{maximize}$) and there not exists a sequence $s' \in S, s' \neq s$, such that $s' \subset s$ (resp. $s' \supset s$).

Definition 6 (XPath extraction rule). An *XPath extraction rule* is defined as $r = \langle EF, as, rs \rangle$, where $EF = f_1 \vee \ldots \vee f_m$ is a disjunction of extraction filters, as and rs are external filters. □

For any sequence s of nodes, the application of an XPath extraction rule $r = \langle EF, as, rs \rangle$ to s yields a sequence of node sequences $r(s)$, which is constructed as follows. Firstly, we build the ordered sequence $EF(s) = [s_1, \ldots, s_k] = \cup_{i=1}^{m} f_i(s)$, that is the sequence obtained by merging the sequences produced by each extraction filter $f_i \in EF$ applied to s. Secondly, we derive the sequence of node sequences $S' = [s_{i1}, \ldots, s_{ih}], h \leq k$ by removing from $EF(s)$ all the sequences $s_i \in EF(s)$ such that $as(s_i)$ is false. Finally, we obtain $r(s)$ by removing from S' all the sequences $s_{ij} \in S'$ such that $rs(s_{ij}, S')$ is false.

Example 1. Suppose we are given an extraction rule $r = \langle f_1 \vee f_2, (2,4), \mathsf{minimize}\rangle$, where filters f_1 and f_2 are defined respectively as:

$$f_1 = \langle \$c : \texttt{//a} \twoheadrightarrow \$t,$$
$$\{\$t : \texttt{[child::*[last()][name()='c']]} \rightarrow \$v_1,$$
$$\$t : \texttt{[child::*[position()=1][name()='d']]} \rightarrow \$v_2\}\rangle,$$

$$f_2 = \langle \$c : \texttt{//a/b} \twoheadrightarrow \$t$$
$$\{\$t : \texttt{[child::*[last()][name()='d']]} \rightarrow \$v_1,$$
$$\$t : \texttt{[child::*[count(*)=2]]} \rightarrow \$v_2\}\rangle.$$

Consider now the document tree sketched below, and suppose we apply the rule r to the sequence of nodes $s = [1, 2, 3]$.

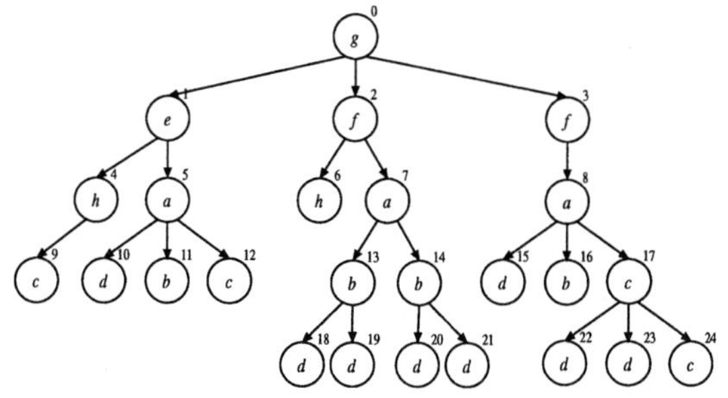

The target predicate of f_1 returns the sequence $[[5], [5,7], [5,7,8], [7], [7,8], [8]]$, which is turned into $[[5], [5,8], [8]]$ by applying conditions in f_1. Analogously, the target predicate of f_2 returns the sequence $[[11], [11,13], [11,13,14], [11,13,14,16], [13], [13,14], [13,14,16], [14], [14,16], [16]]$, which is simplified in $[13,14]$. The union between f_1 and f_2 is computed as $f_1 \vee f_2 = [[5], [5,8], [8], [13,14]]$. By applying the external filters it can straightforwardly derived that the resulting sequence is $[[5,8], [13,14]]$. ▷

4 Wrapper Semantics

In this section we provide a clean declarative semantics for schema-based wrappers. This is accomplished by introducing the notion of extraction models for source HTML documents with respect to a given wrapper. Extraction models are essentially collections of extraction events. An extraction event models the extraction of a subsequence by means of an extraction rule which is applied to a context, that is a specific sequence of nodes. However, not all the extraction events turn out to be useful for the construction of the XML document dedicated to contain the extracted information: extraction models are able to identify those events that can be profitably exploited in building an XML document.

4.1 Extraction Events and Models

The notion of extraction model relies strictly on the notion of extraction event. An extraction event happens whenever an extraction rule is applied. We assume that each extraction event is associated with a unique identifier.

Definition 7 (Extraction event). Given a target element name e_t and an associated node sequence s_t, an *extraction event* ε is a tuple $\varepsilon = \langle pid, id, e_t, s_t, pos \rangle$, where *id* and *pid* denote the identifiers of the current and parent extraction event, respectively, and *pos* denotes the position of ε relative to event *pid*. □

In order to build an XML document to be extracted by a wrapper, we have to consider sets of extraction events. However, only some sets of extraction events correspond to a valid document. Therefore, we have to carefully characterize such sets of extraction events. To this purpose, let us introduce some preliminary definitions on properties of sets of extraction events.

To begin with, a set $\mathcal{E}$ of extraction events is said to be *well-formed* if the following conditions hold:

- there not exist two events $\langle pid, id, e_t, s_t, pos \rangle$ and $\langle pid', id, e'_t, s'_t, pos' \rangle$ in $\mathcal{E}$ such that $pid \neq pid' \vee e_t \neq e'_t \vee s_t \neq s'_t \vee pos \neq pos'$, i.e. an extraction event must have a unique identifier;
- there not exist two events $\langle pid, id, e_t, s_t, pos \rangle$ and $\langle pid, id', e'_t, s'_t, pos \rangle$ such that $id \neq id'$, i.e. two sibling events cannot refer to the same position;
- there not exist two events $\langle pid, id, e_t, s_t, pos \rangle$ and $\langle pid, id', e_t, s_t, pos' \rangle$ such that $id \neq id'$, i.e. two identical node sequences cannot be associated to the same element.

Notations for handling well-formed sets of extraction events are introduced next. Given a set $\mathcal{E}$ of extraction events and a specific event $\varepsilon_p \in \mathcal{E}$ identified by *pid*, we denote with $\mathcal{E}(pid) \subseteq \mathcal{E}$ the set containing all the extraction events which are children of ε_p, i.e. $\mathcal{E}(pid) = \{\varepsilon \mid \varepsilon = \langle pid, id, e_t, s_t, pos \rangle \in \mathcal{E}\}$. We further describe two simple functions, namely *elnames* and *linearize*, that provide flat versions of a set of extraction events. Given an event identifier *pid* and a set $\mathcal{E}$ of extraction events, we denote with *linearize*$(\mathcal{E}(pid))$ the list of extraction events in $\mathcal{E}(pid)$ such that the events are ordered by position. Moreover, we denote with *elnames*$(\mathcal{E}(pid))$ the sequence of element names corresponding to *linearize*$(\mathcal{E}(pid))$: formally, *elnames*$(\mathcal{E}(pid)) = [e^0_t, \ldots, e^k_t]$, where *linearize*$(\mathcal{E}(pid)) = [\langle pid, id^0, e^0_t, s^0_t, pos^0 \rangle, \ldots, \langle pid, id^k, e^k_t, s^k_t, pos^k \rangle]$.

Extraction events need to be characterized with respect to their conformance to a given regular expression specifying an element type. Given a regular expression α on an alphabet of element names, and an event identifier *pid*, we say that $\mathcal{E}(pid)$ is *valid* for α if *elnames*$(\mathcal{E}(pid))$ spells α, i.e. the string formed by concatenating element names in *elnames*$(\mathcal{E}(pid))$ belongs to the language $L(\alpha)$.

We are now able to characterize the *validity* of a set of extraction events with respect to the definition of an element. Let $\mathcal{D} = \langle El, P, e_r \rangle$ be a DTD and $\mathcal{WR} = \langle \mathcal{D}, w \rangle$ be a wrapper. We say that a well-formed set $\mathcal{E}$ of extraction events is *valid* for an element name $e \in El$ if the following conditions hold:

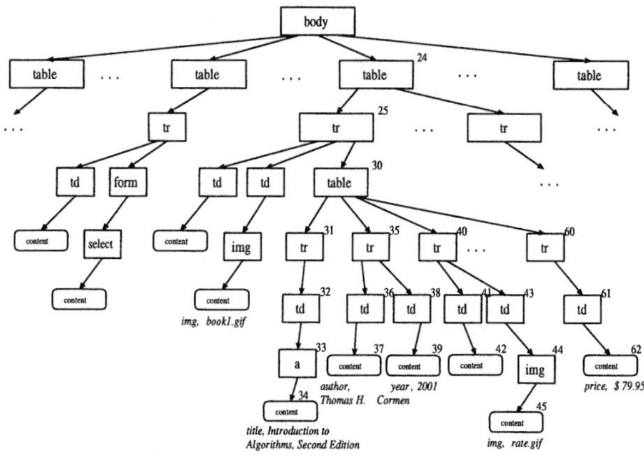

Fig. 2. Sketch of HTML parse tree of page in Fig.1

– $P(e) = \texttt{EMPTY}$, or $P(e) = \#\texttt{PCDATA}$, or
– for each extraction event $\langle ppid, pid, e, s, pos \rangle \in \mathcal{E}$:
  • $\mathcal{E}(pid)$ is valid for $P(e)$, and
  • for each event $\langle pid, id, e_t, s_t, pos \rangle \in \mathcal{E}(pid)$, $s_t \in w(e, e_t)(s)$, and
  • there not exist two extraction events $\langle pid, id, e_t, s_t, pos \rangle$ and $\langle pid, id', e_t, s'_t, pos' \rangle$ in $\mathcal{E}(pid)$ such that $pos \geq pos'$ and s_t does not precede s'_t in $w(e, e_t)(s)$, and
  • $\mathcal{E}(pid)$ contains k extraction events such that $linearize(\mathcal{E}(pid)) = [\langle pid, id^0, e^0, s_t^0, pos^0 \rangle, ..., \langle pid, id^k, e^k, s_t^k, pos^k \rangle], pos^i < pos^{i+1}, i \in [0, k-1]$.

An *extraction model* is essentially a well-formed set of extraction events that conform to the definition of all the elements appearing in the DTD specified within a wrapper. Moreover, an extraction model can be represented by a tree of extraction events.

Definition 8 (Extraction Model). Let $\mathcal{D} = \langle El, P, e_r \rangle$ be a DTD, $\mathcal{WR} = \langle \mathcal{D}, w \rangle$ be a wrapper, *doc* be an XHTML document, and $\mathcal{E}$ be a well-formed set of extraction events. $\mathcal{E}$ is said to be an *extraction model* of *doc* with respect to $\mathcal{WR}$ (for short, $\mathcal{E}$ is an extraction model of $\mathcal{WR}(doc)$) if:

– $\mathcal{E}$ corresponds to a tree $T = \langle r, N, E, \lambda \rangle$, where $r = \langle 0, 0, e_r, [0], 0 \rangle \in \mathcal{E}$, N is the set of extraction events, E is formed by pairs $(\varepsilon_i, \varepsilon_j)$ such that $\varepsilon_i, \varepsilon_j \in \mathcal{E}$ and ε_i is the parent event of ε_j, and λ is a function associating an identifier to each extraction event;
– for each extraction event $\langle pid, id, e_t, s_t, pos \rangle \in \mathcal{E}$, $\mathcal{E}(id)$ is valid for e_t. □

Example 2. Consider again the *Amazon* page displayed in Fig.1, and suppose that such a page is subject to a wrapper based on the DTD presented in the Introduction. The extraction rules used by this wrapper are reported on the third column of Table 1; we assume that $(1, 1)$ and minimize are adopted as default

external filters. The first column reports the target element names associated to each rule, whereas the parent element names can be deduced by the DTD. Extraction events occurring in the example model are reported on the second column of the table. For the sake of simplicity, we focus only on a portion of the document *doc* corresponding to the page of Fig.1; the parse tree associated with *doc* is sketched in Fig.2. Therefore, we consider only some events, according to the portion of page we have chosen. Event $\varepsilon_0 = \langle 0, 0, \texttt{doc}, [0], 0 \rangle$ occurs implicitly in the model under consideration, thus it is not extracted by any rule.
Offered books are stored into a unique table, which is extracted by event ε_1 using filter f_{store}. This filter fulfills the requirement that the book table has to be preceded by a simpler table containing a selection list. Information about any book is stored into a separate table which consists of two parts: the first one contains a book picture, while the second one is another table divided into eight rows, one for each specific information about the book.
Let us consider the first instance of book, whose subtree is rooted in node 25 of the parse tree. The book, which is identified by event ε_2 using filter f_{book}, has information on title, (one) author, year, customer rate, and price. The set of events which are children of ε_2 is built as $\mathcal{E}(2) = \{\varepsilon_3, \varepsilon_4, \varepsilon_5, \varepsilon_6, \varepsilon_8, \varepsilon_9\}$. Even though information on customer rate is available from the first instance of book, we can observe that event ε_8 happens for element `no_rate`: however, such an event cannot appear in the model, because $\mathcal{E}(2)$ would not be a valid content for an element of type `book`.
It is worth noting that rules for extracting information on both availability and unavailability of customer rate have been intentionally defined as identical in this example. However, both kinds of extraction events occur only in any book having customer rate, while only event for element `no_rate` is extracted from any book which has not customer rate. This happens since it is not possible that an event for `rate` occurs as a child of an event for `no_rate`. ▷

An extraction model is implicitly associated with a unique XML document, which is valid with respect to a previously specified schema. Given a DTD $\mathcal{D} = \langle El, P, e_r \rangle$, a wrapper $\mathcal{WR} = \langle \mathcal{D}, w \rangle$, an XHTML document *doc*, and an extraction model $\mathcal{E}$ of $\mathcal{WR}(doc)$, we define the function *buildDoc* which takes $\mathcal{E}$ and an event $\varepsilon \in \mathcal{E}$ as input and returns the XML fragment relative to ε. For any event $\varepsilon = \langle pid, id, e, s, pos \rangle$, $buildDoc(\mathcal{E}, \varepsilon)$ is recursively defined as follows:

- if $P(e) =$ `EMPTY` then $buildDoc(\mathcal{E}, \varepsilon) =$ `<e/>`;
- if $P(e) =$ `#PCDATA` then $buildDoc(\mathcal{E}, \varepsilon) =$ `<e>`$text(s)$`</e>`;
- if $P(e)$ is a regular expression then $buildDoc(\mathcal{E}, \varepsilon) =$ `<e>`$buildDoc(\mathcal{E}, \varepsilon_1) + \ldots + buildDoc(\mathcal{E}, \varepsilon_k)$`</e>`, where $linearize(\mathcal{E}(id)) = [\varepsilon_1, \ldots, \varepsilon_k]$.

In the above definitions, $text(s)$ denotes the concatenation of the string values of the nodes in s, and symbol '+' is used to indicate the concatenation of strings. Moreover, we denote with $buildDoc(\mathcal{E})$ the application of *buildDoc* to the root extraction event in $\mathcal{E}$.

Definition 9 (Extracted XML document). Given a wrapper $\mathcal{WR} = \langle \mathcal{D}, w \rangle$ and an XHTML document *doc*, an XML document *xdoc* is extracted from *doc*

Table 1. Elements, events and rules in a wrapper for *Amazon* pages

element	events	rules
store	$\varepsilon_1 = \langle 0, 1, \texttt{store}, [24], 1 \rangle$	$f_{store} = \langle$\$doc : /table ↠ \$store, {\$store : preceding-sibling::*[1]//select → \$list}$\rangle$
book	$\varepsilon_2 = \langle 1, 2, \texttt{book}, [30], 1 \rangle$ $\varepsilon_{10} = \langle 1, 10, \texttt{book}, [68], 2 \rangle$ $\varepsilon_{17} = \langle 1, 17, \texttt{book}, [106], 3 \rangle$ ...	$f_{book} = \langle$\$store : /tr/table ↠ \$book, {\$book : preceding-sibling::*[1]//img → \$image}$\rangle$
title	$\varepsilon_3 = \langle 2, 3, \texttt{title}, [32], 1 \rangle$ $\varepsilon_{11} = \langle 10, 11, \texttt{title}, [70], 1 \rangle$ ...	$f_{title} = \langle$\$book : /tr/td ↠ \$title, {\$title : //a → \$anchor_text}$\rangle$
author	$\varepsilon_4 = \langle 2, 4, \texttt{author}, [36], 2 \rangle$ $\varepsilon_{12} = \langle 10, 12, \texttt{title}, [74], 2 \rangle$ ...	$f_{author} = \langle$\$book : /tr/td ↠ \$author, {\$author : .[contains(content.text(),'author') or contains(content.text(),'editor')] → \$v}$\rangle$ $r_{author} = \langle f_{author}, (1, \infty), \text{maximize} \rangle$
year	$\varepsilon_5 = \langle 2, 5, \texttt{year}, [38], 3 \rangle$ $\varepsilon_{13} = \langle 10, 13, \texttt{year}, [76], 3 \rangle$ ...	$f_{year} = \langle$\$book : /tr/td ↠ \$year, {\$year : .[contains(content.text(),'year')] → \$y}$\rangle$
customer_rate	$\varepsilon_6 = \langle 2, 6, \texttt{customer\_rate}, [43], 4 \rangle$ $\varepsilon_{21} = \langle 17, 21, \texttt{customer\_rate}, [120], 4 \rangle$ ...	$f_{crate} = \langle$\$book : /tr[3]/td ↠ \$customer_rate$\rangle$
rate	$\varepsilon_7 = \langle 6, 7, \texttt{rate}, [44], 1 \rangle$ $\varepsilon_{22} = \langle 21, 22, \texttt{rate}, [121], 1 \rangle$ ...	$f_{rate} = \langle$\$customer_rate : /img ↠ \$rate$\rangle$
no_rate	$\varepsilon_8 = \langle 2, 8, \texttt{no\_rate}, [43], 5 \rangle$ $\varepsilon_{15} = \langle 10, 15, \texttt{rate}, [120], 5 \rangle$ ...	$f_{norate} = \langle$\$book : /tr[3]/td ↠ \$no_rate$\rangle$
price	$\varepsilon_9 = \langle 2, 9, \texttt{price}, [61], 6 \rangle$ $\varepsilon_{16} = \langle 10, 16, \texttt{year}, [99], 6 \rangle$ ...	$f_{price} = \langle$\$book : /tr/td ↠ \$price, {\$price : .[contains(content.text(),'Buy new')] → \$p}$\rangle$

by applying $\mathcal{WR}$ (hereinafter referred to as $\mathcal{WR}(doc) \rightsquigarrow xdoc$) if there exists an extraction model $\mathcal{E}$ of $\mathcal{WR}(doc)$ such that $xdoc = buildDoc(\mathcal{E})$.
Moreover, we denote with $XDoc(\mathcal{WR}(doc))$ the set of all the XML documents $xdoc$ such that $\mathcal{WR}(doc) \rightsquigarrow xdoc$. □

Theorem 1. Let $\mathcal{WR} = \langle \mathcal{D}, w \rangle$ be a wrapper and *doc* be an XHTML document. If $\mathcal{D}$ is not recursive and all the extraction rules in $\mathcal{WR}$ are monotonic then:

1. each extraction model $\mathcal{E}$ of $\mathcal{WR}(doc)$ is finite, and the cardinality of $\mathcal{E}$ is bounded by a polynomial with respect to the size of *doc*;
2. the set $XDoc(\mathcal{WR}(doc))$ is finite. □

4.2 Preferred Extraction Models

Extraction models provide us a characterization of the set of XML documents that encode the information extracted by a wrapper $\mathcal{WR}$ from a given XHTML document *doc*, i.e. the set $XDoc(\mathcal{WR}(doc))$. Each document in this set represents a candidate result of the application of $\mathcal{WR}$ to *doc*. However, this should not be a desirable property for a wrapping framework.

In this section we investigate the requirements to identify a unique document which is preferred with respect to all the candidate XML extracted documents.

Firstly, we introduce an order relation between sets of extraction events having the same parent element type. Consider two extraction models $\mathcal{E}_1$ and $\mathcal{E}_2$ of $\mathcal{WR}(doc)$, and two events $\langle ppid_1, pid_1, e, s, pos\rangle \in \mathcal{E}_1$ and $\langle ppid_2, pid_2, e, s, pos\rangle \in \mathcal{E}_2$. We say that $\mathcal{E}_1(pid_1)$ precedes $\mathcal{E}_2(pid_2)$ (hereinafter referred to as $\mathcal{E}_1(pid_1) \prec \mathcal{E}_2(pid_2)$) if the following conditions hold:

- $elnames(\mathcal{E}_1(pid_1))$ precedes $elnames(\mathcal{E}_2(pid_2))$ in the language $L(P(e))$, or
- $elnames(\mathcal{E}_1(pid_1))$ is equal to $elnames(\mathcal{E}_2(pid_2))$, and there exists a position pos such that
  - for each $i < pos$, if $\langle pid_1, id_1, e_1, s_1, i\rangle \in \mathcal{E}_1$ and $\langle pid_2, id_2, e_2, s_2, i\rangle \in \mathcal{E}_2$ then $e_1 = e_2$ and $s_1 = s_2$, and
  - if $\langle pid_1, id_1, e_1, s_1, pos\rangle \in \mathcal{E}_1$ and $\langle pid_2, id_2, e_2, s_2, pos\rangle \in \mathcal{E}_2$ then s_1 precedes s_2 in $w(e, e_1)(s)$, or
- $elnames(\mathcal{E}_1(pid_1))$ is equal to $elnames(\mathcal{E}_2(pid_2))$ and there exists a position pos such that
  - for each $i < pos$, if $\langle pid_1, id_1, e_1, s_1, i\rangle \in \mathcal{E}_1$ and $\langle pid_2, id_2, e_2, s_2, i\rangle \in \mathcal{E}_2$ then $e_1 = e_2$ and $s_1 = s_2$, and $\mathcal{E}_1(id_1) \not\prec \mathcal{E}_2(id_2)$ and $\mathcal{E}_1(id_2) \not\prec \mathcal{E}_2(id_1)$
  - if $\langle pid_1, id_1, e_1, s_1, pos\rangle \in \mathcal{E}_1$ and $\langle pid_2, id_2, e_1, s_1, pos\rangle \in \mathcal{E}_2$ then $\mathcal{E}_1(id_1) \prec \mathcal{E}_2(id_2)$.

The above order relation allows us to define an order relation between sets of extraction events, and consequently between extracted documents. Given two extraction models $\mathcal{E}_1$ and $\mathcal{E}_2$ of $\mathcal{WR}(doc)$, we have that $\mathcal{E}_1$ precedes $\mathcal{E}_2$ ($\mathcal{E}_1 \prec \mathcal{E}_2$) if $\mathcal{E}_1(0) \prec \mathcal{E}_2(0)$. Moreover, given two XML documents $xdoc_1$ and $xdoc_2$ generated from $\mathcal{E}_1$ and $\mathcal{E}_2$, respectively, we say that $xdoc_1$ precedes $xdoc_2$ ($xdoc_1 \prec xdoc_2$) if, for each model $\mathcal{E}_2$ of $xdoc_2$, there exists a model $\mathcal{E}_1$ of $xdoc_1$ such that $\mathcal{E}_1 \prec \mathcal{E}_2$.

Definition 10 (Preferred extracted document). Let $\mathcal{D} = \langle El, P, e_r\rangle$ be a DTD, $\mathcal{WR} = \langle \mathcal{D}, w\rangle$ be a wrapper, *doc* be an XHTML document and *xdoc* be an XML document in $XDoc(\mathcal{WR}(doc))$. *xdoc* is *preferred* in $XDoc(\mathcal{WR}(doc))$ if, for each document $xdoc' \in XDoc(\mathcal{WR}(doc))$, $xdoc \prec xdoc'$ holds. □

Theorem 2. Let $\mathcal{D} = \langle El, P, e_r\rangle$ be a DTD, $\mathcal{WR} = \langle \mathcal{D}, w\rangle$ be a wrapper, and *doc* be an XHTML document. There exists a unique preferred extracted document *pxdoc* in $XDoc(\mathcal{WR}(doc))$. □

5 Conclusions and Future Work

In this work, we posed the theoretical basis for exploiting the schema of the information to be extracted in a wrapping process. We provided a clean declarative semantics for schema-based wrappers, through the definition of extraction models for source HTML documents with respect to a given wrapper. We also addressed the issue of wrapper evaluation, developing an algorithm which works in polynomial time with respect to the size of a source document; the reader is referred to [5] for detailed information.

We are currently developing a system that implements the proposed wrapping approach. As ongoing work, we plan to introduce enhancements to extraction schema. In particular, we are interested in considering XSchema constraints and relaxing the one-unambiguous property.

References

1. R. Baumgartner, S. Flesca, and G. Gottlob. Visual Web Information Extraction with Lixto. In *Proc. 27th VLDB Conf.*, pages 119–128, 2001.
2. V. Crescenzi, G. Mecca, and P. Merialdo. RoadRunner: Towards Automatic Data Extraction from Large Web Sites. In *Proc. 27th VLDB Conf.*, pages 109–118, 2001.
3. D. W. Embley, C. Tao, and S. W. Liddl. Automatically Extracting Ontologically Specified Data from HTML Tables of Unknown Structure. In *Proc. 21st ER Conf.*, pages 322–337, 2002.
4. S. Flesca and S. Greco. Partially Ordered Regular Languages for Graph Queries. In *Proc. 26th ICALP*, pages 321–330, 1999.
5. S. Flesca and A. Tagarelli. Schema-based Web Wrapping. Tech. Rep., DEIS - University of Calabria, 2004. Available at `http://www.deis.unical.it/tagarelli/`.
6. D. Freitag and N. Kushmerick. Boosted Wrapper Induction. In *Proc. 17th AAAI Conf.*, pages 577–583, 2000.
7. G. Gottlob and C. Koch. Monadic Datalog and the Expressive Power of Languages for Web Information Extraction. In *Proc. 21st PODS Symp.*, pages 17–28, 2002.
8. J. Hammer, J. McHugh, and H. Garcia-Molina. Semistructured Data: The TSIMMIS Experience. In *Proc. 1st ADBIS Symp.*, pages 1–8, 1997.
9. C.-H. Hsu and M.-T. Dung. Generating Finite-State Transducers for Semistructured Data Extraction from the Web. *Information Systems*, 23(8):521–538, 1998.
10. D. Kim, H. Jung, and G. Geunbae Lee. Unsupervised Learning of mDTD Extraction Patterns for Web Text Mining. *Information Processing and Management*, 39(4):623–637, 2003.
11. N. Kushmerick. Wrapper Induction: Efficiency and Expressiveness. *Artificial Intelligence*, 118(1–2):15–68, 2000.
12. N. Kushmerick, D. S. Weld, and R. Doorenbos. Wrapper Induction for Information Extraction. In *Proc. 15th IJCAI*, pages 729–737, 1997.
13. A. H. F. Laender, B. A. Ribeiro-Neto, and A. S. da Silva. DEByE - Data Extraction By Example. *Data & Knowledge Engineering*, 40(2):121–154, 2002.
14. L. Liu, C. Pu, and W. Han. XWRAP: An XML-Enabled Wrapper Construction System for Web Information Sources. In *Proc. 16th ICDE*, pages 611–621, 2000.
15. W. May, R. Himmeröder, G. Lausen, and B. Ludäscher. A Unified Framework for Wrapping, Mediating and Restructuring Information from the Web. In *ER Workshops*, pages 307–320, 1999.
16. X. Meng, H. Lu, H. Wang, and M. Gu. Data Extraction from the Web Based on Pre-Defined Schema. *JCST*, 17(4):377–388, 2002.
17. I. Muslea, S. Minton, and C. Knoblock. Hierarchical Wrapper Induction for Semistructured Information Sources. *Autonomous Agents and Multi-Agent Systems*, 4(1/2):93–114, 2001.
18. A. Sahuguet and F. Azavant. Building Intelligent Web Applications Using Lightweight Wrappers. *Data & Knowledge Engineering*, 36(3):283–316, 2001.
19. World Wide Web Consortium – W3C. Extensible Markup Language 1.0, 2000.
20. World Wide Web Consortium – W3C. XML Path Language 2.0, 2003.

Web Taxonomy Integration Using Spectral Graph Transducer

Dell Zhang[1,2], Xiaoling Wang[3], and Yisheng Dong[4]

[1] Department of Computer Science, School of Computing, National University of Singapore
S15-05-24, 3 Science Drive 2, Singapore 117543

[2] Computer Science Programme, Singapore-MIT Alliance
E4-04-10, 4 Engineering Drive 3, Singapore 117576
dell.z@ieee.org

[3] Department of Computer Science & Engineering, Fudan University
220 Handan Road, Shanghai, 200433, China
wxling@fudan.edu.cn

[4] Department of Computer Science & Engineering, Southeast University
2 Sipailou, Nanjing, 210096, China
ysdong@seu.edu.cn

Abstract. We address the problem of integrating objects from a source taxonomy into a master taxonomy. This problem is not only currently pervasive on the web, but also important to the emerging semantic web. A straightforward approach to automating this process would be to train a classifier for each category in the master taxonomy, and then classify objects from the source taxonomy into these categories. Our key insight is that the availability of the source taxonomy data could be helpful to build better classifiers in this scenario, therefore it would be beneficial to do transductive learning rather than inductive learning, i.e., learning to optimize classification performance on a particular set of test examples. In this paper, we attempt to use a powerful transductive learning algorithm, Spectral Graph Transducer (SGT), to attack this problem. Noticing that the categorizations of the master and source taxonomies often have some semantic overlap, we propose to further enhance SGT classifiers by incorporating the affinity information present in the taxonomy data. Our experiments with real-world web data show substantial improvements in the performance of taxonomy integration.

1 Introduction

A taxonomy, or directory or catalog, is a division of a set of objects (documents, images, products, goods, services, etc.) into a set of categories. There are a tremendous number of taxonomies on the web, and we often need to integrate objects from a source taxonomy into a master taxonomy.

This problem is currently pervasive on the web, given that many websites are aggregators of information from various other websites [1]. A few examples will illustrate the scenario. A web marketplace like Amazon[1] may want to combine goods from multiple vendors' catalogs into its own. A web portal like NCSTRL[2] may want to combine documents from multiple libraries' directories into its own. A company may want to merge its service taxonomy with its partners'. A researcher may want to

[1] http://www.amazon.com/

[2] http://www.ncstrl.org/

P. Atzeni et al. (Eds.): ER 2004, LNCS 3288, pp. 300–312, 2004.

merge his/her bookmark taxonomy with his/her peers'. Singapore-MIT Alliance[3], an innovative engineering education and research collaboration among MIT, NUS and NTU, has a need to integrate the academic resource (courses, seminars, reports, softwares, etc.) taxonomies of these three universities.

This problem is also important to the emerging semantic web [2], where data has structures and ontologies describe the semantics of the data, thus better enabling computers and people to work in cooperation. On the semantic web, data often come from many different ontologies, and information processing across ontologies is not possible without knowing the semantic mappings between them. Since taxonomies are central components of ontologies, ontology mapping necessarily involves finding the correspondences between two taxonomies, which is often based on integrating objects from one taxonomy into the other and vice versa [3, 4].

If all taxonomy creators and users agreed on a universal standard, taxonomy integration would not be so difficult. But the web has evolved without central editorship. Hence the correspondences between two taxonomies are inevitably noisy and fuzzy. For illustration, consider the taxonomies of two web portals Google[4] and Yahoo[5]: what is "Arts/ Music/ Styles/" in one may be "Entertainment/ Music/ Genres/" in the other, category "Computers_and_Internet/ Software/ Freeware" and category "Computers/ Open_Source/ Software" have similar contents but show non-trivial differences, and so on. It is unclear if a universal standard will appear outside specific domains, and even for those domains, there is a need to integrate objects from legacy taxonomy into the standard taxonomy.

Manual taxonomy integration is tedious, error-prone, and clearly not possible at the web scale. A straightforward approach to automating this process would be to formulate it as a classification problem which has being well-studied in machine learning area [5].

Our key insight is that the availability of the source taxonomy data could be helpful to build better classifiers in this scenario, therefore it would be beneficial to do transductive learning rather than inductive learning, i.e., learning to optimize classification performance on a particular set of test examples. In this paper, we attempt to use a powerful transductive learning algorithm, Spectral Graph Transducer (SGT) [6], to attack this problem. Noticing that the categorizations of the master and source taxonomies often have some semantic overlap, we propose to further enhance SGT classifiers by incorporating the affinity information present in the taxonomy data. Our experiments with real-world web data show substantial improvements in the performance of taxonomy integration.

The rest of this paper is organized as follows. In §2, we review the related work. In §3, we give the formal problem statement. In §4, we present our approach in detail. In §5, we conduct experimental evaluations. In §6, we make concluding remarks.

2 Related Work

Most of the recent research efforts related to taxonomy integration are in the context of ontology mapping on semantic web. An ontology specifies a conceptualization of a domain in terms of concepts, attributes, and relations [7]. The concepts in an ontology

---

[3] http://web.mit.edu/sma/

[4] http://www.google.com/

[5] http://www.yahoo.com/

are usually organized into a taxonomy: each concept is represented by a category and associated with a set of objects (called the extension of that concept). The basic goal of ontology mapping is to identify (typically one-to-one) semantic correspondences between the taxonomies of two given ontologies: for each concept (category) in one taxonomy, find the most similar concept (category) in the other taxonomy. Many works in this field use a variety of heuristics to find mappings [8-11]. Recently machine learning techniques have been introduced to further automate the ontology mapping process [3, 4, 12-14]. Some of them derive similarities between concepts (categories) based on their extensions (objects) [3, 4, 12], therefore they need to first integrate objects from one taxonomy into the other and vice versa (i.e., taxonomy integration). So our work can be utilized as a basic component of an ontology mapping system.

As explained later in §3, taxonomy integration can be formulated as a classification problem. The Rocchio algorithm [15, 16] has been applied to this problem in [3]; and the Naïve Bayes (NB) algorithm [5] has been applied to this problem in [4], without exploiting information in the source taxonomy.

In [1], Agrawal and Srikant proposed the Enhanced Naïve Bayes (ENB) approach to taxonomy integration, which enhances the Naïve Bayes (NB) algorithm [5]. In [17], Zhang and Lee proposed the CS-TSVM approach to taxonomy integration, which enhances the Transductive Support Vector Machine (TSVM) algorithm [18] by the distance-based Cluster Shrinkage (CS) technique. They later proposed another approach in [19], CB-AB, which enhances the AdaBoost algorithm [20-22] by the Co-Bootstrapping (CB) technique. In [23], Sarawagi, Chakrabarti and Godboley independently proposed the Co-Bootstrapping technique (which they named Cross-Training) to enhance the Support Vector Machine (SVM) [24, 25] for taxonomy integration, as well as an Expectation Maximization (EM) based approach EM2D (2-Dimensional Expectation Maximization).

This paper is actually an straightforward extension of [17]. Basically, the approach proposed in this paper is similar to ENB [1] and CS-TSVM [17], in the sense that they are all motivated by the same idea: to bias the learning algorithm against splitting source categories. In this paper, we compare these two state-of-the-art approaches with ours both analytically and empirically. Comparisons with other approaches are left for future work.

3 Problem Statement

Taxonomies are often organized as hierarchies. In this work, we assume for simplicity, that any objects assigned to an interior node really belong to a leaf node which is an offspring of that interior node. Since we now have all objects only at leaf nodes, we can flatten the hierarchical taxonomy to a single level and treat it as a set of categories [1].

Now we formally define the taxonomy integration problem that we are solving. Given two taxonomies:

- a master taxonomy $\mathcal{M}$ with a set of categories C_1, C_2, …, C_M each containing a set of objects, and
- a source taxonomy $\mathcal{N}$ with a set of categories S_1, S_2, …, S_N each containing a set of objects,

we need to find the category in $\mathcal{M}$ for each object in $\mathcal{N}$.

To formulate taxonomy integration as a classification problem, we take C_1, C_2, …, C_M as classes, the objects in $\mathcal{M}$ as training examples, the objects in $\mathcal{N}$ as test examples, so that taxonomy integration can be automatically accomplished by predicting the class of each test example.

It is possible that an object in $\mathcal{N}$ belongs to multiple categories in $\mathcal{M}$. Besides, some objects in $\mathcal{N}$ may not fit well in any existing category in $\mathcal{M}$, so users may want to have the option to form a new category for them. It is therefore instructive to create an ensemble of binary (yes/no) classifiers, one for each category C in $\mathcal{M}$. When training the classifier for C, an object in $\mathcal{M}$ is labeled as a positive example if it is contained by C or as a negative example otherwise. All objects in $\mathcal{N}$ are unlabeled and wait to be classified. This is called the "one-vs-rest" ensemble method.

4 Our Approach

Here we present our approach in detail. In §4.1, we review transductive learning and explain why it is suitable to our task. In §4.1, we review Spectral Graph Transducer (SGT). In §4.3, we propose the similarity-based Cluster Shrinkage (CS) technique to enhance SGT classifiers. In §4.4, we compare our approach with ENB and CS-TSVM.

4.1 Transductive Learning

Regular learning algorithms try to induce a general classifying function which has high accuracy on the whole distribution of examples. However, this so-called inductive learning setting is often unnecessarily complex. For the classification problem in taxonomy integration situations, the set of test examples to be classified are already known to the learning algorithm. In fact, we do not care about the general classifying function, but rather attempt to achieve good classification performance on that particular set of test examples. This is exactly the goal of transductive learning [26].

The transductive learning task is defined on a fixed array of n examples $X = (\mathbf{x}_1, \mathbf{x}_2, ..., \mathbf{x}_n)$. Each example has a desired classification $Y = (y_1, y_2, ..., y_n)$, where $y_i \in \{+1, -1\}$ for binary classification. Given the labels for a subset $Y_l \subset [1..n]$ of $|Y_l| = l < n$ (training) examples, a transductive learning algorithm attempts to predict the labels of the remaining (test) examples in X as accurately as possible.

Several transductive learning algorithms have been proposed. A famous one is Transductive Support Vector Machine (TSVM), which was introduced by [26] and later refined by [18, 27].

Why can transductive learning algorithms excel inductive learning algorithms? Transductive learning algorithms can observe the examples in the test set and potentially exploit structure in their distribution. For example, there usually exists a clustering structure of examples: the examples in same class tend to be close to each other in feature space, and such kind of knowledge is helpful to learning, especially when there are only a small number of training examples.

Most machine learning algorithms assume that both the training and test examples come from the identical data distribution. This assumption does not necessarily hold in the case of taxonomy integration. Intuitively, transductive learning algorithms seem to be more robust than inductive learning algorithms to the violation of this assumption, since transductive learning algorithms takes the test examples into account for learning. This interesting issue needs to be stressed in the future.

4.2 Spectral Graph Transducer

Recently, Joachims introduced a new transductive learning method, Spectral Graph Transducer (SGT) [6], which can be seen as a transductive version of the k nearest-neighbor (kNN) classifier.

SGT works in three steps. The first step is to build the k nearest-neighbor (kNN) graph G on the set of examples X. The kNN graph G is similarity-weighted and symmetrized: its adjacency matrix is defined as $A = A' + A'^T$, where

$$A'_{ij} = \begin{cases} \dfrac{sim(\mathbf{x}_i, \mathbf{x}_j)}{\sum_{\mathbf{x}_k \in knn(\mathbf{x}_i)} sim(\mathbf{x}_i, \mathbf{x}_k)} & \text{if } \mathbf{x}_j \in knn(\mathbf{x}_i) \\ 0 & \text{else} \end{cases}.$$

The function $sim(\cdot,\cdot)$ can be any reasonable similarity measure. In the following, we will use a common similarity function

$$sim(\mathbf{x}_i, \mathbf{x}_j) = \cos\theta = \frac{\langle \mathbf{x}_i \bullet \mathbf{x}_j \rangle}{\|\mathbf{x}_i\| \|\mathbf{x}_j\|},$$

where θ represents the angle between $\mathbf{x}_i$ and $\mathbf{x}_j$ The second step is to decompose G into spectrum, specifically, compute the smallest 2 to $d+1$ eigenvalues and corresponding eigenvectors of G's normalized Laplacian $L = B^{-1}(B - A)$, where B is the diagonal degree matrix with $B_{ii} = \sum_j A_{ij}$. The third step is to classify the examples. Given a set of training labels Y_l, SGT makes predictions by solving the following optimization problem which minimizes the normalized graph cut with constraints:

$$\begin{aligned} \min_{\mathbf{y}} \quad & \frac{cut(G^+, G^-)}{|\{i : y_i = +1\}| |\{i : y_i = -1\}|} \\ s.t. \quad & y_i = +1, \text{ if } i \in Y_l \text{ and positive} \\ & y_i = -1, \text{ if } i \in Y_l \text{ and negative} \\ & \mathbf{y} = \{+1, -1\}^n, \end{aligned}$$

where G^+ and G^- denote the set of examples (vertices) with $y_i = +1$ and $y_i = -1$ respectively, and the cut-value $cut(G^+, G^-) = \sum_{i \in G^+} \sum_{j \in G^-} A_{ij}$ is the sum of the edge weights across the cut (bi-partitioning) defined by G^+ and G^-. Although this optimization problem is known to be NP-hard, there are highly efficient methods based on the spectrum of the graph that give good approximation to the global optimal solution [6].

For example, consider a classification problem with 6 examples $X = (\mathbf{x}_1, \mathbf{x}_2, \mathbf{x}_3, \mathbf{x}_4, \mathbf{x}_5, \mathbf{x}_6)$ whose kNN graph G is shown in Figure 1 (adopted from [6]) with line thickness indicating edge weight. Given a set of training labels $Y_l = \{1,6\}$: $y_1 = +1$ and $y_6 = -1$, SGT predicts y_2 and y_3 to be positive whereas predicts y_4 and y_5 to be negative, because cutting G into $G^+ = \{\mathbf{x}_1, \mathbf{x}_2, \mathbf{x}_3\}$ and $G^- = \{\mathbf{x}_4, \mathbf{x}_5, \mathbf{x}_6\}$ gives the minimal normalized cut-value while keeping $\mathbf{x}_1 \in G^+$ and $\mathbf{x}_6 \in G^-$.

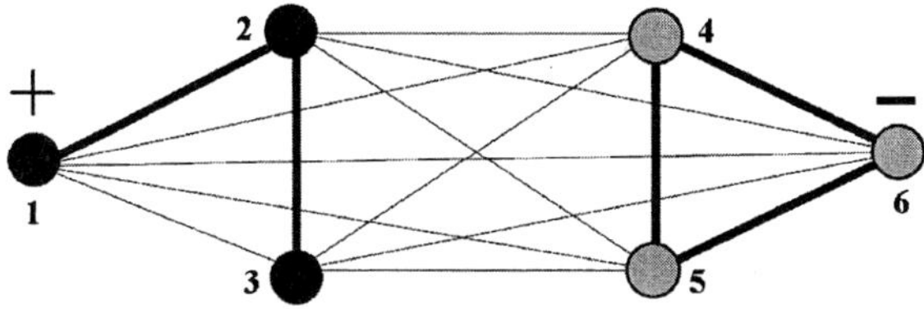

Fig. 1. SGT does classification through minimizing the normalized graph cuts with constraints

Unlike most other transductive learning algorithms, SGT does not need any additional heuristics to avoid unbalanced splits [6]. Furthermore, since SGT has a meaningful relaxation that can be solved globally optimally with efficient spectral methods, it is more robust and promising than existing methods.

4.3 Similarity-Based Cluster Shrinkage

Applying SGT to taxonomy integration, we can effectively use the objects in $\mathcal{N}$ (test examples) to boost classification performance. However, thus far we have completely ignored the categorization of $\mathcal{N}$.

Although $\mathcal{M}$ and $\mathcal{N}$ are usually not identical, their categorizations often have some semantic overlap. Therefore the categorization of $\mathcal{N}$ contains valuable implicit knowledge about the categorization of $\mathcal{M}$. For example, if two objects belong to the same category S in $\mathcal{N}$, they are more likely to belong to the same category C in $\mathcal{M}$ rather than to be assigned into different categories. We hereby propose the similarity-based Cluster Shrinkage (CS) technique to further enhance SGT classifiers by incorporating the affinity information present in the taxonomy data.

4.3.1 Algorithm

Since SGT models the learning problem as a similarity-weighted kNN-graph, it offers a large degree of flexibility for encoding prior knowledge about the relationship between individual examples in the similarity function. Our proposed similarity-based CS technique takes all categories as clusters and shrinks them by substituting the regular similarity function $sim(\cdot,\cdot)$ with the CS similarity function $cs\text{-}sim(\cdot,\cdot)$.

Definition 1. The center of a category S is $\mathbf{c} = \frac{1}{|S|}\sum_{\mathbf{x}\in S}\mathbf{x}$.

Definition 2. The CS similarity function $cs\text{-}sim(\cdot,\cdot)$ for two examples $\mathbf{x}_i \in S_i$ and $\mathbf{x}_j \in S_j$ is defined as $cs\text{-}sim(\mathbf{x}_i,\mathbf{x}_j) = \gamma \cdot sim(\mathbf{c}_i,\mathbf{c}_j) + (1-\gamma) \cdot sim(\mathbf{x}_i,\mathbf{x}_j)$, $0 \le \gamma \le 1$, where $\mathbf{c}_i$ and $\mathbf{c}_j$ are the centers of S_i and S_j respectively,.

When an example $\mathbf{x}$ belongs to multiple categories $S^{(1)}, S^{(2)}, \ldots, S^{(g)}$ whose centers are $\mathbf{c}^{(1)}, \mathbf{c}^{(2)}, \ldots, \mathbf{c}^{(g)}$ respectively, its corresponding category center in the above formula should be amended to $\mathbf{c} = \left(\sum_{h=1}^{g} \mathbf{c}^{(h)} \right) \Big/ g$.

We name our approach that uses SGT classifiers enhanced by the similarity-based CS technique as CS-SGT.

4.3.2 Analysis

Theorem 1. For any pair of examples $\mathbf{x}_i$ and $\mathbf{x}_j$ in the same category S, $cs\text{-}sim(\mathbf{x}_i,\mathbf{x}_j) \ge sim(\mathbf{x}_i,\mathbf{x}_j)$.

Proof: Suppose the center of S is $\mathbf{c}$, we get

$cs\text{-}sim(\mathbf{x}_i,\mathbf{x}_j) = \gamma \cdot sim(\mathbf{c},\mathbf{c}) + (1-\gamma) \cdot sim(\mathbf{x}_i,\mathbf{x}_j)$

Since $sim(\mathbf{c},\mathbf{c}) \ge sim(\mathbf{x}_i,\mathbf{x}_j)$ and $\gamma \ge 0$, we get

$\gamma \cdot sim(\mathbf{c},\mathbf{c}) \ge \gamma sim(\mathbf{x}_i,\mathbf{x}_j)$, therefore

$\gamma \cdot sim(\mathbf{c},\mathbf{c}) + (1-\gamma) \cdot sim(\mathbf{x}_i,\mathbf{x}_j) \ge \gamma \cdot sim(\mathbf{x}_i,\mathbf{x}_j) + (1-\gamma) \cdot sim(\mathbf{x}_i,\mathbf{x}_j)$, i.e.

$cs\text{-}sim(\mathbf{x}_i,\mathbf{x}_j) \ge sim(\mathbf{x}_i,\mathbf{x}_j)$.

From the above theorem, we see that CS-SGT increases the similarity between examples that are known in the same category, consequently puts more weight to the edge between them in the kNN graph. Since SGT seeks the minimum normalized graph cut, stronger connection among examples in the same category directs SGT to avoid splitting that category, in other words, to reserve the original categorization of the taxonomies to some degree while doing classification. Through substituting the regular similarity function with the CS similarity function, the CS-SGT approach can not only make effective use of the objects in $\mathcal{N}$ like SGT, but also make effective use of the categorization of $\mathcal{N}$.

The CS similarity function $cs\text{-}sim(\mathbf{x}_i,\mathbf{x}_j)$ is actually a linear interpolation of $sim(\mathbf{x}_i,\mathbf{x}_j)$ and $sim(\mathbf{c},\mathbf{c})$. The linear interpolation parameter $0 \le \gamma \le 1$ controls the influence of the original categorization on the classification. When $\gamma = 1$, CS-SGT classifies all objects belonging to one category in $\mathcal{N}$ as a whole into a specific category in $\mathcal{M}$. When $\gamma = 0$, CS-SGT is just the same as SGT. As long as the value of γ is set appropriately, CS-SGT should never be worse than SGT because it includes SGT as a special case. The optimal value of γ can be found using a tune set (a set of objects whose categories in both taxonomies are known). The tune set can be made available via random sampling or active learning, as described in [1].

4.4 Comparison with ENB and CS-TSVM

Both ENB and CS-TSVM outperform conventional machine learning methods in taxonomy integration, because they are able to leverage the source taxonomy data to improve classification. CS-SGT also follows this idea to enhance SGT for taxonomy integration.

ENB [1] is based on NB [5] which is an inductive learning algorithm. In contrast, CS-TSVM is based on TSVM [18] which is a transductive learning algorithm. It has been shown that CS-TSVM is more effective than ENB [17] in taxonomy integration. However, CS-TSVM is not as efficient as ENB because TSVM runs much slower than NB.

CS-SGT is based on the recently proposed transductive learning algorithm SGT [6]. We think CS-SGT should achieve similar performance as CS-TSVM, because in theory SGT connects to a simplified version of TSVM, and both of them attempt to incorporate the affinity information present in the taxonomy data into learning. This has been confirmed by our experiments. On the other hand, CS-SGT is much more efficient than CS-TSVM because of the following three reasons.

(1) CS-TSVM is based on TSVM that uses computational-expensive greedy search to get a local optimal solution. In contrast, CS-SGT is based on SGT that uses efficient spectral methods to get the global optimal solution.

(2) CS-TSVM must run SVM first to get a good estimation of the fraction of the positive examples in the test set [17] because TSVM requires that fraction to be fixed a priori [18]. In contrast, CS-SGT does not need this kind of extra-computation due to the merit of SGT in automatically avoiding unbalanced splits [6].

(3) CS-TSVM requires training a TSVM classifier from scratch for each master category, using the "one-vs-rest" ensemble method for multi-class multi-label classification (as stated in §2). In contrast, CS-SGT (or SGT) needs to build and decompose the kNN graph only once for a specific set of examples (dataset), hence saves a lot of time. It has been observed that construction of the kNN graph is the most time-consuming step of SGT, but it can be sped up using appropriate data structures like inverted indices or kd-trees [6].

The CS-SGT approach's prominent advantage in efficiency has also been confirmed by our experiments.

In summary, the CS-SGT approach is able to achieve similar performance as CS-TSVM in taxonomy integration while holding high efficiency as ENB.

5 Experiments

We conduct experiments with real-world web data, to demonstrate the advantage of our proposed CS-SGT approach to taxonomy integration. To facilitate comparison, we use exactly the same datasets and experimental setup as [17].

5.1 Datasets

We have collected 5 datasets from Google and Yahoo: *Book, Disease, Movie, Music* and *News*. One dataset includes the slice of Google's taxonomy and the slice of Yahoo's taxonomy about websites on one specific topic.

In each slice of taxonomy, we take only the top level directories as categories, e.g., the "Movie" slice of Google's taxonomy has categories like "Action", "Comedy", "Horror", etc.

In each category, we take all items listed on the corresponding directory page and its sub-directory pages as its objects. An object (listed item) corresponds to a website on the world wide web, which is usually described by its URL, its title, and optionally a short annotation about its content.

The set of objects occurred in both Google and Yahoo covers only a small portion (usually less than 10%) of the set of objects occurred in Google or Yahoo alone, which suggests the great benefit of automatically integrating them. This observation is consistent with [1].

The number of categories per object in these datasets is 1.54 on average. This observation confirms our previous statement in §3 that an object may belong to multiple categories, and justifies our strategy to build a binary classifier for each category in the master taxonomy.

The category distributions in all theses datasets are highly skewed. For example, in Google's Book taxonomy, the most common category contains 21% objects, but 88% categories contain less than 3% objects and 49% categories contain less than 1% objects. In fact, skewed category distributions have been commonly observed in real-world applications [28].

5.2 Tasks

For each dataset, we pose 2 symmetric taxonomy integration tasks: G←Y (integrating objects from Yahoo into Google) and Y←G (integrating objects from Google into Yahoo).

As described in §3, we formulate each task as a classification problem. The objects in $G \cap Y$ can be used as test examples, because their categories in both taxonomies are known to us [1]. We hide the test examples' master categories but expose their source categories to the learning algorithm in training phase, and then compare their hidden master categories with the predictions of the learning algorithm in test phase. Suppose the number of the test examples is n. For G←Y tasks, we randomly sample n objects from the set G-Y as training examples. For Y←G tasks, we randomly sample n objects from the set Y-G as training examples. This is to simulate the common situation that the sizes of $\mathcal{M}$ and $\mathcal{N}$ are roughly in same magnitude. For each task, we do such random sampling 5 times, and report the classification performance averaged over these 5 random samplings.

5.3 Features

For each object, we assume that the title and annotation of its corresponding website summarizes its content. So each object can be considered as a text document composed of its title and annotation[6].

The most commonly used feature extraction technique for text data is to treat a document as a bag-of-words [18, 25]. For each document d in a collection of documents D, its bag-of-words is first pre-processed by removal of stop-words and

[6] Note that this is different with [1, 23] which take actual Web pages as objects.

stemming. Then it is represented as a feature vector $\mathbf{x} = (x_1, x_2, ..., x_m)$, where x_i indicates the importance weight of term w_i (the *i*-th distinct word occurred in D). Following the TF×IDF weighting scheme, we set the value of x_i to the product of the term frequency $TF(w_i, d)$ and the inverse document frequency $IDF(w_i)$, i.e., $TF(w_i, d) \times IDF(w_i)$. The term frequency $TF(w_i, d)$ means the number of occurrences of w_i in d. The inverse document frequency is defined as $IDF(w_i) = \log\left(\frac{|D|}{DF(w_i)}\right)$, where $|D|$ is the total number of documents in D, and $DF(w_i)$ is the number of documents in which w_i occur. Finally all feature vectors are normalized to have unit length.

5.4 Measures

As stated in §3, it is natural to accomplish a taxonomy integration task via an ensemble of binary classifiers, each for one category in $\mathcal{M}$. To measure classification performance, we use the standard *F*-score (F_1 measure) [15]. The *F*-score is defined as the harmonic average of precision (*p*) and recall (*r*), $F = 2pr/(p+r)$, where precision is the proportion of correctly predicted positive examples among all predicted positive examples, and recall is the proportion of correctly predicted positive examples among all true positive examples. The *F*-scores can be computed for the binary decisions on each individual category first and then be averaged over categories. Or they can be computed globally over all the $M \times n$ binary decisions where M is the number of categories in consideration (the number of categories in $\mathcal{M}$) and n is the number of total test examples (the number of objects in $\mathcal{N}$). The former way is called *macro-averaging* and the latter way is called *micro-averaging* [28]. It is understood that the micro-averaged *F*-score (*miF*) tends to be dominated by the classification performance on common categories, and that the macro-averaged *F*-score (*maF*) is more influenced by the classification performance on rare categories [28]. Since the category distributions are highly skewed (see §5.1), providing both kinds of scores is more informative than providing either alone.

5.5 Settings

We use the SGT software implemented by Joachims[7] with the following parameters : "-k 10", "-d 100", "-c 1000 –t f –p s". We set the parameter γ for CS similarity function to 0.2. Fine-tuning γ using tune sets would decisively generate better results than sticking with a pre-fixed value. In other words, the performance superiority of CS-SGT is under-estimated in our experiments.

5.6 Results

The experimental results of SGT and CS-SGT are shown in Table 1. We see that CS-SGT really can achieve much better performance than SGT for taxonomy integration.

---

[7] http://sgt.joachims.org/

We think this is because CS-SGT makes effective use of the affinity information present in the taxonomy data.

Table 1. Experimental Results of SGT and CS-SGT

		SGT		CS-SGT	
		maF	*miF*	*maF*	*miF*
G←Y	Book	0.2191	0.5161	0.3167	0.6502
	Disease	0.4429	0.4639	0.6602	0.7269
	Movie	0.1388	0.3175	0.2976	0.6373
	Music	0.2371	0.3461	0.4148	0.5766
	News	0.2992	0.4916	0.4499	0.6955
Y←G	Book	0.3608	0.4132	0.4894	0.5844
	Disease	0.4162	0.4222	0.5778	0.7431
	Movie	0.2516	0.3934	0.4162	0.6071
	Music	0.2655	0.2901	0.5464	0.7479
	News	0.3612	0.4698	0.5113	0.6521

In Figure 2 and 3, we compare the experimental results of CS-SGT and those of ENB and CS-TSVM which come from [17]. We see that CS-SGT outperforms ENB consistently and significantly. We also find that CS-SGT's macro-averaged *F*-scores are slightly lower than those of CS-TSVM, and its micro-averaged *F*-scores are comparable to those of CS-TSVM. On the other hand, our experiments demonstrated that CS-SGT was much faster than CS-TSVM: CS-TSVM took about one or two days to run all the experiments while CS-SGT finished in several hours.

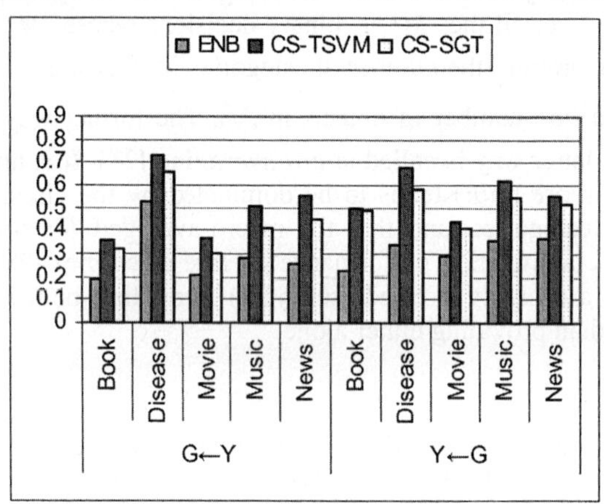

Fig. 2. Comparing the macro-averaged F-scores of ENB, CS-TSVM and CS-SGT

6 Conclusion

Our main contribution is to show how Spectral Graph Transducer (SGT) can be enhanced for taxonomy integration tasks. We have compared the proposed CS-SGT approach to taxonomy integration with two existing state-of-the-art approaches, and demonstrated that CS-SGT is both effective and efficient.

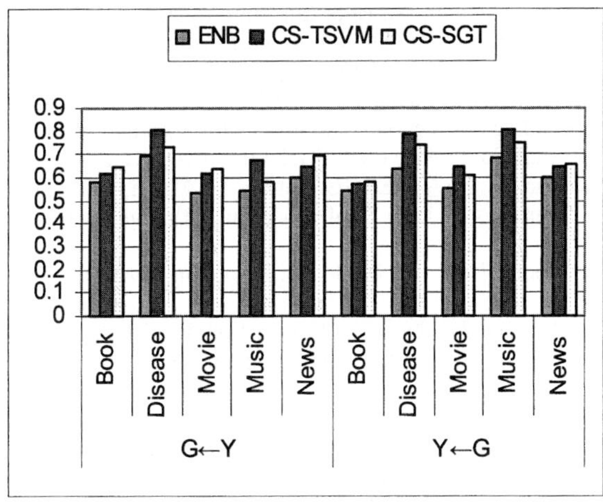

Fig. 3. Comparing the micro-averaged F-scores of ENB, CS-TSVM and CS-SGT

The future work may include: comparing with the approaches in [19, 23], incorporating commonsense knowledge and domain constraints into the taxonomy integration process, extending to full-functional ontology mapping systems, and so forth.

References

1. Agrawal, R., Srikant, R.: On Integrating Catalogs. In: Proceedings of the 10th International World Wide Web Conference (WWW). (2001) 603-612
2. Berners-Lee, T., Hendler, J., Lassila, O.: The Semantic Web. Scientific American (2001)
3. Lacher, M. S., Groh, G.: Facilitating the Exchange of Explicit Knowledge through Ontology Mappings. In: Proceedings of the Fourteenth International Florida Artificial Intelligence Research Society Conference (FLAIRS). (2001) 305-309
4. Doan, A., Madhavan, J., Domingos, P., Halevy, A.: Learning to Map between Ontologies on the Semantic Web. In: Proceedings of the 11th International World Wide Web Conference (WWW). (2002) 662-673
5. Mitchell, T.: Machine Learning. international edn. McGraw Hill, New York (1997)
6. Joachims, T.: Transductive Learning via Spectral Graph Partitioning. In: Proceedings of the 20th International Conference on Machine Learning (ICML). (2003) 290-297
7. Fensel, D.: Ontologies: A Silver Bullet for Knowledge Management and Electronic Commerce. Springer-Verlag (2001)
8. Chalupsky, H.: OntoMorph: A Translation System for Symbolic Knowledge. In: Proceedings of the 7th International Conference on Principles of Knowledge Representation and Reasoning (KR). (2000) 471-482
9. McGuinness, D. L., Fikes, R., Rice, J., Wilder, S.: The Chimaera Ontology Environment. In: Proceedings of the 17th National Conference on Artificial Intelligence (AAAI). (2000) 1123–1124
10. Mitra, P., Wiederhold, G., Jannink, J.: Semi-automatic Integration of Knowledge Sources. In: Proceedings of The 2nd International Conference on Information Fusion. (1999)
11. Noy, N. F., Musen, M. A.: PROMPT: Algorithm and Tool for Automated Ontology Merging and Alignment. In: Proceedings of the National Conference on Artificial Intelligence (AAAI). (2000) 450-455

12. Ichise, R., Takeda, H., Honiden, S.: Rule Induction for Concept Hierarchy Alignment. In: Proceedings of the Workshop on Ontologies and Information Sharing at the 17th International Joint Conference on Artificial Intelligence (IJCAI). (2001) 26-29
13. Noy, N. F., Musen, M. A.: Anchor-PROMPT: Using Non-Local Context for Semantic Matching. In: Proceedings of the Workshop on Ontologies and Information Sharing at the 17th International Joint Conference on Artificial Intelligence (IJCAI). (2001) 63-70
14. Stumme, G., Maedche, A.: FCA-MERGE: Bottom-Up Merging of Ontologies. In: Proceedings of the 17th International Joint Conference on Artificial Intelligence (IJCAI). (2001) 225-230
15. Baeza-Yates, R., Ribeiro-Neto, B.: Modern Information Retrieval. Addison-Wesley, New York, NY (1999)
16. Rocchio, J. J.: Relevance Feedback in Information Retrieval. In: G. Salton, (ed.) The SMART Retrieval System: Experiments in Automatic Document Processing. Prentice-Hall (1971) 313-323
17. Zhang, D., Lee, W. S.: Web Taxonomy Integration using Support Vector Machines. In: Proceedings of the 13th International World Wide Web Conference (WWW). (2004)
18. Joachims, T.: Transductive Inference for Text Classification using Support Vector Machines. In: Proceedings of the 16th International Conference on Machine Learning (ICML). (1999) 200-209
19. Zhang, D., Lee, W. S.: Web Taxonomy Integration through Co-Bootstrapping. In: Proceedings of the 27th Annual International ACM SIGIR Conference on Research and Development in Information Retrieval (SIGIR). (2004)
20. Freund, Y., Schapire, R. E.: A Decision-theoretic Generalization of On-line Learning and an Application to Boosting. Journal of Computer and System Sciences 55 (1997) 119-139
21. Schapire, R. E., Singer, Y.: BoosTexter: A Boosting-based System for Text Categorization. Machine Learning 39 (2000) 135-168
22. Schapire, R. E., Singer, Y.: Improved Boosting Algorithms Using Confidence-rated Predictions. Machine Learning 37 (1999) 297-336
23. Sarawagi, S., Chakrabarti, S., Godbole, S.: Cross-Training: Learning Probabilistic Mappings between Topics. In: Proceedings of the 9th ACM SIGKDD International Conference on Knowledge Discovery and Data Mining (KDD). (2003) 177-186
24. Cristianini, N., Shawe-Taylor, J.: An Introduction to Support Vector Machines. Cambridge University Press, Cambridge, UK (2000)
25. Joachims, T.: Text Categorization with Support Vector Machines: Learning with Many Relevant Features. In: Proceedings of the 10th European Conference on Machine Learning (ECML). (1998) 137-142
26. Vapnik, V. N.: Statistical Learning Theory. Wiley, New York, NY (1998)
27. Bennett, K.: Combining Support Vector and Mathematical Programming Methods for Classification. In: B. Scholkopf, C. Burges, and A. Smola, (eds.): Advances in Kernel Methods-Support Vector Learning. MIT-Press (1999)
28. Yang, Y., Liu, X.: A Re-examination of Text Categorization Methods. In: Proceedings of the 22nd ACM International Conference on Research and Development in Information Retrieval (SIGIR). (1999) 42-49

Contextual Probability-Based Classification

Gongde Guo[1,2], Hui Wang[2], David Bell[3], and Zhining Liao[2]

[1] School of Computer Science
Fujian Normal University, Fuzhou, 350007, China
[2] School of Computing and Mathematics
University of Ulster, BT37 0QB, UK
{G.Guo,H.Wang,Z.Liao}@ulster.ac.uk
[3] School of Computer Science
Queen's University Belfast, BT7 1NN, UK
DA.Bell@qub.ac.uk

Abstract. The k-Nearest-Neighbors (kNN) method for classification is simple but effective in many cases. The success of kNN in classification depends on the selection of a "good value" for k. In this paper, we proposed a contextual probability-based classification algorithm (CPC) which looks at multiple sets of nearest neighbors rather than just one set of k nearest neighbors for classification to reduce the bias of k. The proposed formalism is based on probability, and the idea is to aggregate the support of multiple neighborhoods for various classes to better reveal the true class of each new instance. To choose a series of more relevant neighborhoods for aggregation, three neighborhood selection methods: distance-based, symmetric-based, and entropy-based neighborhood selection methods are proposed and evaluated respectively. The experimental results show that CPC obtains better classification accuracy than kNN and is indeed less biased by k after saturation is reached. Moreover, the entropy-based CPC obtains the best performance among the three proposed neighborhood selection methods.

1 Introduction

kNN is a simple but effective method for classification [1]. For an instance to be classified, its k nearest neighbors are retrieved, and this forms a neighborhood of t. Majority voting among the instances in the neighborhood is commonly used to decide the classification for t, with or without consideration of the distance-based weighting. Despite its conceptual simplicity, kNN performs as well as any other possible classifier when applied to non-trivial problems. Over the last 50 years, this simple classification method has been extensively used in a broad range of applications such as medical diagnosis, text categorization [2], pattern recognition [3], data mining [4], and e-commerce. However, to apply kNN we need to choose an appropriate value for k, and the success of classification is very much dependent on this value. In a sense, kNN is biased by k. There are many ways of choosing the k value, and a simple one is to run the algorithm many times with different k values and choose the one with the best performance. But this is not a pragmatic method in real applications.

P. Atzeni et al. (Eds.): ER 2004, LNCS 3288, pp. 313–326, 2004.

In order for kNN to be less dependent on the choice of k, we propose to look at multiple sets of nearest neighbors rather than just one set of k nearest neighbors. As we know that for an instance t each neighborhood bears support for different possible classes. The proposed formalism is based on contextual probability [5], and the idea is to aggregate the support of multiple sets of nearest neighbors for various classes to give a more reliable support value, which better reveals the true class of t. However, in practice the given data set is usually a sample of the underlying data space, it is impossible to gather all the neighborhoods to aggregate the support for classifying a new instance. On the other hand, even if it is possible to gather all the neighborhoods of a given new instance for classification, the computational cost could be unbearable. In a sense, the classification accuracy of CPC depends on a given number of chosen neighborhoods. So methods used to select more relevant neighborhoods for aggregation in the process of picking up neighborhoods are important. Having identified the existing problems of CPC, we propose three neighborhood selection methods in this paper, aimed at choosing a set of neighborhoods as informative as possible for classification to further improve the classification accuracy of CPC.

The rest of the paper is organized as follows: Section 2 describes the contextual probability-based classification method. Section 3 introduces the three neighborhood selection methods: distance-based, symmetric-based, and entropy-based neighborhood selection methods. The experimental results are described and discussed in Section 4. Section 5 ends the paper with a summary, linking on existing problems and further research directions.

2 Contextual Probability-Based Classification

Let Ω be a finite set called a frame of discernment. A *mass* function is $m : 2^{\Omega} \rightarrow [0,1]$ such that

$$\sum_{X \subseteq \Omega} m(X) = 1 \tag{1}$$

The mass function is interpreted as a *representation* (or *measure*) of *knowledge or belief* about Ω, and $m(A)$ is interpreted as a degree of support for $A \subset \Omega$ [6, 7]. To extend our knowledge to an event, A, that we cannot evaluate explicitly for m, we define a new function $G : 2^{\Omega} \rightarrow [0,1]$ such that for any $A \subseteq \Omega$

$$G(A) = \sum_{X \subseteq \Omega} m(X) \frac{|A \cap X|}{|X|} \tag{2}$$

This means that the knowledge of event A may not be known explicitly in the representation of our knowledge, but we know explicitly some events X that are related to it (i.e. A overlaps with X or $A \cap X \neq \phi$). Part of the knowledge about X, $m(X)$, should then be shared by A, and a measure of this part is $|A \cap X|/|X|$. The mass function can be interpreted in different ways. In order to solve the *aggregation problem*, one interpretation is made as follows.

Let S be a finite set of class labels, and Ω be a finite data set each element of which has a class label in S. The labelling is denoted by a function $f{:}\Omega \rightarrow S$ so that for $x \in \Omega$, $f(x)$ is the class label of x.

Consider a class $c \in S$. Let $N = |\Omega|, N_c = |x \in \Omega| : f(x) = c|$, and $M_c = \sum_{X \in \Omega} P(c|X)$. The mass function for c is defined as $m_c : 2^{\Omega} \rightarrow [0,1]$ such that, for $A \subseteq \Omega$,

$$m_c(A) = \frac{P(c|A)}{\Sigma_{X \subseteq \Omega} P(c|X)} = \frac{P(c|A)}{M_c} \tag{3}$$

clearly $\sum_{X \subseteq \Omega} m_c(X) = 1$, and if the distribution over Ω is uniform, then $M_c = \frac{N_c}{N}(2^N - 1)$. Based on the mass function, the aggregation function for c is defined as $G_c : 2^{\Omega} \rightarrow [0,1]$ such that, for

$$G_c(A) = \sum_{X \subseteq \Omega} m_c(X) \frac{|A \cap X|}{|X|} \tag{4}$$

When A is singleton, denoted as a, equation (4) can be changed to equation (5).

$$G_c(a) = \sum_{X \subseteq \Omega} m_c(X) \frac{|a \cap X|}{|X|} \tag{5}$$

If the distribution over Ω is uniform then, for $a \in \Omega$ and $c \in S, G_c(a)$ can be represented as equation (6).

$$G_c(a) = P(c|a)\alpha_c + \beta \tag{6}$$

Let C_N^n represent the number of ways of picking n unordered outcomes from N possibilities, then,

$$\alpha_c = \frac{1}{M_c} \sum_{i=1}^{N} \frac{1}{i^2}(C_{N-1}^{i-1} - C_{N-2}^{i-2}) \text{ and } \beta = \frac{N_c}{M_c} \sum_{i=1}^{N} \frac{1}{i^2}(C_{N-2}^{i-2})$$

Let t be an instance to be classified. If we know $P(c|t)$ for all $c \in S$ then we can assign t to the class c that has the largest $P(c|t)$. Since the given data set is usually a sample of the underlying data space we may never know the true $P(c|t)$. All we can do is to approximate $P(c|t)$. Equation (6) shows the relationship between $P(c|t)$ and $G_c(t)$, and the latter can be calculated from some given events. If the set of events is complete, i.e. 2^{Ω}, we can accurately calculate $G_c(t)$ and hence $P(c|t)$; otherwise if it is partial, i.e. a subset of 2^{Ω}, $G_c(t)$ is a approximate and so is $P(c|t)$. From equation (5) we know that the more we know about a the more accurate $G_c(a)$ (and hence $P(c|a)$) will be. As a result, we can try to gather as many relevant events about a as possible. In the spirit of kNN we can deem the neighborhood of a as relevant. Therefore we can take neighborhoods of t as events. But in practice, the more neighborhoods chosen for classification, the more computational cost it takes. With limited computing time, the choice of the more relevant neighborhoods is non-trivial. This is one reason that motivated us to seek a series of more relevant neighborhoods to aggregate the support for classification. Also in the spirit of kNN, for an instance t to be classified, the closer an instance is to t, the more contribution the instance donates for classifying t. Based on this understanding, for a given number of neighborhoods (for example, k) chosen for aggregation, we choose a series of specific neighborhoods, which we think are relevant to an instance to be classified, for classification.

Summarizing the above discussion we propose the following procedure for CPC.

1. Determine N and N_c for every class c $\in S$, and then calculate β and M_c. These numbers are valid for any $t \in \Omega$.
2. Select a number of neighborhoods $A_1, A_2, \cdots, A_k$.
3. Calculate $m_c(A_i) = |A_i^c|/(|A_i| \times M_c)$ for all $c \in S$ and $i = 1, 2, \cdots, k$.
4. Calculate $G_c(t) = \sum_{i=1}^{k} m_c(A_i)/|A_i|$ for every $c \in S$.
5. Calculate $P(c|t)$ for every $c \in S$.
6. Classify t for c that has the largest $P(c|t)$.

In its simplest form kNN is majority voting among the k nearest neighbors of $t \in \Omega$. In our terminology kNN can be described as follows:

Select one neighborhood A of t, calculate $m_c(A) = |\{x \in A| : f(x) = c\}|/|A| = |A_c|/|A|$, then calculate $G_c = m_c(A)/|A| = |A^c|/|A|^2$, and then finally classify t by largest $G_c(t)$. We can see that kNN considers only one neighborhood, and it does not take into account the proportion of instances in a class. In this sense, therefore, kNN is a special case of our classification procedure.

3 Neighborhood Selection

In practice, a given data set is usually a sample of the underlying data space. It is impossible to gather all the neighborhoods to aggregate the support for classifying a new instance. On the other hand, even if it is possible to gather all neighborhoods for classification, the computational cost could be unbearable. So methods used to select more relevant neighborhoods for aggregation in the process of picking up neighborhoods are quite important. In this section, we describe the three proposed neighborhood selection methods: distance-based, symmetric, and entropy-based neighborhood selection methods which have been implemented in our prototype.

3.1 Distance-Based Neighborhood Selection

For a new instance t to be classified, distance-based neighborhood selection proceeds by choosing k nearest neighbors with different k as neighborhoods. One simple way, for example, is to ensure that for each i $(i = 0, 1, \cdots, k-1)$ its i nearest neighbors make up of a neighborhood called A_i. With this convention, we have $A_i \subset A_{i+1}$ and $|A_i| + 1 = |A_{i+1}|$, where $i = 0, 1, \cdots, k-2$. $|A_i|$ represents the number of neighbors within A_i. This is the simplest neighborhood selection method.

Figure 1 demonstrates the first four neighborhoods using the distance-based neighborhood selection method.

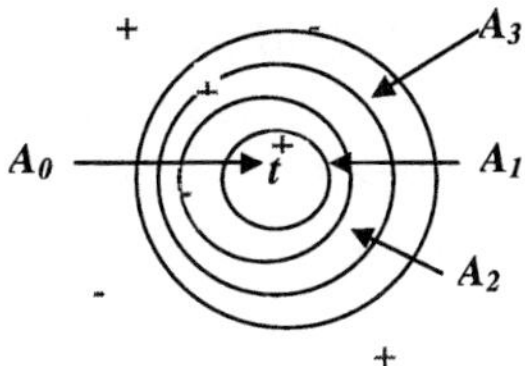

Fig. 1. The first four distance-based neighborhoods around t

3.2 Symmetric-Based Neighborhood Selection

Let S be a finite set of class labels denoted as $S = \{c_1, c_2, \cdots, c_m\}$ and Ω be a finite data set denoted as $\Omega = \{d_1, d_2, \cdots, d_N\}$. Each instance d_i in Ω denoted as $d_i = (d_{i1}, d_{i2}, \cdots, d_{in})$ has a class label in S. The labelling is denoted by a function $f\colon \Omega \to S$ so that for $d_i \in \Omega, f(d_i)$ is the class label of d_i.

Firstly, we project data set Ω into n-dimensional space. Each instance is represented as a point in the n-dimensional space. Then we partition the n-dimensional space into grids. The partitioning process proceeds as follows:

For each dimension of n-dimensional space, if feature a_i is ordinal, we partition $4\sigma_i$ into ρ equal intervals, where σ_i is the standard deviation of the values occurring for the feature a_i. ρ is a parameter whose value is application dependent. We use symbol Δ_i to represent the length of each cell of feature a_i, i.e. $\Delta_i = 4\sigma_i/\rho$. If feature a_i is nominal, its discrete values provide a natural partition. At the end of the partitioning process all the instances in data set Ω are distributed into the grids.

Assume t is an instance to be classified denoted as $t = (t_1, t_2, \cdots, t_n)$, the initial cell location of t denoted by G^0, can be calculated as follows:

- For ordinal feature a_j in cell G^0, it is represented as an interval $[t_j - \Delta_j/2, t_j + \Delta_j/2]$;
- For nominal feature a_j in cell G^0, it is represented as a set $\{t_j\}$.

All the instances covered by cell G^0 make up of the first neighborhood A_0.

Strictly speaking, each cell in grids, e.g. G^0 is a *hypertuple*. A hypertuple is a tuple where entries are sets for nominal features, and intervals for ordinal features instead of single values [10].

Assume A_i is the ith neighborhood and $G^i = (g_1^i, g_2^i, \cdots, g_n^i)$ is the corresponding hypertuple, to generate the next neighborhood A_{i+1} the hypertuple G^i is expanded in the following way:

- An ordinal feature a_j in G^i which is represented as an interval $g_j^i = [g_{j1}^i, g_{j2}^i]$, is expanded to $[g_{j1}^i - \Delta_j, g_{j2}^i + \Delta_j]$;
- An nominal feature a_j in G^i which is represented as a set $g_j^i = \{g_{j1}^i, g_{j2}^i, \cdots, g_{jq}^i\}$, is expanded to $g_j^i \cup \{x\}$, where $x \in dom(a_j)$ and $x \notin g_j^i$.

where $dom(a_i)$ is a set which represents all the values of feature a_j that occur in the training instances. All the instances covered by the newly generated hypertuple G^{i+1} make up of A_{i+1}. Figure 2 is an example of three symmetric hypertuples around t which are denoted as $G^0(blank), G^1(Striped)$, and $G^2(wavy)$ respectively. In Figure 2, G^0 is covered by G^1, and both G^0, G^1 are covered by G^2. All the instances covered by hypertuples $G^0(G^1, G^2)$ make up of the neighborhood $A_0(A_1, A_2$ respectively, where $A_0 \subset A_1 \subset A_2$.

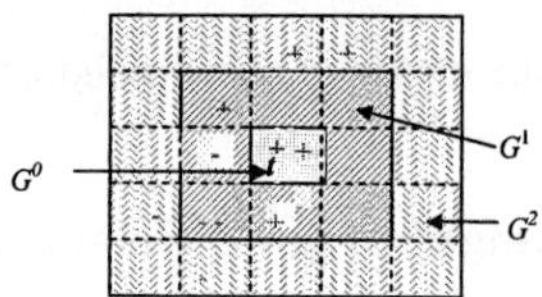

Fig. 2. Three symmetric neighborhoods

3.3 Entropy-Based Neighborhood Selection

We proposed an entropy-based neighborhood selection method by selecting a given number of neighborhoods with as much information for classification as possible. Our goal is to improve the classification accuracy of CPC. This is a neighborhood-expansion method by which the next neighborhood is generated by expanding the previous one. Obviously, the earlier one is covered by the later one. In each neighborhood expansion process, we calculate the entropy of each possible expansion (candidate) and select the one with minimal entropy as our next neighborhood. The smaller the entropy of a neighborhood, the more imbalance there is in the class distribution of the neighbors, and the more relevant the neighbors are to the instance to be classified.

Assume A_i is the ith neighborhood and $G^i = (g_1^i, g_2^i, \cdots, g_n^i)$ is the corresponding hypertuple in n-dimensional space. Consider feature a_j. If it is ordinal, then g_j^i is an interval denoted as $g_j^i = [g_{j1}^i, g_{j2}^i]$. The set of all the instances covered by hypertuple $(g_1^i, \cdots, [g_{j1}^i - \Delta_j, g_{j2}^i], \cdots, g_n^i)$ and the set of all the instances covered by hypertuple $(g_1^i, \cdots, [g_{j1}^i, g_{j2}^i + \Delta_j], \cdots, g_n^i)$ will be two candidates for the next neighborhood selection. If feature a_j is nominal, g_j^i is a set denoted as $g_j^i = \{g_{j1}^i, g_{j2}^i, \cdots, g_{jq}^i\}$. For every instance $x \in dom(a_j)$, where $x \notin g_j^i$, the set of all the instances covered by hypertuple $(g_1^i, \cdots, g_j^i \cup \{x\}, \cdots, g_n^i)$ will be a candidate for the next neighborhood selection. We then calculate each candidate's entropy according to equation (7), and choose the candidate with minimal entropy as G^{i+1}.

The entropy E^i is defined as follows:

$$E^i = I_{A_i}(c_1, c_2, \cdots, c_m) \tag{7}$$

$$I_{A_i}(c_1, c_2, \cdots, c_m) = -\sum_{j=1}^{m} p_j \log_2(p_j), \text{ where } p_j = \frac{|\{d_k | \forall d_k \in A_i, f(d_k) = c_j\}|}{|A_i|} \tag{8}$$

In equation (7), m is the number of classes; $c_1, c_2, \cdots, c_m$ are class labels. p_j in equation (8) is determined by counting the number of instances in the candidate A_i that belongs to class c_j, and presented this as a percentage of the total number of instances in this candidate. All the instances covered by G^{i+1} make up of A_{i+1}.

Suppose that a new instance $t = (t_1, t_2, \cdots, t_n)$ to be classified initially falls into a cell in grids represented as a hypertuple $G^0 = (g_1^0, g_2^0, \cdots, g_n^0)$, i.e. t is covered by G^0. For hypertuple G^0, if t_j is ordinal, g_j^0 represents an interval, denoted by $g_j^0 = [g_{j1}^0, g_{j2}^0]$, where $g_{j1}^0 = t_j - \Delta_j/2, g_{j2}^0 = t_j + \Delta_j/2$. Obviously, t_j satisfies $g_{j1}^0 \leq t_j \leq g_{j2}^0$; if t_j is nominal, g_j^0 is a set, denoted by $g_j^0 = \{t_{jq}^0\}$, where $t_j = g_{jq}^0$. All the instances covered by hypertuple G^0 make up of a set denoted by A_0, which is the first neighborhood of our algorithm. The detailed entropy-based neighborhood selection algorithm is described as follows:

1. Set $A_0 = \{d_i | d_i \text{ is covered by } G^0\}$
2. For i=1 to k-1
   {Find the ith neighborhood with minimal entropy E^i among all the candidates expanding from A_{i-1}}

Suppose that $A_i^{'}$ and $A_i^{''}$ are two neighborhoods of t having the same amount of entropy, i.e.

$$I_{A_i^{'}}(c_1, c_2, \cdots, c_m) = I_{A_i^{''}}(c_1, c_2, \cdots, c_m).$$

If $|A_i^{'}| < |A_i^{''}|$, where $|A_i^{'}|$ represents the cardinality of $A_i^{'}$, we believe that $A_i^{'}$ is more relevant to t than $A_i^{''}$, so in this case, we prefer to choose $A_i^{'}$ as the next neighborhood. Otherwise, we prefer to choose the one with minimal E^i as the next neighborhood.

According to equation (7), the smaller a neighborhood's entropy is, the more imbalance its class distribution is, and consequently the more information it has for classification. So, in our algorithm, we adopt equation (7) to be the criteria for neighborhoods selection. In each neighborhood expanding process, we select a candidate with minimal E^i as the next neighborhood.

To illustrate the method we consider an example here. For simplicity, we describe our entropy-based neighborhood selection method in 2-dimensional space.

Suppose that an instance x to be classified locates at cell [3, 3] in the leftmost graph of Figure 3. We collect all the instances, which are covered by cell [3, 3] (G^0), into a set called A_0 as the first neighborhood. Then we try to expand our cell G^0 one step in each of 4 different directions (up, down, left, and right) respectively and choose a candidate with minimal E^i as a new expanded area,

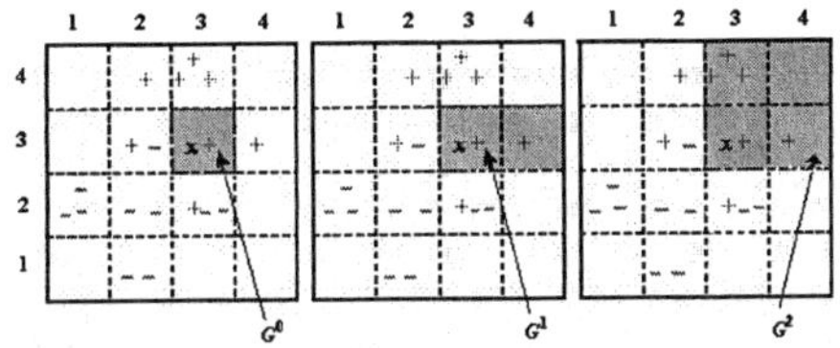

Fig. 3. Neighborhood expansion process (1)

e.g. G^1. Then we look up, down, left, right again and select a new area (e.g. G^2 in the rightmost graph of Figure 3). All the instances covered by the expanded area G^1 make up of the next neighborhood called A_1 and so on. At the end of the procedure, we obtain a series of neighborhoods e.g. $A_2, A_3, \cdots$, as shown in Figure 3 from left to right.

If an instance y to be classified locates at cell [2, 3] in the leftmost graph of Figure 4, the selection process of three neighborhoods is demonstrated by Figure 4 from left to right.

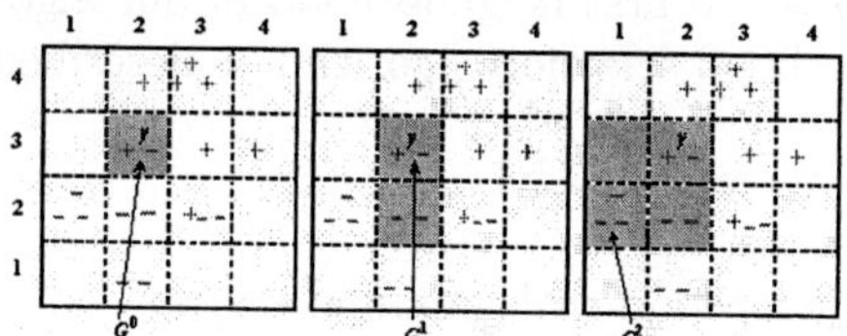

Fig. 4. Neighborhood expansion process (2)

4 Experiment and Evaluation

One motivation of this work is the fact that kNN for classification is heavily dependent on the choice of a 'good' value for k. The objective of this paper is therefore to come up with a method in which this dependence is reduced. A contextual probability-based classification method is proposed to solve this problem, which works in the same spirit as kNN but needs more neighborhoods. For simplicity we refer to our classification procedure presented in the section 2 as *nok*NN. To distinguish between three different neighborhood selection methods, we refer to distance-based neighborhood selection method as *nok*NN(d), symmetric neighborhood selection method as *nok*NN(s), and entropy-based neighborhood selection method as *nok*NN(e).

Here we experimentally evaluate the classification procedures of *nok*NN(d), *nok*NN(s), and *nok*NN(e) with real world data sets in order to verify our expectations and to see if and how aggregating different neighborhoods improves the classification accuracy of kNN.

4.1 Data Sets

In experiment, we used fifteen public data sets available from the UC Irvine Machine Learning Repository. General information about these data sets is shown in Table 1. The data sets are relatively small but scalability is not an issue when data sets are indexed.

In Table 1, the meaning of the column headings is follows, NF-Number of Features, NN-Number of Nominal features, NO-Number of Ordinal features, NB-Number of Binary features, NI-Number of Instances, and CD-Class Distribution.

Table 1. Some information about the data sets

Data set	NF	NN	NO	NB	NI	CD
Australian	14	4	6	4	690	383:307
Colic	23	16	7	0	368	232:136
Diabetes	8	0	8	0	768	268:500
Glass	9	0	9	0	214	70:17:76:0:13:9:29
HCleveland	13	3	7	3	303	164:139
Heart	13	3	7	3	270	120:150
Hepatitis	19	6	1	12	155	32:123
Ionosphere	34	0	34	0	351	126:225
Iris	4	0	4	0	150	50:50:50
LiverBupa	6	0	6	0	345	145:200
Sonar	60	0	60	0	208	97:111
Vehicle	18	0	18	0	846	212:217:218:199
Vote	16	0	0	16	435	267:168
Wine	13	0	13	0	178	59:71:48
Zoo	16	16	0	0	90	37:18:3:12:4:7:9

4.2 Experiments

Experiment 1. kNN and *nok*NN(d) were implemented in our prototype. In the experiment, 30 neighborhoods were used and for every data set. kNN was run with varying number of neighbors ranging from 1 to 88 with step 3 for k, and *nok*NN(d) was run with varying number of neighborhoods ranging from 1 to 30 with step 1 for N. Each set of k nearest neighbors (k=1,4,$\cdots$,88 for kNN) makes up a neighborhood. There are totally 30 neighborhoods corresponding to different k ranging from 1 to 88 with step 3.

The comparison of kNN and *nok*NN(d) in classification accuracy is shown in Figure 5. Each value in horizontal axis, e.g. N=i, represents the number of neighborhoods used for aggregation for *nok*NN(d) and the ith neighborhood used for kNN. The k value for kNN with respect to the ith neighborhood is $3 \times i - 2$.

The detailed experimental results for kNN and *nok*NN(d) are presented in two separate tables: Table 2 for *nok*NN(d) and Table 3 for kNN, where N is varied from 1 to 10 for both kNN and *nok*NN(d).

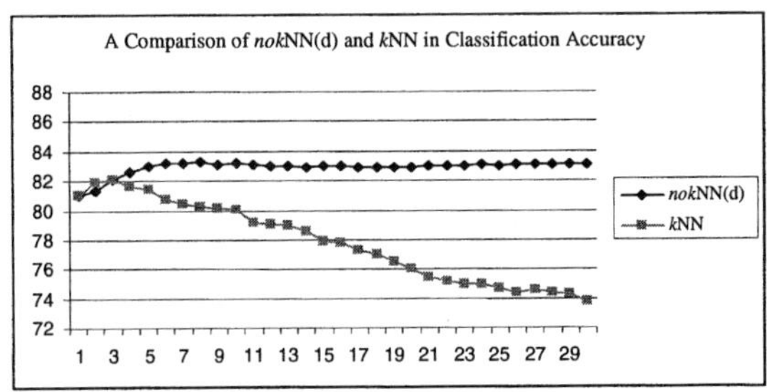

Fig. 5. A comparison of *nok*NN(d) and kNN in average classification accuracy

Table 2. Classification accuracy of *nok*NN(d) in 10-fold cross validation

Data set	N=1	N=2	N=3	N=4	N=5	N=6	N=7	N=8	N=9	N=10
Australian	79.42	80.22	83.04	84.06	84.64	85.07	85.36	85.22	85.36	85.51
Colic	78.89	78.94	81.94	83.33	83.61	83.39	83.89	83.33	83.05	83.33
Diabetes	70.92	71.42	71.97	72.24	72.63	73.29	73.55	73.68	73.82	74.47
Glass	68.10	68.30	67.62	66.67	68.57	68.57	69.05	69.52	70.00	70.00
HCleveland	78.33	78.45	80.00	81.67	82.67	82.67	82.67	83.00	83.33	83.67
Heart	76.30	77.80	78.15	79.63	81.48	81.85	81.85	82.22	81.48	81.48
Hepatitis	80.67	81.25	83.33	83.33	82.67	82.67	82.00	82.67	81.33	82.00
Ionosphere	87.14	87.14	86.29	85.14	84.86	84.57	84.57	84.57	84.29	84.00
Iris	95.33	95.55	96.00	96.00	96.00	96.00	96.00	96.00	96.00	96.00
LiverBupa	60.00	60.21	63.24	65.29	65.88	66.47	66.76	66.18	65.59	65.59
Sonar	88.00	88.06	87.50	87.50	87.50	88.00	88.00	88.00	88.00	87.00
Vehicle	68.57	68.60	68.57	70.48	70.12	71.07	71.43	71.43	71.31	71.31
Vote	91.30	91.39	91.74	91.74	91.74	91.74	91.74	91.74	91.74	92.17
Wine	95.88	95.88	95.88	95.88	95.88	95.29	94.71	94.71	94.71	94.71
Zoo	96.67	96.67	96.67	96.67	96.67	96.67	96.67	96.67	96.67	96.67
Average	81.03	81.33	82.13	82.64	82.99	83.19	83.22	83.26	83.11	83.19

Table 3. Classification accuracy of *k*NN in 10-fold cross validation

Data set	N=1	N=2	N=3	N=4	N=5	N=6	N=7	N=8	N=9	N=10
Australian	79.42	84.49	85.22	85.80	85.51	85.80	86.23	86.09	85.51	85.51
Colic	78.89	83.33	82.50	84.44	84.17	85.00	84.44	83.89	84.72	85.00
Diabetes	70.92	73.42	74.34	73.68	74.34	74.21	74.74	74.34	74.61	74.34
Glass	68.10	65.71	66.19	62.86	61.90	60.48	59.05	59.05	59.05	60.00
HCleveland	78.33	79.33	80.33	81.00	78.67	80.33	80.33	80.33	80.33	79.33
Heart	76.30	79.26	80.37	79.63	80.74	78.52	78.15	79.26	79.63	79.63
Hepatitis	80.67	80.67	83.33	83.33	85.33	84.67	85.33	84.00	84.00	84.00
Ionosphere	87.14	86.57	83.14	84.57	84.57	84.29	82.86	83.14	80.86	82.00
Iris	95.33	96.67	96.00	96.00	95.33	95.33	95.33	96.00	96.67	96.00
LiverBupa	60.00	63.53	66.76	63.24	66.18	64.12	66.76	65.29	67.94	66.18
Sonar	88.00	85.00	83.50	83.00	78.50	79.00	75.00	73.50	72.00	76.50
Vehicle	68.57	68.81	69.17	70.95	68.81	68.69	67.86	69.05	68.21	66.67
Vote	91.30	93.04	92.17	92.17	92.17	91.74	91.74	91.30	90.87	91.30
Wine	95.88	95.53	94.12	91.76	94.12	93.53	95.29	95.29	95.29	94.71
Zoo	96.67	95.56	94.44	92.22	91.11	85.56	83.33	83.33	82.22	78.89
Average	81.03	81.93	82.11	81.64	81.43	80.75	80.43	80.26	80.13	80.00

In Table 2, heading $N{=}i$ represents the number of neighborhoods used for aggregation.

In Table 3, heading $N = i$ represents the ith neighborhoods used for kNN. The ith neighborhood contains $3 \times i - 2$ neighbors, i.e. $k = 3 \times i - 2$.

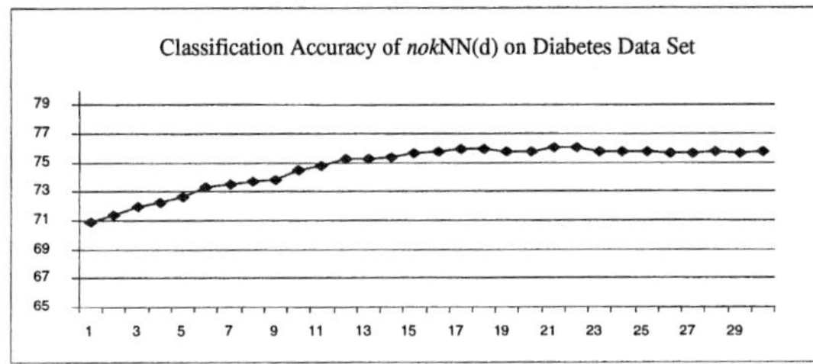

Fig. 6. Classification accuracy of *nok*NN(d) testing on Diabetes data set

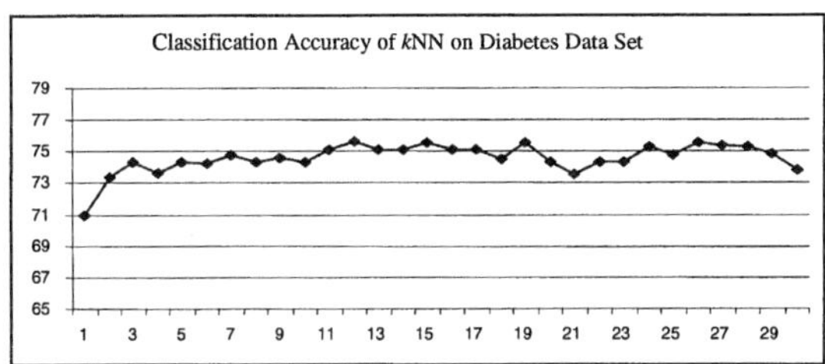

Fig. 7. Classification accuracy of kNN testing on Diabetes data set

Figure 6 and Figure 7 show the full details of the performance of *nok*NN(d) and kNN testing on the Diabetes data set where the number of neighborhoods varies from 1 to 30.

We also give the worst and best performance of kNN together with the corresponding "N" values, and the performance of *nok*NN(d) in Table 4 when ten neighborhoods are used for aggregation. In this experiment, we use the 10-fold cross validation method for evaluation.

The experimental results show that the performance of kNN varies when different neighborhoods are used while the performance of *nok*NN(d) improves with increasing number of neighborhoods, but stabilizes after a certain number of stages (k=6 in Figure 5). Furthermore the stabilized performance of *nok*NN(d) is comparable (in fact slightly better in our experiment on fifteen data sets) to the best performance of kNN within 10 neighborhoods.

Experiment 2 In this experiment, our goal is to test whether or not the entropy-based neighborhood selection method can improve the classification accuracy of CPC. In the experiment, for each value of N, e.g. N=i, *nok*NN(e) represents the average classification accuracy obtained when i neighborhoods are used for aggregation, and kNN represents the average classification accuracy obtained when testing on the ith neighborhood. A comparison of entropy-based *nok*NN(e) and kNN with respect to classification accuracy using 10-fold cross validation is shown in Figure 8.

To further verify our aggregation method, we also implemented a symmetric neighborhood selection method. Refer to section 3.2 for more details.

Table 4. A comparison of kNN and *nok*NN(d) in 10-fold cross validation

Data set	kNN Worse case (N=10)	kNN Best case (N=3)	*nok*NN(d) (N=10)
Australian	85.51	85.22	85.51
Colic	85.50	82.50	83.33
Diabetes	74.34	74.34	74.47
Glass	60.00	66.19	70.00
HCleveland	79.33	80.33	83.67
Heart	79.63	80.37	81.48
Hepatitis	84.00	83.33	82.00
Ionosphere	82.00	83.14	84.00
Iris	96.00	96.00	96.00
LiverBupa	66.18	66.76	65.59
Sonar	76.50	83.50	87.00
Vehicle	66.67	69.17	71.31
Vote	91.30	92.17	92.17
Wine	94.71	94.12	94.71
Zoo	78.89	94.44	96.67
Average	80.00	82.11	83.19

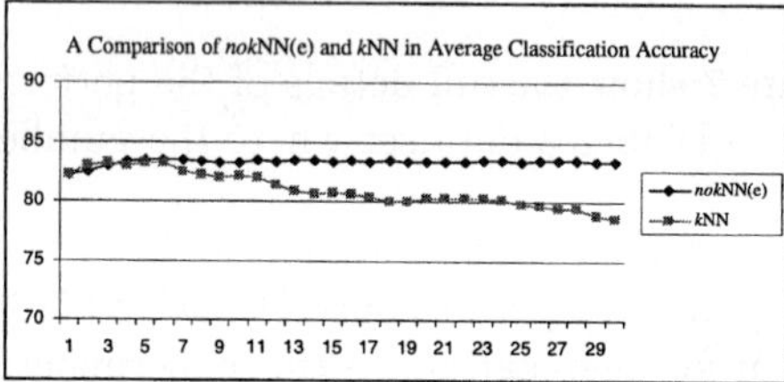

Fig. 8. A comparison of *nok*NN(e) and kNN in classification accuracy

Figure 9 shows that the similar results are obtained using the symmetric neighborhood selection method.

A comparison of entropy-based *nok*NN(e) with symmetric-based *nok*NN(s), and distance-based *nok*NN(d) in classification accuracy is shown in Figure 10

It is obvious that the entropy-based CPC obtains better classification accuracy than the symmetric-based CPC and the distance-based CPC, especially when the number of neighborhoods for aggregation is relatively small, e.g. $k < 10$. The experimental results justify our hypotheses: (1) the bias of k can be removed by CPC, and (2) the entropy-based neighborhood selection method indeed improves the classification accuracy of CPC.

5 Conclusions

In this paper we have discussed the issues related to the kNN method for classification. In order for kNN to be less dependent on the choice of k, we looked at

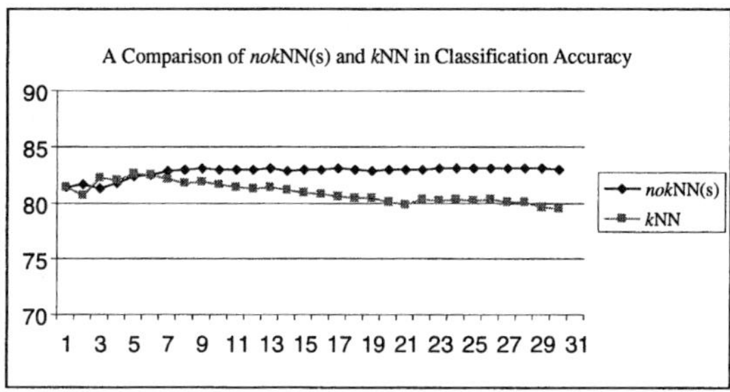

Fig. 9. A comparison of *nok*NN(s) and *k*NN in classification accuracy

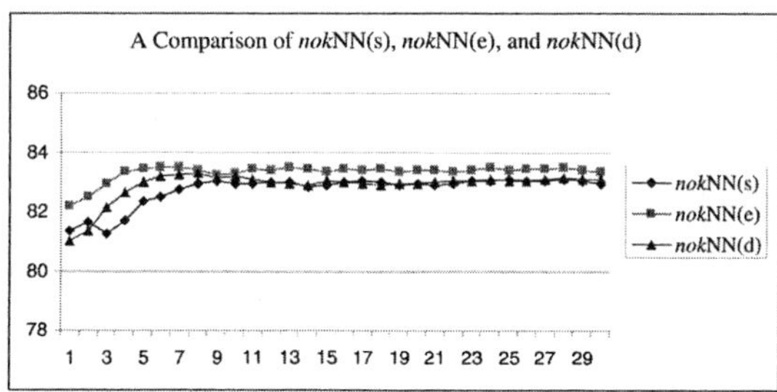

Fig. 10. A comparison of *nok*NN(d), *nok*NN(s), and *nok*NN(d)

multiple sets of nearest neighbors rather than just one set of k nearest neighbors. A set of neighbors is called a neighborhood. For an instance t each neighborhood bears support for different possible classes. We have presented a novel formalism based on probability to aggregate the support for various classes to give a more reliable support value, which better reveals the true class of t. Based on this idea, for specific neighborhoods used in kNN, which always surround around the instance t to be classified, we have proposed a contextual probability-based classification method together with three different neighborhood selection methods. To choose a given number of neighborhoods with as much information for classification as possible, the proposed entropy-based neighborhood selection method which partitions a multidimensional data space into grids and expands neighborhood each time with minimal information entropy among all candidates in this grids. This method is independent on "distance metric" or "similarity metric".

Experiments on some public data sets have shown that using *nok*NN (whether *nok*NN(d), *nok*NN(s), or *nok*NN(e)) the classification accuracy increases as the number of neighborhoods increases, but stabilizes after a small number of neighborhoods; using kNN, however, the classification performance varies when different neighborhoods are used. Experiments also have shown that the stabilized performance of *nok*NN(d) is comparable to the best performance of kNN. The comparison of entropy-based, symmetric-based, and distance-based CPC has shown that the entropy-based CPC obtains the highest classification accuracy.

References

1. Hand, D., Mannila, H., and Smyth, P. Principles of Data Mining, The MIT Press, 2001.
2. Sebastiani, F. Machine Learning in Automatic Text Categorization, In ACM Computing Survey, Vol.34, No. 1, pages.1-47, March 2002.
3. Ripley, B. Pattern Recognition and Neural Networks. Cambridge University Press, 1996.
4. Mitchell, T. Machine Learning, MIT Press and McGraw-Hill, 1997.
5. Wang, H. Contextual Probability, Journal of Telecommunications and Information Technology, 4(3), pages 92-97, 2003.
6. Guan, J. and Bell, D. Generalization of the Dempster-Shafer Theory. Proc. IJCAI-93, pages 592-597, 1993.
7. Shafer, G. A Mathematical Theory of Evidence, Princeton University Press, Princeton, New Jersey, 1976.
8. Feller, W. An Introduction to Probability Theory and Its Applications, Wiley, 1968.
9. Michie, D., Spiegelhalter, D. J., and Taylor, C. C. Machine Learning, Neural and Statistical Classification. Ellis Horwood, 1994.
10. Wang, H., Duntsch, I. and Bell, D. Data Reduction Based on Hyper Relations. Proc. of KDD98, New York, pages 349-353, 1998.

Improving the Performance of Decision Tree: A Hybrid Approach

LiMin Wang[1], SenMiao Yuan[1], Ling Li[2], and HaiJun Li[2]

[1] College of Computer Science and Technology, JiLin University, ChangChun 130012, China
jeffreywlm@sina.com
[2] School of Computer, YanTai University, YanTai 264005, China

Abstract. In this paper, a hybrid learning approach named Flexible NBTree is proposed. Flexible NBTree uses Bayes measure δ to select proper test and applies post-discretization strategy to construct decision tree. The finial decision tree nodes contain univariate splits as regular decision trees, but the leaf nodes contain General Naive Bayes, which is a variant of standard Naive Bayesian classifier. Empirical studies on a set of natural domains show that Flexible NBTree has clear advantages with respect to the generalization ability when compared against its counterpart, NBTree.

Keywords: Flexible NBTree; Bayes measure δ; General Naive Bayes; post-discretization

1 Introduction

Decision tree based methods of supervised learning represent one of the most popular approaches within the AI field for dealing with classification problems. They have been widely used for years in many domains such as web mining, data mining, pattern recognition, signal processing, etc. But standard decision tree learning algorithm [1] has difficulty in obtaining the relation between continuous-valued data points. It is a key issue in research to learn from data consisting of both continuous and nominal variables.

Some researchers indicate that hybrid approaches can take advantage of both symbolic and connectionist models to handle tough problems. Much research has addressed the issue of combining decision tree with other learning algorithm to construct hybrid model. Baldwin et al. [2] used mass assignment theory to translate attribute values to probability distribution over the fuzzy partitions, then introduced probabilistic fuzzy decision trees in which fuzzy partitions were used to discretize continuous test universes. Tsang et al.[3] used a hybrid neural network to refine fuzzy decision tree and extracts a fuzzy decision tree with parameters, which is equivalent to a set of fuzzy production rules. Based on variable precision rough set theory, Zhang et al. [4] introduced a new concept of generalization and employed the variable precision rough sets (VPRS) model to construct multivariate decision tree.

P. Atzeni et al. (Eds.): ER 2004, LNCS 3288, pp. 327–335, 2004.

By redefining test selection measure, this paper proposes a novel hybrid approach, Flexible NBTree, which attempts to utilize the advantage of decision tree and Naive Bayes. The final classifier resembles Kohavi's NBTree [5] but in two respects: 1. NBTree pre-discretizes the data set by applying an entropy based algorithm. Flexible NBTree applyies post-discretization strategy to construct decision tree. 2. NBTree uses standard Naive Bayes at the leaf node to handle pre-discretized and nominal attributes. Flexible NBTree uses General Naive Bayes (GNB), which is a variant of standard Naive Bayes, at the leaf node to handle continuous and nominal attributes in the subspace.

The remainder of this paper is organized as follows: Section 2, 3 introduce the post-discretization strategy and GNB, respectively. Section 4 illustrates Flexible NBTree in detail. Section 5 presents the corresponding experimental results of compared performance with regarding to Flexible NBTree and NBTree. Section 6 sums up whole paper.

2 The Post-discretization Strategy

When applying post-discretization strategy to construct decision tree, at each internal node in the tree, we first select the test which is the most useful for improving classification accuracy, then apply discretization of continuous tests.

2.1 Bayes Measure δ

In this discussion we use capital letters such as X, Y for variable names, and lower-case letters such as x, y to denote specific values taken by those variables. Let $P(\cdot)$ denote the probability, $p(\cdot)$ refer to the probability density function.

Suppose the training set T consists of predictive attributes $\{X_1, \cdots, X_n\}$ and class attribute C. Each attribute X_i is either continuous or nominal. The aim of decision tree learning is to construct a tree model which can describe the relationship between the predictive attributes $\{X_1, \cdots, X_n\}$ and class attribute C.

$$\text{Tree Model: } \{X_1, \cdots, X_n\} \to C$$

That is, the classification accuracy of the tree model on data set T should be the highest. Correspondingly the Bayes measure δ, which is introduced in this section as a test selection measure, is also based on this criterion.

Let X_i represent one of the predictive attributes. According to Bayes theorem, if X_i is nominal then:

$$P(c|x_i) = \frac{P(c)P(x_i|c)}{P(x_i)} \propto P(c)P(x_i|c). \tag{1}$$

Otherwise if X_i is continuous then:

$$P(c|x_i) = \frac{P(c)p(x_i|c)}{p(x_i)} \propto P(c)p(x_i|c). \tag{2}$$

The aim of Bayesian classification is to decide and choose the class that maximizes the posteriori probability. When some instances satisfy $X_i = x_i$, their class labels are most likely to be:

$$c_i^* = \begin{cases} \arg\max_{c \in C} P(c)P(x_i|c) \text{ (if } X_i \text{ is nominal)} \\ \arg\max_{c \in C} P(c)p(x_i|c) \text{ (if } X_i \text{ is continuous)} \end{cases} \tag{3}$$

Definition 1. *Suppose X_i has m distinct values. We define the Bayes measure δ as:*

$$\delta = \frac{\sum_{j=1}^{m} Count(X_i = x_{ij} \wedge C = c_j^*)}{N}. \tag{4}$$

where N is the size of set T. Intuitively spoken, δ is the classification accuracy when classifier consists of attribute X_i only. It describes the extent to which the model constructed by attribute X_i fits class attribute C. The predictive attribute which maximizes δ is the one that is most useful for improving classification accuracy.

2.2 Discretization of Continuous Tests

The aim of discretization is to partition the values of continuous test X_i into a nominal set of intervals. According to (3), we have:

$$c_i^* = \arg\max_{c \in C} P(c)p(x_i|c). \tag{5}$$

where conditional probability density function $p(x_i|c)$ is continuous. Given arbitrary values x_a and x_b of attribute X_i, when $x_a \to x_b$, there will be

$$P(c)p(x_a|c) \to P(c)p(x_b|c).$$

So, the class labels inferred from (3) will not change within a small interval of the values of X_i. For clarification, suppose the relationship between the distribution of X_i and C is shown in Fig. 1.

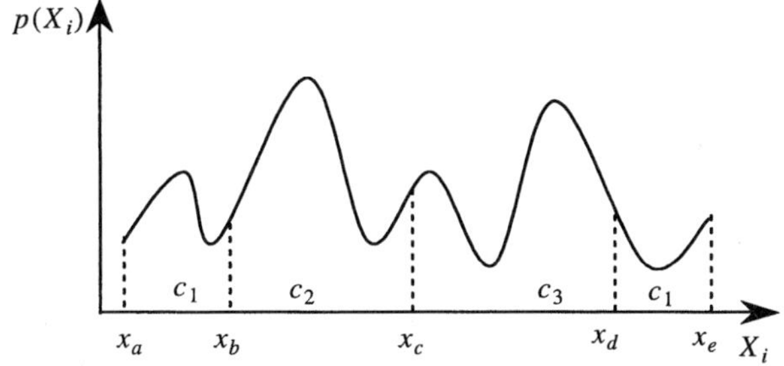

Fig. 1. The relationship between the distribution of X_i and C

We can see from Fig. 1 that,

$$\begin{cases} C = c_1 \ (x_a \leq X_i < x_b \ or \ x_d \leq X_i \leq x_e) \\ C = c_2 \ (x_b \leq X_i < x_c) \\ C = c_3 \ (x_c \leq X_i < x_d) \end{cases} \tag{6}$$

Note that the attribute values c_1, c_2, c_3 are inferred from (3), not the true class labels of training instances. And in the current example, there are three candidate boundaries corresponding to the values of X_i at which the value of C changes: x_b, x_c, x_d. If we use these boundaries to discretize attribute X_i, the classification accuracy after discretization will be equal to δ. So, the process of computing δ is also the process of discretization. The Bayes measure δ can also be used to automatically find the most appropriate boundaries for discretization and the number of intervals.

Although this kind of discretization method can retain classification accuracy, it may lead to too many intervals. The Minimum Description Length (MDL) principle is used in our experimental study to control the number of intervals.

Suppose we have sorted sequence S into ascending order by the values of X_i. Such a sequence is partitioned by boundary B to two subsets S_1, S_2. The class information entropy of the partition denoted by $E(X_i, B; S)$ is given by:

$$E(X_i, B; S) = \frac{|S_1|}{|S|} Ent(S_1) + \frac{|S_2|}{|S|} Ent(S_2)$$

where $Ent(\cdot)$ denotes the entropy function,

$$Ent(S_i) = -\sum_{c \in C} P(c, S_i) \log_2 P(c, S_i)$$

and $P(c, S_i)$ stands for the proportion of the instances in S_i that belong to class c.

According to MDL principle, the partitioning within S is reasonable iff

$$Gain(X_\imath, B; S) \geq \frac{\log_2(N-1)}{N} + \frac{\Delta(X_i, B; S)}{N}$$

where $Gain(X_i, B; S) = Ent(S) - E(X_i, B; S)$ is the information gain, which measures the decrease of the weighted average impurity of the partitions S_1, S_2, compared with the impurity of the complete set S. N is the number of instances in set S, $\Delta(X_i, B; S) = \log_2(3^k - 2) - [k \cdot Ent(S) - k_1 \cdot Ent(S_1) - k_2 \cdot Ent(S_2)]$, k_i is the number of class labels represented in set S_i. This approach can then be applied recursively to all adjacent partitions of attribute X_i, thus create the final intervals.

3 General Naive Bayse (GNB)

Naive Bayes comes originally from work in pattern recognition and is based on one assumption that predictive attributes $X_1, \cdots, X_n$ are conditionally independent given the class attribute C, which can be expressed as follows:

$$P(x_1, \cdots, x_n|c) = \prod_{i=1}^{n} P(x_i|c).$$

But when instance space contains continuous attributes, the situation is different. For clarity, we first just consider two attributes: X_1(continuous) and X_2(nominal). Suppose the values of X_1 have been discretized into a set of intervals, each corresponding to a nominal value. Then the independence assumption should be:

$$P(x_1 \leq X_1 \leq x_1 + \triangle, x_2|c) = P(x_1 \leq X_1 \leq x_1 + \triangle|c)P(x_2|c). \quad (7)$$

where $[x_1, x_1 + \triangle]$ is arbitrary interval of the values of attribute X_1. This assumption, which is the basis of GNB, supports very efficient algorithms for both classification and learning. By the definition of a derivative,

$$\begin{aligned} P(c|x_1 \leq X_1 \leq x_1 + \triangle, x_2) &= \frac{P(c)P(x_1 \leq X_1 \leq x_1 + \triangle|c)P(x_2|c)}{P(x_1 \leq X_1 \leq x_1 + \triangle|x_2)P(x_2)} \\ &= \frac{P(c)p(\zeta|c)\triangle P(x_2|c)}{p(\eta|x_2)\triangle P(x_2)} \\ &= \frac{P(c)p(\zeta|c)P(x_2|c)}{p(\eta|x_2)P(x_2)}. \end{aligned} \quad (8)$$

where $x_1 \leq \zeta, \eta \leq x_1 + \triangle$. When $\triangle \to 0$, $P(c|x_1 \leq X_1 \leq x_1 + \triangle, x_2) \to P(c|x_1, x_2)$ and $\zeta, \eta \to x_1$, hence

$$\lim_{\triangle \to 0} P(c|x_1 \leq X_1 \leq x_1 + \triangle, x_2) = P(c|x_1, x_2) = \frac{P(c)p(x_1|c)P(x_2|c)}{p(x_1|x_2)P(x_2)}. \quad (9)$$

We now extend (9) to handle a much more common situation. Suppose the first k of n attributes are continuous and the remaining attributes are nominal. Similar to the induction process of (9), we will have

$$\begin{aligned} P(c|x_1, \cdots, x_n) &= \frac{P(c)\prod_{i=1}^{k} p(x_i|c)\prod_{j=k+1}^{n} P(x_j|c)}{p(x_1, \cdots, x_k|x_{k+1}, \cdots, x_n)P(x_{k+1}, \cdots, x_n)} \\ &\propto P(c)\prod_{i=1}^{k} p(x_i|c) \prod_{j=k+1}^{n} P(x_j|c). \end{aligned} \quad (10)$$

Then the classification rule of GNB is:

$$c^* = \arg\max_{c \in C} P(c|x_1, \cdots, x_n) = \arg\max_{c \in C} P(c)\prod_{i=1}^{k} p(x_i|c)\prod_{j=k+1}^{n} P(x_j|c). \quad (11)$$

The probability $P(c)$, $P(x_j|c)$ in (11) are estimated by using the Laplace-estimate and M-estimate [6], respectively.

Kernel-based density estimation [7] is the most widely used non-parametric density estimation technique. Compared with parametricdensity estimation technique, it does not make any assumption of data distribution. In this paper we choose it to estimate conditional probability density $p(x_i|c)$ in Eq.(11):

$$\hat{p}(x_i|c) = \frac{1}{nh}\sum_{k=1}^{n} K(\frac{x_i - x_k}{h}) \tag{12}$$

where $x_k(k = 1, \cdots, n)$ is the corresponding value of attribute X when $C = c$, $K(\cdot)$ is a given kernel function $K(t) = (2\pi)^{-1/2}e^{-t^2/2}$. And h is the corresponding kernel width, n is the number of training instances when $C = c$.

This estimate converges to the true probability density function if the kernel function obeys certain smoothness properties and the kernel width are chosen appropriately. One way of measuring the difference between the true $p(x_i|c)$ and the estimated $\hat{p}(x_i|c)$ is the expected cross-entropy:

$$CV_{CE} = -\frac{1}{n}\sum_{k=1}^{n} \log(\frac{1}{(n-1)h} \sum_{i=1, i\neq k}^{n} K(\frac{x_i - x_k}{h}))$$

where $h = c_X/\sqrt{n}$ and c_X is chosen to minimize the estimated cross-entropy. In our experiments, we use an exhaustive grid search where grid width is 0.01 and the search is over $c_X \in [0.2, 0.8]$ [8].

4 Flexible NBTree

Kohavi proposes NBTree as a hybrid approach combining the Naive Bayes and decision tree. It has been shown that NBTree frequently achieves higher accuracy than either a Naive Bayes or a decision tree. Like NBTree, Flexible NBTree also uses a tree structure to split the instance space into subspaces and generates one Naive Bayes in each subspace. However, it uses a different discretization strategy and different version of Naive Bayes.

The Flexible NBTree learning algorithm is shown as follows.

Input: a training set T of pre-classified instances.
Output: a hybrid decision tree with GNB at the leaves.
1. From predictive attribute set $\{X_1, \cdots, X_n\}$, select test X_i which maximizes δ.
2. If X_i is continuous, partition its value into a set of intervals according to subsection 2.2.
3. Partition T according to the value of X_i. If X_i is continuous, a multi-way split is made for all possible nominal intervals; If X_i is nominal, a multi-way split is made for all possible values.
4. If the descendant node satisfies specific stopping criterions, create a GNB as the leaf node and return. If the descendant node belongs to the same class, create a class label as the leaf node and return.
5. For each descendant node, the entire process is recursively repeated on the portion of T that matches the test leading to the node.

Table 1. Average classification accuracy and standard deviation

Data set	NBTree	Flexible NBTree
Anneal	98.3125 ± 1.5284	$98.6837 \pm 1.2854\surd$
Audiology	77.3044 ± 7.5284	$82.7827 \pm 6.8173\surd$
Australian	85.6257 ± 4.0733	83.2843 ± 4.1834
Breast-w	93.6726 ± 2.6743	$94.5274 \pm 2.1827\surd$
German	71.3381 ± 3.2943	$75.2732 \pm 2.7511\surd$
Glass	67.6621 ± 9.3321	65.4732 ± 8.7038
Heart-c	76.9315 ± 6.9162	$83.1621 \pm 6.4923\surd$
Heart-h	80.2725 ± 8.0183	$85.2521 \pm 6.3358\surd$
Ionosphere	89.7836 ± 4.4932	88.1610 ± 3.3275
Iris	94.7162 ± 5.3942	$96.3832 \pm 4.9832\surd$
Kr-vs-Kp	99.4035 ± 0.4927	97.4582 ± 0.8368
Pima-indians	74.5120 ± 5.3637	$77.1105 \pm 4.5374\surd$
Primary-tumor	41.4158 ± 6.9217	$46.7932 \pm 6.2033\surd$
Segment	96.8937 ± 1.6038	95.4382 ± 1.5927
Sick-enthyroid	98.7892 ± 0.6948	96.7042 ± 0.5134
Soybean	91.8824 ± 3.2948	$93.5172 \pm 2.7283\surd$
Vehicle	72.3943 ± 4.2036	$80.4983 \pm 3.4943\surd$
Zoo	92.6462 ± 7.6494	$94.8285 \pm 6.7932\surd$

5 Experiments

In order to evaluate the performance of Flexible NBTree and compare it against its counterpart, NBTree, we conducted an empirical study on 18 data sets from the UCI machine learning repository[1]. Each data set consists of a set of classified instances described in terms of varying numbers of continuous and nominal attributes. For comparison purpose, the stopping criterions in our experiments are the same: the relative reduction in error for a split is less than 5% and there are no more than 30 instances in the node.

The classification performance was evaluated by ten-folds cross-validation for all the experiments on each data set. Table 1 shows classification accuracy and standard deviation for Flexible NBTree and NBTree, respectively. '$\surd$' indicates that the accuracy of Flexible NBTree is higher than that of NBTree at a significance level better than 0.05 using a two-tailed pairwise t-test on the results of the 20 trials in a data set.

From Table 1, the significant advantage of Flexible NBTree over NBTree in terms of the higher accuracy can be clearly seen. In order to investigate the reason(s), we analyze the experimental results on data set Breast-w in particular. Figure 2 shows the comparison of classification accuracy for Flexible NBTree and NBTree.

When N (the training size of data set Breast-w) < 650, the tree structures that learned from these two algorithms are almost the same. But when

[1] ftp://ftp.ics.uci.edu/pub/machine-learning-databases

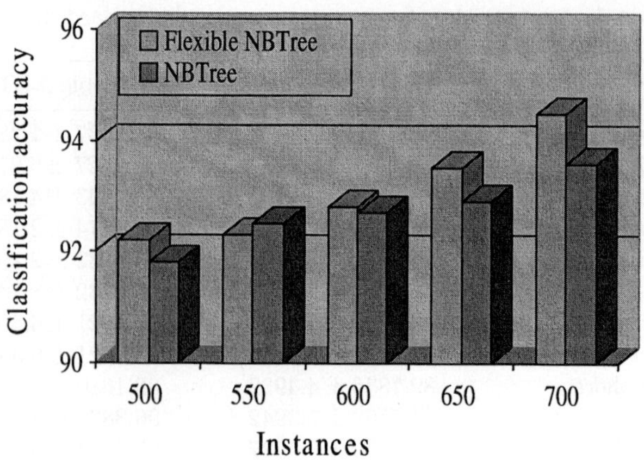

Fig. 2. Comparison of the classification accuracy

$N \geq 650$, the decision node in the second layer of Flexible NBTree contains univariate test <Bare Nuclei> and that learned from NBTree contains test <Cell Shape>. Correspondingly from Fig. 2 we can see that, when $N = 600$ Flexible NBTree achieves 92.83% accuracy on the test set while NBTree reaches about 92.73%. When $N = 650$ Flexible NBTree achieves 93.51% accuracy while NBTree reaches about 92.92%. The error reduction increases from 1.38% to 8.33%. We attribute this improvement to the effectiveness of post-discretization strategy. Since no information-lossless discretization procedure is available, some helpful information may lose in the transformation from infinite numeric area to finite subintervals. We conjecture that pre-discretization does not take full advantage of the information that continuous attributes supply and this may affect the cutting points of continuous test or even test selection in the process of tree construction, thus degrade the classification performance to some extent. But post-discretization strategy applies discretization only when necessary, thus the possibility of information loss can be reduced to minimum.

6 Summary

Pre-discretization is a common choice for handling continuous attributes in machine learning. But the information loss may affect classification performance negatively. In this paper, we propose a novel learning approach, Flexible NBTree, which is hybrid of decision tree and Naive Bayes. Flexible NBTree applies post-discretization strategy to mitigate the negative effect of information loss. Experiments with natural domains showed that Flexible NBTree generalizes much better than NBTree.

References

1. Quinlan, J. R.: Discovering rules from large collections of examples: A case study. Expert Systems in the Micro Electronic Age, Edinburgh University Press, (1979)
2. Baldwin, JF., Sachin, B. Karale.: Asymmetric Triangular Fuzzy Sets for Classification Models. Proceedings of the 7th International Conference on Knowledge-Based Intelligent Information and Engineering Systems, KES 2003 Oxford, UK, (2003) 364-370
3. Tsang, ECC., Wang, XZ., Yeung, YS.: Improving learning accuracy of fuzzy decision trees by hybrid neural networks. IEEE Transactions on Fuzzy Systems, 8 (2000) 601-614
4. Zhang, L., Ye-Yun, M., Yu, S., Ma-Fan, Y.: A New Multivariate Decision Tree Construction Algorithm Based on Variable Precision Rough Set. Advances in Web-Age Information Management, (2003) 238-246
5. Kohavi, R.: Scaling up the accuracy of naive-bayes classifiers: A decision-tree hybrid. Proceedings of the 2th International Conference on Knowledge Discovery and Data Mining, Menlo Park, CA, (1996) 202-207
6. Cestnik, B.: Estimating probabilities: A crucial task in machine learning. Proceedings of the 9th European Conference on Artificial Intelligence, (1990) 147-149
7. Chen, H., Meer, P.: Robust Computer Vision through Kernel Density Estimation. Proceedings of the 7th European Conference on Computer Vision, Copenhagen, Denmark, (2002) 236-246
8. Smyth, P., Gray, A., Fayyad, U.: Retrofitting decision tree classifiers using kernel density estimation. Proceedings of the 12th International Conference on Machine Learning, Morgan Kaufmann Publishers, (1995) 506-514

Understanding Relationships: Classifying Verb Phrase Semantics*

Veda C. Storey[1] and Sandeep Purao[2]

[1] J. Mack Robinson College of Business, Georgia State University,
Atlanta, GA 30302
vstorey@gsu.edu

[2] School of Information Sciences & Technology, The Pennsylvania State University,
University Park, PA 16801-3857
spurao@ist.psu.edu

Abstract. Relationships are an essential part of the design of a database because they capture associations between things. Comparing and integrating relationships from heterogeneous databases is a difficult problem, partly because of the nature of the relationship verb phrases. This research proposes a multi--layered approach to classifying the semantics of relationship verb phrases to assist in the comparison of relationships. The first layer captures fundamental, primitive relationships based upon well-known work in data abstractions and conceptual modeling. The second layer captures the life cycle of natural progressions in the business world. The third layer reflects the context-dependent nature of relationships. Use of the classification scheme is illustrated by comparing relationships from various application domains with different purposes.

1 Introduction

Comparing and integrating databases is an important problem, especially in an increasingly networked world that relies on inter-organizational coordination and systems. With this, is the need to develop new methods to design and integrate disparate databases. Database integration, however, is a difficult problem and one for which semi-automated approaches would be useful. One of the main difficulties is comparing relationships because their verb phrases may be generic or dependent upon the application domain. Being able to compare the semantics of verb phrases in relationships would greatly facilitate database design comparisons. It would be even more useful if the comparison process could be automated. Fully automated techniques, however, are unlikely so solutions to integration problems should aid integrators, but require minimal work on their part [Biskup and Embley, 2003]. The objective of this research is to: *propose an ontology for understanding the semantics of relationship verb phrases by mapping the verb phrases to various categories that capture different interpretations.* Doing so requires that a classification scheme be developed that captures both the domain-dependent and domain independent nature of verb phrases. The contribution of this research is to provide a useful approach to classifying verb phrases so relationships can be compared in a semi-automated way.

---

* This research was partially supported by J. Mack Robinson College of Business, Georgia State University and Pennsylvania State University.

P. Atzeni et al. (Eds.): ER 2004, LNCS 3288, pp. 336–347, 2004.

2 Related Work

The design of a database involves representing the universe of discourse in a structure in such a way that it accurately reflects reality. Conceptual modeling of databases is, therefore, concerned with things (entities) and associations among things (relationships) [Chen 1993; Wand et al. 1999]. A relationship R, can be expressed as A verb phrase B (A vp B), where A and B are entities. Most database design practices use simple, binary associations that capture these relationships between entities. A verb phrase, which is selected by a designer with the application domain in mind, can capture much of the semantics of the relationship. Semantics, for this research, is defined as the meaning of a term or a mapping from the real world to a construct. Understanding a relationship, therefore, requires that one understand the semantics of the accompanying verb phrase. Consider the relationships from two databases:

Customer (entity) buys (verb) Product (entity)
Customer (entity) purchases (verb) Product (entity)

These relationships reflect the same aspect of the universe of discourse, and use synonymous verb phrases. Therefore, the two relationships may be mapped to a similar interpretation, recognized as identical, and integrated. Next, consider:

Customer reserves Car
Customer rents Car.

These relationships reflect different concepts from the universe of discourse. The first captures the fact that a customer wants to do something; the second, that the customer has done it. These may be viewed as different states in a life cycle progression, but the two underlying relationships cannot be considered identical. Thus, they could not be mapped to the same semantic interpretation. Finally, consider:

Manager considers Agreement
Manager negotiates Agreement.

The structures of the relationships suggest that both relationships represent an interaction. However, "negotiates" implies changing the status, whereas "considers" involves simply viewing the status. On the other hand,

Manager makes Agreement
Manager writes Agreement

may capture an identical notion of creation. These examples illustrate the importance of employing and understanding how a verb phrase captures the semantics of the application domain. The interpretation of verbs depends upon the nouns (entities) that surround them [Fellbaum, 1998].

Research has been carried out on defining and understanding ontology creation and use. There are different definitions and interpretations of ontologies [Weber 2002]. In general, though, ontologies deal with capturing, representing, and using surrogates for the meanings of terms. This research adopts the approach of Dahlgren [1988] who developed an ontology system as a classification scheme for speech understanding and implemented it as an interactive tool. Work on ontology development has been carried out in database design (Embley et al. [1999], Kedad and Metais [1999], Dullea and Song [1999], Bergholtz and Johannesson [2001]). These efforts provide useful insights and build upon data abstractions. However, no comprehensive ontology for classifying relationships has been proposed.

3 Ontology for Classifying Relationships

This section proposes an ontology for classifying the verb phrases of relationships. The ontology is of the type developed by Dahlgren [1988] which operates as an interactive system to classify things. The most important part is the classification scheme. It is the focus of this research and is divided into three layers (Figure 1). The layers were developed by considering: 1) prior research in data modeling, in particular, data abstractions and the inherent business life cycle; 2) the local context of the entities; and 3) the domain-dependent nature of verb phrases.

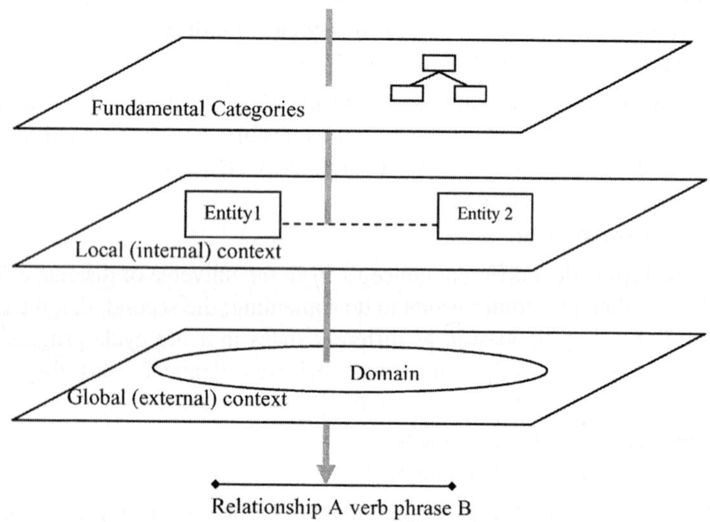

Fig. 1. Relationship classification levels

3.1 Fundamental Categories

The fundamental categories are primitives that reflect a natural division in the real world. This category has three general classes that form the basis of how things in the real world can be associated with each other: *status, change in status*, and *interaction* as shown in Figure 2.

Status: the orientation of one entity towards the other entity. e.g. A <is-owner-of> B **Change of status:** change of one entity with respect the other. e.g. A <becomes-owner-of> B. **Interaction**: communication or operation between entities that does not result in a change of status. e.g. A <sends-message-to> B.

Fig. 2. Fundamental Categories

Status captures the fact that one thing has a status with respect to the other. These are primitive because they describe a permanent, or durable, association of one entity with another, expressing the fact that A <is something> with respect to B. Business applications follow a natural life cycle of conception or creation through to ownership and, eventually, destruction. The *change of status* category describes this transition from one status to another. Relationships in this category express the fact that A is transitioning from *A <is something> with respect to B* to *A <is something else> with respect to B.* An *interaction* does not necessarily lead to a change of status of either entity. This happens when the effect of an interaction is worth remembering. Consider the verb phrase, 'create.' In some cases, it is useful to remember this as a status <is-creator-of> as in *Author writes Book.* In other cases, the interaction itself is important, even if it does not result in a change of status. The interaction category, therefore, expresses the fact that A <is doing something> with respect to B.

These fundamental categories are sufficiently coarse that all verb phrases will map to them. They are also coarse enough to warrant finer categories to distinguish among the large set of relationships in each category. Thus, further refinement is needed for each fundamental category.

3.1.1 Refining the Category: Status

The 'Status' category has been extensively studied by research on *data abstractions,* which focuses on the structure of relationships as a surrogate for understanding their semantics. Most data abstractions associate entities at different levels of abstraction (sub/superclass relationships) [Goldstein and Storey, 1999]. Since data abstractions infer semantics based on the structure of relationships, they, thus, provide a good start point for understanding the semantics of relationships. Research on understanding natural language also provides verb phrase categories such as auxiliary, generic and other types.

The first layer captures fundamental differences between kinds of relationships and was build by considering prior, well-accepted research on data abstractions and other frequently-used verb phrases whose interpretation is unambiguous. These are independent of context. This category, thus, captures the fundamental ways in which things in the real world are related so the categories in this level can be used to distinguish among the fundamental types. Additional results from research on patterns [Coad, 1995] and linguistic analysis [Miller, 1990] results in a hierarchical classification with defined primitives at the leaves of the tree. Figure 3 shows this finer classification of the category 'Status.'

Examples of primitive status relationships are shown in Table 1. There are two variations of one thing being assigned to another: *is-assigned-to* and *is-subjected-to.* In *A is-subjected-to B,* A does not have a choice with respect to its relationship with B, whereas it might in the former. Temporal relationships capture the sequence of when things happen and can be clearly categorized as before, during, and after.

3.1.2 Refining the Category: Change of Status

The change-of-status primitives, in conjunction with the status primitives, capture the lifecycle transitions for each status. Although the idea of a lifecycle has been alluded

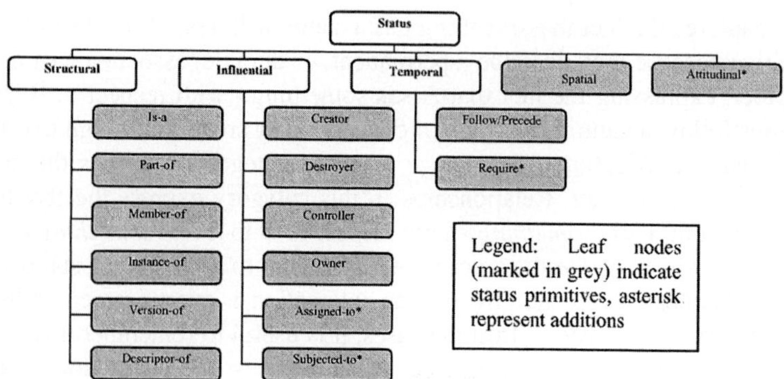

Fig. 3. Primitives for the Category 'Status'

Table 1. Primitives for 'Status' category

	Primitive	Example	Source
1	A is-a B	Pilot <is an> Employee	[Brachman 1983]
2	A is-member-of B	Professor <is member of> Department	[Brodie 1981]
3	A is-part-of B	Car <has> Engine	[Smith and Smith 1977]
4	A is-instance-of B	Video Tape <is copy of> Movie	[Motsching-Pitrik and Mylopoulous 1992]
5	A is-version-of B	Draft <is version of> Manuscript	[Motsching-Pitrik, 2000]
6	A is-descriptor-of B	Document <defines> Task	[Larmon 1997, p. 156]
7	A is-creator-of B	Author <writes> Book	[Gamma et al. 1995, p. 87]
8	A is-destroyer-of B	Tennant <terminates> Lease	[Gamma et al. 1995, p. 266]
9	A is-owner-of B	Company <owns> Building	[Larmon 1997, p. 157]
10	A is-in-control-of B	Manager <leads> Team	[Larmon 1997, p. 156]
11	A is-assigned-to B	Employee <assigned to> Project	*Added*
12	A is-subjected-to B	Industry <regulated by> Law	*Added*
13	A follows-or-precedes B	Rental <follows> Reservation	[Hay 1996, Chp. 5]
14	A requires B	Construction <requires> Approval	*Added*
15	A is-next-to B	San Andreas Fault <is-next-to> Los Angeles	[Larmon 1997, p. 156; Hay 1996, p. 36]
16	A has-attitude-towards B	Customer <likes> Product	*Added*

to previously [Hay 1996], prior research has not systematically recognized the lifecycle concept. Our conceptualization of the 'Change of Status' category is based on an extension and understanding of each primitive in the 'Status' category during the business lifecycle. Consider verb phrases that deal with acquiring something, as is typical of business transactions related to the status primitive 'is-owner-of.' The lifecycle for this status primitive has the states shown in Figure 4.

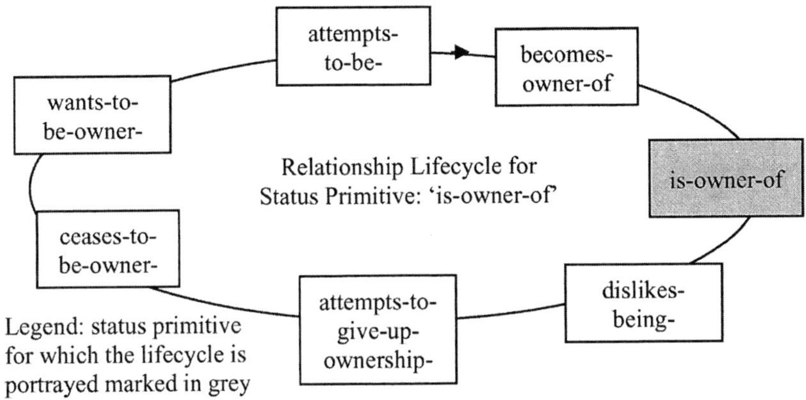

Fig. 4. The Relationship Life Cycle

Each state may, in turn, be mapped to different status primitives. For example, the lifecycle starts with needing something ('has-attitude-towards' and 'requires') which is followed by intending to become an owner ('acquire' or 'create'), owning ('owner' or 'in-control-of') and giving up ownership ('seller' or 'destroyer'). The primitives therefore illustrate a lifecycle that goes through creation or acquisition, ownership, and destruction. The life cycle can be logically divided into: intent, attempt to acquire, transition to acquiring, intent to give up, attempt to give up, and transition to giving up. Table 2 shows this additional information superimposed on the different states within the lifecycle. The sub-column under the change-of-status primitives shows the meanings captured in each: intent, attempt and the actual transition.

Table 2. Primitives for the Category 'Change of Status'

Primitive		Example
A wants-to-be B	*intent*	Customer <wants to own> Product
A attempts-to-become owner of B	*attempt*	Customer <orders> Product
A becomes B	*transition*	Customer <receives> Product
Status Primitive: Customer <owns> Product		
A dislikes-being B	*intent*	Company <wants to sell> Product
A attempts-to-give-up B	*attempt*	Company <offers> Product
A gives-up ownership-of B	*transition*	Company <sells> Product

3.1.3 Refining the Category: Interaction

'Interaction' describes communication of short duration between two entities or an operation of one entity on another. The interaction may cause a change in one of the entities. For example, one entity may 'manipulate' another [Miller, 1990], or cause movement of the other through time or space ('transmit,' 'receive'). Two entities may interact without causing change to either ('communicate with,' 'observe'). One entity may interact with another also by way of performance ('operate,' 'serve'). Figure 5 shows the primitives for 'Interaction' with examples given in Table 3.

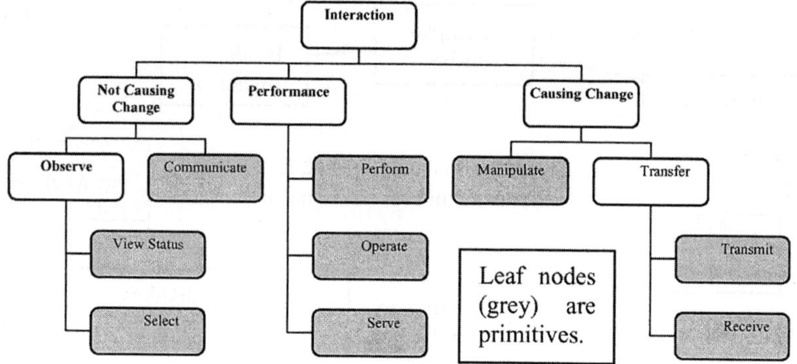

Fig. 5. Primitives for the Category 'Interaction'

Table 3. Primitives for the Category 'Interaction'

	Primitive	**Example**
1	View Status	Analyst <analyses> Requirements
2	Select	Customer <selects> Product
3	Communicate	Modem <negotiates with> Phone Line
4	Perform	Developer <tests> Software
5	Operate	Pilot <flies> Plane
6	Serve	Employee <serves> Customer
7	Manipulate	Instructor <grades> Exam
8	Transmit	Bank <remits> Payment
9	Receive	Warehouse <receives> Shipment

3.2 The Local (Internal) Context

The second category captures internal context by taking into account the nature of the entities surrounding the verb phrase, highlighting the need to understand the nouns that surround verb phrases [Fellbaum, 1998]. For this research, entities are classified as: actor, action, and artifact. Actor entities are capable of performing independent actions. Action represents the performance of an act. Artifact represents an inanimate object not capable of independent action. After entities have been classified, valid primitives can be specified for each pair of entity types. For example, it does not make sense to allow the primitive 'perform' for two entities of the kind 'Actor.' On the other hand, this primitive is appropriate when one of the entities is classified as 'Actor' and the other as 'Action.' The argument can be applied both to the 'Status' and 'Interaction' primitives. Because the 'Change of Status' primitives capture the lifecycle of 'Status' primitives, constraints identified for 'Status' primitives apply to the 'Change of Status' primitives as well. Table 4 shows these constraints for 'Status' primitives. Similar constraints have been developed for the 'Interaction' primitives.

Table 4. Valid 'Status' Primitives based on Entity Context

Entity 1	Entity 2	Valid Status Primitives
Actor	Actor	control, creates/destructor, attitude, sequence, structure
Actor	Action	control, creates/destructor, attitude, not causing change
Actor	Artifact	control, creates/destructor, causing change, not causing change, transfer, exchange
Action	Action	control, creates/destructor, attitude, sequence, not causing change, 3E
Action	Artifact	control, creates/destructor, structure, causing change, not causing change
Artifact	Artifact	control, creates/destructor, structure, causing change, not causing change, transfer, exchange

3.3 Global (External) Context

The third level captures the external context, that is, the domain in which the relationship is used, reflecting the domain-dependent nature of verb phrases. Although attempts have been made to capture taxonomies of such domain-dependent verbs, a great deal of manual effort has been involved. This research takes a more pragmatic approach where a knowledge base of domain-dependent verb phrases may be constructed over time when the implemented ontology is being used. When the user classifies a verb phrase, its classification and application domain should be stored. Consider the use of 'opens' in a theatre database versus a bank database. The relationship *Character <opens> Door* in the theatre domain maps to the interaction primitive <manipulates>. In the bank application, *Teller <opens> Account* maps to the status primitive <is-creator-of>; *Customer <opens> Account* maps to <is-owner-of>. If a verb phrase has already been classified by a user, it can be suggested as a preliminary classification for additional users, who are interested in classifying it. If a verb phrase has already been classified by a different user for the same application domain, then that classification should be displayed to the user who would agree with the classify-cation or provide a new classification. New classifications will also be stored. Ideally, consensus will occur over time. This way the knowledge base builds up, ensuring that the verbs important to different domains are captured appropriately. The following will be stored:

[Relationship, Verb phrase classification, Application Domain, User]

3.4 Use of the Ontology

The ontology can be used for comparing relationships across two databases by first comparing the entities, followed by classification of the verb phrases accompanying the relationships. Examples are shown in Table 5.

The ontology consists of a verb phrase classification scheme, a knowledge base that stores the classified verb phrases, organized by user and application, and a user-questioning scheme as mentioned above. The user is instructed to classify the entities of a relationship as actor, action, or artifact. The next step is to classify the verb

Table 5. Relationship comparison considering classification of entities

Relationship 1	Relationship 2	Relationship Comparison
Contractor builds Bridge (Actor–Artifact)	Builder Constructs Tree house (Actor–Artifact)	Entities similar; compare verb phrases
Contractor builds Bridge (Actor–Artifact)	Contractor has Employee (Actor–Actor)	Entities differ, do not compare verb phrases)
Contract builds Bridge (Actor–Artifact)	Worker does Raking (Actor–Action)	Relationships differ
Manager has Employee (Actor–Actor)	Manager employs Worker (Actor–Actor)	Entities similar; compare verb phrases
Manager gets Employee (Actor–Actor)	Manager gets Contract (Actor–Artifact)	Entities differ; do not compare verb phrases
Employee finds Apprentice (Actor–Actor)	Employ does Allocation (Actor–Action)	Entities differ; do not compare verb phrases

phrase. First, the user is asked to select one the three categories: 'Status,' 'Interaction,' or 'Change of Status.' Based on this selection, and the constraints provided by the entity types, primitives within each category are presented to the user for an appropriate classification. Suppose a user classifies a relationship as 'Status.' Then, knowing the nature of the entities, only certain primitives are presented as possible for the classification of the relationship. Furthermore, identifying that a verb phase is either status, change or status, or interaction restricts the subset of categories from which an appropriate classification can be obtained and, hence, the options presented to the user. If the verb phrase cannot be classified in this way, then, the other levels are checked to see if they are needed.

4 Assessment

Assessing an ontology is a difficult task. A plausible approach to assessment of an ontology is suggested by Gruninger and Fox [1995]. They suggest evaluating the 'competency' of an ontology. One of the ways to determine this 'competency' is to identify a list of queries that a knowledge-base, which builds on the ontology, should be able to answer (competency queries). Based on these queries, the ontology may be evaluated by posing questions such as: Does the ontology contain enough information to answer these types of queries? Do the answers require a particular level of detail or representation of a particular area? Noy and McGuiness [2001] suggest that the competency questions may be representative, but need not be exhaustive. Following our intent of classifying relationships for the purpose of comparison across databases, we attempted to assess whether the classification scheme of the ontology can provide a correct and complete classification of relationship verb phrases. To do so, a study was carried out which involved the following steps: 1) generation of the verb phrases to be classified; 2) generation of relationships using the verb phrases in different application domains; and 3) classification of all verb phrases.

Step 1: Generation of Verb Phrase

Only business-related verbs were used because the intent of the relationship ontology is use for business databases. Furthermore, it restricts the scope of the research. Since the SPEDE verbs [Cottam, 2000] were developed for business applications, these automatically became part of the sample set. The researchers independently selected business-related verbs from a set of 700 generated randomly from WordNet. The verbs that were common to the selections made by both researchers were added to the list from SPEDE. The same procedure was carried out from a set of 300 verbs that were randomly selected by people who support the online dictionary http://dictionary.cambridge.org/. This resulted in a total of 211 business verbs.

Step 2: Generation of Relationships Containing Verbs by Application Domain

For each verb, a definition was obtained from the on-line dictionary. Dictionaries provide examples for understanding and context, which helped to generate the relationships. Relationships were generated for seven application domains (approximately 30 verbs in each): 1) education, 2) business management, 3) manufacturing, 4) airline, 5) service, 6) marketing, 7and) retail. Examples are shown in Table 6.

Table 6. Sample test relationships

Verb phrase	Source	Meaning(s)	Domain	Generated Example
Import	SPEDE	to buy or bring in (products) from another country	Manufacturing	Manufactures import Cars
Obtain	SPEDE	to get (something), esp. by asking for it, buying it, working for it or producing it from something else	Education	Students obtain Degrees
Collect	SPEDE	to gather together from a variety of places or over time	Airline	Agent collects Ticket
Accept	SPEDE	to agree to take (something), or to take (something) as satisfactory, reasonable, true	Retail	Supermarkets accept Credit Cards
Hire	SPEDE	to pay to use (something) for a short period or to pay (someone) to do a job temporarily	Service	Travelers hire Cars

After generating the relationships, the researchers independently classified them using the relationship ontology. First, 30 verbs were classified and the researches agreed on 80% of the cases. The remaining verbs were then classified. The next step involved assessing how many of the ontology classifications the set of 211 verbs covered to test for completeness. The researchers generated additional relationships for ten subclasses for a total of 225. Sample classifications are shown in Table 7.

The results of this exercise were encouraging, especially given our focus on evaluating the competency of the ontology [Gruninger and Fox 1995]. The classification scheme worked well for these sample relationships. It allowed for the classification of all verb phrases. The biggest difficulty was in identifying whether to move from one level to the next. For example, *Student acquires Textbook* is immediately classifiable

Table 7. Sample classifications of relationships

Entity 1	Verb Phrase	Entity 2	Classification
Manufacturer	Imports	Part	receives
Student	acquires	Textbook	becomes-owner-of
Air traffic controller	establishes	Flight path	becomes-creator-of
Salesperson	converts	Competitor-customer	manipulates
Customer	enters-into	Sales agreement	becomes-subjected-to
Caterer	Delivers-to	Plane	is-assigned-to
Teacher	distributes	Handout	sends
Airline	Adjusts	Schedule	manipulates

by the primitives. In other cases, the next layer was necessary. Further research is needed to design a user interface that can explain the use and categories to the user so they can be effectively applied. A preliminary version of a prototype has been developed. This will be completed and an empirical test carried out with typical end-users, most likely, database designers.

5 Conclusion

A classification scheme for comparing relationship verb phrases has been presented. It is based upon results obtained from research on conceptual modeling, common sense knowledge of a typical life cycle, and the domain-dependent nature of relationships. Further research is needed to complete the ontology system for which the classification scheme will be a part. Then, it needs to be expanded to allow for multiple classifications and the user interface refined.

References

1. Bergholtz, M., and Johnannesson, P., "Classifying the Semantics of Relationships in Conceptual Modelling by Categorization of Roles," *Proceedings of the 6th International Workshop on Applications of Natural Language to Information Systems (NLDB'01)*, 28-29 June 2001, Madrid, Spain.
2. Biskup, J. and Embley, D.W., "Extracting Information from Heterogeneous Information Sources using Ontologically Specified Target Terms," *Information Systems*, Vol.28, No.3, 2003.
3. Brachman, R.J., "What IS-A is and Isn't: An Analysis of Taxonomic Links in Semantic Networks," *IEEE Computer,* October, 1983.
4. Brodie, M., "Association: A Database Abstraction," *Proceedings of the Entity-Relationship Conference*, 1981.
5. Chen, P., "The Entity-Relationship Approach", *In Information Technology in Action: Trends and Perspectives,* Englewood Cliffs: Prentice Hall, 1993, pp.13-36.
6. Coad, P. et al. 1995. Object Models: Strategies, Patterns, & Applications. Prentice Hall.
7. Cottam, H., "Ontologies to Assist Process Oriented Knowledge Acquisition," http://www.spede.co.uk/papers/papers.htm, 2000.
8. Dahlgren, K., *Naive Semantics for Natural Language Understanding*, Kluwer Academic Publishers, Hingham, MA, 1988.

9. Dullea, J. and Song, I.-Y., "A Taxonomy of Recursive Relationships and Their Structural Validity in ER Modeling," in Akoka, J. et al. (eds.), *Conceptual Modeling – ER'99, 18th International Conference on Conceptual Modeling, Lecture Notes in Computer Science 1728*, Paris, France, 15-18 November 1999, pp.384-389.
10. Embley, D., Campbell, D.M., Jiang, Y.S., Ng, Y.K., Smith, R. D., Liddle, S.W. and Quass, D.W., "A Conceptual-modeling Approach to Web Data Extraction," *Data & Knowledge Engineering*, 1999.
11. Fellbaum, V., "Introduction," in *Wordnet: An Electronic Lexical Database*, The MIT Press, Cambridge, Mass., 1998, pp.1-19.
12. Gamma, E., Helm, R., Johnson, R., and Vlissides, J., *Design patterns: elements of reusable object-oriented software*. Addison-Wesley Longman Publishing Co., Inc., Boston, MA., 1995.
13. Goldstein, R.C. and Storey, V.C., "Data Abstractions: "Why and How", *Data and Knowledge Engineering*, Vol.29, No.3, 1999, pp. 1-18.
14. Gruninger, M. and Fox, M.S. Methodology for the Design and Evaluation of Ontologies. In: *Proceedings of the Workshop on Basic Ontological Issues in Knowledge Sharing, IJCAI-95*, Montreal.
15. Hay, D. C., and Barker, R. *Data Model Patterns: Conventions of Thought.* Dorset House, 1996.
16. Kedad, Z., and Metais, E., "Dealing with Semantic Heterogeneity During Data Integration," in Akoka, J. et al. (eds.), *Conceptual Modeling – ER'99, 18th International Conference on Conceptual Modeling, Lecture Notes in Computer Science 1728*, Paris, France, 15-18 November 1999, pp.325-339.
17. Larmon, C., *Applying UML and Patterns*. Prentice-Hall, 1997.
18. Miller, G.A., Beckwith, R., Fellbaum, C., Gross, D. and Miller, K.J., "Introduction to WordNet: An On-line Lexical Database," *International Journal of Lexicography*, Vol. 3, No. 4, 1990, pp. 235-244.
19. Motschnig-Pitrik, R. and Myloppoulos, J., "Class and Instances," *International Journal of Intelligent and Cooperative Systems*, Vol.1, No.1, 1992, pp.61-92.
20. Motschnig-Pitrik, R., "A Generic Framework for the Modeling of Contexts and its Applications," *Data and Knowledge Engineering*, Vol. 32, 2000, pp.145-180.
21. Noy, N. F., and McGuinness, D. L. 2001. Ontology Development 101: A Guide to Creating Your First Ontology. Available at http://protege.stanford.edu/publications/ontology_development/ontology101-noy-mcguinness.html. Accessed 15 March 2004
22. Smith, J., Smith, D. "Database Abstractions: Aggregation and Generalization," *ACM Transactions on Database Systems*. Vol.2, No.2, 1977, pp. 105-133.
23. Wand, Y., Storey, V.C. and Weber, R., "Analyzing the Meaning of a Relationship," *ACM Transactions on Database Systems*, Vol.24, No.4. December, 1999, pp.494-528.
24. Weber, R., "Ontological Issues in Accounting Information Systems," Sutton, S. and Arnold, V., (Eds.), *Researching Accounting as an Information Systems Discipline,* 2002.

Fast Mining Maximal Frequent ItemSets Based on FP-Tree

Yuejin Yan*, Zhoujun Li, and Huowang Chen

[1] School of Computer Science, National University of Defense Technology,
Changsha 410073, China
Tel: 86-731-4532956
yanyuejin2003@hotmail.com
http://www.nudt.edu.cn

Abstract. Maximal frequent itemsets mining is a fundamental and important problem in many data mining applications. Since the MaxMiner algorithm introduced the enumeration trees for MFI mining in 1998, there have been several methods proposed to use depth-first search to improve performance. This paper presents FIMfi, a new depth-first algorithm based on FP-tree and MFI-tree for mining MFI. FIMfi adopts a novel item ordering policy for efficient lookaheads pruning, and a simple method for fast superset checking. It uses a variety of old and new pruning techniques to prune the search space. Experimental comparison with previous work reveals that FIMfi reduces the number of FP-trees created greatly and is more than 40% superior to the similar algorithms on average.

1 Introduction

Since the frequent itemsets mining problem (FIM) was first addressed [1], frequent itemsets mining in large database have been an important problem for it enables essential data mining such as discovering association rules, data correlations, sequential patterns, etc.

There are two types of algorithms to mine frequent itemsets. The first one is candidate set generate-and-test approach [1]. The basic idea is to generate and test the candidate itemsets. Each candidate itemset with $k+1$ items is only generated from frequent itemsets with k items. This process is repeated in bottom-up fashion until no candidate itemset can be generated. In each level, all the frequencies of the candidate itemsets are tested by scanning the database. But this method requires scanning the database several times. In the worst case, the number of the scan is equal to the maximal length of the frequent itemsets. Besides this, lots of candidate itemsets is generated, most of them would be infrequent. Another method is data transformation approach [2, 4]: it avoids the cost of generating and testing a large number of candidate sets by growing a frequent itemset from its prefix. It constructs a sub database related to each frequent itemset h such that all frequent itemsets that have h as prefix can be mined only using the sub database.

* Corresponding author.

P. Atzeni et al. (Eds.): ER 2004, LNCS 3288, pp. 348–361, 2004.

The number of frequent itemsets increases exponentially with the increasing of frequent itemsets' length. So large length of frequent itemsets leads to no feasible of FI mining. However, since frequent itemsets are upward closed, it is sufficient to discover only all maximal frequent itemsets. As a result, researchers now turn to find MFI (maximal frequent itemsets) [5,6,9,10,4,7]. A frequent itemset is called maximal if it has no frequent superset. Given a set of MFI, it is easy to analyze some interesting properties of the database, such as the longest pattern, the overlap of the MFI, etc. Also, there are applications where the MFI is adequate, for example, the combinatorial pattern discovery in biological applications [3].

This paper focuses on the MFI mining problems based on data transformation approach. We use FP-tree to represent sub database containing all relevant frequency information, and MFI-tree are used to store information of discovered MFI that is useful for *superset frequency* pruning. With these two data structure, our algorithm takes a novel item ordering policy, and integrates a variety of old and new prune strategies. It also uses a simple but fast superset checking method along with some other optimizations.

The remaining of this paper is organized as follows. In section 2, we briefly review the MFI mining problem and introduce the related works. Section 3 gives the MFI mining algorithm, FIMfi, which does the MFI mining based on FP-tree and MFI-tree. In this section we also introduce our novel item ordering policy, the prune strategies we applied and the simple but fast superset checking that is needed in efficient "*lookaheads*" pruning. In section 4, we compare our algorithm with some previous works. Finally, section 5 gives the conclusions.

2 Preliminaries and Related Work

This section will formally describe the MFI mining problem and the set enumeration tree that represents the searching space. Also the related works and two important data structure, FP-tree and MFI-tree, which is used in our scheme, will be introduced in this section.

2.1 Problem Revisit

Let $I = \{i_1, i_2, \ldots, i_m\}$be a set of m distinct items. Let D denote a database of transactions, where each transaction contains a set of items. A set $X \subseteq I$ is also called an *itemset*. An itemset with k items is called a k-itemset. The support of an itemset X, denoted as $sup(X)$, is the number of transactions in which X occurs as a subset. For a given D and the threshold min_sup, itemset X is *frequent* if $sup(X) \geq min\_sup$. If $sup(X) \geq min\_sup$ and for any $Y \supseteq X$, we have $sup(Y) < min\_sup$, then X is called maximal frequent itemset. From the definitions we can have two lemmas as follows:

Lemma 1: A restricted subset of any frequent itemset is not a maximal frequent itemset.

Lemma2: A subset of any frequent itemset is a frequent itemset, a superset of any infrequent itemset is not a frequent itemset.

Given a transactional database *D*, supposed *I* is an itemset of it, then any combination of the items in *I* would be frequent and all these combinations compose the search space, which can be represented by set enumeration tree [5]. For example, supposed *I* = {*a*,*b*,*c*,*d*,*e*,*f*} is sorted in firm lexicographic order, then the searching tree can be shown as Figure 1. To avoid the tree too big, we use *subset infrequency* pruning and *superset frequency* pruning technique in the tree, and we will introduce the two pruning techniques in next section. The root of the tree represents the empty itemset, and the nodes at level *k* contain all of the *k*-itemsets. The itemset associated with each node, *n*, will be referred as the node's *head* (*n*). The possible extensions of the itemset is denoted as *con_tail*(*n*), which is the set of items after the last item of *head*(*n*). The frequent extensions denoted as *fre_tail*(*n*) is the set of items that can be appended to *head*(*n*) to build the longer frequent itemsets. In depth-first traversal of the tree, *fre_tail*(*n*) contains only the frequent extensions of *n*. The itemset associated with each children node of node *n* is build by appended one of *fre_tail*(*n*) to *head* (*n*). As example in Figure1, suppose node *n* is associated with {*b*}, then *head* (*n*) = {*b*} and *con_tail*(*n*) = {*c*,*d*,*e*,*f*}. We can see that {*b*,*f*} is not frequent, *fre_tail*(*n*) = {*c*,*d*,*e*}. The children node of *n*, {*b*,*e*}, is build by appending *e* from *fre_tail*(*n*) to {*b*}.

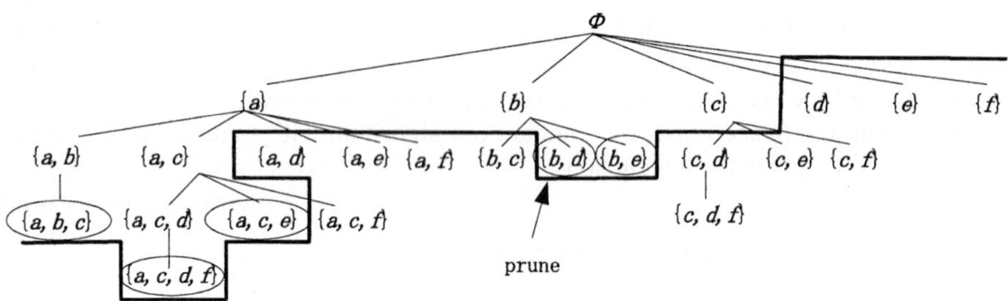

Fig. 1. Search space tree

The problem of MFI mining can be thought as to find a border of the tree, all the elements above the border are frequent itemsets, and others are not. All MFIs is near the border. As our examples in Figure1, itemsets in ellipses are MFI.

2.2 Related Work

Given the set enumeration tree, we can describe the most recent approaches to MFI mining problem.

The MaxMiner [5] employs a breadth-first traversal policy for the searching. To reduce the search space according to lemma 1, it performs not only *subset infrequency* pruning to skip over the itemset that have an infrequent subset, but also *superset frequency* pruning (also called *lookaheads* pruning). To increase the effectiveness of *superset frequency* pruning, MaxMiner dynamically reorders the children nodes, which was used in all the MFI algorithms after it [4,6,7,9,10]. Normally depth-first approach have better performance on *lookaheads*, but MaxMiner uses a breadth-first approach instead to limit the number of passes over the database.

DepthProject performs a mixed depth-first traversal, and do the *subset infrequency* pruning and a variation of *superset frequency* pruning [6] to the tree. Also it uses an improved counting method based on transaction projections along its branches. The original database and the projections are represented as a bitmap. The experiment results in [6] show that DepthProject outperforms MaxMiner by more than one time.

Mafia [7] is another depth-first algorithm, it also uses a vector bitmap representation, where the count of an itemset is based on the column in the bitmap. Besides the two pruning methods we mentioned above, another novel pruning technique called *PEP* (Parent Equivalence Pruning) in [8] is also used in Mafia, The experiments in [7] shows that *PEP* prunes the search space greatly.

Both DepthProject and Mafia mine a superset of the MFIs, and require a post-pruning to eliminate non-maximal frequent itemsets. GenMax [9] integrates the pruning with the mining and finds the exact MFIs by using two strategies. First, just like transaction database is projected on current node, the discovered MFI set can also be projected on the node (Local MFI) and thus yields fast superset checking; Second, GenMax uses *Diffset* propagation to do fast frequency computation.

AFOPT [3] uses a data structure called AFOPT tree in which items are ascending frequency ordered to store the transactions in original database. It also uses *subset infrequency* pruning, *superset frequency* pruning and *PEP* pruning to reduce the search space. And it employs LMFI generated by pseudo projection technique to test whether a frequent itemset is subset of one of it.

FPMax* is an extension of the FP-growth method, for MFIs mining only. It uses a FP-tree to store the transaction projection of the original database for each node in the tree. In order to test whether a frequent itemset is the subset of any discovered MFI in *lookaheads* pruning, another tree structure (MFI-tree) is utilized to keep the track of all discovered MFI, this makes effective superset checking. FPMax* uses an array for each node to store the counts of all 2-itemsets that are subset of the frequent extensions itemset, this makes the algorithm scan each FP-tree only once for each recursive call emanating from it. The experiment results [10] shows that FPMax* has the best performance for almost all the tested database.

2.3 FP-Tree and MFI-Tree

The FP-growth method [2] builds a data structure called the FP-tree (Frequent Pattern tree) for each node of the search space tree. FP-tree is a compact representation of all relevant frequency information of current node, each of its path from the root to a node represents an itemset, and the nodes along the paths are stored according to the order of the items in *fre_tail*(n). Each node of the FP-tree also stores the number of transactions or conditional pattern bases which containing the itemset represented by the path. Compression is achieved by building the tree in such a way that overlapping itemsets share prefixes of the corresponding branches.

Each FP-tree of the nodes is associated with a header table. Single items in tail and the support of itemset that is the union of head and the item are stored in the header table in decreasing order of the support. The entry for an item also contains the head of a list that links to all the corresponding nodes of the FP-tree.

To construct FP-tree of node n, the FP-growth method first finds all the frequent items in *fre_tail*(n) by an initial scan of the database or the *head*(n)'s conditional pattern base that comes from FP-tree of its parent node. And then these items are inserted into the header table in the order of items in *fre_tail*(n). In the next and the last scan, frequent itemset which is subset of the tail are inserted into the FP-tree as a branch. If a new itemset shares a prefix with another itemset that is already in the tree, then the new itemset will share the branch that representing the common prefix with the existing itemset. For example, for the database and *min_sup* shown in Figure2 (a), the FP-tree of root and itemset {f} is shown as Figure2 (b) and (c).

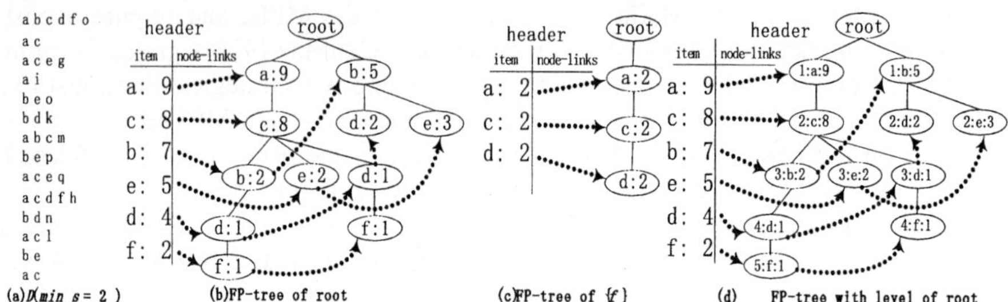

Fig. 2. Examples of FP-tree

FPMax* uses an array for each node along with the FP-tree to avoid the first scan of the conditional pattern bases. For each 2-itemsets $\{a,b\}$ in frequent extensions itemset, an array entry is used to store the support of $head(n) \cup \{a,b\}$, then when extending the tree from a node to one of its children, we can build the header of the children' FP-tree according to the array, and avoid scanning the FP-tree of current node again.

Considering a given MFI M at node n in the depth-first MFI mining, if we have $head(n) \cup fre\_tail\ (n) \subset M$, then all the children of n will not be considered according to lemma 1. This is the *superset frequency* pruning, also called *lookaheads* in [5]. *Lookaheads* needs to access some information in discovered MFI relevant to current node for pruning. FPMax* uses another FP-tree (MFI-tree) to map the need. The differences between the MFI-tree and the FP-tree of the same node are as follows: first, the nodes do not record frequency information, but they store the length of the itemset represented by the path from the root to the current node. Second, for each itemset S represented by a path, $head(n) \cup S$ is subset of a certain discovered MFI. In addition, when considering an offspring node of a node, the MFI-tree of the node will be updated as soon as a new MFI is found. Figure3 shows several examples of MFI-tree.

3 Mining Maximal Frequent Itemsets by FIMfi

In this section, we discuss our algorithm FIMfi in details and explain why it is faster than some previous schemes.

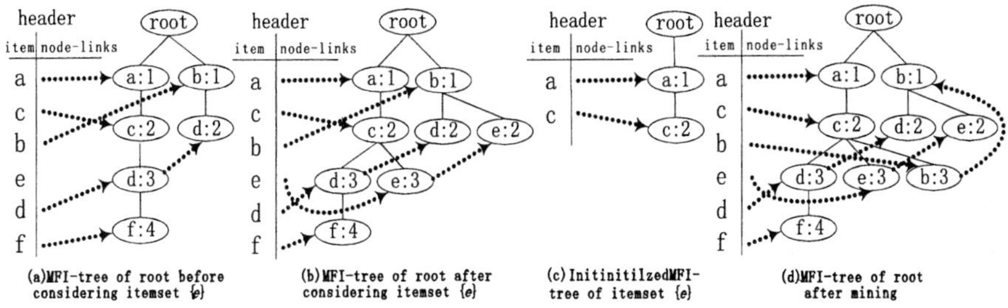

(a)MFI-tree of root before considering itemset {e}

(b)MFI-tree of root after considering itemset {e}

(c)InitinitilzedMFI-tree of itemset {e}

(d)MFI-tree of root after mining

Fig. 3. Examples of MFI-tree

3.1 Pruning Techniques

Subset Infrequency Pruning: Supposed *n* is a node in the search space tree, then for each item *x* in *con_tail*(*n*) that is possible to become an item in *fre_tail*(*n*), we need to compute the support of the itemset *head*(*n*) ∪ {*x*}. If *sup*(*head*(*n*) ∪ {*x*}) < *min_sup*, then we don't add it into *fre_tail*(*n*) and the node identified by itemset *head*(*n*) ∪ {*x*} will not be considered any more. This is based on lemma 2: all itemsets that is superset of *head*(*n*) ∪ {*x*} are not frequent.

Superset Frequency Pruning: Superset frequency pruning is also called *lookaheads* pruning. Considering a node *n*, if itemset *head*(*n*) ∪ *fre_tail*(*n*) is frequent, then all the children node of *n* should be pruned (lemma 1).

There are two existing methods for determining whether the itemset *head*(*n*) ∪ *fre_tail*(*n*) is frequent. The first is to count the support of *head*(*n*) ∪ *fre_tail*(*n*) directly, this method is normally used in an bread-first algorithms such as in MaxMiner. The second one is to check if a superset of *head*(*n*) ∪ *fre_tail*(*n*) has been already in the discovered MFIs. It is commonly used by the depth-first MFI algorithms [4,7,9,10]. Also there are some other techniques, such as LMFI and MFI projection that is used to reduce the cost of checking. For example, in the MFI-tree situation, we can just check if a superset of *fre_tail*(*n*) can be found in all conditional pattern bases of *head*(*n*), and then finish the superset checking. Here we propose a new way to do lookaheads pruning based on FP-tree. For a given node, we can get all the conditional pattern bases of the *head*(*n*) from the FP-tree of its parent node, and then our algorithm tries to find a superset of *fre_tail*(*n*) in a collection of conditional pattern bases, and the last items' counts of these bases are no less than minimum support. If we find one, *S*, then we know *head*(*n*) ∪ *S* being frequent, so *head*(*n*) ∪ *fre_tail*(*n*) is frequent based on lemma 2. For example, when considering itemset {*b*}, the *fre_tail* of {*b*} is {*a*,*c*}, there is a conditional pattern base of {*b*} as *a*3,*c*3 (Figure2 (b)), then we know {*b*,*c*,*a*} frequent, all the children of {*b*} will be pruned. If FIMfi finds a superset of *fre_tail*(*n*) in FP-tree and *head*(*n*) ∪ *fre_tail*(*n*) is an undiscovered MFI, FIMfi needs to update MFI-trees with *head*(*n*) ∪ *fre_tail*(*n*) as described before.

In addition, we also do superset frequency pruning with itemset *head*(*n*) ∪ *con_tail*(*n*). Before generating *fre_tail*(*n*) from *con_tail*(*n*), our algorithm will check if there is a superset of *con_tail*(*n*) in FP-tree, this is because our scheme will use a very simple and fast method to do the superset checking (see section 3.2).

Parent Equivalence Pruning: Also the FIMfi uses the *PEP* for its efficiency. As an example, taking any item x from *fre_tail*(n), then there is $sup(head(n) \cup \{x\}) = sup(head(n))$. So if any frequent itemset Z, which contains Y but does not contain x, has the frequent superset $Z \cup \{x\}$. Since we only want to get MFI, it is not necessary to count itemsets which contain Y but do not contain x. Therefore, we can move item x from *fre_tail*(n) to *head*(n). From the experiment result we find that the *PEP* can greatly reduce the number of FP-trees' comparing to the FPMax*.

3.2 Superset Checking

As discussed before, superset checking is a main operation in lookaheads pruning. This is because that each new MFI needs to be checked before being added into the MFIs. MaxMiner needs scan all the discovered MFIs, and tries to map *head*(n) ∪ *fre_tail*(n) item by item for each discovered MFI. Though GenMax uses LMFI to store all the relevant MFIs, it also needs mapping item by item. As for FPMax*, it only needs map *fre_tail*(n) item by item for all conditional pattern bases of *head*(n) in MFI-tree. Our simple but fast superset checking method of *head*(n) ∪ *fre_tail*(n) is based on the lemmas as follows:

Lemma 3: If there is one conditional pattern base of *head*(n) in MFI-tree and its length is equal to the length of *fre_tail*(n), then *head*(n) ∪ *fre_tail*(n) is frequent.

Proof: Let S be the itemset represented by the base, then *head*(n) ∪ S is frequent. And for each item x in S, $sup(head(n) \cup \{x\}) \geq min\_sup$, $x \in fre\_tail(n)$, $S \subseteq fre\_tail(n)$. For the bases of same length, there is $S = fre\_tail(n)$. Hence, we obtain the lemma.

Lemma 4: If there is one conditional pattern base of *head*(n) in MFI-tree and its length is equal to the length of *con_tail*(n), then *head*(n) ∪ *con_tail*(n) or is frequent.

Proof: Let S be the itemset represented by the base, then *head*(n) ∪ S is frequent. Since *con_tail*(n) includes all possible extensions of *head*(n), there is $S \subseteq con\_tail(n)$. For the bases of same length, there is $S = con\_tail(n)$. Hence, we obtain the lemma.

Lemma 5: Suppose y is a conditional pattern base of *head*(n) in FP-tree. If the counter associated with the last item of y is no less than *min_sup*, and the length of y is equal to the length of *fre_tail*(n), then *head*(n) ∪ *fre_tail*(n) is frequent.

Proof: Similar as Lemma3.

Lemma 6: Suppose y is a conditional pattern base of *head*(n) in FP-tree. If the counter associated with the last item of y is no less than *min_sup*, and the length of y is equal to the length of *con_tail*(n), then *head*(n) ∪ *con_tail*(n) is frequent.

Proof: Similar as Lemma4.

According to lemma 3 and lemma 4, the superset checking needs not to map item by item, and can just be done by checking the length of itemsets. Here the level of the last item in the base can be used as the length of the base. For more efficient lengths checking, the only change of FIMfi for the MFI-tree is storing the node links of items to the header table in the decreasing order of the bases' level. Now the superset checking is very simple for it only needs to check the length of two itemsets.

Similarly, the superset checking based on FP-tree can also be simple according to lemma 5 and lemma 6. In this situation, we add a level to each node of the FP-tree, with the level representing the length of the path from the node in question to root. And the node links, whose counts are no less than *min_sup*, are stored in decreasing order of the levels. The example is shown in Figure2 (d). Therefore, this superset checking is also simple for it needs only to check the length of two itemsets. Let's revisit the example in section 3.1, when doing the superset checking of $\{b\} \cup \{a,c\}$, we need only compare the length of the conditional pattern base $a3{:}c3$ to the length of itemset $\{a,c\}$.

3.3 Item Ordering Policy

Item ordering policy firstly appears in [5], and is used by almost all the follow MFI algorithms for it can increase the effectiveness of superset frequency pruning. As we know, items with higher frequency are more likely to be members of lone frequent itemsets and subset of some discovered MFIs. As for node *n*, after *fre_tail*(*n*) is generated and before extending to the children, the traditional scheme can sort the items at the tail in the decreasing order of $sup(head(n) \cup \{x\})$ ($x \in fre\_tail(n)$). This makes the most frequent items appear in more itemsets that are frequent extensions of some nodes *n*'s offspring. Therefore, there will be more such pruned offspring nodes. In general, this type of item order policy works better in *lookaheads* by scanning the database to count the support of $head(n) \cup fre\_tail(n)$ in breath-first algorithms, such as in MaxMiner. All the recently proposed depth-first algorithms do the superset checking instead to implement the *lookaheads* pruning, for the counting support of $head(n) \cup fre\_tail(n)$ costs high in depth-first policy.

Since superset checking of FIMfi is based on MFI-tree and/or FP-tree, we try to find an item ordering policy to make use of the information of MFI-tree and/or FP-tree. As we know, if *S* is a subset of tail, and $head(n) \cup S$ is frequent, then we can prune the nodes identified by itemset $head(n) \cup s$ ($s \subseteq S$), this is because the itemsets corresponding to the nodes and their offspring are not maximal (lemma 1). Based on FP-tree and MFI-tree, when a policy can let *S* be the maximal subset of *fre_tail*(*n*), we can achieve maximal pruning at the node in question.

Supposed there are two itemsets S_1 and S_2. S_1 is represented by the conditional pattern base whose length is maximal in MFI-tree. S_2 is represented by the conditional pattern base, whose length is maximal among a collection of conditional pattern bases in FP-tree, here the last item's count of these bases is no less than *min_sup*. Let *S* be the longest one of S_1 and S_2, and we put the items in *S* to the head of *fre_tail*(*n*), then we can attain the maximal pruning. For example, when considering the node *n* identified by $\{e\}$, we know $fre\_tail\ (n) = \{a,c,b\}, S_1 = \Phi$ and $S_2 = \{a,c\}$ as in Figure2(b), then the sorted items in *fre_tail*(*n*) is in sequence of *a,c,b*, the old decreasing order of supports is *b,a,c*. FPMax* using the old decreasing order policy has to build FP-trees for nodes $\{e\}$, $\{e,a\}$, and $\{e,c\}$, but FIMfi with the new order policy only need to build FP-trees for nodes $\{e\}$ and $\{e,a\}$. Similarly, when considering the node $\{d\}$, we know $fre\_tail(n) = \{a,c,b\}$, $S_1 = \{a,c\}$ as in Figure3(b) and $S_2 = \Phi$, the sorted items in *fre_tail*(*n*) is in sequence of *a*,*c*,*b*, the old decreasing order of supports is *b*,*a*,*c*. The experiments results of these two policies will be illustrated in section 4 for comparison purpose.

Furthermore, for the items in *fre_tail*(*n*)-*S*, we also sort them in the decreasing order of *sup*(*head*(*n*) ∪ {*x*}) (*x*∈ *fre_tail*(*n*)-*S*).

3.4 Optimizations

FIMfi uses the same array technique for counting frequency as the one in FPMax*, but FIMfi doesn't count the whole triangle array as FPMax* do. Suppose, that at node *n*, sorted *fre_tail*(*n*) is $i_1, i_2, \ldots, i_l, i_{l+1}, \ldots, i_m$, with that *head*(*n*) ∪ { $i_1, i_2, \ldots, i_l$ } is frequent. When we extend the nodes corresponding to the items less than i_{l+1}, the superset checking will return true and those nodes will be pruned. So, for the 2-itemsets which are subsets of { $i_1, i_2, \ldots, i_l$ }, the corresponding cells will not be used any more. Therefore, FIMfi will not count those cells when building the array. By this way, FIMfi costs less than FPMax* does when counting the array. And it is obvious that the bigger the *l* is, the more counting time saved.

We also use the memory management described in [10] to reduce the time consumed in allocating and deallocating space for FP-trees and MFI-trees.

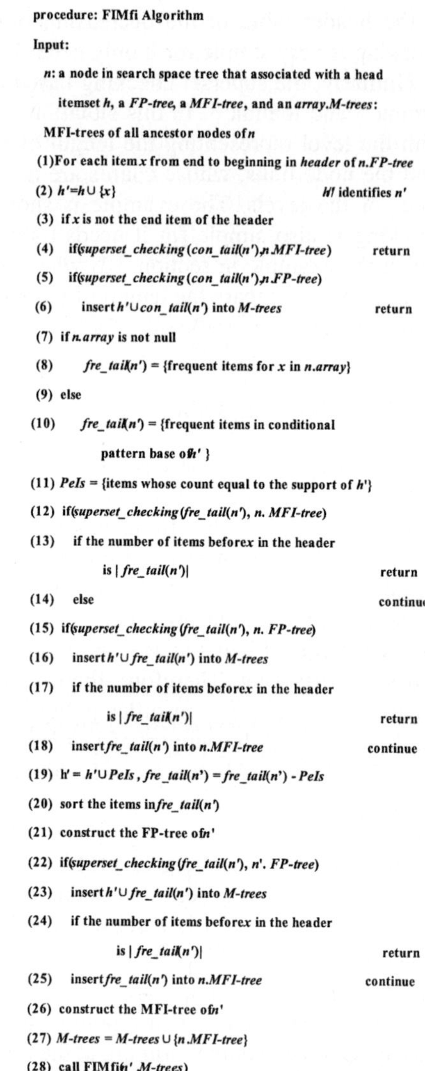

```
procedure: FIMfi Algorithm
Input:
  n: a node in search space tree that associated with a head
     itemset h, a FP-tree, a MFI-tree, and an array.M-trees:
  MFI-trees of all ancestor nodes of n
(1)For each item x from end to beginning in header of n.FP-tree
(2) h'=h ∪ {x}                                          //h' identifies n'
(3) if x is not the end item of the header
(4)   if(superset_checking(con_tail(n'),n.MFI-tree)          return
(5)   if(superset_checking(con_tail(n'),n.FP-tree)
(6)      insert h'∪con_tail(n') into M-trees                  return
(7) if n.array is not null
(8)      fre_tail(n') = {frequent items for x in n.array}
(9) else
(10)     fre_tail(n') = {frequent items in conditional
            pattern base of h' }
(11) PeIs = {items whose count equal to the support of h'}
(12) if(superset_checking(fre_tail(n'), n. MFI-tree)
(13)   if the number of items before x in the header
            is | fre_tail(n')|                               return
(14)   else                                                  continue
(15) if(superset_checking(fre_tail(n'), n. FP-tree)
(16)   insert h'∪ fre_tail(n') into M-trees
(17)   if the number of items before x in the header
            is | fre_tail(n')|                               return
(18)   insert fre_tail(n') into n.MFI-tree                   continue
(19) h' = h'∪PeIs , fre_tail(n') = fre_tail(n') - PeIs
(20) sort the items in fre_tail(n')
(21) construct the FP-tree of n'
(22) if(superset_checking(fre_tail(n'), n'. FP-tree)
(23)   insert h'∪ fre_tail(n') into M-trees
(24)   if the number of items before x in the header
            is | fre_tail(n')|                               return
(25)   insert fre_tail(n') into n.MFI-tree                   continue
(26) construct the MFI-tree of n'
(27) M-trees = M-trees ∪ {n.MFI-tree}
(28) call FIMfi(n' ,M-trees)
```

Fig. 4. Pseudo-code of Algorithm FIMfi

3.5 FIMfi

Based on section 3.1-3.4, here we show the pseudo-code of FIMfi in Figure 4. In each call procedure, each newly found MFI may be used in superset checking for ancestor nodes of the current node, so we use a parameter called *M-trees* to access MFI-tree of the ancestor nodes. And when the top call (FIMfi(*root*,∅)) is over, all the MFIs to be mined are stored in the MFI-tree of *root* in the search space tree.

From line (4) to line (6), FIMfi does *superset frequency* pruning for itemset *con_tail*(*n*'). When *x* is the end item of the header, there is no need to do the pruning, for the pruning has already been done by the procedure calling current one in line (12) and/or line (22). Lines from (7) to (10) use the optimization array technique. The *PEP* technique is used in line (11) and line (19). The *superset frequency* pruning for itemsets *fre_tail*(*n*') is done in lines from (12) to (18), when the condition at line (17) is true, all the children nodes of *n*' are pruned and *fre_tail*(*n*') need not to be inserted into *n.MFI-tree* any more. Line (20) uses our novel item ordering policy. Line (21) builds a new FP-tree: *n*'*.FP-tree*. Lines from (22) to (25) do another *superset frequency* pruning for *fre_tail*(*n*') in the tree. The *return* statements in line (4), (6), (13), (17) and (24) mean that all the children nodes after *n*' of *n* are pruned there. And the *continue* statements in line (14), (18) and (25) tell us that node *n*' will be pruned, then we can go to consider the next child of *n*. After the constructing of *n*'*.FP-tree* and *n*'*.MFI-tree* and the updating of *M-trees*, FIMfi will be called recursively with the new node *n*' and the new *M-trees*.

Note that the algorithm doesn't employ single path trimming used in FPMax* and AFOPT. If, by constructing *n*'*.FP-tree*, we can find out that *n*'*.FP-tree* only has a single path, the superset checking at line (20) will return *true*, there will be a *superset frequency* pruning instead of a single path trimming.

4 Experimental Evaluations

In the first Workshop on Frequent Itemset Mining Implementations (FIMI'03) [11], which took place at ICDM'03 (The Third IEEE International Conference on Data Mining), there are several recently presented algorithms that are good for mining MFI, such as FPMax*, AFOPT, Mafia and etc, we now present the performance comparisons of our FIMfi with them. All the experiments were conducted on 2.4 GHZ Pentium IV with 1024 MB of DDR memory running Microsoft Windows 2000 Professional. The codes of other four algorithms were downloaded from [12] and all codes of the five algorithms were complied using Microsoft Visual C++ 6.0. Duo to the lack of space, only the results for three real dense datasets and one real sparse dataset are shown here. The datasets we used are also selected from all the 11 real datasets of FIMI'03[12], they are BMS-WebView-2 (sparse), Connect, Mushroom and Pumsb_star, and their data characteristics can be found in [11].

4.1 Comparison of FP-Trees' Number

The item ordering policy and *PEP* technology are the main improvement of FIMfi. To test their performance in pruning, we build two sub algorithms: FIMfi-order and FIMfi-pep here. Comparing with FIMfi, FIMfi-order just doesn't use *PEP* for pruning, and FIMfi-pep discards our novel item ordering policy along with the optimization array technique.

We take FPMax* as the benchmark algorithm, because it is also an MFI mining algorithm based on FP-tree and MFI-tree which does the MFI Mining best for almost all the datasets in FIMI'03 [11].

The numbers of FP-tree created by the four algorithms are shown in Figure 5. On the datasets Mushroom, Connect and Pumsb_star FIMfi-order and FIMfi-pep both generate less than half number of the FP-trees than that of FPMax*. The combination of the ordering policy and *PEP* into FIMfi creates the least number of FP-trees in the four algorithms. In fact, at the lowest support of Mushroom, FPMax* creates more than 3 times number of FP-trees than FIMfi does.

Note that in Figure 5, there is no result of BMS-WebView-2, it is because that all the four algorithms generate only one tree for BMS-WebView-2, then we omit it.

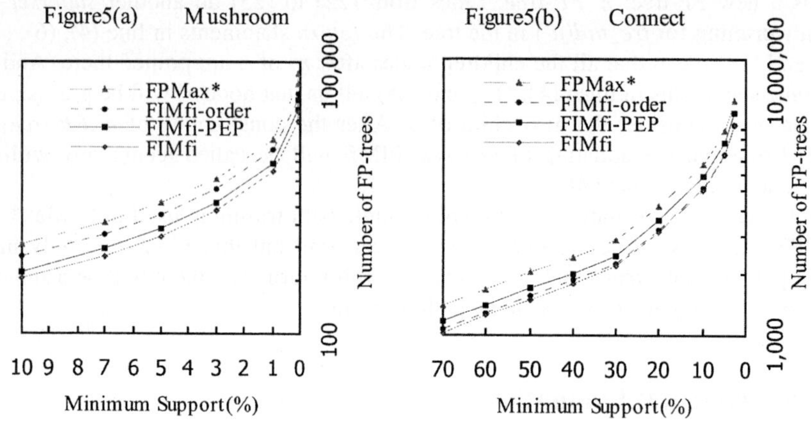

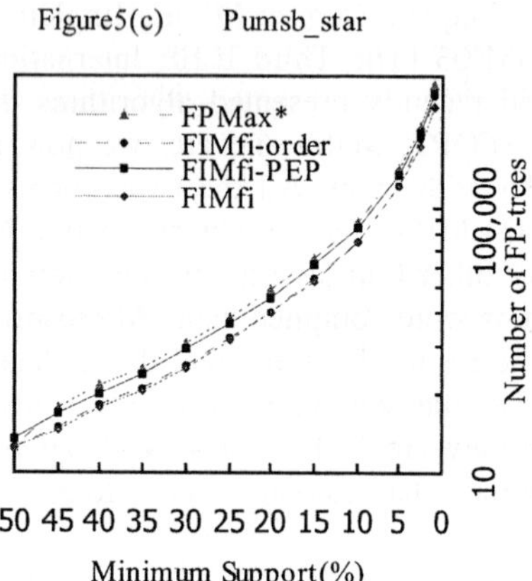

Fig. 5. Comparison of FP-trees' Number

4.2 Performance Comparisons

The performance comparisons of FIMfi, FPMax*, AFOPT and Mafia on sparse data BMS-WebView-2 are shown in Figure 6. FIMfi is faster than AFOPT at the higher supports that are no less than 50%, and FPMax* is always defeated by AFOPT at not only lower but also higher supports. FIMfi outperforms FPMax* about 20% to 40% at all supports and Mafia more than 20 times.

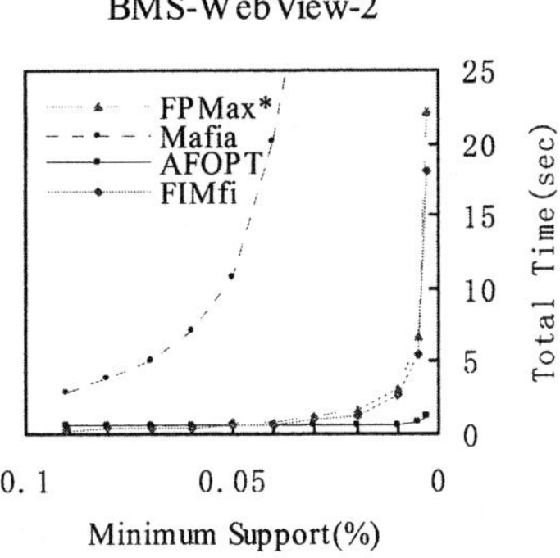

Fig. 6. Performance on Sparse Datasets

Figure 7 gives the results of comparison the four algorithms on dense data. For all supports on dense datasets, FIMfi has the best performance. FIMfi runs around 40% - %60 faster than FPMax* on all of the dense datasets. AFOPT is the slowest algorithm on Mushroom and Pumsb_star and runs from 2 to 10 times worse than FIMfi on all of the datasets across all supports. Mafia is the slowest algorithm on Connect, it runs between 2 to 5 times slower than FIMfi on Mushroom and Connect across all supports. On Pumsb_star, Mafia is outperformed by FIMfi for all the supports though it outperforms FPMax* at lower supports.

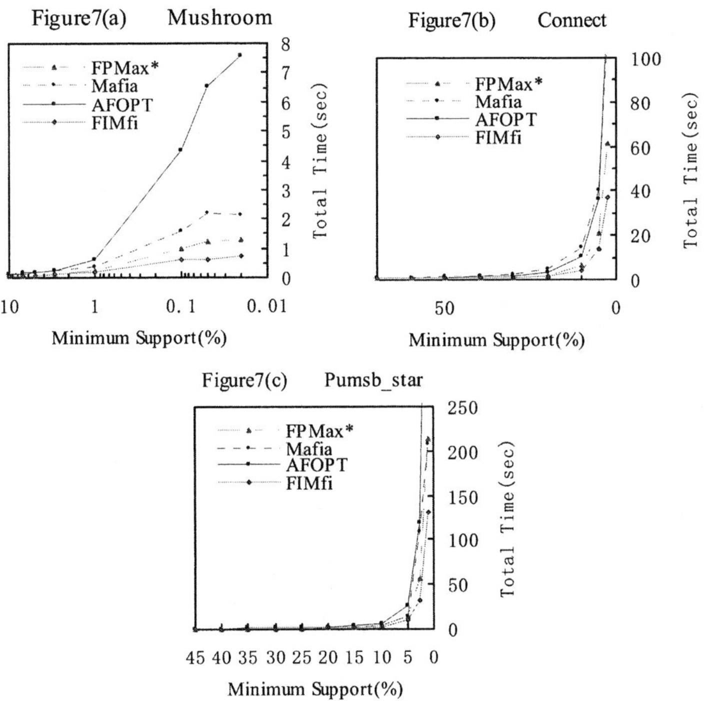

Fig. 7. Performance on Dense Datasets

5 Conclusions

Different from the traditional item ordering policy in which the items are sorted on the decreasing order of supports, this paper introduces a novel item ordering policy based on FP-tree and MFI-tree. The policy can guarantee maximal pruning of each node in the search space tree, and then greatly reduces the number of FP-trees created. The experimental comparison of FP-trees' number reveals that FIMfi will generate less than half number of FP-trees than the traditional one does for dense datasets.

We have found a simple method for fast superset checking. The method simplifies the superset checking to check only the equivalence of two integral, therefore makes the cost of superset checking less.

Several old and new pruning techniques are integrated into FIMfi. Among the new ones, the *superset frequency* pruning based on FP-tree is first introduced and makes the cutting of search space more efficiently. The *PEP* technique used in FIMfi greatly reduces the number of FP-tree created comparing with FPMax* by experimental results in section 4.1.

In FIMfi we also present a new optimization in array technique and use the memory management to further reduce the run time.

Our experimental results demonstrate that FIMfi is more optimized for mining MFI and outperforms FPMax* by 40% averagely, and on dense data it outperforms AFOPT and Mafia more than 2 times to 20 times.

Acknowledgements

We would like to thank Jianfei Zhu for providing the executable of FPMax and the code of FPMax* before the download website being available. We also thank Guimei Liu for providing the code of AFOPT and Doug Burdick for providing the website of downloading the code of Mafia.

References

1. R. Agrawal and R. Srikant. Fast algorithms for mining association rules. In Proceedings of the 20th VLDB Conference, Santiago, Chile, 1994.
2. J. Han, J. Pei, and Y. Yin. Mining Frequent Patterns without Candidate Generation, Proc. 2000 ACM-SIGMOD Int. Conf. on Management of Data (SIGMOD'00), Dallas, TX, May 2000.
3. L. Rigoutsos and A. Floratos: Combinatorial pattern discovery in biological sequences: The Teiresias algorithm.Bioinformatics 14, 1 (1998), 55-67.
4. Guimei Liu, Hongjun Lu, Jeffrey Xu Yu, Wei Wang and Xiangye Xiao. AFOPT: An Efficient Implementation of Pattern Growth Approach. In Proceedings of the IEEE ICDM Workshop on Frequent Itemset Mining Implementations Melbourne, Florida, USA, November 19, 2003.
5. Roberto Bayardo. Efficiently mining long patterns from databases. In ACM SIGMOD Conference, 1998.

6. R. Agarwal, C. Aggarwal and V. Prasad. A tree projection algorithm for generation of frequent itemsets. Journal of Parallel and Distributed Computing, 2001.
7. D. Burdick, M. Calimlim, and J. Gehrke. MAFIA: A Performance Study of Mining Maximal Frequent Itemsets. In Proceedings of the IEEE ICDM Workshop on Frequent Itemset Mining Implementations Melbourne, Florida, USA, November 19, 2003.
8. M. J. Zaki and C.-J. Hsiao. CHARM: An efficient algorithm for closed association rule mining. TR 99-10, CS Dept., RPI, Oct. 1999.
9. K. Gouda and M. J. Zaki. Efficiently Mining Maximal Frequent Itemsets. Proc. of the IEEE Int. Conference on Data Mining, San Jose, 2001.
10. Gösta Grahne and Jianfei Zhu. Efficiently Using Prefix-trees in Mining Frequent Itemsets. In Proceedings of the IEEE ICDM Workshop on Frequent Itemset Mining Implementations Melbourne, Florida, USA, November 19, 2003.
11. Bart Goethals and M. J. Zaki. FIMI'03: Workshop on Frequent Itemset Mining Implementations. In Proceedings of the IEEE ICDM Workshop on Frequent Itemset Mining Implementations Melbourne, Florida, USA, November 19, 2003.
12. Codes and datasets available at http://fimi.cs.helsinki.fi/.

Multi-phase Process Mining: Building Instance Graphs

B.F. van Dongen and W.M.P. van der Aalst

Department of Technology Management, Eindhoven University of Technology
P.O. Box 513, NL-5600 MB, Eindhoven, The Netherlands
{b.f.v.dongen,w.m.p.v.d.aalst}@tm.tue.nl

Abstract. Deploying process-driven information systems is a time-consuming and error-prone task. *Process mining* attempts to improve this by automatically generating a process model from event-based data. Existing techniques try to generate a complete process model from the data acquired. However, unless this model is the ultimate goal of mining, such a model is not always required. Instead, a good visualization of each individual process instance can be enough. From these individual instances, an overall model can then be generated if required. In this paper, we present an approach which constructs an *instance graph* for each individual process instance, based on information in the entire data set. The results are represented in terms of Event-driven Process Chains (EPCs). This representation is used to connect our process mining to a widely used commercial tool for the visualization and analysis of instance EPCs.

Keywords: Process mining, Event-driven process chains, Workflow management, Business Process Management.

1 Introduction

Increasingly, process-driven information systems are used to support operational business processes. Some of these information systems enforce a particular way of working. For example, Workflow Management Systems (WFMSs) can be used to force users to execute tasks in a predefined order. However, in many cases systems allow for more flexibility. For example transactional systems such as ERP (Enterprise Resource Planning), CRM (Customer Relationship Management) and SCM (Supply Chain Management) are known to allow the users to deviate from the process specified by the system, e.g., in the context of SAP R/3 the reference models, expressed in terms of Event-driven Process Chains (EPCs, cf. [13, 14, 19]), are only used to guide users rather than to enforce a particular way of working. Operational flexibility typically leads to difficulties with respect to performance measurements. The ability to do these measurements, however, is what made companies decide to use a transactional system in the first place.

To be able to calculate basic performance characteristics, most systems have their own built-in module. For the calculation of basic characteristics such as the average flow time of a case, no model of the process is required. However, for more complicated characteristics, such as the average time it takes to transfer work

P. Atzeni et al. (Eds.): ER 2004, LNCS 3288, pp. 362–376, 2004.

from one person to the other, some notion of causality between tasks is required. This notion of causality is provided by the original model of the process, but deviations in execution can interfere with causalities specified there. Therefore, in this paper, we present a way of defining certain causal relations in a transactional system. We do so without using the process definition from the system, but only looking at a so called process log. Such a process log contains information about the processes as they actually take place in a transactional system. Most systems can provide this information in some form and the techniques used to infer relations between tasks in such a log is called *process mining*.

The problem tackled in this paper has been inspired by the software package *ARIS PPM* (Process Performance Monitor) [12] developed by IDS Scheer. ARIS PPM allows for the visualization, aggregation, and analysis of process instances expressed in terms of *instance EPCs* (i-EPCs). An instance EPC describes the the control-flow of a case, i.e., a single process instance. Unlike a trace (i.e., a sequence of events) an instance EPC provides a graphical representation describing the causal relations. In case of parallelism, there may be different traces having the same instance EPC. Note that in the presence of parallelism, two subsequent events do not have to be causally related. ARIS PPM exploits the advantages of having instance EPCs rather than traces to provide additional management information, i.e., instances can be visualized and aggregated in various ways. In order to do this, IDS Scheer has developed a number of adapters, e.g., there is an adapter to extract instance EPCs from SAP R/3. Unfortunately, these adapters can only create instance EPCs if the actual process is known. For example, the workflow management system Staffware can be used to export Staffware audit trails to ARIS PPM (Staffware SPM, cf. [20]) by taking projections of the Staffware process model. As a result, it is very time consuming to build adapters. Moreover, the approaches used only work in environments where there are explicit process models available.

In this paper, we do not focus on the visualization, aggregation, and analysis of process instances expressed in terms of instance EPC or some other notation capturing parallelism and causality. Instead we focus on the construction of *instance graphs*. An instance graph can be seen as an abstraction of the instance EPCs used by ARIS PPM. In fact, we will show a mapping of instance graphs onto instance EPCs. Instance graphs also correspond to a specific class of Petri nets known as *marked graphs* [17], *T-systems* [9] or *partially ordered runs* [8, 10]. Tools like VIPTool allow for the construction of partially ordered runs given an ordinary Petri net and then use these instance graphs for analysis purposes. In our approach we do not construct instance graphs from a known Petri net but from an event log. This enhances the applicability of commercial tools such as ARIS PPM and the theoretical results presented in [8, 10]. The mapping from instance graphs to these Petri nets is not given here. However, it will become clear that such a mapping is trivial.

In the remainder of this paper, we will first describe a common format to store process logs in. Then, in Section 3 we will give an algorithm to infer causality at an instance level, i.e. a model is built for each individual case. In Section 4 we will provide a translation of these models to EPCs. Section 5 shows a concrete example and demonstrates the link to ARIS PPM. Section 6 discusses related work followed by some concluding remarks.

2 Preliminaries

This section contains most definitions used in the process of mining for instance graphs. The structure of this section is as follows. Subsection 2.1 defines a process log in a standard format. Subsection 2.2 defines the model for one instance.

2.1 Process Logs

Information systems typically log all kinds of events. Unfortunately, most systems use a specific format. Therefore, we propose an XML format for storing event logs. The basic assumption is that the log contains information about specific *tasks* executed for specific *cases* (i.e., process instances). Note that unlike ARIS PPM we do not assume any knowledge of the underlying process. Experience with several software products (e.g., Staffware, InConcert, MQSeries Workflow, FLOWer, etc.) and organization-specific systems (e.g., Rijkswaterstaat, CJIB, and several hospitals) show that these assumptions are justified.

Figure 1 shows the schema definition of the XML format. This format is supported by our tools, and mappings from several commercial systems are available. The format allows for logging multiple processes in one XML file (cf. element "Process"). Within each process there may be multiple process instances (cf. element "ProcessInstance"). Each "ProcessInstance" element is composed of "AuditTrailEntry" elements. Instead of "AuditTrailEntry" we will also use the terms "log entry" or "event". An "AuditTrailEntry" element corresponds to a single event and refers to a "WorkflowModelElement" and an "EventType". A "WorkflowModelElement" may refer to a single task or a subprocess. The "EventType" is used to indicate the type of event. Typical events are: "schedule" (i.e., a task becomes enabled for a specific instance), "assign" (i.e., a task

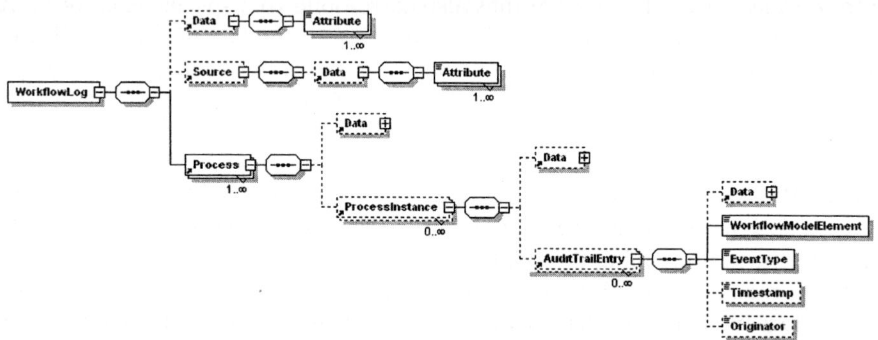

Fig. 1. XML schema for process logs.

instance is assigned to a user), "start" (the beginning of a task instance), " complete" (the completion of a task instance). In total, we identify 12 events. When building an adapter for a specific system, the system-specific events are mapped on these 12 generic events.

As Figure 1 shows the "WorkflowModelElement" and "EventType" are mandatory for each "AuditTrailEntry". There are three optional elements "Data", "Timestamp", and "Originator". The "Data" element can be used to store data related to the event of the case (e.g., the amount of money involved in the transaction). The "Timestamp" element is important for calculating performance metrics like flow time, service times, service levels, utilization, etc. The "Originator" refers to the actor (i.e., user or organization) performing the event. The latter is useful for analyzing organizational and social aspects. Although each element is vital for the practical applicability of process mining, we focus on the "WorkflowModelElement" element. In other words, we abstract from the "EventType", "Data", "Timestamp", and "Originator" elements. However, our approach can easily be extended to incorporate these aspects. In fact, our tools deal with these additional elements. However, for the sake of readability, in this paper events are identified by the task and case (i.e., process instance) involved.

Table 1. A process log.

case identifier	task identifier
case 1	task S
case 2	task S
case 1	task A
case 1	task B
case 2	task B
case 2	task A

Table 1 shows an example of a small log after abstracting from all elements except for the "WorkflowModelElement" element (i.e., task identifier). The log shows two cases. For each case three tasks are executed. Case 1 can be described by the sequence SAB and case 2 can be described by the sequence SBA. In the remainder we will describe process instances as sequences of tasks where each element in the sequence refers to a "WorkflowModelElement" element. A process log is represented as a bag (i.e., multiset) of process instances.

Definition 2.1. (Process Instance, Process Log) Let T be a set of log entries, i.e., references to tasks. Let T^+ define the set of sequences of log entries with length at least 1. We call $\sigma \in T^+$ a process instance (i.e., case) and $W \in T^+ \rightarrow \mathbb{N}$ a process log.

If $\sigma = t_1 t_2 \dots t_n \in T^+$ is a process instance of length n, then each element t_i corresponds to "AuditTrailEntry" element in Figure 1. However, since we abstract from timestamps, event types, etc., one can think of t_i as a reference to a task. $|\sigma| = n$ denotes the length of the process instance and σ_i the i-th element. We assume process instances to be of finite length. $W \in T^+ \rightarrow \mathbb{N}$ denotes a bag, i.e., a multiset of process instances. $W(\sigma)$ is the number of times a process instance of the form σ appears in the log. The total number of instances in a bag is finite. Since W is a bag, we use the normal set operators where convenient. For example, we use $\sigma \in W$ as a shorthand notation for $W(\sigma) > 0$.

2.2 Instance Nets

After defining a process log, we now define an instance net. An instance net is a model of one instance. Since we are dealing with an instance that has been executed in the past, it makes sense to define an instance net in such a way that no choices have to be made. As a consequence of this, no loops will appear in an instance net. For readers familiar with Petri nets it is easy to see that instance nets correspond to "runs" (also referred to as occurrence nets) [8].

Since events that appear multiple times in a process instance have to be duplicated in an instance net, we define an instance domain. The instance domain will be used as a basis for generating instance nets.

Definition 2.2. (Instance domain) Let σ be a process instance such that $\sigma = t_1 t_2 \ldots t_n \in T^+$, i.e., $|\sigma| = n$. We define $D_\sigma = \{1 \ldots n\}$ as the domain of σ.

Using the domain of an instance, we can link each log entry in the process instance to a specific task, i.e., $i \in D_\sigma$ can be used to represent the i-th element in σ. In an instance net, the instance σ is extended with some ordering relation $\dashv_\sigma$ to reflect some causal relation.

Definition 2.3. (Instance net) Let $N = (\sigma, \dashv_\sigma)$ such that σ is a process instance. Let D_σ be the domain of σ and let $\dashv_\sigma$ be an ordering on D_σ such that:

- $\dashv_\sigma$ is irreflexive, asymmetric and acyclic,
- $\forall_{i,j \in D_\sigma}(i < j \Rightarrow j \not\dashv_\sigma i)$,
- $\forall i,j \in D_\sigma(i \dashv_\sigma j \Rightarrow \not\exists_{k \in D_\sigma}(i \dashv_\sigma^+ k \wedge k \dashv_\sigma^+ j)$, where $\dashv_\sigma^+$ is the smallest relation satisfying: $i \dashv_\sigma^+ j$ if and only if $i \dashv_\sigma j$ or $\exists_k(i \dashv_\sigma k \wedge k \dashv_\sigma^+ j)$
- $\forall i,j \in D_\sigma(t_i = t_j \Rightarrow (i \dashv_\sigma^+ j) \vee (j \dashv_\sigma^+ i))$

We call N an instance net.

The definition of an instance net given here is rather flexible, since it is defined only as a set of entries from the log and an ordering on that set. An important feature of this ordering is that if $i \dashv j$ then there is no set $\{k_1, k_2, \ldots, k_n\}$ such that $i \dashv k_1, k_1 \dashv k_2, \ldots, k_n \dashv j$. Since the set of entries is given as a log, and an instance mapping can be inferred for each instance based on textual properties, we only need to define the ordering relation based on the given log. In Section 3.1 it is shown how this can be done. In Section 4 we show how to translate an instance net to a model in a particular language (i.e., instance EPCs).

3 Mining Instance Graphs

As seen in Definition 2.3, an instance net consists of two parts. First, it requires a sequence of events $\sigma \in T^+$ as they appear in a specific instance. Second, an ordering $\dashv$ on the domain of σ is required. In this section, we will provide a method that infers such an ordering relation on T using the whole log. Furthermore, we will present an algorithm to generate *instance graphs* from these *instance nets.*

3.1 Creating Instance Nets

Definition 3.1. (Causal ordering) Let W be a process log over a set of log entries T, i.e., $W \in T^+ \to \mathbb{N}$. Let $b \in T$ and $c \in T$ be two log entries. We define a causal ordering $\to_W$ on W in the following way:

- $b >_W c$ if and only if there is an instance σ and $i \in D_\sigma \setminus \{|\sigma|\}$ such that $\sigma \in W$ and $\sigma_i = b$ and $\sigma_{i+1} = c$,
- $b \Delta_W c$ if and only if there is an instance σ and $i \in D_\sigma \setminus \{|\sigma| - 1, |\sigma|\}$ such that $\sigma \in W$ and $\sigma_i = \sigma_{i+2} = b$ and $\sigma_{i+1} = c$ and $b \neq c$ and not $b >_W b$,
- $b \to_W c$ if and only if $b >_W c$ and ($c \not>_W b$ or $b \Delta_W c$ or $c \Delta_W b$), or $b = c$.

The basis of the causal ordering defined here, is that two tasks A and B have a causal relation $A \to B$ if in some process instance, A is directly followed by B and B is never directly followed by A. However, this can lead to problems if the two tasks are in a loop of length two. Therefore, $A \to B$ also holds if there is a process instance containing ABA or BAB and A nor B can directly succeed themselves. If A directly succeeds itself, then $A \to A$. For the example log presented in Table 1, $T = \{S, A, B\}$ and causal ordering inferred on T is composed of the following two elements $S \to_W A$ and $S \to_W B$.

By defining the $\to_W$ relation, we defined an ordering relation on T. This relation is not necessarily irreflexive, asymmetric, nor acyclic. This $\to_W$ relation however can be used to induce an ordering on the domain of any instance σ that has these properties. This is done in two steps. First, an asymmetric order is defined on the domain of some σ. Then, we prove that this relation is irreflexive and acyclic.

Definition 3.2. (Instance ordering) Let W be a process log over T and let $\sigma \in W$ be a process instance. Furthermore, let $\to_W$ be a causal ordering on T. We define an ordering $\succ_\sigma$ on the domain of σ, D_σ in the following way. For all $i, j \in D_\sigma$ such that $i < j$ we define $i \succ_\sigma j$ if and only if $\sigma_i \to_W \sigma_j$ and $\nexists_{i<k<j}(\sigma_i \to_W \sigma_k)$ or $\nexists_{i<k<j}(\sigma_k \to_W \sigma_j)$.

The essence of the relation defined here is in the final part. For each entry within an instance, we find the *closest* causal predecessor and the *closest* causal successor. If there is no causal predecessor or successor then the entry is in parallel with all its predecessors or successors respectively. It is trivial to see that this can always be done for any process instance and with *any* causal relation.

In the example log presented in Table 1 there are two process instances, case 1 and case 2. From here on, we will refer to case 1 as σ_1 and to case 2 as σ_2. We know that $\sigma_1 = SAB$ and that $D_{\sigma_1} = \{1, 2, 3\}$. Using the causal relation $\to$ the relation $\succ_{\sigma_1}$ is inferred such that $1 \succ_{\sigma_1} 2$ and $1 \succ_{\sigma_1} 3$. For σ_2 this also applies.

It is easily seen that the ordering relation $\succ_\sigma$ is indeed irreflexive and asymmetric, since it is only defined on i and j for which $i < j$. Therefore, it can easily be concluded that it is *irreflexive* and *acyclic.* Furthermore, the third property holds as well. Therefore we can now define an instance net as $(\sigma, \succ_\sigma)$.

3.2 Creating Instance Graphs

In this section, we present an algorithm to generate an instance graph from an instance net. An instance graph is a graph where each node represents one log entry of a specific instance. These instance graphs can be used as a basis to generate models in a particular language.

Definition 3.3. (Instance graph) Consider a set of nodes N and a set of edges $E \subseteq N \times N$. We call $G = (N, E)_\sigma$ an instance graph of an instance net $(\sigma, \succ_\sigma)$ if and only if the following conditions hold.

1. $N = D_\sigma \cup \{0, |D_\sigma| + 1\}$ is the set of nodes.
2. The set of edges E is defined as $E = E_{rel} \cup E_{initial} \cup E_{final}$, where
$E_{rel} = \{(n_1, n_2) \in N \times N | (n_1 \succ_\sigma n_2)\}$ and
$E_{initial} = \{(0, n) \in N \times N | \not\exists_{n_1} (n_1 \succ_\sigma n)\}$ and
$E_{final} = \{(n, |N| - 1) \in N \times N | \not\exists_{n_1} (n \succ_\sigma n_1)\}$

An instance graph as described in Definition 3.3 is a graph that typically describes an execution path of some process model. This property is what makes an instance graph a good description of an instance. It not only shows causal relations between tasks but also parallelism if parallel branches are taken by the instance. However, choices are not represented in an instance graph. The reason for that is obvious, since choices are made at the execution level and do not appear in an instance. With respect to these choices, we can also say that if the same choices are made at execution, the resulting instance graph is the same. Note, that the fact that the same choices are made does not imply that the process instance is the same. Tasks that can be done in parallel within one instance can appear in any order in an instance without changing the resulting instance graph.

For case 1 of the example log of Table 1 the instance graph is drawn in Figure 2. Note that in this graph, the nodes 1,2 and 3 are actually in the domain of σ_1 and therefore, they refer to entries in Table 1. It is easily seen that for case 2 this graph looks exactly the same, although the nodes refer to different entries.

In order to make use of instance graphs, we will show that an instance graph indeed describes an instance such that an entry in the log can only appear if all predecessors of that entry in the graph have already appeared in the instance.

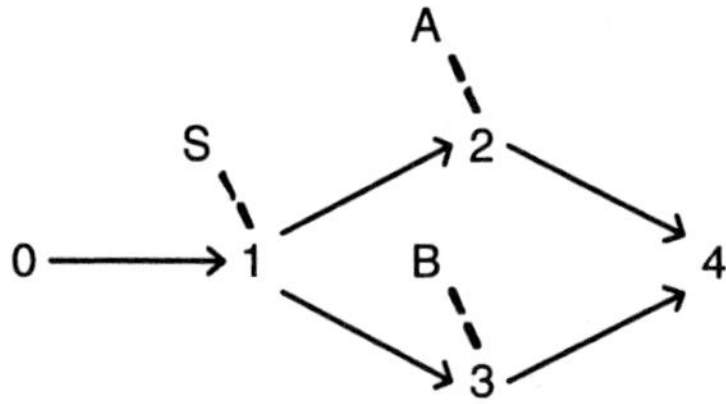

Fig. 2. Instance graph for σ_1.

Definition 3.4. (Pre- and postset) Let $G = (N, E)_\sigma$ be an instance graph and let $n \in N$. We define $\bullet_G n$ to be the preset of n such that $\bullet_G n = \{n' \in N | (n', n) \in E\}$. We define $n \bullet_G$ to be the postset of n such that $n \bullet_G = \{n' \in N | (n, n') \in E\}$.

Property 3.5. (Instance graphs describe an instance) Every instance graph $G = (N, E)_\sigma$ of some process instance σ describes that instance in such a way that for all $i, j \in N$ holds that for all $j \in \bullet_G i$ implies that $j < i$. This ensures that every entry in process entry σ occurs only after all predecessors in the instance graph have occurred in σ.

Proof. To prove that this is indeed the case for instance graph $G = (N, E)_\sigma$, we consider Definition 3.3 which implies that for "internal nodes" we know that $(n_1, n_2) \in E$ if and only if $n_1 \succ_\sigma n_2$. Furthermore, from the definition of $\succ_\sigma$ we know that $n_1 \succ_\sigma n_2$ implies that $n_1 < n_2$. For the source and sink nodes, it is also easy to show that $n_1 \in \bullet_G n_2$ implies that $n_1 < n_2$ because 0 is the smallest element of N while $|N| - 1$ is the largest. □

Property 3.6. (Strongly connectedness) For every instance graph $G = (N, E)_\sigma$ of some process instance σ holds that the short circuited graph $G' = (N, E \cup \{(|N| - 1, 0)\})$ is strongly connected.[1]

Proof. From Definition 3.3 we know that for all $i \in D_\sigma$ such that there does not exist a $j \in D_\sigma$ such that $j \succ_\sigma i$ holds that $(0, i) \in E$. Furthermore, we know that for all $i \in D_\sigma$ such that there does not exist a $j \in D_\sigma$ such that $i \succ_\sigma j$ holds that $(i, |\sigma| + 1) \in E$. Therefore, the graph is strongly connected if the edge $(|N| - 1, 0)$ is added to E. □

In the remainder of this paper, we will focus on an application of instance graphs. In Section 4 a translation from these instance graphs to a specific model are given.

4 Instance EPCs

In Section 3 instance graphs were introduced. In this section, we will present an algorithm to generate instance EPCs from these graphs. An instance EPC is a special case of an EPC (Event-driven Process Chain, [13]). For more information on EPCs we refer to [13, 14, 19]. These instance EPCs (or i-EPCs) can only contain AND-split and AND-join connectors, and therefore do not allow for loops to be present. These i-EPCs serve as a basis for the tool ARIS PPM (Process Performance Monitor) described in the introduction.

In this section, we first provide a formal definition of an instance EPC. An instance EPC does not contain any connectors other than AND-split and AND-joins connectors. Furthermore, there is exactly one initial event and one final event. Functions refer to the entries that appear in a process log, events however do not appear in the log. Therefore, we make the assumption here that each

[1] A graph is strongly connected if there is a directed path from any node to any other node in the graph.

event uniquely causes a function to happen and that functions result in one or more events. An exception to this assumption is made when there are multiple functions that are the start of the instance. These functions are all preceded by an AND-split connector. This connector is preceded by the initial event. Consequently, all other connectors are preceded by functions and succeeded by events.

Definition 4.1. (Instance EPC) Consider a set of events E, a set of functions F, a set of connectors C and a set of arcs $A \subseteq ((E \cup F \cup C) \times (E \cup F \cup C)) \setminus ((E \times E) \cup (F \times F))$. We call (E, F, C, A) an instance EPC if and only if the following conditions hold.

1. $E \cap F = F \cap C = E \cap C = \emptyset$
2. Functions and events alternate in the presence of connectors: $\forall_{n_1,n_2 \in E \cup F} \forall_{(c_1,c_2) \in (A \cap (C \times C))^+ \cup I}((n_1, c_1) \in A \;\wedge\; (c_2, n_2) \in A) \Rightarrow (n_1 \in E \Leftrightarrow n_2 \in F)$, where $I = \{(c, c) \mid c \in C\}$.
3. The graph $(E \cup F \cup C, A)$ is acyclic.
4. There exists exactly one event $e_i \in E$ such that there is no element $n \in F \cup C$ such that $(n, e_i) \in A$. We call e_i the initial event.
5. There exists exactly one event $e_f \in E$ such that there is no element $n \in F \cup C$ such that $(e_f, n) \in A$. We call e_f the final event.
6. The graph $(E \cup F \cup C, A \cup \{(e_f, e_i)\})$ is strongly connected.
7. For each function $f \in F$ there are exactly two elements $n_1, n_2 \in E \cup C$ such that $(f, n_1) \in A$ and $(n_2, f) \in A$. Functions only have one input and one output.
8. For each event $e \in E / \{e_i, e_f\}$ there are exactly two elements $n_1, n_2 \in F \cup C$ such that $(e, n_1) \in A$ and $(n_2, e) \in A$. Events only have one input and one output, except for the initial and the final event. For them the following holds. For e_i there is exactly one element $n \in F \cup C$ such that $(e_i, n) \in A$ and for e_f there is exactly one element $n \in F \cup C$ such that $(n, e_f) \in A$.

4.1 Generating Instance EPCs

Using the formal definition of an instance EPC from Definition 4.1, we introduce an algorithm that produces an instance EPC from an instance graph as defined in Definition 3.3. In the instance EPC generated it makes sense to label the functions according to the combination of the task name and event type as they appear in the log. The labels of the events however cannot be determined from the log. Therefore, we propose to label the events in the following way. The initial event will be labeled "initial". The final event will be labeled "final". All other events will be labeled in such a way that it is clear which function succeeds it. Connectors are labeled in such a way that it is clear whether it is a split or a join connector and to which function or event it connects with the input or output respectively.

Definition 4.2. (Converting instance graphs to EPCs) Let W be a process log and let $G = (N_G, E_G)_\sigma$ be an instance graph for some process instance

$\sigma \in W$. To create an instance EPC, we need to define the four sets E, F, C and A.

- The set of functions F is defined as $F = \{f_i \mid i \in D_\sigma\}$. In other words, for every entry in the process instance, a function is defined.
- The set of events E is defined as $E = \{e_{f_i} \mid f_i \in F \text{ and } \exists_{j \in D_\sigma}(j \succ_\sigma i)\} \cup \{e_{initial}, e_{final}\}$. In other words, for every function there is an event preceding it, unless it is a minimal element with respect to $\succ_\sigma$. Furthermore, there is an initial event $e_{initial}$ and a final event e_{final}.
- The set of connectors C is defined as $C = C_{split} \cup C_{join} \cup C_i \cup C_f$ where
  $C_{split} = \{c_{(split,f_i)} \mid f_i \in F \wedge |i \bullet_G| > 1\}$ and
  $C_{join} = \{c_{(join,e_{f_i})} \mid e_{f_i} \in E \wedge |\bullet_G i| > 1\}$ and
  $C_i = \{c_{(split,e_{initial})} \mid |0 \bullet_G| > 1\}$ and
  $C_f = \{c_{(join,e_{final})} \mid |\bullet_G (|N_G| - 1)| > 1\}$.
  Here, the connectors are constructed in such a way that connectors are always preceded by a function, except in case the process starts with parallel functions, since then the event $e_{initial}$ is succeeded by a split connector.
- The set of arcs A is defined as $A = A_{ef} \cup A_{fe} \cup A_{split} \cup A_{join} \cup A_i \cup A_f$ where
  $A_{ef} = \{(e_{f_i}, f_i) \in (E \times F)\}$ and
  $A_{fe} = \{(f_i, e_{f_j}) \in (F \times E) \mid (i,j) \in E_G \wedge |i \bullet_G| = 1 \wedge |\bullet_G j| = 1\}$

$$\begin{aligned}
A_{split} = &\{(f_i, c_{(split,f_i)}) \in (F \times C_{split})\} \cup \\
&\{(c_{(split,f_i)}, e_{f_j}) \in (C_{split} \times E) \mid (i,j) \in E_G \wedge |\bullet_G j| = 1\} \cup \\
&\{(c_{(split,f_i)}, c_{(join,e_{f_j})}) \in (C_{split} \times C_{join}) \mid (i,j) \in E_G\} \text{ and} \\
A_{join} = &\{(c_{(join,e_{f_i})}, e_{f_i}) \in (C_{join} \times E)\} \cup \\
&\{(f_i, c_{(join,e_{f_j})}) \in (F \times C_{join}) \mid (i,j) \in E_G \wedge |i \bullet_G| = 1\} \text{ and} \\
A_i = \;&\{(e_{initial}, c_{(split,e_{initial})}) \in (E \times C_i)\} \cup \\
&\{(c_{(split,e_{initial})}, f_i) \in (C_i \times F) | (0,i) \in E_G\} \text{ and} \\
A_f = \;&\{(c_{(join,e_{final})}, e_{final}) \in (C_f \times E)\} \cup \\
&\{f_i, (c_{(join,e_{final})}) \in (F \times D_f) | (i, (|N_G| - 1)) \in E_G\}.
\end{aligned}$$

It is easily seen that the instance EPC generated by Definition 4.2 is indeed an instance EPC, by verifying the result against Definition 4.1.

In definitions 3.3 and 4.1 we have given an algorithm to generate an instance EPC for each instance graph. The result of this algorithm for both cases in the example of Table 1 can be found in Figure 3. In Section 5 we will show the practical use of this algorithm to ARIS PPM.

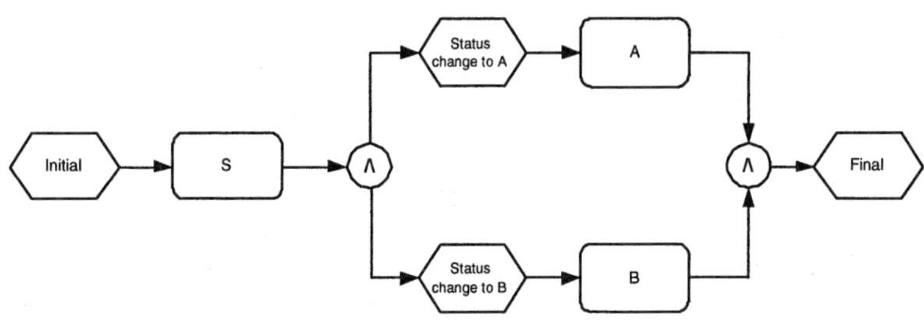

Fig. 3. Instance EPC for σ_1.

5 Example

In this section, we present an example illustrating the algorithms described in sections 3 and 4. We will start from a process log with some process instances. Then, we will run the algorithms to generate a set of instance EPCs that can be imported into ARIS PPM.

5.1 A Process Log

Consider a process log consisting of the following traces.

Table 2. A process log.

case identifier	task executions
case 1	$S_1, A_2, B_3, F_4, C_5, D_6, H_7, G_8, T_9$
case 2	$S_1, A_2, C_3, B_4, E_5, H_6, F_7, G_8, T_9$
case 3	$S_1, A_2, D_3, B_4, C_5, F_6, H_7, G_8, T_9$
case 4	$S_1, A_2, E_3, B_4, C_5, H_6, F_7, G_8, T_9$
case 5	$S_1, A_2, B_3, D_4, F_5, H_6, C_7, G_8, T_9$
case 6	$S_1, A_2, B_3, E_4, F_5, H_6, C_7, G_8, T_9$
case 7	$S_1, A_2, B_3, F_4, D_5, C_6, H_7, G_8, T_9$
case 8	$S_1, A_2, B_3, F_4, E_5, C_6, H_7, G_8, T_9$
case 9	$S_1, A_2, D_3, C_4, B_5, H_6, F_7, G_8, T_9$
case 10	$S_1, A_2, C_3, E_4, H_5, B_6, F_7, G_8, T_9$

The process log in Table 2 shows the execution of tasks for a number of different instances of the same process. To save space, we abstracted from the original names of tasks and named each task with a single letter. The subscript refers to the position of that task in the process instance.

Using this process log, we will first generate the causal relations from Definition 3.1. Note that casual relations are to be defined between tasks and not between log entries. Therefore, the subscripts are omitted here. This definition leads to the following set of causal relations: $\{S \to A,\ A \to B,\ A \to C,\ A \to D,\ A \to E,\ B \to F,\ D \to H,\ E \to H,\ F \to G,\ C \to G,\ H \to G,\ G \to T\}$.

Using these relations, we generate instance graphs as described in Section 3 for each process instance. Then, these instance graphs are imported into ARIS PPM and a screenshot of this tool is presented (cf. Figure 5).

5.2 Instance Graphs

To illustrate the concept of instance graphs, we will present the instance graph for the first instance, "case 1". In order to do this, we will follow Definition 3.2 to generate an instance ordering for that instance. Then, using these orderings, an instance graph is generated. Applying Definition 3.2 to case 1 in the log presented in Table 2 using the casual relations given in Section 5.1 gives the following instance ordering: $0 \succ 1, 1 \succ 2,\ 2 \succ 3,\ 3 \succ 4,\ 4 \succ 8,\ 8 \succ 9,\ 2 \succ 5,\ 5 \succ 8,\ 2 \succ 6,\ 6 \succ 7,\ 7 \succ 8,\ 8 \succ 9, 9 \succ 10$.

Using this instance ordering, an instance graph can be made as described in Definition 3.3. The resulting graph can be found in Figure 4. Note that the instance graphs of all other instances are isomorphic to this graph. Only, the numbers of the nodes change.

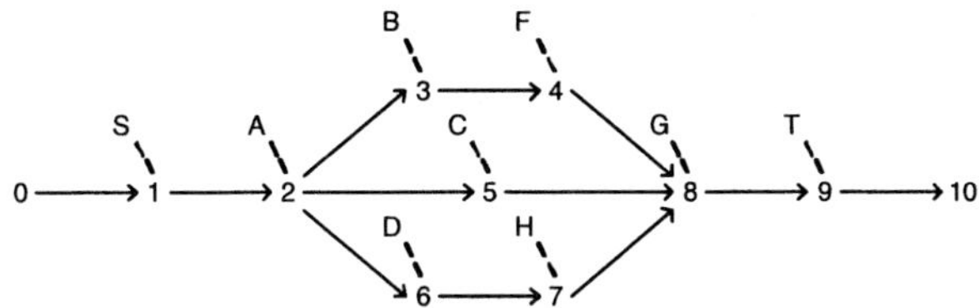

Fig. 4. Instance graph for case 1.

For each process instance, such an instance graph can be made. Using the algorithm presented in Section 4 each instance can than be converted into an instance EPC. These instance EPCs can be imported directly into ARIS PPM for further analysis. Here, we would like to point out again that our tools currently provide an implementation of the algorithms in this paper, such that the instance EPCs generated can be imported into ARIS PPM directly. A screenshot of this tool can be found in Figure 5 where "case 1" is shown as an instance EPC. Furthermore, inside the boxed area, the aggregation of some cases is shown. Note that this aggregation is only part of the functionality of ARIS PPM. Using graphical representations of instances, a large number of analysis techniques is available to the user. However, creating instances without knowing the original process model is an important first step.

6 Related Work

The idea of process mining is not new [1,3,5–7,11,12,15,16,18,21] and most techniques aim at the control-flow perspective. For example, the α-algorithm allows for the construction of a Petri net from an event log [1,5]. However, process mining is not limited to the control-flow perspective. For example, in [2] we use process mining techniques to construct a social network. For more information on process mining we refer to a special issue of Computers in Industry on process mining [4] and a survey paper [3]. In this paper, unfortunately, it is impossible to do justice to the work done in this area. To support our mining efforts we have developed a set of tools including EMiT [1], Thumb [21], and MinSoN [2]. These tools share the XML format discussed in this paper. For more details we refer to www.processmining.org.

The focus of this paper is on the mining of the control-flow perspective. However, instead of constructing a process model, we mine for instance graphs.

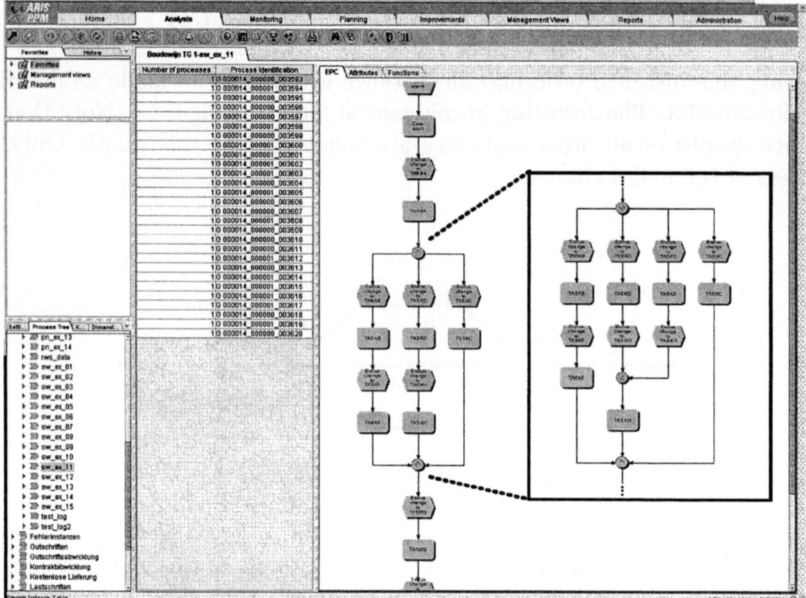

Fig. 5. ARIS PPM screenshot.

The result can be represented in terms of a Petri net or an (instance) EPC. Therefore, our work is related to tools like ARIS PPM [12], Staffware SPM [20], and VIPTool [10]. Moreover, the mining result can be used as a basis for applying the theoretical results regarding partially ordered runs [8].

7 Conclusion

The focus of this paper has been on mining for instance graphs. Algorithms are presented to describe each process instance in a particular modelling language. From the instance graphs described in Section 3, other models can be created as well. The main advantage of looking at instances in isolation is twofold. First, it can provide a good starting point for all kinds of analysis such as the ones implemented in ARIS PPM. Second, it does not require any notion of completeness of a process log to work. As long as a causal relation is provided between log entries, instance graphs can be made. Existing methods such as the α-algorithm [1, 3, 5] usually require some notion of completeness in order to rediscover the entire process model. The downside thereof is that it is often hard to deal with noisy process logs. In our approach noise can be filtered out before implying the causal dependencies between log entries, without negative implications on the result of the mining process.

ARIS PPM allows for the aggregation of instance EPCs into an aggregated EPC. This approach illustrates the wide applicability of instance graphs. However, the aggregation is based on simple heuristics that fail in the presence of complex routing structures. Therefore, we are developing algorithms for the integration of multiple instance graphs into one EPC or Petri net. Early experiments suggest that such a two-step approach alleviate some of the problems existing process mining algorithms are facing [3, 4].

References

1. W.M.P. van der Aalst and B.F. van Dongen. Discovering Workflow Performance Models from Timed Logs. In Y. Han, S. Tai, and D. Wikarski, editors, *International Conference on Engineering and Deployment of Cooperative Information Systems (EDCIS 2002)*, volume 2480 of *Lecture Notes in Computer Science*, pages 45–63. Springer-Verlag, Berlin, 2002.
2. W.M.P. van der Aalst and M. Song. Mining Social Networks: Uncovering interaction patterns in business processes. In M. Weske, B. Pernici, and J. Desel, editors, *International Conference on Business Process Management*, volume 3080 of *Lecture Notes in Computer Science*, pages 244–260. Springer-Verlag, Berlin, 2004.
3. W.M.P. van der Aalst, B.F. van Dongen, J. Herbst, L. Maruster, G. Schimm, and A.J.M.M. Weijters. Workflow Mining: A Survey of Issues and Approaches. *Data and Knowledge Engineering*, 47(2):237–267, 2003.
4. W.M.P. van der Aalst and A.J.M.M. Weijters, editors. *Process Mining*, Special Issue of Computers in Industry, Volume 53, Number 3. Elsevier Science Publishers, Amsterdam, 2004.
5. W.M.P. van der Aalst, A.J.M.M. Weijters, and L. Maruster. Workflow Mining: Discovering Process Models from Event Logs. QUT Technical report, FIT-TR-2003-03, Queensland University of Technology, Brisbane, 2003. (Accepted for publication in IEEE Transactions on Knowledge and Data Engineering.).
6. R. Agrawal, D. Gunopulos, and F. Leymann. Mining Process Models from Workflow Logs. In *Sixth International Conference on Extending Database Technology*, pages 469–483, 1998.
7. J.E. Cook and A.L. Wolf. Discovering Models of Software Processes from Event-Based Data. *ACM Transactions on Software Engineering and Methodology*, 7(3):215–249, 1998.
8. J. Desel. Validation of Process Models by Construction of Process Nets. In W.M.P. van der Aalst, J. Desel, and A. Oberweis, editors, *Business Process Management: Models, Techniques, and Empirical Studies*, volume 1806 of *Lecture Notes in Computer Science*, pages 110–128. Springer-Verlag, Berlin, 2000.
9. J. Desel and J. Esparza. *Free Choice Petri Nets*, volume 40 of *Cambridge Tracts in Theoretical Computer Science*. Cambridge University Press, 1995.
10. J. Desel, G. Juhas, R. Lorenz, and C. Neumair. Modelling and Validation with VipTool. In W.M.P. van der Aalst, A.H.M. ter Hofstede, and M. Weske, editors, *International Conference on Business Process Management (BPM 2003)*, volume 2678 of *Lecture Notes in Computer Science*, pages 380–389. Springer-Verlag, 2003.
11. J. Herbst. A Machine Learning Approach to Workflow Management. In *Proceedings 11th European Conference on Machine Learning*, volume 1810 of *Lecture Notes in Computer Science*, pages 183–194. Springer-Verlag, Berlin, 2000.
12. IDS Scheer. ARIS Process Performance Manager (ARIS PPM). http://www.ids-scheer.com, 2002.

13. G. Keller, M. Nüttgens, and A.W. Scheer. Semantische Processmodellierung auf der Grundlage Ereignisgesteuerter Processketten (EPK). Veröffentlichungen des Instituts für Wirtschaftsinformatik, Heft 89 (in German), University of Saarland, Saarbrücken, 1992.
14. G. Keller and T. Teufel. *SAP R/3 Process Oriented Implementation.* Addison-Wesley, Reading MA, 1998.
15. A.K.A. de Medeiros, W.M.P. van der Aalst, and A.J.M.M. Weijters. Workflow Mining: Current Status and Future Directions. In R. Meersman, Z. Tari, and D.C. Schmidt, editors, *On The Move to Meaningful Internet Systems 2003: CoopIS, DOA, and ODBASE*, volume 2888 of *Lecture Notes in Computer Science*, pages 389–406. Springer-Verlag, Berlin, 2003.
16. M. zur Mühlen and M. Rosemann. Workflow-based Process Monitoring and Controlling - Technical and Organizational Issues. In R. Sprague, editor, *Proceedings of the 33rd Hawaii International Conference on System Science (HICSS-33)*, pages 1–10. IEEE Computer Society Press, Los Alamitos, California, 2000.
17. T. Murata. Petri Nets: Properties, Analysis and Applications. *Proceedings of the IEEE*, 77(4):541–580, April 1989.
18. M. Sayal, F. Casati, and M.C. Shan U. Dayal. Business Process Cockpit. In *Proceedings of 28th International Conference on Very Large Data Bases (VLDB'02)*, pages 880–883. Morgan Kaufmann, 2002.
19. A.W. Scheer. *Business Process Engineering, Reference Models for Industrial Enterprises.* Springer-Verlag, Berlin, 1994.
20. Staffware. Staffware Process Monitor (SPM). http://www.staffware.com, 2002.
21. A.J.M.M. Weijters and W.M.P. van der Aalst. Rediscovering Workflow Models from Event-Based Data using Little Thumb. *Integrated Computer-Aided Engineering*, 10(2):151–162, 2003.

A New XML Clustering for Structural Retrieval*

Jeong Hee Hwang and Keun Ho Ryu

Database Laboratory, Chungbuk National University, Korea
{jhhwang,khryu}@dblab.chungbuk.ac.kr

Abstract. XML becomes increasingly important in data exchange and information management. Starting point for retrieving the information and integrating the documents efficiently is clustering the documents that have similar structure. Thus, in this paper, we propose a new XML document clustering method based on similar structure. Our approach first extracts the representative structures of XML documents by sequential pattern mining. And then we cluster XML documents of similar structure using the clustering algorithm for transactional data, assuming that an XML document as a transaction and the frequent structure of documents as the items of the transaction. We also apply our technique to XML retrieval. Our experiments show the efficiency and good performance of the proposed clustering method.

Keywords: Document Clustering, XML Document, Sequential Pattern, Structural Similarity, Structural Retrieval

1 Introduction

XML(eXtensible Markup Language) is a standard for data representation and exchange on the Web, and we will find large XML document collection on the Web in the near future. Therefore, it has become crucial to address the question of how we can efficiently query and search XML documents. Meanwhile, the hierarchical structure of XML has a great influence on the information retrieval, the document management system, and data mining[1,2,3,4].

Since an XML document is represented as a tree structure, one can explore the relationship among XMLs using various tree matching algorithms[5,6]. A closely related problem is to find trees in a database that "match" a given pattern or query tree[7]. This type of retrieval often exploits various filters that eliminate unqualified data trees from consideration at an early stage of retrieval. The filters accelerate the retrieval process. Another approach to facilitating a search is to cluster XMLs into appropriate categories.

We propose a new XML clustering technique based on similar structure in this paper. We first extract the representative structures of frequent patterns including hierarchical structure information from XML documents by the sequential pattern mining method[8]. And then we perform the document clustering by considering both the CLOPE algorithm[9] and large items[10], assuming that an XML document as a transaction and the extracted frequent structures from documents as the items of the transaction. We also apply our method to structural retrieval of XML documents in order to verify the efficiency of proposed technique.

* This work was supported by University IT Research Center Project and ETRI in Korea.

P. Atzeni et al. (Eds.): ER 2004, LNCS 3288, pp. 377–387, 2004.

The remaining of the paper is organized as follows. Section 2 reviews the previous researches related to the structure of XML documents. Section 3 describes the method extracting the representative structures of XML documents. In section 4, we define our clustering criterion using large items, and we describe about updating the cluster, and section 5 explains how to apply our clustering method to XML retrieval. Section 6 shows the experiment results of clustering algorithm and the result of XML retrieval, section 7 concludes the paper.

2 Related Works

Recently, as XML documents with various structures are increasing, it is needed to study the method that classifies the similar structure documents and retrieves the documents [3,4].

[11] considered XML as a tree and analyzed the similarity among the documents by taking account of semantics. [12] referred the necessity to manage the increasing XML documents and proposed the clustering method about element tags and the text of XML documents using k-means algorithm.

In [3,4,13], they say that there are two kinds of structure mining technique for extracting the XML document structure; intra-structured mining for one document and inter-structured mining for various documents. But the concrete algorithm is not described.

[14] proposed the clustering method about the DTD based on the similarity of elements as the way to find out the mediate DTD to integrate DTDs. But it can just be applied to the DTDs with the same application domain. [15] concentrated on finding out the common structure of the tree, but not cosidering the document clustering. [16] grouped trees about the same pairs of labels occurring frequently, and then finds a subset of the frequent trees. But the multi relational tree structure can't be detected, because it is based on the label pairs. [17] proposed the method for clustering the XML documents using the bit map indexing, but it requires too much space for a large amount of documents.

In this paper, we use the CLOPE algorithm[9] adding the notion of large items for document clustering. The CLOPE algorithm uses only the rate of the common items, not considering individual items in a cluster. Therefore, it can have some problems that the similarity between clusters may be higher, and it mayn't control the number of clusters. In order to address this problem, we add the notion of large items about a cluster to CLOPE algorithm.

3 Extracting the Representative Structure of XML Documents

XML document has sequential and hierarchical structure of elements. Therefore, the orders of the elements and the elements themselves have the feature that can distinguish the XML documents [11,13]. Thus, we use the sequential pattern mining that considers both the frequency and the order of elements.

3.1 Element Path Sequences

We first extract representative structures of each document based on the path from the root to the element about elements having content value. Figure 1 is an example XML document to show how to find out the representative structures from the documents.

```
<bookinventory>
  <book>
    <title>Great Expectations</title>
    <author>
      <name>Charles Dickens</name>
      <born>1812</born>
      <died>1879</died>
      <nationality>English</nationality>
    </author>
    <count>10 </count>
  </book>
</bookinventory>
```

Fig. 1. An XML document

element	rename	element	rename
bookinventory	a	name	d1
book	b	born	d2
title	c1	died	d3
author	c2	nationality	d4
count	c3		

Fig. 2. Element mapping table

We rename each element with alphabet to easily distinguish elements using the element mapping table, as shown in Figure 2. Based on the renamed element by Figure 2, the element paths having contents value is represented as Figure 3, in which element paths are regarded as the sequences and each element contained in sequence is considered to be the items. And then we find out the frequent sequence structures that satisfy the given minimum support by the sequential pattern mining algorithm.

X_id	X_path
1	a/b/c1
2	a/b/c2/d1
3	a/b/c2/d2
4	a/b/c2/d3
5	a/b/c2/d4
6	a/b/c3

Fig. 3. Element path sequences

3.2 The Sequential Pattern Algorithm to Extract The Frequent Structure

To extract the frequent structures, we use the PrefixSpan algorithm[8] about Figure 3. To do this, we define the frequent structure minimum support as follows.

Definition 1 (Frequent Structure Minimum Support). Frequent structure minimum support is the least frequency that satisfies the rate of the frequent structure among the whole paths in a document, and the path sequences that satisfy this condition are the frequent structures. The formula of this is as follows.

FFMS = frequent structure rate * the number of path of the whole documents
(0 < frequent structure rate < 1)

If the frequent structure rate is 0.2, FFMS of sequence set of Figure 3 is 2 (0.2 * 6). And the element frequency of the length-1 satisfying the FFMS is a: 6, b: 6, c2: 4. Starting from this length-1 sequential pattern, we extract the frequent pattern structures using the projected DB(refer to [8] for the detail algorithm). According to this method, the maximal frequent structure in Figure 3 is <a/b/c2>, and this path is occurred at the rate of about 66%(4/6) to the whole document.

We also include the structures of length over the regular rate to the maximal frequent structure (e.g. the most frequent length 5 * 80% = the frequent structure length 4) to the representative structures as the input data for clustering. The reason is that it can avoid frequent structures missing, in case there are various subjects in a document.

4 Large Item Based Document Cluster

The frequent structures of each XML document are basic data for clustering. We assume the XML documents as a transaction, the frequent structures extracted from each document as the items of the transaction, and then we perform the document clustering using the notion of large items.

4.1 A New Clustering Criterion

The item set included all the transaction is defined as $I = \{i_1, i_2, .. i_n\}$, cluster set as $C = \{C_1, C_2 .., C_m\}$, and transaction set that represents the document as $T = \{t_1, t_2, t_3 .., t_k\}$. As a criterion to allocate a transaction to the appropriate cluster, we define the cluster allocation gain.

Definition 2 (Cluster Allocation Gain). The cluster allocation gain is the sum of the ratio of the total occurrences to the individual items in every cluster. The following equation expresses this.

$$Gain(C) = \frac{\sum_{i=1}^{m} G(Ci) \times |Ci(Tr)|}{\sum_{i=1}^{m} |Ci(Tr)|} = \frac{\sum_{i=1}^{m} \frac{T(Ci)}{W(Ci)^2} \times |Ci(Tr)|}{\sum_{i=1}^{m} |Ci(Tr)|} \quad (1)$$

where G is the occurrence rate(H) to individual item(W) in a cluster, H = T (the total occurrence of the individual items) / W (the number of the individual items), $G = T/W^2$.

Gain is a criterion function for cluster allocation of the transaction, and the higher the rate of the common items, the more the cluster allocation gain. Therefore we allocate a transaction to the cluster to be the largest *Gain*.

However if we use only the rate of the common items, not considering the individual items like CLOPE, it causes some problems as follows.

Example 1. Assume that transaction t4 = {f, c} is to be inserted, under the condition of the cluster C1 = {a:3, b:3, c:1}, C2 = {d:3, e:1, c:3} including three transactions respectively. If t4 is allocated to C1 or C2, then *Gain* is $\frac{\frac{9}{4^2}\times 4 + \frac{7}{3^2}\times 3}{7} = 0.654$. Other while, if t4 is allocated to a new cluster, then *Gain* is $\frac{\frac{7}{3^2}\times 3 + \frac{7}{3^2}\times 3 + \frac{2}{2^2}\times 1}{7} = 0.738$. Thus, t4 is allocated a new cluster by Definition 2. As you see in this example, we can get the considerably higher allocation grain about a new cluster, because *Gain* about a new cluster equals W/W^2. Due to this, it causes the production of many clusters over the regular size, so that it may reduce cluster cohesion. In order to address this problem, we define the large items and the cluster participation as follows.

Definition 3 (Large Items). Item support of cluster Ci is defined as the number of the transactions including item i_j ($j <= n$) in the cluster Ci, about the minimum support determined by the user, θ ($0 < \theta <= 1$). If the number of the transactions including item i_j in cluster Ci is over the item support, Sup = θ * |Ci(Tr)|, the item i_j is the large item in the cluster Ci.

$$Ci(L)i_j = |Ci(Tr)i_{j \in I}| >= Sup$$

where |Ci(Tr)| is the number of the whole transactions in Ci, $|Ci(Tr)i_{j \in I}|$ is the number of the transactions including the item i_j in the cluster Ci.

Definition 4 (Cluster Participation). It is the ratio of the common items to the number of items of transaction t_k composed of the frequent structure and the large items in the cluster Cj. And it means the probability of transaction t_k to be assigned to cluster Cj. We represent it as followings.

$$P\_Allo(t_k \Rightarrow Cj) = \frac{|t_k| \cap Cj(L)}{t_k} \geq \omega_1 \tag{2}$$

$$(0 < \omega_1 < 1: \text{minimum participation})$$

$|t_k|$ is the number of the items of the transaction t_k. In example 1, if there is any cluster that satisfies the given minimum participation about insertion of t4, our approach does not produce a new cluster, but allocate t4 to the cluster with maximum participation. Therefore, cluster participation can control the number of clusters. When ω_1 is small, the production of the cluster is suppressed.

Definition 5 (Cluster Cohesion). The cluster cohesion(*Coh*(Ci)) is the ratio of the large items to the whole items T(Ci) in the cluster Ci. This is calculated by the following formula, and if it is near 1, it is the good quality cluster.

$$Coh(Ci) = \frac{Ci(L)}{T(Ci)} \tag{3}$$

Definition 6 (Inter-cluster Similarity). The inter-cluster similarity based on the large items is the rate of the common large items of the cluster Ci, Cj. We calculate the inter-cluster similarity by the following formula, and if it is near 0, it is the good clustering.

$$Sim(Ci,Cj) = \frac{L(Ci \cap Cj) \times \frac{|L(Ci \cap Cj)|}{|L(Ci + Cj)|}}{Ci(L) + Cj(L)} \tag{4}$$

where L(Ci∩Cj) is the number of common large items in the cluster Ci and Cj, |L(Ci∩Cj)| is the total occurrence number of the common large items, and |L(Ci+Cj)| is that of the large items of cluster Ci, Cj.

4.2 Cluster Allocation Using Difference Operation

Once a new document is inserted, we first extract the representative structures of the document by a method described in section 3. And then it can easily be allocated to the cluster of the largest *Gain* through calculating the difference operation about current *Gain* as follows.

Definition 7 (Difference Operation). The difference operation is the different *Gain* of the inserted transaction to the existing cluster. We use inserted difference (*diff_Gain*(Δ^+)).

$$\begin{aligned} & \textit{diff\_Gain}(\Delta^{+}) = \textit{New\_Gain}(\text{Ci}) - \textit{Old\_Gain}(\text{Ci}) \\ & = \frac{T'(Ci)}{W'(Ci)^{2}} \times (|\,Ci\,(Tr\,)\,| + 1) - \frac{T\,(Ci\,)}{W\,(Ci\,)^{2}} \times |\,Ci\,(Tr\,)\,| \end{aligned} \quad (5)$$

W' is the number of the individual items and T' is the total number of individual items when the transaction is inserted. We can compute the change value of the current *Gain* by (5).

We use difference operation, but it takes too much time to compute the *Gain* for all the clusters. Therefore, we reuse the cluster participation(Definition 4), used to control the production of new cluster, to fast predict the allocation probability, and compute the *diff_Gain* about the only clusters that satisfy the newly given cluster participation ω_2. Even though small ω_2 yields better clustering, it takes much time to perform clustering because the number of cluster to compute *diff_Gain* increases.

We allocate the transaction to the cluster that has the largest *diff_Gain*. The XML document clustering algorithm by difference operation is shown in Figure 4.

```
Insert transaction t

 while not end of the existing cluster and p_Allo(C)  >= ω2
                                                   // (ω2=0.2)
     find a cluster(Ci) maximizing diff_Gain(C);
     find a cluster(Cj) maximizing p_Allo(C);
     if diff_Gain((Ck)   > diff_Gain(Ci)      // new cluster Ck
        if p_Allo(Cj) >= ω1 //(ω1=0.5),an existing cluster Ci
           allocate t to an existing cluster Cj;
        else allocate t to an new cluster Ck;
     else allocate t to an existing cluster Ci;
```

Fig. 4. Similar structure-based XML document clustering algorithm using the difference operation

5 XML Retrieval Based on Clustering

The clustering of XML documents based on similar structure can be used as a preprocessing for structure retrieval of XML. The reason is that it reduces the space of retrieval into a similar cluster. Therefore we can obtain the retrieval result fast.

The XML retrieval based on the clustering is composed of three basic steps as follows.

1. Simplify query into simple structure by using the element mapping table.
2. Reduce the search space to the cluster of similar structure, finding the most similar cluster by comparing structure of the large item in each cluster with the query.
3. Display the ranked XML documents by computing the similarity between query and documents in the similar cluster.

It is necessary to compute the similarity for retrieving the XML document of similar structure. An XML is composed of elements with hierarchical structure and it is represented by edges of parent–child relation in the tree structure. Therefore, in order to compute the structural similarity between query tree and XML documents, we consider both edges and paths from the root node to the node currently considering.

Here, path means the structural feature of elements in an XML document. To do this, we formulate the computing measure, edge similarity and path similarity, as follows.

Definition 8 (Edge Similarity). Given an ordered labeled tree T and Query tree Q, edge similarity is defined by the ratio of the number of common edge to the total number of edge between T and Q. if there is an edge u→v and u'→v' in the T and Q respectively, and also u=u' and v=v', we say that u→v and u'→v' are matched. We can get the edge similarity by following formula.

$$EdgeSim(Q, T) = \frac{|E_Q \cap E_T|}{|E_Q \cup E_T|}$$

Example 2. Figure 5 denotes two XML document trees to show how to compute edge similarity.

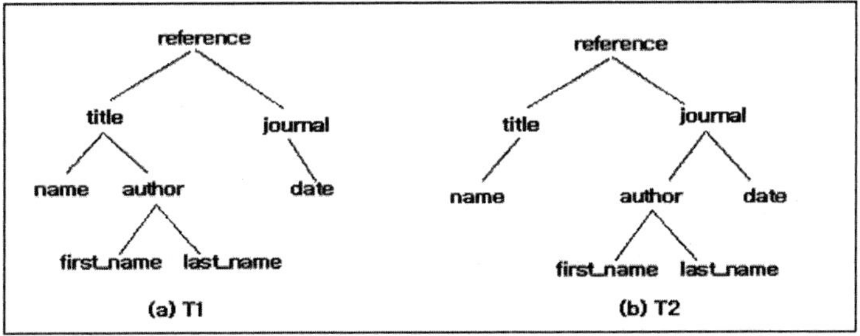

Fig. 5. Example of similar XML document trees

We can obtain the following edge sets in tree T1 and T2(the element name is replaced by the first alphabet).

$$E_{T1} = \{r \to t, r \to j, t \to n, t \to a, j \to d, a \to f, a \to l\}$$
$$E_{T2} = \{r \to t, r \to j, t \to n, j \to a, j \to d, a \to f, a \to l\}$$

So the edge similarity between T1 and T2 by definition 6 is computed as follows.

$$EdgeSim(T1, T2) = \frac{|E_{T1} \cap E_{T_2}|}{|E_{T_1} \cup E_{T_2}|} = \frac{6}{8}$$

Definition 9 (Path Similarity). Given an ordered labeled tree T and Query tree Q, a path is denoted by consecutive edge from the root node to the particular node with the different depth(i.e., $v_1 \to v_2$, $v_1 \to v_2 \to v_3$, $v_1 \to v_2 \to \ldots \to v_n$) and path similarity is defined by the ratio of the number of common path to the total number of path between T and Q. if there are paths $v_1 \to v_2 \to v_3$ and $v_1' \to v_2' \to v_3'$ in the T and Q respectively, and also $v_1 = v_1'$, $v_2 = v_2'$, and $v_3 = v_3'$, we say that $v_1 \to v_2 \to v_3$ and $v_1' \to v_2' \to v_3'$ are matched. We can get the path similarity by following formula.

$$PathSim(Q, T) = \frac{Max_{com} |P_Q \cap P_T|}{Max_{path} |P_Q, P_T|}$$

where $Max_{path}|P_Q, P_T|$ is the largest path length among paths in the T, Q and $Max_{path}|P_Q \cap P_T|$ is the largest common path length in the T, Q.

We can obtain the following path sets in tree T1, T2 in Figure 5.

$$PathSim(\mathrm{T1, T2}) = \frac{Max_{com} \mid P_{T_1} \cap P_{T_2} \mid}{Max_{path} \mid P_{T_1}, P_{T_2} \mid} = \frac{3}{4}$$

According to above definition, the formula for computing similarity between Q and T that considers both edge similarity and path similarity is defined as following.

$$Sim(\mathrm{Q,T}) = \alpha * EdgeSim(\mathrm{Q, T}) + \beta * PathSim(\mathrm{Q, T}) \quad (\alpha + \beta = 1, \alpha \geq 0, \beta \geq 0) \tag{6}$$

where $\alpha > \beta$ gives more emphasis to the edge similarity, and $\alpha < \beta$ gives more emphasis to the path similarity, by default $\alpha = 0.5$, $\beta = 0.5$.

Therefore, the similarity of tree T1 and T2 by equation (6) in Figure 5 is (0.5*6/8 + 0.5*3/4 = 0.75).

We can estimate the degree of structural matching among trees by similarity measure considering both edge similarity and path similarity, and if it is near 1, it means that the similarity is large.

When detecting the most similar cluster by comparing the representative structure of clusters with the given query tree Q, we compute the similarity between the structures of large items in each cluster and query tree Q by equation (6). After that, we calculate similarity between XML documents in the detected cluster and the given query tree Q in the same manner, and the search result is displayed to user, with the XML document list close to the query according to ranked similarity.

6 Experiments and Implementation

In this section, we evaluate the efficiency of the proposed clustering method and show the result of XML retrieval based on the method.

6.1 The Clustering Experiments

For our performance analysis, we have conducted some experiments, comparing our method XML_C with CLOPE. The used data were total 400 XML documents, selected from 8 topics (i.e., book, club, play, auction, company, department, actor, movies), taken from the Wisconsin's XML data bank [18]. We first extracted the representative structures of each document by the frequent structure rate 20% to the whole documents. The average length and number of the frequent structures extracted about a document are 5.4 and 4.9 respectively.

And we performed clustering, including the frequent structures of length over 80% of the maximal frequent structure length without redundancy.

The comparison about the performance time according to the number of the documents is shown in Figure 6.

In Figure 6, we can see that the CLOPE takes more time than the XML_C in average time. Examining Figure 6 more closely, we notice that XML_C takes more time even though the difference is little in the first stage of experiment. This means that it requires more time to construct the large items of each cluster. But, as the documents size increases, XML_C by the cluster participation using the notion of the large items comes into effect on the performance in contrast to CLOPE.

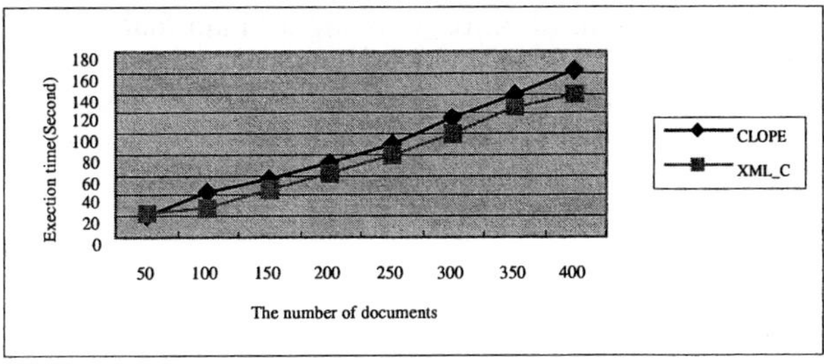

Fig. 6. Execution time

We experiment how many documents are included in the cluster except outlier, which is related to the number of the produced cluster. The result of this experiment is shown in Figure 7.

The number of cluster by CLOPE is averagely 1.3 times larger than that of XML_C. It means that CLOPE produces clusters over the regular size that contain the small number of documents than XML_C because it considers only the common rate of the items in the cluster, while we consider both the rate of common items and individual item using the notion of large items.

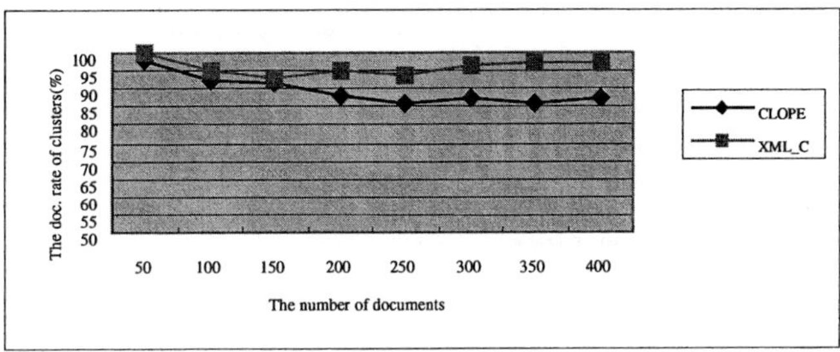

Fig. 7. The document rate of clustering

We also experiment the cluster cohesion and the inter-cluster similarity, about the total 400 documents. In order to compare with CLOPE, we extract the large items based on support from the clustering results, after running CLOPE. The result of the cluster cohesion and the inter-cluster similarity according to the minimum support is shown together in Figure 8.

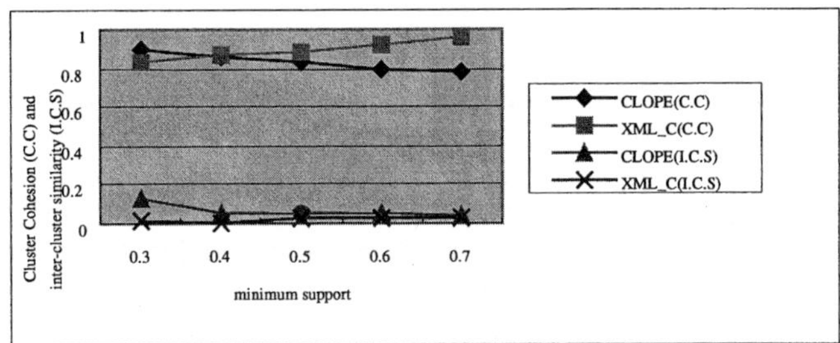

Fig. 8. Cluster cohesion and inter-cluster similarity

It is found that the cohesion of XML_C is higher than that of CLOPE, and inter-cluster similarity is lower than that of CLOPE, as can be easily noted in Figure 8. Therefore these experimental results also show that XML_C produces the better quality clusters than CLOPE. This is because our method considers not only the rate of common items but also the rate of individual item in a cluster.

6.2 Implementation

To retrieve XML document, we have implemented the user interface in which user can input at most three elements of ordered hierarchical structure in the left part of window. Figure 9 shows search result of the ranked similar structured XML documents about query 'book/title' in the right window. And also the contents of XML document selected by user are displayed under right corner of window.

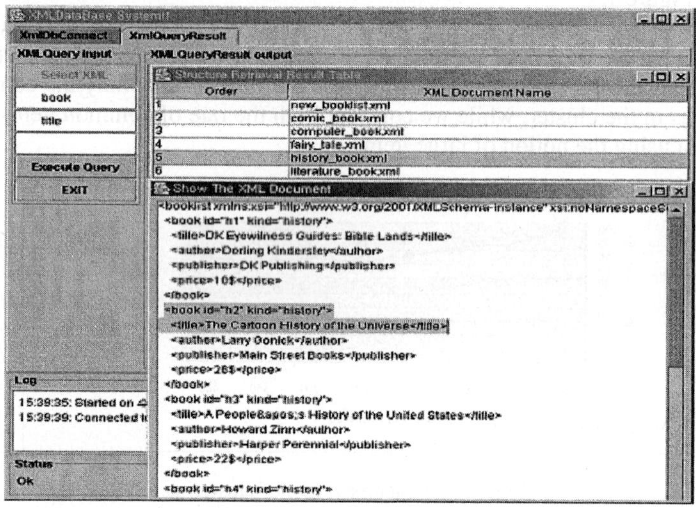

Fig. 9. A query and search result for retrieving XML documents

In summary, the clustering of XML documents based on similar structure is efficient to search XML structure fast, and also it is effective in classifying XML document by the structure pattern in the large XML database.

7 Conclusions

In this paper we proposed a new similar structured based XML document clustering method that is quite different from the existing method. We first extracted the representative structures of XML documents using the sequential pattern mining, which focused on element paths of including hierarchal element information in the XML document. And then we performed clustering based on similar structure using notion of large items to improve cluster quality and performance, assuming that an XML document as a transaction and the extracted frequent structures from documents as the items of the transaction. Our experiments showed that our approach could get the higher cluster cohesion and the lower inter-cluster similarity, taking less time to perform than CLOPE. We also showed the effectiveness of our approach, applying into XML retrieval which is performed by computing similarity considering edge similarity and path similarity between XML documents and query tree. Therefore, our method is efficiently applicable to XML document management and classification in large size XML documents.

References

1. P. Kotasek and J. Zendulka. *An XML Framework Proposal for Knowledge Discovery in Database*. 4th European Conference on Principles and Practice Knowledge Discovery in Databases, 2000.
2. K. Wang and H. Liu. *Discovery Typical Structures of Documents: A Road Map Approach.* Prof. of the ACM SIGIR, 1998.
3. J. Widom. *Data Management for XML: Research Directions.* IEEE Computer Society Technical Commitee on Data Engineering, 1999.
4. R. Nayak, R. Witt, and A. Tonev. *Data Mining and XML Documents.* International Conference on Internet Computing, 2002.
5. D. Shasha, J. T. L. Wang, H. Shan, and K. Zhang. *TreeGrep: Approximate Searching in Unordered Trees.* Proc. of the 14th International Conference on Scientific and Statistical Database Management, 2002.
6. R. Cole, R. Hariharan, and P. Indyk. *Tree Pattern Matching and Subset Matching in Deterministic $O(nlog^3m)$ Time.* Prof. of the 10th Annual ACM-SIAM symposium on discrete algorithms, 1999.
7. J. T. Wang, D. Shasha, and G. J. S. Chang. *Structural Matching and Discovery in Document Databases.* International Conference ACM SIGMOD on Management of Data, 1997.
8. J. Pei, J. Han, B. M. Asi, and H. Pinto. *PrefixSpan: Mining Sequential Pattern Efficiently by Prefix-Projected Pattern Growth.* International Conference Data Engineering(ICDE), 2001.
9. Y. Yang, X. Guan, and J. You. *CLOPE: A Fast and Effective Clustering Algorithm for Transaction Data.* Proc. of the 8th ACM SIGKDD International Conference on Knowledge Discovery and Data Mining, 2002.
10. K. Wang and C. Xu. *Clustering Transactions Using Large Items.* Proc. of ACM CIKM-99, 1999.
11. J. W. Lee, K. Lee, and W. Kim. *Preparation for Semantics-Based XML Mining.* IEEE International Conference on Data Mining(ICDM), 2001.
12. A.Doucet, and H. A. Myka. *Naive Clustering of a Large XML Document Collection.* Proc. of the 1st INEX, Germany, 2002.
13. T. Asai, K. Abe, S. Kawasoe, H. Arimura, and H. Sakamoto. *Efficient Substructure Discovery from Large Semi-structured Data.* Proc. of the Second SIAM International Conference on Data Mining, 2002.
14. M. L. Lee, L. H. Yang, W. Hsu, and X. Yang. *XClust: Clustering XML Schemas for Effective Integration.* Proc. 11th ACM International Conference on Information and Knowledge Management, 2002.
15. M. Zaki. *Efficiently Mining Frequent Tree in a Forest.* 6th ACM SIGKDD International Conference, 2002.
16. A. Termier, M. C. Rouster, and M. Sebag. *TreeFinder: A First Step towards XML Data Mining.* IEEE International Conference on Data Mining (ICDM), 2002.
17. J. Yoon, V. Raghavan, and V. Chakilam. *BitCube: Clustering and Statistical Analysis for XML Documents.* Proc. of the 13th International Conference on Scientific and Statistical Database Management, 2001.
18. NIAGARA query engine. *http://www.cs.wisc.edu/niagara/data.html.*

Link Patterns for Modeling Information Grids and P2P Networks

Christopher Popfinger, Cristian Pérez de Laborda, and Stefan Conrad

Institute of Computer Science
Heinrich-Heine-Universität Düsseldorf
D-40225 Düsseldorf, Germany
{popfinger,perezdel,conrad}@cs.uni-duesseldorf.de

Abstract. Collaborative work requires, more than ever, access to data located on multiple autonomous and heterogeneous data sources. The development of these novel information platforms, referred to as information or data grids, and the evolving databases based on P2P concepts, need appropriate modeling and description mechanisms. In this paper we propose the Link Pattern Catalog as a modeling guideline for recurring problems appearing during the design or description of information grids and P2P networks. For this purpose we introduce the Data Link Modeling Language, a language for describing and modeling virtually any kind of data flows in information sharing environments.

1 Introduction

With the rise of filesharing systems like Napster or Gnutella the database community started to seriously adopt the idea of P2P systems to the formerly known loosely coupled databases. While the original systems were only designed to share simple files among a huge amount of peers, we are not restricted to these data sources any more. New developments allow peers to share virtually any data, no matter if it is originated from a relational, object-oriented, or XML database. In fact, the data may still come from ordinary flat files.

Apparently we have to deal with a very heterogeneous environment of data sources sharing data, referred to as an information or data grid [4]. If we allow participants to join or leave information grids at any time (e.g. using P2P concepts [3]), we must take a constantly changing constellation of peers into account. Any information grid built up by these peers can either evolve dynamically or be planned beforehand. In both cases we need a concept in order to describe and understand the interactions among the peers involved. Having such a mechanism, we could not only detect single data exchanges, but even model and optimize complex data flows of the entire system.

In this paper we adopt commonly used methods for designing data exchanges among peers as *Link Patterns*, suitable especially for information grids and P2P networks. Analogous to the intention of the Design Pattern Catalog used for object-oriented software development [8] we want to provide modeling guidelines for engineers and database designers, engaged in understanding, remodeling, or

P. Atzeni et al. (Eds.): ER 2004, LNCS 3288, pp. 388–401, 2004.

building up an information grid. Thus information grid architects are provided with a common vocabulary for design and communication purposes.

Up to now data flows in information grids were designed without having a formal background leading to individual solutions for a specific problem. These were only known to a circlet of developers involved into that project. Other designers, engaged with a similar problem would never get in contact with these results and thus make the same mistakes again. Different modeling techniques make it difficult to exchange successfully implemented solutions.

Link Patterns do not claim to introduce novel techniques for sharing, accessing, or processing data in shared environments, but a framework for being able to understand, describe, and model their data flows. They provide a description of basic interactions between data sources and operations on the data exchanged, resulting in a catalog of reusable conceptual units.

A developer may choose Link Patterns to model and describe complex data flows, to identify a single point of failure, or to avoid or consciously insert redundant data exchanges. The composition of Link Patterns is an essential feature of our design method. It gives us the possibility to represent a structured visualization not only of single data linkages, but of the entire information platform.

The remainder of this paper is organized as follows. In section 2 we introduce DLML, a language for modeling data flows, followed by a structural description of the Link Patterns in section 3. Section 4 specifies the Link Pattern Catalog, followed by an example. Section 6 catches up some related work and section 7 concludes.

2 The Data Link Modeling Language (DLML)

2.1 Introduction

The Data Link Modeling Language (DLML) is based on the *Unified Modeling Language* (UML) [8] notation, but slightly modifies existing components, adds additional elements, and thus extends its functionality. It is a language for modeling, visualizing, and optimizing virtually any kind of data flows in information sharing environments.

Modeling: DLML is a language, suitable for modeling, planning, and re-engineering data flows in information sharing environments, e.g. information grids, systematically. A Data Link Model built up using this language reflects the logical and not the physical structure of the entire system. It enables the developer to specify the properties and the behavior of existing and novel systems, in order to describe and understand their basic functionalities.

Visualizing: Visualizing data flows is an important assistance in understanding the structure and behavior of an information platform. The impact of ER [13] and UML has proven, that a system is easier to grasp and less error-prone, if a graphical visualization technique is provided, which uses a well-defined set of graphical symbols, understood by a broad community. Especially within the analysis of systems with distributed information, it is favorable to have a method, suitable for drawing up a map of relationships between the participating peers, in order to depict global data flows.

Optimizing: Besides the modeling and visualization of an information sharing environment, DLML can be useful to optimize the whole distributed data management. Redundant data flows and data stocks can systematically be detected and removed, leading to a higher performance of the entire system. Of course, redundancy may explicitly be wanted, in order to achieve a higher fail-safety or a faster access to the data.

Due to the characteristics mentioned above, the Data Link Modeling Language is especially suitable for visualizing data flows in distributed information grids. It may furthermore be employed to model data management in enterprise information systems, data integration and migration scenarios, or data warehouses, i.e. wherever data has to be accessed across multiple different data sources.

2.2 Components

Since DLML is based on UML, its diagrams are constructed in an analogous manner, using a well-defined set of building blocks according to specific rules. The following components may be used in DLML (Fig. 1) to build up a Data Link Model:

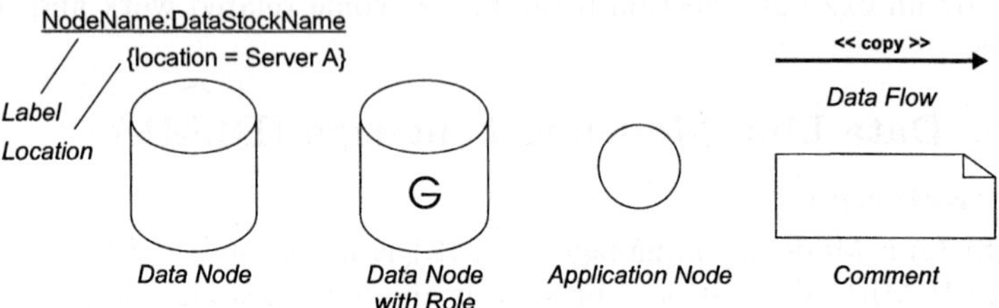

Fig. 1. DLML Components

Nodes: Nodes are data sources, data targets, or applications, usually involved in a data exchange process. They may either be isolated or connected through at least one *data flow*. A data source may be a database (e.g. relational), a flat file (e.g. XML), or something similar, offering data, whereas a data target receives data and stores it locally. An application is a software unit, which accesses or generates data, without maintaining an own physical data stock. Physical data stocks are represented in DLML by *Data Nodes*, applications by *Application Nodes*.

Label: Each node can have a label. It consists of generally two parts separated by a colon: the *node name* and the *data stock name* or *application name* respectively. The data stock name identifies the combination of data and schema information stored at this node. If this data is replicated as an exact and complete copy to another node, the data target has to use the same data stock name. The application is identified by the application name. Analogous to the data stock name, any further instances of the same application have the same application name. In both cases we use the node name to distinguish nodes with the same data stock or application name. Otherwise the node name is optional.

Location: The optional location tagged value specifies the physical location of the node. It either specifies an IP address, a server name, or a room number, helping the developer to locate the Data or Application Node.

Role: A node providing a certain functionality on the data processed, may have a functional role (e.g. filtering or integrating data). This role will usually be implemented as a kind of application, operating directly on the incoming or outgoing data. The name of the role or its abbreviation is placed directly inside the symbol of the node. This information is not only useful for increasing the readability of the model, but also for being able to identify complex relationships.

Data Flow: The data exchange between exactly one data source and one data target is called data flow. The arrow symbolizes the direction, in which data is being sent. A node may have multiple incoming and outgoing data flows. Optionally each data flow may be labeled concerning its behavior, i.e. if the data is being replicated (<<copy>>) to the data target or if it is just accessed (<<access>>). If data is being synchronized, both data flow arrows may be replaced by one single arrow with two arrowheads.

Comment: A comment may be attached to a component, in order to provide additional information about a node or a data flow. These explanations may concern a node's role, filter criteria, implementation hints, data flow properties, or further annotations important for the comprehension of the model.

2.3 Example

We now illustrate the usage of the Data Link Modeling Language with a simplified example. Consider a worldwide operating wholesaler, with an autonomous overseas branch. The headquarters is responsible for maintaining the product catalog (hq:products) with its price list, while the customers database (:customers) is administrated by the branch itself (Fig. 2).

The overseas branch is connected to the headquarters by a dial-up connection, not sufficient for accessing the database permanently. For this reason, the product catalog is replicated to the branch twice a day (branch:products), where the data may be accessed by the local employees. The branch management uses a special application (:managementApp) to access both data stocks in order to generate the annual report for the headquarters.

3 Link Patterns

In order to be able to provide a catalog of essential Link Patterns it is necessary to understand what a Link Pattern is. Therefore we present the elements a Link

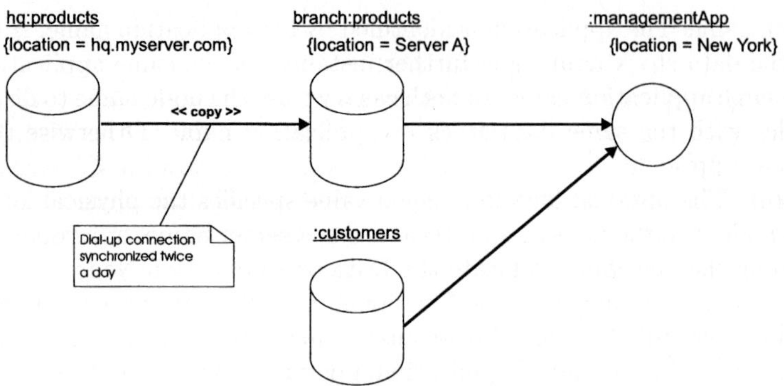

Fig. 2. DLML Example

Pattern is composed of, including its name, its classification, or its description. For graphical representation we use the Data Link Modeling Language, specified above.

3.1 Elements of a Link Pattern

In this section we present the description of the Link Pattern structure. It is based on the Design Pattern Catalog of Gamma et al. [8], which has reached great acceptance within the software engineering community. Thus a developer is able to quickly understand and adopt the main concept of each Link Pattern for his own purposes. Each Link Pattern is described by the following elements:

Name: The name of a Link Pattern is its unique identifier. It has to give a first hint on how the pattern should be used. The name is substantial for the communication between or within groups of developers.

Classification: A Link Pattern is classified according to the categories described in section 3.2. The classification organizes existing and future patterns depending on their functionality.

Motivation: Motivating the usage of the pattern is very important, since it explains the developer figuratively the basic functionality. This is done using a small scenario, which illustrates a possible application field of the pattern. Therewith the developer is able to understand and follow the more detailed descriptions in the further sections.

Graphical Representation: The most important part of the pattern description is the graphical representation. It is a DLML diagram and describes the composition and intention of the pattern in an intuitive way. The developer is advised to adopt this representation, wherever he has identified the related functionality in his own information grid model.

Description: The composition of the Link Pattern is described in-depth in this section, including every single component and its detailed functionality. The explanation of the local operations on each node and data flows between the components involved, points up the intended functionality of the whole pattern described. This description shall give the user both, a guidance through the identification process and instructions for its proper usage.

Challenges: Besides the general instructions given in the prior section, this section shall give hints for sources of error in the implementation process of this pattern. The developer shall get ideas, of how to identify and avoid pitfalls, arising in a certain context (e.g. interaction with other Link Patterns).

3.2 Classification

A classification of the Link Pattern Catalog shall provide an organized access to all Link Patterns presented. Patterns situated in the same class have similar structural or functional properties, depending on the complexity of their implementation. Although a categorization of a very limited number of patterns may seem superfluous, we have decided to include this into our Link Pattern Catalog, since it shall help developers to allocate and evaluate the pattern required. Furthermore it should stimulate the developer to find and rate novel patterns, not yet included in the catalog.

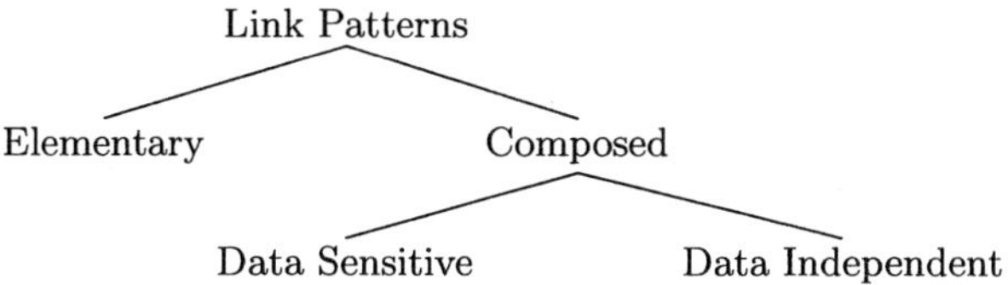

Fig. 3. Link Pattern Catalog Classification

Figure 3 depicts the classification of our Link Pattern Catalog we have chosen. The patterns presented can be divided into two main categories, *Elementary Link Patterns* and *Composed Link Patterns.* In fact this classification is not completed, but shall provide a starting point for further extension.

Elementary Link Pattern: An Elementary Link Pattern is the smallest unit for building up an information grid model. It consists of exclusively one single node and at least one data flow connected to it. Each Data Link Model is composed of several Elementary Link Patterns, linked together with data flows in an appropriate way. Please note, that a single Elementary Link Pattern is not yet a reasonable Data Link Model, since any data flow must have at least one node offering data and one node receiving data.
Elementary Link Patterns are easy to understand and easy to implement, since they concern only a single node, a small set of data flows, and do not include basically any data processing logic. It must be pointed out, that the Elementary Link Patterns consist only of two main patterns, the *Basic Data Node* and the *Basic Application Node*, and its derivatives (e.g. Publisher and Generator, discussed in section 4).

Composed Link Pattern: Composed Link Patterns are built up by combining at least two Elementary Link patterns in a specific way, in order to realize a particular functionality. A Composed Link Pattern may hereby be composed out of both, Elementary or other Composed Link Patterns. A pattern has to represent a prototype or solution for a recurring sort of problem. Please keep in mind, that an arbitrary combination of different patterns will not automatically lead to a reasonable Composed Link Pattern.
In contrast to the Elementary Link Patterns, we have to deal in this context with a more complex kind of patterns. They do not only include more nodes, but may even represent a quite sophisticated way of linking them. Besides, each node may additionally process the data received or sent. The fact, that it may act differently depending on the data involved, is an essential property of Composed Link Patterns and justifies the creation of two subclasses:

Data Sensitive Link Pattern: As soon as a node included in a Composed Link Pattern acts depending on the data it processes, the entire pattern is called a Data Sensitive Link Pattern. This data processing logic implemented on such a node may depend on and be applied to incoming and/or outgoing data. The operations of this application can either create, alter, or filter data.

Data Independent Link Pattern: Any Composed Link Pattern, not classified as Data Sensitive, belongs to this class. In contrast to the patterns described above, data is not being modified, but sent or received as is. A rather crucial topic is the topology of the nodes and data flows involved, which is most relevant for the creation and functionality of this kind of patterns.

3.3 Usage

This section describes how Link Patterns can be useful to develop, maintain, analyze, or optimize both, straightforward and complex data flows in information grids. There are basically two methods, how Link Patterns can improve the work of developers:

Analyzing existing systems: Many existing information grids have arisen during the years without being planned centrally or consistently. Even if they were planned initially, they usually tend to spread in an uncontrolled way. In such an environment it is vital to have supporting tools, helping to understand and later optimize an existing system.
First of all a map or model of the existing system has to be created, e.g. with DLML presented in section 2. Afterwards we examine successively smaller parts of the model, in order to match them to existing Link Patterns of the Catalog. As a result we get a revised model containing basic information on the composition and functionality of subsystems, including their data processing and data flows. With this information in mind, we are now able to derive information on data flows and interaction of nodes inside the Data

Link Model. This enables us to perform optimizations like detecting and eliminating vulnerabilities or handling redundancies.
Link Patterns may thus not replace human expertise for understanding existing information grids, but give support in the process of recognizing global data flows and therewith interpret the purpose of the entire system.

Composing new models: As already mentioned a Link Pattern may not only improve the process of understanding an existing information grid, but is also a support for modeling new systems. An information grid architect needs to have a clear idea of what the system should do. Depending on the data sources available, the local requirements on the nodes, and the results he wants to achieve, he can combine nodes and data flows, according to Link Patterns, until the entire system realizes the intended functionality. Link Patterns hereby guarantee a common language, understood by other developers, not yet involved in the modeling. Each developer is thus able to quickly get a general idea of the system modeled at any time. Furthermore they accelerate the development process, since they provide well tried solutions for recurring problems, leading to a performant system of high quality.

4 Link Pattern Catalog

In this section we finally give an introduction into the Link Pattern Catalog. This includes a graphical overview over the main Link Patterns in DLML, as well as a detailed description of selected patterns. As mentioned beforehand the Link Patterns can be classified according to the classification presented in section 3.2. Since any Composed Link Pattern either belongs to the Data Sensitive or to the Data Independent Link Patterns, we organize the catalog as follows:

Elementary Link Patterns

The Elementary Link Patterns are the basic building blocks of a Data Link Model. They consist of the two basic patterns, described below, and its derivatives. All Elementary Link Patterns are depicted in Figure 4.

Basic Data Node

Classification: Elementary Link Pattern

Motivation: This pattern is one of the basic building blocks of a Data Link Model. Each incoming or outgoing data flow of a Data Node is modeled using this Link Pattern.

Graphical Representation: See Figure 4

Description: A Basic Data Node is a DLML Data Node, which receives data through incoming data flows, stores it locally, and simultaneously propagates data, held in its own data stock. If a Basic Data Node does only have outgoing or incoming data flows, it applies the *Publisher Pattern* or the *Subscriber Pattern* respectively. If it does neither have any incoming, nor any outgoing data flows, the Data Node is called *isolated.*

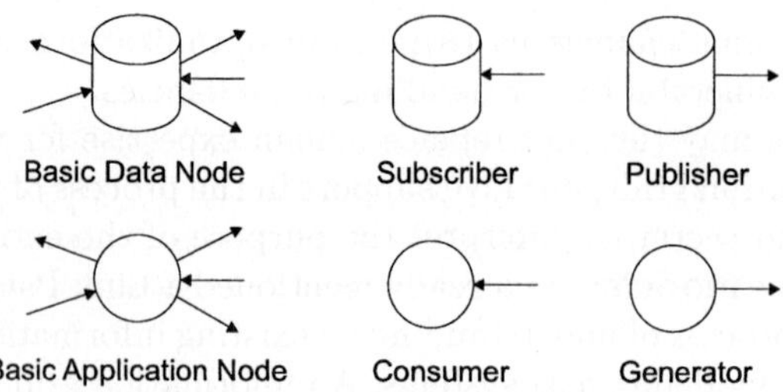

Fig. 4. Elementary Link Patterns

Challenges: One of the main challenges to take in this pattern is the proper coordination of incoming and outgoing data flows. At first all incoming data has to be stored permanently on the local data stock, without violating any constraints, before it may be propagated again to other nodes.

Basic Application Node

Classification: Elementary Link Pattern

Motivation: This pattern is one of the basic building blocks of a Data Link Model. All applications, relevant for a Data Link Model, are based on this pattern.

Graphical Representation: See Figure 4

Description: An application interacting with arbitrary Data or Application Nodes, is represented by this pattern. The application does not only receive, but also propagate data. If a Basic Application Node does only have outgoing or incoming data flows, it applies the *Generator Pattern* or the *Consumer Pattern* respectively. If it does neither have any incoming nor any outgoing data flows, the Application Node is called *isolated.*

Challenges: Propagated data can either be received or generated. All data manipulations on incoming data, which have to be propagated, have to be processed in real-time, without storing data locally.

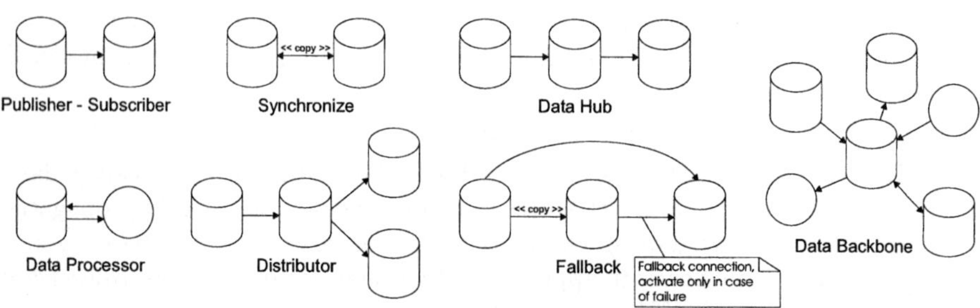

Fig. 5. Data Independent Link Patterns

Data Independent Link Patterns

The Data Independent Link Patterns belong to the Composed Link Patterns. These patterns describe a functionality, which only depends on their structure, i.e. the way nodes and data flows are combined. A graphical overview of the patterns in this class is given in Figure 5, of which the *Data Backbone* is described exemplarily.

Data Backbone

Classification: Data Independent Link Pattern

Motivation: A Data Backbone is used, wherever a centralization of data sharing or data access has to be realized. This is typically required, if data stocks are re-centralized, a central authority wants to keep track on all data flows, or data exchanges have to be established among multiple data stocks and applications.

Graphical Representation: See Figure 5

Description: The Data Backbone Pattern consists of several nodes, linked together in a specific way. A designated node, called Data Backbone, is either data source or data target for all data flows in this pattern. All nodes, including the Data Backbone itself, can be data stocks or applications. Data is always propagated from data sources to the Data Backbone, where it may be accessed or propagated once again to other target nodes. Direct data flows between nodes, which are not the Data Backbone, are avoided.

Challenges: Since the Data Backbone is involved in all data flows, it has a crucial position in this part of the information grid. Thus, a Data Backbone node has to provide a high quality of service, concerning disk space, network connection, and processing performance. If the quality of service required cannot be provided, the Data Backbone may easily become a bottleneck. Furthermore a breakdown of this node could lead to a collapse of the entire data sharing infrastructure, which makes it to a single point of failure.

Data Sensitive Link Patterns

Contrary to the Data Independent Link Patterns, the patterns described in this section are not only classified according to their structural properties, but particularly because of their data processing functionality. A graphical representation of these Data Sensitive Link Patterns can be found in Figure 6, while a detailed description is only given for the *Gatekeeper Pattern.*

Gatekeeper

Classification: Data Sensitive Link Pattern

Motivation: A Gatekeeper is used to control data flows according to specific rules (e.g. Access Control Lists), stored separately from the data processed. It is responsible for providing the target nodes with the accessible data required. The application of this pattern is not limited to data security matters. It may actually be applied to any node, which has to supply different target nodes with specific (e.g. manipulated or filtered) data flows.

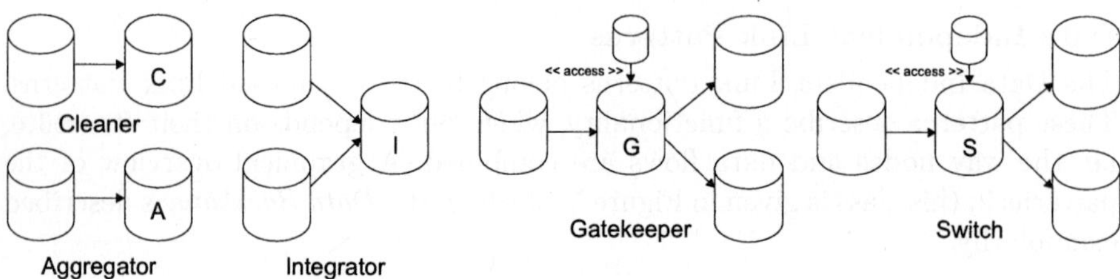

Fig. 6. Data Sensitive Link Patterns

Graphical Representation: See Figure 6

Description: A Gatekeeper is a designated node, which distributes data according to specific rules, eventually stored separately. Local or incoming data of a Gatekeeper is accessed by target nodes. Before this access can be admitted, the Gatekeeper has to check the permissions. Thus, corresponding to the rules processed, neither all data stored in the Gatekeeper, nor all data requested by the target nodes has to be transmitted.

Challenges: The rules and techniques, which are used by the Gatekeeper in order to secure access to the data, have to be robust and safe. The Gatekeeper needs a mechanism to identify and authenticate the source and target nodes (e.g. IP address, public key, username and password, or identifiers [11]), which may be stored in a separated data stock. Due to its vital position in the exchange process, this information has to be protected from unauthorized access. The Gatekeeper must be able to rely on the correctness, authenticity, and availability of the rules required.

5 Example

This section provides an example of how to model a new information grid of a worldwide operating company. The headquarters of the company are located in New York. It has additionally branches in Düsseldorf (head office of the European branches), Paris, Bangalore, and Hong Kong. Each branch maintains its own database containing sales figures, collected by local applications. For backup and subsequent data analysis, this data has to be replicated to the headquarters. Additionally, the Düsseldorf branch needs to be informed about the ongoing sales activities of the Paris branch. To simplify the centralized backup, the company has decided to forbid any data exchanges between the single branches.

The central component of this infrastructure is the backup system in New York. It collects the sales data from all branches, without integrating them. Additionally it provides the Düsseldorf branch with all the information required from Paris. Since the headquarters in New York want to analyze the entire data stock of the company, a data warehouse, based on the data of the backup system, is set up. Having a certain local autonomy, the data provided by the European branches and the remaining branches have some structural differences. For this reason, the data has to be integrated prior to the aggregation required for the data warehousing analysis.

Using the Link Patterns proposed in this paper, we are now able to model the enterprise information grid as depicted in Figure 7.

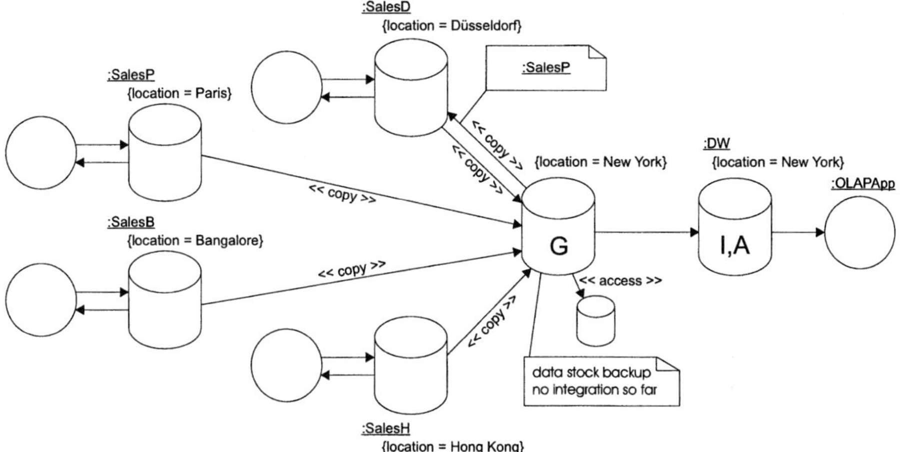

Fig. 7. Example using Link Patterns

The local applications, which maintain the local sales databases, are modeled using the *Data Processor*. This data is replicated to the backup system in New York, realized as a *Gatekeeper*. It thus controls the data flows from the branches to the data warehouse and to the Düsseldorf branch. It must be guaranteed, that the data targets get only their designated data, i.e. neither data from Bangalore, nor from Hong Kong is accessible for the European head office in Düsseldorf. The data warehouse is realized by a node, which integrates several data sources using common integration strategies (*Integrator Pattern*) and aggregates the data afterwards (*Aggregator Pattern*), in order to provide OLAP applications with a homogenous data stock.

Please keep in mind, that the Data Link Model presented in Figure 7 reflects the logical structure of the information platform, not the physical. This means, that the nodes of the model do not have to be located on different machines.

6 Related Work

Data Flow analysis and modeling has been a focus of researchers for decades. Earlier work concentrates mainly on data flows in computer architectures and software components (e.g. [15, 5]). Later on, data flows were also used for query processing and optimization in database systems. For instance, Teeuw and Blanken [14] compare control versus data flow mechanisms controlling the execution of database queries on parallel database systems.

Dennis and Misunas present in [6] a Basic Data-Flow language, which expresses graphically the data dependencies within a program. In this data flow graph model, instructions are represented by nodes and paths stand for data or control flows. Although this language was originally designed for software development, it may be seen as an early forerunner, in designing data flows among different data sources. A specialized data flow graph is introduced by Eich and Wells [7], which can be used for scheduling database queries within multiprocessor environments or databases distributed over a network [1]. Thus, both approaches apply data flow concepts to database processing.

The Link Patterns are tightly coupled to the Design Patterns of the object-oriented software design [8, 2] and Enterprise Application Integration (EAI) [10], since they represent prototypes or solutions for recurring problems. Contrary to these patterns, Link Patterns are not intended to solve recurring problems in software design or EAI, but to provide modeling and description guidelines for information grids, focusing exclusively on data flows.

As a possible application field of our Link Patterns we suggest modeling or visualizing information grids, i.e. heterogeneous environment of data sources sharing data, or modern information infrastructures, based on P2P concepts (e.g. [9] or [12]).

7 Conclusion and Future Work

In this paper we have presented Link Patterns as guidelines for modeling and describing data flows between nodes in information sharing environments. The Link Pattern Catalog consists of prototypes or solutions for recurring problems and therewith supports developers to model, describe, and understand complex information grids. Furthermore the Link Patterns provide a common vocabulary for design and communication purposes, enabling developers to exchange successfully implemented solutions.

Additionally we have introduced the Data Link Modeling Language (DLML) for modeling, visualizing, and optimizing data flows, especially suitable for information grids. This language based on UML consists of a well-defined set of building blocks, representing data nodes, application nodes and data flows between them. They can be combined according to specific rules, to build up the Data Link Model of an information sharing environment.

The concepts we have presented in this paper are ideal to generate a static model of data and application nodes with their corresponding data flows. In future work we have to consider dynamically changing and evolving environments, in which nodes constantly join or leave the grid. This may not only affect the Link Pattern Catalog, but also the Data Link Modeling Language. Furthermore the Catalog has to be enhanced, in order to include novel Link Patterns, not yet identified. The entire Link Pattern Catalog shall provide developers with an extensive reference guideline for modeling information sharing environments.

References

1. Lubomir Bic and Robert L. Hartmann. AGM: A Dataflow Database Machine. *ACM Transactions Database Systems*, 14(1):114–146, 1989.
2. Frank Buschmann, Regine Meunier, Hans Rohnert, Peter Sommerlad, and Michael Stal. *Pattern-Oriented Software Architecture: A System of Patterns.* John Wiley & Sons, Inc., 1996.
3. Mario Cannataro and Domenico Talia. Semantics and knowledge grids: Building the next-generation grid. *IEEE Intelligent Systems*, 19(1):56–63, 2004.
4. Ann Chervenak, Ian Foster, Carl Kesselman, Charles Salisbury, and Steven Tuecke. The Data Grid: Towards an Architecture for the Distributed Management and Analysis of Large Scientific Datasets. *Journal of Network and Computer Applications*, 23(3):187–200, 2000.
5. Lori A. Clarke, Andy Podgurski, Debra J. Richardson, and Steven J. Zeil. A Formal Evaluation of Data Flow Path Selection Criteria. *IEEE Trans. Softw. Eng.*, 15(11):1318–1332, 1989.
6. Jack B. Dennis and David P. Misunas. A Preliminary Architecture for a Basic Data-Flow Processor. In *Proceedings of the 2nd Annual Symposium on Computer Architecture*, pages 126–132. ACM Press, 1975.
7. Margaret H. Eich and David L. Wells. Database Concurrency Control Using Data Flow Graphs. *ACM Transactions Database Systems*, 13(2):197–227, 1988.
8. Erich Gamma, Richard Helm, Ralph Johnson, and John Vlissides. *Design Patterns: Elements od Reusable Object-Oriented Software.* Addison-Wesley Professional Computing Series. Addison-Wesley Publishing Company, New York, NY, 1995.
9. Alon Y. Halevy, Zachary G. Ives, Peter Mork, and Igor Tatarinov. Piazza: Data Management Infrastructure for Semantic Web Applications. In *Proceedings of the twelfth international conference on World Wide Web*, pages 556–567, Budapest, Hungary, 2003.
10. Gregor Hohpe and Bobby Woolf. *Enterprise Integration Patterns.* Addison-Wesley, 2003.
11. Cristian Pérez de Laborda and Stefan Conrad. A Semantic Web based Identification Mechanism for Databases. In *Proceedings of the 10th International Workshop on Knowledge Representation meets Databases (KRDB 2003), Hamburg, Germany, September 15-16, 2003*, volume 79 of *CEUR Workshop Proceedings*, pages 123–130. Technical University of Aachen (RWTH), 2003.
12. Cristian Pérez de Laborda, Christopher Popfinger, and Stefan Conrad. DÍGAME: A Vision of an Active Multidatabase with Push-based Schema and Data Propagation. In *Proceedings of the GI-/GMDS-Workshop on Enterprise Application Integration (EAI'04)*, volume 93 of *CEUR Workshop Proceedings*, 2004.
13. Peter Pin-Shan Chen. The entity-relationship model-toward a unified view of data. *ACM Transactions on Database Systems (TODS)*, 1(1):9–36, 1976.
14. Wouter B. Teeuw and Henk M. Blanken. Control versus Data Flow in Parallel Database Machines. *IEEE Transactions on Parallel and Distributed Systems*, (4):1265–1279, 1993.
15. Elizabeth Winey. Data Flow Architecture. In *Proceedings of the 16th annual Southeast regional conference*, pages 103–108. ACM Press, 1978.

Information Retrieval Aware Web Site Modelling and Generation

Keyla Ahnizeret, David Fernandes, João M.B. Cavalcanti, Edleno Silva de Moura, and Altigran S. da Silva

Department of Computer Science
Federal University of Amazonas, Brazil
{keyla,john,david,edleno,alti}@dcc.fua.br

Abstract. Design and maintenance of large corporate Web sites have become a challenging problem due to the continuing increase in their size and complexity. One particular feature present in the majority of this sort of Web sites is searching for information. However the solutions provided so far, which is based on the same techniques used for search in the open Web, have not provided a satisfactory performance to specific Web sites, often resulting in too much irrelevant content in a query answer. This paper proposes an approach to Web site modelling and generation of intrasite search engines, combining application modelling and information retrieval techniques. Our assumption is that giving search engines access to the information provided by conceptual representations of the Web site improves their performance and accuracy. We demonstrate our proposal by describing a Web site modelling language that represent both traditional modelling features and information retrieval aspects, as well as presenting experiments to evaluate the resulting intrasite search engine generated by our method.

1 Introduction

The continuing increase in size and complexity of Web sites has turned their design, construction and maintenance into a challenging problem. It often involves access to databases, complex cross referencing between information and sophisticated user interaction. This is particularly true for data-intensive Web sites, which are subjected to frequent content updates.

In the same way, finding the desired information among the pages of large and complex Web sites is an important problem. This is why one of the most popular and useful feature in any large data-intensive Web site is allowing to search its content by means of a search engine. We refer to this sort of information retrieval (IR) system as *intrasite* search engine. Such systems represent an alternative for the navigation-based access and currently is present in most corporate Web sites with many commercial products available. However the effectiveness of these systems is questionable. In fact, recent studies show that current intrasite search engines usually fail in satisfying user queries by providing too much irrelevant answers in the result [17, 33].

P. Atzeni et al. (Eds.): ER 2004, LNCS 3288, pp. 402–419, 2004.

The major problem faced by intrasite search engines is that there are few information available to reason about the relevance of a page to a user query. Intrasite search engines are usually developed using the same techniques applied by conventional global search engines, such as Google or Altavista. However, some important sources of evidence that determine the relevance of a page in a global search engine are usually not available in intrasite search. For instance, relevance metrics based on link analysis such as Pagerank [2] or HITS [24] make no contribution to improve the quality of the retrieval over small portions of the Web [18].

On the other hand, most corporate Web sites and Intranets are developed based on data models that define conceptual, logical and physical (i.e., navigational and presentational) features of the Web site prior to the generation of the pages. These data models are rich sources of information that we believe can be used as evidences to determine the relevance of Web pages given a user query. Although there are several research work on Web site modelling and automated generation [28, 26, 11, 6, 15], to our knowledge none of these methods provide means for using modelling-related information to cope with intrasite search engines. Similarly, no current intrasite search systems available use information retrieval models that are able to make use of the Web site modelling to provide better results.

In Web site design, a principle accepted by many authors is separation between information content, navigation structure and visualization [12, 28]. This idea promotes a better understanding of the data requirements (content), the underlying architecture of the site (navigation) and an appropriate user interface (visualization). Furthermore it makes maintenance tasks easier as each of those components can be managed separately [5, 30]. Recent technologies such as XML, XSL and style sheets also promote separation between content and visualization, encouraging and facilitating the development of methods for Web site construction based on those concepts.

Our proposal for Web site development is based on these ideas but innovates by modelling IR aspects of the application. Our assumption is by modelling specific information retrieval attributes of the information content of a Web site, it is possible to develop search engines that reach a significative improvement in the overall ranking quality. In the experiments presented here, our approach has given a 48% of improvement in the average precision when compared with traditional implementations of intrasite search engines. Our proposal merges an IR aware methodology and a model aware intrasite search engine development.

Throughout the paper, we use the terms Web site and Web site application interchangeably because our method can be applied to both of them. However, due to space limitation the description of forms and operations (dynamic pages), which are the main characteristic of Web site applications, is not described in detail here. We focus on modelling information retrieval aspects and generation of intrasite search engines.

The following section discusses some related work either on Web site application development or on information retrieval for individual Web sites. Section 3 presents our intermediate representation language and Section 4 discusses the details of generating search engines using the proposed approach. Section 5 presents experiments carried out based on an example Web site and search engine. Finally, Section 6 presents some final remarks.

2 Related Work

In this section we discuss some existing methods for development and maintenance of Web site applications as well as information retrieval work addressing intrasite or Intranet searching.

2.1 Web Site Development Methods

There is a general agreement amongst most recent work on some core concepts regarding Web Site Development, such as separation between information content, navigation structure and visualization; declarative specifications, by means of high-level conceptual data models or declarative languages; and automated or semi-automated generation of Web site by means of CASE tools.

The main differences between the proposals are in the emphasis given to particular aspects of the development process. Most work focus on modelling aspects such as Araneus [26], Strudel [11], OOHDM [28], OO-H [15] and WebML [6]. There are also work based on semantic descriptions such as OntoWebber [21] and SeAL [25]. Our approach is a data-driven approach, which focuses on the generation of different visualizations and on an associated search engine.

Where the work is driven by modelling most approaches are based on traditional conceptual data models, such as the entity-relationship model (ER) [8] and its extensions or object-oriented data models. In this category we can include Araneus, WebML, OO-H and OOHDM. WebML proposes a structural model compatible with the ER model, ODMG object-oriented data model and UML class diagrams. The OO-H method is based on an object-oriented model. OOHDM is also an object-oriented extension to HDM [13], a method for modelling hypermedia applications. Strudel models a Web site as graphs. OntoWebber and SEAL are based on DAML+OIL and RDF, respectively, which are used to define ontologies describing the application domain. Our approach can support different conceptual data models. We advocate the idea of using existing data models, provided the appropriate mapping procedures to our intermediate representation.

Although existing methods such as those discussed above are appropriate for modelling and creating Web sites, to our knowledge, the issue of information retrieval in Web sites is not addressed by any Web site development method. Our work is distinct by offering a framework for Web site modelling and construction including information retrieval aspects. This feature makes it possible to automatically generate a suitable search engine related to the Web site constructed.

2.2 Information Retrieval Approaches to Intrasite Searching

The problem of searching in small portions of the Web has been directly or indirectly addressed in several recent works [20, 10]. In general, there is an agreement that current techniques applied for traditional global Web search, such as anchor text information [10, 9], URL level [31] and link analysis [23, 14], have little contribution for the ranking quality when applied for small portions of the Web, which is the case of intrasite search. The reasons for that are multifold. For instance, anchor text and link analysis rely on citations made from pages to other pages. However, this is only effective due to the inherent diversity of the content generate by the collectivity of the global Web. Additionally, as pages of data-intensive sites are in most cases generated dynamically, URLs exhibits no level information. Thus, the URL level technique is not applicable.

Currently, several products have also been made available for intrasite search. Some examples of such products are the Cha-Cha intrasite search engine [7], the *Google Search Appliance*[1] and the *AltaVista Enterprise* search engine[2], to name a few. However, based on their available documentation, these products do not consider any underlying Web site modelling as a source of evidence for computing their search results. In fact, no considerations are made regarding possible specific requirements of intrasite search. Google Search Appliance, for instance, is said to "use the same technology that powers Google search engine into intranets and corporate Web sites". This may explain why the quality of results provided by most of the current intra sitesearch systems is close to the results obtained by the vector space model [27] (which is commonly used as the baseline model for information retrieval systems), while global search engines usually outperform by far this model.

A more recent work presented by Xue et. al. [33] has proposed an approach for improving the quality of results in intrasite search systems by mining users' access patterns. Their result has improved the precision in 16% for the top matches by constructing artificial links between the site Web pages and applying a variation of Pagerank to compute the importance of each page in the Web site. This idea is completely orthogonal to what we present here, and the two techniques can even be use in a complementary way to improve the quality of the results provided by the intrasite search systems.

3 Modelling Information Retrieval Aware Web Sites

Systematic approaches can bring many benefits to Web site construction, making development more methodical and maintenance less time consuming. One way to tackle this problem is by providing a high-level description of a Web site application independent from any particular implementation. This allows the designer to concentrate on the application description rather than on the mechanics for producing the Web site.

[1] http://www.google.com/appliance/

[2] http://www.searchtools.com/tools/altavista.html

The proposed approach begins with a high level description of an application. For this task several existing data models such as the entity-relationship model [8] and its extensions or UML class diagrams can be used. From the application description an intermediate representation is (semi-)automatically derived. Depending on the data model used different mapping procedures must be defined in order to generate the intermediate representation. In [4] mapping rules for transforming ER diagrams into a logic-based Web site representation are proposed.

In this paper we focus on the intermediate representation and the further steps to create Web applications. We assume that modelling and an appropriate mapping procedure from the data model concepts to our intermediate representation language has already been performed. Conceptual modelling using known data models and mapping procedures to intermediate representation is a common approach used by most techniques described in Section 2

An intermediate representation is useful for several reasons. It provides a declarative specification of the application, still independent from the implementation language but closer to Web site constructs, such as pages and links, than the original data model [3]. It also provides flexibility for generating different views of a Web site, either in different target languages (HTML, XML, WML, etc) or different visualizations, for example by grouping pieces of information using different criteria or using different styles. Automated generation of Web sites is also easier with an intermediate representation which is combined with a visualization description in order to generate a corresponding Web site. Figure 1 illustrates this idea.

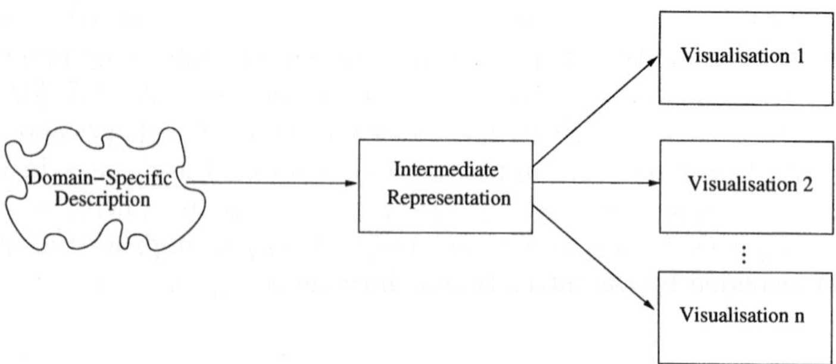

Fig. 1. General Architecure of Web site Generator

As discussed earlier our approach also follows the idea of separation between content, navigation and visualization. Information content refers to data to be displayed on the Web pages. Navigation structure defines the organization of the site and how items of information are related to each other. Finally, visualization concerns how the information will be presented on the Web pages comprising the site. Therefore, any notation for specifying such applications should provide mechanisms for representing those concepts. Another design principle is to define a Web site application in a declarative way. This facilitates automated generation of Web site applications.

In addition, we are also aiming at describing content relevance and other information retrieval aspects in order to produce a search engine associated to the Web site constructed. As a result the search engine will be able to use some "knowledge" about the Web site modelling, which gives more accurate results than other search engines within that particular Web site. Experiments with an example Web site and an associated search engine are discussed in Section 5. Following in this section we give the details of the proposed modelling language used to specify a Web site application according to our approach.

3.1 An IR-Aware Web Site Modelling Language

In our view, a Web site is a collection of *pieces of information* which are organised in *display units* related by *transitions*. These are the basic components of our modelling language which are detailed below.

Pieces of information are structured "chunks" of data having an identifier and a type. Its actual content value (instance) often is described from a database or other data source. The appropriate access mechanisms to retrieve values for a piece of information must also be defined. We have defined types for pieces of information. Types are useful for choosing an appropriate visualization style for each piece of information, such as lists and tables. Hence it is important to note that we do not propose a data type system as traditionally defined in programming languages. The types defined are *simple*, *list*, *tuple*, *table*, *form* and *searchInfo*.

The general format of a piece of information is $info(Id, Type, Datum)$ where Id is a unique identifier for the piece of information, $Type$ is one of the pre-defined types and $Datum$ denotes an actual value of the piece of information. Note that a piece of information might have several instances depending on the instances in the data source. Figure 2 depicts the specification of a simple type piece of information using XML schema.

Note that "Access" refers to the access method to the data source and "InfoStyle" refers to the visualization style for that piece of information. Other types of pieces of information are also defined in a similar fashion. A *list* denotes a piece of information composed of more than one data item of same simple type. A *tuple* refers to a list of related data items of different types and *table* is a list of tuples. *Form* refers to elements for data entry. This is a choice for facilitating the generation of pages with forms, since specific elements for constructing forms are usually offered by languages such as HTML and WML. Similarly, we have defined type *searchInfo* which refers to the input parameters to the intrasite search engine. A typical implementation is a text box associated with a submit button that triggers the execution of the query.

Display units are containers of pieces of information that will be presented to users in a visualization style defined by the designer. Display units can also be seen as classes of pages, where each page corresponds to an instance of a display unit. Therefore, a display unit might result in several pages of the same

```
<xs:element name="SimpleInfo" id="SimpleInfo">
    <xs:complexType>
        <xs:sequence>
            <xs:element name="Datum" id="Datum">
              <xs:complexType>
                <xs:simpleContent>
                    <xs:extension base="xs:string">
                      <xs:attribute ref="Comment"/>
                      <xs:attribute ref="Type"/>
                    <xs:extension>
                <xs:simpleContent>
              </xs:complexType>
            </xs:element>
            <xs:element ref="Detail" minOccurs="0"/>
        </xs:sequence>
        <xs:attribute ref="Id"/>
        <xs:attribute ref="Access"/>
        <xs:attribute ref="InfoStyle"/>
    </xs:complexType>
</xs:element>
```

Fig. 2. XML Schema for Simple Pieces of Information

type, having the same pieces of information and visualization style, each page presenting different instances of pieces of information. Formally a display unit is defined as *Display(Id, Info*$_1$*, Info*$_2$*, ..., Info*$_n$*)* where *Id* is a unique identifier and *Info*$_i$ corresponds to an identifier of a piece of information. Important attributes of display units related to information retrieval are *IRDisplayContentType* and *IRSignificance* which will be detailed in Section 3.2. A definition of display unit is presented in Figure 3.

Similar to display units *Transitions* define classes of links. A transition is defined by an origin and a target. Origin of a transition can be a piece of information or a display unit. The first defines links that have a data item as the link anchor, whereas the latter refers to simple navigation links, without related pieces of information. Given that both sorts of links and operations result in a display unit, the target is always a display unit. Operations are also considered as a type of transition, since it represents a link from a page to another via some computation. There are several issues related to representation and automated generation of operations which are left out here due to space restrictions. The definition of transitions is presented in Figure 4.

3.2 Modelling Information Retrieval Aspects

Our Web site modelling language supports the representation of information retrieval aspects by defining special attributes of pieces of information and display units. These attributes are related to measuring the importance information.

```
<xs:element name="Display" id="Display">
    <xs:complexType>
        <xs:sequence>
            <xs:element name="Info" id="Info" maxOccurs="unbounded">
              <xs:complexType>
                <xs:simpleContent>
                    <xs:extension base="xs:string">
                      <xs:attribute ref="Id"/>
                      <xs:attribute ref="IRSignificance"/>
                    <xs:extension>
                <xs:simpleContent>
              </xs:complexType>
            </xs:element>
        </xs:sequence>
        <xs:attribute ref="Id"/>
        <xs:attribute ref="Access"/>
        <xs:attribute ref="IRDisplayContentType"/>
    </xs:complexType>
</xs:element>
```

Fig. 3. XML Schema for Display Units

There are two basic attributes used so far: *IRDisplayContentType* and *IRSignificance*, as defined in Figure 5.

IRDisplayContentType allows the categorisation of display units with respect to its pieces of information. Possible values for *IRDisplayContentType* are:

- *Entry* - A display unit is an entry point to the Web site when it includes a number of links to "sub-pages" and as a result pages of this type do not focus on any particular information content.
- *Content* - This sort of display unit refers to those pages that include specific content often related to a particular subject. Each "sub-page" linked from the homepage or from an "Entry" page is usually a "Content" page.
- *Irrelevant* - This denotes those pages that should be discarded by the search engine, since they do not provide any relevant content.

As examples, the homepage of a University is an *entry* display unit, a page with a list of courses offered by an academic department is a *content* display unit and an error page such as "invalid login" is defined as *irrelevant.*

IRSignificance supports the specification of the degree of importance of a piece of information with respect to the display unit it is presented. This is very important to search engines since it provides a measurable means to evaluate how a piece of information is related to the subject of its page. This means that the same piece of information can have different degree of importance if presented in another display unit. This is a key concept to develop search engines more adequate to intrasite search than using global search engine techniques for intrasite search. *IRSignificance* allows the search engine to make a distinction between information by their actual importance degree as modelled by the Web

```
<xs:element name="Transition" id="Transition">
    <xs:complexType>
        <xs:sequence>
            <xs:element name="Origin" id="Origin">
              <xs:complexType>
                 <xs:simpleContent>
                     <xs:extension base="xs:string">
                        <xs:attribute ref="Id"/>
                     <xs:extension>
                 <xs:simpleContent>
              </xs:complexType>
            </xs:element>
            <xs:element name="DisplayUnit" id="DisplatUnit">
              <xs:complexType>
                 <xs:simpleContent>
                     <xs:extension base="xs:string">
                        <xs:attribute ref="Id"/>
                     <xs:extension>
                 <xs:simpleContent>
              </xs:complexType>
            </xs:element>
        </xs:sequence>
    </xs:complexType>
</xs:element>
```

Fig. 4. XML Schema for Transitions

site designer instead of "guessing" it by their position in the page (text, header, title, footnote, etc). We have defined the following degrees of importance to pieces of information in a display unit:

- *High* - assigned to pieces of information of higher priority to the process of information retrieval. Usually refers to content directly related to the main subject of the page where it is presented.
- *Medium* - assigned to pieces of information that are not directly related to the main subject of the Web page. For example the name of a lecturer is "high" if it is placed in his/her personal homepage. However it can be defined as "medium" if the lecturer name is presented in a course page.
- *Low* - assigned to pieces of information which low priority to search engines.
- *Irrelevant* - assigned to pieces of information that can be discarded by the search engine.

An example of a Web site modelling including the intrasite search engine design is presented in Section 5. In the next section we show how an intrasite search engine can make use of our modelling method discussed here.

```
<xs:attributename="RIDisplayContentType" default="content" id="RIDisplayContentType">
    <xs:simpleType>
        <xs:restriction base="xs:string">
            <xs:enumeration value="entry"/>
            <xs:enumeration value="content"/>
            <xs:enumeration value="irrelevant"/>
        </xs:restriction>
    </xs:simpleType>
</xs:attribute>
<xs:attribute name="RISignificance" default="irrelevant" id="Significance">
    <xs:simpleType>
        <xs:restriction base="xs:string">
            <xs:enumeration value="high"/>
            <xs:enumeration value="medium"/>
            <xs:enumeration value="low"/>
            <xs:enumeration value="irrelevant"/>
        </xs:restriction>
    </xs:simpleType>
</xs:attribute>
```

Fig. 5. XML Schema for IR Aspects

4 Modelling-Aware Intrasite Search Engines

The creation of the intrasite search engine is accomplished by taking into account specific annotations present in Web pages generated. These annotations derive from specifications of attributes *IRDisplayContentType* and *IRSignificance* defined in the intermediate representation. This allows the immediate access to the information needed by the search engine to appropriately index the Web site content. This also avoids the need for accessing the intermediate representation to gather IR-related specifications. All information are properly annotated in the resulting Web pages written in a target language.

In our experiments, we have used HTML as the target language. The IR annotations are found in each page as HTML comments (<!- - and - ->). In order to define the scope of each IR annotation, we have defined both opening and closing tags for *IRSignificance*. This is necessary because significance of a piece of information is relative to the page where it is presented. The same piece of information might have a different degree of relevance if presented in a different page. Since *IRDisplayContentType* is unique for each page, its annotation is placed before the tag <html> and its closing tag is placed after the tag </html>.

Based on the IR annotations the intrasite search engine can improve the quality and accuracy of query results. Only pages which have *IRDisplayContentType* equal to "content" are indexed. Pages defined as "entry" represent those pages which are entry points to the Web site. Notice that the distinction between content and entry pages is necessary because user queries can also be classified in two categories [22, 29]: (1) bookmark queries, which refer to locating an entry page for a specific site portion. For example, searching for the entry page of the economy section of a newspaper Web site. (2) content queries, which are the most common sort, denote user queries that result in single content pages. For example, finding a page that describes how the stock market operates.

Pages with *IRDisplayContentType* "irrelevant" are automatically discarded. Annotating irrelevant pages is important as it makes the system to index pages with relevant content only, making the resulting search engine more efficient and accurate.

Each piece of information has a level of significance defined by the value given to the attribute *IRSignificance*. This feature specify the importance of a particular piece of information with respect to the page where it is placed. This means that the same piece of information might have a different level of significance when placed in another page. In the indexing process the system stores each piece of information, their location and their *IRSignificance* value. In addition, the number of occurrences of each term present in the piece of information is also stored.

This information is used by our information retrieval model to compute the ranking of documents for each user query submitted to the intrasite search engine. The information retrieval model adopted here is an extension of the well know Vector Space Model [27]. This model is based on identifying the importance how related is each term (word) t to each document (page) d, which should be expressed as a function $w(d,t)$. The queries in this document are modelled in the same way, and the function w is used to represent each element modelled as a vector in a space determined by the set of all distinct terms. The ranking in this model is computed by the score function for each document d in the collection and a given query q as in the equation below.

$$Sim(d,q) = \frac{\sum_{i=1}^{t} w(d,t) \cdot w(q,t)}{\sqrt{\sum_{i=1}^{t} w(d,t)^2}\sqrt{\sum_{i=1}^{t} w(q,t)^2}} \quad (1)$$

which is the cosine between vectors $\boldsymbol{d}$ and $\boldsymbol{q}$ and expresses how similar is document d to the query q. The documents which have similarity $Sim(d,q)$ higher than zero are presented to the users in a descending order.

The function $w(d,t)$ in Equation 1 gives a measurement of how related term t and document d are. This value is usually computed as $tf(d,t) \times idf(t)$, where $idf(t)$ is the inverse document frequency and measures the importance of term t for the whole set of documents, while $tf(d,t)$ expresses the importance of term t for document d.

The idf value is usually computed as

$$idf(t) = \log(\frac{\#docs}{f(t)}) \quad (2)$$

where $\#docs$ is the number of documents (pages) in the collection and $f(t)$ is the number of documents where term t occurs.

The tf value can be computed in several ways. However, it is always a function of the term frequency in the document. Common formulae directly compute number of occurrences of t in d [16]. We here propose the use of information provided from the Web site modelling to define the function tf based not only on the term frequency, but also in the *IRSignificance* described during the Web site modelling. Given a Web page d composed of s different pieces of information $\{d_1, ..., d_s\}$, we define

$$tf(d,t) = \sum_{i=1}^{s} freq(d_i,t) \times IRSignificance(d_i) \quad (3)$$

where $freq(d_i, t)$ gives the number of occurrences of term t in the piece of information d_i and $IRSignificance(d_i)$ assigns values 0,1,2 or 3 corresponding to *irrelevant, low, medium* or *high*, respectively, for piece of information d_i derived from the Web site modelling.

By using this equation, the system assigns to each piece of information a precise importance value, allowing ranking the pages according to the terms used in a query that match the most significant pieces of information.

4.1 Generating a Web Site and Its Associated Intrasite Search Engine

A high-level specification of an application must be provided as the starting point of the development process. Existing conceptual models can be used for this task as discussed earlier. Since issues related to mapping a data model constructs to our intermediate representation language are not in the scope of this paper, we assume that this task has been already carried out. Details of mapping procedures from an ER schema to our intermediate representation can be found in [4].

Once an intermediate representation of the Web site application is provided, the next step is the generation of the pages and the search engine. The steps to perform a complete generation involve:

1. Instantiation of pieces of information, what usually involves access to databases.
2. Creation of pages. For each display unit a number of corresponding pages are created depending on the number of instances of its pieces of information.
3. Instantiation of links.
4. Translation of all intermediate representation to a target language, such as HTML.
5. Application of visualization styles to all pieces of information and pages, based on style and page templates definitions.
6. Creation of additional style sheets, as CSS specifications.
7. Creation of the intrasite search engine.

Visualization is described by individual pieces of information styles, page styles (stylesheet) and page templates. A suitable interface should be offered to the designer in order to input all necessary. Currently, a standard CSS stylesheet is automatically generated including definitions provided by the designer. The reason to make use of stylesheets is to keep the representation for our visualization styles simple. Without a stylesheet, all visual details would have to be included as arguments to the mapping procedure which translates a visualization style to HTML.

As for the creation of the intrasite search engine, its code is automatically incorporated as part of the resulting Web site. Furthermore its index is generated along with the Web site pages, according to the *IRDisplayContentType* and *IRSignificance* specifications.

5 Experiments

In this section we present experiments to evaluate the impact of our new integrated strategy for designing Web sites and intrasite search engines. For these experiments we have constructed two intrasite search systems for the Brazilian Web portal "ultimosegundo", indexing 12,903 news Web pages.

The first system was constructed without considering information provided by the application data model and it has been implemented using the traditional vector space model [27].

The second system was constructed using our IR-aware data model described in Section 4. To construct the second system we first modelled the Web site using our IR-aware methodology, generating a new version where the *IRDisplayContentType* of each page and the *IRSignificance* of the semantic pieces of information that compose each page are available. Figure 6 illustrates a small portion of the intermediate representation of the Web site modelled using our modelling language. The structure and content of this new site is equal to the original version, preserving all pages and keep them with the same content.

The first side effect of our methodology is that only pages with useful content are indexed. In the example only pages derived from the display unit *NewsPage*

```
<Info>
    <SimpleInfo Id="NewsOfTheHour" Access="BDQuery">   ...   </SimpleInfo>
    <SimpleInfo Id="NewsTitle" Access="BDQuery">   ...   </SimpleInfo>
    <ListInfo Id="RecentNews" Access="BDQuery" Type="string"> ... </ListInfo>
           ...
</Info>
<Display Id="HomePage" IRDisplayContentType="entry">
    <InfoId Id="NewsOfTheHour" IRSignificance="high"/>
    <InfoId Id="RecentNews" IRSignificance="medium"/>
    <InfoId Id="OtherNews" IRSignificance="irrelevant"/>
</Display>
<Display Id="NewsPage" IRDisplayContentType="content">
    <InfoId Id="NewsTitle" IRSignificance="high"/>
    <InfoId Id="NewsSummary" IRSignificance="medium"/>
    <InfoId Id="NewsText" IRSignificance="low"/>
    <InfoId Id="OtherNews" IRSignificance="irrelevant"/>
</Display>
    ...
<Transition>
    <Origin Id="NewsOfTheHour"/>
    <DisplayUnit Id="NewsPage"/>
</Transition>
    ...
```

Fig. 6. Example of a Partial Intermediate Representation of a Web Site

are indexed. Furthermore, pieces of information that do not represent useful information are also excluded from the search system. For instance, each news Web page in the site have links to related news (*OtherNews*), these links are considered as non-relevant pieces of information because they are included in the page as a navigation facility, not as content. As a result, the final index size was only 43% of the index file created to index the original site, which means our intrasite search version uses less storage space and is faster when processing user queries.

The experiments evaluating the quality of results were performed using a set of 50 queries extracted from a log of queries on new Web sites. The queries were randomly selected from the log having an average length of 1.5 terms, as the majority of queries are composed of one or two terms. In order to evaluate the results, we have used a precision recall curve, which is the most applied method for evaluating information retrieval systems [1]. The precision at any point of this curve computed using the set of relevant answers for each query (N) and the set of answers given by each system this query (R). The formulae for computing precision and recall are described in Equations 4. For further details about precision recall curve the interested reader is referred to [1, 32].

$$Precision = \frac{\#(R \cap N)}{\#R} \qquad Recall = \frac{\#(R \cap N)}{\#N} \tag{4}$$

To obtain the precision recall curve we need to use human judgment for determining the set of relevant answers for each query evaluated. This set was determined here using the pooling method used for the Web-based collections of TREC [19]. This method consists of retrieving a fix number of top answers from each of the system options evaluated and then make a pool of answers which is used for determining the set of relevant documents. Each answer in the pool is analyzed by humans and is classified as relevant or non relevant for the given user query. After analyzing the answers in the pool, we use the relevant answers identified by humans as the set N in the Equations 4.

For each of the 50 queries of our experiments, we composed a query pool formed by the top 50 documents generated by each of the 2 intra site search systems evaluated. The query pools contained an average of 62.2 pages (some queries had less than 50 documents in the answer). All documents in each query pool were submitted to a manual evaluation. The average number of relevant pages per query pool is 28.5.

Figure 7 shows the precision recall curve obtained in our experiment for both systems. Our Modelling-aware intrasite search is labelled in the figure as "Modelling-aware", while the original vector space model is labelled as "Conventional". This Figure shows that the quality of the ranking results of our system was superior in all points of recall. The precision at the first points in the curve was roughly 96% in our system, against 86.5% which means an improvement of almost 11% in the precision. For higher levels of recall the difference becomes ever higher, being roughly 20% at 50% of recall and 50% at 100%. This last result indicates that our system found in average 50% more relevant documents in this experiment. The average precision for the 11 points were 56% for the

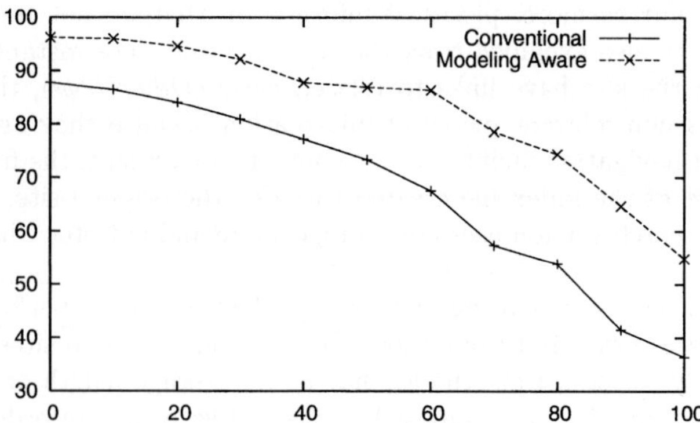

Fig. 7. Comparison of average precision versus recall curves obtained when processing the 50 queries using the original vector space model and the IR-aware model

conventional system and 84% for the Modelling-aware system, which represents an improvement of 48%.

Another important data about the experiment is that our system has returned on the average only 209.8 documents per query (from these, we selected 50 for evaluating) while the original system has returned 957.66 results on the average. This difference is again due to the elimination of non relevant information from the index. To give an example, the original system gave almost all pages as a result for the query "september 11th", while our system gives less than 300 documents. This difference happened because almost all pages in the site had a footnote text linking a special section about this topic in the site.

6 Conclusions

We have presented a new modelling technique for Web site design that transfers information about the model to the Web pages generated. We also presented a new intrasite search model that uses this information to improve the quality of results presented to users and to reduce the size of the indexes generated for processing queries. In our experiments we have presented one particular example of application of our method that illustrates its viability and effectiveness. The gains obtained in precision and storage space reduction may vary for different Web sites. However this example has shown a good indication that our method can be effectively deployed to solve the problem of intrasite and Intranet search. For the site modelled we had an improvement of 48% in the average precision and at the same time a reduction in the index size, occupying only 43% of the space used by the traditional implementation. That means our method produces faster and more precise intrasite search systems.

As future work we are planning to study the application of our method to other Web sites in order to evaluate in more detail the gains obtained and to refine our approach. We are also studying strategies for automatically compute the *IRSiginificance* of pieces of information and for automatically determining the weights of each piece of information for each display unit. These automatic methods will allow the use of our approach for non-modelled Web sites which may be used for extending the benefits of our method to global search engines.

The paradigm described here opens new possibilities for designing better intrasite search systems. Another future research direction is defining new modelling characteristics that can be useful for intrasite search systems. For instance, we are interested in finding ways for determining the semantic relations between Web pages during the modelling phase and use this information to cluster these pages in a search system. The idea is to use the cluster properties for improving the knowledge about the semantic meaning of each Web page in the site.

Acknowledgements

This paper is the result of research work done in the context of the SiteFix and Gerindo projects sponsored by the Brazilian Research Council - CNPq, grants no.55.2197/02-5 and 55.2087/05-5. The work was also supported by a R&D grant by Philips MDS-Manaus. The second author was sponsored by The Amazonas State Research Foundation - FAPEAM. The fourth author is sponsored by the Brazilian Research Council - CNPq, grant no.300220/2002-2.

References

1. Baeza-Yates, R., and Ribeiro-Neto, B. *Modern Information Retrieval*, 1st ed. Addison-Wesley-Longman, 1999.
2. Brin, S., and Page, L. The anatomy of a large-scale hypertextual web search engine. In *Proceedings of the 7th International World Wide Web Conference* (Brisbane, Australia, April 1998), pp. 107–117.
3. Cavalcanti, J., and Robertson, D. Synthesis of Web Sites from High Level Descriptions. In *Web Engineering: Managing Diversity and Complexity in Web Application Development*, S. M. . Y. Deshpande, Ed., vol. 2016 of *Lecture Notes in Computer Science*. Springer-Verlag, Heidelberg, Germany, 2001, pp. 190–203.
4. Cavalcanti, J., and Robertson, D. Web Site Synthesis based on Computational Logic. *Knowledge and Information Systems Journal (KAIS) 5*, 3 (Sept. 2003), 263–287.
5. Cavalcanti, J., and Vasconcelos, W. A Logic-Based Approach for Automatic Synthesis and Maintenance of Web Sites. In *Proceedings of the 14th International Conference on Software Engineering and Knowledge Engineering - SEKE'02* (Ischia, Italy, July 2002), pp. 619–626.
6. Ceri, S., Fraternali, P., and Bongio, A. Web Modeling Language (WebML): a Modeling Language for Designing Web Sites. In *Proceedings of the WWW9 conference* (Amsterdam, the Netherlands, May 2000), pp. 137–157.
7. Chen, M., Hearst, M., Hong, J., and Lin, J. Cha-cha: a system for organizing intranet search results. In *Proceedings of the 2nd USENIX Symposium on Internet Technologies and Systems* (Boulder,USA, October 1999).
8. Chen, P. The entity-relationship model: toward a unified view of data. *ACM Transactions on Database Systems 1*, 1 (1976).

9. CRASWELL, N., HAWKING, D., AND ROBERTSON, S. Effective site finding using link anchor information. In *Proceedings of the 24th Annual International ACM SIGIR Conference on Research and Development in Information Retrieval* (New Orleans, USA, September 2001), pp. 250–257.
10. EIRON, N., AND MCCURLEY, K. S. Analysis of anchor text for web search. In *Proceedings of the 26th Annual International ACM SIGIR Conference on Research and Development in Information Retrieval* (Toronto, Canada, July 2003), pp. 459–460.
11. FERNÁNDEZ, M., FLORESCU, D., KANG, J., LEVY, A., AND SUCIU, D. Catching the Boat with Strudel: Experience with a A Web-site Management System. *SIGMOD Record 27*, 2 (June 1998), 414–425.
12. FLORESCU, D., LEVY, A., AND MENDELZON, A. Database Techniques for the World-Wide Web: A Survey. *SIGMOD Record 27*, 3 (Sept. 1998), 59–74.
13. GARZOTTO, G., PAOLINI, P., AND SCHWABE, D. HDM - A Model-Based Approach to Hypertext Application Design. *TOIS 11*, 1 (1993), 1–26.
14. GEVREY, J., AND RÜGER, S. M. Link-based approaches for text retrieval. In *The Tenth Text REtrieval Conference (TREC-2001)* (Gaithersburg, Maryland, USA, November 2001), pp. 279–285.
15. GÓMEZ, J., CACHERO, C., AND PASTOR, O. Conceptual Modeling of Device-Independent Web Applications. *IEEE Multimedia 8*, 2 (Apr. 2001), 26–39.
16. G.SALTON, AND BUCKLEY, C. Term-weighting approaches in automatic text retrieval. *Information Processing & Management 5*, 24 (1988), 513–523.
17. HAGEN, P., MANNING, H., AND PAUL, Y. Must Search Stink ? The Forrester Report, June 2000.
18. HAWKING, D., CRASWELL, N., AND THISTLEWAITE, P. B. Overview of TREC-7 very large collection track. In *The Seventh Text REtrieval Conference (TREC-7)* (Gaithersburg, Maryland, USA, November 1998), pp. 91–104.
19. HAWKING, D., CRASWELL, N., THISTLEWAITE, P. B., AND HARMAN, D. Results and challenges in web search evaluation. *Computer Networks 31*, 11–16 (May 1999), 1321–1330. Also in Proceedings of the 8th International World Wide Web Conference.
20. HAWKING, D., VOORHEES, E., BAILEY, P., AND CRASWELL, N. Overview of trec-8 web track. In *Proc. of TREC-8* (Gaithersburg MD, November 1999), pp. 131–150.
21. JIN, Y., DECKER, S., AND WIEDERHOLD, G. OntoWebber: Model-driven ontology-based Web site management. In *Proceedings of the first international semantic Web working symposium (SWWS'01)* (Stanford, CA, USA, July 2001).
22. KANG, I.-H., AND KIM, G. Query type classification in web document retrieval. In *Proceedings of the 26th Annual International ACM SIGIR Conference on Research and Development in Information Retrieval* (Toronto, July 2003), pp. 64–71.
23. KANUNGO, T., AND ZIEN, J. Y. Integrating link structure and content information for ranking web documents. In *The Tenth Text REtrieval Conference (TREC-2001)* (Gaithersburg, Maryland, USA, November 2001), pp. 237–239.
24. KLEINBERG, J. M. Authoritative sources in a hyperlinked environment. In *Proceedings of the 9th Annual ACM-SIAM Symposium on Discrete Algorithms* (San Francisco, California, USA, January 1998), pp. 668–677.
25. MAEDCHE, A., STAAB, S., STOJANOVIC, N., STUDER, R., AND SURE, Y. SEAL - A framework for developing semantic Web portals. In *Proceedings of the 18th British national conference on databases (BNCOD 2001)* (Oxford, England, UK, July 2001).

26. MECCA, G., ATZENI, P., MASCI, A., MERIALDO, P., AND SINDONI, G. The ARANEUS Web-Base Management System. *SIGMOD Record (ACM Special Interest Group on Management of Data) 27*, 2 (1998), 544.
27. SALTON, G., AND MCGILL, M. J. *Introduction to Modern Information Retrieval*, 1st ed. McGraw-Hill, 1983.
28. SCHWABE, D., AND ROSSI, G. The Object-oriented Hypermedia Design Model. *Communications of the ACM 38*, 8 (Aug. 1995), 45–46.
29. UPSTILL, T., CRASWELL, N., AND HAWKING, D. Query-independent evidence in home page finding. *ACM Transactions on Information Systems - ACM TOIS 21*, 3 (2003), 286–313.
30. VASCONCELOS, W., AND CAVALCANTI, J. An Agent-Based Approach to Web Site Maintenance. In *Proceedings of the 4th International Conference on Web Engineering and Knowledge Engineering - ICWE 2004. To Appear.* (Munich, Germany, July 2004).
31. WESTERVELD, T., KRAAIJ, W., AND HIEMSTRA, D. Retrieving Web pages using content, links, URLs and anchors. In *The Tenth Text REtrieval Conference (TREC-2001)* (Gaithersburg, Maryland, USA, November 2001), pp. 663–672.
32. WITTEN, I., MOFFAT, A., AND BELL, T. *Managing Gigabytes*, second ed. Morgan Kaufmann Publishers, New York, 1999.
33. XUE, G.-R., ZENG, H.-J., CHEN, Z., MA, W.-Y., ZHANG, H.-J., AND LU, C.-J. Implicit link analysis for small web search. In *Proceedings of the 26th Annual International ACM SIGIR Conference on Research and Development in Information Retrieval* (Toronto - Canada, July 2003), pp. 56–63.

Expressive Profile Specification and Its Semantics for a Web Monitoring System*

Ajay Eppili, Jyoti Jacob, Alpa Sachde, and Sharma Chakravarthy

Information Technology Laboratory
Computer Science and Engineering, UT Arlington, Texas, USA
{eppili,jacob,sachde,sharma}@cse.uta.edu

Abstract. World wide web has gained a lot of prominence with respect to information retrieval and data delivery. With such a prolific growth, a user interested in a specific change has to continuously retrieve/pull information from the web and analyze it. This results in wastage of resources and more importantly the burden is on the user. Pull-based retrieval needs to be replaced with a push-based paradigm for efficiency and notification of relevant information in a timely manner. WebVigiL is an efficient profile-based system to monitor, retrieve, detect and notify specific changes to HTML and XML pages on the web. In this paper, we describe the expressive profile specification language along with its semantics. We also present an efficient implementation of these profiles. Finally, we present the overall architecture of the WebVigiL system and its implementation status.

1 Introduction

Information on the Internet, growing at a rapid rate, is spread over multiple repositories. This has greatly affected the way information is accessed, delivered and disseminated. Users, at present, are not only interested in the new information available on web pages but also in retrieving changes of interest in a timely manner. More specifically, users may only be interested in particular changes (such as keywords, phrases, links etc). Push and Pull paradigms [1] are traditionally used for monitoring the pages of interest. Pull Paradigm is an approach where the user performs an explicit action in the form of a query, transaction execution on a periodic basis on the pages of interest. Here, the burden of retrieving the required information is on the user and may result in changes being missed when a large number of web sites need to be monitored. In the push paradigm, the system is responsible for accepting user needs and informs the user (or a set of users) when something of interest happens. Although this approach reduces the burden on the user, naive use of a push paradigm results in informing users about the changes to web pages irrespective of the user's interest. At present most of the systems use a mailing list to send the same compiled changes to all its subscribers.

---

* This work was supported, in part, by the Office of Naval Research & the SPAWAR System Center–San Diego & by the Rome Laboratory (grant F30602-01-2-05430), and by NSF (grant IIS-0123730).

P. Atzeni et al. (Eds.): ER 2004, LNCS 3288, pp. 420–433, 2004.

Hence, an approach is needed which replaces periodic polling and notifies the user of the relevant changes in a timely manner. The emphasis in WebVigiL is on selective change notification. This entails notifying the user about the changes to the web pages based on user specified interest/policy. WebVigiL is a web monitoring system, which uses an appropriate combination of push and intelligent pull paradigm with the help of active capability to monitor customized changes to HTML and XML pages. WebVigiL intelligently pulls the information using a learning-based algorithm [2] from the web server based on user profile and propagates/pushes only the relevant information to the end user. In addition, WebVigiL is a scalable system, designed to detect even composite changes for a large number of users. An overview of the paradigm used and the basic approach taken for effective monitoring is discussed in [3].

This paper concentrates on the expressiveness of change specification, its semantics, and its implementation. In order for the user to specify notification and monitoring requirements, an expressive change specification language is needed.

The remainder of the paper is organized as follows. Section 2 discusses related work. Section 3 discusses the syntax and semantics of the change specification language which captures the monitoring requirements of the user and in addition supports inheritance, event-based duration and composite changes. Section 4 gives an overview of the current architecture and status of the system. Section 5 concludes the paper with an emphasis on future work.

2 Related Work

Many research groups have been working to address detecting changes to documents. *GNU diff* [4] detects changes between any two text files. Most of the previous work in change detection has dealt only with flat-files [5] and not structured or unstructured web documents. Several tools have been developed to detect changes between two versions of unstructured HTML documents [6]. Some change–monitoring tools such as *ChangeDetection.com* [7] have been developed using the push-pull paradigm. But these tools detect changes to the entire page instead of user specified components and the changes can be tracked only on limited pages.

2.1 Approaches for User Specification

Present day users are interested in monitoring changes to pages and want to be notified based on his/her profile. Hence, an expressive language is necessary to specify user-intent on fetching, monitoring and propagating changes. *WebCQ* [8] detects customized changes between two given HTML pages and provides an expressive language for the user to specify his/her interests. But WebCQ only supports changes between the last two pages of interest. As a result, flexible and expressive compare options are not provided to the user. AT&T Internet Difference Engine [9] views a HTML document as a sequence of sentences and sentence-breaking markups. This approach may be expensive computationally as each sentence may need to be compared with all sentences in the document. *WYSIGOT* [10] is a commercial application that can be used to detect changes to HTML pages. It has to be installed on the local machine, which is not always possible. This system gives an interface to specify the specifications for monitoring a web page. It has the feature to monitor an HTML page and also all the pages that it points to. But the granularity of change detection is at the page level.

In [11], the authors allow the user to submit monitoring requests and continuous queries on the XML documents stored in the Xyleme repository. WebVigiL supports a life-span for change monitoring request which is akin to a continuous query. Change detection is continuously performed over the life-span. To the best of our knowledge, customized changes, inheritance, different reference selection or correlated specifications cannot be specified in Xyleme.

3 Change Specification Language

The present day web user's interest has evolved from mere retrieval of information to monitoring the changes on web pages that are of interest. As the web pages are distributed over large repositories, the emphasis is on selective and timely propagation of information/changes. Changes need to be notified to the user in different ways based on their profiles/policies. In addition, the notification of these changes may have to be sent to different devices that have different storage and communication bandwidths. The language for establishing the user policies should be able to accommodate the requirements of a heterogeneous distributed large network-centric environment. Hence, there is a need to define an expressive and extensible specification language wherein the user can specify details such as the web page(s) to be monitored, the type of change (keywords, phrases etc.) and the interval for comparing occurrence of changes. User should also be able to specify how, when, and where to be notified taking into consideration the quality of service factors such as timeliness, size vs. quality of notification.

WebVigiL provides an expressive language with well-defined semantics for specifying the monitoring requirements of a user pertaining to the web [12]. Each monitoring request is termed a Sentinel. The change specification language developed for this purpose allows the user to create a monitoring request based on his/her requirements. The semantics of this language for WebVigiL have been formalized. Complete syntax of the language is shown in Fig 1.

Following are a few monitoring scenarios that can be represented using the above sentinel specification language.

Example 1: Alex wants to monitor *http://www.uta.edu/spring04/cse/classes.htm* for the keyword "cse5331" to take a decision for registering the course cse5331. The sentinel starts from May 15, 2004 to August 10, 2004 (summer semester) and she wants to be notified as soon as a change is detected. Sentinel (s1) for this scenario is as follows:

Create Sentinel s1 Using http://www.uta.edu/ spring04/cse/classes.htm
Monitor keyword (cse5331)
Fetch 1 day
From 05/15/04 To 08/10/04

Notify By email alex@aol.com Every best effort
Compare pairwise
ChangeHistory 3
Presentation dual frame

Example 2: Alex wants to monitor the same URL as in *Example 1* for regular updates on new courses getting added but is not interested in changes to images. As it is correlated with sentinel s1, the duration is specified between the start of s1 and the end of s1. The sentinel (s2) for the above scenario is:

Create Sentinel s2 Using s1
Monitor Anychange AND (NOT) images
Presentation only change

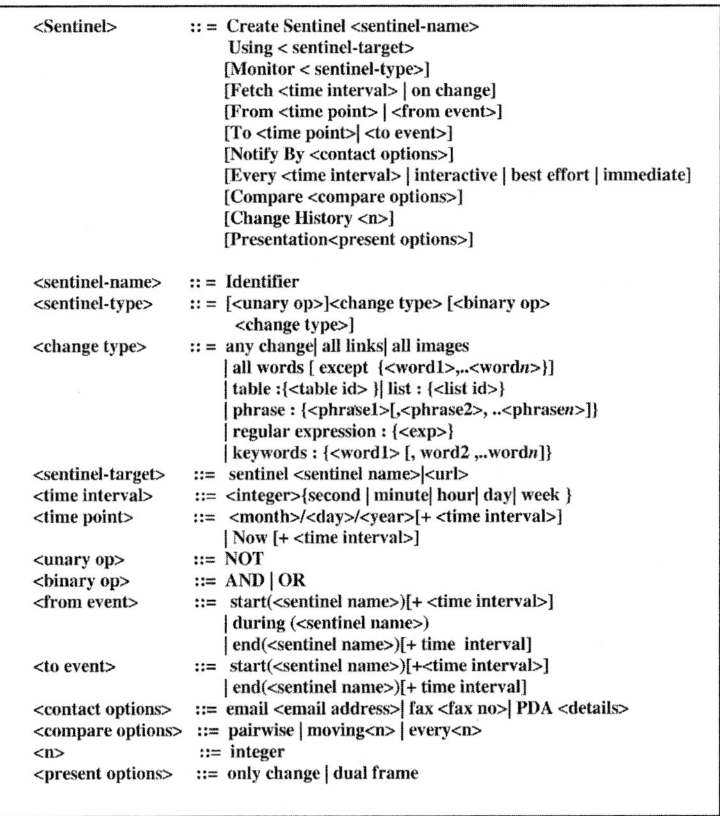

```
<Sentinel>           :: = Create Sentinel <sentinel-name>
                          Using < sentinel-target>
                          [Monitor < sentinel-type>]
                          [Fetch <time interval> | on change]
                          [From <time point> | <from event>]
                          [To <time point>| <to event>]
                          [Notify By <contact options>]
                          [Every <time interval> | interactive | best effort | immediate]
                          [Compare <compare options>]
                          [Change History <n>]
                          [Presentation<present options>]

<sentinel-name>      :: = Identifier
<sentinel-type>      :: = [<unary op>]<change type> [<binary op>
                           <change type>]
<change type>        :: = any change| all links| all images
                          | all words [ except {<word1>,..<wordn>}]
                          | table :{<table id> }| list : {<list id>}
                          | phrase : {<phrase1>[,<phrase2>, ..<phrasen>]}
                          | regular expression : {<exp>}
                          | keywords : {<word1> [, word2 ,..wordn]}
<sentinel-target>    ::=  sentinel <sentinel name>|<url>
<time interval>      ::=  <integer>{second | minute| hour| day| week }
<time point>         ::=  <month>/<day>/<year>[+ <time interval>]
                          | Now [+ <time interval>]
<unary op>           ::= NOT
<binary op>          ::= AND | OR
<from event>         ::=  start(<sentinel name>)[+ <time interval>]
                          | during (<sentinel name>)
                          | end(<sentinel name>)[+ time  interval]
<to event>           ::=  start(<sentinel name>)[+<time interval>]
                          | end(<sentinel name>)[+ time interval]
<contact options>    ::= email <email address>| fax <fax no>| PDA <details>
<compare options>    ::= pairwise | moving<n> | every<n>
<n>                  ::= integer
<present options>    ::= only change | dual frame
```

Fig. 1. Sentinel Syntax

3.1 Sentinel Name

This is to specify a name for user's request. The syntax of sentinel name is *Create Sentinel <sentinel-name>*. For every sentinel, the WebVigiL system generates a unique identifier. In addition, the system also allows the user to specify a sentinel name. The user is required to specify a distinct name for all his sentinels. This name identifies a request uniquely. Further it facilitates the user to specify another sentinel in terms of his/her previously defined sentinels.

3.2 Sentinel Target

The syntax of sentinel target is *Using <sentinel- target>*. The sentinel-target could be either a URL or a previously defined sentinel S_i. If the new sentinel S_n, specifies the sentinel target as S_i, then S_n inherits all properties of S_i, unless the user overrides those properties in the current specification.

In *Example 1*, Alex is interested in monitoring the course web page for the keyword 'cse5331'. Alex should be able to specify this URL as the target on which the system monitors the changes on the keyword cse5331. Later Alex wants to get updates on the new classes being added to the page, as this may affect her decision for registering for the course cse5331. She should place another sentinel for the same URL but with different change criteria. As the second case is correlated with the first case, Alex can specify s1 as the sentinel target with a different change type.

Sentinels are correlated if they inherit run time properties such as start and end time of a sentinel. Otherwise, they merely inherit static properties (e.g., URL, change type, etc. of the sentinel). The language allows the user to specify the reference web page or a previously placed sentinel as the target.

3.3 Sentinel Type

WebVigiL allows the detection of customized changes in the form of sentinel type and provides explicit semantics for the user to specify his/her desired type of change. The syntax of sentinel type is given as: *Monitor <sentinel-type>*, where sentinel type is *sentinel-type= [<unary op>]<change type> [<binary op> <change type>]*

In *Example 1*, Alex is interested in 'cse5331'. Detecting changes to the entire page leads to wasteful computations and further sends unwanted information to Alex.

In *Example 2*, Alex is interested in any change to the class web page but is not interested in the changes pertaining to images.

WebVigiL handles such requests by introducing change type and operators in its change specification language. The contents of a web page can be any combination of objects such as set of words, links and images. Users can specify such objects using change type and use operators over these objects. Change Specification Language defines Primitive change and Composite change for a sentinel type.

Primitive change: It is the detection of a single type of change between two versions of the same page. For keyword change, the user must specify a set of words. An exception list can also be given for any change. For phrase change, a set of phrases is specified. For regular expressions, a valid regular expression is given.

Composite change: It comprises of a combination of distinct primitive change(s) specified on the same page, using one of the binary operators AND and OR. The semantics of composite change formed by the use of an operator can be defined as follows (Note that Λ, V, and ~ are Boolean AND, OR, and NOT operators, respectively).

3.4 Change Type

If V_1 and V_2 are two different versions of the same page, then Change C_t on V_2 with reference to V_1, is defined as:

$C_t(V_1, V_2)$ = True if the change type t is detected as insert in V_2 or delete in V_1.

False otherwise.

The sentinel-type is the change type t selected from the set T where
T = {any change, links, images, all words except <set of words>, phrase:<set of phrases>, keywords:<set of words>, table: <table id>, list :<list id>, regular expression: <exp> }.

Based on the form of information that is usually available on web pages change types may be classified as links, images, keywords, phrases, all words, table, list, regular expression and any change based on the form of information.

Links: Corresponds to a set of hypertext references. In HTML, links are presentation-based objects represented between the hypertext tag (<A href=".”>). Given two versions of a page, if any of the old links are deleted in the new version or new links are inserted, a change is flagged.

Images: Corresponds to a set of image references extracted from the image source. In HTML, images are represented by the image source tag (< IMG src=".”>). The changes detected are similar to the links except that the images are monitored.

Keywords<set of words>: Corresponds to a set of unique words from the page. A change is flagged when any of the keyword (mentioned in the set of words) appears or disappears in a page with respect to the previous version of the same page.

Phrase<set of phrases>: Corresponds to a set of contiguous words from the page. A change is flagged on the appearance or disappearance of a given phrase in a page with respect to the previous version of the same page. Update to a phrase is also flagged depending on the percentage of words that has been modified in a phrase. If the number of words changed exceeds above a threshold, it is deemed as a delete (or disappearance).

Table: Corresponds to the content of the page represented in a tabular format. Though the table is a presentation object, the changes are tracked on the contents of the table. Hence, whenever the table contents are changed, it is flagged as a table change.

List: Corresponds to the contents of a page represented in a list format. The list format can be bullets or numbered. Any change detected on the set of words represented in a list format is flagged as a change.

Regular expression <exp>: Expressed as valid regular expression syntax for querying and extracting specific information from the document data.

All words: A page can be divided into a set of words, links and images. Any change to the set of words between two versions of the same page is detected as all words change.

All words encompass phrases, keywords and words in the table and list. While considering changes to all words, the presentation objects such as table and list are not considered and only the content in these presentation objects are taken into consideration.

Anychange: Anychange encompasses all the above given types of changes. Changes to any of the defined set (i.e., all words, all links and all images) are flagged as anychange. Hence, the granularity is limited to a page for anychange. Any change is the superset of all changes.

3.5 Operators

Users may want to detect more than one type of change on a given page or the non-occurrence of a type of change. To facilitate such detections the change specification language includes unary and binary operators.

NOT: A unary operator, which detects the non-occurrence of a change type. For a given change type t on version V_2 with reference to version V_1 of the same page the semantics of NOT are: $(\text{NOT } C_t)(V_1,V_2) = \sim C_t\ (V_1,V_2)$

OR: A binary operator representing disjunction of change types. It is denoted by C_t^1 OR C_t^2 for two primitive changes C_t^1 and C_t^2 specified on version V_2 with reference to version V_1 of the same page. A change is detected if either C_t^1 is detected or C_t^2 is detected. Formally, $(C_t^1 \text{ OR } C_t^2)\ (V_1,V_2) = C_t^1(V_1,V_2) \vee C_t^2(V_1,V_2)$, where t1, t2 are the types of changes and t1<>t2

AND: A binary operator representing conjunction of change types. It is denoted by C_t^1 AND C_t^2 for two primitive changes C_t^1 and C_t^2 specified on version V_2 with reference to version V_1 of the same page. A change is detected when both C_t^1 and C_t^2 are detected. Formally,$(C_t^1 \text{ AND } C_t^2)\ (V_1,V_2) = C_t^1\ (V_1,V_2) \wedge C_t^1(V_1,V_2)$, where t1, t2 are types of changes and t1 <>t2

The unary operator NOT can be used to specify a constituent primitive change in a composite change. For example, for a page containing the list of fiction books, a user can specify a change type as: All words AND NOT phrase {" Lord of the Rings"}. A change will be flagged only if given two versions of a page, at least some words may change such as insertion of a new book and author etc. but the phrase "Lord of the Rings" has not changed. Hence, the user is interested in monitoring the arrival of new books or removal of old books, only as long as the book "Lord of the Rings" is available.

3.6 Fetch

Changes can be detected for a web page only when a new version of the page is fetched. New versions can be fetched based on the freshness of the page. The page properties (or meta-data) of a web page, such as the last modified date for static pages or checksum for dynamic pages define whether a page has been modified or not. The syntax of fetch is *Fetch <time interval>| on change.* User can specify a 'time interval' indicating how often a new page should be fetched, or can specify 'on change' to indicate that he/she is unaware of the change frequency of the page.

On change: This option relieves the user of knowing when the page changes. WebVigiL's fetch module uses a heuristic-based fetch algorithm called Best Effort Algorithm [13] to determine the interval with which a page should be fetched. This algorithm uses change history and meta-data of the page.

Fixed Interval <time interval> t_d: User can specify a fixed user-defined fetch interval when a page is fetched by the system, t_d can be in terms of minutes, hours, days or weeks (a non-negative integer).

3.7 Sentinel Duration

WebVigiL monitors a web page for changes during the lifespan of the sentinel. The lifespan of a sentinel is a closed interval formed by the start time and end time of sentinel. This is defined as:

From <timepoint>| <from event>   To   <timepoint>|<to event>

Let the timeline be an equidistant discrete time domain having "0" as the origin and each time point as a positive integer as defined in [14]. Defining it in terms of the timeline, occurrences of the created Sentinel S are specific points on the time line and the duration (lifespan) defines the closed interval within which S occurs. The 'From' modifier denotes the start of a sentinel S and the 'To' modifier denotes the end of S. The start and end times of a sentinel can be specific times or can depend upon the attributes of other correlated sentinels. The user has the flexibility to specify the duration as one of the following: (a) Now (b) Absolute time (c) Relative time (d) Event-based time

Now: A system-defined variable that keeps track of the current time.

Absolute time: Denoted as time point T, it can be specified as a definite point on the time line. The format for specifying the time point is MM/DD/YYYY.

Relative time: It is defined as an offset from a time point (either absolute or event-based). The offset can be specified by the time interval t_d defined in Section 3.6.

Event-based time: Events, such as the start and end of a sentinel can be mapped to specific time points and can be used to trigger the start or end of a new sentinel. Start of a sentinel can also depend on the active state of another sentinel and is specified by the event 'during'. During s_i defines that a sentinel should be started in the closed interval of s_i and the start should be mapped to *Now*. When a sentinel inherits from another sentinel having a start time of *Now*, as the properties are inherited, the time of the current sentinel will be mapped to the current time.

3.8 Notification

Users need to be notified of detected changes. How, when and where to notify is an important criterion for notification and should be resolved by the change specification semantics.

Notification Mechanism: The mechanism selected for notification is important especially when multiple types of devices with varying capabilities are involved. The syntax for specifying the notification mechanism is given by: *Notify By <contact options>*. The *<contact options>* allows the users to select the appropriate mechanism for notification from a set of options *O = {email, fax, PDA}*. The default is email.

Notification Frequency: The notification module has to ensure that the detected changes are presented to the user at the specified frequency. The system should incorporate the flexibility to allow users to specify the desired frequency of notification. The syntax of notification frequency has been defined as: *best effort | immediate | interactive| <time interval>* where <time interval> is as defined in the Section 3.6. *Immediate* denotes immediate (without delay) notification on change detection. *Best effort* is defined as notify as soon as possible after change detection. Hence, best effort is equivalent to immediate but will have lesser priority than immediate for notification. *Interactive* is a navigational style notification approach where the user visits the WebVigiL dashboard to retrieve the detected changes at his/her convenience.

3.9 Compare Options

One of the unique aspects of WebVigiL is its compare option and its efficient implementation. Changes are detected between two versions of the same page. Each fetch of the same page is given a version number. The first version of the page will be the first page fetched after a sentinel starts. Given a sequence of versions V_1, V_2 ......V_n, of the same page, the user may be interested in knowing changes with respect to different references. In order to facilitate this, the change specification language allows users to specify three types of compare options. The syntax of compare options is: *Compare <compare options>* where compare options can be selected from a set *P = {pairwise, moving n, every n}*.

Pairwise: The default is pairwise, which will allow change comparison between two chronologically adjacent versions as shown in Fig 2.

Every n: Consider an example where the user is aware of the changes occurring on a page such as a web developer or administrator and is interested in the cumulative changes between only n versions. This compare option allows detecting changes between versions V_i and V_{i+n}. For the next comparison, the nth page becomes the reference page. For example if a user wants to detect changes between every 4 versions of the page, the versions for comparing will be selected as shown in Fig 2.

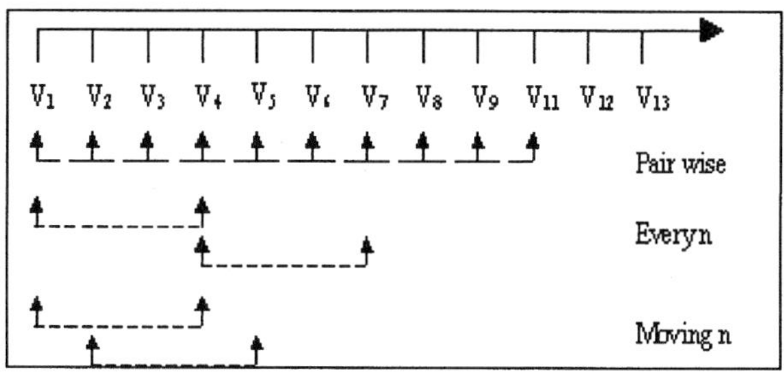

Fig. 2. Compare Options

Moving n: This is a moving window concept for tracking changes. When a user wants to monitor the trend of a particular stock where meaningful change detection is only possible between particular set of pages occurring in a moving window.

For moving n, If a user specifies the compare option of moving n where n=4, as shown in Fig 2, V_1 will be the reference page for V_4. The next comparison will be between V_2 and V_5.

WebVigiL believes in giving the users more flexibility and options for change detection and hence has incorporated several compare options for change specification along with efficient change detection algorithms. By default, the previous page (based on user-defined fetch interval where appropriate) and the current page are used for change detection.

3.10 Change History

The syntax of Change History is *ChangeHistory <n>*. Change Specification language facilitates the user to specify the number of previous changes to be maintained by the system. User should be able to view last n changes detected for a particular request (sentinel). WebVigiL provides an interface to users to view and manage the sentinels they have placed. A user dashboard is provided for this purpose. *Interactive* option is a navigational style notification approach where the users visit the WebVigiL dashboard to retrieve the detected changes at their convenience. Through the WebVigiL dashboard users can view and query the changes generated by their sentinels. Change history, mentioned by the user will be used by the system to maintain detected changes.

3.11 Presentation

Presentation semantics are included in the language to present the detected changes to users in a meaningful manner. In *Example 1* Alex is interested in viewing the content cse5331 along with the context, but in *Example 2* she is interested in getting a brief overview of the changes occurring to the page. To support these, change specification language facilitates the users with two types of presentations. In *change only* approach, changes, to the page along with the type (insert/delete/update) of change information are displayed in an HTML file using a tabular representation. *Dual Frame* approach shows both documents (involved in the change) on the same page in different frames side-by-side, highlighting the changes between the documents. The syntax is *Presentation <presentation options* > where presentation options is specified as *<presentation options> change-only | dual-frame approach.*

3.12 Desiderata

All of the above expressiveness is of not much use if they are not implemented efficiently. One of the focuses of WebVigiL was to design efficient ways of supporting the sentinel specification, provide a truly asynchronous way of notification and managing the sentinels using the active capability developed by the team earlier. In the following sections, we describe the overall WebVigiL architecture and the current status of the working system. The reader is welcome to access the system at *http://berlin.uta.edu:8081/webvigil/* and test the usage of the system.

4 WebVigiL Architecture and Current Status

WebVigiL is a profile-based change detection and notification system. The high-level block diagram shown in Fig 3 details the architecture of WebVigiL. WebVigiL aims at investigating the specification, management and propagation of changes as requested by the user in a timely manner while meeting the quality of service requirements [15]. All the modules shown in the architecture (Fig 3) have been implemented.

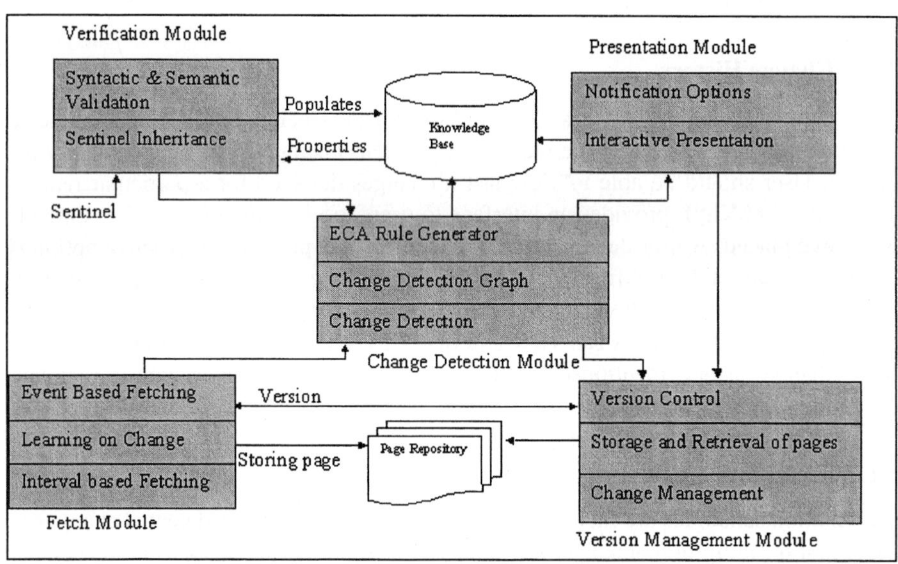

Fig. 3. WebVigiL Architecture

User specification module provides an interface for the first time users to register with the system and a dashboard for registered users to place, view, and manage their sentinels. Sentinel captures the user's specification for monitoring a web page. Verification module is used to validate user-defined sentinels before sending the information to the Knowledgebase. The Knowledgebase is used to persist meta-data about each user and his/her sentinels. Change detection module is responsible for generating ECA rules [16] for the run time management of a validated sentinel.

Fetch module is used to fetch pages for all active or enabled sentinels. Currently fetch module supports fixed interval and best effort approaches for fetching the web pages. Version management module deals with a centralized server based repository service that retrieves, archives, and manages versions of pages. A page is saved in the repository only if the latest copy in the repository is older than the fetched page. Subsequent requests for the web page can access the page from the cache instead of repeatedly invoking the fetch procedure. [3] discusses how each URL is mapped to a unique directory and how all the versions of this URL are stored in this directory. Versions are checked for deletion periodically and versions no longer needed are deleted.

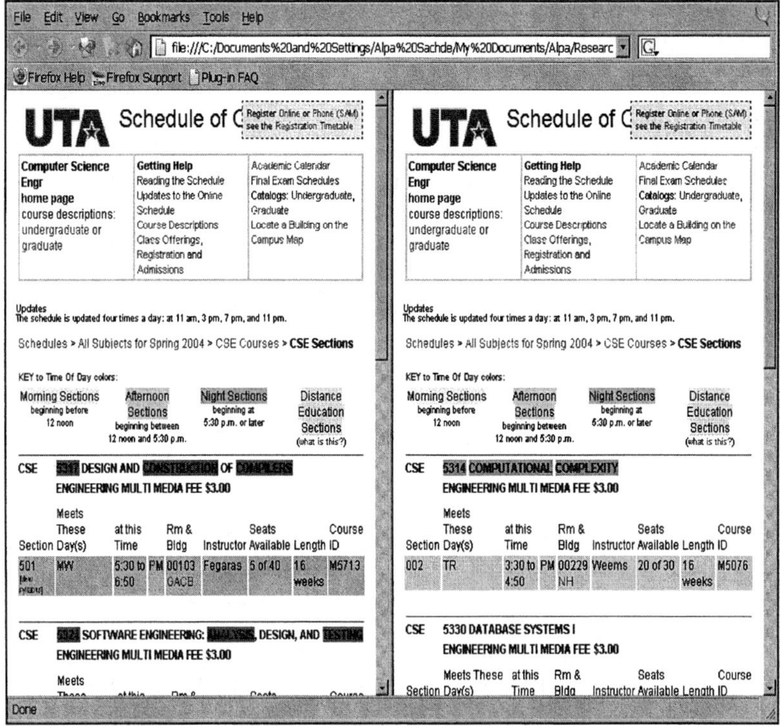

Fig. 4. Presentation using dual frame approach for a html page

The change detection module [17] builds a change detection graph to efficiently detect and propagate the changes. The graph captures the relationship between the pages and sentinels, and groups the sentinels based on the change type and target web page. Change detection is performed over the versions of the web page and the sentinels associated with the groups are informed about the detected changes. Currently, grouping is performed only for sentinels that follow best effort approach for fetching pages. WebVigiL architecture can support various page types such as XML, HTML, and TEXT in a uniform way. Currently changes are detected between HTML pages using specifically developed CH-Diff [2] module and XML pages using CX-Diff [18] module. Change detection modules for new page types can be added or current modules for HTML and XML page types can be replaced by efficient modules without disturbing the rest of the architecture. Among the change types discussed above in Section 0 all change types except Table, List and Regular expressions are currently supported by WebVigiL.

Currently notification module propagates the detected changes to users via email. Presentation module supports both change-only and dual-frame approaches for presenting the detected changes. A screenshot of the notification using dual frame approach for html pages is shown in Fig 4. This approach is visually intuitive and enhances user interpretation since changes are presented along with the context.

5 Conclusion and Future Work

In this paper we have discussed the rationale for an expressive change specification language, its syntax as well as its semantics. We have given a brief overview of WebVigiL architecture and have discussed the current status of the system, which included a complete implementation of the language presented. We are currently working on several extensions. The change specification language can be extended to provide the capability of supporting sentinels on multiple URLs. The current fetch module is being extended to a distributed fetch module to reduce the network traffic. The deletion algorithm for the cached versions discussed in Section 0 is being improved to efficiently delete the no longer needed pages as soon as possible instead of the slightly conservative approach used currently.

References

1. Deolasee, P., et al., Adaptive Push-Pull: Disseminating Dynamic Web Data. in Proceeding of the 10th International WWW Conference. Hong Kong: p. 265-274, 2001.
2. Pandrangi, N., et al., WebVigiL: User Profile-Based Change Detection for HTML/XML Documents. in Twentieth British National Conference on Databases. Coventry, UK. pages 38 - 55, 2003,
3. Chakravarthy, S., et al., WebVigiL: An approach to Just-In-Time Information Propagation In Large Network-Centric Environments. in Second International Workshop on Web Dynamics. Hawaii, 2002.
4. GNUDiff. http://www.gnu.org/software/diffutils/diffutils.html,
5. Hunt, J.W. and Mcllroy, M.D. An algorithm for efficient file comparison, in Technical Report. Bell Laboratories. 1975.
6. Zhang, K., A New Editing based Distance between Unordered Labeled Trees. Combinatorial Pattern Matching, vol. **1** p. 254-265, 1993.

7. Changedetection. http://www.changedetection.com,
8. Liu, L., et al., Information Monitoring on the Web: A Scalable Solution. in World Wide Web: p. 263-304, 2002.
9. Douglis, F., et al., The AT&T Internet Difference Engine: Tracking and Viewing Changes on the Web, in World Wide Web. Baltzer Science Publishers. p. 27-44. 1998.
10. WYSIGOT. http://www.wysigot.com/,
11. Nguyen, B., et al., Monitoring XML Data on the Web. in Proceedings of the 2001 ACM SIGMOD International Conference on Management of Data, 2001.
12. Jacob, J. WebVigiL: Sentinel specification and user-intent based change detection for Extensible Markup Language (XML), in MS Thesis. The University of Texas at Arlington. 2003.
13. Chakravarthy, S., et al., A Learning-Based Approach to fetching Pages in WebVigiL. in Proc of the 19th ACM Symposium on Applied Computing, March 2004.
14. Chakravarthy, S. and Mishra, D., Snoop: An Expressive Event Specification Language for Active Databases. Data and Knowledge Engineering, vol. **14**(10): p. 1--26, 1994.
15. Jacob, J., et al., WebVigiL: An approach to Just-In-Time Information Propagation In Large Network-Centric Environments(to be published), in Web Dynamics Book. Springer-Verlag. 2003.
16. Chakravarthy, S., et al., Composite Events for Active Databases: Semantics, Contexts and Detection, in Proc. Int'l. Conf. on Very Large Data Bases VLDB: Santiago, Chile. p. 606--617. 1994.
17. Sanka, A. A Dataflow Approach to Efficient Change Detection of HTML/XML Documents in webVigiL, in MS Thesis. The University of Texas at Arlington, August 2003.
18. Jacob, J., Sachde, A., and Chakravarthy, S., CX-DIFF: A Change Detection Algorithm for XML Content and change Presentation Issues for WebVigiL, ER Workshops October 2003: 273-284.

On Modelling Cooperative Retrieval Using an Ontology-Based Query Refinement Process

Nenad Stojanovic[1] and Ljiljana Stojanovic[2]

[1] Institute AIFB, Research Group Knowledge Management, University of Karlsruhe, 76128 Karlsruhe, Germany
nst@aifb.uni-karlsruhe.de

[2] FZI - Research Center for Information Technologies at the University of Karlsruhe, 76128 Karlsruhe, Germany
Stojanovic@fzi.de

Abstract. In this paper we present an approach for the interactive refinement of ontology-based queries. The approach is based on generating a lattice of the refinements, that enables a step-by-step tailoring of a query to the current information needs of a user. These needs are implicitly elicited by analysing the user's behaviour during the searching process. The gap between a user's need and his query is quantified by measuring several types of query ambiguities, which are used for ranking of the refinements. The main advantage of the approach is a more cooperative support in the refinement process: by exploiting the ontology background, the approach supports finding "similar" results and enables efficient relaxing of failing queries.

1 Introduction

Although a lot of research was dedicated to improving the cooperativeness of an information access process [1], almost all of them were focused on resolving the problem of an empty answer set. Indeed, either due to false presuppositions concerning the content of the knowledge base which lead to the *stonewalling* behaviour of the retrieval system, or due to the misconceptions (concerning the schema of the domain) which cause mismatches between a user's view on the world and the concrete conceptualisation of the domain, when a query fails it is more cooperative to identify the *cause* of failure, rather than just to report the empty answer set. If there is no a cause per se for the query's failure it is then worthwhile to report the part of the query which failed. Further, some types of query's generalizations [2] or relaxations [3], [4] were proposed for weakening a user's query in order to allow him to find some relevant results.

The growing nature of the web information content implies a users behaviour's pattern that should be treated in a more collaborative way in the modern retrieval systems: users tend to make short queries which they refine (expand) subsequently. Indeed, in order to be sure to get any answer to a query, a user forms as short as possible query and depending on the list of answers, he tries to narrow his query in several refinement steps. Probably the most expressive examples are product catalogue applications that serve as web interfaces to the large product databases. The main problem here is that a user cannot express clearly his need for a product by using only 2-3 terms, i.e. a user's query represents just an approximation of his information need [5]. Therefore, a user tries in several refinement steps to filter the list of retrieved products, so that only the products which are most relevant for his information need

P. Atzeni et al. (Eds.): ER 2004, LNCS 3288, pp. 434–449, 2004.

remain. Unfortunately, most of the retrieval systems do not provide a cooperative support in the query refinement process, so that a user is "forced" to change his query on his own in order to find the most suitable results. Indeed, although in an interactive query refinement process [6] a user is provided with a list of terms that appear frequently in retrieved documents, a more semantic analysis of the relationships between these terms is missing. For example, if a user made a query for a metallic car, then the refinements that include the value of the car's colour of the car can be treated more relevant than the refinements regarding the speed of the car, since the feature metallic is strongly related to the colour. At least, such reasoning can be expected from a human shop assistant. Obviously, if a retrieval system has more information about the model of the underlying product data, then a more cooperative (human-like) retrieval process can be created.

In our previous work we have developed a query refinement process, called Librarian Agent Query Refinement process, that uses an ontology for modelling an information repository [7],[8]. That process is based on incrementally and interactively tailoring a query to the current information need of a user, whereas that need is discovered implicitly by analysing the user's behaviour during the search process. The gap between the user's query and his information need is defined as the query ambiguity and it is measured by several ambiguity parameters that take into account the used ontology as well as the content of the underlying information repository. In order to provide a user with suitable candidates for the refinement of his query, we calculate the so-called Neighbourhood of that query. It contains the query's direct neighbours regarding the lattice of queries defined by considering the inclusion relation between query results.

In this paper we extend this work by involving more user's-related information in the query refinement phase of the query refinement process. In that way our approach ensures continual adaptation of the retrieval system to the changing preferences of users. Due to the reluctance of users to give explicit information about the quality of the retrieval process, we base our work on the implicit user's feedback, a very popular information retrieval technique for gathering user's preferences [9]. From a user's point of view, our approach provides more cooperative retrieval process: In each refinement step a user is provided with a complete but minimal set of refinements, which enables him to develop/express his information need in a step-by-step fashion. Secondly, although all users' interactions are anonymous, we personalize the searching process and achieve the so-called *ephemeral personalization* by implicitly discovering a user's need. The next benefit is the possibility to anticipate which alternative resources can be interesting for the user. Finally, this principle enables coping with a user's requests that cannot be fulfilled in the given repository (i.e. the requests that returns zero results), a hard-solvable problem for existing information retrieval approaches.

The paper is organised as follows: In the second Section we present the extended Librarian Agent Query Refinement process and discuss its cooperative nature. Section 3 provides related work and Section 4 contains concluding remarks.

2 Librarian Agent Query Refinement Process

The goal of the Librarian Agent Query Refinement process [8] is to enable a user to efficiently find results relevant for his information need in an ontology-based information repository, even if some problems we sketched in the previous section appear in the searching process. These problems lead to some misinterpretations of a user's need in his query, so that either a lot of irrelevant results and/or only a few relevant results are retrieved. In the Librarian Agent Query Refinement process, potential ambiguities (i.e. misinterpretations) of the initial query are firstly discovered and assessed (cf. the so-called *Ambiguity-Discovery* phase). Next, these ambiguities are interpreted regarding the user's information need, in order to estimate the effects of an ambiguity on the fulfilment of the user's goals (cf. the so-called *Ambiguity-Interpretation* phase). Finally, the recommendations for refining the given query are ranked according to their relevance for fulfilling the user's information need and according to the possibility to disambiguate the meaning of the query (cf. the so-called *Query Refinement* phase). In that way, the user is provided with a list of relevant query refinements ordered according to their capabilities to decrease the number of irrelevant results or/and to increase the number of relevant results. In the next three subsections we explain these three phases further, whereas the first phase is just sketched here, since its complete description is given in [8].

In order to present the approach in a more illustrative way, we refer to examples based on the ontology presented in Fig. 1. Table 1 represents a small product catalog, indexed/annotated with this ontology. Each row represents the features assigned to a product (a car), e.g. product P8 is a cabriolet, its colour is green metallic and it has an automatic gear changing system. The features are organised in an isA hierarchy, for example the feature (concept) "BlueColor" has two specializations "DarkBlue" and "WhiteBlue" which means that a dark or white blue car is also a blue colour car.

isA(SportsCar, Car), isA(FamilyCar, Car) isA(MiniCar, Car), hasFeature(Car, Feature) isA(Colour, Feature)*, isA(Luxury, Feature) isA(GearChanging, Feature), isA(Petrol, Feature) isA(MerchantFeature, Feature), isA(Price, MerchantFeature) hasColourValue(Colour, ColourValue) sub(ColourValue, ColourValue) hasColourType(Colour, ColourType) hasLuxuryType(Luxury, LuxuryType) hasGearChangingType(GearChanging, GearChangingType),	hasPetrolType(Petrol, PetrolType) spendLitters(Petrol, Value) hasPriceValue(Price, Value) ColourValue("BlueColor"), ColourValue("DarkBlue") ColourValue("WhiteBlue"), ColourValue("GreenColor") sub("BlueColor", "DarkBlue"), sub("BlueColor", "WhiteBlue") ColourType("Metallic"), ColourType("Standard") ColourType("Protected"), LuxuryType("Cabriolet") GearChangingType("Automatic"), PetrolType("Diesel")

* It means that a Colour is a type of Features.

Fig. 1. The car-feature ontology used throughout the paper

2.1 Phase 1: Ambiguity Discovery

We define query ambiguity as an indicator of the gap between the user's information need and the query that results from that need. Since we have found two main factors that cause the ambiguity of a query: the vocabulary (ontology) and the information repository, we define two types of the ambiguity that can arise in interpreting a query: (i) the *semantic ambiguity*, as the characteristic of the used ontology and (ii) the *content-related ambiguity*, as the characteristic of the repository. In the next two subsections we give more details on them.

Table 1. A product catalog based on Fig. 1

	Blue Color	Dark Blue	White Blue	Green Color	Metallic	Cabriolet	Automatic	Diesel	Price
P1	X	X			X	X			10 k
P2	X	X					X		8 k
P3	X	X							7 k
P4	X		X					X	8 k
P5	X		X		X	X	X		11 k
P6	X		X				X		8 k
P7				X					5 k
P8				X	X	X	X		11 k

2.1.1 Semantic Ambiguity

The goal of an ontology-based query is to retrieve the set of all instances which fulfil all constraints given in that query. In such a logic query the constraints are applied on the *query variables*. For example in the query:

```
∀ x ← Colour(x) and hasColorValue(x,BlueColour)
```

`x` is a *query variable* and `hasColorValue(x,BlueColour)` is a *query constraint.* The stronger these constraints are (by assuming that all of them correspond to the user's need), the more relevant the retrieved instances are for the user's information need.

Since an instance in an ontology is described through (i) the concept it belongs to and (ii) the relations to other instances, we see two factors which determine the semantic ambiguity of a query variable:

- the concept hierarchy: How general is the concept the variable belongs to
- the relation-instantiation: How descriptive/strong are constraints applied to that variable

Consequently, we define the following two parameters in order to estimate these values:

Definition 1: *Variable Generality*
$VariableGenerality(X) = Subconcepts(Type(X)) + 1$, where *Type*(*X*) is the concept the variable *X* belongs to, *Subconcepts*(*C*) is the number of subconcepts of the concept *C*.

Definition 2: *Variable Ambiguity*

$$VariableAmbiguity(X,Q) = \frac{|Relation(Type(X))| + 1}{|AssignedRelations(Type(X),Q)| + 1} \cdot \frac{1}{|AssignedConstraints(X,Q)| - |AssignedRelations(Type(X),Q)| + 1}, \quad (1)$$

where *Relation*(*C*) is the set of all relations defined for the concept *C* in the ontology, *AssignedRelations*(*C,Q*) is the set of all relations defined in the set *Relation(C)* and which appear in the query *Q*. *AssignedConstraints*(*X,Q*) is the set of all constraints related to the variable *X* that appear in the query *Q*.

The total ambiguity of a variable is calculated as the product of these two parameters, in order to model uniformly the directly proportional effect of both parameters to the ambiguity. Note that the second parameter is typically less than 1. We now define the ambiguity as follows:

$$Ambiguity(X,Q) = VariableGenerality(X) \cdot VariableAmbiguity(X,Q) \quad (2)$$

Finally, the *Semantic Ambiguity* for the query Q is calculated as follows:

$$SemanticAmbiguity(Q) = \sum_{x \in Var(Q)} Ambiguity(x,Q)\text{'}$$

where *Var*(*Q*) represents the set of variables that appear in the query *Q*. By analysing these ambiguity parameters it is possible to discover which of the query variables introduces the highest ambiguity in a query. Consequently, this variable should be refined in the query refinement phase.

2.1.2 Content-Related Ambiguity

An ontology defines just a model how the entities from a real domain should be structured. If there is a part of that model that is not instantiated in the given domain, then that part of the model cannot be used for calculating ambiguity. Therefore, we should use the content of the information repository to prune the results from the ontology-related analyses of a user's query.

2.1.2.1 Query Neighbourhood

We introduce here the notation for ontology-related entities that are used in the rest of this subsection:

- *Q*(*O*) is a query defined against the ontology *O*. The setting in this paper encompasses positive conjunctive queries. However, the approach can be easily extended to queries that include negation and disjunction.
- Ω(*O*) is the set of all possible elementary queries (queries that contain only one constraint) for an ontology *O*.
- *KB*(*O*) is the set of all relation instances (facts) which can be proven in the given ontology *O*. It is called the knowledge base.
- *A*(*Q*(*O*)) is the set of answers (in the logical sense) for the query *Q* regarding the ontology *O*.

Definition 3: Ontology-based information repository

An Ontology-based information repository *IR* is the structure (*R, O, ann*), where:

- *R* is a set of elements r_i that are called resources, $R=\{r_i\}$, $1 \leq i \leq n$;
- *O* is an ontology, which defines the vocabulary used for annotating these resources. We say that the repository is annotated with ontology *O* and a knowledge base *KB*(*O*);
- *ann* is a binary relation between a set of resources and a set of facts from the knowledge base *KB*(*O*), $ann \subseteq R\text{x}KB(O)$. We write $ann(r, k_i)$, meaning that a fact k_i is assigned to the resource *r* (i.e. a resource *r* is annotated with a fact k_i).

Definition 4: Resources-Attributes group (*user's request*)

A Resources-Attributes group (ς) in an *IR=(R, O, ann)* is a tuple $\varsigma = (Q', R')$, where

- $Q' \subset \Omega(O)$, is called a set of *ς_attributes*,
- $R' \subseteq R$, is called a set of *ς_resources*. It follows: $R' = \{r \in R \mid \forall i \in A(Q') : ann(r,i)\}$, i.e. this is the set of resources which are annotated with all attributes of the query *Q'*.

Definition 5: Structural equivalence (=) between two user's requests ς_1, ς_2, is defined by: $(Q_1', R_1') = (Q_2', R_2') \leftrightarrow R_1' = R_2'$. It means that two user's requests are structurally equivalent if their sets of result resources (ς*_resources*) are equivalent.

Definition 6: Cluster of users' queries (in the rest of text: *Query cluster*) is a set of all structurally equivalent user's requests $\Delta = (Q_x, R_y)$, where

- $Q_x \subseteq \Omega(O)$, Q_x is called the set of Δ*_attributes* (attribute set) and contains the union of attributes of all requests that are equivalent. For a user's request ς_u it is calculated in the following manner $Q_x = \{ \bigcup_{\forall \zeta_i \; \zeta_i = \zeta_u} \zeta_i\_attributes \}$.

It holds: $\forall \zeta_1, \zeta_2 \;\; \zeta_1 = \zeta_2 \wedge (\zeta_1\_attributes \subset Q_x) \rightarrow \zeta_2\_attributes \subset Q_x$.

- $R_y \subseteq R$, R_y is called the set of Δ*_resources* (resource set) and is equal to the ς*_resources* set of the query Q_x. Formally: $R_y = \{ r \in R | \; \forall i \in A(Q_x) \rightarrow ann(r,i) \}$.

The Query cluster which contains all existing resources in *IR* (i.e. a cluster for which R_y=*R*) is called the *root cluster*. The set of all Query clusters Δ is denoted by Δ(*IR*).

Definition 7: Structural subsumption (parent-child relation) (<) between two query clusters is defined by: $(Q_{x1}, R_{y1}) < (Q_{x2}, R_{y2}) \leftrightarrow R_{y1} \subset R_{y2}$ or $(Q_{x1}, R_{y1}) < (Q_{x2}, R_{y2}) \leftrightarrow Q_{x1} \supset Q_{x2}$.

A Query cluster Δ_2 subsumes another cluster Δ_1 if the set of resources of Δ_2 is a superset of the resource set of the cluster Δ_1, or if the set of attributes of Δ_2 is a subset of the set of attributes of Δ_1. Note that this relation is irreflexive, anti-symmetric and transitive.

We define a special subsumption relation ($<_{dir}$) on the set of Query clusters:

$$\Delta_1 <_{dir} \Delta_2 \leftrightarrow \Delta_1 < \Delta_2 \wedge \neg \exists \Delta_i, \Delta_1 < \Delta_i < \Delta_2 .$$

In that case we call Δ_2 a direct_parent cluster of Δ_1 and Δ_1 a direct_child cluster of Δ_2. The sets of direct_parent and direct_child clusters of a Query cluster Δ_1 are calculated in the following way:

DirectParents(Δ_1)={ $\Delta_i \in \Delta(IR) | \;\; R_{x1} \subset R_{yi} \wedge \neg \exists \Delta_j, R_{y1} \subset R_{yj} \subset R_{yi} \wedge \exists q \in Q_{yi} \wedge q \notin Q_{rest-i}$ },

where Q_{rest-i} is the set of all query terms that belong to direct_parents clusters, excluding the cluster Δ_i and

DirectChildren(Δ_1) = { $\Delta_i \in \Delta(IR) | \;\; Q_{x1} \subset Q_{xi} \wedge \neg \exists \Delta_j, Q_{x1} \subset Q_{xj} \subset Q_{xi} \wedge \exists r \in R_{yi} \wedge r \notin R_{rest-i}$ },

where R_{rest-i} is the set of all resources that belong to direct_children clusters, excluding the child Δ_i.

The conditions regarding rest-i sets in above-mentioned definitions ensure the minimal cardinality of the both direct neighbour sets.

Moreover the partial order of Query clusters induces many properties that are important for the efficient manipulation of user's queries:

Definition 8: Structural-similarity (siblings relation) (~)
We define two kinds of structural similarity between two Query clusters Δ_1 and Δ_2:

- common_parent ($\sim_{\text{parent}}$): $\Delta_1 \sim_{parent} \Delta_2 \leftrightarrow \exists \Delta_i \quad \Delta_1 <_{dir} \Delta_i \wedge \Delta_2 <_{dir} \Delta_i \wedge \neg(\Delta_1 = \Delta_2)$
- common_child ($\sim_{\text{child}}$): $\Delta_1 \sim_{child} \Delta_2 \leftrightarrow \exists \Delta_i \quad \Delta_i <_{dir} \Delta_1 \wedge \Delta_i <_{dir} \Delta_2 \wedge \neg(\Delta_1 = \Delta_2)$.

Definition 9: Disjoint Query clusters ($<>$) are clusters which have no resources in common, i.e. $\Delta_1 <> \Delta_2 \leftrightarrow R_{y1} \cap R_{y2} = \{\}$.

Definition 10: Query Neighbourhood
The Neighbourhood of a user's request ς_u is the structure $N := (E, P, C, \gamma, \eta)$, where

- $E := \{\varsigma_i \mid \varsigma_i = \varsigma_u\}$, i.e. the set of all user's requests equivalent to ς_u. Consequently, all requests from E form the *starting cluster* $\Delta_{start}(\varsigma_u)$ for ς_u, i.e. $E = \Delta_{start}(\varsigma_u)$.
- $P := \{\Delta_i \mid \Delta_{start}(\varsigma_u) <_{dir} \Delta_i\}$, i.e. the set of all direct_parent clusters of $\Delta_{start}(\varsigma_u)$.
- $C := \{\Delta_i \mid \Delta_i <_{dir} \Delta_{start}(\varsigma_u)\}$, i.e. the set of all direct_child clusters of $\Delta_{start}(\varsigma)$.
- $\gamma: P \rightarrow \Re$, is the relevance function for direct_parent clusters (it is used for ranking direct_parent clusters) and
- $\eta: C \rightarrow \Re$, is the relevance function for direct_child clusters (it is used for ranking direct_child clusters) ($\Re$ denotes the set of real numbers)

The ranking of direct_child (direct_parent) clusters is discussed in section 2.3.1.

2.1.2.2 Quantifying Content-Related Ambiguity

We define several properties which characterise the content ambiguity of a query [7], but due to the lack of space we focus here only on two which are used in the subsequent sections.

Max_equal_request of a user's request ς_a is the set of attributes found in its largest (regarding *ς_attributes*) structurally equivalent request, $\varsigma_{a\,max}$. $\varsigma_{a\,max}$ is equal to the starting cluster $\Delta_{start}(\varsigma_a)$ (see Definition 10), or Δ_a as a shorthand here. This cluster is calculated as $\Delta_a = (Q_{xa}, R_{ya})$ so that $Q_{xa} \supset Q'_a \wedge \neg\exists\, \Delta_i, \Delta_a <_{dir} \Delta_i, Q_{xi} \supset Q'_a$. Note that Q_a' is the set of attributes in the query ς_a.

Min_equal_request is the set of attributes found in the smallest (regarding *ς_attributes*) equivalent request for the given user's request, $\varsigma_{a\,min}$. There can be several such groups. They are calculated in the following way:
$\varsigma_{a\,min} \in \{(\times(Q_{xi} \cap Q_a')) \mid \Delta_a <_{dir} \Delta_i, i = 1,..n\}$, where $\Delta_a = \Delta_{start}(\varsigma_a)$.

2.2 Phase 2: Interpretation of Query Ambiguities

The previously defined parameters estimate the ambiguity of a query regarding the underlying ontology and the information repository. However, the problems in the meaning of a query have to be analysed regarding the user's needs, i.e. regarding the resource(s) the user is searching for.

2.2.1 Importance of a Query' Constraint for a User's Need

Despite the fact that in most IR systems, users do not quantify the importance of a constraint (attribute) in a query, a user does have his local preferences regarding these constraints, i.e. some constraints in a user's request are more relevant for his need than other. However, the crucial problem is how to discover the differences in user's preferences regarding a request, without to force a user to give explicitly a feedback about those preferences. In our approach we rely on the so-called implicit relevance feedback, a very popular information retrieval technique for gathering user's preferences [9]. However, we expand and extend these methods according to the different nature of our ontology-based querying process. We define two parameters that describe the importance of a constraint for the user's need: *Interpretability* and *Actuality*.

Interpretability. The general assumption is that a user forms a query according to his current information need, i.e. that all parts of the query correspond, to some extent, to his need. However, it is possible that a query is interpreted in a repository in an unexpected manner, i.e. the execution of a query can be interpreted ambiguously: either as a more general or a more specific query. For example, if a user is searching for a Cabriolet-car against the given product catalog (Table 1), due to the content of the underlying dataset, the system will retrieve the same results as for the query ?"*Cabriolet, Metallic*", which is the *Max_equal_request* (See Section 2.1.2.2.) for the request ?"Cabriolet". It means that the constraint *Metallic* is interpreted as an additional constraint in the user's query, but it might be not aligned to his need. Consequently, the importance of that parameter for refining should be reduced. Therefore if a constraint is a part of the *Max_equal_request* of a user's query, but not of that query, then its *Interpretability* is very low (= 0). Otherwise if a user is searching for a Cabriolet- and Metallic-car, the system will retrieve the same results as for the query ?"*Cabriolet*" or for the query ?"*Metallic*", which can be interpreted as the "ignorance" of one of these constraints in the searching process. Consequently, the importance of these constraints should be increased. Since the reduced queries belong to the *Min_equal_requests* of the initial query, by considering the constraints from the initial query that are not contained in the *Min_equal_requests* we get the set of constraints with a high *Interpretability* (=1). Therefore:

$$Interpretability(c,\varsigma_a)=\begin{cases}0, & c\in Max\_equal\_request(\varsigma_a)\wedge c\notin\varsigma_a\\ 1, & c\notin Min\_equal\_request(\varsigma_a)\wedge c\in\varsigma_a\\ 0.5, & others\end{cases},$$

where c is a constraint from a user's query ς_a.

Actuality. The *Actuality* parameter reflects the phenomena, accounted in the IR research [10], that a user may change the criteria about the relevance of a query term, when encountering newly retrieved results. In other words, the constraints most recently introduced in a user's query are more indicative of what the user currently finds relevant for his need. We model it using the analogy to the ostensive relevance [10]:

$Actuality(c,Qs)=\dfrac{1}{num\_session(c,Qs)+1}$, where c is a constraint (Δ_attribute), Qs is the current query session and *num_session*(c, Qs) is the number of refinement steps, which the constraint c is involved in.

2.2.2 Relevance of a Query Constraint for a User's Need

The theory about the implicit relevance feedback postulates that if a user selects a resource from the list of retrieved results, then this resource corresponds, to some extent, to his information need. However, a click on a particular resource in the resulted list cannot be treated as an absolute relevance judgement, since users typically scan only the top l ranked ($l \approx 10$) resources. For example, maybe a document ranked much lower in the list was much more relevant, but the user newer saw it. It appears that users click on the (relatively) most promising resources in the top l, independent of their absolute relevance. However, if we assume that a user scans the list of results from top to bottom, the relative relevance is evident: all non-clicked-on resources placed above a clicked-on resource are less relevant than the clicked-on resource. Obviously, the relevance is related to some feature that are contained in the clicked-on resource and not contained in non-clicked-on resources. It means that by analysing the commonalities in the attributes of results a user clicked/not clicked, we can infer more information about the intension of the user in the current query session. In order to achieve this, we define the relation *preferred ranking* as

$R_i <_{rQ^*} R_j$ for all pairs $1 <= j < i$, with $i \in C$ and $j \notin C$,

where $(R_1, R_2, R_3, \ldots)$ is a ranked list of resources, set C contains the ranks of the clicked-on resources and Q is the posted query.

ImplicitRelevance. By analysing the difference between the features (attributes, constraints) of the clicked-on and non-clicked-on resources we get a set of so called *Preferred* constraints for a query Q in the following manner:

$$Preferred(Q) = \{con \mid con \in \cup_j\, Preferred_j(Q)\}, \text{ where}$$
$$Preferred_j(Q) = \{el \mid el \in Attr(R_j) \setminus \cup_i Attr(R_i),\ \forall i\ R_i <_{rQ^*} R_j\},$$

$Attr(R_x)$ is the set of constraints (attributes) that are defined for the resource R_x.

Therefore, the set of constraints that seems to be relevant for a user in a query Q_s can be calculated as:

$$ImplRel(c, Qs) = \begin{cases} 0, & c \notin Preferred(Qs) \\ \dfrac{1}{n} \sum\limits_{i=1,n} \dfrac{1}{num\_sessions(c, Q_S, i)}, & c \in Preferred(Qs) \end{cases}, \quad (3)$$

where $num\_sessions(c, Qs, i)$ is the number of refinement steps which the constraint c is involved as a preferred constraint in, whereas n is the total number of times the constraint c is treated as a preferred constraint in the current session Qs.

In this way we decrease the likelihood that a preferred constraint is still relevant if it was suggested as relevant in a previous refinement step, but was not selected by the user as relevant in the subsequent refinement step (see (3)). Therefore, our approach has the self-improvement nature – it learns from its failures.

ImplicitIrrelevance. Since the recommended refinements are presented to a user in the decreasing order of relevance, one can assume that if a user has selected n-th ranked results, then the first n-1 ranked results (constraints) are wrongly ranked on the top of the list of the refinements. We call these constraint *implicit irrelevant*. They are calculated in similar manner as implicit relevant constraints:

$$ImplIrrel(c,Qs) = \begin{cases} 0, & c \notin Nonpreferred(Qs) \\ \sum_{i=1,n} \frac{1}{num\_sessions(c,Q_S,i)}, & c \in Nonpreferred(Qs) \end{cases}, \quad (4)$$

where $NonPreferred(Q) = \{con \mid con \in \cup_j NonPreferred_j(Q)\}$

$NonPreferred_j(Q) = \{el \mid el \in \cup_i Attr(R_i) \backslash Attr(R_j), \forall i\ R_i <rQ^*\ R_j\}$.

The definition of *num_sessions*(*c, Qs, i*) is analogue to (3), but regarding implicit irrelevance.

Similar to (3), formula (4) enables the correction of false assumptions (regarding the preferences of the current user) made in the ranking process.

Formulas (3) and (4) ensures the self-adaptivity of the ranking system, e.g. they do not allow that the system repeatedly ranks a non-interesting refinement highly. Finally, the calculated implicit relevance of a refinement *c* looks like:

$$Relevance(c,Qs) = \frac{ImplRel(c,Qs)+1}{ImplIrrel(c,Qs)+1} \quad (5)$$

The previously defined parameters estimate the ambiguity of a query regarding the underlying ontology and the information repository. However, the problems in the meaning of a query have to be analysed regarding the user's needs, i.e. regarding the resource(s) the user is searching for.

2.3 Phase 3: Query Refinement

This is the last phase in the query refinement process, which processes previously defined ambiguity parameters in order to help a user in finding more relevant resources in a shorter period of time. Primarily, we provide three types of support:

1. Recommending query refinements that can lead to better fulfilment of the user's need;
2. Recommending resources which can be treated as alternatives for the resource a user selected for further processing;
3. Recommending modifications of the query in case of zero results.

2.3.1 Ranking of Recommendations (Refinements)

The presented approach supports step-by-step query refinement, which means that a user is provided with all and only relevant refinements. In other words, the set of provided refinements is (1) minimal and (2) complete regarding the relevant resources. Due to the lack of space we give the proof only for the first one statement.

Proof for (1): Let us assume that for a user's query $\Delta_{start}(\zeta_u)$ (see Definition 10), there is a refinement Δ_x that belongs to the set of children $C := \{\Delta_i \mid \Delta_i <_{dir} \Delta_{start}(\varsigma_u)\}$, but that could be omitted from the children without disabling the retrieval of some relevant resources. It means that there are some refinements from the set *C*, let us assume Δ_a and Δ_b, that retrieve parts of the R_x (results of the refinement Δ_x), let us say R_{xa} and R_{xb}, respectively. Therefore, $R_a \subset R_{xa}$, $R_b \subset R_{xb}$ and $R_{xa} \cup R_{xb} = R_x$. According to the formula for the calculation of the set *DirectChildren* (below Definition 7) this is not possible, since each refinement from *C* has to have a unique element in its list of result. It means - the starting assumption is false □.

In the step-by-step query refinement we assume that with every decision taken by the user can be used as information about the user's intensions and background. For example, each transition (refinement) from the query *e* to query *d* involves a conscious choice by the user by preferring the constraints contained in *d* to the other options in the constraint *e*. The probability of a constraint *d* being the target of the navigation process is related to the distance fluctuations while travelling the navigation path. Recent fluctuations have more impact then past fluctuations. Typically, the farther removed a constraint is from the path, the less likely that it is the target of the search. This is captured by the probability of *d* being the search target, after having traversed search path *p*. For this purpose we will transform the search space into a transition network, allowing the use of Markov chains theory. First, the set of states is defined as the set of *query constraints* augmented with a special state called *stop*. This state represents the termination of the search process. The transition between states are defined as follows: if constraints *x* and *y* are connected regarding the ontology structure, then they are connected in the transition network.

We assume for each transaction *e* a probability $q_e > 0$ of occurring. In a transition network, for each state *a*: $\sum_{b:a\to b} q_{a\to b} = 1$. The transition matrix T is defined as

$$T(x,y)=\begin{cases} q_s & \text{if } x\in Related(y) \\ 0 & \text{otherwise} \end{cases},$$

where q_s is uniformly distributed over all related constraints and *Related*(*c*) is a function that retrieves constraints that are related to *c* regarding the underlying ontology. For example, `Car` and `Motorbike` are related to each other through the superconcept `Vehicle`.

Further, $T^i(x,y)$ is the probability of reaching *y* starting from *x* in *i* transitions. $T^0 =$ *I*, the identity matrix. Thus, the sum $\sum_{i=0}^{\infty} T^i(e,d)$ is the probability of reaching *d* from *e* in any number of steps. Next we focus on the probability *Pr*(*d* | *e*) of a constraint *d* being the search target of a navigation path. The destination probability for *d* after traversing a path from *e* is defined as follows: $Pr(d\,|\,e)=\sum_{i=0}^{\infty} T^i(e,d)\cdot T(d,stop)$.

The infinite sum converges to $(I-T)^{-1}(e,d)$ (see [11]). This requires the calculation of the inverse matrix of an $|\Omega(O)|$ x $|\Omega(O)|$ matrix, where $\Omega(O)$ is the set of elementary constraints regarding given ontology *O*. Note that this operation can be calculated off-line.

However, in a step-by-step refinement a user is navigating through queries Q_x that contain several constraints. In that case we expand the probability to include this information as follows:

$$Pr(Q_d\,|\,Q_e)=\frac{1}{|Q_d|}\cdot\sum_{d\in Q_d}\frac{1}{|Q_e|}\cdot\sum_{e\in Q_e} Pr(d\,|\,e),$$

where *d* and *e* are constraints from queries Q_d and Q_e respectively. $|\,Q_d\,|$ depicts the number of constraints in Q_d.

We use this destination probability function as a starting point for computing which neighbours bring the user most direct towards the highest probable destination constraint. Indeed, as we mentioned above the refinement process depends on the searching history (parameters *Actuality* and *Relevance*) and the content of the repository (parameters *Interpretability*).

This is formalized by assigning the coefficient *Rank* to each query Q_d that belongs to the lattice of the refinement for the query Q_e:

$$Rank(Q_d \mid Q_e) = \frac{1}{|Q_d|} \cdot \sum_{d \in Q_d} \frac{1}{|Q_e|} \cdot \left(\sum_{e \in Q_e} Pr(d \mid e) \cdot \left(\frac{\lambda \cdot Relevance(d) \cdot Actuality(e) + Interpretability(e, Q_e)}{\lambda + 1} \right) \right),$$

where λ is a forgetfulness coefficient that model the impact on the past user's behaviour on the ranking process: $\lambda = 0$ - the past is forgotten, $\lambda < 1$ - the past carries less weight then the present, usually $\lambda = ½$.

Therefore our approach prioritises highly relevant refinements, i.e. the refinements that are related to the very characteristic (regarding a query) constraints and tailored to the user's need.

2.3.2 Finding Alternative Results

An alternative result for a query is a result that does not fulfil all constraints from the query perfectly (but fulfils some of them), but has (many) suitable features from a user's point of view (e.g. usability). In the domain of e-commerce such features are often called merchant characteristics (like price of a product, warranty, time of delivery). However the problem is how to find which characteristics can be relaxed in the user's query and which not. Our approach supports this decision by analysing implicitly discovered user's need. The query neighbourhood is used as a snapshot of the repository where relevant alternatives can be found. Briefly, we define the function *Alternatives*(R_p, *M*, *level*), which finds all resources from the neighbourhood of the cluster in which the user selected the resource R_p, for which the merchant characteristic *M* is in the offset *level* of the value for the resource R_p. The system checks all resources contained in sibling clusters which satisfy the offset of the selected merchant characteristic. A user should set offset according to his preferences. The default value is 0,1. Formally,

$$Alternatives(R_p, M, level) = \{ R_{pi} \mid R_{pi} \subset \bigcup_{\forall \Delta_i,\ \Delta_i \sim \Delta_p} R_{yi} \ \wedge |M(R_p) - M(R_{pi})| < level \},$$

where Δ_p is the current cluster that contains the product R_p selected by the user. The alternative results are ranked according to the relevance to the current elicitated user's need. Moreover, using the parameter *Importance*, our approach "knows" which attributes are relevant for the user's need and tries firstly to find alternative products that retain these attributes.

2.3.3 Resolving Failing Queries

A query is said to fail whenever its evaluation produces the empty set. An empty answer is surprising to the user since the user expects that there exist answers to the asked query. So when a query fails, a system could be more cooperative by helping to trace the reason for the query's failure, or at least to pinpoint to the failure. However, the main problem is that it is possible to have a huge number of (independent) causes of a failure in a query. Consequently, finding all of them can require exponential time in worst case. Therefore, an efficient "repairing" system has to select only the most relevant *repairs* of a failing query. In our approach the relevance of a repair is calculated according to the lost in information that is caused by replacing/eliminating a query constraint. In that way we ensure that the interpretation of the new (satisfiable) query is close to the user's information need expressed in the original query.

The degradation of a user's information need caused by eliminating a constraint C_i from his initial (failing) request ς_x, is proportional to the ambiguity (see Section 2.1.1) introduced by this constraint and inverse proportional to the number of query's constraints that are related to C_i:

$$InfContent(C_i, \varsigma_x) = \sum_{r \in Var(C_i)} Ambiguity(r, Q_x) \cdot \frac{1}{|\{f \mid f \in Q_x \ \wedge \ f \in Related(C_i)\}|},$$

where ς_x is a user's request in the form $\{Q_x, R_x\}$. *Var*(*c*) is the function that returns the variable contained in the constraint *c* and *a*, *b*, *d* are weighting factors which are by default set to 1. *Related*(*c*) is a function that retrieves constraints that are related to *c* regarding the underlying ontology. Particularly, we treat the constraints defined on the same domain as related to each other, e.g. the constraints *Metallic* and *BlueColour* are related since the both of them are defined on the concept Colour (see Fig. 1).

The following procedure searches for the most suitable repairs regarding a user's query:

Let assume that a query ς has *n* constraints.

Step 1. Create *n* subqueries by eliminating (each) one constraint from the query.
Evaluate these queries.
If one of these subqueries does not fail *Then* go to Step2.
Else Calculate the *InfContent* for each constraint and select the subquery that corresponds to (i.e. misses) the least informative constraint. Repeat Step1 starting with that subquery.

Step 2.
If more subqueries did not fail,
Then Calculate the *InfContent* of the missing constraint in each subquery and select that subquery which corresponds to the least informative one (it is most close to the original query), e.g. ς_i.

Calculate the starting cluster $\Delta_{start}(\varsigma_i)$ and determine all direct_child clusters of that cluster.

If one of these direct_child clusters (e.g. Δ_k) contains an attribute (constraint), that is different from $\Delta_{start}(\varsigma_i)$ but it is in relation to the constraint eliminated by generating ς_i, then that cluster is a candidate for the query repair. Formally, *Candidates*$(\varsigma, \varsigma_i) = \{x \mid x \in Q_a \wedge x \notin \varsigma \wedge \exists R_a \{Q_a, R_a\} \in DirectChildren(\Delta_{start}(\varsigma_i)) \wedge x \in$ *Related*(y) $\wedge\, y \in \{\varsigma \setminus \varsigma_i\}\}$. These candidates are ranked according to the ontology-based similarity (function *Related*) between a candidate and the eliminated constraint.

Example: Let us suppose that a user is interested in a "Cabriolet" car that has an "Automatic" gear changing system and has "DarkBlue" colour. However, in the underlying product catalog (Table 1) there is no car which fulfils these constraints. According to the previous algorithm: ς = ?"Cabriolet" +"DarkBlue" + "Automatic", ς_i = "Cabriolet" + "Automatic" and *Candidates*(ς, ς_i) = {"WhiteBlue"}, since "White-

Blue" and the eliminated constraint, "DarkBlue", are *related* (i.e. have a common parent). Therefore, the new query is ?"Cabriolet" +"WhiteBlue" + "Automatic". It conveys the initial user's need very well.

Since our approach finds only several, most relevant, repairs, the complexity of the approach is low. We perform a depth-first search, such that in at most n steps (n is the number of constraints) we find a non-failing subquery. In the i-th step from the beginning we perform $(n - i)$ tests in order to find the most suitable subquery. Therefore the worst time-complexity of the Step1 is $O(n^2)$. The complexity of the Step2 is equal to the complexity of finding direct_child clusters of a query that is discussed in the next section.

3 Related Work

1. Ontology-Based Recommender Systems. Our system can be considered as a content-based recommender system. From that point of view we see three main advantages of applying our approach: (i) basically, our system does not provide just a ranked list of results, but it recommends the set of possible refinements of the initial user's request as well, (ii) by using an ontology for indexing an information repository, our system can discover some implicitly presented similarities between information resources and therefore can provide better, semantic-based recommendations and (iii) by analysing the users' implicit relevance feedback, our system learns on-line (short-term) users' profiles, avoiding capturing and processing large log-files. Due to the ontology-based backbone of our system, it can be seen as a prototype of a recommender system for the **Semantic Web**, i.e. as an example how traditional on-line shopping portals can benefit from moving to the Semantic Web. The benefits regarding the integration between various product catalogs, e.g. using a common ontology, are not discussed here. A similar, ontology-based, recommender is the Quickstep system [12], which recommends on-line research papers to the academic community. However, it is primarily focused on using an ontology for profile bootstrapping in order to overcome the cold start problem by generating recommendations for a novel user.

2. Cooperative Answering / Personal Assistant / Interface Agents. From an end user point of view, our approach can be seen as a personal assistant [13] who analyses the user's behaviour and interacts with him in order to provide more relevant solutions for his initial task. Our approach differs from existing approaches for such a cooperative answering in two directions: (i) the cooperation is based not only on processing the query a user posts, but rather on understanding what the user is searching for (i.e. a query is treated as an approximation of a user's need) and (ii) the cooperation helps not only in resolving failure situation (no result for a query), but in suggesting the user some better alternatives for the given results.

3. Concept Lattice. Conceptually, the most similar approach to our query refinement system is Query By Navigation QBN [14], an approach for the navigation through a hyperindex of query terms. The hyperindex search engine supprts users to add, delete or substitute a term from the initial query by providing the minimal query refinements/enlargements. However, the variety of the analyses, especially regarding the ambiguity of the query and the query equivalence, is missing. Visualization similar to ours can be found in the REFINER system [15], which combines Boolean information retrieval and content-based navigation with concept lattices. For a Boolean query REFINER builds and displays a portion of the concept lattice associated with the documents being searched centred around the user's query. The cluster network displayed by the system shows the result of the query along with a set of minimal query refinements/enlargements. However, it (as QBN) does not use an ontology as background what limits its possibilities for proposing the refinements. Moreover, it does not tailor refinements to a user's need.

4 Conclusion

In this paper we presented a comprehensive approach for the refinement of ontology-based queries, which takes into account problems reported in traditional information retrieval. It extends our previous work in the ontology-based query refinement by involving more users' related information in the query refinement process. In that way our approach provides more cooperative retrieval process: In each refinement step a user is provided with a complete but minimal set of refinements, which enables him to develop/express his information need in a step-by-step fashion. Secondly, although all users' interactions are anonymous, we tailor the querying process to a user's preferences by using implicit user's feedback. Next, it is possible to anticipate which alternative resources can be interesting for the user. Finally, this principle enables coping with a user's requests that cannot be fulfilled in the given repository (i.e. the requests that returns zero results), a hard-solvable problem for existing information retrieval approaches.

Applied on Web searching our approach enables a new paradigm for presenting results to users in the Semantic Web by meta-organizing the retrieved list of results, by clustering these results in the groups which are ranked according to the relevance for the user's need.

Acknowledgement

Research for this paper was partially financed by BMBF in the project "SemIPort" (08C5939) and EU in projects "KnowledgeWeb" (507482) and "OntoGov" (507237).

References

1. Gaasterland, T., Godfrey, P., Minker, J.: An overview of cooperative answering, *Journal of Intelligent Information Systems*, 1(2) (1992) 123-157
2. Chaudhuri, S.: Generalization and a Framework for Query Modification, In IEEE ICDE, Los Angeles, CA, (1990)
3. Chu, W.W., Chiang, K., Hsu, C.-C., Yau. H.: Error-based Conceptual Clustering Method for Providing Approximate Query Answers. Comm. ACM, 39(12) (1996) 216–230
4. Lee, D.: Query Relaxation for XML Model Dongwon Lee, In Ph.D Dissertation, University of California, Los Angeles, (2002)
5. Saracevic, T.: Relevance: A Review of and a framework for the thinking on the notion in information science. Journal of the American Society for Information Science, 26(6) (1975) 321-343
6. Efthimiadis, E.N.: User choices: A new yardstick for the evaluation of ranking algorithms for interactive query expansion. Information Processing and Management, 31(4) (1995) 605-620

7. Stojanovic, N.: An Approach for Using Query Ambiguity for Query Refinement: The Librarian Agent Approach, 22nd International Conference on Conceptual Modeling (ER 2003), Chicago, Illinois, USA, Springer (2003)
8. Stojanovic, N., Studer, R., Stojanovic, Lj.: An Approach for Step-By-Step Query Refinement in the Ontology-based Information Retrieval, WI 2004, Beijing, in press
9. Salton, G., Buckley, C.: Improving retrieval performance by relevance feedback. Journal of the American Society for Information Science. 41(4) (1990) 288-297
10. Ruthven, I., Lalmas, M., van Rijsbergen, C.J.: Incorporating user search behaviour into relevance feedback, Journal of the American Society for Information Science and Technology, 54. 6. (2003) 528-548
11. Trividi K.S.: Probability and Statistics with Reliability, Queuing and Computer Science Applications. Prentice-Hall, Englewood Cliffs, New Jersey (1982)
12. Middleton, S.E. Alani, H. Shadbolt, N.R. De Roure, D.C.: Exploiting Synergy Between Ontologies and Recommender Systems, WWW2002, Semantic Web Workshop 2002, Hawaii, USA (2002)
13. Maes, P.: Agents that reduce work and information overload, *Communications of the ACM* 37(7) (1994)
14. Bruza, P.D., Dennis, S.: Query Reformulation on the Internet: Empirical Data and the Hyperindex Search Engine, RIAO97, Montreal (1997)
15. Carpineto, C., Romano, G.: Effective reformulation of boolean queries with concept lattices. In Flexible Query Answering Systems FQAS'98, Berlin, Springer (1998) 277-291

Load-Balancing Remote Spatial Join Queries in a Spatial GRID

Anirban Mondal and Masaru Kitsuregawa

Institute of Industrial Science
University of Tokyo, Japan
{anirban,kitsure}@tkl.iis.u-tokyo.ac.jp

Abstract. The explosive growth of spatial data worldwide coupled with the emergence of GRID computing provides a strong motivation for designing a spatial GRID which allows transparent access to geographically distributed data. While different types of queries may be issued from any node in such a spatial GRID for retrieving the data stored at other (remote) nodes in the GRID, this paper specifically addresses spatial join queries. Incidentally, skewed user access patterns may cause a disproportionately large number of spatial join queries to be directed to a few 'hot' nodes, thereby resulting in severe load imbalance and consequently increased user response times. This paper focusses on load-balanced spatial join processing in a spatial GRID.

1 Introduction

The explosive growth of spatial data worldwide coupled with the prevalence of spatial applications has made efficient management of geographically distributed spatial data a necessity. Spatial applications often arise in town planning, cartography, resource management, GIS (Geographic Information Systems), CAD (Computer-Aided Design) and computer vision. Incidentally, the emergence of GRID computing [4], which is associated with the massive integration and virtualization of geographically distributed computing resources, provides a strong motivation for designing a spatial GRID [11] which allows transparent access to geographically distributed data. While different types of queries (e.g., spatial select queries[1], nearest neighbour queries, similarity search queries and spatial join queries) may be issued from any node in the GRID for retrieving the data stored at other (remote) nodes of the GRID, this paper specifically addresses spatial joins on remote data since such queries constitute a typically expensive as well as popular class of query in spatial databases. Incidentally, a spatial join query retrieves from two spatial relations all the tuple pairs satisfying a given spatial predicate.

Now let us understand the importance of optimizing remote spatial joins with the help of an example. This year's Olympic Games is expected to attract tens of

[1] Our previous work [11] studied load-balancing of spatial select queries in a spatial GRID.

P. Atzeni et al. (Eds.): ER 2004, LNCS 3288, pp. 450–463, 2004.

thousands of visitors to Athens and many of these visitors would possibly wish to find a hotel near a bus station for the purpose of convenient transportation. Such visitors may issue the following query from their respective home countries which may be quite far away from Athens: *Find all the hotels in Athens which are near to any bus station.* Assuming there are two relations *'Hotels'* (containing details, such as location, rental charges, of all the hotels in Athens) and *'Bus Stations'* (containing information concerning all the bus stations in Athens), this translates to a remote spatial join operation. Interestingly, the above scenario is also *equally* applicable to any major international event that attracts people from various countries. Notably, the recent trend of increased globalization has significantly increased the importance as well as the performance demands of such global applications. Unfortunately, the current state-of-the-art does *not* allow a user to perform this kind of operation efficiently.

Skews in initial data distributions, skewed user access patterns and changing popularities of data regions may cause a disproportionately large number of spatial join queries to be directed to a few 'hot' nodes, thereby resulting in severe load imbalance and consequently increased user response times. From our example, given the huge number of queries from potential visitors to Athens, the nodes containing the data of Athens would quickly become overloaded, thereby necessitating a load-balancing mechanism for processing remote spatial joins efficiently. Several factors such as wide-area communication overheads, node heterogeneity and lack of centralization make the problem of load-balanced spatial join processing in GRIDs significantly more complex than that of load-balanced spatial join processing in traditional distributed environments such as clusters. However, we believe that the time has come to deal head-on with this problem. The main contributions of our proposal are as follows.

- We present a dynamic data placement strategy involving *online* data replication in GRIDs, the objective being to bring the data closer to the node from which it is frequently queried.
- We propose a novel load-balancing strategy for speeding up spatial joins in GRID environments.

Our performance evaluation demonstrates the effectiveness of our proposed approach in reducing the response times of spatial joins in GRIDs. To our knowledge, this work is one of the earliest attempts at addressing the load-balancing of remote spatial joins via *online* data replication in GRID environments. The remainder of this paper is organized as follows. Section 2 discusses related work, while Section 3 presents the system overview. Issues concerning load-balancing in spatial GRIDs are presented in Section 4. The proposed strategy for load-balancing spatial joins in GRIDs is discussed in Section 5, while Section 6 reports our performance evaluation. Finally, we conclude in Section 7.

2 Related Work

Important ongoing GRID computing projects such as the European DataGrid [2], the Grid Physics Network (GriPhyN) [13] and the Earth Systems Grid (ESG)

[6] aim at efficient distributed handling of huge amounts of data (in terabyte or petabyte range).

Issues concerning spatial databases with GIS applications can be found in [15], while a comprehensive survey on spatial indexes has been presented in [5]. Parallel spatial join processing has been extensively researched in the traditional domain. The proposals in [7] and [1] discuss synchronous traversal of generalization trees and R*-trees respectively. The work in [1] investigates parallel *load-balanced* spatial join processing using R*-trees on a shared-virtual-memory architecture. The PBSM (Partition Based Spatial-Merge) algorithm [12] first partitions the inputs into smaller chunks and uses a computational geometry based plane-sweeping technique to obtain a set of candidate pairs and then the tuples corresponding to the candidate set are fetched from disk to determine whether the join condition is actually satisfied. The work in [10] proposes a parallel non-blocking spatial join algorithm which uses duplicate avoidance and addresses main memory issues. Several dynamic [16] load-balancing techniques for clusters have also been proposed specifically for *clusters*. Notably, neither the the existing spatial join techniques nor the existing load-balancing strategies consider GRID-related issues such as heterogeneity and wide-area communication overheads essentially because these issues do *not* arise in traditional environments.

Incidentally, our proposal amounts to some form of caching of the results. Recent works on caching include [9, 14]. The work in [9] analyzes the effects of different design choices involving cache structure, cache capacity, and timeouts for caching previously discovered routes in demand routing protocols for wireless ad hoc networks. In [14], a semantic caching scheme has been proposed for accessing location-dependent data in mobile environments.

3 System Overview

We envisage the spatial GRID as comprising several clusters, where each cluster comprises nodes that belong to the same Local Area Network (LAN) [11]. This facilitates the separation of concerns between intra-cluster and inter-cluster load-balancing issues. Given that intra-cluster issues have been extensively researched, this paper specifically focusses on inter-cluster issues. For each cluster, the most reliable and best administered node is selected as the cluster leader, any ties being resolved arbitrarily. A cluster leader's job is to coordinate the activities (e.g., load-balancing, searching) of the nodes in its cluster. We define distance between two clusters as the communication time τ between the cluster leaders and if the value of τ for two clusters is less than a pre-defined threshold, the clusters are regarded as *neighbours*. A cluster C_i is considered to be *relevant* to a query Q_i if C_i contains at least a non-empty subset of the answers to Q. Given that the number of queries waiting in node N_i's job queue is W_i and taking the heterogeneity in node processing capacities into account, we define L_{N_i}, the load of N_i, as follows:

$$L_{N_i} = W_i \times (CPU_{N_i} \div CPU_{Total}) \tag{1}$$

where CPU_{N_i} denotes the CPU power of N_i and CPU_{Total} stands for the total CPU power of the cluster in which N_i is located. The *load of a cluster* is calculated as $\sum L_{N_i}$ i.e, the sum of the loads of its individual members. Given that the loads of two clusters C_i and C_j are L_{C_i} and L_{C_j} respectively and assuming without loss of generality that $L_{C_i} > L_{C_j}$, the normalized load difference Δ between C_i and C_j is computed as follows:

$$\Delta = ((L_{C_i} \times TC_i) - (L_{C_j} \times TC_j))/(TC_i + TC_j) \qquad (2)$$

where TC_i is the sum of the CPU power of all the members of C_i. Similarly, TC_j is the sum of the CPU power of all the members of C_j.

Spatial indexing mechanisms may vary across clusters. Hence, we propose a generalized indexing scheme which is built on top of the existing index at a cluster node. The indexing scheme in each cluster comprises three index structures, namely IID (Index structure for Internal Data), IED (Index structure for External Data) and IRD (Index structure for Replicated Data). Note that we distinguish between a cluster's *internal data* (the data which is originally stored at a cluster) and its replicated data because it may *not* be possible to integrate the replicated data smoothly into the existing index structure (for the internal data) of the cluster as the replicated data may be far apart in space from the cluster's internal data. Such separation of concerns between internal data and replicated data also makes it easier to periodically delete infrequently accessed replicas for optimizing disk space usage. IID is a *generalized* two-tier indexing mechanism, the first-tier of which resides at the cluster leader C_i and is essentially a list, each entry of which is of the form (*region,node_id*), where *region* represents a specific region and *node_id* stands for the node in the cluster at which the region is located. At the second tier, every node has its own independent index structure for the data allocated to it. For example, in case of R-trees [8], rectangular-shaped regions would be stored in the first-tier at C_i, while the second-tier would comprise R-trees at the individual nodes. IED and IRD are hierarchical tree-based index structures, which reside at the cluster leader. In our example, IED/IRD would be R-tree-like structures except that their leaf nodes would contain cluster IDs of neighbouring clusters' data regions instead of pointers to objects in the database. Updates to IED/IRD are periodically exchanged between neighbouring cluster leaders preferably via piggybacking onto other messages. Notably, in this paper, we have used the R-tree as an example, but our proposed technique may also be applicable to other spatial indexing structures albeit with certain modifications. Hence, in the near future, we also plan to investigate the use of other spatial indexing structures for performing spatial joins in GRIDs.

When a cluster leader C_i receives a query Q, it first checks its IID and IRD to ascertain whether any of its cluster nodes is relevant to Q. If C_i finds that *none* of its nodes is relevant to Q, it checks its IED and sends Q to its neighbouring cluster leaders which are relevant to Q. In case *none* of its neighbouring cluster leaders contain the answers to Q, C_i broadcasts Q to *all* of them. This process continues till either the answers to Q are retrieved or Q is timed-out. Assume the existence of n clusters in the GRID, $C_1, C_2, C_3, ...C_n$. Now suppose cluster C_i issues a spatial join query Q_i for the data in cluster C_j. A straightforward solution would be for C_j to process Q_i and return the results to C_i, but this solution would *not* be efficient in scenarios where many spatial join queries, which attempt to retrieve data from the same regions in C_j, are issued from C_i to C_j. Our primary focus is to reduce the response times of such spatial join queries on remote data via replication.

4 Issues Concerning Load-Balancing of Spatial Joins via Replication in GRIDs

This section addresses important issues which need to be addressed when supporting load-balancing of spatial joins via replication in GRIDs.

Hotspot Detection

The heat of data regions should be defined with respect to clusters which issue queries for these regions. For example, if cluster C_S issues a large number of queries pertaining to data region D_i of cluster C_T, but cluster C_O issues no queries for D_i, D_i will be considered a 'hot' region only w.r.t. C_S (but *not* w.r.t. C_O). Understandably, many different clusters accessing D_i infrequently would make D_i a 'hot' region in the conventional sense, but replicating D_i at any of these clusters may *not* necessarily be useful for reducing response times and may indeed be counter-productive owing to replication-related overheads. For hotspot detection purposes, every node within a cluster maintains its own access statistics comprising a list $HotList$, each entry of which is of the form ($data$,ptr_{access}). Here $data$ represents a specific data region and ptr_{access} is a pointer to a three-dimensional array of the form (cluster_id,num,$avgtime$), where cluster_id stands for the ID of the particular cluster which accessed $data$, num indicates the number of times that cluster accessed $data$ and $avgtime$ represents the average processing time it took for a node to perform spatial join on $data$. The value of $avgtime$ is used in ascertaining the benefit of replicating a specific data region as we shall see in Section 5. This information is periodically sent by every node to its cluster leader, thereby enabling the cluster leader to determine the 'popularity' of different data regions with respect to different clusters.

For reflecting *current* hotspots accurately in dynamic GRID environments, we propose that $HotList$ should be initialized periodically i.e., the information in $HotList$ should be deleted periodically and then $HotList$ should be populated with fresh access information. Additionally, whenever an overloaded source cluster node N_i has completed offloading some part of its load to a node at another cluster, N_i refreshes its own $HotList$ by deleting those entries in $HotList$ which triggered the replication so that $HotList$ reflects hotspots concerning which action has *not* yet been taken. Moreover, we maintain access statistics information at the granularity of the respective leaf node levels of the index structures at the nodes. Throughout this paper, we shall use the term **data region** to indicate the spatial region corresponding to the Minimum Bounding Rectangle (MBR) of the data stored at a leaf node of the IID at a particular node. An interesting question which arises here is: *Given that several different kinds of queries can be issued to a real system, how do we know whether the leaf node accesses are being* *made specifically for a spatial join query?* Incidentally, at the leaf node level, it is *not* feasible to determine the type of query for which the leaf node is being accessed, but this information can be found at the query engine level.

What to Replicate?

Once a 'popular' region D_i w.r.t. a specific cluster C_i has been detected, our strategy is to replicate the *results of the spatial join operation on* D_i at C_i. Note that replicating the results (as opposed to replicating the data itself) can significantly benefit those subsequent spatial join queries whose spatial select windows have considerable overlap with D_i since C_i will *not* need to do any processing at all for a significant part of these queries. Additionally, replicating the results can reduce communication cost significantly if join selectivity of D_i is low. Even in case of high join selectivity of D_i, intuitively we can understand that the communication cost of replicating the result tuples can never exceed that of replicating the data itself. Our strategy assumes that the datasets are relatively static. Note that we use 'data replication' and 'replication of result tuples' interchangeably throughout this paper to imply replication of result tuples.

Exploiting Overlap Between Different Spatial Join Queries

Interestingly, every spatial join query has an associated MBR associated with it either explicitly or implicitly. We shall designate this MBR as SPJMBR (Spatial Join's Minimum Bounding Rectangle). For example, the join query *"Find a hotel near a station in Athens within a 5 km radius of X, where X is a certain landmark in Athens"* explicitly specifies the SPJMBR associated with the join query, while the query *"Find a hotel near a bus station in Athens"* implicitly specifies that the SPJMBR for this query corresponds to the MBR of Athens. Intuitively, efficient exploitation of overlaps between different spatial join queries requires a mechanism for storing the replicas in a manner which enables quick identification of overlap between spatial join queries and existing replicas.

In our proposed system, whenever a replica of result tuples is stored at a cluster, the cluster leader also stores the SPJMBR corresponding to that replica. Identification of overlap between an SPJMBR and a spatial join query Q can be classified into 3 cases: (a) Q's MBR does *not* intersect with SPJMBR: This implies that there is *no* overlap between the query and the existing replica. (b) Q's MBR is fully contained within the SPJMBR: This means that all the results tuples requested by Q are already in the stored replica and only a spatial select query using Q's MBR as the spatial select condition should be run on the replicated data to obtain the answers to Q. We propose to run this spatial select condition on the replicated data at the cluster C_{Rep} where the replicated data exists (if C_{Rep} is *not* overloaded and has sufficient disk space) to save communication costs. However, if C_{Rep} is overloaded and/or C_{Rep} has insufficient available disk space, the replica is sent to the cluster C_{Issue} which issued Q and C_{Issue} needs to run Q's MBR as the spatial select query on the replica to obtain the query results. (c) Q's MBR partially intersects with SPJMBR:

The implication is that the results of Q already exist for the intersecting part between Q's MBR and SPJMBR, but for the non-intersecting parts, the results need to be computed. In this case, the tuples in the intersecting part are sent to the query issuing peer, while a spatial join operation needs to be run to get the result tuples in the non-intersecting parts between Q's MBR and SPJMBR. This spatial join operation involving the non-intersecting parts of Q's MBR and SPJMBR should be run at C_{Rep} if C_{Rep}'s load is low, otherwise it should be executed at C_{Issue}.

Whenever a spatial join query Q arrives at a cluster leader, the cluster leader traverses its list of SPJMBRs and identifies and exploits overlaps (if any) in the manner stated above. Additionally, in order to optimize disk space usage, each cluster leader keeps track of the replicas in its cluster nodes as well as the number of accesses made to each of the replicas during recent time intervals. Replicas whose access frequency during recent time intervals falls below a pre-defined threshold are deleted because the valuable disk space consumed by such unused replicas can be put to better use by storing 'hot' data, thereby improving system performance.

5 Load-Balancing Strategy for Spatial Joins in GRIDs

In our proposed strategy, a cluster leader determines itself to be overloaded if its load exceeds the average loads of its neighbouring clusters by more than $y\%$. (The value of y is application-dependent and in our case, we assume $y = 15\%$.) When a cluster leader determines itself to be overloaded, it periodically checks the frequency with which its **data regions**[2] are being queried by other cluster leaders during the recent time intervals. Based on this information, the cluster leader C_i creates a set ψ comprising all cluster leaders which have issued more than η queries for *any* of its regions. (η is a threshold parameter which influences the sensitivity of load-balancing.) C_i sends a message to each member of set ψ informing its own disk space requirement (i.e., the amount of disk space required to store the replicated data) and requesting information concerning their load status, list of neighbours and whether their available disk space is sufficient to store the replicated data. After receiving the necessary status information of ψ's members, C_i evaluates their replies one-by-one. Members of ψ whose available disk space is too low to store the replicated data or whose normalized load difference with C_i (Δ) falls below a pre-specified threshold are deleted from ψ. For such members, C_i adds their list of neighbouring clusters to ψ. For these neighbouring clusters, clusters with low disk space or those with low normalized load difference with C_i are deleted from ψ. The remaining members of ψ are candidates for replication. For each member α of ψ, C_i traverses each hot data region H that has been queried by α and decides whether to replicate the spatial join result tuples associated with H on a case-by-case basis. Now let us see how C_i makes this decision.

[2] Recall that 'data region' refers to the spatial region corresponding to the MBR of the data stored at a leaf node of the IID at a particular node.

The total cost C_H of replicating H from C_i at α consists of the cost $Extr_H$ of extracting H from IID at C_i, the communication cost Cm_H of transferring H and the bulkloading cost $Bulk_H$ of integrating H into the IRD of α. Hence, C_H is given by the following formula:

$$C_H = Extr_H + Cm_H + Bulk_H \tag{3}$$

Recall that every cluster leader maintains information concerning the average processing time and the accesses made to each data region from each of the clusters in the system. Let n_H denote the number of times H has been accessed by α and $avgtime_H$ represents the average processing time of H. Hence, the benefit B_H of replicating H at α can be estimated as follows:

$$B_H = (n_H \times avgtime_H) \tag{4}$$

From (3) and (4), we have the following formula:

$$Decide_H = (B_H - C_H \geq TH_{min}) \tag{5}$$

where TH_{min} is a pre-defined threshold parameter which is essentially application-dependent and on which the degree of load-balancing depends and $Decide_H$ is a boolean variable. Every member α of ψ for which $Decide_H$ returns 'TRUE' is put into a temporary list data structure which we shall designate as *'temp'*. The data structure of 'temp' is essentially a list structure where for each 'hot' data region H, the corresponding destination candidates (those members of ψ for which $Decide_H$ had returned 'TRUE') for H are stored in a linked list. Using the 'temp' data structure, the overloaded cluster leader uses a function **Select_dest_from_temp( )** which selects (as the destination cluster) the least loaded member in 'temp' (corresponding to each H) for each H. The load-balancing algorithm executed by an overloaded source cluster leader is depicted in Figure 1, while the load-balancing algorithm executed by a potential destination cluster leader is presented in Figure 2.

Observe that in contrast with existing works in traditional environments, our strategy does *not* use the value of normalized load difference when deciding upon the amount of data to replicate. This is because in our scenario, the increase in load at α owing to spatial join queries on H is negligible (even in case of spatial select conditions) as compared to the decrease in load for C_i especially since the join has already been computed. Moreover, note that replication is initiated from C_i to α whenever the normalized load difference between C_i and α exceeds a given threshold, irrespective of whether C_i is *really* overloaded or not. Even if C_i is *not* overloaded, we believe it is still reasonable to replicate at α since bringing the data closer to the cluster from where the data are being frequently queried implies a reduction in network overheads (as well as response times) for future spatial joins on the same data.

6 Performance Study

This section reports the performance evaluation of our proposed inter-cluster load-balancing technique via replication of result tuples of spatial join queries.

```
Algorithm LB_OverloadedSource( )
Create a set ψ comprising cluster leaders that issued more than η queries for any of its regions
if (ψ is an empty set) {
  exit
} else {
  for each element α in set ψ {
     Send message to α and asking α's disk space, load and neighbours' list
     Receive reply from α
     if ( ( α's disk space is NOT sufficient ) OR ( Δ ≤ LOAD_THRESHOLD ) ) {
     /* Δ is the normalized load difference between itself and α */
        Delete α from set ψ and Add members of List_Neighbours to ψ
        for each member NG of List_Neighbours {
           Send message to NG asking NG's disk space availability and current load
           Receive reply from NG
           if ( ( NG's disk space is NOT sufficient ) OR ( Δ ≤ LOAD_THRESHOLD ) ) {
              Delete NG from ψ
           }
        }
     }
  }
  for each element α in ψ {
     for each data region H queried by α {
        if ( Decide_H = = TRUE ) {
           Put α into a temporary list designated as 'temp'
        }
     }
  }
  Select_dest_from_temp( )
}
end
```

Fig. 1. Load-balancing Algorithm executed by an overloaded source cluster leader

Note that we consider performance issues associated *only* with inter-cluster load-balancing since a significant body of research work pertaining to efficient intra-cluster load-balancing algorithms already exists. Hence, for our experiments, we use a cluster size of 1. The machine used for the experiments had processing capacity of 1.7 GHz (Pentium-4), main memory of 768 Mbytes and disk space of 40GB. We ran the experiments under the Redhat Linux (version 7.3) operating system using LAM-MPI (version 7.00) for message-passing. In order to model inter-cluster communication in a wide area network environment, we assigned transfer rates for communication between cluster leaders randomly in the range of 0.8 Megabit/second to 1.2 Megabit/second. We used a maximum of 3 neighbouring cluster leaders corresponding to each cluster leader. The number of clusters simulated in our experiments was 24. The interarrival time between queries arriving at a cluster was fixed at 10 milliseconds and the value of TH_{min} was set to 5 seconds. We have used two *real-life* datasets [3] for our experiments. The first dataset is the set of roads in Germany, while the second one is a dataset of railway lines in Germany. The first dataset comprises MBRs of 30,674 streets of Germany, while the second one consists of MBRs of 36,334 railroad lines in Germany. We had enlarged each of these datasets by translating and mapping the data for the purpose of our experiments. For our experiments, each of the

Algorithm LB_PotentialDestination( )

Receive message from overloaded source cluster leader SRC
/ The message contains disk space requirement of SRC */*
Send a Broadcast message to all the nodes in its cluster asking each node for its current load and disk space
Receive replies concerning current load and disk space of each node
Nodes with sufficient available disk space and load below a pre-defined threshold λ are put into a set $Candidate$
if ($Candidate$ is an empty set) {
  Send message to SRC stating that its disk space is insufficient and informing SRC about its list of neighbours
} else {
    Send message to SRC informing SRC about its sufficient disk space, its current load and its list of neighbours
}
Receive reply from SRC
if (SRC has selected it as the destination cluster) {
  Send a Broadcast message to the nodes in $Candidate$ for their current load status
  Receive the corresponding replies and select the least loaded node MIN from $Candidate$
  Send a message to SRC to replicate the data at MIN
}
end

Fig. 2. Load-balancing algorithm executed by each potential destination cluster leader

clusters had more than 200000 rectangles for each of the relations. We used two R-trees at each cluster, one for each dataset. We assumed that one R-tree node fits in a disk page (page size = 4096 bytes). Hence, R-tree node capacity is the same as page size in our case. The height of each of the R-trees was 3 and the fan-out was 64. We generated queries for each cluster by using a spatial select (window query) condition in conjunction with the spatial join. Note that this is in consonance with real-world scenarios where spatial joins may be quite often accompanied by certain select conditions. The selectivity of each spatial join query was fixed at 40%. Assuming n queries for a particular cluster C_i, let us designate the queries as $Q_1, Q_2, ...Q_n$. We generated the n queries for C_i such that the queries had *at least* 75% overlap with each other. This overlap was generated by shifting the respective spatial select query windows in such a manner that each query had $x\%$ (where $x \geq 75\%$) overlap with the other queries.

For performing the spatial join operation at each cluster, we use an existing approach where the data from the smaller fragment is extracted and used to probe the index structure corresponding to the larger fragment. For the sake of convenience, we shall refer to our proposed technique as LBREP (Load-balancing via replication). Since *no* work on load-balanced processing of remote spatial joins in GRIDs exists, we shall compare the performance of LBREP with a technique which performs spatial join without load-balancing. We designate this reference technique as NOLB (No load-balancing). For all our experiments, we had run the system for an initial period of time to obtain access statistics information and once the system had reached a stable state (after the replication of result tuples have been performed), we noted down the results. We only present results associated with the stable state of the system.

C_{Source}	$C_{Destination}$
1	24, 15
2	23,17
3	22, 14
4	21, 18
6	20, 15
8	19, 14
9	18, 10
11	17,15
12	16, 14
13	14, 10

(a) Table indicating replication

N	C_E	$C_Q(f)$
16	1	24(9),15(7)
12	2	23(6), 17(6)
12	3	22(6), 14(6)
4	4	21(3), 18(1)
4	6	20(3),15(1)
4	8	19(3), 14(1)
4	9	18(3), 10(1)
4	11	17(3),15(1)
4	12	16(3), 14(1)
4	13	14(3), 10(1)

(b) $QD1$

N	C_E	$C_Q(f)$
16	1	15(10), 24(6)
12	2	17(4), 23(8)
12	3	14(3), 22(9)
4	4	18(3), 21(1)
4	6	15(3), 20(1)
4	8	14(3), 19(1)
4	9	10(3), 18(1)
4	11	15(3), 17(1)
4	12	14(3), 16(1)
4	13	10(3), 14(1)

(c) $QD2$

Fig. 3. Replication table and $QD1$ and $QD2$ for a 24-cluster GRID

The replications that have already been performed (based on access statistics information) prior to the system reaching stable state are depicted in Figure 3(a). In Figure 3(a), C_{Source} represents the IDs of the source cluster whose data (spatial join result tuples) have been replicated, while $C_{Destination}$ stands for the IDs of the destination clusters where C_{Source}'s data has been replicated. For example, the first row of the table indicates that a portion of cluster 1's data has been replicated at clusters 24 and 15. Similarly, a part of cluster 2's data has been replicated at clusters 23 and 17 and so on. Note that the portions of cluster 1's data that have been replicated at clusters 24 and 15 need *not* necessarily be the same, even though overlap is possible between the replicated data of cluster 1 at cluster 24 and cluster 15. This is because the replication performed was based on previous access statistics, thereby implying that the replicated data at different clusters depends upon the queries that these clusters had issued during the past. Now we shall evaluate the relative performance of LBREP and NOLB by using different query distributions. Even though we had used several query distributions to test the robustness of LBREP, in the interest of space, here we present only two such distributions. For the sake of convenience, we shall refer to these query distributions as $QD1$ and $QD2$ respectively. Figures 3b and 3c summarize $QD1$ and $QD2$. In Figure 3b, N denotes the number of queries, C_E indicates the ID of the cluster which processed the queries, C_Q represents the IDs of the clusters which issued those queries and f stands for the number of queries issued by a cluster. Note that the sequence of the queries arriving at each cluster is also specified by Figure 3b. For example, the first row of the table in Figure 3b indicates that 16 queries (let us designate them as $Q1$ to $Q16$) were processed by cluster 1. $Q1$ to $Q9$ were issued by cluster 24, $Q10$ to $Q16$ were issued by cluster 15. In contrast, the first row in Figure 3c indicates that $Q1$ to $Q10$ were issued by cluster 15, while cluster 24 issued $Q11$ to $Q16$. Owing to space constraints, we are *not* able to present the detailed results concerning *all* the queries in the system. Note that the selectivity of each spatial join query in case of both $QD1$ and $QD2$ was fixed at 40%. In all our experiments, cluster 1 is

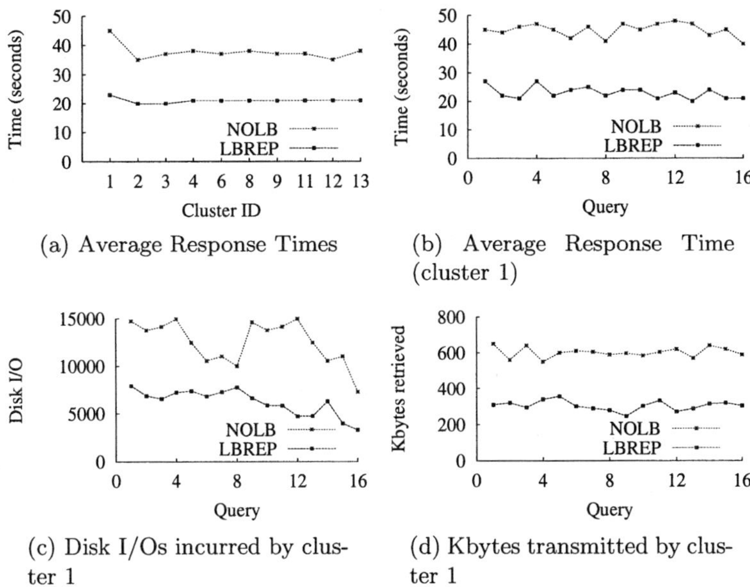

Fig. 4. Results on $QD1$ for a 24-cluster GRID

the most overloaded (hot) cluster and also it was the last cluster in the GRID to complete processing. Hence, we shall examine details concerning the processing of queries that were directed to cluster 1.

Figures 4 and 5 depict the results corresponding to $QD1$ and $QD2$ respectively. Figure 4a indicates the average response times of *all* the queries directed to each cluster. The results demonstrate that LBREP is indeed able to decrease the average response times for each of the clusters significantly, especially decreasing the average response time of cluster 1 by upto 48%. The reduction in average response times occurs because of the reduction in disk I/O overhead at the query executing clusters as well as the reduction in communication overhead arising from transmission of result tuples to the clusters which issued the respective queries. To put things into perspective, we take a closer look at the processing of the 16 queries that were directed to cluster 1. Figure 4b depicts the individual response times of each of the 16 queries that were directed to cluster 1 for $QD1$, while Figure 4c shows the corresponding disk I/Os incurred for each query at cluster 1 for the same experiment. Figure 4d indicates the number of KBytes for each query that cluster 1 had to transmit to the cluster which had issued the query.

Observe that Figure 4b indicates that for *all* the queries directed to cluster 1, LBREP's performance is superior to that of NOLB in terms of response times. Such reductions occur because part of the results of the spatial join have already been replicated at clusters which issued these queries (clusters 24 and 15 in this case). The implication is that cluster 1 did *not* need to process a significant part of each of these queries, thereby resulting in reduction of disk I/O cost incurred

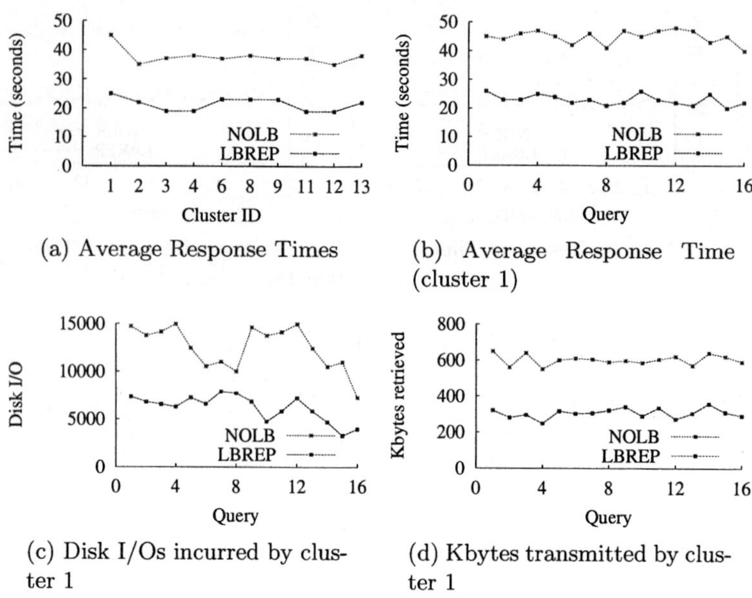

(a) Average Response Times (b) Average Response Time (cluster 1) (c) Disk I/Os incurred by cluster 1 (d) Kbytes transmitted by cluster 1

Fig. 5. Results on $QD2$ for a 24-cluster GRID

by cluster 1. Moreover, since clusters 24 and 15 already had a part of the results associated with the queries that they issued, the number of result tuples that cluster 1 had to transmit to such clusters was also reduced, thereby reducing the communication overhead. Detailed investigation of the experimental results revealed that the reduction in disk I/O cost varied between 45% to 54%, while reduction in the total size of result tuples transmitted to the querying clusters varied between 46% to 52%. However, note that the price LBREP pays for improvements in response time is additional disk space usage since replication causes redundant usage of disk space. We believe that the overhead of additional disk space usage is justifiable because of the significant improvement in response times of spatial joins that LBREP provides.

The explanations for Figure 4 also hold good for the results in Figure 5. Observe that the performance of NOLB remains same in case of Figures 4 and 5 because in case of NOLB, no data has been replicated at the querying clusters, thereby implying that every query is completely processed at the query executing cluster and then the results are sent back to the querying clusters. We also find that the results in Figures 4 and 5 differ to some extent for LBREP. This is because the portions of cluster 1's data replicated at clusters 24 and 15 were *not* exactly the same, even though there was overlap between those portions.

7 Conclusion

Huge amounts of available spatial data worldwide and the prevalence of spatial applications, coupled with the emergence of GRID computing, provides a strong motivation for designing a spatial GRID. Skewed user access patterns may cause severe load imbalance in the system, thereby degrading system performance significantly. Our proposal has specifically focussed on speeding up remote spatial joins in this environment via a novel dynamic load-balancing strategy which deploys online replication. In the near future, we plan to address issues concerning dynamic data. Incidentally, for dynamic data, query results may change, thereby requiring updates to be propagated to the clusters containing the old replicated result tuples. Moreover, we shall investigate scalability issues concerning larger number of clusters. Additionally, we also plan to examine the use of other spatial index structures for performing spatial joins in GRIDs.

Acknowledgements

We wish to express our sincere thanks to the JSPS (Japanese Society for the Promotion of Science) for supporting this work.

References

1. T. Brinkhoff, H.P. Kriegel, and B. Seeger. Efficient processing of spatial joins using R-trees. *Proc. ACM SIGMOD*, pages 237–246, 1993.
2. European DataGRID. http://eu-datagrid.web.cern.ch/eu-datagrid/.
3. Datasets. http://dias.cti.gr/~ytheod/research/datasets/spatial.html.
4. I. Foster and C. Kesselman. The GRID: Blueprint for a new computing infrastructure. *Morgan-Kaufmann*, 1999.
5. V. Gaede and O. Gunther. Multidimensional access methods. *ACM Computing Surveys*, 30(2):170–231, 1998.
6. Earth Systems GRID. http://www.earthsystemgrid.org/.
7. O. Gunther. Efficient computation of spatial joins. *Proc. ICDE*, pages 50–59, 1993.
8. A. Guttman. R-trees: A dynamic index structure for spatial searching. *Proc. ACM SIGMOD*, pages 47–57, 1984.
9. Y.C. Hu and D.B. Johnson. Caching strategies in on-demand routing protocols for wireless Ad Hoc networks. *Proc. MOBICOM*, pages 231–242, 2000.
10. G. Luo, J. F. Naughton, and C. Ellmann. A non-blocking parallel spatial join algorithm. *Proc. ICDE*, 2002.
11. A. Mondal, K. Goda, and M. Kitsuregawa. Effective load-balancing via migration and replication in spatial GRIDs. *Proc. DEXA*, 2003.
12. J. Patel and D. DeWitt. Partition based spatial-merge join. *Proc. ACM SIGMOD*, pages 259–270, 1996.
13. GriPhyN Project. http://www.griphyn.org/index.php.
14. Q. Ren and M.H. Dunham. Using semantic caching to manage location dependent data in mobile computing. *Proc. MOBICOM*, pages 210–221, 2000.
15. P. Rigaux, M. Scholl, and A. Voisard. Spatial databases with application to GIS. *Morgan Kaufmann ISBN 1-55860-588-6*, 2001.
16. P. Scheuermann, G. Weikum, and P. Zabback. Disk cooling in parallel disk systems. *IEEE Bulletin of the Technical Committee on Data Engineering*, 17(3):29–40, 1994.

Expressing and Optimizing Similarity-Based Queries in SQL

(Extended Abstract)*

Like Gao[1], Min Wang[2], X. Sean Wang[1], and Sriram Padmanabhan[2]

[1] CS Dept., University of Vermont, VT
{lgao,xywang}@emba.uvm.edu
[2] IBM T.J. Watson Research Center, NY
{min,srp}@us.ibm.com

Abstract. Searching for similar objects (in terms of near and nearest neighbors) of a given query object from a large set is an essential task in many applications. Recent years have seen great progress towards efficient algorithms for this task. This paper takes a query language perspective, equipping SQL with the near and nearest search capability by adding a user-defined-predicate, called NN-UDP. The predicate indicates, among a set of objects, if an object is a near or nearest-neighbor of a given query object. The use of the NN-UDP makes the queries involving similarity searches intuitive to express. Unfortunately, traditional cost-based optimization methods that deal with traditional UDPs do not work well for such SQL queries. Better execution plans are possible with the introduction of a new operator, called NN-OP, which finds the near or nearest neighbors from a set of objects for a given query object. An optimization algorithm proposed in this paper can produce these plans that take advantage of the efficient search algorithms developed in recent years. To assess the proposed optimization algorithm, this paper focuses on applications that deal with streaming time series. Experimental results show that the optimization strategy is effective.

1 Introduction

In many applications, searching for similar objects of a given query object from a large given set is important. Similarity measure is best intuited as some distance and similarity is then usually expressed in terms of near and nearest neighbors. When complex objects such as time series are involved and object sets are large, the task of finding near and nearest neighbors becomes rather costly. A large body of research has been devoted to reducing this cost and efficient algorithms and indexing structures have been developed (see, e.g., [13, 12, 1, 5, 11, 10]).

To the best of our knowledge, however, there has not been any systematic study on how to incorporate near and nearest neighbor searches into the popular query language SQL and, more important, how to optimize the resulting queries. The purpose of this paper is to initiate such a study, considering the two aspects of the query language, namely expression and optimization, when it needs to deal with similarity searches.

* This is an abbreviated version of the technical report [6].

P. Atzeni et al. (Eds.): ER 2004, LNCS 3288, pp. 464–478, 2004.

As an example application, consider the problem of monitoring different sources of time series data to detect certain events (e.g., onset of a flu season). Assume we have collected many patterns (in the form of time series) from historical data on school attendance and flu-related medicine sales at pharmacies. Using data analysis tools, we may have learned the strong correlation between the presence of certain events and the appearance of certain patterns in school and pharmacy data. For example, a sharp decrease in school attendance accompanied by a sharp increase in pharmacy sales three days in a row is a strong indication of the beginning of a flu season. Based on such learned "rules" and the time series data reported everyday regarding current school attendance and pharmacy sales, we may detect the appearance of certain events.

To be more specific, suppose we have two sets of historical patterns, S for school attendance and P for pharmacy sales. For simplicity, let us assume $S = \{\mathsf{s1}, \mathsf{s2}, \mathsf{s3}\}$ and $P = \{\mathsf{p1}, \mathsf{p2}, \mathsf{p3}\}$, respectively. We can store the rules learned from historical data in a relation called *Events* shown in Figure 1. Each row in the relation represents a rule learned from the historical data. For example, the first row says that when school attendance data matches pattern s1 and pharmacy data matches pattern p1, it usually indicates the peak of a flu season.

EID	*eName*	*School*	*Pharmacy*
e1	Flu_peak	s1	p1
e2	Flu_start	s2	p2
e3	Flu_end	s3	p3

Fig. 1. *Events* table with the rules learned from historical data

The meaning of "match" in the above example can be in terms of near and nearest neighbor based on a similarity (or distance) measure. Near neighbors are defined in terms of the distance between a pair of objects (e.g., time series) irrespective of the existence of other objects, while nearest neighbor is a relative notion, defined with respect to a set. Both notions are best used together. Thus, that the current school data matches pattern s1 may indicate that among all the school patterns, s1 is closest to the current school data (nearest neighbor notion), and *at the same time*, they are not too far away from each other (near neighbor notion).

Clearly, algorithms and data structures that can provide efficient evaluation of near and nearest neighbors can be very helpful in the above example application. However, it is also very important that the users should have an intuitive language to express these types of queries. At the same time, the system should figure out how to efficiently answer these queries, invoking efficient algorithms and indexing structures. For this purpose, we propose to add a user-defined-predicate (UDP) to SQL for users to express the notion of near and nearest neighbors in their queries. The UDP, called NN-UDP, indicates, among a set of objects, if an object is a near/nearest-neighbor of a query one.

The use of the NN-UDP makes the queries involving near/nearest neighbors easy to express, since the user can intuitively treat it as a selection condition. However, when the query is evaluated, we probably do not always want the predicate as a selection condition. Indeed, we would like to take advantage of the algorithms and data structures for finding near and nearest neighbors. For example, in our detection application, we may want to report the corresponding event name by performing the following three steps:

1. In pattern set S, find the nearest neighbor (call it si) of the current school series.
2. In pattern set P, find the nearest neighbor (call it pj) of the current pharmacy series.
3. Issue an SQL to select the $eName$ of table $Events$ with $School =$ si and $Pharmacy$ = pj as the conditions.

Here, we use the direct method to find the near/nearest neighbors from sets of objects instead of using the NN-UDP as selection conditions. Obviously, various strategies can apply to each of the above steps.

However, the above strategy may not always be the best. For example, once the school pattern si is found from Step 1, the number of tuples in the *Events* relation that satisfy the condition $School =$ si may be so small that, in fact, a near/nearest neighborhood test of (in contrast to search for) the corresponding patterns from the Pharmacy column will be more beneficial.

In order to make the correct decision on selecting the appropriate evaluation strategy, we introduce a heuristic optimization method which is based on a new operator NN-OP and the derived algebraic equivalence rules involving NN-UDP and NN-OP. Our experiments have confirmed the superiority of this systematic cost-based approach.

By treating each NN-UDP in the query either as a traditional UDP or as the output of NN-OP, our proposed optimization method can find better execution plans than those appearing in previous work on UDP query optimization [4, 9, 3, 2], In [4], Chimenti et al. propose an algorithm for LDL system to optimize the queries with UDPs. In LDL, each UDP is treated as a relation during the query optimization process. However, since it uniformly treats each UDP as a relation, it may fail to consider some efficient plans. Hellerstein and Stonebraker propose Predicate Migration algorithm [9, 8] that improves the LDL approach by pushing down selections on both operands of a join. Later, Chaudhuri and Shim present several efficient algorithms that are able to guarantee the optimal plan over the desired execution space and show these proposed algorithms can either find the optimal plan or efficiently find a plan that is very close to the optimal one [3]. However, all these algorithms uniformly treat UDPs as selection conditions.

Our work is also related to [2] by Chaudhuri and Gravano, which deals with query optimization when external searches are involved. They study the optimization of queries over multimedia repositories, and assume that query predicates are independent. However, in this paper, the similarity searches on different sources are less likely to be independent since they are involved in the detection of the same event.

The contribution of this paper can thus be summarized as follows. Firstly, we take a query language perspective to deal with similarity searches. The novelty of our language is on the incorporation of the nearest neighbor searches. This makes similarity-based queries easy to write and provides a powerful tool for various related tasks. Secondly, we provide a heuristic optimization algorithm to derive efficient evaluation plans for these queries, fully taking advantage of the efficient algorithms and index structures for near/nearest neighbor for evaluation. Thirdly, we use experiments to demonstrate the effectiveness of our optimization algorithm for the (streaming) time series case.

The remainder of the paper is organized as follows. In Section 2, we define our extension of SQL, called SQL/sim, to incorporate the similarity search capability into SQL. In Section 3, we discuss our optimization algorithm, including algebraic equivalence rules, and our heuristic method for deriving optimized evaluation plans. We report experimental results in the (streaming) time series case in Section 4, and in Section 5, we conclude our paper with some future research directions.

2 SQL/sim

In this section, we provide a simple extension of SQL, called SQL/sim, that offers the capability of expressing similarity searches in RDBMSs. We start with defining the similarity between pairs of objects.

Definition Given two objects p and q, the similarity measure, denoted $sim(\mathsf{p}, \mathsf{q})$, is a non-negative real number.

The similarity metrics might have a positive or inverse relationship with respect to the similarity of two objects. For example, Correlation Coefficient is positive, i.e., the large the metric value, the more similar the objects are. On the other hand, Euclidean Distance is inversely related to the similarity of objects, i.e., the smaller the metric value, the more similar the objects are. Without loss of generality, in this paper, we assume that if two objects are more similar, then the similarity metric is smaller. In this case, similarity measure is more like a distance measure.

Definition Let α be a non-negative real number. Given a *query* object q, an object p is said to be its *α-near neighbor* if $sim(\mathsf{p}, \mathsf{q}) \leq \alpha$.

In the above definition, the number α is called the nearness *threshold.* This near-neighbor definition relates similar objects independently of the existence of other objects. In some situations, it is meaningful to obtain similarity between the query object and an object relative to a set of objects. We call this relative measure as the k-nearest neighbors defined as follows:

Definition Let $k \geq 1$ be an integer, $\mathsf{P} = \{\mathsf{p}_1, \mathsf{p}_2, \ldots, \mathsf{p}_m\}$ a set of objects, and q a query object. An object p_i in P is said to be *one of the k-nearest neighbors of* q in P if there are at most $k - 1$ objects p_j $(j \neq i, 1 \leq j \leq m)$ such that $sim(\mathsf{p}_j, \mathsf{q}) < sim(\mathsf{p}_i, \mathsf{q})$.

Integer k above is called the *rank of similarity*[1]. For $k = 1$, the 1-nearest neighbor of q is normally abbreviated as the *nearest neighbor of* q.

2.1 Required Relations

In order to model the notions of objects and object sets for the purpose of near/nearest-neighbor searches in a RDBMS, an application needs to set up at least two relations. One corresponds to the set of all (pattern) objects (abstractly called *Patterns*), and the other to the collection of (pattern) object sets (called *PatternSets*). Each pattern set must be a subset of the *Patterns*.

[1] For simplicity, we assume no two pairs of objects will have exactly the same similarity measure. In real applications, we remark it's easy to lift this restriction.

For our running example, the *Patterns* are all the historical patterns and the *PatternSets* are those collections of historical patterns related to specific types of events (e.g., all the patterns related to school attendance are collected into *schoolSet*).

In terms of relation schemas, the relation for *Patterns* should have an ID attribute (PID) that is the primary key of the relation; and the relation for *PatternSets* should have two attributes that are for the ID of the sets (SID) and the ID of the Pattern (PID). The primary key must be these two attributes together, and the PID must reference to the ID of the *Patterns* relation. These two relations only need to use the identifiers of the objects and the object sets, while the objects themselves may be stored elsewhere inside or outside of the relational database. For example, the objects themselves may be stored as BLOBS in a RDBMS.

The relations corresponding to our running example are shown in Figure 2. Here, the two required relations are given by *Patterns* and *PatternSets*, respectively. We assume that all patterns in the *Event* relation (under the attributes *School* and *Pharmacy*) in Figure 1 all refer to attribute *PID* in the *Patterns* relation.

Patterns (P)

PID	pName
s1	$Fast\_Up$
s2	Up_Down
s3	$Slow\_Up$
p1	$Slow\_Down$
p2	$Quick\_Change$
p3	$Fast\_Down$

PatternSets (PS)

SID	PID
$schoolSet$	s1
$schoolSet$	s2
$schoolSet$	s3
$pharmacySet$	p1
$pharmacySet$	p2
$pharmacySet$	p3

Fig. 2. For our running example, the required *Patterns* and *PatternSets* relations

Query objects need not belong to relation P. They can be stored in relations or can be constant IDs that are understood by SQL/sim. In this paper, we will use constant IDs.

2.2 NN-UDP

To equip SQL with the near/nearest-neighbor search capability, we introduce a user-defined-predicate (UDP) as follows.

Definition NN is a 5-ary predicate such that for each given query object QID, pattern set SID (from relation PS), pattern PID (from relation P and in the set SID), integer RK ≥ 1, and real number TH ≥ 0,

$$NN(\mathsf{QID}, \mathsf{SID}, \mathsf{PID}, \mathsf{RK}, \mathsf{TH}) = \textbf{True}$$

if and only if PID is one of the RK-nearest neighbors of QID in the pattern set SID, and the similarity measure between them is no greater than TH. NN is called the NN-UDP.

For example, NN('s', '*schoolSet*', 's1', 1, 0.2)=**True** if and only if s1 is the nearest neighbor of s in *schoolSet*, and the similarity measure of s1 and s is no greater than 0.2. Unlike most other proposals, NN-UDP incorporates both near and nearest neighbor tests.

In the above definition, the input relation takes five parameters. Among them, QID and PID are specific values, while SID, RK and TH can take NULL values. The semantics of these three attributes with NULL values are:

1. If SID=NULL, the pattern set is all patterns in P.
2. If RK=NULL, the similarity rank is infinity.
3. If TH=NULL, the similarity threshold is infinity.

Therefore, SID=NULL is a special case to take all the patterns as a "global" set for the purpose of nearest neighbor test. Furthermore, by allowing NULL either for RK or TH, we can use NN-UDP for either near or nearest neighbor tests, respectively. In the cases where both RK and TH are NULL, $NN(\text{QID}, \text{SID}, \text{PID}, \text{RK}, \text{TH})$ =**True** means that PID is in the set SID. On the other hand, if neither RK nor TH is NULL, then $NN(\text{QID}, \text{SID}, \text{PID}, \text{RK}, \text{TH})$ =**True** means that PID is both a near and nearest neighbor of QID.

2.3 SQL/sim Examples

With SQL/sim, users can write similarity-based queries in an intuitive manner. Here we give two example queries. The first corresponds to the flu detection scenario mentioned in the introduction.

Example 1. Report the event name based on the observed school time series s and pharmacy time series p. More specifically, the event name is decided by: (1) the nearest neighbor of school attendance time series in *schoolSet* with similarity measure no greater than 0.2; (2) the nearest neighbor of pharmacy time series in *pharmacySet*; and (3) the rules in the *Events* table, as described in Figure 2. The query in SQL/sim is:

```
SELECT E.eName
FROM   Events E
WHERE  NN('s', 'schoolSet', E.School, 1, 0.2)
  AND  NN('p', 'pharmacySet', E.Pharmacy, 1, NULL)
```

The result is a list of event names.

Example 2. As another example, we want to find the PIDs of the nearest neighbor of the school attendance time series s in *schoolSet* if this nearest neighbor satisfies the following two conditions: (1) the similarity measure is no greater than 0.2; and (2) according to the rules in table *Events*, this nearest neighbor pattern is correlated to the event named Flu_peak, i.e., this nearest neighbor appears in a row of *Events* table with eName='Flu_peak'. The query is as follows, and the result is a list of school IDs.

```
SELECT E.School
FROM   Events E
WHERE  E.eName= 'Flu_peak'
  AND  NN('s', 'schoolSet', E.School, 1, 0.2)
```

3 Optimizing SQL/sim

In this section, we develop a strategy to optimize queries in SQL/sim. We start with an example to show various options for evaluating queries in SQL/sim. We then describe a heuristic method that can, in many cases, automatically take the best option when evaluating a query.

Consider the query in Example 1. Using traditional optimization methods for UDPs, two execution plans are possible:

(1) One may consider the order of applying the two NN-UDPs in the query. Cost and selectivity should both be considered for this ordering as in [3, 9].
(2) Another method is to consider each NN-UDP as a relation as in [4]. In this case, both occurrences of NN will be evaluated on the entire relation and the results are joined together (with *Events* relation again). The join order needs to be carefully considered as in [4].

Each of the above strategies has its advantages in particular situations as explained below. This is due to the fact that, in most situations, algorithms that test if an object is a near/nearest neighbor are faster than those that search for near/nearest neighbors[2]. More specifically, in our example, if the number of patterns in *Events* under the *School* attribute is large, then it is beneficial to find the nearest neighbor (with RK=1 and TH=0.2) of the query object s by using some indexing method. Since at most one school attendance pattern will be found by this process, once this is done, we can select the tuples in the *Events* relation that contain that particular school attendance pattern, and project out the patterns under the *Pharmacy* attribute in these tuples. If the number of the resulting patterns is small, we can then use the NN-UDP to test each one. If the number is still large, we can use an index-based algorithm to find the nearest neighbor of p, and join back to the relation *Events* to obtain the final result. (This last case, where index-based algorithms are used twice, corresponds to the strategy found in [4]). Of course, this whole process can be done starting with the second occurrence of the NN-UDP.

Another possibility is that there are only a few tuples in *Events*. Then testing each one of them using the two NN predicates will probably be the best strategy. Here, the strategy of [3, 9] should be considered.

The above example shows that each of the traditional methods mentioned previously may be best in certain situations. However, a combination of these methods may be called for in certain other situations. The choice must be made by considering the cost, selectivity and sizes of the involved operations and intermediate results.

3.1 Near/Nearest-Neighbor Operator

From the above example, we can see that we cannot simply treat NN-UDPs as selection conditions or their output as relations. Rather, we need to choose different plans for different query instances. Sometimes we need to use index-based algorithms to directly find near/nearest-neighbors, and sometimes we may use the NN-UDP directly.

---

[2] For example, we used a scan method for both testing and searching in our experiments. In our scan method, search needs to look through the entire pattern set, while test can stop much earlier when a nearer object is found and hence is faster in general. If multidimensional index is used for multidimensional objects, a test is only to ask whether there is any object that is within a range and hence is generally faster than searching for the exact objects that are the near/nearest neighbors.

$R =$

QID	SID	RK	TH
s	*schoolSet*	1	0.4
p	*pharmacySet*	1	0.5

$D(R) =$

QID	SID	PID	RK	TH
s	*schoolSet*	s1	1	0.4
p	*pharmacySet*	p3	1	0.5

Fig. 3. Example of NN-OP, assuming s1 is the near/nearest neighbor of s in *schoolSet* (with RK $=$ 1 and TH $=$ 0.4), and p3 is the near/nearest neighbor of p in *pharmacySet* (with RK $=$ 1 and TH $=$ 0.5)

In order to derive such optimized evaluation plans, we need to define an operator that encodes the use of an indexing algorithm for finding near/nearest-neighbors.

Definition Let $S = \{\mathsf{QID}, \mathsf{SID}, \mathsf{RK}, \mathsf{TH}\}$. The relational operator D is defined as follows: For each relation R whose schema contains all the attributes in S, $D(R)$ is the relation with the schema $S \cup \{\mathsf{PID}\}$ such that a tuple t is in $D(R)$ if and only if (1) $t[S]$ is in $\pi_S(R)$, and (2) $NN(t[\mathsf{QID}], t[\mathsf{SID}], t[\mathsf{PID}], t[\mathsf{RK}], t[\mathsf{TH}])$ = **True**. Operator D is called the NN-OP.

Intuitively, for each tuple t in R, D finds the near/nearest neighbors for the query object $t[\mathsf{QID}]$ among the patterns in the set $t[\mathsf{SID}]$ with rank and threshold RK and TH, respectively. Figure 3 shows an example of the D operator.

The above definition of D is extended to relations that have some of the attributes in S missing. More specifically, R may not contain any of the attributes SID, RK, TH. In these cases, the output of D will not have these attributes either, and the condition (2) in the above definition will take NULL value in place of $t[\mathsf{SID}], t[\mathsf{RK}], t[\mathsf{TH}]$.

It should be noted that the output size of NN-OP may be even bigger than that of the input relation. For example, if RK $= k$, then for each tuple in R, $D(R)$ may contain k tuples derived from it.

3.2 Equivalence Rules

As explained in the beginning of this section, our goal is to use the NN-OP in place of some NN-UDPs in evaluating a query. In this section, we give a set of transformation rules for this purpose.

Our transformation rules work on the relational algebra expression derived from SQL/sim. In a relational algebra expression, in a natural way, we treat NN-UDP as a selection condition on a relation R containing attributes QID, SID, PID, RK, and TH, written as $\sigma_{NN}(R)$. If R does not have any of the attribute SID, RK, TH, the corresponding value is treated as NULL.

As an example, let R_1 be a relation with schema {QID, SID, RK, TH} that contains only one tuple ('s', '*schoolSet*', 1, 0.2) and R_2 be a relation with schema {QID, SID, RK} that contains only one tuple ('p', '*pharmacySet*', 1). The SQL/sim query in Example 1 can be written in relational algebra form as $\pi_{eName}(R_1'' \bowtie R_2'')$, where

$$R_1'' = \pi_{EID,eName}(\sigma_{NN}(R_1')) \text{ with } R_1' = \rho_{School \rightarrow PID}(\, R_1 \times Events), \text{ and}$$
$$R_2'' = \pi_{EID,eName}(\sigma_{NN}(R_2')) \text{ with } R_2' = \rho_{Pharmacy \rightarrow PID}(R_2 \times Events).$$

Note that ρ is the renaming operator.

In the following, R can be any relation with the implied attributes. For notational convenience, in these rules and the later plans, we will indicate the ordering of the operators by nested algebraic expressions.

Figure 4 shows the equivalence rules. Rule 1 gives the equivalence transformation between σ_{NN} and D. Rule 2 shows how to move a selection operator σ inside the NN-OP D. Likewise, we can exchange the order of join and NN-UDP as in Rule 3. Rules 4-7 are useful to prune some operators and the associated relations from the plan. Note that Rule 4 and 5 are different since in Rule 4, relation PS refers to the *PatternSets* relation which contains attribute PID, while in Rule 5, the schema of R does not contain PID.

Rule 1	$\sigma_{NN}(\text{R}) \equiv R \bowtie D(R)$
Rule 2	$\sigma_c(D(R)) \equiv D(\sigma_c(R))$, if c only refers to attribute(s) in $\{\text{QID, SID, RK, TH}\}$.
Rule 3	$R_1 \bowtie D(R_2) \equiv R_1 \bowtie D(R_1 \bowtie R_2)$
Rule 4	$PS \bowtie D(R \bowtie PS) \equiv D(R \bowtie PS)$
Rule 5	$R \bowtie D(R \bowtie PS) \equiv D(R \bowtie PS)$ if R's schema is a subset of $\{\text{QID, SID, RK, TH}\}$.
Rule 6	$\pi_p(\text{D}(R)) \equiv \pi_p(R)$ if p is a set of attribute that does not contain PID.
Rule 7	$D(\pi_p(R)) \equiv D(R)$ if p is the subset of $\{\text{QID, SID, RK, TH}\}$ appearing in R's schema.

Fig. 4. Equivalence rules (PS is *PatternSets*)

With the set of equivalence rules shown in Figure 4, we can transform a query plan involving NN-UDPs into equivalent ones with NN-OPs only or a combination of NN-UDPs and NN-OPs. We use the query in Example 1 to illustrate how to use these rules to obtain different query plans.

At the beginning of this subsection, we represent the query as $\pi_{eName}(R_1'' \bowtie R_2'')$. This expression corresponds to the straightforward way of executing the query by testing the two NN-UDPs independently, joining the two testing results on attribute EID, and projecting out the interested attribute.

Alternatively, we can use the equivalence rules to generate another query plan: $\pi_{eName}(R_1'' \bowtie R_2'')$

$\equiv \pi_{eName}(\pi_{EID,eName}(\sigma_{NN}(R_1')) \bowtie \pi_{EID,eName}(\sigma_{NN}(R_2')))$

$\equiv \pi_{eName}(\pi_{EID,eName}(\sigma_{NN}(R_1')) \bowtie \sigma_{NN}(R_2'))$ *//standard equivalence*

$\equiv \pi_{eName}(\pi_{EID,eName}(R_1' \bowtie D(R_1')) \bowtie \sigma_{NN}(R_2'))$ *// Rule 1*

$\equiv \pi_{eName}(\pi_{EID,eName}(R_1' \bowtie D(R_1)) \bowtie \sigma_{NN}(R_2'))$

//since $D(\pi_{\text{QID,SID,RK,TH}}(R_1')) = D(R_1')$ *by Rule 7, and* $\pi_{\text{QID,SID,RK,TH}}(R_1') = R_1$

$\equiv \pi_{eName}(\sigma_{NN}(\pi_{EID,eName}(R_1' \bowtie D(R_1)) \bowtie R_2'))$ *//standard equivalence*

The resulting expression corresponds to the following query plan: We first use an index-based algorithm to discover the nearest neighbor of s in the pattern set *schoolSet* (this corresponds to $D(R_1)$). We then find the events that use that particular school pattern (i.e., the first join $R_1' \bowtie D(R_1)$). We then join the result with R_2', the input relation of the second NN-UDP, on attribute EID and $eName$. Finally, we test the second NN-UDP on the join output and project out the interested attribute $eName$.

Naturally, we can get another plan in a symmetrical way: $\pi_{eName}(\sigma_{NN}(\pi_{EID,eName}(R_2' \bowtie D(R_2)) \bowtie R_1'))$.

As another possibility, we may continue the above transformation as follows (picking up from the second to the last step):

$$\pi_{eName}(R_1'' \bowtie R_2'')$$
$$\equiv \pi_{eName}(\pi_{EID,eName}(R_1' \bowtie D(R_1)) \bowtie \sigma_{NN}(R_2'))$$
$$\equiv \pi_{eName}(\pi_{EID,eName}(R_1' \bowtie D(R_1)) \bowtie \pi_{EID,eName}(R_2' \bowtie D(R_2)))$$
//same as done to $\sigma_{NN}(R_1')$

The resulting expression corresponds to the following query plan: We first use an index-based algorithm to discover the nearest neighbor of s in the pattern set *schoolSet*, as well as the nearest neighbor of p in the pattern set *pharmacySet*. We then join the results with R_1' and R_2', respectively, to find the corresponding events, and finally obtain the common events by a join.

In the above plans, we have only used Rules 1 and 7. For other queries, e.g., pattern sets IDs are from a relation instead of being a constant, other rules will be useful.

3.3 Optimization Procedure

From the example given in the beginning of the section, we can see that a good execution plan is more likely to combine the use of both NN-UDPs and NN-OPs. Even though the equivalence rules of the previous subsection, together with the standard equivalence rules from the relational algebra, can be used to search through all the execution plans, it is obviously a very large space for an exhaustive search.

Instead of using exhaustive search, we give an optimization algorithm, called the *UdpOp* algorithm. The major steps of the *UdpOp* algorithm are outlined in Figure 5.

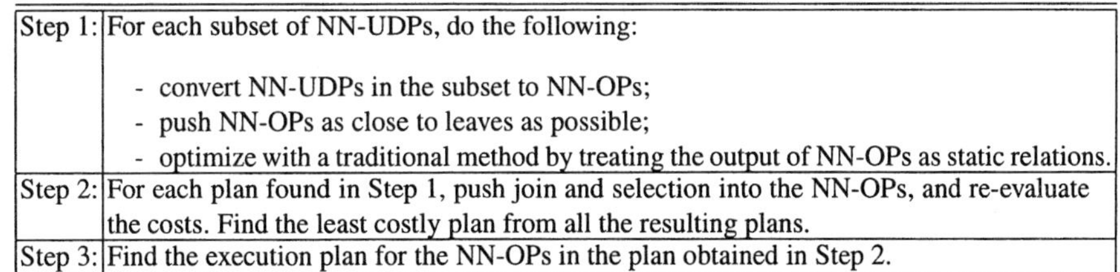

Step 1:	For each subset of NN-UDPs, do the following: - convert NN-UDPs in the subset to NN-OPs; - push NN-OPs as close to leaves as possible; - optimize with a traditional method by treating the output of NN-OPs as static relations.
Step 2:	For each plan found in Step 1, push join and selection into the NN-OPs, and re-evaluate the costs. Find the least costly plan from all the resulting plans.
Step 3:	Find the execution plan for the NN-OPs in the plan obtained in Step 2.

Fig. 5. Major steps of the *UdpOp* algorithm

Step 1 of *UdpOp* is to select a subset of the NN-UDPs to be converted to NN-OPs. In this step, we enumerate all subsets of the NN-UDPs in a query. We argue this is not too much overhead since in real applications with similarity-based queries, the numbers of UDPs should not be too large. In special cases where there are many UDPs, heuristics may need to be adopted to reduce the search space.

For each possible choice of converting NN-UDP to NN-OP, we push NN-OPs as much down to the leaves as possible. This is done for two reasons. The first is to give more flexibility for the traditional optimization algorithms (that deal with UDPs, i.e., all the remaining NN-UDPs). The second is that in an evaluation plan, the cost of an NN-OP does not usually depend where it is performed (there are exception, see below). We then treat each NN-OP as a static relation and hand over the query to an optimizer. This optimizer will treat NN-UDP as traditional UDPs.

obtaining the plan using *UdpOp* optimization algorithm. Note that UDP may be treated as NN-UDP or NN-OP in (3), depending on the statistics.

In the experiment, we vary the size of relation *Events* so that the number of tuples that are fed into the UDP varies from 10% to 100% of the size of pattern set *schoolSet*. For each case, we execute the query using each of the three plans and measure the cost. We also measure the cost of the "best plan", which is obtained by trying all possible plans and choosing the least-costly one.

The results are shown in Figure 6, which are normalized by the maximum cost for the respective input sizes, ranging from 5ms (for the "10% of pattern set" case) to 120 ms (the "whole pattern set" case). We can see that both (1) and (2) may result in very costly plans in some cases while our *UdpOp* algorithm always achieves good plans.

Experiment 2. In the second experiment, we change the schema of relation *Events* to represent more complicated rules. The new schema is (EID, eName, A1, A2, ..., An), where attribute Ai ($1 \leq i \leq n$) refers to patterns in pattern set set_i. We then populate the *Events* table and consider the following query for streaming time series d1, d2, ..., dn.

```
SELECT E.eName
FROM   Events E
WHERE  NN('d1', 'set1', E.A1, K1, TH1)
  AND  NN('d2', 'set2', E.A2, K2, TH2)
       ...
  AND  NN('dn', 'setn', E.An, Kn, THn)
```

We consider two independent pairs of stream and pattern set, and hence two UDPs. We set up the data so that, dependent on the data in the *Events* table, the near/nearest-neighbor patterns discovered for one of the two streams may or may not help to narrow down the scope of the patterns to be considered for the other stream. More specifically, we generate multiple *Events* relations by using random subsets of the Cartesian Product of two sets (each having 10^5 patterns), one for each of the two Ai columns. The ranks in both UDPs are NULL and the thresholds are both set to 0.07. Two streaming time series are randomly chosen from a set of streams.

There are three possible optimization methods for comparison with the *UdpOp* algorithm, which are, (1) 2-NN-UDP Method: both UDPs are NN-UDPs, (2) 2-NN-OPs Method: both UDPs are converted into NN-OPs, and (3) 1-UDP/1-NN-OP Method, that is, we always convert one UDP into NN-OP and keep the other as NN-UDP.

We run this experiment 300 times. For each run, we use one of the randomly generated *Events* relations and the randomly chosen streaming time series and continuously evaluate the query for all 500 time positions. We take the average cost of these 300 runs as the performance measure for each optimization method. In addition, we also get the performance of the best plan, the least cost plan obtained by trying all possibilities. The result is in Figure 7, with all costs normalized by the maximum cost of 15 milliseconds. From this graph, it is clear that the performance of the *UdpOp* algorithm is very close to the best one.

Experiment 3. In this experiment, we use the same setup as for Experiment 2, i.e., we use the same schema of relation *Events* and the same SQL query. In contrast to Experiment 2, we test the scalability of our algorithm when the number of UDPs goes up in the following situation. All UDPs deal with the same pattern set but with a different

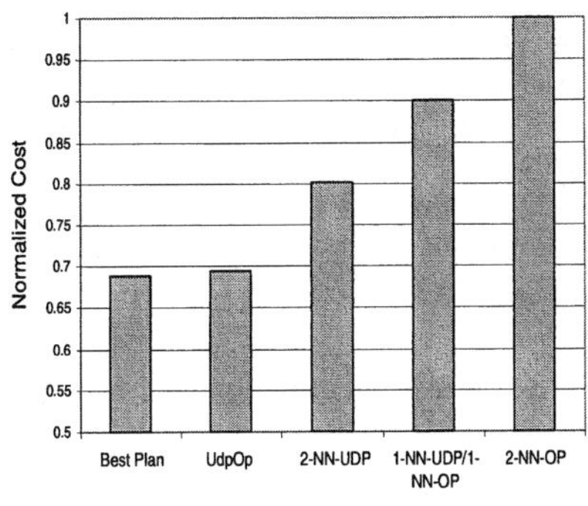

Fig. 7. Optimization comparison for Exp. 2

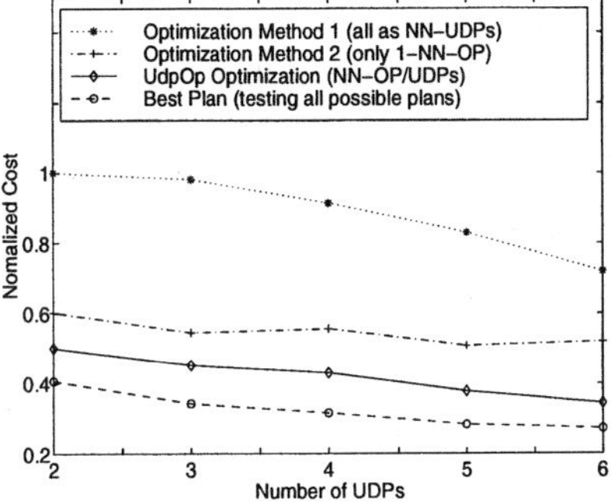

Fig. 8. Optimization comparison for Exp. 3

stream, and all thresholds are 0.07 and the rank of similarity is 1. Hence, we look for the pattern in the pattern set that is similar to *all* the streams. We vary the number of UDPs from 2 to 6, and set the size of the *Events* as 20% of the pattern set. We generate the *Events* relation such that no value appears twice in the same column. This guarantees that if we find a nearest neighbor with the evaluation of one UDP (under one column), then there is only one tuple in relation *Events* which needs to be fed into other UDPs. Clearly, in the optimized plan, other UDPs should remain NN-UDPs since only one tuple needs to be verified, and the ordering of UDPs and which UDP being converted into NN-OP will determine the performance.

Given the number of UDPs, we randomly pick up the same number of streams. Two other optimization methods are used for comparison. The first one is to treat all UDPs as selections, i.e., none of the UDPs are converted to NN-OP. Then we use the algorithm proposed in paper [3] to obtain a plan. More specifically, we use the estimation models to find the *rank*, as defined in [3], for each UDP and then get the ordering among them. The second optimization method will always convert only one NN-UDP into NN-OP, which is the one estimated to have the least cost among all possibly converted NN-OPs.

The performance comparison is shown in Figure 8, as the average cost of 210 runs for each number of UDPs. Again, we normalized all costs by a maximum value that is roughly 15 milliseconds. We can see that the performance of the plans obtained by the *UdpOp* algorithm is close to the best one.

5 Conclusion

In this paper, we introduced a user-defined predicate (UDP) for expressing queries involving similarity searches. We provided an optimization algorithm to derive efficient evaluation plans. In the (streaming) time series cases, our experiments demonstrated the good performance of our optimization algorithm.

We mainly focused on the situation where there are only a few query objects (e.g., time series and streaming time series). In our examples, we mostly used constants to represent them. We believe in real applications, this is mostly the case. However, for applications where the query series are massive, there are opportunities to further optimize the queries. For example, when NN-OP is applied to many combinations of query series and pattern sets, many combinations may not find any pattern within the required threshold. This finding can be useful to optimize other NN-OPs in the same query. Same observation applies to the number of pattern sets.

References

1. R. Agrawal, C. Faloutsos, and A. N. Swami. Efficient similarity search in sequence databases. In *FODO*, pages 69–84, 1993.
2. Surajit Chaudhuri and Luis Gravano. Optimizing queries over multimedia repositories. In *SIGMOD Conference*, pages 91–102, 1996.
3. Surajit Chaudhuri and Kyuseok Shim. Optimization of queries with user-defined predicates. *ACM Transactions on Database Systems*, 24(2):177–228, 1999.
4. D. Chimenti, R. Gamboa, and R. Krishnamurthy. Towards an open architecture for LDL. In *VLDB Conference*, 1989.
5. C. Faloutsos, M. Ranganathan, and Y. Manolopoulos. Fast subsequence matching in time-series databases. In *SIGMOD Conference*, pages 419–429, 1994.
6. L. Gao, M. Wang, X. S. Wang, and S. Padmanabhan. Expressing and optimizing similarity-based queries in SQL. Technical Report CS-04-06, University of Vermont, http://www.cs.uvm.edu/csdb/techreport.shtml, March, 2004.
7. L. Gao, X. S. Wang, M. Wang, and S. Padmanabhan. A learning-based approach to estimate statistics of operators in continuous queries: a case study. In *Workshop on Research Issues in Data Mining and Knowledge Discovery (DMKD)*, 2003.
8. Joseph M. Hellerstein. Practical predicate placement. In *SIGMOD Conference*, pages 325–335, 1994.
9. Joseph M. Hellerstein and Michael Stonebraker. Predicate migration: optimizing queries with expensive predicates. In *SIGMOD Conference*, pages 267–276, 1993.
10. Eamonn J. Keogh, Kaushik Chakrabarti, Sharad Mehrotra, and Michael J. Pazzani. Locally adaptive dimensionality reduction for indexing large time series databases. In *SIGMOD Conference*, 2001.
11. D. Rafiei and A. Mendelzon. Similarity-based queries for time series data. In *SIGMOD Conference*, pages 13–25, 1997.
12. N. Roussopoulos, S. Kelley, and F. Vincent. Nearest neighbor queries. In *SIGMOD Conference*, pages 71–79, 1995.
13. T. Seidl and H.-P. Kriegel. Optimal multi-step k-nearest neighbor search. In *SIGMOD Conference*, pages 154–165, 1998.

XSLTGen: A System for Automatically Generating XML Transformations via Semantic Mappings

Stella Waworuntu and James Bailey

Department of Computer Science, The University of Melbourne,
Victoria 3053, Australia
{stellavw,jbailey}@cs.mu.oz.au

Abstract. XML is rapidly emerging as a dominant standard for representing and exchanging information. The ability to transform and present data in XML is crucial and XSLT is a relatively recent programming language, specially designed to support this activity. Despite its utility, however, XSLT is widely considered a difficult language to learn.
In this paper, we present *XSLTGen: An Automatic XSLT Generator*, a novel system that automatically generates an XSLT stylesheet, given a source XML document and a desired output HTML or XML document. It allows users to become familiar with and learn XSLT, based solely on their knowledge of XML or HTML. Our method is based on the use of semantic mappings between the input and output documents. We show how such mappings can be first discovered and then employed to create XSLT stylesheets. The results of our experiments show that XSLTGen works well with different varieties of XML and HTML documents.

1 Introduction

XML is rapidly emerging as the new standard for data representation and exchange on the Web. As the medium for communication between applications, an ability to transform XML to other data representations is essential. This data conversion can be performed by XSLT (eXtensible Stylesheet Language: Transformations) [3]. XSLT plays an important role in transforming XML into HTML, text, or other types of XML[1]. However, XSLT is a relatively new language, which is widely considered difficult to learn [8]. Rendering to HTML using XSLT requires skills of XSLT programming as well as Web page styling. Hence, we focus on developing a tool that can automatically generate XSLT stylesheets, given a source XML document and a target HTML document, provided by the users.

Automatic XSLT generation is an extremely useful facility for students and Web developers in the process of learning XSLT. Such a tool enables them to see and understand how the XSLT stylesheet should look, in order to transform a

[1] This paper focuses on XML to HTML transformations since we are motivated by publishing applications, but our techniques are also applicable for XML to XML transformations.

P. Atzeni et al. (Eds.): ER 2004, LNCS 3288, pp. 479–492, 2004.

particular XML document into a desired HTML document. This tool is also useful in the XSLT development process. Programmers may use the automatically generated XSLT stylesheet as a starting point for something more complex.

In this paper, we present *XSLTGen: An Automatic XSLT Generator*, a novel system that automatically generates an XSLT stylesheet, given a source XML document, and a desired output HTML document. The generated XSLT stylesheet contains rules for transforming the given XML document to the HTML document, and can be applied to other XML documents with similar structure. The important feature of this system is that users can generate an XSLT stylesheet based solely on their knowledge of XML and HTML, i.e. users only need to create a desired output HTML document based on an input XML document. Moreover, users do not have to know anything about the syntax or programming of XSLT, or be aware of the XSLT rule generation process.

A naive solution to the problem of automatic XSLT generation is to create an XSLT stylesheet consisting of only one template rule, which matches the XML root element and contains the HTML document markup (i.e., create a stylesheet which is very specific to the desired output). This approach has a major drawback in terms of reusability, since this kind of stylesheet could not be used to transform other XML documents having similar structure as the input XML document. In contrast, we are interested in generating a more generic stylesheet, which can then be reused to transform other XML documents with similar structure.

This paper shows how XSLT stylesheets can be generated via semantic mappings between the input and output. Our contributions are:

- We describe *text matching* and *structure matching*, techniques for finding semantic mappings between an XML and an HTML documents.
- We introduce *sequence checking* to the matching context, which enables our system to not only discover 1-1 mappings, but also 1-m mappings.
- We describe a fully automatic XSLT generation system that generates XSLT rules based on the semantic mappings found.
- We describe a technique for refining the XSLT stylesheet generated, which examines the differences between the original HTML document and the one produced by applying the generated stylesheet back to the XML document.
- We conduct experiments to validate the matching accuracy and the quality of XSLT stylesheets generated by XSLTGen. The results show that XSLTGen works well with different varieties of XML and HTML documents.
- This is the first paper that we are aware of that describes completely automatic XSLT generation from an XML source and an HTML destination.

2 XSLTGen System

We now present an overview of the XSLTGen system. Due to lack of space, we describe the necessary algorithms informally. We use Soccer[2] as our running example. Before that, we introduce important definitions and terminology used.

[2] http://www.wrox.com/books/0764543814.shtml

2.1 Definitions and Terminology

We assume familiarity with XSLT language. Both *XSLT Version 1.0 Specification* [3], and *XSLT Programmer's Reference* [6] provide good background.

Let $m : (m.p, m.x, m.h)$ denote a mapping from an element in the XML document (source) to one or more elements in the HTML document (destination). The XML component of m is denoted by $m.x$, while the HTML component of m is denoted by $m.h$. If $m.x$ is an ATTRIBUTE_NODE, we define the term *owner node*, denoted by $m.p$, to be the XML node that owns $m.x$, otherwise it is *null*.

Two mappings m_1 and m_2 are *distinct* if $m_1.x.name \neq m_2.x.name$ and $m_1.h.name \neq m_2.h.name$ (where *name* refers to the tag name of the element).

An *exact mapping* is a mapping e, where $e.x$ is a TEXT_NODE or an ATTRIBUTE_NODE, $e.h$ is a TEXT_NODE, and the text value of $e.x$ is identical to the text value of $e.h$, i.e. $e.x.value = e.h.value$.

A *substring mapping* is a mapping s, where $s.x$ is a TEXT_NODE or an ATTRIBUTE_NODE, $s.h$ is a TEXT_NODE, $s.x.value$ is a substring of $s.h.value$, and

- if $s.x.value$ starts with a non-letter and non-digit character, then the character preceding its occurrence in $s.h.value$ (if any) must be either a letter or a digit; otherwise, it must be both non-letter and non-digit. And,
- if $s.x.value$ ends with a non-letter and non-digit character, then the character following its occurrence in $s.h.value$ (if any) must be either a letter or a digit; otherwise, the following character must be both non-letter and non-digit.

Special HTML elements are used to separate text in HTML, e.g. `br` and `hr`.

An *extra node* is a node that does not have any matching node in the other document. *Extra XML nodes* are those XML nodes that are ignored when generating the HTML document, while *extra HTML nodes* are those HTML nodes that are added at the time the HTML document was generated and are not constructed from any part of the XML document.

Let N be an XML or HTML node. The *precise node* of N, *precise*(N), is the node used to represent a transformation in the XSLT template rule. For a mapping m, if $m.x$ is a TEXT_NODE, $precise(m.x)$ is the parent of $m.x$ and $precise(m.p)$ is *null*, whereas if $m.x$ is an ATTRIBUTE_NODE, $precise(m.x) = m.x$ and $precise(m.p) = m.p$. The precise node for $m.h$ is:

- If the next sibling of $m.h$ is a *special* HTML ELEMENT_NODE h_s, then $precise(m.h) = m.h \mathbin{++} h_s$
- If $m.h$ has no next sibling or the next sibling of $m.h$ is not *special* and $m.h$ has ELEMENT_NODE siblings, then $precise(m.h) = m.h$
- Otherwise, $precise(m.h)$ is the highest ancestor of $m.h$ such that each node on the path between $precise(m.h)$ and $m.h$ only has one *non-extra* child.

The *sequence* of N, *seq*(N), is a DTD of N if N is the root of a document. Otherwise, let D' be a DTD of the parent of N. *seq*(N) is then equal to $trim_N(D')$, where $trim_N$ is a function which removes both the largest prefix not containing N and the largest suffix not containing N from its argument.

2.2 System Architecture

The architecture of the XSLTGen system is illustrated in Fig. 1. Two documents, a source XML document and a desired target HTML document, are given to XSLTGen in order to initiate the stylesheet generation process. The output of XSLTGen is an XSLT stylesheet consisting of rules for transforming the given XML document to the supplied HTML document. As shown in the figure, the system consists of six main components described next. Fig. 2 shows an example of fragments of XML DOM and HTML DOM for the Soccer example.

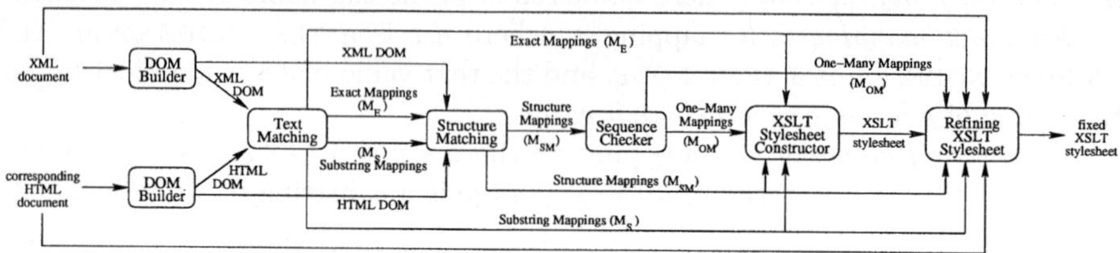

Fig. 1. Architecture of the XSLTGen system

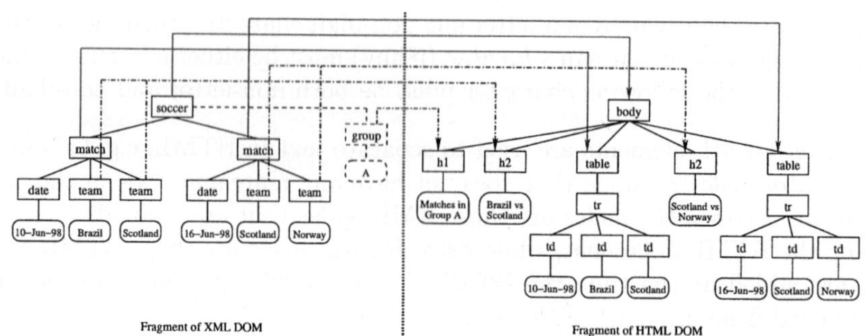

Fig. 2. Soccer example

Text Matching. The goal of the text matching subsystem is to discover a set of *exact mappings* and *substring mappings*. As the content of the HTML document is created based on the content of the XML document, it is important to find both exact and substring mappings between the two documents, since there must be HTML elements that have the same string or substring as the XML elements.

The starting point to find a mapping is to compare nodes having a *value* attribute, i.e. TEXT_NODEs and ATTRIBUTE_NODEs. In this paper, we only compare an XML TEXT_NODE with an HTML TEXT_NODE and an XML ATTRIBUTE_NODE with an HTML TEXT_NODE. We ignore HTML ATTRIBUTE_NODEs since the attribute value of those nodes is usually specific to the display of the HTML document in the Web browsers and is not generated from the text within the XML document. In the Soccer example of Fig. 2,

- Exact mapping occurs between XML TEXT_NODE "10-Jun-98" and HTML TEXT_NODE "10-Jun-98", because their *value*s are the same.
- Substring mapping occurs between XML TEXT_NODE "A" and HTML TEXT_NODE "Matches in Group A", since only part of the *value* of the HTML TEXT_NODE, i.e. "A", is identical to the value of the XML TEXT_NODE.

As mentioned earlier, text matching takes two inputs: an XML DOM x and an HTML DOM h. It discovers as many text mappings as possible between the nodes in x and h. The text matching procedure is called twice, once to discover all EXACT mappings between the nodes in x and h and again to discover all SUBSTRING mappings. The output of our text matching algorithm is: a list of EXACT mappings (M_E) and a list of SUBSTRING mappings (M_S).

Our text matching process is implemented using a top-down approach by visiting each node in the XML DOM in pre-order and using the same traversal to find a matching node in the HTML DOM. Note that in order to create an XSLT template rule, the XML node should be an ELEMENT_NODE (not a text node). Therefore, we need to determine for each exact and substring mapping found, the *precise node* of its XML and HTML component that best describes the transformation. This approach allows us to discover more precise mappings between the XML and HTML documents. Moreover, we require that every HTML node that has been matched to an XML node during the exact matching process, cannot be considered as a matching candidate in the substring matching process.

In Fig. 2, some of the text mappings are: (`<soccer>...</soccer>`,`group="A"`, `<h1>Matches in Group A</h1>`); (*null*,`<team>Brazil</team>`,`<td>Brazil</td>`); and (*null*,`<team>Brazil</team>`,`<h2>Brazil vs Scotland</h2>`).

Structure Matching. This subsystem discovers all structure mappings between elements in the XML and HTML DOMs. We adopt two constraints used in GLUE system [4] as a guide to determine whether two nodes are structurally matched:

- *Neighbourhood Constraint*: "two nodes match if nodes in their neighbourhood also match", where the neighbourhood is defined to be the children.
- *Union Constraint*: "if every child of node A matches node B, then node A also matches node B".

Note that there could be a range of possible matching cases, depending on the completeness and precision of the match. In the ideal case, all components of the structures in the two nodes fully match. Alternatively, only some of the components are matched (a partial structural match). In the case of partial structure matching between two nodes, there are some *extra nodes*, i.e. children of the first node that do not match with any children of the second node; and/or vice versa. Since *extra nodes* do not have any match in the other document, they are ignored in the structure matching process. Therefore, the above constraints need to be modified to construct the definition of structure matching which accommodates both partial and full structure matching:

- *Neighbourhood Constraint*: "XML node X structurally matches HTML node H if H is not an *extra* HTML node and every *non-extra* child of H either text matches or structurally matches a *non-extra* descendant of X".
- *Union Constraint*: "X structurally matches H if every *non-extra* child of H either text matches or structurally matches X".

As stated in the above constraints, we need to examine the children of the two nodes being compared in order to determine if a structure matching exists. Therefore, structure matching is implemented using a bottom-up approach that visits each node in the HTML DOM in post-order and searches for a matching node in the entire XML DOM. If the list of substring mappings M_{SM} is still empty after the structure matching process finishes, we add a mapping from the XML root element to the HTML body element, if it exists, or to the HTML root element, otherwise. Revisiting the Soccer example (Fig. 2), some of the discovered structure mappings are: (*null*,`match`, `tr`) (neighbourhood constraint), (*null*,`match`, `table`) (union constraint) and (*null*,`soccer`, `body`).

Sequence Checking. Up to this point, the mappings generated by the text matching and structure matching subsystems are limited to 1-1 mappings. In cases where the XML and HTML documents have more complex structure, these mappings may not be accurate and this can affect the quality of the XSLT rules generated from these mappings. Consider the following example:

In Fig. 2, the sequence of the children of XML node `soccer` is made up of nodes with the same name, `match`; whereas the sequence of the children of the matching HTML node `body` follows a specific pattern: it starts with `h1` and is followed repetitively by `h2` and `table`. Using only the discovered 1-1 mappings, it is not possible to create an XSLT rule for `soccer` that resembles this pattern, since `match` maps only to `table` according to structure matching. In other words, there will be no template that will generate the HTML node `h2`.

Focusing on the structure mapping (`match`,`table`) and the substring mappings {(`team[1]`,`h2`), (`team[2]`,`h2`)}, we can see in the DOM trees that the children of `match`, i.e. `team[1]` and `team[2]`, are not mapped to the descendant of `table`. Instead, they map to the sibling of `table`, i.e. `h2`. Normally, we expect that the descendant of `match` maps only to the descendant of `table`, so that the notion of 1-1 mapping is kept. In this case, there is an intuition that `match` should not only map to `table`, but also to `h2`. In fact, `match` should map to the concatenation of nodes `h2` and `table`, so that the sequence of the children of `body` is preserved when generating the XSLT rule. This is called a 1-m mapping, where an XML node maps to the concatenation of several HTML nodes.

The 1-m mapping (`match`,`h2 ++ table`) can be found by examining the subelement sequence of `soccer` and the subelement sequence of `body` described above. Note that the subelement sequence of a node can be represented using a regular expression, which is a combination of symbols representing each subelement and metacharacters: $|, *, +, ?, (,)$. To obtain this regular expression, XTRACT [5], a system for inferring a DTD of an element, is employed. In our example, the regular expression representing the subelement sequence of `soccer` is $match*$, whereas the one representing subelement sequence of `body` is $h_1(h_2, table)*$. We then check whether the elements in the first sequence conform to the elements in the second sequence, as follows: According to the substring mapping (`soccer`,`group`,`h1`), element h_1 conforms to an attribute of `soccer` and thus, we ignore it and remove h_1 from the second sequence. Comparing $match*$ with $(h_2, table)*$, we can see that element $match$ should conform to elements $(h_2, table)$ since the sequence $match*$ corresponds directly to the sequence $(h_2, table)*$, i.e. they both are in repetitive pattern, denoted by $*$. However, element $match$ conforms only to element $table$, as indicated by the structure matching (`match`,`table`). The verification therefore fails, which indicates that the structure matching (`match`,`table`) is not accurate. Consequently, based on the sequences $match*$ and $(h_2, table)*$, we deduce the accurate 1-m mapping: (*null*,`match`,`h2 ++ table`).

The main objective of the sequence checking subsystem is to discover 1-m mappings using the technique of comparing two sequences described above.

XSLT Stylesheet Generation. This subsystem constructs a template rule for each mapping discovered in M_E, M_{SM}, and M_{OM} (the list of 1-m mappings); and puts them together to compose an XSLT stylesheet. We do not consider the substring mappings in M_S, because in substring mappings, it is possible to have a situation where the text *value* of the HTML node is a concatenation of text *values* from two or more XML nodes. Hence, it is impossible to create template rules for those XML nodes. Moreover, the HTML text *value* may contain substrings that do not have matching XML text *value* (termed as *extra string*). Considering these situations, we implement a procedure that generates a *template* for each distinct HTML node in M_S.

The XSLT stylesheet generation process begins by generating the list of substring rules. We then construct a stylesheet by creating the `<xsl:stylesheet>` root element and subsequently, filling it with template rules for the 1-m mappings in M_{OM}, the structure mappings in M_{SM} and the exact mappings in M_E. The template rules for the 1-m mappings have to be constructed first, since within that process, they may invalidate several mappings in M_{SM} and M_E and thus, the template rules for those omitted mappings do not get used . In each mapping list (M_{OM}, M_{SM}, and M_E), the template rule is constructed for each *distinct* mapping, to avoid having some conflicting template rules.

In the next three subsections, we give more detail on the XSLT generation process. Discussion of 1-m mappings is left out due to space constraints.

Substring Rule Generation. The substring rule generator creates a template from an XML node or a set of XML nodes to each distinct HTML node presented in the substring mapping list M_S. The result of this subsystem is a list of substring rules SUB_RULES, where each element of the list is a tuple (*html_node*, *rule*). Due to space constraints, we omit the detailed description of our algorithm for generating the substring rule itself. The following example illustrates how substring rule generation works.

Consider the following substring mappings discovered in the Soccer example (Fig. 2): (*null*,`<team>Scotland</team>`,`<h2>Brazil vs Scotland</h2>`) and (*null*,

`<team>Brazil</team>,<h2>Brazil vs Scotland</h2>`). The HTML string is "`Brazil vs Scotland`", while the set of XML strings is {"`Brazil`,"`Scotland`"}. By replacing parts of the HTML string that appear in the set of XML strings with the corresponding XSLT instruction, the substring rule is:

```
<xsl:value-of select="team[1]"/> vs <xsl:value-of select="team[2]"/>,
```

where "`vs`" is an *extra string*.

Constructing a Template Rule for an Exact Mapping in M_E. Each template rule begins with an XSLT `<xsl:template>` element and ends by closing that element. For a mapping m, the pattern of the corresponding template rule is $m.x.name$ and the only XSLT instruction used in the template is `<xsl:value-of>`. In this procedure, we only construct a template rule when m is a mapping between an XML ELEMENT_NODE to an HTML node or a concatenation of HTML nodes. The reason that we ignore mappings involving XML ATTRIBUTE_NODEs is that the template for this mapping will be generated directly within the construction of the template rule for structure mapping and 1-m mapping. In text matching, there could be mappings from an XML node to a concatenation of HTML nodes, hence, we need to create a template for each HTML node h_i in $m.h$. E.g., the template rule for an exact mapping (*null*,`line`,`text() ++ br`) is:

```
<xsl:template match="line">
  <xsl:value-of select="."/><br/>
</xsl:template>
```

Constructing a Template Rule for a Structure Mapping in M_{SM}. Recall that in structure matching, one of the mappings in M_{SM} must be the mapping whose XML component is the root of the XML document. Let r denote this special mapping. The template for r begins with copying the root of the HTML document and its subtree, excluding the HTML component $r.h$ and its subtree.

The next step in constructing the template for mapping r follows the steps performed for the other mappings in M_{SM}. For any mapping m in M_{SM}, the opening tag for $m.h$ is created, then a template for each child c_i of $m.h$ is created, and finally, the $m.h$ tag is closed. E.g., Suppose there is a structure mapping (`null`,`match`,`table`) discovered in Soccer (Fig. 2). And suppose we have exact mappings (*null*,`date`,`td[1]`), (*null*,`team[1]`,`td[2]`), (*null*,`team[2]`,`td[3]`) in M_E. The template rule representing this structure mapping is:

```
<xsl:template match="match">
  <tr><xsl:apply-templates select="./date"/>
      <xsl:apply-templates select="./team[1]"/>
      <xsl:apply-templates select="./team[2]"/></tr>
</xsl:template>
```

Refining the XSLT Stylesheet. In some cases, the (new) HTML document obtained by applying the generated XSLT stylesheet to the XML document may not be accurate, i.e. there are differences between this (new) HTML document and the original (user-defined) HTML document. By examining those differences, we can improve the accuracy of the XSLT stylesheets generated. This step is applicable when we have a set of complete and accurate mappings between the XML and HTML documents, but the generated XSLT stylesheet is erroneous. If the discovered mappings themselves are incorrect or incomplete, then this refinement step is not effective and it is better to address the problem by improving the matching techniques. An indicator that we have complete and accurate mappings is that each element in the new HTML document corresponds exactly to the element in the original HTML document at the same depth.

One possible factor that can cause the generated XSLT stylesheet to be inaccurate, is the wrong ordering of XSLT instructions within a template. This situation typically occurs when we have XML nodes with the same name but different order or sequence of children. Therefore, the main objective of the refinement step is to fix the order of the XSLT instructions within the template matches of the generated XSLT stylesheet, so that the resulting HTML document is closer to or exactly the same as the original HTML document.

A naive approach to the above problem is to use brute force and attempt all possible orderings of instructions within templates until the correct one is found (there exist no differences between the new HTML and the original HTML). However, this approach is prohibitively costly. Therefore, we adopt a heuristic approach, which begins by examining the differences between the original HTML document and the one produced by the generated XSLT stylesheet. We employ a change-detection algorithm [2], that produces a sequence of edit operations needed to transform the original HTML document to the new HTML document. The types of edit operations returned are insert, delete, change, and move.

To carry out the refinement, the edit operation that we focus on is the move operations, since we want to swap around the XSLT instructions in a template match to get the correct order. In order for this to work, we require that there are no missing XSLT instructions for any template match in the XSLT stylesheet.

After examining all move operations, this procedure is started over using the fixed XSLT stylesheet. This repetition is stopped when no move operations are found in one iteration; or, the number of move operations found in one iteration is greater than those found in the previous iteration. The second condition is there to prevent the possibility of fixing the stylesheet incorrectly. We want the number of move operations to decrease in each iteration until it reaches zero.

3 Empirical Evaluation

We have conducted experiments to study and measure the performance of XSLT-Gen. To give the reader some idea on how our system performs, we evaluated XSLTGen on four examples taken from a popular XSLT book[3] and a real-life data taken from MSN Messenger chat history. These datasets exhibit a wide variety of characteristics ranging from 10 - 244 element nodes. Originally, they were pairs of (XML document, XSLT stylesheet). To get the HTML document associated with each dataset, we apply the original XSLT stylesheet to the XML

[3] http://www.wrox.com/books/0764543814.shtml

document using Xalan[4] XSLT processor. We then manually determined the correct mappings between the XML and HTML DOMs in each dataset.

For each dataset, we applied XSLTGen to find the mappings between the elements in the XML and HTML DOMs, and generate the corresponding XSLT stylesheet. We then measured the *matching accuracy*, i.e. the percentage of the manually determined mappings that XSLTGen discovered, and the quality of the XSLT stylesheet inferred by XSLTGen. To evaluate the quality of the XSLT stylesheet generated by XSLTGen in each dataset, we applied the generated XSLT stylesheet back to the XML document using Xalan and then compared the resulting HTML with the original HTML document using HTMLDiff[5]. HTMLDiff is a tool for analysing changes made between two revisions of the same file. It is commonly used for analysing HTML and XML documents. The differences may be viewed visually in a browser, or be analysed at the source level.

The results of the matching accuracy are impressive. XSLTGen achieves high matching accuracy across all five datasets. Exact mappings reach 100% accuracy in four out of five datasets. In the dataset *Chat Log*, exact mappings reach 86% accuracy. This is caused by the undiscovered mappings from XML ATTRIBUTE NODEs to HTML ATTRIBUTE NODEs, which violates our assumption in Section 2.2 that the value of an HTML ATTRIBUTE_NODE is usually specific to the display of the HTML document in Web browsers and is not generated from a text within the XML document. Substring mappings achieve 100% accuracy in the datasets *Itinerary* and *Soccer*. In contrast, substring mappings achieve 0% accuracy in the dataset *Poem*. This poor performance is caused by incorrectly classifying substring mappings as exact mappings during the text matching process. In the datasets *Books* and *Chat Log*, substring mappings do not exist. Structure mappings achieve perfect accuracy in all datasets except *Poem*. In the dataset *Poem*, structure mappings achieves 80% accuracy because an XML node is incorrectly matched with an HTML TEXT_NODE in text matching, while it should be matched with other HTML node in structure matching. Following the success of the other mappings, 1-m mappings achieve 100% accuracy in the datasets *Itinerary* and *Soccer*. In the datasets *Books, Poem* and *Chat Log*, there are no 1-m mappings. This results indicate that in most of these cases, the XSLTGen system is capable of discovering complete and accurate mappings.

The results returned by HTMLDiff are also impressive. The new HTML documents have a very high percentage of correct nodes. In the datasets *Itinerary* and *Soccer*, the HTML documents being compared are identical, which is shown by the achievement of 100% in all types of nodes. In the dataset *Poem*, the two HTML documents have exactly the same appearance in Web browsers, but according to HTMLDiff, there are some missing whitespaces in each line within the paragraphs of the new HTML document. That is why the percentage of correct TEXT_NODEs in this dataset is very low (14%). The reason of this low percentage is that in the text matching subsystem, we remove the leading and trailing whitespaces of a string before the matching is done. The improvement

[4] http://xml.apache.org/xalan-j/index.html

[5] http://www.componentsoftware.com/products/HTMLDiff/

stage does not fix the stylesheet since there are no move operations. In the dataset *Books*, the difference occurs in the first column of the table. In the original HTML document, the first column is a sequence of numbers 1, 2, 3 and 4; whereas in the new HTML document, the first column is a sequence of 1s. The numbers 1, 2, 3 and 4 in the original HTML document are represented using four *extra nodes*. However, our template rule constructor assumes that all *extra nodes* that are cousins (their parent are siblings and have the same node name) have the same structure and values. Since the four *extra nodes* have different text values in this dataset, the percentage of correct TEXT_NODEs in the new HTML document is slightly affected (86%). Lastly, the differences between the original and the new HTML documents in the dataset *Chat Log* are caused by the undiscovered mappings mentioned in the previous paragraph. Because of this, it is not possible to fix the XSLT stylesheet. However, the percentage of correct ATTRIBUTE_NODEs is still acceptable (75%).

We have tested XSLTGen on many other examples and the results are very similar to those obtained in this experiment. However, there are some problems that prevent XSLTGen from obtaining even higher matching accuracy. First, in a few cases, XSLTGen is not able to discover some mappings between XML ATTRIBUTE_NODEs and HTML ATTRIBUTE_NODEs because these mappings violate our assumption stated in Section 2.2. This problem can be alleviated by considering HTML ATTRIBUTE_NODEs in the matching process. Undiscovered mappings are also caused by incorrectly matching some nodes, which is the second problem faced in the matching process. Incorrect matchings typically occur when an XML or an HTML TEXT_NODE has some ELEMENT_NODE siblings. In some cases, these nodes should be matched during the text matching process, while in other cases they should be matched in structure matching. Here, the challenge will be in developing matching techniques that are able to determine whether a TEXT_NODE should be matched during text matching or structure matching. The third problem concerns with incorrectly classified mappings. This problem only occurs between a substring mapping and an exact mapping, when the compared strings have some leading and trailing whitespaces. Determining whether whitespaces should be kept or removed is a difficult choice.

Besides this, as the theme of our text matching subsystem is text-based matching (matching two strings), the performance of the matching process decreases if the supplied documents contain mainly numerical data. In this case, the mappings discovered, especially substring mappings, are often inaccurate and conflicting, i.e. more than one HTML node is matched with an XML node.

Finally, the current version of XSLTGen does not support the capability to automatically generate XSLT stylesheets with complex functions (e.g. sorting). This is a very challenging task and an interesting direction for future work.

4 Related Work

There is little work in the literature about automatic XSLT stylesheets generation. The only prior work of which we are aware of is XSLbyDemo [10], a system that generates an XSLT stylesheet by example. In this system, the process of generating XSLT stylesheet begins with transforming the XML document to an *initial HTML page*, which is an HTML page using a manually created XSLT stylesheet, taking into account the DTD of the XML document. The user then modifies the initial HTML page using a WYSIWYG editor and their actions are recorded in an operation history. Based on the user's operation history, a new stylesheet is generated. Obviously, this system is not automatic, since the user is directly involved at some stages of the XSLT generation process. Hence, it is not comparable to our fully automatic XSLTGen system. Specifically, our approach differs from XSLbyDemo in three key ways: (i) Our algorithm produces a stylesheet that transforms an XML document to an HTML document, while XSLbyDemo generates transformations from an initial HTML document to its modified HTML document. (ii) Our generated XSLT can be applied directly to other XML documents from the same document class, whereas using XSLbyDemo, the other XML documents have to be converted to their initial HTML pages before the generated stylesheet can be applied. (iii) Finally, our users do not have to be familiar with a WYSIWYG editor and the need of providing structural information through the editing actions. The only thing that they need to possess is knowledge of a basic HTML tool.

In the process of generating XSLT, semantic mappings need to be found. There are a number of algorithms available for tree matching. Work done in [12, 13] on the tree distance problem or tree-to-tree correction problem and in [2] known as the change-detection algorithm, compare and discover the sequence of edit operations needed to transform the source tree into the result tree given. These algorithms are mainly based on structure matching, and their input comprises of two labelled trees of the same type, i.e. two HTML trees or two XML trees. The text matching involved is very simple and limited since it compares only the labels of the trees. Clearly, these algorithms do not accommodate our needs, since we require an algorithm that matches an XML tree with an HTML tree. However, these algorithms are certainly useful in our refinement stage since within that subsystem, we are comparing two HTML documents.

In the field of semantic mapping, a significant amount of work has focused on schema matching (refer to [11] for survey). Schema matching is similar to our matching problem in the sense that two different schemas are compared, which have different sets of element names and data instances. However, the two schemas being compared are mostly from the same domain and therefore, their element names are different but comparable. Besides using structure matching, most of the schema mapping systems rely on element name matchers to match schemas. The TransSCM system [9] matches schema based on the structure and names of the SGML tags extracted from DTD files by using concept of labelled graphs. The Artemis system [1] measures similarity of element names, data types and structure to match schemas. *In XSLTGen, it is impossible to compare the element names since XML and HTML have completely different tag names.*

XMapper [7] is another system for finding semantic mappings between structured documents within a given domain, particularly XML sources. This system uses an inductive machine learning approach to improve accuracy of mappings for XML data sources, whose data types are either identical or very similar, and the tag names between these data sources are significantly different. In essence, this system is suitable for our matching process in XSLTGen since the tag names of XML and HTML documents are absolutely different. However, this system requires the user to select one matching tag between two documents, which violates our principle intention of creating a fully automatic system.

Recent work in the area of ontology matching also focuses on the problem of finding semantic mappings between two ontologies. One ontology matching system that we are aware of is GLUE system [4]. GLUE also employs machine learning techniques to semi-automatically create such semantic mappings. Given two ontologies: for each node in one ontology, the purpose is to find the most similar node in the other ontology using the notions of *Similarity Measures* and *Relaxation Labelling*. Similar to our matching process, the basis used in the *similarity measure* and *relaxation labelling* are data values and the structure of the ontologies, respectively. However, GLUE is only capable of finding 1-1 mappings whereas our XSLTGen matching process is able to discover not only 1-1 mappings but also 1-m and sometimes m-1 mappings (in substring mappings).

The main difference between mapping in XSLTGen and other mapping systems, is that in XSLTGen we believe that mappings exist between the elements in the XML and HTML documents, since the HTML document is derived from the XML document by the user; whereas in other systems, the mapping may not exist. Moreover, the mappings generated by the matching process in XSLTGen are used to generate code (an XSLT stylesheet) and that is why the mappings found have to be accurate and complete, while in schema matching and ontology matching, the purpose is only to find the most similar nodes between the two sources, without further processing of the results. To accommodate the XSLT stylesheet generation, XSLTGen is capable of finding 1-1 mappings, 1-m mappings and sometimes m-1 mappings; whereas the other mapping systems focus only on discovering 1-1 mappings. Besides this, the matching subsystem in XSLTGen has the advantage of having very similar and related data sources, since the HTML data is derived from the XML data. Hence, they can be used as the primary basis to find the mappings. In other systems, the data instances in the two sources are completely different, the only association that they have is that the sources come from the same domain. Following this argument, XSLTGen discovers the mappings between two different types of document, i.e. an XML and an HTML document, whereas the other systems compare two documents of the same type. Finally, another important aspect which differs XSLTGen from several other systems, is that the process of discovering the mappings which will then be used to generate XSLT stylesheet is completely automatic.

5 Conclusion

With the upsurge in data exchange and publishing on the Web, conversion of data from its stored representation (XML) to its publishing format (HTML) is increasingly important. XSLT plays a prominent role in transforming XML documents into HTML documents. However, it is difficult for users to learn.

We have devised XSLTGen, a system for automatically generating an XSLT stylesheet, given an XML document and its corresponding HTML document. This is useful for helping users to learn XSLT. The main strong characteristics of the generated XSLT stylesheets are accuracy and reusability. We have described how the text matching, structure matching and sequence checking enables XSLTGen to discover not only 1-1 semantic mappings between the elements in the XML document and those in the HTML document, but also 1-m mappings and sometimes m-1 mappings. We have also described a fully automatic XSLT generation system that generates XSLT rules based on the mappings found. Our experiments showed that XSLTGen can achieve high matching accuracy and produce high quality stylesheets.

References

1. S. Bergamaschi, S. Castano, S.D.C.D. Vimeracati, and M. Vincini. An Intelligent Approach to Information Integration. In *Proceedings of the 1st International Conference on Formal Ontology in Information Systems*, pages 253–267, Trento, Italy, June 1998.
2. S.S. Chawathe, A. Rajaraman, H. Garcia-Molina, and J. Widom. Change Detection in Hierarchically Structured Information. In *Proceedings of the 1996 International Conference on Management of Data*, pages 493–504, Montreal, Canada, June 1996.
3. J. Clark. *XSL Transformation (XSLT) Version 1.0.* W3C Recommendation, November 1999. *http://www.w3.org/TR/xslt.*
4. A. Doan, J. Madhavan, P. Domingos, and A. Halevy. Learning to Map between Ontologies on the Semantic Web. In *Proceedings of the 11th International Conference on World Wide Web*, pages 662–673, Honolulu, USA, May 2002.
5. M. Garofalakis, A. Gionis, R. Rastogi, S. Seshadri, and K. Shim. XTRACT: Learning Document Type Descriptors from XML Document Collections. *Data Mining and Knowledge Discovery*, 7(1):23–56, January 2003.
6. M. Kay. *XSLT Programmer's Reference.* Wrox Press Ltd., 2000.
7. L. Kurgan, W. Swiercz, and K.J. Cios. Semantic Mapping of XML Tags using Inductive Machine Learning. In *Proceedings of the 2002 International Conference on Machine Learning and Applications*, pages 99–109, Las Vegas, USA, June 2002.
8. M. Leventhal. XSL Considered Harmful. *http://www.xml.com/pub/a/1999/05/xsl/xslconsidered_1.html*, 1999.
9. T. Milo and S. Zohar. Using Schema Matching to Simplify Heterogeneous Data Translation. In *Proceedings of 24th International Conference on Very Large Data Bases*, pages 122–133, New York, USA, August 1998.
10. K. Ono, T. Koyanagi, M. Abe, and M. Hori. XSLT Stylesheet Generation by Example with WYSIWYG Editing. In *Proceedings of the 2002 International Symposium on Applications and the Internet*, Nara, Japan, March 2002.
11. E. Rahm and P.A. Bernstein. A Survey of Approaches to Automatic Schema Matching. *VLDB Journal*, 10(4):334–350, December 2001.
12. S.M. Selkow. The Tree-to-Tree Editing Problem. *Information Processing Letters*, 6(6):184–186, December 1977.
13. K.C. Tai. The Tree-to-Tree Correction Problem. *Journal of the ACM*, 26(3):422–433, July 1979.

Efficient Recursive XML Query Processing in Relational Database Systems

Sandeep Prakash[1], Sourav S. Bhowmick[1], and Sanjay Madria[2]

[1] School of Computer Engineering
Nanyang Technological University
Singapore
assourav@ntu.edu.sg

[2] Department of Computer Science
University of Missouri-Rolla
Rolla, MO 65409
madrias@umr.edu

Abstract. There is growing evidence that schema-conscious approaches are a better option than schema-oblivious techniques as far as XML query performance is concerned in relational environment. However, the issue of recursive XML queries for such approaches has not been dealt with satisfactorily. In this paper we argue that it is possible to design a schema-oblivious approach that outperforms schema-conscious approaches for certain types of recursive queries. To that end, we propose a novel schema-oblivious approach called SUCXENT++ that outperforms existing schema-oblivious approaches such as XParent by up to 15 times and schema-conscious approaches (Shared-Inlining) by up to 3 times for recursive query execution. Our approach has up to 2 times smaller storage requirements compared to existing schema-oblivious approaches and 10% less than schema-conscious techniques. In addition, existing schema-oblivious approaches are hampered by poor query plans generated by the relational query optimizer. We propose optimizations in the XML query to SQL translation process that generate queries with more optimal query plans.

1 Introduction

Recursive XML queries are considered to be quite significant in the context of XML query processing [3] and yet this issue has not been addressed satisfactorily in existing literature. Recursive XML queries are XML queries that contain the descendant axis (//). The use of the '//' is quite common in XML queries due to the semi-structured nature of XML data [3]. For example, consider the XML document in Figure 2. The element `item` could occur either under `europe` or `africa`. Consider the scenario where a user needs to retrieve all `item` elements. The user will have to execute the path expression Q = /site//item. Another scenario could be that the document structure is not completely known to the user except that each `item` has a `name` and `price`. Suppose, the user needs to

P. Atzeni et al. (Eds.): ER 2004, LNCS 3288, pp. 493–510, 2004.

find out the price of the `item` with `name` `"Gold Ignot"`. Q = //item[name="Gold Ignot"]/price will be the corresponding path expression.

Efficient execution of XML queries, recursive or otherwise, is largely determined by the underlying storage approach. There has been a substantial research effort in storing and processing XML data using existing relational databases [1, 6, 2]. These approaches can be broadly classified as: (a) *Schema-conscious approach:* This method first creates a relational schema based on the DTD of the XML documents. Examples of such approach is the inlining approach [5]. (b) *Schema-oblivious approach:* This method maintains a fixed schema which is used to store XML documents irrespective of their DTD. Examples of schema-oblivious approaches are the Edge approach [1], XRel [7] and XParent [2]. Schema-oblivious approaches have obvious advantages such as the ability to handle XML schema changes better as there is no need to change the relational schema and a uniform query translation approach. Schema-conscious approaches, on the other hand, have the advantage of more efficient query processing [6]. Also, no special relational schema needs to be designed for schema-conscious approaches as it can be generated on the fly based on the DTD of the XML document(s).

In this paper, we present an efficient approach to process recursive XML queries using a schema-oblivious approach. At this point, one would question the justification of this work for two reasons. First, this issue may have already been addressed. Surprisingly, this is not the case as highlighted in [3]. Second, a growing body of work suggests that schema-conscious approaches perform better than schema-oblivious approaches. In fact, Tian et al. have demonstrated in [6] that schema-conscious approaches generally perform substantially better in terms of query processing and storage size. However, the Edge approach [1] was used as the representative schema-oblivious approach for comparison. Although the Edge approach is a pioneering relational approach, we argue that it is not a good representation of the schema-oblivious approach as far as query processing is concerned. In fact, XParent [2] and XRel [7] have been shown to outperform the Edge approach by up to 20 times, with XParent outperforming XRel [2]. However, this does not mean that XParent outperforms schema-conscious approaches. In fact as we will show in Section 6, schema-conscious approaches still outperform XParent. Hence, it may seem that schema-conscious generally outperforms schema-oblivious in terms of query processing. In this paper we argue that it is indeed possible to design a schema-oblivious approach that can outperform schema-conscious approaches for certain types of *recursive queries.*

To justify our claim, we propose a novel schema-oblivious approach, called SUCXENT++ (**S**chema **U**n**c**oncious **XML** **En**abled Sys**t**em (pronounced "succinct++")), and investigate the performance of recursive XML queries. We only store the leaf nodes and the associated paths together with two additional attributes for efficient query processing (details follow in Section 3). SUCXENT++ outperforms existing schema-oblivious techniques, such as XParent, by up to 15 times and shared-inlining - a schema-conscious approach - by up to 3 times for recursive queries with characteristics described in Section 6. In addition,

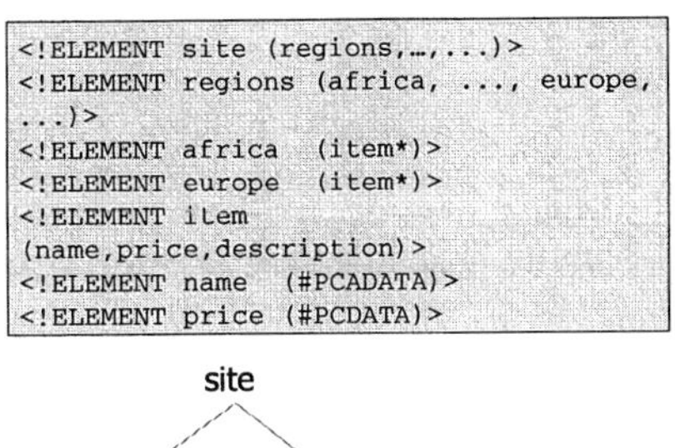

```
<!ELEMENT site (regions,…,...)>
<!ELEMENT regions (africa, ..., europe,
...)>
<!ELEMENT africa  (item*)>
<!ELEMENT europe  (item*)>
<!ELEMENT item
(name,price,description)>
<!ELEMENT name  (#PCADATA)>
<!ELEMENT price (#PCDATA)>
```

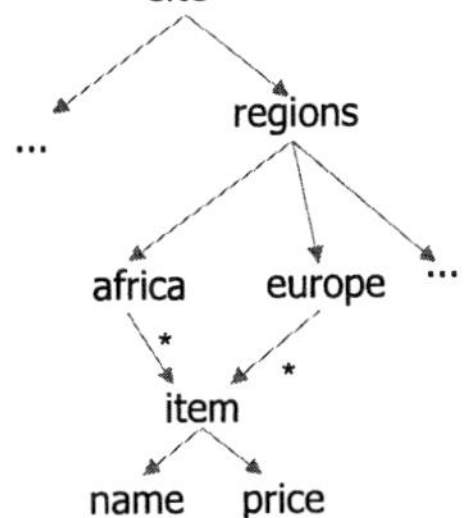

Fig. 1. Sample DTD.

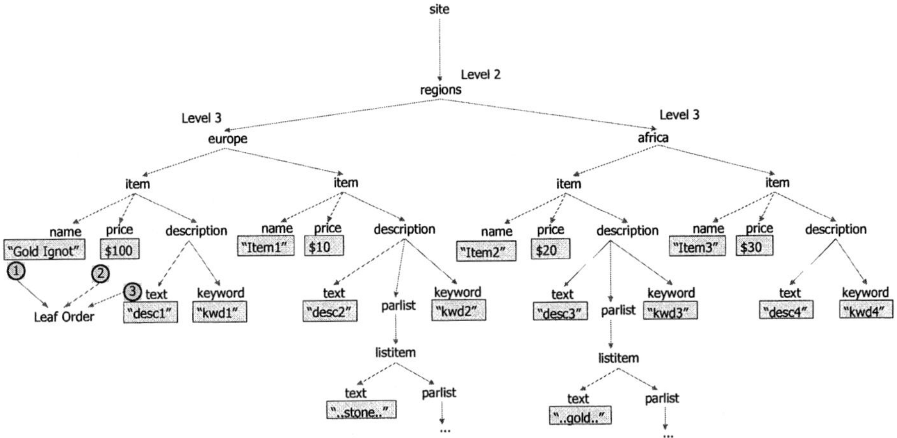

Fig. 2. Sample XML document.

SUCXENT++ can reconstruct shredded documents up to 2 times faster than Shared-Inlining. The main reasons SUCXENT++ performs better than existing approaches are 1) Significantly lower storage size and, consequently, lower I/O-cost associated with query processing, 2) Fewer number of joins in the corresponding SQL queries and, 3)Additional optimizations, discussed in Section 5, that are made to improve the query plan generated by the relational query optimizer. In summary, the main contributions of this paper are: (1) A novel schema-oblivious approach whose storage size depends only on the number of leaf nodes in the document. (2) Optimizations to improve the query plan generated by the relational query optimizer. Traditional schema-oblivious approaches have been hampered by the poor query plan selection of the underlying relational query optimizer[6, 8]. (3) To the best of our knowledge, this is the first attempt to show that it is indeed possible to design a schema-oblivious approach that can outperform schema-conscious approaches as far as the execution of certain types of recursive XML queries is concerned.

2 Related Work

All existing schema-oblivious approaches store, at the very least, every node in the XML document. The Edge approach [1] essentially captures edge information of the tree that represents the XML document. However, resolving ancestor-descendant relationships requires the traversal of all the edges from the ancestor to the descendant (or vice-versa). The system proposed by Zhang et. al in [8] labels each node with its preorder and postorder traversal numbers. Then, ancestor-descendant relationships can be resolved in constant time using the property $preorder(ancestor) < preorder(descendant)$ and $postorder(ancestor) > postorder(descendant)$. It still results in as many joins as there are path separators.

To solve the problem of multiple joins, XRel [7] stores the path of each node in the document. Then, the resolution of path expressions only requires the paths (which can be represented as strings) to be matched using string matching operators. However, the XRel approach still makes use of the containment property mentioned above to resolve ancestor-descendant relationships. It involve joins with $\theta(< or >)$ operators that have been shown to be quite expensive due to the manner in which an RDBMS processes joins [8]. In fact, special algorithms such as the Multi-predicate merge sort join algorithm [8] have been proposed to optimize these operations. However, to the best of our knowledge there is no off-the-shelf RDBMS that implements these algorithms.

XParent [2] solves the problem of θ-joins by using an Ancestor table that stores all the ancestors of a particular node in a single table. It then replaces θ-joins with *equi*-joins over this set of ancestors. However, this approach results in an explosion in the database size as compared to the original document. The number of relational joins is also quite substantial. XParent requires a join between the LabelPath, DataPath, Element and Ancestor tables for each path in the query expression. The joins are quite expensive especially when the Ancestor table is involved as it can be quite large in size.

SUCXENT++ is different from existing approaches in that it only stores leaf nodes and their associated paths. We store two additional attributes, called `BranchOrder` and `BranchOrderSum`, for each leaf node that capture the relationship between leaf nodes. Essentially, they allow the determination of common nodes between the paths of any two leaf nodes in a constant time. This results in a substantial reduction in storage size and query processing time. In addition, we propose optimizations that enable the underlying relational query optimizer to generate near-optimal query plans for our approach, resulting in a substantial performance improvement. Our studies indicate that these optimizations can be applied to other schema-oblivious approaches as well.

LabelPath (ID, Len, Path)
DataPath (Pid, Cid)
Element (PathID, Did, Ordinal)
Data (PathID, Did, Ordinal, Value)
Ancestor (Did, Ancestor, Level)

Fig. 3. XParent schema.

Document (DocId, Name)
Path (PathId, CPathId, PathExp, Length)
PathValue (DocId, PathId, LeafOrder, BranchOrder, BranchOrderSum, LeafValue)
DocumentRValue(DocId, Level, Rvalue)

Fig. 4. SUCXENT++ schema.

Document

DocId	Name
1	Auction.xml
2	..

Path

PathId	PathExp	CPathId	Length
1	site.regions.africa.item.description.keyword	1	6
2	site.regions.africa.item.description.text	3	6
3	site.regions.africa.item.name	5	5
4	site.regions.africa.item.price	7	5
5	site.regions.europe.item.description.keyword	2	6
6	site.regions.europe.item.description.text	4	6
7	site.regions.europe.item.name	6	5
8	site.regions.europe.item.price	8	5

PathValue

DocId	PathId	CPathId	LeafOrde	BranchOrder	BranchOrderSum	LeafValue
1	7	6	1	0	0	Gold Ignot
1	8	8	2	4	3	$100
1	6	4	3	4	6	desc1
1	5	2	4	5	8	kwd1
1	...	...	...	...	...	...
1	3	5	13	3	85	Item3
1	4	7	14	4	88	$30
1	2	3	15	4	91	desc4
1	1	1	16	5	93	kwd4

DocumentRValue

DocId	Level	RValue
1	1	329
1	2	41
1	3	10
1	4	3
1	5	2
1	6	1

Fig. 5. SUCXENT++: XML data in RDBMS.

Schema-oblivious approaches are not influenced by recursion in the schema. However, the Edge approach uses *recursive SQL queries* using the SQL99 `with` construct to evaluate recursive XML queries. XParent and XRel handle recursive queries like any other query. Unlike these schema-oblivious approaches, schema-conscious strategies have to treat recursion in both schema and queries as special cases. In [3], the authors propose a generic algorithm to translate recursive XML queries for schema-conscious approaches using the SQL99 `with` construct. However, no performance evaluation of the resulting SQL queries is presented and it is assumed that schema-conscious approaches will outperform schema-oblivious approaches. SUCXENT++ also treats recursive XML queries like other queries. It also implements optimizations to generate SQL translations of recursive XML queries that enable the relational query optimizer to produce better query plans resulting in significant performance gains.

3 Storing XML Data

In this section, we first discuss the SUCXENT++ schema. This will be followed by a formal algorithm to reconstruct XML documents from their relational form. The document in Figure 2 is used as a running example.

3.1 SUCXENT++ Schema

The schema is shown in Figure 4 and the shredded document in Figure 5. The semantics of the schema is as follows. The `Document` table is used for storing the names of the documents in the database. Each document has unique id recorded in `DocID`. `Path` is used to record the path of all the leaf nodes. For example, the path of the first leaf node *name* in Figure 2 is `/site/regions/europe/item/name`. This table maintains `path_ids`, relative path expressions and their length recorded as instances of `PathID`, `PathExp` and `Length` respectively. This is to reduce the storage size so that we only need to store `path_id` in the `PathValue` table. The `Length` attribute is useful for resolving recursive queries.

`PathValue` stores only the leaf nodes. The `DocID` attribute indicates which XML document a particular leaf node belongs to. The `PathID` attribute maintains the `id` of the path of a particular leaf node as stored in `Path`. `LeafOrder` records the *node order* of leaf nodes in an XML tree. For example, when the sample XML document is parsed, the leaf node *name* with value `"Gold Ignot"` is encountered as the first leaf node. Therefore, it is assigned a `LeafOrder` value of `1`. `BranchOrder` of a leaf node is the level at which it intersects the preceding leaf node i.e., it is the level of the highest common ancestor of the leaf nodes under consideration. Consider the leaf node with `LeafOrder=2` in Figure 2. This leaf node intersects the leaf node with `LeafOrder=1` at the node *item* which is at level 4. So, the `BranchOrder` value for this node is 4. Similarly, the node *name* with value `"Item2"` has `BranchOrder=2` (intersecting the node to the left at *regions*). `PathValue` stores the textual content of the leaf nodes in the column `LeafValue`. The attribute `BranchOrder` in this table is useful for reconstructing the XML documents from their shredded relational format as discussed in Section 3.2. The significance of `DocumentRValue` and `BranchOrderSum` in `PathValue` is elaborated in Section 4 and `CPathId` in `Path` is discussed in Section 5. For the remainder of the paper, we will refer to `LeafOrder` and `BranchOrder` as `Order` information.

3.2 Extraction of XML Documents

The algorithm for reconstruction is presented in Figure 6. The input to the algorithm is a list of leaf nodes arranged in ascending `LeafOrder`. Each leaf node path is first split into its constituent nodes (lines 5 to 7). If the document construction has not yet started (line 10) then the first node obtained by splitting the first leaf node path is made the root (lines 11 to 15). When the next leaf node is processed we only need to look at the nodes after `BranchOrder` of that node as the nodes up to this level have already been added to the document

```
Input: L = {n_1, ..., n_k}, a list of leaf nodes arranged in order of
   LeafOrder values
Output: D is the document to be returned.
1: c is an XML node.
2: c ← φ
3: C ← list of XML nodes.
4: for all n_i in L do
5:    /* /book/authors/author would give p = [book,authors,author]*/
6:    p is the array of nodes in a path.
7:    p = n_i.Path.GetNodes()
8:    /*s is a counter*/
9:    s ← 0
10:   if c = φ then
11:      /* c has not been assigned a value yet. */
12:      c ← new XmlDocumentNode( p[0] )
13:      /* Make c the root. This happens only once. */
14:      D.AddNode( c )
15:      C.Add( c )
16:      s ← 1
17:   else if
      then
18:      s ← n_i.BranchOrder()
19:   end if
20:   /* Keep only those nodes in C that are
      common between n_{i-1} and n_i. */
21:   C.ClearFromIndex( s )
22:   q is an XML node
23:   /* assign c to a temporary variable q.
      Need to keep it as the starting node for processing n_{i+1} */
24:   q ← c
25:   while s < p.Length() do
26:      m ← new XmlDocumentNode(p[s])
27:      q.AppendChild( m )
28:      C.Add( m)
29:      q ← m
30:      s++
31:   end while
32: end for
```

Fig. 6. Extraction algorithm.

(lines 20 to 22). The remaining are now added to the document (lines 27 to 32). Document extraction is completed once all the leaf nodes have been processed. In addition to reconstructing the whole document, this algorithm can be used to construct a document fragment given a partial list of consecutive leaf nodes.

4 Recursive Query Processing

Consider the recursive query *XQuery 1* in Figure 7. A tree representation of the query is shown in Figure 8. This query returns those *price* leaf nodes that intersect the constraint-satisfying *text* leaf node at *item*. Consider how XParent resolves this query. The schema for XParent is shown in Figure 3. XParent evaluates this query by locating leaf nodes from the Data table that satisfy the constraint on *text*. This involves a join between the LabelPath and Data to satisfy the path constraint `/site/regions/africa/item//text` and a predicate on the Data to satisfy the value constraint. Next, LabelPath and Data tables are joined again to obtain those leaf nodes that satisfy `/site/regions/africa/item/price`. These two results sets are joined using the Ancestor table to find nodes that have a common ancestor at level 4 (at `item`). Thus, the final SQL query involves five joins - two between the LabelPath and Data, two between the Data and Ancestor and one between two Ancestor tables (SQL query translation details for XParent can be found in [2]). These joins can be quite expensive due to the large size of Ancestor. XRel follows a similar approach to

```
For                                                         XQuery 1
  $b in document( "auction" )/site/regions/africa/item
Where
  contains($b//text, "Gold Ignot")
Return
  <price>$b/price</price>
```

```
SELECT                                                      SQL 1
v2.* from PathValue v1, Path p1, PathValue v2, Path p2,
DocumentRValue r
Where
p1.PathExp LIKE '/site/regions/africa/item/%/text'
AND p2.PathExp = '/site/regions/africa/item/price'
AND v1.PathId = p1.PathId and v2.PathId = p2.PathId
AND v1.LeafValue LIKE '%Gold Ignot%'
AND v1.DocId = v2.DocId and r1.Level=4
AND abs(v1.BranchOrderSum - v2.BranchOrderSum) < r1.RValue
```

Fig. 7. Running example.

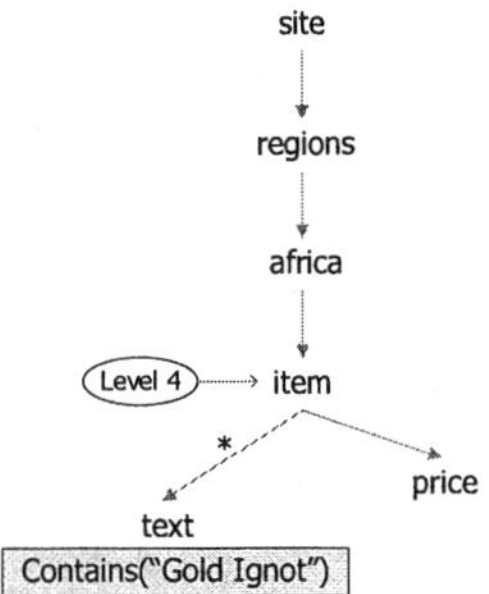

Fig. 8. Query Tree.

resolving path expressions except that it uses the *ancestor-descendant* containment property instead of an Ancestor table. This produces θ-joins resulting in performance worse than XParent. A detailed evaluation of XRel vs. XParent can be found in [2].

4.1 The SUCXENT++ Approach

In order to reduce the I/O cost involved in query evaluation, SUCXENT++ only stores the leaf nodes of a document. However, the attributes discussed till now are insufficient for query processing. The schema needs to be extended as follows. An attribute `BranchOrderSum`, denoted as s_n, is assigned to a leaf node with `LeafOrder` n. In addition, we store an attribute `RValue`, r_l in the DocumentRvalue table for each level, l, in the document. Essentially, these allow the determination of common nodes between the paths of any two leaf nodes in a constant time. This results in a substantial reduction in storage size and query processing time. Given an XML document with maximum depth D the `RValue` and `BranchOrderSum` assignment is done as follows. (1) `RValue` is assigned recursively based on the equation: $r_i = r_{i+1} \times c_{i+1} + 1$ where (a) c_k is the maximum number of *consecutive* leaf nodes with `BranchOrder` $\geq k$ (b) $r_D = 1$. (2) Let us denote the `BranchOrder` of a node with `LeafOrder` n as b_n. Then, the `BranchOrderSum` of this node is $s_n = \sum_{i=1}^{i \leq n} r_{b_i}$.

We illustrate the above attributes with an example. Consider the document in Figure 2. For simplicity, ignore the *parlist* element. Then, the depth of the document in 6. So, $r_6 = 1$ and $c_6 = 1$. This means that $r_5 = 1 \times 1 + 1 = 2$. The maximum number of *consecutive* leaf nodes with `BranchOrder` ≥ 5 is 1. Therefore, $r_4 = 2 \times 1 + 1 = 3$. The maximum number of *consecutive* leaf nodes with `BranchOrder` ≥ 4 is 3 (e.g., *price, text, keyword* under the first *item* element). So, $r_3 = 3 \times 3 + 1 = 10$. `BranchOrderSum` of the first leaf node is 0. Since `BranchOrder` of the second leaf node is 4 and $r_4 = 3$, `BranchOrderSum` of the second leaf node is 3. The values for the complete document are shown in DocumentRValue and PathValue of Figure 5.

Lemma 1. *If $s_d = |s_n - s_m| < r_l$, then nodes with* LeafOrders *n and m intersect at a level greater than l. That is, $|s_n - s_m| < r_L \Rightarrow I(n, m) > L$ where $I(n, m)$ is the level at which nodes with leaf orders n and m intersect.* ∎

The proof for the above lemma is not presented here due to space constraints. The attributes `RValue` and `BranchOrderSum` allow the determination of the intersection level between any two leaf nodes in a more or less *constant time*, whereas in XParent, it depends on the size of the Ancestor and Data tables as a join between these tables is required to determine the ancestor node at a particular level. This reduces the query processing time drastically. Since this is achieved without storing separate ancestor information, the storage requirements are also reduced significantly.

We will now discuss how these attributes are useful in query processing. Consider *XQuery1*. The `BranchOrderSum` value for the first constraint satisfying *text* is 6. The `BranchOrderSum` value for the first *price* node is 3. Also, $r_3 =$

10. Using the property proven above we conclude that these two nodes have ancestors till a level ≥ 3, since $|3 - 6| < 10$. Since, *item* is at level 4 in both cases it is clear that they have a common *item* node and, therefore, satisfy the query. Similarly, we can conclude that the first *text* node and the *item* node with *name* `Item3` intersect at a level > 1 (since $r_1 = 329$ and $|85 - 3| < 329$) and therefore do not form a part of the query result.

4.2 SQL Translation

We have implemented an algorithm to translate XQuery queries to SQL in SUCXENT++. Due to space constraints we discuss the translation procedure informally. Consider the recursive query of Figure 7 (**XQuery 1**) and its corresponding SQL translation (**SQL 1**). The translation can be explained as follows: (1) Lines 5, 7 and 8 translate the part of the query that seeks an entry with `contains(text, "Gold Ignot")`. Note that we store only the leaf nodes, their textual content and `path_id`) in the PathValue table. The actual path expression corresponding to the leaf node is stored in the `Path` table. Therefore, we need to join the two to obtain leaf nodes that correspond to the path `/site/regions/africa/item//text` and contain the phrase `"Gold Ignot"`. Notice that the corresponding SQL translation has the `LIKE` clause to resolve the // relationship. This is how recursive queries are handled in SUCXENT++. (2) Lines 6 and 7 do the same for the extraction of leaf nodes that correspond to the path `/site/regions/africa/item/price`. (3) Line 9 ensures that the leaf nodes extracted in Lines 5 to 8 belong to the same document. (4) Line 10 ensures that the two sets of leaf nodes intersect at least level 4. The reason a level 4 ancestor is needed is that the two paths in the query intersect at level 4. It calculates the absolute value of the difference between the `BranchOrderSum` values and ensures that it is below the `RValue` for level 4. (5) Line 1 returns the properties of the leaf nodes corresponding to the *price* element. These properties are needed to construct the corresponding XML fragment based on the algorithm in Figure 6. Say, the `return` clause in Figure 7 was `<item>$b</item>`. Then, line 6 in the translation would change to `p2.PathExp LIKE '/site/regions/africa/item%'` to extract all leaf nodes that have paths **beginning** with `$b`. This way, elements and their children can be retrieved.

Compared to XParent, SUCXENT++ uses only the PathValue, Path and DocumentRValue tables to evaluate a query. The size of the PathValue and Path tables is the same as that of the Data and LabelPath tables in XParent. DocumentRValue has the same number of rows as the depth of the document as compared to the **Ancestor** table in XParent which stores the ancestor list of every node in the document. This results in substantially better query performance in addition to much smaller storage size.

5 Optimizations

A preliminary performance evaluation using the above translation procedure yielded some interesting results. We checked the query plans generated by the

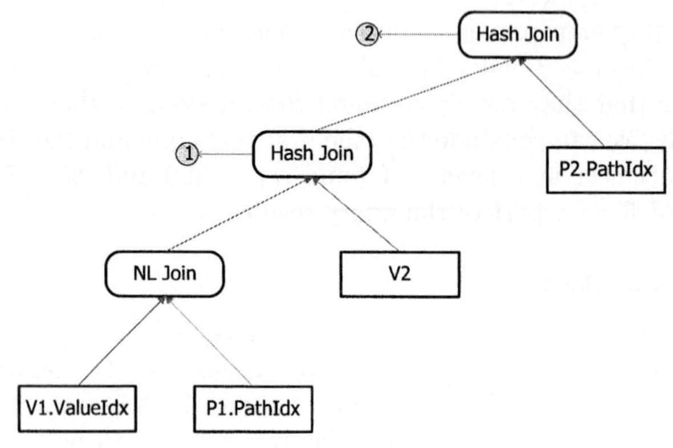

Fig. 9. Initial query plan.

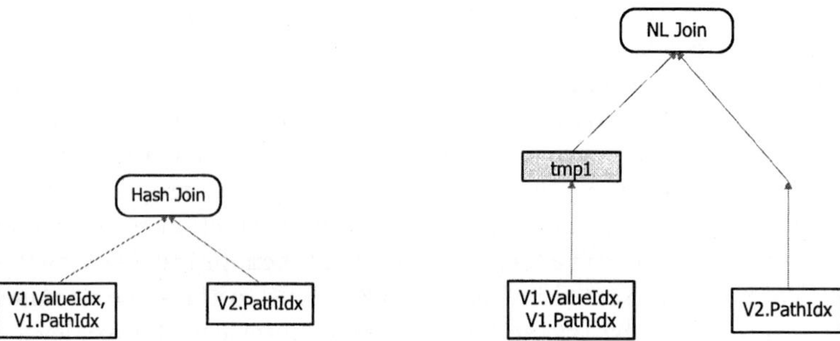

Fig. 10. Path optimization.

Fig. 11. Multiple-queries optimization.

query optimizer and noticed that the join between the Path and PathValue tables took a significant portion of the query processing time. This was because for most of the queries this join was being performed last. For example, in SQL 1 of Figure 7 the joins in lines 8 to 10 were evaluated first and only then was the join between Path and PathValue tables performed. The initial query plan is shown in Figure 9. We have not shown the `DocumentRValue` table in the plan, even though the query optimizer includes it, as it does not influence the optimization. The two Hash-Joins (labelled 1 and 2) in this plan are both very expensive. The first takes the PathValue table (with alias `v2`) as one of its inputs. The second join takes the result of this join as one of its inputs. Both these inputs are quite substantial in size resulting in very expensive join operations. In order to improve the above query plans we propose three optimizations that are discussed below.

Optimization for Simple Path Expressions. The join expression `v1.PathId = p1.Id and p1.PathExp =` ***path*** is replaced with `v1.PathId = n` where `n` is the `PathId` value corresponding to ***path*** in the table `Path`. Similarly, `v1.PathId = p1.Id and p1.PathExp LIKE` ***path%*** is replaced with `v1.PathId >= n and v1.PathId <= m`. For the second case `PathIds` are assigned in lexicographic order

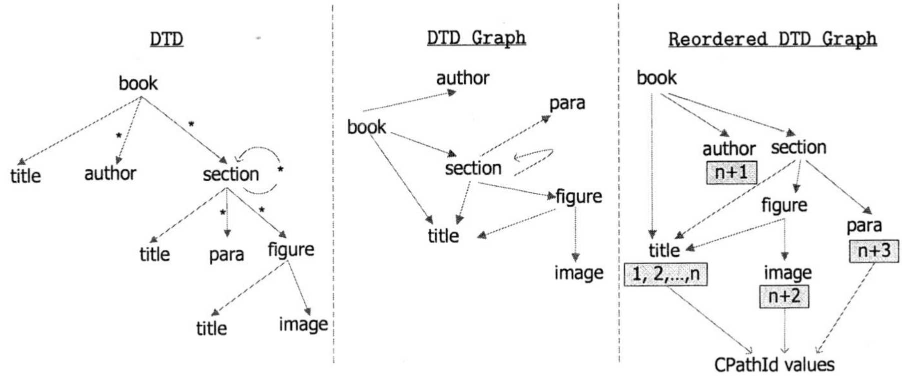

Fig. 12. DTD graph and path numbering.

```
SELECT                                                   SQL 1.1
v1.* into tmp1 from PathValue v1, Path p1
Where p1.PathExp = '/site/regions/africa/item/%/text'
AND v1.PathId = p1.PathId
AND v1.LeafValue LIKE '%Gold Ignot%'
```

```
SELECT                                                   SQL 1.2
t2.* from tmp1 t1, tmp2 t2, DocumentRValue r1
Where t1.DocId = t2.DocId and t1.DocId = r1.DocId
AND r1.Level = 4 AND
abs(t1.BranchOrderSum-t2.BranchOrderSum) < r1.RValue
```

Fig. 13. Multiple queries.

and `(n, m)` correspond to the first and last occurrences of expressions that have the prefix *path*. This changes the query plan to the one in Figure 10. Since there is no join between the `PathValue` and `Path` tables anymore, the joins in Lines 9 and 10 now get executed the last. The `PathId` and `LeafValue` predicates are evaluated earlier resulting in smaller inputs to the join operations. This optimization resulted in an improvement of up to 60% in query execution time as shown in Section 6.

Optimization for Recursive Path Expressions. A lexicographic numbering of paths is not sufficient for recursive expressions when the DTD structure is a graph. Figure 12 shows an example of such a DTD. It has a graph structure due to the recursion on the *section* element. If only lexicographic `PathId` is available, expressions such as `//title` cannot be optimized i.e., converted to a range expression instead of a join. We assign another `pathId`, called `CPathId`, to a `Path` based on the following rules: (1) Elements in the DTD graph are ordered by the number of incoming edges. Lexicographic ordering is followed within this ordering. Figure 12 shows the "reordered" graph. The element *title* is ordered first as it has the highest number of incoming edges. $1 \ldots n$ are the `CPathId` values for paths ending in *title.* (2) Cycles in the DTD graph are handled by clustering paths with the same non-recursive element after the end of the cycle.

Based on this rule, `/book/section/title`, `/book/section/section/title`,..., `/book/section/../section/title` would all occur consecutively for the DTD in Figure 12. This allows the replacement of paths such `//section//title` with range expressions in the SQL translation.

The SUCXENT++ schema has to be extended to incorporate the `CPathId` attribute together with the existing `PathId` column in PathValue (Figure 5). Any recursive path expression can be now be converted to a range query on the `CPathId` attribute. Consider the following examples: (1) `//title` is replaced by `(p.CPathId >= 1 and p.CPathId <= n)` as all paths ending in `title` have `CPathId` values between `1` and `n`. (2) Consider the path `//section/title`. To begin with, the first and last `CPathId` values of `%section/title` in the Path table are obtained. Say, these are n_f and n_l, respectively. Then, the join expression is replaced by `(p.CPathId >=` n_f `and p.CPathId <=` n_l`)`.

Optimization Using Multiple Queries. After performing the above two optimizations the new query plans still had one major limitation. The last two join expressions (lines 9 and 10 in Figure 7) were still being evaluated using Hash-Joins. The analysis of the two intermediate results used for the evaluation of the join expression found that Nested-Loop would be a better option.

Forcing a Nested-Loop-based query plan is not a good choice as there are cases where Hash-Join (or Merge-Sort join) is still a better option. Our conclusion was that we should separate the pre-join results, execute a separate join query on these temporary results and let the query optimizer decide. We materialized one of the results into a separate temporary table and then executed a join on this temporary table and PathValue. The query optimizer now generated a better plan for all queries. This optimization resulted in an improvement of up to 7 times as shown in Section 6. The final set of queries for the given example, in order of execution, is shown in Figure 13. SQL 1.1 corresponds to the intermediate result. The resulting query plan is shown in Figure 11.

6 Performance Evaluation

SUCXENT++ was developed using Java JDK1.5 and a commercial RDBMS[1]. The experiments were conducted on a P4 1.4GHz machine with 256MB of RAM and a 40GB (7200rpm) IDE hard disk. The operating system was Windows 2000 Professional. We experimented with the data sets shown in Figure 17 and the queries shown in Figure 14 which also indicates the sources of these data sets. Note that the DTD graph of the ODP dataset contains cycles. Also, in order to measure the insertion/extraction times we use a small subset of the DBLP data set with documents that vary in size from 11KB to 1MB.

Storage Size. Figure 17 shows the relative database sizes for the three approaches. Note that, as expected, XParent has by far the largest database size

[1] Our licensing agreement disallows us from naming the product

Query	Database	Query Features
Q1: FOR $b in document("odp.xml")//topic WHERE $b/Title = "Photography" RETURN $b/Description	ODP[1]	- Recursive schema - One // axis in query
Q2: FOR $b in document("odp.xml")//topic WHERE $b//Title = "Photography" RETURN $b/Description	ODP	- Recursive schema - Two // axis in query
Q3: FOR $b in document("odp.xml")//topic WHERE month($b/lastUpdate) >= 10 RETURN $b/Description	ODP	- Recursive schema - One // axis in query - typecast
Q4: FOR $b in document("odp.xml")//topic WHERE month($b//lastUpdate) >= 10 RETURN $b/Description	ODP	- Recursive schema - Two // axis in query - typecast
Q5: FOR $b in document("auction.xml")/site/regions RETURN count($b//item)	Xmark[10]	- One // axis - Aggregate function
Q6: FOR $b in document("auction.xml")/site RETURN count($b//description)+count($b//annotation)+count($b//email)	XMark	- One // axis with respect to root - Aggregate function
Q7: FOR $b in document("auction.xml")/site/regions/africa/item WHERE contains($b//description,"gold") RETURN $b/name	XMark	- One // axis on Recursive portion of schema - Text search
Q8: FOR $b in document("sprot.xml")/sptr/entry WHERE $b/reference//authorList/person[@name="Mueller P."] RETURN $b/accession	Swiss-Prot[2]	- One // axis - Distant return and where clause
Q9: FOR $b in document("sprot.xml")/sptr/entry WHERE $b/reference//person[@name="Hermann R."] RETURN $b/reference	Swiss-Prot	- One // axis - Distant return and where clause - Shallow return clause
Q10: FOR $b in document("sprot.xml")/sptr/entry WHERE $b/reference//@type="journal article" RETURN $b/accession	Swiss-Prot	- One // axis - Large result size

[1]The Open Directory Project. http://dmoz.org.
[2]The Swiss-Prot Database. http://us.expasy.org

Fig. 14. Queries and their features.

among the three approaches and SUCXENT++ has the smallest. In the Shared-Inlining approach indexes are created on all columns to aid in query processing. We did notice that the non-indexed database size for the Shared-Inlining approach was by far the smallest among the three. This means that indexing all columns in the inlining approach is not a good strategy as far as storage is concerned and should instead be based on the query workload.

Decomposition/Extraction Times. Figures 15 shows the results for document load performance which is dependent on the number of tuples inserted. As expected, XParent takes the longest for inserting documents. The performance of SUCXENT++ and the inlining approach is quite comparable.

Extraction time depends on the time taken to extract the relevant tuples and main-memory processing time to reconstruct the document. The results in Figure 16 show that SUCXENT++ performs marginally better than XParent and up to 40% better than Shared-Inlining. The inlining approach has to join several tables to get all the data needed for document reconstruction. As an indication of the data fragmentation consider that 34 tables are created for the Swiss-Prot data set. In addition, the main-memory processing time is also higher due to the fragmented nature of the retrieved data.

The extraction performance of SUCXENT++ is only slightly better than XParent. Even though the time taken to extract the relevant tuples (only leaf nodes) is smaller than the corresponding operation in XParent (that involves

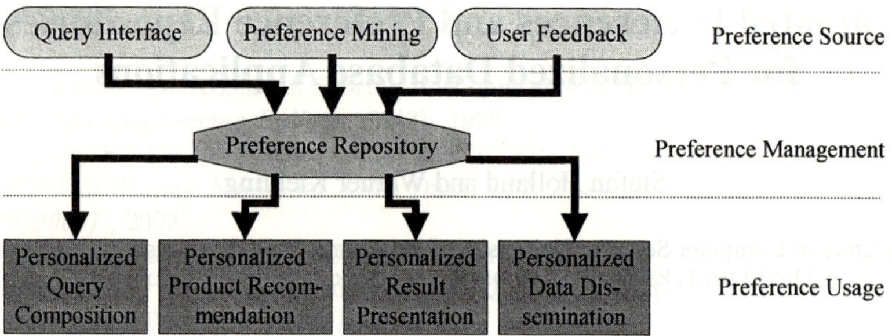

Fig. 1. Preference-centered architecture for personalized applications

financial services. As a fact of life the user preferences in such applications do not always hold in general but may depend on underlying situations. For instance, a customer may have different shopping preferences depending on his location (being at work or at home) or on the time of day [15]. In order to integrate such situations into preferences a generic approach on situation modeling has to be developed.

Initially let us consider some related work. So far in conceptual modeling and database technology only little research on situation models has been done. The pragmatic approach of computer scientists is usually focused on the needs of the underlying application. For instance, in [26] information like the user's position, timestamp, or weather is used to define the user's current situation. In [25] the so-called context-aware mobile computing distinguishes situations w.r.t. "where you are", "who you are with", and "what resources are nearby". Other context-aware applications consider only selected aspects of situations like the timestamp or the user's location [2, 5].

In cognitive science a few work on situation modeling has been done in the past. Barwise and Perry developed the idea that a situation is composed of a collection of entities, whereby each entity may have a set of properties associated with it [1]. The entities of a situation can be any meaningful object, such as person, inanimate object, or abstract idea. Furthermore, there can be some relations within these entities. These relations include, but are not limited to, spatial, temporal, or ownership relations [22].

With these ideas as foundation we develop an entity-relationship based meta model for situations in this work. Since its introduction to the database community in 1976 by [4], the entity-relationship modeling technique has established as a major design tool for the development of database applications. The main advantages are the semantically rich nature and the easily interpretable structure of the resulting ER models. With our extensions on situated ER models we follow this philosophy by providing an intuitive framework for the integration of situations into the ER models of personalized applications.

The rest of the paper is organized as follows: In Section 2 we describe our novel meta model for situations, give examples for situation models in personalized applications, and introduce the concept of situated preferences. Section 3 describes the preference repository as the major component for the storage and management of long-term and situated preferences. Situated preferences introduced in Section 2 are not restricted to a specific preference model, whereas in Section 3 we use a strict partial order approach for modeling preferences. We conclude our paper with a summary and outlook in Section 4.

2 Situated Preferences

Preferences and wishes are key components of personalized applications. In real life a user's preferences are typically not changeless but vary due to different situations. For instance, a user may have various news preferences depending on the temporal situation: on Friday he is interested in the current exchange rates of his stocks and on the other days his preferred news categories are politics and science. In this section we introduce an appropriate approach on modeling such situations for personalized applications.

2.1 The Meta Model for Situations

The Oxford Advanced Learner's Dictionary (http://www.oup.com/elt/oald) defines a situation as "all the circumstances and things that are happening at a particular time and in a particular place". This definition as well as Barwise's and Perry's work in [1] denote location and time as important aspects of situations. Our meta model considers spatial-temporal entities as important, too, but also includes further – often application-specific – entities for describing situations. We define our meta model for situations with entity-relationship modeling techniques.

Fig. 2 represents the meta model of situation-oriented entities and relationships. Thereby the *Situation* is the most general entity type of situation models. It can contain any attributes describing the situational context of people, agents, applications, etc. *Timestamp* denotes the date and time of situations and the entity type *Location* can describe the current position. Attributes for *Timestamp* can be SQL data types like date, time, time zone, etc. It can also be described in more detail using temporal ER modeling techniques [9]. Attributes for the *Location* are, for example, city, zip-code, or global positioning system coordinates (GPS). *Influences* describes other aspects affecting a situation. *Personal Influences* denotes human factors of a situation like physical state or current emotion. *Surrounding Influences* describes outer influences like weather condition or other people the current user is together with. Each situation can consist of one timestamp and of one location but it can have one or more influences (e.g. a personal and a surrounding influence). A timestamp, location, or influence can be part of more than one situation. *Personal Influences* and *Surrounding Influences* are sub-entities of *Influences*.

This framework for modeling situations can be integrated into existing ER-models that need to be enhanced with situational context. For instance, personalized applications typically have an entity like *user*, which can be connected – with appropriate relationships – to entities describing the user's situation. If required, above meta model can be extended with further situated sub-entities.

2.2 Use Cases for Situation Models

COSIMA is an online application providing electronic bargaining for computer hardware products [8]. During the bargaining process it is very important to notice the customer's current situation – like being angry or pleased – and to react appropriately.

Fig. 3 describes a situation model for the COSIMA application. For each customer the personal role is noticed [23], since it is a difference for COSIMA, if she is bargaining with an ordinary or a chief purchaser. The emotion of the customer is also important so that COSIMA can react to the current constitution of her counterpart.

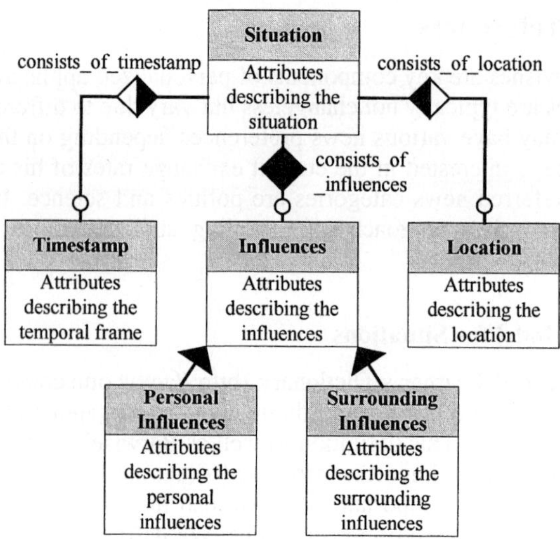

Fig. 2. Extensible meta model for situations

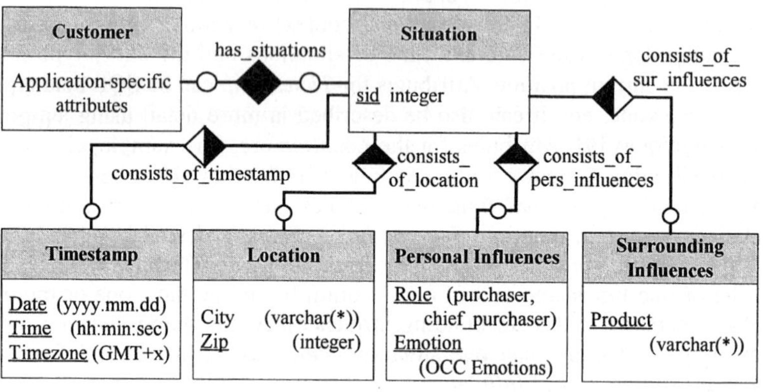

Fig. 3. Situated ER-model for COSIMA

The OCC emotion model introduced in [20] can be used as underlying domain. The product of the current bargaining process is the most important attribute of the surrounding influences, because it is a great difference whether COSIMA is bargaining for a PC mouse or for a workstation. Additionally, the situation includes information about the current time and date and the location of the purchaser. A situation can be identified with a situation identifier *sid*. Application-specific attributes for the customer can be modeled with common standards (e.g. xCIL [19]).

As a second case study we design a situation model for personalized web sites. Assume a web portal provides personalized information like sports news, current stock quotations, weather forecast, etc. It would be a great added value for the users to get such information not only personalized but also with respect to the current situation.

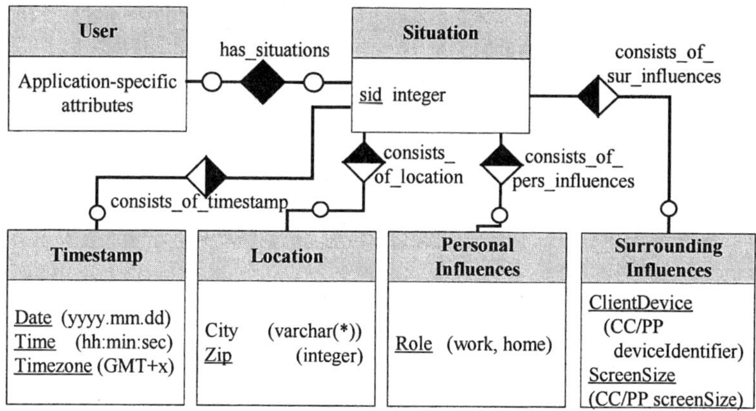

Fig. 4. Situated ER-model for personalized web sites

Fig. 4 represents a potential situation model for such a situation-based personalized web portal. The role is used to decide whether the user is at home or at work [23]. The timestamp helps to present the right news categories at the right time. The spatial information can be used to deliver regional weather forecast or regional sports results. The user's device and the according screen size allow the adaptation of the web contents and the layout to the user's current technical environment. For instance, the resolution should be reduced and the contents should be arranged appropriately, if he uses a mobile phone. Browsing device and screen size can be specified with the CC/PP framework defined by the W3C consortium [17]. An instance of such an ER model defines a concrete situation (Fig. 5).

situation.sid = 212	
timestamp.date = 2003.01.12 timestamp.time = 20:56:19 timestamp.timezone = GMT+1	location.city = Munich location.zip = 80469 personal_influences.role = home
surrounding_influences.client_device = pda	surrounding_influences.screen_size = 320 x 240

Fig. 5. Instance of a situation

Such values for an actual situation can be queried from the system, calculated with GPS technologies (global positioning system), or gained with the help of some meta information.

2.3 Modeling Situated Preferences

Since situations can have great influence on the user's preferences, we consider situated preferences in this section. There are various frameworks for preference models (see [6, 14] for a discussion on preference models). Our following approach is kept independent from the underlying preference model.

In the previous situation modeling examples we stated an identifier for situations. This *sid* can be used to refer to situations. For instance, *sid* = 212 corresponds to the situation described in Fig. 5. Preferences are specified with a *pid*. For example, a preference like "I like notebooks manufactured by HP and Dell" may be identified with *pid* = 29. Before we can model situated preferences we have to consider the various possibilities of situated preferences since some user preferences may hold in general, whereas other preferences are only valid in one or more situations. We identify three types of preferences:

- Long-term preference: this preference holds generally.
- Singular preference: this preference holds in exactly one situation.
- Non-singular preference: this preference holds in more than one situation.

We model such situated preferences as N:M relationships between situations and preferences. A concrete situated preference can be considered as a tuple (*sid*, *pid*) expressing that the preference *pid* holds in the situation *sid*. By convention a long-term preference is identified with *sid* = 0.

Example 1. Classification of situated preferences
We consider the tuples {(0, 12), (0, 13), (127, 22), (128, 22), (212, 29), (212, 30)} of situated preferences. In this example we have two long-term preferences, namely the preferences 12 and 13. In the two situations with *sid* = 127 and *sid* = 128 the preference 22 holds. The preferences 29 and 30 are valid, if the situation 212 occurs. ♦

The preference repository introduced in Section 3 stores and manages such N:M relationships between situations and preferences.

3 The Preference Repository

The preference repository defines a general storage structure to manage long-term and situated preferences for personalized database applications. We use the strict partial order approach for modeling preferences introduced in [14], where an intuitive, powerful, and flexible constructor-based framework for preferences is given. We define the preference repository using the extended markup language. An XML-based schema extension for user preferences is already specified within the MPEG-7 standard [13]. For two reasons this approach is not appropriate for a preference repository. Firstly, it is focused on MPEG-7 documents and therefore general preferences of other domains cannot be recorded in a natural way. Secondly, MPEG-7 uses scores to describe user wishes leading to preferences with very limited semantic expressiveness compared to the general strict partial order approach.

3.1 Preference Constructors and the BMO Query Model

In this section we revisit those concepts of the preference model of [14] that are relevant for the scope of this paper. A preference P is defined as a strict partial order P = (A, $<_P$), where A = {A_1, …, A_k} denotes a set of attributes with corresponding domains dom(A_i). The domain of A is defined as Cartesian product of the dom(A_i), $<_P \subseteq \text{dom}(A) \times \text{dom}(A)$, and x $<_P$ y is interpreted as "y is better than x".

For an intuitive preference modeling a set of preference constructors is defined. These constructors include POS(A, pos-set), and POS/POS(A, pos1-set; pos2-set) on categorical domains and LOWEST(A) on numerical domains. The pos-set $\subseteq$ dom(A) of a POS preference defines a set of favorite values that are better than all other values of dom(A). A POS/POS preference distinguishes between optimal (pos1-set) and alternative values (pos2-set). For a LOWEST preference lower values are better. Preferences can inductively be combined with complex preference constructors. Relevant for this paper is the Pareto preference $P = P_1 \otimes P_2$, which treats the underlying preferences as equally important. Precise definitions can be found in [14].

Such preferences can be evaluated on SQL or XML databases using the query languages Preference SQL or Preference XPATH, respectively [16]. These query engines return those database elements that match best to the strict partial order specified in the preference expression. This behavior is called best-matches-only (BMO) query model [14]. It accomplishes a suitable match-making between wishes and reality. For instance, applying the preference P = POS/POS(manufacturer, {HP}; {Dell}) items produced by HP are delivered, if they exist in the database. Otherwise, if products manufactured by Dell exist, they are returned. Otherwise, products from different vendors are delivered. Several real-life applications use this preference model for describing user wishes [8, 15].

3.2 Preference Repository Document Type Definition

Using an XML-based preference repository has several advantages. By defining recursive elements in the according document type definition combined preferences of any complexity can be recorded. A clear specification avoids the storage of preferences not conform to the preference algebra defined in [14]. Furthermore, an XML-based preference repository can be accessed either via XPATH and Preference XPATH [16] or from object-oriented programming languages like Java or C++ using the document object model (DOM). Another aspect is the interchangeability of XML documents. Preference repositories based on XML can be interchanged between various personalized applications.

In this section we describe some interesting details of the preference repository. The key tags of the document type definition are given in Fig. 6. The element *PrefRepository* is the root element of a preference repository XML document. Preferences are stored for each user separately. As proposed in [13] a user is denoted with a *UserId* element, where the user's name must be unique indicated with the XML type *ID*. A *UserId* can also represent a user group or a whole domain, where the latter can be used for storing domain preferences. For details on modeling user groups and stereotypes see [23]. For each user several (situated) preferences can be recorded as *PrefData* elements. The *Preference* elements consist of the various preference con-

```
<!ELEMENT PrefRepository (UserId*)>
<!ELEMENT UserId (PrefData*)>
   <!ATTLIST UserId name ID #REQUIRED>
<!ELEMENT PrefData (Preference*, Source?, Situation*>
   <!ATTLIST PrefData name ID #REQUIRED>
<!ELEMENT Situation (Condition*)>
   <!ATTLIST Situation sid ID #REQUIRED>
<!ELEMENT Condition (EMPTY)>
   <!ATTLIST Condition key CDATA #REQUIRED>
   <!ATTLIST Condition value CDATA #REQUIRED>
```

Fig. 6. Main elements of the preference repository

structors as sub-elements, whereby for each preference relevant additional information – like the pos-set of a POS preference – has to be recorded. Combined preferences of any complexity can be stored with the recursive definition of the corresponding XML elements. For the detailed description of all preference elements in the preference repository see [11]. A *PrefData* element contains zero, one, or more preferences and zero, one, or more situations representing the N:M relationship between preferences and situations introduced in Section 2.3. Situations are stored as conditions with key-value pairs representing the allocation of the attributes of the situation model with concrete values. The *Source* denotes the origin of a preference. The origin could be, e.g., preference mining [11, 12] or preference query languages like Preference SQL or Preference XPath [16].

We consider the COSIMA application for an example of a preference repository XML document (Fig. 7). In her role as purchaser Laverne has a LOWEST(price) preference if she is bargaining for a notebook and is feeling satisfied. If she has the same emotion and the same role but is bargaining for a desktop pc, she has a POS(installed_software, {Windows XP, Acrobat Reader}) preference.

3.3 The Preference Repository Query Interface

The methods for querying the preference repository are twofold. One the one hand we define a set of useful operations like "get all preferences of a specific customer" and on the other hand we provide a Preference XPATH interface [11]. With it the application developer can query the preference repository using the full functionality of XPATH and Preference XPATH.

In personalized applications it is important to know, which user preferences are valid w.r.t. a specific situation, so that the application can react appropriately. For the

```
<PrefRepository> <UserId name="Laverne">
  <PrefData name="Laverne1">
    <Preference pid=31> <LOWEST att="price"/> </Preference>
    <Situation sid=127>
      <Condition key="product" value="notebook"/>
      <Condition key="role" value="purchaser"/>
      <Condition key="emotion" value="satisfied"/>
    </Situation> </PrefData>
  <PrefData name="Laverne2">
    <Preference pid=35> <POS att="installed_software">
      <POSSet> <Value val="Windows XP"/>
               <Value val="Acrobat Reader"/>
      </POSSet> </POS> </Preference>
    <Situation sid=128>
      <Condition key="product" value="desktop"/>
      <Condition key="role" value="purchaser"/>
      <Condition key="emotion" value="satisfied"/>
    </Situation> </PrefData>
</UserId> </PrefRepository>
```

Fig. 7. Preference repository example

finding of singular and non-singular situated preferences we postulate the following requirements:

1. It should be possible to get preferences that belong to a given situation.
2. It should be possible to get preferences, whose situations match best to a given situation.

The former requirement can be fulfilled with appropriate XPATH requests on the preference repository. These requests are exact-match-queries with the structure

```
Situation/Condition[@key=attribute_name and
                    @value=attribute_value]
```

where the situation – described as condition – can be specified by using the full XPATH functionality. In the latter case we use Preference XPATH, since this query language implements the BMO query model (see Section 3.1). The given situation is considered as preference expression and Preference XPATH computes those *PrefData* elements with best matching situations. Our access operations include already a Preference XPATH interface, so such queries can be executed without any additional effort.

3.4 Query Examples

Below we give some examples for XPATH and Preference XPATH queries. They are based on the preference repository in Fig. 7.

Example 2. Querying long-term preferences
At first, we want to get Laverne's long-term preferences stored in the preference repository.

```
UserId[@name='Laverne']/PrefData[Situation[@sid=0]]
```

Long-term preferences are identified with *sid* = 0 (see Section 2.3). The corresponding preferences can be queried with XPATH using a hard condition (`[@sid = 0]`). ♦

Example 3. Querying situated preferences using hard conditions
Assume Laverne is bargaining for a notebook. We know with mimic recognition [21] that she is feeling satisfied. Furthermore, her current role is chief purchaser. We are interested in those preferences that are relevant in this situation.

```
UserId[@name='Laverne']/PrefData
[Situation/Condition[@key='product' and
                     @value='notebook']]
[Situation/Condition[@key='emotion' and
                     @value='satisfied']]
[Situation/Condition[@key='role' and
                     @value='chief_purchaser']]
```

In this XPATH query the situation is specified as a hard condition. Applying this query on our repository example (Fig. 7) an empty result is delivered since there is no exact match. ♦

Example 4. Querying situated preferences using soft conditions
The embarrassing empty result effect occurring in the previous example is caused by the exact-match query model of XPATH. Using Preference XPATH with BMO query

semantics we can avoid this effect. If perfect matches do not exist, preferences with best-matching situations are returned.

For each attribute of the situation the attribute name is specified with a hard condition that must be fulfilled (e.g. `@key='product'`). The value is considered as soft condition that should be fulfilled (e.g. `POS(value, {'notebook'})`). The components of the query are assembled with Pareto accumulation ('⊗'-operator). Soft conditions are denoted with '`#[`' and '`]#`' in Preference XPATH syntax.

```
UserId[@name='Laverne']/PrefData
#[Situation/Condition[@key='product'] #[POS(value,
                                        {'notebook'})]#
⊗ Situation/Condition[@key='emotion'] #[POS(value,
                                       {'satisfied'})]#
⊗ Situation/Condition[@key='role'] #[POS(value,
                                   {'chief_purchaser'})]#]#
```

If available, Preference XPATH delivers perfect matches. Otherwise, best alternatives are returned. Using our repository example (Fig. 7) the preference with *pid* = 31 is returned since the situation *sid* = 127 is best-matching to the given situation. ♦

Such queries for situated preferences can additionally be improved by using semantic knowledge of the underlying domain stored in an appropriate ontology [7]. We discuss this in the following example.

Example 5. Querying situated preferences using ontologies
Assume a simple ontology for computer hardware products is given (Fig. 8). We know that Laverne is currently bargaining for a pda, and therefore we are interested in relevant situated preferences. Our repository example in Fig. 7 contains only situated preferences for notebooks and desktops. Using an ontology-based "broaden" mechanism within the Preference XPATH query related situated preferences can be delivered.

```
UserId[@name='Laverne']/PrefData[Situation/Condition
[@key='product'] #[POS/POS(value, {pda};broaden(pda))]#
```

```
<Subject name="computing systems">
  <Topic name="pda"> </Topic>
  <Topic name="workstation"> </Topic>
  <Topic name="notebook"> </Topic>
  <Topic name="tablet pc"/> </Topic>
  <Topic name="desktop"> </Topic>
</Subject>
```

Fig. 3. Ontology example

The function `broaden(term)` computes the set of ontology elements that have the same parent node as `term`. Above Preference XPATH query delivers now the situated preferences that hold if Laverne is bargaining for a pda. If none exists, situated preferences for the products workstation, notebook, tablet pc, and desktop are delivered. ♦

3.5 Updating the Preference Repository

User preferences and situations can change over time. Assume Laverne states that there is no situation, in which she has a preference for installed software. Furthermore, she informs us that her LOWEST(price) preference holds generally. Finally, the Preference Miner detects a situated POS(manufacturer, {Dell}) preference that holds, if her role is chief purchaser.

Such changes of the user's preferences can be gained from preference query languages [16], user feedback or preference mining [11, 12]. Details about the varying situations can be queried from the system (timestamp), calculated with GPS technologies (location), or transmitted with an appropriate data transfer protocol (client device). The emotion can be detected with the application of mimic recognition [21].

Updates of situations and preferences can easily be managed by using the preference repository interface. The predefined methods for inserts, updates, and deletions have several benefits for the application developer. If he uses these access operations, he does not have to care about the detailed structure of the preference repository. Preferences of any complexity can be stored in the preference repository and it is guaranteed that they are inserted and updated correctly. Query interfaces typically produce a large amount of preferences. Using the predefined access operations they can be inserted and managed in the preference repository in a comfortable way.

4 Summary and Outlook

In this paper we presented a novel framework for modeling situated preferences and preference repositories. We defined an extensible meta model for situations so that well-designed situation models can be created and integrated into existing ER models. Modifications of situated ER-models are uncomplicated and therefore changes in the situation model can also be handled. With it we support a straightforward software development process for situated and personalized database applications.

The preference repository holds an eminent place for personalized applications. It allows the storage and management of the users' long-term and situated preferences. The stored preferences can be applied for personalized query composition, user-centric product recommendations, or personalized result presentation. With the Preference XPATH interface preferences best-matching to a given situation can be queried. This approach allows e-applications to react flexibly and personalized to the changing situations of their customers. The preference repository is already in practical use in the intelligent e-procurement prototype COSIMA^{B2B} [15], which is part of the interdisciplinary Bavarian research cooperation FORSIP on "Situated, Individualized, and Personalized Human-Computer Interaction" (http://www.forsip.de).

This paper has introduced innovations on situated preferences and preference repositories that suggest several promising directions for future research. One direction is the dealing with dynamic situations. In personalized applications a user's situation may change during a session. For example, his role or his emotional state may change during a shopping tour. The integration of such dynamic situations into our situated meta model forms an interesting research task. The consideration of a user's interaction history [10] may also enrich our situation models noticeably. Another direction deals with the detection of situated preferences. A promising approach is the adaptation of preference mining algorithms. Preference mining works on the user's log data containing information about requested articles or bought products. In order to detect situated preferences the log has to be extended with situation-specific data, so that for each transaction details about the current situation (timestamp, location, emotion, client device, etc.) is recorded. This allows the invocation of the preference mining algorithms for each situation separately and with it situated preferences can be detected. Another interesting task is the application of our techniques on situation modeling and preference repositories in new domains. For instance, the fast-growing area of personalized mobile services (e.g. online banking, route planning, or electronic shopping) requires a comprehensive knowledge about the situated preferences of the mobile users [27]. For example, a user may have different preferences on text length or image resolution whether he is using his notebook or his pda. Therefore our techniques will find a broad application area in personalized mobile environments.

References

1. J. Barwise and J. Perry. *Situations and Attitudes*. Cambridge, Massachusetts, MIT Press, 1983.
2. P. Beadle, B. Harper, G. Q. Maguire, and J. Judge. *Location Aware Mobile Computing*. Proc. of IEEE Intl. Conference on Telecommunications, Melbourne, Australia, 1997.
3. J. S. Breese, D. Heckerman, and C. Kadie. *Empirical Analysis of Predictive Algorithms for Collaborative Filtering*. In Proc. Fourteenth Annual Conf. on Uncertainty in Artificial Intelligence, pp. 43-52, Madison, Wisconsin, USA, 1998.
4. P. P. Chen. *The Entity-Relationship Model – Toward a Unified View of Data*. ACM Transactions on Database Systems, vol. 1 (1), pp. 9-36, 1976.
5. G. Chen and D. Kotz. *A Survey of Context-Aware Mobile Computing Research*. Technical Report TR2000-381, Dept. of Computer Science, Dartmouth College, Hanover, New Hampshire, USA, 2000.
6. J. Chomicki. *Preference Formulas in Relational Queries*. ACM Transactions on Database Systems, vol. 28 (4), pp. 1-39, 2003.
7. D. Fensel, F. van Harmelen, I. Horrocks, D. L. McGuinness, P. F. Patel-Schneider. *OIL: An Ontology Infrastructure for the Semantic Web*. IEEE Intelligent Systems, vol. 16 (2), pp. 38-45, 2001.
8. S. Fischer, W. Kießling, S. Holland, and M. Fleder. *The COSIMA Prototype for Multi-Objective Bargaining*. Proc. First International Joint Conference on Autonomous Agents and Multiagent Systems (AAMAS 2002), pp. 1364-1371, Bologna, Italy, 2002.
9. H. Gregersen and C. S. Jensen. *Temporal Entity-Relationship Models - A Survey*. Knowledge and Data Engineering, vol. 11 (3), pp. 464-497, 1999.
10. A. Hinze and A. Voisard. *Location- and Time-Based Information Delivery in Tourism*. Advances in Spatial and Temporal Databases: 8th International Symposium (SSTD 2003), pp. 489-507, Santorini Island, Greece, 2003.
11. S. Holland. *Preference Mining and Preference Repositories: Design, Algorithms and Personalized Applications*. Phd-thesis, ibidem-Verlag, Stuttgart, Germany, 2004. ISBN 3-89821-352-8.
12. S. Holland, M. Ester, and W. Kießling. *Preference Mining: A Novel Approach on Mining User Preferences for Personalized Applications*. Proc. 7th European Conference on Principles and Practice of Knowledge Discovery in Databases (PKDD 2003), pp. 204-216, Dubrovnik, Croatia, 2003.
13. ISO/IEC 15938-5. *Information Technology - Multimedia Content Description Interface - Part 5 Multimedia Description Schemes*. International Organization for Standardization (ISO), International Electrotechnical Commission (IEC), 2001.

14. W. Kießling. *Foundations of Preferences in Database Systems.* Proc. 28th Inter. Conference on Very Large Data Bases (VLDB 2002), pp. 311-322, Hong Kong, China, 2002.
15. W. Kießling, S. Fischer, and S. Döring. *COSIMA^{B2B} – Sales Automation for E-Procurement.* 6th IEEE Conference on E-Commerce Technology (CEC 2004). San Diego, CA, USA, 2004.
16. W. Kießling, B. Hafenrichter, S. Fischer, and S. Holland: *Preference XPATH: A Query Language for E-Commerce.* Proc. 5th International Conference Wirtschaftsinformatik, pp. 427-440, Augsburg, Germany, 2001.
17. G. Klyne, F. Reynolds, C. Woodrow, H. Ohto, J. Hjelm, M. H. Butler, and L. Tran. *Composite Capability/Preference Profiles (CC/PP): Structure and Vocabularies.* 2003. http://www.w3.org/TR/CCPP-struct-vocab/.
18. G. Koutrika and Y. Ioannidis. *Personalization of Queries in Database Systems.* Proc. 20th International Conference on Data Engineering, Boston, USA, 2004.
19. OASIS. XML Standards for "Global" Customer Information Managaement. http://www.oasis-open.org/committees/ciq/ciq.shtml.
20. A. Ortony, G. Clore, and A. Collins. *The Cognitive Structure of Emotions.* Cambridge University Press, 1988.
21. M. Pantic and L. J. M. Rothkrantz. *Automatic Analysis of Facial Expressions: The State of the Art.* IEEE Transactions on Pattern Analysis and Machine Intelligence, vol. 22(12), pp. 1424-1445, 2000.
22. G. A. Radvansky and R. T. Zacks. *The Retrieval of Situation-Specific Information.* Cognitive Models of Memory, pp. 173-213, 1997.
23. E. Rich. *User Modeling via Stereotypes.* Cognitive Science, vol. 3(4), pp. 329-354, 1979.
24. G. Rossi, D. Schwabe, and R. Guimaraes. *Designing Personalized Web Applications.* Proc. 10th International World Wide Web Conference (WWW 2001), pp. 275-284, Hong Kong, China, 2001.
25. B. Schilit, N. Adams, and R. Want. *Context-Aware Computing Applications.* In Workshop on Mobile Computing Systems and Applications, pp. 85-90, Santa Cruz, California, USA, 1994.
26. L. Suryanarayana and J. Hjelm. *Profiles for the Situated Web.* Proc. 11th International World Wide Web Conference (WWW 2002), pp. 200-209, Honolulu, Hawaii, USA, 2002.
27. M. Wagner, W.-T. Balke, R. Hirschfeld, and W. Kellerer. *A Roadmap to Advanced Personalization of Mobile Services.* Proc. 10th International Conference on Cooperative Information Systems (CoopIS 2002), Irvine, CA, USA, 2002.

Analysis and Management of Web Service Protocols

Boualem Benatallah[1], Fabio Casati[2], and Farouk Toumani[3]

[1] CSE, UNSW, Sydney NSW 2052, Australia
boualem@cse.unsw.edu.au
[2] Hewlett-Packard Laboratories, Palo Alto, CA, 94304 USA
casati@hpl.hp.com
[3] LIMOS Laboratory, ISIMA, UBP Clermont-Ferrand, France
ftoumani@isima.fr

Abstract. In the area of Web services and service-oriented architectures, business protocols are rapidly gaining importance and mindshare as a necessary part of Web service descriptions. Their immediate benefit is that they provide developers with information on how to write clients that can correctly interact with a given service or with a set of services. In addition, once protocols become an accepted practice and service descriptions become endowed with protocol information, the middleware can be significantly extended to better support service development, binding, and execution in a number of ways, considerably simplifying the whole service life-cycle. This paper discusses the different ways in which the middleware can leverage protocol descriptions, and focuses in particular on the notions of protocol compatibility, equivalence, and replace-ability. They characterise whether two services can interact based on their protocol definition, whether a service can replace another in general or when interacting with specific clients, and which are the set of possible interactions among two services.

1 Introduction

Web services, and more in general service-oriented architectures (SOAs), are emerging as the technologies and architectures of choice for implementing distributed systems and performing application integration within and across companies' boundaries. The basic principles of SOAs consist in modularizing functions and exposing them as services, that are typically specified using (de jure or de facto) standard languages and interoperate through standard protocols. Web service technology is characterized by two trends that were not part of conventional (e.g., CORBA-like) middleware services and that are relevant to the topics discussed in this paper. The first is that, from a technology perspective, all interacting entities are considered to be (Web) services, even when they are in fact requesting and not providing services. This allows uniformity in the specification language (for example, the interface of both requestor and providers will be described using the Web Services Description Language – WSDL) and uniformity in the development and runtime support tools.

P. Atzeni et al. (Eds.): ER 2004, LNCS 3288, pp. 524–541, 2004.

The second trend, that is gathering momentum and mindshare, is that of including, as part of the service description, not only the service interface but also the *business protocol* supported by the service, i.e., the specification of which message exchange sequences (called *conversations* in the following) are supported by the service [3]. This is important, as it rarely happens that service operations can be invoked at will independently from one another. The interactions between clients and services are always structured in terms of a set of operation invocations, whose order typically has to obey certain constraints for clients to be able to obtain the service they need. In the following, we use the term *external specification* to refer to the combination of the interface and business protocol specifications, that define the externally visible behavior of a service [1, 12]. In addition to the business protocol[1], a service may be characterized by other protocols, such as security (e.g., trust negotiation) or transaction protocols that also need to be exposed as part of the service description so that clients know how to interact with a service [3, 10].

If two or more services need to interoperate, their protocols must be *compatible*. For example, a bookseller's business protocol may require customer's Web services to first invoke the *orderBook* operation and then the *makePayment* operation. If a requestor wishes to interact with this service, then its business protocol will need to include the invocation of the *orderBook* operation followed at some point by the invocation of the *makePayment* operation. If this is not the case, then the interaction between the two entities will result in an error. Hence, it is essential that requestors are only bound, statically or dynamically, to providers that have compatible protocols.

This paper analyzes protocol compatibility and similarity in Web services. In particular, we define and characterize different types of protocol compatibility, corresponding to different capabilities of services to interoperate, and we show how, given two services and their external specifications, it is possible to formally identify their compatibility level. In addition, we discuss similarities and differences between protocols, to understand if two services exhibit the same behavior or if one can be used instead of another when serving a certain client. In doing the analysis, our motivation and goal is to devise protocol management primitives that support and simplify service development. This complements our earlier efforts aiming at designing and developing a complete CASE tool supporting the Web service lifecycle [3, 2, 10]. Indeed, and as discussed in this paper, the primitives presented here can be used by service development and runtime environment to: i) assist developers in creating and evolving Web services that are compatible with other services of interest or with standard protocol specifications; ii) identify (statically or dynamically) services that can interoperate with a given service; iii) manage non-compatibility situations.

This paper does not discuss other aspects that are in general relevant to identifying whether two services can interact to achieve the desired goals. For example, we do not deal with quality of service issues, or with structural and semantic interoperability of messages [6]. While we believe that these issues are also important, the (syntactic) protocols compatibility and similarity analysis

[1] In this paper we will use "business protocol" and "protocol" interchangeably.

discussed here is complex enough in itself to deserve the whole paper (and indeed many aspects still remain to be addressed). Finally, we observe that, although to make the presentation more concrete we will introduce the concepts based on a specific protocol language, the results presented here can be applied to any protocol language, such as WSCI or BPEL.

The outline of the paper is as follows: Section 2 introduces a protocol model and some notations and concepts used throughout the paper. Section 3 defines a collection of protocol management operators that allow understanding commonalities and differences between protocols, as well as whether two protocols can interact with each other. Section 4 introduces compatibility and similarity classes, and shows how the model and operators developed in the previous sections can be used to analyze and understand the kind of compatibility or similarity that two protocols exhibit. Finally, Section 5 concludes the paper with a discussion of possible applications of the proposed protocol analysis.

2 Preliminaries

2.1 Business Protocols Modeling

Following our previous work [3], we choose to model a service business protocol (protocol for short) as a non-deterministic finite state machine, where the states represent the different phases that a service may go through during its interaction with a requestor. Transitions are triggered by messages sent by the requestor to the provider or vice versa (hence, transitions are labeled with either input or output messages). A message corresponds to the invocation of a service operation or to its reply. Note that each service may be simultaneously involved in several message exchanges (conversations) with different clients, and therefore can be characterized by multiple concurrent instantiations of the protocol state machine. The purpose of the protocol is essentially to specify the set of conversations that are supported by the service. The reason for using a state machine-based model is because it a formalism that is fairly easy to understand for users, it is suitable to describe reactive behaviors, and it has the notion of state which is useful for monitoring service executions. Furthermore, there are a number of models and tools (some developed by the authors [2]), that enable protocol modelling by means of state machines. The need for non-determinism comes from the observation that a service may respond in different ways to a certain message, based on internal business logic that is not exposed as part of the protocol. For example, in response to an "approval request" message, a service may move to different states based on whether the request is approved or rejected. However, the criteria by which the service moves to this or that state is hidden from the user as it is internal business logic that the provider does not want to expose as part of the protocol definition.

As an example, Figure 1(a) shows a graphical representation of a protocol, called $\mathcal{P}_1$, that describes the external behavior of a store service. Each transition is labeled with a message name followed by the message polarity[2], that

[2] The notion of message polarity is borrowed from [13].

is, whether the message is incoming (plus sign) or outgoing (minus sign). For instance, it specifies that the store service is initially in the Start state, and that clients begin using the service by sending a login message, upon which the service moves to the Logged state (transition (login(+)). We next provide a formal definition of a protocol.

Definition 1. ***(Business protocol)***
A business protocol is a tuple $\mathcal{P} = (\mathcal{S}, s_0, \mathcal{F}, \mathtt{M}, \mathcal{R})$ which consists of the following elements:

- *$\mathcal{S}$ is a finite set of states.*
- *$s_0 \in \mathcal{S}$ is the initial state.*
- *$\mathcal{F} \subseteq \mathcal{S}$ is a set of final states. If $\mathcal{F} = \emptyset$, then $\mathcal{P}$ is said to be an empty protocol.*
- *$\mathtt{M}$ is a finite set of messages. For each message $m \in \mathtt{M}$, we define a function $Polarity(\mathcal{P}, m)$ which will be positive $(+)$ if m is an input message in $\mathcal{P}$ and negative $(-)$ if m is an output message in $\mathcal{P}$. In the sequel, we use the notation $m(+)$ (respectively, $m(-)$) to denote the polarity of a message m.*
- *a finite set $\mathcal{R} \subseteq \mathcal{S}^2 \times \mathtt{M}$ of transitions. Each transition (s, s', m) identifies a source state s, a target state s' and either an input or an output message m that is either consumed or produced during this transition. In the sequel, we note $\mathcal{R}(s, s', m)$ instead of $(s, s', m) \in \mathcal{R}$.*

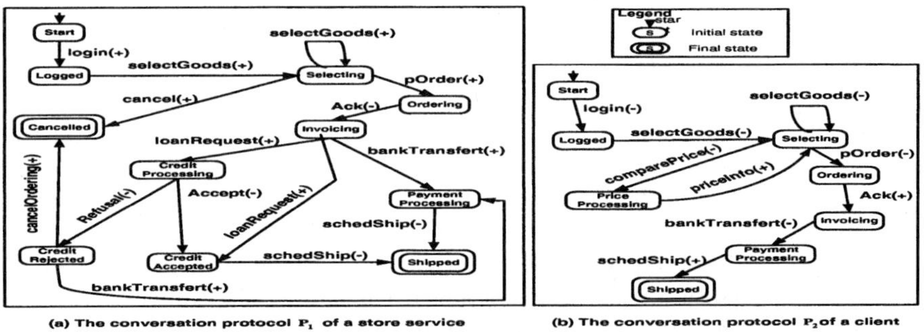

(a) The conversation protocol P_1 of a store service (b) The conversation protocol P_2 of a client

Fig. 1. Business protocols.

2.2 Execution Paths and Execution Trees

In this subsection, we introduce some important concepts and definitions that are used to define the semantics of the protocol model defined above[3]. A protocol defines all the possible conversations that a service supports in terms of alternating sequences of states and messages. We call these sequences *executions paths.* For example, the sequence Start.login(+).Logged.selectGoods(+).Selecting is an execution path of protocol $\mathcal{P}_1$. We are particularly interested in the *complete execution paths* (i.e., paths that start from an initial state and ends at a final state)

[3] See [8] for details on the various process model semantics.

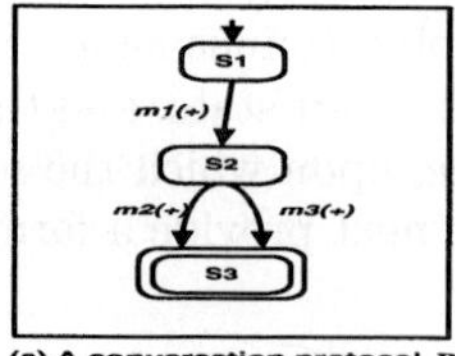

(a) A conversation protocol P

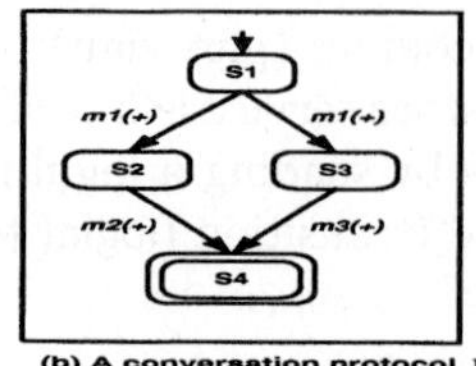

(b) A conversation protocol P'

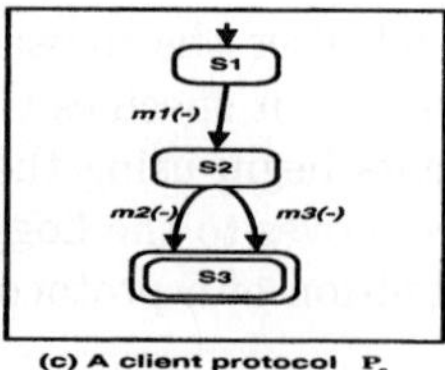

(c) A client protocol P_c

Fig. 2. Comparing protocols with respect to their branching structures.

as they denote the set of correct conversations supported by a service. For example, the execution path Start.login(+).Logged.selectGoods(+).Selecting.cancel(+). Cancelled corresponds to a complete execution path of protocol $\mathcal{P}_1$. The sequence of message exchanges login(+).selectGoods(+).selectGoods(+).cancel(+), extracted from the complete execution path depicted at Figure 3(d), represents a conversation which is *compliant* with (i.e., is allowed by) protocol $\mathcal{P}_1$ of Figure 1(a).

Since protocols are represented using non-deterministic state machines, execution paths are not enough to capture the branching structures of protocols. As an example, Figures 2(a) and (b) show two protocols $\mathcal{P}$ and $\mathcal{P}'$ that specify exactly the same set of compliant conversations (the conversations m1(+).m2(+) and m1(+).m3(+)). However, we can observe that after sending a message m1 in protocol $\mathcal{P}$, a client interacting with $\mathcal{P}$ will have a choice to either send the message m2 or m3, while a client interacting with protocol $\mathcal{P}'$ will not have such a choice. For example, the client protocol $\mathcal{P}_\mathcal{C}$ depicted in Figure 2(c) can interact correctly with the protocol $\mathcal{P}$. However, the interaction of $\mathcal{P}_\mathcal{C}$ with protocol $\mathcal{P}'$ may result in an error (e.g., if $\mathcal{P}_\mathcal{C}$ sends the messages m1 and then m2, while protocol $\mathcal{P}'$ decides to move to the state S3 after receiving the message m1).

To compare protocols with respect to their branching structures, we adopt the well known branching-time approach [8] to describe business protocol semantics. In this approach, the possible conversations allowed by a protocol are characterized in terms of trees, called *execution trees*, instead of paths. The execution trees of a protocol are used to derive what we call *conversation trees.* In a nutshell, conversation trees of a protocol $\mathcal{P}$ capture all the conversations that are compliant with $\mathcal{P}$ (i.e, message exchanges that occur in accordance with the constraints imposed by $\mathcal{P}$) as well as the branching structures of $\mathcal{P}$ (i.e., which messages are allowed at each stage of a conversation).

To formally define the notions of execution and conversation trees, we use the following definition of a tree as in [9]: A tree is a set $\tau \subseteq \mathbb{N}^*$ such that if $xn \in \tau$, for $x \in \mathbb{N}^*$ and $n \in \mathbb{N}$, then $x \in \tau$ and $xm \in \tau$ for all $0 \leq m < n$. The elements of τ represent nodes: the empty word ϵ is the root of τ, and for each node x, the nodes of the form xn, for $n \in \mathbb{N}$, are children of x. Given a pair of set S and M, an $\langle S, M\rangle$-labeled tree is a triple (τ, λ, δ), where τ is a tree, $\lambda : \tau \rightarrow S$ is a node labeling function that maps each node of τ to an element in S, and $\delta : \tau \times \tau \rightarrow M$ is an edge labeling function that maps each edge (x, xn) of τ to an element in M. Then, every path $\rho = \epsilon, n_0, n_0n_1, \ldots$ of τ generates a sequence $\Gamma(\rho) = \lambda(\epsilon).\delta(\epsilon, n_0).\lambda(n_0).\delta(n_0, n_0n_1).\lambda(n_0n_1)\ldots.$ of alternating labels from S and M.

Informally, if S and M correspond to the sets of states and messages, we can use an $\langle S, M\rangle$-labeled tree to characterize protocol semantics. In particular, the branches of the tree (once mapped with the labeling functions) represent execution paths, and the tree hierarchy reflects the branching structures of the protocol.

Definition 2. ***(Execution trees and conversation trees)***

Let $\mathcal{P} = (\mathcal{S}, s_0, \mathcal{F}, \mathtt{M}, \mathcal{R})$ be a business protocol.

(a) *An execution tree of $\mathcal{P}$ is a $\langle \mathcal{S}, \mathtt{M}\rangle$-labeled tree $T = (\tau, \lambda, \delta)$ such that:*
   - $\lambda(\epsilon) = s_0$, *and*
   - *for each edge (x, xn) of τ, we have $\mathcal{R}(\lambda(x), \lambda(xn), \delta(x, xn))$*

   An execution tree $T = (\tau, \lambda, \delta)$ is a complete execution tree of the protocol $\mathcal{P}$ if for every leave $x \in \tau$ we have $\lambda(x) \in \mathcal{F}$.

(b) *If $T = (\tau, \lambda, \delta)$ is a complete execution tree of a protocol $\mathcal{P}$, then $T^C = (\tau, \lambda^C, \delta)$ where $\lambda^C(x) = \emptyset, \forall x \in \tau$, is a conversation tree which is compliant with protocol $\mathcal{P}$.*

For example, Figures 3(a) and (c) show complete execution trees of the protocols $\mathcal{P}$ and $\mathcal{P}'$ of Figure 2. Figure 3(d) shows two complete execution trees which are compliant with the protocol $\mathcal{P}_1$ of Figure 1. Figure 3(b) shows a conversation tree which is compliant with the protocol $\mathcal{P}$ (shown at Figure 2(a)). This conversation tree describes the message exchanges that are accepted by $\mathcal{P}$ (i.e., m1(+).m2(+) and m1(+).m3(+)) as well as the branching choice allowed by $\mathcal{P}$ after receiving the message m1. Conversation trees of a protocol are derived from complete execution trees by removing labels corresponding to the states. For instance, the conversation tree of Figure 3(b) is derived from the complete execution tree of Figure 3(a) by removing the labels of the states $s1$, $s2$, and $s3$. In this paper we use complete execution trees to represent conversations that are compliant with a protocol.

2.3 Protocol Simulation

The notion of *simulation* is used in the literature as a relation to compare labeled transition systems with respect to their branching structures [8, 9]. Simulation is a preorder relation on labeled transition systems that identifies whether a given system has the same branching structures as another one. Here, we introduce a slightly adapted notion of simulation between protocols that will be used to compare protocols with respect to their complete execution trees.

Definition 3. ***(Protocol Simulation)***
Let $\mathcal{P} = (\mathcal{S}, s_0, \mathcal{F}, \mathtt{M}, \mathcal{R})$ and $\mathcal{P}' = (\mathcal{S}', s'_0, \mathcal{F}', \mathtt{M}', \mathcal{R}')$ be two protocols.

- *A relation $\Gamma \subseteq \mathcal{S} \times \mathcal{S}'$ is a protocol simulation between protocols $\mathcal{P}$ and $\mathcal{P}'$ if whenever $(s_1, s'_1) \in \Gamma$ then the following holds:*
   - $\forall \mathcal{R}(s_1, s_2, m)$ *there is an s'_2 such that $\mathcal{R}'(s'_1, s'_2, m)$, $Polarity(\mathcal{P}, m) = Polarity(\mathcal{P}', m)$ and $(s_2, s'_2) \in \Gamma$.*
   - $\forall (s, s') \in \Gamma$, *if $s \in \mathcal{F}$ then $s' \in \mathcal{F}'$*

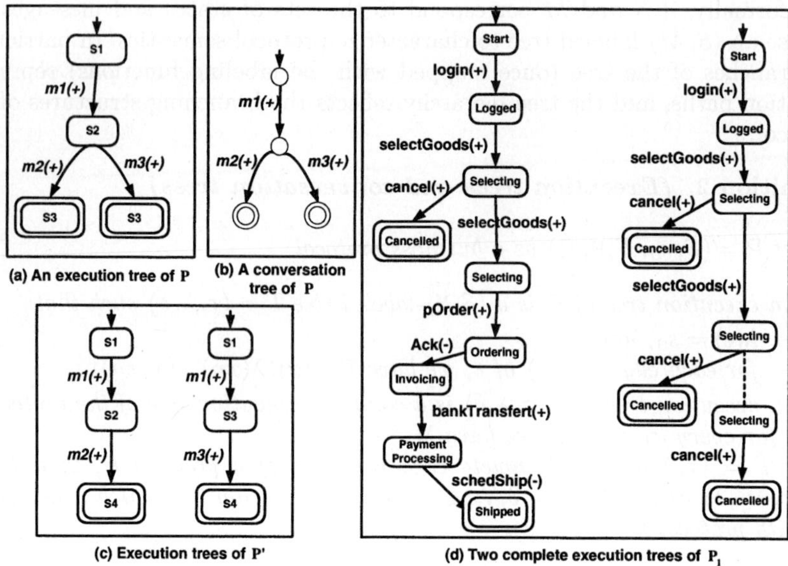

Fig. 3. Example of execution trees of the protocol $\mathcal{P}_1$.

- *We use notation* $s_1 \lesssim s'_1$ *to say that there is a protocol simulation* Γ *such that* $(s_1, s'_1) \in \Gamma$.
- *We say that protocol* $\mathcal{P}$ *is simulated by* $\mathcal{P}'$ *(noted* $\mathcal{P} \lesssim \mathcal{P}'$*) iff* $s_0 \lesssim s'_0$.
- *We say that two protocols* $\mathcal{P}$ *and* $\mathcal{P}'$ *are* similar *(noted* $\mathcal{P} \cong \mathcal{P}'$*) iff* $\mathcal{P} \lesssim \mathcal{P}'$ *and* $\mathcal{P}' \lesssim \mathcal{P}$.

The following lemma[4] states that the simulation relation allows to compare protocols with respect to their complete execution trees.

Lemma 1. *Let* $\mathcal{P}_1 = (\mathcal{S}^1, s_0^1, \mathcal{F}^1, \mathtt{M}^1, \mathcal{R}^1)$ *and* $\mathcal{P}_2 = (\mathcal{S}^2, s_0^2, \mathcal{F}^2, \mathtt{M}^2, \mathcal{R}^2)$ *be two protocols.*

(i) $\mathcal{P}_1 \lesssim \mathcal{P}_2$ *iff there exists a node labeling function* $\lambda^2 : \tau \rightarrow \mathcal{S}^2$ *such that for each complete execution tree* $T = (\tau, \lambda, \delta)$ *of* $\mathcal{P}_1$, $T' = (\tau, \lambda^2, \delta)$ *is a complete execution tree of* $\mathcal{P}_2$ *and* $Polarity(\mathcal{P}_1, \delta(x, x_n)) = Polarity(\mathcal{P}_2, \delta(x, x_n))$ *for each edge* (x, x_n) *of* τ.
(ii) $\mathcal{P}_1 \cong \mathcal{P}_2$ *iff* $\mathcal{P}_1$ *and* $\mathcal{P}_2$ *have exactly the same set of complete execution trees, modulo the name of the states.*

2.4 Protocol Interactions

In the previous subsections we focused on representing a protocol supported by a given service and comparing two service protocols using the simulation relation. We now address the joint analysis of two protocols, that of a requestor and that

[4] It should be noted that lemma proofs are not presented due to space reasons.

of a provider, to see if interactions between them are compatible. By defining the constraints on the ordering of the messages that a web service accepts, a business protocol makes explicit to clients how they can *correctly* interact with the service (i.e., without generating errors due to incorrect sequencing of messages)[5] [13, 3]. For example, a service that supports the reversed protocol $\bar{\mathcal{P}_1}$ obtained from $\mathcal{P}_1$ of Figure 1(a) by reversing the direction of the messages (i.e., input messages becomes outputs and vice versa) can interact correctly with the store service. Interactions between two given protocols can also be characterized in terms of execution paths and trees.

As an example, consider again the protocol $\mathcal{P}_1$ depicted in Figure 1(a) and its reversed protocol $\bar{\mathcal{P}_1}$. As the two protocols have exactly the same states, if s is a state in the protocol $\mathcal{P}_1$, we use $\bar{s}$ to denote the corresponding state in the protocol $\bar{\mathcal{P}_1}$. The path $(\texttt{Start}, \bar{\texttt{Start}}).\texttt{login}.(\texttt{Logged}, \bar{\texttt{Logged}})$ corresponds to a possible interaction between protocols $\mathcal{P}_1$ and $\bar{\mathcal{P}_1}$. This path indicates that, at the beginning, the two protocols $\mathcal{P}_1$ and $\bar{\mathcal{P}_1}$ are respectively at the states `Start` and $\bar{\texttt{Start}}$. Then, protocol $\bar{\mathcal{P}_1}$ sends message `login` and goes to state $\bar{\texttt{Logged}}$ while protocol $\mathcal{P}_1$ receives message `login` and goes to state `Logged`. The path $(\texttt{Start}, \bar{\texttt{Start}}).\texttt{login}.(\texttt{Logged}, \bar{\texttt{Logged}})$ is called an *interaction path* of protocols $\mathcal{P}_1$ and $\bar{\mathcal{P}_1}$. Each state in this interaction path consists of a state of $\mathcal{P}_1$ together with a state of $\bar{\mathcal{P}_1}$. The transition `login` indicates that an input `login` message of one of the protocols coincides with an output `login` message of the other protocol. Consequently, the polarity of the messages that appear in an interaction path is not defined.

Correct interactions between two protocols are captured by using the notion of *complete interaction trees*, i.e., interaction trees in which both protocols start at an initial state and end at a final state. For example, the complete interaction tree of Figure 4(a) describes a possible correct interaction between the protocols $\mathcal{P}_1$ of Figure 1(a) and its reversed protocol $\bar{\mathcal{P}_1}$. The notion of *interaction tree* is formally defined below.

Definition 4. ***(interaction tree)*** *An interaction tree between two protocols* $\mathcal{P}_1 = (\mathcal{S}^1, s_0^1, \mathcal{F}^1, \mathtt{M}^1, \mathcal{R}^1)$ *and* $\mathcal{P}_2 = (\mathcal{S}^2, s_0^2, \mathcal{F}^2, \mathtt{M}^2, \mathcal{R}^2)$ *is a* $\langle(\mathcal{S}^1 \times \mathcal{S}^2, \mathtt{M}^1 \cap \mathtt{M}^2)\rangle$*-labeled tree* $I = (\tau, \lambda, \delta)$ *such that:*

- $\lambda(\epsilon) = (s_0^1, s_0^2)$*, and*
- *For* $x \in \tau$*,* $\lambda(x) = (s_x^1, s_x^2)$ *such that* $s_x^1 \in \mathcal{S}^1$ *and* $s_x^2 \in \mathcal{S}^2$*. Then, for each edge* (x, xn) *of* τ*, we have:* $\mathcal{R}^1(s_x^1, s_{xn}^1, \delta(x, xn))$ *and* $\mathcal{R}^2(s_x^2, s_{xn}^2, \delta(x, xn))$*, and* $Polarity(\mathcal{P}_1, \delta(x, xn)) \neq Polarity(\mathcal{P}_2, \delta(x, xn))$
  An interaction tree $I = (\tau, \lambda, \delta)$ *is a complete interaction tree of the protocols* $\mathcal{P}_1$ *and* $\mathcal{P}_2$ *if for every leave* $x \in \tau$ *we have* $\lambda(x) \in \mathcal{F}^1 \times \mathcal{F}^2$*.*

In the sequel, an interaction between two protocols is characterized by the set of the complete interaction trees of these protocols.

It should be noted that the notions of simulation and interactions defined above focus on comparing protocols based on their structure and their messages,

[5] Recall that structural and semantics interoperability [6] are outside the scope of this paper.

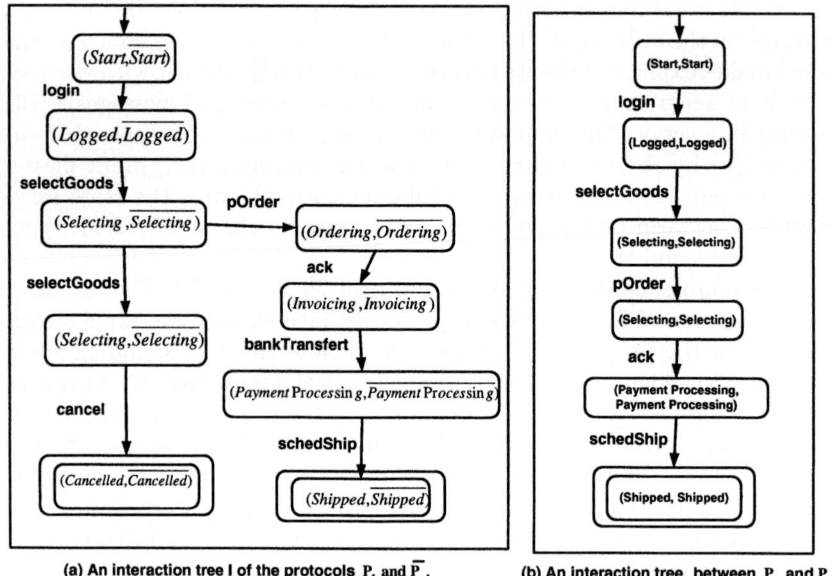

Fig. 4. Interaction trees.

regardless of how states are named. Specifically, when in the formal definition we place conditions on the two protocols having the same message (with the same or opposite polarity), we mean that they have to refer to the same WSDL message, as defined by its fully qualified name. Naming of the states is instead irrelevant, as it has no effect on identifying the conversations allowed by a protocol.

3 Protocol Management Operators

To assess commonalities and differences between protocols, as well as whether two protocols can interact with each other, we define a set of generic operators to manipulate business protocols, namely: *compatible composition* of protocols, *intersection* of protocols, *difference* between protocols, and *projection* of protocol on a given role. The proposed operators take protocols as their operands and return a protocol as their result. Although the proposed operators are generic in the sense that they can be useful in several tasks related to management and analysis of business protocols, we will show in the next section how these operators can be used for analysing protocols compatibility and replaceability. Effecient algorithms that implement the proposed operators as well as correctness proofs are given in [4].

3.1 Compatible Composition

The operator *compatible composition* allows to characterize possible interactions between two protocols, that of a requestor and that of a provider (i.e., the result-

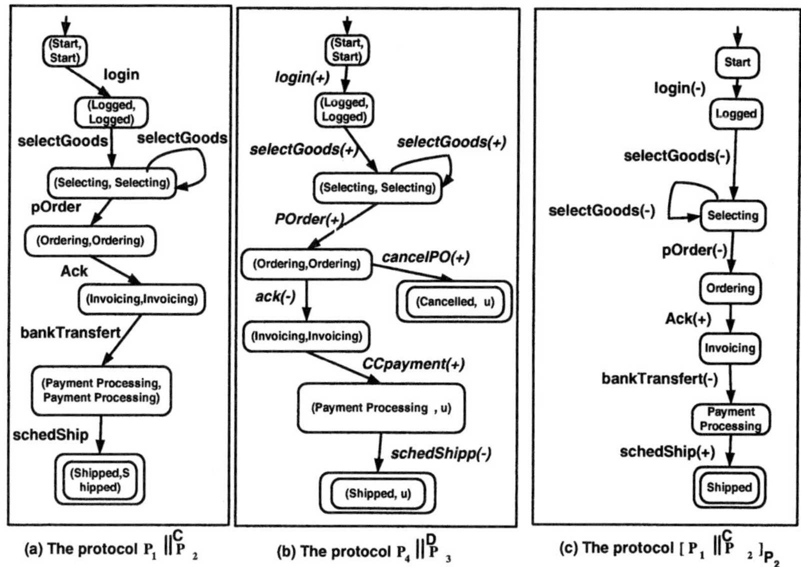

Fig. 5. Examples of protocol management operators.

ing protocol describes all the interaction trees between the considered protocols, and therefore characterizes the possible conversations that can take place between the requestor and the provider). This operator, denoted as $||^{\mathsf{C}}$, takes as input two business protocols and returns a protocol, called a *compatible composition protocol*, that describes the set of complete interactions trees between the input protocols. Informally, the initial state of the resulting protocol is obtained by combining the initial states of the input protocols, final states are obtained by combining the final states of the input protocols, while intermediate states are constructed by combining the intermediate states of the input protocols. The resulting protocol is constructed by considering messages of the two input protocols which have same names but opposite polarities, and that allow execution paths to flow from the start state to end states of the new protocol. All the states that are not reachable from the initial state of the resulting protocol as well as the states that cannot lead to a final state are removed from the resulting protocol. If the result of a compatible composition of two protocols is empty, this means that no conversation is possible between two services that support these protocols. Otherwise, the result is the identification of possible interactions between these protocols.

As an example, Figure 5(a) shows protocol $\mathcal{P}_1||^{\mathsf{C}}\mathcal{P}_2$ that describes all the possible complete interaction trees between protocols $\mathcal{P}_1$ of Figure 1(a) and $\mathcal{P}_2$ of Figure 1(b).

Definition 5. *(Compatible composition)*
Let $\mathcal{P}_1 = (\mathcal{S}^1, s_0^1, \mathcal{F}^1, \mathtt{M}^1, \mathcal{R}^1)$ *and* $\mathcal{P}_2 = (\mathcal{S}^2, s_0^2, \mathcal{F}^2, \mathtt{M}^2, \mathcal{R}^2)$ *be two protocols. The compatible composition* $\mathcal{P} = \mathcal{P}_1||^{\mathsf{C}}\mathcal{P}_2$ *is a protocol* $(\mathcal{S}, s_0, \mathcal{F}, \mathtt{M}, \mathcal{R})$ *where:*

- $\mathcal{S} \subseteq \mathcal{S}^1 \times \mathcal{S}^2$ *is a finite set of states,*
- $s_0 = (s_0^1, s_0^2)$ *is the initial state,*
- $\mathcal{F} \subseteq \mathcal{F}^1 \times \mathcal{F}^2$ *is a set of final states,*
- $\mathtt{M} \subseteq \mathtt{M}^1 \cap \mathtt{M}^2$ *is a set of messages. Note that, the polarity function is not defined for the messages in an a compatible composition protocol.*
- $\mathcal{R}((s^1, s^2), (q^1, q^2), m)$ *iff* $\mathcal{R}^1(s^1, q^1, m)$ *and* $\mathcal{R}^2(s^2, q^2, m)$ *and* $Polarity(\mathcal{P}_1, m) \neq Polarity(\mathcal{P}_2, m)$.
- $\forall (s^1, s^2) \in \mathcal{S}^1 \times \mathcal{S}^2$, *the state* $(s^1, s^2) \in \mathcal{S}$ *iff* (s^1, s^2) *belongs to a complete execution path of* $\mathcal{P}$ *(i.e., a path that goes from the initial state* (s_0^1, s_0^2) *to a final state* $(s_i^1, s_j^2) \in \mathcal{F}$*).*

3.2 Intersection

The intersection operator allows the computation of the largest common part between two protocols. The intersection operator, denoted as $||^{\mathtt{I}}$, takes as input two business protocols and returns a protocol that describes the set of complete execution trees that are common between the two input protocols. The resulting protocol is called an *intersection protocol.* This operator combines the two input protocols as follows: states of the resulting protocols are constructed using the same procedure as in the compatible composition operator. However, unlike compatible composition, the intersection protocol is constructed by considering messages of the input protocols which have same names and polarities.

Definition 6. *(Intersection)*
Let $\mathcal{P}_1 = (\mathcal{S}^1, s_0^1, \mathcal{F}^1, \mathtt{M}^1, \mathcal{R}^1)$ *and* $\mathcal{P}_2 = (\mathcal{S}^2, s_0^2, \mathcal{F}^2, \mathtt{M}^2, \mathcal{R}^2)$ *be two protocols. The intersection* $\mathcal{P} = \mathcal{P}_1||^{\mathtt{I}}\mathcal{P}_2$ *is a protocol* $(\mathcal{S}, s_0, \mathcal{F}, \mathtt{M}, \mathcal{R})$ *where:*

- $\mathcal{S} \subseteq \mathcal{S}^1 \times \mathcal{S}^2$,
- $s_0 = (s_0^1, s_0^2)$,
- $\mathcal{F} \subseteq \mathcal{F}^1 \times \mathcal{F}^2$,
- $\mathtt{M} \subseteq \mathtt{M}^1 \cap \mathtt{M}^2$.
- $\mathcal{R}((s, q), (s', q'), m)$ *iff* $\mathcal{R}^1(s, s', m)$ *and* $\mathcal{R}^2(q, q', m)$ *and* $Polarity(\mathcal{P}_1, m) = Polarity(\mathcal{P}_2, m)$.
- $\forall (s^1, s^2) \in \mathcal{S}^1 \times \mathcal{S}^2$, *the state* $(s^1, s^2) \in \mathcal{S}$ *iff* (s^1, s^2) *belongs to a complete execution path of* $\mathcal{P}$ *(i.e., a path that goes from the initial state* (s_0^1, s_0^2) *to a final state* $(s_i^1, s_j^2) \in \mathcal{F}$*).*

Note that the intersection protocol preserves the polarity of the messages (i.e., $\forall m \in \mathtt{M}, Polarity(\mathcal{P}_1||^{\mathtt{I}}\mathcal{P}_2, m) = Polarity(\mathcal{P}_1, m) = Polarity(\mathcal{P}_2, m)$).

3.3 Difference

While the intersection identifies common aspects between two protocols, the *difference operator*, denoted as $||^{\mathtt{D}}$, emphasizes their differences. This operator takes as input two protocols $\mathcal{P}_1$ and $\mathcal{P}_2$, and returns a protocol called *difference protocol*, whose purpose is to describe the set of all complete execution trees of $\mathcal{P}_1$ that are not common with $\mathcal{P}_2$. As shown below, we compute the difference as a protocol where states are combination of states of $\mathcal{P}_1$ and $\mathcal{P}_2$, as opposed to deriving the subset of $\mathcal{P}_1$ that is not part of $\mathcal{P}_2$. This will allow us to reuse procedures similar to those developed for computing results of previous operators.

Definition 7. *(Difference)*
Let $\mathcal{P}_1 = (\mathcal{S}^1, s_0^1, \mathcal{F}^1, \mathtt{M}^1, \mathcal{R}^1)$ *and* $\mathcal{P}_2 = (\mathcal{S}^2, s_0^2, \mathcal{F}^2, \mathtt{M}^2, \mathcal{R}^2)$ *be two protocols and let* $\mu \notin \mathcal{S}^1 \cup \mathcal{S}^2$ *be a new state name. The difference* $\mathcal{P} = \mathcal{P}_1 ||^{\mathtt{D}} \mathcal{P}_2$ *is a protocol* $(\mathcal{S}, s_0, \mathcal{F}, \mathtt{M}, \mathcal{R})$ *where:*

- $\mathcal{S} \subseteq \mathcal{S}^1 \times (\mathcal{S}^2 \cup \{\mu\})$,
- $s_0 = (s_0^1, s_0^2)$,
- $\mathcal{F} \subseteq \mathcal{F}^1 \times ((\mathcal{S}^2 \cup \{\mu\}) \setminus \mathcal{F}^2)$,
- $\mathtt{M} \subseteq \mathtt{M}^1$.
- $\mathcal{R}((s,q),(s',q'),m)$, *with* $q, q' \in \mathcal{S}^2$, *iff* $\mathcal{R}^1(s,s',m)$, $\mathcal{R}^2(q,q',m)$ *and* $Polarity(\mathcal{P}_1, m) = Polarity(\mathcal{P}_2, m)$,
- $\mathcal{R}((s,q),(s',\mu),m)$, *with* $q \in \mathcal{S}^2$, *iff* $\mathcal{R}^1(s,s',m)$ *and not exists* $q' \in \mathcal{S}^2$ *such that* $\mathcal{R}^2(q,q',m)$ *and* $Polarity(\mathcal{P}_1, m) = Polarity(\mathcal{P}_2, m)$,
- $\mathcal{R}((s,\mu),(s',\mu),m)$ *iff* $\mathcal{R}^1(s,s',m)$.
- $\forall (s^1, s^2) \in \mathcal{S}^1 \times \mathcal{S}^2$, *the state* $(s^1, s^2) \in \mathcal{S}$ *iff* (s^1, s^2) *belongs to a complete execution path of* $\mathcal{P}$ *(i.e., a path that goes from the initial state* (s_0^1, s_0^2) *to a final state* $(s_i^1, s_j^2) \in \mathcal{F}$*).*

As an example, Figure 5(b) shows the difference protocol $\mathcal{P}_4 ||^{\mathtt{D}} \mathcal{P}_3$ that describes all the complete execution trees of the protocol $\mathcal{P}_4$ of Figure 6(b) that are not allowed by the protocol $\mathcal{P}_3$ of Figure 6(a). From this, it can be inferred, e.g, that the sequence of messages login(+).selectGoods(+).POrder(+).cancelPO(+), which is derived from a complete execution path of the difference protocol, is a conversation which is allowed by the protocol $\mathcal{P}_4$ but it is not allowed by $\mathcal{P}_3$.

3.4 Projection

In this section, we discuss the projection of a protocol obtained by using one of the previous operators (i.e, compatible composition, intersection, or difference) on a participant protocol. In the case of compatible composition, the projection of $\mathcal{P}_1 ||^{\mathtt{C}} \mathcal{P}_2$ on the protocol $\mathcal{P}_1$, denoted as $[\mathcal{P}_1 ||^{\mathtt{C}} \mathcal{P}_2]_{\mathcal{P}_1}$, allows to identify the part of the protocol $\mathcal{P}_1$ that is able to interact correctly with the protocol $\mathcal{P}_2$. While a compatible composition protocol $\mathcal{P}$ allows to characterize the possible interactions between two business protocols each defining the behavior of a service playing a certain *role* in a collaboration, the projection of $\mathcal{P}$ allows the extraction of a protocol that defines the role a service plays in a collaboration (e.g., a customer) defined by $\mathcal{P}$. This is very important since the expected behavior of a service in a collaboration constitutes an important part of the requirements for the implementation.

As an example, Figure 5(c) shows the projection of protocol $\mathcal{P}_1 ||^{\mathtt{C}} \mathcal{P}_2$ of Figure 5(a) on protocol $\mathcal{P}_2$. The obtained protocol describes the part of protocol $\mathcal{P}_2$ that can be used to interact correctly with $\mathcal{P}_1$ (i.e, the role of $\mathcal{P}_2$ in $\mathcal{P}_1 ||^{\mathtt{C}} \mathcal{P}_2$).

Briefly stated, the projection of a protocol obtained using an intersection or a difference is defined as follows. In the case of intersection, the projection

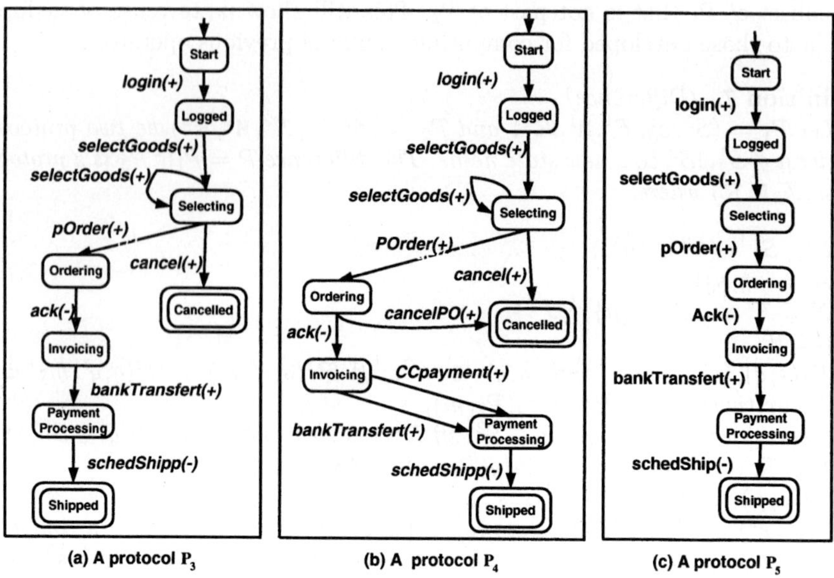

Fig. 6. Business protocols of two other store services.

$[\mathcal{P}_1||^{\mathtt{I}}\mathcal{P}_2]_{\mathcal{P}_1}$ allows to identify the part of the protocol $\mathcal{P}_1$ that is common with the protocol $\mathcal{P}_2$. In the case of difference, the projection $[\mathcal{P}_1||^{\mathtt{D}}\mathcal{P}_2]_{\mathcal{P}_1}$ allows to identify the part of the protocol $\mathcal{P}_1$ that is not supported by the protocol $\mathcal{P}_2$. Below, we give the formal definition of the projection of a protocol obtained by using compatible composition, intersection, or difference.

Definition 8. *(Projection) Let $\mathcal{P} = (\mathcal{S}, s_0, \mathcal{F}, \mathtt{M}, \mathcal{R})$ be a protocol obtained using compatible composition, intersection, or difference of two protocols $\mathcal{P}_1$ and $\mathcal{P}_2$ (e.g., $\mathcal{P} = \mathcal{P}_1||^{\mathtt{C}}\mathcal{P}_2$). A projection of $\mathcal{P}$ on the protocol $\mathcal{P}_1$, denoted as $[\mathcal{P}]_{\mathcal{P}_1}$, is a protocol $(\mathcal{S}', s'_0, \mathcal{F}', \mathtt{M}, \mathcal{R})$ obtained from $\mathcal{P}$ by projecting the states of $\mathcal{P}$ on $\mathcal{P}_1$ (i.e., replacing each state $(s^1_i, s^2_j) \in \mathcal{S}$ by the state s^1_i in $\mathcal{S}'$) and by defining the polarity function of the messages as follows: $Polarity([\mathcal{P}]_{\mathcal{P}_1}, m) = Polarity(\mathcal{P}_1, m), \forall m \in \mathtt{M}$.*

4 Taxonomy of Protocols Compatibility and Replaceability

This section analyzes service protocols compatibility and replaceability. Service compatibility refers to capabilities of services to interoperate while service replaceability refers to the ability of a given service to be used instead of another service, in such a way that the change is transparent to external clients. We define and characterize several types of protocols compatibility (respectively, replaceability). We show how, given two services and the corresponding protocols, it is possible to identify their compatibility (respectively, replaceability) levels using the operators introduced in section 3. Instead of simple black and white compatibility and replaceability measures (i.e, whether two services are compatible or not, whether a service can replace another or not), we propose to consider different classes of protocols compatibility and replaceability.

4.1 Compatibility Classes

We identify two classes of protocols compatibility which provide basic building blocks for analysing complex interactions between service protocols.

- *Partial compatibility* (or simply, compatibility): A protocol $\mathcal{P}_1$ is partially compatible with another protocol $\mathcal{P}_2$ if there are some executions of P1 that can interoperate with P2, i.e., if there is at least one possible conversation that can take place among two services supporting these protocols
- *Full compatibility*: a protocol $\mathcal{P}_1$ is fully compatible with another protocol $\mathcal{P}_2$, if all the executions of $\mathcal{P}_1$ can interoperate with $\mathcal{P}_2$, i.e., any conversation that can be generated by $\mathcal{P}_1$ is understood by $\mathcal{P}_2$.

These notions of compatibility are very useful in the context of Web services. For example, it does not make sense to have interactions with services for which there is no (partial or total) compatibility, as no meaningful conversation can be carried on. Furthermore, if there is only partial compatibility, the developer and the Web service middleware need to be aware of this, as the service will not be able to exploit its full capabilities when interacting with the partially compatible one: indeed, in this case, it is not sufficient that a service implementation is compliant with its advertised protocol, as additional constraints are posed by the fact that the service is interacting with another one whose protocols is only partially compatible, and hence some conversations are disallowed.

As an example, Protocol $\mathcal{P}_1$ of Figure 1(a) can interact with the its reversed protocol $\bar{\mathcal{P}_1}$ without generating errors and, hence, $\mathcal{P}_1$ is *fully compatible* with $\bar{\mathcal{P}_1}$. However, this is not the case for the protocol $\mathcal{P}_1$ of Figure 1(a) and the protocol $\mathcal{P}_2$ of Figure 1(b). When the protocol $\mathcal{P}_2$ is at the state Selecting, it can send a message comparePrice, e.g., to look for the best price of a given product, and goes into a state Price Processing where it waits for an input message priceInfo. These two transitions do not coincide with the transitions of the protocol $\mathcal{P}_1$ (i.e., the protocol $\mathcal{P}_1$ does not accept an input message comparePrice at the state Selecting nor it is able to generate an output message priceInfo). Clearly, there are some executions of the protocol $\mathcal{P}_2$ that cannot interact with the protocol $\mathcal{P}_1$. However, we can observe that there are some cases where the protocol $\mathcal{P}_2$ is able to interact correctly with the protocol $\mathcal{P}_1$ (i.e., there are some executions of $\mathcal{P}_2$ that are compatible with executions of the protocol $\mathcal{P}_1$). An example of such an interaction is given by the complete interaction tree between $\mathcal{P}_1$ and $\mathcal{P}_2$ depicted at Figure 4(b). Hence, the protocols $\mathcal{P}_1$ and $\mathcal{P}_2$ are(partially) compatible.

We use the boolean operator *P-compat*$(\mathcal{P}_1, \mathcal{P}_2)$ (respectively, *F-compat*$(\mathcal{P}_1, \mathcal{P}_2)$) to test if the protocol $\mathcal{P}_1$ is partially compatible (respectively, fully compatible) with the protocol $\mathcal{P}_2$. The following lemma gives necessary and sufficient conditions to identify the compatibility level between two protocols.

Lemma 2. *Let $\mathcal{P}_1$ and $\mathcal{P}_2$ be two business protocols, then*

(i) P-compat$(\mathcal{P}_1, \mathcal{P}_2)$ iff $\mathcal{P}_1 ||^C \mathcal{P}_2$ is not an empty protocol (i.e., the set of its final states is not empty).
(ii) F-compat$(\mathcal{P}_1, \mathcal{P}_2)$ iff $[\mathcal{P}_1 ||^C \mathcal{P}_2]_{\mathcal{P}_1} \cong \mathcal{P}_1$

Note that *full compatibility* is not a symmetric relation, i.e., *F-compat*$(\mathcal{P}_1, \mathcal{P}_2)$ does not imply *F-compat*$(\mathcal{P}_2, \mathcal{P}_1)$ (however, *F-compat*$(\mathcal{P}_1, \mathcal{P}_2)$ implies *P-compat*$(\mathcal{P}_2, \mathcal{P}_1)$).

4.2 Replaceability Classes

Repleacability analysis helps us identify if we can use a service supporting a certain protocol in place of a service supporting a different protocol, both in general and when interacting with a certain client. It also helps developer to manage service evolution, as when a service is modified there is the need for understanding if it can still support all conversations the previous version supported. We identify four replaceability classes between protocols, namely: equivalence, subsumption, replaceability with respect to a client protocol and replaceability with respect to an interaction role. These replaceability classes provide basic building blocks for analysing the commonalities and differences between service protocols.

1. *Protocols equivalence*: two business protocols $\mathcal{P}_1$ and $\mathcal{P}_2$ are equivalent if they are mutually substituable, i.e., the two protocols can be interchangeably used in any context and the change is transparent to clients. We use the boolean operator *Equiv*$(\mathcal{P}_1, \mathcal{P}_2)$ to test the equivalence of protocols $\mathcal{P}_1$ and $\mathcal{P}_2$.
2. *Protocol subsumption*: a protocol $\mathcal{P}_1$ is subsumed by another protocol $\mathcal{P}_2$, if the externally visible behavior of $\mathcal{P}_1$ encompasses the externally visible behavior of $\mathcal{P}_2$, i.e., if $\mathcal{P}_1$ supports at least all the conversations that $\mathcal{P}_2$ supports. In this case, protocol $\mathcal{P}_1$ can be transparently used instead of $\mathcal{P}_2$ but the opposite is not necessarily true. We use the boolean operator *Subs*$(\mathcal{P}_1, \mathcal{P}_2)$ to test if $\mathcal{P}_2$ subsumes $\mathcal{P}_1$. It should be noted that equivalence is stronger than subsumption (i.e., *Equiv*$(\mathcal{P}_1, \mathcal{P}_2)$ implies *Subs*$(\mathcal{P}_1, \mathcal{P}_2)$ and *Subs*$(\mathcal{P}_2, \mathcal{P}_1)$). The protocol $\mathcal{P}_1$ of Figure 1(a) is subsumed by the protocol $\mathcal{P}_3$ of Figure 6(a).
3. *Protocol replaceability with respect to a client protocol*: The previous definitions discussed replaceability in general. However, it may be important to understand if a service can be used to replace another one when interacting with a certain client. This leads to a weaker definition of replaceability: a protocol $\mathcal{P}_1$ can replace another protocol $\mathcal{P}_2$ with respect to a client protocol Pc, denoted as *Repl*$_{[\mathcal{P}_c]}(\mathcal{P}_1, \mathcal{P}_2)$, if $\mathcal{P}_1$ behaves similarly as $\mathcal{P}_2$ when interacting with a specific protocol Pc. Hence, if *Repl*$_{[\mathcal{P}_c]}(\mathcal{P}_1, \mathcal{P}_2)$ than $\mathcal{P}_1$ can replace $\mathcal{P}_2$ to interact with $\mathcal{P}_c$ and this change is transparent to the client $\mathcal{P}_c$. It should be noted that, this replaceability class is also weaker than subsumption (i.e., *Subs*$(\mathcal{P}_1, \mathcal{P}_2)$ implies *Repl*$_{[\mathcal{P}_c]}(\mathcal{P}_1, \mathcal{P}_2)$ for any protocol $\mathcal{P}_c$). For example, Protocol $\mathcal{P}_1$ of Figure 1(a) is not subsumed by protocol $\mathcal{P}_4$ of Figure 6(b), as $\mathcal{P}_4$ allows a client to cancel an order (message cancelPO(+) at

state Ordering) and also accept payments by credit card (message CCpayment(-) at state Invoicing) while $\mathcal{P}_1$ does not support these two possibilities. Hence, $\mathcal{P}_1$ cannot replace $\mathcal{P}_4$ for arbitrary clients. However, we can observe that $\mathcal{P}_1$ can replace $\mathcal{P}_4$ when interacting with the protocol $\mathcal{P}_2$ of Figure 1(b) as this client never cancel an ordering and it also always performs its payments by bank transfer.

4. *Protocol replaceability with respect to an interaction role*: Let $\mathcal{P}_R$ be a business protocol. A protocol $\mathcal{P}_1$ can replace another protocol $\mathcal{P}_2$ with respect to a role $\mathcal{P}_R$, denoted as $Repl\_Role_{[\mathcal{P}_R]}(\mathcal{P}_1, \mathcal{P}_2)$, if $\mathcal{P}_1$ behaves similarly as $\mathcal{P}_2$ when $\mathcal{P}_2$ behaves as $\mathcal{P}_R$. This replaceability class allows to identify executions of a protocol $\mathcal{P}_2$ that can be replaced by the protocol $\mathcal{P}_1$ even in the case when $\mathcal{P}_1$ and $\mathcal{P}_2$ are not comparable with respect to any of the previous replaceability classes. The class $Repl\_Role_{[\mathcal{P}_R]}(\mathcal{P}_1, \mathcal{P}_2)$ is the weakest replaceability class (i.e., $Repl_{[\mathcal{P}_R]}(\mathcal{P}_1, \mathcal{P}_2)$ implies $Repl\_Role_{[\mathcal{P}_R]}(\mathcal{P}_1, \mathcal{P}_2)$).
For example, consider the protocol $\mathcal{P}_2$ of Figure 1(b) and its reversed protocol $\bar{\mathcal{P}}_2$. Protocol $\mathcal{P}_4$ of Figure 6(b) cannot replace protocol $\bar{\mathcal{P}}_2$ when interacting with client $\mathcal{P}_2$ (i.e., $Repl_{[\mathcal{P}_2]}(\mathcal{P}_4, \bar{\mathcal{P}}_2)$ does not hold). This is because protocol $\mathcal{P}_4$ does not accept an input message comparePrice at the state Selecting. However, even in this case, a client $\mathcal{P}_2$ may be interested to know for which executions it can use $\mathcal{P}_4$ instead of $\bar{\mathcal{P}}_2$. For example, we can observe that $\mathcal{P}_4$ can replace $\bar{\mathcal{P}}_2$ in all the interactions in which $\bar{\mathcal{P}}_2$ behaves as the protocol $\mathcal{P}_5$ of Figure 6(c) (i.e., $Repl\_Role_{[\mathcal{P}_5]}(\mathcal{P}_4, \bar{\mathcal{P}}_2)$). In other words, the protocol $\mathcal{P}_5$ exhibits to a given client executions of $\bar{\mathcal{P}}_2$ for which it is possible to use $\mathcal{P}_4$ instead of $\bar{\mathcal{P}}_2$.

The following lemma characterizes the replaceability levels of two given protocols using the operators introduced in previous sections.

Lemma 3. *Let $\mathcal{P}_1$, $\mathcal{P}_2$, $\mathcal{P}_c$ and $\mathcal{P}_R$ be business protocols.*

1. *$Equiv(\mathcal{P}_1, \mathcal{P}_2)$ iff $\mathcal{P}_1 \cong \mathcal{P}_2$*
2. *$Subs(\mathcal{P}_1, \mathcal{P}_2)$ iff $\mathcal{P}_2 \lesssim \mathcal{P}_1$*
3. *$Repl_{[\mathcal{P}_c]}(\mathcal{P}_1, \mathcal{P}_2)$ iff $[\mathcal{P}_c ||^{\mathrm{C}} \mathcal{P}_2]_{\mathcal{P}_2} \lesssim \mathcal{P}_1$ (or equivalently, iff $\mathcal{P}_c ||^{\mathrm{C}} [\mathcal{P}_2 ||^{\mathrm{D}} \mathcal{P}_1]_{\mathcal{P}_2}$ is an empty protocol)*
4. *$Repl\_Role_{[\mathcal{P}_R]}(\mathcal{P}_1, \mathcal{P}_2)$ iff $P_R \lesssim [\mathcal{P}_1 ||^{\mathrm{I}} \mathcal{P}_2]_{\mathcal{P}_1}$.*

Note that this lemma provides two equivalent characterizations of class $Repl_{[\mathcal{P}_c]}(\mathcal{P}_1, \mathcal{P}_2)$ (item 3 of the lemma). The second characterization (i.e., $\mathcal{P}_c ||^{\mathrm{C}} [\mathcal{P}_1 ||^{\mathrm{D}} \mathcal{P}_2]_{\mathcal{P}}$) can be useful to check whether $\mathcal{P}_2$ can be used instead of $\mathcal{P}_1$ with respect to a client $\mathcal{P}_c$ in those cases where the protocol $\mathcal{P}_2$ is not fully accessible (e.g., $\mathcal{P}_2$ is hidden for security reasons). Furthermore, such a characterization may be interesting for change support as it allows to incrementally check whether a given client protocol $\mathcal{P}_c$ used to interact with a protocol $\mathcal{P}_1$ can still interact correctly with a new version $\mathcal{P}_2$ of the protocol $\mathcal{P}_1$.

5 Discussion

We believe that the effective use and widespread adoption of Web service technologies and standards requires: (i) high-level frameworks and methodologies for supporting automated development and interoperability (e.g., code generation, compatibility), and (ii) identification of appropriate abstractions and notations for specifying service requirements and characteristics. Service protocol management as proposed in this paper offers a set of mechanisms for the automation of services development and interoperability.

Several efforts recognize aspects of protocol specifications in component-based models [7, 13]. These efforts provide models (e.g., pi-calculus -based languages for component interface specifications) and algorithms (e.g., compatibility checking) that can be generalized for use in Web service protocol specifications and management. Indeed, various efforts in the general area of formalizing Web service description and composition languages emerged recently [5, 11]. However, in terms of managing the Web service development life-cycle, technology is still in the early stages. The main contribution of the work presented in this paper is a framework that leverages emerging Web services technologies and established modeling notation (state machine-based formalism) to provide high-level support for analyzing degrees of commonalities and differences between protocols as well interoperation possibilities of interacting Web services. In the following we briefly discuss how the framework presented in this paper can be leveraged to better support the service lifecycle management.

Development-time support. During service development, protocol analysis can assist in assessing the compatibility of the newly created service (and service protocol) with the other services with which it needs to interact. The protocol analysis will in particular help users to identify which part of the protocol are compatible and which are not, therefore suggesting possible areas of modifications that we need to tackle if we want to increase the level of compatibility with a desired service.

Runtime support. In terms of runtime support, the main application of compatibility analysis is in dynamic binding. In fact, just like for static binding, the benefit of protocol analysis is that search engines can restrict the services they return to those that are compatible. This is essential, as there is no point in returning services that are not protocol-compatible, since no interoperation will be possible (unless there is a mediation mechanism that can make interaction possible, as discussed below).

Change Support. Web services operate autonomously within potentially dynamic environments. In particular, component or partner services may change their protocols, others may become unavailable, and still others may emerge. Consequently, services may fail to invoke required operations when needed. The proposed operators allow to statically and dynamically identify alternative services based on behavior equivalence and substitution. Protocols analysis and management provide also opportunities to: (i) help understanding mismatch between protocols, (ii) help understand if a new version of a service protocol is compatible with the intended clients, and the like.

The framework presented in this paper is one of the components of a broader CASE tool, partially implemented, that manages the entire service development lifecycle [2, 3, 10]. In this paper, we focused on analysing and managing Web service protocols. Another component (presented in [2]) of this framework features a generative approach where conversation protocols are specified using an extended state machine model, composition models are specified using statecharts, and executable processes are described using BPEL. Through this component, users can visually edit service conversation and composition models and automatically generate the BPEL skeletons, which can then be extended by the developers and eventually executed using BPEL execution engine such as the IBM's BPWS4J (www.alphaworks.ibm.com/tech/bpws4j). We are also considering the extension of the proposed approach to cater for trust negotiation and security protocols in Web services, by exploring the leverages between conversation and trust negotiation protocols [10], that can both be specified through state machines, although at different levels of abstractions. The proposed framework supports also lifecycle management of trust negotiation protocols [10]. We introduced a set of change operations that are used to modify protocol specifications. Strategies are presented to allow migration of ongoing negotiations to a new protocol specification. Details about these features of framework can be found in [2, 10]. Finally, our current research also includes addressing the problem of designing and testing for compatibility, trying in particular to understand how to develop test cases that can test that two services can interact and how to devise a methodology for service development that facilitates protocol compatibility.

References

1. G. Alonso, F. Casati, H. Kuno, and V. Machiraju. *Web Services Concepts, Architectures and Applications*. Springer Verlag, 2004.
2. K. Baina, B. Benatallah, F. Casati, and F. Toumani. Model-Driven Web Service Development. In *CAiSE'04*, volume 3084 of *LNCS*, Riga, Latvia, 2004. Springer.
3. B. Benatallah, F. Casati, and F. Toumani. Web Service Conversation Modeling: A Cornerstone for e-Business Automation. *IEEE Internet Computing*, 6(1), 2004.
4. B. Benatallah, F.Casati, and F. Toumani. A Framework for Modeling, Analyzing, and Managing Web Service Protocols. Technical Report 0430, CSE-UNSW, August, 2004.
5. T. Bultan, X. Fu, R. Hull, and J. Su. Conversation specification: a new approach to design and analysis of e-service composition. In *WWW'03*. ACM, 2003.
6. C. Bussler. *B2B Integration: Concepts and Architecture*. Springer Verlag, 2003.
7. C. Canal, L. Fuentes, E. Pimentel, J. M. Troya, and A. Vallecillo. Adding Roles to CORBA Objects. *IEEE TSE*, 29(3):242–260, March 2003.
8. R.J. van Glabbeek. The Linear Time – Branching Time Spectrum (extended abstract). In *CONCUR'90*, volume 458 of *LNCS*, pages 278–297. Springer, 1990.
9. T.A. Henzinger, S. Qadeer, S.K. Rajamani, and S. Tasiran. An assume-guarantee rule for checking simulation. *ACM Trans. Prog. Lang. Syst.*, 24(1):51–64, Jan' 02.
10. H.Skogsrud, B.Benatallah, and F.Casati. Model-Driven Trust Negotiation for Web Services. *IEEE Internet Computing*, 7(6), October 2003.
11. M. Mecella, B. Pernici, and P. Craca. Compatibility of e -Services in a Cooperative Multi-platform Environment. In *VLDB-TES'01*, Rome, Italy, 2001. Springer.
12. M. P. Papazoglou and D. Georgakopoulos. Special issue on service oriented computing. *Commun. ACM*, 46(10):24–28, 2003.
13. D.M. Yellin and R.E. Storm. Protocol Specifications and Component Adaptors. *ACM Trans. Program. Lang. Syst.*, 19(2):292–333, March 1997.

Semantic Interpretation and Matching of Web Services

Chang Xu, Shing-Chi Cheung, and Xiangye Xiao

Department of Computer Science
Hong Kong University of Science and Technology
Clear Water Bay, Kowloon, Hong Kong
{changxu,scc,xiaoxy}@cs.ust.hk

Abstract. A major issue in the study of semantic Web services concerns the matching problem of Web services. Various techniques for this problem have been proposed. Typical ones include *FSM* modeling, *DAML-S* ontology matching, description logics reasoning, and *WSDL* dual operation composition. They often assume the availability of concept semantic relations, based on which the capability satisfiability is evaluated. However, we find that the use of semantic relations alone in the satisfiability evaluation may lead to inappropriate results. In this paper, we study the problem and classify the existing techniques of satisfiability evaluation into three approaches, namely, set inclusion checking, concept coverage comparison and concept subsumption reasoning. Two different semantic interpretations, namely, capacity interpretation and restriction interpretation, are identified. However, each of the three approaches assumes only one interpretation and its evaluation is inapplicable to the other interpretation. To address this limitation, a novel interpretation model, called *CRI* model, is formulated. This model supports both semantic interpretations, and allows the satisfiability evaluation to be uniformly conducted. Finally, we present an algorithm for the unified satisfiability evaluation.

1 Introduction

Much attention has been paid to the study of semantic Web services [5], which aims to explore a better way to describe and implement Web services, making them accessible to automated agents. Ontology plays a key role in the Semantic Web by providing common vocabularies shared by applications. Currently, the Web Services Description Language (*WSDL*) [19] does not support semantic descriptions for Web services [4], and the Universal Description, Discovery and Integration (*UDDI*) [20] also cannot provide adequate documentation of Web service capabilities [4]. To address their limitations, ontology languages (e.g., *DAML+OIL* [15]) have been proposed whose goal is to facilitate the automation of tasks including Web service discovery, execution, composition and interoperation.

Capability matching of Web services is a major research issue in this field. Generally, when an agent is given a service request, it tries to match it against available service advertisements stored in its Web service repository. The matching is conducted in terms of capabilities based on the underlying semantics of the concepts involved. A variety of techniques have been proposed. Popular ones include finite-state machine (*FSM*) modeling [2], *DAML-S* [16] ontology matching [11], Description Logics (*DLs*) [1] reasoning [4], and *WSDL* dual operation composition [6].

A service advertisement is said to be matched for a service request only when the capabilities of this advertisement satisfy the requirements of this request. The match-

P. Atzeni et al. (Eds.): ER 2004, LNCS 3288, pp. 542–554, 2004.

ing process is called *satisfiability evaluation*. We classify existing techniques in the satisfiability evaluation into three approaches:

- **Set Inclusion Checking:** In this approach, each set contains available resources or required resources. The goal of checking is to find inclusion relations between sets. For example, if B_1 = {"*SOAP*"} [18] and B_2 = {"*SOAP*", "*HTTP*"}, B_2 is said to be able to satisfy B_1 [6].
- **Concept Coverage Comparing:** This approach uses concepts to represent capabilities or requirements. In comparison, a more general concept can satisfy a more specific concept. For example, concept *Vehicle* satisfies concept *Car* [11].
- **Concept Subsumption Reasoning:** In this approach, capabilities or requirements are represented in *DL* clauses. In reasoning, a more specific *DL* clause can satisfy a more general *DL* clause. For example, $\forall item.(PC \cap \geq_{256} memorySize)$ satisfies $\forall item.(PC \cap \geq_{128} memorySize)$ [4].

The first two approaches are essentially equivalent. To illustrate this, we assume that *Vehicle* has two sub-concepts: *Car* and *Bus*. After we rewrite *Vehicle* as {*Car*, *Bus*} and *Car* as {*Car*}, *Vehicle* satisfies *Car* iff {*Car*, *Bus*} includes {*Car*}. Next, the last two approaches have opposite criteria for the satisfiability evaluation. The reason is that each *DL* clause can be regarded as a concept. Finally, all the three approaches make use of semantic relations between concepts.

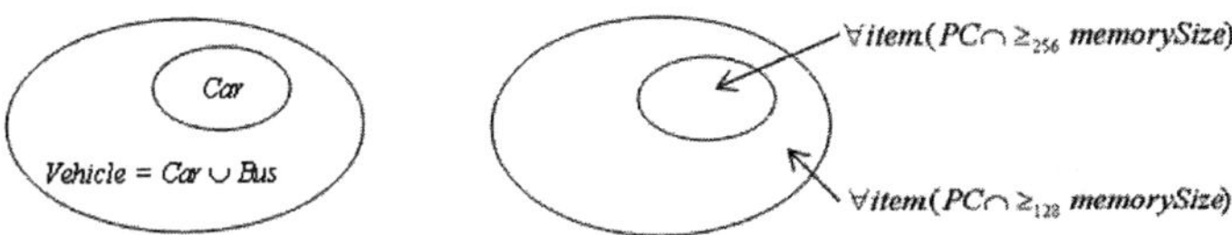

Fig. 1. The *Vehicle* and *PC* Examples

However, the use of concept semantic relations alone in the satisfiability evaluation may lead to inappropriate results. It is because a concept can be subject to multiple interpretations under different contexts. The *Vehicle* example actually adopts the *capacity interpretation* of *Vehicle* that refers to the semantics of *Vehicle* and all its sub-concepts. *Vehicle* can satisfy *Car* under this context. But the *PC* example adopts *restriction interpretations* of two *DL* clauses: $\forall item.(PC \cap \geq_{256} memorySize)$ and $\forall item.(PC \cap \geq_{128} memorySize)$. Under this context, the former is more restrictive than the latter. Therefore, the requirement of a *PC* with memory larger than 128MB can be satisfied by the offering of a *PC* with memory larger than 256MB (Fig. 1).

The above two examples indicates that an offering labeled by a more general concept does not necessarily satisfy a requirement labeled by a more specific concept, and vice versa. The satisfiability evaluation should depend on how the involved concepts are semantically interpreted. We call this *semantic interpretation* which can be based on either capacity or restriction. More rigorous definitions for these interpretations will be given later.

Each of the three approaches discussed actually assumes only one semantic interpretation, and its satisfiability evaluation is inapplicable to the other semantic interpretation. To address this limitation, we propose a unified capability matching model for Web services, in which the satisfiability evaluation can be performed uniformly based on two semantic interpretations.

The remainder of this paper is organized as follows. Section 2 introduces related work. Section 3 proposes our solution to the Web service capability matching problem. Section 4 discusses how to implement the capability matching system. Section 5 evaluates our system using four well-known criteria, and presents our two extra features. In the last section, we conclude our contributions and explore future work.

2 Related Work

Various studies have been conducted on the service capability matching issue. Gao et al. [2] formally defined *exact match* and *plug-in match* for Web service capabilities based on abstract *FSM* models. They also proposed a capability description language *SCDL* and a solution for comparing service capabilities. However, the work focuses mainly on signature matching rather than semantic matching. Moreover, it is difficult to use the *FSM* approach to precisely describe Web service capabilities.

Paolucci et al. [11] suggested semantic matching for Web services and proposed a solution based on *DAML-S*. The work presents a matching framework to examine every advertisement and request pair. It also suggests flexible matching by providing four matching degrees based on a predefined taxonomy tree. However, the work only considers capacity interpretations of concepts. Furthermore, the technique addresses mainly *is-a* relations between concepts.

Li and Horrocks [4] described a service matchmaking prototype using a *DAML-S* ontology and a *DL* reasoner. This approach is useful to describe the semantics of service adverts and queries. However, each *DL* expression can be regarded as a conjunction of several restriction clauses. If a given advert and query contain different restriction clauses at some corresponding position, the algorithm cannot work well. To address this problem, they proposed to minimize the *DL* expression under examination by moving unimportant *providedBy* and *requestedBy* clauses out of the *profile* that participates in comparison. This adjustment only partially solves the problem because the remaining part of the *profile* may also include some information that will affect the matching result. Another limitation of the work is that the authoring of *DL* expressions requires users' familiarity of formal logics.

Medjahed et al. [6] proposed an ontology-based framework for Web service composition. Several composability rules are deployed to compare the syntactic and semantic features of Web services. A composability model that covers from low-level binding mode to high-level composition soundness was formulated. In the satisfiability evaluation, the framework only adopts simple set inclusion checking. Essentially, the approach is based on the capacity interpretations of concepts.

Other related work includes *LARKS* [12] and *ARLAS* [10] matchmaking systems. *LARKS* defines five techniques for service matchmaking. Those techniques mostly compare service text descriptions, signatures, and logical constraints about inputs and outputs [6]. *ATLAS* defines two methods to compare services for functional attributes and capabilities [6].

Generally, existing techniques decide matching results based on relations between compared concept pairs. In our approach, these relations are used as the intermediate result in the satisfiability evaluation. To accurately perform capability matching, we take into account the semantic interpretations of concepts involved. Our satisfiability evaluation differs from others in that it uniformly performs multiple satisfiability evaluations based on semantic interpretations of concepts. Therefore, the final matching result is a synthesis of multiple satisfiability evaluations.

3 Semantic Interpretation and Capability Matching

Let us first overview some preliminary concepts on conceptual modeling before presenting our satisfiability evaluation technique, which is based on semantic interpretations of concepts. A capability matching algorithm will be subsequently formulated.

3.1 Preliminary

Definition 1 (Concept-Instance Structure): *A concept-instance (CI) structure CIS = (C, I, cimap) is a triple where:*

- *C is a set of concepts;*
- *I is a set of instances;*
- *Total function cimap:* $C \rightarrow 2^I$ *relates a concept in C with a non-empty set of instances in I.*

Fig. 2 gives the graphical representation of an illustrative example. The following is the corresponding *CI* structure:

$CIS = (C, I, cimap)$
$C = \{Vehicle, Bus, Car, Sedan, SUV\}$
$I = \{b_1, b_2, se_1, se_2, suv\}$
$cimap(Vehicle) = \{b_1, b_2, se_1, se_2, suv\}$
$cimap(Bus) = \{b_1, b_2\}$
$cimap(Car) = \{se_1, se_2, suv\}$
$cimap(Sedan) = \{se_1, se_2\}$
$cimap(SUV) = \{suv\}$

Definition 2 (Equivalent, subsumed, including, intersecting and disjoint): *In a CI structure CIS, any two concepts* c_1 *and* c_2 *are subject to one of the following relations:*

- *equivalent: if* $cimap_{CIS}(c_1) = cimap_{CIS}(c_2)$;
- *subsumed: if* $cimap_{CIS}(c_1) \subset cimap_{CIS}(c_2)$;
- *including: if* $cimap_{CIS}(c_1) \supset cimap_{CIS}(c_2)$;
- *disjoint: if* $cimap_{CIS}(c_1) \cap cimap_{CIS}(c_2) = \phi$;
- *intersecting: otherwise.*

Definition 3 (Descendent concept): *If concepts* c_1 *and* c_2 *have an equivalent or subsumed relation,* c_1 *is said to be a descendent concept of* c_2.

Since the equivalent relation is reflexive, a concept is a descendent concept of itself. Tables 1 and 2 give the concept relations and the descendent concepts, respectively, for the example of Fig. 2.

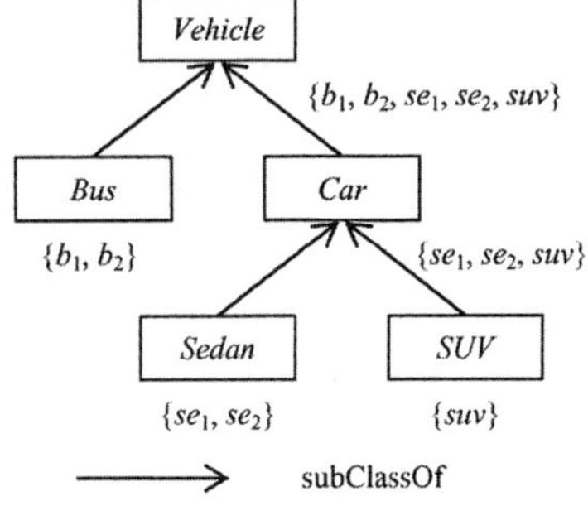

Fig. 2. An illustrative example

Table 1. The concept relation table (c_1 to c_2)

c_1 \ c_2	*Vehicle*	*Bus*	*Car*	*Sedan*	*SUV*
Vehicle	equivalent	including	including	including	including
Bus	subsumed	equivalent	disjoint	disjoint	disjoint
Car	subsumed	disjoint	equivalent	including	including
Sedan	subsumed	disjoint	subsumed	equivalent	disjoint
SUV	subsumed	disjoint	subsumed	disjoint	equivalent

Table 2. The descendent concept table

For *Vehicle*	*Vehicle, Bus, Car, Sedan, SUV*
For *Bus*	*Bus*
For *Car*	*Car, Sedan, SUV*
For *Sedan*	*Sedan*
For *SUV*	*SUV*

Definition 4 (Coverage): *Suppose that $c_1,\ldots, c_n$ are concepts in a CI structure CIS. If I is a set of instances that satisfies* $I \subseteq cimap_{CIS}(c_1) \cup \ldots \cup cimap_{CIS}(c_n)$ *and* $(\exists e \in cimap_{CIS}(c_1), e \in I) \wedge \ldots \wedge (\exists e \in cimap_{CIS}(c_n), e \in I)$, *I is said to have a coverage relation with $\{c_1, \ldots, c_n\}$, written as: $I\ R_{cov}\ \{c_1, \ldots, c_n\}$.*

If I has a coverage relation with $\{c_1, \ldots, c_n\}$, it means that I is subject to some relation with each concept in set $\{c_1, \ldots, c_n\}$. Some coverage relations for the example in Fig. 2 are given below:

$\{b_1\}\ R_{cov}\ \{BUS\}$ $\quad \{b_2\}\ R_{cov}\ \{BUS\}$ $\quad \{b_1, b_2\}\ R_{cov}\ \{BUS\}$
$\{se_1, suv\}\ R_{cov}\ \{Sedan, SUV\}$ $\quad \{se_2, suv\}\ R_{cov}\ \{Sedan, SUV\}$
$\{se_1, se_2, suv\}\ R_{cov}\ \{Sedan, SUV\}$

3.2 Satisfiability Evaluation

3.2.1 Semantic Interpretation

Definition 5 (Restriction interpretation): *If c is a concept in a CI structure CIS, the restriction interpretation $\vartheta^R_{CIS}(c)$ of c is the set of all sets that has a coverage relation with $\{c\}$: $\vartheta^R_{CIS}(c) = \{I \mid I\ R_{cov}\ \{c\}\}$.*

Definition 6 (Capacity interpretation): *If c is a concept in a CI structure CIS, the capacity interpretation $\vartheta^C_{CIS}(c)$ of c is the set of all sets that has a coverage relation with the set of all descendent concepts of c: $\vartheta^C_{CIS}(c) = \{I \mid I\ R_{cov}\ \{c_1,\ldots,c_n\}$, $c_1,\ldots,c_n$ are all descendant concepts of c$\}$.*

The restriction interpretation of a concept represents the semantics of this concept, while the capacity interpretation of a concept represents the semantics of all descendent concepts of this concept. Some restriction interpretations and capacity interpretations for the example in Fig. 2 are given below:

$\vartheta^R_{CIS}(Sedan) = \{\{se_1\}, \{se_2\}, \{se_1, se_2\}\}$ $\quad \vartheta^C_{CIS}(Sedan) = \{\{se_1\}, \{se_2\}, \{se_1, se_2\}\}$
$\vartheta^R_{CIS}(SUV) = \{\{suv\}\}$ $\quad \vartheta^C_{CIS}(SUV) = \{\{suv\}\}$
$\vartheta^R_{CIS}(Car) = \{\{se_1\}, \{se_2\}, \{suv\}, \{se_1, se_2\}, \{se_1, suv\}, \{se_2, suv\}, \{se_1, se_2, suv\}\}$
$\vartheta^R_{CIS}(Car) = \{\{se_1, suv\}, \{se_2, suv\}, \{se_1, se_2, suv\}\}$

Definition 7 (Semantic interpretation): *An interpretation is a semantic interpretation iff it is a restriction interpretation or a capacity interpretation.*

Semantic interpretation is used for the satisfiability evaluation in Web service capability matching. Each concept has two semantic interpretations: restriction interpretation and capacity interpretation.

3.2.2 Semantics Satisfiability

Definition 8 (Semantics satisfiability): *The evaluation for semantics satisfiability compares the semantic interpretations of concepts. Given two concepts c_1 and c_2 in a CI structure CIS and their semantic interpretations $\vartheta_{CIS}(c_1)$ and $\vartheta_{CIS}(c_2)$,*

- *If* $\forall e_2 \in \vartheta_{CIS}(c_2), \exists e_1 \in \vartheta_{CIS}(c_1), e_1 \subseteq e_2$, $\vartheta_{CIS}(c_1)$ *is said to be satisfied by* $\vartheta_{CIS}(c_2)$.
- *Otherwise,* $\vartheta_{CIS}(c_1)$ *is said not to be satisfied by* $\vartheta_{CIS}(c_2)$.

Definition 8 unifies the impact of two different semantic interpretations so that the satisfiability evaluation can be done uniformly under different contexts. Let us denote $\lhd$ as the "*is satisfied by*" relation. Some semantics satisfiability results for the example in Fig. 2 are given below:

$\vartheta^{C}_{CIS}(Bus) \lhd \vartheta^{C}_{CIS}(Vehicle)$ $\quad\quad$ $\vartheta^{C}_{CIS}(Sedan) \lhd \vartheta^{C}_{CIS}(Car)$
$\vartheta^{R}_{CIS}(Vehicle) \lhd \vartheta^{R}_{CIS}(Bus)$ $\quad\quad$ $\vartheta^{R}_{CIS}(Car) \lhd \vartheta^{R}_{CIS}(Sedan)$
$\vartheta^{C}_{CIS}(Sedan) \lhd \vartheta^{R}_{CIS}(Sedan)$ $\quad\quad$ $\vartheta^{C}_{CIS}(SUV) \lhd \vartheta^{R}_{CIS}(SUV)$
$\vartheta^{R}_{CIS}(Sedan) \lhd \vartheta^{C}_{CIS}(Car)$ $\quad\quad$ $\vartheta^{R}_{CIS}(Car) \lhd \vartheta^{C}_{CIS}(Sedan)$

3.2.3 Satisfiability Result

Given two concepts, the result of the satisfiability evaluation depends on two factors: (i) the relation between them and (ii) the semantic interpretations of them. The following satisfiability result table can be derived from Definition 8:

Table 3. The result of satisfiability evaluation of $\vartheta_{CIS}(c_1)$ and $\vartheta_{CIS}(c_2)$

Relation (c_1 and c_2)	equivalent			subsumed			including			intersecting			disjoint		
Figure	c_1 c_2			c_1 c_2			c_1 c_2			c_1 c_2			c_1 c_2		
Satisfiability result	c_1 \ c_2	R	C	c_1 \ c_2	R	C	c_1 \ c_2	R	C	c_1 \ c_2	R	C	c_1 \ c_2	R	C
	R	√	√	R	×	√	R	√	√	R	×	$*_2$	R	×	×
	C	$*_1$	√	C	×	√	C	×	×	C	×	×	C	×	×

Notes:

- R: restriction interpretation; C: capacity interpretation.
- √: $\vartheta_{CIS}(c_1) \lhd \vartheta_{CIS}(c_2)$; ×: $\neg(\vartheta_{CIS}(c_1) \lhd \vartheta_{CIS}(c_2))$.
- $*_1$: $\vartheta_{CIS}(c_1) \lhd \vartheta_{CIS}(c_2)$ iff all descendent concepts of c_1 and c_2 are equivalent; $*_2$: $\vartheta_{CIS}(c_1) \lhd \vartheta_{CIS}(c_2)$ iff c_1 has descendent concepts other than itself and each descendent concept c satisfies $cimap_{CIS}(c) \cap cimap_{CIS}(c_1) \cap cimap_{CIS}(c_2) \neq \phi$.

3.2.4 Satisfiability Theorems and Transitive Law

To effectively use the satisfiability result table in Web service capability matching, we generalize the following four satisfiability theorems and a transitive law:

Theorem 1. *The restriction interpretation / capacity interpretation of a concept can satisfy the restriction interpretation / capacity interpretation of any concept equivalent to this concept.*

Theorem 2. *The capacity interpretation of a concept can satisfy the restriction interpretation of any concept equivalent to this concept.*

Theorem 3. *The capacity interpretation of a concept can satisfy the capacity interpretation of any descendent concept of itself.*

Theorem 4. *The restriction interpretation of a concept can be satisfied by the restriction interpretation of any descendent concept of itself.*

Theorem 5. *Transitive law applies to semantics satisfiability.*

Theorems 1 and 2 concern the equivalent part of Table 3, while theorems 3 and 4 concern the subsumed part and the including part of the table, respectively. The proof of Theorem 1 is naturally followed from the definitions of capacity and restriction interpretations. The proofs for the other four theorems can be found in [13].

3.2.5 Satisfiability Evaluation

Suppose that c_1, …, c_n are concepts in a CI structure *CIS*, such that c_n is a descendent concept of c_{n-1}, …, and c_2 is a descendent concept of c_1. Note that c_n has no descendent concept other than itself. We have two satisfiability sequences: $\vartheta^R_{CIS}(c_1) \lhd \ldots \lhd \vartheta^R_{CIS}(c_n)$, and $\vartheta^C_{CIS}(c_n) \lhd \ldots \lhd \vartheta^C_{CIS}(c_1)$, where $\vartheta^R_{CIS}(c_n) = \vartheta^C_{CIS}(c_n)$ (Fig. 3).

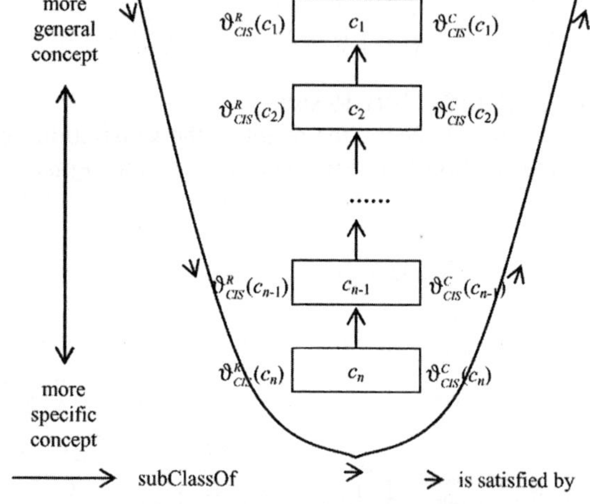

Fig. 3. A satisfiability sequence

The first sequence gives the satisfiability evaluation result between restriction interpretations. A more specific concept can satisfy a more general concept under this semantic interpretation. It is what the concept subsumption reasoning approach is to achieve. The second sequence gives satisfiability evaluation result between capacity interpretations. A more general concept can satisfy a more specific concept under this semantic interpretation. It is what the concept coverage comparing approach is to achieve.

Our satisfiability evaluation generalizes the above two approaches by supporting both restriction and capacity inter-interpretations. In addition, it allows dynamic specification of semantic interpretations. This feature is use-useful. Let us assume a binding protocol ontology in Fig. 4. A service provider, which supports

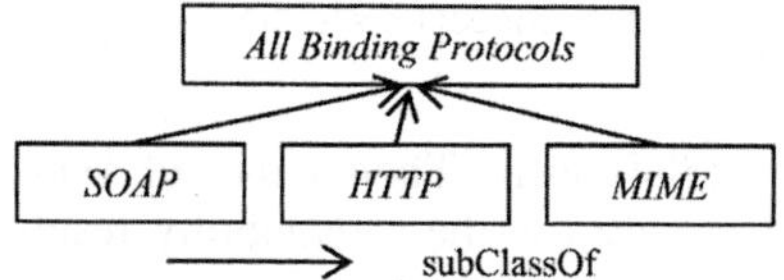

Fig. 4. A binding protocol ontology

SOAP, *HTTP* and *MIME*, advertises his protocols as *All Binding Protocols* using a capacity interpretation. Users looking for a service supporting all binding protocols can make a request for *All Binding Protocols* using a capacity interpretation. However, if users are happy with any binding protocol, they can select a restriction interpretation instead. Dynamic specification of semantic interpretations enables service providers and users to flexibly express their capabilities and requirements.

3.3 CRI Models

Fig. 5 defines an ontology describing the semantics of service advertisements and requests using the Ontology Web Language (*OWL*). This ontology is similar to the latest *OWL-S* 1.0 [17] (*OWL-S* is an *OWL*-based Web service ontology).

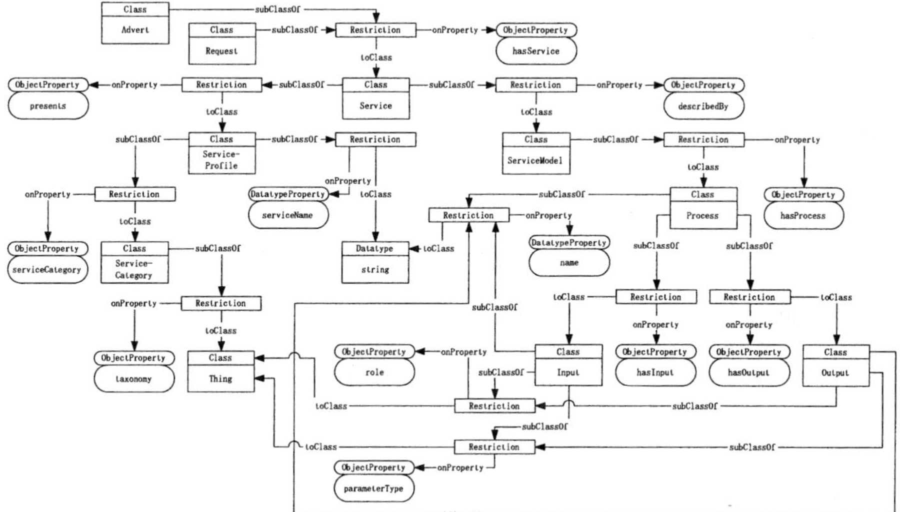

Fig. 5. The ontology for describing Web service advertisements and requests

The ontology presents a meta-model of Web service descriptions. Important concepts that participate in the satisfiability evaluation are specified using capacity interpretation or restriction interpretation. Each important concept is also assigned a specific satisfiability evaluation process. The specification of semantic interpretations and the assignment of satisfiability evaluation processes are described by means of *CRI* models.

Definition 9 (CRI model): *A Capacity-Restriction Interpretation (CRI) model, CRIM = (O, imap, emap), is a capability matching oriented structure, where:*

- *O is a Web service ontology (e.g., the one defined in Fig. 5) for describing the semantics of service advertisements and requests.*
- *imap: C → {capacity, restriction} is a partial function that relates a concept with a semantic interpretation (capacity interpretation or restriction interpretation). C is a concept defined in O.*

- *emap: C → {equivalence, plug-in, subsumption} is a partial function that relates a concept with a satisfiability evaluation process (equivalence evaluation, plug-in evaluation, or subsumption evaluation). C is a concept defined in O.*

Different satisfiability evaluation processes result in different impacts on capability matching. Subsumption evaluation requires that a concept from the request should subsume or equivalent to the corresponding concept from the advertisement (like the concept subsumption reasoning approach), while plug-in evaluation has a right opposite criterion (like the concept coverage comparing approach). Finally, equivalence evaluation asks for an equivalent relation between two involved concepts.

CRI models are used to describe Web service semantics, especially focusing on the specification of semantic interpretations and the assignment of satisfiability evaluation processes. Its significance lies in that it is the first time, to our best knowledge, to explicitly separate the assignment of satisfiability evaluation processes from the semantics representation of Web services, such that the satisfiability evaluation can be changed or improved independent of the service semantics representation. Many researches implicitly think that all concepts have capacity interpretations, and therefore, the satisfiability evaluation is fixed to the comparison of concept coverage. Some researches adopting *DLs* lack a flexible assignment mechanism for different satisfiability evaluation processes, only allowing concept subsumption reasoning. *CRI* models improve the matching accuracy by allowing dynamic specification of semantic interpretations and flexible assignment of satisfiability evaluation processes.

In a *CRI* model, the ontology, semantic interpretations and satisfiability evaluation processes are dynamically bound. The deciding of the most appropriate assignment of satisfiability evaluation processes mostly depends on the semantic interpretations of concepts involved, but the concept meanings and the related matching requirements also have their impacts. At present, our research suggests the following *CRI* model:

- *O*: The ontology defined in Fig. 5.
- *imap*: (1) *ServiceCategory*, *taxonomy*, ***Thing*** → capacity; (2) *Input*, *parameterType*, ***Thing*** → restriction; (3) *Output*, *parameterType*, ***Thing*** → restriction.
- *emap*: (1) *ServiceCategory*, *taxonomy*, ***Thing*** → plug-in; (2) *Input*, *role*, ***Thing*** → equivalence; (3) *Input*, *parameterType*, ***Thing*** → subsumption; (4) *Output*, *role*, ***Thing*** → equivalence; (5) *Output*, *parameterType*, ***Thing*** → subsumption.

Note that the bold literals are concepts under consideration. We use a prefix before each *Thing* concept to specify which *Thing* we are referring to (Fig. 5). Explanations for this suggested *CRI* model are given below.

The term *taxonomy* represents service category. A more general *taxonomy* means a more powerful service (e.g. *renting_vehicle* can satisfy *renting_car*). We specify *taxonomy* with a capacity interpretation. *parameterType* represents range restriction for an input/output parameter (e.g. we may need an *integer* input, or we plan to produce a *float* output). We specify both *parameterTypes* to have restriction interpretations.

The assignment of satisfiability evaluation processes has close relations with semantic interpretations specified by function *imap*. Realizing that the *taxonomy* has a capacity interpretation, we examine Table 3 with both c_1 and c_2 subject to capacity interpretations. We find that c_1 is satisfied by c_2 only when they have equivalent or subsumed relations. As such, concept *taxonomy* matches successfully only when the *taxonomy* from a service request could be plugged in or equivalent to the corresponding *taxonomy* from a service advertisement. Theorem 1 and Theorem 3 can infer this conclusion in a more convenient way. Therefore, we assign plug-in evaluation process to *taxonomy*. Similarly, we assign subsumption evaluation process to *parameterType*. This time we check Table 3 based on restriction interpretations of c_1 and c_2. Alternatively, we use Theorem 1 and Theorem 4 to infer it directly.

We have two more mappings about *role*. A *role* represents the business role of *Inputs* or *Outputs* of a Web service process. In the satisfiability evaluation, two *roles* from an advertisement and a request respectively should be similar or equal in meaning. We assign equivalence evaluation process to them.

3.4 Capability Matching Algorithm

The capability matching algorithm examines each advertisement in the Web service repository to find whether there is one fully or partially satisfying the given request. For each advertisement and request pair, the algorithm does the satisfiability evaluation based on the *ServiceProfile* and *ServiceModel* semantics (Fig. 5). For the *ServiceProfile* part, the algorithm performs plug-in evaluation for *taxonomy* as our *CRI* model suggests. But for the *ServiceModel* part, it is more complex.

A *ServiceModel* can have several *Process*es, and each *Process* may have multiple *Inputs*/*Outputs*. For full capability matching, the algorithm checks whether for each *Process* declared in the request, the advertisement can offer a satisfying *Process*. However, for partial capability matching, the criterion is reduced to whether there is at least one *Process* declared in the request such that the advertisement can offer a satisfying *Process*. Partial capability matching serves for service compositions.

No matter whether using full or partial capability matching, the algorithm checks all *Inputs* and *Outputs* in the *Process* pair being examined. A match is recognized when the following two conditions are met: (i) for each *Input* in the *Process* from the advertisement, there is a matched *Input* in the *Process* from the request (it guarantees that the request can provide sufficient *Inputs*); (ii) for each *Output* in the *Process* from the request, there is a matched *Output* in the *Process* from the advertisement (it guarantees that the advertisement can provide sufficient *Outputs*).

For the *Input*/*Output* part, the algorithm performs equivalence evaluation for *role* and subsumption evaluation for *parameterType*, following our *CRI* model. Due to space limitation, only the pseudo code for full capability matching algorithm is given below.

```
List capabilityMatching(req) {
  List result = new List();
  forall adv in advertisement_repository do {
    if checkProfile(getProfile(req), getProfile(adv)) == true
      && checkModel(getModel(req), getModel(adv)) == true
    then result.add(adv);
  }
  return result;
}
boolean checkProfile(reqProfile, advProfile) { ... }
boolean checkModel(reqModel, advModel) {
  forall reqProcess in getAllProcesses(reqModel) do {
    if not exists(advProcess) in getAllProcesses(advModel)
      such that checkProcess(reqProcess, advProcess) == true
```

```
      then return false;
    }
    return true;
  }
  boolean checkProcess(reqProcess, advProcess) {
    forall advInput in getAllInputs(advProcess) do {
      if not exists(reqInput) in getAllInputs(reqProcess
        such that checkInput(advInput, reqInput) == true
      then return false;
    }
    forall reqOutput in getAllOutputs(reqProcess) do { ... }
    return true;
  }
  boolean checkInput(advInput, reqInput) {
    if equivalent(getRole(advInput), getRole(reqInput)) == true
      && subsuming(getParamType(advInput),
      getParamType(reqInput)) == true
    then return true else return false;
  }
  boolean checkOutput(reqOutput, advOutput) { ... }
```

4 Implementation

Our Web service capability matching system adopts a three-tier architecture as illustrated in Fig. 6. *System Service Layer* provides four functionalities: advertisement browsing, advertisement/request consistency checking, request matching, and service composition. *Ontology Matching Layer* realizes ontology consistency checking and ontology structure matching for Web services based on *xlinkit* technology. *Satisfiability Evaluation Layer* is responsible for the satisfiability evaluation.

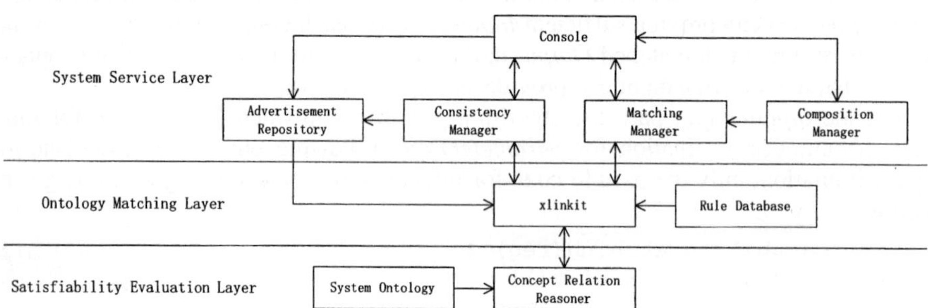

Fig. 6. The architecture of our Web service capability matching system

Detailed implementation considerations including the adaptation of *xlinkit* to service matching purposes are explained in [13]. The applications of *xlinkit* in the software engineering field can be found in [7][8][9].

5 Evaluation

Paolucci proposed four criteria in [11] for evaluating a service capability matching system: (i) the system should support semantics matching between advertisements and requests based on ontology; (ii) the system should minimize false positives and false negatives; (iii) the system should encourage service providers and users to be honest with their descriptions at the cost of paying the price of either not being matched or being matched inappropriately; and (iv) the matching process should be efficient.

Our matching system strives to satisfy all the four criteria. Firstly, the matching is based on an *OWL* ontology. The system can perform semantic inferences leading to the recognition of capability matching despite of their syntactic differences. Secondly, the use of *OWL* also supports accuracy: no matching is recognized when the satisfiability criteria cannot be met for a given advertisement and request pair. Thirdly, dishonesty behaviors (e.g. arbitrarily aggrandizing capabilities) by service providers and users will lead to no matching or inappropriate matching, which will harm them eventually. Finally, in order to increase performance, our system adopts an efficient *xlinkit* tool for performing ontology structure matching between advertisements and requests, and uses a special concept relation reasoner for the kernel satisfiability evaluation.

In addition, our matching system has two more features: (i) the use of the notation of capacity interpretation and restriction interpretation to adapt to different contexts for improving the accuracy of semantics representation; and (ii) utilization of *CRI* models to support flexible assignment of satisfiability evaluation processes for improving the accuracy of satisfiability evaluation.

6 Conclusions and Future Work

In this paper, we studied several Web service capability matching models, and classified their satisfiability evaluation techniques into three approaches. We analyzed their limitations under two semantic interpretations: restriction interpretation and capacity interpretation. To address these limitations, we proposed a unified Web service capability matching model, in which the satisfiability evaluation can be performed in a uniform way based on semantic interpretations of concepts. On the basis of the satisfiability result table and satisfiability theorems, we have proposed *CRI* models as a promising solution to the Web service capability matching problem. The corresponding algorithm can be implemented based on *xlinkit* technology.

At present, our implementation is subject to a communication bottleneck between the *Ontology Matching Layer* and the *Satisfiability Evaluation Layer*. We are working at various means to alleviate this problem such that our prototype could be refined into a practical semantic Web service tool. More features (e.g., satisfiability evaluation between capacity interpretation and restriction interpretation) will be incorporated in the refined *CRI* model. We also plan to extend the proposed semantic evaluation to the support of mobile and pervasive services [3][14].

Acknowledgements

This work was supported by a grant from the Research Grants Council of the Hong Kong Special Administrative Region, China, under Project HKUST6170/03E. The authors would also like to thank Min Ye (csmarco@cs.ust.hk) for his assistance with the system implementation.

References

1. F. Baader, D. Calvanese, D. McGuinness, D. Nardi, P. Patel-Schneider, *The Description Logic Handbook*, Cambridge University Press, 2002.
2. Xiang Gao, Jian Yang, Mike P. Papazoglou, The Capability Matching of Web Services, *Proceedings of the 4th International Symposium on Multimedia Software Engineering (MSE'02)*, Newport Beach, California, USA, Dec 2002.
3. Dickson K.W. Chiu, S.C. Cheung, Eleanna Kafeza and H.F. Leung, A Three-tier View-based Methodology for M-Services Adaptation, *IEEE Transactions on Systems, Man, and Cybernetics (Part A)*, 33 (6), November 2003, pp. 725-741.
4. Lei Li, Ian Horrocks, A Software Framework for Matchmaking Based on Semantic Web Technology, *Proceedings of the WWW 2003 Conference*, Budapest, May 2003, pp 331-339.
5. S.A. Mcllraith, T.C. Son, H. Zeng, Semantic Web Services, *IEEE Intell Sys 16*(2): 46-53.
6. Brahim Medjahed, et al, Composing Web Services on the Semantic Web, *VLDB Journal (2003) (Special Issue on the Semantic Web) 12*: 333-351.
7. C. Nentwich, W. Emmerich, A. Finkelstein, Consistency Management with Repair Actions, *Proceedings of the 25th International Conference on Software Engineering (ICSE'03)*, Portland, Oregon, USA, May 2003.
8. C. Nentwich, et al, xlinkit: A Consistency Checking and Smart Link Generation Service, *ACM Transactions on Internet Technology 2*(2): 151-185, May 2002.
9. C. Nentwich, W. Emmerich, A. Finkelstein, Static Consistency Checking for Distributed Specifications, *Proceedings of the 16th International Conference on Automated Software Engineering (ASE)*, pp 115-124, Coronado Island, CA, Nov 2001.
10. T.R. Payne, et al, Advertising and Matching DAML-S Service Descriptions, *Proceedings of the International Semantic Web Working Symposium*, Stanford, CA, July, 2001.
11. Massimo Paolucci, Takahiro Kawamura, Terry R. Payne, Katia Sycara, Semantic Matching of Web Services Capabilities, *Proceedings of the 1st International Semantic Web Conference*, Sardinia, Italy, June 2002, pp 318-332.
12. Katia Sycara, Mattheus Klusch, Seth Widoff, Janguo Lu, Dynamic Service Matchmaking among Agents in Open Information Environments, *ACM SIGMOD Record (Special Issue on Semantic Interoperability in Global Information System) 28(1)*: 47-53, 1999.
13. Chang Xu, S.C. Cheung, Xiangye Xiao, Capability Matching of Web Services, *Technical Report HKUST-CS04-08*, Department of Computer Science, Hong Kong University of Science and Technology, Clear Water Bay, Hong Kong, July 2004.
14. Chang Xu, S.C. Cheung, Cindy Lo, K.C. Leung, Jun Wei, Cabot: On the Ontology for the Middleware Support of Context-Aware Pervasive Applications, *Proceedings of the Workshop of Building Intelligent Sensor Networks (BISON'04)*, October 2004, Wuhan, China.
15. DAML+OIL Language, http://www.daml.org/2001/03/daml+oil-index.html, 2001.
16. DAML-S: Semantic Markup for Web Services, http://www.daml.org/services/daml-s/0.9/daml-s.html, May 2003.
17. OWL-S: Semantic Markup for Web Services, http://www.daml.org/services/owl-s/1.0/owl-s.html, Nov 2003.
18. W3C (2003) Simple Object Access Protocol (SOAP), http://www.w3.org/TR/soap.
19. W3C Web Service Description Language (WSDL), http://www.w3.org/TR/wsdl.
20. W3C Universal Description, Discovery, and Integration (UDDI), http://www.uddi.org.

Intentional Modeling to Support Identity Management*

Lin Liu[1] and Eric Yu[2]

[1]School of Software, Tsinghua University,
Beijing 100080, China
linliu@tsinghua.edu.cn

[2]Faculty of Information Studies, University of Toronto,
Toronto, M5S 3G6, Canada
yu@fis.utoronto.ca

Abstract. Identity management has arisen as a major and urgent challenge for internet-based communications and information services. Internet services involve complex networks of relationships among users and providers - human and automated - acting in many different capacities under interconnected and dynamic contexts. There is a pressing need for frameworks and models to support the analysis and design of complex social relationships and identities in order to ensure the effective use of existing protection technologies and control mechanisms. Systematic methods are needed to guide the design, operation, administration, and maintenance of internet services, in order to address complex issues of security, privacy, trust and risk, as well as interactions in functionality. All of these rely on sophisticated concepts for identity and techniques for identity management.

We propose using a requirements modeling framework GRL to facilitate identity management for Internet Services. Using this modeling approach, we are able to represent different types of identities, social dependencies between identity users and owners, service users and providers, and third party mediators. We may also analyze the strategic rationales of business players/stakeholders in the context of identity management. This modeling approach will help identity management technology vendors to provide customizable solutions, user organizations to form integrated identity management solution, system operators and administrators to accommodate changes, and policy auditors to enforce information protection principles, e.g., Fair Information Practice Principles.

1 Introduction

Networks, and businesses, are about relationships. As a result of the convergence brought about by IP technologies, numerous Internet services are now available on a common network. Internet services thus involve complex networks of relationships among users and providers - human and automated - acting in many different capacities under interconnected and dynamic contexts. A typical user may employ many services, concurrently or at different times. Many services are complementary and may invoke each other to achieve functionalities, while others could have adverse interactions. Thus, identity management has arisen as a major and urgent challenge for internet-based communications and information services.

Identity management concepts and technologies have been developed in the computer security area in a traditional internal enterprise context. They are currently being

---

* This research was conducted at the University of Toronto.

P. Atzeni et al. (Eds.): ER 2004, LNCS 3288, pp. 555–566, 2004.

extended to deal with the much more complex, open IP-network environment. While advances in fundamental technologies and mechanisms are crucial, there is a pressing need for frameworks and models to support the analysis and design of complex social relationships and identities in order to ensure the effective use of these technologies and mechanisms. Systematic methods are needed to guide the design, operation, administration, and maintenance of internet services, in order to address complex issues of security, privacy, trust and risk, as well as interactions in functionality. All of these rely on sophisticated concepts for agent identity and techniques for identity management. Thus, effective identity management is crucial for the successful transition to IP-based integrated communication and information services.

Based on our previous work on trust analysis [14], security and privacy requirements modeling [13,6], we propose using a modeling framework to facilitate the identity management for Internet services. By using this modeling approach, we are able to represent identities of different natures, describe social dependencies between identity users and owners, service users and providers, third party mediators. We may also analyze the strategic rationales of these business players/stakeholders in the setting of identity management. With the support of this modeling approach, vendors, who involve in the development and sale of identity management, privacy and security products and service, will be able to provide customizable solutions to different users. Organizations, who want to deploy identity management in its business settings, will be able to form an integrated solution that addresses all competing high-level concerns at the same time. System operators and administrators will be able to accommodate to changes in the system and environments and maintain the security levels at run time. Policy makers and auditors, who want to enforce certain principles, e.g., Fair Information Practice Principles, will be able to evaluate whether a proposed identity management solution complies with such intended principles by using various model analysis techniques.

In section 2, we introduce identity modeling structures based on GRL, illustrating the basic concepts and how they can help understand and analyze the basic settings of identity management. Section 3 provides a systematic approach for identity design, in which a general design model is given. Section 4 concludes the work and discusses related work and future directions.

2 Towards an Intentional Identity Management Modeling Framework

Identity management is a difficult process that can be facilitated by the use of technology. However, it is not just a matter a developing a piece of technology that people can use to manage their identities. There are already a wide range of products and mechanisms that can help – passwords, smart-cards, personal organizers, to name but a few. What is in much urgent need is a framework within which these products can fit into, and within which new products and services can be developed where required.

In this section and next, we use GRL modeling constructs to build a generic identity management meta-model, with which the requirements for identity management, the environment within which it must exist, and the architectural designs that have been proposed so far can be analyzed at an intentional level.

Although conventional entity-relationships modeling can provide the foundation for identity management and access control, it does not provide constructs to describe the intentions of ID owners and users. Thus, it is very hard to define and reason about the context and the motivation. As a consequence, the design of the identity management and access control solutions is hard to be related to the specific concerns and preferences of stakeholders, as well as operational constraints of a specific situation.

The Goal-oriented Requirements Language (GRL) [7] was originally developed to describe users' needs from a higher level of abstraction. It is an elaborated and evolving version of a strategic actors modeling framework *i** [12]. By using concepts such as actor, goal, softgoal, tasks, dependencies, resources, users' requirements and specific existing technology solutions can be explicitly related. Alternative solutions can be traded off based on their impacts to the requirements according to user set priorities.

2.1 Dealing with Identities in GRL: Actor, Agent, Role, and Position

The right hand side of Figure 1 shows the basic modeling constructs of GRL in terms of identity. Actor is a general concept that covers all kinds of intentional entities that is identifiable. However, not all identities were created equal. There are in fact at least three different types of identities, each having different attributes and each kind is likely to experience different adoption characteristics and market longevity.

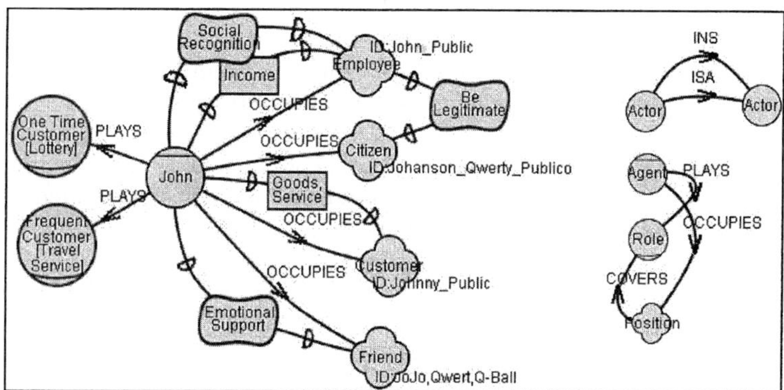

Fig. 1. Identities Modeling

These three kinds of IDs are defined as follows:

- ➢ Agent (***Personal***) Identity: is both timeless and unconditional. They are the true personal digital identity and are owned and controlled entirely by the individual, for his/her sole benefit. Agent identities exist for people as well as for devices & programs, with the exception that a device or program operates in Agent mode only, meaning, it is reflecting the identity and intention of another person who is controlling the device.
- ➢ Position (***Organizational***) Identity: is both conditional and temporary in its issuance to the individual. We typically denote these identities as being assigned or issued, and they typically refer to the person in the context of a business relationship. For example, nearly every 'identity' we have with a business is a position identity, our job title, our cell phone, our air miles card, our social insurance are all Position IDs. These IDs comprise the bulk of the digital identities today.

- Role (***Attribute***) Identity: is abstract. This type of identities speaks to the way in which companies aggregate customers into different buckets for the purposes of advertising or communicating. For example, an agent is either a 'frequent buyer' or a 'one time customer' etc. Role ids are typically based upon the agents' demographics or behavior in their interactions with business. The entire CRM market caters to such identities. Role IDs usually has specific attributes or preferences attached.

Also shown on the diagram are the different types of actor association links, amongst which, INS is used when an actor is an instance of another actor (class). ISA will be used if one actor (class) is the subclass of another actor (class). Plays will be used to connect an agent with the abstract roles it is playing. Occupies will be used to relate an agent with his/her official occupations represented by a position. Covers is used when one position is associated with multiple roles. With these links, we will be able to create a network structure for the players involved in a system with these links. This forms the basis of our identity management modeling framework.

In traditional identity management, the concept of role is most widely understood in the context of role-based access control (RBAC) [10]. Access privileges on a system are grouped into roles, and users are attached to roles as a convenient mechanism to manage their privileges.

In contrast, we are more interested in reasoning about a system entity's intentions and capabilities. In managing identity across multiple systems, users may play multiple roles, each involving different intentions and implying different capabilities. Beyond addressing issues of user classification, role definition and conflict resolution, we are able to explore system vulnerabilities and opportunities in the identity management context.

The left hand side of Figure 1 shows a typical set of related user identities. It allows for many different types of systems and relationships, depending upon the context. This type of model explores the implications and relationships of the multiple IDs used by an individual (John). From this example, we know that John has needs as a physical entity (*Agent*), he obtains different IDs/names for his different organizational positions in order to satisfy the corresponding needs. His name as an Employee is "John_Public", Citizen ID is "Johanson_Qwerty_Publico", while Customer ID is "Johnny_Public". As a Friend, he has many nicknames, such as, JoJo, Qwert, and Q-ball [8]. Sometimes, an ID is needed when applying for other ID e.g., to become an employee, he has to be a legitimate citizen first. In the meantime, he is identified by Lottery Service as One Time Customer, while Travel Service as Frequent Customer. Linking those identities would have to be done based on certain predetermined principle: always ask for the consent of the individual, through a trusted authority, link within a circle of trust, etc.

2.2 Proceed with a General Social Dependency Model of Identity Management – Why and How Do We Manage Identity?

In the Internet service setting, a fundamental relationship between interactive parties is the user-provider relationship. In the social dependency model in Figure 2, the user of an Internet service and the provider of the service are represented as two position actors: User[Service] and Provider[Service]. The two actors depend on each other to fulfill their own goals. First of all, the user depends on the provider for a service, which is represented as a goal dependency: Be Provided [Service]. In the other direction, the provider depends on the user's legitimacy as a user of the service, which is shown as a softgoal dependency Legitimacy [User [Service]]. The user may also prefer that the service be personalized, which is modeled as another softgoal dependency - Be Personalized [Service]. These two softgoal dependency relationships are the major motivating requirements for identity management.

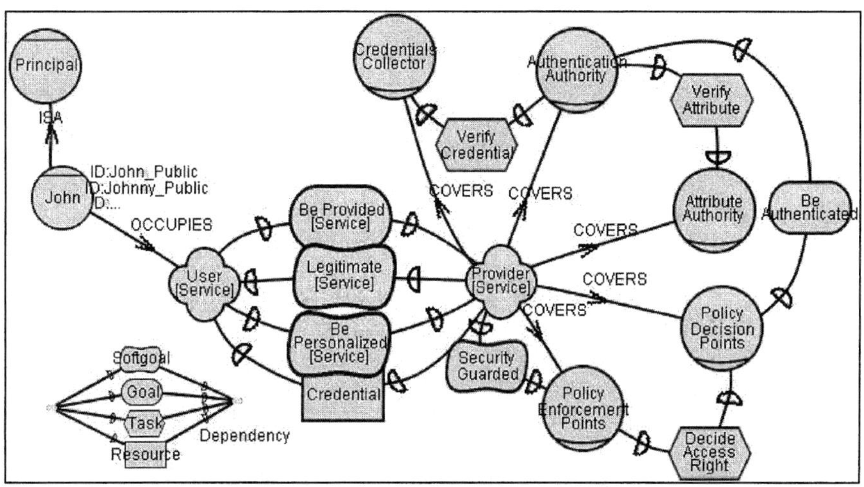

Fig. 2. A Generic Social Dependency (SD) model

In GRL, dependencies are distinguished into four different types. As Goal dependency represents an abstract functional requirement of one actor imposed on another actor. For example, Be Provided [Service] is a functional goal dependency. Softgoal dependency represents an abstract non-functional requirement. Be Personalized[Service] is modeled as non-functional dependency since it doesn't affect the system's normal functioning, but they will have some subtle, indirect effects to the business. Other dependency relationships are task dependency, through which the depending party delegates a course of action to the depended party, and resource dependency, which means the depending party asks for the delivery of certain information entity or business asset from the depended party. Resource is data contained in an information system, or a service provided by a system, or a system capability such as processing power or communication bandwidth, or an item of system equipment, or a facility that houses system operations and equipment.

Figure 2 illustrates some of the features of generic identity management architectures [8, 9]. Here each User is a Principal, who can have multiple Credentials, which can be transferred or presented to establish a claimed principal identity. Principal uses Credential to sign-on to Credentials Collector, who Verifies Credential. Authentication Authority performs authentication of a principal at a particular time using a particular method of authentication, e.g. password, token, smart card, biometrics, etc. Attribute Authority verifies Attribute about a principal, based upon to-be-determined inputs. Examples of attributes are: group, role, title, contract code, etc. Policy Decision Point makes decision as a result of evaluating the user's identity, the requested operation, and the requested resource in light of applicable security policies. Policy Enforcement

Point enforces the decision made by access decision function upon each access control request. In this single service setting, all of the roles other than Principal are played by the service provider. So the dependencies between the roles are likely to be dependable. However, this is not always the case. In the multiple service case to be discussed in section 2.3, the dependability of roles needs to be evaluated.

2.3 Continue with a Social Dependency Model on Single Sign-On

Using the generic model developed above, we now consider a more complex situation. One of the most demanded features in identity management is Single Sign-On. In this kind of setting, a user authenticates with one Web service provider, then, is able to use a secured resource from another service provider, without further authentication.

Using GRL, we are able to explicitly describe what the social dependency relationships between different system entities are, so that configurations of the future system can be explored and traded off. Figure 3 is a representation of one possible mode to support Single Sign-On. In this case, the travel service provider (travel.com) will only provide discount ticket to an employee of company.com. Thus, each time it receives a service request, it will pull the authentication information from the Employer (played by company.com) based on IDs provided by the User (John). In this scenario, company.com acts as a Credentials Collector, Authentication Authority, and Attribute Authority. John is the Principal. Travel.com plays Policy Decision Point and Policy Enforcement Point. Comparing to the single service situation, there is distributed trust between Travel.com and Company.com. In other words, Travel.com has to trust Company.com to authenticating the customer.

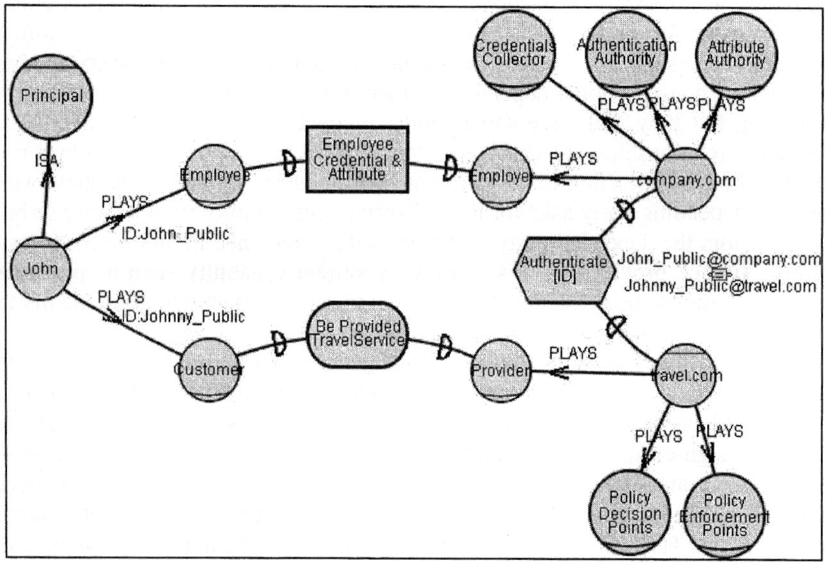

Fig. 3. Single Sign-On: A Social Dependency model

The key distinction of such a model from conventional ones is that from the distribution of roles, one can infer distribution of trust and dependency relationships. A special case is when multiple services are provided by different branches of the same company which trust each other, e.g. Bell residential phone service, Bell wireless phone service, Bell Sympatico high-speed internet service, and Bell ExpressVu satellite TV can share customer information with each other since they are operating within the same trusted jurisdiction.

A variation on the above Single Sign-On model is that a third party security service provider (e.g., Microsoft .Net Passport, Novell DigitalMe) provides authentication assertions for the user. In this case, Microsoft as a centralized intermediary has many competitive advantages in terms of customer management (or control). At the same time, it also creates a vulnerable point of security, risk of privacy infringement, and issues of scalability due to its centralized nature.

2.4 Reasoning Further upon the Generic Model – Revealing Potential Conflict of Interests

Identity management as a business model and business enabler is fairly new and unproven. On the one hand, it may bring great opportunities to organizations that own information, and the customers and partners who want to share such information. This also highlights the importance of adhering to emerging privacy standards and data regulations. Identity is at the core of online business and data transactions. It is interwoven into most business processes, including granting access to information and systems, enabling customer relationships managements, and driving relationships with business partners and suppliers. Besides just presenting credentials for authenticated access to systems and services, an identity includes attributes that make for more targeted and productive use of the services. However, unwanted scenarios such as customer lock-in and privacy violations may also happen. We want to analyze these different viewpoints and conflicts of interest as well.

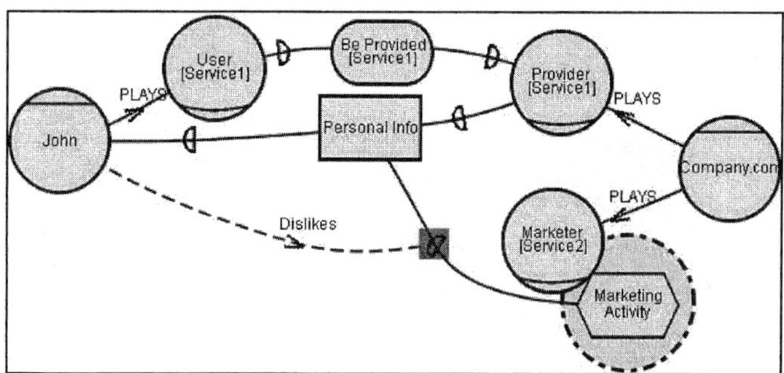

Fig. 4. A SD model revealing potential conflict-of-interest

Figure 4 shows that company.com has obtained the Personal Info of John through its capacity as a Provider [Service1]. Being a Marketer [Service2] in the meantime, company.com may put this information into secondary use and recommend new services to its current customer. This is a beneficial identity management scenario from the service provider's viewpoint. However, this may be frustrating or threatening to customers who do not want to be the target of marketing activity. We represent such side effects with a dotted link with a textual label (e.g. *Dislike*). The focal point is highlighted. A focal point can either be a link or an element, where the inconsistencies between different viewpoints, or conflicts of interest between different agents come to the surface.

3 Design for Identity and Access Management – Towards a Systematic Approach

In designing an identity management systems, some basic questions need to be answered:

- Who is involved? i.e., what are the types of users the organization will manage?
- What are the objectives of the stakeholders? i.e., what are the high-level concerns of the system players and system designers, particularly, the non-functional ones?
- What are the resources/services to be accessed and controlled?
- What kinds of ID are needed?
- What kinds of ID management procedure or mechanism are needed?
- What are the implications of each of these specific ID management solutions towards the high-level concerns?

3.1 What Does the Stakeholder Have in Mind? – Strategic Rationales Modeling

By building a social dependency model, we are able to analyze the inter-actor relationships relevant to identity management. However, to better understand each stakeholder's requirements, a strategic rationale (SR) model such as the one shown in Figure 5 provides the desired details.

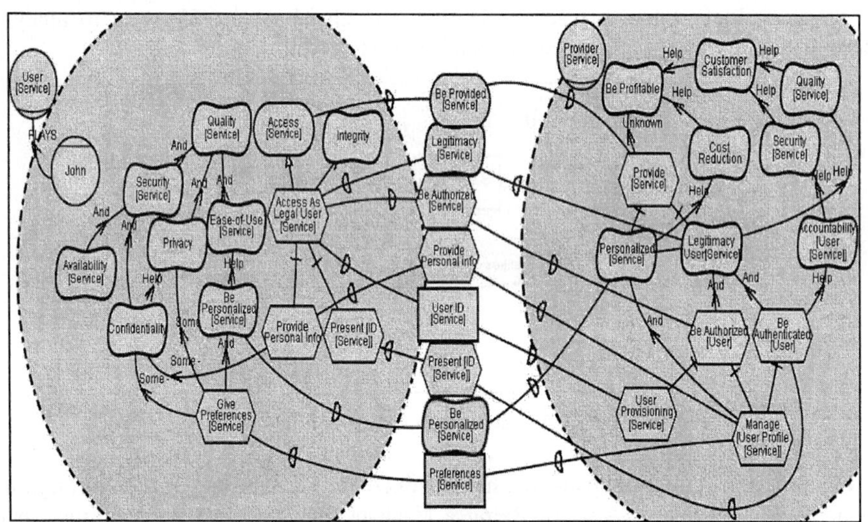

Fig. 5. A Strategic Rationale model – Stakeholders' intentions

In a strategic rationale model, an actor's high-level concerns are elaborated and refined into lower-level goals, operable tasks or concrete information entities. For example, an agent John who *plays* service user (User[Service]) has the following requirements: access the service (Access[Service]), and the service is of good quality (Quality[Service]). Furthermore, quality of service can be elaborated into concerns on Security, Respect to Privacy, and Ease-of-Use, which are further refined into Availability, Confidentiality, and Be Personalized. On the functional side, Access[Service] is operationalized into the tasks to be performed by the user: Provide Personal Info, and Present [ID[Service]]. In order to provide personalized service, John needs to Give Preferences for the desired Service.

Similar analysis happens on the provider side. This refinement process goes on until sufficient information is obtained. Thus, the previously isolated external dependencies in the SD model can be interconnected through the hierarchical goal refinement structures within the actor boundaries of the SR model.

3.2 Competing Non-functional Requirements and Alternative Solutions

Having understood the concerns of the agents involved, we may now begin to look for design solutions. In Figure 6, we combine the requirements of the service user and the provider. Knowledge from a system designer viewpoint are also added – for example, knowledge about the various building blocks of an identity management system for Internet service. In the figure we see that, there are competing non-functional requirements: Security, User Productivity, Privacy, Cost Reduction, Accountability, Ease-of-use, and so on.

The major modeling constructs used include goals, softgoals and tasks. They are linked together with means-ends links (—▷—), decompositions links (—+), and contribution links (→). In the design modeling setting, means-ends are used to indicate alternative techniques, while decompositions are used to identify necessary components. Contributions are used to represent the impacts to a softgoal. An impact can be positive or negative; partial, sufficient, or unknown.

In figure 5, building blocks of identity management systems are modeled. This kind of knowledge is usually obtained from domain experts [3]. To generate a satisficing design, the impacts of the chosen solution to these non-functional requirements represented with softgoal need to be evaluated and traded-off. Here we use a qualitative approach to represent and propagate the impacts across the graph. Details about the evaluation algorithm are in [2]. Then by combining the favorable alternatives from each design decision making process, we obtain a design blueprint.

4 Discussion and Conclusion

We have outlined an approach for modeling and analyzing identity management issues. The approach is based on an intentional and social ontology that is centered on strategic actor relationships. This ontology allows us to go beyond entity relationships and mechanistic behavior, to deal with the opportunistic behavior of strategic actors. Interdependencies among actors place constraints on their freedom of action. Nevertheless, constraints can be violated due to agent autonomy (unlike in mechanistic systems) as in the conflict-of-interest example. Strategic actors seek to achieve goals (hard and soft) by obtaining new identities from service providers, taking into account the opportunities and vulnerabilities arising from various dependency relationships, as illustrated in the generic identity modeling example.

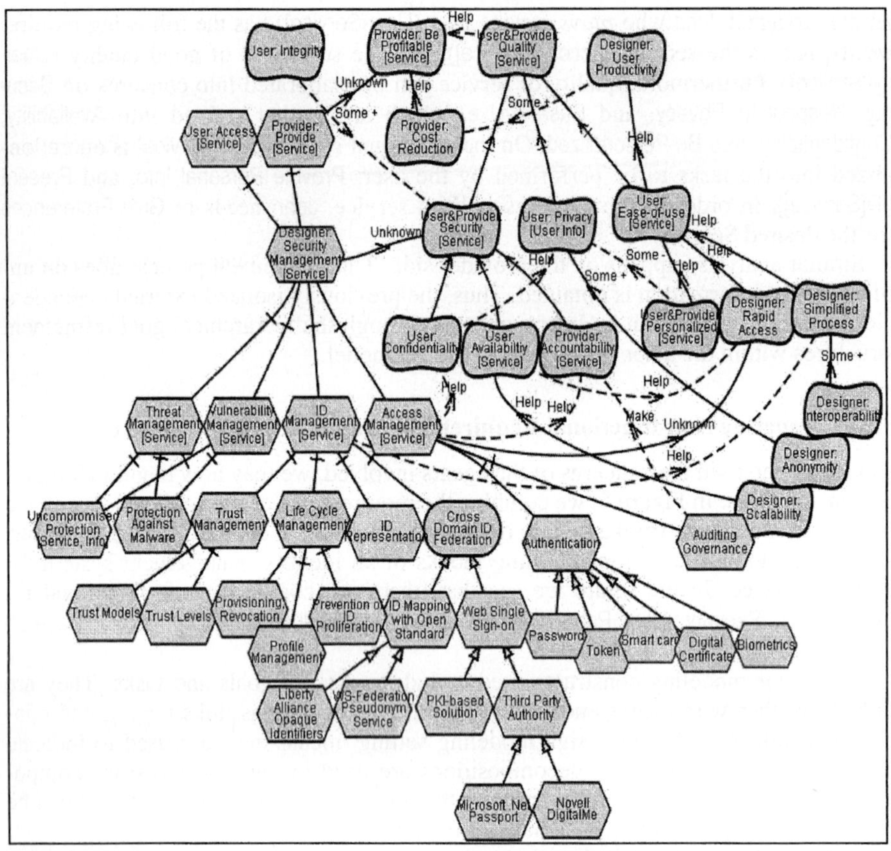

Fig. 6. Requirements and building blocks of identity management

Our approach is complementary to existing frameworks and techniques for identity management. Recent approaches have emphasized taking a systematic and holistic view towards identity and security management processes [11] and the business value that identity management can bring [1, 3]. There is also increasing use of new technology and business models, e.g., single sign-on, third-party intermediaries in authentication or trust [1]. Our approach emphasizes the systematic analysis of relationships among strategic actors and their intentions by extending conceptual modeling techniques. It supports the exploration and management of structural alternatives, based on a balanced consideration of all competing requirements, thus complementing the various point solutions of recent identity management techniques.

Identity management is increasingly connected with other activities in enterprise management. The strategic modeling approach provides a way of linking identity related analysis to business strategy analysis and technology analysis. An intentional conceptual modeling approach can thus provide a unifying framework for enterprise information systems, supporting decision making and the management of change across technical system development, business development, and identity and security management [16].

In information systems and software engineering research, organizational modeling has been of interest, often in connection with requirements engineering. Goal-oriented approaches have been used in this context, and agents or actors are often part of the modeling ontology [4, 5]. However, the GRL approach is distinctive in its treatment of agents/actors as being strategic [12], and thus readily adaptable to the identity management analysis domain illustrated in this paper. A related technique was used earlier to model intellectual property in a business analysis setting [14].

While this paper has outlined some basic modeling concepts, much remains to be done. There is much potential in the synergy between strategic modeling and the foundational principles in conceptual modeling. For example, in analyzing the implications of an identity, one would like to model the inter-relatedness among their subject matters. The interaction between intentional concepts and relationships (e.g., strategic actors, intentional dependencies) and non-intentional ones (e.g., processes, information assets, time, etc.) need to be detailed. Libraries of reusable design knowledge about identity management would be very helpful during modeling and analysis. These are topics of ongoing research.

Acknowledgements

Financial support from Bell Canada University Labs and the Natural Sciences and Engineering Research Council of Canada are gratefully acknowledged.

References

1. Buell, D.A., Sandu, R. eds. Special Issue on: Identity Management. IEEE Internet Computing, November/December, 2003. pp.26-52.
2. Chung, L., Nixon, B. A., Yu, E. and Mylopoulos, J. Non-Functional Requirements in Software Engineering. Kluwer Academic Publishers, 2000.
3. Damiani, E., Vimercati, S.D.C., Damarati, P. Managing Multiple and Dependable Identities. IEEE Internet Computing, November/December, 2003. pp.29-37.
4. Gans, G., M. Jarke, S. Kethers, G. Lakemayer, E. Ellrich, C. Funken. Requirements Modeling for Organization Networks: A (Dis-)Trust –Based Approach, in Int. Symp. Requirements Engineering, 2001.
5. Lamsweerde, A. Requirements Engineering in Year 2000 – A Research Perspective, in Proceeding of 22nd International Conference on Software Engineering(ICSE 2000), Limerick, ACM Press, 2000. Also available at: //ftp.info.ucl.ac.be/pub/publi/2 000/icse2000-avl.pdf.
6. Liu, L., E. Yu and J. Mylopoulos. Security and Privacy Requirements Analysis within a Social Setting. Proceedings of International Conference on Requirements Engineering (RE'03), Monterey, California, September 2003. pp.151-161.
7. Liu, L., E. Yu. Designing Information Systems in Social Context: A Goal and Scenario Modelling Approach. Information Systems, Vol.29, No.2. 2003, Elsevier Ltd. pp.187-203.
8. The National Electronic Commerce Coordinating Council. Identity Management: A White Paper. Available at: http://www.ec3.org/Downloads/2002/id_management.pdf.
9. OASIS SAML 1.0 Domain Model. Available at: http://www.oasis-open.org/committees/security/docs/draft-sstc-use-domain-05.pdf.
10. Sandhu, R. S., Coyne, E.J., Feinstein, H.L., Youman, C.E. Role-Based Access Control Models. IEEE Computer, Vol.29, No.2, Feburary 1996. pp. 38-47.
11. Schneier, B., Beyond Fear, Thinking Sensibly About Security in an Uncertain World. Copernicus Books, 2003.

12. Yu, E. Towards Modeling and Reasoning Support for Early-Phase Requirements Engineering. Proceedings of the 3rd IEEE International Symposium on Requirements Engineering (RE'97) Jan. 6-8, 1997, Washington D.C., USA. pp. 226-235.
13. Yu, E., Cysneiros, L. Designing for Privacy and Other Competing Requirements. 2nd Symposium on Requirements Engineering for Information Security (SREIS'02). Raleigh, North Carolina, October 16, 2002.
14. Yu, E. and Liu, L. Modeling Trust for System Design Using the *i** Strategic Actors Framework. In: Trust in Cyber-Societies - Integrating the Human and Artificial Perspectives. R. Falcone, M. Singh, Y.H. Tan, eds. LNAI-2246. Springer, 2001. pp.175-194.
15. Yu, E., Liu, L., Li, Y. Modeling Strategic Actor Relationships to Support Intellectual Property Management. 20th International Conference on Conceptual Modeling (ER-2001). Yokohama, Japan, November 27-30, 2001. LNCS 2224 Spring Verlag. pp. 164-178.
16. Yu, E. Information Systems. In: Practical Handbook of Internet Computing, M.P. Singh, ed. CRC Press. 2004.

WUML: A Web Usage Manipulation Language for Querying Web Log Data*

Qingzhao Tan, Yiping Ke, and Wilfred Ng

Department of Computer Science
The Hong Kong University of Science and Technology,
Hong Kong
{ttqqzz,keyiping,wilfred}@cs.ust.hk

Abstract. In this paper, we develop a novel Web Usage Manipulation Language (WUML) which is a declarative language for manipulating Web log data. We assume that a set of trails formed by users during the navigation process can be identified from Web log files. The trails are dually modelled as a transition graph and a navigation matrix with respect to the underlying Web topology. A WUML expression is executed by transforming it into Navigation Log Algebra (NLA), which consists of the sum, union, difference, intersection, projection, selection, power and grouping operators. As real navigation matrices are sparse, we perform a range of experiments to study the impact of using different matrix storage schemes on the performance of the NLA.

1 Introduction

The topology of a Web site is constructed according to the designers' conceptual view of the Web information. There may be a mismatch, however, between the users' behavior and the expectation of the designers. Therefore, we propose and develop a query language on Web log data. We assume that the Web usage information can be generated from log files through a cleaning process [11, 4]. Based on our earlier work in [11], we model a collection of user sessions on a given Web topology as a weighted directed graph, called a *transition graph*. A corresponding navigation matrix is then computed using knowledge of the underlying Web topology.

Herein, we extend the four basic operators of `sum`, `union`, `intersection` and `difference` from [11] on *valid navigation matrices* to a more comprehensive set of operators: `sum`, `union`, `intersection`, `difference`, `projection`, `selection`, `power` and `grouping`. We call these operators collectively the Navigation Log Algebra (the NLA). Navigation matrices generated from real Web log files are sparse. We therefore carry out a spectrum of experiments to study the performances of the NLA operators on synthetically generated navigation matrices. The results indicate that the storage schemes affect the performances differently.

* This work is supported in part by grants from the Research Grant Council of Hong Kong, Grant Nos DAG01/02.EG05 and HKUST6185/02E.

P. Atzeni et al. (Eds.): ER 2004, LNCS 3288, pp. 567–581, 2004.

To gain better insight regarding navigation behavior from the log data, we further develop a novel declarative language termed *Web Usage Manipulation Language* (*WUML*), which allows users to specify queries on navigation matrices. The WUML expressions are implemented as a sequence of NLA operations. Using WUML, a Web designer is able to better understand navigation details over the site structure based on the analysis of querying results. For example, the overall usage of the site can be generated by a WUML query that combines all user categories, while the deviation analysis can be generated by a WUML query that finds out the contrast between the designer's expectation and user navigation behaviors. WUML also enables the designers to view the overall performance of a set of closely-related pages using `grouping`.

Our Contributions. (1) We define the NLA on navigation matrices, which are a comprehensive set of operators of `sum`, `union`, `intersection`, `difference`, `projection`, `selection`, `power` and `grouping`. (2) We propose a validation algorithm called VALID, which is able to preserve the validity of the navigation matrix when executing some of the operations. Essentially, this is to avoid isolated sets of pages happening in NLA operations. (3) We develop a novel declarative language WUML on navigation matrices. WUML can be transformed into a corresponding sequence of operations. (4) We study three different storage schemes to deal with the sparse nature in navigation matrices. By carrying out a spectrum of experiments on synthetic Web log data, we clarify the effects of storage schemes on individual NLA operators.

Related Work. There has been a lot of research related to applying data mining techniques on the Web log data. A mass of Web usage mining tools [1,2,5, 14,13,7] have been developed to help the designers improve Web sites, attract visitors, or provide users with a personalized and adaptive service. Several mining languages, such as WUM's MINT [13] and WEBMINER's query language [7], are also proposed for these objectives. However, these languages are based on mining techniques for association rules and sequential patterns. Our WUML is developed to specify a query which is sufficiently expressive to query log data represented as a transition graph, or equivalently a navigation matrix.

The rest of this paper is organized as follows. In Sect. 2, we give preliminary definitions related to Web usage analysis. NLA for the navigation matrices is discussed in Sect. 3. We propose WUML and discuss the transformation of a WUML expression into an NLA expression in Sect. 4. In Sect. 5, three storage schemes for navigation matrices are introduced. A set of experimental results on the NLA using different storage schemes are analyzed in Sect. 6. Finally, we give our concluding remarks in Sect. 7.

2 Preliminaries

A Web topology W is defined as a directed graph, in which each node represents one Web page and each directed link represents the hyperlink between pages. A user session is a sequence of page requests from the same user such that no two consecutive requests are separated by more than X minutes. In a user session, two consecutive pages should have a link in the Web topology.

A transition graph is a weighted directed graph constructed from W by adding two special pages: the starting page S and the finishing page F. Given a set of user sessions, we define the weight of the link from S to any other page as the number of times that the page is first requested. Similarly, the weight of the link from any page to F is the number of times that the page is last requested. As for links between any other two pages in W, called *internal links*, the weight is the number of times that two pages appear as consecutive pages in user sessions. We dually model a transition graph as a *navigation matrix* [11]. A navigation matrix is defined as the *adjacency matrix* of a transition graph. A one-to-one correspondence exists between transition graphs and navigation matrices.

Now, we discuss the notion of validity of a transition graph. A node in a transition graph is said to be *balanced* if the total weights of its in-links equal to the total weights of its out-links. And the *node degree* is the total weights of in-links and out-links. A transition graph is said to be *valid* if it satisfies the following four conditions. (1) In-degree of S, out-degree of F and the link weight from S to F are zero; (2) Every internal link having non-zero weight is also a link in the Web topology, (Note that this excludes self-looping in the graph.); (3) Every node except S and F should be balanced; (4) Every node which has non-zero degree should be reachable from S.

The validity of the navigation matrix is equivalent to the validity of the transition graph. That is, a navigation matrix is said to be valid if and only if its corresponding transition graph is valid. As we can see in the subsequent sections, after execution of some NLA operators, such as `difference`, `intersection` and `power`, the output navigation matrix may not be valid. There may be nodes with non-zero degree which cannot be reached from S. However, the validity in outcomes is essential since it ensures that the operations continue in a procedural manner. It is thus necessary to guarantee the output navigation matrix is valid.

We outline an algorithm, VALID, as shown in Algorithm 1, which employs DFS strategy, to keep the validity of a navigation matrix. The input of the algorithm is a navigation matrix whose nodes are balanced. Using VALID, connected components of the transition graph can be found. If there is more than one component, we add a link from S to the root of that component and also a link from that root to F to keep it balanced. The output matrix is then valid since all pages with non-zero degree are reachable from S.

Note that VALID needs three extra arrays (namely, color, parent and tag), each with size of $n+2$, the space complexity is $O(n)$. The time determining steps are the two nested loops over $n+2$ in Lines 1 and 3 in Algorithm 1, which takes $O(n^2)$ time. As for the execution of the DFS-VISIT procedure, it takes $O(E)$ time, where E is the number of edges in the transition graph corresponding to the input navigation matrix. In the worst case, E equals to $(n+2)^2$. To conclude, the time complexity for running VALID is $O(n^2)$.

3 Navigation Log Algebra

In this section, we define the Navigation Log Algebra (the NLA). For more illustrated examples on using some operations, the readers may refer to [11].

Algorithm 1 VALID Algorithm

Input: Matrix M with $n+2$ dimensions

```
VALID(M)
FOR all 0 ≤ i ≤ n+1                                 //Initialization
    DO color[i] := WHITE; parent[i] := NIL; tag[i] := 0;
        FOR all 0 ≤ j ≤ n+1
            DO IF M[i][j] != 0
                THEN tag[i] := 1; break;//tag indicates pages with non-zero degree
tag[0] := 1;               //Make sure DFS starts from page S
FOR all 0 ≤ i ≤ n+1                                 //DFS: Find connected components
    DO IF tag[i] = 1 and color[i] = WHITE
        THEN DFS-VISIT(i);
FOR all 1 ≤ i ≤ n
    DO IF tag[i] = 1 and parent[i] = NIL                //Ensure validity by adding
        THEN M[0][i] += 1; M[i][n+1] += 1;  //links from S and links to F
DFS-VISIT(i)            //Recursively search to form connected components
color[i] := GRAY
FOR all 0 ≤ j ≤ n+1
    DO IF M[i][j] != 0 and color[j] = WHITE
        THEN parent[j] := i; DFS-VISIT(j);
```

Output: The valid matrix of M

Sum. The sum of two navigation matrices M_1 and M_2, denoted as $M_1 + M_2$, is defined as a navigation matrix M_3 such that, for all $i, j \in \{0, \ldots, n+1\}$, $(a_{ij})_3 = (a_{ij})_1 + (a_{ij})_2$. Actually, sum is exactly the generic sum of two matrices. Trivially, the outcome M_3 remains to be valid.

Union. The union of two navigation matrices M_1 and M_2, denoted as $M_1 \bigcup M_2$, is defined as a navigation matrix M_3 such that, for all $i, j \in \{1, \ldots, n\}$, $(a_{ij})_3 = max((a_{ij})_1, (a_{ij})_2)$; $(a_{0j})_3 = max((a_{0j})_1, (a_{0j})_2) + max(0, \sum_{k=1}^{n+1} max((a_{jk})_1, (a_{jk})_2) - \sum_{k=0}^{n} max((a_{kj})_1, (a_{kj})_2))$; $(a_{i(n+1)})_3 = max((a_{i(n+1)})_1, (a_{i(n+1)})_2) + max(0, \sum_{k=0}^{n} max((a_{ki})_1, (a_{ki})_2) - \sum_{k=1}^{n+1} max((a_{ik})_1, (a_{ik})_2))$; and all other elements are zero. For union, we do not need to use VALID because the max function used in union is able to maintain the reachability of nodes from S.

Difference. The difference of two navigation matrices M_1 and M_2, denoted as $M_1 - M_2$, is defined as a navigation matrix M_3 such that, for all $i, j \in \{1, \ldots, n\}$, $(a_{ij})_3 = max(0, ((a_{ij})_1 - (a_{ij})_2))$; $(a_{0j})_3 = max(0, ((a_{0j})_1 - (a_{0j})_2)) + max(0, \sum_{k=1}^{n+1} max(0, ((a_{jk})_1 - (a_{jk})_2)) - \sum_{k=0}^{n} max(0, ((a_{kj})_1 - (a_{kj})_2)))$; $(a_{i(n+1)})_3 = max(0, ((a_{i(n+1)})_1 - (a_{i(n+1)})_2)) + max(0, \sum_{k=0}^{n} max(0, ((a_{ki})_1 - (a_{ki})_2)) - \sum_{k=1}^{n+1} max(0, ((a_{ik})_1 - (a_{ik})_2)))$; and all other elements are zero. As the result may be invalid, we run VALID after executing the above operation.

Intersection. The intersection of two navigation matrices M_1 and M_2, denoted as $M_1 \bigcap M_2$, is defined as a navigation matrix M_3 such that, for all $i, j \in \{1, \ldots, n\}$,$(a_{ij})_3 = min((a_{ij})_1, (a_{ij})_2)$; $(a_{0j})_3 = min((a_{0j})_1, (a_{0j})_2) + max(0, \sum_{k=1}^{n+1} min((a_{jk})_1, (a_{jk})_2) - \sum_{k=0}^{n} min((a_{kj})_1, (a_{kj})_2))$; $(a_{i(n+1)})_3 =$

$min((a_{i(n+1)})_1, (a_{i(n+1)})_2) + max(0, \sum_{k=0}^{n} min((a_{ki})_1, (a_{ki})_2) - \sum_{k=1}^{n+1} min((a_{ik})_1, (a_{ik})_2))$; and all other elements are zero. We run the VALID algorithm on the intermediate answer from executing `intersection`.

Projection. The `projection` of one navigation matrix M_1, denoted as $\prod_P(M_1)$ where P is a set of Web pages, is defined as a navigation matrix M_3 such that, for all $P_i, P_j \in P$, $(a_{ij})_3 = (a_{ij})_1$; $(a_{0j})_3 = (a_{0j})_1 + \sum_{k=1,\ldots,n; P_k \notin P}(a_{kj})_1$; $(a_{i(n+1)})_3 = (a_{i(n+1)})_1 + \sum_{k=1,\ldots,n; P_k \notin P}(a_{ik})_1$; and all other elements are zero. `Projection` does not need the VALID algorithm.

Selection. The `selection` of one navigation matrix M_1, denoted as $\sigma_{\theta x}(M_1)$, where θ is a comparator such as $>$, $<$, $>=$, $<=$, or $=$, and x is a positive integer, is defined as a navigation matrix M_3 such that, for all $i, j \in \{1, \ldots, n\}$, $if(a_{ij})_1 \theta x, (a_{ij})_3 = (a_{ij})_1$; $(a_{0j})_3 = (a_{0j})_1 + \sum_{k=1,\ldots,n;(a_{kj})_1 \bar{\theta} x}(a_{kj})_1$; $(a_{i(n+1)})_3 = (a_{i(n+1)})_1 + \sum_{k=1,\ldots,n;(a_{ik})_1 \bar{\theta} x}(a_{ik})_1$; and all other elements are zero. The notation $\bar{\theta}$ denotes the complement of θ (e.g. $\bar{\theta}$ is "<=" when θ is ">"). The output is already valid, so it does not need to be processed through VALID.

Power. The `power` of one navigation matrix M_1, denoted as $(M_1)^x$, where x is a non-negative integer, is defined as a navigation matrix M_3 such that $M_3 = 0_{(n+2)\times(n+2)}$ if $x = 0$; $M_3 = M_1$ if $x = 1$; and $M_3 = M_1 \cdot (M_1)^{x-1}$ if $x \geq 2$. Herein, the operator "$\cdot$" denotes the multiplication of two matrices. The result M_3 may not be valid, since we need to ignore the possible non-zero values in its diagonal and at $(a_{0(n+1)})_3$. We should maintain the pages balance and run VALID. The semantics for non-zero entry $(a_{ij})_3$ in $M_3 = (M_1)^x$ is that there is a trail from P_i to P_j with the length of x in M_1. If $(a_{ij})_3$ is large, it indicates that many users have traversed from P_i to P_j. If there is no link from P_i to P_j in the Web topology, the designer may add this link to facilitate better navigation.

Grouping. The `grouping` of a navigation matrix M_1, denoted as $G_P(M_1)$, where P is a set of pages in W, returns a navigation matrix M_3 which is an aggregated view of M_1. `Grouping` groups all the pages in P as a single page in M_3 by ignoring the links within the pages in P and adding up the weight of links from and to the outside pages, respectively. By grouping a set of pages which are closely related in semantics, we are able to understand the navigation in terms of *information units* [9]. Our approach is to view `grouping` as an aggregation of log information. Therefore, we do not define ungrouping here, since ungrouping introduces uncertainty in log information which needs further study.

The following properties follow from the definitions of the NLA operators. We will see later these properties pave the way for choosing an efficient execution plan for a given WUML expression. We only state the following properties where we assume $\delta_1 \in \{+, \cup, \cap\}$ and $\delta_2 \in \{\cup, \cap\}$, since the proof is straightforward.

Associative Property. $(M_1 \; \delta_1 \; M_2) \; \delta_1 \; M_3 = M_1 \; \delta_1 \; (M_2 \; \delta_1 \; M_3)$.

Commutative Property. $M_1 \; \delta_1 \; M_2 = M_2 \; \delta_1 \; M_1$; $\Pi_P(\sigma_{\theta x}(M)) = \sigma_{\theta x}(\Pi_P(M))$

Distributive Property. $\Pi_P(M_1 \; \delta_1 \; M_2) = \Pi_P(M_1) \; \delta_1 \; \Pi_P(M_2)$; $G_P(M_1 \; \delta_1 \; M_2) = G_P(M_1) \; \delta_1 \; G_P(M_2)$; and $\sigma_{\theta x}(M_1 \; \delta_2 \; M_2) = \sigma_{\theta x}(M_1) \; \delta_2 \; \sigma_{\theta x}(M_2)$.

4 The Web Usage Manipulation Language

We now introduce a declarative language on navigation matrices termed the Web Usage Manipulation Language (WUML). A WUML expression is executed via the NLA operators defined in Sect. 3, which shares the same principle of translating a SQL expression into a sequence of relational algebra operations. We now define the WUML syntax in Backus Naur Form (BNF):

<query> :: = <selectClause><fromClause>[<conditionClause>][<groupClause>]
<selectClause> :: = SELECT <pageList>
<queryList> :: = query [, query...]
<fromClause> :: = FROM <matrixIdentifier> | FROM <operator> <matrixList>
<conditionClause> :: = WHERE LINKWT <compOp> integer
<groupClause> :: = GROUP BY <pageList>
<pageList> :: = pageIdentifier [, pageIdentifier...]|*
<matrixList> :: = matrixIdentifier [, matrixIdentifier...]
<operator> :: = SUM|UNION|DIFF|INTERSECT|POWER integer
<compOp> :: = | <= | >= | < | =

There are four main clauses in a query expression: the *select*, *from*, *condition*, and *group* . Among them the *select* and the *from* clauses are compulsory, while the *condition* and the *group* clauses are optional. Similar to SQL, WUML is a simple declarative language but is powerful enough to express query on the log information stored as navigation matrices.

We execute a WUML expression by translating it into a sequence of NLA operations using Algorithm 2. Suppose $\mathcal{P} = \{P_1, P_2, \ldots, P_l\}$ is a set of l Web pages in the select clause, $\mathcal{M} = \{M_1, M_2, \ldots, M_m\}$ is a set of m matrices in the

---

Algorithm 2 TRANS Algorithm

Input: A WUML expression q
LET q = <selectClause><fromClause>[<conditionClause>][<groupClause>]
<selectClause> := "SELECT $\mathcal{P}$ | $*$"
<fromClause> := "FROM $OPER\ \mathcal{M}$"
<conditionClause> := "WHERE LINKWT θx"
<groupClause> := "GROUP BY P_G"
Procedure:
Step 1 : For the fromClause, **CASE** $OPER$ **OF**:
$\epsilon : TEMP :=$ "M_1"
$SUM : TEMP :=$ "$M_1 + M_2 + \cdots + M_m$"
$UNION : TEMP :=$ "$M_1 \bigcup M_2 \bigcup \cdots \bigcup M_m$"
$DIFF : TEMP :=$ "$M_1 - M_2 - \cdots - M_m$"
$INTERSECT : TEMP :=$ "$M_1 \bigcap M_2 \bigcap \cdots \bigcap M_m$"
$POWER\ \alpha : TEMP :=$ "$(M_1)^\alpha$"
Step 2 : For the selectClause:
IF "$*$" **THEN** $TEMP := TEMP$
ELSE $TEMP :=$ "$\Pi_{\mathcal{P}}(TEMP)$"
Step 3 : **IF** there is a whereClause **THEN** $TEMP :=$ "$\sigma_{\theta x}(TEMP)$"
Step 4 : **IF** there is a groupClause **THEN** $TEMP :=$ "$G_{P_G}(TEMP)$"
Output: $TEMP$ expression

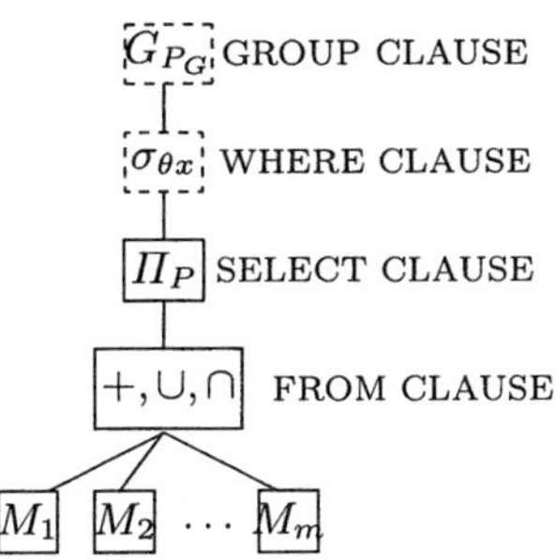

Fig. 1. WUML query tree

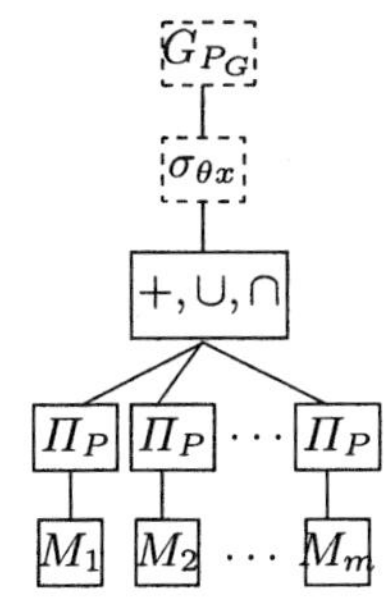

Fig. 2. Optimized WUML query tree

from clause, $P_G = \{P_1, P_2, \ldots, P_n\}$ is a set of n Web pages in the group clause, $OPER \in \{\epsilon$, SUM, $UNION$, $DIFF$, $INTERSECT$, $POWER\ \alpha\ \}$, x and α are two non-negative integers. Note that the input WUML query expression is assumed to be syntactically valid. If $OPER = \epsilon$ or $POWER\ \alpha$, then $m = 1$. Fig. 1 depicts a query tree which illustrates the basic idea.

Now, we present a set of examples, which illustrates the usage of the WUML expressions and the translation into the corresponding sequence of NLA operations. Let M, M_1, M_2 and M_3 be navigation matrices.

Q_1: We want to know how frequently the pages P_1 and P_2 were visited.
WUML expression: SELECT P_1, P_2 FROM SUM M_1, M_2.
NLA operation: $\Pi_{\{P_1,P_2\}}(M_1 + M_2)$.

Q_2: We want to find out the essential difference of preferences between the two groups of users in M_1 and M_2. We consider those links having the weight > 3.
WUML expression: SELECT * FROM DIFF M_1, M_2 WHERE LINKWT > 3. *NLA operation*: $\sigma_{>3}(M_1 - M_2)$.

Q_3: We want to get the navigation details in an *information unit* [9] consisting of the pages P_1, P_2, and P_3. We may gain insight to decide whether it is better to combine these three Web pages or not. So we consider them as a group.
WUML expression: SELECT * FROM SUM M_1, M_2 GROUP BY P_1, P_2, P_3.
NLA operation: $G_{\{P_1,P_2,P_3\}}(M_1 + M_2)$.

Q_4: We want to know whether some pages were visited by users after 3 clicks. If they were seldom visited or lately visited in a user session, we may decide to remove or update them to make them more popular.
WUML expression: SELECT P_1, P_2, P_3 FROM POWER 3 M.
NLA operation: $\Pi_{\{P_1,P_2,P_3\}}(M)^3$.

Q_5: Now we want to get the specific information of a particular set of Web pages.
WUML expression: SELECT P_1, P_2, P_3, P_4, P_5 FROM INTERSECT M_1, M_2, M_3 WHERE LINKWT > 6.
NLA operation: $\sigma_{>6}(\Pi_{\{P_1,P_2,P_3,P_4,P_5\}}(M_1 \bigcap M_2 \bigcap M_3))$.

Let us again consider the query, Q_5. We will see in Sect. 6 that the running time of NLA operators are proportional to the number of non-zero elements in the executed matrix. Therefore, the optimal plan is to first execute the NLA operators which can minimize the number of non-zero elements in the matrix. For the sake of efficiency, the `projection` (Π) should be executed as early as possible. So a better NLA execution plan of Q_5 can be obtained as follows: $Q_6 : \sigma_{>6}(\Pi_{\{P_1,P_2,P_3,P_4,P_5\}}(M_1) \bigcap \Pi_{\{P_1,P_2,P_3,P_4,P_5\}}(M_2) \bigcap \Pi_{\{P_1,P_2,P_3,P_4,P_5\}}(M_3))$.

We now summarize some optimization rules as depicted in Fig. 2. First, `projection` should be done as early as possible since it can eliminate some non-zero elements. Note that `projection` is not distributive under `difference` and `power`. Second, since `selection` is not distributive under some binary operators such as `difference`, we do not change the execution order. Finally, `grouping` creates a view different from the underlying Web topology. Therefore, it should be done at the last step except some operators taking another navigation matrix whose structure is the same as the grouped one. Note that these rules are simple heuristics to sort NLA operations. We still need to find out a more systematic way to generate an optimized execution plan for a given WUML expression.

5 Storage Schemes for Navigation Matrices

As the navigation matrices generated from the Web log files are usually sparse, the storage scheme of a matrix greatly affects the performance of WUML. In this section we introduce three storage schemes, COO, CSR, and CSC, to study their impacts on the NLA operations.

In literature, the technique of storing sparse matrices has been intensively studied [3, 8]. In our WUML environment, we store the navigation matrix as three separate parts: the first row (i.e. the weights of the links starting from S), the last column(i.e. the weights of the links ending in F) and the square matrix despite the rows and columns of S and F. We employ two vectors, S_{vector} and F_{vector}, which contains an array for the non-zero values as well as corresponding indices, to store the first row and the last column. Table 2 and 3 show examples using the matrix in Table 1. As for the third part, we implement the storage schemes proposed in [8]. We illustrate the schemes using the matrix in Table 1.

The Coordinate (COO) storage scheme is the most straightforward structure to represent a sparse matrix. As illustrated in Table 4, it records each nonzero

Table 1. Navigation Matrix

	S	P_1	P_2	P_3	P_4	F
S	0	3	1	0	0	0
P_1	0	0	2	2	0	0
P_2	0	1	0	0	0	3
P_3	0	0	0	0	3	0
P_4	0	0	1	1	0	1
F	0	0	0	0	0	0

Table 2. S_{vector}

Non-zero	3	1
Column	1	2

Table 3. F_{vector}

Non-zero	3	1
Column	2	4

Table 4. COO Scheme

Non-zero	2	2	1	3	1	1
Column	2	3	1	4	2	3
Row	1	1	2	3	4	4

entry together with its column and row index in three arrays in row-first order. Similar to COO, the Compressed Sparse Row (CSR) storage scheme also consists of three arrays. It differs from COO in the Compressed Row array which stores the location of the first non-zero entry in that row. Table 5 shows the structure of CSR. The Compressed Sparse Column (CSC) storage scheme, as shown in Table 6, is similar to CSR. It has three arrays: Nonzero array to hold the non-zero values in column-first order, Compressed Column array to hold the location of the first non-zero entry of that column, Row array for the row indices. CSC is the *transpose* of CSR. There are also other sparse matrix storage schemes, such as Compressed Diagonal Storage (CDS) and Jagged Diagonal Storage (JDS) [12]. However, they are used for storing a *banded sparse matrix*. In reality, the navigation matrix should not be banded. Therefore, these schemes are not studied in our experiments.

Table 5. CSR Scheme

Non-zero	2	2	1	3	1	1
Column	2	3	1	4	2	3
Compressed Row	0	2	3	4		

Table 6. CSC Scheme

Non-zero	1	2	1	2	1	3
Compressed Column	0	1	3	5		
Row	2	1	4	1	4	3

6 Experimental Results and Analysis

We carry out a set of experiments to compare the performances of the three storage schemes introduced in Sect. 5. We also study the usability and efficiency of WUML on different data sets. The data set we used is a set of synthetic Web logs on different Web topology, which are generated by a log generator designed in [10]. The parameters used to generate the log files are described in Table 7. Among these four parameters, PageNum and MeanLink are dependent on the underlying Web topology while the other two are not. These experiments are run on Pentium 4, 2.5GHz, and 1G of RAM machine configuration.

Table 7. Parameters for Data Set

LogSize	The number of log records in a log file.
UserNum	The number of users traversing the Web site.
PageNum	The number of pages in the Web topology.
MeanLink	The average number of links per page in the Web topology.

6.1 Construction Time of Storage Schemes

We choose three data sets: $D_1 = (2500, 1500, 1500, 3)$, $D_2 = (5000, 3000, 3000, 5)$ and $D_3 = (10000, 6000, 6000, 10)$, in which the components represent the parameters LogSize, UserNum, PageNum and MeanLink, respectively. Then we construct three storage schemes based on the generated log files from D_1 to D_3.

Our measurement of the system response time includes I/O processing time and CPU processing time. As shown in Fig. 3, the response time grows significantly as the parameters increase. Since most of the time is consumed in reading the log files, the construction time for the same given data set varies slightly among the three storage schemes. But it still takes more time to construct COO than the other two schemes, since there is no compressed array for COO. CSC needs more time than CSR because the storage order in CSC is column-first while reading in the file is in row-first order.

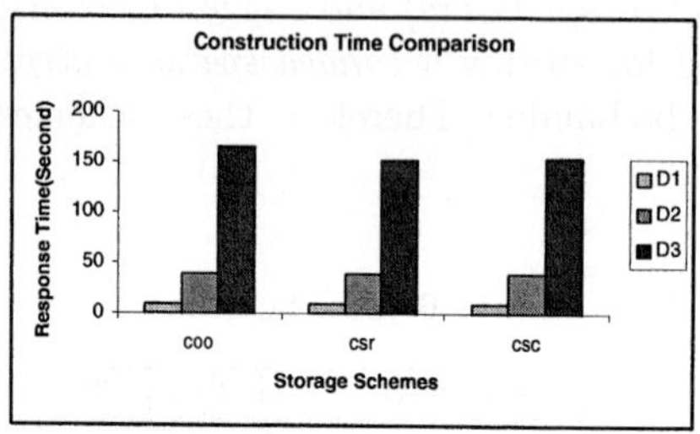

Fig. 3. Construction Time

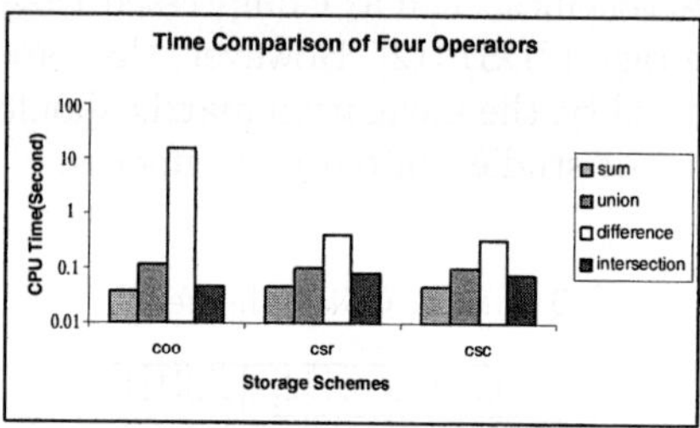

Fig. 4. Running Four Operators

6.2 Processing Time of Binary Operators

We present the CPU processing time results of four binary operators: `sum`, `union`, `difference` and `intersection`. Each time we tune one of the four parameters to see how the processing time changes on COO, CSR and CSC storage schemes. For each parameter, we carry out experiments on ten different sets of Web logs. We first compare the processing time of each single operator under different storage schemes. Then we present the processing time of each storage scheme under different operators.

Tuning LogSize. We set UserNum and PageNum as 3000, MeanLink as 5. The results are shown in Fig. 5. When LogSize increases, the processing time of the same operator on each storage scheme also increases. The reason is that the number of non-zero elements in the navigation matrix grows with the increase of LogSize, and therefore it needs more time to do the operations.

Tuning PageNum. We set LogSize as 5000, UserNum as 3000, and MeanLink as 5. The results are presented in Fig. 7. With the growth of PageNum, the CPU time for each operator on specified storage scheme grows quickly. It is because PageNum is a significant parameter when constructing the navigation matrix. The more pages in the Web site, the larger dimension of a navigation matrix, and consequently, the more time needed to construct the navigation matrix.

Tuning UseNum. Figure 6 shows the results when LogSize is 5000, PageNum is 3000 and MeanLink is 5. The processing time remains almost unchanged when UserNum grows. The main reason is that, although different user may have different behavior when traversing the Web site, the number of non-zero elements in navigation matrix is roughly the same due to the fixed LogSize.

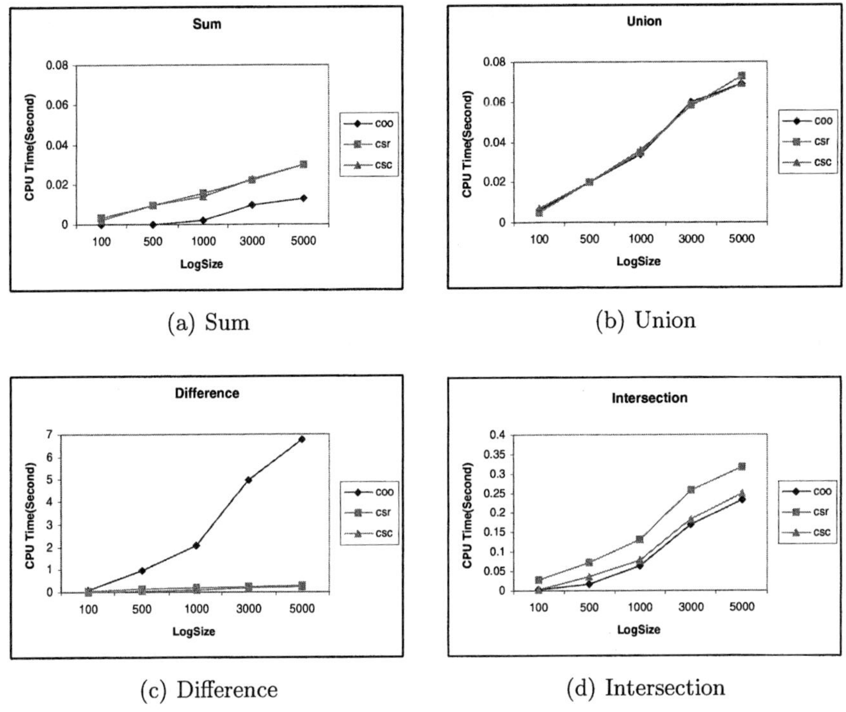

(a) Sum

(b) Union

(c) Difference

(d) Intersection

Fig. 5. The CPU time by tuning LogSize

Tuning MeanLink. We use the log files with LogSize of 5000, UserNum of 3000 and PageNum of 3000. The results are shown in Fig. 8 which indicates that, with the increase of MeanLink, the processing time decreases.

Note that for `sum`, COO always outperforms others, while CSR and CSC perform almost the same (see Fig. 5(a), 6(a), 7(a) and 8(a)). The similar phenomenon can be observed in Fig. 5(d), 6(d), 7(d) and 8(d) for `intersection`. As shown in Fig. 5(b), 6(b), 7(b) and 8(b), the processing time for `union` on three storage schemes has no significant difference. Finally, from Fig. 5(c), 6(c), 7(c) and 8(c), the performances of CSR and CSC are much better than COO for `difference`. Note also that from Fig. 4, `difference` requires the most processing time, and `sum` needs the least. The Web logs used are of 5000 LogSize, 1000 UserNum, 3000 PageNum and 5 MeanLink. The reason for this result is as follows. As we have mentioned, we do not need to check the balance of Web pages and the validity of the navigation matrix for `sum`. Therefore, it takes the least time. For `union`, we only need to check the balance of Web pages without checking the validity of the output matrix. But for `difference` and `intersection`, we have to check both the page balance and matrix validity, which is rather time-consuming. It can be found that `intersection` does not need much time since there are very few non-zero elements in the output matrix.

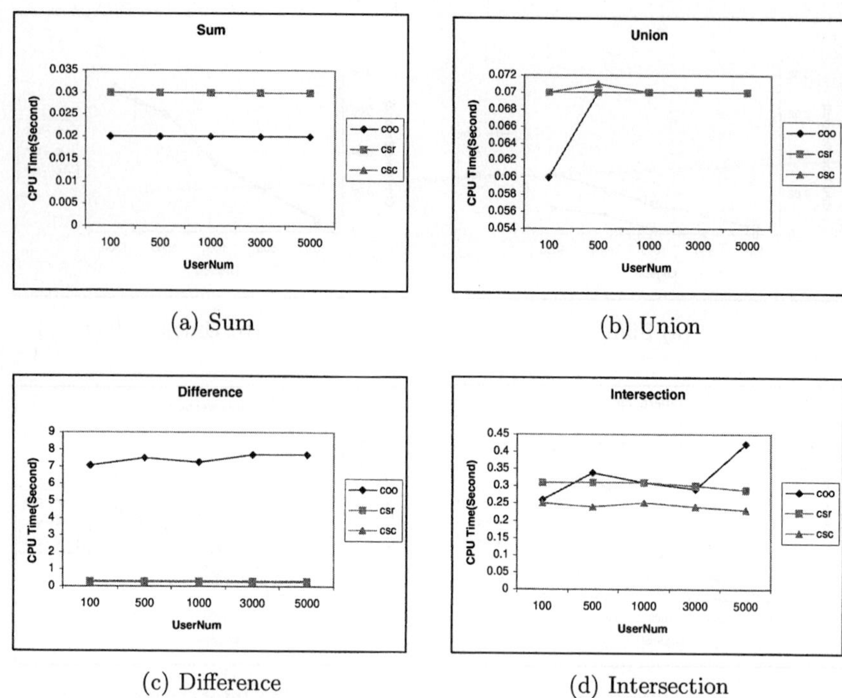

(a) Sum (b) Union

(c) Difference (d) Intersection

Fig. 6. The CPU time by tuning UserNum

6.3 Performance of Unary Operators

Power. We use log files with 5000 LogSize, 3000 UserNum, 5 MeanLink, (100, 500, 1000) PageNum. Each matrix multiplies twice (i.e. power = 2). As shown in Fig. 9, COO performs much worse than CSR and CSC. We also see that `power` is a rather time-consuming operator.

Projection and Selection. Since `projection` and `selection` are commutative, we study the time cost by swapping them on the navigation matrix with 5000 LogSize, 5000 PageNum, 3000 UserNum and 5 MeanLink. As shown in Fig. 10, doing `projection` before `selection` is more efficient than doing `selection` and then `projection`. According to this result, we can do some optimization when interpreting some queries. Moreover, COO outperforms CSR and CSC.

From the experimental results shown above, we have the following observations. First, from construction point of view, CSR is the best. Second, COO is the best for `sum` and `intersection`. Third, CSR and CSC perform almost the same for `difference` and `power`, and greatly outperform COO. Finally, COO, CSR and CSC perform the same for `union`. Taking these observations into consideration, CSR is the best for our WUML expressions. Although COO performs better in `sum` and `intersection`, it needs too much time for `difference` which is intolerant. Although the performance of CSC is the same as CSR with respect to the operations, CSC needs more time to be constructed. We also observe that

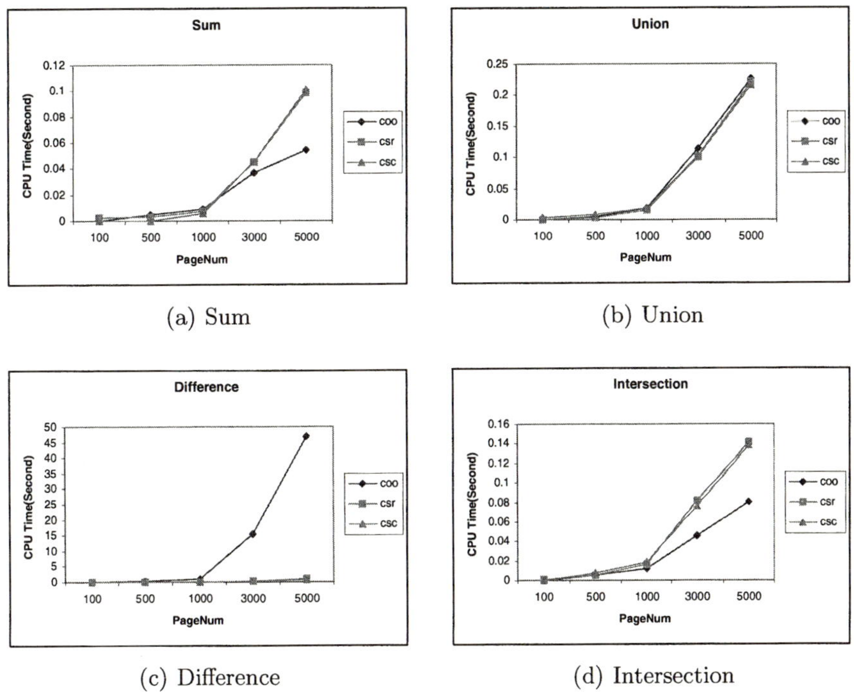

(a) Sum (b) Union

(c) Difference (d) Intersection

Fig. 7. The CPU time by tuning PageNum

the time growth for each operator is linear to the growth of parameters, which indicates that the usability and scalability of WUML is acceptable in practice.

7 Concluding Remarks

We presented NLA which consists of a set of operators on navigation matrices and proposed an efficient algorithm VALID ($O(n)$ space and $O(n^2)$ time complexities) to ensure the validity of an output matrix by NLA operators. Within NLA, we develop a query language WUML and study the mapping between the WUML statements and NLA expressions. To choose an efficient storage scheme for the sparse navigation matrix, we carried out a set of experiments on different synthetic Web log data sets, which are generated by tuning different parameters such as the number of pages, the number of mean links and the number of users. By the experimental results on three storage schemes of COO, CSC and CSR, we can see that the CSR scheme is relatively efficient for NLA. As for future work, we plan to develop a full-fledged WUML system to preform both analyzing and mining the real Web log data sets. We are also studying a more complete set of optimization heuristic rules for the NLA operators in order to generate a better execution plan for an input WUML expression.

provide high availability, reliability, and scalability in the face of high degrees of autonomy and heterogeneity with which services are deployed and managed on the web [3]. The use of intelligent agents has been suggested to handle the challenges.

2.2 Intelligent Agents for Web Service Composition

There is increasing recognition that web services and intelligent agents represent a natural match. It has been argued that both represent a form of "modularized intelligence" [7]. The analogy has been carried further to articulate the ultimate challenge as the creation of effective frameworks, standards and software for automating web service discovery, execution, composition and interoperation on the web [13]. Following the discussion of web service composition above, the role of intelligent agents may be identified as on-demand planning, and proactively responding to changes in the environment. In particular, planning techniques have been applied to web services composition. Kay [14] describes the ATL Postmaster system that uses agent-based collaboration for service composition. A drawback of the system is that the ATL postmaster is not fault-tolerant. If a node fails, the agents residing in it are destroyed and state information is lost. Maamar and et. al. [15] propose a framework based on software agents for web services composition, but fail to tie their framework to web services standards. It is not clear how their framework will function with BPEL4WS and other web services standards and handle exceptions. Srivastava and Koehler [4], while discussing use of planning approaches to web services composition, indicate planning alone is not sufficient; and useful solutions must consider failure handling as well as composition with multiple partners. Effective web service composition, thus, requires expertise regarding available services, as well as process decomposition knowledge. A particular flavor of intelligent agents, called team-based agents, allows expertise to be distributed, making them a more appropriate fit for web services composition.

Team-based agents are a special kind of intelligent agents with distributed expertise (knowledge) and emphasize on cooperativeness and proactiveness in pursuing their common goals. Several computational models of teamwork have been proposed including GRATE* [16], STEAM [17] and CAST [6]. These models allow multiple agents to solve (e.g., planning, task execution) complex problems collaboratively. In web services composition, team-based agents can facilitate a distributed approach to dynamic composition, which can be scalable, facilitate learning about specific types of services across multiple compositions, and allow proactive failure handling. In particular, the CAST architecture (Collaborative Agents for Simulating Teamwork) [6] offers a feasible solution for dynamic web services composition. Two key features of CAST are (1) CAST agents can work collaboratively using a shared mental model of the changing environment; (2) CAST agents proactively inform each other of changes that they perceive to handle any exceptions that arise in achieving a team goal. By collaboratively monitoring the progress of a shared process, a team of CAST agents can not only initiate helping behaviors proactively but can also adjust their own behaviors to the dynamically changing environment.

In the rest of this paper, we first propose a generic team-based agent framework for dynamic web-service composition, and then extend the existing CAST agent architecture to realize the framework.

3 A Methodology for Interleaved Composition and Execution

We illustrate the proposed methodology with the help of an example that demonstrates how team-based agents may help with dynamic web services composition.

The example concerns dynamic service outsourcing in a virtual software development organization, called 'VOSoft'. VOSoft possesses expertise in designing and developing software packages for customers from a diversity of domains. It usually employs one of two developing methodologies (or software processes): prototype-based approach (Mp) is preferred for software systems composed of tightly-coupled modules (integration problems reveal earlier), and unit-based approach (Mu) is preferred for software systems composed of loosely-coupled modules (more efficient due to parallel tasks).

Suppose a customer "WSClient" engages VOSoft to develop CAD design-software for metal casting patterns. It is required that the software is able to (a) read AutoCAD drawings automatically, (b) develop designs for metal casting patterns, and (c) maintain all the designs and user details in a database. Based on its expertise, VOSoft designs the the software as being composed of three modules: database management system (DMS), CAD, and pattern design. Assume VOSoft's core competency is developing the application logic that is required for designing metal casting patterns, but it cannot develop CAD software and the database module. Hence, VOSoft needs to compose a process where the DMS and CAD modules could be outsourced to competent service providers.

In this scenario, several possible exceptions may be envisioned. We list three below to illustrate the nature and source of these exceptions. First, non-performance by a service provider will result in a service failure exception, which may be resolved by locating another service to perform the task. Second, module integration exceptions may be raised if two modules cannot interact with each other. This may be resolved by adding tasks to develop common APIs for the two modules. Third, the customer may change or add new functionality, which may necessitate the change of the entire process.

It is clear that both internal (capability of web services) as well as external (objectives being pursued) changes can influence the planning and execution of composite web services in such scenarios. It thus requires an approach being able to monitor service execution and proactively handle services failures.

3.1 Composing with Team-Based Agents

A team-based agent A is defined in terms of (a) a set of capabilities (service names), denoted as C_A, (b) a list of service providers SP_A under its management, and (c) an acquaintance model M_A (a set of agents known to A, and their respective capabilities: $M_A = \{\langle i, C_i \rangle\}$).

An agent in our framework may play multiple roles. First, every agent is a Web-service manager. An agent A knows which providers in SP_A can offer a service S ($S \in C_A$), or at least knows how to find a provider for S (e.g. by searching the UDDI registry) if none of the providers in SP_A are capable of performing the service. Services in C_A are primitive to agent A in the sense that it can directly delegate the services to appropriate service providers. Second, an agent becomes a service composer upon being requested of a complex service. An agent is responsible for composing a process using known services when it receives a user request that falls beyond its capabilities. In such situations, the set of acquaintances, M_A, forms a community of contacts available to agent A. The acquaintance model is dynamically modified based on the agent's collaboration with other agents (e.g., assigning credit to those with successful collaborations). This additional, local knowledge supplements the global knowledge about publicly advertised web services (say, on the UDDI registry). Third, an agent becomes a team leader when it tries to forming a team to honor a complex service.

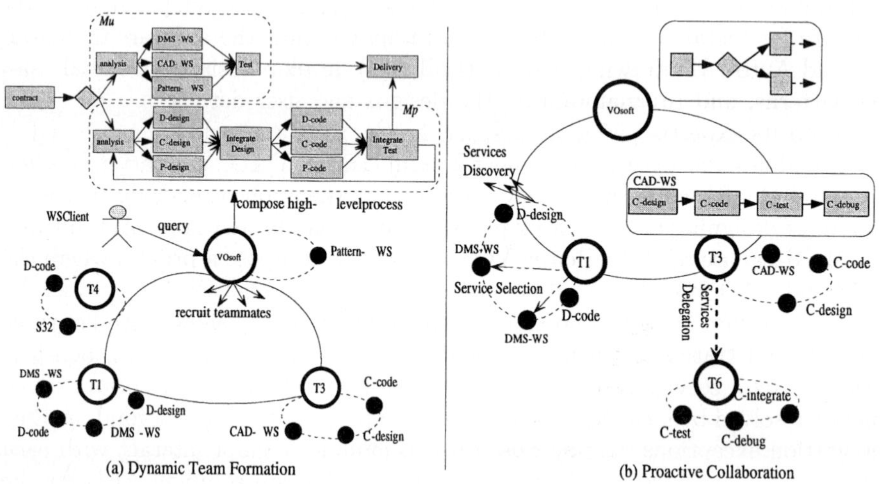

Fig. 1. Team formation and Collaboration

3.2 Responding to Request for a Complex Service

An agent, upon receiving a complex service request, initiates a team formation process:
(1) The agent (say, C) adopts "offering service S" as its persistent goal.
(2) If $S \in C_C$ (i.e., S is within its capabilities), agent C simply delegates S to a competent provider (or first finds a service provider, if no provider known to C is competent).

(3) If $S \notin C_C$ (i.e., agent C cannot directly serve S), then C tries to compose a process (say, H) using its expertise and the services in $C_C \cup \bigcup_{\langle i, C_i \rangle \in M_C} C_i$ (i.e., it considers its own capabilities and the capabilities of those agents in its acquaintance model), then starts to form a team:

i. Agent C identifies teammates by examining agents in its acquaintance model who have the capability to contribute to the process (i.e. $A \in M_C$, and $S_H \cap C_A \neq \emptyset$, where S_H is the set of services used in process H).
ii. Agent C chooses willing and competent agents from M_C (e.g., using contract-net protocol [18]) as teammates, and shares the process H with them with a view to working together as a team jointly working on H.

(4) If the previous step fails, then agent C either fails in honoring the external request (is penalized), or, if possible, may proactively discover a different agent (either using M_A or a using UDDI) and delegate S to it.

[**Example**] Suppose agent $VOSoft$ composes a top-level process as shown in Figure 1(a). In the process, the "contract" service is followed by a choice point, where $VOSoft$ needs to make a decision on which methodology (Mp or Mu) to choose. If Mu is chosen, then services DMS-WS, CAD-WS and Pattern-WS are required; if Mp is chosen, then services need to be more refined so that interactions between service providers in the software development process could be carried out frequently to avoid potential integration problems at later stages. Now, suppose $VOSoft$ chooses branch Mu, and manages to form a team including agents $T1$, $T3$ and $VOSoft$ to collaboratively satisfy the user's request. It is possible that agent $T4$ was asked but declined to join the team for certain reason (e.g., lack of interest or capacity). After the team is formed, each agent's responsibility is determined and mutually known. As a team leader, agent $VOsoft$ is responsible for coordinating others' behavior to work towards their common goal, and making decisions at critical points (e.g., adjust the process if service fails). Agent $T1$ is responsible for service DMS-WS; and agent $T3$ is responsible for service CAD-WS. As service managers, both $T1$ and $T3$ are responsible for choosing an appropriate service provider for service DMS-WS and CAD-WS, respectively.

3.3 Collaborating in Service Execution

The sharing of high-level process enables agents in a team to perform proactive teamwork behaviors during service execution.

Proactive Service Discovery: Knowing the joint responsibility of the team and individual responsibility of team members, one agent can help another find web services. For example, in Figure 1(b), agent $T1$ is responsible for contributing service D-design. Agent $T3$, who happened to identify a service provider for service D-design while interacting with the external world, can proactively inform $T1$ about the provider. This can not only improve $T1$'s competency regarding service D-design, but also can enhance $T3$'s credibility in $T1$'s acquaintance model.

Proactive Service Delegation: An agent can proactively contract out services to competent teammates. For example, suppose branch Mu is selected and service CAD-WS is a complex service for $T3$, who has composed a process for CAD-WS as shown in Figure 1(b). Even though $T3$ can perform C-design and C-code, services C-test and C-debug are beyond its capabilities. In order to provide the committed service CAD-WS, $T3$ can proactively form another team and delegate the services to the recruited agents (i.e., $T6$). It might be argued that agent $VOSoft$ would have generated a high-level process with more detailed decomposition, say, the sub-process generated by $T3$ for CAD-WS were embedded (in the place of CAD-WS) as a part of the process generated by $VOSoft$. If so, $T6$ would have been recruited as $VOSoft$'s teammate, and no delegation will be needed. However, the ability to derive a process at all decomposition levels is too stringent a requirement to place on any single agent. One benefit of using agent teams is that one agent can leverage the knowledge (expertise) distributed among team members even though each of them only have limited resources.

Proactive Information Delivery: Proactive information delivery can occur in various situations. (i) A complex process may have critical choice points where several branches are specified, but which one will be selected depends on the known state of the external environment. Thus, teammates can proactively inform the team leader about those changes in states that are relevant to its decision-making. (ii) Upon making a decision, other teammates will be informed of the decision so that they can better anticipate potential collaboration needs. (iii) A web service (say, the service Test in branch Mu) may fail due to many reasons. The responsible agent can proactively report the service failures to the leader so that the leader can decide how to respond to the failure: choose an alternative branch (say, Mp), or request the responsible agent to re-attempt the service from another provider.

4 The CAST-WS Architecture

We have designed a team-based agent architecture CAST-WS (Collaborative Agents for Simulating Teamwork among Web Services) to realize our methodology (see Figure 2). In the following, we describe the components of CAST-WS and explain their relationships.

4.1 Core Representation Decisions

The core representation decisions that drive the architecture involve mapping concepts from team-based agents to composition and execution of complex web services with an underlying representation that may be common to both domains. Such a representation is found in Petri nets [19]. The CAST architecture utilizes hierarchical predicate-transition nets as the underlying representation for specifying plans created and shared among agents. In the web service domain, the dominant standard for specifying compositions, BPEL4WS can also be interpreted based on a broad interpretation of the Petri net formalism. Another

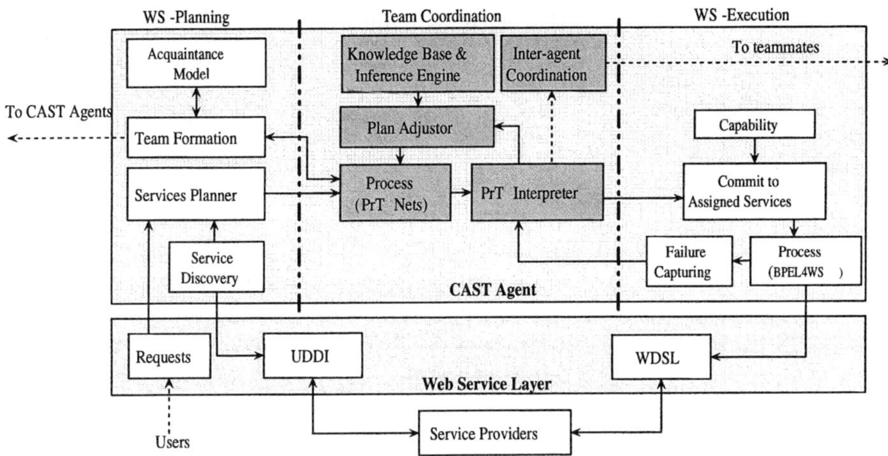

Fig. 2. The CAST-WS Architecture

key building block for realizing complex web services, protocols for conversations among web services [20], uses state-based representations that may be mapped to Petri-net based models for specifying conversation states and their evolution. As a conceptual model, therefore, a control-oriented representation of workflows, complex web services and conversations can share the Petri-net structure, with the semantics provided by each of the domains. The mapping between team-based agents and complex web services is summarized in Table 1 below.

Table 1. Mapping between Team-based Agents and Complex Web Services

Team-based Agents	**Complex Web Services**	**Representation**
Agent	Service provider	entity
Plan	Process Specification	MALLET, BPEL4WS
Goal	requests/tasks	predicates
Agent Capability	Services	WSDL
Agent Interaction	Conversations	Petri Net
Process knowledge	No corresponding concept	Petri Net
Environment knowledge	No corresponding concept	Horn clauses

Following this mapping, we have devised the following components of the architecture: service planning (i.e. composing complex web services), team coordination (i.e. knowledge sharing among web services), and executing (i.e. realizing the execution of complex web services).

4.2 WS-Planning Component

The Planning component is responsible for composing services and forming teams. This component includes three modules. The service discovery module is used by service planner to lookup in UDDI registry for required services. The team formation module, together with acquaintance model, is used to find team agents who can support the required services. A web service composition starts from user's request. The agent who gets the request is the composer agent, who is in charge of fulfilling the request. Upon receiving a request, the composer agent turns the request into its persistent goal and invokes its service planner module to generate a business process for it.

The architecture uses hierarchical predicate-transition nets (PrT nets) to represent and monitor business processes. PrT Nets consists of the following components: (1) a set P of token places for controlling the process execution; (2) a set T of transitions, which represent either an abstraction of a sub PrT net (i.e. an invocation of some sub-plans), or an operation (e.g., primitive web service). A transition is associated with preconditions (predicates), which is used to specify conditions for continuing the process. (3) a set of arcs over $P \times T$ that describes the order of execution that the team will follow; and (4) a labeling function on arcs, which are tuples of agents and bindings for variables.

The services that are used by the service planner for composing a process come from two sources: the UDDI directory and the acquaintance model. Assume from the requested service we can derive a set of expected effects, which will be the goals to be achieved by CAST agents. Given any set of goals G, a partial order (binary relation) can be defined over G: $\forall g1 \in G, g2 \in G, g3 \in G$,

(1) $g1 \leq g1$;
(2) $g1 \leq g2, g2 \leq g1 \Rightarrow g1 = g2$;
(3) $g1 \leq g2, g2 \leq g3 \Rightarrow g1 \leq g3$.

Given $\langle G, \leq \rangle$, $\forall g \in G$, its pre-set, denoted as $\bullet g$, is defined as $\{g' \in G | g' \leq g, \text{and } \nexists g'' \neq g \text{ such that } g' \leq g'' \leq g\}$; its post-set, denoted as $g\bullet$, is defined as $\{g' \in G | g \leq g', \text{and } \nexists g'' \neq g \text{ such that } g \leq g'' \leq g'\}$. Given $\langle G, \leq \rangle$, any $G1 \subset G, G2 \subset G$, $G1$ and $G2$ are *independent* iff $\forall g \in G1$, $\nexists g' \in G2$ such that $g \leq g'$ or $g' \leq g$, and vice versa. Element $g \in G$ is *indetachable* from G iff $\exists g' \in G$ such that $g \leq g'$ or $g' \leq g$.

The following algorithm is used by the service planner to generate a Petri-net process for a given goal (service request).

Algorithm: ServicePlanning(Goal g)

1. Let $G = \{g\}$
2. If g can be divided into $\{g_1, g_2, \cdots, g_k\}$ then Let $G = \{g_1, g_2, \cdots, g_k\}$
3. Partition G into G_1, G_2, $\cdots$, G_m such that they are pairwisely independent, and any goal in G_i $(1 \leq i \leq m)$ is indetatchable from G_i. Since each G_i is an ordered set, we denoted them as $\langle G_i, \leq \rangle$.
4. Create a PrT net PN with a parallel construct where G_i $(1 \leq i \leq m)$ are the branches;
5. For i from 1 to m DO
   If (expandFurther is $True$) then
      sub_net = Expanding(G_i, $\leq$)
      Replace G_i in PN with sub_net
6. return PN.

Algorithm: Expanding(GoalSet G, Order $\leq$)

1. Create a net SN for G based on the order information:
   a. If $g2$ depends on $g1$, use *sequential* construct SEQ;
   b. If the chosen of $g1$ and $g2$ depends on the truth value of some condition, use *conditional* construct IF;
   c. If a goal (or sequence of goals) needs to be done repeatedly, use *iterative* construct $WHILE$;
   d. If two or more goals can be done in parallel, use *parallel* construct PAR;
   e. Make sure for any $g \in G$, there is a token place between g and any goal in $g\bullet$.
2. For any g in net SN
   a. If a service can achieve g then replace g with the service (name);
   b. If a plan (process) can achieve g then replace g with the plan;
   c. If more than one plan (process) can achieve g then replace g with a *choice* construct $CHOICE$;
   d. Otherwise, if (expandFurther is $True$) then $Serviceplanning(g)$;
3. return SN.

4.3 The Team Coordination Component

The team coordination component is used to coordinate with other agents during service execution. This component includes an inference engine with a built-in knowledge base, a process shared by all team members, a PrT interpreter, a plan adjustor, and an inter-agent coordination module. Knowledge base holds the (accumulated) expertise needed for service composition. The inter-agent coordination module, embedded with team coordination strategies and conversation policies [21], is used for behavior collaboration among teammates. Here we mainly focus on the process interpreter and the plan adaptor.

Each agent in a team uses its PrT net interpreter to interpret the business process generated by its service planner, monitor the progress of the shared process and takes its turn to perform tasks assigned to it. If the assigned task is a primitive web service, the agent invokes the service through its BPEL4WS process controller. If a task is assigned to multiple agents, the responsible agents coordinate their behavior (e.g., not compete for common resources) through the inter-agent coordination module. If an agent faces an unassigned task, it evaluates constrains associated with the task and tries to find a competent teammate for the task. If the assigned task is a complex service (i.e. further decomposition required) and is beyond its capabilities, the agent treats it as an internal request, composes a sub-process for the task, and forms another team to solve it.

The plan adjustor uses the knowledge base and inference engine to adjust and repair the process whenever an exception or a need for change in the process arises. The algorithm used by the plan adjustor utilizes the failure handling policy implemented in CAST. Due to the hierarchical organization of the team process, each CAST agent maintains a stack of active process and sub-processes. A sub-process returns the control to its parent process when its execution is completed. Failure handling is interleaved with (abstract) service executing: execute a service; check termination conditions; handle failures, and propagate failures to the parent process if needed. The algorithm captures four kinds of termination modes resulting from a service execution. The first (i.e. return 0) result indicates the service is completed successfully. The second (i.e. return 1) indicates that the process is terminated abnormally but the expected effects from the service has already been achieved "magically" (e.g. by proactive help from teammates). The third (i.e., return 2) indicates that the process is not completed and is likely at an impasse. In this case, if the current service is just one alternative of a choice point, another alternative can be selected to re-attempt the service. Otherwise, the failure is propagated to the upper level. The fourth (i.e. return 3) indicates that the process is terminated because the service has become irrelevant. This may happen if the goal or context changes. In this case, the irrelevance is propagated to the parent service, which checks its own relevance. The plan adjustor algorithm is shown below.

Algorithm: ServiceExecution(Level i, Service S)

1. Let P be the process(plan) for S
2. $SS = getNextService(P)$
3. While SS is not null /*P is not completed
   terminateCode= $ServiceExecution(i+1, SS)$
   if terminateCode !=0
     if terminateCode =1
       $SS = getNextService(P)$
     if terminateCode =2
       if SS is one branch of a choice point C
         $SS = chooseAnotherWay(P, C)$
       else return 2
     if terminateCode =3
       if (the execution of S is irrelevant) return 3
       else $SS = getNextService(P)$
4. end while
5. return 0

4.4 The WS-Execution Component

A service manager agent executes the primitive services (or a process of primitive services) through the WS-Execution component. The WS-Execution component consists of a commitment manager, a capability manager, a BPEL4WS process controller, an active process, and a failure detector. The capability manager maps services to known service providers. The commitment manager is used to schedule the services assigned to it in an appropriate order.

An agent ultimately needs to delegate those contracted services to appropriate service providers. The process controller generates a BPEL4WS process based on the WSDL of the selected service providers and the sequence indicated in the PrT process. The failure detector identifies execution failure by

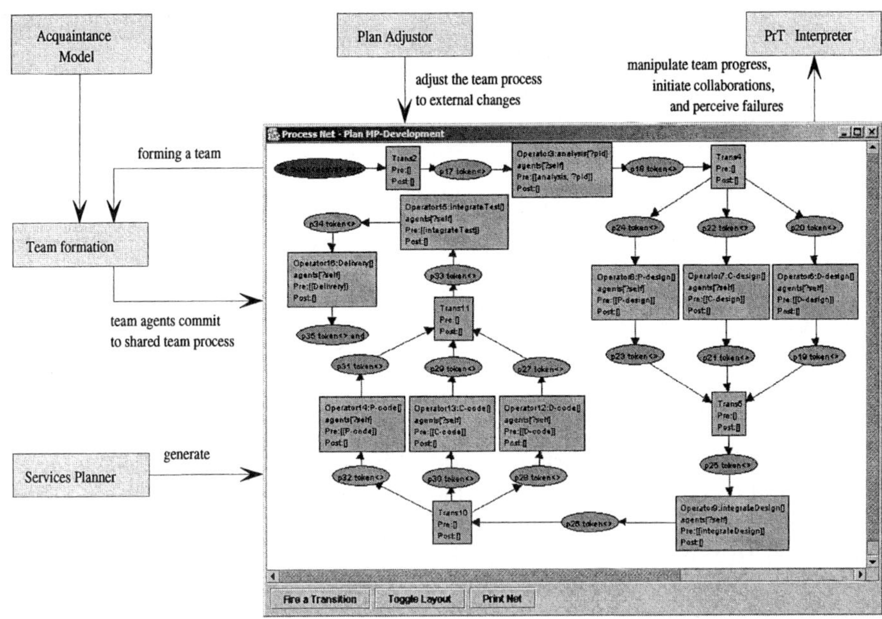

Fig. 3. The relations between generated team process and other modules

checking the termination conditions associated with services. If a termination condition has been reached, the failure detector throws an error and the plan adjustor module is invoked. If it is a service failure, the plan adjustor simply asks the agent to choose another service provider and re-attempt the service; if it is a process failure (unexpected changes make the process unworkable), the plan adjustor back-tracks the PrT process, tries to find another (sub-)process that would satisfy the task, and uses it to fix the one that failed.

4.5 The Example Revisited

Figure 3 shows how web service composition for VOSoft may be performed with interleaved planning and execution. The figure shows the core (hierarchical) Petri net representation used by the CAST architecture, and the manner in which each of the modules in the architecture use this representation. Due to the dynamic nature of the process, it is not feasible to show all possible paths that the execution may take. Instead, we show one plausible path, indicating the responsibilities for each of the modules in the architecture such as planning, team formation, undertaking execution, sensing changes in the internal or external environment (that may lead to exceptions), proactive information sharing, and how these will allow adapting the process to changes in the environment (proactive exception handling). The result is an interleaved process that includes planning and execution. The figure shows mapping to elements of the web service technology stack (e.g. BPEL4WS specification), which allows use of the proposed architecture with current proposals from W3C.

5 Discussion

As business processes, specified as workflows and executed with web services, need to be adaptive and flexible, approaches are needed to facilitate this evolution. The methodology and architecture we have outlined addresses this concern by pushing the burden of ensuring this flexibility to the web services participating in the process. To achieve this, we have adapted and extended research in the area of team-based agents. A key consequence of this choice is that our approach allows interleaving of execution with planning, providing several distinct advantage over current web service composition approaches to facilitate adaptive workflows. First, it supports an adaptive process that suitable for the highly dynamic and distributed manner in which web services are deployed and used. The specification of a joint goal allows each team member to contribute relevant information to the composer agent, who can make decisions at critical choice points. Second, it elicits a hierarchical methodology for process management where a service composer can compose a process at a coarse level appropriate to its capability and knowledge, leaving further decomposition to competent teammates. Third, it interleaves planning with execution, providing a natural vehicle for implementing adaptive workflows.

Our work in this direction so far has provided us with the fundamental insight that further progress in effective and efficient web service composition can be made by better understanding how *distributed* and *partial knowledge* about the availability and capabilities of web services, and the environment in which they are expected to operate, can be shared among the team of agents that must collaborate to perform the composed web service. Our current work involves extending the ideas to address these opportunities and concerns, and reflecting the outcomes in the ongoing implementation.

References

1. Heuvel, v.d., Maamar, Z.: Moving toward a framework to compose intelligent web services. Communications of the ACM **46** (2003) 103–109
2. Allen, R.: Workflow: An introduction. In Fisher, L., ed.: The Workflow Handbook 2001. Workflow Management Coalition (2001) 15–38
3. Pires, P., Benevides, M., Mattoso, M.: Building reliable web services compositions. In: Web, Web-Services, and Database Systems 2002. LNCS-2593. Springer (2003) 59–72
4. Koehler, J., Srivastava, B.: Web service composition: Current solutions and open problems. In: ICAPS 2003 Workshop on Planning for Web Services. (2003) 28–35
5. Oberleitner, J., Dustdar, S.: Workflow-based composition and testing of combined e-services and components. Technical Report TUV-1841-2003-25, Vienna University of Technology, Austria (2003)

6. Yen, J., Yin, J., Ioerger, T., Miller, M., Xu, D., Volz, R.: CAST: Collaborative agents for simulating teamworks. In: Proceedings of IJCAI'2001. (2001) 1135–1142
7. Bernard, B.: Agents in the world of active web-services. Digital Cities (2001) 343–356
8. Manes, A.T.: Web services: A manager's guide. Addison-Wesley Information Technology Series (2003) 47–82
9. Casati, F., Shan, M.C.: Dynamic and adaptive composition of e-services. Information Systems **26** (2001) 143–163
10. Sheng, Q., Benatallah, B., Dumas, M., Mak, E.: SELF-SERV: A platform for rapid composition of web services in a peer-to-peer environment. In: Demo Session of the 28th Intl. Conf. on Very Large Databases. (2002)
11. McIlraith, S., Son, T.C.: Adopting Golog for composition of semantic web services. In: Proceedings of the International Conference on knowledge representation and Reasoning (KR2002). (2002) 482–493
12. Chakraborty, D., Joshi, A.: Dynamic service composition: State-of-the-art and research directions. Technical Report TR-CS-01-19, Department of Computer Science and Electrical Engineering, University of Maryland, Baltimore, USA (2001)
13. Ermolayev, V.: Towards cooperative distributed service composition on the semantic web. Talks at Informatics Colloquium (2003)
14. Kay, J., Etzl, J., Rao, G., Thies, J.: The ATL postmaster: a system for agent collaboration and information dissemination. In: Proceedings of the second international conference on Autonomous agents, ACM (1998)
15. Maamar, Z., Sheng, Q., Benatallah, B.: Interleaving web services composition and execution using software agents and delegation. In: AAMAS'03 Workshop on web Services and Agent-based Engineering. (2003)
16. Jennings, N.R.: Controlling cooperative problem solving in industrial multi-agent systems using joint intentions. Artificial Intelligence **75** (1995) 195–240
17. Tambe, M.: Towards flexible teamwork. Journal of Artificial Intelligence Research **7** (1997) 83–124
18. Smith, R.G.: The contract net protocol: High-level communication and control in a distributed problem solver. IEEE Transactions on Computers **29** (1980) 1104–1113
19. van der Aalst, W., vanHee, K.: Workflow Management: Models, Methods, and Systems. MIT Press (2002)
20. Hanson, J.E., Nandi, P., Kumaran, S.: Conversation support for business process integration. In: Proc. of the IEEE International Enterprise Distributed Object Computing Conference. (2002) 65–74
21. Umapathy, K., Purao, S., Sugumaran, V.: Facilitating conversations among web services as speech-act based discourses. In: Proceedings of the Workshop on Information Technologies and Systems. (2003) 85–90

A Probabilistic QoS Model and Computation Framework for Web Services-Based Workflows

San-Yih Hwang[1,2,*], Haojun Wang[2,**], Jaideep Srivastava[2], and Raymond A. Paul[3]

[1] Department of Information Management
National Sun Yat-sen University, Kaohsiung 80424, Taiwan
syhwang@mis.nsysu.edu.tw

[2] Department of Computer Science
University of Minnesota, Minneapolis 55455, USA
{haojun,srivasta}@cs.umn.edu

[3] Department of Defense, United States

Abstract. Web services promise to become a key enabling technology for B2B e-commerce. Several languages have been proposed to compose Web services into workflows. The QoS of the Web services-based workflows may play an essential role in choosing constituent Web services and determining service level agreement with their users. In this paper, we identify a set of QoS metrics in the context of Web services and propose a unified probabilistic model for describing QoS values of (atomic/composite) Web services. In our model, each QoS measure of a Web service is regarded as a discrete random variable with probability mass function (PMF). We describe a computation framework to derive QoS values of a Web services-based workflow. Two algorithms are proposed to reduce the sample space size when combining PMFs. The experimental results show that our computation framework is efficient and results in PMFs that are very close to the real model.

1 Introduction

Web services have become a de facto standard for achieving interoperability among business applications over the Internet. In a nutshell, a Web service can be regarded as an abstract data type that comprises a set of operations and data (or message types). Requests to and responses from Web service operations are transmitted through SOAP (Simple Object Access Protocol), which provides XML-based message delivery over an HTTP connection. The existing SOAP protocol uses synchronous RPC for invoking operations in Web services. However, in response to an increasing need to facilitate long running activities new proposals have been made to extend SOAP to allow asynchronous message exchange (i.e., requests and responses are not synchronous). One notable proposal is ASAP (Asynchronous Service Access Protocol) [1], which allows the execution of long-running Web service operations,

* San-Yih Hwang was supported in part by Fulbright Scholarship.
** Haojun Wang was supported in part by the NSF under grant ISS-0308264.

P. Atzeni et al. (Eds.): ER 2004, LNCS 3288, pp. 596–609, 2004.

and also non-blocking Web services invocation, in a less reliable environment (e.g., wireless networks). In the following discussion, we use the term Web service, to refer to *an atomic activity*, which may encompass either a single Web service operation (in the case of asynchronous Web services) or a pair of invoke/respond operations (in the case of synchronous Web services), and the term *WS-workflow* to refer to a workflow composed of a set of Web service invocations threaded into a directed graph.

Several languages have been proposed to compose Web services into workflows. Notable examples include WSFL (Web Service Flow Language) [13] and XLANG (Web Services for Business Process Design) [16]. The ideas of WSFL and XLANG have converged and been superceded by BPEL4WS (Business Process Execution Language for Web Services) specification [2]. Such Web services-based workflows may subsequently become (composite) Web services, thereby enabling nested Web Services Workflows (WS-workflows).

While the syntactic description of Web services can be specified through WSDL (Web Service Description Language), their semantics and *quality of service* (QoS) are left unspecified. The concept of QoS has been introduced and extensively studied in computer networks, multimedia systems, and real-time systems. QoS was mainly considered as an overload management problem that measures non-functional aspects of the target system, such as timeliness (e.g., message delay ratio) and completeness (e.g., message drop percentage). More recently, the concept of QoS is finding its way into application specification, especially in describing the level of service provided by a server. Typical QoS metrics at the application level include throughput, response time, cost, reliability, fidelity, etc [12]. Some work has been devoted to the specification and estimation of workflow QoS [3, 7]. However, previous work in workflow QoS estimation either focused on the static case (e.g., computing the average or the worst case QoS values) or relied on simulation to compute workflow QoS in a broader context. While the former has limited applicability, the later requires substantial computation before reaching stable results. In this paper, we propose a probability-based QoS model on Web services and WS-workflows that allows for efficient and accurate QoS estimation. Such an estimation serves as the basis for dealing with *Web services selection problem* [11] and *service level agreement (SLA) specification problem* [6].

The main contributions of our research are:

1. We identify a set of QoS metrics tailored for Web services and WS-workflows and give an anatomy of these metrics.
2. We propose a probability-based WS-workflow QoS model and its computation framework. This computation framework can be used to compute QoS of a complete or partial WS-workflow.
3. We explore alternative algorithms for computing probability distribution functions of WS-workflow QoS. The efficiency and accuracy of these algorithms are compared.

This paper is organized as follows. In Section 2 we define the QoS model in the context of WS-workflows. In Section 3 we present the QoS computation framework for WS-workflows. In Section 4 we describe algorithms for efficiently computing the

QoS values of a WS-workflow. Section 5 presents preliminary results of our performance evaluation. Section 6 reviews related work. Finally, Section 7 concludes this paper and identifies directions for future research.

2 QoS Model for Web Services

2.1 Web Services QoS Metrics

Many workflow-related QoS metrics have been proposed in the literature [3, 7, 9, 11, 12]. Typical categories of QoS metrics include performance (e.g., response time and throughput), resources (e.g., cost, memory/cpu/bandwidth consumption), dependability (e.g., reliability, availability, and time to repair), fidelity, transactional properties (e.g., ACID properties and commit protocols), and security (e.g., confidentiality, non-repudiation, and encryption).

Some of the proposed metrics are related to the system capacity for executing a WS-workflow. For example, metrics used to measure the power of servers, such as throughput, memory/cpu/bandwidth consumption, time to repair (TTR), and availability, falls in the category called *system-level QoS*. However, the capacities of servers for executing Web services (e.g., man power for manual activities and computing power for automatic activities) are unlikely to be revealed due to autonomy consideration, and may change over time without notification. These metrics might be useful in some workflow context such as intra-organizational workflows (for determining the amount of resources to spend on executing workflows). For inter-organizational workflows, where a needed Web service may be controlled by another organization, QoS metrics in this category generally cannot be measured, and are thus excluded from further discussion. Another QoS metrics require all instances of the same Web service to share the same values. In this case, it is better to view these metrics as *service classes* rather than quality of service. Metrics of service class include those categorized as transactional properties and security. In this paper we focus on those WS-workflow QoS metrics that measure a WS-workflow instance and whose value may change across instances. These metrics, called *instance-level QoS* metrics, include response time, cost, reliability, and fidelity rating. Note that *cost* is a complicated metric and could be a function of both service class and/or other QoS values. For example, a Web service instance that imposes weaker security requirements or incurs longer execution time might be entitled to lower cost. Some services may adopt a different pricing scheme that charges based on factors other than usage (e.g., membership fee or monthly fee). In this paper, we consider the *pay-per-service* pricing scheme, which allows us to include cost as an instance-level QoS metric.

In summary, our work considers four metrics: **Response time** (i.e., time elapsed from the submission of a request to the receiving of the response)**, Reliability** (i.e., the probability that the service can be successfully completed)**, Fidelity** (i.e., reputation rating) and **Cost** (i.e., the amount of money paid for executing an activity), which can be equally applicable to both atomic Web services and WS-workflows (also called composite Web services). These QoS metrics are defined such that different instances of the same Web service may have different QoS values.

2.2 Probabilistic Modeling of Web Services QoS

We use a probability model for describing Web service QoS. In particular, we use *probability mass function* (PMF) on finite scalar domain as the QoS probability model. In other words, each QoS metric of a Web service is viewed as a discrete random variable, and the PMF indicates the probability that the QoS metric assumes a particular value. For example, the fidelity F of an example Web service with five grades (1-5) may have the following PMF:

$$f_F(1) = 0.1, f_F(2) = 0.2, f_F(3) = 0.3, f_F(4) = 0.3, f_F(5) = 0.1$$

Note that it is natural to describe Reliability, Fidelity rating and Cost as random variables and to model them as PMFs with domains being {0 (fail), 1 (success)}, a set of distinct ratings, and a set of possible costs respectively. However, it is less intuitive to use PMF for describing response time whose domain is inherently continuous. By viewing response time at a coarser granularity, it is possible to model response time as a discrete random variable. Specifically, we partition the range of response time into a finite sequence of sub-intervals and use a representative number (e.g., the mean) to indicate each sub-interval. For example, suppose that the probabilities of a Web service being completed in one day, two to four days, and five to seven days, are 0.2, 0.6, and 0.2, respectively. The PMF of its response time X is represented as follows:

$f_X(1)=0.2, f_X(3)=0.6$ (3 is the mean of [2, 4]), and $f_X(6)=0.2$ (6 is the mean of [5, 7])

As expected, finer granularity on response time will yield more accurate estimation with higher overhead in representation and computation. We explore these tradeoffs in our experiments.

2.3 WS-Workflow Composition

For an atomic Web service, its QoS PMFs can be derived from its past records of invocations. For a newly developed WS-workflow that is composed of a set of atomic Web services, we need a way to determine its QoS PMFs. Different workflow composition languages may provide different constructs for specifying the control-flow among constituent activities (e.g., see [14, 15] for a comparison of the expressive powers of various workflow and Web services composition languages). Kiepuszewski *et al.* [8] define a structured workflow model that consists of only four constructs: sequential, or-split/or-join, and-split/and-join, and loop, which allows for recursive construction of larger workflows. Although it has been shown that this structured workflow model is unable to model arbitrary workflows [8], it is nevertheless powerful enough to describe many real-world workflows. In fact, there exist some commercial workflow systems that support only structured workflows, such as SAP R/3 and Filenet Visual workflo.

In this paper, as an initial step of the study, we focus our attention on structured workflows. To distinguish between *exclusive or* and (*multiple choice*) *or*, which is crucial in deriving WS-workflow QoS, we extend the structured workflow model to include five constructs:

1. ***sequential***: a sequence of activities ($a_1, a_2, \ldots, a_n$).
2. ***parallel*** (and split/and join): multiple activities ($a_1, a_2, \ldots, a_n$) that can be concurrently executed and merged with synchronization.
3. ***conditional*** (exclusive split/exclusive join): multiple activities ($a_1, a_2, \ldots, a_n$), among which only one activity can be executed.
4. ***fault-tolerant*** (and split/exclusive join): multiple activities ($a_1, a_2, \ldots, a_n$) that can be concurrently executed but merged without synchronization.
5. ***loop***: a block of activities a guarded by a condition "*LC*". Here we adopt *while* loop in our following discussion.

3 Computing QoS Values of WS Compositions

We now describe how to compute the WS-workflow QoS values for each composition construct introduced earlier. We identify five basic operations for manipulating random variables, namely (i) addition, (ii) multiplication, (iii) maximum, (iv) minimum, and (v) conditional selection. Each of these operations takes as input a number of random variables characterized by PMFs and produces a random variable characterized by another PMF. The first four operations are quite straightforward, and their detailed descriptions are omitted here due to space limitations. For their formal definitions, interested readers are referred to [5]. The conditional selection, denoted as $\underset{1 \le i \le n}{CS}(X_i, p_i)$, is defined as following[1]. Let $X_1, X_2, \ldots, X_n$ be n random variables, with p_i, $1 \le i \le n$, being the probability that X_i is selected by the conditional selection operation *CS*. Note the selection of any random variable is exclusive, i.e., exactly one of these would be selected. The result of $\underset{1 \le i \le n}{CS}(X_i, p_i)$ is a new random variable Z with $Dom(Z) = \bigcup_{1 \le i \le k} Dom(X_i)$. Specifically, the PMF $f_Z()$ of Z is as follows:

$$f_Z(Z = z) = \sum_{z \in Dom(X_j)} p_j \cdot f_{X_j}(z), \, z \in Dom(Z).$$

For each activity a, we consider four QoS metrics, namely response time, cost, reliability, and fidelity, denoted $T(a)$, $C(a)$, $R(a)$, and $F(a)$ respectively[2]. A WS-workflow composed of activities $a_1, a_2, \ldots, a_n$ using some composition construct is denoted $w(a_1, a_2, \ldots, a_n)$. The QoS values of w, under various composition constructs, are shown in Table 1.

We assume that the fidelity of w using sequential or parallel composition is a weighted sum of the fidelities of its constituent activities. The fidelity weight of each

---

[1] Ensure not to confuse the conditional selection by the weighted sum ∑pi·Xi. The weighted sum results in a random variable whose domain may not be the union of the domains of the constituent activities. While weighted sum is used for computing the average value of a set of scalar values, it should not be used to compute the PMF resulted from the conditional selection of a set of random variables.

[2] Note that each QoS metric of an activity is NOT a scalar value but a discrete random variable characterized by a PMF.

activity can be either manually assigned by the designer, or automatically derived from past history, e.g. by using linear regression. For the conditional construct, exactly one activity will be selected at run-time. Thus, the fidelity of w is the conditional selection of the fidelity of its constituent activities with the associated probabilities. For the fault-tolerant construct, the fidelity of the activity that is the first to complete becomes the fidelity of w. Thus, $F(w) = \underset{1\le i\le n}{CS}(F(a_i), p_f(a_i))$, where

$$p_f(a_i) = \prod_{k\neq i} P(T(a_k) > T(a_i)).$$

A loop construct is defined as a repetition of a block guarded by a condition "*LC*", i.e., this block is repetitively executed till the condition "*LC*" no longer holds. Cardoso et al. assumed a geometric distribution on the number of iterations [3]. However, the memoryless property of the geometric distribution fails to capture a common phenomenon that a repeated execution of a block usually has a better chance to exit the loop. Gillmann et al [7] assumed the number of iterations to be uniformly distributed, which again may not hold in many applications. In this paper, rather than assuming a particular distribution, we simply regard the number of iterations as a PMF with a finite scalar domain. Let $f_{L(a)}(l), 0\le l\le c$, be the PMF of the number of iterations of a loop structure L defined on a block a, where c is the maximum number of iterations. Let $T(a)$, $C(a)$, $R(a)$, $F(a)$ denote the PMFs of the response time, cost, reliability, and fidelity of a respectively. If a is executed for l times, the response time $T_a(l)$ is $T_a(l) = \sum_{1\le i\le l} T(a)$. The response time of L is the *conditional selection* on $T_a(l)$ with probabilities $f_{L(a)}(l)$, $0\le l\le c$. Thus, the response time of L is $T(L) = \underset{1\le l\le c}{CS}(T_a(l), f_{L(a)}(l))$. Similar arguments can be applied to the computation of cost and reliability. Regarding fidelity, **let** p_1 be the probability of executing at least one iteration and p_0=1-p_1. When a is executed at least once, the fidelity of a loop structure, in our view, is determined simply by its last execution of a. Let F_a(T) denote the fidelity that a is executed at least once (i.e., F_a(T)=$F(a)$) and F_a(F) be the fidelity that a is not executed. The fidelity of L is therefore computed as follows:

$$F(L) = \underset{i\in\{F,T\}}{CS}(F_a(i), p_i).$$

4 Efficient Computation of WS-Workflow QoS

4.1 High Level Algorithm

A structured WS-workflow can be recursively constructed by using the five basic constructs. Figure 1 shows an example WS-workflow, namely *PC order fulfillment*. This WS-workflow is designed to tailor-make and to deliver personal computers at a customer's request. At the highest level, the WS-workflow is a sequential construct that consists of *Parts procurement*, *Assembly*, *Test*, *Adjustment*, *Shipping*, and *Cus-*

Table 1. The QoS values of a WS-workflow *w* under various composition constructs

Composition Construct	Cost: $C(w)$)	Response time: $T(w)$	Reliability: $R(w)$	Fidelity: $F(w)$
Sequential	$\sum_{i=1}^{n} C(a_i)$	$\sum_{i=1}^{n} T(a_i)$	$\prod_{i=1}^{n} R(a_i)$	$\sum_{i=1}^{n} w_i F(a_i)$
Parallel	$\sum_{i=1}^{n} C(a_i)$	$\underset{i}{Max}\{T(a_i)\}$	$\prod_{i=1}^{n} R(a_i)$	$\sum_{i=1}^{n} w_i F(a_i)$
Conditional	$\underset{1 \le i \le n}{CS}(C(a_i), p_i)$	$\underset{1 \le i \le n}{CS}(T(a_i), p_i)$	$\underset{1 \le i \le n}{CS}(R(a_i), p_i)$	$\underset{1 \le i \le n}{CS}(F(a_i), p_i)$
Fault-tolerant	$\sum_{i=1}^{n} C(a_i)$	$\underset{i}{Min}\{T(a_i)\}$	$1 - \prod_{i=1}^{n} (1 - R(a_i))$ where $f_{1\text{-}R}(0) = f_R(1)$ and $f_{1\text{-}R}(1) = f_R(0)$	$\underset{1 \le i \le n}{CS}(F(a_i), p_f(a_i))$ where $p_f(a_i) = \prod_{k \ne i} P(T(a_k) > T(a_i))$
Loop	$\underset{1 \le l \le c}{CS}(C_a(l), f_{L(a)}(l))$ where $C_a(l) = \sum_{1 \le i \le l} C(a)$	$\underset{1 \le l \le c}{CS}(T_a(l), f_{L(a)}(l))$ where $T_a(l) = \sum_{1 \le i \le l} T(a)$	$\underset{1 \le l \le c}{CS}(R_a(l), f_{L(a)}(l))$ where $R_a(l) = \prod_{1 \le i \le l} R(a)$	$\underset{i \in \{F,T\}}{CS}(F_a(i), p_i)$ where F_b(T)=$F(a)$) and F_a(F) be the fidelity that *a* is not executed.

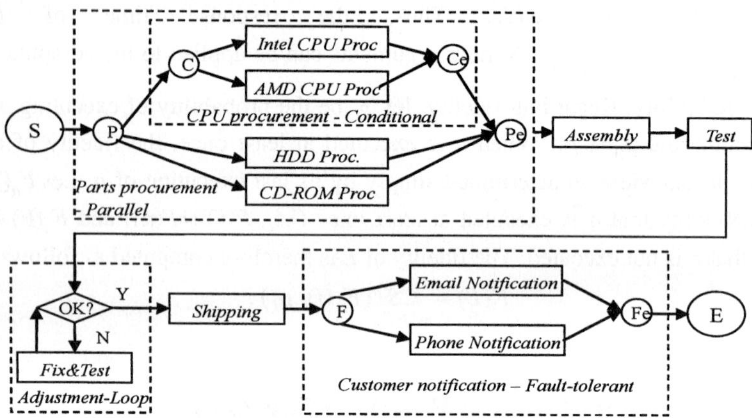

Fig. 1. An example WS-workflow *PC order fulfillment*

Customer notification. Parts procurement is a parallel construct that comprises of *CPU procurement*, *HDD procurement*, and *CD-ROM procurement*. CPU procurement in turn is a conditional construct composed of *Intel CPU procurement* and *AMD CPU procurement*. Adjustment is a loop construct on *Fix&Test*, which is iteratively executed until the quality of the PC is ensured. Customer notification is a fault-

```
ComputeQoS(A: a WS-workflow activity)
{
    IF A.type ≠ ATOMIC THEN {
        FOR (each activity t∈A.activities) DO
                        ComputeQoS(t);
        IF A.construct = SEQUENTIAL THEN
                        A.QoS = SequentialQoS(A.activities);
        ELSEIF A.construct = PARALLEL THEN
                        A.QoS = ParallelQoS(A.activities);
        ELSEIF A.construct = CONDITIONAL THEN
                        A.QoS = ConditionalQoS(A.activities);
        ELSEIF A.construct = FAULT_TOLERANT THEN
                        A.QoS = FaultTolerantQoS(A.activities);
        ELSE // A.construct = LOOP
                        A.QoS = LoopQoS(A.activities);
    }
    ELSE Estimate the QoSs of A and put them in A.QoS;
};
```

Fig. 2. Pseudo code for computing QoS of a WS-workflow

tolerant construct that consists of *Email notification* and *Phone notification*. The success of either notification marks the completion of the entire WS-workflow.

The QoS of the entire WS-workflow can be recursively computed. The pseudo-code is listed in Figure 2. Note that ***SequentialQoS***(*A*.activities), ***ParallelQoS*** (*A*.activities), ***ConditionalQoS***(*A*.activities), ***FaultTolerantQoS***(*A*.activities), ***LoopQoS***(*A*.activities) are used to compute the four QoS metric values for sequential, parallel, conditional, fault tolerant, and loop constructs respectively. Their pseudo codes are quite clear from our discussion in Section 3 and omitted here for brevity.

4.2 Sample Space Reduction

When combining PMFs of discrete random variables with respect to a given operation, the sample space size of the resultant random variable may become huge. Consider adding k discrete random variables each having n elements in their respective domains. The sample space size of the resultant random variable, in the worst case, is of the order of n^k. In order to keep the domain of a PMF after each operation at a reasonable size, we propose to group the elements in the sample space. In other words, several consecutive scalar values in the sample space will be represented by a single value and the aggregated probability is computed. The problem is formally described below.

Let the domain of X be $\{ x_1, x_2, ..., x_s \}$, where $x_i < x_{i+1}, 1 \le i < s$, and the PMF of X be f_X. We called another random variable Y an *aggregate random variable* of X if there exists a partition $(j_0, j_1, j_2, \ldots, j_m)$ of $(x_1, x_2, ..., x_s)$, where $1=j_0<j_1<j_2< \ldots <j_{m-1}<j_m=s+1$, such that domain of Y is

$$\{y_r : y_r = \sum_{k=j_{r-1}}^{j_r-1} \left(x_k \cdot f_X(x_k)\right) \Big/ \sum_{k=j_{r-1}}^{j_r-1} f_X(x_k), 1 \le r \le m\}$$

and the PMF for Y is $f_Y(y_r)=\sum_{k=j_{r-1}}^{j_r-1} f_X(x_k)$, $1\leq r\leq m$. The aggregate error of Y with respect to X, denoted *aggregate_error*(Y, X), is the mean square error defined as follows:

$$aggregate\_error(Y, X)=\sum_{r=1}^{m}\sum_{k=j_{r-1}}^{j_r-1} f_X(x_k)\cdot(x_k-y_r)^2 .$$

Aggregate Random Variable Problem
Given a random variable X of domain size s and a desired domain size m, the problem is to find an aggregate random variable Y of domain size m such that its aggregate error with respect to X is minimized.

Dynamic Programming Method
An optimal solution to this problem can be obtained by formulating it as a dynamic program. Let $e(i, j, k)$ be the optimal aggregate error of partitioning $x_i, x_{i+1},\ldots, x_j$ into k subsequences. We have the following recurrence:

$$e(i,j,k)=\min_{i\leq a<j,1\leq b<k}(e(i,a,b)+e(a+1,j,k-b)) \text{ if } j\text{-}i\text{+}1>k \text{ and } k>1$$

$$e(i, j, k) = 0 \text{ if } j\text{-}i\text{+}1=k$$

$$e(i, j, 1) = error(i, j),$$

where *error*(i, j) is the aggregated error introduced in representing $\{x_i, x_{i+1},\ldots, x_j\}$ by a single value. Specifically, $error(i, j)=\sum_{i\leq k\leq j} f_X(x_k)\cdot(x_k-\overline{x})^2$, where

$$\overline{x}=\frac{\sum_{i\leq k\leq j} f_X(x_k)\cdot x_k}{\sum_{i\leq k\leq j} f_X(x_k)} .$$

The time complexity of the dynamic programming algorithm is $O(s^3m^2)$, and its space complexity is $O(s^2m)$.

Greedy Method
To reduce the computation overhead, we propose a heuristic method for solving this problem. The idea is to continuously merge the adjacent pair of samples that gives the least error until a reasonable sample space size is reached. When an adjacent pair (x_i, x_{i+1}) is merged, a new element x' is created to replace x_i and x_{i+1}, where

$$x'=\frac{f_X(x_i)\cdot x_i+f_X(x_{i+1})\cdot x_{i+1}}{f_X(x_i)+f_X(x_{i+1})} \text{ and } f_X(x')=f_X(x_i)+f_X(x_{i+1}) .$$

The error of merging (x_i, x_i+1), denoted *pair_error*(x_i, x_i+1), is computed as follows:

$$pair\_error(x_i, x_{i+1}) = f_X(x_i)\cdot(x_i - x')^2 + f_X(x_{i+1})\cdot(x_{i+1} - x')^2 .$$

We can use a priority queue to store the errors of merging adjacent pairs. In each iteration, we perform the following steps:

1. Extract an adjacent pair with the least *pair_error*() value from the priority queue, say (x_i, x_{i+1}).
2. Replace x_i and x_{i+1} by the new value x' in the domain of X.
3. Compute *pair_error*(x_{i-1},x') if i>1 and *pair_error*(x', x_{i+2}) if i<n-1. Delete *pair_error*(x_{i-1},x_i) and *pair_error*(x_{i+1},x_{i+2}) from the priority queue, and insert *pair_error*(x_{i-1},x') and *pair_error*(x', x_{i+2}) into the priority queue.

In each iteration, step 1 and 3 takes O(lg$s$) time while step 2 takes only constant time. The total number of iterations is s-m. Thus, the time complexity of this greedy approach is O($s$lg$s$).

When it comes to combining the QoS values of n activities, we can perform pair-wise QoS combinations n-1 times and apply a sample space reduction method as described above after each combination. Suppose each random variable has the same domain size m. The addition of two random variables may result in a new random variable with domain size up to m^2. We then apply some sample space reduction technique to reduce the domain size down to m before combining the next random variable. Although there exist a large number of possible orders in which one can combine the n activities, we have concluded from our preliminary experiments that different orders of activity combination has little effect on the resultant aggregate errors. Therefore, we simply choose an arbitrary order for pair-wise combinations.

5 Performance Evaluation

In this section we report the results of our initial evaluation of the proposed probabilistic QoS computation framework. Due to space limitation, we only show the experimental results on one QoS metric, namely the *response time*. Other metrics exhibit similar trends.

This first set of experiments aims to show how the two proposed sample space size reduction techniques, namely dynamic programming and the greedy method, impact the accuracy of the resultant PMFs. Consider a simple workflow that consists of only two sequential activities. Let Z be the response time of the workflow, and X and Y be the response times of the two activities. Obviously Z=X+Y. For ease of comparison, we assumed that the generative models for both X and Y are both normal distributions, which allows us to theoretically compute the generative model of Z. The performance metric considered is *cumulative distribution function* (CDF). The CDF of Z, denoted as $F_Z(z)$, is defined as Pr($Z \le z$). We exercised 100 values for z ranging from 100 to 270. Figure 3(a) shows the CDFs obtained by using dynamic programming and the greedy method, with the theoretical method serving as the benchmark, which is directly computed from the generative model of Z. As can be seen, the CDFs ob-

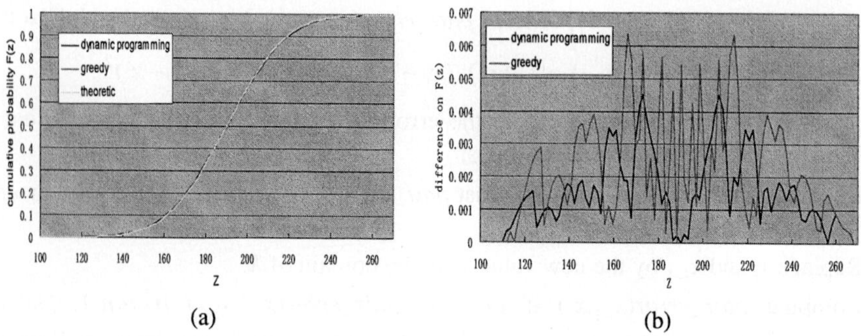

(a) (b)

Fig. 3. (a) CDFs of the dynamic programming and the greedy method with the theoretical method serving as the benchmark; (b) the CDF difference of each method from the theoretical method

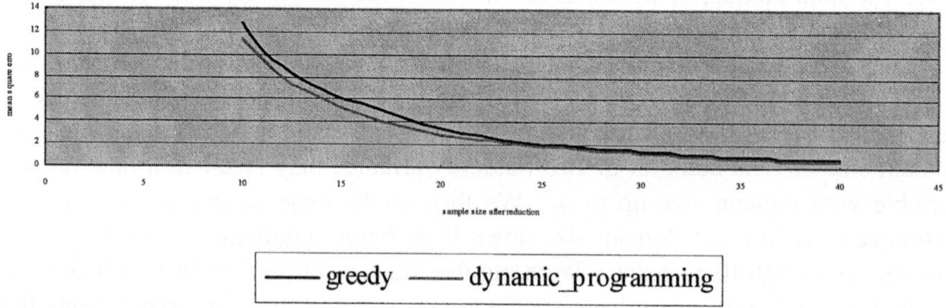

Fig. 4. Mean square errors of dynamic programming and greedy methods over different sample space sizes

tained from dynamic programming and greedy methods are very close to the theoretical CDF. To show the subtle differences, we plotted the CDF differences of dynamic programming and greedy methods obtained from substracting the theoretical CDF from both CDFs, which are shown in Figure 3(b). Although the differences are indeed very small (less than 0.01), it can still be seen that dynamic programming in general leads to better CDF with the mean probability error of 0.001494, compared to 0.002136 for the greedy method.

We next vary the domain size of the aggregate random variable Z and compare the mean square errors incurred by both dynamic programming and greedy methods. Figure 4 shows the experimental results. As expected, a larger domain size leads to a smaller mean square error. Besides, the greedy method constantly incurs slightly higher mean square errors over different domain sizes.

We finally apply the proposed framework to compute the response time of the example WS-workflow shown in Section 4.1, namely PC order fulfillment. The generative model of each atomic activity is assumed to be the normal distribution with minimum and maximum value constraints. To evaluate the PMF of the example WS-workflow computed by our framework, we ran simulation and generated 1 million instances. Thus, we were able to get a stable PMF of the total response time that is

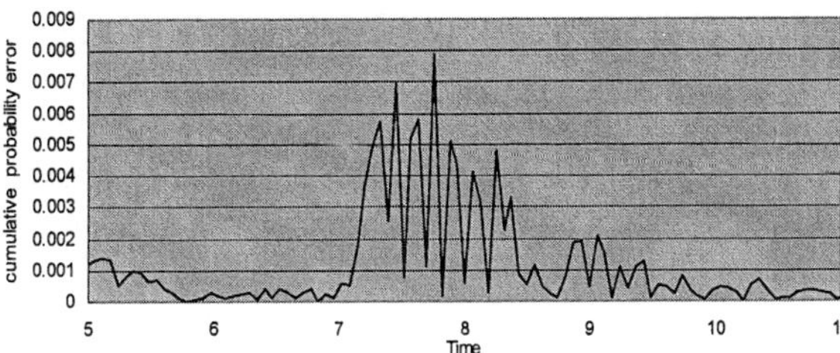

Fig. 5. Cumulative probability error of response time of PC order fulfillment (aggregate sample space size = 30)

very close to the real one. We then used the PMF generated by simulation as the benchmark. Figure 5 shows the difference between the cumulative probabilities computed using the greedy method and the benchmark, when the aggregate sample space size is set to 30. It can be seen that the difference is very small, i.e., no higher than 0.008. In contrast, the running time difference is substantial. Our experimental platform was a PC server equipped with Intel P4 2.66 GHz CPU and 512 MB main memory. The simulation program took about 3.5 seconds to generate one million instances, while the greedy method based approach took only about 3 ms to compute the response time PMF of the example WS-workflow.

6 Related Work

QoS-based Web service selection has attracted a lot of attention in recent years. While previous work attempted to optimize the selection for a single activity, recent work has focused on the selection of Web services in order to satisfy the QoS requirements of a WS-workflow. Patel et al. [11] proposed an approach to select a number of Web services for a given activity, and to distribute activity instances to these Web services according to their QoS values. Menasce [10] proposed a scheme to estimate the throughput of a composite Web service from those of its constituent Web services, which serves as a basis for selecting Web services. However, the derivation of various QoS values of a composite Web service was not a focus of these efforts. Zeng et al. [17] identified a set of QoS metrics and proposed to apply linear programming to select an execution plan that has the optimal QoS value. However, the workflow constructs considered in their work are limited and do not include loop and fault-tolerance. Besides, only deterministic QoS values are computed.

Our work is closest to the Stochastic workflow reduction technique [3], which iteratively applies a set of reduction rules until a single workflow is reached. Furthermore, Cardoso [3] identified the same four QoS measures as used in our work. However, the mathematical approach proposed there can only be used to compute deterministic QoS values (e.g., average response time), while our probability-based QoS model enables the estimation of a probability distribution function for a given workflow, which allows broader applicability.

Finally, several previous efforts have proposed using simulation to measure the QoS of a workflow [3, 6, 7], with a major focus on timeliness measures. The simulation approach models a workflow as a queuing system with transition probabilities associated with conditional branches. In addition to its high computation overhead, this approach requires the specification of server capacities. In other words, processing time and number of servers associated with each activity have to be specified. While such a requirement causes little problem for an (intra-organizational) workflow, it is impossible to do so for a WS-workflow that spans the boundaries of several autonomous enterprises.

CPM (Critical Path Method) and PERT (Program Evaluation Review Technique) are project management techniques for project Planning, Scheduling and Control [4]. The key idea of CPM/PERT is to identity the critical path, which is the longest path through the activity network controlling the entire project. In CPM, the time of each activity is deterministic. PERT assumes Beta distribution and independence of the time of each activity. It uses three parameters, namely the Most Optimistic, Most Likely, and Most Pessimistic estimates, to determine the mean value μ and standard deviation σ for the execution time of an activity using the following formulae:

μ= (Most Optimistic + (4 $\times$ Most Likely) + Most Pessimistic)/6
σ = (Most Pessimistic - Most Optimistic)/6

Compared to the structure of business processes, the network of CPM/PERT is much simpler and does not contain conditional and loop structures. It is more suitable for describing manufacturing processes, whose component activities are usually deterministic. CPM/PERT is focused on the computation of process time and the tradeoffs between the time and cost, while in WS-workflows, other QoS metrics, such as fidelity and reliability, need to be supported.

7 Conclusions

In this paper, we have identified a number of QoS metrics for Web services and proposed a probability-based QoS model. A QoS metric of a (atomic or composite) Web service is described as a probability mass function. We have described algorithms to compute the QoS values of a WS-workflow from those of its constituent Web services. We introduced the problem of computing the least error PMF of a composite WS-workflow, and show that the search space is very large. We provided a dynamic programming formulation for the optimal solution, and an efficient approximation heuristic for it. Preliminary experimental results show that our proposed algorithm achieves high accuracy and is computationally efficient.

The proposed model and framework can be used to estimate the QoS values of a WS-workflow at design time. However, we foresee the need of a WS-workflow monitoring service that can alert the owner or users of a WS-workflow about the possible violation of some QoS objective at the early stage. Such an alert function serves as an early notification of potential violation of the service level agreement (SLA) and allows the responsible entities to carry out compensatory activities. Although our QoS computation framework has been shown to be efficient, further optimization is needed in order to meet the high efficiency requirements of the run-time monitoring service. We are currently investigating the issues and techniques in implementing the monitoring service.

References

1. OASIS, Asynchronous Service Access Protocol, available at http://www.oasis-open.org/committees/tc_home.php?wg_abbrev=asap.
2. S. Thatte, Business Process Execution Language for Web Services 1.1, 2003, available at http://www-106.ibm.com/developerworks/webservices/library/ws-bpel/.
3. J. Cardoso, "Quality of Service and Semantic Composition of Workflows," Ph.D. Dissertation, Department of Computer Science, University of Georgia, Athens, GA, 2002.
4. F. S. Hillier, G.. J. Lieberman, Introduction to Operations Research, McGraw-Hill Science/Engineering/Math; 7th ed., 2002.
5. S.-Y. Hwang, H.-J. Wang, J. Srivastava, "A Probabilistic QoS Model and Computation Framework for Web Services-Based Workflows," Tech. Report, Department of Computer Science, U. of Minnesota.
6. L.Jin, V. Machiraju, A. Sahai, "Analysis of Service Level Agreement," HP Labs Tech. Report HPL 2002-180, 2002, available at http://www.hpl.hp.com/techreports/2002/HPL-2002-180.pdf.
7. M. Gillmann, G. Weikum, W. Wonner, "Workflow Management with Service Quality Guarantees," Proc. of ACM SIGMOD Int. Conf. on Management of Data, 2002.
8. B. Kiepuszewski, A.H.M. ter Hofstede, and C. Bussler, "On Structured Workflow Modelling," Proc. of the 12th Int. Conference on Advanced Information Systems Engineering (CAiSE00), 2000.
9. A. Mani, A. Nagarajin, "Understanding quality of service for Web services," 2002, available at http://www-106.ibm.com/developerworks/webservices/library/ws-quality.html.
10. D. A. Menasce, "QoS Issues in Web Services," IEEE Internet Computing, Nov/Dec., 2002.
11. C. Patel, K. Supekar, Y. Lee, "A QoS Oriented Framework for Adaptive Management of Web Service based Workflows," Proc. of Int. Conf. on Database and Expert Systems (DEXA2003), 2003.
12. B. Sabata, S. Chatterjee, M.Davis, J. Sydir, and T.F Lawrence. "Taxonomy for QoS specification," Proc. of Workshop on Object-oriented Real-time Dependable Systems, 1997.
13. IBM Software Group, Web Services Flow Language 1.0, 2001, available at http://www-306.ibm.com/software/solutions/webservices/pdf/WSFL.pdf
14. Workflow Patterns, http://tmitwww.tm.tue.nl/research/patterns/.
15. P. Wohed, W.M.P. van der Aalst, M. Dumas, A. H. M. ter Hofstede, "Analysis of Web Services Composition Languages," Proc. of 22nd Int. Conf. on Conceptual Modeling (ER2003), 2003.
16. S. Thatte, Web Services for Business Process Design, 2001, available at http://www.gotdotnet.com/team/xml_wsspecs/xlang-c/default.htm.
17. L. Zeng, B. Benatallah, M. Dumas, J. Kalagnanam, Q. Sheng, "Web Engineering: Quality driven Web Services Composition,", Proc. of 12'th Int. Conf. on World Wide Web, 2003.

Lossless Conditional Schema Evolution

Ole G. Jensen[1] and Michael H. Böhlen[2]

[1] Department of Computer Science, Aalborg University, Fredrik Bajers Vej 7E, DK-9220 Aalborg Øst, Denmark
guttorm@cs.aau.dk

[2] Faculty of Computer Science, Free University of Bozen-Bolzano, Dominikanerplatz 3, I-39100 Bolzano, Italy
boehlen@inf.unibz.it

Abstract. Conditional schema changes change the schema of the tuples that satisfy the change condition. When the schema of a relation changes some tuples may no longer fit the current schema. Handling the mismatch between the intended schema of tuples and the recorded schema of tuples is at the core of a DBMS that supports schema evolution. We propose to keep track of schema mismatches at the level of individual tuples, and prove that evolving schemas with conditional schema changes, in contrast to database systems relying on data migration, are lossless when the schema evolves. The lossless property is a precondition for a flexible semantics that allows to correctly answer general queries over evolving schemas. The key challenge is to handle attribute mismatches between the intended and recorded schema in a consistent way. We provide a parametric approach to resolve mismatches according to the needs of the application. We introduce the mismatch extended completed schema (MECS) which records attributes along with their mismatches, and we prove that relations with MECS are lossless.

1 Introduction

Schema evolution occurs when the schema of a populated database is changed. After the schema of a relation has evolved some tuples no longer fit the schema. The mismatch between the intended schema of a tuple and the recorded schema of the tuple, i.e., the schema used to record the tuple in the database, is inherent to evolving schemas. Handling this mismatch is at the very core of a DBMS that supports schema evolution.

The paper considers conditional schema evolution. A *conditional schema change* is an operation that changes the schema of the tuples that satisfy the condition. Conditional schema changes properly subsume regular (i.e., unconditional) schema changes, since it is always possible to have the condition select the entire extent of a relation. The main difference is that conditional schema evolution results in several current and equally important schemas.

As a first step towards a foundation for conditionally evolving database schemata, we present a theoretical framework for conditional evolution at the level of the relational model. The framework is based on evolving schemas consisting of a set of schema segments (akin to versions) where each segment defines the intended schema of a subset of tuples. We show that in contrast to current commercial database systems evolving schemas are lossless models. The lossless property ensures that schema changes can be

P. Atzeni et al. (Eds.): ER 2004, LNCS 3288, pp. 610–623, 2004.

rolled back and that tuple updates and schema changes are orthogonal operations, i.e., we never have to resort to data migration to deal with schema mismatches.

After the schema of a relation has evolved the intended and recorded schema of some tuples are out of sync. The attribute mismatches between the intended and recorded schemas of tuples have to be resolved systematically to get sensible answers to queries. We suggest a parametric approach that resolves attribute mismatches according to the needs of the application.

We propose the *mismatch extended completed schema* (MECS) which records both attributes and their corresponding attribute mismatches. We prove that relations with MECS are lossless evolution models. One of the salient features of such relations is that schema changes can be dealt with as standard tuple updates. We introduce parametric mismatch resolution of relations with MECS and establish the upper bound on its time complexity to be proportional to the size of the relation.

2 Preliminaries

2.1 Evolving Schemas

An *evolving schema*, $E = \{S_1, \ldots, S_n\}$, generalizes a relation schema and is defined as a set of schema segments. A *schema segment*, $S = (\mathcal{A}, P)$, consists of a schema $\mathcal{A}$ and a qualifier P. Throughout, we write $\mathcal{A}_S$ and P_S to directly refer to the schema and qualifier of segment S, respectively. As usual, a *schema*, $\mathcal{A} = \{A_1, \ldots, A_n\}$, is defined as a set of attributes. For the purpose of this paper, no distinction is made between schemas and sets of attributes. A *qualifier* P is either TRUE, FALSE, or a conjunction/disjunction of attribute constraints. An *attribute constraint* is a predicate of the form $A\theta c$ or $\neg(A\theta c)$, where A is an attribute, $\theta \in \{<, \leq, =, \neq, \geq, >\}$ is a comparison predicate, and c is a constant. An evolving schema may have segments with different schemas. Consequently, some tuples may be missing attributes that appear in other segments. In order to evaluate attribute constraints on such tuples, $A\theta c$ is an abbreviation for $\exists v(A/v \in t \wedge v\theta c)$ where t is a tuple. Likewise, $\neg(A\theta c)$ is an abbreviation for $\neg\exists(A/v \in t \wedge v\theta c)$. Note that this implies that the constraints $\neg(A = c)$ and $A \neq c$ are not equivalent.

A tuple t is a set of attribute values where each attribute value is an attribute/value pair: $\{A_1/v_1, \ldots, A_n/v_n\}$. The value must be an element of the domain of the attribute, i.e., if $dom(A)$ denotes the domain of attribute A, then $\forall A, v, t(A/v \in t \Rightarrow v \in dom(A))$. A tuple t *qualifies* for a segment S, $qual(t, S)$, iff t satisfies the qualifier P_S. A tuple satisfies a qualifier, $P(t)$, iff the qualifier is TRUE or the tuple makes the qualifier true under the standard interpretation. If a tuple t qualifies for a segment S in an evolving schema E, then $\mathcal{A}_S$ is the *intended schema* of t, i.e., $\forall t, S, E(S \in E \wedge qual(t, S)) \Rightarrow is(t, E) = \mathcal{A}_S)$. A tuple t *matches* a segment S iff the schema of S and t are identical: $match(t, S)$ iff $\forall A(A \in \mathcal{A}_S \Leftrightarrow \exists v(A/v \in t))$. If a tuple t matches a segment S in the evolving schema E, then $\mathcal{A}_S$ is the *recorded schema* of t, i.e., $\forall t, S, E(S \in E \wedge match(t, S) \Rightarrow rs(t, E) = \mathcal{A}_S)$.

2.2 Conditional Schema Changes

A *conditional schema change* is an operation that changes the set of segments of an evolving schema. The condition determines the tuples that are affected by the schema change. A *condition* C is either TRUE, FALSE, an attribute constraint, or a conjunction of attribute constraints. For the purpose of this paper we consider two conditional schema changes: adding an attribute, $\alpha(A, E, C)$, and deleting an attribute, $\beta(A, E, C)$. An extended set of schema changes that includes mappings between attributes and a discussion of their completeness can be found elsewhere [9].

$\alpha(A, E, C)$: An attribute A is added to the schemas of all segments that do not already include the attribute. For each such segment two new segments are generated: a segment with a schema that does not include the new attribute and a segment with a schema that includes the new attribute. Segments with a schema that already includes A are not changed.

$\beta(A, E, C)$: The attribute A is deleted from the schemas of all segments that include the attribute. For each such segment two new segments are generated: a segment with a schema that still includes the attribute and a segment with a schema that does not include the attribute. Segments with a schema that does not include A are not changed.

The precise formal definitions of conditional attribute additions and deletions are given in Figure 1.

$$\alpha(A, \emptyset, C) = \emptyset$$
$$\alpha(A, \{(\mathcal{A}, P)\} \cup E, C) = \begin{cases} \{(\mathcal{A}, P)\} \cup \alpha_A(E, C) & \text{iff } A \in \mathcal{A} \\ \{(\mathcal{A} \cup \{A\}, P \wedge C), (\mathcal{A}, P \wedge \neg C)\} \cup \alpha_A(E, C) & \text{iff } A \notin \mathcal{A} \end{cases}$$

$$\beta(A, \emptyset, C) = \emptyset$$
$$\beta(A, \{(\mathcal{A}, P)\} \cup E, C) = \begin{cases} \{(\mathcal{A}, P)\} \cup \beta_A(E, C) & \text{iff } A \notin \mathcal{A} \\ \{(\mathcal{A} \setminus \{A\}, P \wedge C), (\mathcal{A}, P \wedge \neg C)\} \cup \beta_A(E, C) & \text{iff } A \in \mathcal{A} \end{cases}$$

Fig. 1. Adding ($\alpha(A, E, C)$) and Deleting ($\beta(A, E, C)$) Attribute A on Condition C

2.3 Running Example

Assume a schema that models students: $\mathit{Student} = (\mathit{Name}, \mathit{Major}, \mathit{Level}, \mathit{Grade})$. The schema requires a name, major, level, and grade for each student. We consider two conditional schema changes.

$$\alpha(\mathit{sUpervisor}, \mathit{Student}, \mathit{Level} = grad) \tag{1}$$
$$\beta(\mathit{Grade}, \mathit{Student}, \mathit{Major} = bio),\ \alpha(\mathit{Credits}, \mathit{Student}, \mathit{Major} = bio) \tag{2}$$

The first conditional schema change assigns a supervisor to graduate students. Therefore, a $\mathit{sUpervisor}$ attribute is added to the schema of graduate students: $(\mathit{Name}, \mathit{Major}, \mathit{Level}, \mathit{Grade}, \mathit{sUpervisor})$. The schema $(\mathit{Name}, \mathit{Major}, \mathit{Level}, \mathit{Grade})$ remains valid for undergraduate students. Note that we are left with *two* current and equally important schemas.

The second conditional schema change requires that a new credit system is used for students with a major in biology. The credit system replaces the old grading system. Thus, biology students need to be recorded with a $\mathit{Credits}$ attribute instead of a Grade attribute. Obviously, biology students may be enrolled as undergraduate or graduate students. Therefore, the schema change applies to the schema of graduate and undergraduate students. This yields an evolving schema with a total of four segments:

$$S_1 = (\{N, M, L, G\}, \neg(L = grad) \wedge \neg(M = bio))$$
$$S_2 = (\{N, M, L, G, U\}, L = grad \wedge \neg(M = bio))$$
$$S_3 = (\{N, M, L, C\}, \neg(L = grad) \wedge M = bio)$$
$$S_4 = (\{N, M, L, C, U\}, L = grad \wedge M = bio)$$

An example instance of the evolving S_{tudent} schema is illustrated in Figure 2. Each tuple is shown as specified by the user, i.e., with values for the attributes of the recorded schema. The intended schema (is) is shown to the right. Note that only tuples t_3 and t_5 match on their recorded and intended schema. For the other three tuples the recorded and intended schema do not match. For example, tuple t_1 has the recorded schema $rs = (N, M, L, G)$ and the intended schema $is = (N, M, L, C)$.

t1 = (N/john,M/bio,L/ugrad, G/9.2) is = (N,M,L,C)
t2 = (N/anne,M/math,L/grad, G/8.7) is = (N,M,L,G,U)
t3 = (N/tom,M/math,L/ugrad, G/5.9) is = (N,M,L,G)
t4 = (N/kim,M/bio,L/grad, G/7.1,U/rick) is = (N,M,L,C,U)
t5 = (N/rita,M/bio,L/grad, C/31,U/mike) is = (N,M,L,C,U)

Fig. 2. An Instance of the S_{tudent} Schema

3 Lossless Schema Evolution

This section develops a framework that can be used to decide whether an evolving database model is *lossless*. Intuitively, a model is lossless iff at each point it can be used to determine the intended schema of tuples. This also means that schema changes can be rolled back. We use the evolving schema from Section 2.1 as a yardstick. Essentially, a lossless model must be able to determine the intended schema with at least the same degree of precision as the evolving schema.

A key issue with evolving schemas is that after several schema changes the schema may no longer permit to correctly determine the intended schema. To see this assume a model that preserves deleted attributes so it is possible to roll back to previous states (this is a common technique that is also used by commercial database systems). In order to replace grades with credits we drop the grade attribute and add a credit attribute. With dropped attributes being preserved we end up with the schema (N, M, L, G, C). This is clearly not the intended schema, and without extra information it is impossible to figure out that the credit attribute is supposed to replace the grade attribute. Thus, the model is lossy.

Evolving schema preserves qualification of tuples. Thus, tuples with an intended schema are guaranteed to also have an intended schema after the schema has evolved. Moreover, this intended schema is unique. The proofs have been omitted due to space consideration, but can be found in full detail in [10].

Lemma 1. *Let E be an evolving schema, t be a tuple, and $\gamma(A, E, C)$ be a conditional schema change where $\gamma \in \{\alpha, \beta\}$. If t qualifies for a segment in E, then t also qualifies for a segment in $\gamma(A, E, C)$, i.e., $\forall E, S, t, \gamma(S \in E \wedge qual(t, S) \Rightarrow \exists S'(S' \in \gamma(A, E, C) \wedge qual(t, S')))$.*

Lemma 2. *Let E and E' be evolving schemas, and $\gamma \in \{\alpha, \beta\}$ be a conditional schema change such that $\gamma(A, E, C) = E'$. Let t be a tuple that qualifies for a single segment in E, then the qualifying segment of t in E' is* unique.

Lemma 1 and 2 guarantee that the evolving schema always uniquely determines the intended schema of each tuple in a relation. This is required to accurately answer general queries over evolving relations (cf. Section 5). Moreover, for each tuple the evolving schema provides an intended schema that is consistent with the schema changes applied, i.e., a conditional schema change only changes the intended schema of a tuple if the tuple satisfies the corresponding condition.

We characterize an evolution model $M = (D, \Gamma, is)$ by a database schema D, a set of schema change operations Γ, and a function $is : t \times D \rightarrow \mathcal{A}$ that given a tuple t and a database schema D determines the intended schema of t. Each schema change operation $\gamma \in \Gamma$ is a function $\gamma : D \times C \rightarrow D$ that given a database schema and a condition applies the conditional schema change to produce a new database schema. An evolution model that associates the same intended schemas with tuples as the evolving schema is *lossless* iff it continues to do so after a conditional schema change has been applied.

Definition 1. (lossless) *Let E be an evolving schema and M be an evolution model. Let t be a tuple and $\gamma(A, E, C)$ be a conditional schema change. M is* lossless *iff*

$$\begin{aligned}
&\forall t, \gamma, C, E, M(\\
&\quad M = (D, \Gamma, is') \wedge \gamma \in \Gamma \wedge \\
&\quad is(t, E) = is'(t, D) \Rightarrow is(t, \gamma(A, E, C)) = is'(t, \gamma(A, D, C))
\end{aligned}$$

Example 1. Consider the evolution model $M = (D, \Gamma, is)$ based on the completed schema. The completed schema $D = \mathcal{A}$ contains all attributes $\mathcal{A}$ ever introduced, i.e., only attribute additions change the schema. The schema change operations Γ on the completed schema are therefore defined as follows: $\alpha(A, \mathcal{A}, C) = \mathcal{A} \cup \{A\}$ and $\beta(A, \mathcal{A}, C) = \mathcal{A}$. A property of the completed schema is that the intended and actual schema of tuples are synchronized, i.e., $is(t, \mathcal{A}) = \mathcal{A}$. Clearly, the completed schema is not lossless, since attribute deletions do not change the intended schema of tuples as required by the evolving schema.

4 Attribute Mismatches

This section investigates the mismatch between the recorded and intended schema of tuples. We illustrate the four type of mismatches that may occur at the level of individual attributes, and establish the relationship between conditional schema changes and attribute mismatches.

A *history* $H = [\gamma_1(A_1, E, C_1), \ldots, \gamma_n(A_n, E, C_n)]$ is a sequence of conditional schema changes where $\gamma_i \in \{\alpha, \beta\}$. Any schema can be constructed by adding each attribute unconditionally. E.g. $\alpha(G, \alpha(L, \alpha(M, \alpha(N, E_0, \text{TRUE}), \text{TRUE}), \text{TRUE}), \text{TRUE})$ constructs the initial student schema where $E_0 = \{(\{\}, \text{TRUE})\}$ is an evolving schema with a single empty segment. We assume that segments with FALSE qualifiers are removed which will yield an evolving schema with a single segment having the intended schema. It follows that any evolving schema can be constructed from a history by first constructing the initial schema and then adding in sequence the same conditional schema changes applied to the evolving schema. We write E_H to denote the evolving schema defined by H.

4.1 Mismatches Types

Let H be a history and $\mathcal{A}_H$ be the schema containing all attributes added by schema changes in H. Let t be a tuple with recorded schema $\mathcal{A}_r$ and intended schema $\mathcal{A}_i = is(t, H)$. Only attributes in $\mathcal{A}_H$ can be queried. Since $\mathcal{A}_r \subseteq \mathcal{A}_H$ and $\mathcal{A}_i \subseteq \mathcal{A}_H$ (otherwise t would not be a valid tupel for H) an attribute $A \in \mathcal{A}_H$ causes one of four possible types of mismatches depending on its membership of $\mathcal{A}_r$ and $\mathcal{A}_i$, respectively:

- **No mismatch** ($M_1 : A \in \mathcal{A}_r \wedge A \in \mathcal{A}_i$) The attribute appears in both the recorded and intended schema of a tuple. For example, for Kim (tuple t_4 in Figure 2) there is no mismatch for attributes N, M, E, and U.
- **Not recorded** ($M_2 : A \notin \mathcal{A}_r \wedge A \in \mathcal{A}_i$) The attribute appears only in the intended schema of the tuple. These mismatches occur when schema changes add new attributes. For example, John (tuple t_1 in Figure 2) was not recorded with a value for the Credits attribute, which was added after the tuple was inserted into the database.
- **Not available** ($M_3 : A \in \mathcal{A}_r \wedge A \notin \mathcal{A}_i$) A tuple is recorded with the attribute, but the attribute does not appear in the intended schema of the tuple. Mismatches of this kind are the result of attribute deletions. For example, John (tuple t_1 in Figure 2) is recorded with a grade of 9.2, but according to the intended schema is not supposed to have a grade attribute.
- **Not applicable** ($M_4 : A \notin \mathcal{A}_r \wedge A \notin \mathcal{A}_i$) The attribute neither appears in the recorded nor the intended schema of the tuple. Such mismatches occur e.g. for tuples that do not satisfy the condition for an attribute addition. For example, the Credits and sUpervisor attributes are not available to Tom (tuple t_3).

Table 1 shows the attribute mismatches and attribute values (where available) for each tuple in Figure 2. Note that the recorded and intented schema of a tuple can be determined directly from the attribute mismatches of the tuple. The mismatch type of each attribute determines whether that attribute appears in both schemas (M_1 type mismatches), only in the intented schema (M_2 type mismatches), only in the recorded schema (M_3 type mismatches), or in neither schema (M_4 type mismatches).

Table 1. Attribute Mismatches and Attribute Values for the Evolving Student Schema

Name	Major	Level	Grade	Credits	sUpervisor
$M_1/john$	M_1/bio	$M_1/ugrad$	$M_3/9.2$	M_2	M_4
$M_1/anne$	$M_1/math$	$M_1/grad$	$M_1/8.7$	M_4	M_2
M_1/tom	$M_1/math$	$M_1/ugrad$	$M_1/5.9$	M_4	M_4
M_1/kim	$M_1/math$	$M_1/grad$	$M_3/7.1$	M_2	$M_1/rick$
$M_1/rita$	M_1/bio	$M_1/grad$	M_4	$M_1/31$	$M_1/mike$

4.2 Mismatches and Conditional Schema Changes

Conditional schema changes change the set of attributes in the intended schema of tuples. Because the intented schema can be determined from the set of attribute mismatches, conditional schema changes also change the attribute mismatches of tuples.

The following two lemmas establish this relationship between attribute mismatches and conditional schema changes.

Let A be an attribute, t be a tuple, H be a history, and M_i be an attribute mismatch with $i \in \{1, \ldots, 4\}$. If the attribute mismatch between t and $is(t, E_H)$ on attribute A is M_i, then $m(A, t, E_H) = M_i$. Note that $m(A, t, \emptyset)$ is M_3 iff $\exists v(A/v \in t)$ otherwise M_4, since the intended schema of t is empty.

Lemma 3. *Let H be a history and t be a valid tuple of E_H with $m(A, t, E_H) = M_i$. Let $\alpha(A, E_H, C)$ be a conditional attribute addition, then*

$$m(A, t, \alpha(A, E_H, C)) = \begin{cases} M_{i-2} & \textit{iff } i \in \{3, 4\} \wedge C(t) \\ M_i & \textit{otherwise} \end{cases}$$

Lemma 4. *Let H be a history and t be a valid tuple of E_H with $m(A, t, E_H) = M_i$. Let $\beta(A, E_H, C)$ be a conditional attribute deletion, then*

$$m(A, t, \beta(A, E_H, C)) = \begin{cases} M_{i+2} & \textit{iff } i \in \{1, 2\} \wedge C(t) \\ M_i & \textit{otherwise} \end{cases}$$

5 Mismatch Resolution

When querying an evolving database, the DBMS has to systematically resolve attribute mismatches. We discuss three sensible and intuitive policies to resolve attribute mismatches at the level of individual attributes (it would be easy to add other policies).

- **Projection:** Resolves the mismatch by using the recorded attribute value. Clearly, this is only possible if the attribute appears in the recorded schema of the tuple. Therefore, projection can only be used to resolve M_1 and M_3 attribute mismatches.
- **Replacement:** Resolves the mismatch by replacing the (missing) attribute value with a specified value.
- **Exclusion:** Resolves the mismatch by excluding the tuple entirely for the purpose of the query.

To illustrate the resolution policies we provide a series of examples.

Example 2. Assume we want to count the number of students who got assigned a supervisor although they are not intended to have one. This means that we need to count the supervisors of tuples with an M_3 mismatch for the supervisor attribute. The query $\pi[cnt(U)](students)$ together with the policies M1:exclusion, M2:exclusion, M3:projection, and M4:exclusion answers the query, since only tuples with M_3 mismatches are included after resolution of the policies. The result is 0 (cf. Table 1).

Example 3. Assume we want to print all the grades that ever have been assigned. This means we also want to see the grades of students who got a grade before they transitioned to the credit system. With the policies M1:projection, M2:exclusion, M3:projection, and M4:exclusion for G_{rade}, the query $\pi[G](students)$ answers the query. After resolution only tuples with an actual value of the G_{rade} attribute are included. The result is $\{9.2, 8.7, 5.9, 7.1\}$.

Example 4. Assume we want to count the number of students who are supposed to have a supervisor but have not got assigned one yet. With the policies: M1:exclusion, M2:replacement, M3:exclusion, and M4:exclusion for ${}_sU_{\text{pervisor}}$, $\pi[cnt(U)](students)$ answers the query. Only tuples with M_2 mismatches are included after resolution of the policies. Since M_2 mismatches indicate that the tuples have no actual value stored, a replacement policy is used to introduce a value that can be counted by the query. The result is 1.

Note the generality of our approach. The key advantage of the proposed resolution approach is that it *decouples* schema definition and querying phases. This means that the above examples do not depend on the specifics of the database schema. For example, the exact reason why someone should (not) have a supervisor does not matter. Queries and resolution policies are conceptual solutions that do not depend on the conditional schema changes. This is a major difference to approaches that exploit the conditions of the schema changes (or other implicit schema information) to formulate special purpose queries to answer the example queries.

6 Mismatch Extended Completed Schema

In this section we introduce the *mismatch extended completed schema* (MECS). To support conditional schema evolution and policies, the DBMS must be able to determine and maintain the recorded and intended schema of tuples. We show that relations with MECSs (referred to as evolving instances) can accomplish this task, and give the algorithms to perform both conditional schema evolution and mismatch resolution. Finally, we show that an evolving instance is a lossless evolution model.

A MECS is a schema $\{A_1, \ldots, A_n, M_1, \ldots, M_n\}$ where for each attribute A_i there is an attribute M_i recording the attribute mismatch of A_i. The domain of M_i indicate the current type of attribute mismatch of A_i: 1 (no mismatch), 2 (not recorded), 3 (not available), and 4 (not applicable). MECSs are used by *evolving instances* to record both the attribute values and the attribute mismatches of tuples:

Definition 2. (evolving instance) *Let H be a history and $\{A_1, \ldots, A_n\}$ be the schema containing all attributes added by schema changes in H. Let I be a relation with the MECS $(A_1, \ldots, A_n, M_1, \ldots, M_n)$ as its schema. If, for all tuples $t \in I$ and all $i \in \{1, \ldots, n\}$, M_i is the attribute mismatch given by $m(A_i, t, E_H)$, then I is an* evolving instance *of H.*

Table 2 shows the evolving instance for the Student example.

In Section 4 we showed that the attribute mismatches of a tuple encode both the recorded and the intended schema of that tuple. Moreover, conditional schema changes

Table 2. The Evolving Student Instance

N	M	L	G	C	U	M_N	M_M	M_L	M_G	M_C	M_U
john	*bio*	*ugrad*	9.2			1	1	1	3	2	4
anne	*math*	*grad*	8.7			1	1	1	1	4	2
tom	*math*	*ugrad*	5.9			1	1	1	1	4	4
kim	*math*	*grad*	7.1		*rick*	1	1	1	3	2	1
rita	*bio*	*grad*		31	*mike*	1	1	1	4	1	1

can be applied directly to the attribute mismatches. It is therefore sufficient for a DBMS to maintain the attribute mismatches of tuples instead of their intended and recorded schemas. This is desireable for two reasons. First, to apply policies the DBMS needs to determine the attribute mismatches of tuples anyway. Second, while the mismatch type for an attribute may differ between tuples, each tuple in the same evolving relation has defined a mismatch type for the exact same set of attributes; namely one for each attribute added by conditional schema changes. The attribute mismatches of all tuples can therefore be recorded in a single relation. In contrast, tuples have different recorded and intended schemas with respect to both number and composition of attributes.

By definition, an evolving instance records the tuples and all their attribute mismatches. The missing attribute values in Table 2 occur only for attributes with mismatch type M_2 or M_4. We require that attribute mismatches are resolved before queries are answered, and since the projection policy is only applicable to attribute mismatches of type M_1 and M_3, the missing attributes in an evolving instance are never directly accessed, so their content is irrelevant.

6.1 Applying Conditional Schema Changes to Evolving Instances

Lemma 3 and 4 from Section 4.2 establish the relationship between conditional schema changes and attribute mismatches. The operations for conditional attribute addition and deletion on evolving instances are based on those two lemmas. The main point is that conditional schema changes do not modify the schema of the evolving instance, but rather update the attribute values for the mismatch attributes of tuples satisfying the change condition. Conditional schema changes can therefore be handled by the DBMS in the same way as standard tuple updates.

Figure 3 gives the formal definitions of conditional addition and deletion of an attribute A_i for a tuple t in an evolving instance. Both operations assume that the attribute A_i is in the schema of the evolving instance. Intuitively, deleting an attribute that does not appear in the schema has no effect. Moreover, if we consider the set of all possible attributes $\mathbf{A}$, then any schema is a subset of $\mathbf{A}$. The MECS of an evolving instance I contains exactly all the attributes (and their corresponding mismatches) added by conditional schema changes applied to I. Therefore, only attributes in the MECS of I can appear in the intended schemas of tuples in I. The recorded schemas of tuples in I are similarly bounded. This means that for any attribute $A \in \mathbf{A}$ that does not appear in the MECS of I, the attribute mismatch is M_4 for all tuples in I. According to Figure 3 applying an attribute deletion to tuples with an M_4 mismatch type for that attribute has no effect.

$$\alpha(A_i, t, C) = \begin{cases} (t \setminus \{M_i/v_i\}) \cup \{M_i/v_i - 2\} & \text{iff } t[M_i] \in \{3, 4\} \wedge C(t) \\ t & \text{otherwise} \end{cases}$$

$$\beta(A_i, t, C) = \begin{cases} (t \setminus \{M_i/v_i\}) \cup \{M_i/v_i + 2\} & \text{iff } t[M_i] \in \{1, 2\} \wedge C(t) \\ t & \text{otherwise} \end{cases}$$

Fig. 3. Attribute Addition and Deletion Operations on Tuples in Evolving Instances

When adding an attribute A_{n+1} that does not already appear in the evolving instance I, we have to extend the MECS of I with that attribute and its corresponding mismatch attribute M_{n+1}, before applying the attribute addition:

$$\alpha_{A_{n+1}}(t, C) = \alpha_{A_{n+1}}(t \cup \{A_{n+1}/\omega, M_{n+1}/4\}, C) \text{ iff } A_{n+1}/v_{n+1} \notin t$$

Note that the mismatch type for the new attribute is M_4 (as described in the previous paragraph) and ω can be any value in the domain of the attribute (which value is irrelevant as it will never be used). Operations that add a new column (either empty or with a default value) to an existing and populated table are already supported by commercial DBMSs such as Oracle9.

Theorem 1. *An evolving instance is lossless.*

6.2 Mismatch Resolution for Evolving Instances

The three policies presented in the previous section are functions that resolve attribute mismatches at the level of individual attributes.

Let I be an evolving instance and t be a tuple in I. Let A_i be an attribute in the schema of I and M be a mismatch type, then projection, replacement, and exclusion policies are functions defined as follows:

$$f_{proj}(t, A_i, M) = \begin{cases} undef & \text{iff } t[M_i] \in \{2, 4\} \\ t & \text{otherwise} \end{cases}$$

$$f_{repl}^{c}(t, A_i, M) = \begin{cases} (t \setminus \{A_i/v_i\}) \cup \{A_i/c\} & \text{iff } t[M_i] = M \\ t & \text{otherwise} \end{cases}$$

$$f_{excl}(t, A_i, M) = \begin{cases} \emptyset & \text{iff } t[M_i] = M \\ t & \text{otherwise} \end{cases}$$

An *attribute policy* $P = (A, [f_1, \ldots, f_n])$ where $f_i \in \{f_{proj}, f_{repl}^{c}, f_{excl}\}$ specifies a policy for each of the four mismatch types of A, i.e., $f_1, \ldots, f_4$ are used to resolve the attribute mismatches of A of type $M_1, \ldots, M_4$, respectively. Intuitively, an attribute policy specifies how the DBMS resolves all the attribute mismatches of a given attribute. We write P_A as a shorthand for $P = (A, [f_1, \ldots, f_4])$.

We can now define the *mismatch resolution* $\rho[P_A]I$ of an evolving instance I given attribute policy P_A.

Definition 3. (mismatch resolution) *Let I be an evolving instance, A_i be an attribute in the MECS of I, P_{A_i} be the attribute policy of A_i, and t be a tuple in I. Then the* mismatch resolution ρ *is given by:*

$$\rho[P_{A_i}]I = \{t' | t \in I \wedge M = t[M_i] \wedge t' = f_M(t, A_i, M)\}$$

Intuitively, for each tuple in the evolving instance the mismatch resolution considers the mismatch type of attribute A_i and applies the corresponding policy function (f_1 for M_1 mismatches, f_2 for M_2 mismatches, etc.) to derive the resolved tuple t'.

To illustrate mismatch resolution and attribute policies, we review the examples from Section 5.

Example 5. Example 2 resolves mismatches with the attribute policy $P_U = (U, [f_{excl}, f_{excl}, f_{proj}, f_{excl}]$. Table 2 contains no tuples with 3 as their M_U attribute value, so all tuples are excluded by the mismatch resolution. The result to $\pi[cnt(U)]I_{Student}$ is therefore 0.

Example 6. Example 3 uses an attribute policy on G: $P_G = (G, [f_{proj}, f_{excl}, f_{proj}, f_{excl}])$, excluding tuples with M_2 and M_4 mismatches for attribute G. Mismatch resolution results in Table 3. The answer to the query $\pi[G]I_{Student}$ is $\{9.2, 8.7, 5.9, 7.1\}$.

Table 3. Mismatch Resolution for Example 3

N	M	L	G	C	U	M_N	M_M	M_L	M_G	M_C	M_U
john	*bio*	*ugrad*	9.2			1	1	1	3	2	4
anne	*math*	*grad*	8.7			1	1	1	1	4	2
tom	*math*	*ugrad*	5.9			1	1	1	1	4	4
kim	*math*	*grad*	7.1		*rick*	1	1	1	3	2	1

Example 7. Example 4 uses the same query as Example 2, but resolves mismatches according to a different attribute policy: $P_U = (U, [f_{excl}, f^{jd}_{repl}, f_{excl}, f_{excl}])$. The result is shown in Table 4. The policy has replaced the missing $_sU_{pervisor}$ attribute value with jd (john doe) for all tuples with M_2 mismatches, and excluded all other tuples. The result of the query is 1.

Table 4. Mismatch Resolution for Example 4

N	M	L	G	C	U	M_N	M_M	M_L	M_G	M_C	M_U
anne	*math*	*grad*	8.7		*jd*	1	1	1	1	4	2

Mismatch resolution can apply any number of attribute policies (on different attributes) to an evolving instance at the same time (cf. Lemma 5).

Lemma 5. *Let $P_{A_1}, \ldots, P_{A_m}$ be policies on different attributes. Let I be an evolving instance and t be a tuple in I. Then:*

$$\rho[P_{A_1}] \ldots \rho[P_{A_m}]I = \{t' | t \in I \wedge t' = \rho_{A_1} \times \ldots \times \rho_{A_m}(\{t\})$$

Lemma 5 also establishes the upper bound on time complexity of mismatch resolution of evolving instances to be proportional to the size of the evolving instance, i.e., $O(|I|)$.

For query purposes, this corresponds to resolving all attribute mismatches and then apply the query to the resolved relation. For applications with fixed policies, a view can be created for the resolved relation. However, for applications using ad hoc attribute policies, we want to minimize the number of attributes and tuples that have to be resolved in order to answer a given query.

7 Related Work

Conditional schema evolution has been investigated in the context of temporal databases, where proposals have been made for the maintenance of schema versions along one [13, 17, 20] or more time dimensions [6]. Because schema change conditions are restricted to one or two time recording attributes the exponential explosion of the number of schemas segments are avoided.

In temporal databases schema evolution has been analyzed in the context of temporal data models [7, 1], and schema changes are applied to explicitly specified versions [22, 5]. This requires an extension to the query language and forces schema semantics (such as missing or inapplicable information) down into attribute values [18, 14]. In order to preserve the convenience of a single global schema for each relation null values have been used [14, 8]. In particular, it is possible to use inapplicable nulls if an attribute does not apply to a specific tuple [2, 3, 11, 12]. This leads to completed schemas [18] with an enriched semantics for null values. The approach does not scale to an ordered sequence of conditional evolution steps with multiple current schemas. It is also insufficient for attribute deletions if we do not want to overwrite (and thus loose) attribute values. In response to this it has been proposed to activate and deactivate attributes rather than to delete them [19].

Unconditional schema evolution has also been investigated in the context of OODBs, where several systems have been proposed. *Orion* [4], CLOSQL [15], and *Encore* [21] all use a versioning approach. Typically, a new version of the object instances is constructed along with a new version of the schema. The *Orion* schema versioning mechanism keeps versions of the whole schema hierarchy instead of the individual classes or types. Every object instance of an old schema can be copied or converted to become an instance of the new schema. The class versioning approach CLOSQL provides update/backdate functions for each attribute in a class to convert instances from the format in which the instance is recorded to the format required by the application. The *Encore* system provides exception handlers for old types to deal with new attributes that are missing from the instances. This allows new applications to access undefined fields of legacy instances. In general, the versioning approach for unconditional schema changes cannot be applied to conditional schema changes, because the number of versions that has to be constructed grows exponentially.

Views have been proposed as an approach to schema evolution in OODBs [23]. [16] propose the Transparent Schema Evolution approach, where schema changes are specified on a view schema rather than the underlying global schema. They provide algorithms to compute the new view that reflects the semantics of the schema change. The approach allows for schema changes to be applied to a single view without affecting other views, and for the sharing of persistent data used by different views.

8 Summary and Future Research

The paper defines the lossless property for general models of evolving schemas, and show that the solutions offered by current commercial database systems are not lossless. The main problem is to resolve the mismatches between the recorded and intended schemas of tuples systematically. We propose a parametric approach where mismatches are resolved according to the needs of the query. We propose the mismatch extended completed schema (MECS) which records both attributes and their mismatches. We show that relations with MECS (called evolving instances) are lossless, and by exploiting the relationship between attribute mismatches and conditional schema changes we can treat conditional schema changes as tuple updates. Finally, we establish an upper bound on the cost of parametric mismatch resolution of evolving instances.

Ongoing and future work includes the optimization of mismatch resolution. Specifically, we investigate techniques to minimize the amount of data that has to be resolved. By defining mismatch resolution as an algebraic operator, we are currently developing algebraic transformation rules to be used by the query optimizer. Preliminary results indicate that mismatch resolution can be delayed until the recorded attribute values are required by other operators which can substantially reduce the cost of resolution.

References

1. G. Ariav. Temporally Oriented Data Definitions: Managing Schema Evolution in Temporally Oriented Databases. *Data Knowledge Engineering*, 6(6):451–467, 1991.
2. P. Atzeni and V. de Antonellis. *Relational Database Theory*. Benjamin/Cummings, 1993.
3. P. Atzeni and N. M. Morfuni. Functional dependencies in relations with null values. *Information Processing Letters*, 18(4):233–238, 1984.
4. J. Banerjee, W. Kim, H.-J. Kim, and H.F. Korth. Semantics and Implementation of Schema Evolution in Object-Oriented Databases. In *ACM SIGMOD International Conference on Management of Data*, pages 311–322. ACM Press, 1987.
5. C.D. Castro, F. Grandi, and M.R. Scalas. *On Schema Versioning in Temporal Databases. In: Recent Advances in Temporal Databases*. Springer, 1995.
6. C.D. Castro, F. Grandi, and R.R. Scalas. Schema Versioning for Multitemporal Relational Databases. *Information Systems*, 22(5):249–290, 1997.
7. J. Clifford and A. Croker. The Historical Relational Data Model (HRDM) and Algebra based on Lifespans. In *3rd International Conference of Data Engineering, Los Angeles, California, USA, Proceedings*, pages 528–537. IEEE Computer Society Press, 1987.
8. G. Grahne. The Problem of Incomplete Information in Relational Databases. In *Springer LNCS No. 554*, 1991.
9. O. G. Jensen and M. H. Böhlen. Evolving Relations. In *Database Schema Evolution and Meta-Modeling*, volume 9th International Workshop on Foundations of Models and Languages for Data and Objects of *Springer LNCS 2065*, page 115 ff., 2001.
10. O.G. Jensen. *Multi-Dimensional Conditional Schema Evolution in Relational Databases*. PhD thesis, Aalborg University, 2004.

11. A. M. Keller. Set-theoretic problems of null completion in relational databases. *Information Processing Letters*, 22(5):261–265, 1986.
12. N. Lerat and W. Lipski. Nonapplicable Nulls. *Theoretical Computer Science*, 46:67–82, 1986.
13. L.E. McKenzie and R.T. Snodgrass. Schema Evolution and the Relational Algebra. *Information Systems*, 15(2):207–232, 1990.
14. R. van der Meyden. *Logical Approaches to Incomplete Information: a Survey. In: Logics for Databases and Information Systems (chapter 10)*. Kluwer Academic Publishers, 1998.
15. Simon R. Monk and Ian Sommerville. Schema Evolution in OODBs using Class Versioning. *SIGMOD Record*, 22(3):16–22, 1993.
16. Young-Gook Ra and Elke A. Rundensteiner. A transparent object-oriented schema change approach using view evolution. In Philip S. Yu and Arbee L. P. Chen, editors, *Proceedings of the Eleventh International Conference on Data Engineering, March 6-10, 1995, Taipei, Taiwan*, pages 165–172. IEEE Computer Society, 1995.
17. J.F. Roddick. SQL/SE - A Query Language Extension for Databases Supporting Schema Evolution. *ACM SIGMOD Record*, 21(3):10–16, 1992.
18. J.F. Roddick. A Survey of Schema Versioning Issues for Database Systems. *Information Software Technology*, 37(7):383–393, 1995.
19. J.F. Roddick, N.G. Craske, and T.J. Richards. A Taxonomy for Schema Versioning based on the Relational and Entity Relationship Models. In *12th International Conference on Entity-Relationship Approach, Arlington, Texas, USA, December 15-17, 1993, Proceedings*, pages 137–148. Springer-Verlag, 1993.
20. J.F. Roddick and R.T. Snodgrass. *Schema Versioning. In: The TSQL92 Temporal Query Language*. Noewell-MA: Kluwer Academic Publishers, 1995.
21. Andrea H. Skarra and Stanley B. Zdonik. The Management of Changing Types in an Object-Oriented Database. In *OOPSLA, 1986, Portland, Oregon, Proceedings*, pages 483–495, 1986.
22. R.T. Snodgrass et al. TSQL2 Language Specification. *ACM SIGMOD Record*, 23(1), 1994.
23. Markus Tresch and Marc H. Scholl. Schema transformation without database reorganization. *SIGMOD Record*, 22(1):21–27, 1993.

Ontology-Guided Change Detection to the Semantic Web Data

Li Qin and Vijayalakshmi Atluri

MSIS Dept. and Center for Information Management, Integration and Connectivity (CIMIC)
Rutgers University
{liqin,atluri}@cimic.rutgers.edu

Abstract. The Semantic Web is envisioned as the next generation web in which data instances are enriched with metadata defined in ontologies to describe the meaning of its instances. In this paper, we present an approach that exploits ontologies in guiding the change detection to their data instances. Inference rules are identified based on the semantic relationships among concepts, properties and instances as well as their change behaviors. Starting with changes to some seed instances, a reasoning engine is designed to fire the pre-defined rule set and act on ontologies to project some semantically associated concepts as target concepts. Certain instances of these target concepts are further selected as target instances, which have a high likelihood of having changed. Our approach is specifically oriented toward the Semantic Web, thus it has intelligence to exploit the semantic associations among data instances and make smart decisions.

1 Introduction

Change detection is to find out whether and what changes have occurred to data of interest, especially those owned and updated by autonomous sources. For example, a search engine has to detect changes to data published by autonomous sources in order to synchronize its local copies and its index with their sources. The major challenge confronting change detection lies in the conflict between limited availability of resources for change detection and the enormity of the data available. As an extension of WWW, the Semantic Web [2] will continue to be decentralized with its information space projected to increase at a much faster pace than resource availability. Therefore, change detection as well as management of versions and changes will be essential to data warehouses, search engines, cache maintenance and knowledge archival applications for the Semantic Web. Earlier approaches on change detection to web pages rely on the link structure among web pages or statistics estimated offline such as their change frequencies [7,11]. In this paper, we present an approach that exploits the ontologies, in particular, the relationships among concepts, in guiding the change detection to their data instances.

Under the Semantic Web, data instances are enriched with metadata, which describes the meaning of its instances. The metadata used for annotating data instances are defined as concepts and properties in ontologies so that data instances can be interpreted and processed by machines. Semantic Web technologies, e.g. RDF [12], RDF Schema [13] and OWL [9], provide methods and standards that enable abstracting from syntactic idiosyncrasies into semantically meaningful description of data and services, accurate access to information as well as flexibility to comply with the needs of users or agents. It has promised flexibility, scalability and quality in data and service provision, which the current web cannot possibly achieve.

P. Atzeni et al. (Eds.): ER 2004, LNCS 3288, pp. 624–638, 2004.

The Semantic Web will no longer be about pages and links, but semantic relationships between things. Under this context, we present an approach that exploits ontologies in guiding the change detection to their data instances. Our semantics-based approach gives higher priority to data instances related to the instances to which changes have been recently found, as it believes those semantically related data are more likely to have changed as the result of the efforts by the same or even different information sources to maintain freshness and consistency. An inference engine is designed to reason on the basis of some detected changes and ontologies, and to make intelligent decisions on what to visit next so that changes to the Semantic Web data can be detected in a more efficient way. To this end, the inference engine needs to take advantage of inferences rules, which are identified based on the ontologies and specified among concepts, properties, and instances of concepts as well as their changes. Given changes detected to seed instances, these rules are essentially used by the reasoning engine to generate a profile for locating the target instances that are likely to have changed and therefore should be visited. The profile for the target instances also contains target concepts that target instances belong to, and target properties that target instances should or should not instantiate based on the change type.

With our ontology-guided approach, not only more changes may be detected, but also these changes are more semantically related. Changes detected to related, but independent sources may reveal something interesting not discovered by observing each change separately. For example, if consistent changes are witnessed to multiple independent sources, this may increase the trust-worthiness of the detected changes so that they can be trusted to identify more changes. Change detection can ultimately become a focused, well-controlled process in the sense that, instead of visiting pages in a blind way, it targets more accurately the pages it wants to visit, e.g. those related to a specific topic. Besides, techniques for our semantics-based approach can provide insights into utilizing semantic association in other applications such as guiding information discovery for agents, consistency maintenance among distributed information sources, and so on.

In summary, our work is an attempt to design intelligent change detection techniques guided by ontologies, combining inference and search for target instances under the infrastructure of the Semantic Web. Other related work on change detection includes studies on the change dynamics of web pages [3,5,6] and diff algorithms developed to accommodate data formats such as HTML and XML [4,8,14]. Compared to the earlier proposals, our approach is specifically oriented toward the Semantic Web, thus it has intelligence to exploit the semantic associations among data instances and make smart decisions in an ad-hoc manner with no assumptions about the contents of data or changes.

This paper is organized as follows. Section 2 is an overview of our approach. We present preliminaries in section 3, and elaborate the types of changes to the Semantic Web data and profiles in section 4. Section 5 and 6 present inference rules along with our intelligent change detection. Section 7 provides conclusions and our future work.

2 Overview of the Proposed Approach

Our approach begins with identifying different types of inference rules based on certain semantic relationships in ontologies and these rules are exploited by the reasoning engine in guiding the change detection process. Our change detection approach is ontology-guided since all these rules act based on the ontologies. Essentially, the change detection process takes a set of seed instances to which changes have been detected, and derives a set of target instances which should also have changed. We identify five categories of inference rules: (1) **Change Inference Rules**: Given changes to seed instances, these rules imply changes to their semantically related instances. (2) **Profile Inference Rules**: Once any change inference rule is fired, i.e. changes to certain semantically related instances are implied, the corresponding profile inference rule is used to derive a profile for these instances with descriptions of target concepts possibly in terms of eq[c] and sub[c], target instances in terms of eq[i] and da[i], and target properties in terms of eq[p] and sup[p] (These operators are formally introduced in section 5.). (3) **Concept Inference Rules**: If the description of target concepts contains eq[c] or sub[c], concept inference rules are called to derive the specific target concepts. (4) **Property Inference Rules**: If the description of target properties contains eq[p] or sup[p], property inference rules are called to derive the specific target properties. (5) **Instance Inference Rules**: If the description of target instances contains eq[i] or da[i], instance inference rules are called to derive the specific target instances.

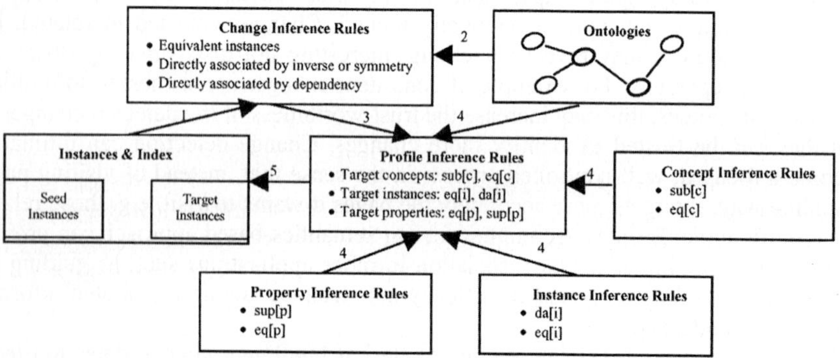

Fig. 1. Information used by the reasoning engine

Fig. 1 shows the components involved in the reasoning. It starts with some seed instances and finds changes to them. These changes become input to the change inference rules, as indicated by step 1 in Fig. 1. Assume that the webpage for the MSIS Dept. of Rutgers, which is an instance of concept 'Department', is visited and the 'address' of the department is found updated. Given these change(s), the reasoning engine comes into play by checking the **change inference rules** and fires those relevant to the detected change(s) and the ontologies, shown as step 2 in Fig. 1. Let us assume one of the change inference rules is stated as follows: "If dependency[1] exists from any property of the semantically associated concepts to this 'address' property, then instances specifically associated with this department instance should have that property value changed." Then, the reasoning engine visits the ontology this department instance points to, and finds out 'address' property is defined to concept 'Aca-

[1] If *dependency* exists from property p_i of concept c_i to p_j of concept c_j, where c_i and c_j are directly associated, then when the value to p_j of an instance of c_j has changed, the value to p_i of the directly associated instances of c_i should also have changed.

demic Unit', of which concept 'Department' is defined as a specialization, concept 'Employee' associates itself with 'Academic Unit' through object property 'worksFor', and dependency exists from the 'business address' property of 'Employee' to the 'address' property of 'Academic Unit'. This means if the 'address' property of an instance of 'Department' has changed, then the value to the 'Business Address' of all the instances of 'Employee' directly associated with this 'Department' instance should also have changed. As a result, the above change inference rule is fired. Since the fired change inference rule implies possible changes to some semantically related instances, the corresponding **profile inference rules** are triggered, indicated by step 3 in Fig. 1. In our example, the profile inference rule for semantically related instances by dependency is triggered. Shown as step 4 in Fig. 1, the profile inference rules generate a profile for the target instances, which have a high likelihood of having been changed, therefore, should be visited next. This profile consists of target concepts, target instances and target properties with each set described by certain operators we define. In our example, if concept 'Employee' has subclass concepts 'Faculty', 'Staff'', 'Ph.D Student' with each possibly having their own subclass concepts, then the target concepts will contain the operator for subclass concepts as sub(Employee). The operators for concepts, instances and properties in the profile will call **concept inference rules, instance inference rules** and **property inference rules,** respectively, to derive their specific elements. For our example, the concept inference rules will be called to derive the specific concepts constituting sub(Employee), which includes concepts 'Faculty', 'Staff', 'Ph.D Student' as well as their subclass concepts if exist. After that, the reasoning engine finally derives a profile for the target instances to be the instances of concepts in sub(Employee), which are directly associated with the MSIS Department by taking it as the value to its 'worksFor' property and have its 'business address' instantiated. The profile is used to locate the actual target instances if the profile contains or is satisfiable by certain instances, shown as step 5 in Fig. 1. The target data instances for our example may be located in the personal web pages of the department's faculty members, the faculty list page on the department's web site, and so on.

3 Preliminaries

Ontologies: *"An ontology defines the terms used to describe and represent an area of knowledge."* [10] Generally, an ontology defined for a domain contains a description of important concepts in the domain, properties of each concept as well as restrictions or axioms upon properties. Fig. 2 is an example of an ontology (the part above the horizontal line), available at http://cimic.rutgers.edu/ontologies/university, and some instances (the part below the horizontal line). The dashed lines across these two parts indicate the correspondence between the instances and ontologies.

An ontology o_i consists of the following elements: (1) **Concepts**: The set of *concepts* $\mathbf{C[o_i]}=\{c_1,c_2,\ldots,c_n\}$. C[http://cimic.rutgers.edu/ontologies/university]={Student, Ph.D Student, Course, Faculty} for the ontology in Fig. 2. (2) **Properties**: $\forall\, c \in C[o_i]$, there exists a set of *properties* $\mathbf{P[c]} = DP[c] \cup OP[c]$ where $\mathbf{DP[c]} = \{dp_1,dp_2,\ldots,dp_m\}$ are **datatype properties** of concept c, each taking a primitive data type as the value, and $\mathbf{OP[c]} = \{op_1,op_2,\ldots,op_n\}$ are **object properties**, each taking some concept(s) as the value. We use $\mathbf{dp_i[c]}$ to represent the value taken by the datatype property dp_i of concept c, and $\mathbf{op_i[c]}$ to denote the concept(s) taken by object property op_i of concept c. In Fig. 2, P[Ph.D Student] = {*subClassOf*, quaExamDate, advisedBy}, with DP[Ph.D Student] = {quaExamDate} where quaExamDate[Ph.D Student] = xsd:date and OP[Ph.D Student] ={*subClassOf*, advisedBy}. Object properties can be **domain-independent** or **domain-specific**. While the domain-independent object properties have pre-defined meaning that does not vary from one ontology to another, the meaning of domain-specific object properties depends on the context in which it is defined. We use $\mathbf{OP_{DI}[c]}$ and $\mathbf{OP_{DS}[c]}$ to denote the domain-independent and domain-specific object properties of concept c, respectively. For example, OP_{DI}[Ph.D Student] = {*subClassOf*} where *subclassOf*[Ph.D Student] = Student and OP_{DS}[Ph.D Student] = {advisedBy} where advisedBy[Ph.D Student] = Faculty. (3) **Restrictions:** For all $p \in DP[c]$ or $p \in OP_{DS}[c]$ where $c \in C[o_i]$, there exists a set of *restrictions* on the value or cardinality of the property, denoted by $\mathbf{R[p]} = \{r_1,\ldots,r_w\}$ where $\mathbf{r_k[p]}$ is the value to the restriction r_k of property p. For example, R[quaExamDate] = {*maxCardinality*} where *maxCardinality*[quaExamDate] = 2. (4) **Axioms:** For all $p \in DP[c]$ or $p \in OP_{DS}[c]$ where $c \in C[o_i]$, there exists a set of *axioms* with each defined by itself (unary) or in relation to another property (binary), denoted by $\mathbf{A[p]}=\{a_1,a_2,\ldots a_n\}$. If a_i is binary, $\mathbf{a_i[p]}$ denotes the property related to p through axiom a_i. Fig. 2 shows that *inverseOf*[advisedBy] = supervises, where supervises[Faculty] = Ph.D Student.

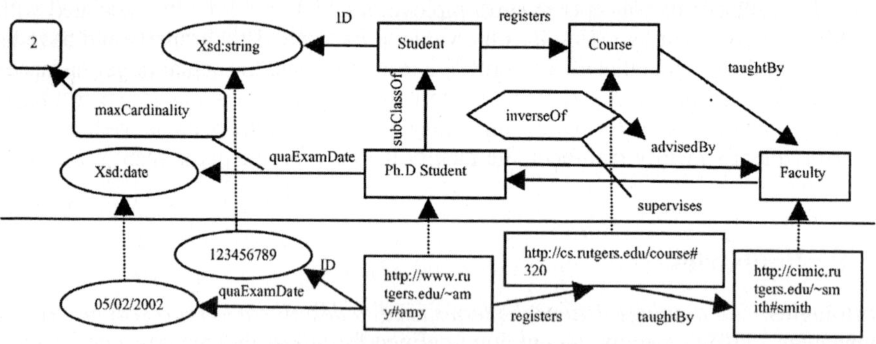

Fig. 2. Example for ontology and instances

Different ontology languages may support different types of domain-independent object properties, restrictions and axioms upon properties. For instance, OWL supports domain-independent object properties such as *subClassOf*, *equivalentClass*, restrictions such as *cardinality*, and axioms such as *subPropertyOf*, *equivalentProperty*, *TransitiveProperty*, *SymmetricProperty*, *FunctionalProperty*, *InverseFunctionalProperty*, *inverseOf*, and so on. Though our approach is not limited to any specific ontology language, we will resort to the OWL vocabulary [9] to simplify our discussion.

Instances: Ontologies provide interpretations to the content of the Semantic Web data since ontologies define and relate concepts used to annotate the web data, which are instances to the concepts in ontologies. Different elements of ontologies serve different functions: concepts along with their datatype properties and domain-specific object properties are what can be instantiated by instances, restrictions upon properties specify what requirements instantiation should satisfy in order to be valid, and domain-independent object properties and the axioms of properties provide powerful mechanisms for enhanced reasoning about instances. A semantic document contains instances of different concepts with some or all of the properties instantiated, and pointers to the ontologies where concepts used for annotation are defined.

In ontologies, a property is only specified to the most general concept to which it applies; the subclass concepts of this general concept can inherit all of its properties. Therefore, the instances of these subclass concepts can instantiate these inherited properties as well as their own. For a concept c_i, we use $P'[c_i]$ to represent all the properties that instances of concept c_i can instantiate. Therefore, $P'[c_i] = DP[c_i] \cup OP_{DS}[c_i] \cup DP[c_j] \cup OP_{DS}[c_j]$ for any c_j where $c_i \in sub[c_j]$ or $c_i \in eq[c_j]$. Similarly, $DP'[c_i]$ and $OP'_{DS}[c_i]$ represent the set of datatype properties and domain-specific object properties that instance i can instantiate where $i \in I[c_i]$, respectively. $R'[p]$ will be the set of restrictions on property p. Based on Fig. 2, since *subclassOf*[Ph.D Student]=Student, P′[Ph.D Student]={quaExamDate, advisedBy, ID, registers}.

If c_i is a subclass of c_j, then instances of c_i are also instances of c_j. To be clear, we use the following notation: I[c] for the instances which are asserted to belong to concept c, and $i \in I[c]$ only if an instance i is asserted to belong to a concept c; $I'[c]$ to refer to all the instances of concept c by explicit assertion and by inheritance, in which case, $I'[c] = I[c] \cup I[c_i]$ for any c_i, where $c_i \in sub[c]$ or $c_i \in eq[c]$. For instance, *subclassOf*[Ph.D Student]=Student and 'http://www.rutgers.edu/~amy#amy'$\in$ I[Ph.D student]. Therefore, 'http://www.rutgers.edu/~amy#amy'$\in$ I′[student]. For an instance i, we use C[i] to represent the set of concepts, where $i \in I'[c]$. Therefore, C['http://www.rutgers.edu/~amy#amy'] = {Student, Ph.D Student}.

Each concept c_i has a set of instances $I[c_i] = \{i_1, \ldots, i_n\}$ and $\forall\, i \in I[c_i]$, the description of i may include: (1) **URI**: A Universal Resource identifier (URI) by which i can be universally identified and other instances can refer to it. (2) **Concept**: $\mathbf{c_i}$, the concept that i is asserted to instantiate. (3) **Datatype property instantiation**: $\forall\, dp \in DP'[c_i]$, dp takes a specific value v, denoted as **i:dp=v**, where the instantiation is *valid* if $R'[dp]$ are satisfied. (4) **Object property instantiation**: $\forall\, op \in OP'_{DS}[c_i]$ and $op[c_i]=c_j$, op takes an instance i_j as its value, denoted as **i:op=$\mathbf{i_j}$** where $i_j \in I'[c_j]$. This instantiation is *valid* if $R'[op]$ are satisfied. Note that the instantiation of an object property of a concept taking another concept as its value represents a mapping (direct association) between the instances belonging to these two concepts.

We use P[i], DP[i] and OP[i] to denote the set of properties, datatype properties and object properties instantiated by instance i. If $i \in I[c]$, $p \in P[i]$, then $p \in P'[c]$. Also, if $i \in I[c]$, then $P[i] \subset P'[c]$, $DP[i] \subset DP'[c]$, $OP[i] \subset OP'[c]$. Take the instance of concept 'Ph.D Student' in Fig. 2 as an example. The URI for this instance is http://www.rutgers.edu/~amy#amy and the concept it belongs to is 'Ph.D Student'. P['http://www.rutgers.edu/~amy#amy']={ID, quaExamDate, registers}.

Relationships: Given two concepts c_i and c_j, we say c_i and c_j are *directly associated* through op_i if $op_i[c_i]=c_j$ or $op_i[c_j]=c_i$. We use $da[c_i]$ to denote the set of concepts that are directly associated with concept c_i and $da[c_i{:}op_i]$ to denote the concept directly associated with concept c_i through object property op_i. For example, da[Ph.D Student]={Student, Faculty} where da[Ph.D Student:*subClassOf*]= Student.

The relationship between two instances can be directly associated, indirectly associated or not associated. We will first discuss equivalence between instances as a special category, whose transitivity allows it to be either directly associated or indirectly associated. In this paper, we focus only on direct association between instances because our change and profile inference rules are mainly specified upon directly associated instances. The relationship between instances covers both *explicit* and *implicit* relationships. By *explicit* relationship, we mean the relationship between the instances is asserted explicitly by content creators while the *implicit* relationship between two instances can be derived through reasoning. The equivalence between instances we discuss below is implicit, if it is evaluated based on the value of its identification property.

Each instance should be given a URI by its owner for identifying the instance and for other instances to refer to it. URIs are decentralized and "Two URIs are different unless they are the same character for character."[1] However, different URIs may be *equivalent* if they refer to the same real world object. We notice that equivalent instances published in different sources may be matched based on the value of some *identification* or *quasi-identification* property (or a combination of multiple properties), similar to the primary key in a relational database table. Sometimes, instances of different concepts may be equivalent. For instance, the same international Ph.D student may be instantiated as an instance of concepts such as 'Student', 'International Student', 'Graduate Student' or 'Ph.D Student'. In particular, if concepts share a property defined to be *owl:InverseFunctionalProperty*, then instances that have the same value for this property are equivalent. In other words, a property, whose axiom defines it to be an *owl:InverseFunctionalProperty*, is an identification property. Besides, equivalence between instances can also be explicitly indicated using *owl:sameIndividualAs*.

Equivalence between instances: Two instances are equivalent if they refer to the same entity in the real world. This definition will be the foundation for the instance inference rule on equivalent instances discussed in section 5. We use $eq[i_m]$ for the set of equivalent instances of i_m with i_m itself included. If instances $i_m \in I[c_i]$ and $i_n \in I[c_j]$ are equivalent, c_i and c_j refer to the same concept, or c_i is an equivalent or subclass concept of c_j, or c_j is a subclass concept of c_i; c_i and c_j share an identification datatype property dp_k such that $i_m{:}dp_k = i_n{:}dp_k$ or an identification object property op_k such that $i_m{:}op_k = i_n{:}op_k$ (or $i_m{:}op_k \in eq[i_n{:}op_k]$).

Direct association between instances: For instances i_i and i_j where $i_i \in I'[c_i]$, $i_j \in I'[c_j]$, if there exists $op_i \in OP'[c_i]$ such that $op_i[c_i]=c_k$, $c_k \in C[i_j]$ and $i_i{:}op_i=i_j$, then i_i and i_j are directly associated instances through op_i. For instance i, we use da[i] for the set of instances directly associated with i, and da[i:op] represents the set of instances directly associated with i through op. Take an instance from Fig. 2 as an example, da['http://www.rutgers.edu/~amy#amy':registers]= 'http://cs.rutgers.edu/course#320'.

4 Changes to the Semantic Web Data and Profiles

Detecting changes to the Semantic Web data requires one to first identify whether a change has occurred to the instantiation of concepts along with their properties. If a change has occurred, then the change detection needs to identify the actual changes to the instances and their properties. A change to the Semantic Web data is denoted by Δ. Three types of changes are significant to our approach: addition of property instantiation (denoted by Δ^A), deletion of property instantiation (Δ^D) and update to property instantiation value (Δ^U). We define $\Delta^A(\Delta^D)$ = **⟨i, c, p, v⟩**, where i is the instance involved in the addition (deletion), c the concept to which i belongs, i.e. $i \in I(c)$, p the property added or deleted in the change, and v the value of p involved in the addition (deletion); Δ^U = **⟨i, c, p, ov, nv⟩**, where i is the instance being updated, c the concept to which i belongs, i.e. $i \in I(c)$, p the property being updated, ov the old value of p before the update, and nv the new value of p after the update.

Given a specific change Δ, we use i[Δ], c[Δ], p[Δ], dp[Δ], op[Δ] to denote the instance, the concept to which the instance belongs, the property, the datatype property and object property involved in the change, respectively. We use v[Δ^A] to denote the value to p[Δ^A] added in the change, v[Δ^D] to denote the value to p[Δ^D] deleted by the change, ov[Δ^U] to denote the old value of p[Δ^U] before the change and nv[Δ^U] denotes the new value of p[Δ^U] after the change.

Based on the changes to the Semantic Web data, the reasoning engine fires the appropriate change inference rules and profile inference rules to generate a profile for the target instances. We describe the components of a profile below.

Profile: A profile generated by the reasoning engine consists of: Target instances (**TI**): instances identified explicitly by its URI or instances whose properties take specific values; Target concepts (**TC**): set of concept(s) that target instances belong to; Target Properties (**TP**): set of properties that target instances may or may not instantiate, based on the type of the change. Specifically, TP are instantiated if the change is Δ^U or Δ^D, but they are not instantiated if the change is Δ^A. We use EXISTS and NOT EXISTS to indicate whether or not TP are instantiated. The profile predicted for the target instances describes their common characteristics in terms of concepts, instances as well as their properties, and is further used to locate these instances.

5 Inference Rules

Based on some detected changes and ontologies, the reasoning engine makes smart decisions about what instances should have changed and describes them in terms of target concepts, instances and properties. The reasoning process relies on different types of inference rules triggered in a specific sequence: it first fires the change inference rules based on the changes to seed instances and ontologies, then the profile inference rules to generate the profile, in which concept inference rules, property inference rules and instance inference rules may be triggered.

The components of an ontology described in section 3 are based on what is explicitly stated in the ontology. The significance of ontologies definitely goes beyond its components by allowing for reasoning, entailed particularly by domain-independent object properties and axioms of properties. Domain-independent object properties such as *subClassOf* and *equivalentClass* have their own axioms such as transitivity. For a concept c_i, we use sub[c_i] to represent the set of concepts which are subclass of c_i and eq[c_i] to represent the set of concepts which are equivalent to c_i, either by definition or by inference. These operators will be used in the profile inference rules to represent the target concepts for a profile. The concept inferences rules specify how the set of equivalent and subclass concepts can be generated for a given concept based on the ontology.

Concept Inference Rules: We identify the following inference rules for identifying sub[c] and eq[c] for a given concept c. Let c_i, c_j and c_k be three concepts. (1) (*equivalentClass*[c_k]=c_i $\vee$ *equivalentClass*[c_k]=c_j where $c_j \in$ eq[c_i]) $\Rightarrow$ ($c_k \in$ eq[c_i]). This means, if c_k is asserted as *equivalentClass* of c_i or *equivalentClass* of c_j such that c_j belongs to the set of concepts equivalent to c_i, then c_k belongs to the set of concepts equivalent to c_i. (2) ($c_k \in$ eq[c_i]) $\Rightarrow$ ($c_i \in$ eq[c_k]). If c_k belongs to the set of concepts equivalent to c_i, then c_i also belongs to the set of concepts equivalent to c_k. (3) (*subclassOf*[c_k]=c_i $\vee$ *subclassOf*[c_k]=c_j where $c_j \in$ sub[c_i]) $\Rightarrow$ ($c_k \in$ sub[c_i]); and ($c_i \in$ *intersectionOf*[c_k] $\vee$ $c_k \in$ *unionOf*[c_i])$\Rightarrow$(*subclassOf*[c_k]=c_i). This means, if c_k is asserted as *subClassOf* c_i or *subClassOf* c_j such that c_j belongs to the set of subclass concepts of c_i, then c_k belongs to the set of subclass concepts of c_i. Moreover, c_k is a subclass of c_i can also be implied if c_k is the intersection of c_i and some other concepts, or if c_i is the union of c_k and some other concepts. (4) ($c_k \in$ eq[c_j] $\wedge$ $c_k \in$ sub[c_i]) $\Rightarrow$ ($c_j \in$ sub[c_i]). This means, if c_k belongs to the set of concepts equivalent to c_j and the set of subclass concepts of c_i, then c_j also belongs to the set of subclass concepts of c_i. (5) ($c_k \in$ eq[c_j] $\wedge$ $c_i \in$ sub[c_k]) $\Rightarrow$ ($c_i \in$ sub[c_j]). This mean, if c_i belongs to the set of subclass concepts of c_k and c_k belongs to the set of equivalent concepts of c_j, then c_i also belongs to the set of subclass concepts of c_j.

Similar rules for sup[p] and eq[p] can be built based on *subPropertyOf*() and *equivalentProperty*(). The property inference rules below would help us identify the target properties from the set of properties where initial changes are detected. For a property p, we use sup[p] to represent the super-properties of p, i.e. the properties to which p is a sub-property, and eq[p] to represent the properties equivalent to p.

Property Inference Rules: We identify the following inference rules for identifying sup(p) and eq(p) for a given property p. Let p_i, p_j and p_k be three properties. (1) (*equivalentProperty*[p_k]=p_i $\vee$ *equivalentProperty*[p_k]=p_j where $p_j \in$ eq[p_i]) $\Rightarrow$ ($p_k \in$ eq[p_i]). This means, if p_k is asserted as *equivalentProperty* of p_i, or that of p_j such that p_j belongs to the set of properties equivalent to p_i, then p_k belongs to the set of properties equivalent to p_i. (2) ($p_k \in$ eq[p_i]) $\Rightarrow$ ($p_i \in$ eq[p_k]). This means, if p_k belongs to the set of properties equivalent to p_i, then p_i also belongs to the set of properties equivalent to p_k. (3) (*subPropertyOf*[p_k]=p_i $\vee$ *subPropertyOf*[p_k]=p_j where

$p_i \in sup[p_j]) \Rightarrow (p_i \in sup[p_k])$. This means, if p_k is asserted as *subPropertyOf* p_i or that of p_j such that p_i belongs to the set of super-properties of p_j, then p_i belongs to the set of super-properties of p_k. (4) $(p_k \in eq[p_j] \wedge p_k \in sup[p_i]) \Rightarrow (p_j \in sup[p_i])$. This means, if p_k belongs to the set of properties equivalent to p_j and the set of super-properties of p_i, then p_j also belongs to the set of super-properties of p_i. (5) $(p_k \in eq[p_j] \wedge p_i \in sup[p_k]) \Rightarrow (p_i \in sup[p_j])$. This means, if p_k belongs to the set of properties equivalent to p_j and p_i belongs to the set of super-properties of p_k, then p_i also belongs to the set of super-properties of p_j.

Instance inference rules used by the reasoning engine can identify eq[i] and da[i] for a given instance i. The complexity of identifying equivalent instances results from the distributed nature of the web, where owners of information sources are allowed to instantiate equivalent instances by resorting to even different concepts and properties. The target instances in the profile generated by the profile inference rules may call the rules defined below to get the instances.

Equivalent Instance Inference Rule: We identify the following inference rule for identifying eq(i) for a given property i. Let i_i be an instance. Given $i_i \in I[c_i]$, $eq(i_i)=\{i|(i \in I[c_j]$ such that $c_j=c_i$, $c_j \in eq[c_i]$, $c_i \in sub[c_j]$ or $c_j \in sub[c_i]) \wedge (i{:}p_k=i_i{:}p_k \vee i{:}p_k=eq[i_i{:}p_k]$ such that *InverseFunctionalProperty*$\in A[p_k])\}$. This rule states that given i_i is an instance of concept c_i, the equivalent instances of i_i will be those that are instances of c_i or an equivalent concept of c_i or a subclass concept of c_i or a concept to which c_i is a subclass concept, and take the same value for its identification property as that for i_i.

Directly Associated Instance Inference Rules: We identify the following inference rules for identifying da(i) for a given instance i. (1) Given $i_i \in I'[c_i]$, if $op_i[c_k]=c_j$ (or $op_i[c_j]=c_k$) where $c_k \in C[i_i]$ and *SymmetricProperty* $\notin A[op_i]$, where A[p] as the set of axioms over property p, then $da[i_i{:}op_i] = \{i|i \in I'[c_j] \wedge (i_m{:}op_i=i_j$ where $i_m \in eq[i_i]$ and $i_j \in eq[i])$ (or $i_j{:}op_i=i_m$ where $i_m \in eq[i_i]$ and $i_j \in eq[i])\}$. This rule states that, given i_i is an instance (by assertion or inference) of concept c_i, c_i is directly associated with concept c_j through object property op_i and op_i is not a symmetric property, then the directly associated instances of i_i through op_i belong to concept c_j (by assertion or inference), and these instances or their equivalent instances are taken as the value to object property op_i of i_i or its equivalent instances. It also implies that, if c_j is directly associated with c_i through object property op_i, then the directly associated instances of i_i through op_i belong to concept c_j (by assertion or inference), and these instances or their equivalent instances take i_i or the equivalent instances of i_i as the value to object property op_i. (2) Given $i_i \in I'[c_i]$, if $op_i[c_k]=c_j$(or $op_i[c_j]=c_k$) where $c_k \in C[i_i]$ and *SymmetricProperty*$\in A[op_i]$, then $da[i_i{:}op_i]=\{i|i \in I'[c_j] \wedge (i_m{:}op_i=i_j \vee i_j{:}op_i=i_m$ where $i_m \in eq[i_i]$ and $i_j \in eq[i])\}$. This states that, given i_i is an instance of concept c_i, c_i is directly associated with concept c_j through object property op_i (or c_j is directly associated with c_i through object property op_i) and op_i is a symmetric property, then the

also. They define a higher-order logic language, SchemaSQL, which handles both data integration and schema evolution in relational multi-database systems. In contrast, our approach uses a simple set of schema transformation primitives, augmented with a functional query language, both of which are uniformly applicable to multiple data models. Other previous work on schema evolution, e.g. [1–4], has also presented approaches in terms of just one data model.

AutoMed is a heterogeneous data transformation and integration system which offers the capability to handle data integration across multiple data models[1]. In [7] we discussed how AutoMed metadata can be used to express the schemas and the cleansing, transformation and integration processes in heterogeneous data warehouse environments, supporting both schema heterogeneity and model heterogeneity. We discussed how this metadata can be used to populate and incrementally maintain the warehouse, and any data marts derived from it, and also to trace the lineage of data in the warehouse or the data marts. It is clearly advantageous to be able to reuse this kind of metadata if a schema evolves. In this paper we show how this can be achieved.

Earlier work [16] has shown how the AutoMed framework readily supports schema evolution in *virtual* data integration scenarios. In this paper we address the problem of schema evolution in *materialised* data integration scenarios, including both evolution of a source schema and of the warehouse schema, and also the impact on any data marts derived from the warehouse. This scenario is more complex than with virtual data integration, since both schemas and materialised data may be affected by an evolution.

The outline of the paper is as follows. Section 2 gives an overview of the AutoMed framework. Section 3 describes how AutoMed transformations can be used to express a schema evolution if either the schema changes, or the data model changes, or both. Section 4 describes the actions that are taken in order to evolve these transformations and the materialised data if the warehouse schema or a local schema evolves. Section 5 discusses the benefits of our approach and gives our concluding remarks.

2 Overview of AutoMed

AutoMed supports a low-level hypergraph-based data model (HDM). Higher-level modelling languages are defined in terms of this HDM. For example, previous work has shown how relational, ER, OO [15], XML [21], flat-file [5] and multidimensional [7] data models can be so defined. An HDM schema consists of a set of nodes, edges and constraints, and each modelling construct of a higher-level modelling language is specified as some combination of HDM nodes, edges and constraints. For any modelling language $\mathcal{M}$ specified in this way (via the API of AutoMed's Model Definitions Repository [5]), data source wrappers translate data source schemas expressed in $\mathcal{M}$ into their AutoMed representation, without loss of information. AutoMed also provides a set of primitive schema transformations that can be applied to schema constructs expressed in $\mathcal{M}$. In particular, for

[1] See `http://www.doc.ic.ac.uk/automed/`

every construct of $\mathcal{M}$ there is an add and a delete primitive transformation which add to/delete from a schema an instance of that construct. For those constructs of $\mathcal{M}$ which have textual names, there is also a rename primitive transformation.

In AutoMed, schemas are incrementally transformed by applying to them a sequence of primitive transformations $t_1, \ldots, t_r$. Each primitive transformation adds, deletes or renames just one schema construct. Thus, intermediate schemas may contain constructs of more than one modelling language.

Each add or delete transformation is accompanied by a query specifying the extent of the new or deleted construct in terms of the rest of the constructs in the schema. This query is expressed in a functional query language IQL (see Section 2.1). Also available are contract and extend transformations which behave in the same way as add and delete except that they indicate that their accompanying query may only partially construct the extent of the new/removed schema construct. Moreover, their query may just be the constant Void, indicating that the extent of the new/removed construct cannot be derived even partially, in which case the query can be omitted.

We term a sequence of primitive transformations from one schema S_1 to another schema S_2 a transformation *pathway* from S_1 to S_2, denoted $S_1 \rightarrow S_2$. All source, intermediate, and integrated schemas, and the pathways between them, are stored in AutoMed's Schemas & Transformations Repository [5].

The queries present within transformations that add or delete schema constructs mean that each primitive transformation t has an automatically derivable *reverse transformation*, $\bar{t}$. In particular, each add/extend transformation is reversed by a delete/contract transformation with the same arguments, while each rename transformation is reversed by swapping its two arguments. Thus, AutoMed is a **both-as-view** (BAV) data integration system. As discussed in [17], BAV subsumes the global-as-view (GAV) and local-as-view (LAV) approaches [13], since it is possible to extract a definition of each global schema construct as a view over source schema constructs, and it is also possible to extract definitions of source schema constructs as views over the global schema. We refer the reader to [9] for details of AutoMed's GAV and LAV view generation algorithms.

Figure 1 illustrates the general integration scenario with AutoMed. Each data source is described by a local schema LS_i. Each LS_i is first conformed into a schema CS_i (which may or may not be expressed in the same modelling language as LS_i) by means of a transformation pathway T_i. Not all of the information within a local schema LS_i need be transferred into the global schema and this is asserted by means of contract transformation steps within T_i. Conversely, there may be information within the global schema which is not semantically derivable from LS_i, and this is asserted by the pathway from CS_i to a 'union-schema' US_i which consists of the necessary extend transformations[2].

All the union schemas US_1, ..., US_n are syntactically identical and this is asserted by creating a sequence of id transformations between each pair US_i and US_{i+1}, of the form id $US_i : c$ $US_{i+1} : c$ for each schema construct c. An id transformation signifies the semantic equivalence of syntactically identical

[2] If there are none, then this pathway is empty and CS_i and US_i are the same schema

There are several algebraic properties of IQL's operators that we can use in order to incrementally compute materialised data and to reason about IQL expressions, specifically for the purposes of this paper in a schema/data evolution context (note that the algebraic properties of `fold` below apply to all the operators defined in terms of `fold`):

(a) `e ++ [] = [] ++ e = e, e -- [] = e, [] -- e = [],`
`distinct [] = sort [] = []`
for any list-valued expression `e`. Since `Void` represents a construct for which no data is obtainable from a data source, it has the semantics of the empty list, and thus the above equivalences also hold if `Void` is substituted for `[]`.
(b) `fold f op e [] = fold f op e Void = e`, for any `f, op, e`
(c) `fold f op e (b1 ++ b2) = (fold f op e b1) op (fold f op e b2)`
for any `f, op, e, b1, b2`. Thus, we can always incrementally compute the value of fold-based functions if collections expand.
(d) `fold f op e (b1 -- b2) = (fold f op e b1) op' (fold f op e b2)`
provided there is an operator `op'` which is the inverse of `op` i.e. such that `(a op b) op' b = a` for all `a,b`. For example, if `op` = `+` then `op'` = `-`, and thus we can always incrementally compute the value of aggregation functions such as `count`, `sum` and `avg` if collections contract. Note that this is not possible for `min` and `max` since `lesser` and `greater` have no inverses. Although IQL is list-based, if the ordering of elements within lists is ignored then its operators are faithful to the expected bag semantics, and within AutoMed we generally do assume bag semantics. Under this assumption,
`(xs ++ ys) -- ys = xs`
for all `xs,ys` and thus we can incrementally compute the value of `flatmap` and all its derivative operators if collections contract[4].

2.2 An Example

We will use schemas expressed in a simple relational data model and a simple XML data model to illustrate our techniques. However, we stress that these techniques are applicable to schemas defined in *any* data modelling language that has been specified within AutoMed's Model Definitions Repository.

In the simple relational model, there are two kinds of schema construct: Rel and Att. The extent of a Rel construct ⟨⟨R⟩⟩ is the projection of the relation R onto its primary key attributes $k_1, ..., k_n$. The extent of each Att construct ⟨⟨R, a⟩⟩ where a is an attribute (key or non-key) of R is the projection of relation R onto $k_1, ..., k_n, a$. For example, the schema of table `MAtab` in Figure 2 consists of a Rel construct ⟨⟨MAtab⟩⟩, and four Att constructs ⟨⟨MAtab, Dept⟩⟩, ⟨⟨MAtab, CID⟩⟩, ⟨⟨MAtab, SID⟩⟩, and ⟨⟨MAtab, Mark⟩⟩. We refer the reader to [15] for an encoding of a richer relational data model, including the modelling of constraints.

In the simple XML data model, there are three kinds of schema construct: Element, Attribute and NestSet. The extent of an Element construct ⟨⟨e⟩⟩ consists

[4] The `distinct` operator can also be used to obtain set semantics, if needed

of all the elements with tag e in the XML document; the extent of each Attribute construct ⟨⟨e, a⟩⟩ consists of all pairs of elements and attributes x, y such that element x has tag e and has an attribute a with value y; and the extent of each NestSet construct ⟨⟨p, c⟩⟩ consists of all pairs of elements x, y such that element x has tag p and has a child element y with tag c. We refer the reader to [21] for an encoding of a richer model for XML data sources, called XMLDSS, which also captures the ordering of children elements under parent elements and cardinality constraints. That paper gives an algorithm for generating the XMLDSS schema of an XML document. That paper also discusses a unique naming scheme for Element constructs so as to handle instances of the same element tag occurring at multiple positions in the XMLDSS tree.

Figure 2 illustrates the integration of three data sources LD_1, LD_2, and LD_3, which respectively store students' marks for three departments MA, IS and CS.

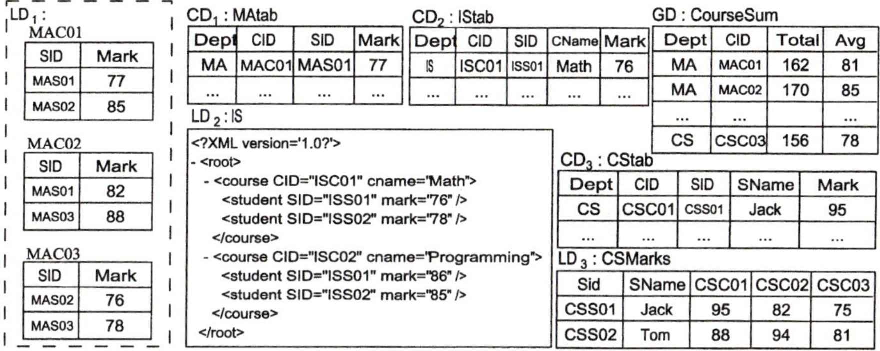

Fig. 2. An example integration

Database LD_1 for department MA has one table of students' marks for each course, where the relation name is the course ID. Database LD_2 for department IS is an XML file containing information of course IDs, course names, student IDs and students' marks. Database LD_3 for department CS has one table containing one row per student, giving the student's ID, name, and mark for the courses CSC01, CSC02 and CSC03. CD_1, CD_2, and CD_3 are the materialised conformed databases for each data source. Finally, the global database GD contains one table CourseSum(Dept,CID,Total,Avg) which gives the total and average mark for each course of each department. Note that the virtual union schema US (not shown) combines all the information from all the conformed schemas and consists of a virtual table Details(Dept,CID,SID,CName,SName,Mark).

The following transformation pathways express the schema transformation and integration processes in this example. Due to space limitations, we have not given the remaining steps for deleting/contracting the constructs in the source schema of each pathway (note that this 'growing' and 'shrinking' of schemas is characteristic of AutoMed schema transformation pathways):

one primitive transformation. If $S \rightarrow S^{new}$ is a composite transformation, then it is handled as a sequence of primitive transformations. Our discussion below assumes that the primitive transformation being handled is adding, removing or renaming a construct of S that has an underlying data extent. We do not discuss the addition or removal of constraints here as these do not impact on the materialised data, and we make the assumption that any constraints in the pathway $S \rightarrow S^{new}$ have been verified as being valid.

4.1 Evolution of the Global Schema

Suppose the global schema GS evolves by means of a primitive transformation t into GS^{new}. This is expressed by the step t being appended to the pathway T_u of Figure 1. The new global schema is GS^{new} and its associated extension is GD^{new}. GS is now an intermediate schema in the extended pathway $T_u; t$ and it no longer has an extension associated with it. t may be a rename, add, extend, delete or contract transformation. The following actions are taken in each case:

1. If t is rename c c', then there is nothing further to do. GS is semantically equivalent to GS^{new} and GD^{new} is identical to GD except that the extent of c in GD is now the extent of c' in GD^{new}.
2. If t is add c q, then there is nothing further to do at the schema level. GS is semantically equivalent to GS^{new}. However, the new construct c in GD^{new} must now be populated, and this is achieved by evaluating the query q over GD.
3. If t is extend c, then the new construct c in GD^{new} is populated by an empty extent. This new construct may subsequently be populated by an expansion in a data source (see Section 4.2).
4. If t is delete c q or contract c, then the extent of c must be removed from GD in order to create GD^{new} (it is assumed that this a legal deletion/contraction, e.g if we wanted to delete/contract a table from a relational schema, then first the constraints and then the columns would be deleted/contracted and lastly the table itself; such syntactic correctness of transformation pathways is automatically verified by AutoMed). It may now be possible to simplify the transformation network, in that if T_u contains a matching transformation add c q or extend c, then both this and the new transformation t can be removed from the pathway $US \rightarrow GS^{new}$. This is purely an optimization – it does not change the meaning of a pathway, nor its effect on view generation and query/data translation. We refer the reader to [19] for details of the algorithms that simplify AutoMed transformation pathways.

In cases *2* and *3* above, the new construct c will automatically be propagated into the schema DMS of any data mart derived from GS. To prevent this, a transformation contract c can be prefixed to the pathway $GS \rightarrow DMS$. Alternatively, the new construct c can be propagated to DMS if so desired, and materialised there. In cases *1* and *4* above, the change in GS and GD may impact on the data marts derived from GS, and we discuss this in Section 4.3.

4.2 Evolution of a Local Schema

Suppose a local schema LS_i evolves by means of a primitive transformation t into LS_i^{new}. As discussed in Section 2, there is automatically available a reverse transformation $\bar{t}$ from LS_i^{new} to LS_i and hence a pathway $\bar{t}; T_i$ from LS_i^{new} to CS_i. The new local schema is LS_i^{new} and its associated extension is LD_i^{new}. LS_i is now just an intermediate schema in the extended pathway $\bar{t}; T_i$ and it no longer has an associated extension.

t may be a rename, add, delete, extend or contract transformation. In 1–5 below we see what further actions are taken in each case for evolving the integration network and the downstream materialised data as necessary.

We first introduce some necessary terminology: If p is a pathway $S \rightarrow S'$ and c is a construct in S, we denote by $descendants(c, p)$ the constructs of S' which are directly or indirectly dependent on c, either because c itself appears in S' or because a construct c' of S' is created by a transformation add c' q within p where the query q directly or indirectly references c. The set $descendants(c, p)$ can be straight-forwardly computed by traversing p and inspecting the query associated with each add transformation within in.

1. If t is rename c c', then schema LS_i^{new} is semantically equivalent to LS_i. The new transformation pathway $T_i^{new} : LS_i^{new} \rightarrow CS_i$ is $\bar{t}; T_i$ = rename c' c; T_i. The new local database LD_i^{new} is identical to LD_i except that the extent of c in LD_i is now the extent of c' in LD_i^{new}.
2. If t is add c q, then LS_i has evolved to contain a new construct c whose extent is equivalent to the expression q over the other constructs of LS_i. The new transformation pathway $T_i^{new} : LS_i^{new} \rightarrow CS_i$ is $\bar{t}; T_i$ = delete c q; T_i.
3. If t is delete c q, this means that LS_i has evolved to not include a construct c whose extent is derivable from the expression q over the other constructs of LS_i, and the new local database LD_i^{new} no longer contains an extent for c. The new transformation pathway $T_i^{new} : LS_i^{new} \rightarrow CS_i$ is $\bar{t}; T_i$ = add c q; T_i.

In the above three cases, schema LS_i^{new} is semantically equivalent to LS_i, and nothing further needs to be done to any of the transformation pathways, schemas or databases $CD_1, \ldots, CD_n$ and GD. This may not be the case if t is a contract or extend transformation, which we consider next.

4. If t is extend c, then there will be a new construct available from LS_i^{new} that was not available before. That is, LS_i has evolved to contain the new construct c whose extent is not derivable from the other constructs of LS_i. If we left the transformation pathway T_i as it is, this would result in a pathway T_i^{new} = contract c; T_i from LS_i^{new} to CS_i, which would immediately drop the new construct c from the integration network. That is, T_i^{new} is consistent but it does not utilize the new data.

However, recall that we said earlier that we assume no contract steps in the pathways from local schemas to their union schemas, and that all the data in LS_i should be available to the integration network. In order to achieve this, there are four cases to consider:

(a) c appears in US_i and has the same semantics as the newly added c in LS_i^{new}. Since c cannot be derived from the original LS_i, there must be a transformation extend c, in $CS_i \rightarrow US_i$.
We remove from T_i^{new} the new contract c step and this matching extend c step. This propagates c into CS_i, and we populate its extent in the materialised database CD_i by replicating its extent from LD_i^{new}.

(b) c does not appear in US_i but it can be derived from US_i by means of some transformation T.
In this case, we remove from T_i^{new} the first contract c step, so that c is now present in CS_i and in US_i. We populate the extent of c in CD_i by replicating its extent from LD_i^{new}.
To repair the other pathways $T_j : LS_j \rightarrow CS_j$ and schemas US_j for $j \neq i$, we append T to the end of each T_j. As a result, the new construct c now appears in all the union schemas. To add the extent of this new construct to each materialised database CD_j for $j \neq i$, we compute it from the extents of the other constructs in CS_j using the queries within successive add steps in T.
We finally append the necessary new id steps between pairs of union schemas to assert the semantic equivalence of the construct c within them.

(c) c does not appear in US_i and cannot be derived from US_i.
In this case, we again remove from T_i^{new} the first contract c step so that c is now present in schema CS_i.
To repair the other pathways $T_j : LS_j \rightarrow CS_j$ and schemas US_j for $j \neq i$, we append an extend c step to the end of each T_j. As a result, the new construct c now appears in all the conformed schemas $CS_1, \ldots, CS_n$.
The construct c may need further translation into the data model of the union schemas and this is done by appending the necessary sequence, T, of add/delete/rename steps to all the pathways $LS_1 \rightarrow CS_1, \ldots, LS_n \rightarrow CS_n$. We compute the extent of c within the database CD_i from its extent within LD_i^{new} using the queries within successive add steps in T.
We finally append the necessary new id steps between pairs of union schemas to assert the semantic equivalence of the new construct(s) within them.

(d) c appears in US_i but has different semantics to the newly added c in LS_i^{new}. In this case, we rename c in LS_i^{new} to a new construct c'. The situation reverts to adding a new construct c' to LS_i^{new}, and one of (a)-(c) above applies.

We note that determining whether c can or cannot be derived from the existing constructs of the union schemas in (a)–(d) above requires domain or expert human knowledge. Thereafter, the remaining actions are fully automatic.

In cases (a) and (b), there is new data added to one or more of the conformed databases which needs to be propagated to GD. This is done by computing $descendants(c, T_u)$ and using the algebraic equivalences of Section 2.1 to propagate changes in the extent of c to each of its descendant constructs gc in GS. Using these equivalences, we can in most cases incrementally recompute the extent of gc. If at any stage in T_u there is a transformation add c' q where no equivalence can be applied, then we have to recompute the whole extent of c'.

In cases (b) and (c), there is a new schema construct c appearing in the US_i. This construct will automatically appear in the schema GS. If this is not desired, a transformation contract c can be prefixed to T_u.

5. If t is contract c, then the construct c in LS_i will no longer be available from LS_i^{new}. That is, LS_i has evolved so as to not include a construct c whose extent is not derivable from the other constructs of LS_i. The new local database LD_i^{new} no longer contains an extent for c.
The new transformation pathway $T_i^{new} : LS_i^{new} \rightarrow CS_i$ is $\bar{t}; T_i =$ extend $c; T_i$. Since the extent of c is now Void, the materialised data in CD_i and GD must be modified so as to remove any data derived from the old extent of c.
In order to repair CD_i, we compute $descendants(c, LS_i \rightarrow CS_i)$. For each construct uc in $descendants(c, LS_i \rightarrow CS_i)$, we compute its new extent and replace its old extent in CD_i by the new extent. Again, the algebraic properties of IQL queries discussed in Section 2.1 can be used to propagate the new Void extent of construct c in LS_i^{new} to each of its descendant constructs uc in CS_i. Using these equivalences, we can in most cases incrementally recompute the extent of uc as we traverse the pathway T_i.
In order to repair GD, we similarly propagate changes in the extent of each uc along the pathway T_u.
Finally, it may also be necessary to amend the transformation pathways if there are one or more constructs in GD which now will always have an empty extent as a result of this contraction of LS_i. For any construct uc in US whose extent has become empty, we examine all pathways $T_1, \ldots,$ T_n. If all these pathways contain an extend uc transformation, or if using the equivalences of Section 2.1 we can deduce from them that the extent of uc will always be empty, then we can suffix a contract gc step to T_u for every gc in $descendants(uc, T_u)$, and then handle this case as paragraph 4 in Section 4.1.

4.3 Evolution of Downstream Data Marts

We have discussed how evolutions to the global schema or to a source schema are handled. One remaining question is how to handle the impact of a change to the data warehouse schema, and possibly its data, on any data marts that have been derived from it.

In [7] we discuss how it is possible to express the derivation of a data marts from a data warehouse by means of an AutoMed transformation pathway. Such a pathway $GS \rightarrow DMS$ expresses the relationship of a data mart schema DMS to the warehouse schema GS. As such, this scenario can be regarded as a special case of the general integration scenario of Figure 1, where GS now plays the role of the single source schema, databases $CD_1, \ldots, CD_n$ and GD collectively play the role of the data associated with this source schema and DMS plays the role of the global schema. Therefore, the same techniques as discussed in sections 4.1 and 4.2 can be applied.

5 Concluding Remarks

In this paper we have described how the AutoMed heterogeneous data integration toolkit can be used to handle the problem of schema evolution in heterogeneous data warehousing environments so that the previous transformation, integration and data materialisation effort can be reused. Our algorithms are mainly automatic, except for the aspects that require domain or expert human knowledge regarding the semantics of new schema constructs.

We have shown how AutoMed transformations can be used to express schema evolution within the same data model, or a change in the data model, or both, whereas other schema evolution literature has focussed on just one data model. Schema evolution within the relational data model has been discussed in previous work such as [11, 12, 18]. The approach in [18] uses a first-order schema in which all values in a schema of interest to a user are modelled as data, and other schemas can be expressed as a query over this first-order schema. The approach in [12] uses the notation of a *flat scheme*, and gives four operators UNITE, FOLD, UNFOLD and SPLIT to perform relational schema evolution using the SchemaSQL language. In contrast, with AutoMed the process of schema evolution is expressed using a simple set of primitive schema transformations augmented with a functional query language, both of which are applicable to multiple data models.

Our approach is complementary to work on mapping composition, e.g. [20, 14], in that in our case the new mappings are a composition of the original transformation pathway and the transformation pathway which expresses the schema evolution. Thus, the new mappings are, by definition, correct. There are two aspects to our approach: (i) handling the transformation pathways and (ii) handling the queries within them. In this paper we have in particular assumed that the queries are expressed in IQL. However, the AutoMed toolkit allows any query language syntax to be used within primitive transformations, and therefore this aspect of our approach could be extended to other query languages.

Materialised data warehouse views need to be maintained when the data sources change, and much previous work has addressed this problem at the data level. However, as we have discussed in this paper, materialised data warehouse views may also need to be modified if there is an evolution of a data source schema. Incremental maintenance of schema-restructuring views within the relational data model is discussed in [10], whereas our approach can handle this problem in a heterogeneous data warehousing environment with multiple data models and changes in data models. Our previous work [7] has discussed how AutoMed transformation pathways can also be used for incrementally maintaining materialised views at the data level. For future work, we are implementing our approach and evaluating it in the context of biological data warehousing.

References

1. J. Andany, M. Léonard, and C. Palisser. Management of schema evolution in databases. In *Proc. VLDB'91*, pages 161–170. Morgan Kaufmann, 1991.
2. Z. Bellahsene. View mechanism for schema evolution in object-oriented DBMS. In *Proc. BNCOD'96, LNCS 1094*. Springer, 1996.
3. B. Benatallah. A unified framework for supporting dynamic schema evolution in object databases. In *Proc. ER'99, LNCS 1728*. Springer, 1999.
4. M. Blaschka, C. Sapia, and G. Höfling. On schema evolution in multidimensional databases. In *Proc. DaWaK'99, LNCS 1767*. Springer, 1999.
5. M. Boyd, S. Kittivoravitkul, C. Lazanitis, P.J. McBrien, and N. Rizopoulos. AutoMed: A BAV data integration system for heterogeneous data sources. In *Proc. CAiSE'04*, 2004.
6. P. Buneman *et al.* Comprehension syntax. *SIGMOD Record*, 23(1):87–96, 1994.
7. H. Fan and A. Poulovassilis. Using AutoMed metadata in data warehousing environments. In *Proc. DOLAP'03*, pages 86–93. ACM Press, 2003.
8. E. Jasper, A. Poulovassilis, and L. Zamboulis. Processing IQL queries and migrating data in the AutoMed toolkit. Technical Report 20, Automed Project, 2003.
9. E. Jasper, N. Tong, P. McBrien, and A. Poulovassilis. View generation and optimisation in the AutoMed data integration framework. In *Proc. 6th Baltic Conference on Databases and Information Systems*, 2004.
10. A. Koeller and E. A. Rundensteiner. Incremental maintenance of schema-restructuring views. In *Proc. EDBT'02, LNCS 2287*. Springer, 2002.
11. L. V. S. Lakshmanan, F. Sadri, and I. N. Subramanian. On the logical foundations of schema integration and evolution in heterogeneous database systems. In *Proc. DOOD'93, LNCS 760*. Springer, 1993.
12. L. V. S. Lakshmanan, F. Sadri, and S. N. Subramanian. On efficiently implementing SchemaSQL on an SQL database system. In *Proc. VLDB'99*, pages 471–482. Morgan Kaufmann, 1999.
13. M. Lenzerini. Data integration: A theoretical perspective. In *Proc. PODS'02*, 2002.
14. Jayant Madhavan and Alon Y. Halevy. Composing mappings among data sources. In *Proc. VLDB'03*. Morgan Kaufmann, 2003.
15. P. McBrien and A. Poulovassilis. A uniform approach to inter-model transformations. In *Proc. CAiSE'99, LNCS 1626*, pages 333–348. Springer, 1999.
16. P. McBrien and A. Poulovassilis. Schema evolution in heterogeneous database architectures, a schema transformation approach. In *Proc. CAiSE'02, LNCS 2348*, pages 484–499. Springer, 2002.
17. P. McBrien and A. Poulovassilis. Data integration by bi-directional schema transformation rules. In *Proc. ICDE'03*, pages 227–238, 2003.
18. Renée J. Miller. Using schematically heterogeneous structures. In *Proc. ACM SIGMOD'98*, pages 189–200. ACM Press, 1998.
19. N. Tong. Database schema transformation optimisation techniques for the AutoMed system. In *Proc. BNCOD'03, LNCS 2712*. Springer, 2003.
20. Yannis Velegrakis, Renée J. Miller, and Lucian Popa. Mapping adaptation under evolving schemas. In *Proc. VLDB'03*. Morgan Kaufmann, 2003.
21. L. Zamboulis. XML data integration by graph restrucring. In *Proc. BNCOD'04, LNCS 3112*. Springer, 2004.

Metaprogramming for Relational Databases

Jernej Kovse, Christian Weber, and Theo Härder

Department of Computer Science
Kaiserslautern University of Technology
P.O. Box 3049, D-67653 Kaiserslautern, Germany
{kovse,c_weber,haerder}@informatik.uni-kl.de

Abstract. For systems that share enough structural and functional commonalities, reuse in schema development and data manipulation can be achieved by defining problem-oriented languages. Such languages are often called domain-specific, because they introduce powerful abstractions meaningful only within the domain of observed systems. In order to use domain-specific languages for database applications, a mapping to SQL is required. In this paper, we deal with metaprogramming concepts required for easy definition of such mappings. Using an example domain-specific language, we provide an evaluation of mapping performance.

1 Introduction

A large variety of approaches use SQL as a language for interacting with the database, but at the same time provide a separate problem-oriented language for developing database schemas and formulating queries. A *translator* maps a statement in such problem-oriented language to a series of SQL statements that get executed by the DBMS. An example of such a system is *Preference SQL*, described by Kießling and Köstler [8]. Preference SQL is an SQL extension that provides a set of language constructs which support easy use of *soft preferences*. This kind of preferences is useful when searching for products and services in diverse e-commerce applications where a set of strictly observed hard constraints usually results in an empty result set, although products that approximately match the user's demands do exist. The supported constructs include *approximation* (clauses `AROUND` and `BETWEEN`), *minimization/maximization* (clauses `LOWEST`, `HIGHEST`), *favorites and dislikes* (clauses `POS`, `NEG`), *pareto accumulation* (clause `AND`), and *cascading of preferences* (clause `CASCADE`) (see [8] for examples).

In general, problem-oriented programming languages are also called *domain-specific languages* (DSLs), because they prove useful when developing and using systems from a predefined *domain*. The systems in a domain will exhibit a range of similar structural and functional features (see [4,5] for details), making it possible to describe them (and, in our case, query their data) using higher-level programming constructs. In turn, these constructs carry semantics meaningful only within this domain. As the activity of using these constructs is referred to as programming, defining such con-

P. Atzeni et al. (Eds.): ER 2004, LNCS 3288, pp. 654–667, 2004.

structs and their mappings to languages that can be compiled or interpreted to allow their execution is referred to as *metaprogramming*.

This paper focuses on the application of metaprogramming for relational databases. In particular, we are interested in concepts that guide the implementation of fast mappings of custom languages, used for developing database schemas and manipulating data, onto SQL-DDL and SQL-DML. The paper is structured as follows. First, in Sect. 2, we further motivate the need for DSLs for data management. An overview of related work is given by Sect. 3. Our system prototype (DSL-DA – domain-specific languages for database applications) that supports the presented ideas is outlined in Sect. 4. A detailed performance evaluation of a DSL for the example product line will be presented in Sect. 5. Sect. 6 gives a detailed overview of metaprogramming concepts. Finally, in Sect. 7, we summarize our results and give some ideas for the future work related to our approach.

2 Domain-Specific Languages

The idea of DSLs is tightly related to *domain engineering*. According to Czarnecki and Eisenecker [5], domain engineering deals with collecting, organizing, and storing past experience in building systems in form of *reusable assets*. In general, we can rely that a given asset can be reused in a new system in case this system possesses some structural and functional similarity to previous systems. Indeed, systems that share enough common properties are said to constitute a *system family* (a more market-oriented term for a system family is a *software product-line*). Examples of software product-lines are extensively outlined by Clements and Northrop [4] and include satellite controllers, internal combustion engine controllers, and systems for displaying and tracing stock-market data. Further examples of more data-centric product lines include CRM and ERP systems. Our example *product line for versioning systems* will be introduced in Sect. 4.

Three approaches can be applied to allow the reuse of "assets" when developing database schemas for systems in a data-intensive product line.

Components: Schema components can be used to group larger reusable parts of a database schema to be used in diverse systems afterwards (see Thalheim [16] for an extensive overview of this approach). Generally, the modularity of system specification (which components are to be used) directly corresponds to the modularity of the resulting implementation, because a component does not influence the internal implementation of other components. This kind of specification transformations towards the implementation is referred to as *vertical transformations* or *forward refinements* [5].

Frameworks: Much like software frameworks in general (see, for example, Apache Struts [1] or IBM San Francisco [2]), schema frameworks rely on the user to extend them with system-specific parts. This step is called *framework instantiation* and requires certain knowledge of how the missing parts will be called by the framework. Most often, this is achieved by extending superclasses defined by the framework or implementing *call-back methods* which will be invoked by mechanisms such as *reflection*. In a DBMS, application logic otherwise captured by such methods can be defined by means of constraints, trigger conditions and actions, and stored procedures. A detailed overview of schema frameworks is given by Mahnke [9]. Being more flexible than components, frameworks generally require more expertise from the user. Moreover, due to performance reasons, most DBMSs restrain from dynamic invocation possibilities through method overloading or reflection (otherwise supported in common OO programming languages). For this reason, schema frameworks are difficult to implement without middleware acting as a mediator for such calls.

Generators: Schema generators are, in our opinion, the most advanced approach to reuse and are the central topic of this paper. A schema generator acts much like a compiler: It transforms a high-level specification of the system to a schema definition, possibly equipped with constraints, triggers, and stored procedures. In general, the modularity of the specification does not have to be preserved. Two modular parts of the specification can be interwoven to obtain a single modular part in the schema (these transformations are called *horizontal transformations*; in case the obtained part in the schema is also refined, for example, columns not explicitly defined in the specification are added to a table, this is called an *oblique transformation*, i.e., a combination of a horizontal and a vertical transformation.)

It is important to note that there is no special "magic" associated with schema generators that allows them to obtain a ready-to-use schema out of a short specification. By narrowing the domain of systems, it is possible to introduce very powerful language abstractions that are used at the specification level. Due to similarities between systems, these abstractions aggregate a lot of semantics that is dispersed across many schema elements. Because defining this semantics in SQL-DDL proves labour-intensive, we rather choose to define a special domain-specific DDL (DS-DDL) for specifying the schema at a higher level of abstraction and implement the corresponding mapping to SQL-DDL. The mapping represents the "reusable asset" and can be used with any schema definition in this DS-DDL. The data manipulation part complementary to DS-DDL is called DS-DML and allows the use of domain-specific query and update statements in application programs. Defining custom DS-DDLs and their mappings to SQL-DDL as well as fast translation of DS-DML statements is the topic we explore in this paper.

3 Related Work

Generators are the central idea of the OMG's *Model Driven Architecture* (MDA) [13] which proposes the specification of systems using standardized modeling languages (UML) and automatic generation of implementations from models. However, even OMG notices the need of supporting custom domain-specific modeling languages. As noted by Frankel [6], this can be done in three different ways:

- *Completely new modeling languages*: A new DSL can be obtained by defining a new MOF-based metamodel.
- *Heavyweight language extensions*: A new DSL can be obtained by extending the elements of a standardized metamodel (e.g., the UML Metamodel).
- *Lightweight language extensions*: A new DSL can be obtained by defining new language abstractions *using the language itself*. In UML, this possibility is supported by *UML Profiles*.

The research area that deals with developing custom (domain-specific) software engineering methodologies well suited for particular systems is called *computer-aided method engineering* (CAME) [14]. CAME tools allow the user to describe an own modeling method and afterwards generate a CASE tool that supports this method. For an example of a tool supporting this approach, see MetaEdit+ [11].

The idea of a rapid definition of domain-specific programming languages and their mapping to a platform where they can be executed is materialized in Simonyi's work on *Intentional Programming* (IP) [5,15]. IP introduces an IDE based on *active libraries* that are used to import language abstractions (also called *intentions*) into this environment. Programs in the environment are represented as source graphs in which each node possesses a special pointer to a corresponding abstraction. The abstractions define *extension methods* which are metaprograms that specify the behavior of nodes. The following are the most important extension methods in IP.

- *Rendering and type-in methods.* Because it is cumbersome to edit the source graph directly, rendering methods are used to visualize the source graph in an editable notation. Type-in methods convert the code typed in this notation back to the source graph. This is especially convenient when different notations prove useful for a single source graph.
- *Refactoring methods.* These methods are used to restructure the source graph by factoring out repeating code parts to improve reuse.
- *Reduction methods.* The most important component of IP, these methods reduce the source graph to a graph of low-level abstractions (also called *reduced code* or *R-code*) that represent programs executable on a given platform. Different reduction methods can be used to obtain the R-code for different platforms.

How does this work relate to our problem? Similar as in IP, we want to support a custom definition of abstractions that form both a custom DS-DDL and a custom DS-DML. We want to support the rendering of source graphs for DS-DDL and DS-DML statements to (possibly diverse) domain-specific textual representations. Most importantly, we want to support the reduction of these graphs to graphs representing SQL statements that can be executed by a particular DBMS.

4 DSL-DA System

In our DSL-DA system, the user starts by defining a domain-specific (DS) metamodel that describes language abstractions that can appear in the source graph (the language used for defining metamodels is a simplified variant of the MOF Model) for the DS-DDL. We used the system to fully implement a DSL for the *example product line of versioning systems* which we also use in the next section for the evaluation of our approach. In this product line, each system is used to store and version objects (of some object type) and relationships (of some relationship type). Thus individual systems differ in their type definitions (also called information models [3]) as well as other features illustrated in the DS-DDL metamodel in Fig. 1 and explained below.

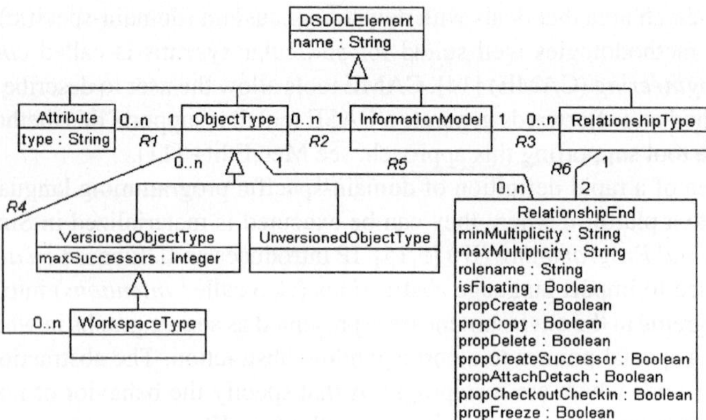

Fig. 1. DS-DDL metamodel for the example product line

- Object types can be *versioned* or *unversioned.* The number of direct successors to a version can be limited to some number (*maxSuccessors*) for a given versioned object type.
- Relationship types connect to object types using either *non-floating* or *floating* relationship ends. A non-floating relationship end connects directly to a particular version as if this version were a regular object. On the other hand, a floating relationship end maintains a user-managed subset of all object versions for each connected object. Such subsets are called *candidate version collections* (CVC) and prove useful for managing configurations. In *unfiltered navigation* from some origin object, all versions contained in every connected CVC will be returned. In *filtered navigation*, a version preselected for each CVC (also called the *pinned version*) will be returned. In case there is no pinned version, we return the latest version from the CVC.
- Workspace objects act as containers for other objects. However, only one version of a contained object can be present in the workspace at a time. In this way, workspaces allow a version-free view to the contents of a versioning system. When executed within a workspace, filtered navigation returns versions from the CVC that are connected to this workspace and ignores the pin setting of the CVC.
- Operations *create object*, *copy*, *delete*, *create successor*, *attach/detach* (connects/ disconnects an object to/from a workspace), *freeze*, and *checkout/checkin* (locks/ unlocks the object) can propagate across relationships.

A model expressed using the DS-DDL metamodel from Fig. 1 will represent a source graph for a particular DS-DDL schema definition used to describe a given versioning system. To work with these models (manipulate the graph nodes), DSL-DA uses the DS-DDL metamodel to generate a *schema editor* that displays the graphs in a tree-like form (see the left-hand side of Fig. 2). A more convenient graphical notation of a source graph for our example versioning system that we will use for the evaluation in the next section is illustrated in Fig. 3.

The metamodel classes define rendering and type-in methods that render the source graph to a textual representation and allow its editing (right-hand side of Fig. 2). More importantly, the metamodel classes define reduction methods that will reduce the

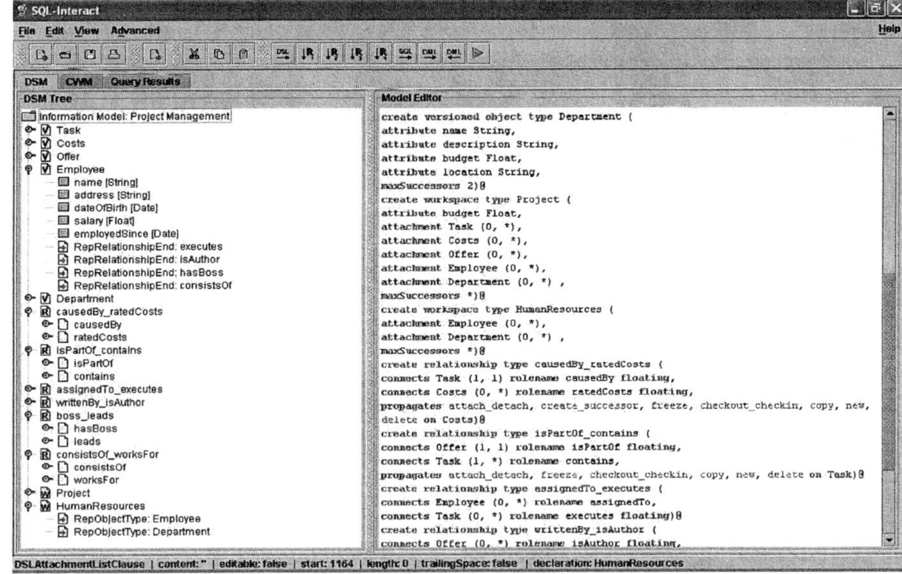

Fig. 2. DS-DDL schema development with the generated editor

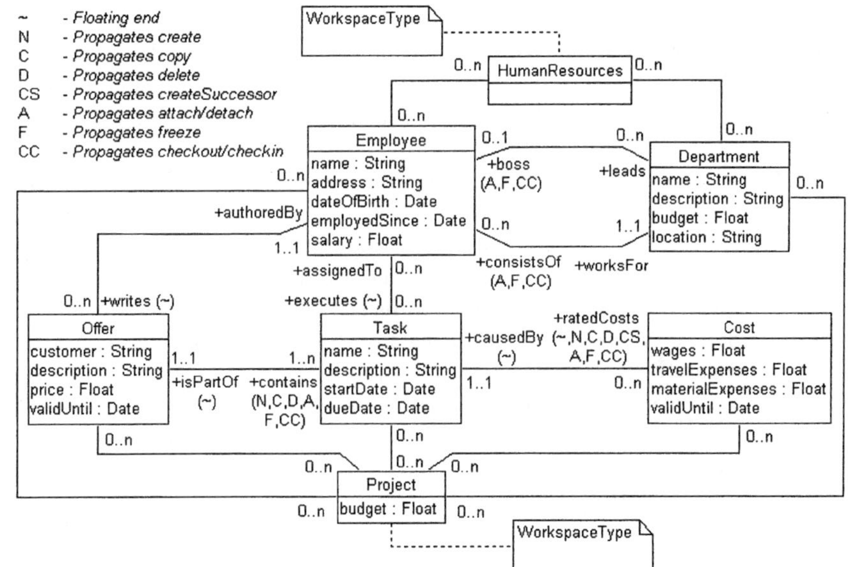

Fig. 3. Example DS-DDL schema used in performance evaluation

source graph to its representation in SQL-DDL. In analogy with the domain-specific level of the editor, the obtained SQL-DDL schema is also represented as a source graph; the classes used for this graph are the classes defined by the package *Relational* of the OMG's Common Warehouse Metamodel (CWM) [12]. The rendering methods of these

Table 1. Examples of DS-DML statements

Statement	Explanation
SELECT Task.* FROM Department-consistsOf->Employee-executes->Task WHERE Department.globalId = 502341	Get all tasks executed by employees of a given department (all three objects are versioned). Note that the fact that the relationship end *executes* is floating (i.e. filtered navigation will be used) is transparent for the user.
CREATE SUCCESSOR OF OBJECT Task USE WORKSPACE Project WHERE globalId = 235711 AND Task WHERE objectId = 982	Create a successor version to a version of a task. The version graph for the task is identified by the *objectId*. The successor is to be created to the version attached to the workspace with a given *globalId*. Note that according to the DS-DDL schema, the operation will propagate to connected costs.
GET ALTERNATIVES OF Employee WHERE globalId = 234229	Get the alternative versions (versions that have the same predecessor) of a given employee version

classes are customizable so that by rendering the SQL-DDL source graphs, SQL-DDL schemas in SQL dialects of diverse DBMS vendors can be obtained.

Once an SQL-DDL schema is installed in a database, how do we handle statements in DS-DML (three examples of such statements are given by Table 1)? As for the DS-DDL, there is a complementary DS-DML metamodel that describes language abstractions of the supported DS-DML statements. This metamodel can be simply defined by first coming up with an EBNF for DS-DML and afterwards translating the EBNF symbols to class definitions in a straightforward fashion. The EBNF of our DS-DML for the sample product line for versioning systems is available through [17]. DS-DML statements can then be represented as source graphs, where each node in the graph is an instance of some class from the DS-DML metamodel. Again, metamodel classes define reduction methods that reduce the corresponding DS-DML source graph to an SQL-DML source graph, out of which SQL-DML statements can be obtained through rendering.

DS-DML is used by an application programmer to embed domain-specific queries and data manipulation statements in the application code. In certain cases, the general structure of a DS-DML statement will be known at the time the application is written and the parameters of the statement will only need to be filled with user-provided values at run time. Since these parameters do not influence the reduction, the reduction from DS-DML to SQL-DML can take place using a *precompiler*. Sometimes, however, especially in the case of Web applications, the structure of the DS-DML query will depend on the user's search criteria and other preferences and is thus not known at compile time. The solution in this case is to wrap the native DBMS driver into a *domain-specific driver* that performs the reduction at run time, passes the SQL-DML statements to the native driver, and restructures the result sets before returning them to the user, if necessary. To handle both cases where query structure is known at compile time and when it is not, DSL-DA can generate both the precompiler and the domain-specific driver from the DS-DML metamodel, its reduction methods, and its rendering methods for SQL-DML. We assumed the worst-case scenario in which all SQL-DML statements need to be reduced at run time for our evaluation in the next section to examine the effect of run time reduction in detail.

5 Evaluation of the Example Product Line

The purpose of the evaluation presented in this section is to demonstrate the following.

- Even for structurally complex DS-DML statements, the reduction process carried out at run time represents a very small proportion of costs needed to carry out the SQL-DML statements obtained by reduction.
- DS-DDL schemas that have been reduced to SQL-DDL with certain optimizations in mind imply reduction that is more difficult to implement. Somewhat surprisingly, this does not necessarily mean that such reduction will also take more processing time. Optimization considerations can significantly contribute to a faster execution of DS-DML statements once reduced to SQL-DML.

To demonstrate both points, we implemented four very different variants of both DS-DDL and DS-DML reduction methods for the example product line. The DS-DDL schema from Fig. 3 has thus been reduced to four different SQL-DDL schemas. In all four variants, object types from Fig. 3 are mapped to tables (called *object tables*) with the specified attributes. An object version is then represented as a tuple in this table. The identifiers in each object table include an *objectId* (all versions of a particular object, i.e., all versions within the same version tree, possess the same *objectId*), a *versionId* (identifies a particular version within the version tree) and a *globalId*, which is a combination of an *objectId* and a *versionId*. The four reductions differ in the following way.

- *Variant 1*: Store all relationships, regardless of relationship type, using a single "generic" table. For a particular relationship, store the *origin globalId*, *objectId*, *versionId* and the *target rolename*, *globalId*, *objectId*, and *versionId* as columns. Use an additional column as a flag denoting whether the target version is pinned.
- *Variant 2*: Use separate tables for every relationship type. In case a relationship type defines no floating ends or two floating ends, this relationship type can be represented by a single table. In case only one relationship end is floating, such relationship type requires two tables, one for each direction of navigation.
- *Variant 3*: Improve *Variant 2* by considering maximal multiplicity of *1* on non-floating ends. For such ends, the *globalId* of the connected target object is stored as a column in the object table of the origin object.
- *Variant 4*: Improve *Variant 3* by considering maximal multiplicity of *1* of floating ends. For such ends, the *globalIds* of the pinned version and the latest version of the CVC for the target object can be stored as columns in the object table of the origin object.

Our benchmark, consisting of 141,775 DS-DML statements was then run using four different domain-specific drivers corresponding to four different variants of reduction. To eliminate the need of fetching metadata from the database, we assumed that, once defined, the DS-DDL schema does not change, so each driver accessed the DS-DDL schema defined in Fig. 3 directly in the main memory. The overall time for executing a DS-DML statement is defined as $t_{DS}= t_{par}+t_{red}+t_{ren}+t_{SQL}$, where t_{par} is the required DS-DML parsing time, t_{red} the time required for reduction, t_{ren} the time required for rendering all resulting SQL-DML statements, and t_{SQL} the time used to carry out these statements. Note that t_{par} is independent of the variant, so we were mainly interested in the remaining three times as well as the overall time. The average t_{DS}, t_{red}, t_{ren} and t_{SQL}

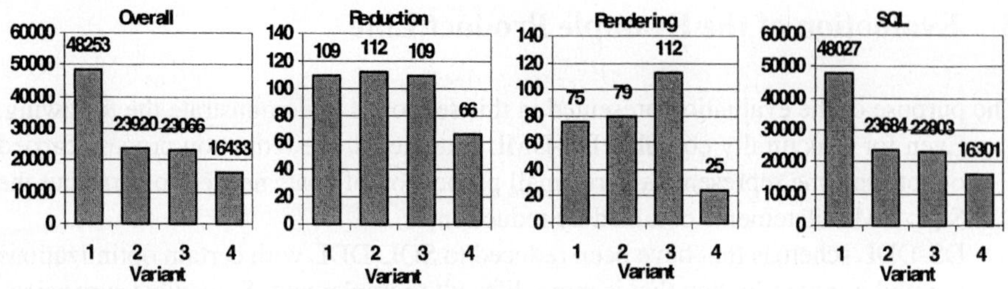

Fig. 4. Execution times for the category of *select* statements

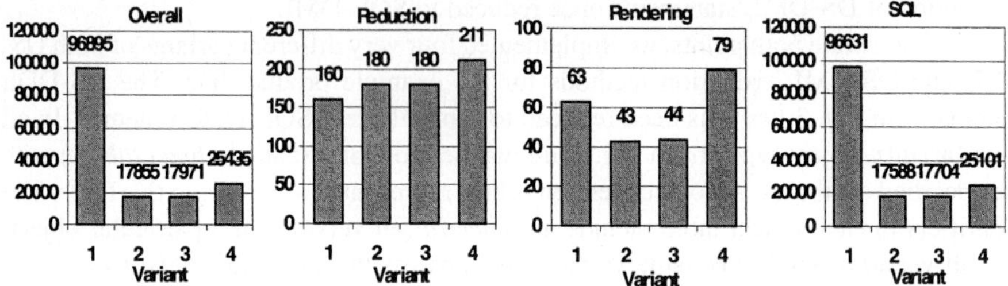

Fig. 5. Execution times for the category of *create relationship* statements

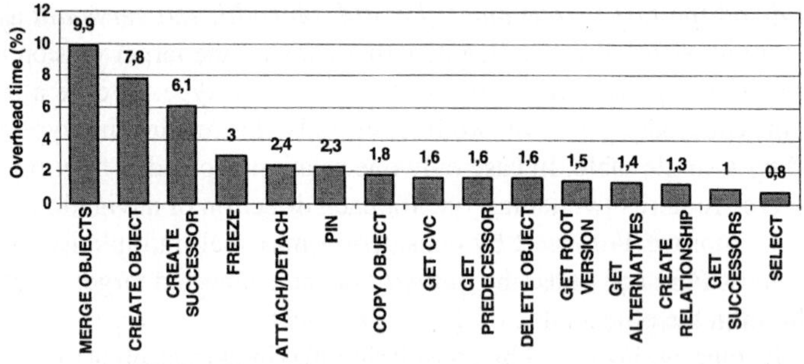

Fig. 6. Overhead due to DS-DML parsing, reduction and rendering

values (in μs) for the category of *select* statements are illustrated in Fig. 4. This category included queries over versioned data within and outside workspaces that contained up to four navigation steps. As evident from Fig. 4, *Variant 4* demonstrates a very good t_{SQL} performance and also allows the fastest reduction. On the other hand, due to materialization of the *globalIds* of pinned and latest versions for CVCs in *Variant 4*, *Variant 2* proves faster for manipulation (i.e., creation and deletion of relationships). The values for the category of *create relationship* statements are illustrated in Fig. 5.

Most importantly, the overhead time required due to the domain-specific driver $t_{dr}=t_{par}+t_{red}+t_{ren}$ proves to be only a small portion of t_{DS}. As illustrated in Fig. 6, when using *Variant 4*, the portion t_{dr}/t_{DS} is lowest (0.8%) for the category of *select* statements

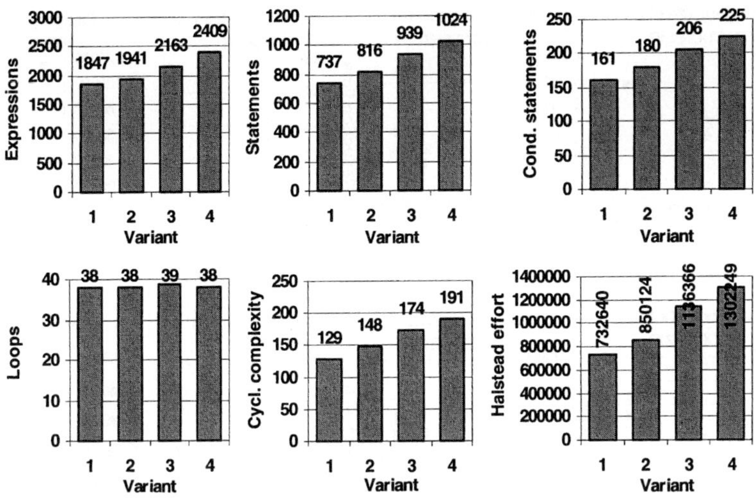

Fig. 7. Properties of reduction methods

and highest (9.9%) for *merge* statements. When merging two versions (denoted as primary and secondary version), their attribute values have to be compared to their so-called *base (latest common) version* in the version graph to decide which values should be used for the result of the merging. This comparison, which is performed in the driver, accounts for a high t_{red} value (9.1% of t_{DS}). Note that t_{SQL} is the minimal time an application spends executing SQL-DML statements in any case (with or without DS-DML available) to provide the user with equivalent results: Even without DS-DML, the programmer would have to implement data flows to connect sequences of SQL-DML statements to perform a given operation (in our evaluation, we treat data flows as part of t_{red}).

How difficult is it to implement the DS-DML reduction methods? To estimate this aspect, we used measures such as the count of expressions, statements, conditional statements, loops, as well as McCabe's cyclomatic complexity [10] and Halstead effort [7] on our Java implementation of reduction methods. The summarized results obtained using these measures are illustrated by Fig. 7. All measures, except for the count of loops confirm an increasing difficulty to implement the reduction (e.g., the Halstead effort almost doubles from *Variant 1* to *Variant 4*). Is there a correlation between the Halstead effort for writing a method and the times t_{red} and t_{SQL}? We try to answer this question in Fig. 8. Somewhat surprisingly, a statement with a reduction more difficult to implement will sometimes also reduce faster (i.e., an increase in Halstead effort does not necessarily imply an increase in t_{red}), which is most evident for the category of *select* statements. The explanation is that even though the developer has to consider a large variety of different reductions for a complex variant (e.g., *Variant 4*), once the driver has found the right reduction (see Sect. 6), the reduction can proceed even faster than for a variant with less optimization considerations (e.g., *Variant 1*). For all categories in Fig. 8, a decreasing trend for t_{SQL} values can be observed. However, in categories that manipulate the state of the CVC (note that operations from the category

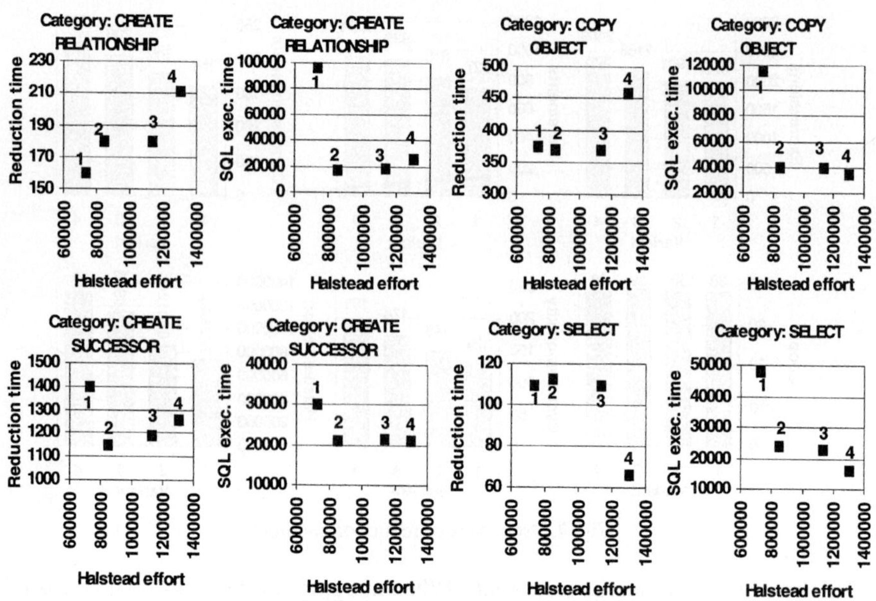

Fig. 8. Correlation of t_{red} and t_{SQL} to the Halstead effort

copy object propagate across relationships and thus manipulate the CVCs), impedance due to materializing the pin setting and the latest version comes into effect and often results in only minor differences in t_{SQL} values among *Variants 2-4*.

6 Metaprogramming Concepts

Writing metacode is different and more difficult than writing code, because the programmer has to consider a large variety of cases that may occur depending on the form of the statement and the properties defined in the DS-DDL schema.

Our key idea to developing reduction methods is the so-called *reduction polymorphism.* In OO programming languages, polymorphism supports dynamic selection of the "right" method depending on the type of object held by a reference (since the type is not known until run time, this is usually called *late binding*). In this way, it is possible to avoid disturbing conditional statements (explicit type checking by the programmer) in the code. In a similar way, we use reduction polymorphism to avoid explicit use of conditional statements in metacode. This means that for an incoming DS-DML statement, the domain-specific driver will execute reduction methods that (a) match the syntactic structure of the statement and (b) apply for the specifics of the DS-DDL schema constructs used in the statement. We illustrate both concepts using a practical example.

Suppose the following DS-DML statement.

```
SELECT Cost.*
FROM Offer-contains->Task-ratedCosts->Cost
USE WORKSPACE Project WHERE globalId = 435532 AND Offer WHERE objectId = 122;
```

Using our DS-DDL schema from Fig. 3 and reduction *Variant 4*, the statement gets reduced to the following SQL-DML statement (`OT` denotes object table, `ATT` the attachment relationship table, `F` a floating end, and `NF` a non-floating end).

```
 1: SELECT CostOT.globalId, CostOT.objectId, CostOT.versionId, CostOT.wages, CostOT.travelExpenses,
 2:     CostOT.materialExpenses, CostOT.validUntil, CostOT.isFrozen
 3: FROM OfferOT, TaskOT, CostOT, isPartOfF_containsNF, causedByF_ratedCostsF,
 4:     ProjectOT, Project_OfferATT, Project_TaskATT, Project_CostATT
 5: WHERE OfferOT.globalId = isPartOfF_containsNF.isPartOfGlobalId
 6:     AND isPartOfF_containsNF.containsGlobalId = TaskOT.globalId
 7:     AND TaskOT.globalId = causedByF_ratedCostF.causedByGlobalId
 8:     AND causedByF_ratedCostF.ratedCostsGlobalId = CostOT.globalId
 9:     AND Project_OfferATT.projectGlobalId = 435532
10:     AND Project_OfferATT.offerGlobalId = OfferOT.globalId
11:     AND Project_TaskATT.projectGlobalId = 435532
12:     AND Project_TaskATT.taskGlobalId = TaskOT.globalId
13:     AND Project_CostATT.projectGlobalId = 435532
14:     AND Project_CostATT.costGlobalId = CostOT.globalId
15:     AND Offer.objectId = 122
```

First, any `SELECT` statement will match a very generic reduction method that will insert `SELECT` and `FROM` clauses into the SQL-DML source graph. A reduction method on the projection clause (`Cost.*`) will reduce to a projection of identifiers (*globalId*, *objectId*, and *versionId*), user-defined attributes and the flag denoting whether the version is frozen. Note that because the maximal multiplicity of the end *causedBy* pointing from *Cost* to *Task* is *1*, the table `CostOT` also contains the materialization of a pinned or latest version of some *task*, but the column for this materialization is left out in the projection, because it is irrelevant for the user. Next, a reduction method is invoked on the DS-DML `FROM` clause, which itself calls reduction methods on two DS-DML subnodes, one for each navigation step. Thus, the reduction of `Offer-contains->Task` results in conditions in lines 5–6 and the reduction of `Task-ratedCosts->Cost` results in conditions in lines 7–8. The reductions carried out in this example rely on two mechanisms, *DS-DDL schema divergence* and *source-graph divergence*.

DS-DDL schema divergence is applied in the following way. The relationship type used in the first navigation step defines only one floating end while the one used in the second navigation step defines both ends as floating. Thus in the reduction of DS-DDL, we had to map the first relationship type to two distinct tables (because relationships with only one floating end are not necessarily symmetric). Therefore, the choice of the table we use (`isPartOfF_containsNF`) is based on the direction of navigation. The situation would be even more different in case the multiplicity defined for the non-floating end would be *1*, where we would have to use a foreign key column in the object table. Another important situation where schema divergence is used in our example product line is operation propagation. To deal with DS-DDL schema divergence, each reduction method for a given node comes with a set of preconditions related to DS-DDL schema that have to be satisfied for method execution.

Source-graph divergence is applied in the following way. In *filtered navigation within a workspace*, we have to use the table `causedByF_ratedCostsF` to arrive at *costs*. The obtained versions are further filtered in lines 9, 11, and 13 to arrive only at *costs* attached to the workspace with *globalId* 435532. The situation would be different *outside a workspace*, where another table which stores the materialized *globalIds* of versions of costs that are either pinned or latest in the corresponding CVC would have to be used for the join. Thus the reduction of the second navigation step depends on whether the clause `USE WORKSPACE` is used. To deal with source-graph divergence, each reduction method for a given node comes with a set of preconditions related to node neighborhood in the source graph that have to be satisfies for method execution.

Due to source-graph divergence, line 3 of the DS-DML statement gets reduced to lines 9–15 of the SQL-DML statement.

Obviously, it is a good choice for the developer to shift decisions due to divergence to many "very specialized" reduction methods that can be reused in diverse superordinated methods and thus abstract from both types of divergence. In this way, the subordinated methods can be explicitly invoked by the developer using generic calls and the driver itself selects the matching method. Four different APIs are available to the developer within a reduction method.

- *Source tree traversal.* This API is used to explicitly traverse the neighboring nodes to make reduction decisions not automatically captured by source-graph polymorphism. The API is automatically generated from the DS-DML metamodel.
- *DS-DDL schema traversal.* This API is used to explicitly query the DS-DDL schema to make reduction decisions not automatically captured by DS-DDL schema polymorphism. The API is automatically generated from the DS-DDL metamodel.
- *SQL-DML API.* This API is used to manipulate the SQL-DML source graphs.
- *Reduction API.* This API is used for explicit invocation of reduction methods on subordinated nodes in the DS-DML source graph.

7 Conclusion and Future Work

In this paper, we examined the topic of custom schema development and data manipulation languages which facilitate increased reuse within database-oriented software product lines. Our empirical evaluation, based on an example product line for versioning systems, shows that the portion of time required for mapping domain-specific statements to SQL at run time is below 9.9%. For this reason, we claim that domain-specific languages introduce great benefits in terms of raising the abstraction level in schema development and data queries at practically no cost.

There is a range of topics we want to focus on in our future work. Is there a way to make DS-DMLs even faster? Complex reduction methods can clearly benefit from the following ideas.

- Source graphs typically consist of an unusually large number of objects that have to be created at run time. Thus the approach could benefit from *instance pools* for objects to minimize object creation overhead.
- Caching of SQL-DML source graphs can be applied to reuse them when reducing upcoming statements.
- Would it be possible to use parameterized stored procedures to answer DS-DML statements? This makes the reduction of DS-DML statements simpler, because a statement can be reduced to a single stored procedure call. On the other hand, it makes the reduction of DS-DDL schema more complex, because stored procedures capable of answering the queries have to be prepared. We assume this approach is especially useful when many SQL-DML statements are needed to execute a DS-

DML statement. Implementing a stored procedure for a sequence of statements avoids excessive communication between (a) the domain-specific and the native driver and (b) between the native driver and the database.

- In a number of cases where a sequence of SQL-DML statements is produced as a result of reduction, these statements need not necessarily be executed sequentially. Thus developers of reduction methods should be given the possibility to explicitly mark situations where the driver could take advantage of parallel execution.

In addition, dealing with DS-DDL schemas raises two important questions.

- *DS-DDL schema evolution.* Clearly, supplementary approaches are required to deal with modifications in a DS-DDL schema which imply a number of changes in existing SQL-DDL constructs.
- *Product-line mining.* Many companies develop and market a number of systems implemented independently despite their structural and functional similarities, i.e., without the proper product-line support. Existing schemas for these systems could be mined to extract common domain-specific abstractions and possible reductions, which can afterwards be used in future development of new systems.

References

1. Apache Jakarta Project: Struts, available as: http://jakarta.apache.org/struts/
2. Ben-Natan, R., Sasson, O.: IBM San Francisco Developer's Guider, McGraw-Hill, 1999
3. Bernstein, P.A.: Repositories and Object-Oriented Databases, in: SIGMOD Record 27:1 (1998), 34-46
4. Clements, P., Northrop, L.: Software Product Lines, Addison-Wesley, 2001
5. Czarnecki, K., Eisenecker, U.W.: Generative Programming: Methods, Tools, and Applications, Addison-Wesley, 2000
6. Frankel, D.S.: Model Driven Architecture: Applying MDA to Enterprise Computing, Wiley Publishing, 2003.
7. Halstead, M.H.: Elements of Software Science, Elsevier, 1977
8. Kießling, W., Köstler, G.: Preference SQL – Design, Implementation, Experiences, in: Proc. VLDB 2002, Hong Kong, Aug. 2002, 990-1001
9. Mahnke, W.: Towards a Modular, Object-Relational Schema Design, in: Proc. CAiSE 2002 Doctoral Consortium, Toronto, May 2002, 61-71
10. McCabe, T.J.: A Complexity Measure, in: IEEE Transactions on Software Engineering 2:4 (1976), 308-320
11. MetaCase: MetaEdit+ Product Website, available as: http://www.metacase.com/mep/
12. OMG: Common Warehouse Metamodel (CWM) Specification, Vol. 1, Oct. 2001
13. OMG: Model Driven Architecture (MDA) – A Technical Perspective, July 2001
14. Saeki, M.: Toward Automated Method Engineering: Supporting Method Assembly in CAME, presentation at EMSISE'03 workshop, Geneva, Sept. 2003
15. Simonyi, C.: The Death of Computer Languages, the Birth of Intentional Programming, Tech. Report MSR-TR-95-52, Microsoft Research, Sept. 1995
16. Thalheim, B.: Component Construction of Database Schemes, in: Proc. ER 2002, Tampere, Oct. 2002, 20-34
17. Weber, C., Kovse, J.: A Domain-Specific Language for Versioning, Jan. 2004, available as: http://wwwdvs.informatik.uni-kl.de/agdbis/staff/Kovse/DSVers/DSVers.pdf

Incremental Navigation: Providing Simple and Generic Access to Heterogeneous Structures*

Shawn Bowers[1] and Lois Delcambre[2]

[1] San Diego Supercomputer Center at UCSD, La Jolla CA 92093, USA
bowers@sdsc.edu

[2] OGI School of Science and Engineering at OHSU, Beaverton OR 97006, USA
lmd@cse.ogi.edu

Abstract. We present an approach to support *incremental navigation* of structured information, where the structure is introduced by the data model and schema (if present) of a data source. Simple browsing through data values and their connections is an effective way for a user or an automated system to access and explore information. We use our previously defined Uni-Level Description (ULD) to represent an information source explicitly by capturing the source's data model, schema (if present), and data values. We define generic operators for incremental navigation that use the ULD directly along with techniques for specifying how a given representation scheme can be navigated. Because our navigation is based on the ULD, the operations can easily move from data to schema to data model and back, supporting a wide range of applications for exploring and integrating data. Further, because the ULD can express a broad range of data models, our navigation operators are applicable, without modification, across the corresponding model or schema. In general, we believe that information sources may usefully support various styles of navigation, depending on the type of user and the user's desired task.

1 Introduction

With the WWW at our fingertips, we have grown accustomed to easily using unstructured and loosely-structured information of various kinds, from all over the world. With a web browser it is very easy to: (1) view information (typically presented in HTML), and (2) download information for viewing or manipulating in tools available on our desktops (e.g., Word, PowerPoint, or Adobe Acrobat files). In our work, we are focused on providing similar access to structured (and semi-structured) information, in which data conforms to the structures of a representation scheme or data model.

There is a large and growing number of structural representation schemes being used today including the relational, E-R, object-oriented, XML, RDF, and Topic Map models along with special-purpose representations, e.g., for exchanging scientific data. Each representation scheme is typically characterized by its choice of constructs for representing data and schema, allowing data engineers to select the representation best suited for their needs. However, there are few tools that allow data stored in different representations to be viewed and accessed in a standard way, with a consistent interface.

* This work supported in part by NSF grants EIA 9983518 and ITR 0225674.

P. Atzeni et al. (Eds.): ER 2004, LNCS 3288, pp. 668–681, 2004.

The goal of this work is to provide generic access to structured information, much like a web browser provides generic access to viewable information. We are particularly interested in browsing a data source where a user can select an individual item, select a path that leads from the item, follow the path to a new item, and so on, *incrementally* through the source.

The need for incremental navigation is motivated by the following uses. First, we believe that simple browsing tools provide people with a powerful and easy way to access data in a structured information source. Second, generic access to heterogeneous information sources supports tools that can be broadly used in the process of data integration [8, 10]. Once an information source has been identified, its contents can be examined (by a person or an agent) to determine if and how it should be combined (or integrated) with other sources.

In this paper, we describe a generic set of incremental-navigation operators that are implemented against our Uni-Level Description (ULD) framework [4, 6]. We consider both a low-level approach for creating detailed and complete specifications as well as a simple, high-level approach for defining specifications. The high-level approach exploits the rich structural descriptions offered by the ULD to automatically generate the corresponding detailed specifications for navigating information sources. Thus, our high-level specification language allows a user to easily define and experiment with various navigation styles for a given data model or representation scheme. The rest of this paper is organized as follows. In Section 2 we describe motivating examples and Section 3 briefly presents the Uni-Level Description. In Section 4, we define the incremental navigation operators and discuss approaches to specifying their implementation. Related work is presented in Section 5 and in Section 6 we discuss future work.

2 Motivating Examples

When an information agent discovers a new source (e.g., see Figure 1) it may wish to know: (1) what data model is used (is it an RDF, XML, Topic Map, or relational source?), (2) (assuming RDF) whether any classes are defined for the source (what is the source schema?), (3) which properties are defined for a given class (what properties does the *film* class have?), (4) which objects exist for the class (what are the instances of the *film* class?) and (5) what kinds of values exist for a given property of a particular object of the class (what *actor* objects are involved in this *film* object?).

This example assumes the agent (or user) understands the data model of the source. For example, if the data model used was XML (e.g., see Figure 2) instead of RDF, the agent could have started navigation by asking for all of the available element types (rather than RDF classes). We call this approach *data-model-aware navigation*, in which the constructs of the data model can be used to guide navigation.

In contrast, we also propose a form of browsing where the user or agent need not have any awareness of the data-model structures used in a data source. The user or agent is able to navigate through the data and schema directly. As an example (again using Figure 1), the user or agent might ask for: (1) the kind of information the source contains, which in our example would include "films," "actors," and "awards," etc., (2) (assuming the crawler is interested in films) the things that describe films, which

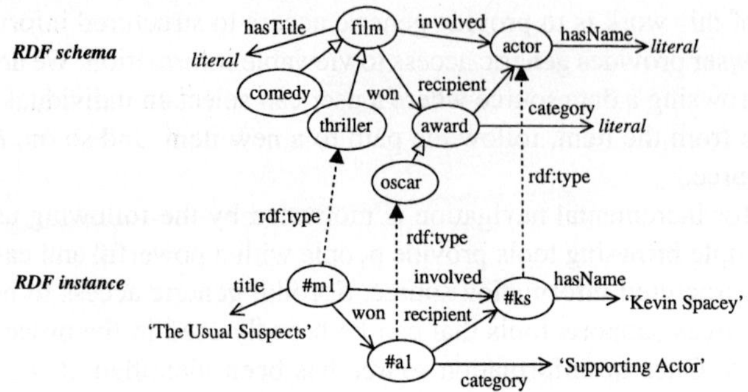

Fig. 1. An example of an RDF schema and instance.

XML DTD:

```
<!ELEMENT moviedb (movie*)>
<!ELEMENT movie (title,studio,genre*,actor*)>
<!ELEMENT title (#PCDATA)>
<!ELEMENT studio (#PCDATA)>
<!ELEMENT genre (#PCDATA)>
<!ELEMENT actor (#PCDATA)>
<!ATTLIST actor role CDATA #REQUIRED>
```

XML Instance:

```
<?xml version=''1.0''?>
<moviedb>
 <movie>
  <title>The Usual Suspects</title>
  <studio>Gramercy</studio>
  <genre>Thriller</genre>
  <actor role=''supporting actor''>
    Spacey, Kevin
  </actor>
 </movie>
 ...
</moviedb>
```

Fig. 2. An example XML DTD (left) and instance document (right).

would include "titles" and relationships to awards and actors, (3) the available films in the source, and (4) the actors of a particular film, which is obtained by stepping across the "involved" link for the film in question. We call this form of browsing *simple navigation*.

3 The Uni-level Description

The Uni-Level Description (ULD) is both a *meta-data-model* (i.e., capable of describing data models) and a distinct representation scheme: it can directly represent both schema and instance information expressed in terms of data-model constructs. Figure 3 shows how the ULD represents information, where a portion of an object-oriented data model is described. The ULD is a flat representation in that all information stored in the ULD is uniformly accessible (e.g., within a single query) using the logic-based operations described in Table 1.

Information stored in the ULD is logically divided into three layers, denoted *meta-data-model*, *data model*, and *schema and data instances*. The ULD meta-data-model, shown as the top level in Figure 3, consists of *construct types* that denote structural primitives. The middle level uses the structural primitives to define both data and schema *constructs*, possibly with *conformance relationships* between them. Constructs are necessarily instances of construct types, represented with ct-inst instance-of links.

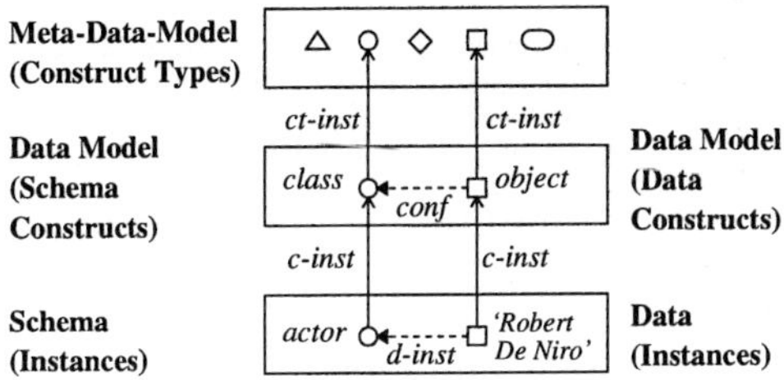

Fig. 3. The ULD meta-data-model architecture.

Table 1. The ULD operations expressed as logical formulas.

Operations for defining instance-of relationships	
ct-inst(c, ct)	Construct c is a *ct-inst* of construct-type ct.
c-inst(d, c)	Construct instance d is a *c-inst* of construct c.
d-inst(d_1, d_2)	Construct instance d_1 is a *d-inst* of instance d_2.
conf(d, r, c_1, c_2)	Instances of construct c_1 can conform to instances of construct c_2 as required by domain d and range r cardinality constraints (exactly one 1, zero or one ?, zero or many *, or one or many +).
Operations for restricting construct instances	
$c_1.s\text{->}c_2$	Instances of construct c_1 have selectors s with instances of construct c_2 as values.
setof(c_1, c_2)	Instances of construct c_1 are sets whose members are construct c_2 instances.
bagof(c_1, c_2)	Instances of construct c_1 are bags whose members are construct c_2 instances.
listof(c_1, c_2)	Instances of construct c_1 are lists whose members are construct c_2 instances.
unionof(c_1, c_2)	Instances of construct c_2 are also construct c_1 instances.
Operations for accessing instance structures	
$d_1.s{:}d_2$	Construct instance d_1 has value d_1 for selector s.
$d_1 \in d_2$	Construct instance d_1 is a member of collection d_2.
$d_1[i]{=}d_2$	Construct instance d_2 is at the i-th position in the list d_1.
$\|d_1\|{=}n$	The length of the collection construct instance d_1 is n.
$d_1 {\in\in} d_2{=}n$	Construct instance d_1 is a member of the bag d_2 n times.

Similarly, every item introduced in the bottom layer, denoting actual data or schema items, is necessarily an instance of a construct in the middle layer, represented with c-inst instance-of links. An item in the bottom layer can be an instance of another item in the bottom layer, represented with *d-inst* instance-of links, as allowed by the conformance relationships specified in the middle layer. For example, in Figure 3, the *class* and *object* constructs are related through a conformance link, labeled *conf*, and their corresponding construct instances in the bottom layer, i.e., *actor* and the object with the name 'Robert De Niro' are related through a data instance-of link, labeled *d-inst*.

The ULD offers flexibility through the conf and d-inst relationships. For example, an XML element that does not have an associated element type can be represented in the ULD; the element would simply not have a d-inst link to any XML element type.

The ULD represents an information source as a *configuration* containing the constructs of a data model, the construct instances (both schema and data) of a source, and the associated conformance and instance-of relationships. A configuration can be viewed as an instantiation of Figure 3. Each configuration uses a finite set of identifiers to denote construct types, constructs, and construct instances as well as a finite set of ct-inst, c-inst, conf, and d-inst facts. We note that a configuration can be implemented as a logical view over an information source, and is not necessarily "materialized."

The ULD meta-data-model contains primitive structures for tuples, i.e., sets of name-value pairs; set, list, and bag collections; atomics, for scalar values such as strings and integers; and unions, for representing non-structural, generalization relationships

schema constructs:

ct-inst(elemType, struct-ct)	ct-inst(pcdata, atomic-ct)	elemType.hasModel->contentDef
ct-inst(attDefSet, set-ct)	ct-inst(cdata, atomic-ct)	setof(attDefSet, attDef)
ct-inst(attDef, struct-ct)	elemType.hasName->uldString	attDef.hasName->uldString
ct-inst(contentDef, set-ct)	elemType.hasAtts->attDefSet	setof(contentDef, elemType)

data constructs:

ct-inst(element, struct-ct)	conf(*, ?, element, elemType)	element.hasChildren->content
ct-inst(attSet, set-ct)	conf(*, ?, attribute, attDef)	setof(attSet, attribute)
ct-inst(attribute, struct-ct)	unionof(node, element)	attribute.hasName->uldString
ct-inst(content, list-ct)	element.hasTag->uldString	attribute.hasVal->cdata
ct-inst(node, union-ct)	element.hasAtts->attSet	listof(content, node)
unionof(node, pcdata)		

Fig. 4. The XML with DTD data model.

among constructs. The construct-type identifiers for these structures are denoted *struct-ct*, *set-ct*, *list-ct*, *bag-ct*, *atomic-ct*, and *union-ct*, respectively.

Figures 4, 5, and 6 give example descriptions of simplified versions of XML with DTDs, RDF with RDF Schema, and sample schema and data (from Figure 1) for the RDF model, respectively[1]. We note that there are potentially many ways to describe a data model in the ULD, and these examples show only one choice of representation.

The XML data model shown in Figure 4 includes constructs for element types, attribute types, elements, attributes, content models, and content, where element types contain attribute types and content specifications, elements can optionally conform to element types, and attributes can optionally conform to attribute types. We simplify content models to sets of element types for which a conforming element must have at least one subelement for each corresponding type.

The RDF data model with RDF Schema (RDFS) of Figure 5 includes constructs for classes, properties, resources, and triples. A triple in RDF contains a subject, predicate, and object, where a predicate can be an arbitrary resource, including a defined property. In RDFS, `rdf:type`, `rdfs:subClassOf`, and `rdfs:subPropertyOf` are considered special RDF properties for denoting instance and specialization relationships. However, we model these properties using conformance and explicit constructs. For example, a subclass relationship is represented by instantiating a `subClassOf` construct as opposed to using the special `rdfs:subClassOf` RDF property[2].

A ULD query is expressed as a Datalog program [1] and is executed against a configuration. As an example, the first query below finds all available class names within an RDF configuration. Note that upper-case terms denote variables and lower-case terms denote constants. The rule is read as "If C is an RDF class and the label of C is X, then X is a classname." The second query returns the property names of all classes in an RDF configuration. This query, like the first, is expressed solely against the schema of the source. The third query below is expressed directly against data, and returns the URI of all RDF resources used as a property in at least one triple, where the resource may or may not be associated with schema.

1 We use `uldValue` and `uldValuetype` as special constructs to denote scalar values and value types [4,6]. Also, `uldString` and `uldURI` are default atomic constructs provided by the ULD.

2 This ULD representation of RDF allows properties and isa relationships to be decoupled (compared with RDF itself). This approach does not limit the expressibility of RDF: partial, optional, and multiple levels of schema are still possible.

schema constructs:

ct-inst(resource, union-ct)	conf(*, *, class, class)	simpleRes.hasURI->uldURI
ct-inst(rdfType, union-ct)	conf(*, *, prop, rdfType)	class.hasURI->uldURI
ct-inst(simpleRes, struct-ct)	unionof(rangeVal, class)	class.hasLabel->uldString
ct-inst(class, struct-ct)	unionof(rangeVal, uldValueType)	prop.hasURI->uldURI
ct-inst(prop, struct-ct)	subClass.hasSub->class	prop.hasLabel->uldString
ct-inst(rangeVal, union-ct)	unionof(resource, rdfType)	prop.hasDomain->class
ct-inst(subClass, struct-ct)	unionof(resource, simpleRes)	prop.hasRange->rangeVal
ct-inst(subProp, struct-ct)	unionof(rdfType, class)	subClass.hasSuper->class
conf(*, *, simpleRes, class)	unionof(rdfType, prop)	subProp.hasSub->prop
subProp.hasSuper->prop		

data constructs:

ct-inst(triple, struct-ct)	unionof(objVal, resource)	triple.hasObj->objVal
ct-inst(objVal, union-ct)	triple.hasPred->resource	unionof(objVal, literal)
ct-inst(literal, atomic-ct)	triple.hasSubj->resource	

Fig. 5. The RDF with RDF Schema data model.

schema:

c-inst(film, class)	thriller.hasURI:'#thriller'	prop.hasLabel:'#hasTitle'
c-inst(title, prop)	filmthril.hasSub:thriller	prop.hasRange:'literal'
c-inst(thriller, class)	film.hasURI:'#film'	thriller.hasLabel:'thriller'
c-inst(filmthril, subclass)	film.hasLabel:'film'	filmthril.hasSuper:film
prop.hasDomain:film	prop.hasURI:'#title'	

data:

c-inst(m1, simpleRes)	d-inst(m1, film)	t1.hasSubj:m1
c-inst(t1, triple)	m1.hasURI:'#m1'	t1.hasObj:'The Usual Suspects'
d-inst(m1, thriller)	t1.hasPred:title	

Fig. 6. Portion of schema and data for RDF(S).

classname(X) ← c-inst(C, class), C.hasLabel:X.
hasProp(X, Y) ← c-inst(C, class), c-inst(P, prop), P.hasDomain:C, C.hasLabel:X, P.hasLabel:Y.
dataprop(X) ← c-inst(T, triple), T.hasPred:P, P.hasURI:X.

The following three queries are similar to the previous three, but are expressed against an XML configuration. The first query finds the names of all available element types in the source, the second finds, for each element-type name, its corresponding attribute-definition names, and the last finds all available attribute names as a data query.

elemtype(X) ← c-inst(E, elemType), E.hasName:X.
atttype(X,Y) ← c-inst(E, elemType), E.hasName:X, E.hasAtts:AL, AT∈AL, AT.hasName:Y.
atts(X) ← c-inst(A, attribute), A.hasName:X.

Finally, the following query returns all constructs that serve as *struct-ct* schema constructs and their component selectors. This query is solely expressed against the data-model constructs.

schemastruct(SC, P) ← ct-inst(SC, struct-ct), conf(DC, SC, X, Y), SC.P->C.

4 Navigation Operators

The ULD presents a complete, highly detailed description of a data source, with interconnected model, schema, and data information. In the ULD, each construct type, construct, and instance is represented by an id and every id, in turn, has an associated value. The value can be either an atomic value (such as a literal in RDF) or a structured value (such as a set or bag of ids).

We view navigation as a process of traversing a graph consisting of *locations* (nodes) and *links* (bi-directional edges), superimposed over a ULD source file. A location is either a construct type, construct, or instance in the ULD; thus a location is anything with an id. A link is a (simple or compound) path, from one location to another, through the connections in the ULD.

A navigation binding consists of an implementation for the following functions. For a binding, we assume a finite set of location names $\mathcal{L}$ and a finite set of link names $\mathcal{N}$, where both $\mathcal{L}$ and $\mathcal{N}$ consist of atomic string values. Navigation consists of moving from one location name to another. The binding should include only those locations that are meaningful to the intended user community, with appropriate links.

Starting Points. The operator $sloc : \mathcal{P}(\mathcal{L})$ returns all available entry points into an information source. We require the result of *sloc* to be a set of locations (as opposed to links). Note that $\mathcal{P}(\mathcal{L})$ stands for the power set of $\mathcal{L}$.

Links. The operator $links : \mathcal{L} \rightarrow \mathcal{P}(\mathcal{N})$ returns all out-bound links available from a particular location. For some locations, there may not be any links available, i.e., the *links* operator may return the empty set.

Following Links. The operator $follow : \mathcal{L} \times \mathcal{N} \rightarrow \mathcal{P}(\mathcal{L})$ returns the set of locations that are at the end of a given link. We use the *follow* operator to prepare to move to a new location from our current location. Given the set of locations returned by the *follow* operator, the user or agent directing the navigation can choose one as the new location.

Types. The operator $types : \mathcal{L} \rightarrow \mathcal{P}(\mathcal{L})$ returns the (possibly empty) set of types for a given location. We use the *types* operator to obtain locations that represent the schema for a data item. A particular location may have zero, one, or many associated types.

Extents. The operator $extent : \mathcal{L} \rightarrow \mathcal{P}(\mathcal{L})$ returns the (possibly empty) set of instances for a given location. The *extent* operator computes the inverse of the *types* operator.

As a simple example, the following (partial) navigation binding can be defined for the data shown in Figure 6

sloc = {'class', 'property', 'subClass', 'resource', 'triple', ...}
extent('class') = {'film', 'comedy', 'thriller', ...}
links('thriller') = {'title'}
extent('thriller') = {'#m1', ...}
follow('#m1', 'title') = {'The Usual Suspects'}

We express the navigation functions in Datalog using the predicates described below. An operator binding is a set of ULD queries, where the head of each query is a navigation operation (expressed as a predicate). Thus, operator bindings are defined as global-as-view mappings from the ULD (typically, over any configuration of a data model) to the navigation operations. We propose two ways to specify a navigation binding: as a set of low-level ULD queries and as a high-level specification that is used to automatically generate the appropriate navigation bindings.

- *sloc*(r), where r represents a starting location.
- *links*(l, k), where k is a link from location l.

- *follow*(l, k, r), where r is a location that is found by following link k from some location l.
- *types*(l, r), where l is a location of type r.
- *extent*(l, r), where r is in the extent of l.

To illustrate, the following low-level binding queries present a view of an RDF configuration, where we only allow navigation from data items with corresponding schema. Thus, this example supports simple browsing. The starting locations are classes and the available links from a class are its associated properties and its associated instances. The definition uses an additional intensional predicate *subClassClosure* for computing the transitive closure of the RDF subclass relationship.

```
sloc(L)          ← c-inst(C, class), C.hasLabel:L.
links(L, K)      ← c-inst(C, class), C.hasLabel:L, c-inst(P, property),
                   P.hasLabel:K, P.hasDomain:C′, subClassClosure(C, C′).
links(L, K)      ← c-inst(C, class), d-inst(O, C), O.hasURI:L, c-inst(T, triple), T.hasPred:X,
                   T.hasSubj:O, c-inst(X, property), X.hasLabel:K, X.hasDomain:C′,
                   subClassClosure(C, C′).
follow(L, K, R) ← c-inst(C, class), C.hasLabel:L, c-inst(T, property), T.hasLabel:K,
                   T.hasDomain:C′, T.hasRange:C″, C″.hasLabel:R, subClassClosure(C, C′).
follow(L, K, R) ← c-inst(C, class), C.hasLabel:L, c-inst(T, property), T.hasLabel:K,
                   T.hasDomain:C′, T.hasRange:R, R='literal', subClassClosure(C, C′).
follow(L, K, R) ← c-inst(C, class), d-inst(O, C), O.hasURI:L, c-inst(T, triple), T.hasPred:X,
                   T.hasSubj:O, T.hasObj:R, c-inst(R, literal), c-inst(X, property), X.hasLabel:K,
                   X.hasDomain:C′, subClassClosure(C, C′).
follow(L, K, R) ← c-inst(C1, class), d-inst(O1, C1), O1.hasURI:L, c-inst(T, triple), T.hasPred:X,
                   T.hasSubj:O1, T.hasObj:O2, O2.hasURI:R, c-inst(X, property), X.hasLabel:K,
                   X.hasDomain:C′, subClassClosure(C, C′).
extent(L, R)     ← c-inst(C, class), C.hasLabel:L, d-inst(O, C), O.hasURI:R.
type(L, R)       ← c-inst(C, class), C.hasLabel=R, d-inst(O, C), O.hasURI:L.

subClassClosure(C, C)   ← c-inst(C, class).
subClassClosure(C1, C3) ← c-inst(S, subClass), S.hasSub:C1, S.hasSuper:C2,
                          subClassClosure(C2, C3).
```

In general, with low-level binding queries a user can specify detailed and exact descriptions of the navigation operations for data sources. To specify higher-level bindings, a user selects certain constructs as locations and certain other constructs as links. Using this specification, the navigation operators are automatically computed by traversing the appropriate instances of locations and links in the configuration. Figure 7 shows an example of a high-level binding definition for RDF, where RDF classes, resources, and literals are considered sources for locations and RDF properties and triples are considered sources for links (Figure 10 shows a similar binding for XML, which we discuss later).

We define a high-level binding specification as a tuple (L, N, S, F). The disjoint sets L and N consist of construct identifiers such that L is the set of constructs used as locations and N is the set of constructs used as links. The set $S \subseteq L$ gives the entry points of the binding. Finally, the set F contains *link definitions* (described below).

Each construct in L and N has an associated naming definition that describes how to compute the name of an instance of the construct. The name would typically be viewed by the user during navigation. The naming definitions serve to map location and

RDF Binding:
$B = (L, N, S, F)$
$L =$ class, resource, literal
$N =$ property, triple
$S =$ class
$F =$ triple : resource [triple/hasSubj] $\Rightarrow$ literal [triple/hasObj],
triple : resource [triple/hasSubj] $\Rightarrow$ resource [triple/hasObj],
property : class [property/hasDomain] $\Rightarrow$ class [property/hasRange],
property : class [property/hasDomain] $\Rightarrow$ literal [property/hasRange]

name(X, N) $\leftarrow$ c-inst(X, class), X.hasLabel:N.
name(X, N) $\leftarrow$ c-inst(X, resource), X.hasURI:N.
name(N, N) $\leftarrow$ c-inst(N, literal).
name(X, N) $\leftarrow$ c-inst(X, property), X.hasLabel:N.
name(X, N) $\leftarrow$ c-inst(X, triple), X.hasPred:R, c-inst(R, property), R.hasLabel:N.

Fig. 7. A high-level binding for simple navigation of RDF.

link instances to appropriate string values. For example, in Figure 7, RDF classes and properties are named by their labels, resources are named by their URI values, a literal value is used directly as its name, and the name of a triple is the name of its associated predicate value.

The incremental operators in a high-level binding specification are computed automatically by traversing connected instances. We define the following generic rules to compute when two instances are connected. (Note that these connected rules only perform single-step traversal, and can be extended to allow an arbitrary number of steps, which we discuss at the end of this section.)

connected(X_1, X_2) $\leftarrow$ c-inst(X_1, C), ct-inst(C, struct-ct), X_1.S:X_2.
connected(X_1, X_2) $\leftarrow$ c-inst(X_1, C), ct-inst(C, bag-ct), $X_2 \in X_1$.
connected(X_1, X_2) $\leftarrow$ c-inst(X_1, C), ct-inst(C, list-ct), $X_2 \in X_1$.
connected(X_1, X_2) $\leftarrow$ c-inst(X_1, C), ct-inst(C, set-ct), $X_2 \in X_1$.
connected(X_2, X_1) $\leftarrow$ connected(X_1, X_2).

A connected formula is true when there is a structural connection between two instances. Note that the rules above do not consider the case when two items are linked by a *d-inst* relationship. Instead, the *d-inst* relationship is directly used by the *types* and *extent* operators, whereas connections are used by the *links* and *follow* operators.

The link definitions of F have the form $c_k : c_1[p_1] \Rightarrow c_2[p_2]$ where:

- The behavior of the link construct $c_k \in N$ is being described by the rest of the expression. For example, in Figure 7, the first link definition is for triple constructs.
- For $c_1, c_2 \in L$, the construct c_k can serve to link an instance of c_1 to an instance of c_2. Thus, we can traverse from instances of c_1 to instances of c_2 via an instance of c_k. For example, in Figure 7, the first link definition says that we can follow a resource instance to a literal instance if they are connected by a triple.
- The expressions p_1 and p_2 further restrict how instances of c_k can be used to link c_1 and c_2 instances, respectively. For example, in Figure 7, the first link definition states that triples link resources and literals through the triple's hasSubj and hasObj selector, respectively.

We define the *linkSource*(f, i_1, i_k) and *linkTarget*(f, i_k, i_2) clauses as follows. Given a link definition $f \in F$ and a connection from i_1 to i_k such that connected(i_1, i_k) is true (where i_k is the link instance), *linkSource*(f, i_1, i_k) is true if $f = c_k : c_1[p_1] \Rightarrow c_2[p_2]$ such that i_1 is an instance of c_1 (that is, c-inst(i_1, c_1) is true), i_k is an instance of

sloc(R) ← B_S(S), c-inst(X, S), name(X, R).
links(L, K) ← name(X, L), connected(X, Y), B_F(F), linkSource(F, X, Y), name(Y, K).
follow(L, K, R) ← name(X, L), connected(X, Y), B_F(F), linkSource(F, X, Y), name(Y, K), connected(Y, Z), linkTarget(F, Y, Z), name(Z, R).
type(L, R) ← name(X, L), c-inst(X, P), B_L(P) d-inst(X, Y), c-inst(Y, Q), B_L(Q), name(Y, R).
extent(L, R) ← name(Y, L), c-inst(Y, Q), B_L(Q), d-inst(X, Y), c-inst(X, P), $B_L(P)$, name(X, R).

Fig. 8. Datalog rules to compute links and locations.

c_k (that is, c-inst(i_k, c_k) is true where c_k is a link construct), and i_1 and i_k are connected according to the expression p_1. Similarly, for an $f \in F$, *linkTarget(*f, i_k, i_2*)* is true if $f = c_k : c_1[p_1] \Rightarrow c_2[p_2]$ such that i_k is an instance of c_k (a link construct), i_2 is an instance of c_2, and i_k and i_2 are connected according to the expression p_2.

Given the above definitions, we automatically compute each navigation operator using the Datalog queries in Figure 8. We assume each operator is represented as an intensional predicate (as before) and the binding specification $B = (L, N, S, F)$ is stored as a set of unary extensional predicates B_L, B_N, B_S, and B_F. For example, the expression $B_L(X)$ binds X to a location in L for binding B. We also assume that the *name* predicate is stored as an intensional formula (as defined in the binding).

The first rule in Figure 8 finds the set of entry points: It obtains a construct in the set of starting locations, finds an instance of the construct, and then computes the name of the instance. The second rule finds the locations with links. For each named instance in the configuration that is connected to another instance, we use the *linkSource* predicate to check if it is a valid connection, we check to make sure that the link instance (represented as the variable Y) is valid, and then compute the name of the instance. The third rule is similar to the second, except it additionally uses the *linkTarget* to determine the new location. Finally, the last two rules use the *d-inst* relationship to find types and extents, respectively.

To demonstrate the approach, we use the binding definition of Figure 7 and the sample configuration of Figure 9. This configuration shows part of Figure 1 as a graph whose nodes are construct instances and edges are either connections between structures or $d\text{-}inst$ links. Consider the following series of invocations.

1. *sloc* = {'film','thriller'}. According to the binding definition, the *sloc* operator returns all the labels of *class* construct instances. As shown in Figure 9, the only *class* construct instances are *thriller* and *film*.
2. *links*('film') = {'title'}. The *links* operator is computed by considering each connected construct instance of *film* until it finds a construct instance whose associated construct is in N. As shown, the only such instance is *title*, which is an RDF property.
3. *extent*('film') = {'#m1'}. The *extent* operator looks for the *d-inst* links of the given instance. As shown, the only such link for *film* is to *m1*.
4. *follow*('#m1', 'title') = {'The Usual Suspects'}. The *follow* operator starts in the same way as the *links* operator by finding instances (whose constructs are in N) that are connected to the given instance. For the given item, the only such instance in Figure 9 is *t1*. The *follow* operator then returns the *hasObj* component of *t1*, according to the link definition for *triple*.

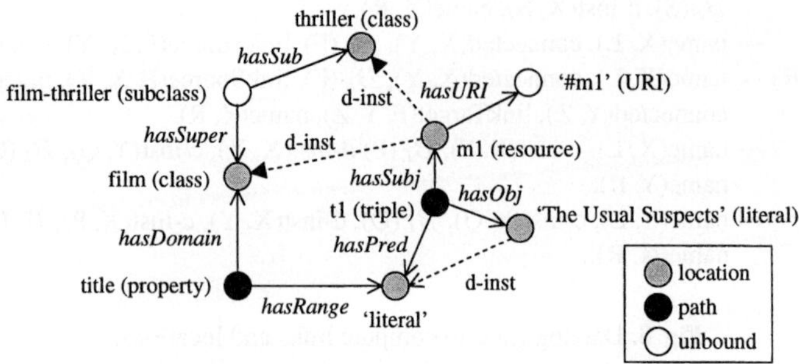

Fig. 9. An example of labeled instances for RDF.

Note that for this example, the rules for computing the *follow* and *links* operators only consider instances that are directly connected to each other (through the *connected* predicate). Thus, invoking the operator links('thriller') will not return a result (for our example) because there are no link construct instances directly connected to the associated RDF class. However, the properties of a class in RDF also include the properties of its superclasses. We can include such information by expanding the set of connection rules. One approach is to allow the navigation specifier to add a connected rule specifically for the subclass case. Alternatively, we can extend the connection definition to compute the transitive closure (of connections) using the following rule.

$\text{connected}(X_1, X_3) \leftarrow \text{connected}(X_1, X_2), \text{connected}(X_2, X_3).$

We also allow binding specifications to include multiple-step path expressions in F. For example, we add the following link definitions to the RDF binding specification to correctly support subclasses.

property : class [property/hasDomain/hasSuper/hasSub] ⇒ class [property/hasRange]
property : class [property/hasDomain/hasSuper/hasSub] ⇒ literal [property/hasRange]

Finally, Figure 10 shows a high-level binding specification for the XML data model of Figure 4. The binding specification assumes the transitive connection relation defined above. Element types, elements, and atomic data serve as locations, with element types as starting locations. Attribute definitions, attributes, content definitions, and content serve as links. We use 'hasChildType' and 'hasChild' strings as the names of the links for content definitions and element content, respectively. Note the attDef link definition is a special case in which attDef links always lead to an empty set of locations (denoted using the empty set in Figure 10). Also, the ending '/' in a link-definition path denotes traversal into the elements of a collection structure (as opposed to denoting the collection structure itself).

5 Related Work

A number of approaches provide browsing capability for traditional databases. Motro [14] seeks to enable users who are (1) not familiar with the data model of the system, (2)

XML Binding:
$B = (L, N, S, F)$
$L =$ elemType, element, cdata, pcdata
$N =$ attDef, attribute, contentDef, content
$S =$ elemType
$F =$ attDef : elemType [elemType/hasAtts/] $\Rightarrow \{\}$,
attribute : element [element/hasAtts/] $\Rightarrow$ cdata [attribute/hasVal],
contentDef : elemType [elemType/hasModel] $\Rightarrow$ elemType [contentDef/],
content : element [element/hasChildren] $\Rightarrow$ element [content/],
content : element [element/hasChildren] $\Rightarrow$ pcdata [content/]

name(X, N) $\leftarrow$ c-inst(X, elemType), X.hasName:N.
name(X, N) $\leftarrow$ c-inst(X, element).
name(X, X) $\leftarrow$ c-inst(X, cdata).
name(X, X) $\leftarrow$ c-inst(X, pcdata).
name(X, N) $\leftarrow$ c-inst(X, attDef), X.hasName:N.
name(X, N) $\leftarrow$ c-inst(X, attribute), X.hasName:N.
name(X, N) $\leftarrow$ c-inst(X, contentDef), N='hasChildType'.
name(X, N) $\leftarrow$ c-inst(X, content), N='hasChild'.

Fig. 10. A high-level binding for direct navigation of XML.

not familiar with the organization of the database (i.e., the schema), (3) not proficient with the use of the system (i.e., the query language), (4) not sure what data they are looking for (but are looking for something interesting or suitable), and/or (5) not clear how to construct the desired query. As more structured information finds its way on the Web, we believe these issues become more pressing for users as well as for software agents wishing to exploit structured information.

Database browsing typically assumes a fixed data model [2, 14, 12, 17, 3, 8, 18] (either relational, E-R, or object-oriented). Only a few systems allow browsing schema and data in isolation [3, 12, 14], where most support browsing data only through schema (i.e., navigating data using items of the schema). Hypertext systems, including those with structured data models, also use browser-based interfaces [15, 13]. These systems, as in database approaches, are developed for a single data model, and support limited browsing styles.

The links and locations abstraction used by incremental navigation is similar in spirit to the graph-based model of RDF and RDF Schema. The Object Exchange Model (OEM) – the semi-structured representation of TSIMMIS [11, 16] – is another simple abstraction. Both TSIMMIS and some database browsing systems [2, 9, 14, 8] support user navigation mixed with user queries, which we would like to explore as an extension to our current navigation operators. Finally, Clio [18] provides some support for navigation, specifically to help users build data-transformation queries. Clio supports "data walks," which display example data involved in each potential join path between two relations, and "data chases," which display all occurrences of a specific value within a database.

6 Conclusion and Future Work

We believe incremental navigation provides a simple, generic abstraction, consisting of *links* and *locations* (and *types* and *extents* when applicable), that can be applied over arbitrary data models. More than that, with the high-level binding approach, it becomes relatively straightforward to specify the links and locations for a data model, thus enabling generic and uniform access to information represented in any underlying data model (described in the ULD). We believe that this approach can be extended beyond navigation to include querying information sources (i.e., querying links and locations) and for specifying high-level mappings between data sources.

We have implemented a prototype browser [5] to demonstrate incremental navigation, both for data-model aware and simple navigation of RDF, XML, Topic Map, and relational sources. In addition, some of the ideas of incremental navigation appear in the Superimposed Schematics browser [7], which allows users to incrementally navigate an ER schema and data source. Based on these experiments, we believe incremental navigation is viable, and helps reduce the work required to develop such browsing tools.

For future work, we intend to investigate whether additional ULD information can be used, such as data-model constraints, to help validate and generate operator bindings. We are also interested in defining a language to express path-based queries over the links and locations abstraction offered by incremental navigation. One issue is to determine whether algorithms and optimizations can be defined to efficiently compute (i.e., unfold) the binding-specification rules to answer such path queries. Finally, we believe that the incremental-navigation operators can be easily expressed as a standard web-service interface (where information sources have corresponding web-service implementations), providing generic, web-based access to heterogeneous information.

References

1. S. Abiteboul, R. Hull, and V. Vianu. *Foundations of Databases*. Addison-Wesley Publishing Company, 1995.
2. B. Aditya, G. Bhalotia, S. Chakrabarti, A. Hulgeri, C. Nakhe, and P. Sudarshan. BANKS: Browsing and keyword searching in relational databases. In *Proceedings of the Twenty-Eighth Very Large Data Bases (VLDB) Conference*, 2002.
3. R. Agrawal, N. Gehani, and J. Srinivasan. OdeView: The graphical interface to Ode. In *Proceedings of the 1990 ACM SIGMOD International Conference on Management of Data*, pages 34–43, 1990.
4. S. Bowers. *The Uni-Level Description: A Uniform Framework for Managing Structural Heterogeneity*. PhD thesis, OGI School of Science and Engineering, OHSU, December 2003.
5. S. Bowers and L. Delcambre. JustBrowsing: A generic API for exploring information. In *Demo Session at the 21st International Conference on Conceptual Modeling (ER)*, 2002.
6. S. Bowers and L. Delcambre. The uni-level description: A uniform framework for representing information in multiple data models. In *Proceedings of the 22nd International Conference on Conceptual Model (ER)*, volume 2813 of *Lecture Notes in Computer Science*, pages 45–58. Springer-Verlag, 2003.
7. S. Bowers, L. Delcambre, and D. Maier. Superimposed schematics: Introducing E-R structure for *in-situ* information selections. In *Proceedings of the 21st International Conference on Conceptual Model (ER)*, volume 2503 of *Lecture Notes in Computer Science*, pages 90–104. Springer-Verlag, 2002.
8. M. J. Carey, L. M. Haas, V. Maganty, and J. H. Williams. PESTO: An integrated query/browser for object databases. In *Proceedings of 22nd International Conference on Very Large Data Bases (VLDB)*, pages 203–214. Morgan Kaufmann, 1996.
9. T. Catarci, G. Santucci, and J. Cardiff. Graphical interaction with heterogeneous databases. *The VLDB Journal*, 6(2):97–120, 1997.

10. W. W. Cohen. Some practical observations on integration of web information. In *Informal Proceedings of the ACM SIGMOD Workshop on the Web and Databases (WebDB)*, pages 55–60, 1999.
11. J. Hammer, H. Garcia-Molina, K. Ireland, Y. Papakonstantinou, J. D. Ullman, and J. Widom. Information translation, mediation, and mosaic-based browsing in the TSIMMIS system. In *Proceedings of the 1995 ACM SIGMOD International Conference on Management of Data*, page 483. ACM Press, 1995.
12. M. Kuntz and R. Melchart. Ergonomic schema design and browsing with more semantics in the Pasta-3 interface for E-R DBMSs. In *Proceedings of the Eight International Conference on Enity-Relationship Approach*, pages 419–433, 1989.
13. C. C. Marshall, F. M. Shipman III, and J. H. Coombs. VIKI: Spatial hypertext supporting emergent structure. In *European Conference on Hypertext Technology (ECHT)*, pages 13–23. ACM Press, 1994.
14. A. Motro. BAROQUE: A browser for relational databases. *ACM Transactions on Office Information Systems*, 4(2):164–181, 1986.
15. J. Nanard and M. Nanard. Should anchors be typed too? An experiment with macweb. In *Proceedings of Hypertext*, pages 51–62, 1993.
16. Y. Papakonstantinou, H. Garcia-Molina, and J. Widom. Object exchange across heterogeneous information sources. In *Proceedings of the Eleventh International Conference on Data Engineering*, pages 251–260. IEEE Computer Society, 1995.
17. T. Rogers and R. Cattell. Entity-Relationship databases user interfaces. In *Sixth International Conference on Entity-Relationship Approach*, pages 353–365, 1997.
18. L. L. Yan, R. J. Miller, L. M. Haas, and R. Fagin. Data-driven understanding and refinement of schema mappings. In *Proceedings of the 2001 ACM SIGMOD International Conference on Management of Data*. ACM Press, 2001.

Agent Patterns for Ambient Intelligence

Paolo Bresciani, Loris Penserini, Paolo Busetta, and Tsvi Kuflik

ITC-irst
via Sommarive 18
I-38050 Trento-Povo, Italy
{bresciani,penserini,busetta,kuflik}@itc.it

Abstract. The realization of complex distributed applications, required in areas such as e-Business, e-Government, and ambient intelligence, calls for new development paradigms, such as the Service Oriented Computing approach which accommodates for dynamic and adaptive interaction schemata, carried on on a per-to-peer level. Multi Agent Systems offer the natural architectural solutions to several requirements imposed by such an adaptive approach.
This work discusses the limitation of common agent patterns, typically adopted in distributed information systems design, when applied to service oriented computing, and introduces two novel agent patterns, that we call *Service Oriented Organization* and *Implicit Organization Broker* agent pattern, respectivelly. Some design aspects of the Implicit Organization Broker agent pattern are also presented. The limitations and the proposed solutions are demonstrated in the development of a multi agent system which implements a pervasive museum visitors guide. Some of the architecture and design features serve as a reference scenario for the demonstration of both the current methods limitations and the contribution of the newly proposed agent patterns and associated communication framework.

1 Introduction

Complex distributed applications emerging in areas such as e-Business, e-Government, and the so called *ambient intelligence* (i.e., "intelligent" pervasive computing [7]), needs to adopt forms of group communication that are deeply different from classical client-server and Web-based models (see, for instance, [13]). This strongly motivates forms of application-level peer-to-peer interaction, clearly distinct from the request/response style commonly used to access distributed services such as, e.g., Web Services adopting SOAP, XML, and RPC as communication protocol [6, 12]. The so called service oriented computing (SOC) is the paradigm that accommodates for the above mentioned more dynamic and adaptive interaction schemata.

Service-oriented computing is applicable to ambient intelligence as a way to access environmental services, e.g., accessing sensors or actuators close to a user. Multi Agent Systems (MAS) naturally accommodate for the SOC paradigm. In fact, each service can be seen as an autonomous agent (or an aggregation of autonomous agents), possibly without global visibility and control over the global system, and characterized by unpredictable/intermitted connections with other agents of the system. However, we argue that some domain specificities – such as the necessity to continuously monitor the environment for understanding the context and adapting to the user needs, and the speed

P. Atzeni et al. (Eds.): ER 2004, LNCS 3288, pp. 682–695, 2004.

at which clients and service providers come and go within a physical environment populated with mobile devices – impose new challenging system architecture requirements that are not satisfied by traditional agent patterns proposed for request/response interactions. Moreover, in ambient intelligence applications, we often need to effectively deal with service composition based on dynamic agreements among autonomous peers, because group of peers collaborate at different levels and times during the *service providing process life-cycle*, analogously to the product life-cycle process introduced by Virtual Enterprise scenarios [14]. This group communication styles should be used as architectural alternatives or extensions to middle agents (e.g., *matchmakers* and *brokers*), simplifying the application logic and moving context-specific decision-making from high-level applications or intermediate agents down to the agents called to achieve a goal. For these reasons, in this paper, we propose novel agent patterns, which allow for dynamic, collective, and collaborative reconfiguration of service providing schemata.

To illustrate our approach, we use the notion of service oriented organization. We call *service oriented organization* (SOO) a set of autonomous software agents that, in a given location at a given time, coordinate in order to provide a service; in other words, a SOO is a team of agents whose goal is to deliver a service to its clients. Examples of SOO are not restricted to Web Services and ambient intelligence; for instance, they include *virtual enterprises* or *organizations* [14, 8], the name of which reflect the application area in which they have been adopted, i.e., e-Business. As well, this paper focuses on a special type of SOO that we call *implicit organization broker* (IOB), since it exploits a form of group communication called *channelled multicast* [3] to avoid explicit team formation and dynamically agree on the service composition. We will compare SOO and IOB to traditional agent patterns based on brokers or matchmakers. As a reference example to illustrate our ideas, we adopt an application scenario from Peach [15], an ongoing project for the development of an interactive museums guide. Using the Peach system, users can request information about exhibits; these may be provided by a variety of information sources and media types (museum server, online remote servers, video, etc.). As well, we adopt the Tropos software design methodology [5, 2] to illustrate and compare the different agent patterns.

Tropos adopts high-level requirements engineering concepts founded on notions such as actor, agent, role, position, goal, softgoal, task, resource, belief and different kinds of social dependency between actors [5, 2, 11]. Therefore, Tropos allows for a modeling level more abstract than other current methodologies as, e.g., UML and AUML [1]. Such properties well fit with our major interest, which is in modeling environmental constraints that affect and characterize agents' roles and their intentional and social relationships, rather than in implementation and/or technological issues.

Section 2 briefly recalls some background notions on Tropos, on service oriented computing, and on agent patterns. Section 3 describes and discusses an excerpt of the Peach project, adopted as a reference case to illustrate our arguments. Section 5.1 tries to overcome some limitations of traditional patterns by proposing two new agent patterns: the *Service Oriented Organization* and the *Implicit Organization Broker*. Section 5.2 aims at justifying group communication as fundamental to effectively deal with the proposed patterns, providing a rationale view and describing dynamic aspects. Some conclusions are given in Section 6.

2 Background

Tropos. The Tropos methodology [2,5] adopts ideas from Multi Agents Systems technologies and concepts from requirements engineering through the ***i**** framework. ***i**** is an organizational modeling framework for early requirements analysis [18], founded on notions such as *actor, agent, role, goal, softgoal, task, resource*, and different kinds of social dependency between actors. Actors represents any active entity, either individual or collective, and either human or artificial. Thus, an actor may represent a person or a social group (e.g., an enterprise or a department) or an artificial system, as, e.g., an interactive museum guide or each of its components (both hardware and software) at different levels of granularity. *Actors* may be further specialized as *roles* or *agents*. An *agent* represents a physical (human, hardware or software) instance of actor that performs the assigned activities. A *role*, instead, represents a specific function that, in different circumstances, may be executed by different agents – we say that the agent *plays* the role. Actors (agents and roles) are used in Tropos to describe different social dependency and interaction models. In particular, Actor Diagrams (see Figures 1, 3, and 4) describe the network of social dependencies among actors. An Actor Diagram is a graph, where each node may represent either an actor, a goal, a softgoal, a task or a resource. Links between nodes may be used to form paths like: *depender* → *dependum* → *dependee*, where the *depender* and the *dependee* are actors, and the *dependum* is either a goal, a softgoal, a task or a resource. Each path between two actors indicates that one actor depends on the other for something (represented by the dependum) so that the former may attain some goal/softgoal/task/resource. In other terms, a dependency describes a sort of "agreement" between two actors (the depender and the dependee), in order to attain the dependum. The depender is the depending actor, and the dependee the actor who is depended upon. The type of the dependum describes the nature of the dependency. Goal dependencies are used to represent delegation of responsibility for fulfilling a goal; softgoal dependencies are similar to goal dependencies, but their fulfillment cannot be defined precisely (for instance, the appreciation is subjective, or the fulfillment can occur only to a given extent); task dependencies are used in situations where the dependee is required to perform a given activity; and resource dependencies require the dependee to provide a resource to the depender. As exemplified in Figure 1, actors are represented as circles[1]; dependums – goals, softgoals, tasks and resources – are represented as ovals, clouds, hexagons and rectangles, respectively. Goals and softgoals introduced with Actor Diagrams can be further detailed and analyzed by means of the so called Goals Diagrams [2], in which the rationale of each (soft)goal is described in terms of goal decompositions, means-end-analysis and the like, as, e.g., in Figure 5.

Tropos spans four phases of Requirements Engineering and Software Engineering activities [5,2]: Early Requirements Analysis, Late Requirements Analysis, Architectural Design, and Detailed Design. Its key premise is that agents and goals can be used as fundamental concepts for all the phases of the software development life cycle. Actor and Goal Diagrams are adopted from Early Requirements Analysis to architectural design. Here, we use them to describe the agent patterns we are interested in.

[1] We do not adopt any graphical distinction between agents and roles: when needed, we clarify it in the text.

Service oriented computing. *Service Oriented Computing* (SOC) [12] provides a general, unifying paradigm for diverse computing environments such as grids, peer-to-peer networks, ubiquitous and pervasive computing. A *service* encapsulates a component made available on a network by a provider. The interaction between a client and a service normally follows a straightforward request/response style, possibly asynchronous; this is the case with Web Services, which adopt SOAP, XML, and RPC [6, 12] as communication protocol. Two or more services can be aggregated to offer a single, more complex, service or even a complete business process; the process of aggregation is called *service composition*.

As already noticed, MAS naturally accommodate for the SOC paradigm. Since each agent in a MAS may be either an arbiter or an intermediary for the user's requested service, two common agent patterns that appear to be appropriate are the *matchmaker* and the *broker* (see, e.g., [10, 16]).

Agent patterns for SOC. To accommodate the different settings and agents that can be involved, and with the different roles that – from time to time – can be played by each agent, a *pattern based* approach for the description and design of the MAS architectures for SOC systems can be adopted. An agent pattern can be used to describe a problem commonly found in MAS design and to prescribe a flexible solution for that problem, so to ease the reuse of that solution [11, 17, 9]. The literature on Tropos adopts ideas from social patterns [5, 11] to focus on social and intentional aspects that are recurrent in multi-agent or cooperative systems. Here, we adopt Actor and Goal Diagrams to characterize MAS design patterns, focusing on how the goals assigned to each agent[2] are fulfilled [2, 11], rather than on how agents communicate with each other. In the very spirit of Tropos, which naturally carries out the importance of analyzing each problem at a high abstraction level, allowing to reduce and easily manage at 'design time' the system components complexity, we aim at enhancing the reuse of design experience and knowledge by means of the adoption of agent patterns.

In our context, such patterns have to cope with the important issue of locating information/service providers, which is an architectural requirement. Indeed, as also investigated in [13], such a requirements strongly affect coordination issues in decentralized (pure) peer-to-peer scenarios. Thus, to support the peer-to-peer scenario, the matchmaker agent pattern (see Figure 1a) play a key/centric role in order to allow the whole system for the searching and matching capabilities, e.g., see [16].

At the same time, the focus on the *service providing process life-cycle* puts the consumer in the center, and when the consumer demands novel services the system architecture should provide them without overwhelming her with additional interactions. Moreover, in a decentralized scenario, it may have several local failures may happen, when trying to locate new services; hence, a huge number of interactions, before reaching the related provider, are possible. Of course, the reduction of the interaction complexity decreases the customer overload. Such a requirement calls for a broker pattern too, as detailed in Figure 1b (e.g., see [10]).

[2] Indeed, accordingly with the Tropos terminology, we should speak about roles, but we drop, here, this distinction, to ease the reading of the diagrams.

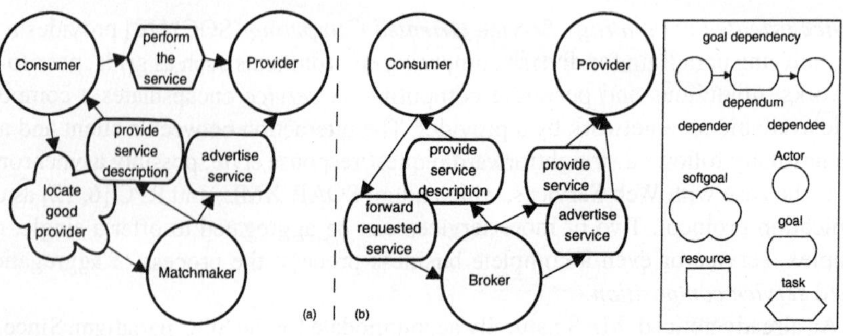

Fig. 1. a) Matchmaker agent pattern; b) Broker agent pattern, depicted by means of the Tropos Actor Diagrams.

The Tropos diagram, of Figure 1.a, shows that each time a user's information/service request arrives[3], Consumer depends on Matchmaker to locate good provider. On the contrary, Figure 1.b shows that Consumer depends on Broker in order to forward requested service, that is, Broker plays an intermediary role between Provider and Consumer. In essence, both Broker and Matchmaker depend on Provider to advertise service(s). Namely, the two patterns skills consist of mediating, among both consumers and providers, for some synergic collaborations to satisfy global goals. In particular, Matchmaker lets Consumer directly interact with Provider, while Broker handles all the interactions between Consumer and Provider.

3 A Reference Scenario

The Peach project [15] focuses on the development of a mobile museum visiting guide system. The whole system is a MAS, which has been developed following the Tropos methodology. Indeed, agents perform their actions while situated in a particular environment that they can sense and affect. More specifically, in the typical Peach museum visiting guide scenario, a user (the visitor) is provided with several environmental interaction devices. The most evident to her is a personal hand-held mobile I/O device, namely a PDA. Other devices include: i) passive localization hot-spots, based on triangularization of signals coming from the PDA; ii) (pro)active stationary displays of different sizes and with different audio output quality. Depending on the dimensions, the displays may be used to deliver visual/audio information (images and/or motion pictures possibly with audio comments; text) to a single user at a time, or to a group of users.

Given this environment, let us start from the following possible user–system interaction scenario:

Example 1 (explicit communication). A museum visitor requests some information during her tour by using her mobile device. To deliver on such a goal, the PDA con-

[3] In the context of our simplified Peach example (see below), the Consumer is the role plaid by the software agent acting as the interface for the human user, that is the *User Assistant*.

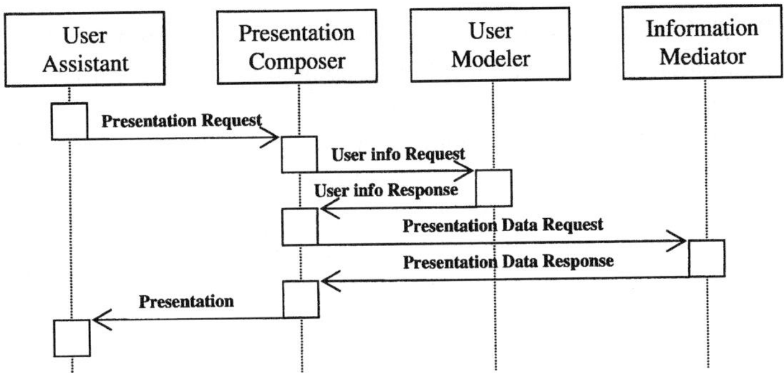

Fig. 2. Overview of the actor interactions.

tains an agent (the *User Assistant*) which, on behalf of the user, sends a presentation request to the museum central system. Here, three system actors take the responsibility of generating a presentation: the *Presentation Composer*, the *User Modeler* and the *Information Mediator*.

Still using Tropos, we can get to detailed design and model the communication dimension of the system actors. To this end, Tropos adopts AUML [1] interaction diagrams. The communication diagram of Figure 2 presents the sequence of events from the time a request for presentation is issued until the presentation is presented to the user. The *User Assistant*, the *Presentation Composer*, and the *User Modeler* are generic roles that may be played by different software agents, e.g., there may be several different information mediators (for video, audio, text, pictures, animation, local and remote information sources and more), there may be several user assistants with different capabilities (hand-held devices, desk-top stations, wall mounted large plasma screens and more), and there may also be several different user modelers implementing various techniques to get users' profiles.

In any case, here, we are not interested in the specific agents implementing such functionalities (i.e., playing the assigned role), but, instead, in the roles themselves. In fact, they – i.e., the *User Assistants*, the *Presentation Composer*, and the *Information Mediator* – form ad-hoc service-oriented organizations, in order to achieve the service goal. Each SOO is characterized by members that collaborate at different levels and times during the *service providing process life-cycle*. After the goal is satisfied, the organization is dissolved and a new one will be formed – possibly including different agents, provided they play the listed roles – to serve a new request.

3.1 Discussion

The previous section motivates the need of some agent patterns to effectively deal with distributed computing issues (e.g., see [11, 17, 16, 10]).

Nevertheless, if we proceed by adopting traditional agent patterns, as, e.g., the matchmaker and broker introduced in Section 2, probably we could not be able to capture few but interesting and vital architectural requirements that arise from our ambient intelligence scenario, specially if we want to fully exploit the flexibility – in terms of self organizing presentation delivery channels – that can be provided.

In particular, to motivate our assertion, let us consider the following new scenario:

Example 2 (implicit communication). Let us assume that, while walking around, the user is approaching some presentation devices that are more comfortable and suitable to handle the presentation than the mobile device (*User Assistant*), e.g., in terms of pixel resolution and audio quality. So, we may assume the *User Assistant* is autonomously capable to exploit its intelligent behavior by negotiating the most convenient presentation, on behalf of its human owner. Let us also assume that there are several different *Presentation Composers* for each single device (capable to generate video, text, animated explanation, audio, etc.) and that each *Presentation Composer* relies on different *Information Mediators* to provide the information required for presentation generation. Moreover, we may also assume that each *Presentation Composer* is able to proactively propose its best services (in terms of available or conveniently producible presentations) to the *User Assistant*, possibly through some mediation interface. As well, we expect that all the services (negotiated or proposed) are "dynamically validated", that is, due to the fact that the environment and the user location are quickly changing, only the appropriate services are considered.

Such a scenario calls for architecture flexibility in terms of dynamic group reconfiguration to support SOOs involvement. Traditional approaches allow for intentional relationships and request/response communication protocols among single agents only, and not among group of agents [9–11, 17]. More specifically, we may assume that the *User Assistant* starts an interaction session that triggers the involvement of a group of system actors all with the ability of *Presentation Composer*, which in turn trigger the involvement of a group of system actors all with the ability of *Information Mediator*. Each *Presentation Composer*, instead, relays on the *User Modeler* to know the user profile to correctly build up a user-tailored presentation.

Therefore, such an architecture has to adopt group communication in order to support an 'intelligent' pervasive computing model among users' assistant devices and the system actor information/service providers. To cope with these new challenges, we can imagine that the system agents exploit a form of 'implicit communication', where they can autonomously build up SOOs in order to satisfy a request at the best they can do at that time. This is not possible by means of traditional approaches that adopt simple request/response based communication styles (e.g., [16]). In fact, as shown in Figure 1, using classical matchmaker and broker approaches, we assume that there is an advertise service dependency (e.g., based on a preliminary registration phase) forcing the system actors to rely on a centralized computing model.

4 Agent Patterns-Based Detailed Design

The discussion above highlights the limits of traditional patterns when applied to our ambient intelligence pervasive computing scenario; hence, the necessity of characterizing our system architecture by means of new agent patterns.

4.1 The Service Oriented Organization

In distributed computing and especially in *'intelligent' pervasive* computing based scenarios, each time an information consumer explicitly or implicitly causes a specific

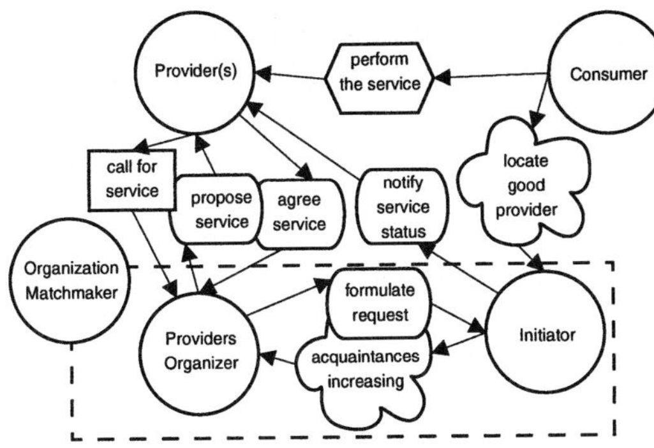

Fig. 3. Actor Diagram for the *Service Oriented Organization* pattern.

service request, it inherently needs a searching capability in order to locate the service provider. In particular, in our scenario, when the *User Assistants* is looking for a *Presentation Composer* in order to ask for a personalized presentation, a matchmaker (e.g., the one presented in Section 2) or a facilitator architecture is required [10, 11, 13, 16].

As previously discussed, the matchmaker pattern illustrated in Section 2 does not completely fit the requirements of our pervasive computing scenario (Example 2). Here, we define a new agent pattern – the *Service Oriented Organization* pattern – illustrated in Figure 3, which extends and adapts the matchmaker pattern of Figure 1.a. Here, the actor Matchmaker is replaced by Organization Matchmaker, which is further decomposed in two component system actors: Service oriented Organization and Initiator. The dependencies between Consumer and Organization Matchmaker (or, more specifically, Initiator) and between Consumer and Provider(s) are as before. The main difference, instead, is that now there is no advertise service goal dependency between Organization Matchmaker and Provider(s). In fact, our scenario call for dynamic group reconfiguration, which cannot be provided on the basis of a pre-declared and centrally recorded set of service capabilities, as foreseen in the classical matchmaker approach. The solution we propose, instead, is based on a proactive and, specially, dynamic capability of service proposal, on the basis of the actual, current requests or needs of services. In particular, our system low level communication infrastructure is based on a group communication, which has been designed to support channelled multicast [3]. That is, a form of group communication that allows messages addressed to a single agent or a group of agents (Provider(s)) to be received by everybody tuned on the channel, i.e., the agent "introspection" capability described in Section 5. Thus, Provider(s) depends now on Organization Matchmaker, or, more specifically, on Providers Organizer to have a call for service. That is, because of each SOO member adopts an IP channelled multicast approach that allows to overhear on channels (see Section 5 for details), the organizer simply sends its service request message on a specific channel and it waits for some providers offers[4]. On the basis of such calls, Provider(s) may notify their current services availability. Thus, the Providers Organizer depends on Provider(s) for propose service and,

[4] In fact, channels are classified by topics and each provider is free to overhear on the preferred channels according to its main interest and capabilities.

vice-versa, Provider(s) depend on the Providers Organizer for the final agreement on service provision (goal agree service). Moreover, in an 'intelligent' pervasive computing based scenario, the system awareness allows to proactively propose services to the consumer without any explicit service request. Thus, Initiator acts as interface towards Consumer. It is able to interpret Consumer's requests and, specially, proactively propose not explicitly requested services, on the basis of Consumer's profile and previous interaction history[5]. To this end, Initiator depends on Providers Organizer to get new acquaintances about Provider(s) and their services, while Providers Organizer depends on the Initiator to formulate request. In this way, we can drop the dependency Provide service description between Matchmaker and Consumer, which is instead present in the traditional matchmaker pattern. Finally, Initiator requires that Provider(s) timely notify service status in order to only propose active services.

4.2 The Implicit Organization Broker

As observed in Section 1, ambient intelligence environments are often characterized by intermitted communication channels. This problem is even more relevant when proactive broadcasting is adopted, as in the scenario suggested by Example 2. In this case communications to/from the *User Assistant* need to be reduced at a minimum. To this end, we propose here to exploit the *implicit communication* paradigm towards the adoption of an *implicit organizations broker* (IOB) agent pattern that is inspired to the implicit organization introduced by [4]. That is, we define the IOB as a SOO formed by all the agents tuned on the same channel to play the same *role* (i.e., having same communication API) and willing to coordinate their actions. The term 'implicit' highlights the fact that there is no group formation phase – since joining an organization is just a matter of tuning on a channel – and no name for it – since the role and the channel uniquely identify the organization. Its members play the same role but they may do it in different ways; redundancy (as in fault tolerant and load balanced systems) is just a particular case where agents happen to be perfectly interchangeable. In particular, we can consider to have *implicit organizations* playing a kind of broker role. In other terms, each time the system perceives the visitor's information needs, the system actors set up a SOO (as described in Section 4.1), which, in addition to the already presented matchmaking capabilities, can also manage the whole service I/O process; that is, the SOO is able to autonomously and proactively cope with the whole *service providing process life cycle*. Such a system ability enhances the ambient intelligence awareness, a system requirement that cannot be captured by adopting traditional agent patterns [10, 11].

Figure 4 introduces a IOB pattern as a refinement/adaptation of the SOO pattern introduced in Section 4.1. Provider(s) are now part of the organization itself, which plays the role of an Organization Broker. Thus, the latter include both Providers Organizer and Provider(s) (see the inside of the dashed-line rectangle). It is worth noticing that the IOB members are characterized by the same (required) skill (see ahead Section 5).

The differences between the two traditional agent patterns of Figure 1 are naturally reflected also between the two patterns illustrated in Figures 3 and 4. In particular, Fig-

[5] For example, every system actor, through environmental sensors, can perceive and profile users during their visits across museum media services, as in the scenario of Example 2.

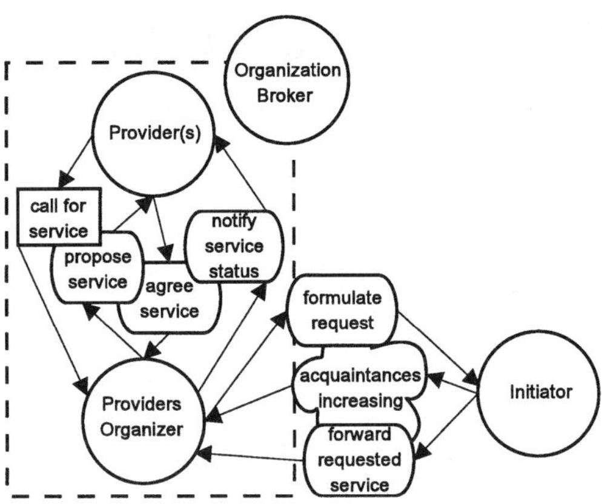

Fig. 4. Actor Diagram for the *Implicit Organization Broker* (IOB) pattern.

ure 3 tries to capture intentional aspects for more general group communication scenarios, i.e., general SOO. On the contrary, Figure 4 gives a level of pattern based detailed design focusing more on special kind of SOO, tailor-made for ambient intelligence scenarios. In other words, Figure 3 does not consider a strictly 'intelligent' pervasive computing scenario that, on the contrary, characterizes our IOB of Figure 4.

As well, it is worth noticing that the IOB pattern incorporate in the Initiator role both the roles of Consumer and Initiator of the SOO pattern. As already said, this is a consequence of the fact that, in ambient intelligence, some system actors concurrently play the consumer and initiator roles, which allows the system to enhance autonomy and proactivity skills. Moreover, and similarly to what happen in Figure 1.b between the Consumer and the Broker, in Figure 4, the Initiator depends on the Organization Broker – or, more specifically, on the Providers Organizer – to forward requested service, in order to avoid *User Assistant* message/interaction overloading. Nevertheless, the IOB pattern allows for acquaintance increasing (for Initiator), so to consent a more precise service requests during future interactions, as already foreseen for the generic *Service Oriented Organization* pattern.

5 Supporting Implicit Organization Brokers

The two agent patterns *Service Oriented Organization* and the *Implicit Organization Broker* presented so forth have been experimented within the Peach project to build an interactive, pervasive, museum guide. As mentioned, our patterns require a group communication infrastructure. To this end, we adopt the *LoudVoice* [4] experimental communication infrastructure based on channelled multicast and developed at our institute. Specifically, LoudVoice uses the fast but inherently unreliable IP multicast – which is not a major limitation in our domain, since the communication media in use are unreliable by their own nature. However, we had to deal with message losses and temporary network partitions by carefully crafting protocols and using time-based mechanisms to ensure consistency of mutual beliefs within organizations.

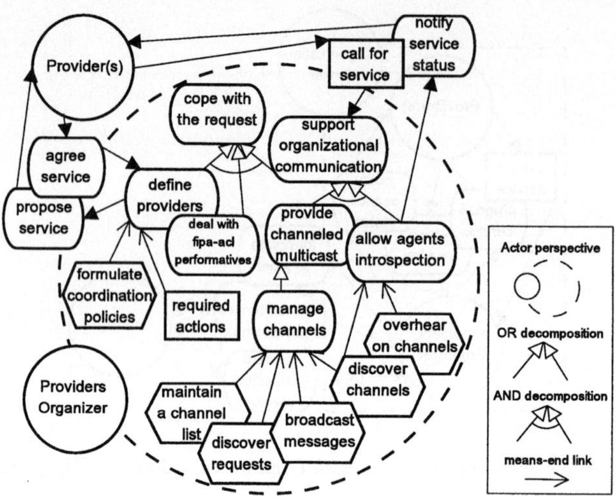

Fig. 5. Goal Diagram for an agent's role characterization by means of its capabilities.

5.1 Agent Roles Characterization

Analyzing agent roles means figuring out and characterizing its main capabilities (e.g., internal and external services) required to achieve its intentional dependencies already identified by the agent patterns analysis of Section 4. Note that, a capability (or skill) is not necessarily justified by external requests (like a service), but it can be an internal agent characteristic, required to enhance its autonomous and proactive behavior. To deal with the rationale aspects of an agent at 'design time', that is, in order to look inside and to understand how an agent exploits its capabilities, we adopt the *Goal Modeling Activity* of Tropos [2]. In Figure 5, we adopt the *means-end* and *AND/OR decomposition* reasoning techniques of the Goal Modeling Activity [2, 5, 18]. Means-end analysis aims at identifying goals, tasks, and resources that provide means for achieving a given goal. AND/OR decomposition analysis combines AND and OR decompositions of a root goal into subgoals, modeling a finer goal structure. Notice that, we have modeled every agent capability as a goal to be achieved.

For the sake of briefness, here we consider only the IOB pattern. According to Figures 5 and 4, each time Initiator formulates a request, Providers Organizer achieves its main goal cope with the request (i.e., the goal that Providers Organizer internally adopts to satisfy Initiator's request) relying on its three principal skills: define providers, deal with fipa-acl performatives, and support organizational communication. The principal goal success depends on the satisfaction of all the three goals (i.e., AND decomposition). For the sake of simplicity, Figure 5 does not consider Initiator and its intentional relationships. An adequate organizational communication infrastructure is used to enhance the system actor autonomous and proactive behavior by means of group communication based on channelled multicast [3] (see goal provide channelled multicast) that allows messages to be exchanged over open channels identified by topic of conversation. Thus, a proper structuring of conversations among agents allows every listener to

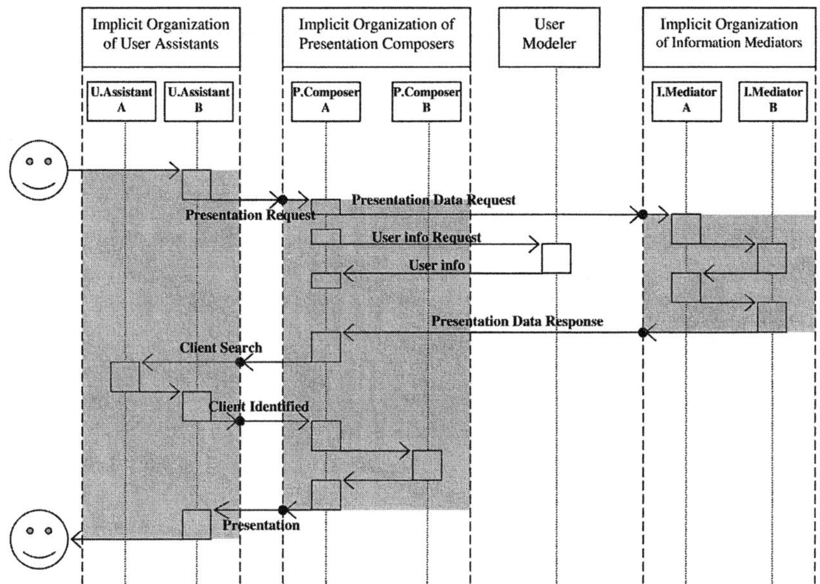

Fig. 6. Interaction of organizations.

capture its partner intentions without any explicit request, thanks to its agent introspection skill (see goal allow agents introspection). Indeed, each actor is able to overhear on specific channels every ongoing interaction; hence, it can choose the best role to play in order to satisfy a goal, provide a resource, perform a task, without any external decision control, but only according to its internal beliefs and desires.

Exploiting the provide channelled multicast ability, each actor can decide by itself what channels to listen to, by means of a subscription phase (represented by the tasks discover channels and maintain a channel list). This communication mechanisms well support group communication for service oriented and implicit organizations composed by members with the same interests or skills. Such organizations assist the *User Assistant* avoiding it to know how directly interact with the museum multi-media services.

5.2 Group Communication: Dynamics

As described earlier, the museum visitor guide system is composed of several different types of agents. Rather than by individual agents, most components are formed by a group of coordinated agents, as presented by Example 2 of Section 3. Modeling this example requires the representation of implicit organizations, which cannot be done by a regular AUML communication diagram, as presented, e.g., in [2, 5]. Therefore, in Figure 6, we propose a new type of diagram that deals with the group communication features required by the scenario introduced with Example 2. Here, the shaded rectangles and the dashed lines below them represent the implicit organizations, and the gray rectangles represent the communication internal to implicit organizations. Requests sent to an organization are presented as arrows terminating in a dot at the border of the organization; the organization reply is presented by an arrow starting from a dot on the organization border. Obviously, we consider an asynchronous message-based communication model.

In the example diagram of Figure 6, the request for presentation is initiated by a certain *User Assistant* on behalf of a specific user. The request is addressed to the *Implicit Organization of Presentation Composers*. Presentation composers have different capabilities and require different resources. Hence every presentation composer requests user information on the user model and presentation data (availability, constraints, etc.) from the *Implicit Organization of Information Mediators*. In turn, the implicit organization of information mediators holds an internal conversation. Each member suggests the service it can provide. The "best" service is selected and returned, as a group decision, to the requesting presentation composer. At this stage, the presentation composers request additional information to the *Implicit Organization of User Assistants*, regarding the availability of assistants capable to show the presentation being planned. When all the information has been received, the implicit organization of presentation composers can reason and decide on the best presentation to prepare. This will be sent from the composers as a group response to the selected (user) assistant.

6 Conclusions

Ambient intelligence scenarios characterized by service oriented organizations, where group of agents collaborate at different levels and times during the service providing life-cycle, generates new software architectural requirements that traditional agent patterns cannot satisfy. For example, 'intelligent' pervasive computing and peer-to-peer computing models naturally support group communication for ambient intelligence, but they also call for architecture flexibility in terms of dynamic group reconfiguration. Traditional request/response communication protocols are not appropriate to cope with service negotiation and aggregation that must be 'dynamically validate', since the environment conditions and the user location are quickly changing.

For such reasons, we propose two new agent patterns (Service Oriented Organization and Implicit Organization Broker) and compare them with traditional patterns [10, 11]. Specifically, we adopt the agent oriented software development methodology Tropos [2, 5], to effectively figure out the new requirements. For example, using Tropos, we can keep the agent conversation and social levels independent from complex coordination activities, thanks to an inherently pure *peer-to-peer* computing model [13]. Such a way of modeling has been thought for enriching the Tropos methodology detailed design phase with new capabilities, more oriented towards sophisticated software agents, which requires advanced modeling mechanisms to better fit group communication, goals, and negotiations. Thus, we have been able to capture important aspects of ambient intelligence requirements and to build up new agent patterns, more flexible and reusable than the traditional ones.

References

1. B. Bauer, J. P. Muller, and J. Odell. Agent uml: A formalism for specifying multiagent software systems. *International Journal of Software Engineering and Knowledge Engineering*, 11(3):1–24, 2001.

2. P. Bresciani, P. Giorgini, F. Giunchiglia, J. Mylopoulos, and A. Perini. TROPOS: An agent-oriented software development methodology. *Autonomous agents and Multi-agent Systems (JAAMAS)*, 8(3):203–236, May 2004.
3. P. Busetta, A. Donà, and M. Nori. Channeled multicast for group communications. In *Proceedings of the first international joint conference on Autonomous agents and multiagent systems*, pages 1280–1287. ACM Press, 2002.
4. P. Busetta, M. Merzi, S. Rossi, and F. Legras. Intra-role coordination using group communication: A preliminary report. In F. Dignum, editor, *Advances in Agent Communication*, LNAI. Springer Verlag (to Appear), 2003.
5. J. Castro, M. Kolp, and J. Mylopoulos. Towards requirements-driven information systems engineering: The tropos project. *Information Systems (27)*, pages 365–389, Elsevier, Amsterdam, The Netherlands, 2002.
6. F. Curbera, R. Khalaf, N. Mukhi, S. Tai, and S. Weerawarana. The next step in web services. *Commun. ACM*, 46(10):29–34, 2003.
7. K. Ducatel, M. Bogdanowicz, F. Scapolo, J. Leijten, and J.-C. Burgelman. Scenarios for ambient intelligence in 2010. Technical report, Information Society Technologies Programme of the European Union Commission (IST), Feb. 2001. `http://www.cordis.lu/ist/`.
8. U. J. Franke. *Managing Virtual Web Organizations in the 21th century: Issues and Challenges*. Idea Group Publishing, Pennsylvania, 2001.
9. S. Hayden, C. Carrick, and Q. Yang. Architectural design patterns for multiagent coordination. In *Proc. of the 3rd Int. Conf. on Agent Systems (Agents'99)*, 1999.
10. M. Klusch and K. Sycara. Brokering and matchmaking for coordination of agent societies: A survey. In A. Omicini, F. Zambonelli, M. Klusch, and R. Tolksdorf, editors, *Coordination of Internet Agents: Models, Technologies, and Applications*, pages 197–224. Springer-Verlag, Mar. 2001.
11. M. Kolp, P. Giorgini, and J. Mylopoulos. A goal-based organizational perspective on multi-agents architectures. In *Proceedings of the Eighth International Workshop on Agent Theories, architectures, and languages (ATAL-2001)*, 2001.
12. M. P. Papazoglou and D. Georgakopoulos. Introduction to the special section on Service Oriented Computing. *Commun. ACM*, 46(10):24–28, 2003.
13. L. Penserini, L. Liu, J. Mylopoulos, M. Panti, and L. Spalazzi. Cooperation strategies for agent-based p2p systems. *WIAS: Web Intelligence and Agent Systems: An International Journal*, IOS Press, 1(1):3–21, 2003.
14. L. Penserini, L. Spalazzi, and M. Panti. A p2p-based infrastructure for virtual-enterprise's supply-chain management. In *Proc. of the Sixth Int. Conference on Enterprise Information Systems (ICEIS-04)*. INSTICC-Institute for Systems and Technologies of Information, Control and Communication, vol.4, pp 316-321, 2004.
15. O. Stock and M. Zancanaro. Intelligent Interactive Information Presentation for Cultural Tourism. In *Proc. of the International CLASS Workshop on Natural Intelligent and Effective Interaction in Multimodal Dialogue Systems*, Copenhagen, Denmark, 28-29 June 2002.
16. K. Sycara, S. Widoff, M. Klusch, and J. Lu. Larks: Dynamic matchmaking among heterogeneous software agents in cyberspace. *Autonomous Agents and Multi-Agent Systems*, 5(2):173–203, 2002.
17. Y. Tahara, A. Ohsuga, and S. Honiden. Agent system development method based on agent patterns. In *Proc. of the 21st Int. Conf. on Software Engineering (ICSE'99)*. IEEE Computer Society Press, 1999.
18. E. Yu. *Modeling Strategic Relationships for Process Reengineering*. PhD thesis, Department of Computer Science, University of Toronto, Toronto, Canada, 1995.

Modeling the Semantics of 3D Protein Structures

Sudha Ram and Wei Wei

Department of Management Information Systems, Eller College of Management,
The University of Arizona, Tucson, AZ 85721, USA
{ram,wwei}@eller.arizona.edu

Abstract. The post Human Genome Project era calls for reliable, integrated, flexible, and convenient data management techniques to facilitate research activities. Querying biological data that is large in volume and complex in structure such as 3D proteins requires expressive models to explicitly support and capture the semantics of the complex data. Protein 3D structure search and comparison not only enable us to predict unknown structures, but can also reveal distant evolutionary relationships that are otherwise undetectable, and perhaps suggest unsuspected functional properties. In this work, we model 3D protein structures by adding spatial semantics and constructs to represent the contributing forces such as hydrogen bonds and high-level structures such as protein secondary structures. This paper makes a contribution to modeling the specialty of life science data and develops methods to meet the novel challenges posed by such data.

1 Introduction

The Human Genome Project and its concomitant research have provided the scientific community with data that is increasing in volume and complexity. It has generated a precious information pool that can be used to support the best interests of human beings. To exploit this information, we need new ways to manage, integrate, and present the data so complex questions can be answered effectively. To do so, we need expressive data models that can capture the semantics of the wide variety of biological data.

Proteins are large biological molecules with complex structure and they constitute much of the bulk of living organisms. In order to understand the life processes of an organism, it is necessary to first know the functions of the proteins. Since the function of a protein in a given environment is determined by its structure, we need to know the structure of the molecule to fully understand its function. The success of the Human Genome Project generated multiple protein databases including protein sequence databases and protein 3D structure databases [8]. Each 3D structure stored in the databases is either determined by experimental methods such as X-ray crystallography and Nuclear Magnetic Resonance or by computational chemistry [22]. Researchers need to search these databases for specific structures or compare structures with each other to seek similarities. Similar sequences can result in similar 3D structures, and similar structures perform similar functions. Therefore, protein structure similarities may be predicted based on sequence similarities. More importantly, search for similar protein structures can help us find homologs that sequence searches cannot discover, and, homologs often conserve structure more strongly than sequence. Also,

P. Atzeni et al. (Eds.): ER 2004, LNCS 3288, pp. 696–708, 2004.

we can explore protein evolution because similar protein folds can be used to support different functions [13]. Meanwhile, if we can identify conserved core elements of protein folding, the information can be used to model related proteins of unknown structures. Being able to determine, search and compare 3D protein structures, rather than just comparing sequences, is thus becoming very important in the life sciences. However, structure comparisons are currently a big challenge. We address this issue in our research by developing a semantic model. We believe our semantic model can facilitate the development of techniques and operators for 3D structure searching and comparison. In this paper, we extend our previous work on semantic modeling of DNA sequences and primary protein sequences to three-dimension (3D) protein structures with semantics that are novel using extended Entity-Relationship Modeling [10]. When studying proteins, scientists investigate not only the amino acids subunits that form a protein and their order, but also how the sequences fold into 3D structures in certain ways due to chemical forces. Currently, protein structure data is stored in plain text files that record the three-dimensional coordinates of each non-hydrogen atom as well as a small part of the substructures. The text file formatted data doesn't capture biological meaning. Comparison and search over structure data have to be done using visualization tools and extra software tools running on various algorithms.

We define the semantics of primary, secondary, tertiary and quaternary structures of proteins by describing their components, chemical bonding forces, and spatial arrangement. To model the 3D structure of a protein and its formation, we need to explicitly represent the spatial arrangement of each component in addition to its sequential order, along with its associated biological information. Our semantic model captures the semantics of protein data and specifies it using an annotation-based approach to capture all of this semantic information in a straightforward way.

The rest of the paper is organized as follows. Section 2 provides a brief background about proteins and their various levels of structures, and describes the semantics of such structures. In section 3 we describe entity classes and new constructs to represent the semantics of protein structures and develop annotations to capture their spatial arrangement and biological characteristics. Also, we briefly review related research and justify why it is necessary to develop new semantic constructs to model protein structures. In section 4, we describe the utility of our semantic model, demonstrate its application and point out extensibility of the model for other similar fields. We conclude with a discussion of future research directions in section 5.

2 Background

2.1 Protein Structures

Proteins are the most important macromolecules in the factory of living cells that perform various biological tasks. Basically, a protein is composed of various numbers of 20 kinds of amino acids, also known as subunits or residues (see Figure 1). These residues are arranged in a specific order or sequence; each amino acid is denoted by a letter of the English alphabet [6].

Multiple amino acids bond together through condensation reaction to form amino bonds (see Figure 2) which connect subunits into a protein sequence. One protein sequence can range from 10 to 1000 amino acids (residues). The actual proteins are not linear sequences; rather they are 3-D structures. Knowing this 3-D structure is a key to understanding the protein's functions and for using it to improve human lives.

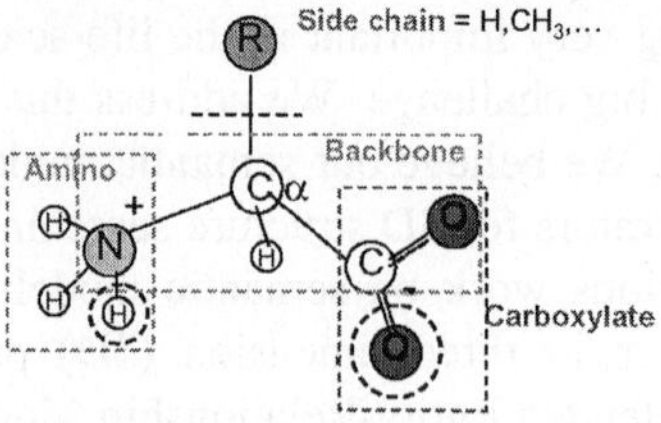

Fig. 1. General Structure of Amino Acids. Different side chain-R determines the type of amino acid. Each amino acid contains an amino group and a carboxylate group. Hydrogen atom on amino group reacts with hydroxyl on carboxylate group through condensation to form amino bonds

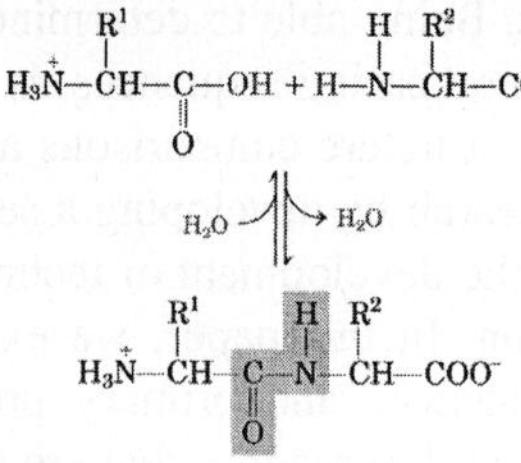

Fig. 2. Structure of Amino Bonds. Two amino acid residues (subunits) are shown

The general principle that protein sequences follow to fold into 3-D structures is that "The three-dimensional structure of a native protein in its normal physiological milieu is the one in which the Gibbs free energy of the whole system is lowest; that is, the native conformation is determined by the totality of inter-atomic interactions and hence by the amino acid sequence, in a given environment" [11]. Following are descriptions for the four levels of protein structures [6].

Primary Structure. The primary structure of a protein refers to the exact sequence of amino acids in a protein. Hence the primary structure is linear in nature; it says nothing about the spatial arrangement of amino acids or their atoms. It merely shows the specific amino acids used to compose the protein and their linear order.

M-H-G-A-Y-R-T-P-R-S-K-T-D-A-Y-G-C

Fig. 3. Primary Protein Structure

Secondary Structure. The covalently linked amino acids are further organized by forming regularly repeating patterns such as α helix and β sheet and other less popular structures [16]. A hydrogen bond is the cause of the secondary structure. More specifically, it is the spatial interaction between a hydrogen atom in an N-H group and a nearby highly electro-negative carbonyl oxygen as shown in Figure 4. Each atom participating in the formation of a hydrogen bond is from a different residue, the distance between these residues determines the possible category of its secondary structure. The secondary structure is the base on which tertiary and quaternary structures are formed. 3D structure search and com-

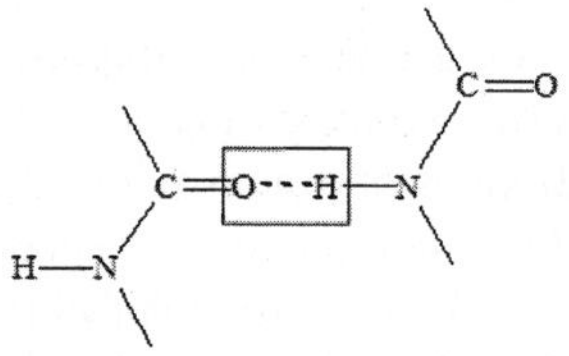

Fig. 4. Formation of Hydrogen Bond

parison start from the secondary structure level [19]. One protein sequence or a chain can contain multiple different secondary structures. Each of these secondary structures is formed on a segment of the primary sequence. Several adjacent secondary structures form a motif and motifs can group to form domains.

Tertiary Structure. Several motifs typically combine to form a compact globular structure referred to as a domain. The tertiary structure is used to describe the way motifs are arranged into domain structures and the way a single polypeptide chain folds into one or several domains. The side chain interactions contributing to the formation of domains or tertiary structures include: (a) Hydrogen bonds between polar side chain groups; (b) Hydrophobic interactions among non-polar groups; (c) Salt bridges between acidic and basic side chains; and, (d) Disulfide bridges. Here, each "chain" is a protein sequence recorded in protein sequence databases.

Quaternary Structure. For proteins with more than one chain, interactions can occur between the chains themselves. The forces contributing to the quaternary structure are of the same kinds as those for tertiary structures, but they are between chains, not within chains.

To summarize, various inter- and intra-molecular forces work together to decide the least energy/most stable structure of the proteins. The structure determines how various biological tasks are performed. It is therefore important to represent the semantics of these structures so they can be queried easily.

2.2 Current Protein Structure Databases and Usage

The Protein Data Bank, PDB (http://www.rcsb.org/pdb/) is the only worldwide archive of experimentally determined (using X-ray Crystallography and Nuclear Magnetic Resonance techniques) three-dimensional structures of proteins [2]. It is operated by the Research Collaboratory for Structural Bioinformatics (RCSB). There are 26485 structures stored in PDB as of now with the number and complexity of the structures increasing rapidly.

The format of data stored in PDB consists of a HEADER followed by the data. There are two major categories of data. The first category includes the identifier of each protein, the experiment (which determined its structure), the authors, keywords and references etc. The other more important category is the x, y and z coordinates of each non-hydrogen atom (heavy atom) in the structure. This format records the protein sequence and the composition of its secondary structure. It does not record the tertiary and quaternary structures, which as stated earlier, are very important parts of the protein structure. The core of the protein data lies in its coordinate data or its spatial arrangement. However, spatial coordinates by themselves depict nothing more than the shape and provide no biological value, unless they can be related to other information such as the shape, the strength (or energy), and the length of the chemical bonds between the various subunits of a protein. This is very important in structural genomics [12] and is used to connect spatial data with whole-genome data and to relate it to various biological activities.

Researchers use experimental methods or computational calculation to determine or predict the structure of proteins, and submit their data to PDB [5, 23], PDB processes the data based on the mmCIF (Macromolecular Crystallographic Information File standard) dictionary that is an ontology of 1700 terms that define the macromolecular structure and the crystallographic experiment [4]. Then the data is stored in the core database.

Structure data stored in flat files poses challenges to effective and efficient data retrieval and analysis. Because data in flat file formats is not machine-processable, specialized structure search and comparison software tools are required to access and analyze the data. Each of the tools available has its own interface supporting slightly different invocation, processing and data semantics. This makes using the tools difficult because the input must be guaranteed to be in the correct format with the correct semantics and the tools must be invoked in specific, non-standard ways [7]. Primary protein structure or protein sequence search and comparison software tools use the BLAST (Basic Local Alignment Search Tool) algorithm [1], while 3D structure search and comparison software tools use more or less similar algorithms [15, 20] based on VAST (Vector Alignment Search Tool) [18]. Meanwhile, co-existence of multiple search tools makes one-stop search impossible. Inefficient structure search and comparison has become the bottleneck for high throughput experiments. Our research focuses on how to represent 3D structure semantics in a conceptual model which can be used for seamless interoperation of multiple resources [21]. More importantly, operators [9] can be developed based on the semantic model to facilitate query and analysis of structure data. Therefore, using extra software tools would become unnecessary and the bottlenecks can be eliminated.

In this paper, we propose new constructs to explicitly represent the semantics of protein structures. We believe our model will help facilitate the ability of scientists to understand and detect the link between protein structures and their biological functions. Our proposed model provides formally defined constructs to represent the semantics of protein structure data. The spatial elements are represented using annotations. Our semantic model will also aid the development of tools to process ad hoc queries about protein structures. It can also be used as a canonical model to virtually unify protein structure data [3, 23].

3 Proposed Semantic Model

3.1 Entity Classes

Atoms. This entity class is used to model chemical atoms (C, H, O, N and heteroatoms such as S) in the protein structure with each of them identified uniquely by an ID. Each atom in the structure can be represented by a 3-tuple A <*as, an, ty*>. The *as* element represents the atom's serial number and $as \in$ AS where AS is the collection of all atom serial numbers. The *an* element is the atom name and $an \in$ AN where AN = {C, H, O, N, S}. The last element *ty* is the atom type and $ty \in$ TY where TY= {C_α, N, C_c, O_c, H_s, H_n, $H_{c\alpha}$, S}. Each element in TY is a representative category of atoms in an amino acid. C_α is α carbon, N is the nitrogen atom, C_c is the carboxylate carbon, O_c is the carboxylate oxygen and H_s, H_n, $H_{c\alpha}$ are side chain hydrogen, amino hydrogen and C_α hydrogen respectively. S is sulfur atom that contributes to structure formation such as disulfur bridges.

Residues. Each residue (amino acid subunit) is an aggregate of a set of component atoms and a set of intra-residue bonds. Each residue can be represented using a 4-tuple R < *rs*, *rn*, $\{a_i \mid a_i \in A\}$, $\{B(a_i, a_j), BL, BE \mid a_i, a_j \in A\}$ >. Element *rs* is the residue serial number, and $rs \in N \wedge rs \leq SL$, where SL is the length of the protein sequence or the total number of residues. The second element *rn* is the residue name, $rn \in AA$ where AA is the set of all types of amino acid residues. AA = {A, R, N, D, C, E, Q, G, H, I, L, K, M, F, P, S, T, W, Y, V}. $\{a_i \mid a_i \in A\}$ is the set of atoms in the residue identified by their atom serial numbers. $\{B(a_i, a_j), BL, BE \mid a_i, a_j \in A\}$ is the set of internal bonds in the residue. $B(a_i, a_j)$ is the bond between atom i and atom j. BL and BE are used to record the bond length and bond energy. This structure data is determined by experimental or computational methods.

Primary Structure. The Primary structure of a protein is the sequence of amino acids comprising the protein. It describes what amino acids subunits are used in which order to form specific protein sequence. It can be represented as a 3-tuple PS < *psid, pn, psl* >, where *psid* is the unique identifier for each protein sequence record in the database, *pn* is the biological name of the protein and *psl* is the length of the protein sequence. At the same time, $psid \in PSID$ where PSID is the collection of all available identifiers for protein sequences. Also, $pn \in PN$ where PN is the collection of the names of all proteins.

Segment. A complete protein sequence can be fragmented into several segments and each segment is folded to form certain higher-level structures. A segment is defined as seg <*segid*> where $segid \in N$ and $seg \in SEG$. SEG is the set of all segments fragmented from a single protein sequence. More information about each segment is represented by the Fragment relationship between Primary Structure and Segment.

Forces. This entity class represents the four chemical forces that contribute to the formation of secondary structures, namely, hydrogen bonds, disulfur bridges, salt bridges, and hydrophobic interactions. FORCES is a superclass with four subclasses where each of them represents one of the four types of chemical forces. Hydrogen bond is the focus of our study, but by capturing the other three types of forces in our model, we allow for future expansion.

Hydrogenbonds. A hydrogen bond is modeled as an entity class because it is the main cause of secondary structures based on which protein sequences fold into specific spatial arrangements. HYDROGENBONDS as a superclass has two subclasses – BACKBONE and SIDECHAIN. BACKBONE represents hydrogen bonds formed by backbone hydrogen atoms. SIDECHAIN represents hydrogen bonds formed by non-backbone hydrogen atoms. We focus on backbone hydrogen bonds in this paper; sidechain hydrogen bonds are included in the model for future investigation. Each hydrogen bond in the structure can be depicted as a 3-tuple hb < (H_{ni}, O_{cj}), BL, BE>.

The first element records the hydrogen bond formed between a hydrogen atom from an amino group and an oxygen atom from a carboxylate group. *i* is the serial number of the residue which donates the hydrogen atom and *j* is the serial number of the residue which donates the oxygen atom where $| i - j | \geq 3$ because the two residues have to be at least 3 units away from each other to form a hydrogen bond. Different distances between amino acids cause different forms of secondary structures [16]. For each protein structure, there is a set of hydrogen bonds formed within the structure HB and $HB=\{ hb_m \mid hb_m = < (H_{ni}, O_{cj}), BL, BE> \wedge i, j, m \in N \wedge i, j \leq SL \wedge | i-j| \geq 3 \}$.

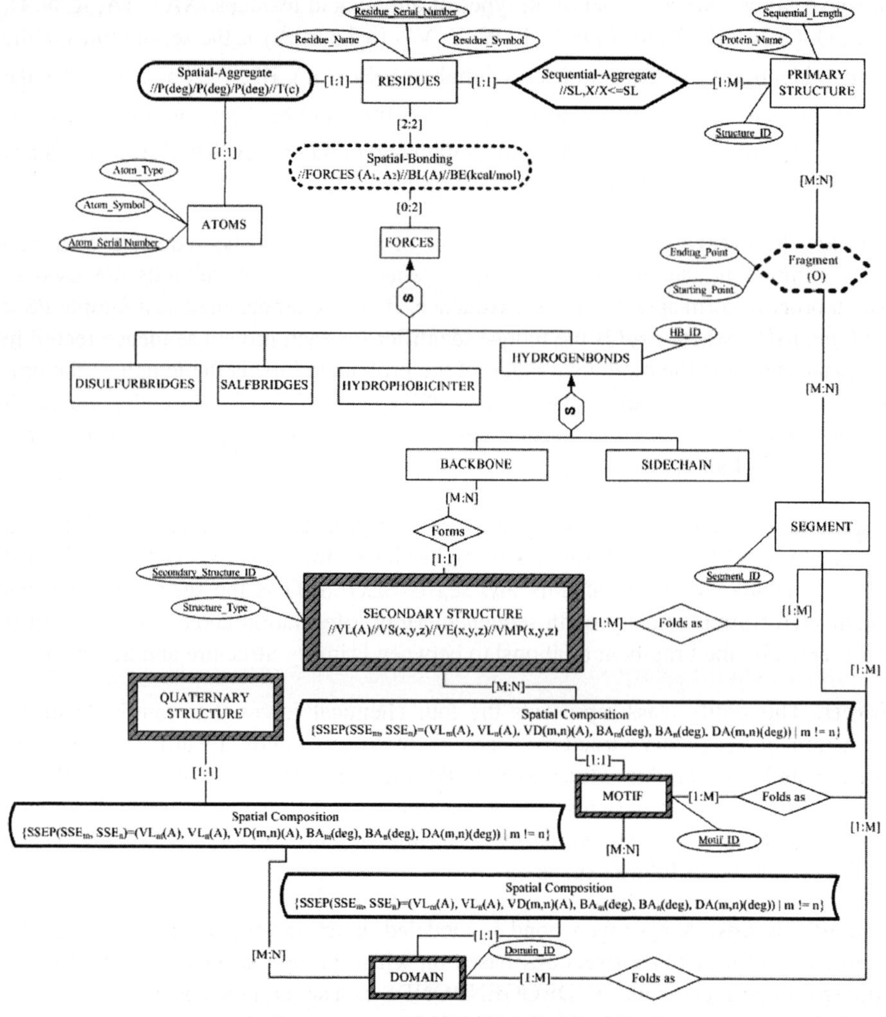

Fig. 5. Semantic model of protein 3D structure

Secondary Structure. A secondary structure is formed by hydrogen bonding. Multiple hydrogen bonds make a segment of the protein sequence fold in specific ways. Therefore, each secondary structure corresponds to a set of hydrogen bonds. The type of hydrogen bonds in the set determines the type of the secondary structure i.e. α helix and β sheet. The contributing hydrogen bond set is defined as a set HB_n where $HB_n \subseteq HB$. If $| i - j | = n$ and $n \in \{3,4,5\}$, then the resulting structure is called n-turn. Multiple adjacent turns form a α helix. Minimal helices overlapping can form longer helices. Other types of structures can also be defined using i and j. The geometry of a secondary structure can be represented as a vector which is the basis for VAST. Each vector is represented as a 4-tuple <VL(A), VS(x,y,z), VE(x,y,z), VMP(x,y,z)>. VL is the vector length in angstrom, VS(x,y,z) are the internal coordinates of the starting point of the vector, VE(x,y,z) are the internal coordinates of the ending point of the vector and VMP(x,y,z) are the internal coordinates of the middle point of the vector. These values of a secondary structure element (SSE) need to be defined because structure comparison is based on vector geometry. Within each protein structure, all SSEs group together to form a set SSE where $SSE = \{ sse_i \mid sse_i = \langle VL(A), VS(x,y,z), VE(x,y,z), VMP(x,y,z)\rangle \wedge i \in N \}$.

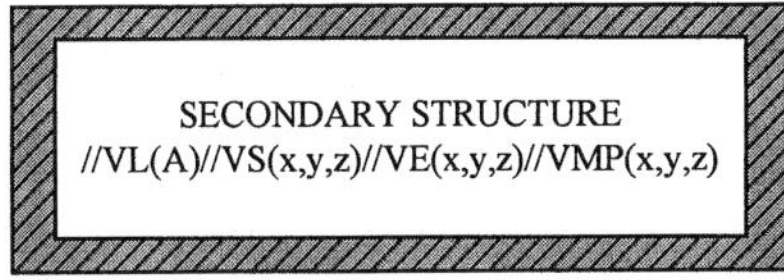

Fig. 6. Secondary Structure Entity Class

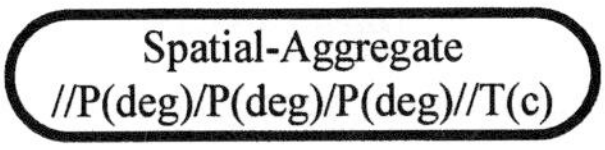

Spatial-Aggregate
//P(deg)/P(deg)/P(deg)//T(c)

Fig. 7. Spatial-Aggregate Relationship

Motif. Secondary structure elements usually arrange themselves in simple motifs. Motifs are formed by packing side chains from adjacent secondary structures such as α helices and β sheets that are close to each other. Therefore, a motif is a cluster of SSEs and we define it as $M=\{sse_j|sse_j = \langle VL(A), VS(x,y,z), VE(x,y,z), VMP(x,y,z)\rangle \wedge j \in N \}$ and $M \subseteq SSE$. The relative spatial relationship between pairs of SSEs can be defined by six geometrical variables (see Figure 12).

Domain and Quaternary Structure. This entity class represents a compact globular structure composed of several motifs. It is defined as $D = \{ M_k \mid M_k \in M \wedge M \subseteq SSE \wedge k \in N \}$. When the protein of interest actually has more than one polypeptide chain, the interaction among chains will fold them further to form quaternary structures.

3.2 Relationships

Spatial-Aggregate. This construct (see Figure 7) is defined to capture the spatial arrangement of each atom in an amino acid to form the protein's 3-D structure. This is similar to the normal aggregate in existing spatial semantic models only in this case we want to represent the x, y and z coordinates of each atom. Each atom can be depicted as a point. *//P(deg)/P(deg)/P(deg)* suggesting that the position of this point can be measured using x, y and z coordinate in degrees. *//T(c)* is another dimension denoting the temperature (Celsius) at the time the structure was determined, because temperature changes affects the activities of atoms and relative positions change depending on the temperature. The relationship can be more concretely represented as

$spa < a_i, r_j, <x, y, z>>$ and $spa \in SPA$ where SPA is the complete set of spatial aggregate relationships within each structure, $SPA = \{ spa_l \mid spa_l = < a_i, r_j, <x, y, z>> \wedge a_i \in A \wedge r_j \in R \wedge l \in N\}$. The constraint $a_i \in A \wedge r_j \in R$ states which atom composes a which residue at what position, where x, y and z are the coordinates of each atom.

Sequential Aggregate. This is a concept borrowed from our previous work to model DNA sequences and primary protein sequences. This construct represents the fact that multiple amino acids/residues are bonded together in a specific linear order to form a sequence. $sea <r_i, ps_j, X>$ represents which residue is at which position of which protein sequence where $sea \in SEA$ and $SEA = \{ sea_m \mid sea_m = <r_i, ps_j, X> \wedge r_i \in R \wedge ps_j \in PSID \wedge X \leq SL \wedge m \in N \}$. *SL* represents the sequence length and *X* is an integer that represents the position of this residue in the sequence, where the position number has to be less than or equal to the length of the sequence.

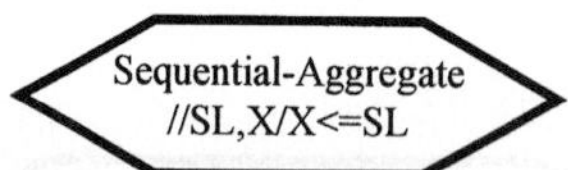

Fig. 8. Sequential-Aggregate Relationship

Ending_Point
Starting_Point
Fragment
(O)

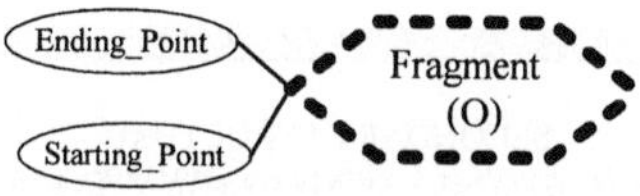

Fig. 9. Fragment Construct

Fragment. This relationship can be considered the exact opposite of the aggregation relationship. The "O" in this relationship represents the fact that segments can overlap, or one segment can contain another. The formal definition of this relationship is $frag < psid, segid, sp, ep>$ and $frag \in FRAG$ where $FRAG = \{ frag_n \mid frag_n = <psid, segid, sp, ep> \wedge psid \in PSID \wedge segid, n \in N, sp, ep \leq SL \}$. It says which segment is fragmented from which protein sequence starting and ending at what points. The length of the segment can be easily derived by subtracting the starting point from the ending point. A complete protein sequence contains several segments at different levels, where each segment contributes to a higher-level structure. For example, a segment of size 4 can form a 4-turn, several adjacent 4-turns can group together to form a helix. Helices further can group together to form motifs.

Spatial-Bonding. This relationship is used to describe how atoms in the structure form forces that contribute to the formation of secondary structure. A1 and A2 are the two atoms participating in the force. For hydrogen bonds. it specifies which two residues contribute to the bond. This is specified as: //HB (Hi, Oj)//BL(A)//BE(kcal/mol). BL records the bond length and BE is bond energy of the chemical force. From the value of i and j, the type of fold (i.e. α and β) can be determined.

Spatial-Bonding
//FORCES (A_1, A_2)//BL(A)//BE(kcal/mol)

Fig. 10. Spatial-Bonding Relationship

Spatial Composition
{SSEP(SSE_m, SSE_n)=(VL_m(A), VL_n(A), VD(m,n)(A), BA_m(deg), BA_n(deg), DA(m,n)(deg)) | m != n}

Fig. 11. Spatial Composition Relationship

Spatial Composition. This is a very complicated relationship that captures all geometrical data required to compare 3D structures based on the arrangement of secondary structures. As mentioned earlier, each secondary structure can be geometrically represented by a vector. Consider the two vectors Vm and V_n in Figure 12 as an example. Each of them has its own length denoted by VL_m and VL_n. Since the mid-point of each vector is recorded, the distance VD (m, n) between two vectors can be measured using the distance between the mid-points of the two vectors. Together with the two bond angles BA_m and BA_n as well as the dihedral angle between the two vectors DA (m, n), these variables can strictly define how two vector or secondary structure elements are arranged spatially. If there is a pair of SSEs (SSEP) in another protein structure that display the same geometrical arrangement, structure similarities may be inferred. With further analysis, the SSE pairs can be enlarged to accommodate more secondary structure elements to infer higher-level structure similarities. We can think of SSEPs as SSE groups of the finest granularity.

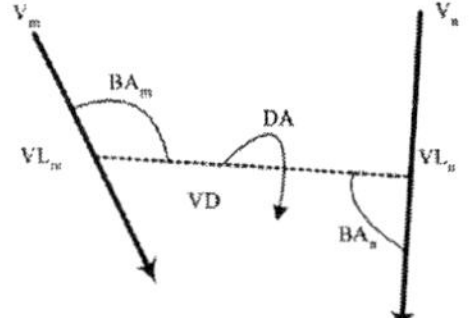

Fig. 12. Internal coordinates that represent spatial arrangements of a pair of vectors

4 Contributions and Utility of Our Semantic Model

We believe our model makes significant contributions because it brings out the hidden meaning behind the spatial arrangement of protein structures. This information is even more powerful when it is associated with the structure and formation of the bonding forces. Our model can facilitate easier data retrieval and analysis by the scientific community in following ways.

4.1 Database Integration

Being able to use structure data effectively and efficiently is the core of structural genomics [22] especially when there are number of resources using different data models. Ontologies are being developed in the field of bioinformatics to support data integration [14]. Most of this work is aimed at describing DNA sequence with particular focus on their function and how they react with other biological entities. Not much research has been directed at representing the structural complexity of biological data. Our model can serve as a canonical model for unifying different sources of protein structure data with all the semantics captured. This would save a lot of time and human resource in data curating and enable one-stop shopping.

4.2 Revolutionize Structure Search and Comparison

Current protein structure data is stored in flat files that cannot be easily queried or examined. Our model can represent the semantics of the data and facilitate development of user-friendly tools to browse, search, and extract protein structures. For instance, a model such as ours can be used to ask queries of the following type " For a specific protein with ID 1SHA, find all of its motifs, and retrieve the structural composition of each motif".

Protein structure prediction can be improved or perhaps even speeded up and also made easier by deploying our model. Instead of building various software tools and developing algorithms to compare and search structure on the top of flat file data, we can explore the possibility of extending an object-relational DBMS with specialized operators targeted at structure data. This approach is currently being explored by the latest Oracle 10g database management system that embeds data mining functionality for classification, prediction and association mining. One of the new features is that it incorporates the BLAST algorithm supporting sequence matching and alignment searches. But there is an obvious difference between the Oracle approach and our work presented in this paper. In Oracle 10g, the sequence data is still recorded as a text field. The BLAST operator is merely an interface based on flat files without capturing the semantics of sequence data.

As to the application of our proposed model, we can implement VAST or similar algorithms based on our semantic model into the DBMS. At the same time, new structure search and comparison operators can also be developed to extend SQL (Structured Query Language). For example, using our semantic model we capture the spatial composition of each secondary structure element in a protein. We can now define operators to compare the different SSEs based on their vector variables. Such a comparison operator can include thresholds for determining similarity. That is, if the vector length, vector angle, vector distance and vector dihedral angle comparison results are all within the corresponding thresholds then the SSEPs can be determined to be similar. Once such an operator is defined and implemented, we can extend it further to easily compare two 3D structures to find out what structures two proteins share in common and therefore determine the overall similarity between proteins. This will allow scientific users to easily query the data without having to learn advanced SQL operators and procedural languages.

4.3 Utility in Other Fields

Besides its application in bioinformatics, our semantic model can benefit other related fields such as Chemoinformatics [17]. Chemoinformatics is concerned with the application of computational methods to tackle chemical problems, with particular emphasis on the manipulation of chemical structure information. Therefore, it is essential in Chemoinformatics that researchers have effective and efficient approaches to store, search, and compare large quantities of complicated 2D or 3D structures of various chemical compounds. We are planning to extend our model for this field.

5 Future Research

The number of protein structures that are determined or calculated is increasing rapidly. Searching for and comparing structures is currently very complicated and have become major obstacles in the development of structural genomics.

Our work focuses on the semantics of bioinformatics data to understand and model 3-D protein structures. With this model, we hope to pave the way for standard and useful software tools for performing protein structure search more effectively and efficiently. We are continuing to extend this model to make it more complete. For example, we are elaborating on the chemical forces that contribute to the formation of secondary structures beyond hydrogen bonds. Other semantics are also being explored including the effects of solvent molecules. Based on our semantic model, a relational schema is being developed, and we are proposing new structure comparison and search operators. Even though implementation is not the focus of our research, we will be developing a prototype system as a proof-of-concept.

References

1. Altschul, S.F., Gish, W., Miller, W., Myers, E.W. and Lipman, D.J. Basic Local Alignment Search Tool. *Journal of Molecular Biology, 215*. 1990, 403-410.
2. Berman, H., Westbrook, J., Feng, Z., Gilliland, G., Bhat, T.N., Weissig, H., Shindyalov, I. and Bourne, P. The Protein Data Bank. *Nucleic Acids Research, 28* (1). 2000, 235-242.
3. Bhat, T.N., Bourne, P., Feng, Z., Gilliland, G., Jain, S., Ravichandran, V., Schneider, B., Schneider, K., Thanki, N., Weissig, H., Westbrook, J. and Berman, H. The PDB data uniformity project. *Nucleic Acids Research, 29* (1). 2001, 214-218.
4. Bourne, P., Berman, H., Mcmahob, B., Watenpaugh, K., Weissig, H. and Fitzgerald, P. The macromolecular CIF dictionary. *Meth, Enzymol,, 227* (571-590). 1997.
5. Bourne, P.E., Addess, K., Bluhm, W., Chen, L., Deshpande, N., Feng, Z., Fleri, W., Green, R., Merino-Ott, J., Townsend-Merino, W., Weissig, H., Westbrook, J. and Berman, H. The distribution and query systems of the RCSB Protein Data Bank. *Nucleic Acids Research,, 32* (Database Issue). 2004, D223-D225.
6. Branden, C. and Tooze, J. *Introduction to Protein Structure*. Garland Publishing, 1999.
7. Buttler, D., Coleman, M., Critchlow, T., Fileto, R., Han, W., Liu, L., Pu, C., Rocco, D. and Xiong, L. Querying Multiple Bioinformatics Information Sources: Can Semantic Web Research Help? *SIGMOD Record, 31* (4). 2002.
8. Chen, J., Anderson, J.B., DeWeese-Scott, C., Fedorova, N.D., Geer, L.Y., He, S. and Hurwitz, D.I. MMDB: Entrez's 3D-structure database. *Nucleic Acids Research, 31* (1). 2003, 474-477.
9. Chen, J.Y. and Carlis, J.V., Similar_Join: Extending DBMS with a Bio-specific Operator. in *Proceedings of the 2003 ACM Symposium on Applied Computing*, (Melbourne, FL, USA, 2003), 109-114.
10. Chen, P.P.-S. The Entity-Relationship Model-Toward a Unified View of Data. *ACM Transactions on Database Systems, 1* (1). 1976, 9-36.
11. Epstein, C.J., Goldberger, R.F. and Anfinsen, C.B. Cold Spring Harbor Symp. Speech. *Quant. Biol., 28*. 1963, 439.
12. Gerstein, M. Integrative database analysis in structural genomics. *Nature Structural Biology, Structural genomics supplement*. 2000.

13. Gibrat, J.-F., Madej, T. and Bryant, S.H. Surprising similarities in structure comparison. *Current Opinion in Structural Biology, 6*. 1996, 377-385.
14. Greer, D., Westbook, J. and Bourne, P. An ontology driven architecture for derived representations of macromolecular structure. *Bioinformatics, 18* (9). 2002, 1280-1281.
15. Holm, L. and Sander, C., 3-D Lookup: Fast Protein Structur Database Searches at 90% Reliability. in *Third International Conference on Intelligent Systems for Molecular Biology*, (Robinson College, Cambridge, England, 1995), AAAI Press, 179-187.
16. Kabsch, W. and Sander, C. Dictionary of Protein Secondary Structure: Pattern Recognition of Hydrogen-Bonded and Geometrical Features. *Biopolymers, 22*. 1983, 2577-2683.
17. Leach, A. and Gillet, V. *An Introduction to Chemoinformatics*. Kluwer Academic Publishers, 2003.
18. Madej, T., Gibrat, J.-F. and Bryant, S.H. Threading a Databse of Protein Cores. *Proteins: Structure, Function, and Genetics, 23*. 1995, 356-369.
19. Mizuguchi, K. and Go, N. Comparison of spatial arrangements of secondary structural elements in proteins. *Protein Engineering, 8* (4). 1995, 353-362.
20. Murthy, M.R.N. A fast methods of comparing protein structures. *FEBS, 168* (1). 1984, 97-102.
21. Stone, J., Wu, X. and Greenblatt, M. A Semantic Network for Modeling Biological Knowledge in Multiple Databases, University of Vermont Computer Science Technical Report, 2003.
22. Westbrook, J., Feng, Z., Chen, L., Yang, H. and Berman, H. The Protein Data Bank and Structural genomics. *Nucleic Acids Research, 31* (1). 2003, 489-491.
23. Westbrook, J., Feng, Z., Jain, S., Bhat, T.N., Thanki, N., Ravichandran, V., Gilliland, G., Bluhm, W., Weissig, H., Greer, D., Bourne, P. and Berman, H. The Protein Data Bank: unifying the archive. *Nucleic Acids Research, 30* (1). 2002, 245-248.

Risk-Driven Conceptual Modeling of Outsourcing Decisions*

Pascal van Eck[1], Roel Wieringa[1], and Jaap Gordijn[2]

[1] Department of Computer Science, University of Twente
P.O. Box 217, 7500 AE Enschede, The Netherlands
{vaneck,roelw}@cs.utwente.nl

[2] Department of Computer Science, Vrije Universiteit Amsterdam
De Boelelaan 1081, 1081 HV Amsterdam, The Netherlands
gordijn@cs.vu.nl

Abstract. In the current networked world, outsourcing of information technology or even of entire business processes is often a prominent design alternative. In the general case, outsourcing is the distribution of economically viable activities over a collection of networked organizations. To evaluate outsourcing decision alternatives, we need to make a conceptual model of each of them. However, in an outsourcing situation, many actors are involved that are reluctant to spend too many resources on exploring alternatives that are not known to be cost-effective. Moreover, the particular risks involved in a specific outsourcing decision have to be identified as early as possible to focus the decision-making process. In this paper, we present a risk-driven approach to conceptual modeling of outsourcing decision alternatives, in which we model just enough of each alternative to be able to make the decision. We illustrate our approach with an example.

1 Introduction

Current network technology reduces the cost of outsourcing automated tasks to such an extent that it is often cheaper to outsource the automated task than to perform it in-house. Automation decisions thereby become outsourcing decisions. In the simplest case, outsourcing is the delegation of value activities from one organization to another, but in the general case, it is the distribution of a set of value activities over a collection of networked organizations. Organization involved in negotiating about outsourcing must know as early as possible whether some allocation of activities to organizations is profitable. This precludes them from the costly modeling of functionality, data, behavior, communication structure and quality attributes of each possible alternative. To reduce this cost, a just-enough approach to conceptual modeling of possible solutions is needed, which allows a selection among alternatives without elaborate conceptual models of each.

In this paper, we present a risk-driven approach to conceptual modeling of alternatives in outsourcing decisions. The main advantage of our approach is that it provides,

* This work is part of the Freeband A-MUSE project. Freeband (http://www.freeband.nl) is sponsored by the Dutch government under contract BSIK 03025.

P. Atzeni et al. (Eds.): ER 2004, LNCS 3288, pp. 709–723, 2004.

with relatively little effort, a *problem structuring* of the outsourcing decision. The approach itself involves only very simple diagramming techniques, just enough to capture the structure of the problem while simple enough to present to stakeholders who do not have a background in conceptual modelling. The approach helps in identifying the parts of the problem for which we need to develop more detailed conceptual models using well-known techniques such as provided by the UML.

We illustrate our approach by a case study that is introduced in Section 2. The first step in our approach is based on the e^3*-value* method, which is presented in Section 3. The e^3*-value* method, which has been developed earlier by the third author, can be used to model and evaluate innovative business models for networked businesses (in this paper: outsourcing options) from the perspective of value created by each participant in a networked business. The e^3*-value* method is based on accepted conceptual notions from marketing, business science and axiology. It deliberately limits the number of modeling constructs such that the method is easy to learn and apply in practice. Using e^3*-value* , outsourcing decision alternatives for the case study are developed in Section 4. In Section 5, we present a systematic approach to identify risks associated with each option, which is applied to our case study and discussed in Section 6. Section 7 concludes the paper.

2 The NGO Example

We illustrate our approach with a real-life example of a collection of European Non-Governmental Organizations (NGOs) in the domain of international voluntary service. Each NGO sends out volunteers from its own country to projects offered by NGOs in other countries (as well as to its own projects) and accepts volunteers from other countries in its own projects. The purpose is to create possibilites for learning from other cultures and to help in local social development. The NGOs maintain contact with each other about projects offered and about volunteers, and there is a supranational umbrella organization that loosely coordinates the work of the (independent) NGOs. Some of the NGOs receive government subsidies, most do not. In the projects offered, only work is done that cannot be performed commercially.

Each NGO has a web site, a general ledger system for the financial administration, a simple workflow management system (WFM) to manage the workflow for matching each volunteer to a project, a project database of running projects, and a customer relationship management system (CRM) to manage information about volunteers that have shown interest in voluntary service. Since the NGOs vary widely in age, size and level of professionalism, and since they are independent, the implementations of these systems also vary widely and do not provide compatible interfaces. Recently, an application service provider (ASP) has offered to handle the WFM/CRM systems of all NGOs. The question to be solved is how this can be done such that the ASP makes money, while the NGOs are better off in terms of costs, quality, or both and the risks associated with the outsourcing solution chosen are manageable.

3 The e^3*-value* Method

The e^3*-value* methodology is specifically targeted at the design of business networks, as for example in e-commerce and e-business. Business networks jointly produce, distribute and consume things of economic value. The rapid spread of business networks, and of large enterprises that organize themselves as networks of profit and loss responsible business units, is enabled by the capability to interconnect information systems of various businesses and business units. In all cases, the trigger of an application of e^3*-value* are the networking opportunities perceived to be offered by information and communication technology (ICT). The use of e^3*-value* is then to explore whether the networking idea can really be made profitable for all actors involved. We do so by thoroughly conceptualizing and analyzing such a networked idea, to increase shared understanding of the idea by all stakeholders involved. The results of an e^3*-value* track are sufficiently clear to start requirements engineering for software systems. In the following, we will indicate networks of businesses and networks of business units by the blanket term *networked enterprises*. We will also call the software systems that support business processes *business systems*. Examples of business systems are information systems, workflow management systems and enterprise-specific application software.

Before the requirements on the information technology used by networked enterprises can be understood, the goals of the network itself need to be understood. More precisely, before specifying the business systems and communications between these, it is important to understand how various enterprises in the network create, distribute and consume objects of economic value. The e^3*-value* method has been developed in a number of action research projects as a method to determine the economic structure of a networked enterprise. These are real life projects in which the researcher uses the technique together with business partners, followed by a reflection on and improvement of the technique. For the business partners, these projects are not research but commercial projects where they pay for the results. The researcher has the dual aim to do a job for the business and to learn something from doing so.

We illustrate the concepts of e^3*-value* using Fig. 1, which shows a value model of the current network of NGOs.

Actor. An actor is perceived by its environment as an independent economic (and often also legal) entity. An actor intends to make a profit or to provide a non-profit service. In a sound, sustainable business model each actor should be capable of creating a net

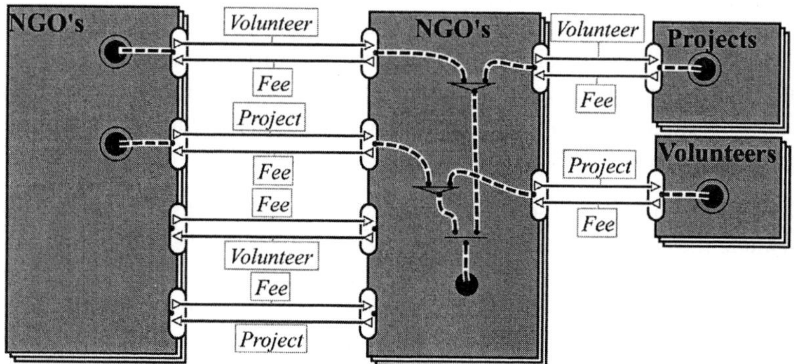

Fig. 1. Value Model of the current NGO network.

value. Commercial actors should be able to make a profit, and non-profit actors should be able to create a value that in monetary terms exceeds the costs of producing it in order to sustain. Each NGO, the umbrella organization, each project and each volunteer in our example is an actor.

Although this example is about non-profit organizations, the arguments to enter the network of cooperating NGOs are stated in terms of value added and costs saved by the members in this cooperation. This makes e^3-*value* a useful technique to solve the business problem whether a cooperation can be organized in such a way that value is added for all concerned.

Value Object. Actors exchange value objects, which are services, products, money, or even consumer experiences. A value object is of value to at least one actor. In Fig. 1, Assigned volunteer and Assigned project are value objects.

Value Port. An actor uses a value port to show to its environment that it wants to provide or request value objects. A value port has a direction, namely outbound (e.g. a service provision) or inbound (e.g. a service consumption). A value port is represented by a small arrowhead that represents its direction.

Value Transfer. A value transfer connects two equidirectional value ports of different actors with each other. It is one or more potential trades of value objects between these value ports. A value transfer is represented by a line connecting two value ports. Note that a value transfer may be implemented by a complex business interaction containing data transmissions in both directions [1]. The direction of a value transfer is precisely that: the direction in which value is transfered, not the direction of data communications underlying this transfer.

Value exchange. Value transfers come in economic reciprocal pairs, which are called value exchanges. This models 'one good turn deserves another': you offer something to someone else only if you get adequate compensation for it.

Value Interface. A value interface consists of ingoing and outgoing ports of an actor. Grouping of ingoing and outgoing ports model economic reciprocity: an object is delivered via a port, and another object is expected in return. An actor has one or more value interfaces, each modelling different objects offered and reciprocal objects requested in return. The exchange of value objects across one value interface is atomic. A value interface is represented by an ellipsed rectangle.

Market segment. A market segment is a set of actors that, for one or more of their value interfaces, ascribe value to objects in the same way from an economic perspective. Naturally, this is a simplification of the real world, but choosing the right simplifications is exactly what modeling is about. A market segment is represented by a stack of actor symbols. NGOs is an example of such a market segment.

With the concepts introduced so far, we can describe who exchanges values with whom. If we include the end consumer as one business actor, we would like to show all value exchanges triggered by the occurrence of one end-consumer need. This considerably enhances a shared understanding of the networked enterprise idea by all stakeholders. In addition, to assess the profitability of the networked enterprise, we would like to do profitability computations. But to do that, we must *count* the number of value exchanges triggered by one consumer need. To create an end-consumer need and do profitability computations, we include in the value model a representation of *dependency paths* between value exchanges. A dependency path connects value interfaces in an actor and represents triggering relations between these interfaces. A dependency path has a direction. It consists of dependency nodes and connections.

Dependency node. A dependency node is a stimulus (represented by a bullet), an AND-fork or AND-join (short line), an OR-fork or OR-join (triangle), or an end node (bull's eye). As explained below, a stimulus represents a trigger for the exchange of economic value objects, an end node represents a model boundary.
Dependency connection. A dependency connection connects dependency nodes and value interfaces. It is represented by a link.
Dependency path. A dependency path is a set of connected dependency nodes and connections with the same direction, that leads from one value interface to other value interfaces or end nodes of the same actor. The meaning of the path is that if a value exchange occurs across a value interface I, then value interfaces pointed to by the path that starts at interface I are triggered according to the and/or logic of the dependency path. If a branch of the path points to an end node, then this says "don't care".

Dependency paths allow one to reason about a network as follows: When an end consumer generates a stimulus, this triggers a number of value interfaces of the consumer as indicated by the dependency path starting from the triggering bullet inside the consumer. These value interfaces are connected to value interfaces of other actors by value exchanges, and so these other value interfaces are triggered too. This in turn triggers more value interfaces as indicated by dependency paths inside those actors, and so on.

Our value model now represents two kinds of coordination requirements: Value exchanges represent the need to coordinate two actors in their exchange of a value object, and dependency paths indicate the need for internal coordination in an actor. When an actor exchanges value across one interface, it must exchange value across all value interfaces connected to this interface. This allows us to trace the value activities and value exchanges in the network triggered by a consumer need, and it also allows us to estimate profitability of responding to this need in this way for each actor. For each actor we can compute the net value of the value objects flowing in and those flowing out according to the dependency path. The concept of a dependency path is reminiscent to that of use case maps [2], but it has a different meaning. A use case map represents a sequential scenario. Dependency paths represent coordination of value interfaces, and dependency paths in different actors may among each other not have an obvious temporal ordering, even if triggered by the same stimulus.

4 Example: Outsourcing Options for the NGO's

4.1 Current Value Model

In order to explore possibilities for outsourcing, we first discuss the current value model of the NGOs as presented in Fig. 1. The diagram shows the NGO market segment twice, because we want to show that there exists interaction between NGOs. An NGO serves two types of actors: Volunteers and projects. The task of a NGO is to match a volunteer to a project. If a match is successful, the project obtains a volunteer, and a volunteer obtains a project. Both the volunteer as well as the project pay a fee for this service. Volunteers need a project to work for; Projects need volunteers. These needs are shown in Fig. 1 by stimuli.

The match itself is represented as an AND-join. Following the paths connected to the join, it can be seen that for a match, a volunteer and a project is needed. These volunteers and projects can be obtained from the NGO's own customer base, or can be obtained from other NGO's as is represented by OR-joins.

Note that Fig. 1 shows only part of the dependency path. Specifically we represent that for matching purposes the rightmost NGO uses volunteers and projects from its own base or from other NGO's. However, the leftmost NGO's do also matching. Paths associated with these matchings are not presented. We skip the profitability estimations for this example, because these play no role in the following argument. The interested reader can find examples in earlier publications [3,4]. The e^3-*value* method includes tools to check well-formedness of models and to perform profitability analysis.

4.2 Option (1): ICT Outsourcing

A main concern for NGOs and the umbrella organization is to have cost-effective ICT support for their processes, while preserving or improving the quality of service offered to volunteers. Specifically, NGOs have indicated that the different WFM and CRM systems present in the NGOs are candidates for cost-cutting operations. We saw in our current problem analysis that each NGO exploits its own WFM and CRM. One option for cost-cutting is therefore to replace all these WFM and CRM systems by one system, to be used by all NGOs. This system can be placed at the unbrella organization, who then acts as an Application Service Provider (ASP). This means that NGOs connect to the Internet, and use the WFM and CRM system owned by the umbrella organization. To keep costs low, NGOs use a browser to interact with the WFM and CRM system of the umbrella. This leads to the value model in Fig. 2.

The exchanges introduced in Fig. 1 remain intact. The umbrella organization acting as ASP is introduced in the value model. In the value model we see that the ASP offers a matching service, i.e. the ASP offers an information system with the same main functionality as the old WFM and CRM application. Each NGO still has to perform the matching function (using the information system offered by the ASP). Thus, this is a case of IT outsourcing but not of business process outsourcing (BPO) This implies that the NGO interacts from a value perspective exactly the same as in Fig. 1.

4.3 Option (2): Business Process Outsourcing

A second option is to outsource the matching function itself to the umbrella organization (business process outsourcing, which includes ICT outsourcing). Fig. 3 show the value model of this. The matching is now done for all NGOs using the same base of volunteers and projects. This allows for doing global matching, rather than doing local matching for each NGO separately. In this solution, there is a drastic change in the value exchanges: Each NGO pays for a match to the umbrella organization. The role of a NGO is not so much the matching itself, but attracting volunteers and projects

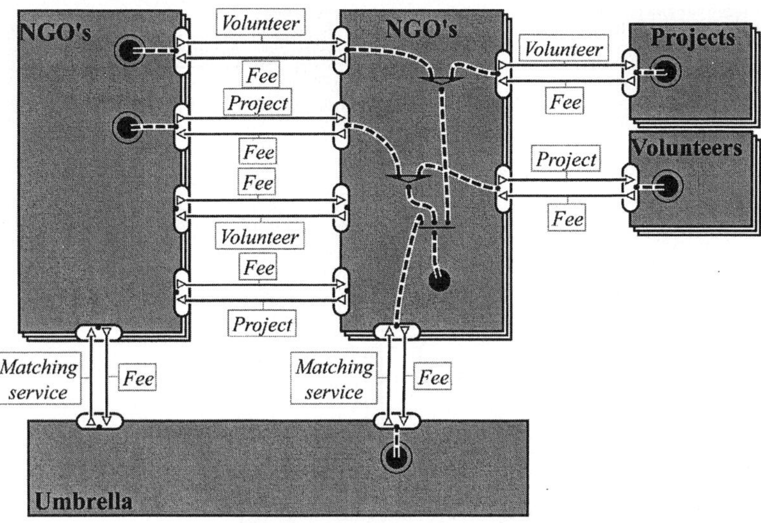

Fig. 2. Value Model for an ICT outsourcing solution.

in their specific region. So, exchanges between NGOs disappear. They exchange now value objects using the umbrella organization as an intermediate.

5 Concerns and Risks

In order to implement a value model, we need to model business processes, information manipulated by these processes, and other aspects of the technology support of the model. To prevent us from spending a lot of time on models that will not be used after an outsourcing option is chosen, we identify current business goals that will be used to discriminate different options. The goals are identified by listing current business issues, as illustrated in table 1. This table is explained later. Each outsourcing option will be evaluated with respect to these goals.

Furthermore, we will use a **concern matrix,** that lists all relevant system aspects that we possibly would want to model, and set this off against the major cost factor of each option, namely maintenance. Table 2 shows a concern matrix, that we will discuss later. We use a concern matrix to identify the risks asssociated with each option, where a risk is the likelihood of a bad consequence, combined with the severity of that consequence. Each cell in the concern matrix is evaluated by asking (i) what the risk is that this option cannot be realized, and (ii) what the risk is that the option under consideration will not achieve the business goals in this area.

The concern matrix allows us to reduce conceptual modeling costs in two ways. First, it prevents us from modeling in detail options that will not be chosen, and second, for the chosen option it will point us at aspects that need not be modelled because no risk is associated with them. Use of the issue/goal list and of the concern matrix are two tools in our method engineering approach to conceptual modeling. They allow us to select system aspects for which we will make conceptual models.

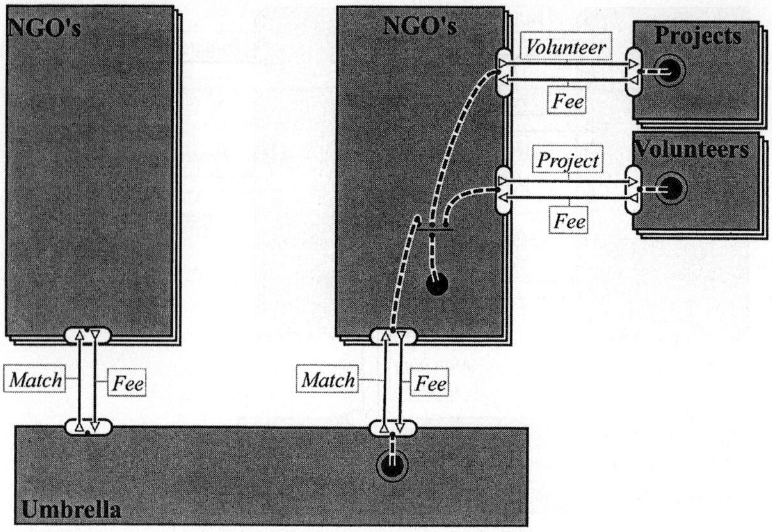

Fig. 3. Value Model for a business process outsourcing solution.

We now explain the two dimensions of the concern matrix in more detail. The horizontal dimension of the matrix distinghuishes five general aspects of any system. The universality of these aspects is motivated extensively in earlier publications [5, 6]. The relevance of these aspects follows from the fact that any specification of a system to be outsourced, must specify these aspects. Note that in this paper, a system equals an outsourcing option, i.e. outsourced ICT and/or business processes together with their context in an organization. We now briefly explain the system aspects.

- The *services* (or functions) provided by the system;
- The *data* (or information) processed and provided by the system;
- The *behaviour of a system*: the temporal order of interactions during delivery of these services.
- *Communication*: the communication channels through which the system interacts with other systems during service delivery.
- The *composition* of the system in terms of subsystems;

Our earlier publications [5, 6] distinguish a sixth aspect: the non-functional or *quality* aspect. In this paper, this aspect consists of attributes of the other aspects.

The vertical dimension of our concern matrix consists of several types of maintenance. *Maintenance* in this paper is defined as all activities that need to be performed to manage, control and maintain the ICT systems and procedures of an organization. Maintenance in this sense is also called IT service management. We need to consider maintenance because this embodies most of the costs of the entire system costs, and therefore contains most of the risk of an outsourcing option. By the same token, design and implementation of ICT systems (i.e., the work done by software engineers) is only a small part of the entire system cost and therefore contain only a small part of the risk of a design alternative. In addition, in the context of outsourcing, design and implementation are even less relevant: If existing ICT systems are outsourced, design and implementation have already been completed; if new business processes are outsourced, design and implementation of ICT systems that support these processes is the responsibility of the organization to which these processes are outsourced.

The maintenance dimension distinghuises three kinds of maintenance, namely functional, application and infrastructure [7], explained next.

- *Functional maintenance* consists both of maintenance of the set of services that an information system provides, as well as of supporting users in getting the most out of the set of services offered. This involves providing some form of helpdesk and user handholding, but also personnel and procedures to collect user requirements and turn them into a specification of required services. Functional maintenance is a responsibility of the user organization and is often performed by non-IT personel. Some of the users are partially freed from their normal duties and instead are given the task to help other users, perform acceptance tests, etc.
- *Application maintenance* consists of maintenance of the software that implements an information system (as well as, to a lesser extent, user support, e.g. providing a third-line helpdesk). Application maintenance is carried out mostly by IT personel, specifically programmers. Tasks include fixing bugs, implementing new functions, version and release management. ASL (Application Service Library) is a standard process model for application maintenance [8].
- *Infrastructure maintenance* comprises all tasks needed to provide the computer and networking infrastructure needed for the information systems of an organisation to run: configuration management, capacity management, incident management (including user support). ITIL (IT Infrastructure Library is a standard process model for application maintenance [9].

The maintenance dimension contains maintenance aspects of the outsourcing options, not of maintenance itself. This means for instance that the behaviour aspect is involved with the processes an outsourced system executes and not with processes needed for maintenance such as described by ASL and ITIL.

Table 1. NGO ICT policy goals and the issues they address.

Issue	Goal
Low quality of end-user support (personnel in primary processes)	**G1** Improve end-user support
Functionality inadequate due to long application release turnarounds: – Ad-hoc queries – Information exchange with other applications	Improve speed of adding new functionality: **G2a** Ad-hoc queries can be performed with short turnaround time. **G2b** Information exchange functions with other applications can be provided in months, not years.
Data pollution	**G3** Improve means for cleaning up data, either by end users or by databases administrator
Possible future European consolidation	**G4** Robustness w.r.t. future changes in fundamental way of working

Table 2. Concerns matrix for NGO. Changes in risks as opposed to the current situation. All entries name issues that lead to increased risk unless indicated otherwise.

	Services	Data	Behaviour	Communication	Composition
Functional maintenance	Options 1 & 2: helpdesk quality **(G1)**	Options 1 & 2: Ad hoc queries **(G2a)**	Option 1: none option 2: fundamental change in way of working Both: **G4**		
Application maintenance	Options 1 & 2: quality and availability of adaptive and corrective maintenance **(G2b)**	Options 1 & 2: DBA availability and quality **(G3)**		Options 1 & 2: interfaces with systems that are not outsourced **(G2b)**	
Infrastructure maintenance	Options 1 & 2: ASP network connection quality	Options 1 & 2: no DBMS needed (decreased risk)			

6 Example: NGO Outsourcing Concerns

Table 1 lists the goals with respect to which we will decide what concerns us in the outsourcing options. For each cell in the matrix, we ask whether it will help bring us closer to the goals, and what the risk is that it take us farther away from the goals. The resulting concern matrix is shown in Table 2. We now discuss the columns of the matrix.

6.1 The Behaviour Aspect

The current business processes operating in the NGOs are these:

- Core processes
  - — acquisition of own projects
  - — acquisition of own volunteers
  - — matching:
    - — placement of incoming volunteers in own projects
    - — placement of own volunteers in projects of other NGOs
  - — volunteer preparation (training)
- Management of the network of NGOs
  - — Entry and exit of an NGO in the NGO network
- Financial processes
- ICT support processes
- ICT management processes
- HRM processes
- Controlling processes
  - — policy making
  - — quality control
  - — incident response

At this moment, there is no need to elaborate this simple conceptual model of business processes, because we can already see what is the issue. In option (1), the ASP solution, has no impact on the business processes. However, in option (2), the BPO solution, one of the core processes (matching) no longer has to be executed. We can now ask the NGOs to decide whether this is good (more time to focus on project and volunteer acquisition and preparation) or bad (loss of strategic advantage).

Looking at our list of goals (table 1), we see that a second question to the NGO's is whether Options 1 and 2 facilitate possible future European consolidation.

6.2 The Communication Aspect

Fig. 4 shows the currently available business systems in each NGO. The figure shows a number of business systems in NGO1. Each system consists of people and technology, such as software, paper, telephones, fax, etc. Each NGO has systems with the same functionality, but different NGOs may use different people-technology combinations to implement this functionality. The diagram also shows a number of communication channels between these systems. We have labeled them to be able to refer to them below. Each communication channel is a means to share information between two actors. The meaning of the diagram is that each channel is reliable and instantaneous; if we want to include an unreliable communication channel with delays, we should include the channel as system in the diagram and connect it with lines to the systems communicating through the channel; the remaining lines then represent reliable instantaneous communication channels. The WFM system of NGO1 communicates with WFM systems in all other NGOs through channel E. Not shown is the fact that the communication between WFMs of different NGOs currently is done mostly by telephone, fax, email and paper mail. Fig. 4 also shows the context of NGO1, which consists of volunteers and projects (and other NGOs).

Option (1), the ASP solution, impacts the technology situation, as shown in the context diagram of Fig. 5(a). From an ICT perspective, there is now only one WFM/CRM application (instead of many different ones), but there are still as many instances of it as there were applications in the old situation, only they are now provided by one party, and they are all exactly the same. By doing so, the umbrella organization can exploit economies of scale and thus yield a more cost-effective ICT service for the NGOs. Interface E is now simplified because it is an interface between different instances of the same system. However, the other interfaces need to be redesigned, as the WFM/CRM application offered by the ASP is most probably different from the one the NGO used before. This means that either the ASP or each NGO has to manage integration middleware. Cross-organizational integration of enterprise applications is a relatively new phenomenon and is known to be complicated. Thus, the need for this technology adds considerable risk to outsourcing. The NGOs use the WFM/CRM applications exactly in the same way as before; their business processes do not have to change.

From an ICT perspective, option (2), the business process outsourcing solution, has one matching (WFM/CRM) system for all NGOs (Fig. 5(b)). Interface E now dis-

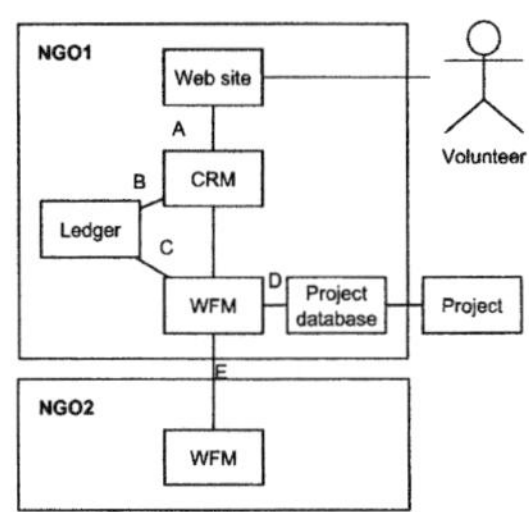

Fig. 4. Communication diagram of current situation.

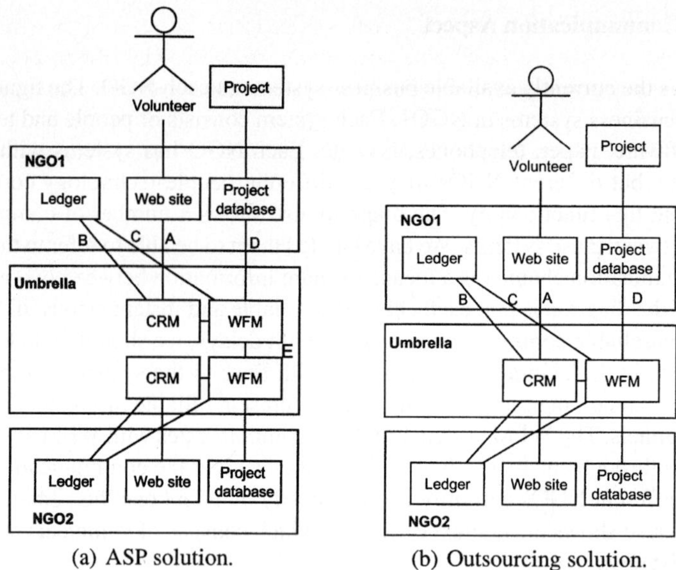

Fig. 5. Communication diagrams of software systems in the ASP and the outsourcing solutions.

appears. However, as in the ICT outsourcing option, the other interfaces have to be adapted.

6.3 The Services Aspect

Functional support/maintenance. The question in both outsourcing options is how user support ('handholding') is organised. One possibility is that the ASP provides a first-line helpdesk, either as part of a package deal (fixed price), or billed per incident. In this case, each NGO has to ask itself whether it thinks the ASP knows enough of this NGO to actually by able to understand user questions and respond to them in a helpful way (language is an issue here as well). For the ASP, this helpdesk is a new value object that can be added to the value models in Fig. 2 and Fig. 3 to get a more complete model. If the ASP does not offer a first-line helpdesk, each NGO has to appoint someone (most probably a 'power user') to provide support for other users. This person is then supported by a second-line helpdesk provided by the ASP.

Application support/maintenance. In application maintenance, often a distinction is made between corrective maintenance (fixing bugs, no new functions) and adaptive maintenance (implementing new user needs by adapting or building new functions).

- Corrective maintenance is equivalent with fixing bugs. It can be expected that in both options, the ASP is responsible for this. The NGO needs to convince itself that the ASP is up to this task.
- Adaptive maintenance. It can be expected that each NGO from time to time needs new functions. The ASP may provide a service that consists of building new func-

tions in the application provided, for instance billed by the hour or at a fixed, pre-negotiated price (this is a value object that the ASP may offer). The ASP may also use a collaborative, open-source based method. The ASP may also not offer adaptive maintenance. In this case all added functionality has to be implemented outside of the application offered by the NGOs themselves, which has implications for interfaces A–D.

Infrastructure support/maintenance. Infrastructure support/maintenance does not change significantly for the NGOs if the CRM/WFM application is outsourced to the ASP. Each NGO still needs to provide a local infrastructure to its personel consisting of workstations, a local area network, operating systems and personal productivity software. If the CRM/WFM application is outsourced, the NGO no longer needs to provide e.g. a database or application server (assuming it was only used for the CRM/WFM application), but maintenance of the Internet uplink becomes more important as it is a single point of failure: If it is unavailable, the outsourced application cannot be used.

6.4 The Data Aspect

Functional support/maintenance. The issue here are ad-hoc queries. From time to time, each NGO may want to do some one-time analysis of its data. (A realistic example is checking whether the NGO qualifies for a certain form of subsidy, e.g. related to the average age of its volunteers.) Strictly speaking, this belongs to the function aspect, as it requires a new function. In practice, however, it is not possible to treat a one-time analysis as a new function: there is not enough time to wait for a new release. The ASP may offer a kind of extended datatbase administration service that can run ad-hoc queries, or provide data-level access to the data sets to NGO, which would require a new interface next to A–D.

Application support/maintenance

- Information aspect, corrective maintenance. It is widely known that each and every data set sooner or later gets polluted with incorrect data. It may be the case that the application offered by the ASP provides a set of functions that enables end users to always manipulate all data, no matter what happened to it. It is perhaps more realistic to assume that every now and then, a database administrator is needed to correct things at the database level, either because no function is available for certain corrective actions, or it is more efficient (bulk updates). The ASP may offer a database administrator, either as part of a package deal (fixed price), or billed by the hour. The ASP may also decide to offer access at the database level to the NGOs, or both. For each NGO, this means that it has to decide whether to perform database maintenance itself, or buy it from the ASP.
- Information aspect, adaptive maintenance. This refers to changing the database scheme and most often also requires adapting existing functions to do something useful with the new scheme. Therefore, the same considerations hold as for the function aspect, adaptive maintenance.

Infrastructure support/maintenance. The NGO is able to save some costs as a database management system for the WFM and CRM applications is no longer needed.

6.5 Discussion

The concern matrix identifies issues to be taken into consideration when choosing between options. It also identifies aspects of the chosen option to be elaborated in conceptual models. So it saves us work in two ways: (1) It prevents us from detailed conceptual modeling when choosing options and (2) it prevents us from modeling all aspects of an option once chosen.

Identification of possible outsourcing options (Section 4) and the risks associated with them (Section 6) enabled the NGO to focus its internal decision process as well as discussions with the ASP provider. So far, none of the options have been found to be unacceptable. The next step for the NGO is to further elaborate the options by designing high-level models of support processes and estimating the costs associated with them. Moreover, the NGO needs to look deeper into the interfaces needed with the outsourced application. This will involve modelling the data exchanged to get an idea of the effort needed to design these interfaces. The ASP may, based on discussions with the NGOs, further extend its offerings, which can be modelled with additional e^3*-value* models.

7 Conclusions

We presented an approach to quickly identify alternatives for outsourcing decisions and the risks associated with them, using a few simple diagramming techniques (value models, a bulleted list as a process model, and communication diagrams). The main value of this approach is that it provides, with relatively little effort, insight into the *structure* of the outsourcing *problem* at hand. This insight is needed to identify the parts of the problem that warrant more detailed conceptual modelling efforts using well-known techniques such as entity-relationship modelling. The problem structure also quickly reveals enterprise application integration (EAI) problems introduced by outsourcing.

We plan to further develop our value-based approach to design and analysis of e-business systems. This involves for instance systematic ways of deriving business processes from a value model [1]. Furthermore, we plan to investigate the relation between our approach and Quality Function Deployment (QFD/House of Quality) [10]. QFD provides a systematic way to compare alternative solutions to a design problem with respect to quality attributes. We think that our approach can be used to identify which quality attributes are important in a given outsourcing problem, as well as to identify alternative solutions. In this way, QFD may be usable as an extension to our approach.

References

1. van Eck, P., Gordijn, J., Wieringa, R.: Value-based design of collaboration processes for e-commerce. In Yuan, S.T., Liu, J., eds.: Proceedings 2004 IEEE International Conference on e-Technology, e-Commerce and e-Service, EEE'04, IEEE Press (2004) 349–358

2. Buhr, R.J.A.: Use case maps as architectural entities for complex systems. IEEE Transactions on Software Engineering **24** (1998) 1131–1155
3. Gordijn, J., Akkermans, J.M.: Designing and evaluating e-Business models. IEEE Intelligent Systems - Intelligent e-Business **16** (2001) 11–17
4. Gordijn, J., Akkermans, J.: Value-based requirements engineering: Exploring innovative e-commerce ideas. Requirements Engineering Journal **8** (2003) 114–134
5. Wieringa, R.: A survey of structured and object-oriented software specification methods and techniques. ACM Computing Surveys **30** (1998) 459–527
6. Wieringa, R.J.: Design Methods for Reactive Systems: Yourdon, Statemate, and the UML. Morgan Kaufman (2003)
7. Looijen, M.: Information Systems, management, control and maintenance. Ten Hagen & Stam (1998)
8. van der Pols, R.: ASL , a Framework for Application Management. Van Haren Publishing (2004)
9. Office of Government Commerce: ITIL Service Support. The Stationary Office (2000)
10. Herzwurm, G., Schockert, S., Pietsch, W.: QFD for customer-focused requirements engineering. In Wieringa, R., Chang, C., Sikkel, K., eds.: 11th IEEE International Requirements Engineering Conference (RE'03), IEEE Computer Society Press (2003) 330–340

A Pattern and Dependency Based Approach to the Design of Process Models

Maria Bergholtz, Prasad Jayaweera, Paul Johannesson, and Petia Wohed

Department of Computer and System Sciences
Stockholm University/Royal Institute of Technology
Forum 100, SE-164 40 Kista, Sweden
{maria,prasad,pajo,petia}@dsv.su.se

Abstract. In this paper an approach for building process models for e-commerce is proposed. It is based on the assumption that the process modeling task can be methodologically supported by a designers assistant. Such a foundation provides justifications, expressible in business terms, for design decisions made in process modeling, thereby facilitating communication between systems designers and business users. Two techniques are utilized in the designers assistant, namely process patterns and action dependencies. A process pattern is a generic template for a set of interrelated activities between two agents, while an action dependency expresses a sequential relationship between two activities.

1 Introduction

Conceptual models have become important tools for designing and managing complex, distributed and heterogeneous systems, e.g. in e-business and e-commerce, [2, 17]. In e-commerce it is possible to identify two basic types of conceptual models: business models and process models. A business model focuses on the *what* in an e-commerce system, identifying agents, resources, and exchanges of resources between agents. Thus, a business model provides a high-level view of the activities taking place in e-commerce. A process model, on the other hand, focuses on the *how* in an e-commerce system, specifying operational and procedural aspects of business communication. The process model moves into a more detailed view on the choreography of the activities carried out by agents.

A business model has a clearly declarative form and is expressed in terms that can be easily understood by business users. Therefore, business models function well for supporting communication between systems designers and business users. In contrast, a process model has a more procedural form and is at least partially expressed in terms, like sequence flows and gateways, that are not immediately familiar to business users. Furthermore, it is often difficult to understand why a process model has been designed in a certain way and what consequences alternative designs would have. In order to overcome these limitations, we believe that process models should be complemented by and be based on a more declarative foundation. Such a foundation would provide justifications, expressible in business terms, for design decisions made in process modeling, thereby facilitating communication between systems designers and business users. In this paper, we propose a designers assistant that provides a declarative foundation for process modeling suggests a method for gathering domain knowledge. The work reported in this paper extends the work of [1] and [10] in that we propose two instruments for a declarative foundation of process models:

P. Atzeni et al. (Eds.): ER 2004, LNCS 3288, pp. 724–739, 2004.

process patterns and action dependencies. A process pattern is a generic template for a set of interrelated activities between two agents, while an action dependency expresses a sequential relationship between two actions.

The rest of the paper is organized as follows. Section 2 presents the notions of business models and process models. Section 3 introduces process patterns and makes a distinction between transaction patterns and collaboration patterns. Section 4 discusses action dependencies. Section 5 proposes a designers assistant that supports a designer in the construction of a process model. Section 6 concludes the paper and gives suggestions for further research.

2 Business Models and Process Models

For illustrating business and process models, a small running case is introduced. It is a simplified version of the Drop-Dead Order business case described in [8]. In this business scenario, a Customer requests an amount of fried chicken from a Distributor. The Distributor then requests formal offers from a Chicken Supplier and a Carrier. Furthermore, the Distributor requests a down payment from the Customer before accepting the offers from the Chicken Supplier and Carrier. As the Customer completes the down payment to the Distributor, the Distributor accepts the offer from the Chicken Supplier by also paying a down payment and the offer from Carrier. When the Chicken Supplier has provided the fried chicken and the Carrier has delivered them to the Customer, the Distributor has thereby fulfilled the Customer's order. After that, the Customer settles the final payment to the Distributor. Finally, the Distributor settles the Chicken Supplier's final payment and the payment for the Carrier.

2.1 Business Models

As a foundation for business models, we will use the REA ontology [13], which has been widely used for business modeling in e-Commerce, [17]. The REA framework is based on three main components: Resources, Economic Events, and Agents, see Fig. 1[1]. An Agent is a person or organization that is capable of controlling Resources and interacting with other Agents. A Resource is a commodity, e.g. goods or services that is viewed as being valuable by Agents. An Economic Event is the transfer of control of a Resource from one Agent to another one. Each Economic Event has a counterpart, i.e. another Economic Event that is performed in return and realizing an exchange. For instance, the counterpart of a delivery of goods may be the payment of the same goods. This connection between Economic Events is modeled through the relationship *Duality*.

Furthermore, a Commitment is a promise to execute a future Economic Event, for example fulfilling an order by making a delivery. The Duality between Economic Events is inherited by the Commitments, where it is represented by the association *Reciprocal*. In order to represent collections of related Commitments, the concept of Contract is used. A Contract is an aggregation of two or more reciprocal Commitments. An example of a Contract is a purchase order composed of one or several

[1] Due to space restrictions and for the purpose of readability we use abbreviated forms of the terms in the original REA ontology. This is done by dropping the term 'Economic' for Economic Contract, Economic Commitment, Economic Resource, and Economic Agent.

order lines, each one representing two Commitments (the goods to be delivered and the money to be paid for the goods, respectively).

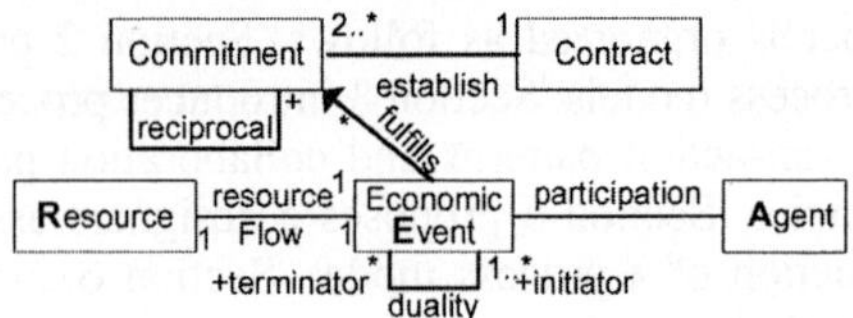

Fig. 1. REA basis for business models

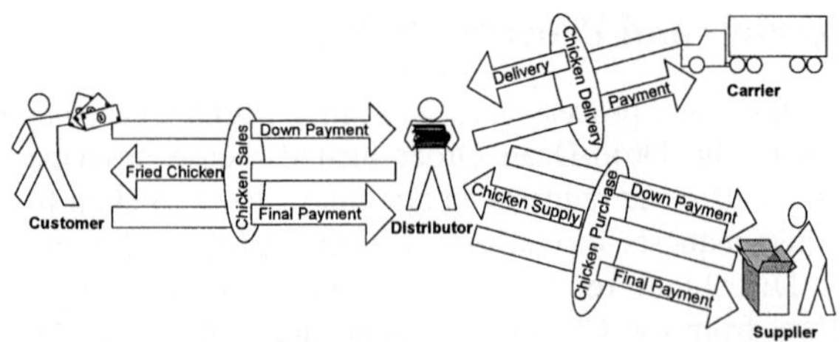

Fig. 2. Business Model for the Fried Chicken Business Case

A business model based on REA will consist of instances of the classes Resource, Economic Event and Agent as well as the associations between these. The business model for the running case described above can be visualized as in Fig. 2. Here, arrows represent Economic Events labeled with relevant Resources. The transfer of resource control from one Agent to another is represented by the direction of arrows. Ellipses represent relationships between Economic Events belonging to the same Duality.

2.2 Process Models

The notation we will use for process models is BPMN [4], a standard developed by the Business Process Management Initiative (BPMI) [3]. The goal of BPMN is to be a easily comprehensible notation for a wide spectrum of stakeholders ranging from business domain experts to technical developers. A feature of BPMN is that BPMN specifications can be readily mapped to executable XML languages for process specification such as BPEL4WS, [2].

In this paper, a selected set of core elements from BPMN have been used. These elements are Activities, Events, Gateways, Sequence flows, Message flows, Pools and Lanes. Activity is a generic term for work that an Agent can perform. In a BPMN Business Process Diagram (abbreviated BPMN diagram), an Activity is represented by a rounded rectangle. Events, represented as circles, are something that "happens" during the course of a business process. There exist three types of Events: Start, End and Intermediate Events. Activities and Events are connected via Sequence Flows that show the order in which Activities will be performed in a process. Gateways are used to control the sequence flows by determining branching, forking, merging, and joining of paths. In this paper we will restrict our attention to XOR and AND branching, graphically depicted as a diamond with an 'X' or a '+', respectively. Lanes and Pools are graphical constructs for separating different sets of Activities from each other. A

Lane is a sub-partition within a Pool used to organize and categorize Activities. Message flows depicted as dotted lines are used for communication between Activities in different Pools. (An example of them appear later in Fig. 12)

An example of a BPMN diagram is shown in Fig. 3. The diagram shows a single Business Transaction in one pool with three lanes. A Business Transaction is a unit of work through which information and signals are exchanged (in agreed format, sequence and time interval) between two Agents [17]. A Business Transaction consists of two Activities, one Requesting Activity where one Agent initiates the Business Transaction and one Responding Activity where another Agent responds to the Requesting Activity. (See Fig. 4)

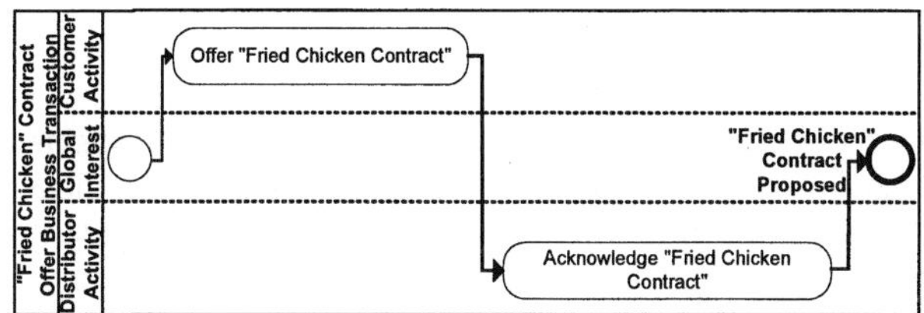

Fig. 3. Example of a BPMN diagram

Several Business Transactions between two Agents can be combined into one binary Business Collaboration. It turns out that it is often fruitful to base binary Business Collaborations on Dualities, i.e. one Business Collaboration will contain all the Business Transactions related to one Duality. This gives a starting point for constructing a process model from a business model. Each Duality in the business model gives rise to one binary Business Collaboration, graphically depicted as a BPMN diagram in a Pool. In this way, a process model will be constructed as a set of interrelated Business Collaborations.

Furthermore, a binary Business Collaboration can naturally be divided into a number of phases. Dietz, [6], distinguishes between three phases. The Ordering phase, in which an Agent requests some Resource from another Agent who, in turn, promises to fulfill the request. The Execution phase, in which the Agents perform Activities in order to fulfill their promises. The Result phase, in which an Agent declares a transfer of Resource control to be finished, followed by the acceptance or rejection by the other Agent. The ISO OPEN-EDI initiative [15] identifies five phases: Planning, Identification, Negotiation, Actualization and Post-Actualization. In this paper, we use only two phases: a *Contract Negotiation phase* in which contracts are proposed and accepted, and an *Execution phase* in which transfers of Resources between Agents occur and are acknowledged. In the next section, we will discuss how a binary Business Collaboration can be constructed utilizing patterns for these phases.

3 Generic Process Patterns

Designing and creating business and process models is a complicated and time consuming task, especially if one is to start from scratch for every new model. A good designer practice to overcome these difficulties is, therefore, to use already proven solutions. A *pattern* is a description of a problem, its solution, when to apply the solution, and when and how to apply the solution in new contexts [11]. The significance of a pattern in e-commerce is to serve as a predefined template that encodes business rules and business structure according to well-established best practices. In this paper such patterns are expressed as BPMN diagrams. They differ from the workflow patterns of [18], [16], [19] by focusing primarily on communicative aspects, while control flow mechanisms are covered on a basic level only.

In the following sub sections, a framework for analyzing and creating transaction- and collaboration patterns is proposed. We hypothesize that most process models for e-commerce applications can be expressed as a combination of a small number of these patterns.

3.1 Modeling Business Transactions

When a transaction occurs, it typically gives rise to effects, i.e. Business Entities like Economic Events/Contracts/Commitments are effected (created, deleted, cancelled, fulfilled). Furthermore, the execution of a transaction may cause the desired effect to come into existence immediately, or only indirectly, depending on the intentions of the interacting Agents. For example, the intention of an Agent in a transaction may be to *propose* a Contract, to *request* a Contract or to *accept* a Contract. In all three cases the business entity is the same (a Contract) but the intention of the Agent differs.

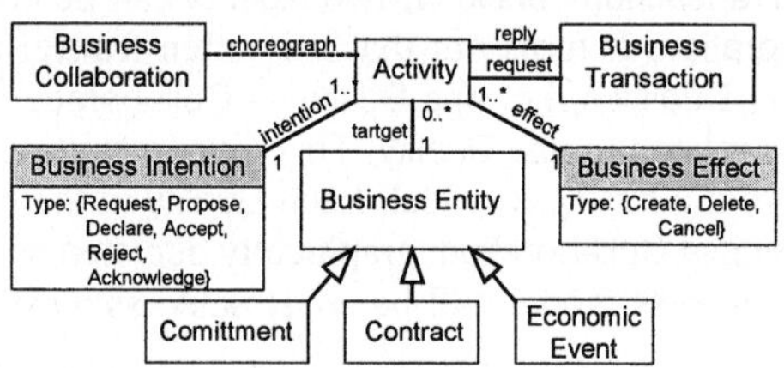

Fig. 4. Business Transaction analysis

Fig. 4 builds on REA and suggests a set of Business- Intentions, Effects and Entities. These notions are utilized in defining transaction patterns and transaction pattern instances as follows.

Definition: A *transaction pattern* (TP) is a BPMN diagram with two Activities, one Requesting Activity and one Responding Activity. Every Activity has a label of the form <Intention, Effect, Business Entity>, where Intention ∈ {Request, Propose, Declare, Accept, Reject, Acknowledge}, Effect ∈ {create, delete, cancel}, and Business Entity ∈ {aContract, anEconomicEvent, aCommitment}. All End Events are labeled according to the Intention and Business Entity of the Activity prior to the sequence flow leading to the End Event.

Intuitively, the components of an activity label mean the following:

- Business Entity tells what kind of object the Activity may effect.
- Effect tells what kind of action is to be applied to the Business Entity – create, delete or cancel.
- Intention specifies what intention the business partner has towards the Effect on the Business Entity.

The meanings of the intentions listed above are as follows:

- Propose – someone offers to create, delete or cancel a Business Entity.
- Request – someone requests other Agents to propose to create,
- delete or cancel a Business Entity.
- Declare – someone unilaterally declare a Business Entity created, deleted or cancelled.
- Accept/Reject – someone answers a previously given proposal.
- Acknowledge – someone acknowledges the reception of a message.

Definition: A *pattern instance* of a transaction pattern is a BPMN diagram derived from the pattern by renaming its Activities, replacing each occurrence of aContract in an activity label with the name of a specific Contract, replacing each occurrence of anEconomicEvent in an activity label with the name of a specific EconomicEvent, and replacing each occurrence of aCommitment in an activity label with the name of a specific Commitment.

3.2 Transaction Patterns (TPs)

In the following sections three basic Contract Negotiation and two Execution TPs are suggested based on the framework described above.

3.2.1 Contract Negotiation TPs

The Contract-Offer TP models one Agent proposing an offer (<propose, Create, aContract>) to another Agent who acknowledges receiving the offer. The acceptance or rejection of an offer is modeled in the Contract-Accept/Reject TP, see Fig. 5.

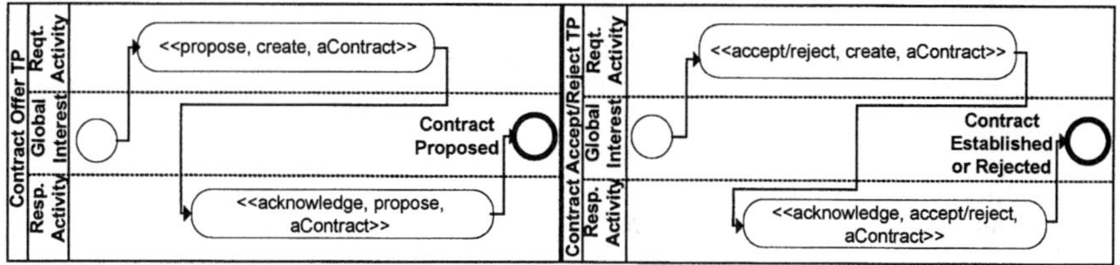

Fig. 5. TPs for Contract Negotiation: Contract-Offer and Contract-Accept/Reject

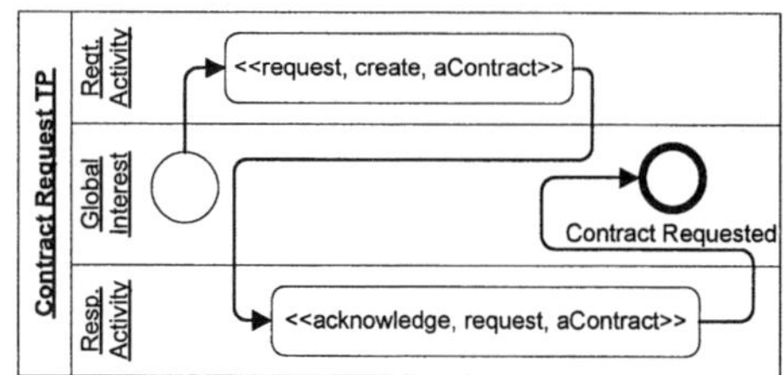

Fig. 6. TP for Contract Negotiation: Contract-Request

Fig. 6 models the Contract Request case where an Agent requests of other Agents to make an offer for aContract on certain Resources.

3.2.2 Execution TPs

We introduce two Execution TPs (see Fig. 7) that specify the execution of an Economic Event, i.e. the transfer of Resource control from one Agent to another. An example is a Chicken Distributor selling Chickens (a Resource) for $3 (another Resource).

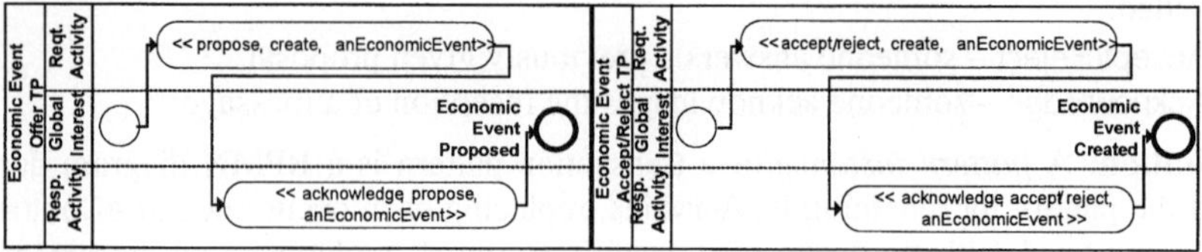

Fig. 7. TPs for Execution: Economic Event Offer and Economic Event Accept

3.3 Assembling Transactions Patterns into Collaboration Patterns

An issue is how to combine the transaction patterns described in the previous section, i.e. how to create larger sequences of patterns. For this purpose, collaboration patterns define the orchestration of Activities by assembling a set of transaction patterns and/or more basic collaboration patterns based on rules for transitioning from one transaction/collaboration to another.

To hide the complexity when TPs are combined into arbitrarily large collaboration patterns, we use a layered approach where the TPs constitute activities in the BPMN diagram of the collaboration patterns.

Definition: A *collaboration pattern* (CP) is a BPMN diagram where the activities consist of transaction and collaboration pattern(s). A CP has exactly two end events representing success or failure of the collaboration, respectively. All end events are labeled according to the Intention and Business Entity of the Activity prior to the sequence flow that led to the end event.

3.3.1 Contract Negotiation CPs

The Contract Establishment CP, see Fig. 8, is assembled from the Contract-Offer and Contract-Accept/Reject TPs. An example scenario is a Chicken Distributor proposing an offer to a customer on certain terms. The contract is formed (or rejected) by the customers acceptance or rejection of the proposed offer.

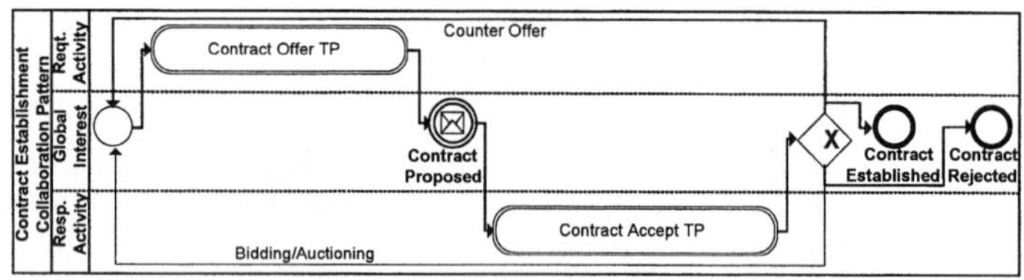

Fig. 8. Contract Establishment CP

The two recursive paths when a contract offer/request has been rejected have a natural correspondence in the business negotiation concepts 'Counter Offer' and 'Bidding' (or 'Auctioning') respectively. 'Counter Offer' refers to the switch of roles between Agents, i.e. when the responding Agent has rejected the requesting Agents offer, the former makes an offer of her own. 'Bidding' is modeled via the other sequence Flow from the gateway, i.e. when the responding Agent has turned down a contract offer, the requesting Agent immediately initiates a new Business Transaction with a new (changed) offer for Contract.

The Contract-Proposal collaboration pattern, Fig. 9[2], is assembled from the Contract-Request TP and the Contract-Establishment CP defined above.

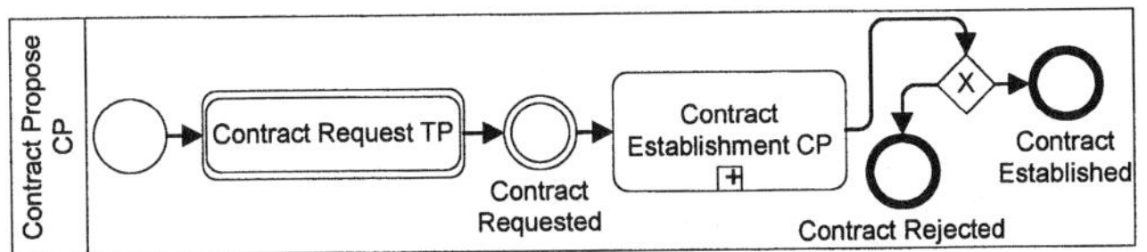

Fig. 9. Contract Propose CP

3.3.2 Execution CP

The execution collaboration pattern specifies relevant TPs and rules for sequencing among these within the completion of an Economic Event. The pattern is assembled from the Offer-Event and Accept/Reject Event TPs.

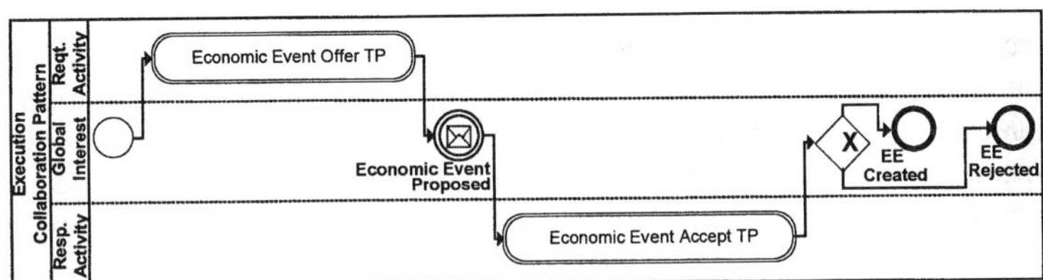

Fig. 10. Execution CP

4 Action Dependencies

The process patterns introduced in the previous section provide a basis for a partial ordering of the activities taking place in a business process, in particular the ordering based on contract negotiation and execution. We will refer to the activities involved in the different phases of a process as *contract negotiation* or *execution* activities respectively. However, the ordering derived from the process patterns only provide a starting point for designing complete process models, i.e. it needs to be complemented by additional interrelationships among the activities. These interrelationships should have a clear business motivation, i.e. every interrelationship between two activities should be explainable and motivated in business terms. We suggest to formalize this idea of business motivation by introducing the notion of action dependencies. An *action dependency* is a pair of actions (either economic events or activities), where the second action for some reason is dependent on the first one. We identify the following four kinds of action dependencies.

Flow dependencies. A flow dependency, [12], is a relationship between two Economic Events, which expresses that the Resources obtained by the first Economic Event are

---

2 When a CP is composed of other CPs, no lanes can be shown as the Requesting and Responding Activities are already encapsulated.

required as input to the second Economic Event. An example is a retailer who has to obtain a product from an importer before delivering it to a customer. Formally, a flow dependency is a pair <A, B>, where A and B are Economic Events from different Dualities.

Trust dependencies. A trust dependency is a relationship between two Economic Events within the same Duality, which expresses that the first Economic Event has to be carried out before the other one as a consequence of low trust between the Agents. Informally, a trust dependency states that one Agent wants to see the other Agent do her work before doing his own work. An example is a car dealer who requires a down payment from a customer before delivering a car. Formally, a trust dependency is a pair <A, B>, where A and B are Economic Events from the same Duality.

Control dependencies. A control dependency is a relationship between an execution Activity and a contract negotiation Activity. A control dependency occurs when one Agent wants information about another Agent before establishing a Contract with that Agent. A typical example is a company making a credit check on a potential customer (i.e. an exchange of the Resources information and money in two directions). Formally, a control dependency is a pair <A, B>, where A is an execution Activity and B is a contract negotiation Activity and where A and B belong to different Dualities.

Negotiation dependencies. A negotiation dependency is a relationship between Activities in the contract negotiation phase from different Dualities. A negotiation dependency expresses that an Agent is not prepared to establish a contract with another Agent before she has established another contract with a third Agent. One reason for this could be that an Agent wants to ensure that certain Resources can be procured before entering into a Contract where these Resources are required. Another reason could be that an Agent does not want to procure certain Resources before there is a Contract for an Economic Event where these Resources are required. Formally, a negotiation dependency is a pair <A, B>, where A and B are contract negotiation Activities in different Dualities.

5 A Designers Assistant

In this section, we will show how a process model can be designed based on process patterns and action dependencies. Designing a process model is not a trivial task but requires a large number of design decisions. In order to support a designer in this task, we propose an automated designers assistant that guides the designer through the task by means of a sequence of questions, divided into four steps, followed by a fifth step where the process model is generated based on the answers to questions in step 1-4, see Fig. 11.

Step 1. during which information is gathered about the Agents involved in the business process, the Resources exchanged between them, and the Economic Events through which these Resources are exchanged. The result from this step is a business model.

Step 2. during which information about the (partial) order between the Economic Events is gathered. The result from this step is an ordering of the Activities in the Execution phase of a process model.

Step 3. during which information about existing negotiation dependencies is gathered. The result from this step is an ordering of the Activities in the Negotiation phase.

Step 4. during which inter phase and inter pool dependencies are established. The result from this step is an ordering of Activities that crosses the Negotiation and Execution phases.

Step 5. during which a set of production rules are applied on the results of the previous steps in order to generate a process model.

Fig. 11. Steps of the Designers Assistant

5.1 Step 1 – Business Model

In order to produce a business model the following four questions need to be answered. Answers according to the running case are given after every question.

1. *Who are the Agents?* Answers: Customer (Cust), Distributor (Dist), Chicken Supplier (Supp), Carrier (Carr)
2. *What are the Resources?* Answers: Money, Chicken, Delivery
3. *What are the Economic Events? Specify them by filling in the following table.*

Table 1. Answers to question 3

Name of Economic event	Transferred Resource	From Agent	To Agent
DownPayToDist	DownPayment	Cust	Dist
FinalPayToDist	FinalPayment	Cust	Dist
ChickenToCust	Chicken	Dist	Cust
DownPayToSupp	DownPayment	Dist	Supp
FinalPayToSupp	FinalPayment	Dist	Supp
ChickenToDist	Chicken	Supp	Dist
DeliveryToDist	Delivery	Carr	Dist
PayToCarr	Payment	Dist	Carr

4. *Group the Economic Events into Dualities by filling in the following table.*

Table 2. The answers to question 4

Economic event	Duality
DownPayToDist	Chicken Sales
FinalPayToDist	
ChickenToCust	
DownPayToSupp	Chicken Purchase
FinalPayToSupp	
ChickenToDist	
DeliveryToDist	Chicken Delivery
PayToCarr	

The answers to these four questions provide sufficient information to produce the business model shown in Fig. 2.

5.2 Step 2 – Execution Phase Order

Having identified the Economic Events, the designer is prompted to determine the dependency orders. In this step only flow and trust dependencies are considered.

5. *Specify* Flow *and* Trust Dependencies *by filling in the table below* (where the row and column headings are Economic Events identified in question 4). *If an* $EconomicEvent_i$ *(in row i) precedes an* $EconomicEvent_j$ *(in column j): put a '<' symbol in the corresponding cell (cell <i,j>). The '<' symbol is to be subscripted with 'f' or 't' depending on the type of dependency.*

Table 3. Answers to the question 5 in the assistant

	DPTD	FPTD	CTC	DPTS	FPTS	CTD	DTD	PTC
DownPayToDist (DPTD)			$<_t$	$<_{f(1)}$				
FinalPayToDist (FPTD)					$<_{f(5)}$			$<_{f(4)}$
ChickenToCust (CTC)		$<_t$						
DownPayToSupp (DPTS)						$<_t$		
FinalPayToSupp (FPTCS)								
ChickenToDist (CTD)			$<_{f(2)}$		$<_t$			
DeliveryToDist (DTD)			$<_{f(3)}$					$<_t$
PayToCarr (PTC)								

The input from this step will be sufficient to roughly sketch the Execution phase in the BPMN diagram See the shaded area in Fig. 12 where for every Duality a pool is created. The numerical notes in the table are used to refer to the resulting sequence and message flows in the model. However, some dependencies, e.g. "$<_{f(1)}$" are later on overridden by refined orders and are then reduced from the final model.

5.3 Step 3 – Contract Negotiation Phase Order

After having gathered sufficient information to produce the BPMN diagram for the Execution phase, the analysis continues for the Contract Negotiation phase. As there are two ways for initiating a binary Business Collaboration according to the suggested collaboration patterns in Section 3, it is first necessary to identify which of these patterns to use for each binary collaboration.

6. *For each binary Business Collaboration, ask whether*
   (a) a quotation already exists when the binary collaboration starts, or
   (b) the binary collaboration is started by a partner requesting a quotation.

If the answer is (a) then the contract establishment collaboration pattern of Fig. 8 will be chosen. If the answer is (b) then the contract proposal collaboration pattern of Fig. 9 will be chosen.

Below, the answers to question 6 for the running case are given in bold.

6.1 **(a)** ***Does a quotation already exist when the Cust-Dist collaboration starts, or***
(b) *is the Cust-Dist collaboration started by a partner requesting a quotation?*

6.2 (a) *Does a quotation already exist when the Dist–Supp collaboration starts, or*
(b) ***Is the Dist–Supp collaboration started by a partner requesting a quotation?***

6.3 (a) *Does a quotation already exist when the Dist-Carr collaboration starts, or*
(b) ***is the Dist-Carr collaboration started by a partner requesting a quotation?***

Note that abbreviated Agent names are used here in naming the collaborations above. The answers from this question are used to derive the beginning of each binary collaboration (see the white area in Fig. 12). We continue by identifying the negotiation and control dependencies.

7. *Specify the* Control *and* Negotiation Dependencies *by filling in the following table,* (where the row and column headings are pattern instantiations identified in questions 4 and 6). *If an Activity*[3] *(in row i) precedes an Activity (from column j) put a '$<_n$' symbol (for negotiation dependency) or a '$<_c$' symbol (for control dependency) in the corresponding cell (i.e. cell <i,j> in the table).*

Due to space restrictions and since the running case does not contain any control dependencies, we depict contract negotiation Activities only in Table 4.

Table 4. Answers to the running case for question 7

	COCD	CECD	CRDS	CODS	CEDS	CRDC	CODC	CEDC
Contract-Offer:Cust-Distr (COCD)			$<_{n(a)}$			$<_{n(b)}$		
Contract-Accept/Reject:Cust-Distr (CECD)								
Contract-Request:Distr-Supp (CRDS)								
Contract-Offer:Distr-Supp (CODS)		$<_{n(c)}$						
Contract-Accept/Reject:Distr-Supp (CEDS)								
Contract-Request:Distr-Carr (CRDC)								
Contract-Offer: Distr-Carr (CODC)		$<_{n(d)}$						
Contract-Accept/Reject: Distr-Carr (CEDC)								

Note, that the relationships within a binary collaboration are given by the process patterns and we have therefore crossed out the corresponding cells. The results from this question will give input for ordering of the activities from the Contract Negotiation phase across the binary collaborations. The alphabetical notes in the table refer to the resulting flows in the process model in Fig. 12.

5.4 Step 4 – Refined Order

In the first three steps, the Agents and Economic Events were identified. Furthermore, the activities in the Execution phase were ordered within and between binary Busi-

[3] Formally the contents of the rows are *TP instances* (see Section 3.1), but for simplicity, we have referred to each TP instance by its first Activity.

ness Collaborations as well as the activities in the Contract Negotiation phase. In this step, we identify relationships that cross binary collaborations as well as Execution and Contract Negotiation phases.

8. *For each pair of Economic Events <EE_i, EE_j> (see Table 3), such that $EE_i <_f EE_j$: Is it required to perform EE_i before making a contract acceptance for EE_j, (i.e. a Contract Establishment between the Agents in EE_j)?*

The intuition behind this question is that an Agent may want to ensure that she has definite access to certain Resources before she is prepared to enter into a Contract for some product where these Resources are needed as input. It is possible to think about this question as a strengthening of a flow dependency – we say not only that EE_j cannot be performed before we have got the Resources from EE_i, but even that we are not prepared to enter into a Contract for EE_j before we have got the Resources from EE_i.

Below, the implementation of question 8 for the running case is given with answers.

8.1	*Must DownPayToDist be done before establishment of Dist-Supp Contract?*	Yes
8.2	*Must FinalPayToDist be done before establishment of Dist-Supp Contract?*	No
8.3	*Must FinalPaytToDist be done before establishment of Dist-Carr Contract?*	No
8.4	*Must ChickenToDist be done before establishment of Dist-Cust Contract?*	No
8.5	*Must DeliveryToDist be done before establishment of Dist-Cust Contract?*	No

9. *For each triple of Economic Events in table 3, EE_i, EE_j, EE_k, such that $EE_i <t\ EE_j$ and $EE_k <_f EE_j$: Is it required to perform EE_i before making a contract acceptance for EE_k (i.e a Contract Establishment between the Agents in EE_k)?*

This question can be seen as a strengthening of a trust dependency. It says not only that we want to see another Agent perform EE_i before we perform EE_j, but that we want to see our partner to perform EE_i before we even start acquiring resources needed to perform EE_j.

Below, the implementation of question 9 for the running case with answers.

9.1	*Must DeliveryToDist be done before establishment of Cust-Dist Contract?*	No
9.2	*Must ChickenToDist be done before establishment of Cust-Dist Contract?*	No
9.3	*Must DownPayToDist be done before establishment of Dist-Supp Contract[4]?*	No
9.4	*Must DownPayToDist be done before establishment of Dist-Carr Contract?*	Yes

5.5 Business Process Generation

The final step of the proposed designers assistant is the generation of a BPMN diagram based on the answers from steps 1 – 4. This is achieved using the binary collaboration patterns introduced in Section 3 and a set of production rules to interconnect those instantiated binary collaborations into a multi-party collaboration. The set of production rules that are proposed can be categorized into four groups: *Rules for Binary Collaborations* (within a pool), *Rules for Inter-Collaborations* (between pools), *Reduction Rules*, and *Deadlock Prevention Rules*. However, due to space limitations, only the first two categories are summarized informally here.

---

[4] Case 9.3 is already covered by case 8.1 and only shown here for reasons of completeness.

Rules for Binary Collaborations

1. For each duality, introduce a binary collaboration contained in one pool. Such a collaboration will start with an instantiation of the BPMN diagram Contract Propose CP, (Fig. 9), if the answer to question 6 is a), otherwise the binary collaboration starts with an instantiation of the Contract Establish CP, (Fig. 8).
2. The BPMN diagram in a pool continues with instantiations of the Fig. 10 pattern, one for each Economic Event identified through question 5 in the designers assistant. These collaborations will initially be in parallel.
3. For each trust dependency between two Economic Events, introduce a sequence flow between the corresponding execution activities.

Rule for Inter-collaborations

1. For each flow dependency between two Economic Events, introduce a message flow between the corresponding execution activities.
2. For each control and negotiation dependency between two activities, introduce a message flow between these activities.
3. For each positive answer to questions 8 and 9, introduce a message flow between the relevant activities.

The BPMN diagram generated by these rules for the running case is shown in Fig. 12. (A formal definition of the generation via the production rules is found in Chapter 7 of [9])

6 Conclusions and Further Work

In this paper, we have proposed an approach for building process models on a declarative foundation. A starting point of the approach is that the process modeling task can be supported by gradually gathering domain knowledge, initially for the construction of business models and subsequently for their refinement and transformation into process models. The proposed designers assistant is structured on a division of e-commerce interactions into two phases: a Contract Negotiation Phase where a contract for exchanging economic resources is established; and an Execution Phase where the actual exchanges of the economic resources take place. We believe that this phase division provides an adequate starting point, but a topic for further work is to investigate more refined phase divisions, [6], [15].

The proposed approach is based on the concept of process patterns. A framework for representing process patterns is introduced, together with a number of basic process patterns. Two kinds of process patterns are identified: transaction patterns, basically capturing small communication chunks between two agents; and collaboration patterns, which are compositions of transaction patterns facilitating the representation of complex interactions. The value of this framework is not only that it provides an instrument for precise and unambiguous pattern definitions, but also that it gives a basis for motivating design choices in process modeling.

Finally, we also introduce the notion of action dependencies for capturing relationships between the activities within a process. Four kinds of dependencies are identified: flow, trust, control and negotiation dependencies. They can be stated declaratively, have a clear business motivation, and are used for the final derivation of a process model. A topic for further work is to investigate whether additional kinds of action dependencies are required.

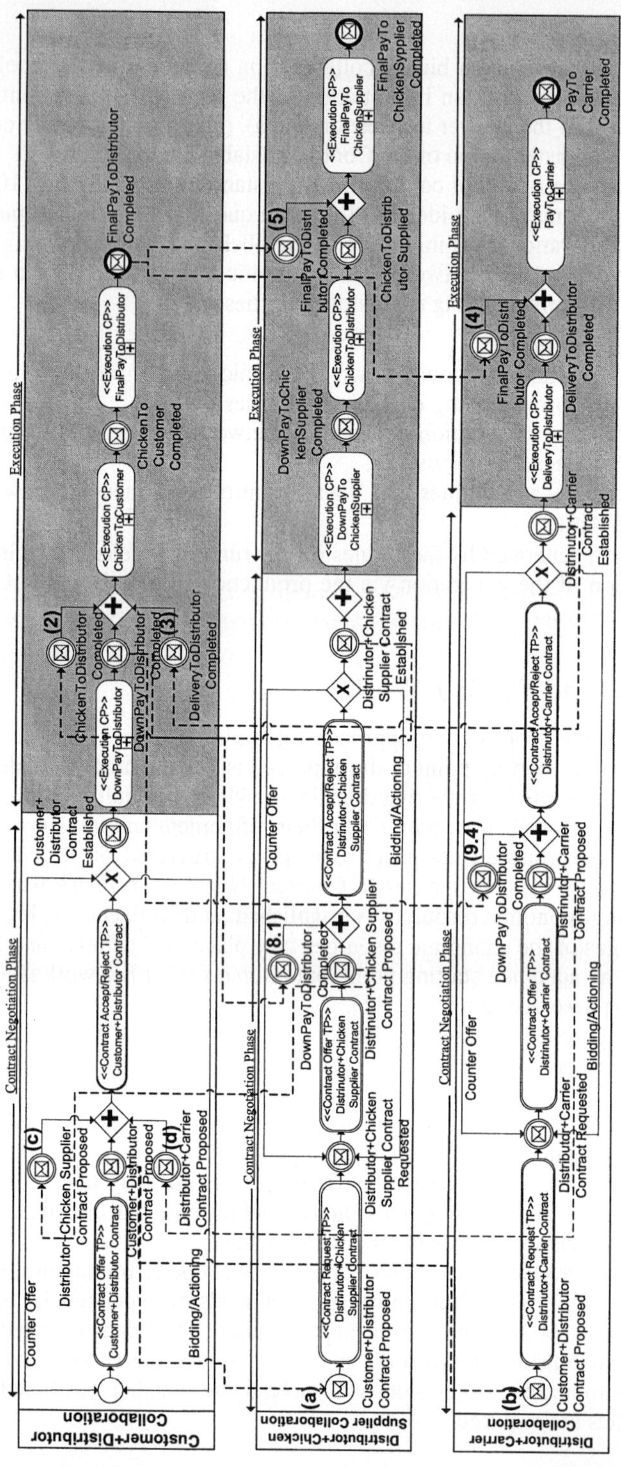

Fig. 12. Final BPNM diagram for Fried Chicken Case

A further line of future work is to examine the quality of the produced models, during which their completeness as well as their logical soundness should be investigated. While the work on completeness can primarily be done through empirical studies, the work on logical soundness can be supported by theoretical work like the one given in [5].

References

1. Bergholtz M., Jayaweera P., Johannesson P., Wohed P., "Reconciling Physical, Communicative and Social/institutional Domains in Agent Oriented Information Systems – a Unified Framework", in Proc. of AOIS'03, held in conjunction with the *22nd, Int. Conference on Conceptual Modeling (ER'2003)*,Chicago, Illinois, USA
2. *Business Process Execution Language for Web Services*, OASIS WS-BPEL Technical Committee, Valid on 20040419, http://www.ebpml.org/bpel4ws.htm
3. *Business Process Management Initiative (BPMI)*, Valid on 20040419, http://www.bpmi.org/
4. *Business Process Modeling Notation (BPMN)*, http://www.bpmn.org/, Valid on 20040419
5. Chrzastowski-Wachtel P., Benatallah B., Hamadi R., O'Dell M., and Susanto A., "A Top-Down Petri Net-Based Approach for Dynamic Workflow Modeling", in Proc. of *Business Process Management Int. Conf.*, W. van der Aalst, A. ter Hofstede and M. Weske (Eds.), LNCS 2678, pp.336-353, Springer, 2003
6. Dietz J., "Deriving Use Cases from Business Process Models", in Proc. of *22nd Int. Conference on Conceptual Modeling (ER'2003)*,Chicago, Illinois, USA. LNCS 2813, pp. 131-143, 2003
7. Gordijn J., Akkermans J. M. and Vliet J. C., "Business Modeling, is not Process Modeling", Proc. of the *1st Int. Workshop on Conceptual Modeling Approaches for e-Business (eCOMO'2000)*, at 19th Int. Conference on Conceptual Modeling (ER'2000), Salt Lake City, Utah, USA
8. Haugen B., Fletcher T., "*Multi-Party Electronic Business Transactions*", Valid on 20040419, http://www.ebpml.org/archive1.htm
9. Jayaweera P., "*A Unified Framework for e-Commerce Systems Development: Business Process Patterns Perspective*", PhD thesis, ISBN 91-7265-938-6, Valid on 20040419, http://www.dsv.su.se/~prasad/Publications/Thesis.pdf
10. Jayaweera P., Johannesson P., Wohed P., "Collaborative Process Patterns for e-Business", *ACM SIGGROUP Bulletin 2001/Vol 22, No. 2*
11. Larman C., "*Applying UML and patterns: an introduction to object oriented analysis and design*", ISBN 0-13-74880-7
12. Malone et al.: "*Towards a handbook of organizational processes*", MIT eBusiness Process Handbook, Valid on 20040419, http://ccs.mit.edu/21c/mgtsci/index.htm
13. McCarthy W. E., "*REA Enterprise Ontology*", Valid on 20040419, http://www.msu.edu/user/mccarth4/rea-ontology/
14. Moore S. A., "A foundation for flexible automated electronic communication", *Information Systems Research*, 12:1 (March 2001)
15. *Open-EDI phases with REA*, UN-Centre for Trade Facilitation and Electronic Business, Valid on 20040419, http://www.unece.org/cefact/docum/download/02bp_rea.doc
16. *The workflow patterns*, Valid on 20040419, http://tmitwww.tm.tue.nl/research/patterns/
17. *UN/CEFACT Modeling Methodology (UMM-N090 Revision 10)*, Valid on 20040419, http://webster.disa.org/cefact-groups/tmg/doc_bpwg.html
18. van der Aalst W.M.P., ter Hofstede A.H.M., Kiepuszewski B., and Barros A.P., "Workflow Patterns", *Distributed and Parallel Databases*, 14(3), pages 5-51, July 2003
19. van Dijk A., "Contracting Workflow and Protocol Patterns", in Proc. of Business Process Management Int. Conf., W. van der Aalst, A. ter Hofstede and M. Weske (Eds.), LNCS 2678, pp.152-167, Springer, 2003

Use of Tabular Analysis Method to Construct UML Sequence Diagrams

Margaret Hilsbos and Il-Yeol Song

College of Information Science and Technology, Drexel University,
Philadelphia, PA 19104, USA
{mhilsbos,song}@drexel.edu

Abstract. A sequence diagram in UML is used to model interactions among objects that participate in a use case. Developing a sequence diagram is complex; our experience shows that novice developers have significant difficulty. In earlier work, we presented a ten-step heuristic method for developing sequence diagrams. This paper presents a tabular analysis method (TAM) which improves on the ten-step heuristic method. TAM analyzes the message requirements of the use case, while documenting the resulting analysis in a tabular format. The resulting table is referenced to build the sequence diagram. This process aids novice modelers by separating the problem analysis from the learning curve of a modeling tool. Building sequence diagrams with the systematic approach of TAM facilitates consistency with the use case model and the class model. We found that developers effectively developed sequence diagrams using TAM.

1 Introduction

A sequence diagram is a type of interaction diagram, which is used in UML to depict a set of messages between objects which participate in a use case [2, 13]. Objects in a sequence diagram are typically instances of classes, and the messages passed between objects invoke operations of the receiving classes [12]. If we accept as axiomatic that the elements of a sequence diagram should be consistent with their corresponding elements in the other diagrams of the system model, then there we need straightforward construction methods which help the modeler achieve this consistency.

While seemingly intuitive, methods for constructing a sequence diagram have not been discussed much in literature. Our experience shows that novice developers have significant trouble in understanding and developing sequence diagrams. Most UML books simply explain the notations and semantics and present pre-built sequence diagrams. Some authors provide simple guidelines for developing sequence diagrams. We found that those simple guidelines are not sufficient for many novice developers. Most research activities on sequence diagrams have focused on real time systems [6, 17], simulation [4] or behavior-driven analysis and design. Very few authors even mentioned possible methods, processes or steps that could be used to develop effective sequence diagrams.

Li [7] proposed using a parser to semi-automatically translate use case steps into "message records" which can be used to construct a sequence diagram. The parser produces a tabular listing of classes, objects, and operations, based on the syntactic structure of each sentence in the use case steps. The modeler can then apply this information to create the sequence diagram. Li's method relies on first "normalizing" the expression of the use case steps to a somewhat rigorous grammatical model. This

P. Atzeni et al. (Eds.): ER 2004, LNCS 3288, pp. 740–752, 2004.

normalization depends on a modeler's English-language skills. Furthermore, although normalization of the vocabulary and expressions of use cases theoretically may be beneficial, it may not always be feasible in real-world projects because the use case is primarily for communication with users, not for input to a computer program.

1 Select the initiating actor and initiating event from the use case description.

2 Identify the primary display screen needed for implementing the use case. Call it the *Primary boundary object.*

3 Create a *use-case controller* (*primary control object*) to handle communication between the primary boundary object and domain objects.

4 If the use case involves any included or extended use case, create one *secondary control object* for each of them.

5 Identify the number of major screens necessary to implement the use case. Create one *secondary boundary object* for each of the major screens and create one *secondary control object* for each of them.

6 From the class diagram, list all *domain* classes participating in the use case by reviewing the use case description. If any class identified from the use case description does not exist in the class diagram, add it to the class diagram.

7 Use those classes just identified as block labels (Column names) in the sequence diagram. List classes in the following order: (1) The primary boundary stereotype, (2) The primary use case controller, (3) Domain classes (list in the order of access), and (4) Secondary control objects and secondary boundary objects in the order of access

8 Identify all problem-solving operations based on the following classifications:

8.1 Instance creation and destruction

8.2 Association forming

8.3 Attribute modification:

8.3.1 Calculation;

8.3.2 Change States

8.3.3 Display or reporting requirements

8.3.4 Interface with external objects or systems

These problem-solving operations can be identified by:

- Identify verbs from the use case description
- Remove verbs used to *describe* the problem; select verbs used to solve the problem. We call these verbs *problem-solving verbs(PSVs).*
- From the problem-solving verbs, select verbs that represent an automatic operation. We call these PSVs *problem-solving operations(PSOs)* and use them in the sequence diagram.

9 Rearrange the sequence of messages among the object classes based on any pre-existing design patterns, when possible.

10 Name each message and supply it with optional parameters. This can be done at design stage as well.

Fig. 1. The Ten-Step heuristics [18]

Song [18] introduced a heuristic-based approach (Figure 1) to constructing sequence diagrams. The technique instructs the modeler to pull appropriate elements from the prerequisite model artifacts (the use case description and the analysis class diagram), and induces some consistency in the resulting model. Our paper proposes an enhancement to the heuristic approach of [18]. Similarly to [7], our proposed method results in a tabular listing of message records. However, while [7] requires "normalization" of the use case steps, our method proposed here requires only that the use case be clear and unambiguous, and that ultimately agreement between the use case and the sequence diagram can be confirmed.

The enhanced method, referred to as the *tabular analysis method* (TAM), consists essentially of reordering the steps of Song's ten-step heuristic (referred to as the "original heuristic"), sequentially applying the reordered steps to each action in the use case activity flow, and documenting the resulting analysis in a tabular format. The tabular data can then be used as a reference to build the diagram relatively quickly in a modeling tool. Some advantages of the tabular method over the original heuristic are:

- The step-by-step process of the TAM is defined in more detail, which should be helpful to novice modelers to conceptualize and visualize the building process.
- With the TAM, a more comprehensive model is relatively easy to construct: the tabular format presents the modeler with all elements to be considered for an operation in an easy-to-read format, which encourages thoroughness in modeling parameters, constraints, etc. – resulting in a more semantically complete model with minimal added effort.
- Tool-independence: the tabular data could be exported to an XMI file (see [10]) and then uploaded into the modeling tool of choice, to create the model elements. A further conversion of the XMI file to an SVG file (see [11]) could fully automate the diagram creation from the table. While the theorized automation capability has not yet been developed, if this potential is realized, the tabular method presented here will have significant added value.

By using the method proposed in this paper, the modeler can express the analysis in a more commonly familiar tool (a word processor or spreadsheet program), and then reference the analysis worksheet while learning how to construct the elements in the CASE tool. In other words, this method separates two analytic processes so that each can be more fully attended to by students or novice modelers.

The rest of this paper is organized as follows. Section 2 discusses issues related to the consistency among UML elements that need to be maintained for the accurate sequence diagrams. Section 3 presents our TAM for constructing sequence diagrams with examples, and Section 4 concludes the paper.

2 Model Consistency

Sequence diagrams share model elements with use cases and class diagrams. In this section, we discuss consistency issues among use case models, class diagrams, and sequence diagrams.

2.1 Consistency with the Use Case Model

A sequence diagram represents the design for fulfilling the requirements expressed in a use case [5]. The use case elements which should be reflected in the sequence diagram are postconditions, actions, and related use cases (included, extending, and specialized). The postconditions in the use case description specify what state of the system must be true upon successful completion of the use case [5]. If the sequence diagram depicts all the behavior required for successful completion of the use case, it follows that each postcondition specified in the use case description must be achieved by some message in the set of sequence diagrams for that use case. Conversely, if the use case postconditions accurately define the system state, it follows that the use case description should identify as postconditions all final states resulting from execution of the use case behavior detailed by the sequence diagram.

Each action specified or implied in the use case description should be detailed in a corresponding message or set of messages in the sequence diagram. Depending on the clarity and completeness of the use case description text, the author of the sequence diagram may need to infer some of the operations. Song [18] presents several categories for identifying operations: instance creation and destruction, association forming, attribute modification, calculation, change of states, display or reporting, and interface with external objects or systems. Each action in the use case description will require one or more of these message types for its fulfillment.

2.2 Consistency with the Class Diagram

From the literature review, we have identified several areas where consistency between class diagrams and sequence diagrams can be easily confirmed: classes, operations, arguments, visibility between objects, and composition responsibility.

Classes. All entity classes used in a sequence diagram must appear in the Class Diagram. Conversely, if sequence diagrams are completed for all use cases within the project scope, all entity classes shown on the design class diagram must be used in at least one sequence diagram, with the exception of some or all abstract classes. Abstract classes *may* be shown in certain cases [9, 15]; but generally the receiver of a message is a concrete class - the lowest class in its hierarchy to which all instances addressed by the message could belong [15].

Operations. For an object to handle a message that it receives, it must have a conforming interface, which is defined in the receiver's class as an operation signature [12, 8]. Therefore, all messages shown on the sequence diagram must map to operations of the receiving class in the class diagram. A temporary message name may be assigned before the class operation has been designed.

Arguments. A sequence diagram message may transfer information to the receiver as arguments. Arguments must represent information that is known to the sender, such as attribute values or constants. Depending on the intended precision of the model, the sequence diagram may not show all the relevant arguments [3]. However, some parameters should always be shown, such as an object or parameter that is being passed among multiple other objects [3]. Some practitioners choose not to show all (or even any) return messages [12]. Pender argues that it is worth the effort to model operations and returns completely, to avoid ambiguity [12].

Visibility (Relationships Between Classes). In order for objects to exchange messages, the sending object must have a handle to the receiving object [15]. Another way of saying this is that the sender must have *visibility* to the receiver. Some authors state or imply that a message between two objects in a sequence diagram requires a permanent association (association, generalization, or aggregation) to be shown between the classes in the class diagram [1]. Others note that there are *four types of visibility* possible between objects – attribute visibility, parameter visibility, local visibility, and global visibility [5, 14] – and that only attribute visibility requires a permanent association [16]. Messages which rely on parameter, local, or global visibility to a class require a *temporary*, or *transient*, association between the classes [16]. A transient association is modeled on the class diagram as a *dependency* instead of an association, with an arrow depicting the direction of the dependency [5, 14]. To summarize, consistency between the class diagram and the sequence diagram requires that for each message in the sequence diagram, the class diagram depicts either a permanent association or a dependency, according to the type of visibility required, between the classes of the sender and receiver. Conversely, if an association depicted on the class diagram is never used in an interaction, then there must be an error in the model [1].

Composition Responsibility. If the class diagram depicts a whole-part (composition, or strict aggregation) relationship between two classes, then the whole should create the part [5, 14]. In the sequence diagram, this is depicted by first creating the composite (probably with a create() message from a controller), then using the composite as the sender for the create() message to the part.

3 Constructing Accurate Sequence Diagrams with TAM

In this section, we present our tabular analysis method (TAM) for constructing accurate sequence diagrams in a manner that enforces consistency with the use case, while promoting consistency with the class diagram as well. The TAM uses the ten-step heuristic introduced in [18] as a starting point, and applies it methodically to each step in the use case description. The TAM takes the procedures expounded in [18] as follows:

- A system sequence diagram (SSD) is constructed first, treating the system as a "black box" and modeling only the actions visible to the actor. These actions are called system events [5].
- Each system event may be documented in one detailed sequence diagram; or details for multiple system events may be combined in one sequence diagram.
- A separate sequence diagram will be constructed for each included or extending use case.
- A separate controller is used for the base use case, and each included or extending use case, and functions as a "connector" between the sequence diagrams.
- Actors communicate with boundary objects, which communicate with controllers, which communicate with the entity objects. Normally, actors do not communicate directly with controller or entity objects.

The TAM uses a tabular format called Sequence Analysis Table (SAT) which captures the list of use case actions by adding columns for source and receiving objects, message names and parameters. Figure 2 shows a condensed version of the empty template. The table used here can also be thought of as a condensed version of the Tabular Notation described in the UML 2.0 specification [13]. A Sequence Analysis Table is created for the primary use case and each included or extending use case. The overall process of the TAM can be summarized as follows:

- From the use case description, create a *system sequence analysis table (SSAT)* to create a system sequence diagram. Note that each line here is an input system event from an actor to a system or an output from the system to an actor.
- Expand each line of SSAT in such a way that each system event or output can be broken into multiple messages that can be represented in a sequence diagram. Into detailed sequence analysis table.
- Each included or expanding use case description results in a different detailed SAT.
- Create a sequence diagram from the detailed sequence analysis table.

Step #	Use case action	Message Name	Parameters	Constraints	Sender	Receiver

Fig. 2. The Template for Sequence Analysis Table (SAT)

Actor Action	System Action
1. Staff starts "New Rental" mode on POS, if POS is not already in the correct mode.	
2.The staff verifies the customer's status by their ID card or number.	3. System finds and displays the customer's information.
	4. INCLUDE Get Overdue Fees. Any overdue items are displayed with tape information, due date, and late fee amount due.
5. The staff records new rental items by scanning the bar codes.	6. System determines rental price and due date and displays with title, date and price for each item.
7. On completion of last item entry, the staff indicates to the POS terminal that the rental is complete.	8. System calculates tax and total rental fee, and records with date out. Late fees determined in prior step are added to the balance due.
9. Staff accepts payment from customer for the balance due.	10. INCLUDE Pay Fees.
	11. IF payment is successful, on-hand inventory is reduced by one for each rented item, and receipt is printed.
12. Staff hands items and receipt to customer and concludes transaction.	

Fig. 3. The Main Success Scenario of Use Case "Process Rents" of VRS Use Case Description

3.1 Getting Started – Designing the System Sequence Diagram (SSD)

In this section, we discuss how to create a system sequence diagram in the TAM. The first step is to copy the actions from the use case description document (UCD) to the empty template. Each input from an actor to the system (called a system event) and an output from the system to the actor forms a row in SAT. Next, for each row, enter a short message name that describes the primary communication. Depending on the quality of the UCD steps, some editing may be required at this point.

The next step is to identify sending and receiving objects as the initiating actor and a boundary object representing the system user interface. Evaluate each subsequent action as "from the actor to the system" or "from the system to the actor". For "system" put "BO"(meaning a boundary object that represents the system being modeled) in the "Sender" or "Receiver" column. It is not necessary to name boundary objects yet.

An example Use Case Description of the use case "Process Rents" for a Video Rental System (VRS) case study is shown in Figure 3 (only the Main Success Scenario is shown). The resulting SSD table is shown in Figure 4; and the resulting SSD diagram is shown in Figure 5. Refer to [18] for the problem statement, the use case diagram, and the class diagram of the VRS case study.

S#	Use case action	Message Name	Parameters	Constraints	Sender	Receiver
1	Staff starts "New Rental" mode on POS, if POS is not already in the correct mode.	start_rental			Staff	BO
2	Staff verifies the customer's status by their ID card or number.	enter_customer			Staff	BO
3	System finds and displays the customer's information.	display_customer			BO	Staff
4	INCLUDE Get Overdue Fees. Any overdue items are displayed with tape information, due date, and late fee amount due.	display_overdue			BO	Staff
5	The staff records new rental items by scanning the bar codes.	enter_rental_items		*[until end_rental received]	Staff	BO
6	System determines rental price and due date and displays with title, date and price for each item.	display_item_data		[enter_rental_items received]	BO	Staff
7	On completion of last item entry, the staff indicates to the POS terminal that the rental is complete.	end_rental			Staff	BO
8	System calculates tax and total rental fee, and records with date out. Late fees determined in prior step are added to the balance due.	display_total_due			BO	Staff
9	Staff accepts payment from customer for the balance due.	n/a			Customer	Staff
10	INCLUDE Pay Fee.	enter_payment			Actor: Staff	BO
11	IF payment is successful, on-hand inventory is reduced by one for each rented item, and receipt is printed.	print_receipt		payment is successful	BO	Staff
12	Staff hands items and receipt to customer and concludes transaction.	n/a		payment is successful	Staff	Customer

Fig. 4. Resulting System Sequence Analysis Table (SSAT) for System Sequence Diagram of the VRS Example

3.2 Defining the Sequence Diagram (SQD) Details

In this section, we show how to build the detailed sequence diagram in the TAM. At this point, the template contains a single line for each system event between the Actor and the System, as shown in Figure 4. Based on the ten-step heuristic, this section shows how to decompose the single interaction into multiple messages at the detailed level, as shown in Figure 6.

A detailed sequence diagram must show the interactions *within* the system, between various objects, as well as the parameters and constraints relevant to the messages. The following steps describe a methodical approach to completing the table. *In the resulting table, there will be one line for each message shown on the sequence diagram.* That means, in completing the detailed information, it will be necessary to *insert lines in the table* wherever multiple messages are required to implement a use case step – which will be true for *almost all* of the use case steps. The steps described below are illustrated in Figure 6 through Figure 8 for the "Enter Customer" system event of the VRS use case.

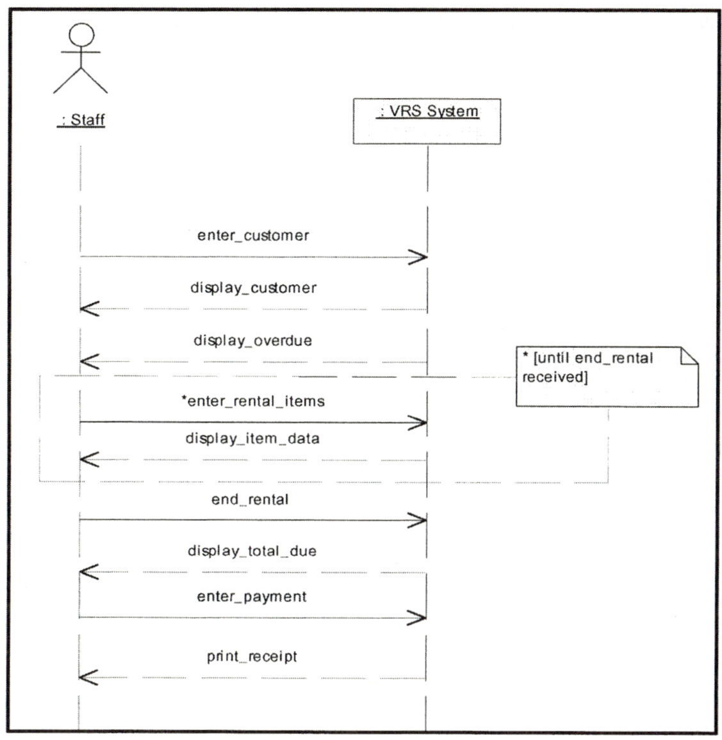

Fig. 5. Resulting System Sequence Diagram (SSD) for use case "Process Rents"

Step #	Use case action	Message Name	Parameters	Constraints	Sender	Receiver
1	Staff starts "New Rental" mode on POS, if POS is not already in the correct mode.	start_rental			Actor: Staff	Rental Window
1.1		start_rental			Rental Window	Rental Handler
1.2		request_cust_id			Rental Handler	Rental Window
2	Staff verifies the customer's status by their ID card or number.	enter_customer	cust_ID		Actor: Staff	Rental Window
2.1		get_cust	cust_ID		Rental Window	Rental Handler
2.2		get_cust	cust_ID		Rental Handler	Customer
2.3			customer_ data		Customer	Rental Handler
2.4			customer_ data		Rental andler	Rental Window
3	System finds and displays the customer's information.	display_customer	cust_ID		Rental indow	Actor: Staff

Fig. 6. Expansion of use case step 2 of Figure 4 for communication with controllers

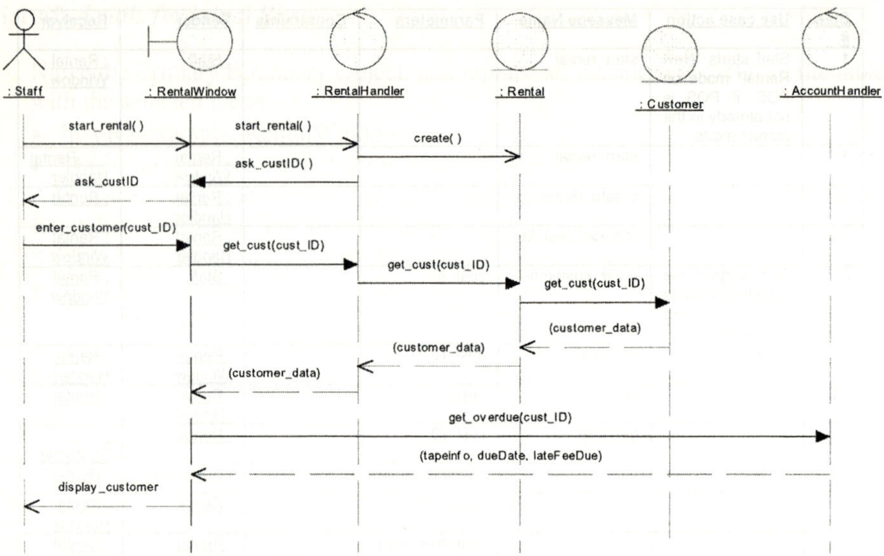

Fig. 8. Sequence Diagram for "Enter Customer" system event

- Indicate iteration of a message with a * (example: *get_item_info).
- Be sure to identify and add to the table, any messages with the same *Sender* and *Receiver* (such as calculations).
- Figure 7 shows how the steps to this point have been applied for the first two use case steps of the table. The expansion of use case step 2 to add communication with controllers and the entity class Customer is outlined in bold.

10. Review the constraints originally entered for the use case steps, and copy these as necessary into the new lines for the added messages.

Throughout the analysis, identify any clarifications needed, or missing or implied steps in the use case. Insert rows and add steps as needed; highlight changes to the use case steps in order to go back and update the UCD for consistency later. If it is apparent that additional major screens will be required, create a secondary boundary object and secondary controller for each major screen that is needed in addition to the main screen for the use case. Insert lines in the table as needed for passing messages from the primary controller to each secondary boundary object.

At this point, the table is complete for the *main success scenario of the primary use case*. Similar tables should be constructed for the included and extending use cases. If it is desired to create a generic sequence diagrams which includes all scenarios, messages and qualifications can be added as necessary by inserting rows in the table, to include the information covered in the "Other Successful Scenarios" and "Unsuccessful Scenarios" sections of the UCD.

Once satisfied that the table represents all data required for the sequence diagram, the modeler can create the diagram by referring to the table. Since the classes have already been modeled, the modeler merely drags the required classes into the sequence diagram. The classes should be ordered in the diagram as proposed in step 7 of the original heuristic. Then the message names, parameters, and qualifications can be copied and pasted from the table into operations in the modeling tool. The messages should be shown on the diagram in the correct relative time order. As mentioned in the Introduction, we envision a future capability to export a table developed with this method into an XMI file which can then be imported into any XMI-compatible tool, thus further simplifying the diagram creation.

4 Conclusion

This paper has proposed the tabular analysis method (TAM) for constructing accurate sequence diagrams.. The proposed method is rigorous and, applied as envisioned, results in a thorough modeling of operation elements. As such it may be considered tedious, but has the advantage of separating model analysis from the vagaries of tool usage. Therefore, it may prove ideal for application in the following circumstances:

- learning environments;
- situations where there is a need for comprehensive sequence diagrams; and
- situations where there may be multiple modeling tools in use, or tool selection is not complete at the time modeling needs to begin.

In addition, the tabular format used in this method is anticipated to be adaptable to automated model interchange in accordance with the OMG specifications for XML Metadata Interchange [10] and UML 2.0 Diagram Interchange [11]. Successful development of conversion scripts to realize this automation will enhance the applicability of the tabular approach, to the point where even experienced modelers may find it useful for quickly documenting interaction sequences.

References

1. Ambler, S. W. (2002) "UML Modeling Style Guidelines" retrieved 8/24/2003 from http://www.modelingstyle.info/classDiagram.html
2. Ambler, S. W. (2003) "UML 2 Sequence Diagram Overview" retrieved 8/24/2003 from http://www.agilemodeling.com/artifacts/sequenceDiagram.htm
3. Chonoles, M. J.; Schardt, J.A. (2003). *UML 2 for Dummies*. Wiley.
4. Kabajunga, C and Pooley, R.. Simulating UML sequence diagrams. *UK Performance Engineering Workshop*, UK PEW 1998, pages 198–207, July 1998.
5. Larman, C. (2002) *Applyng UML and Patterns: An Introduction to Object-Oriented Analysis and Design and the Unified Process.* 2nd ed., Prentice Hall PTR.
6. Li, X. and Lilius, J. Timing Analysis of UML Sequence Diagrams. *UML'99, The Unified Modeling Language. Beyond the Standard.* October 28-30, 1999.
7. Li, L. (2000). "Translating Use Cases to Sequence Diagrams", Automated Software Engineering, 2000. Proceedings ASE 2000. 11-15 Sept. 2000. pp. 293 – 296.
8. Litvak, B., Tyszberowicz, S. and Yehudai, A. (2003) "Behavioral Consistency Validation of UML diagrams", In *Proceedings of the First International Conference on Software Engineering and Formal Methods (SEFM'03).*
9. Martin, R. C. (2003). *Agile Software Development: Principles, Patterns, and Practices.* Prentice Hall.
10. Object Management Group. (May 2003). "XML Metadata Interchange (XMI) Specification Version 2.0" retrieved 03/17/2004 from http://www.omg.org/cgi-bin/doc?formal/2003-05-02.
11. Object Management Group. "UML 2.0 Diagram Interchange draft adopted specification." Retrieved 03/17/2004 from http://www.omg.org/cgi-bin/apps/do_doc?ptc/03-07-03.pdf
12. Pender, T. (2003). *UML Bible*. Wiley.

13. Object Management Group. (August 2003). "UML 2.0 Superstructure Final Adopted specification." Retrieved 9/12/2003 from http://www.omg.org/cgi-bin/doc?ptc/2003-08-02.
14. Oestereich, B. (2002). *Developing Software with UML: Object-Oriented Analysis and Design in Practice.* Addison-Wesley.
15. Page-Jones, M. (2000). *Fundamentals of Object-Oriented Design in UML.* Addison-Wesley.
16. Rumbaugh, J., Jacobson, I., and Booch, G. (1999). *The Unified Modeling Language ReferenceManual.* Addison-Wesley.
17. Seemann, J. and Wvg, J. (1998). Extension of UML Sequence Diagrams for Real-Time Systems, In Proc. *International UML Workshop,* Mulhouse, June 1988.
18. Song, I. (2001). "Developing Sequence Diagrams in UML." In *Proc. of 20th International Conference on Conceptual Modeling (ER2001),* Yokohama, Japan, 2001, pp. 368-382.

An Approach to Formalizing the Semantics of UML Statecharts*

Xuede Zhan and Huaikou Miao

School of Computer Engineering and Science, Shanghai University,
Shanghai, 200072, China
{xdzhan,hkmiao}@mail.shu.edu.cn

Abstract. UML is a language for specifying, visualizing and documenting object-oriented systems. However, UML statecharts lack precisely defined syntax and semantics. This paper provides a method of formalizing semantics of UML statecharts with Z. According to this precise semantics, UML statecharts are transformed into FREE (Flattened Regular Expression) state models. The hierarchical and concurrent structure of states is flattened in the resulting FREE state model. The model helps to determine whether the software design is consistent, unambiguous and complete. It is also beneficial to software testing.

1 Introduction

The Unified Modeling Language (UML) is a de facto standard for documenting the specification and design of object-oriented systems. The continuously growing popularity of this notation has led software developers to use UML to model application domains that were originally out of the language scope. These domains include business processes, Web-based applications, information systems, component-based systems, etc. In general, the rich set of diagrams provided by UML, together with a flexible extension mechanism, allow developers to model all the relevant features of software systems [1]. UML's very advantages are given by a great variety of intuitive and mostly well-known notation for different kind of information to be specified: requirements, static structure, interactive and dynamic behavior as well as physical implementation structures. However, this intuitive appeal comes at the prize of an insufficient definition. Whereas the UML syntax is defined in quite a precise and complete manner, its semantics is not.

Statechart diagrams were originally introduced by David Harel [4] in the mid 80's of the twentieth century. The notation and semantics of UML statecharts were adapted from the Harel's original version with the addition of object-oriented features [1]. UML statechart diagram is an important part of the standard UML language [1]. UML statecharts extend ordinary state transition diagrams with notions of hierarchy and concurrency [1]. They are a visual language and are typically used to model the dynamic behaviour of a class of UML objects. This language has proved useful in modeling complex control aspects of many software systems. UML statechart diagram is a highly expressive hierarchical modelling language with well defined syntax [1]. Unfortunately, its precise semantics are not well formalized.

* This work is supported by the National Natural Science Foundation of China (60173030 60373072) National 973 Program (2002CB312001) and the fourth key subject construction of Shanghai

P. Atzeni et al. (Eds.): ER 2004, LNCS 3288, pp. 753–765, 2004.

However, there are some semantic differences between the two notations of UML statecharts and David Harel's statecharts. One most major difference is that causal paradoxes avoided by introducing the notion of *steps* [3,4,5,7,10,11] in the classical statecharts are not an issue with the *run-to-completion* assumption in UML, which allows that an event only can be dispatched when the processing of the previous event is fully completed (refer to [1] for other semantic differences relative to classical statecharts). For these reasons, although several semantics have been proposed for classical statecharts [3,4,5,7,10,11], it is worthwhile to define a formal semantics for the UML statecharts. A formalization of the state machine package in the UML metamodel using Object-Z was presented in [2]. However, there was not formal syntax and semantics of whole UML statechart in [2]. [8] described a formal semantics of special UML statechart but not general UML statechart, and it didn't consider the concurrent mechanism. [9] described the syntax of UML statecharts with the *Graph-type Definition Language* and specified the semantics of UML statecharts by an *Abstract State Machine* in a heterogeneous modeling environment, but did not describe a formal semantics of UML statecharts in general modeling environment. In [12], starting with a precise textual syntax definition, they developed a structured operational semantics for UML statecharts based on labeled transition systems. In [13], an operational semantics for a subset of UML state machines was proposed. [14, 15] gave a formal syntax and semantics of UML statecharts using mathematics method.

In this paper, we use Z notation rather than "standard mathematics" to formalize UML statechart. Z has been used for precisely describing user's requirements, and has been used for a number of digital systems in a variety of ways to improve the specification of computer-based systems [16]. A lot of textbooks on Z are now available [17]. The teaching of Z has become of increasing interest [18]. The Z notation has many supporting tools for its convenient representation. And it was widely used by many people.

We present the formal definition of the syntax and semantics of UML statecharts, extend the definition of firing priorities between the two conflicting compound transitions based on [1]. In this paper, the transition labels are restricted to that: the only effect of actions is the generation of events.

It's difficult to generate test cases of class directly from the UML statecharts diagrams that contain hierarchical and concurrent structure. According to our precise semantics, a UML statechart diagram can be transformed into FREE state model [6]. For example, a UML statechart diagram shown in Fig.1 can be transformed into a FREE state model shown in Fig. 2. The hierarchical and concurrent structure of states is flattened in the resulting FREE state model. The model helps to determine whether the software design is consistent, unambiguous and complete. A UML model that follows the FREE conventions will be testable [6]. It is beneficial to software testing.

In section 2, the formal semantics of UML statecharts is defined. Section 3 gives FREE state model. Finally, some conclusions are draw.

2 Formal Semantics of UML Statecharts

2.1 Well-Formed UML Statecharts

A set of states at different levels forms a state hierarchy: the states contained within a state are called *substates* of the surrounding state; the surrounding state is called the *composite state* and higher than the states it contains in the hierarchy. The highest state is called the *top state* which is not surrounded by any state. In the example shown in Fig. 1, *S0* is the top state in the state hierarchy *S1* and *S2* are its substates. *S0* is an *ancestor* of *S1* and *S2*.

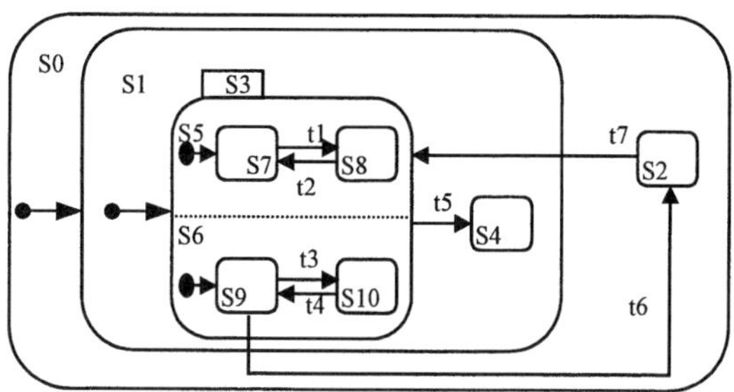

Fig. 1. An Example of UML statechart diagram

State Names and State Types. We postulate a finite, nonempty set of state name Σ and denote the types of states by *TYPE*. We denote non-concurrent composite state by *NCCS*, concurrent composite state by *CCS*, the initial state by *INITIAL* and the final state by *FINAL*.

$$[\Sigma]$$

$$\exists n: \mathbb{N} \bullet \#\Sigma = n$$

$$TYPE ::= SIMPLE \mid NCCS \mid CCS \mid INITIAL \mid FINAL$$

Definition of State Hierarchy. A state hierarchy *STATETREE* consists of the following components: the root *top* of the tree, the finite hierarchy function ρ which assigns a (possibly empty) set of direct substates to an ancestor state and the finite typing function ψ which assigns to each state its type. For example, the direct substates of state *S0* are *initial*, *S1* and *S2*, namely $\rho\,(S0) = \{initial, S1, S2\}$, $\psi\,(S0) = NCCS$, $\psi\,(S2) = SIMPLE$, $\psi\,(S3) = CCS$. The schema *STATETREE* defines these objects is given in next page.

Simple Transition. A *simple transition* connects two states. Simple transition labels in UML statechart have the simple structure

event[guard]/action

STATETREE

$top: \Sigma$

$\rho: \Sigma \mathrel{-\!\!\!+\!\!\!+\!\!\!\!\rightarrow} \mathbb{F}\Sigma$

$\psi: \Sigma \mathrel{-\!\!\!+\!\!\!+\!\!\!\!\rightarrow} TYPE$

$\mathbf{dom}\rho \setminus \bigcup(\mathbf{ran}\rho) = \{top\} \land \psi(top) = NCCS$

$\forall set: \mathbb{F}(\bigcup(\mathbf{ran}\rho)) \bullet (\exists el: set \bullet (\forall st: set \bullet el \notin \rho(st)))$

$\forall s: \bigcup(\mathbf{ran}\rho) \bullet (\exists_1 anc: \mathbf{dom}\rho \bullet s \in \rho\,(anc))$

$\mathbf{dom}\rho = \mathbf{dom}\,\psi$

$\forall s: \mathbf{dom}\rho \bullet ((\psi(s) = SIMPLE \lor \psi(s) = INITIAL \lor \psi(s) = FINAL) \Rightarrow \rho(s) = \phi)$

$\land(\psi(s) = CCS \Rightarrow (\forall sub: \rho(s) \bullet \psi\,(sub) = NCCS \land \#\{\rho(s)\} \geq 2\,))$

$\land(\psi(s) = NCCS \Rightarrow (\exists_1 initial: \rho(s) \bullet \psi(initial) = INITIAL\,))$

where *event* is trigger event, *guard* is a boolean condition, and *action* is an action. All three parameters are optional.

We define a finite set of events.

[*EVE*]

$\exists n: \mathbb{N} \bullet \# EVE = n$

As mentioned above we restrict the action part to the generation of events only. The schema *LABEL* defines the set of labels.

```
┌─ LABEL ──────────────────────────
│ event: EVE
│ guard: BOOLEAN
│ action: seq EVE
└──────────────────────────────────
```

A simple transition leads from a state denoted by *source* to another state denoted by *target*. Simple transitions are labeled. The schema *TRANSITION* defines the set of simple transitions.

```
┌─ TRANSITION ─────────────────────
│ source: Σ
│ target: Σ
│ label: LABEL
└──────────────────────────────────
```

Now we can give a well-defined condition that allows to compose a state hierarchy and a set of simple transitions into a well-defined statechart.

Well-Formed Statecharts. The consistency between the root, the initial state, the final state and the set of simple transitions is as follows:

1. A *simple transition* connects a *source* state to a *target* state. The source and target can be composite state.
2. The *top* state is neither a target nor a source of any simple transition.
3. An initial state has exactly one outgoing simple transition (called *initial transition* and indicated as *initialt*) and no incoming simple transitions.[1]
4. A final state has at least one incoming simple transition (called *final transition* and indicated as *finalt*) and no outgoing simple transitions.

These requirements are formalized in the schema *STATECHARTS*.

```
┌─ STATECHARTS ────────────────────────────────────────
│ tree : STATETREE
│ tset: F₁TRANSITION
├──────────────────────────────────────────────────────
│ ∀t: tset • #{t.source}=1∧#{t.target}=1
│           ∧tree.top∉{t.source, t.target}
│ ∀s:Σ•((ψ(s)=INITIAL⇒(s∉{t: tset • t.target})
│                       ∧(∃₁initialt: tset • initialt.source= s))
│   ∧(ψ(s)=FINAL⇒(s∉{t: tset•t.source})∧(∃finalt: tset•finalt.target=s)))
└──────────────────────────────────────────────────────
```

2.2 State Configurations

When dealing with composite state, the simple term "current state" may be quite confusing. In UML statecharts more than one state can be active at once. The current active "state" is actually represented by a tree of states starting with the single top state at the root down to individual simple states at the leaves. We refer to such a state tree as a state *configuration* such as {*S0, S1, S4*}, {*S0, S1, S3, S5, S6, S7, S9*}. Except during transition execution, only one state configuration is active, and the following invariants always apply to state configurations [1]:

- If a non-concurrent composite state is active, exactly one of its substates is active.
- If a concurrent composite state is active, all of its substates (regions) are active.

We introduce functions to reason about state hierarchy and we identify a relation between a set of states and an ancestor state. This relation helps us to define the state configuration function *confset*.

Substates and Ancestors. We define extensions of ρ: its reflexive, transitive closure ρ^* and its non-reflexive, transitive closure ρ^+. The ancestor relation is expressed by *ancestor*. The strict ancestor relation is expressed by *strancestor*.

$$\rho^*, \rho^+ : \Sigma \times STATETREE \twoheadrightarrow \mathbb{F}\Sigma$$
$$ancestor\_,\ strancestor\_ : \mathbb{F}_1(\Sigma \times \mathbb{F}_1\Sigma \times STATETREE)$$
$$\forall s: \Sigma,\ tree: STATETREE \bullet$$
$$\rho^*(s, tree) = \{ s \} \cup \bigcup \{ sub: tree.\rho(s) \bullet \rho^*(sub, tree) \}$$
$$\wedge \rho^+(s, tree) = \rho^*(s, tree) \setminus \{ s \}$$
$$\forall anc: \Sigma;\ set: \mathbb{F}_1\Sigma;\ tree: STATETREE \bullet$$
$$(ancestor(anc, set, tree) \Leftrightarrow set \subseteq \rho^*(anc, tree))$$
$$\wedge (strancestor(anc, set, tree) \Leftrightarrow set \subseteq \rho^+(anc, tree))$$

State Configurations. Given a *STATETREE tree* and a state *s* that isn't an initial state neither a final state, let *CONF* be a set of state configurations containing *s*, every configuration in *CONF* is a set of states *conf* obeying the following rules:

- conf contains tree.top.
- If conf contains a state st that is not tree.top, it must also contain the ancestor of st.
- If conf contains a state st of type NCCS, it must also contain exactly one of st's substates.
- If conf contains a state st of type CCS, it must also contain all of st's substates.

The only states that are in *conf* are those that are required by the above rules. Obviously, a configuration must contain at least one simple state. Generally, a configuration must not contain a pseudostate and a final state. The following definition is a direct interpretation of the rules above. Let *CONF* be a set of configuration that contains *s*.

$$confset: \Sigma \times STATETREE \twoheadrightarrow \mathbb{F}_1\mathbb{F}_1\Sigma$$
$$\mathbf{dom}(confset) = \{\forall s: \Sigma;\ tree: STATETREE \mid s \neq tree.top$$
$$\wedge tree.\psi(s) \neq INITIAL \wedge tree.\psi(s) \neq FINAL\}$$
$$\forall s: \Sigma;\ tree: STATETREE;\ CONF: \mathbb{F}_1\mathbb{F}_1\Sigma \bullet confset(s, tree) = CONF \Leftrightarrow$$
$$\forall conf: CONF \bullet tree.top \in conf \wedge s \in conf$$
$$\wedge (\forall st: conf \bullet (tree.\psi(st) = NCCS \Rightarrow (\exists_1 sub: tree.\rho(st) \bullet sub \in conf))$$
$$\wedge (tree.\psi(st) = CCS \Rightarrow tree.\rho(st) \subseteq conf)$$
$$\wedge (st \neq tree.top \wedge \forall anc: \Sigma \bullet ancestor(anc, \{st\}, tree)) \Rightarrow anc \in conf)$$

pound transition *ct32* (refer to Fig.2) is the set of states {*S0*, *S1*, *S3*, *S5*, *S6*, *S8*} and scope of a compound transition *ct54* is the set of state {*S0*, *S1*}. Since more than one compound transition may be enabled by the same current event, being enabled is a necessary but not sufficient condition for the firing of a compound transition. Two compound transitions are said to *conflict* if they both originate from the same configuration, both triggered by the same event and both guard conditions are true. In case of conflicting compound transitions, only one of them will fire in a run-to-completion step. For example, two compound transitions *ct32* and *ct54* (refer to Fig.2) that originate from the same state configuration {*S0*, *S1*, *S3*, *S5*, *S6*, *S8*, *S9*} are conflicting if they both triggered by the same event and both guarded conditions are true.

$$
\begin{array}{|l}
scope : COMTRAN \twoheadrightarrow \mathbb{F}_1\Sigma \\
conflicting\_ : \mathbb{F}(COMTRAN \times COMTRAN \times \mathbb{F}_1\Sigma) \\
\hline
\forall ct : COMTRAN \bullet scope(ct) = ct.souconf \cap ct.tarconf \\
\exists conf : \mathbb{F}_1\Sigma; \forall ct1, ct2 : COMTRAN \bullet conflicting(ct1,ct2,conf) \Leftrightarrow \\
\qquad (ct1 \neq ct2 \wedge ct1.souconf = conf \wedge ct2.souconf = conf \\
\qquad \wedge ct1.cl.event = ct2.cl.event \wedge ct1.cl.guard \wedge ct2.cl.guard)
\end{array}
$$

Firing Priorities. The *firing priorities* between the two conflicting compound transitions are determined by comparing the scope of two conflicting compound transitions. For two conflicting compound transition, if scope of a compound transition is a proper subset of the other one, then its compound transition firing priority is lower than the other one. For example, a compound transition *ct32* (refer to Fig.2) has higher firing priority than other compound transition *ct54* if they both are conflicting. Only higher firing priority of a compound transition will fire for two conflicting compound transitions. These priorities resolve some of the compound transition conflicts, but not all of them. In the case of more conflicting compound transitions and the same firing priority, one of them can be chosen to fire in a run-to-completion step.

2.4 Definition of the Run-to-Completion Step

Status of a Statechart. The set of run-to-completion steps of UML statecharts *STEP* are sequences of statuses. A status consists of three components: active state configuration, current event and event queue.

actconf: a state configuration in which the system currently resides;
curevent: a current event that was dequeued and dispatched in the previous step
evequeue: an event queue that holds incoming event instances until they are dispatched.

The schema *STATUS* defines these objects.

$$
\begin{array}{|l}
\hline
STATUS \\
actconf : \mathbb{F}_1\Sigma \\
curevent : EVE \\
evequeue : \mathbf{seq}\ EVE \\
\hline
\end{array}
$$

Initial Status. We will define a special configuration $conf_0$ that contains initial state. The only active state configuration in the first status of UML statecharts *STEP* is the initial configuration $conf_0$ that contains tree.top and initial state *($conf_0$={tree.top, initial})*. The current event and the event queue are empty. We define an event constant, empty event empevent before schema initial status *INITSTATUS* is presented as follows.

empevent: *EVE*

```
┌─ INITSTATUS ──────────────────────────
│ STATUS
├──────────────
│ actconf = conf₀
│ curevent = empevent
│ evequeue = < >
└───────────────────────────────────────
```

$$actconf = conf_0$$
$$curevent = empevent$$
$$evequeue = \langle\,\rangle$$

Definition of the Run-to-Completion Step. The *run-to-completion* step is the passage between two state configurations of the UML statecharts [1]. We postulate that the event queue is a first-in first-out queue. Events are generated as a result of some action either within the system or in the environment surrounding the system. The events are added to the event queue *evequeue.*

The semantics of event processing is based on the *run-to-completion* assumption, interpreted as run-to-completion processing. Run-to-completion processing means that an event can only be dequeued and dispatched if the processing of the previous current event is fully completed.

The following list is our remarks that explain how it relates to our definition in the Z schema *STEP*.

- Compute the set of enabled compound transitions (corresponds to the set *ECT*).
- Remove from this set all compound transitions that are in conflict with an enabled compound transition of higher priority (corresponds to the set *ETHP*).
- If there are no enabled compound transitions then the step is empty, else there choose one compound transition nondeterministically for execution. Let *ct* be the choice. The action of compound transition *ct* is executed.
- The action event queue *ct.cl.action* that were generated by the action of the executed compound transition are catenated the back of the event queue *evequeue*. The front event in the event queue *evequeue* is removed and became the current event *curevent* in the next step if the event queue *evequeue* is not empty.

(This corresponds to the assignments to the variables *actconf*, *curevent*' and *evequeue*'.)

STEP

$\Delta STATUS$

$evequeue1 : \mathbf{seq}\ EVE$

$$ECT \mathrel{\hat=} \{ct : COMTRAN \mid enabled(ct, actconf, curevent)\} \bullet$$
$$ETHP \mathrel{\hat=} \{ct : ECT \mid (\forall ect : ECT \bullet scope(ct) \not\subset scope(ect))\} \bullet$$
$$(\#ETHP = 0 \Rightarrow (actconf' = actconf$$
$$\wedge ((\#evequeue = 0 \Rightarrow curevent' = empevent \wedge evequeue' = \langle\,\rangle)$$
$$\wedge (\#evequeue \neq 0 \Rightarrow curevent' = \mathbf{head}\ evequeue$$
$$\wedge evequeue' = \mathbf{tail}\ evequeue))))$$
$$\wedge (\#ETHP \neq 0 \Rightarrow (\exists_1\ ct : ETHP \bullet (evequeue1 = evequeue ^\frown ct.cl.action \bullet$$
$$actconf' = ct.tarconf$$
$$\wedge ((\#evequeue1 = 0 \Rightarrow curevent' = empevent$$
$$\wedge evequeue' = \langle\,\rangle)$$
$$\wedge (\#evequeue1 \neq 0 \Rightarrow curevent' = \mathbf{head}\ evequeue1$$
$$\wedge evequeue' = \mathbf{tail}\ evequeue1)))))$$

3 FREE State Model

3.1 Definition of FREE State Model

In the formalism of Mealy model, event and action can be associated to a transition, and state is static. Whereas in the formalism of Moore model, event was associated to a transition and action was associated to a state that isn't static. Both Mealy model and Moore model can be implemented in UML statechart. This mixture in UML statechart easily leads to errors and low efficiency. This mixture in FREE model is forbidden. In section 2, we consider UML statechart that adopt only Mealy model, which seems to reduce the expressiveness. But in fact, the actions in states were transformed into the actions of the self-transition, it can sufficiently express the information of More model. It's difficult to generate test cases of class directly from the UML statecharts diagrams that contain hierarchical and concurrent structure. According to our precise semantics, a UML statechart diagram can be transformed into FREE state model [6]. To flatten the hierarchical and concurrent structure of states in UML statecharts diagram a FREE state model is generated in the transformation. A UML model that follows the FREE conventions will be testable [6].

FREE State Model. A FREE state model is an extended FSM, a tuple <*CONF*, $conf_0$, *CT*> such that

- *CONF* is a set of configurations.
- $conf_0 \in CONF$ is the *initial configuration.*
- *CT* is a set of compound transitions

The set of configurations *CONF1* is the union of the sets of configurations by applying the function *confset* (refer to section 2.2) to each of the states of the UML statechart diagram. In section 2.4 we defined the initial configuration $conf_0$ that contains *tree.top* and *initial* state ($conf_0$={*tree.top*, *initial*}). The set of configurations *CONF* is the union of the set of configurations *CONF1* and the initial configuration $conf_0$. The set of compound transitions *CT* is calculated by applying schema *COMTRAN* (refer to section 2.3).

3.2 Example of FREE State Model

From a given UML statechart diagram, we can construct a FREE state model which is equivalent to the UML statechart. In our example, there are seven configurations in Fig. 1 and these constitute *CONF* of FREE state model in Fig. 2.

In Fig. 1, six configurations are calculated by applying function *confset.* These six configurations and the initial configuration $conf_0$ make up the set of configurations *CONF*. In Fig. 1, there are fifteen compound transitions calculated by applying schema *COMTRAN*. The fifteen compound transitions and the initial compound transition make up the set of compound transitions *CT.*

We give two examples that the compound transition is calculated by applying schema *COMTRAN*:

A simple transition *t1* in Fig. 1 corresponds to two compound transitions *ct11* and *ct12* in Fig. 2 because there are two state configurations in state *S7,* the source state of transition *t1*. The state *S7* maps into the set of state configurations {{*S0*, *S1*, *S3*, *S5*, *S6*, *S7*, *S9*}, {*S0*, *S1*, *S3*, *S5*, *S6*, *S7*, *S10*}} by applying function *confset.* In this example, *gds=S7*, *DS*={*S7*}, *gas=S8*, *defaconf* (*S8*, *tree*)= {*S8*}, *AS* = ρ^*(*gas*, *tree*) ∩*defaconf* (*t.target*, *tree*) = {*S8*}, if *souconf* = {*S0*, *S1*, *S3*, *S5*, *S6*, *S7*, *S9*}, then *tarconf* = (*souconf* *DS*) ∪*AS* =({*S0*, *S1*, *S3*, *S5*, *S6*, *S7*, *S9*}\{*S7*})∪{*S8*}={*S0*, *S1*, *S3*, *S5*, *S6*, *S8*, *S9*}; if *souconf* = {*S0*, *S1*, *S3*, *S5*, *S6*, *S7*, *S10*}, then *tarconf*= (*souconf* *DS*) ∪*AS* =({*S0*, *S1*, *S3*, *S5*, *S6*, *S7*, *S10*}\{S7}) ∪{S8}={*S0*, *S1*, *S3*, *S5*, *S6*, *S8*, *S10*}.

As another example, a simple transition *t6* in Fig. 1 corresponds to two compound transitions *ct61* and *ct62* in Fig. 2 because there are two state configurations in state *S9*, the source state of transition *t6*. The state *S9* maps into the set of state configurations {{*S0*, *S1*, *S3*, *S5*, *S6*, *S7*, *S9*}, {*S0*, *S1*, *S3*, *S5*, *S6*, *S8*, *S9*}} by applying function *confset*. In this example, *gds=S1*, *DS*={*S1*, *S3*, *S4*, *S5*, *S6*, *S7*, *S8*, *S9*, *S10*}, *defaconf* (*S2*, *tree*)= {*S2*}, *gas=S2*, *AS* = ρ^*(*gas*, *tree*)∩*defaconf* (*t.target*, *tree*) = {*S2*}, if *souconf* = {*S0*, *S1*, *S3*, *S5*, *S6*, *S7*, *S9*}, then *tarconf* = (*souconf* *DS*) ∪*AS* =({*S0*, *S1*, *S3*, *S5*, *S6*, *S7*, *S9*}\{*S1*, *S3*, *S4*, *S5*, *S6*, *S7*, *S8*, *S9*, *S10*})∪{*S2*}={*S0*, *S2*}; if *souconf* = {*S0*, *S1*, *S3*, *S5*, *S6*, *S8*, *S9*}, then *tarconf* = (*souconf* *DS*) ∪*AS* =({*S0*, *S1*, *S3*, *S5*, *S6*, *S8*, *S9*}\{*S1*, *S3*, *S4*, *S5*, *S6*, *S7*, *S8*, *S9*, *S10*})∪{*S2*}={*S0*, *S2*}.

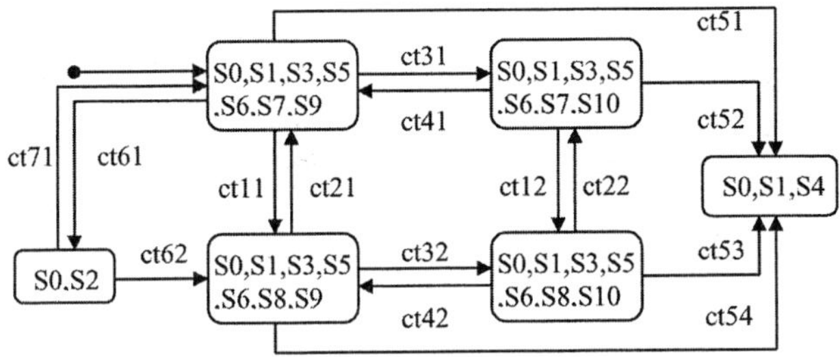

Fig. 2. An example of FREE state model

3.3 Computation of FREE Models

The above FREE state model abstracts from the specific environment the UML statechart is interacting with. The environment events that were sent over environment and other object were saved event queue *evequeue* (refer to section 2.4). We use the notation $\mathbf{s_i} \xrightarrow{\mathbf{STEP}} \mathbf{S_{i+1}}$ to denote that the pair of statuses (s_i, s_{i+1}) is in relation *STEP*.

Definition 3.1 (Computation). A computation for FREE model is an infinite or finite sequence of statuses $c_i \in STATUS$ ($i \in \mathbb{N}$), such that:

$$\forall i\colon \mathbb{N} \bullet ((\exists s{:}STATUS \bullet (s.curevent = \mathbf{head}\ s_i.evequeue$$

$$\wedge\ s_i.actconf = s.actconf$$

$$\wedge\ s \xrightarrow{STEP} S_{i+1}))$$

$$\wedge\ (\exists k\colon \mathbb{N} \bullet (i<k \Rightarrow (\exists s{:}STATUS \bullet$$

$$(s.curevent = \mathbf{head}\ s_i.evequeue$$

$$\wedge\ s_i.actconf = s.actconf$$

$$\wedge\ s \xrightarrow{STEP} S_{i+1})))$$

$$\wedge\ (i{=}k \Rightarrow (\nexists s{:}STATUS \bullet$$
$$(s.curevent = \textbf{head}\ s_{i+1}.evequeue$$
$$\wedge\ s_{i+1}.actconf = s.actconf$$
$$\wedge\ s_k \xrightarrow{STEP} S\ )))))$$

In above definition, the first case of computation is infinite; the second case of computation is finite (maximum $k \in \mathbb{N}$). This definition captures the interplay with the environment: environment steps, which possibly provide new events, alternate with steps of the system. This definition records both internally generated events as well as those events provided by the environment. In order to understand the computations of FREE state model, we let *t1*, *t2*, *t3*, *t4*, *t5*, *t6* and *t7* in Fig.1 be *e1/e2*, *e3/e4*, *e2/e4*, *e4/e5*, *e4/*, *e5/e3* and *e3/e4*. The event queue *evequeue* is initialized with event *e1*. An example of the interaction of FREE state model of Fig. 2 is given in Fig. 3.

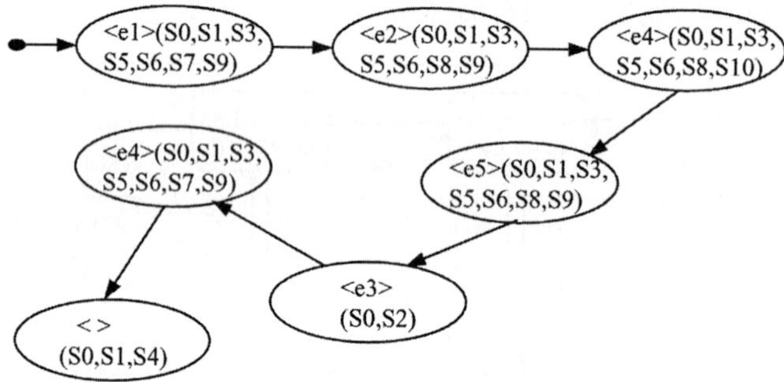

Fig. 3. An Example of the Interaction of FREE State Model

Obviously, computations are mathematical abstractions for test runs. It is highly advantageous to the automatic derivation of test cases from UML statecharts.

4 Conclusions and Further Work

We give a formal semantics definition for UML statecharts described in [1]. This paper provides a method of formalizing semantics of UML statecharts with Z, extends the definition of firing priorities between the two conflicting compound transitions based on [1]. A simple transition in UML statechart corresponds to one or more compound transitions in FREE state model if the simple transition is neither an initial transition nor a final transition. According to this precise semantics, a UML statechart can be transformed into a FREE state model. The hierarchical and concurrent structure of states is flattened in the resulting FREE state model. The model helps to determine whether the software design is consistent, unambiguous and complete. The work presented in this paper is beneficial to the development of methods for the automatic derivation of test cases from UML statecharts models. The study and development of such methods is a first item for further research.When we will discuss the application of statecharts in UML to class testing, we only require discussing FREE state model to class testing.

References

1. OMG *UML Specification*, version 2.0, Nov 2003, http://www.omg.org .
2. S-K. Kim and D. Carrington, A formal metamodeling approach to a transformation between the UML state machine and object-Z, In Proceedings of International Conference on Formal Engineering Methods 2002, Springer Verlag, LNCS 2495.
3. E. Mikk, Y. Lakhnech, C. Petersohn and M. Siegel, On Formal Semantics of Statecharts as Supported by STATEMATE, In 2nd BCS-FACS Northern Formal Methods Workshop. Springer-Verlag, July 1997.
4. D. Harel and A. Naamad. The STATEMATE semantics of statecharts. ACM Transactions on Software Engineering and Methodology (Also available as technical report of Weizmann Institute of Science, CS95-31), 5(4):293–333, Oct 1996.
5. D. Harel, A. Pnueli, J.P. Schmidt and R. Sherman. On the Formal Semantics of Statecharts. In Proc. 2nd IEEE Symp. on Logic in Computer Science, pages 56–64. IEEE Press, 1987.
6. Robert V. Binder. Testing Object-Oriented System:Models, Patterns, and Tools. Addison Wesley Longman, Inc. 2000.
7. Pnueli and M. Shalev, What is in a step: on the semantics of statscharts, Proceedings of International Conference on Theoretical Aspects of Computer Science, Lecture Notes in Computer Science, Vol. 298, pages 245–264,Springer-Verlag, 1991.
8. Huaikou Miao, Ling Liu, and Li Li, Formalizing UML Models with Object-Z, In Proceedings of International Conference on Formal Engineering Methods 2002, Springer-Verlag, LNCS 2495, p. 523
9. Y. Jin, R. Esser and J. W. Janneck. Describing the syntax and semantics of UML Statecharts in a heterogeneous modeling environment. Proceedings DIAGRAMS 2002, 2002.
10. Uselton and S. Smolka. A compositional semantics for Statecharts using labeled transition systems. In CONCUR '94, volume 836 of LNCS, pages 2-17. Springer-Verlag, 1994.
11. Huizing, R. Gerth, and W.P. de Roever. Modeling Statecharts behavior in a fully abstract way. In CAAP '88, volume 299 of LNCS, pages 271-294. Springer-Verlag, 1988.
12. M.v.d. Beeck. Formalization of UML-Statecharts. M. Gogolla and C. Kobryn (Eds.): «UML» 2001, LNCS 2185,pp.406-421,2001. Springer 2001.
13. S. Kuske. A Formal Semantics of UML State Machines Based on Structured Graph Transformation. M. Gogolla and C. Kobryn (Eds.): «UML» 2001, LNCS 2185, pp.406-421, 2001. Springer 2001.
14. Li Liuying,Wang Ji, Qi Zhichang. An Operational Semantics for UML Statechart Diagrams. Journal of Software, Vol. 12, pages 1864-1873, 2001.
15. issertation] (in Chinese). National University of Defense Technology, Changsha, 2000.
16. Bowen, J. P. Formal Specification and Documentation Using Z: A Case Study Approach. International Thomson Computer Press, 1996.
17. Jacky, J. The Way of Z: Practical Programming with formal Methods. Cambridge University Press, 1997.
18. Bowen, J. P. Experience Teaching Z with Tool and Web Support. Technical Report SBU-CISM-00-30, SCISM, South Bank University, London, UK, 2000.

Applying the Application-Based Domain Modeling Approach to UML Structural Views

Arnon Sturm[1] and Iris Reinhartz-Berger[2]

[1] Department of Information System Engineering,
Ben-Gurion University of the Negev, Beer Sheva 84105, Israel
sturm@bgumail.bgu.ac.il

[2] Department of Management Information Systems,
University of Haifa, Haifa 31905, Israel
iris@mis.hevra.haifa.ac.il

Abstract. Being part of domain engineering, domain analysis enables identifying domains and capturing their ontologies in order to assist and guide system developers to design domain-specific applications. Several studies suggest using metamodeling techniques for modeling domains and their constraints. However, these techniques use different notions, and sometimes even different notations, for defining domains and their constraints and for specifying and designing the domain-specific applications. We propose an Application-based DOmain Modeling (ADOM) approach in which domains are treated as regular applications that need to be modeled before systems of those domains are specified and designed. This way, the domain models enforce static and dynamic constraints on their application models. The ADOM approach consists of three-layers and defines dependency and enforcement relations between these layers. In this paper we describe the ADOM architecture and validation rules focusing on applying them to UML static views, i.e., class, component, and deployment diagrams.

1 Introduction

Domain Engineering is a software engineering discipline concerned with building reusable assets and components in a specific domain [4], [5], [6]. We refer to a *domain* as a set of applications that use a common jargon for describing the concepts and problems in that domain. The purpose of domain engineering is to identify, model, construct, catalog, and disseminate a set of software artifacts that can be applied to existing and future software in a particular application domain [21]. As such, it is an important type of software reuse, verification, and validation [15].

Similarly to software engineering, domain engineering includes three main activities: domain analysis, domain design, and domain implementation. *Domain analysis* identifies a domain and captures its ontology [26]. Hence, it should specify the basic elements of the domain, organize an understanding of the relationships among these elements, and represent this understanding in a useful way [4]. *Domain design* and *domain implementation* are concerned with mechanisms for translating requirements into systems that are made up of components with the intent of reusing them to the highest extent possible.

Domain analysis is especially crucial because of two main reasons. First, analysis is one of the initial steps of the system development lifecycle. Avoiding syntactic and semantic mistakes at this stage (using domain analysis principles) helps to reduce

P. Atzeni et al. (Eds.): ER 2004, LNCS 3288, pp. 766–779, 2004.

development time and to improve product quality and reusability. Secondly, the core elements of a domain and the relations among them usually remain unchanged, while the technologies and implementation environments are in progressive improvement. Hence, domain analysis models usually remain valid for long periods.

Several methods and architectures have been developed to support domain analysis. Some of them rely on Unified Modeling Language (UML) [3] and metamodeling techniques [27], for example Catalysis [11]. Using standard notations and techniques has many advantages, including accessibility, reliability, and uniformity. However, most of the suggested works to domain analysis use different notions, and sometimes even different notations, for defining domains and their constraints and for specifying and designing applications, weakening the mentioned standardization benefits. Other techniques (e.g., [7], [25]) use UML extension mechanisms, more accurately stereotypes. Yet, this mechanism provides no formal definition of domain models.

In this paper we present the Application-based DOmain Modeling (ADOM) approach, which enables modeling domains as if they were regular applications. This approach enables the validation of domain-specific application models against their domain models. The ADOM approach consists of three layers: the application layer, the domain layer, and the (modeling) language layer. In the application layer, the required application is modeled as composed of classes, associations, collaborations, etc. In the domain layer, the domain elements and relations are modeled as if the domain itself is an application. Finally, the language layer includes metamodels of modeling languages (or methods). We also provide a set of validation rules between the different layers: the domain layer enforces constraints on the application layer, while the language layer enforces constraints on both the application and domain layers. Thus, the contribution of this paper is twofold. First, we provide an approach for modeling various aspects of domains and for validating application models against domain models. This approach uses a single, standard modeling language, UML, and a standard technique, metamodeling. Secondly, applying the ADOM approach to UML, we provide a formal framework for defining and constraining stereotypes.

The structure of the rest of the paper is as follows. Section 2 reviews existing works within the domain analysis area, dividing them into single-level and two-level domain analysis approaches. Section 3 introduces our three-level ADOM approach. In this section, we elaborate on applying ADOM to UML class, component, and deployment diagrams, exemplifying the approach stages and validation rules on a domain of Web applications and a Web-based glossary application. Finally, Section 4 summarizes the strengths of this approach and refers to future research plans.

2 Domain Analysis – Literature Review

Referring to domain analysis as an engineering approach, Argano [1] suggested that domain analysis should consist of conceptual analysis combined with infrastructure specification and implementation. Meekel et al. [15] suggested that in addition to its static definition, domain analysis may be conceived of as a development process which identifies a domain scope, builds a domain model, and validates that model. Since the domain keeps evolving as the product users within its scope generate new requirements, domain analysis in not a one-shot affair [5], [6]. Gomaa and Kerschberg [13] agreed that the domain model lifecycle is constantly evolving via an iterative process. Supporting this domain evolution concept, Drake and Ett [10] claimed that domain analysis gives rise to two concurrent, mutually dependent lifecycles that should be correlated: the fundamental system lifecycle and the domain lifecycle. Becker and Diaz-Herrera [2] proposed that the two concurrent streams are the design for reuse (i.e., the domain model) and the design with reuse (i.e., the application model). Following this spirit, the Model-Driven Architecture (MDA) [19], which originally aimed to separate business or application logic from underlying platform technology, observes that system functionality will gradually become more knowledge-based and capable of automatically discovering common properties of dissimilar domains. In other words, the aim of MDA is to eventually build systems in which considerable amount of domain knowledge is pushed up into higher abstraction levels. However, this vision is supported in a conceptual level and not (yet) in a practical one.

Several methods and techniques have been developed to support domain analysis. We classify them into two categories: single-level and two-level domain analysis approaches.

2.1 Single-Level Domain Analysis Approaches

In the single level domain analysis approaches, the domain engineer defines domain components, libraries, or architectures. The application designer reuses these domain artifacts and can change them in the application model. Meekel et al. [15], for example, propose a domain analysis process that is based on multiple views. They used Object Modeling Technique (OMT) [24] to produce a domain-specific framework and components. Gomaa and Kerschberg [13] suggest that a system specification will be derived by tailoring the domain model according to the features desired in the specific system.

Feature-Oriented Domain Analysis (FODA) [14] defines several activities to support domain analysis, including context definition, domain characterization, data analysis and modeling, and reusable architecture definition. A specific system makes use of the reusable architecture but not of the domain model.

Clauss [7] suggests two stereotypes for maintaining variability within a domain model: <<variation point>>, which indicates the variability of an element, and <<variant>>, which indicates the extension part. These stereotypes seems to be weak when defining a domain model and validating a specific application model of that domain.

Catalysis [11] is an approach to systematic business-driven development of component-based systems. It defines a process to help business users and software developers share a clear and precise vocabulary, design and specify component interfaces so they plug together readily, and reuse domain models, architectures, interfaces, code, etc. Catalysis introduced two types of mechanisms for separating different subject areas: package extension and package template. Package extension allows definitions of fragments of language to be developed separately and then merged to form complete languages. Package templates, on the other hand, allow patterns of language definition to be distilled and then applied consistently across the definition of languages and their components. Both package extension and package template mechanisms deal basically with classes and packages and enable renaming of the structural elements when reusing them in particular systems. In addition, that work does not address the application model validation against its domain model(s).

2.2 Two-Level Domain Analysis Approaches

In the two-level domain analysis approaches, connection is made between the domain model and its usage in the application model. Contrary to the single-level domain analysis approaches, the domain and application models in the two-level domain analysis approaches remain separate, while validation rules between them are defined. These validation rules enable avoiding syntactic and semantic mistakes during the initial stages of the application modeling, reducing development time and improving system quality. Petro et al. [20], for example, present a concept of building reusable repositories and architectures, which consist of correlated component classes, connections, constraints, and rationales. When modeling a specific system, the system model is validated with respect to the domain model in order to check that no constraint has been violated.

Schleicher and Westfechtel [25] discuss static metamodeling techniques in order to define domain specific extensions. They divide these extensions into descriptive stereotypes for expressing the elements of the underlying domain metamodel, restrictive stereotypes for attaching constraints to stereotyped model elements, regular metamodel extensions, and restrictive metamodel extensions. They mostly deal with packages and classes, but not with behavioral elements. Furthermore, the semantics and constraints of the stereotypes used in this work are expressed in a natural language, weakening the formality of this approach.

Gomma and Eonsuk-Shin [12] suggest a multiple view metamodeling method for software product lines. They solve model commonalty and variability problems within the product line domain by defining special stereotypes which are used in the use case, class, collaboration, statechart, and feature model views. These stereotypes are modeled in the metamodel level by class diagrams, while the relations among them are specified in Object Constraint Language (OCL) [028]. The main shortcoming of this method is in using a new dialect of UML for modeling the domain elements and constraints (e.g., adding alternating paths).

Morisio et al. [16] propose an extension to UML that includes a special stereotype indicating that a class may be altered within a specific system. The extension is demonstrated by applying it to UML class diagrams. The validation of an application model with respect to its domain model entails checking whether a class appears in the application model along with its associate classes, but not if the class is correctly connected.

The Institute for Software Integrated Systems (ISIS) at Vanderbilt University suggested a metamodeling technique for building a domain-specific model using UML and OCL [17]. The application models are created from the domain metamodel, enabling validation of their consistency and integrity in terms of the domain analysis [9]. However, the domain models are specified using UML class diagrams and OCL, while the application models use other notations, conceding the benefits of applying a standard modeling language to the application models as well.

3 The Application-Based Domain Modeling (ADOM) Approach

Application models and domain models are similar in many aspects. An application model consists of classes and associations among them and it specifies a set of possible behaviors. Similarly, a domain model consists of core elements, static constraints, and dynamic relations. The main difference between these models is in their abstraction levels, i.e., domain models are more abstract than application models. Furthermore, domain models should be flexible in order to handle commonalities and differences of the applications within the domain.

The classical framework for metamodeling is based on an architecture with four abstraction layers [18]. The first layer is the information layer, which is comprised of the desired data. The model layer, which is the second layer, is comprised of the metadata that describes data in the information layer. The third metamodel layer is comprised of the descriptions that define the structure and semantics of metadata. Finally, the meta-metamodel layer consists of a description of the structure and semantics of meta-metadata (for example, metaclasses, metaattributes, etc.). Following this general architecture, we divide our Application-based DOmain Modeling (ADOM) approach into three layers: the application layer, the domain layer, and the (modeling) language layer. The application layer, which is equivalent to the model layer (M1), consists of models of particular systems, including their structure (scheme) and behavior. The domain layer, i.e., the metamodel layer (M2), consists of specifications of various domains. The language layer, which is equivalent to the meta-metamodel layer (M3), includes metamodels of modeling languages. The modeling languages may be graphical, textual, mathematical, etc. In addition, the ADOM approach explicitly enforces constraints among the different layers: the domain layer enforces constraints on the application layer, while the language layer enforces constraints on both the application and domain layers.

Figure 1 depicts the architecture of the ADOM approach. The application layer in this figure includes three examples of applications: *Amazon*, which is a Web-based book store, *eBay*, which is an auction site supported by agents, and *Kasbah*, which is a multi-agent electronic marketplace. Each one of these systems may have several models in different modeling languages. The domain layer in Figure 1 includes two domains: *Web applications* and *multi agent systems*, while the language layer in this example includes only one modeling language, *UML*. Since UML is the current standard (object-oriented) modeling language, we apply the ADOM approach to UML.

Figure 1 shows also the relations between the layers. The black arrows indicate constraint enforcement of the domain models on the application models, while the grey arrows indicate constraint enforcement of the language metamodels on the application and domain models.

The rest of this section elaborates on the domain and application layers, while the language layer is restricted to the UML metamodel [3] except of two minor changes:

1. A model element (e.g., attribute, operation, message, etc.) has an additional feature, called "multiplicity", which represents how many times the model element can appear in a particular system. This feature appears as <<min..max>> before a relevant domain element in a domain model, while <<1..1>> is the default (and, hence, does not appear).
2. A model element can have several stereotypes, which are separated by commas.

3.1 Applying UML Structural Views to the Domain Layer of the ADOM Approach

When referring to the static views of a domain, the domain engineer can use UML class, component, and deployment diagrams for specifying the domain elements and

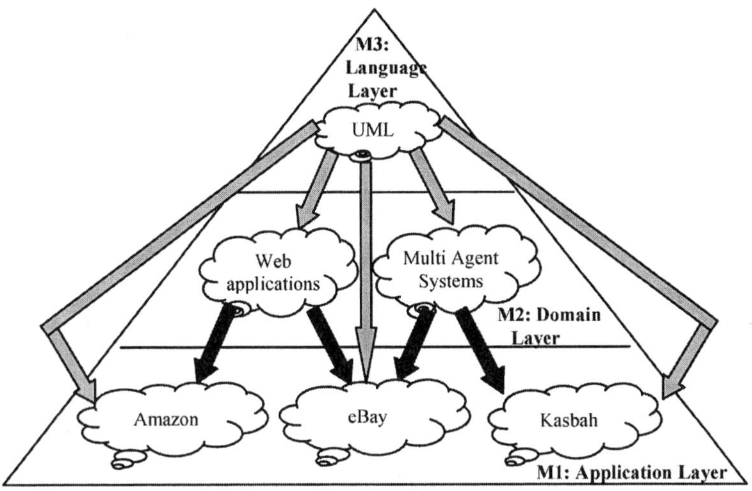

Fig. 1. The Application-based DOmain Modeling (ADOM) architecture

the (structural) constraints among them. In what follows, we demonstrate the ADOM approach on a part of the Web application domain as defined by Conallen [8]. Figure 2 cites a definition of a server page given by Conallen.

1. A server page represents a web page that has scripts which are executed by the server.
2. These scripts interact with resources on the server (databases, business logic, external systems, etc).
3. The object's operations represent the functions in the script, and its attributes represent the variables that are visible in the page's scope (accessible by all functions in the page).
4. Server pages can only have relationships with objects on the server.

Fig. 2. A part of Conallen's specification for the Web application domain – A Server Page definition

As can be seen, the definition in Figure 2 includes logical and physical elements (classes, components, and nodes). Hence, modeling this particular domain element, a server page, requires UML class, component, and deployment diagrams.

Figure 3 is a partial class diagram that models the logical aspects of a server page: A **server page** is specified as a class the attributes of which are classified as **variables**. A **server page** may have any number (including 0) of **variables** which can be of any type recognized in UML. These constraints are modeled in the domain model as the attribute "**<<0..m>> variable: anyType**" of the **server page** class. Since these **variables** are visible only within the server page's scope (including its scripts), their scope is defined to be "package" in the domain model. The order of scopes (from the least restricted to the most restricted) is public, package, protected, and private. A scope of a model element defined in a domain model is the least restricted scope that this element can get in any application model of that domain[1]. In particular, a **variable** scope within an application model can be package, protected, or private.

[1] Enforcing a specific scope on a model element (e.g., public) can be done by defining an OCL constraint.

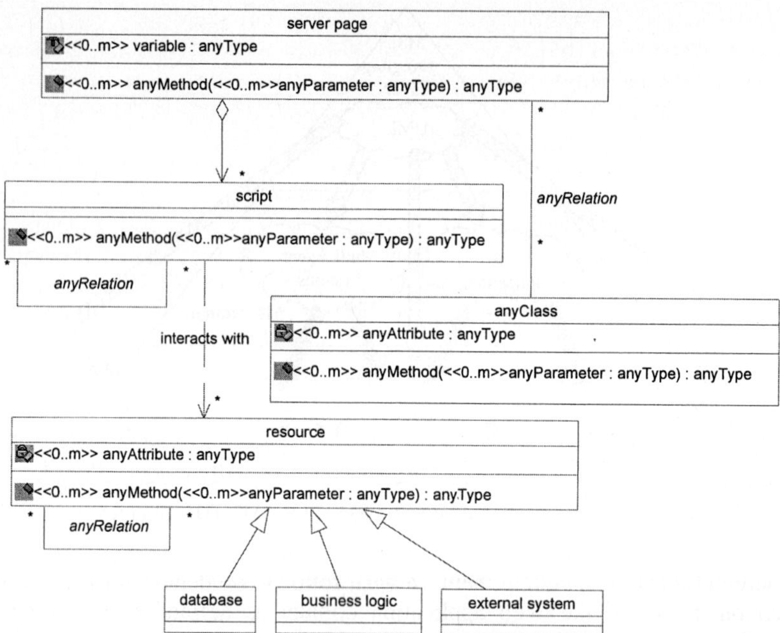

Fig. 3. A partial class diagram of a Server Page within the Web application domain

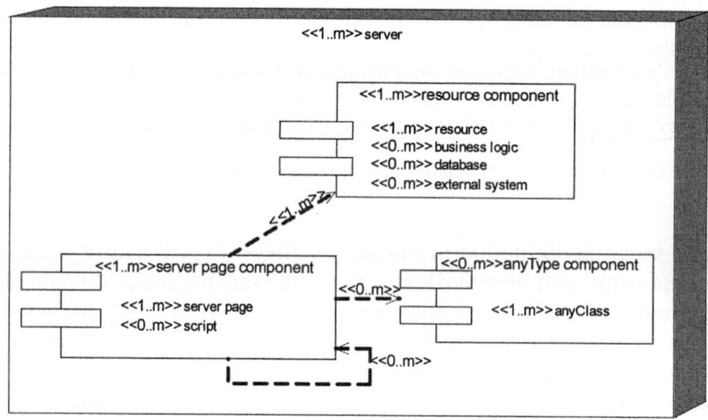

Fig. 4. A partial merged component and deployment diagram describing the physical constraints on a Server Page within the Web application domain

Figure 3 also specifies that a **server page** may have any number of operations regardless of their signatures as indicated by "**<<0..m>> anyMethod (<<0..m>> anyParameter :anyType): anyType**" declaration. All the operations of a **server page** (as all the operations in this domain model) are defined as public in the domain model and, hence, their scopes are not limited in the application models, i.e., they can be public, package, protected, or private. A **server page** may have relations with any class (on the server, as will be constrained next), as indicated by the association between **server page** and **anyClass**. In addition, a **server page** may aggregate any number of **scripts**. A **script** has any number of operations regardless of their signatures, may have any relations with other scripts, as indicated by the self association labeled **anyRelation**, and interacts with any number of **resources** (on the server), as indicate by the dependency relation labeled "**interacts with**".

Similarly to scopes, the ADOM approach defines a precedence order between relations. The most general relation is an association, followed by a navigational association, an aggregation, a navigational aggregation, a composition, and a navigational composition. A relation specified in a domain model is the most general relation possible between the two model elements in any application model of that domain. Enforcing a specific relation type (e.g., aggregation) requires definition of a new type of an OCL constraint.

Figure 3 does not limit the structure of a **resource** element, i.e., it may have any attributes, any operations, and any relations with other **resources**. However, this figure defines the hierarchy of resources: a **resource** is specialized into **database**, **business logic**, and **external system**, each of which is a special type of **resources**.

Figure 4 presents a component diagram merged into a deployment diagram. The merged diagram expresses the physical constraints of the domain on server pages. The main domain node is a **server** from which at least one physical node exists as indicated by the multiplicity feature (**<<1..m>>**). The **server** hosts at least one **resource component** and at least one **server page component**. It may also host components of any type each of which implements at least one class (of any type). A **resource component** implements at least one **resource** class and may implement any number of other **resource** classes, i.e., **business logic**, **database**, and/or **external system**. A **server page component** implements at least one **server page** class and any number (including 0) of **script** classes. Figure 4 also defines dependency constraints among components: a **server page component** depends on at least one **resource component** and may depend on other components of any type, including other **server page components**.

3.2 Applying UML Structural Views to the Application Layer of the ADOM Approach

An application model uses a domain model as a validation template. All the constraints enforced by the domain model should be applied to any application model of that domain. In order to achieve this goal, any element in the application model is classified according to the elements declared in the domain model using UML stereotype mechanism. As defined in UML user guide [3], a *stereotype* is a kind of a model element whose information content and form are the same as the basic model element, but its meaning and usage are different. The ADOM approach requires that a model element in an application model will preserve the relations of its stereotypes in the relevant domain model(s).

Returning to our example of the Web application domain, we describe in this section a partial model of a Web-based glossary application (GLAP) in that domain. The GLAP system [8] provides an online version of a software development project's glossary of terms. The project's team members can access the database of terms, using a common Web browser. Team members may also update, add entries to the database, and remove entries from it, using the same browser interface. Figure 5 is a partial class diagram of the GLAP system. Following the server page definition in the Web application domain, shown in Figure 3, the GLAP system defines two types of server pages: **process search**, which uses the glossary API to search the glossary for words (or descriptions) that match a string, and **edit entry**, which builds an edit page for a specific entry in the glossary. **Process search** consists of **writeEntry** (classified as a script) and **getEntries** (also classified as a script). It also has four variables (attributes): **searchWord**, **searchDescription**, **nl** (the new line string), and **messageWord** (the word searched for, modified for use as a hyperlink parameter). All the variables of **process search** are of type string. The **Edit entry** server page consists of **getEntry** (classified as a script) and has three variables (**id**, **word**, and **description**). The **getEntries** script consists of a **getEntry** script. The **writeEntry** and **getEntries** scripts interact with the **glossary DB** (classified as a database), which in turn consists of many **glossary entries** (classified as "database" elements).

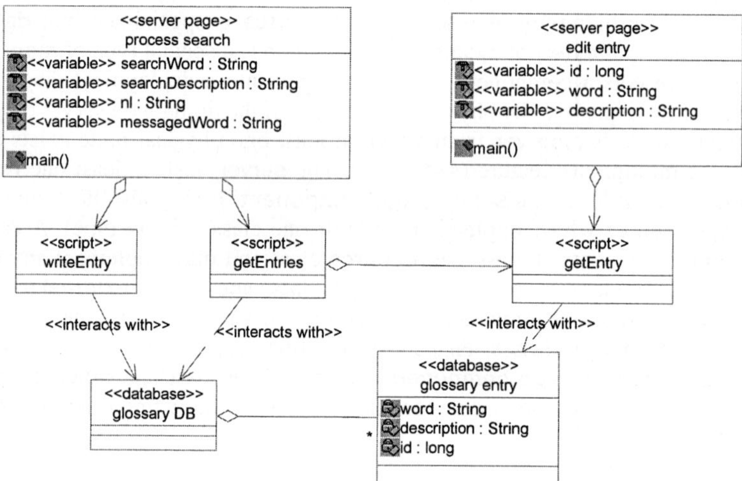

Fig. 5. A partial class diagram of the GLAP system – A description of **process search** and **edit entry** server pages

The ADOM approach validates the structure of each application class and the relations among them using the domain model. Table 1 summarizes the domain constraints of the Web application elements, and how these are correctly fulfilled in the class diagram of the GLAP system. For each domain class, the table lists its features (in the "Feature Name" column), scope or relation type constraints (in the "Feature Constraint" column), and multiplicity constraints (in the "Allowed Feature Multiplicity" column). In addition, the table summaries the actual features of each class in the application model (in the "Actual Features" column). As can be seen, none of the constraints expressed in the domain model, shown in Figure 3, are violated by the application model, specified in Figure 5.

Figure 6 depicts the implementation view of the GLAP system. This diagram follows the guidelines of the Web application domain for components and their deployment as expressed in Figure 4. The ADOM approach validates the existence of the defined classes and their associations to components and nodes. It also validates the relationships among the various model elements and their multiplicities.

Table 1. The Web application domain constraints and their fulfillment in the GLAP system model – comparing the class diagrams

Class	Feature Name	Feature Constraint	Allowed Feature Multiplicity	Actual Features
Server page	variable	Max scope: package	0..∞	• 4 package variables for process search • 3 package variables for edit entry
	general operation	Max scope: public	0..∞	• 1 public operation for each server page (process search & edit entry)
	relation to script	Type: navigational aggregation	0..∞	• 2 navigational aggregations for process search (writeEntry and getEntries) • 1 navigational aggregation for edit entry (getEntry)
	relation to any class	Type: association	0..∞	• 0 relation to other classes for both process search & edit entry
script	general attribute	None	0	• 0 attributes for both process search and edit entry
	general operation	Max scope: public	0..∞	• 0 public operations for each script
	relation to script	Type: association	0..∞	• 1 navigational aggregation for getEntries • 0 relations for the other scripts
	dependency to resource	None	0..∞	• 1 dependency relation for each script
resource	general attribute	Max scope: private	0..∞	• 0 attributes for glossary DB • 3 private attributes for glossary entry
	general operation	Max scope: public	0..∞	• 0 public operations for each resource
	relation to resource	Type: association	0..∞	• 1 aggregation for glossary DB • 0 relations for the other resources

Table 2 summarizes the physical constraints of the Web application domain (specified in Figure 4) and shows that none of them is violated by the GLAP system. For each component or node, the domain constraints (the "Feature Constraints" column) and the relevant features in the application model (the "Actual Features" column) are listed side-by-side.

4 Summary and Future Work

The Application-based DOmain Modeling (ADOM) approach enables domain engineers to define structural and behavioral constraints that are applicable to all the systems within a specific domain. When developing a system in ADOM, its domain (or domains) is first defined in order to enforce domain restrictions on particular systems. Then, the application models are validated against their domain models in order to detect semantic errors in early development stages. These errors cannot be automatically found when using syntactic modeling language alone.

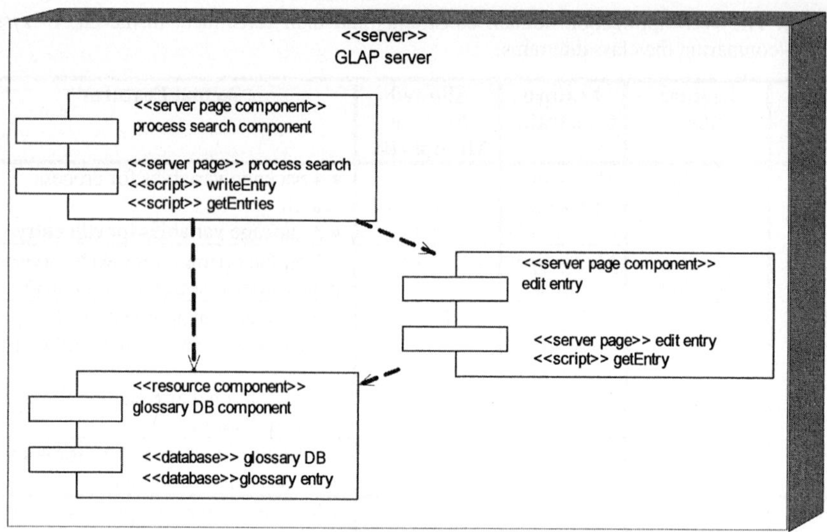

Fig. 6. A partial merged component and deployment diagram of the GLAP system – Allocating the **process search** and **edit entry** server pages into components and nodes

Two major techniques are usually used when applying UML to the domain analysis area: stereotypes and metamodeling. The main limitation of the stereotypes technique is the need to define the basic elements of a domain outside the model via a natural language, as was done, for example, by Conallen for the Web application domain [8]. While using natural languages is more comprehensible to humans, it lacks the needed formality for defining domain elements, constraints, and usage contexts. The ADOM approach enables modeling the domain world in a (semi-) formal UML model. This model is used to validate domain-specific application models.

While applying a metamodeling technique, the basic elements of the domain and the relations among them are modeled. Usually, the domain and application models are specified using different notions (and even different notations). In the case of UML, the domain models are expressed using class diagrams, while the application models are expressed using various UML diagram types. This unreasonably limits the expressiveness of domain models. In the ADOM approach, the domain and application models are specified using the same notation and ontology. In other words, the ADOM approach enables specification of physical and behavioral constraints in the domain level (layer). Furthermore, keeping the same notation and ontology for the entire development team (which includes domain engineers and system engineers) improves collaboration during the development process.

In this paper, we applied the ADOM approach to UML static views. In [22], we have also applied the ADOM approach to UML interaction diagrams. In the future, we plan to develop a domain validation tool that will check a system model against its domain model and will even guide system developers according to given domain models. An experiment is planned to classify domain-specific modeling errors when using the ADOM approach and other domain analysis methods. This experiment will also check the adoption of several different domains within the same application utilizing the ADOM approach.

Table 2. The domain constraints and their fulfillment in the GLAP system model – comparing the component and deployment diagrams

Component/ Node	Feature Constraints	Actual Features
server	At least one node	One server called **GLAP server**
	Includes at least one resource component	One resource component called **glossary DB component**
	Includes at least one server page component	Two server page components called **process search component** and **edit entry component**
	Includes 0 or more components of any type	No other components
server page component	Includes at least one server page class	• The **process search component** includes one server page class (**process search**) • The **edit entry component** includes one server page class (**edit entry**)
	Includes 0 or more script classes	• The **process search component** includes two script classes (**writeEntry** and **getEntries**) • The **edit entry component** includes one script class (**getEntry**)
	Depends on at least one resource component	• The **process search component** depends on one resource component (**glossary DB component**) • The **edit entry component** depends on one resource component (**glossary DB component**)
	Depends on 0 or more server page components	• The **process search component** depends on one server page component (**edit entry component**) • The **edit entry component** does not depend on other server page components
	Depends on 0 or more other components of any type	• Neither the **process search component** nor the **edit entry component** depends on other components
resource component	Includes at least one resource class	The **glossary DB component** includes two resource classes of type database (**glossary DB** and **glossary entry**)
	Includes 0 or more business logic classes	The **glossary DB component** includes 0 business logic classes
	Includes 0 or more database classes	The **glossary DB component** includes two database classes (**glossary DB** and **glossary entry**)
	Includes 0 or more external system classes	The **glossary DB component** includes 0 external system classes

References

1. Arango, G. "Domain analysis: from art form to engineering discipline", Proceedings of the Fifth International Workshop on Software Specification and Design, p.152-159, 1989.
2. Becker, M. and Diaz-Herrera, J. L. "Creating domain specific libraries: a methodology, design guidelines and an implementation", Proceedings of the Third International Conference on Software Reuse, pp. 158-168, 1994.

3. Booch, G., Rumbaugh, J., and Jacobson, I. The Unified Modeling Language User Guide, Addison-Wesley, 1998.
4. Carnegie, M. “Domain Engineering: A Model-Based Approach”, Software Engineering Institute, http://www.sei.cmu.edu/domain-engineering/, 2002.
5. Champeaux, D. de, Lea, D., and Faure, P. Object-Oriented System Development, Addison Wesley, 1993.
6. Cleaveland, C. “Domain Engineering”, http://craigc.com/cs/de.html, 2002.
7. Clauss, M. "Generic Modeling using UML extensions for variability", Workshop on Domain Specific Visual Languages, Object-Oriented Programming, Systems, Languages, and Applications (OOPSLA'01), 2001.
8. Conallen, J., Building Web Applications with UML, First Edition, Addison-Wesley, Reading, MA, 1999.
9. Davis, J. “Model Integrated Computing: A Framework for Creating Domain Specific Design Environments”, The Sixth World Multiconference on Systems, Cybernetics, and Informatics (SCI), 2002.
10. Drake, R. and Ett, W. “Reuse: the two concurrent life cycles paradigm”, Proceedings of the conference on TRI-ADA '90, p.208-221, 1990.
11. D’Souza, D. F., Wills, A.C. Objects, Components, and Frameworks with UML – The CatalysisSM Approach. Addison-Wesley, 1999.
12. Gomma, H. and Eonsuk-Shin, M. "Multiple-View Meta-Modeling of Software Product Lines", Proceedings of the Eighth IEEE International Confrerence on Engineering of Complex Computer Systems, 2002.
13. Gomaa, E. and Kerschberg, L. "Domain Modeling for Software Reuse and Evolution", Proceedings of Computer Assisted Software Engineering Workshop (CASE 95), 1995.
14. Kang, K., Cohen, S., Hess, J., Novak, W., and Peterson, A.,”Feature-Oriented Domain Analysis (FODA) Feasibility Study”, CMU/SEI-90-TR-021 ADA235785, 1990.
15. Meekel, J., Horton, T. B., France, R. B., Mellone, C., and Dalvi, S. “From domain models to architecture frameworks”, Proceedings of the 1997 symposium on Software reusability, pp. 75-80, 1997.
16. Morisio, M., Travassos, G. H., and Stark, M. “Extending UML to Support Domain Analysis”, Proceedings of the Fifth IEEE International Conference on Automated Software Engineering, pp. 321-324, 2000.
17. Nordstrom, G., Sztipanovits, J., Karsai, G., and Ledeczi, A. “Metamodeling - Rapid Design and Evolution of Domain-Specific Modeling Environments”, Proceedings of the IEEE Sixth Symposium on Engineering Computer-Based Systems (ECBS), pp. 68-74, 1999.
18. OMG, “Meta-Object Facility (MOF™)”, version 1.4, 2003, http://www.omg.org/docs/formal/02-04-03.pdf
19. OMG, "Model Driven Architecture (MDA™)", version 1.0.1, 2003, http://www.omg.org/docs/omg/03-06-01.pdf
20. Petro, J. J., Peterson, A. S., and Ruby, W. F. “In-Transit Visibility Modernization Domain Modeling Report Comprehensive Approach to Reusable Defense Software” (STARS-VC-H002a/001/00). Fairmont, WV: Comprehensive Approach to Reusable Defense Software, 1995.
21. Pressman, R.S. "Software Engineering: A Practitioner's Approach", 5th Edition, New York: McGraw-Hill, 2000.
22. Reinhartz-Berger, I. and Sturm, A. Behavioral Domain Analysis – The Application-based Domain Modeling Approach, accepted to UML'2004, 2004.
23. Rix, M. “Case study of a Successful Firmware Reuse Program”, HP Software Productivity Conference, 1992.
24. Rumbaugh, J., Blaha, M., Premerlani, W., Eddy, F., and Lorensen, W. Object-Oriented Modeling and Design, Prentice-Hall International, Inc., Englewood Cliffs, New Jersey, 1991

25. Schleicher, A. and Westfechtel, B. "Beyond Stereotyping: Metamodeling Approaches for the UML", Proceedings of the Thirty Fourth Annual Hawaii International Conference on System Sciences, pp. 1243-1252, 2001.
26. Valerio, A., Giancarlo, S., and Massimo, F. "Domain analysis and framework-based software development", ACM SIGAPP Applied Computing Review, 5 (2), 1997.
27. Van Gigch, J. P. System Design Modeling and Metamodeling. Kluwer Academic Publishers, 1991.
28. Warmer, J. and Kleppe, A. The Object Constraint Language: Precise Modeling with UML. Addison-Wesley, 1998.

A Model Driven Approach for XML Database Development*

Belén Vela, César J. Acuña, and Esperanza Marcos

Kybele Research Group
Rey Juan Carlos University
Madrid, Spain
{bvela,cjacunia,emarcos}@escet.urjc.es

Abstract. In this paper we propose a methodological approach for the development of XML databases. Our proposal is framed in MIDAS, a model driven methodology for the development of Web Information Systems (WISs) based on the Model Driven Architecture (MDA) proposed by the Object Management Group (OMG). So, in this framework, the proposed data Platform Independent Model (PIM) is the conceptual data model and the data Platform Specific Model (PSM) is the XML Schema model. Both of them will be represented in UML, therefore we also summarize in this work an extension to UML for XML Schema. Moreover, we define the mappings to transform the data PIM into the data PSM, which will be the XML database schema. The development process of the XML database will be shown by means of a case study: a WIS for the management of medical images stored in the XML DB of Oracle.

Keywords: XML Database Development, XML Schema, UML, Mappings, Database Design, Model Driven Engineering.

1 Introduction

The development of a database (DB) depends on different features. On the one hand it depends on the previous existence of the DB or if it is necessary to start from scratch. On the other hand we have to take into account the selected data repository, that is, if we want to use an object-relational (OR) DB or an XML DB. We have proposed a general framework and a specific process for each of the cases when modeling a Web DB taking into account the previous features; in [13] we have defined a methodological approach for the development of OR DBs, including the proposed tasks, models, notations and mapping rules to obtain the final implementation of the OR DB in a product (Oracle); and, in this paper we go deeply into the development of XML DBs. XML [3] is the current standard for the information exchange and data transportation between heterogeneous applications. Traditionally the XML documents information were stored in conventional DB systems, but now the XML DBs are emerging as the best alternative to store and manage XML documents. There exist different solutions

* This research is carried out in the framework of the projects: *EDAD* (07T/0056/2003 1) financed by Autonomous Community of Madrid (Spain) and *DAWIS*, financed by the Spanish Ministry of Science and Technology (TIC 2002-04050-C02-01).

P. Atzeni et al. (Eds.): ER 2004, LNCS 3288, pp. 780–794, 2004.

for the XML documents storage, which could be roughly categorized according to [20] into two main groups: native XML DBs like Tamino [17], X-Hive/DB [21], eXcelon XIS [7], eXist [6] or ToX [2]; and XML DB extensions enabling the storage of XML documents within conventional, usually relational or object-relational DataBase Management Systems (DBMSs) like Oracle [16], which includes since version 9*i* new features, collectively referred to as Oracle XML DB, IBM DB2 XML Extender [8] or Microsoft SQLXML [14]. In [20] a study of different XML DB solutions is made.

Nonetheless, good technology is not enough to support complex XML data and applications. It is necessary to provide methodologies that guide designers in the XML DB design task, in the same way as it has been traditionally done with relational or object-relational DBs [5]. There are a few works in this research line, for example, [9] proposes some rules to obtain an XML Schema from a UML class diagram, but unfortunately, this proposal is not included in a methodological framework and does not give specific guidelines for the design of XML DBs. So, in spite of existing a lot of XML DB solutions as we have mentioned before, to the best of our knowledge, there is no methodology for the systematic design of XML DBs.

For this reason, in this work we show a methodological approach for the development XML DBs in the framework of MIDAS, a model driven methodology for the development of Web Information Systems (WISs). In our approach the proposed data Platform Independent Model (PIM) is the conceptual data model and the data Platform Specific Model (PSM) is the XML Schema model, which will be defined both in UML. For this purpose, we summarize the extension to UML for representing XML Schemas, based on the preliminary work presented in [18]. Moreover, we propose the mappings to transform the data PIM into the data PSM in XML Schema. The obtained data PSM will be the XML DB.

The rest of the paper is organized as follows: section 2 is an overview of the MIDAS framework, including its model driven architecture and its process; in section 3 we focus on the XML DB development in MIDAS, showing the specific part of the process, the summarized UML extension and the mappings to obtain the data PSM from the data PIM; in section 4 we present part of a case study for the management of medical images. We focus on the development of the XML DB, showing the obtained data PIM and data PSM, as well as a small part of the final implementation in Oracle's XML DB; finally, section 5 sums up the main conclusions as well as the future work.

2 MIDAS Framework

MIDAS [12] is a model driven methodology for the development of WISs with an incremental and iterative process model based on prototyping. It also proposes some techniques based on agile methodologies, as for example, eXtreme Programming. Its architecture is based on the Model Driven Architecture (MDA) proposed by the Object Management Group (OMG) [15]. The methodology specifies some Computation Independent Models, PIMs, PSMs and mappings between them. The MIDAS architecture (see figure 1) considers the aspects of *content*, *hypertext* and *behavior* at the PIM and PSM levels to model the system [4]. In this work we focus on the *content* aspect, where the used data PIM is the conceptual data model and the used PSM is the

OR or the XML Schema model. The *hypertext* and *behavior* aspects are out of the scope of this paper and are described in detail in other works [10].

MIDAS proposes to use standards in the development process, and, therefore, it is based on UML, XML and SQL:1999. UML is used to model the whole system in a unique notation. As UML provides some extension mechanisms, it can be extended to be used for all the necessary techniques when modeling a WIS. MIDAS proposes to use some of the existing extensions for Web modeling and it also defines new ones whenever it is necessary, for example, the UML extension for OR DB design [11,13] or the UML extensions for XML technology, including one for XML Schemas [18].

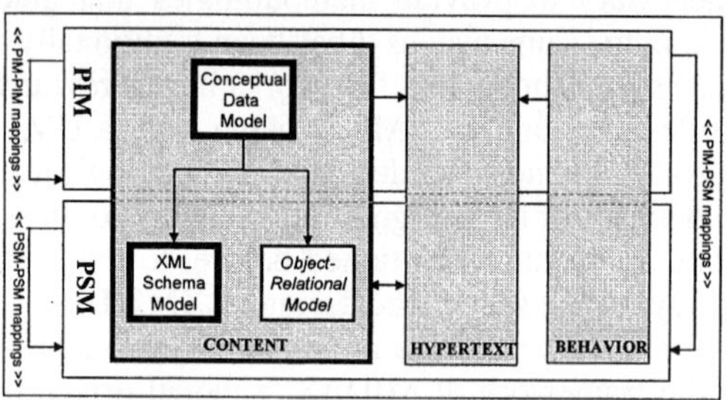

Fig. 1. MIDAS Architecture

MIDAS process defines different steps and at the end of each step a new version of the product is obtained. In the first step the user requirements and the architecture have to be defined. In the second step, MIDAS/PR, a first PRototype of the WIS is developed with static Web pages. This prototype permits validating the specified user requirements with the customer and obtaining a first version of the product in a short time. In the third step, MIDAS/ST, the STructural dimension of the WIS is carried out. Taking the first version of the hypertext obtained in the previous step, a new version of the Web hypertext is implemented using XML technology. The dynamic Web pages in XML extract the information from the DB, which is also built in this step. There are also another step, MIDAS/BH, to model the services and the BeHaviour of the WIS, as well as another one for testing the system. Each step defines the specific tasks, models and notations to be carried out.

This work deals specifically with the MIDAS/ST step of the MIDAS methodology, where the structural dimension of a WIS is carried out, which includes the content aspect. This aspect, on which we focus in this paper, corresponds to the traditional concept of a DB. Figure 2 shows the specific process for the development of the DB (XML or OR) and its specific tasks: at the PIM level the conceptual data design task has to be carried out and at the PSM level the logical data design task has to be realized using XML or OR technology. A detailed description of the MIDAS process and its tasks, models and notation can be found in [4,12,13].

3 XML Database Development

In this work we concentrate our attention on the XML database development in the **MIDAS/ST** step of the MIDAS methodology, which is responsible for the development of the structural dimension of a WIS. This dimension includes the content aspect, which corresponds to the traditional concept of a DB. The development of the

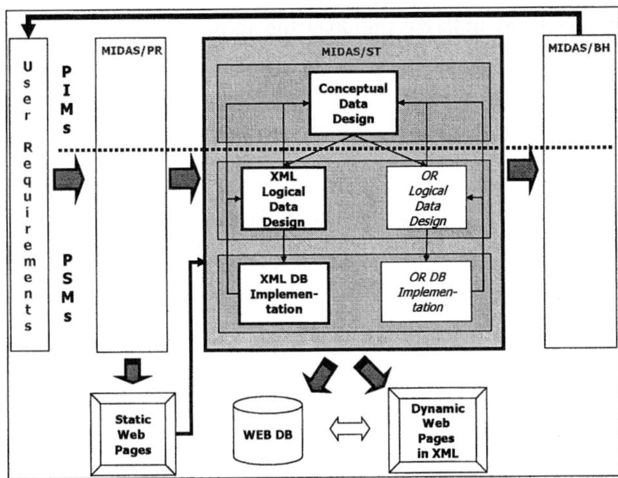

Fig. 2. MIDAS Process for the DB development

DB can be carried out in different ways: case a) there exists already a DB in the organization and we have to integrate it with the WIS; case b) we want to use an OR DB; case c) we want to use an XML DB.

In this section we will show how to carry out the XML DB development starting from scratch, including the necessary techniques and models. We will see at first the specific development process for XML DBs, then we will sum up the UML extension to represent XML Schemas based on the preliminary work presented in [18], and finally, we will show the mappings to transform a data PIM into a data PSM defined with an XML Schema.

3.1 XML Database Development Process

The proposed process for the development of XML DBs includes several activities, but we will show just the specific ones for XML DBs development: analysis, design and implementation.

- The **analysis activity** is independent of the way in which the DB is developed and the used technology. The data PIM obtained in the previous step MIDAS/PR will be refined taking into account new user requirements and the feedback provided by the use of the prototype obtained at the end of the previous step. The data PIM will be represented with a UML class diagram.

The tasks that are carried out in the **design** and **implementation activities** depend mainly on the way we want to develop the DB, but we will only show the activities related with the development of an XML DB.

- In the **design activity** we have to obtain the logical data design. The logical design of the DB is carried out starting from the data PIM obtained in the analysis activity of the current step. From this data PIM we obtain the XML Schema at the PSM level represented in extended UML for XML Schemas, summed up in the next section 3.2, applying the mappings defined in section 3.3. The obtained XML Schema is the logical design of the DB.

- The **implementation activity** includes the implementation of the DB, using an XML DB to store the obtained XML Schemas.

3.2 Representing XML Schemas with Extended UML

In MIDAS we propose to use the XML Schema model as the data PSM. An XML Schema [19] is the definition of a specific XML structure. The W3C XML Schema language specifies how each type of element is defined in the schema and the data type that the element has associated. The XML Schema itself is a special kind of XML document that is written according to the rules given by the W3C XML Schema specification. These rules constitute a language, known as the XML Schema definition language; for a detailed description see [19].

The proposed notation to represent the XML Schema model is extended UML. So, next we sum up our UML extension to represent XML Schemas, which is based on the preliminary work presented in [18]. The extension defines a set of stereotypes, tagged values and constraints that enable us to represent in graphical notation in UML all the components of an XML Schema, keeping the associations, the specified order and nesting between them.

According to the proposed UML extension, an **XML schema** is represented by means of an UML package stereotyped with <<Schema>>, which will include all the components of the XML schema. The name of the schema will be the name of the package. The attributes of the XML Schema will be tagged values of the package.

The **XML elements** are represented with stereotyped classes named as the value of the attribute *name* of the element. The attributes of the element will be tagged values of the class. The appearance order of the element in the XML Schema, including as a prefix the order number of the element to which it belongs, will also be a tagged value of the class and it will be represented next to the name of the class.

The **XML attributes** are represented by means of UML attributes of the class that represent the XML element to which the XML attributes belong to. The base type of an XML attribute will be represented as the data type of the corresponding UML attribute. The constraints to be satisfied by the attribute (required, optional) and the default or fixed value will be represented as tagged values.

A ***compositor*** **composition** is a special kind of composition stereotyped with the kind of compositor: <<Choice>>, <<Sequence>> or <<All>>. It can only be used to join an element (composite) with the elements that compose the father element (parts). The compositors can be used to represent nameless XML complexTypes.

The **XML complexTypes** have been considered as stereotyped classes with <<complexType>>, if they are named. In this case, the complexType will be related by means of a *uses* association with the element, complexType or simpleType that uses it. If the complexType has no name, it will be represented in an implicit way by the compositor that composes the complexType.

The **XML simpleType** is a type that has no subelements or attributes. The simpleTypes have been considered as classes stereotyped with <<simpleType>> named as the element that contains it. It will be related with its father element with a stereotyped composition with <<simpleType>>.

The **XML complexContent** is a subclass of the complexType that it defines. The complexContent types have been considered as stereotyped classes, which must be related by an inheritance association with the elements or complexTypes that the complexContent redefines.

The **XML simpleContent** is a subclass of the complexType or a simpleType. The simpleContent types have been considered as stereotyped classes that are related with an inheritance association to the father type (simple or complex type) that is redefined by the simpleContent type.

A ***uses* association** is a special kind of unidirectional stereotyped association which joins a named complexType with the element or type (simple or complex) that uses it. A <<uses>> association can also be used to join two elements by means of a *ref* attribute in one of the elements. The direction of the association is represented by an arrow at the end of the element, which is used by the one that contains the corresponding *ref* element.

A **REF element** will be represented by means of an attribute stereotyped with <<REF>> and represents a link to another element. A REF attribute can only refer to a defined element and is associated with the referred element by means of a *uses* association.

In figure 3 the metamodel of the UML extension for XML Schemas is shown.

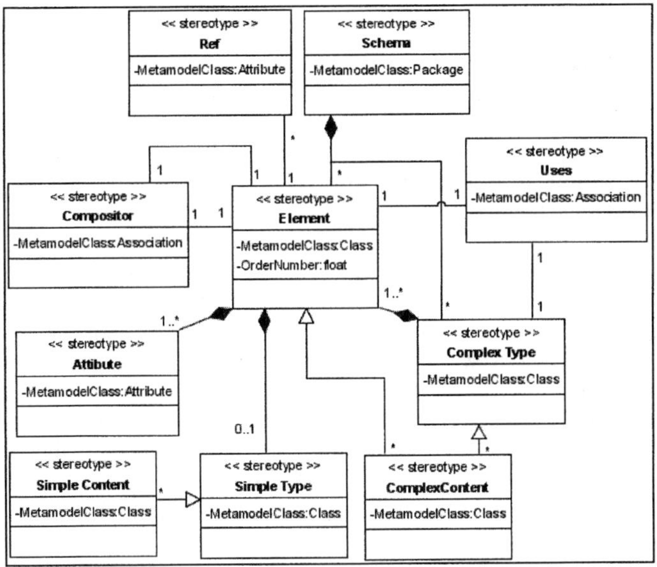

Fig. 3. Metamodel of the UML extension for XML Schemas

3.3 Mappings to Obtain the Data PSM from the Data PIM

In this section we are going to describe the mappings defined to build the data PSM from the data PIM. There exist some other works [9], in which some rules are defined to obtain XML Schemas from the UML class diagram, but, to our knowledge, none of these proposals give specific guidelines for the design of XML DBs.

We will start from the data PIM represented with a UML class diagram and will obtain the data PSM in XML, also represented in extended UML applying the following mapping rules:

- The *complete* **conceptual data model** is transformed, at the PSM level, into an XML schema named '*Data PSM*', including all the components of the data PIM. It will be represented with a UML package stereotyped with <<SCHEMA>> and named '*Data PSM*'. This package will include the components of the data PSM.
- **Transformation of UML classes**
  We can split the **UML classes** into different groups: subclasses of a generalization, classes that represent parts of a composition and finally, the rest of the classes.
  - The first and second groups of UML classes (subclasses and parts) will be transformed by means of named complexTypes.
  - In the third group the classes will be transformed into an element, named as the class name. The abstract classes are mapped into abstract elements.

  The complexTypes generated when transforming UML classes belonging to the first and second group, will be represented in extended UML by means of stereotyped classes with <<complexType>> and named with the name of the subclasses or parts plus "_type". The elements generated when transforming the UML classes belonging to the third group will be represented in extended UML with a class stereotyped with <<ELEMENT>> and named as the class of the data PIM from which it comes.
- **Transformation of UML attributes**
  In order to map the **UML attributes** of the classes, we can transform them in two different ways: into XML attributes or into XML elements. A straightforward mapping is to transform the UML attributes into XML attributes of the element that represents the class. However, in this way the attributes can no be used if they are not single valued, as for example, multivalued or composed ones. Moreover, attributes are usually used to describe the content of the elements and not to be visualized. For these reasons, and as the UML attributes are represented as classes in the UML metamodel, we propose to transform the UML attributes of a class by means of a complexType including as subelements the UML attributes of the class.
  This complexType will be represented in extended UML with composition stereotyped with <<sequence>>, which includes all the attributes as subelements represented with classes stereotyped with <<ELEMENT>>.
  The **attributes of the class** can be transformed according to their type:
  - A ***mandatory*** attribute will be represented with a minimum multiplicity of one at the composition, whereas an ***optional*** attribute will be represented with a minimum multiplicity of zero at the composition.
  - A ***multivalued*** attribute will be represented with a maximum multiplicity of N in the part side of the composition.
  - A ***composed*** attribute will be represented by an element that is related to the composing attributes by means of a complexType
  - An ***enumerated*** attribute will be represented by a simpleType composition, with the stereotyped restriction Enumeration.
  - A ***choice*** attribute will be represented by a simpleType composition, with the stereotyped restriction Choice.

- **Transformation of associations**
  There exist two main aspects to take into account when transforming UML associations into an XML Schema. The first one deals with the direction in which the associations are implemented, that is, if they are unidirectional or bidirectional. The second one deals with the way in which the associations are mapped using XML Schema constructions.
  With regard to the first aspect, UML associations can be represented in an XML schema either as unidirectional or as bidirectional associations. A unidirectional association means that it can be crossed only in one direction whereas a bidirectional one can be crossed in the two directions. If we know that queries require data in both directions of the association, then it is recommended to implement them as bidirectional associations improving in this way the response times. However, we have to take into account that bidirectional associations are not maintained by the system, so the consistence has to be guaranteed in a manual way. Therefore bidirectional associations, despite of improving in some cases the response times, have a higher maintenance cost. The navigability (if it is represented) in a UML diagram shows the direction in which the association should be implemented.
  With regard to the second aspect, the way in which an association could be mapped to XML schema is a crucial issue and there are different ways of transforming UML associations into XML Schema associations within a XML document, each with its advantages and disadvantages. Some criteria to select the best alternative are related to the kind of information, the desirable level of redundancy, etc. In [9] a study of the different alternatives is made. We propose to model the associations by adding association elements within the XML elements that represent the classes implicated in the association. Next, we show how to map the association in a unidirectional way using *ref* elements.
  - **One-to-One.** A one-to-one association will be mapped creating an association subelement of one of the elements that represent the classes implicated in the association. The subelement will be named with the association name. This subelement will include a complexType with an element of a *ref* type that references the other element implicated in the association. If the minimum multiplicity is one, the attribute *minOccurs* will be one, which is the default value and can be omitted, and otherwise it will be zero. As the maximum multiplicity is one, the attribute *maxOccurs* has to be one, which is the default value too and can be omitted.
  - **One-to-Many.** A one-to-many association will be transformed in a unidirectional way creating an association subelement within the element that represents the class with multiplicity N, named as the association, including a complexType within this element with a subelement of a *ref* type that references the other element implicated in the association. If the minimum multiplicity is one, the attribute *minOccurs* will be one, which is the default value and can be omitted, and otherwise it will be zero. As the maximum multiplicity is one in this direction, the attribute *maxOccurs* has to be one, which is the default value and can also be omitted.
  - **Many-to-Many.** Following the same reasoning as in the previous case, a many-to-many association will be transformed defining an association element within one of the elements, including a <<sequence>> complexType of refer-

ence elements to the collection of elements implicated in the association. If the minimum multiplicity is one, the attribute *minOccurs* will be one, which is the default value, otherwise it will be zero. As the maximum multiplicity is N in this direction, the attribute *maxOccurs* has to be N.

- **Transformation of aggregations**
  An aggregation will be mapped creating a subelement of the element which represents the aggregate named as the aggregation. If the aggregation has no name, the name will be "is_aggregated_of". This element (aggregate) will include a complexType with an element of *ref* type that references the parts of the aggregation. If the maximum multiplicity is N, the complexType will include a sequence of references. If the minimum multiplicity is one, the attribute *minOccurs* will be one, which is the default value, otherwise it will be zero.
  It will be represented in extended UML by means of an aggregation stereotyped with <<all>>.
- **Transformation of compositions**
  A composition of classes in the UML class diagram will be mapped including as subelements in the element that represents the compositor the parts of the composition. The subelements will be of the type of the complexType defined to represent the parts of the composition.
  It will be represented in extended UML including in the compositor a part of the stereotyped composition and a *uses* association, which relates the part with the corresponding complexType of the part.
- **Transformation of generalizations**
  A generalization of classes in the UML class diagram will be mapped including the superclass as an element and a complexType of choice type which includes as subelements of a complexType the subclasses of the generalization.
  It will be represented in extended UML by means of a composition stereotyped with <<choice>>.

The proposed mapping rules to obtain the data PSM are summarized in the table 1.

4 A Case Study

The tasks, models and mappings proposed in MIDAS are being defined by means of different case studies. In this paper we present part of the case study of a WIS for medical image management. This WIS is based on DICOM (Digital Image and COmmunications in Medicine) [1], which is the most accepted standard for the medical image exchange. In this paper, the presented case study will only focus on the development of the XML DB. We will show how to build it starting from a conceptual data model. In section 4.1 we present the data PIM and the section 4.2 presents the data PSM, showing how to apply the proposed mappings to obtain it. Finally, section 4.3 shows the XML database implementation in Oracle's XML DB.

4.1 Data PIM

For the sake of brevity we will only present a reduced part of the data PIM obtained in the analysis activity of MIDAS/ST step. This partial data PIM is based on the infor-

Table 1. Mapping rules to pass from the data PIM into the data PSM.

Data PIM	Data PSM
Data PIM	XML Schema
Class	XML Element
Sub class (generalization)	Subelement of complexType
Part class (composition)	Subelement of complexType
Attribute	Subelement
Mandatory	*minOccurs* =1 (default)
Optional	*minOccurs* = 0
Multivalued	*maxOccurs*= N
Composed	(all | sequence) complexType
Choice	choice complexType
Association	
One-To-One	Subelement (of any element) for association with complexType including a REF element
One-To-Many	Subelement (multiplicity N) for association with complexType including a REF to element (multiplicity 1)
Many-To-Many	Subelement (of any element) for association with sequence complexType of REFs to elements
Aggregation	
Maximum Multiplicity: 1	Subelement with complexType with REF element
Maximum Multiplicity: N	Subelement with sequence complexType of REF elements
Composition	ALL composition relating the compositor with the parts
Generalization	Choice complexType

mation model defined in the DICOM standard. As we can see in figure 4, the *Patients* can make one or more *Visits*. Each *Visit* can derive into one or more *Studies*. A Study is formed by several Study Components, which can belong simultaneously to different Studies. A Study Component makes references to several Series, which are a set of Images. There are different kinds of Series like Image, Raw Data, etc. A Result is obtained from a Study and is composed of several Interpretations.

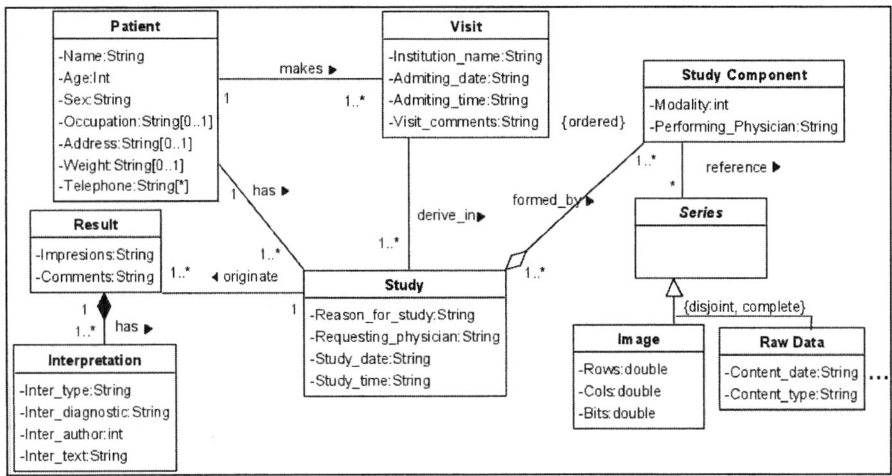

Fig. 4. Partial Data PIM in UML

4.2 Data PSM

To obtain the data PSM from the data PIM we have to apply the mappings defined in section 3.3 and we have to use the extended UML notation resumed in section 3.2, to represent the resulting XML Schema.

Transformation of classes: In order to transform the UML classes we could split them into two groups as follow:

- The first group is the one formed by those classes that are part classes in a composition, as the *Interpretation* class, as well as those classes that are subclasses in a generalization, as the *Image* and *Raw Data* classes. These classes are transformed into XML complexTypes and the attributes of these classes are mapped into subelements of the defined complexTypes. Figure 5 depicts part of the data PSM represented in extended UML. The part remarked with a solid line shows the transformation of the *Interpretation* class by means of a complexType named *Interpretation_type*.
- The other group is formed by the rest of the classes. Each of these classes is mapped into an XML element and its attributes are mapped into subelements of the XML element that represents the class related by means of a composition stereotyped with <<sequence>>. Figure 5 shows the transformation of the class *Result*, which is remarked with a dashed line.

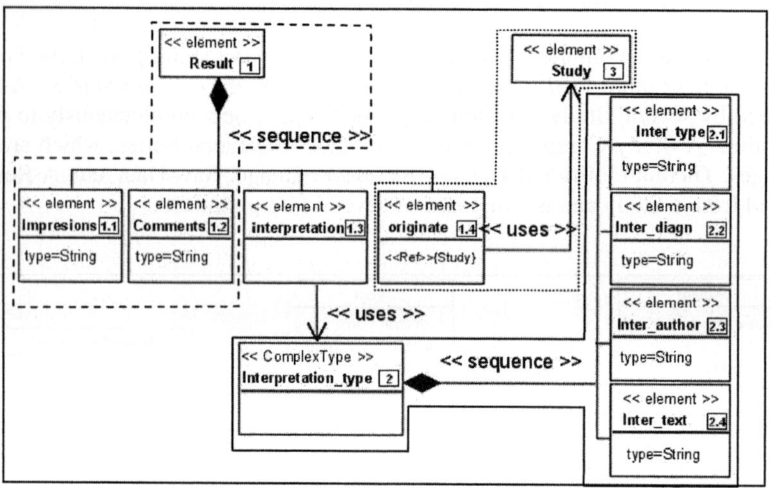

Fig. 5. Partial Data PSM in extended UML

Transformation of associations: In figure 5 the transformation of the one-to-many association between the *Study* and *Result* classes is remarked with a dotted line. For space reasons the *Study* class is not completely represented in this figure and the representation of its UML attributes were omitted. As the mapping rules indicate, the one-to-many association between these classes is transformed adding a subelement to the element that represents the class of the maximum multiplicity N. In this case, we add the subelement *originate* to the element *Result* named as the association, which has a reference to the element that represents the class with the maximum multiplicity one. The subelement *originate* will be related to the *Study* element by means of a *uses* association. Moreover, figure 5 depicts the transformation of the composition between the *Result* and *Interpretation* classes. This association is mapped adding a subelement to the element that represents the compositor class *Result,* named as the part class *Interpretation*. The type of the *Interpretation* element is the complex type *Interpretation_Type* defined when mapping the *Interpretation* class.

Additionally, figure 6 shows the XML Schema code generated from the UML diagram depicted in figure 5.

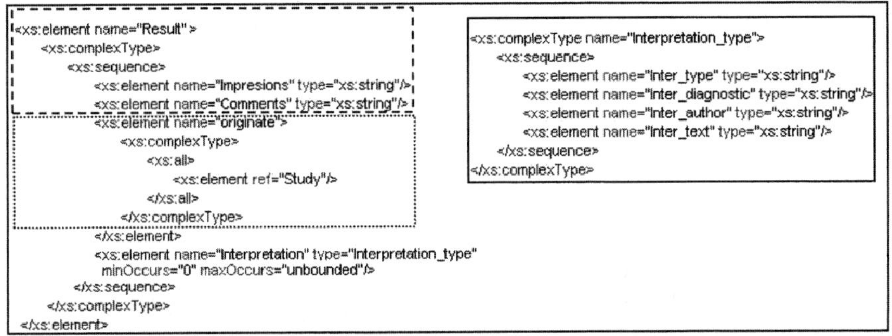

```
<xs:element name="Result" >
    <xs:complexType>
        <xs:sequence>
            <xs:element name="Impresions" type="xs:string"/>
            <xs:element name="Comments" type="xs:string"/>
            <xs:element name="originate">
                <xs:complexType>
                    <xs:all>
                        <xs:element ref="Study"/>
                    </xs:all>
                </xs:complexType>
            </xs:element>
            <xs:element name="Interpretation" type="Interpretation_type"
             minOccurs="0" maxOccurs="unbounded"/>
        </xs:sequence>
    </xs:complexType>
</xs:element>
```

```
<xs:complexType name="Interpretation_type">
    <xs:sequence>
        <xs:element name="Inter_type" type="xs:string"/>
        <xs:element name="Inter_diagnostic" type="xs:string"/>
        <xs:element name="Inter_author" type="xs:string"/>
        <xs:element name="Inter_text" type="xs:string"/>
    </xs:sequence>
</xs:complexType>
```

Fig. 6. XML Schema code

In order to transform the disjoint and incomplete generalization association between the *Series*, *Image* and *Raw Data* classes, an element for each subclass has to be added into the XML choice complexType, within the element that represents the superclass. That is to say, the *Image* and *Raw_data* elements have to be included into the *Series* element. The complexTypes of the added elements are *Image_type* and *Raw_data_type*, respectively. These types were created when transforming the *Image* and *Raw Data* UML classes. Figure 7 shows the resulting transformation in extended UML and figure 8 shows the corresponding XML Schema code generated. In both figures, the subelements of I*mage_type* and *Raw_data_type* were omitted for space reasons.

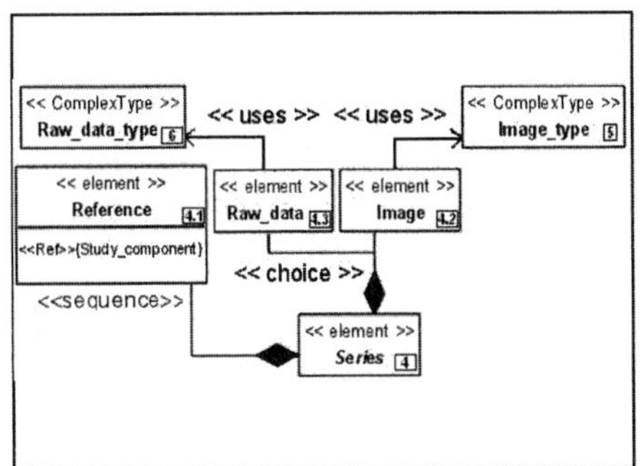

Fig. 7. Partial Data PSM in extended UML (generalization transformation)

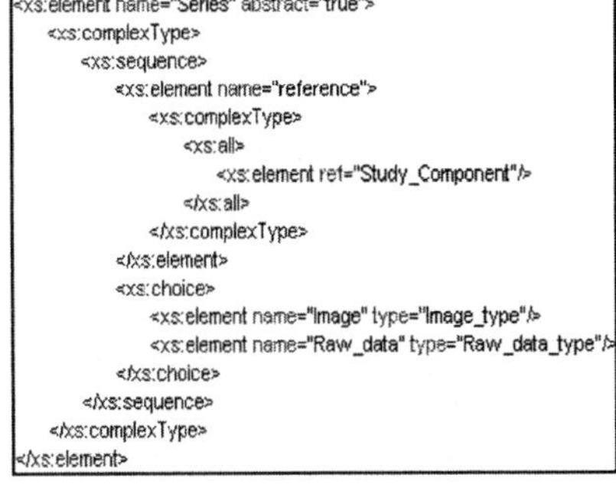

```
<xs:element name="Series" abstract="true">
    <xs:complexType>
        <xs:sequence>
            <xs:element name="reference">
                <xs:complexType>
                    <xs:all>
                        <xs:element ref="Study_Component"/>
                    </xs:all>
                </xs:complexType>
            </xs:element>
            <xs:choice>
                <xs:element name="Image" type="Image_type"/>
                <xs:element name="Raw_data" type="Raw_data_type"/>
            </xs:choice>
        </xs:sequence>
    </xs:complexType>
</xs:element>
```

Fig. 8. 8XML Schema code

4.3 Database Implementation in Oracle XML DB

The XML Schema obtained in the previous section was implemented using Oracle's XML DB. Based on the study of different XML DB solutions made in [20] and on the previous experience of our research group we have chosen Oracle to validate our proposal and to carry out the implementation of the XML DB. But, as we propose to use the standard XML Schema as data storage model in XML, the approach will be applicable to any DBMS that supports XML Schema. The way in which Oracle stores the XML data compliant with the defined XML Schema is shown in figure 9. We use the UML extension for OR DB design proposed in [13] to represent it. For space reasons, in figure 9 we only show the part corresponding to the XML Schema depicted in figure 5.

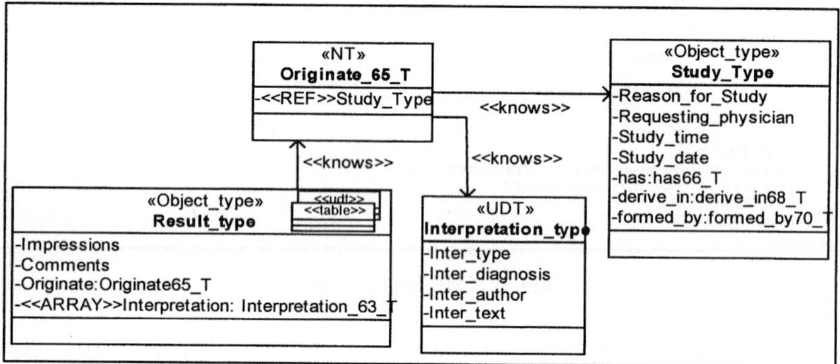

Fig. 9. Implementation in Oracle's XML DB

5 Conclusions and Future Work

Nowadays, there exists different solutions for the storage of XML data, but, in spite of existing several works in this line, there is no methodology for the systematic design of XML databases. In this paper we have described a model driven approach for the development of XML DBs in the framework of MIDAS, a model driven methodology for the development of WIS based on MDA. Specifically, we have focused on the content aspect of the structural dimension of MIDAS, which corresponds to the traditional concept of a DB. There exists different ways of developing a DB. In this paper we have proposed the development process for XML DBs, where the data PIM is the conceptual data model (UML class diagram) and the data PSM the XML Schema model. Both of them will be represented in UML, therefore we have also summarized the UML extension to represent XML Schemas. Moreover, we have defined the mappings to transform the data PIM into the data PSM, which will be the XML database schema.

We have developed different case studies to validate our proposal and in this paper we have shown part of the case study of the development of a XML DB for the management of medical images stored in Oracle's XML DB.

We are working on the implementation of a CASE tool (MIDAS-CASE), which integrates all the techniques proposed in MIDAS for the semiautomatic generation of WIS. The repository of the CASE tool is also being implemented in Oracle's XML

DB, following the approach proposed in this paper. We have already implemented in the tool the XML module, including the part for XML Schema and WSDL. Now, we are implementing on the one hand the automatic generation of the XML Schema code from the corresponding graphical representation of the data PSM in extended UML and on the other hand, the semi-automatic transformation from the data PIM to the data PSM to obtain the code of the XML DB.

References

1. ACR-NEMA. The DICOM Standard. Retrieved from: http://medical.nema.org/, 2003.
2. Barbosa, D., Barta, A., Mendelzon, A., Mihaila, G., Rizzolo, F. and Rodriguez-Gianolli, P. *ToX - The Toronto XML Engine*, International Workshop on Information Integration on the Web, Rio de Janeiro, 2001.
3. Bray, T., Paoli, J, Sperberg-McQu4een, C. M. and Maler, E., *Extensible Markup Language (XML) 1.0 (Second Edition)*, W3C Recommendation. Retrieved from: http://www.w3.org/TR/2000/REC-xml-20001006/, 2000.
4. Cáceres, P., Marcos, E. and Vela, B. *A MDA-Based Approach for Web Information System Development.* Workshop in Software Model Engineering in UML Conference. San Francisco, USA, October, 2003.
5. Case, T., Henderson-Sellers, B. and Low, G.C. *A generic object-oriented design methodology incorporating database considerations.* Annals of Software Engineering. Vol. 2, pp. 5-24, 1996.
6. Chaudhri, A.B., Rashid, A. and Zicari, R. (Eds.). *XML Data Management. Native XML and XML-Enabled Database Systems.* Addison Wesley, 2003.
7. eXcelon Corporation. *Managing DXE. System Documentation Release 3.5.* eXcelon Corporation. Burlington. Retrieved from: www.excelon.corp.com, 2003.
8. IBM Corportation. *IBM DB2 Universal Database -XML Extender Administration and Programming, Product Documentation Version 7.* IBM Corporation, 2000.
9. Krumbein, T. and Kudrass, T. *Rule-Based Generation of XML Schemas from UML Class Diagrams.* Berliner XML Tage 2003, Berlin (Germany). 13-15 October 2003. Ed. R. Tolksdorf and R. Eckstein. Berliner XML Tage. 2003
10. Marcos, E., Cáceres, P, and De Castro, V. *From the Use Case Model to the Navigation Model: a Service Oriented Approach.* CAISE FORUM '04. Riga (Latvia). 10-11 June, 2004. Ed: J. Grabis, A. Persson y J. Stirna. Proceedings, 2004.
11. Marcos E., Vela B. and Cavero, J. M. *Extending UML for Object-Relational Database Design.* Fourth Int. Conference on the Unified Modeling Language, UML 2001. Toronto (Canadá), LNCS 2185, Springer-Verlag, pp. 225-239, October, 2001.
12. Marcos, E. Vela, B., Cáceres, P. and Cavero, J.M. *MIDAS/DB: a Methodological Framework for Web Database Design.* DASWIS 2001. Yokohama (Japan), November, 2001. LNCS 2465, Springer-Verlag, pp. 227-238, September, 2002.
13. Marcos, E., Vela, B. and Cavero J.M. *Methodological Approach for Object-Relational Database Design using UML.* Journal on Software and Systems Modeling (SoSyM). Springer-Verlag. Ed.: R. France and B. Rumpe. Vol. SoSyM 2, pp.59-72, 2003.
14. Microsoft Corporation. *Microsoft SQL Server - SQLXML 2.0*, System Documentation. Microsoft Corporation, 2000.
15. OMG. *Model Driven Architecture.* Document number ormsc/2001-07-01. Ed.: Miller, J. and Mukerji, J. Retrieved from: http://www.omg.com/mda, 2001.
16. Oracle Corporation. *Oracle XML DB. Technical White Paper.* Retrieved from: www.otn.com, January, 2003.
17. Software AG. *Tamino X-Query. System Documentation Version 3.1.1.* Software AG, Darmstadt, Germany. Retrieved from: www.softwareag.com, 2001.

18. Vela, B. and Marcos E. *Extending UML to represent XML Schemas.* The 15th Conference On Advanced Information Systems Engineering. CAISE'03 FORUM. Klagenfurt/Velden (Austria). 16-20 June 2003. Ed: J. Eder, T. Welzer. Short Paper Proceedings, 2003.
19. W3C XML Schema Working Group. *XML Schema Parts 0-2:[Primer, Structures, Datatypes].* W3C Recommendation. Retrieved from: http://www.w3.org/TR/xmlschema-0/, http://www.w3.org/TR/xmlschema-1/ and http://www.w3.org/TR/xmlschema-2/, 2001.
20. Westermann, U. and Klas W. *An Analysis of XML Database Solutions for the Management of MPEG-7 Media Descriptions.* ACM Computing Surveys, Vol. 35 (4), pp. 331-373, December, 2003.
21. X-Hive Corporation. *X-Hive/DB 2.0-Manual. System. Documentation Release 2.0.2.*, X-Hive Corp., Rotherdam, The Neatherlands. Retrieved from: http://www.x-hive.com/,2002.

On the Updatability of XML Views Published over Relational Data

Ling Wang and Elke A. Rundensteiner

Department of Computer Science
Worcester Polytechnic Institute Worcester, MA 01609
{lingw,rundenst}@cs.wpi.edu

Abstract. Updates over virtual XML views that wrap the relational data have not been well supported by current XML data management systems. This paper studies the problem of the existence of a correct relational update translation for a given view update. First, we propose a *clean extended-source theory* to decide whether a translation mapping is correct. Then to answer the question of the existence of a correct mapping, we classify a view update as either *un-translatable*, *conditionally* or *unconditionally translatable* under a given *update translation policy*. We design a graph-based algorithm to classify a given update into one of the three update categories based on schema knowledge extracted from the XML view and the relational base. This now represents a practical approach that could be applied by any existing view update system in industry and in academic for analyzing the translatability of a given update statement before translation of it is attempted.

1 Introduction

Typical XML management systems [5, 9, 14] support the creation of XML wrapping views and the querying against these virtual views to bridge the gap between relational databases and XML applications. Update operations against such wrapper views, however, are not well supported yet.

The problem of updating XML views published over relational data comes with new challenges beyond those of updating relational [1, 7] or even object-oriented [3] views. The first is the *updatability*. That is, the mismatch between the hierarchical XML view model and the flat relational base model raises the question whether the given view update is even mappable into SQL updates. The second is the *translation strategy*. That is, assuming the view update is indeed translatable, how to translate the XQuery updates statements on the XML view into the equivalent tuple-based SQL updates expressed on the relational base.

Translation strategies have been explored to some degree in recent work. [11] presents an XQuery update grammar and studies the execution performance of translated updates. However, the assumption made in this work is that the given update is indeed translatable and that in fact it has already been translated into SQL updates over a relational database, which is assumed to be created by a

P. Atzeni et al. (Eds.): ER 2004, LNCS 3288, pp. 795–809, 2004.

fixed inline loading strategy [8]. Commercial database systems such as SQL-Server2000 [10], Oracle [2] and DB2 [6] also provide system-specific solutions for restricted update types, again under the assumption of given updates always being translatable.

Our earlier work [12] studies the XML view updatability for the "round-trip" case, which is characterized by a pair of invertable lossless mappings for (1) loading the XML documents into the relational bases, and (2) extracting an XML view identical to the original XML document back out of it. We prove that such XML views are always updatable by any update operation valid on the XML view. However, to the best of our knowledge, no result in the literature focuses on a general method to assess the updatability of an *arbitrary* XML view published over an *existing* relational database.

This view updatability issue has been a long standing difficult problem even in the relational context. Using the concept of "clean source", Dayal and Bernstein [7] characterize the *schema conditions* under which a relational view over a single table is updatable. Beyond this result, our current work now analyzes the key factors affecting the view updatability in the XML context. That is, given an *update translation policy*, we classify updates over an XML view as *un-translatable*, *conditionally* or *unconditionally translatable*. As we will show, this classification depends on several features of the XML view and the update statements, including: (a) granularity of the update at the view side, (b) properties of the view *construction*, and (c) types of *duplication* appearing in the view. By extending the concept of a "clean source" for relational databases [7] into "clean extended-source" for XML, we now propose a theory for determining the existence of a correct relational update translation for a given XML view update.

We also provide a graph-based algorithm to identify the conditions under which an XML view over a relational database is updatable. The algorithm depends only on the view and database schema knowledge instead of on the actual database content. It rejects un-translatable updates, requests additional conditions for conditionally translatable updates, and passes unconditionally translatable updates to the later update translation step. The proof of correctness of our algorithm can be found in our technical report [13]. It utilizes our *clean extended-source theory*.

Section 2 analyzes the factors deciding the XML view updatability, which is then formalized in Section 3. In Section 4 we propose the "clean extended-source" theory as theoretical foundation of our proposed solution. Section 5 describes our graph-based algorithm for detecting update translatability. Section 6 provides conclusions.

2 Factors for XML View Updatability

Using examples, we now illustrate what factors affect the view updatability in general, and which features of XML specifically cause new view update translation issues. Recent XML systems [5, 9, 14] use a *default XML view* to define the

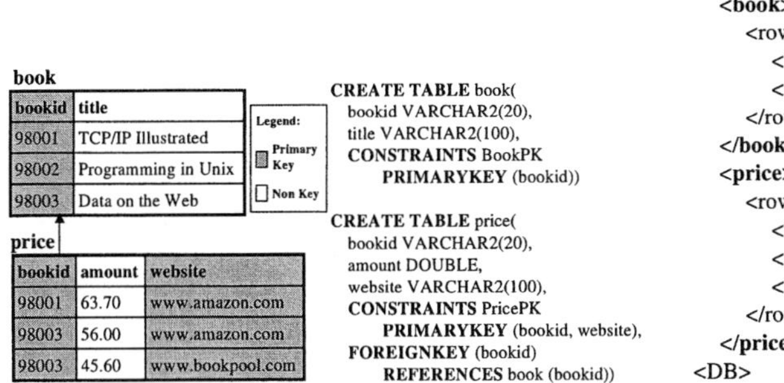

book

bookid	title
98001	TCP/IP Illustrated
98002	Programming in Unix
98003	Data on the Web

price

bookid	amount	website
98001	63.70	www.amazon.com
98003	56.00	www.amazon.com
98003	45.60	www.bookpool.com


```
CREATE TABLE book(
  bookid VARCHAR2(20),
  title VARCHAR2(100),
  CONSTRAINTS BookPK
    PRIMARYKEY (bookid))

CREATE TABLE price(
  bookid VARCHAR2(20),
  amount DOUBLE,
  website VARCHAR2(100),
  CONSTRAINTS PricePK
    PRIMARYKEY (bookid, website),
  FOREIGNKEY (bookid)
    REFERENCES book (bookid))
```

Fig. 1. Relational database

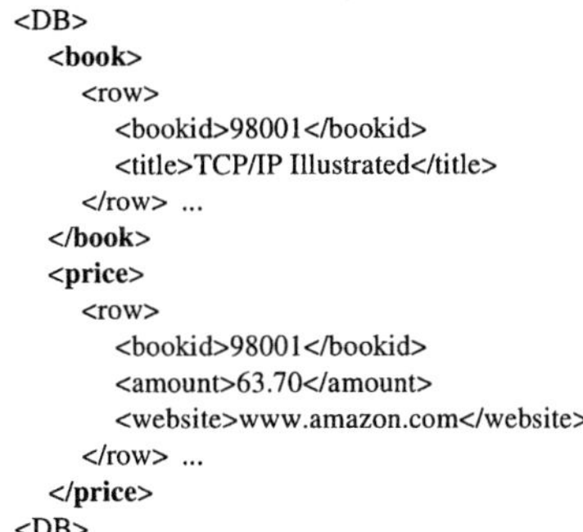

```
<DB>
  <book>
    <row>
      <bookid>98001</bookid>
      <title>TCP/IP Illustrated</title>
    </row> ...
  </book>
  <price>
    <row>
      <bookid>98001</bookid>
      <amount>63.70</amount>
      <website>www.amazon.com</website>
    </row> ...
  </price>
<DB>
```

Fig. 2. Default XML view of database shown in Figure 1

one-to-one XML-to-relational mapping (Fig. 2). A *view query* (Fig. 3) is defined over it to express user-specific XML wrapper views. User updates over the virtual XML views are expressed in XQuery update syntax [11] (Fig. 4). Also, we only consider insertion/deletion in our discussion. A replacement is treated as a deletion followed by an insertion without specifically discussion.

2.1 Update Translation Policy

Clearly, the *update translation policy* chosen for the system is essential for the decision of view updatability. An update may be translatable under one policy, while not under another one. We now enumerate common policies observed in the literature [3, 11] and in practice [14].

Policies for update type selection. (1) Same type. The translated update always must have the same update type as the given view update. (2) Mixed type. Translated updates with a different type are allowed.

Policies for maintaining referential integrity of the relational database under deletion. (1) Cascade. The directly translated relational updates cascade to update the referenced relations as well. (2) Restrict. The relational update is restricted to the case when there are no referenced relations. Otherwise, reject the view update. (3) Set Null. The relational update is performed as required, while the foreign key is set to be NULL in each dangling tuple.

The translatability of a *valid view update* under a given policy can be classified as *unconditionally translatable*, *conditionally translatable* and *un-translatable*. A view update is called *un-translatable* if it cannot be mapped into relational updates without violating some consistency. A view update is *unconditionally translatable* if such a translation always exists under the given policy. Otherwise, we call it *conditionally translatable*. That is, under the current update policy, the given update is not translatable unless additional conditions, such as assumptions or user communication, are introduced to make it translatable.

When not stated otherwise, throughout the paper we pick the most commonly used policy, that is, *same update type* and *delete cascade*. If a different translation

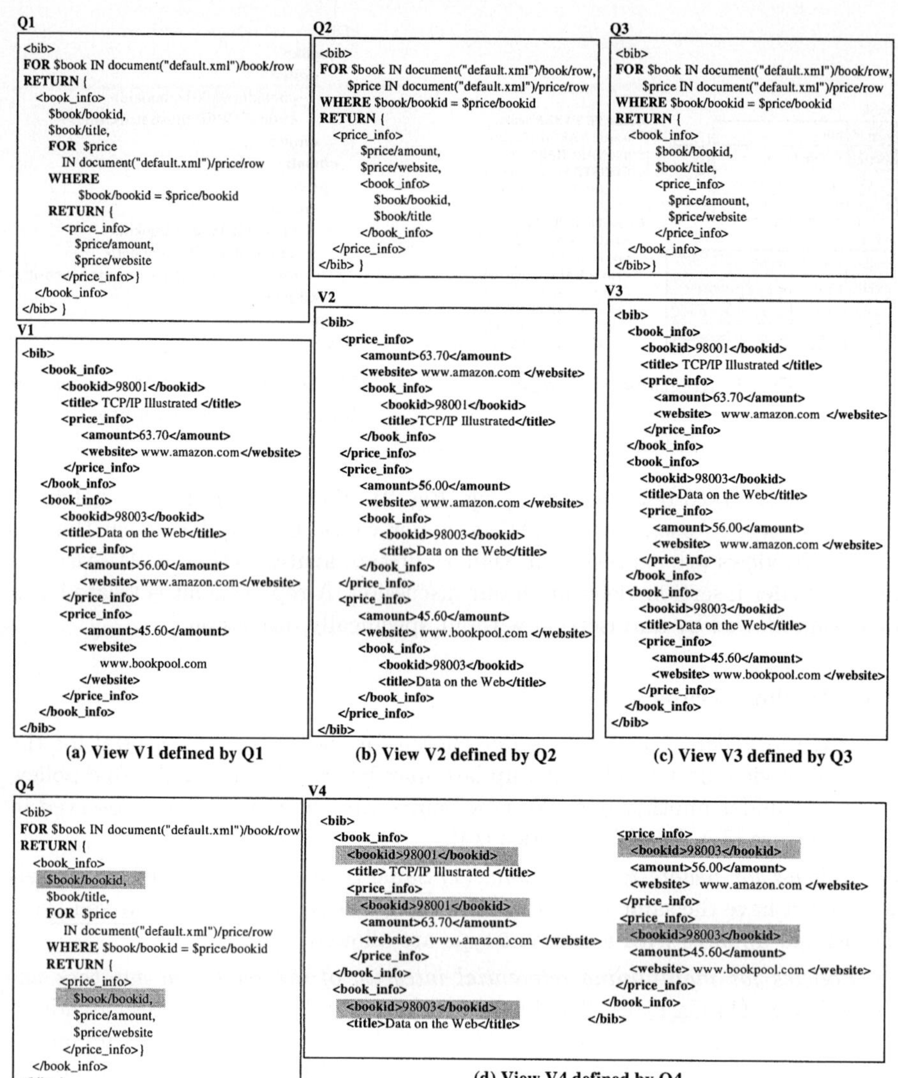

Fig. 3. View V1 to V4 defined by XQuery Q1 to Q4 respectively

policy is used, then the discussion can be easily adjusted accordingly. Also, we do not indicate the order of the translated relational updates. For a given execution strategy, the correct order can be easily decided [1, 11, 12].

2.2 New Challenges Arising from XML Data Model

Example 1 (View construction consistency). Assume two view updates u_1^V and u_2^V (Fig. 4) delete a "book_info" element from $V1$ and $V2$ in Fig. 3 respectively.

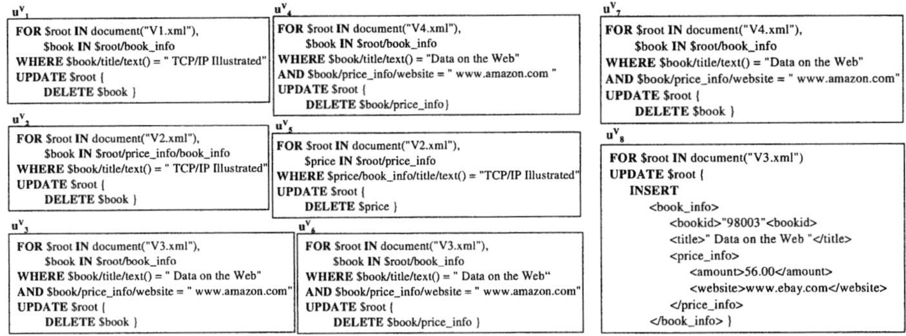

Fig. 4. Update operations on XML views defined in Fig. 3

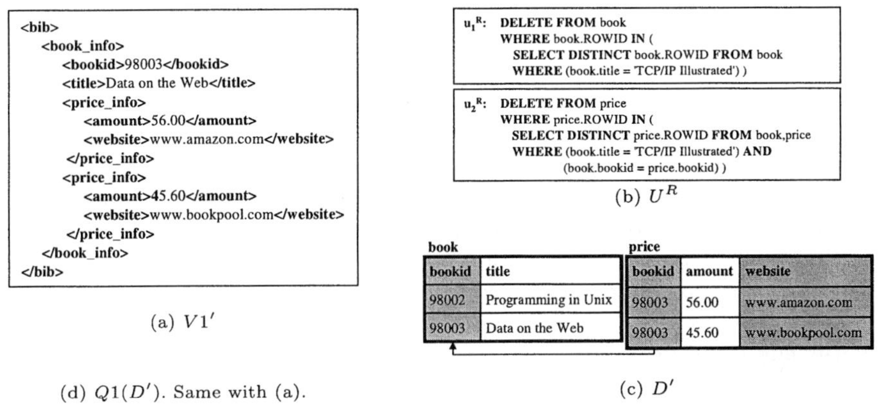

Fig. 5. Translate u_1^V (a) $V1'$: The user expected updated view, (b) U^R: The translated update, (c) D': The updated relational database, (d) $Q1(D')$: The regenerated view

(i) Fig. 5 shows u_1^V is *unconditionally translatable*. The translated relational update sequence U^R in Fig. 5(b) will delete the first book from the "book" relation by u_1^R, and its prices from the "price" relation through u_2^R. By re-applying the view query $Q1$ on the updated database D' in Fig. 5(c), the updated XML view in Fig. 5(d) equals the user *expected* updated view $V1'$ in Fig. 5(a).
(ii) Fig. 6 shows u_2^V is *un-translatable*. First, the relational update u_1^R in Fig. 6(b) is generated to delete the book (bookid=98001) from the "book" relation. Note the foreign key from the "price" relation to the "book" relation (Fig. 1). The second update operation u_2^R will be generated by the update translator to keep the relational database consistent. The regenerated view in Fig. 6(d) is different than the user expected updated view $V2'$ in Fig. 6(a). No other translation is available which could preserve consistency either.

The existence of a correct translation is affected by the *view construction consistency* property, namely, whether the XML view hierarchy agrees with the hierarchical structure implied by the base relational schema.

```
<bib>
  <price_info>
    <amount>63.70</amount>
    <website>www.amazon.com</website>
  </price_info>
  <price_info>
    <amount>56.00</amount>
    <website>www.amazon.com</website>
    <book_info>
      <bookid>98003</bookid>
      <title>Data on the Web</title>
    </book_info>
  </price_info>
  ...
</bib>
```

(a) $V2'$

(b) U^R. Same with Fig.5(b).

(c) D'. Same with Fig.5(c).

```
<bib>
  <price_info>
    <amount>56.00</amount>
    <website>www.amazon.com</website>
    <book_info>
      <bookid>98003</bookid>
      <title>Data on the Web</title>
    </book_info>
  </price_info>
  ...
</bib>
```

(d) $Q2(D')$

Fig. 6. Translate u_2^V (a) $V2'$: The user expected updated view, (b) U^R: The translated update, (c) D': The updated relational database, (d) $Q2(D')$: The regenerated view

Example 2 (Content duplication). Next we compare the two virtual XQuery views $V1$ and $V3$ in Fig. 3. The book (bookid=98003) with two prices is exposed twice in $V3$, while only once in $V1$. The update u_3^V in Fig. 4 will delete the "book_info" element from amazon, while keeping the one from bookpool. Now should we delete the book tuple underneath? It is unclear. An additional condition, such as an extra translation rule like "*No underlying tuple is deleted if it is still referenced by any other part of the view*" could make the update u_3^V translatable by keeping the book tuple untouched. This update is thus called *conditionally translatable.*

This ambiguous *content duplication* is introduced by the XQuery "FOR" expression. This property could also arise in relational *Join* views.

Example 3 (Structural duplication). Given $Q4$ in Fig. 3 with each "bookid" exposed twice in the single "book_info" element. The update u_4^V in Fig. 4, which deletes the first price of the specified book, is classified as *conditionally translatable.* Since the primary key "bookid" is touched by u_4^V, we cannot decide whether to delete the book-tuple underneath. With an additional condition, such as knowledge of the user intention about the update, u_4^V becomes translatable.

Structural duplication, as illustrated above, is special to XML view updating. While it also exists in the relational context, it would not cause any ambiguity. The flat relational data model only allows *tuple-based* view insertion/deletion. The update touches all not just some of the duplicates within a view tuple. Instead of always enforcing an update on the biggest view element "book_info", the flexible hierarchical structure of XML allows a "partial" update on subelements inside it. Inconsistency between the duplicated parts thus occurs.

Example 4 (Update granularity). Compared with the failure of translating u_2^V in Example 1, the update u_5^V in Fig. 4 on the same view $V2$ is *conditionally translatable.* u_5^V deletes the whole "price_info" element instead of just the subelement "book_info". The translated relational update sequence U^R is the same as in Fig. 6(b). The regenerated view is the same as what the user expects. Due to content duplication, u_5^V is said to be *conditionally translatable.*

XML hierarchical structure offers an opportunity for different *update granularity,* an issue that does not arise for relational views.

3 Formalizing the Problem of XML View Updatability

The structure of a relation is described by a **relation schema** $\mathcal{R}(\mathcal{N}, \mathcal{A}, \mathcal{F})$, where $\mathcal{N}$ is the name of the relation, $\mathcal{A} = \{a_1, a_2, ..., a_m\}$ is its attribute set, and $\mathcal{F}$ is a set of constraints. A **relation** R is a finite subset of $dom(\mathcal{A})$, a *product* of all the attribute domains. A **relational database**, denoted as D, is a set of n relations $R_1, ..., R_n$. A **relational update operation** $u^R \in \mho^R$ is a deletion, insertion or replacement on a relation R. A **sequence** of relational update operations, denoted by $U^R = \{u_1^R, u_2^R, ..., u_p^R\}$ is also modeled as a function $U^R(D) = u_p^R(u_{p-1}^R(..., u_2^R(u_1^R(D))))$.

Table 1. Notations for XML view update problem

D	relational database	$\mathcal{R}(\mathcal{N}, \mathcal{A}, \mathcal{F})$	schema of relation
R	relation	$\mho^R$	domain of relational update operations
u^R	relational update operation	U^R	sequence of relational update operations
V	XML view	DEF^V	XML view definition
u^V	view update	$\mho^V$	domain of view update operations

An **XML view** V over a relational database D is defined by a **view definition** DEF^V (an XQuery expression in our case). The domain of the view is denoted by $dom(V)$. Let *rel* be a function to extract the relations in D referenced by DEF^V, then $rel(DEF^V) = \{R_{i_1}, R_{i_2}, ..., R_{i_p}\} \subseteq D$. An **XML view schema** is extracted from both DEF^V and $rel(DEF^V)$. See [13] for details.

Let $u^V \in \mho^V$ be an update on the view V. A **valid view update** (e.g., Fig. 4) is an insertion or deletion that satisfies all constraints in the view schema.

Definition 1. *Given an update translation policy. Let D be a relational database and V be a virtual view defined by* DEF^V*. A relational update sequence* U^R *is a* **correct translation** *of* u^V *iff (a)* $u^V(DEF^V(D)) = DEF^V(U^R(D))$ *and (b) if* $u^V(DEF^V(D)) = DEF^V(D) \Rightarrow U^R(D) = D$.

First, a correct translation means the "rectangle" rule holds (Fig. 7). Intuitively, it implies the translated relational updates do not cause any *view side effects.* Second, if an update operation does not affect the view, then it should not affect the relational base either. This guarantees any modification of the relational base is indeed done for the sake of the view.

Fig. 8 shows a typical partition of the view update domain $\mho^V$. The **XML view updatability** classifies a valid view update as either *unconditionally translatable, conditionally translatable* or *un-translatable.*

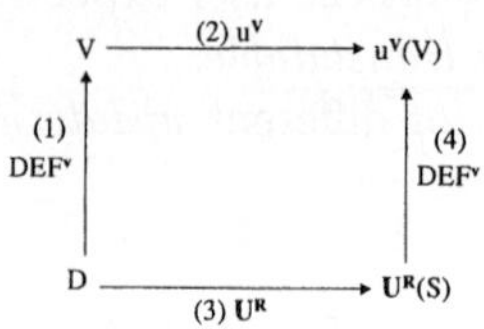

Fig. 7. Correct translation of view update to relational update

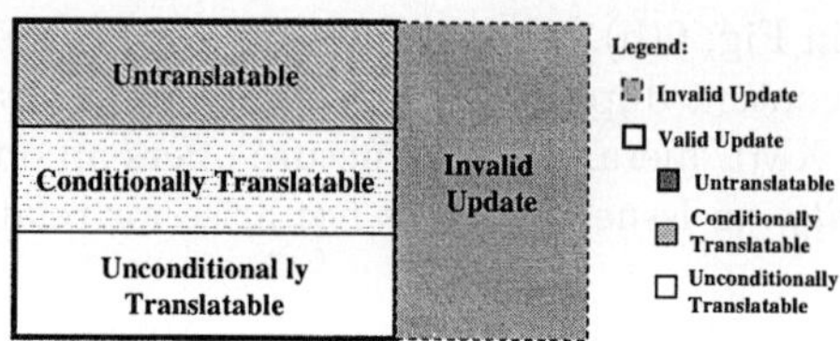

Fig. 8. The partition of view update domain $\mho^V$

4 Theoretical Foundation for XML View Updatability

Dayal and Bernstein [7] show that a correct translation exists in the case of a "clean source", when only considering functional dependencies inside a single relation. In the context of XML views, we now adopt and extend this work to also consider functional dependencies between relations.

Definition 2. *Given a relational database D and an XML view V defined over several relations $rel(DEF^V) \subseteq D$. Let v be a view element of V. Let $g = (t_1, ..., t_p)$ be a generator of v, where $t_i \in R_x$ for $R_x \in rel(DEF^V)$. Then t_i is called a* **source tuple** *in D of v.*

Further, $t_j \in R_y$ is an **extended source tuple** *in D of v iff $\exists t_i \in g$ that $t_i.a_k$ is a foreign key of $t_j.a_z$, where $a_k \in \mathcal{R}_x(\mathcal{A})$, $a_z \in \mathcal{R}_y(\mathcal{A})$ and $R_x, R_y \in rel(DEF^V)$. $g_e = g \cup \{t_j \mid t_j$ is an extended source tuple of $v\}$ is called an* **extended generator** *of v.*

A *source tuple* is a relational row used to compute the view element. For instance, in $V1$ of Fig. 3, the first view element v_1 is *book_info* element with bookid=98001. Let R_1 and R_2 denote the *book* and *price* relations respectively, then the generator g of v_1 is $g = (t_1, t_2)$, where $t_1 \in R_1$ is the book tuple *(98001,TCP/IP Illustrated)* and $t_2 \in R_2$ is the price tuple *(98001, 63.70, www.amazon.com)*. Let the view-element v_2 be the title of v_1. Then the source tuple of v_2 is t_1. Since t_1.*bookid* is a foreign key of t_2.*bookid*, we say t_2 is an extended source tuple of v_2, and $g_e = (t_1, t_2)$ is an extended generator of v_2.

Definition 3. *Let V^0 be a part of a given XML view V. Let $G(V^0)$ be the set of generators of V^0 defined by $G(V^0) = \{g \mid g$ is a generator of a view-element in $V^0\}$. For each $g = (t_1, ..., t_p) \in G(V^0)$, let $H(g)$ be some nonempty subset of $\{t_i \mid t_i \in g\}$. Then any superset of $\cup_{g \in G(V^0)} H(g)$ is a* **source** *in D of V^0. (If $G(V^0) = \emptyset$, then V^0 has no source in D.)*

Similarly, let $G_e(V^0)$ be the set of extended generators for view elements in V^0. Then any superset of $\cup_{g \in G_e(V^0)} H(g)$ is an **extended source** *in D of V^0, denoted by S_e.*

A *source* includes the underlying relational part of a view "portion" V^0 which consists of multiple view-elements. For example, let $V^0 = V1$ (Fig. 3), $G(V^0) = \{g_1, g_2\}$, where $g_1 = \{$*(98001,TCP/IP Illustrated),(98001, 63.70,www.amazon.*

com)}, g_2 = {*(98003,Data on the Web),(98003,56.00,www.amazon.com),(98003, 45.60, www.bookpool.com)*}. That is, $G(V^0)$ includes all the generators for view elements in V^0. Let $H(g_1)$ = {*(98001, TCP/IP Illustrated)*} and $H(g_2)$ = {*(98003, 56.00, www.amazon.com)*}. Then {*(98001, TCP/IP Illustrated),(98003, 56.00, www.amazon.com)*} is a source of V^0, also an extended source of V^0.

Definition 4. *Let $D = \{R_1, ..., R_n\}$ be a relational database. Let V^0 be part of a given XML view V and S_e be an extended source in D of V^0. S_e is a* **clean extended source** *in D of V^0 iff $(\forall v \in V - V^0)$, $(\exists S'_e)$ such that S'_e is an extended source in $(R_1 - S_{e1}, ..., R_n - S_{en})$ of v. Or, equivalently, S_e is a clean extended source in D of V^0 iff $(\forall v \in V - V^0)(S_e$ is not an extended source in D of $v)$.*

A *clean extended source* defines a source that is only referenced by the given view element itself. For instance, given the view-element v in $V2$ (Fig. 3) representing the *book_info* element (bookid = 98001), its extended source {*(98001, TCP/IP Illustrated),(98001, 63.70,www.amazon.com)*} is not a *clean extended source* since it is also an extended source of the *price* element.

The **clean extended source theory** below captures the connection between *clean extended source* and update translatability (Proofs in [13]). It serves as a conservative solution for identifying the (*unconditionally) translatable* updates.

Theorem 1. *Let u^V be the deletion of a set of view elements $V^d \subseteq V$. Let τ be a translation procedure, $\tau(u^V, D) = U^R$. Then τ* **correctly translates** *u^V to D iff U^R deletes a clean extended source of V^d.*

By Definition 1, a correct delete translation is one without any view side effect. This is exactly what deleting a clean extended-source guarantees by Definition 4. Thus Theorem 1 follows.

Theorem 2. *Let u^V be the insertion of a set of view elements V^i into V. Let $V^- = V - V^i$, $V^u = V^i - V$. Let τ be a translation procedure, $\tau(u^V, D) = U^R$. Then τ* **correctly translates** *u^V to D iff (i) $(\forall v \in V^u)(U^R$ inserts a source tuple of $v)$ and (ii) $(\forall v \in dom(V) - (V^u \cup V^-))(U^R$ does not insert a source tuple of $v)$.*

Since $dom(V) - (V^u \cup V^-) = (dom(V) - (V^i \cup V)) \cup (V^i \cap V)$, Theorem 2 indicates a correct insert translation is the one without any duplicate insertion (insert a source of $V^i \cap V$) and any extra insertion (insert a source of $dom(V) - (V^i \cup V)$). That is, it inserts a clean extended source for the new view-element. Duplicate insertion is not allowed by BCNF, while extra insertion will cause a view side effect. For example, for u_8^V in Fig. 4, let u_1^R = {*Insert (98003,Data on the Web) into book*}, u_2^R = {*Insert (98003,56.00,www.ebay.com) into price*}. Then $U^R = \{u_1^R, u_2^R\}$ is not a correct translation since it inserts a duplicate source tuple into *book*. While $U^{R'} = \{u_2^R\}$ is a correct translation.

5 Graph-Based Algorithm for Deciding View Updatability

We now propose a graph-based algorithm to identify the factors and their effects on the update translatability based on our clean extended source theory. We assume the relational database is in the BCNF form. No cyclic dependency caused by integrity constraints among relations exists. Also, the predicate used in the view query expression is a conjunction of *non-correlation* (e.g., *\$price/website* = *"www.amazon.com"*) or *equi-correlation* predicates (e.g., *\$book/bookid* = *\$price/bookid*).

5.1 Graphic Representation of XML Views

Two graphs capture the update related features in the view V and relational base D. The **view relationship graph** $\mathcal{G}_R(N_{\mathcal{G}_R}, E_{\mathcal{G}_R})$ is a forest representing the hierarchical and cardinality constraints in the *XML view schema*. An internal node, represented by a triangle $\triangle$, identifies a view element or attribute labeled by its name. A leaf node (represented by a small circle $\circ$) is an atomic type, labeled by both the XPath binding and the name of its corresponding relational column $R_x.a_k$. An edge $e(n_1, n_2) \in E_{\mathcal{G}_R}$ represents that n_1 is a parent of n_2 in the view hierarchy. Each edge is labeled by the cardinality relationship and condition (if any) between its end nodes. A label "?" means each parent node can only have one child, while "*" shows multiple children are possible. Figures 9(a) to 9(d) depict the view relationship graphs for $V1$ to $V4$ in Fig. 3 respectively.

Definition 5. *The* **hierarchy implied in relational model** *is defined as:*
(1) Given a relation schema $\mathcal{R}(\mathcal{N}, \mathcal{A}, \mathcal{F})$, with $\mathcal{A} = \{a_i | 1 \leq i \leq m\}$, then $\mathcal{N}$ is called the **parent** *of the attribute a_i ($1 \leq i \leq m$).*
(2) Given two relation schemas $\mathcal{R}_i(\mathcal{N}_i, \mathcal{A}_i, \mathcal{F}_i)$ and $\mathcal{R}_j(\mathcal{N}_j, \mathcal{A}_j, \mathcal{F}_j)$, with foreign key constraints defined as $PK(\mathcal{R}_i) \leftarrow FK(\mathcal{R}_j)$, then $\mathcal{N}_i$ is the **parent** *of $\mathcal{N}_j$.*

The **view trace graph** $\mathcal{G}_T(N_{\mathcal{G}_T}, E_{\mathcal{G}_T})$ represents the hierarchical and cardinality constraints in the *relational schema* underlying the XML view. The set of leaf nodes of $\mathcal{G}_T$ correspond to the union of all leaves of $\mathcal{G}_R$. Specially, a leaf node labeled by the primary key attribute of a relation is called a *key node* (depicted by a black circle $\bullet$). An internal node, depicted by a triangle $\triangle$, is labeled by the relation name. Each edge $e(n_1, n_2) \in E_{\mathcal{G}_T}$ means n_1 is the parent of n_2 by Definition 5. An edge is labeled by its foreign key condition (if it is generated by rule (2) in Definition 5), and the cardinality relationship between its end nodes. The view trace graphs of $V1$ to $V4$ are identical (Fig. 10), since they all defined over the same attributes of base relations.

The concept of closure in $\mathcal{G}_R$ and $\mathcal{G}_T$ is used to represent the "effect" of an update on the view and on the relational database respectively. Intuitively, their relationship indicates the updatability of the given view.

The **closure** of a node $n \in N_{\mathcal{G}_R}$, denoted by $n^+_{\mathcal{G}_R}$, is defined as follows: (1) If n is a leaf node, $n^+_{\mathcal{G}_R} = \{n\}$. (2) Otherwise, $n^+_{\mathcal{G}_R}$ is the union of its children's closures grouped by their hierarchical relationship and marked by their cardinality (for

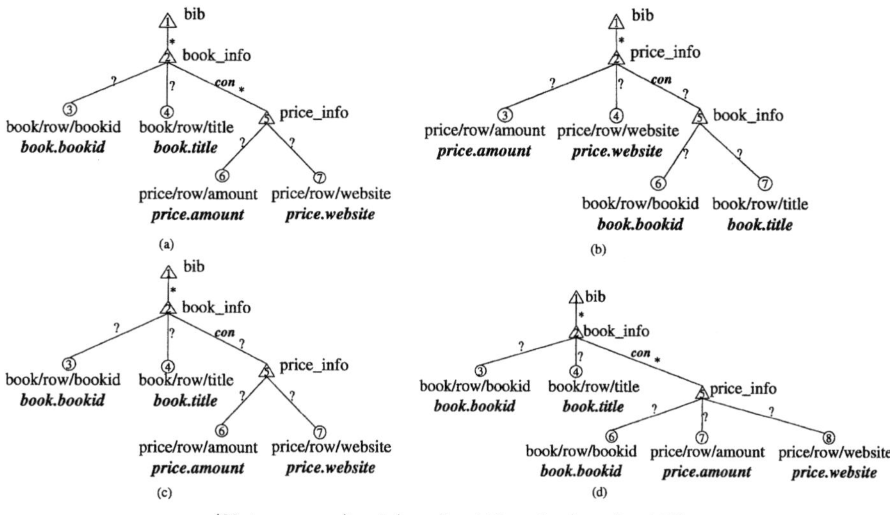

*Note: con = (book/row/bookid=price/row/bookid)

Fig. 9. $\mathcal{G}_R$ of V1 to V4 as shown by (a) to (d)

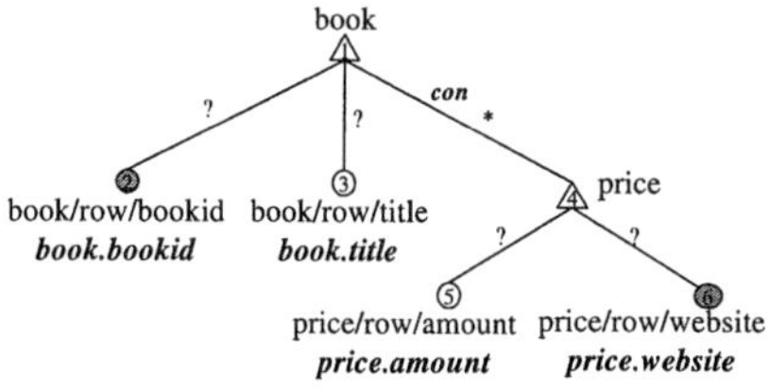

*Note: con = (book.bookid=price.bookid)

Fig. 10. $\mathcal{G}_T$ of V1 – V4

simplicity, not shown when cardinality mark is ?). For example, in Figure 9(a), $(n_3)^+_{\mathcal{G}_R} = \{n_3\}$, while $(n_5)^+_{\mathcal{G}_R} = \{n_6, n_7\}$, $(n_2)^+_{\mathcal{G}_R} = \{n_3, n_4, (n_6, n_7)^*\}$.

The **closure** of a node $n \in N_{\mathcal{G}_T}$ is defined in the same manner as in $\mathcal{G}_R$, except for leaf nodes. Each leaf node has the same closure as its parent node. For instance, in Fig. 10, $(n_2)^+_{\mathcal{G}_T} = (n_3)^+_{\mathcal{G}_T} = (n_1)^+_{\mathcal{G}_T} = \{n_2, n_3, (n_5, n_6)^*\}$. This closure definition in $\mathcal{G}_T$ is based on the pre-selected update policy in Section 2.1. If a different policy were used, then the definition needs to be adjusted accordingly. For example, if we pick the *mixed type*, the closure will be "only the *key node* has the same closure definition as its parent node, while any other leaf node has itself as the closure". Consequently in Fig. 10, $(n_3)^+_{\mathcal{G}_T} = \{n_3\}$, while $(n_2)^+_{\mathcal{G}_T} = \{n_2, n_3, (n_5, n_6)^*\}$. The delete on these non-key leaf nodes can be translated as a replacement on the corresponding relational column.

To reduce the closure definition, the group mark "()" can be eliminated if its cardinality mark is "?". For example, in Figure 9(c), $(n_2)^+_{\mathcal{G}_T} = \{n_3, n_4, (n_6, n_7)\} = \{n_3, n_4, n_6, n_7\}$. The closure of a set of nodes N, denoted by N^+, is defined as

$N^+ = \bigcup_{(n_i \in N)} n_i^+$, where $\bigcup$ is a "Union-like" operation that combines not only the nodes but their shared occurrence. For instance, in Fig. 10, $\{n_2, n_5\}^+_{\mathcal{G}_T} = (n_2)^+_{\mathcal{G}_T} \bigcup (n_5)^+_{\mathcal{G}_T} = \{n_2, n_3, (n_5, n_6)^*\} \bigcup \{n_5, n_6\} = \{n_2, n_3, (n_5, n_6)^*\}$. Two leaf nodes in $\mathcal{G}_R$ or $\mathcal{G}_T$ are *equal* if and only if the relational attribute labels in their respective node labels are the same.

5.2 A Graph-Based Algorithm for View Updatability Identification

Definition 6. *Two closures C_1 and C_2* **match**, *denoted by $C_1 \cong C_2$, iff the node set of C_1 and C_2 are equal. Further, C_1 and C_2 are* **equal**, *denoted by $C_1 \equiv C_2$, iff the node groups, cardinality marks of each group, and conditions on each "*" edge are all the same.*

For two closures to match means that the same view schema nodes are included. While equality indicates that the same instances of XML view elements will be included. For example, $(n_2)^+_{\mathcal{G}_R}$ in Fig. 9(c) and $(n_1)^+_{\mathcal{G}_T}$ in Fig. 10 *match*. That is, both closures include the same XML view schema nodes: *book.bookid, book.title, price.amount, price.website*. However, $(n_2)^+_{\mathcal{G}_R}$ in Figure 9(a) and $(n_1)^+_{\mathcal{G}_T}$ in Figure 10 are *equal*, namely {*book.bookid, book.title, (price. amount, price.website)**}. This is because their group partition (marked by "()"), cardinality mark (* or ?) and conditions for each "*" edge are all the same. Both closures touch exactly the same XML view-element instances.

Theorem 3. *Let V be a view defined by DEF^V over a relational database D with the view relationship graph $\mathcal{G}_R(N_{\mathcal{G}_R}, E_{\mathcal{G}_R})$ and view trace graph $\mathcal{G}_T(N_{\mathcal{G}_T}, E_{\mathcal{G}_T})$. Let $Y \subseteq N_{\mathcal{G}_R}$ and $X \subseteq N_{\mathcal{G}_T}$. ($\forall$ generators g, g' of view elements v and v' respectively, $g[X] = g'[X] \Rightarrow v[Y] = v'[Y]$) iff their closures $X^+_{\mathcal{G}_T} \equiv Y^+_{\mathcal{G}_R}$.*

Theorem 3 indicates that two equal generators always produce the identical view elements iff the respective closures of the view schema nodes in $\mathcal{G}_R$ and $\mathcal{G}_T$ are equal. Theorem 3 now enables us to produce an algorithm for detecting the *clean extended sources* S_e of a view element based on schema knowledge captured in $\mathcal{G}_R$ and $\mathcal{G}_T$.

Theorem 4. *Let $V, DEF^V, D, \mathcal{G}_R, \mathcal{G}_T, Y$ be defined as in Theorem 3. Given a view element $v \in V(Y)$, there is a clean extended source S_e of v in D iff ($\exists X \subseteq N_{\mathcal{G}_T}$) such that $X^+_{\mathcal{G}_T} \equiv Y^+_{\mathcal{G}_R}$.*

Theorem 4 indicates that a given view element v has a clean extended source iff the closure of its schema node in $\mathcal{G}_R$ has an equal closure in $\mathcal{G}_T$. As indicated by Theorems 1 and 2, the existence of a clean extended source for a given XML view element implies that the update touching this element is unconditionally translatable. The following observation thus serves as a general methodology for view updatability determination.

Observation 1 *Let $D, V, \mathcal{G}_R, \mathcal{G}_T, Y$ be defined as in Theorem 3. (1) Updates that touch Y are* **unconditionally translatable** *iff ($\exists X \subseteq N_{\mathcal{G}_T}$) such that $X^+_{\mathcal{G}_T} \equiv Y^+_{\mathcal{G}_R}$. (2) Updates that touch Y are* **conditionally translatable** *iff ($\exists X \subseteq N_{\mathcal{G}_T}$) such that $X^+_{\mathcal{G}_T} \cong Y^+_{\mathcal{G}_R}$. (3) Otherwise, updates on Y are* **un-translatable**.

However, searching all node closures in $\mathcal{G}_T$ to find one equal to the closure of a given view-element is expensive. According to the generation rules of $\mathcal{G}_T$, the nodes in the closure of v also serve as leaf nodes in $\mathcal{G}_T$. We thus propose to start searching from leaf nodes within the closure, thus reducing the search space. Observation 2 utilized the following definition to determine the translatability of a given view update.

Definition 7. *Let n be a node in $\mathcal{G}_R(V)$, with its closure in $\mathcal{G}_R$ denoted by $C_R = n^+_{\mathcal{G}_R}$. Let $C_T = \bigcup_{(n_i \in C_R)} (n_i)^+_{\mathcal{G}_T}$, where $(n_i)^+_{\mathcal{G}_T}$ be the closure of n_i in $\mathcal{G}_T$. We say n is a* **clean node** *iff $C_R \equiv C_T$, a* **consistent node** *iff $C_R \cong C_T$ and an* **inconsistent node** *otherwise.*

For a node to be *inconsistent* means that the effect of an update on the view (node closure in $\mathcal{G}_R$) is different from the effect on the relational side (node closure in $\mathcal{G}_T$) based on the selected policy (closure definition in $\mathcal{G}_T$). It is thus un-translatable. A *clean* node is guaranteed to be safely updatable without any view side-effects. A dirty *consistent* node, however, needs an additional condition to be updatable. For example, n_5 in Fig. 9(a) is a clean node. In Fig. 9(b), n_5 is an inconsistent node and n_2 is a dirty consistent node.

Observation 2 *An update on a clean node is unconditionally translatable, on a consistent node it is conditionally translatable, while on an inconsistent node it is un-translatable.*

Algorithm 1 Optimized Update Translatability Checking Algorithm

```
/*Given G_R and G_T of a view V, determine
the translatability of a view update u*/

Procedure checkTranslatability(u, G_R,
G_T)
Node n = identifyNodeToUpdate(u, G_R)
classifyNode(n, G_R, G_T)
if n is a clean node then
   n is unconditionally translatable
else
   if n is a consistent node then
      n is conditionally translatable
   else
      n is untranslatable
   end if
end if

/*Classify the node n ∈ G_R to be updated*/
Procedure classifyNode (n, G_R, G_T)
Initiate C_R and C_T empty
C_R = computeClosure(n, G_R)
while C_R has more node do
   get the next node n_i ∈ C_R
   C_T = C_T ∪ computeClosure(n_i, G_T)
end while
if C_R ≅ C_T then
   if C_R ≡ C_T then
      n is a consistent node
   else
      n is a clean node
   end if
else
   n is an inconsistent node
end if
```

Algorithm 1 shows our optimized update translatability checking algorithm using Observation 2. It first identifies the deleting/inserting $\mathcal{G}_R$ node. Then, using Definition 7 the procedure *classifyNode* $(n, \mathcal{G}_R, \mathcal{G}_T)$ determines the type of the node to be updated. Thereafter the given view update can be classified as un-translatable, conditionally or unconditionally translatable by Observation 2. Using this optimized update translatability checking algorithm, a concrete case study on the translatability of deletes and inserts is also provided in [13].

6 Conclusion

In this paper, we have identified the factors determining *view updatability* in general and also in the context of XQuery views in particular. The *extended clean-source theory* for determining translation correctness is presented. A graph-based algorithm has also been presented to identify the conditions under which a correct translation of a given view update exists.

Our solution is general. It could be used by an update translation systems such as [4] to identify the translatable update before translation of it is attempted. This way we would guarantee that only a "well-behaved" view update is passed down to the next translation step. [4] assumes the view is always *well-formed*, that is, joins are through keys and foreign keys, and nesting is controlled to agree with the integrity constraints and to avoid duplication. The update over such a view is thus always translatable. Our work is *orthogonal* to this work by addressing new challenges related to the decision of translation existence when conflicts are possible, that is a view cannot always be guaranteed to be well-formed (as assumed in this prior work).

Our view updatability checking solution is based on schema reasoning, thus utilizes only view and database schema and constraints knowledge. Note that the translated updates might still conflict with the actual base data. For example, an update inserting a book (bookid = 98002) to $V1$ is said to be unconditionally translatable by our schema check procedure, while conflicts with the base data in Fig. 1 may still arise. Depending on selected update translation policy, the translated update can then be either rejected or executed by replacing the existing tuple with the newly inserted tuple. This run-time updatability issue can only be resolved at execution time by examining the actual data in the database.

References

1. A. M. Keller. The Role of Semantics in Translating View Updates. *IEEE Transactions on Computers*, 19(1):63–73, 1986.
2. S. Banerjee, V. Krishnamurthy, M. Krishnaprasad, and R. Murthy. Oracle8i - The XML Enabled Data Management System. In *ICDE*, pages 561–568, 2000.
3. T. Barsalou, N. Siambela, A. M. Keller, and G. Wiederhold. Updating Relational Databases through Object-Based Views. In *SIGMOD*, pages 248–257, 1991.
4. V. P. Braganholo, S. B. Davidson, and C. A. Heuser. On the Updatability of XML Views over Relational Databases. In *WEBDB*, pages 31–36, 2003.
5. M. J. Carey, J. Kiernan, J.Shanmugasundaram, E. J. Shekita, and S. N. Subramanian. XPERANTO: Middleware for Publishing Object-Relational Data as XML Documents. In *The VLDB Journal*, pages 646–648, 2000.
6. J. M. Cheng and J. Xu. XML and DB2. In *ICDE*, pages 569–573, 2000.
7. U. Dayal and P. A. Bernstein. On the Correct Translation of Update Operations on Relational Views. In *ACM Transactions on Database Systems*, volume 7(3), pages 381–416, Sept 1982.
8. J. Shanmugasundaram et al. Relational Databases for Querying XML Documents: Limitations and Opportunities. In *VLDB*, pages 302–314, September 1999.

9. M. Fernandez et al. SilkRoute: A Framework for Publishing Relational Data in XML. *ACM Transactions on Database Systems*, 27(4):438–493, 2002.
10. M. Rys. Bringing the Internet to Your Database: Using SQL Server 2000 and XML to Build Loosely-Coupled Systems. In *VLDB*, pages 465–472, 2001.
11. I. Tatarinov, Z. G. Ives, A. Y. Halevy, and D. S. Weld. Updating XML. In *SIGMOD*, pages 413–424, May 2001.
12. L. Wang, M. Mulchandani, and E. A. Rundensteiner. Updating XQuery Views Published over Relational Data: A Round-trip Case Study. In *XML Database Symposium (VLDB Workshop)*, pages 223–237, 2003.
13. L. Wang and E. A. Rundensteiner. Updating XML Views Published Over Relational Databases: Towards the Existence of a Correct Update Mapping. Technical Report WPI-CS-TR-04-19, Computer Science Department, WPI, 2004.
14. X. Zhang, K. Dimitrova, L. Wang, M. EL-Sayed, B. Murphy, L. Ding, and E. A. Rundensteiner. RainbowII: Multi-XQuery Optimization Using Materialized XML Views. In *Demo Session Proceedings of SIGMOD*, page 671, 2003.

XBiT: An XML-Based Bitemporal Data Model

Fusheng Wang and Carlo Zaniolo

Department of Computer Science, University of California, Los Angeles,
Los Angeles, CA 90095, USA
{wangfsh,zaniolo}@cs.ucla.edu

Abstract. Past research work on modeling and managing temporal information has, so far, failed to elicit support in commercial database systems. The increasing popularity of XML offers a unique opportunity to change this situation, inasmuch as XML and XQuery support temporal information much better than relational tables and SQL. This is the important conclusion claimed in this paper where we show that valid-time, transaction-time, and bitemporal databases can be naturally viewed in XML using temporally-grouped data models. Then, we show that complex historical queries, that would be very difficult to express in SQL on relational tables, can now be easily expressed in standard XQuery on such XML-based representations. We first discuss the management of transaction-time and valid-time histories and then extend our approach to bitemporal histories. The approach can be generalized naturally to support the temporal management of arbitrary XML documents and queries on their version history.

1 Introduction

While users' demand for temporal database applications is only increasing with time [1], database vendors are not moving forward in supporting the management and querying of temporal information. Given the remarkable research efforts that have been spent on these problems [2], the lack of viable solutions must be attributed, at least in part, to the technical difficulties of introducing temporal extensions into the relational data model and query languages.

In the meantime, database researchers, vendors and SQL standardization groups are working feverishly to extend SQL with XML publishing capabilities [4] and to support languages such as XQuery [5] on the XML-published views of the relational database [6]. In this context, XML and XQuery can respectively be viewed as a new powerful data model and query language, thus inviting the natural question on whether they can provide a better basis for representing and querying temporal database information. In this paper, we answer this critical question by showing that transaction-time, valid-time and bitemporal database histories can be effectively represented in XML and queried using XQuery without requiring extensions of current standards. This breakthrough over the relational data model and query languages is made possible by (i) the ability of XML to support a temporally grouped model, which is long-recognized

P. Atzeni et al. (Eds.): ER 2004, LNCS 3288, pp. 810–824, 2004.

as natural and expressive [7, 8] but could not be implemented well in the flat structure of the relational data model [9], and (ii) the greater expressive power and native extensibility of XQuery (which is Turing-complete [10]) over SQL. Furthermore, these benefits are not restricted to XML-published databases; indeed these temporal representations and queries can be naturally extended to arbitrary XML documents, and used, e.g., to support temporal extensions for database systems featuring native support for XML and XQuery, and in preserving the version history of XML documents, in archives [11] and web warehouses [12].

In this paper, we build and extend techniques described in previous papers. In particular, support for transaction time was discussed in [13], and techniques for managing document versions were discussed in [12]. However, the focus of this paper is supporting valid-time and bitemporal databases, which pose new complexity and were not discussed in previous papers.

The paper is organized as follows. After a discussion of related work in the next section, we study an example of temporal relations modeled with a temporal ER model. In Section 4 we show that the valid time history of relational database history can be represented as XML, and queried with XQuery. Section 5 briefly reviews how to model transaction-time history with XML. In Section 6, we focus on an XML-based bitemporal data model to represent the bitemporal relational database history, and show that complex bitemporal queries can be expressed with XQuery based on this model, and database update can also be supported. Section 7 concludes the paper.

2 Related Work

Temporal ER Modeling. There has been much interesting work on ER-based temporal modeling of information systems at the conceptual level. For instance, ER models have been supported in commercial products for database schema designs, and more than 10 temporal enhanced ER models have been proposed in the research community [14]. As discussed in the survey by Gregersen and Jensen [14], there are two major approaches of extensions to ER model for temporal support, devising new notational shorthands, or altering the semantics of the current ER model constructs. The recent TIMEER model [15] is based on an ontological foundation and supports an array of properties. Among the temporal ER models, the Temporal EER Model (TEER) [16] extends the temporal semantics into the existing EER modeling constructs.

Temporal Databases. A body of previous work on temporal data models and query languages include [17–20]; thus the design space for the relational data model has been exhaustively explored [2, 21]. Clifford et al. [9] classified them as two main categories: *temporally ungrouped* and *temporally grouped* data models. Temporally grouped data model is also referred to as non-first-normal-form model or attribute time stamping, in which the domain of each attribute is extended to include the temporal dimension [8], e.g., Gadia's temporal data model [22]. It is shown that the temporally grouped representation has more expressive power and is more natural since it is history-oriented [9]. TSQL2 [23] tries to reconcile the two approaches [9] within the severe limitations of the relational tables. Our approach is based on a temporally grouped data model, which dovetails perfectly with the hierarchical structure of XML documents.

The lack of temporal support in commercial DBMS can be attributed to the limitations of SQL, the engineering complexity, and the difficulty to implement it incrementally [24].

Publishing Relational Databases in XML. There is much current interest in publishing relational databases in XML. A middleware-based approach is used in SilkRoute [25] and XPERANTO [6]. For instance, XPERANTO can build a default view on the whole relational database, and new XML views and queries upon XML views can then be defined using XQuery. XQuery statements are then translated into SQL and executed on the RDBMS engine. SQL/XML is emerging as a new SQL standard supported by several DBMS vendors [4, 26], to extend RDBMS with XML support.

Time in XML. Some interesting research work has recently focused on the problem of representing historical information in XML. In [27] an annotation-based object model is proposed to manage historical semistructured data, and a special Chorel language is used to query changes. In [28] a new `<valid>` markup tag for XML/HTML documents is proposed to support valid time on the Web, thus temporal visualization can be implemented on web browsers with XSL. In [29], a dimension-based method is proposed to manage changes in XML documents, however how to support queries is not discussed.

In [30], a data model is proposed for temporal XML documents. However, since a valid interval is represented as a mixed string, queries have to be supported by extending DOM APIs or XPath. Similarly, in [31, 32], extensions of XPath is needed to support temporal semantics. (In our approach, we instead support XPath/XQuery without any extension to XML data models or query languages.) A τXQuery language is proposed in [33] to extend XQuery for temporal support, which has to provide new constructs for the language.

An archiving technique for scientific data using XML was presented in [34], but the issue of temporal queries was not discussed. Both the schema proposed in [34] and our schema are generalizations of SCCS [35].

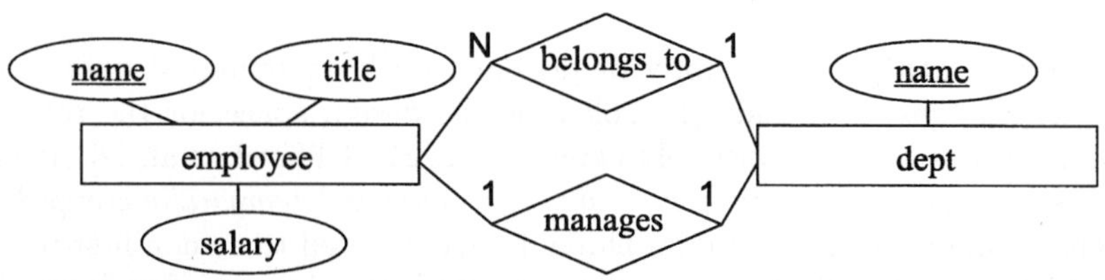

Fig. 1. TEER Schema of Employees and Departments (with Time Semantics Added)

3 An Example

The Temporal EER Model (TEER) [16] extends the temporal semantics into the existing EER modeling constructs, and works for both valid time and transaction time. TEER model associates each entity with a lifespan, and an attribute's value history is grouped together, and assigned with a temporal element (a union of valid temporal spans). Each relationship instance is also associated with a temporal element to represent the lifespan.

This temporal ER model is believed by the authors to be more natural to manage temporal aspects of data than in a tuple-oriented relational data model [16]. Suppose that we have two relations **employees** and **departments**, and each employee has a name, title, salary, and dept (name is the key), and each dept has a name and manager(name is the key). To model the history of the two relations, we use a TEER diagram as shown in Figure 1. (For simplicity, only valid time is considered, and transaction time can be modeled in a similar way.) Figure 1 looks exactly like a normal ER diagram except that the time semantics is added.

In this schema, the entity **employee** (or **e**) will have the following temporal attribute values:

```
SURROGATE(e) = {[1995-01-01,now] -> surrogate_id}
NAME(e)    = {[1995-01-01,now] -> Bob}
TITLE(e)   = {[1995-01-01,1997-12-31] -> Engineer,
              [1998-01-01,now] -> {Sr Engineer} }
SALARY(e)  = {[1995-01-01,1997-12-31]-> 65000,
              [1998-01-01,1999-12-31]-> 70000,
              [2000-01-01,now] -> 85000}
```

Here each attribute value is associated with a valid time lifespan. **surrogate** is a system-defined identifier, which can be ignored if the key doesn't change.

The following is the list of temporal attribute values of entity **dept** (or **d**) :

```
SURROGATE(d) = {[1995-01-01,now] -> surrogate_id}
NAME(d)      = {[1995-01-01,now] -> RD}
```

Similarly, for the instance **rb** of the relationship **belongs_to** between employee 'Bob' and dept 'RD', the lifespan is `T(rb)=[1995-01-01,now]`, and for the instance **rm** of the relationship **manages** between employee 'Mike' and dept 'RD', the lifespan is `T(r)=[1999-01-01,now]`.

In the next section, we show that such temporal ER model can be supported well with XML.

4 Valid Time History in XML

While transaction time identifies when data was recorded in the database, valid time concerns when a fact was true in reality. One major difference is that while transaction time is appended only and cannot be updated, valid time can

Name	Title	Dept	Salary	Start	End
Bob	Engineer	RD	65000	1995-01-01	1997-12-31
Bob	Sr Engineer	RD	70000	1998-01-01	1999-12-31
Bob	Sr Engineer	RD	85000	2000-01-01	now

Fig. 2. Valid Time History of Employees

```
<employees vstart="1995-01-01" vend="now">
  <employee vstart="1995-01-01" vend="now">
    <name vstart="1995-01-01" vend="now">Bob</name>
    <title vstart="1995-01-01" vend="1997-12-31">Engineer</title>
    <title vstart="1998-01-01" vend="now">Sr Engineer</title>
    <dept vstart="1995-01-01" vend="now">RD</dept>
    <salary vstart="1995-01-01" vend="1997-12-31">65000</salary>
    <salary vstart="1998-01-01" vend="1999-12-31">70000</salary>
    <salary vstart="2000-01-01" vend="now">85000</salary>
  </employee>
</employees>
```

Fig. 3. XML Representation of the Valid-time History of Employees(VH-document)

be updated by users. We show that, with XML, we can model the valid time history naturally.

Figure 2 shows a valid time history of employees, where each tuple is timestamped with a valid time interval. This representation assumes valid time homogeneity, and is temporally ungrouped [9]. It has several drawbacks: first, redundancy information is preserved between tuples, e.g., Bob's department appeared the same but was stored in all the tuples; second, temporal queries need to frequently coalesce tuples, which is a source of complications in temporal query languages.

These problems can be overcome using a representation where the timestamped history of each attribute is grouped under the attribute [9]. This produces a hierarchical organization that can be naturally represented by the hierarchical XML view shown in Figure 3 (VH-document). Observe that every element is timestamped using two XML attributes **vstart** and **vend**.

In the VH-document, each element is timestamped with an inclusive valid time interval (vstart, vend). **vend** can be set to *now* to denote the ever-increasing current date, which is internally represented as "9999-12-31" (Section 4.2). Please note that an entity (e.g., employee 'Bob') always has a longer or equal lifespan than its children, thus there is a *valid time covering constraint* that the valid time interval of a parent node always covers that of its child nodes, which is preserved in the update process(Section 4.3).

Unlike the relational data model that is almost invariably depicted via tables, XML is not directly associated with a graphical representation. This creates the challenge and the opportunity of devising the graphical representation most conducive for the application at hand—and implementing it using standard XML

<table>
<tr><th>Name</th><th>Title</th><th>Dept</th><th>Salary</th></tr>
<tr><td rowspan="3">1995-01-01
Bob
now</td><td>1995-01-01
Engineer
1997-12-31</td><td rowspan="3">1995-01-01
RD
now</td><td>1995-01-01
65000
1997-12-31</td></tr>
<tr><td rowspan="2">1998-01-01
Sr Engineer
now</td><td>1998-01-01
70000
1999-12-31</td></tr>
<tr><td>2000-01-01
85000
now</td></tr>
</table>

Fig. 4. Temporally Grouped Valid Time History of Employees

tools such as XSL [36]. Figure 4 shows a representation of temporally grouped tables that we found effective as user interface (and even more so after contrasting colored backgrounds and other browser-supported embellishments).

4.1 Valid Time Temporal Queries

The data shown in Figure 4 is the actual data stored in the database—with the exception of the special "now" symbol discussed later. Thus a powerful query language such as XQuery can be directly applied to this data model. In terms of data types, XML and XQuery support an adequate set of built-in temporal types, including datetime, date, time, and duration [5]; they also provide a complete set of comparison and casting functions for duration, date and time values, making snapshot and period-based queries convenient to express in XQuery. Furthermore, whenever more complex temporal functions are needed, they can be defined using XQuery functions that provide a native extensibility mechanism for the language.

Next we show that we can specify temporal queries with XQuery on the VH-document, such as temporal projection, snapshot queries, temporal slicing, temporal joins, etc.

QUERY V1: Temporal projection: retrieve the history of departments where Bob was employed:

```
<dept>
 for $s in doc("emps.xml")/employees/employee[name="Bob"]/dept
 return $s
</dept>
```

QUERY V2: Snapshot: retrieve the managers of each department on 1999-05-01:

```
for $m in doc("depts.xml")/depts/
   dept/mgrno[vstart(.)<="1999-05-01" and vend(.)>="1999-05-01"]
return $m
```

Here `depts.xml` is the VH-document that includes the history of dept names and managers. `vstart()` and `vend()` are user-defined functions (expressed in

XQuery) that return the starting date and ending date of an element's valid time respectively, thus the implementation is transparent to users.

QUERY V3: Continuous Period: find employees who worked as a manager for more than 5 consecutive years (i.e., 1826 days):

```
for $e in doc("emps.xml")/employees/employee[title="Manager"]
for $t in $e/title[.="Manager"]
let $duration := subtract-dates( vend($t), vstart($t)  )
where dayTimeDuration-greater-than($duration,"P1826D")
return  $e/name
```

Here "P1826D" is a duration constant of 1826 days in XQuery.

QUERY V4: Temporal Join: find employees who were making the same salaries on 2001-04-01:

```
for $e1 in doc("emps.xml")/employees/employee
for $e2 in doc("emps.xml")/employees/employee
where $e1/salary[vstart(.)<='2001-04-01'
  and vend(.)>= '2001-04-01'] =
  $e2/salary[vstart(.)<= '2001-04-01' and vend(.)>='2001-04-01']
  and $e1/name != $e2/name
return ($e1/name , $e2/name)
```

This query will join `emps.xml` with itself. It is also easy to support *since* and *until* connectives of first-order temporal logic [18], for example:

QUERY V5: A Until B: find the employee who was hired and worked in dept "RD" until Bob was appointed as the manager of the dept:

```
for $e in doc("emps.xml")/employees/employee
for $b in doc("emps.xml")/employees/employee[name='Bob']
let $t := $b/title[.='manager']
let $bd := $b/dept[.='RD']
let $d := $e/dept [1][.='RD']
where vmeets($d, $t) and vcontains($bd,$t)
return <employee>{$e/name}</employee>
```

4.2 Temporal Operators

In the temporal queries, we used functions such as `vstart` and `vend` to shield users from the implementations of representing time. Functions predefined include: timestamp referencing functions, such as `vstart, vend`; interval comparison functions, such as `voverlaps, vprecedes, vcontains, vequals, vmeets, voverlapinterval`; and during and date/time functions, such as `vtimespan, vinterval`. For example, `vcontains` is defined as follows:

```
define function vcontains($a, $b){
 if ($a/@vstart<= $b/@vstart and $a/@vend >= $b/@vend )
 then true()
 else false()
}
```

Internally, we use "end-of-time" values to denote the 'now' and 'UC' symbol. For instance for dates we use "9999-12-31." The user does not access this value directly, but accesses it through built-in functions. For instance, to refer to the ending valid time of a node **s**, the user uses the function **vend(s)**, which returns **s**'s end, if this is different from '9999-12-31" and CURRENT_DATE otherwise. The nodes returned in the output, normally use the "9999-12-31" representation used for internal data. However, for data returned to the end-user, two different representations are preferable. One is to return the CURRENT_DATE by applying function *rvend*() that, recursively, replaces all the occurrence of "9999-12-31" with the value of CURRENT_DATE. The other is to return a special string, such as *now* to be displayed on the end-user screen.

These valid-time queries are similar to those transaction time history, as discussed in [13]. However, unlike transaction-time databases, valid time databases must also support explicit update. This is not discussed in [13] and will be discussed next.

4.3 Database Modifications

An update task force is currently working on defining standard update constructs for XQuery [37]; moreover, update constructs are already supported in several native XML databases [38]. Our approach to temporal updates consists in supporting the operations of insert, delete, and update via user-defined functions. This approach will preserve the validity of end-user programs in the face of differences between vendors and evolving standards. It also shields the end-users from the complexity of the additional operations required by temporal updates, such as the coalescing of periods, and the propagation of updates to enforce the covering constraints.

INSERT. When a new entity is inserted, the new employee element with its children elements is appended in the VH-Document; the **vstart** attributes are set to the valid starting timestamp, and **vend** are set to *now*. Insertion can be done through the user-defined function **VInsert($path,$newelement)**. The new element can be created using the function **VNewElement($valueset, $vstart, $vend)**.

For example, the following query inserts Mike as an engineer into RD dept with salary 50K, starting immediately:

```
for $s in doc("emps.xml")/employees/employee[last()]
return VInsert($s, VNewElement(
  ["Mike", "Engineer", "RD", "50000"], current-date(),"now" ))
```

DELETE. There are two types of deletion: deletion without valid time and deletion with valid time. The former assumes a default valid time interval: (current_date, forever), and can be implemented with the user defined function **VNodeDelete($path)**. For deletion with a valid time interval **v** on node **e**, there can be three mutually exclusive cases: (i) **e** is removed if its valid time interval is contained in `v`, (ii) the valid time interval of `e` is extended if the two intervals overlap, but do not contain each other, or (iii) `e`'s interval is split if it properly contains `v`. Deletions on a node are then propagated downward to its children to satisfy the covering constraint. Node deletion (with downward propagation) is supported by the function `vTimeDelete($path, $vstart, $vend)`.

UPDATE. Updates can be on values or valid time, and coalescing is needed. There are two functions defined: `vNodeReplace($path,$newValue)`, and `vTimeReplace($path, $vstart,$vend)`. For value update, propagation is not needed; for valid time update, it is needed to downward update the node's children's valid time. If a valid time update on a child node violates the valid time covering constraint, then the update will fail.

5 Viewing Transaction Time History as XML

In [13] we have proposed an approach to represent the transaction-time history of relational databases in XML using a temporally grouped data model. This approach is very effective at supporting complex temporal queries using XQuery [5], without requiring changes in this standard query language.

In [13] we used these features to show that the XML-viewed transaction time history(TH-document) can be easily generated from the evolving history of the databases, and implemented by either using native XML databases or, after decomposition into binary relations, by relational databases enhanced with tools such as SQL/XML [4]. We also showed that XQuery without modifications can be used as an effective language for expressing temporal queries.

A key issue not addressed in [13] was whether this approach, and its unique practical benefits of only requiring off-the-shelf tools, can be extended to support bitemporal databases. With two dimensions of time, bitemporal databases have much more complexity, e.g., coalescing on two dimensions, explicit update complexity, and support of more complex bitemporal queries. In the next section, we explore how to support a bitemporal data model based on XML.

6 An XML-Based Bitemporal Data Model

6.1 The XBiT Data Model

In practice, temporal applications often involve both transaction time and valid time. We show next that, with XML, we can naturally represent a temporally grouped data model, and provide support for complex bitemporal queries.

Bitemporal Grouping. Figure 5 shows a bitemporal history of employees, using a temporally ungrouped representation. Although valid time and transaction time are generally independent, for the sake of illustration, we assume here that employees' promotions are scheduled and entered in the database four months before they occur.

XBiT supports a temporally grouped representation by coalescing attributes' histories on both transaction time and valid time. Temporal coalescing on two

Name	Title	Dept	Salary	Valid Time	Transaction Time
Bob	Engineer	RD	65000	1995-01-01:now	1995-01-01:1997-08-31
Bob	Engineer	RD	65000	1995-01-01:1997-12-31	1997-09-01:UC
Bob	Sr Engineer	RD	70000	1998-01-01:now	1997-09-01:1999-08-31
Bob	Sr Engineer	RD	70000	1998-01-01:1999-12-31	1999-09-01:UC
Bob	Sr Engineer	RD	85000	2000-01-01:now	1999-09-01:UC

Fig. 5. Bitemporal History of Employees

temporal dimensions is different from coalescing on just one. On one dimension, coalescing is done when: i) two successive tuples are value equivalent, and ii) the intervals overlap or meet. The two intervals are then merged into maximal intervals.

For bitemporal histories, coalescing is done when two tuples are value-equivalent and (i) their valid time intervals are the same and the transaction time intervals meet or overlap; or (ii) the transaction time intervals are the same and the valid time intervals meet or overlap. This operation is repeated until no tuples satisfy these conditions.

For example, in Figure 5, to group the history of titles with value 'Sr Engineer' in the last three tuples, i.e., (title, valid_time, transaction_time), the last two transaction time intervals are the same, so they are coalesced as `(Sr Engineer, 1998-01-01:now, 1999-09-01:UC)`. This one again has the same valid time interval as the previous one: (`(Sr Engineer, 1998-01-01:now, 1997-09-01:1999-08-31)`, thus finally they are coalesced as `(Sr Engineer, 1998-01-01:now, 1997-09-01:UC)`, as shown in Figure 7.

Data Modeling of Bitemporal History with XML. With temporal grouping, the bitemporal history is represented in XBiT as an XML document (BH-document). This is shown in the example of Figure 6, which is snapshot-equivalent to the example of Figure 5. Each employee entity is represented as an employee element in the BH-document, and table attributes are represented as employee element's child elements. Each element in the BH-document is assigned two pairs of attributes `tstart` and `tend` to represent the inclusive transaction time interval, and `vstart` and `vend` to represent the inclusive valid time interval. Elements corresponding to a table attribute value history are ordered by the starting transaction time `tstart`. The value of `tend` can be set to *UC* (until changed), and `vend` can be set to *now*. There is a covering constraint whereby the transaction time interval of a parent node must always cover that of its child nodes, and likewise for valid time intervals.

Figure 7 displays the resulting temporally grouped representation, which is appealing to intuition, and also effective at supporting natural language interfaces, as shown by Clifford [7].

```
<employees vstart="1995-01-01" vend="now" tstart="1995-01-01" tend="UC">
  <employee vstart="1995-01-01" vend="now" tstart="1995-01-01" tend="UC">
    <name vstart="1995-01-01" vend="now" tstart="1995-01-01" tend="UC">Bob</name>
    <title vstart="1995-01-01" vend="now" tstart="1995-01-01" tend="1997-08-31"> Engineer</title>
    <title vstart="1995-01-01" vend="1997-12-31" tstart="1997-09-01" tend="UC"> Engineer</title>
    <title vstart="1998-01-01" vend="now" tstart="1997-09-01" tend="UC">Sr Engineer</title>
    <dept vstart="1995-01-01" vend="now" tstart="1995-01-01" tend="UC">RD</dept>
    <salary vstart="1995-01-01" vend="now" tstart="1995-01-01" tend="1997-08-31">65000</salary>
    <salary vstart="1995-01-01" vend="1997-12-31" tstart="1997-09-01" tend="UC">65000</salary>
    <salary vstart="1998-01-01" vend="now" tstart="1997-09-01" tend="1999-08-31">70000</salary>
    <salary vstart="1998-01-01" vend="1999-12-31" tstart="1999-09-01" tend="UC">70000</salary>
    <salary vstart="2000-01-01" vend="now" tstart="1999-09-01" tend="UC">85000</salary>
  </employee>
</employees>
```

Fig. 6. XML Representation of the Bitemporal History of Employees(BH-document)

6.2 Bitemporal Queries with XQuery

The XBiT-based representation can also support powerful temporal queries, expressed in XQuery without requiring the introduction of new constructs in the language. We next show how to express bitemporal queries on employees.

QUERY B1: Temporal projection: retrieve the bitemporal salary history of employee "Bob":

```
<salary_history>
 for $s in doc("emps.xml")/employees/employee[name="Bob"]/salary
 return $s
</salary_history>
```

This query is exactly the same as query V1, except that it retrieves both transaction time and valid time history of salaries.

QUERY B2: Snapshot: according to what was known on 1999-05-01, what was the average salary at that time?

```
let $s := doc("emps.xml")/employees/employee/salary
where tstart($s)<="1999-05-01" and  tend($s) >=  "1999-05-01"
  and vstart($s)<="1999-05-01" and vend($s) >=  "1999-05-01"
return  avg($s)
```

Here `tstart()`, `tend()`, `vstart()` and `vend()` are user-defined functions that get the starting date and ending date of an element's transaction-time and valid-time, respectively.

QUERY B3: Diff queries: retrieve employees whose salaries (according to our current information) didn't changed between 1999-01-01 and 2000-01-01:

```
let $s := doc("emps.xml")/employees/employee/salary
where tstart($s)<=current-date() and  tend($s)>=current-date()
  and vstart($s)<="1999-01-01" and vend($s)>= "2000-01-01"
return  $s/..
```

<table>
<tr><th>Name</th><th>Title</th><th>Dept</th><th>Salary</th></tr>
<tr><td rowspan="5">t:1995-01-01
v:1995-01-01
Bob
t:UC
v:now</td><td>v:1995-01-01 t:1995-01-01
Engineer
v:now t:1997-08-31</td><td rowspan="5">t:1995-01-01
v:1995-01-01
RD
t:UC
v:now</td><td>v:1995-01-01 t:1995-01-01
65000
v:now t:1997-08-31</td></tr>
<tr><td>v:1995-01-01 t:1997-09-01
Engineer
v:1997-12-31 t:UC</td><td>v:1995-01-01 t:1997-09-01
65000
v:1997-12-31 t:UC</td></tr>
<tr><td rowspan="3">v:1998-01-01 t:1997-09-01
Sr Engineer
v:now t:UC</td><td>v:1998-01-01 t:1997-09-01
70000
v:now t:1999-08-31</td></tr>
<tr><td>v:1998-01-01 t:1999-09-01
70000
v:1999-12-31 t:UC</td></tr>
<tr><td>v:2000-01-01 t:1999-09-01
85000
v:now t:UC</td></tr>
</table>

Fig. 7. Temporally Grouped Bitemporal History of Employees

This query will take a transaction time snapshot and a valid time slicing of salaries.

QUERY B4: Change Detection: find all the updates of employee salaries that were applied retroactively.

```
for  $s in doc("emps.xml")/employees/employee/salary
where tstart($s) > vstart($s) or  tend($s) > vend($s)
```

QUERY B5: find the manager for each current employee, as best known now:

```
for $e in doc("emps.xml")/employees/employee
for $d in doc("depts.xml")/depts/dept/name[.=$e/dept]
where tend($e)="UC" and tend($d)="UC"
 and vend($e)="now" and vend($d)="now"
return $e, $d
```

This query will take the current snapshot on both transaction time and valid time.

6.3 Database Modifications

For valid time databases, both attribute values and attribute valid time can be updated by users, and XBiT must perform some implicit coalescing to support the update process. Note that only elements that are current (ending transaction time as *UC*) can be modified. A modification combines two processes: explicit modification of valid time and values, and implicit modification of transaction time.

Modifications of Transaction Time Databases. Transaction time modifications can also be classified as three types: insert, delete, and update.

INSERT. When a new tuple is inserted, the corresponding new element (e.g., employee 'Bob') and its child elements in BH-document are timestamped with starting transaction time as current date, and ending transaction time as *UC*. The user-defined function `TInsert($node)` will insert the node with the transaction time interval(current date, *UC*).

DELETE. When a tuple is removed, the ending transaction time of the corresponding element and its current children is changed to current time. This can be done by the function `TDelete($node)`.

UPDATE. Update can be seen as a delete followed by an insert.

Database Modifications in XBiT. Modifications in XBiT can be seen as the combination of modifications on valid time and transaction time history. XBiT will automatically coalesce on both valid time and transaction time.

INSERT. Insertion is similar to valid time database insertion except that the added element is timestamped with transaction time interval as (current date, *UC*).

This can be done by the funciton `BInsert($path, $newelement)`, which combines `VInsert` and `TInsert`.

DELETE. Deletion is similar to valid time database insertion, except that the function `TDelete` is called to change `tend` of the deleted element and its current children to current date. Node deletion is done through the function `BNodeDelete($path)`, and valid time deletion is done through the function `BTimeDelete($path, $vstart, $vend)`.

UPDATE. Update is also a combination of valid time and transaction time, i.e., deleting the old tuple with `tend` set to current date, and inserting the new tuple with new value and valid time interval, `tstart` set to current date and `tend` set to *UC*. This is done by the functions `BNodeReplace($path, $newValue)` and `BTimeReplace($path, $vstart, $vend)` respectively.

6.4 Temporal Database Implementations

Two basic approaches are possible to manage the three types of H-documents discussed here: one is to use a native XML database, and the other is to use traditional RDBMS. In [13] we show that a transaction time TH-document can be stored in a RDBMS and has significant performance advantages on temporal queries over a native XML database. Similarly, RDBMS-based approach can be applied to the valid history and bitemporal history. First, the BH-document is shredded and stored into H-tables.

For example, the employee BH-document in Figure 6 is mapped into the following attribute history tables:

```
employee_name(id,name,vstart,vend,tstart,tend)
employee_title(id,title,vstart,vend,tstart,tend)
employee_salary(id,salary,vstart,vend,tstart,tend)
...
```

Since the BH-document and H-tables have a simple mapping relationship, temporal XQuery can be translated into SQL queries based on such mapping relationship, using the techniques discussed in [13].

7 Conclusions

In this paper, we showed that valid-time, transaction-time, and bitemporal databases can be naturally managed in XML using temporally-grouped data models. This approach is similar to the one we proposed for transaction-time data bases in [13], but we have here shown that it also supports (i) the temporal EER model [16], and (ii) valid-time and bitemporal databases with the complex temporal update operations they require. Complex historical queries, and updates, which would be very difficult to express in SQL on relational tables, can now be easily expressed in XQuery on such XML-based representations.

The technique is general and can be applied to historical representations of relational data, XML documents in native XML databases, and version management in archives and web warehouses [12]. It can also be used to support schema evolution queries [39].

Acknowledgments. The authors would like to thank Xin Zhou for his help and comments.
This work was supported by the National Historical Publications and Records Commission and a gift by NCR Teradata.

References

1. R. T. Snodgrass. Developing Time-Oriented Database Applications in SQL. *Morgan Kaufmann*, 1999.
2. G. Ozsoyoglu and R.T. Snodgrass. Temporal and Real-Time Databases: A Survey. *IEEE Transactions on Knowledge and Data Engineering*, 7(4):513–532, 1995.
3. F. Grandi. An Annotated Bibliography on Temporal and Evolution Aspects in the World Wide Web. In *TimeCenter Technical Report TR-75*, 2003.
4. SQL/XML. http://www.sqlx.org.
5. XQuery 1.0: An XML Query Language. http://www.w3.org/XML/Query.
6. M. Carey, J. Kiernan, J. Shanmugasundaram, and et al. XPERANTO: A Middleware for Publishing Object-Relational Data as XML Documents. In *VLDB*, 2000.
7. J. Clifford. *Formal Semantics and Pragmatics for Natural Language Querying.* Cambridge University Press, 1990.
8. J. Clifford, A. Croker, and A. Tuzhilin. On completeness of historical relational query languages. *ACM Trans. Database Syst.*, 19(1):64–116, 1994.
9. J. Clifford, A. Croker, F. Grandi, and A. Tuzhilin. On Temporal Grouping. In *Recent Advances in Temporal Databases*, pages 194–213. Springer Verlag, 1995.
10. S. Kepser. A Proof of the Turing-Completeness of XSLT and XQuery. In *Technical report SFB 441, Eberhard Karls Universitat Tubingen*, 2002.
11. ICAP: Incorporating Change Management into Archival Processes. http://wis.cs.ucla.edu/projects/icap/.
12. F. Wang and C. Zaniolo. Temporal Queries in XML Document Archives and Web Warehouses. In *TIME-ICTL*, 2003.

13. F. Wang and C. Zaniolo. Publishing and Querying the Histories of Archived Relational Databases in XML. In *WISE*, 2003.
14. H. Gregersen and C. S. Jensen. Temporal Entity-Relationship Models - A Survey. *Knowledge and Data Engineering*, 11(3):464–497, 1999.
15. H. Gregersen and C. Jensen. Conceptual Modeling of Time-varying Information. In *TIMECENTER Technical Report TR-35, September 1998.*, 1998.
16. R. Elmasri and G.T.J.Wuu. A Temporal Model and Query Language for ER Databases. In *ICDE*, pages 76–83, 1990.
17. R. T. Snodgrass. *The TSQL2 Temporal Query Language*. Kluwer, 1995.
18. J. Chomicki, D. Toman, and M.H. Böhlen. Querying ATSQL Databases with Temporal Logic. *TODS*, 26(2):145–178, June 2001.
19. M. H. Böhlen, J. Chomicki, R. T. Snodgrass, and D. Toman. Querying TSQL2 Databases with Temporal Logic. In *EDBT*, pages 325–341, 1996.
20. J. Chomicki and D. Toman. Temporal Logic in Information Systems. In *Logics for Databases and Information Systems*, pages 31–70. Kluwer, 1998.
21. C. S. Jensen and C. E. Dyreson (eds). A Consensus Glossary of Temporal Database Concepts - February 1998 Version. *Temporal Databases: Research and Practice*, pages 367–405, 1998.
22. S. K. Gadia and C. S. Yeung. A Generalized Model for a Relational Temporal Database. In *SIGMOD*, 1988.
23. C. Zaniolo, S. Ceri, C.Faloutsos, R.T. Snodgrass, V.S. Subrahmanian, and R. Zicari. *Advanced Database Systems*. Morgan Kaufmann Publishers, 1997.
24. Adam Bosworth, Michael J. Franklin, and Christian S. Jensen. Querying the Past, the Present, and the Future. In *ICDE*, 2004.
25. M. Fernandez, W. Tan, and D. Suciu. SilkRoute: Trading Between Relations and XML. In *8th Intl. WWW Conf.*, 1999.
26. Oracle XML. http://otn.oracle.com/xml/.
27. S.S. Chawathe, S. Abiteboul, and J. Widom. Managing Historical Semistructured Data. *Theory and Practice of Object Systems*, 24(4):1–20, 1999.
28. F. Grandi and F. Mandreoli. The Valid Web: An XML/XSL Infrastructure for Temporal Management of Web Documents. In *ADVIS*, 2000.
29. M. Gergatsoulis and Y. Stavrakas. Representing Changes in XML Documents using Dimensions. In *Xsym*, 2003.
30. T. Amagasa, M. Yoshikawa, and S. Uemura. A Data Model for Temporal XML Documents. In *DEXA*, 2000.
31. C.E. Dyreson. Observing Transaction-Time Semantics with TTXPath. In *WISE*, 2001.
32. S. Zhang and C. Dyreson. Adding valid time to xpath. In *DNIS*, 2002.
33. D. Gao and R. T. Snodgrass. Temporal Slicing in the Evaluation of XML Queries. In *VLDB*, 2003.
34. P. Buneman, S. Khanna, K. Tajima, and W. Tan. Archiving scientific data. *ACM Trans. Database Syst.*, 29(1):2–42, 2004.
35. M.J. Rochkind. The Source Code Control System. *IEEE Transactions on Software Engineering*, SE-1(4):364–370, 1975.
36. The Extensible Stylesheet Language (XSL). http://www.w3.org/Style/XSL/.
37. M. Rys. Proposal for an XML Data Modification Language. In *Microsoft Report*, 2002.
38. Tamino XML Server. http://www.tamino.com.
39. F. Wang and C. Zaniolo. Representing and Querying the Evolution of Databases and their Schemas in XML. In *Intl. Workshop on Web Engineering, SEKE*, 2003.

Enterprise Cockpit for Business Operation Management

Fabio Casati, Malu Castellanos, and Ming-Chien Shan

Hewlett-Packard
1501 Page Mill road
Palo Alto, CA, 94304
{fabio.casati,malu.castellanos,ming-chien.shan}@hp.com

The area of business operations monitoring and management is rapidly gaining importance both in the industry and in the academia. This is demonstrated by the large number of performance reporting tools that have been developed. Such tools essentially leverage system monitoring and data warehousing applications to perform online analysis of business operations and produce fancy charts, from which users can get the feeling of what is happening in the system. While this provides value, there is still a huge gap between what is available today and what users would ideally like to have[1]:

- Business analysts tend to think of the way business operations are performed in terms of high level business processes, that we will call *abstract* in the following. There is no way today for analyst to draw such abstract processes and use them as a metaphor for analyzing business operations.
- Defining metrics of interest and reporting against these metrics requires a significant coding effort. No system provides, out of the box, the facility for easily defining metrics over process execution data, for providing users with *explanations* for why a metric has a certain value, and for *predicting* the future value for a metric.
- There is no automated support for identifying optimal configurations of the business processes to improve critical metrics.
- There is no support for understanding the business impact of system failures.

The Enterprise Cockpit (EC) is an "intelligent" business operation management platform that provides the functionality described above. In addition to providing information and alerts about any business operation supported by an IT infrastructure, EC includes control and optimization features, so that managers can use it to automatically or manually intervene on the enterprise processes and resources, make changes in response to problems, or identify optimizations that can improve business-relevant metrics. In the following, we sketch the proposed solution[2].

The basic layer of EC is the Abstract Process Monitor (APM), that allows users to define abstract processes and link the steps in these processes with *events* (e.g., access to certain Web pages, invocation of SAP interface methods, etc.) occurring in the underlying IT infrastructure In addition to monitoring abstract processes, EC leverages other business operation data, managed by means of "traditional" data warehousing techniques, and therefore not discussed further here.

Once processes have been defined, users can specify metrics or SLAs over them, through the *metric/SLA definer*. For example, analysts can define a *success* metric

---

[1] We name here just a few of the many issues that came out at a requirements gathering workshop held last fall in Palo Alto.

[2] A more detailed paper is available on request.

P. Atzeni et al. (Eds.): ER 2004, LNCS 3288, pp. 825–827, 2004.

stating that a payment process is successful if it ends at the "pay invoice" node and is completed within 4 days from the time the invoice has been received. Metrics are defined by means of a simple web-based GUI and by reusing metric templates either built into APM or developed by consultants at solution deployment time. Once metrics have been defined, the *metric computation engine* takes care of computing their values. In addition, EC computes *distributions* for both process attributes (such as the duration of each step and of the whole process, or the process arrival rate) and metrics. This is done by the *curve fitting* module. For example, users can discover that the duration of the *check invoice* step follows a normal distribution with a given mean and variance, or that the process arrival rate follows an exponential distribution.

EC also provides features to help users make the most out of this information and really understand which things go wrong, why, what is their impact on the business, and how to correct problems. One of these features is *process analysis,* performed by the *analysis and prediction engine*. This consists in providing users with explanation for why metrics have certain values (e.g., why the cost is high or the success rate is low). To this end, EC integrates algorithms that automatically mine the EC databases and extract *decision trees*, which have a graphical formalism that makes it easy, even for business users, to examine correlations between metric values and other process attributes or metrics and identify the critical attributes affecting metric deviations from desired values. For example, users can see that unsuccessful processes are often characterized by invoices from a certain supplier arriving on a certain day. The hard challenge here is how to prepare the data (collected among the ocean of information available by the different data logs) to be fed to the mining algorithm, how to do this in an automated fashion (without human supervision), and in a way that works for every process and every metric. We addressed this challenge by confining the problem (we do analysis and prediction over metric data defined over abstract processes), by leveraging the fact that we have a rich, self-describing process and metric meta-model and therefore could write data preparation programs that can gather all the potentially useful process and metric data, and by leveraging experimental knowledge about which process features are most typically correlated with metric values.

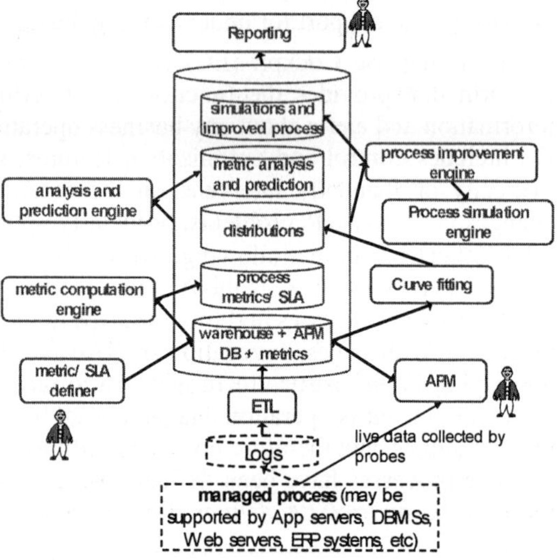

Another feature, essentially based on the same mining technology, is to provide users with a *prediction* of the value that a metric will have at the end of a process, or whether an SLA will be violated or not. Predictions are made at the start of the process and are updated as process execution proceeds. To this end, a family of decision (or regression) trees is built for each abstract process. In addition to the predicted value, users are provided with a confidence value that indicates the probability that the prediction will happen.

Metric analysis and predictions are useful tools in their own right, but they leave the burden of *optimization* to the users. Hence, EC also includes an optimization component, that suggests improvements to the enterprise process based on business goals, expressed in terms of desired metric values defined over abstract processes. This is achieved by leveraging process simulation techniques: Users can state that they want to optimize an abstract process so to minimize or maximize the value of a certain metric. EC will then simulate the execution of several alternative process configurations corresponding to that abstract process (for example, will try to allocate human and automated resources in different ways, while meeting resource constraints defined by the user), will compute metrics out of the simulated data, and will consequently identify the configuration that best meets the user's goals. EC also optimizes the search among the many possible process configurations, although in the current version we use simple heuristics for this purpose.

Finally, we stress that all of the above features are provided in a fully automated fashion, at the click of the mouse. This is in sharp contrast with the way that, for example, data mining or process simulation packages are used today, requiring heavy manual intervention and lengthy consulting efforts.

Modeling Autonomous Catalog for Electronic Commerce

Yuan-Chi Chang, Vamsavardhana R. Chillakuru, and Min Wang

IBM Thomas J. Watson Research Center,
P.O. Box 704, Yorktown Heights, NY 10598, USA

The catalog function is an essential feature in B2C and B2B e-commerce. While catalog is primarily for end users to navigate and search for interested products, other e-commerce functions such as merchandising, order, inventory and aftermarket constantly refer to information stored in the catalog [1]. The billion-dollar mail order business was created around catalog long before e-commerce. More opportunities surface after catalog content previously created on paper is digitized. While catalog is recognized as a necessity for a successful web store, its content structure varies greatly across industries and also within each industry. Product categories, attributes, measurements, languages, and currency all contribute to the wide variations, which create a difficult dilemma for catalog designers.

We have recently encountered a real business scenario that challenges traditional approaches of modeling and building e-catalog. We were commissioned to build an in-store shopping solution for branches in retail store chains. The local catalog at a branch is a synchronized copy of selected enterprise catalog content plus branch specific information, such as item location on the shelf. A key business requirement, which drives up the technical challenge, is that the in-store catalog solution needs to interoperate with the retail chain's legacy enterprise catalog or its catalog software vendor of choice. This requirement reflects the business reality that decisions to pick enterprise software and branch software are usually not made simultaneously nor coordinated. As we learned that hundreds of enterprise catalog software, legacy and recent, is being used in industries such as grocery, clothing, books, office staples and home improvement, our challenge is to create a catalog model that is autonomously adapting to the content of enterprise catalog in any of the industries.

A straightforward answer to the challenge is to build a mapping tool that will convert enterprise catalog content to the pre-designed in-store catalog, but this approach is highly undesirable. The difficulty lies within that it is impossible to predict the content to be stored. A simple example to illustrate the difficulty is by looking at what is stored in catalog for Home Depot, a home furnishing retailer, and by examining what is stored in catalog for Staples, an office equipment retailer. A kitchen faucet sold at Home Depot has information about its size, weight, material, color, and style. On the other hand, a fax machine sold at Staples carries attributes such as speed, resolution, and tone dialing. These attributes need to be stored in the catalog for retrieval and product comparisons. Without knowing where a catalog will be used, our design obviously

P. Atzeni et al. (Eds.): ER 2004, LNCS 3288, pp. 828–830, 2004.

cannot pre-set the storage schema for either faucets or fax machines. Needless to say, there are hundreds of thousands of products whose information needs to be stored in catalogs. Today's catalog solutions in the market also suffer from over design, which leads to wasted storage space, over-normalized schema and poor performance. Multi-language support, currency locale, geological label and access control are commonly embedded and inseparable from the main catalog functions. Suppose a company only operates stores in California. The additional features can turn highlights to burden.

Further enhancing the shortfall of the traditional catalog modeling and mapping approach is the lack of configurability and optimization. Customization made on small delta changes to the catalog data model propagates in a magnified way all the way up to business logic and presentation layers. Furthermore, the vertical schema to store catalog attributes in name-value pairs distorts database statistics and makes catalog queries hard to optimize [3] [4]. We foresee no easy way to continue the traditional methodology for a satisfactory solution to our problem.

In this paper, we propose a set of abstracted catalog semantics to model an autonomous catalog to become the in-store catalog solution. An autonomous catalog exhibits two key properties of autonomic computing: self-configuration and self-optimization [2]. It receives definitions of catalog entities from enterprise catalog to synthesize and create persistent storage schema and programming access interface. It buffers objects for cached retrieval and learns from search history to create index for performance. The use of autonomous catalog requires little learning and training since it morphs into enterprise catalog content structure. Changes can be reflected instantly at storage schema and programmatic interfaces.

We model this autonomous catalog by associations of basic categorical entities. A categorical entity is defined as a named grouping of products that share similar attributes. Instances of a categorical entity are physical, procurable products or services. For example, the kitchen faucet may be declared as a categorical entity and one of its instances is Moen Asceri. A categorical entity may be pointing to one or more categorical entities to establish parent or child category relationship. Attributes in a categorical entity may be completely different from those in another and yet in both cases, they are efficiently stored in a normalized schema without applying the vertical schema.

We define five operations including add, update, delete, search and retrieve on categorical entity. To shield software developers from accessing instances of categorical entities directly, these five catalog operations can only be executed through a programming language interface such as Java. When a new entity is declared by the enterprise catalog in XML Schema expression, new Java classes and interfaces, following a predefined template of these five operations, will be automatically synthesized.

For example, the enterprise may declare an entity named 'Kitchen Faucet' with five attributes. Our autonomous catalog then creates tables in the database to store instances of faucets and synthesizes a Java class with methods to populate, retrieve and search the instances by attribute values. Kitchen faucet may be associated with plumbing and kitchen categories. The Java class has methods to support searches from the associated categories. Revisiting the aforementioned catalog features such as multi-language support, we can easily add new attributes describing kitchen faucet in foreign languages applicable to use cases. There is no unused space for catalog attributes not needed.

Another advantage of the autonomous catalog is its ability to capture more sophisticated modeling semantics at runtime, due to the flexibility of programming language wrapper. For example, in the synthesized Java class, programmatic pointers can reference an external taxonomy or ontology for runtime inferencing. Catalog content linked to a knowledge management system can support more intelligent queries such as 'which kitchen faucets are recommended for water conservation?' This further brings catalog modeling beyond the inclusive entity-relationship diagram.

The modeling of autonomous catalog enables it to re-configure itself while administrators and programmers are shielded from knowing the details in managing the flexible persistent storage. As the Java classes change and evolve to adapt to the enterprise catalog content, one can envision that business logic that invokes these Java classes to be modeled and generated autonomously as well. We are investigating the modeling of merchandising and order tracking to demonstrate the feasibility of autonomous modeling of business logic.

References

1. S. Danish, "Building database-driven electronic catalogs," *ACM SIGMOD Record*, Vol. 27, No. 4, December 1998.
2. J. O. Kephart and D. M. Chess, "The vision of autonomic computing," *IEEE Computer Magazine*, Janurary 2003.
3. S. G. Lee, et.al. "An experimental evaluation of dynamic electronic catalog models in relational database systems," *2002 Information Resources Management Association International Conference*, Vol. 1, May 2002.
4. M. Wang, Y. C. Chang and S. Padmanabhan, "Supporting efficient parametric search of e-commerce data: a loosely-coupled solution," *8th International Conference on Extending Database Technology*, March 2002.

GiSA: A Grid System for Genome Sequences Assembly*

Jun Tang, Dong Huang, Chen Wang, Wei Wang, and Baile Shi

Fudan University, China
{tangjun,032053004,chenwang,weiwang1,bshi}@fudan.edu.cn

Sequencing genomes is a fundamental aspect of biological research. Shotgun sequencing, since introduced by Sanger et al [2], has remained the mainstay in the research field of genome sequence assembly. This method randomly obtains sequence reads (e.g. a subsequence including about 500 characters) from a genome and then assemblies them into contigs based on significant overlap among them. The whole-genome shotgun (*WGS*) approach, generates sequence reads directly from a whole-genome library and uses computational techniques to reassemble them. A variety of assembly programs have been previously proposed and implemented, including *PHRAP* [3] (Green 1994), *CAP3* [4] (1999), *Celera* [5] (2000) etc. Because of great computational complexity and increasingly large size, they incur great time and space overhead. *PHRAP* [3], for instance, which can only run in a stand-alone way, requires many times memory (usually greater than 10) as the size of original sequence data. In realistic applications, sequencing process might come to become unacceptably slow for insufficient memory even with a mainframe with huge RAM.

The *GiSA* (i.e. **G**r**i**d System for Genome **S**equence **A**ssembly) is thus designed to solve the problem. It is based on Globus Toolkit 3.2. With grid framework, it exploits parallelism and distribution for improving scalability. Its architecture is shown in figure 1.

The approach of *GiSA* is designed into a recursive procedure containing two steps. The first step partitions the sequence data into several intermediate-sized groups in which sequence reads are relevant and can potentially be assembled together. Each group can be successfully processed independently in limited memory. The second step will be performed to assemble intermediate results derived from the first steps in the round. In this way, we can handle dramatically large size of biological sequence data.

GiSA is divided into three layers: client, *PHRAP* servers, and servers for management including *BLAST* [1] Data Server and Management Data Server (*MDS*). The client simply sends assembly request through Web Browser. *MDS* of *GiSA* is ready to receive request and then *GiSA* starts working for genome sequence assembly.

PHRAP servers are deployed with Grid Environment (Globus Toolkit 3.2 for Linux in our implementation) and gird services for control and communication.

* This research is supported in part by the Key Program of National Natural Science Foundation of China (No. 69933010 and 60303008), and China National 863 High-Tech Projects (No. 2002AA4Z3430 and 2002AA231041)

P. Atzeni et al. (Eds.): ER 2004, LNCS 3288, pp. 831–833, 2004.

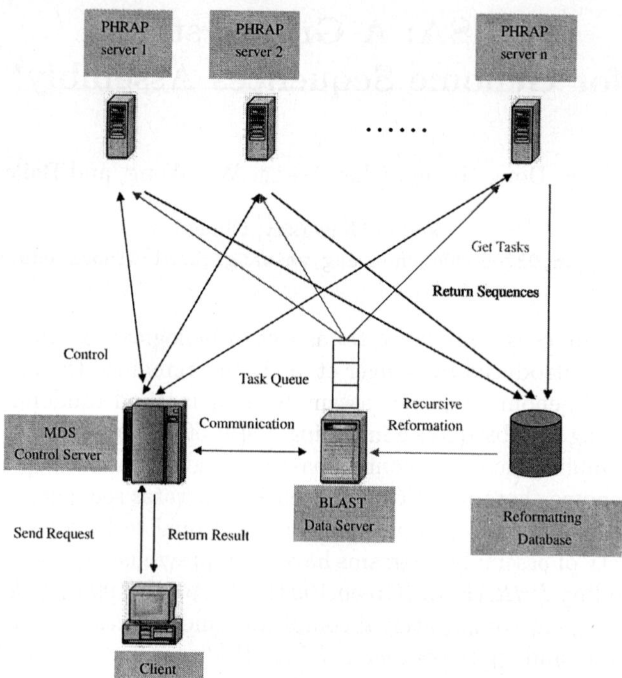

Fig. 1. Grid System for Genome Sequences Assembly

Information about the grid services such as *GSH* (Grid Service Handle) is registered in *MDS*. Each grid service works as a single thread to provide parallelism. *PHRAP* is also installed in each *PHRAP* server to accomplish assembly task. Each server continuously receives task from Task Queue on *MDS* and return locally processed result.

On *MDS*, several important programs are deployed as threads. Main control thread manages all the process variables and schedules the other programs. Queue thread constructs and maintains global Task Queue for workload balance. Dispatching thread dispatches tasks from Task Queue to *PHRAP* servers. And results-receiving thread collects partial results returned from *PHRAP* servers. All the four threads above are finely designed for synchronization.

Genome sequence data are stored in the *BLAST* Data Sever where *BLAST* is available for sequence similarity search.

The whole procedure works as follows. As the client sends assembly request through Web Browser, *GiSA* starts to run in a recursive reformation. First, control thread launches 'formatdb' program in *BLAST* package to construct *BLAST* target db. Then, queue thread randomly selects an unused sequence. *BLAST* use the sequence as a seed for finding sequences which have a promising chance of being joined. These sequences are collected in file and ready to be packed as Task Element into Task Queue. Dispatching thread dispatches tasks to each *PHPAP* server according to their respective capability. If there is no task in queue currently, it will sleep for a while. When a certain Task Element is dispatched to a certain *PHRAP* server, the server receives task and run *PHRAP* to align the sequences. Multiple *PHRAP* servers work independently and concurrently. Local assembly results are generated in plain file format and transferred back to *MDS*. After *MDS* gets the results, it updates server's capability information for future dispatching decision and sequence alignment information for next-round use. When a certain portion of sequences has been processed, next round starts. New data source file and *BLAST* db is reconstructed,. This procedure goes recursively. It does not cease until no contigs be generated any more and returns results to the client.

Additionally, we design a Web progress bar in JSP format as user interface to visualize the undergoing progress.

Obviously, we can benefit a lot from such an architecture and work flow of *GiSA*. The bottleneck of lacking enough RAM in a single computer is overcome by partitioning overall sequence data into smaller clusters. All the available service resources of servers contribute to *GiSA* to accelerate the assembly procedure. This is the common characteristic of grid system. Moreover, when a server finishes earlier than others, it will immediately get another assembly task from Task Queue until it is empty. As a result, the computing ability of each server is well exerted. In summary, this grid system provides new solutions to large scales of genome sequences assembly and it is a meaningful application of Grid in the area of sequence assembly.

References

1. S.F. Altschul, W. Gish, W. Miller, E.W. Myers, and D.J. Lipman. Basic Local Alignment Search Tool. *J. Mol. Biol.*, 215:403-410, 1990.
2. F. Sanger, S. Nicklen, and A.R. Coulsen. DNA Sequencing with Chain Terminating Inhibitors. In *Proc. Natl. Acad. Sci*, 74: 5463-5467, 1977.
3. P. Green. PHRAP Documentation. *http://www.phrap.org*, 1994.
4. X. Huang. and A. Madan. CAP3: A DNA Sequence Assembly Program. *Genome Res.*, 9:868-877, 1999.
5. E.W. Myers, G.G. Sutton, A.L. Delcher, and I.M. Dew, et al. A Whole-genome Assembly of Drosophila. *Science*, 287:2196-2204, 2000.

Analytical View of Business Data: An Example

Adam Yeh, Jonathan Tang, Youxuan Jin, and Sam Skrivan

Microsoft Corporation, One Microsoft Way
Redmond, WA, USA
{adamyeh,jontang,yjin,samsk}@mcirosoft.com

Abstract. This paper describes an example of how the Analytical View (AV) in Microsoft Business Framework (MBF) works. AV consists of three components: Design time Model Service, Business Intelligence Entity (BIE) programming model, and the runtime Intell-Drill for navigation between OLTP and OLAP data sources. Model Service transforms an "object model (transactional view)" to a "multi-dimensional model (analytical view)." It infers dimensionality from the object layer where richer metadata is stored, eliminating the guesswork that a traditional data warehousing process requires. Model Service also generates BI Entity classes that enable a consistent object oriented programming model with strong types and rich semantics for OLAP data. Intelli-Drill links together all the information in MBF using metadata, making information navigation in MBF fully discover-able.

1 Introduction

The goals of the analytical view [1] are to ensure less contention on the transactional databases, easier access of information, and tighter integration with the application framework's programming model, such as Microsoft Business Framework (MBF), with a focus on prescriptiveness [2]. Furthermore, we want to unleash the information and data stored in the application through a set of framework level programming models so they can be fully leveraged for BI, data mining, and information navigation in business applications.

In MBF, Entity-Relational Maps (ER-Maps) describe how each field in a business entity (e.g., a "customer name" in the customer entity) is originated from a column in a database table (e.g., the CustomerName column in the Customers table). The Model Service infers respective OLAP cubes from the MBF object models - business entities in form of metadata. After this model transformation, a set of classes, namely the Business Intelligence (BI) Entities, are code generated as well to objectify the access to the multi-dimensional data in OLAP cubes.

AV automatically infers the corresponding analytical model from the transaction business logic. This process not only enables BI entities to be generated automatically but also preserves the "transformation" logic to offer the full fidelity of the metadata describing relationships between business entities and BI Entities. The end result of this process is a technical break-through that enables BI Entities to drill back to business entities and navigate among them in design and run –time, using metadata. The Intelli-Drill run-time service furthers the idea used by hypermedia [3] for the object transversal in an object graph. Figure 1 illustrates the architecture vision for AV.

P. Atzeni et al. (Eds.): ER 2004, LNCS 3288, pp. 834–837, 2004.

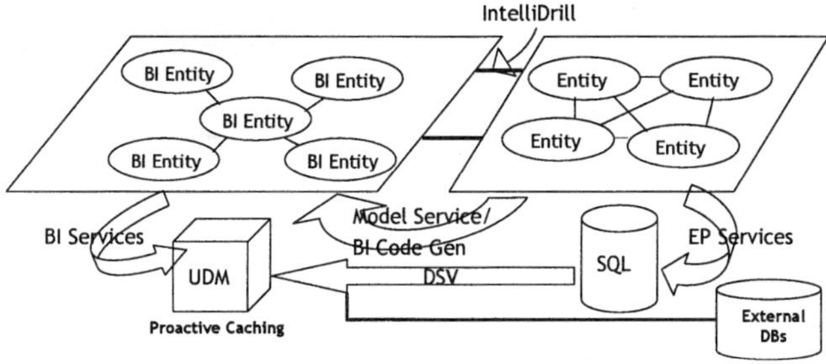

Fig. 1. Our Architecture Vision for Analytical View

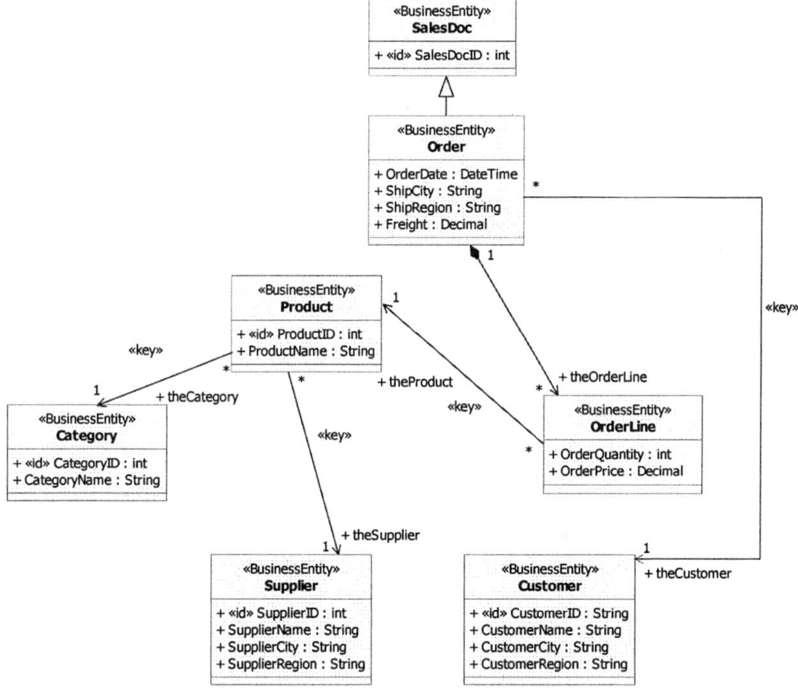

Fig. 2. UML Model for the Example

2 An Example

A developer uses MBF to design an application object model using UML (see Figure 2.) He maps the entities and relationships to relational objects. He runs Model Service to infer the dimensional model from the defined object model and the O-R mapping. The translator uses a rules engine to create dimensions and hierarchies. The translator first examines the model and determines the "reachable" object from all defined measures. A reachable object implies that a path exists to that object through relationships of the correct cardinality, from the measures. This insures that the dimensions that are built can "slice" the measures.

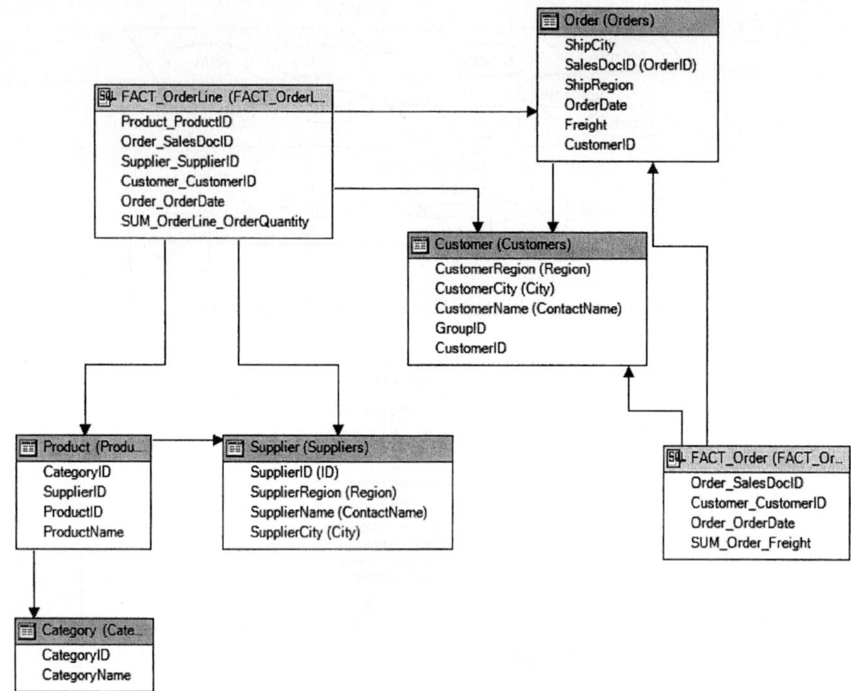

Fig. 3. Inferred Star Schema for the Example

The translation engine then generates a Data Source View [4] which describes the entities as data sources in the OLAP mode. Object relationships such as associations and compositions are emulated by foreign keys understood by the OLAP. Additional objects, known as the FACT objects, are built by traversing the object tree rooted by each focal point following foreign keys in a many-to-one direction.

Finally, the translation engine builds a dimensional model from the Data Source View. A Sales cube is built with two measure groups [4] and dimensions (Figure 3). The measure groups are derived from objects with decorated measures. The rules engine determines the structure of the dimensions, rolling up some entities into a single dimension and constructing hierarchies with the appropriate levels.

The deployment engine of the Model Service deploys the dimensional model on a specified UDM server and generates the BI Entity code for programmatic access.

We also introduced a notion of "Smart Report" to make information more accessible to the end users wherever they are in a business application by leveraging the metadata and Intelli-Drill runtime services. Figure 4 shows a mockup to illustrate the idea. In Smart Report, data points are traversable through Intelli-Drill. E.g., when a user types information about a customer in a sales order, the user can see the credit rating and payment history of this customer.

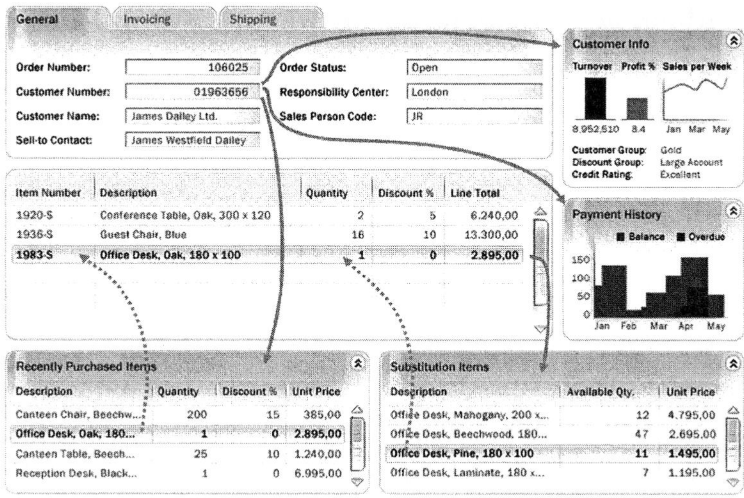

Fig. 4. Sample Smart Report

3 Conclusions and Future Work

Traditionally, converting an object model into a dimensional model is done manually to re-construct the business logic, which could be lost in the process. Importing data from the object model into the dimension model also creates a big overhead for the process of data analysis.

The conversion from an object oriented model to a dimensional model is a new concept in OLAP. Often, the two models are not related to each other because people who deal with them have different backgrounds. Our break-through automates the conversion process and removes the need to reconstruct the business logic. As such, we provide a lowest cost of entry point for application developers to include BI or data mining functionality in their applications. Most work described here has been done and will be part of MBF. We are working diligently to support prescriptive navigation using Intelli-Drill.

References

1. Adam Yeh, Jonathan Tang, Youxuan Jin, Sam Skrivan, Analytical View of Business Data, to be published in ACM SIGKDD 2004 proceedings.
2. Microsoft Business Framework (http:// microsoft.sitestream.com/PDC2003/DAT/ DAT340_files/Botto_files/DAT340_Brookins.ppt)
3. Alejandra Garrido and Gustavo Rossi, A Framework for Extending Object-Oriented Applications with Hypermedia Functionality (http://www.cs.colorado.edu/~kena/classes/7818/f99/framework.pdf).
4. Business Intelligence and Data Warehousing in SQL Server Yukon (http://www.microsoft.com/technet/treeview/default.asp?url=/technet/prodtechnol/sql/next/ DWSQLSY.asp)

Ontological Approaches to Enterprise Applications*

Dongkyu Kim[1], Yuan-Chi Chang[2], Juhnyoung Lee[2], and Sang-goo Lee[3]

[1] CoreLogiX, Inc., Seoul, Korea
dkkim@corelogix.co.kr
[2] IBM T. J. Watson Research Center, Hawthorne, NY, USA
{jyl,yuanchi}@us.ibm.com
[3] Center for e-Business Technology, Seoul National University, Seoul, Korea
sglee@snu.ac.kr

1 Introduction

One of the main challenges in building enterprise applications has been to balance between general functionality and domain/scenario-specific customization. The lack of formal ways to extract, distill, and standardize the embedded domain knowledge has been a barrier to minimizing the cost of customization. Using ontology, as many would hope, will give application builders the much needed methodology and standard to achieve the objective of building flexible enterprise solutions [1, 2].

However, even with a rich amount of research and quite a few excellent results on designing and building ontologies [3, 4], there are still gaps to be filled for actual deployment of the technology and concept in a real life commercial environment. The problems are hard especially in those applications that require well-defined semantics in mission critical operations. In this presentation, we introduce two of our projects where ontological approaches are used for enterprise applications. Based on these experiences we discuss the challenges in applying ontology-based technologies to solving business applications.

2 Product Ontology

In our current project, an ontology system is being built for the Public Procurement Services (PPS) of Korea, which is responsible for procurement for government and public agencies of the country. The main focus is the development of a system of ontologies representing products and services. This will include the definitions, properties, and relationships of the concepts that are fundamental to products and services. The system will supply tools and operations for managing catalog standards, and will serve a standard reference system for e-catalogs. Strong support for semantics of product data and processes will allow for dynamic, real-time data integration, and also real-time tracking and configuration of products, despite differing standards and conventions at each stage.

* This work has been conducted in part under the Joint Study Agreement between IBM T. J. Watson Research Center, USA, and the Center for e-Business Technology, Seoul National University, Korea. D. Kim and S. Lee's work was supported by Ministry of Information & Communications, Korea, under the Information Technology Research Center (ITRC) Support Program.

P. Atzeni et al. (Eds.): ER 2004, LNCS 3288, pp. 838–840, 2004.

An important component of the ontology model will be the semantic model for product classification schemes such as UNSPSC[1], since that alone can be used to enrich the current classification standards to include machine-readable semantic descriptions of products. The model will provide a logical structure in which to express the standards. The added semantics will enhance the accuracy of mappings between classification standards.

3 Performance Monitoring Ontology

We extend our discussions to another domain to argue that the issues and principles in the above project are not specific to product information, but rather can be generally applied to other database applications that deal with diverse semantics.

In this second project, we attempt to create a worldwide monitoring and collaboration platform for petroleum surveillance engineers of a major oil production and distribution company. The job of a surveillance engineer is to constantly monitor multiple time series sensor data, which takes measurements of production equipment outputs as well as natural environmental factors. An ontology to describe operational data and events in association with oil production is expected to serve as the reference to all operational sensor data and all equipment failure monitors. A performance monitoring ontology primarily serves three objectives in our system. First, the ontology organizes the matrix of sensor data in a semantically meaningful way for engineers to navigate and browse. Second, through ontology, the pattern recognizers can be de-coupled from actual sensor data, which may be added, upgraded, and retired in the lifetime of a well. Third, the ontology helps to link treatment actions to pending failure events. The use of ontology for performance monitoring appears through the working loop of sense, alert, decision, and reaction.

4 Discussions and Conclusion

Based on our experiences from the projects described above, we discuss some of the practical issues that hinder widespread use of ontology-based applications in enterprise settings. We came to realize the lack of modeling methodology, domain user tools, persistent storage, lifecycle management and access control for the creation, use, and maintenance of ontology on a large, deployable scale. While our engagement is specific to government procurement and oil production, we believe that one can infer this paradigm to similar business applications in other industries.

Modeling: Level of abstraction problem haunts all aspects of ontology design. Multiple views and taxonomies, often with conflicting semantics, present another challenge for the field engineer.

Ontology – DB Integration: The ontology can be modeled as meta data for the database, where the database alone represents the information content of the system and the ontology is a secondary facility. On the other hand, the ontology can be modeled

---

[1] UNSPSC, *United Nations Standard Products and Services Code*, UNDP, http://www.unspsc.org/

as an integral part of the database, in which case, ontology must be part of all queries and operations. Trade-off includes implementation complexity, semantic richness, and efficiency.

Ontology Lifecycle Management: Populating the ontology is a daunting task which can make or break the project. The job is complicated by multiple formats, semantic mismatches, errors or dirty data in pre-existing information sources. Change management (versions, mergers, decompositions, etc.) is another complicated issue.

Accountability and Control: One of the biggest concerns inhibiting ontology adoption in enterprise applications is its lack of control. When is an ontology complete, in the sense that it holds sufficient content to support all mission critical operations? Is the behavior/performance predictable?

Human Factors: Building and maintaining the ontology requires much more than software engineers. Domain experts must define the concepts and relationships of the domain model. Ontological information model is not a concept easily understood by non-computer/ontology experts. A set of intuitive guidelines must be provided. Easy-to-use tools are also essential.

Through this presentation, we wish to share our experiences on these issues and solutions to some of them. The solutions to these problems are most likely to come as disciplines, guidelines, and tools that implement these guidelines. In our future research, we plan to build a map that links individual ontological requirements to ontology issues, and then to applicable ontology technology.

References

1. D. L. McGuinness: Ontologies Come of Age. In: D. Fensel, et al. (eds.): The Semantic Web: Why, What, and How. MIT Press (2001)
2. N. Guarino: Formal Ontology and Information Systems. Proc. of Formal Ontology in Information Systems, Trento, Italy (1998)
3. P. Spyns, et al: Data Modeling versus Ontology Engineering. SIGMOD Record, Vol. 31(4), ACM (2002)
4. C.W. Holsapple & K.D. Joshi: A Collaborative Approach to Ontology Design. Comm. Of the ACM, Vol. 45(2), ACM (2002)

FASTAXON: A System for FAST (and Faceted) TAXONomy Design

Yannis Tzitzikas[1], Raimo Launonen[1], Mika Hakkarainen[1], Pekka Korhonen[2], Tero Leppänen[2], Esko Simpanen[2], Hannu Törnroos[2], Pekka Uusitalo[2], and Pentti Vänskä[2]

[1] VTT Information Technology, P.O.Box 1201, 02044 VTT, Finland
ytz@info.fundp.ac.be, {Raimo.Launonen,Mika.Hakkarainen}@vtt.fi
[2] Helsinki University of Technology, Finland

Building very big taxonomies is a laborious task vulnerable to errors and management/scalability deficiencies. FASTAXON is a system for building very big taxonomies in a quick, flexible and scalable manner that is based on the *faceted* classification paradigm [4] and the *Compound Term Composition Algebra* [5]. Below we sketch the architecture and the functioning of this system and we report our experiences from using this system in real applications.

Taxonomies, i.e. hierarchies of names, is probably the oldest and most widely used conceptual modeling tool still used in Web directories, Libraries and the Semantic Web (e.g. see XFML [1]). Moreover, the advantages of the taxonomy-based conceptual modeling approach for building large scale *mediators* and *P2P systems* that support semantic-based retrieval services have been analyzed and reported in [7, 6, 8]. However, building very big taxonomies is a laborious task vulnerable to errors and management/scalability deficiencies. One method for building efficiently a very big taxonomy is to first define a *faceted taxonomy* (i.e. a set of independently defined taxonomies called *facets*) like the one presented in Figure 1, and then derive automatically the inferred *compound taxonomy* i.e. the taxonomy of all possible *compound terms* (conjunctions of terms) over the faceted taxonomy. Faceted taxonomies carry a number of well known advantages over single hierarchies in terms of building and maintaining them, as well as using them in multicriteria indexing (e.g. see [3]). FASTAXON is a system for building big (compound) taxonomies based on the above mentioned idea. Using the system, the designer at first defines a number of facets and assigns to each one of them one taxonomy. After that the system can generate dynamically (and on the fly) a navigation tree that allows to the designer (as well to the object indexer or end user) to browse the set of *all* possible compound terms.

A drawback, however, of faceted taxonomies is the cost of avoiding the *invalid* (meaningless) compound terms, i.e. those that do not apply to any object in the domain. Let's consider the faceted taxonomy of Figure 1. Clearly we cannot do any winter sport in the Greek islands (Crete and Cefalonia) as they never have enough snow, and we cannot do any sea sport in Olympus because Olympus is a mountain. For the sake of this example, let us also suppose that only Cefalonia has a Casino. According to this assumption, the partition of the set of compound terms to the set of *valid* (meaningful) and *invalid* (meaningless)

P. Atzeni et al. (Eds.): ER 2004, LNCS 3288, pp. 841–843, 2004.

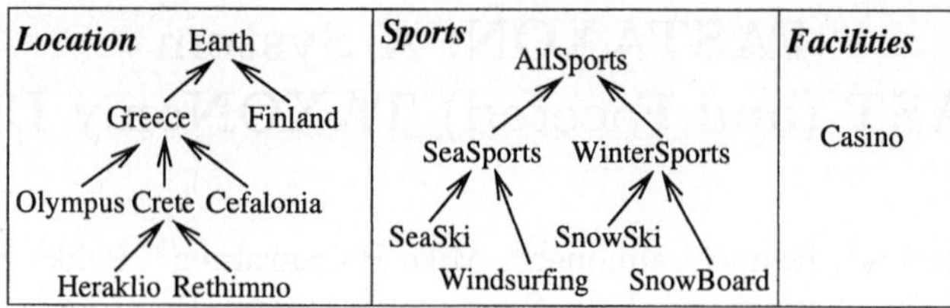

Fig. 1. A faceted taxonomy for indexing hotel Web pages

is shown in Table 1. The availability of such a partition would be very useful during the construction of a materialized faceted taxonomy (i.e. a catalog based on a faceted taxonomy). It could be exploited in the indexing process for *preventing* indexing errors, i.e. for allowing only meaningful compound terms to be assigned to objects. It could also *aid* the indexer during the indexing process, by generating dynamically a single hierarchical navigation tree that allows selecting the desired compound term by browsing *only* the meaningful compound terms. However, even from this toy example, it is more than obvious that the definition of such a partition would be a formidably laborious task for the designer.

FASTAXON allows specifying the meaningful compound terms in a very flexible manner. It is the first system that implements the recently emerged *Compound Term Composition Algebra* (CTCA) [5]. This allows to the designer to use an algebraic expression for specifying the valid compound terms. This involves declaring only a *small* set of valid or invalid compound terms from which other (valid or invalid) compound terms are then *inferred.* For instance, the partition shown in Table 1, can be defined using the expression:
$e = (Location \ominus_N Sports) \oplus_P Facilities$ with the following P and N parameters:
$N = \{\{Crete, WinterSports\}, \{Cefalonia, WinterSports\}\}$,
$P = \{\{Cefalonia, SeaSki, Casino\}, \{Cefalonia, Windsurfing, Casino\}\}$.
Specifically, FASTAXON provides an Expression Builder for formulating CTCA expressions in a flexible, interactive and guided way. Only the expression that defines the desired compound terminology is stored (and not the inferred partition), as an inference mechanism is used to check (in polynomial time) whether a compound term belongs to the compound terminology of the expression.

The productivity obtained using FASTAXON is quite impressive. The so far experimental evaluation has shown that in many cases a designer can define from scratch a compound taxonomy of around 1000 indexing terms in some minutes. FASTAXON has been implemented as a client/server Web-based system written in Java. The server is based on the Apache Web server, the Tomcat application server and uses MySQL for persistent storage. The user interface is based on DHTML (dynamic HTML), JSP (Java Server Pages) and Java Servlet technologies (J2EE). The client only needs a Web browser that support JavaScripts (e.g. Microsoft Internet Explorer 6). Future extensions include modules for importing and exporting XFML [1] and XFML+CAMEL [2] files. FASTAXON will be published under the VTT Open Source Licence within 2004 (for more see http://fastaxon.erve.vtt.fi/).

Table 1. The Valid and Invalid compound terms of the example of Figure 1

Valid		Invalid	
Earth, AllSports	Greece, AllSports	Olympus, SeaSports	
Finland, AllSports	Olympus, AllSports	Crete, WinterSp.	Cefal., WinterSp.
Crete, AllSports	Cefal., AllSports	Reth., WinterSp.	Heraklio, WinterSp.
Reth., AllSports	Heraklio, AllSports	Olympus, SeaSki	Olympus, WindSurf.
Earth, SeaSports	Greece, SeaSports	Crete, SnowB.	Cefal., SnowB.
Finland, SeaSports	Crete, SeaSports	Reth., SnowB.	Heraklio, SnowB.
Cefal., SeaSports	Reth., SeaSports	Crete, SnowSki	Cefal., SnowSki
Heraklio, SeaSports	Earth, WinterSp.	Reth., SnowSki	Heraklio, SnowSki
Greece, WinterSp.	Finland, WinterSp.	Olympus, SeaSports, Cas.	Crete, WinterSp., Cas.
Olympus, WinterSp.	Earth, SeaSki	Cefal., WinterSp., Cas.	Reth., WinterSp., Cas.
Greece, SeaSki	Finland, SeaSki	Heraklio, WinterSp., Cas.	Olympus, SeaSki, Cas.
Crete, SeaSki	Cefal., SeaSki	Olympus, WindSurf., Cas.	Crete, SnowB., Cas.
Reth., SeaSki	Heraklio, SeaSki	Cefal., SnowB., Cas.	Reth., SnowB., Cas.
Earth, WindSurf.	Greece, WindSurf.	Heraklio, SnowB., Cas.	Crete, SnowSki, Cas.
Finland, WindSurf.	Crete, WindSurf.	Cefal., SnowSki, Cas.	Reth., SnowSki, Cas.
Cefal., WindSurf.	Reth., WindSurf.	Heraklio, SnowSki, Cas.	Olympus, AllSports, Cas.
Heraklio, WindSurf.	Earth, SnowB.	Crete, AllSports, Cas.	Reth., AllSports, Cas.
Greece, SnowB.	Finland, SnowB.	Heraklio, AllSports, Cas.	Crete, SeaSports, Cas.
Olympus, SnowB.	Earth, SnowSki	Reth., SeaSports, Cas.	Heraklio, SeaSports, Cas.
Greece, SnowSki	Finland, SnowSki	Olympus, WinterSp., Cas.	Crete, SeaSki, Cas.
Olympus, SnowSki	Earth, AllSports, Cas.	Reth., SeaSki, Cas.	Heraklio, SeaSki, Cas.
Greece, AllSports, Cas.	Cefal., AllSports, Cas.	Crete, WindSurf., Cas.	Reth., WindSurf., Cas.
SeaSports, Cas.	SeaSports, Cas.	Heraklio, WindSurf., Cas.	Olympus, SnowB., Cas.
Cefal., SeaSports, Cas.	Earth, WinterSp., Cas.	Olympus, SnowSki, Cas.	Finland, AllSports, Cas.
Greece, WinterSp., Cas.	Earth, SeaSki, Cas.	Finland, SeaSports, Cas.	Finland, WinterSp., Cas.
Greece, SeaSki, Cas.	Cefal., SeaSki, Cas.	Finland, SeaSki, Cas.	Finland, WindSurf., Cas.
Earth, WindSurf., Cas.	Greece, WindSurf., Cas.	Finland, SnowSki, Cas.	Finland, SnowB., Cas.
Cefal., WindSurf., Cas.	Earth, SnowB., Cas.		
Greece, SnowB., Cas.	Earth, SnowSki, Cas.		
Greece, SnowSki, Cas.			

References

1. "XFML: eXchangeable Faceted Metadata Language". http://www.xfml.org.
2. "XFML+CAMEL:Compound term composition Algebraically-Motivated Expression Language". http://www.csi.forth.gr/markup/xfml+camel.
3. Ruben Prieto-Diaz. "Implementing Faceted Classification for Software Reuse". *Communications of the ACM*, 34(5):88–97, 1991.
4. S. R. Ranganathan. "The Colon Classification". In Susan Artandi, editor, *Vol IV of the Rutgers Series on Systems for the Intellectual Organization of Information.* New Brunswick, NJ: Graduate School of Library Science, Rutgers University, 1965.
5. Y. Tzitzikas, A. Analyti, N. Spyratos, and P. Constantopoulos. "An Algebraic Approach for Specifying Compound Terms in Faceted Taxonomies". In *Information Modelling and Knowledge Bases XV, Procs of EJC'03*, pages 67–87. IOS Press, 2004.
6. Y. Tzitzikas and C. Meghini. "Ostensive Automatic Schema Mapping for Taxonomy-based Peer-to-Peer Systems". In *7th Int. Workshop on Cooperative Information Agents, CIA-2003*, pages 78–92, Helsinki, Finland, August 2003.
7. Y. Tzitzikas, C. Meghini, and N. Spyratos. "Taxonomy-based Conceptual Modeling for Peer-to-Peer Networks". In *Procs of 22th Int. Conf. on Conceptual Modeling, ER'2003*, pages 446–460, Chicago, Illinois, October 2003.
8. Y. Tzitzikas, N. Spyratos, and P. Constantopoulos. "Mediators over Taxonomy-based Information Sources". *VLDB Journal*, 2004. (to appear).

CLOVE: A Framework to Design Ontology Views

Rosario Uceda-Sosa[1], Cindy X. Chen[2], and Kajal T. Claypool[2]

[1] IBM T. J. Watson Research Center, Hawthorne, NY 10532, USA
rosariou@us.ibm.com
[2] Department of Computer Science, University of Massachusetts,
Lowell, MA 01854, USA
{cchen,kajal}@cs.uml.edu

1 Introduction

The management and exchange of knowledge in the Internet has become the cornerstone of technological and commercial progress. In this fast-paced environment, the competitive advantage belongs to those businesses and individuals that can leverage the unprecedented richness of web information to define business partnerships, to reach potential customers and to accommodate the needs of these customers promptly and flexibly. The Semantic Web vision is to provide a standard information infrastructure that will enable intelligent applications to automatically or semi-automatically carry out the publication, the searching, and the integration of information on the Web. This is to be accomplished by semantically annotating data and by using standard inferencing mechanisms on this data. This annotation would allow applications to understand, say, dates and time intervals regardless of their syntactic representation. For example, in the e-business context, an online catalog application could include the expected delivery date of a product based on the schedules of the supplier, the shipping times of the delivery company and the address of the customer. The infrastructure envisioned by the Semantic Web would guarantee that this can be done automatically by integrating the information of the online catalog, the supplier and the delivery company. No changes to the online catalog application would be necessary when suppliers and delivery companies change. No syntactic mapping of metadata will be necessary between the three data repositories.

To accomplish this, two things are necessary: (1) the data structures must be rich enough to represent the complex semantics of products and services and the various ways in which these can be organized; and (2) there must be flexible customization mechanisms that enable multiple customers to view and integrate these products and services with their own categories. Ontologies are the answer to the former, *ontology views* are the key to the latter.

We propose *ontology views* as a necessary mechanism to support the ubiquitous and collaborative utilization of ontologies. Different agents (human or computational) require different organization of data and different vocabularies to suit their information seeking needs, but the lack of flexible tools to customize and evolve ontologies makes it impossible to find and use the right nuggets of

P. Atzeni et al. (Eds.): ER 2004, LNCS 3288, pp. 844–849, 2004.

information in such environments. When using an ontology, an agent should be able to introduce new classes using high level constraints, and define contexts to enable *efficient*, *effective* and *secure* information searching. In this paper we present a framework that enables users to design customized ontology views and show that the views are the right mechanism to enhance the usability of ontologies.

2 Ontology Views

Databases views and XML views [1–3, 5–7], have been used extensively to both tailor data to specific applications and to limit access to sensitive data. Much like traditional views, it is imperative for ontology views to provide a flexible model that meets the demands of different applications as well as different categories of users. For example, consider an online furniture retailer, `OLIE`, that wants to take advantage of ontology-based technologies and provide a flexible and extensible information model for its web-based applications. The retailer creates an ontology that describes the furniture inventory, manufacturers and customer transactions. Let us assume that two primary applications use this ontology. The first application, a *catalog browsing application*, allows customers to browse the furniture catalog and make online purchases, while the second application, a *pricing application*, allows marketing strategists to define sales promotions and pricing. The information needs of these two applications are very different. For example, customers should not be allowed to access the *wholesale price* of a furniture piece. Similarly, an analyst is only concerned with attributes of a furniture piece that describe it as a marketable entity, not those that refer to its dimensions, which are primarily of interest to customers.

The catalog browsing and the pricing applications need to take these restrictions into consideration when querying and displaying the ontology to their respective users. If the ontology changes, regardless of how powerful the inferencing is, the applications will invariably need to change their queries. This hard-coded approach to accessing ontologies is costly in development time and error prone, and underlies the need for a flexible model for ontology views. In this case, it is desirable to be able to define the MarketingView and CustomerView as in the ontology fragment shown in Figure 1.

Despite their similarities with relational database views, ontology views have also differentiating characteristics. First, ontology views need to be first-class citizens in the model, with relations and properties just like regular ontology classes. For example, suppose that the pricing analyst wants to define the PreferredCustomer category, as a customer with a membership card that offers special prices for furniture and accessories. Now the catalog application needs a PreferredCustomerView, similar to the CustomerView defined in Figure 1, adding the promotional price for card holders. It would also be desirable to define the PreferredCustomerView as a subclass of CustomerView, so that whenever some information is added or removed to the CustomerView, the changes are automatically reflected in the PreferredCustomerView. Notice that, in this case, we

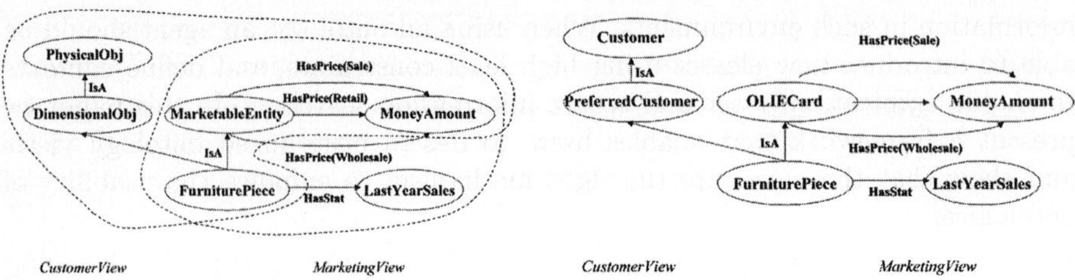

Fig. 1. Two Views of a Furniture Piece.

Fig. 2. Inheritance Hierarchy in Ontology Views.

have an inheritance hierarchy within the views, that is PreferredCustomerView IsA CustomerView, as shown in Figure 2.

Second, views need to be used as contexts to interpret further queries. For example, suppose that the marketing analyst defines the class SeasonalItems as a set of furniture pieces or accessories that have unusually high volume of sales in a given shopping season, based on previous years sales statistics. The analyst also defines ChristmasItems, SummerItems and FallItems as refinements of SeasonalItems. When a customer queries for information on large oval tablecloths in Christmas, items in the ChristmasItems view should be selected, and the information on each item should be filtered through either the CustomerView or the PreferredCustomerView, depending on the type of customer.

It is easy to see that views need to represent structures of the ontology (like CustomerView) as well as new classes defined through constraints, much like OWL [4] class operators. In fact, the views proposed here are extensions to OWL classes and expressions, as discussed in Section 2.1.

2.1 CLOVE – A View Definition Language for OWL

We focus on the systematic description and management of views as first-class objects in ontologies, as described in the scenarios above. To the best of our knowledge, this work is the first of its kind in defining ontology views as first-class objects. In particular, we extend OWL [4], a recently proposed standard of W3C, to describe ontologies and their views. OWL allows the definition of classes from other classes through set operations, thereby providing the basic infrastructure support for defining simple views, like the SeasonalItems category described above. However, it has limitations. First, even though ontology views can be considered as classes that are derived from the underlying ontology, they can also refer to subnetworks or structures of classes and relations (like in the case of the CustomerView), underscoring the need for a language rich enough to define both types of views. Second, we need to define a set of standard rules that govern the creation and management of these views, as well as their scope and visibility. While the later is still an open problem, there are some simple mechanisms that allow adequate view definitions. In this paper, we present an overview of a high level constraint language – CLOVE (*Constraint Language for Ontology View Environments*) that extends OWL constraints. We employ CLOVE as the underlying mechanism to support the creation of OWL views.

A view in CLOVE is defined by a set of (1) *subject* clauses; (2) *object* clauses; and (3) variable definitions. The subject clauses describe the constraints under which the view is valid, as well as the range of instances for which the view is applicable. The subject clauses are used to check whether the view (if declared active) should be used in the current query. CLOVE does not restrict the number of subjects of a view. For example, the CustomerView defines as subjects all types of customers. It is also possible to not specify the subject of a view by using the keyword *ANY*, in which case, the CLOVE runtime system uses the view to filter all queries when the view is active. A subject is defined through a *NavigationExpression* which is described below The objects are expressions that describe the content of a view, and have the form:

```
{INCLUDE|EXCLUDE} NavigationExpression ConstraintExpression
```

where the keywords *INCLUDE* and *EXCLUDE* indicate whether the classes or instances satisfying the clause are included or excluded from the view. The *NavigationExpression* is a Boolean expression of relations or properties that are navigated from the set of currently evaluated classes and instances or from a variable or name included in the expression. For example, *?Object SUBSUMES* and *IS-A* are valid navigation expressions.

The *ConstraintExpression* is an extension of an OWL expression. In its simplest form is just the name of a class or instance, but it can also describe the content of its data (the *WITH CONTENT* in Figure 3) or the data type of the properties of a class or instance (with *WITH TYPE*) among others. In the example below, *Customer* and *MarketableEntity* are valid and very simple- constraint expressions.

CLOVE also defines variables that can be directly used in clauses, as well as it allows users to define their own variables. A variable in CLOVE is preceded by the question mark. In Figure 3, the variable *?object* refers to the currently evaluated content of the view. There is also a pre-defined variable, *?subject* that refers to all the currently evaluated subjects of the view. User-defined variables can be used to define scripts or procedures to calculate data from the existing data, like *LastYearXmSales* in Figure 3, which is evaluated from existing properties of LastYearSales, the November and December sales.

The full specification of CLOVE is beyond the scope of this paper but Figure 3 gives a brief example of the creation of some of the OWL views of the scenarios above using CLOVE.

CLOVE allows arbitrary relations among views, in particular, inheritance (that is, *IsA*). CLOVE also allows the dynamic creation of classes to evaluate views (like the LastYearXmSales as a refinement of LastYearSales in Figure 3. After defining them, views can be activated or de-activated by their authors or by users with administrative privileges. The runtime system requires that every query is tagged with information about the user, which is associated to a class in the ontology. Queries are evaluated with respect to the currently active views in

```
CustomerView{
  Subject:IS-A Customer
  Object: INCLUDE ATTRIBUTE-OF FurniturePiece
  Object: INCLUDE ATTRIBUTE-OF Accessory
  Object: EXCLUDE ?Object SUBSUMES MarketableEntity
  Object: INCLUDE ?Object HAS-PRICE Retail
  Object: INCLUDE ?Object HAS-PRICE Sale
}

PreferredCustomerView IS-A CustomerView{
  Subject: ANY
}

SeasonalItems {
 Subject: FurnitureItem

}

ChristmasItems IS-A SeasonalItems{
  Subject: ANY
  Define: LastYearXmSales IS-A LastYearSales WITH CONTENT
    LastYearSales.November+LastYearSales.December
  Object: Include  ?object HAS-STAT ?LastYearXmSales >
    1.2 * (MarketableEntity HAS-STAT LastYearSales.AvgMonthlySales)
}
```

Fig. 3. Creating views with CLOVE.

the order that they were defined. The result is that queries against the ontology are automatically filtered by one or more views, according to the current user context.

All users with access to the ontology should be able to create views. This is one of the most important design principles of CLOVE. However, not every view should be used to filter every query, thats why the CLOVE runtime system keeps track of view dependencies and who created them, with a simple access control system based on user IDs.

3 Conclusions

The Semantic Web brings forth the possibility of heterogeneous ontologies that are universally accessible to arbitrary agents through the Internet. These agents may not only access these ontologies, but also customize their organization and information with their own knowledge and communicate it in turn to their own users. Hence, the ability to create views and contexts on ontologies becomes as crucial as the view mechanism in traditional database technologies, providing a scope and filtering of information necessary to modularize and evolve ontologies.

However, ontology views are not just straightforward extensions of database views. We have designed and implemented a framework that explores the issues of authoring and management of views and their underlying ontologies. Among them, we have focused on the dual nature of views as classes in the ontology and contexts to interpret new queries. As contextual elements, views are structures of classes and as classes they have relations to other views and even to other classes. We have also implemented a constraint language, CLOVE that takes into account this duality and allows users to both create and query views with an easy-to-use, natural interface.

References

1. S. Abiteboul, R. Hull, and V. V. *Foundations of Databases.* Addison-Wesley Publishing Company, 1995.
2. J. Gilbert. Supporting user views. *Computer Standards and Interfaces*, 13:293–296, 1991.
3. G. Gottlob, P. Paolini, and R. Zicari. Properties and update semantics of consistent views. *ACM Trans. on Database Systems*, vol.13(4):486–524, Dec. 1988.
4. OWL Web Ontology Language. *http://www.w3.org/TR/owl-guide/.*
5. A. Rosenthal and E. Sciore. First-Class Views: A Key to User-Centered Computing. *SIGMOD Record*, 28(3):29–36, May 1999.
6. P. V. S. Cluet and D. Vodislav. Views in a large scale xml repository. In *Proceedings of International Conference on Very Large Data Bases*, pages 271–280, 2001.
7. T. W. L. Y. B. Chen and M. L. Lee. Designing valid xml views. In *Proceedings of International Conference on Conceptual Modeling*, pages 463–478, 2002.

Dr. Rosario Uceda-Sosa is a researcher in intelligent information infrastructures, knowledge representation and usability at IBM T.J. Watson Research Center. She received a BS in Philosophy by the University of Seville (Spain), as well as a MS in Mathematics and a PhD in Computer Science by the University of Michigan. She is currently interested in the usability of ontologies and in ontology query languages.

Dr. Cindy Chen is an assistant professor at Department of Computer Science, University of Massachusetts at Lowell. She received B.S. degree in Space Physics from Peking University, China, M.S. and Ph.D. degrees in Computer Science from University of California, Los Angeles. Her current research interests include Spatio-Temporal Databases, XML, and Data Mining, etc.

Dr. Kajal T. Claypool is an Assistant Professor in the Department of Computer Science at University of Massachusetts - Lowell. She received her B.E. degree in Computer Engineering from Manipal Institute of Technology, India, and her Ph.D degree in Computer Science from Worcester Polytechnic Institute, Worcester MA. Her research interests are Data Integration focused on XML integration and Life Science Integration, Data Stream Engineering, and Software Engineering.

iRM: An OMG MOF Based Repository System with Querying Capabilities

Ilia Petrov, Stefan Jablonski, Marc Holze, Gabor Nemes, and Marcus Schneider

Chair for Database Systems, Department of Computer Science,
University of Erlangen-Nürnberg, Martensstrasse 3, Erlangen, D-91058, Germany
{petrov,jablonski,holze,nemes,schneider}@cs.fau.de
http://www6.informatik.uni-erlangen.de/

Abstract. In this work we present iRM – an OMG MOF-compliant repository system that acts as custom-defined application or system catalogue. iRM enforces structural integrity using a novel approach. iRM provides declarative querying support. iRM finds use in evolving data intensive applications, and in fields where integration of heterogeneous models is needed.

1 Introduction

Repository systems are "shared databases about engineered artifacts" [2]. They facilitate integration among various tools and applications, and are therefore central to an enterprise. Loosely speaking repository systems are data stores with a *customizable system catalogue* – a new and distinguishing feature. Repository systems exhibit an architecture comprising several layers of metadata [3], e.g. repository application's instance data (M_0), repository application's model (M_1), meta-model (M_2) and meta-meta-model (M_3). In comparison to database systems repository systems contain an additional metadata layer, M_3, allowing for a custom definable and extensible system catalogue (M_2). Preserving consistency between the different layers is a major challenge specific to repository systems. A declarative query language with higher order capabilities is needed to provide model (schema) independent querying. Treating data and metadata in uniform manner is a key principle when querying repository objects on different meta-layers. Areas of applications are domain-driven application engineering, scientific repositories, data-intensive Web applications. In this demonstration we present an OMG MOF based repository system developed in the frame of the iRM (Fig. 1) project [1].

2 iRM/RMS Repository System and mSQL Query Language

Structural consistency is one of the key issues in repository systems and must be enforced automatically by the RMS. It ensures that the structure of the repository objects conforms to its definition on the upper meta-layer. Without structural integrity the repository data will be inconsistent (no type conformity), which has profound consequences on any repository applications, since they rely heavily on reflection. The concept of *repository transactions* is an integral part of the structural consistency of the repository data. Repository systems must be able to handle concurrent multi-client access, i.e. concurrent atomic sets of operations from multiple repository cli-

P. Atzeni et al. (Eds.): ER 2004, LNCS 3288, pp. 850–851, 2004.

ents. Implementing isolation requires *extension* of the traditional locking mechanisms, e.g. multi-granularity locking mechanisms in OODB [4]. In iRM/RMS we introduce "instance lattice" in addition to aggregation and class (type) lattices.

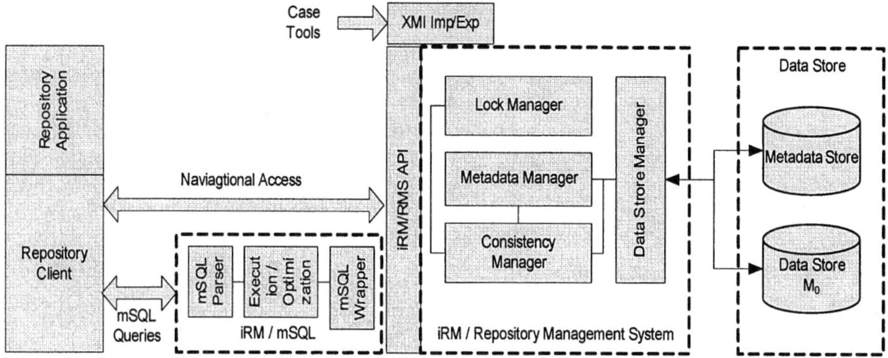

Fig. 1. Logical Architecture of the iRM Project

We introduce mSQL (meta SQL) as a query language-extension of SQL, to account for the specifics of the repository systems. The mSQL syntax is inspired by SchemaSQL [5]. The main value of mSQL lies in its declarative nature – especially beneficial in the context of repository systems. Given only a programmatic access, through the RMS API, a repository application needs additional code to load repository objects. mSQL queries significantly simplify this task and reduce application complexity. mSQL allows model independent querying: querying attributes values in classes on meta-layer instances of a specified meta-class.

3 The Demonstration

The demonstration will show the enforcement of structural integrity in iRM. We will consider several cases: (a) creation of new models and import of data; (b) modification of existing meta-metamodels (M2) with existing M1 models and instance data; (c) concurrent multi-client access. The second and the third cases illustrate the main value of structural integrity. We will showcase mSQL queries' execution, illustrating the value of mSQL to repository applications. We shall demonstrate model independent querying and dynamic schema discovery with mSQL.

References

1. Petrov, I., Jablonski, S.: An OMG MOF based Repository System with Querying Capability - the iRM Project. To appear In Proceedings of iiWAS 2004.
2. Bernstein, P., Dayal, U.: An overview of repository technology. In Proc. of VLDB 1994.
3. Object Management Group: Meta Object Facility Specification Version 1.4.
4. Ozsu, T.: Transaction Models and transaction management in Object-oriented database management systems. In Advances in Object-oriented Data-base Systems, 1994.
5. Lakshmanan, L.V.S., Sadri, F., Subramanian, S.N.: SchemaSQL: An extension to SQL for multidatabase interoperability. TODS, Vol. 26/ 4. Dec 2001.

Visual Querying for the Semantic Web

Sacha Berger, François Bry, and Christoph Wieser

University of Munich, Institute for Informatics
http://www.ifi.lmu.de

This paper presents a demonstration of visXcerpt [BBS03,BBSW03], a visual query language for both, standard Web as well as Semantic Web applications.

Principles of visXcerpt. The Semantic Web aims at enhancing data and service retrieval on the Web using meta-data and automated reasoning. Meta-data on the Semantic Web is heterogeneous. Several formalisms have been proposed. RDF, Topic Maps and OWL, e.g., and some of these formalisms have already a large number of syntactic variants. Like Web data, Web meta-data will be highly distributed. Thus, meta-data retrieval for Semantic Web applications will most likely call for query languages similar to those developed for the standard Web. This paper presents a demonstration of a visual query language for the Web and Semantic Web called **visXcerpt**. visXcerpt is based on three main principles.

First, visXcerpt has been conceived for querying not only Web meta-data, but also all kind of Web data. The reason is that many Semantic Web applications will most likely refer to both, standard Web and Semantic Web data, i.e. to Web data and Web meta-data. Using a single query language well-suited for data of both kinds is preferable to using different languages for it reduces the programming effort and hence costs and it avoids mismatches resulting from interoperating languages. **Second, visXcerpt is a query language capable of inference.** The inferences visXcerpt can perform are limited to simple inference like needed in querying database views, in logic programming, and in usual forms of Semantic Web reasoning. Offering both, inference and querying, in a same language avoids e.g. the impedance mismatch, which is commonly arising when querying and inferencing are performed in different processes. **Third, visXcerpt has been conceived as a mere Hypertext rendering of a textual query language.** This approach to developing a visual language is fully new. It has several advantages. It results in a visual language tightly connected to a textual language, namely the textual language it is a rendering of. This tight connection makes it possible to use both, the visual and the textual language, in the development of applications. Last but not least, a visual query language conceived as an Hypertext application is especially accessible for Web and Semantic Web application developers.

Further principles of visXcerpt are as follows. visXcerpt is **rule-based**. visXcerpt is **referentially transparent** and **answer-closed**. Answers to visXcerpt queries can be **arbitrary XML data**. visXcerpt uses (like the celebrated visual database query language QBE) **patterns** for binding variables in query expressions instead of path expressions – as do e.g. the Web query languages XQuery and XSLT. visXcerpt keeps **queries and constructions separated**.

P. Atzeni et al. (Eds.): ER 2004, LNCS 3288, pp. 852–853, 2004.

Language Visualization as Hypertext Rendering. XML and hence modelling languages for the Semantic Web based on XML like RDF, Topic Maps and OWL, are visualized in visXcerpt as nested, labeled boxes, each box representing an XML element. Graph structures are represented using Hyperlinks. Colors are used for conveying the nesting depth of XML elements. As visXcerpt's query and construction patterns can be seen as samples, the same visualization can be used for query and construction patterns. This makes visXcerpt's visualization of queries and answer constructions very close to the visualization of the data the queries and answer constructions refer to. visXcerpt has **interactive features** helping for a quick understanding of large programs: boxes representing XML elements can be folded and unfolded and semantically related portions of programs like e.g. different occurrences of the same variable), can be highlighted. visXcerpt programs can be composed using a **novel Copy-and-Paste** paradigm specifically designed for tree (or term) editing. **Patterns** are provided as templates to support easy construction of visXcerpt programs without in-depth prior knowledge of visXcerpt's syntax. Today's Web Standards together with Web browsers offer a ideal basis for the implementation of a language such as visXcerpt.The visXcerpt prototype demonstrated is implemented using only well-established techniques like CSS, ECMAScript, and XSL and, of course, the run time system of the textual query language Xcerpt [SB04] (cf. `http://xcerpt.org`).

Demonstrated Application. The application used for demonstrating visXcerpt is based on data inspired by "Friend of a Friend" cf. `http://xmlns.com/foaf/0.1/` expressed in various formats, including plain XML and RDF formats. The demonstration illustrates the following aspects of the visual query language visXcerpt.

Standard Web and Semantic Web data can be retrieved using the same visual query language, visXcerpt. Meta-data formated in various Semantic Web formats are conveniently retrieved using visXcerpt. visXcerpt queries and answer constructions are expressed using patterns that are intuitive and easy to express (cf. [BBS03,BBSW03] for examples). Hypertext features are used by visXcerpt such as Hypertext links for following references forward and backward or different renderings (such as hiding and showing of program components or XML elements) so as to help screening large programs. Recursive visXcerpt programs are presented and evaluated demonstrating that visXcerpt gives rise to a rather simple expression of transitive closures of Semantic Web relations and of recursive traversal of nested Web documents.

This research has been funded within the 6th Framework Programme project REWERSE number 506779 (cf. http://www.rewerse.net).

References

[BBS03] S. Berger, F. Bry, and S. Schaffert. A Visual Language for Web Querying and Reasoning. In *Workshop on Principles and Practice of Semantic Web Reasoning*, LNCS 2901, Springer Verlag, 2003.

[BBSW03] S. Berger, F. Bry, S. Schaffert, and C. Wieser. Xcerpt and visXcerpt: From Pattern-Based to Visual Querying of XML and Semistructured Data. In *29th Intl. Conference on Very Large Data Bases*, 2003.

[SB04] S. Schaffert and F. Bry. Querying the Web Reconsidered: A Practical Introduction to Xcerpt. In *Extreme Markup Languages*, 2004.

Query Refinement by Relevance Feedback in an XML Retrieval System

Hanglin Pan, Anja Theobald, and Ralf Schenkel

Max-Planck-Institute for Computer Science
D-66123 Saarbrücken, Germany
{pan,atb,schenkel}@mpi-sb.mpg.de

1 Introduction

In recent years, ranked retrieval systems for heterogeneous XML data with both structural search conditions and keyword conditions have been developed for digital libraries, federations of scientific data repositories, and hopefully portions of the ultimate Web. These systems, such as XXL [2], are based on pre-defined similarity measures for atomic conditions (using index structures on contents, paths and ontological relationships) and then use rank aggregation techniques to produce ranked result lists. An ontology can play a positive role for term expansion [2], by improving the average precision and recall in the INEX 2003 benchmark [3].

Due to the users' lack of information on the structure and terminology of the underlying diverse data sources, and the complexity of the (powerful) query language, users can often not avoid posing overly broad or overly narrow initial queries, thus getting either too many or too few results. For the user, it is more appropriate and easier to provide relevance judgments on the best results of an initial query execution, and then refine the query, either interactively or automatically by the system. This calls for applying relevance feedback technology in the new area of XML retrieval [1].

The key question is how to appropriately generate a refined query based on a user's feedback in order to obtain more relevant results among the *top-k* result list. Our demonstration will show an approach for extracting user information needs by relevance feedback, maintaining more intelligent personal ontologies, clarifying uncertainties, reweighting atomic conditions, expanding query, and automatically generating a refined query for the XML retrieval system XXL.

2 Stages of the Retrieval Process

a. Query Decomposition and Weight Initialization: A query is composed of weighted (i.e., differently important) atomic conditions, for example, XML element content constrains, XML element name (tag) constrains, path pattern constrains, ontology similarity constrains, variable constrains, search space constrains, and output constrains. In the XXL system, each atomic condition has an initial weight. If some constrains are uncertain, we specify them by the operator '$\sim$'. Concrete examples are shown in the poster.

P. Atzeni et al. (Eds.): ER 2004, LNCS 3288, pp. 854–855, 2004.

b. Retrieval with Ontology based Similarity Computation: Content index and path index structures are pre-computed and used for the relevance score evaluation of result item candidates. The global ontology index is built beforehand as a table of concepts from WordNet, and frequency-based correlations of concepts are computed statistically using large web crawls. To enable efficient query refinement in the following feedback iterations, we have a set of strategies to maintain a query-specified personal ontology which is automatically generated from fragments of the global ontology. This is the source for further query term expansion, as well as ontological similarity computations.

c. Result Navigation and Feedback Capturing: The retrieved ranking list is visualized in a user-friendly way supporting zoom plus focus. Features like group selection and re-ranking are supported in our system, which can capture richer feedback at various levels, i.e., content, path and overall level.

d. Strategy Selection for Query Reweighting and Query Expansion: The strategy selection module will choose an appropriate rank aggregation function over atomic conditions for overall score computation. After each feedback iteration, tuning functions (e.g., minimum weight algorithm, average weight algorithm, as in [4]), are used to derive the relative importance among all atomic conditions, and to update the personal ontology [1].

e. Adaptable Query Reformulation: Our system is adaptable using reweighting and expansion techniques. The open architecture allows us easily add new rank aggregation functions, reweighting strategies, or expansion strategies.

3 Demonstration

The INEX 2003 benchmark [3] consists of a set of content-and-structure queries and content-only queries over 12117 journal articles. Each document in a result set of a query is assigned a relevance assessment score provided by human experts. We run our method on this data set to show the improvement of average precision and recall using relevance feedback with up to four iterations. Our baseline is using only ontology-based expansion [2]. We show the comparison between different strategies of rank aggregation, query reweighting and expansion. We also show our approach to refine structural XML queries based on relevance feedback.

References

1. Hanglin Pan. Relevance feedback in XML retrieval. In: Proceedings of the *ICDE/EDBT* Joint Ph.D. Workshop, Boston, pages 193-202, March 2004. To appear in LNCS 3268, *Current Trends in Database Technology*, Springer, 2004.
2. Ralf Schenkel, Anja Theobald, and Gerhard Weikum. XXL@INEX2003. In: Proceedings of the *2003 INEX* Workshop, Dagstuhl Castle, Germany, December 15-17, 2003.
3. Norbert Fuhr, Mounia Lalmas. Initiative for the evaluation of XML retrieval (INEX), 2003. `http://inex.is.informatik.uni-duisburg.de:2003/`.
4. Michael Ortega-Binderberger, Kaushik Chakrabarti, and Sharad Mehrotra. An approach to integrating query refinement in SQL. In: Proceedings of *EDBT 2002*. In LNCS 2287, *Advances in Database Technology*, Springer, 2002.

Semantics Modeling for Spatiotemporal Databases

Peiquan Jin, Lihua Yue, and Yuchang Gong

Department of Computer Science and Technology,
University of Science and Technology of China, 230027, Hefei, P.R. China

1 Introduction

How to model spatiotemporal changes is one of the key issues in the researches on spatiotemporal databases. Due to the inefficiency of previous spatiotemporal data models [1, 2], none of them has been widely accepted so far.

This paper investigates the types of spatiotemporal changes and the approach to describing spatiotemporal changes. The semantics of spatiotemporal changes are studied and a systematic classification on spatiotemporal changes is proposed, based on which a framework of spatiotemporal semantic model is presented.

2 Semantic Modeling of Spatiotemporal Changes

The framework for modeling spatiotemporal changes is shown in Fig. 1 as an *And/Or Tree*. Spatiotemporal changes are represented by object-level spatiotemporal changes that result in changes of object identities and attribute-level spatiotemporal changes that do not change any objects' identities but only the internal attributes of an object. Attribute-level spatiotemporal changes are spatial attribute changes or thematic attribute changes, which are described by spatial descriptor and attribute descriptor, while object-level spatiotemporal changes are discrete identity changes, which are represented by history topology. The modeling of spatiotemporal changes as shown in Fig.1 is complete. The proof can be found in the reference [3].

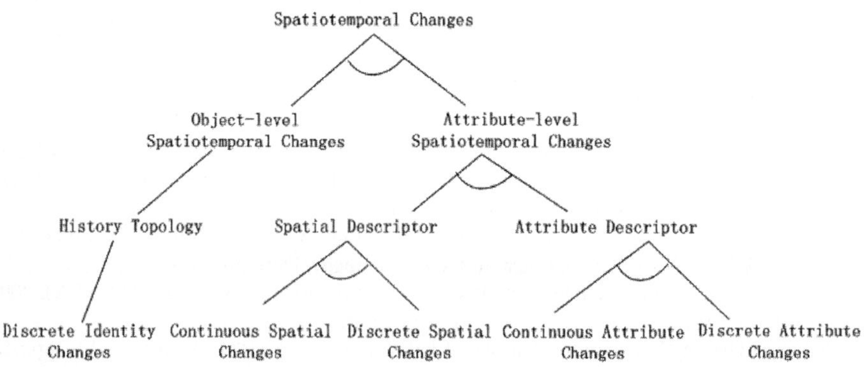

Fig. 1. The framework for modeling spatiotemporal changes

P. Atzeni et al. (Eds.): ER 2004, LNCS 3288, pp. 856–857, 2004.

3 A Framework of Spatiotemporal Semantic Model

The framework of spatiotemporal semantic model is shown in Fig. 2. The circle notation represents identity-level changes, and the triangle notation represents attribute-level changes. The *attribute descriptor* describes the time-varying thematic properties of the spatiotemporal object. The *spatial descriptor* represents the time-varying spatial value of the spatiotemporal object. And the *history topology*, which represents identity-level changes, describes the life cycle of spatiotemporal objects, such as split and mergence. Thus a spatiotemporal object can be defined as a quadruple of object identity, spatial descriptor, attribute descriptor and history topology, which is *O* = < *OID, SD, AD, HT*>. This structure can represent both spatiotemporal data and spatiotemporal changes: a static state of a spatiotemporal object can be determined by inputting a definite time value into *SD*, *AD* and *HT*, while a dynamic state during a period of time can be obtained by the *SD*, *AD* and *HT* in the period.

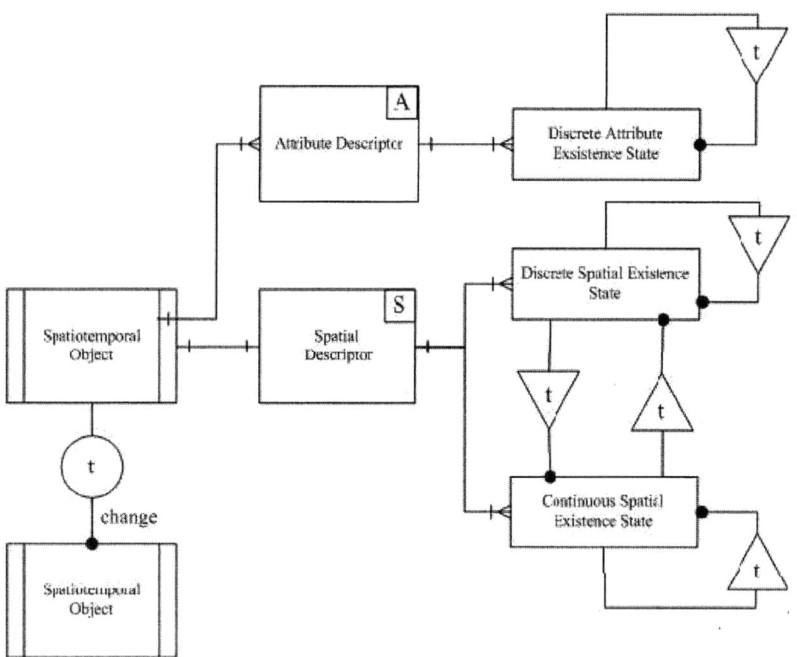

Fig. 2. The spatiotemporal semantic model

References

1. Xiaoyu, W., Xiaofang, Z.: Spatiotemporal data modeling and management: a survey. In Proceedings of the 36th TOOLS Conference, IEEE Press (2000) 202-211
2. Forlizzi, L., Güting, R., Nardelli, E., Schneider, M.: A data model and data structures for moving objects databases. ACM SIGMOD (2000) 319-330
3. Peiquan, J., Lihua Y., Yuchang, G.: Semantics and modeling of spatiotemporal changes. LNCS 2888, CoopIS/DOA/ODBASE, Springer-Verlag, Berlin (2003) 924-933.

Temporal Information Management Using XML

Fusheng Wang, Xin Zhou, and Carlo Zaniolo

Department of Computer Science, University of California, Los Angeles,
Los Angeles, CA 90095, USA
{wangfsh,xinzhou,zaniolo}@cs.ucla.edu

1 Introduction

A closer integration of XML and database systems is actively pursued by researchers and vendors because of the many practical benefits it offers. Additional special benefits can be achieved on temporal information management – an important application area that represents an unsolved challenge for relational databases [1]. Indeed, XML data model and query languages support:

- Temporally grouped representations that have long been recognized as a natural data model for historical information [2], and
- Turing-complete query languages, such as XQuery [3], where all the constructs needed for temporal queries can be introduced as user-defined libraries, without requiring extensions to existing standards.

By contrast, the flat relational tables of traditional DBMSs are not well-suited for temporally grouped representations [4]; moreover, significant extensions are required to support temporal information in SQL and, in the past, they were poorly received by SQL standard committees.

We will show that (i) XML hierarchical structure can naturally represent the history of databases and XML documents via temporally-grouped data models, and (ii) powerful temporal queries can be expressed in XQuery without requiring any extension to current standards. This approach is quite general and, in addition to the evolution history of databases, it can be used to support the version history of XML documents for transaction-time, valid-time, and bitemporal chronicles [5]. We will demo the queries discussed in [5] and show that this approach leads to simple programming environments that are fully-integrated with current XML tools and commercial DBMSs.

2 The Systems ArchIS and ICAP

In our demo, we first show that transaction-time history of relational databases can be effectively published as XML views, where complex temporal queries on the evolution of database relations can be expressed in standard XQuery [6]. Therefore, we will demonstrate our ArchIS prototype that supports these queries efficiently on traditional database systems enhanced with SQL/XML [7]. A temporal library of XQuery functions is used to facilitate the writing of the

P. Atzeni et al. (Eds.): ER 2004, LNCS 3288, pp. 858–859, 2004.

more complex queries and hide some implementation details (e.g., the internal representation of 'now'). We can thus support the complete gamut of historical queries, including snapshot and time-slicing queries, element-history queries, *since* and *until* queries. These temporal queries in XQuery are then mapped and executed as equivalent SQL/XML queries executing on the RDBMS.

The next topic in the demo is the application of our temporal representations and queries to XML documents of arbitrary nesting complexity. In the ICAP project [8], we store the version history of documents of public interest in ways that assure that powerful historical queries can be easily expressed and supported. Examples include successive versions of standards and normative documents, such as the UCLA course catalog [9], and the W3C Xlink specs [10], which are issued in XML form. Toward this objective,

(i) we use structured diff algorithms [11–14] to compute the validity periods of the elements in the multi-version document,
(ii) we use the output generated by the diff algorithm, to build a concise representation history of the document using a temporally grouped data model. Then, on this representation,
(iii) we use XQuery, enhanced with the library of temporal functions, to formulate temporal queries on the evolution of the document and its content.

The ICAP system also provides additional version-support services, including the ability of color-marking changes between versions, and annotating the changes with explanations and useful metainformation.

References

1. G. Ozsoyoglu and R.T. Snodgrass, *"Temporal and real-time databases: A survey"*. in TKDE, 7(4):513–532, 1995.
2. J. Clifford. *Formal Semantics and Pragmatics for Natural Language Querying.* Cambridge University Press, 1990.
3. XQuery 1.0: An XML Query Language. http://www.w3.org/TR/xquery/.
4. J. Clifford, A. Croker, F. Grandi,and A. Tuzhilin, *"On Temporal Grouping"*, in Proc. of the Intl. Workshop on Temporal Databases, 1995.
5. F. Wang and C. Zaniolo. *"XBiT: An XML-based Bitemporal Data Model"*, in ER 2004.
6. F. Wang and C. Zaniolo, *"Publishing and Querying the Histories of Archived Relational Databases in XML"*, in WISE 2003.
7. "SQL/XML. http://www.sqlx.org", http://www.sqlx.org.
8. UCLA ICAP Project. http://wis.cs.ucla.edu/projects/icap/.
9. UCLA Catalog. http://www.registrar.ucla.edu/catalog/.
10. XML Linking Language (XLink). http://www.w3.org/TR/xlink/.
11. S. Chawathe, A. Rajaraman, H. Garcia-Molina, J. Widom, *"Change Detection in Hierarchically Structured Information"*, in SIGMOD 1996.
12. Microsoft XML Diff. http://apps.gotdotnet.com/xmltools/xmldiff/.
13. Gregory Cobena, Serge Abiteboul, Amelie Marian, *"Detecting Changes in XML Documents"*, in ICDE 2002.
14. Y. Wang, D. J. DeWitt, and J. Cai, *"X-Diff: A Fast Change Detection Algorithm for XML Documents"*, in ICDE 2003.

SVMgr: A Tool for the Management of Schema Versioning

Fabio Grandi

Alma Mater Studiorum – Università di Bologna,
Dipartimento di Elettronica, Informatica e Sistemistica,
Viale Risorgimento 2, I-40136 Bologna, Italy
fgrandi@deis.unibo.it

1 Overview of the SVMgr Tool

The SVMgr tool is an integrated development environment for the management of a relational database supporting schema versioning, based on the *multi-pool* implementation solution [2]. In a few words, the multi-pool solution allows the extensional data connected to each schema version (data pool) to evolve independently from each other. The multi-pool solution is more flexible and potentially useful for advanced applications as it allows the coexistence of different full-fledged *conceptual viewpoints* on the mini-world modeled by the database [5], and it has partially been adopted also by other authors [3]. The multi-pool implementation underlying the SVMgr tool is based on the **Logical Storage Model** presented in [4] and allows the underlying multi-version database to be implemented on top of MS Access. The software prototype has been written in Java (it is downward compatible with the 1.2 version) and interacts with the underlying database via JDBC/ODBC on a MS Windows platform.

In order to show the multi-pool approach features in practice and test its potentialities against applications, SVMgr has been equipped with a multi-schema query interface, initially supporting select-project-join queries written in the **Multi-Schema Query Language** MSQL [4, 5]. Hence, the SVMgr prototype represents the first implemented relational database system with schema versioning support *which is able to answer multi-schema queries.* The MSQL language includes two syntax extensions to refer to different schema versions: *naming qualifiers* and *extensional qualifiers* [4, 5]. The former allow users to denote a schema object (e.g. an attribute or relation name) through its name used in different schema versions: for instance, "[SV1:R]" denotes the relation named R in schema version SV1. The latter allow users to denote object values as stored in different data pools: for instance "SV2:S" denotes the instance of relation S in the data pool connected to schema version SV2. Recently, the MSQL language has been further developed with the addition of grouping and ordering facilities: multi-schema extensions of the SQL `GROUP BY`, `HAVING` and `ORDER BY` clauses, and of the SQL aggregate functions are fully supported by the SVMgr tool in its current release.

The SVMgr environment, in its current release (ver 13.02, as of July 2004), supports four main groups of functions:

P. Atzeni et al. (Eds.): ER 2004, LNCS 3288, pp. 860–861, 2004.

Database Content Management, which allow users to inspect and modify the contents of the data pools associated to different schema versions. Also integrity checks on primary key uniqueness (which may be threatened by the execution of schema changes) can be effected.

Schema Version Management, which allow users to effect schema changes and create a new schema version. Supported schema changes are: add, rename, drop a table; add, rename, drop a table column; change the primary key of a table.

Integration Support Tools, which allow users to support the integration activities [1] when the underlying database is used as a data source in an heterogeneous environment.

Multi-schema Queries, which allow users to execute multi-schema SPJ queries, by implementing a MSQL query language interface. MSQL queries are translated into standard SQL queries which are executed via JDBC on the underlying database implementing the Logical Storage Model.

Users of the tool are supposed to be database administrators, which have complete control and responsibility over the database schema and contents, including management of schema versions. Although SVMgr users are supposed to have a reasonable knowledge of the main features of schema versioning with the multi-pool implementation solution, the prototype has been equipped with a user-friendly interface, and requires a minimum knowledge of the underlying data model beyond the intuition. Also several correctness checks have been carefully encoded in all the available user functions to protect, as much as possible, the database integrity from an incorrect use.

References

1. S. Bergamaschi, S. Castano, A. Ferrara, F. Grandi, F. Guerra, G. Ornetti, M. Vincini, Description of the Methodology for the Integration of Strongly Heterogeneous Sources, Tech. Rep. D1.R6, D2I Project, 2002, http://www.dis.uniroma1.it/~lembo/D2I/Prodotti/index.html.
2. C. De Castro, F. Grandi, and M. R. Scalas. Schema Versioning for Multitemporal Relational Databases. *Information Systems*, 22(5):249–290, 1997.
3. R. de Matos Galante, A. Bueno da Silva Roma, A. Jantsch, N. Edelweiss, and C. Saraiva dos Santos. Dynamic Schema Evolution Management Using Version in Temporal Object-Oriented Databases. In *Proceedings of the 13th International Conference on Database and Expert Systems Applications (DEXA 2002)*, pages 524–533, Aix-en-Provence, France, September 2002. Springer Verlag.
4. F. Grandi, "A Relational Multi-Schema Data Model and Query Language for Full Support of Schema Versioning", *Proc. of SEBD 2002*, Portoferraio – Isola d'Elba, Italy, pp. 323-336. 2002.
5. F. Grandi, "Boosting the Schema Versioning Potentialities: Querying with MSQL in the Multi-Pool Approach", 2004 (*in preparation*).

GENNERE: A Generic Epidemiological Network for Nephrology and Rheumatology

Ana Simonet[1], Michel Simonet[1], Cyr-Gabin Bassolet[1], Sylvain Ferriol[1], Cédric Gueydan[1], Rémi Patriarche[1], Haijin Yu[2], Ping Hao[2], Yi Liu[2], Wen Zhang[2], Nan Chen[2], Michel Forêt[5], Philippe Gaudin[4], Georges De Moor[6], Geert Thienpont[6], Mohamed Ben Saïd[3], Paul Landais[3], and Didier Guillon[5]

[1] Laboratoire TIMC-IMAG, Faculté de Médecine de Grenoble, France
{Ana.Simonet, Michel.Simonet}@imag.fr

[2] Rui Jin Hospital, Shanghai, China

[3] LBIM, Université Paris 5 Necker, France

[4] CHU Grenoble, France

[5] AGDUC Grenoble, France

[6] RAMIT, Belgium

Abstract. GENNERE is a networked information system designed to answer epidemiological needs. Based on a French experiment in the field of End-Stage Renal Diseases (ESRD), it has been thought of so as to be adapted to Chinese medical needs and administrative rules. It has been implemented for nephrology and rheumatology at the Rui Jin hospital in Shanghai, but its design and implementation have been guided by genericity in order to make easier its adaptation and extension to other diseases and other countries. The genericity aspects have been considered at the levels of events design, database design and production, and software design. This first experiment in China leads to some conclusions about the adaptability of the system to several diseases and the multilinguality of the interface and in medical terminologies.

1 Introduction

GENNERE, for Generic Epidemiological Network for Nephrology and Rheumatology, is a project supported by the European ASIA-ITC program in 2003-2004. This project come from a cooperation established between partners of the French MSIS-REIN project [1] and the Rui Jin hospital in Shanghai. The main goal of the project is the setting up of a system for the epidemiological follow-up of chronic diseases, following the MSIS-REIN approach, although adapted to China's needs [2]. A secondary objective was to find a methodology to design and implement software that will support an easy adaptation to other chronic diseases and to other countries. To demonstrate the generic aspects which have been emphasized in the GENNERE program, two medical fields have been considered in this experiment: nephrology (as in MSIS-REIN) and rheumatology. In this demonstration we present the GENNERE systems, with an emphasis on genericity aspects in their design and implementation.

2 The GENNERE Project

Genericity, which is the major non-medical objective of the GENNERE project, has been considered mainly at two levels: the design process and the software implemen-

P. Atzeni et al. (Eds.): ER 2004, LNCS 3288, pp. 862–864, 2004.

tation. From the design point of view, the methodology followed was: 1) to highlight the events and functionalities by categories of users, 2) to define the abstract ontological model for chronic diseases, 3) to isolate the data specific to a country, 4) to design the interfaces blocks.

Events. In GENNERE the events for nephrology are the same as the events taken into account in the French MSIS-REIN project. The events model for rheumatology is very similar to that for nephrology, which demonstrates the possibility to constitute a core of minimal events for this kind of system.

Database design. For database design we have used the CASE tool ISIS (Information System Initial Specification) developed at the TIMC laboratory [3]. It enables the designer to work at the conceptual level and specify behavioral aspects rather than implement them directly at the level of relational tables. Moreover, thanks to its ability to check the consistency of a specification and to automatically generate the database (logical and physical schema), the ISIS system has considerably shortened the cycle of knowledge extraction from medical experts and its validation by users.

Views. To ensure the minimum work when modifying the database schema we have been careful to access the database only through views – except for some database updates which were too complex to be supported by the DBMS.

Ontological data model. As in the French model, the core of the conceptual model is centered on three generic concepts: PATIENT, FOLLOW UP and TREATMENT. However, each concept is derived according to a specific structure for each disease. For example, the TREATMENT concept is much more complex for Rhumatoid Arthritis than for ESRD because this illness has several anatomic localizations and can be treated by several means: medicines, local manipulations or traditional Chinese medicine.

Country-specific data. The setting up of the GENNERE system has put into light the data which are specific of a given country, e.g., addresses and insurance for patient, which depend strongly on the geographical and administrative organization of the country; another example is that of Chinese traditional medicine (acupuncture, herbs, massages, etc). These categories of data are much country-specific and will have to be studied anew when a new country is to be considered.

Multilingualism. Dealing simultaneously with several languages, while keeping the possibility of adding a new language, imposes the choice of an encoding system which supports a wide variety of languages [4]. In GENNERE, which must support Chinese, English and French, the choice was UTF8-Unicode, which also supports most known languages, including other Asian languages.

Metadata. To present multilingual interfaces without needing to duplicate the interface code, we built a specific database for the management of the metadata of the GENNERE system (Nephrology and Rheumatology). This database contains the description of the database objects: tables, columns, domain values (for enumerated attributes). It also contains the objects necessary to the various interfaces, e.g., labels used in the Graphical User Interface. Each object has a unique identifier and is associated to as many items as different languages, Chinese, English and French at the present time. Thus, a value or a label may be rapidly retrieved according to the selected language. This method also facilitates the addition of a new language: one must only fill the metadata tables with the corresponding items in this language.

3 Conclusion

Genericity has constituted a major concern in the design and the implementation of the GENNERE information system.

This project showed us a need for tools allowing a cooperative work, especially when the team in charge of conceiving and developing the project is culturally, socially and geographically heterogeneous. This lead to several cycles for knowledge extraction and validation in order to come to a consensus. The CASE tool ISIS [3] played a very important role for reaching consensus more rapidly among the partners.

For the success of the MSIS-REIN the human factor has been determining. Beside technology improvements, didactic efforts have been made and are still necessary to help users and to identify impediments to changes. This factor is at least as important in China.

The GENNERE program in its final development phase will be installed at the Rui Jin hospital in Shanghai at the end of the year 2004 on two servers, one for nephrology and one for rheumatology. During the next phase (2005-2006) data integration from other centres will be carried out and a data warehouse will be implemented, also in a generic way, along with epidemiological and data presentation tools [5]. A Geographical Information System, currently under implementation in France, seems very promising to support public health decision and will be considered in a later phase [6].

References

1. Landais P., Simonet A., et le groupe de travail SIMS@REIN. SIMS@REIN: *Un Système d'Information Multisources pour l'Insuffisance Rénale Terminale.* CR Acad Sci (série (III) Sciences de la Vie). 2002; 325: 515-528
2. Chen N., et al. Shanghai Cooperation group: *The clinical epidemiology of cardiovascular disease in chronic renal failure in Shanghai.* Chin. Journal of Nephrology 2001; 17: 91-94
3. Simonet A., Simonet, M.: *The ISIS Methodology for Object Database Conceptual Modelling.* Poster E/R 99: 18th Conference on Conceptual Modeling, Paris, 15-18 Nov. 99
4. Kumaran A., Haritsa J. R.: *On the costs of multilingualism in database systems.* Procs. of the 29th VLDB Conference, Berlin, Germany, 2003.
5. Simonet A. et al.: *Un entrepôt de données pour l'aide à la décision sanitaire en néphrologie.* Revue des Sciences et Technologies de l'Information, série Ingénierie des Systèmes d'Information, Vol. 8 – N° 1/2003, pp 75-89, HERMES.
6. Simonet M., Toubiana L., Simonet A., Ben Said M., Landais P.: *Ontology and Geographical Information System for End-Stage Renal Disease: the SIGNE.* Workshop on fundamental issues on geographic and spatial ontologies, held with COSIT'03 (Conference on Spatial Information Theory), Ittingen, 23 sept. 2003.

Panel: Beyond Webservices – Conceptual Modelling for Service Oriented Architectures

Peter Fankhauser

Fraunhofer IPSI
64293 Darmstadt, Germany
fankhaus@ipsi.fraunhofer.de

Abstract. Webservices are evolving as the paradigm for loosely coupled architectures. The prospect of automatically composing complex processes from simple services is promising. However, a number of open issues remain: Which aspects of service semantics need to be explicated? Does it suffice to just model datastructures and interfaces, or do we also need process descriptions, behavioral semantics, and quality of service specifications? How can we deal with heterogeneous service descriptions? Should we use shared ontologies or adhoc mappings? This panel shall discuss to which extent established techniques from conceptual modelling can help in describing services to enable their discovery, selection, composition, negotiation, and invocation.

P. Atzeni et al. (Eds.): ER 2004, LNCS 3288, p. 865, 2004.

Author Index

Acuña, César J. 780
Ahnizeret, Keyla 402
Al-Kamha, Reema 150
Atluri, Vijayalakshmi 624

Bailey, James 479
Bassolet, Cyr-Gabin 862
Bell, David 313
Benatallah, Boualem 524
Ben Saïd, Mohamed 862
Berger, Sacha 852
Bergholtz, Maria 724
Bhowmick, Sourav S. 493
Böhlen, Michael H. 610
Bowers, Shawn 668
Bresciani, Paolo 682
Bry, François 852
Busetta, Paolo 682

Cabot, Jordi 69
Casati, Fabio 524, 825
Castellanos, Malu 825
Cavalcanti, João M.B. 402
Chakravarthy, Sharma 420
Chang, Yuan-Chi 828, 838
Chen, Cindy X. 844
Chen, Huowang 348
Chen, Nan 862
Cheung, Shing-Chi 542
Chillakuru, Vamsavardhana R. 828
Claypool, Kajal T. 844
Conesa, Jordi 122
Conrad, Stefan 388

da Silva, Altigran S. 402
Davies, Islay 30
Delcambre, Lois 668
Demetrovics, János 166
De Moor, Georges 862
de Moura, Edleno Silva 402
Dong, Yisheng 300

Embley, David W. 150
Eppili, Ajay 420

Fan, Hao 639
Fan, Xiaocong 582
Fankhauser, Peter 865
Feng, Jiansheng 18
Fernandes, David 402
Fernández-Medina, Eduardo 217
Ferriol, Sylvain 862
Flesca, Sergio 286
Forêt, Michel 862

Gallo, Stan 30
Ganascia, Jean-Gabriel 83
Gao, Like 464
Garcia-Molina, Hector 1
Gaudin, Philippe 862
Goelman, Don 43
Gong, Yuchang 856
Gordijn, Jaap 709
Gosain, Anjana 205
Grandi, Fabio 860
Graupmann, Jens 3
Greco, Gianluigi 231
Green, Peter 30, 110
Gueydan, Cédric 862
Guillon, Didier 862
Guo, Gongde 313
Gupta, Amarnath 55

Härder, Theo 654
Hakkarainen, Mika 841
Hao, Ping 862
He, Qi 245
Hilsbos, Margaret 740
Holland, Stefan 511
Holze, Marc 850
Hu, Dabin 18
Huang, Dong 831
Hwang, Jeong Hee 377
Hwang, San-Yih 596

Indulska, Marta 110

Jablonski, Stefan 850
Jacob, Jyoti 420
Jayaweera, Prasad 724
Jensen, Ole G. 610
Ji, Xiao 18

Jin, Peiquan 856
Jin, Youxuan 834
Johannesson, Paul 724

Ke, Yiping 567
Kießling, Werner 511
Kim, Dongkyu 838
Kitsuregawa, Masaru 450
Korhonen, Pekka 841
Kovse, Jernej 654
Kuflik, Tsvi 682

Landais, Paul 862
Launonen, Raimo 841
Lee, Juhnyoung 838
Lee, Sang-goo 838
Lembo, Domenico 231
Leppänen, Tero 841
Li, HaiJun 327
Li, Ling 327
Li, Shijun 273
Li, Zhoujun 348
Liao, Zhining 313
Liddle, Stephen W. 150
Ling, Tok Wang 245
Liu, Lin 555
Liu, Mengchi 273
Liu, Yi 862
Lu, An 259
Luján-Mora, Sergio 191

Madria, Sanjay 493
Marcos, Esperanza 780
Miao, Huaikou 753
Molnár, András 166
Mondal, Anirban 450

Nemes, Gabor 850
Ng, Wilfred 259, 567

Olivé, Antoni 122, 136

Padmanabhan, Sriram 464
Pan, Hanglin 854
Patriarche, Rémi 862
Paul, Raymond A. 596
Penserini, Loris 682
Pérez de Laborda, Cristian 388
Petrov, Ilia 850
Piattini, Mario 217
Popfinger, Christopher 388
Poulovassilis, Alexandra 639
Prakash, Naveen 205
Prakash, Sandeep 493
Purao, Sandeep 336, 582

Qin, Li 624

Ram, Sudha 696
Raventós, Ruth 69
Reinhartz-Berger, Iris 766
Rosemann, Michael 30, 110
Rundensteiner, Elke A. 795
Ryu, Keun Ho 377

Sachde, Alpa 420
Santini, Simone 55
Schenkel, Ralf 3, 854
Schneider, Marcus 850
Shan, Ming-Chien 825
Shi, Baile 831
Simonet, Ana 862
Simonet, Michel 862
Simpanen, Esko 841
Singh, Yogesh 205
Skrivan, Sam 834
Song, Il-Yeol 43, 740
Srivastava, Jaideep 596
Stojanovic, Ljiljana 434
Stojanovic, Nenad 434
Storey, Veda C. 336
Sturm, Arnon 766

Tagarelli, Andrea 286
Tan, Hee Beng Kuan 180
Tan, Qingzhao 567
Tang, Haidong 18
Tang, Jonathan 834
Tang, Jun 831
Thalheim, Bernhard 166
Theobald, Anja 854
Theobald, Martin 3
Thienpont, Geert 862
Toumani, Farouk 524
Trujillo, Juan 191, 217
Tzitzikas, Yannis 841
Törnroos, Hannu 841

Uceda-Sosa, Rosario 844
Umapathy, Karthikeyan 582
Uusitalo, Pekka 841

van der Aalst, W.M.P. 362
van Dongen, B.F. 362
van Eck, Pascal 709
Vänskä, Pentti 841
Vassiliadis, Panos 191
Vela, Belén 780
Velcin, Julien 83
Vigna, Sebastiano 96
Villarroel, Rodolfo 217

Wang, Chen 831
Wang, Fusheng 810, 858
Wang, Haojun 596
Wang, Hengjie 18
Wang, Hui 313
Wang, LiMin 327
Wang, Ling 795
Wang, Min 464, 828
Wang, Wei 831
Wang, X. Sean 464
Wang, Xiaoling 300
Waworuntu, Stella 479
Weber, Christian 654
Wei, Wanxia 273
Wei, Wei 696
Weikum, Gerhard 3
Wieringa, Roel 709
Wieser, Christoph 852
Wohed, Petia 724

Xiao, Xiangye 542
Xu, Chang 542

Yan, Yuejin 348
Yeh, Adam 834
Yen, John 582
Yu, Eric 555
Yu, Haijin 862
Yuan, SenMiao 327
Yue, Lihua 856

Zaniolo, Carlo 810, 858
Zhan, Xuede 753
Zhang, Dell 300
Zhang, Wen 862
Zhao, Yuan 180
Zhou, Xin 858

Lecture Notes in Computer Science

For information about Vols. 1–3198

please contact your bookseller or Springer

Vol. 3305: P.M.A. Sloot, B. Chopard, A.G. Hoekstra (Eds.), Cellular Automata. XV, 883 pages. 2004.

Vol. 3302: W.-N. Chin (Ed.), Programming Languages and Systems. XIII, 453 pages. 2004.

Vol. 3299: F. Wang (Ed.), Automated Technology for Verification and Analysis. XII, 506 pages. 2004.

Vol. 3294: C.N. Dean, R.T. Boute (Eds.), Teaching Formal Methods. X, 249 pages. 2004.

Vol. 3293: C.-H. Chi, M. van Steen, C. Wills (Eds.), Web Content Caching and Distribution. IX, 283 pages. 2004.

Vol. 3292: R. Meersman, Z. Tari, A. Corsaro (Eds.), On the Move to Meaningful Internet Systems 2004: OTM 2004 Workshops. XXIII, 885 pages. 2004.

Vol. 3291: R. Meersman, Z. Tari (Eds.), On the Move to Meaningful Internet Systems 2004: CoopIS, DOA, and ODBASE. XXV, 824 pages. 2004.

Vol. 3290: R. Meersman, Z. Tari (Eds.), On the Move to Meaningful Internet Systems 2004: CoopIS, DOA, and ODBASE. XXV, 823 pages. 2004.

Vol. 3289: S. Wang, K. Tanaka, S. Zhou, T.W. Ling, J. Guan, D. Yang, F. Grandi, E. Mangina, I.-Y. Song, H.C. Mayr (Eds.), Conceptual Modeling for Advanced Application Domains. XXII, 692 pages. 2004.

Vol. 3288: P. Atzeni, W. Chu, H. Lu, S. Zhou, T.W. Ling (Eds.), Conceptual Modeling – ER 2004. XXI, 869 pages. 2004.

Vol. 3287: A. Sanfeliu, J.F.M. Trinidad, J.A. Carrasco Ochoa (Eds.), Progress in Pattern Recognition, Image Analysis and Applications. XVII, 703 pages. 2004.

Vol. 3286: G. Karsai, E. Visser (Eds.), Generative Programming and Component Engineering. XIII, 491 pages. 2004.

Vol. 3284: A. Karmouch, L. Korba, E.R.M. Madeira (Eds.), Mobility Aware Technologies and Applications. XII, 382 pages. 2004.

Vol. 3281: T. Dingsøyr (Ed.), Software Process Improvement. X, 207 pages. 2004.

Vol. 3280: C. Aykanat, T. Dayar, I. Körpeoğlu (Eds.), Computer and Information Sciences - ISCIS 2004. XVIII, 1009 pages. 2004.

Vol. 3278: A. Sahai, F. Wu (Eds.), Utility Computing. XI, 272 pages. 2004.

Vol. 3274: R. Guerraoui (Ed.), Distributed Computing. XIII, 465 pages. 2004.

Vol. 3273: T. Baar, A. Strohmeier, A. Moreira, S.J. Mellor (Eds.), <<UML>> 2004 - The Unified Modelling Language. XIII, 454 pages. 2004.

Vol. 3271: J. Vicente, D. Hutchison (Eds.), Management of Multimedia Networks and Services. XIII, 335 pages. 2004.

Vol. 3270: M. Jeckle, R. Kowalczyk, P. Braun (Eds.), Grid Services Engineering and Management. X, 165 pages. 2004.

Vol. 3269: J. Lopez, S. Qing, E. Okamoto (Eds.), Information and Communications Security. XI, 564 pages. 2004.

Vol. 3266: J. Solé-Pareta, M. Smirnov, P.V. Mieghem, J. Domingo-Pascual, E. Monteiro, P. Reichl, B. Stiller, R.J. Gibbens (Eds.), Quality of Service in the Emerging Networking Panorama. XVI, 390 pages. 2004.

Vol. 3265: R.E. Frederking, K.B. Taylor (Eds.), Machine Translation: From Real Users to Research. XI, 392 pages. 2004. (Subseries LNAI).

Vol. 3264: G. Paliouras, Y. Sakakibara (Eds.), Grammatical Inference: Algorithms and Applications. XI, 291 pages. 2004. (Subseries LNAI).

Vol. 3263: M. Weske, P. Liggesmeyer (Eds.), Object-Oriented and Internet-Based Technologies. XII, 239 pages. 2004.

Vol. 3262: M.M. Freire, P. Chemouil, P. Lorenz, A. Gravey (Eds.), Universal Multiservice Networks. XIII, 556 pages. 2004.

Vol. 3261: T. Yakhno (Ed.), Advances in Information Systems. XIV, 617 pages. 2004.

Vol. 3260: I.G.M.M. Niemegeers, S.H. de Groot (Eds.), Personal Wireless Communications. XIV, 478 pages. 2004.

Vol. 3258: M. Wallace (Ed.), Principles and Practice of Constraint Programming – CP 2004. XVII, 822 pages. 2004.

Vol. 3257: E. Motta, N.R. Shadbolt, A. Stutt, N. Gibbins (Eds.), Engineering Knowledge in the Age of the Semantic Web. XVII, 517 pages. 2004. (Subseries LNAI).

Vol. 3256: H. Ehrig, G. Engels, F. Parisi-Presicce, G. Rozenberg (Eds.), Graph Transformations. XII, 451 pages. 2004.

Vol. 3255: A. Benczúr, J. Demetrovics, G. Gottlob (Eds.), Advances in Databases and Information Systems. XI, 423 pages. 2004.

Vol. 3254: E. Macii, V. Paliouras, O. Koufopavlou (Eds.), Integrated Circuit and System Design. XVI, 910 pages. 2004.

Vol. 3253: Y. Lakhnech, S. Yovine (Eds.), Formal Techniques, Modelling and Analysis of Timed and Fault-Tolerant Systems. X, 397 pages. 2004.

Vol. 3252: H. Jin, Y. Pan, N. Xiao, J. Sun (Eds.), Grid and Cooperative Computing - GCC 2004 Workshops. XVIII, 785 pages. 2004.

Vol. 3251: H. Jin, Y. Pan, N. Xiao, J. Sun (Eds.), Grid and Cooperative Computing - GCC 2004. XXII, 1025 pages. 2004.

Vol. 3250: L.-J. (LJ) Zhang, M. Jeckle (Eds.), Web Services. X, 301 pages. 2004.

Vol. 3249: B. Buchberger, J.A. Campbell (Eds.), Artificial Intelligence and Symbolic Computation. X, 285 pages. 2004. (Subseries LNAI).

Vol. 3246: A. Apostolico, M. Melucci (Eds.), String Processing and Information Retrieval. XIV, 332 pages. 2004.

Vol. 3245: E. Suzuki, S. Arikawa (Eds.), Discovery Science. XIV, 430 pages. 2004. (Subseries LNAI).

Vol. 3244: S. Ben-David, J. Case, A. Maruoka (Eds.), Algorithmic Learning Theory. XIV, 505 pages. 2004. (Subseries LNAI).

Vol. 3243: S. Leonardi (Ed.), Algorithms and Models for the Web-Graph. VIII, 189 pages. 2004.

Vol. 3242: X. Yao, E. Burke, J.A. Lozano, J. Smith, J.J. Merelo-Guervós, J.A. Bullinaria, J. Rowe, P. Tiňo, A. Kabán, H.-P. Schwefel (Eds.), Parallel Problem Solving from Nature - PPSN VIII. XX, 1185 pages. 2004.

Vol. 3241: D. Kranzlmüller, P. Kacsuk, J.J. Dongarra (Eds.), Recent Advances in Parallel Virtual Machine and Message Passing Interface. XIII, 452 pages. 2004.

Vol. 3240: I. Jonassen, J. Kim (Eds.), Algorithms in Bioinformatics. IX, 476 pages. 2004. (Subseries LNBI).

Vol. 3239: G. Nicosia, V. Cutello, P.J. Bentley, J. Timmis (Eds.), Artificial Immune Systems. XII, 444 pages. 2004.

Vol. 3238: S. Biundo, T. Frühwirth, G. Palm (Eds.), KI 2004: Advances in Artificial Intelligence. XI, 467 pages. 2004. (Subseries LNAI).

Vol. 3236: M. Núñez, Z. Maamar, F.L. Pelayo, K. Pousttchi, F. Rubio (Eds.), Applying Formal Methods: Testing, Performance, and M/E-Commerce. XI, 381 pages. 2004.

Vol. 3235: D. de Frutos-Escrig, M. Nunez (Eds.), Formal Techniques for Networked and Distributed Systems – FORTE 2004. X, 377 pages. 2004.

Vol. 3234: M.J. Egenhofer, C. Freksa, H.J. Miller (Eds.), Geographic Information Science. VIII, 345 pages. 2004.

Vol. 3232: R. Heery, L. Lyon (Eds.), Research and Advanced Technology for Digital Libraries. XV, 528 pages. 2004.

Vol. 3231: H.-A. Jacobsen (Ed.), Middleware 2004. XV, 514 pages. 2004.

Vol. 3230: J.L. Vicedo, P. Martínez-Barco, R. Muñoz, M. Saiz Noeda (Eds.), Advances in Natural Language Processing. XII, 488 pages. 2004. (Subseries LNAI).

Vol. 3229: J.J. Alferes, J. Leite (Eds.), Logics in Artificial Intelligence. XIV, 744 pages. 2004. (Subseries LNAI).

Vol. 3226: M. Bouzeghoub, C. Goble, V. Kashyap, S. Spaccapietra (Eds.), Semantics of a Networked World. XIII, 326 pages. 2004.

Vol. 3225: K. Zhang, Y. Zheng (Eds.), Information Security. XII, 442 pages. 2004.

Vol. 3224: E. Jonsson, A. Valdes, M. Almgren (Eds.), Recent Advances in Intrusion Detection. XII, 315 pages. 2004.

Vol. 3223: K. Slind, A. Bunker, G. Gopalakrishnan (Eds.), Theorem Proving in Higher Order Logics. VIII, 337 pages. 2004.

Vol. 3222: H. Jin, G.R. Gao, Z. Xu, H. Chen (Eds.), Network and Parallel Computing. XX, 694 pages. 2004.

Vol. 3221: S. Albers, T. Radzik (Eds.), Algorithms – ESA 2004. XVIII, 836 pages. 2004.

Vol. 3220: J.C. Lester, R.M. Vicari, F. Paraguaçu (Eds.), Intelligent Tutoring Systems. XXI, 920 pages. 2004.

Vol. 3219: M. Heisel, P. Liggesmeyer, S. Wittmann (Eds.), Computer Safety, Reliability, and Security. XI, 339 pages. 2004.

Vol. 3217: C. Barillot, D.R. Haynor, P. Hellier (Eds.), Medical Image Computing and Computer-Assisted Intervention – MICCAI 2004. XXXVIII, 1114 pages. 2004.

Vol. 3216: C. Barillot, D.R. Haynor, P. Hellier (Eds.), Medical Image Computing and Computer-Assisted Intervention – MICCAI 2004. XXXVIII, 930 pages. 2004.

Vol. 3215: M.G.. Negoita, R.J. Howlett, L.C. Jain (Eds.), Knowledge-Based Intelligent Information and Engineering Systems. LVII, 906 pages. 2004. (Subseries LNAI).

Vol. 3214: M.G.. Negoita, R.J. Howlett, L.C. Jain (Eds.), Knowledge-Based Intelligent Information and Engineering Systems. LVIII, 1302 pages. 2004. (Subseries LNAI).

Vol. 3213: M.G.. Negoita, R.J. Howlett, L.C. Jain (Eds.), Knowledge-Based Intelligent Information and Engineering Systems. LVIII, 1280 pages. 2004. (Subseries LNAI).

Vol. 3212: A. Campilho, M. Kamel (Eds.), Image Analysis and Recognition. XXIX, 862 pages. 2004.

Vol. 3211: A. Campilho, M. Kamel (Eds.), Image Analysis and Recognition. XXIX, 880 pages. 2004.

Vol. 3210: J. Marcinkowski, A. Tarlecki (Eds.), Computer Science Logic. XI, 520 pages. 2004.

Vol. 3209: B. Berendt, A. Hotho, D. Mladenic, M. van Someren, M. Spiliopoulou, G. Stumme (Eds.), Web Mining: From Web to Semantic Web. IX, 201 pages. 2004. (Subseries LNAI).

Vol. 3208: H.J. Ohlbach, S. Schaffert (Eds.), Principles and Practice of Semantic Web Reasoning. VII, 165 pages. 2004.

Vol. 3207: L.T. Yang, M. Guo, G.R. Gao, N.K. Jha (Eds.), Embedded and Ubiquitous Computing. XX, 1116 pages. 2004.

Vol. 3206: P. Sojka, I. Kopecek, K. Pala (Eds.), Text, Speech and Dialogue. XIII, 667 pages. 2004. (Subseries LNAI).

Vol. 3205: N. Davies, E. Mynatt, I. Siio (Eds.), UbiComp 2004: Ubiquitous Computing. XVI, 452 pages. 2004.

Vol. 3204: C.A. Peña Reyes, Coevolutionary Fuzzy Modeling. XIII, 129 pages. 2004.

Vol. 3203: J. Becker, M. Platzner, S. Vernalde (Eds.), Field Programmable Logic and Application. XXX, 1198 pages. 2004.

Vol. 3202: J.-F. Boulicaut, F. Esposito, F. Giannotti, D. Pedreschi (Eds.), Knowledge Discovery in Databases: PKDD 2004. XIX, 560 pages. 2004. (Subseries LNAI).

Vol. 3201: J.-F. Boulicaut, F. Esposito, F. Giannotti, D. Pedreschi (Eds.), Machine Learning: ECML 2004. XVIII, 580 pages. 2004. (Subseries LNAI).

Vol. 3199: H. Schepers (Ed.), Software and Compilers for Embedded Systems. X, 259 pages. 2004.